D0776766

A Time for Courage

A Time for Courage

The Royal Air Force in the European War, 1939–1945

by John Terraine

MACMILLAN PUBLISHING COMPANY
New York

Macmillan Publishing Company
866 Third Avenue, New York, N.Y. 10022

Library of Congress Cataloging in Publication Data

Terraine, John.
  A time for courage.
  1. World War, 1939–1945 – Aerial operations, British.
  2. Great Britain – Royal Air Force – History – World War,
  1939–1945.   I. Title
  D786.T44   1985   940.54′4941   84-17098
  ISBN 0-02-616970-3

Macmillan books are available at special discounts for bulk purchases for sales
promotions, premiums, fund-raising, or educational use. Special editions or book
excerpts can also be created to specification. For details, contact:

Special Sales Director
Macmillan Publishing Company
866 Third Avenue
New York, New York 10022

10 9 8 7 6 5 4 3 2 1

Printed in the United States of America

Contents

PART III:
THE STRAIN
"The only plan is to persevere."

THE BATTLE OF BRITAIN
". . . a few thousand airmen . . ."

THE BATTLE OF THE ATLANTIC (I)
"Anxiety supreme"

THE STRATEGIC AIR OFFENSIVE (I)
"The leading element in bringing about our victory . . ."

Contents

PART IV:
THE VICTORY
"The Air must hold the ring"

THE MEDITERRANEAN
"... Air warfare in its own right ..."

THE BATTLE OF THE ATLANTIC (II)
"... the dominating factor all through the war ..."

Contents

THE STRATEGIC AIR OFFENSIVE (II)
"... they are sowing the wind ..."

VICTORY IN EUROPE
"... the highest degree of intimacy ..."

Contents

Illustration Contents

Acknowledgments
1. By courtesy of the Royal Air Force Museum, Hendon
2. Reproduced with the permission of the Controller of Her Majesty's Stationery Office
3. By courtesy of the Imperial War Museum
4. By courtesy of the BBC Hulton Picture Library
5. By courtesy of Harleyford Publications
6. By courtesy of Air Commodore Voyce
7. By courtesy of Mr David Irving

Foreword

At the Battle of Crécy, on August 26, 1346, the English Army under King Edward III faced apparently hopeless odds. A hard fight, with every possibility of disaster, was at hand. When the king drew up his army, it was to his eldest son, the 16-year-old Black Prince, that Edward "gave the place of honour and greatest danger, commanding the vanguard on the right of the line".* The battle was hard indeed, with the Black Prince's division bearing the brunt of it throughout. The English won, and the boy prince won his spurs, the supreme accolade of chivalry. It is from those distant times that "the right of the line" has come to mean, in battle, "the place of greatest danger" – "the vanguard" – and in ceremony "the place of honour". Thus, when the Army is on parade, it is the Cavalry (whose traditions go back to the age of chivalry) which forms on the right – unless the Royal Horse Artillery is present, in which case the horse Gunners claim the post of honour. When the three Services parade together, the Royal Navy, as the senior Service, takes the right, and the Royal Air Force, as the junior, takes the left. But in this book it is argued that in the war in Europe between 1939 and 1945 the RAF was, in effect, "the vanguard", holding for much of the time the place of honour on the right of the line, as the Black Prince and his men did at Crécy.

This argument will no doubt be considered odd by a number of people, because even now, in the 1980s, so much modern military history continues to be written two-dimensionally, that is to say, from the point of view of the land and sea forces only. And indeed, in World War I, when air warfare made its début, it was the armies and navies which continued to play the overwhelmingly larger part. In World War II the terms of reference were quite different; the Air rôle was always significant, often dominant. In the first half of 1940 the German Air Force ruled the skies of Europe; it is possible that its ten *Panzer* divisions would have enabled the Army to win the Battle of France without the aid of the *Luftwaffe* – possible but, I would suggest, not very likely, because it was the Air arm that produced the fatal demoralization of the Allies, leading to successive surrenders. Thereafter, it can

The Black Prince by Hubert Cole, p. 49, Hart-Davis, MacGibbon, 1976.

certainly be argued that the decline of Germany may be measured by the decline of the *Luftwaffe*. So the importance of the Air arm in Germany's effort is very clear. Meanwhile, as I shall hope to show, on the other side, the Royal Air Force found itself without option shouldering the burden of the war when the Army was in eclipse and the Royal Navy strained to its limits.

That is one of the main threads of this story; the second is my intention, throughout, to place both the war itself and the RAF's part in it firmly in the perspectives to which they truly belong. I do not subscribe to the notion that World War II was a thing apart, without resemblance to anything that had gone before. On the contrary, I see it as belonging to a sequence of great wars (that is, wars of great powers for survival) in the period whose technology was dominated by the First Industrial Revolution. These are: the American Civil War (this connection became very clear indeed in 1942–43), the First World War (so many of whose lessons had to be painfully relearned in the Second) and finally the great conflict of 1939–45. In all three the prime war material was steel, and the prime motive force was steam; but by 1939 a second revolution was well advanced, and it is to that, with its dependence on light metals and the internal combustion engine, that the RAF evidently belongs. From this standpoint it was soon obvious that any narrative of the RAF's war which did not dwell considerably on the products of the technology – the aircraft themselves – would probably be wide of the mark. The RAF, like the Navy, fights entirely with machines; they are of the essence.

The outstanding human aspect of the three great wars of this period is the mobilization of the masses. In World War I this was a totally unfamiliar procedure in Britain (though not in America or Europe), and having raised and maintained a mass army for the first time in their history by splendid and heroic efforts, the British then recoiled from the whole feat with disastrous results when war loomed again. The RAF profited from this recoil by presenting itself as an alternative to mass warfare. How amazed its founders and its champions must have been when they saw the mass air force of nearly one-and-a-quarter million men and women which the war brought forth! 1939–45 was the time of the vast air fleets, the big aircraft with large specialized crews, and the host of people on the ground required to direct and service them. The 1939–45 RAF was not, in other words, by any means the air force that it had expected to be.

The British are notoriously equivocal in their attitudes towards their armed forces. Grudging and parsimonious in peacetime, they try as far as possible to ignore the Services (or, indeed, abuse them), and then as war approaches to see them through the rose-tinted lenses of sentimentality and military ignorance. It came as a great shock in World War I that the Royal Navy, Britain's pride, not only failed to produce another Trafalgar, but suffered grievous losses, and at one stage looked like losing the war at sea. No attempt was made between the wars to strengthen the Navy so that this should not happen again; in 1939 it was far weaker than it had been in 1914 – yet it was expected to "rule the waves" as though nothing had happened since Nelson's famous victory. When the Army met defeat and disaster in 1940, the national instinct was to pretend that no such thing had occurred, and to elevate the Dunkirk débâcle into some kind of "miracle" victory. But the grim fact was that for the next two years the British Army was never able to engage more than four weak German divisions in battle – a hopeless situation.

Delusions about the RAF were – not unnaturally – similar. Even serious students of air power were misled by the prevailing optimistic sentiment. Thus J. M. Spaight, who rightly perceived and stated in 1945 that the Air Force had held the right of the line (as quoted on my title page) in the same passage echoed the national credo. Mistaken pre-war policies, he wrote,

> were reprehensible, but they were atoned for by one great service which was rendered to the nation and indeed to civilization in those years of gathering storm-clouds. The standard of the Royal Air Force was not lowered. The Force was too small in 1939, but for all that it was the finest air force in the world. It was a superb arm of war.**

I leave it to readers to assess that judgment against the condition of the RAF at its "coming of age", as reported by its responsible commanders, Air Chief Marshals Sir Edgar Ludlow-Hewitt and Sir Hugh Dowding, and related in Chapter 8. For the nation, the five and a half years of the war against Hitler were a painful time of awakening from superstition; for the RAF they were equally painful – a time of awakening from false dogma, and learning the practicalities of war. The fact that this was such hard going only makes the achievement greater, the post of honour that much more deserved.

These, then, are the threads that I try to follow. I am conscious of many omissions, and I am sorry about them. Originally, I had intended to include the war against Japan in this account, but as I proceeded I realized that to do so would require another volume and another title, because the texture of the air war in the Far East was (for Britain, at any

**AHB/II/116/17, p. 38.

rate) a very different matter from that in Europe. Yet I regret this gap, because that story is full of interest and drama. I regret the gaps in the Western narrative also – the Commands and functions which here receive bare mention or none at all. To all those who feel left out, I make sincere apologies now. And in addition there are individuals who do not receive their full deserts: members of the Air Council and the Air Staff, Group Commanders, "back-room boys", aircrew and ground-crew. To them, too, I can only apologize – and point to the already great length of the book, uncomplainingly accepted by the publishers.

It will be seen that in writing it I have leaned heavily on the material which exists in the Air Historical Branch of the Ministry of Defence. All this is, of course, also available in the Public Record Office, but it will be understood that great benefit accrues from having one's researches guided – as mine were – by the friendly and knowledgeable members of the Branch. To Air Commodore (rtd) H. A. Probert, the Head of the Branch, for his unfailing encouragement, to Mr Humphrey Wynn, its Senior Historian, for much enlightening discourse, to Mr J. P. Macdonald (now also retired) who went to much trouble on my behalf, to Mr Denis Bateman, Mr Eric Munday and all their obliging colleagues, I wish now to say how deeply grateful I am, and how much I valued their advice and cooperation. I could not have written this book without their aid. I must also add that this was at all times given without any attempt to influence my thoughts or conclusions beyond correcting palpable errors. This is *not* in any way an "official" history; it expresses my personal view, and the Air Historical Branch gave me invaluable assistance in forming it.

Group Captain (rtd) E. B. Haslam, the ex-Head of the Branch, has given me immense support throughout, and I can scarcely express the debt that I owe to him for his careful reading and re-reading of the manuscript, his wise suggestions and his great fund of information. Others on the Air side to whom I owe sincere thanks are Group Captain (rtd) T. P. Gleave, ex-Battle of Britain pilot and an Official Historian with great knowledge and wisdom, Mr Denis Richards, also an Official Historian, whose words are much quoted on the following pages, and Dr Noble Frankland, not merely for his contribution to the three volumes of the Official History of *The Strategic Air Offensive Against Germany*, but also for the penetrating and illuminating lectures which he delivered to the Royal United Services Institute in the wake of that publication. Robert Wright, biographer of Dowding and Sholto Douglas, is an old friend whose support I also value. Two other old friends to whom I owe a debt are Stewart Rodgers and Laurence

Perkins, through whom I have been able to feel a certain intimacy with the ground-crew of the wartime RAF. Mr Tom Potts, though not an ex-airman but an ex-soldier, has been a mine of information on the technical aspects of the air war, and very kindly supplied me with a number of most useful items from his own library. Other soldiers have also been most helpful: Field-Marshal Lord Carver paid me the great compliment of reading the whole manuscript and making valuable comments on it; Major-General J. M. McNeill CB, CBE (rtd) supplied additional information on the important subject of Air Support; it was my friend Brigadier Shelford Bidwell (rtd) who led me to him in the course of some of our consultations which are by now a regular feature of my composition of military history. To all of these, and to others who, perhaps without realizing it, have helped to illuminate these pages, let me now say "Thank you". Finally, I must also thank Ion Trewin, my editor at Hodder & Stoughton, who has been unfailingly encouraging and supportive, Stephanie Darnill, the meticulous copy-editor, and Mary-Lou Nesbitt, who obtained the illustrations.

JOHN TERRAINE
July 1984

Abbreviations

AA = Anti-Aircraft
AASF = Advanced Air Striking Force
AC2 = Aircraftman Second Class
ADGB = Air Defence of Great Britain
AEAF = Allied Expeditionary Air Force
AGRA = Army Group Royal Artillery
AHB = Air Historical Branch
AI = Airborne Interception
ALO = Air Liaison Officer
AOC = Air Officer Commanding
AOC in C = Air Officer Commanding in Chief
AOP = Air Observation Post
ASC = Air Support Control
ASDIC = Allied Submarine Detection Investigation Committee (1917)
ASOS = Air Staff Operations Survey
ASSU = Army Support Signals Unit
ASV = Air to Surface Vessel
ATC = Air Training Corps
BAFF = British Air Forces in France
BAMS = British and Allied Merchant Shipping Code
B-Dienst (Beobachter Dienst) = Observation Service
BEF = British Expeditionary Force
BGS = Brigadier – General Staff
CAS = Chief of the Air Staff
(ACAS = Assistant Chief of the Air Staff
DCAS = Deputy Chief of the Air Staff
VCAS = Vice-Chief of the Air Staff)
CCOR = Combined Central Operations Room
CH = Chain Home (radar stations)
CHL = Chain Home Low
CIGS = Chief of the Imperial General Staff
CNS = Chief of the Naval Staff
COSSAC = Chief of Staff to the Supreme Allied Commander
CRA = Chief of Royal Artillery
CRO = Civilian Repair Organization

DC(M) = Ministerial Committee on Disarmament
D/F = Direction Finding
DFC = Distinguished Flying Cross
DRC = Defence Requirements Committee (1934)
DWI = Directional Wireless Installation
ETA = Estimated Time of Arrival
FASL = Forward Air Support Link
FAT = Flächenabsuchender torpedo
GCC = Group Control Centre
GC & CS = Government Code & Cypher School
GCI = Ground-Control Interception
GOC-in-C = General Officer Commanding in Chief
GR = General Reconnaissance
GRT = Gross Registered Tons
HF/DF ("Huff-Duff") = High-Frequency Direction Finding
IE = Initial Establishment
IR = Initial Reserve
JG (Jagdgeschwader) = Fighter Group
KG (Kampfgeschwader) = Bomber Group
LR = Long-range
MAP = Ministry of Aircraft Production
MASAF = Mediterranean Allied Strategic Air Force
MEW = Ministry of Economic Warfare
MORU = Mobile Operations Room Unit (Group Control Centre)
MT = Motor Transport
NATAF = North African Tactical Air Force
NCO = Non-commissioned officer
OH = Official History
OKH = German Army General Staff
OKW = Oberkommando der Wehrmacht German Armed Forces General Staff
OP = Observation Post

OTU = Operational Training Unit
POG = Committee on Preventing Oil
from reaching Germany
PRU = Photographic Reconnaissance
Unit
RAAF = Royal Australian Air Force
RAFVR = Royal Air Force Volunteer
Reserve
RASL = Rear Air Support Link
RCAF = Royal Canadian Air Force
RDF = Radio Direction Finding
REME = Royal Electrical &
Mechanical Engineers
RFC = Royal Flying Corps
RNZAF = Royal New Zealand Air
Force
R/T = Radio-telephony
SAAF = South African Air Force
SAS = Special Air Service
SASO = Senior Air Staff Officer

SEAC = South-East Asia Command
SHAEF = Supreme Headquarters
Allied Expeditionary Force
TAF = Tactical Air Force
U-boat *(Unterseeboot)* = submarine
USAAF = United States Army
Air Force
USAMEAF = United States Army
Middle East Air Force
USN = United States Navy
USSTAF = United States Strategic
Air Forces
VGO = Vickers Gas Operated (guns)
VHF = Very High Frequency
VLR = Very Long Range
WA = Western Air
WAAF = Women's Auxiliary Air Force
W/T = Wireless telegraphy
ZOAN = *Zone d'Opérations Aériennes
du Nord*

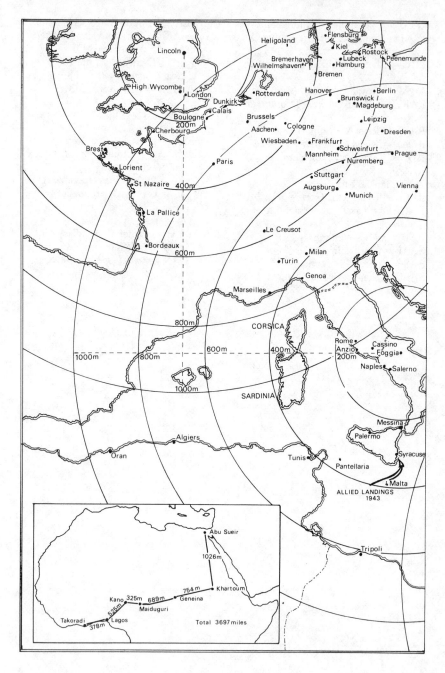

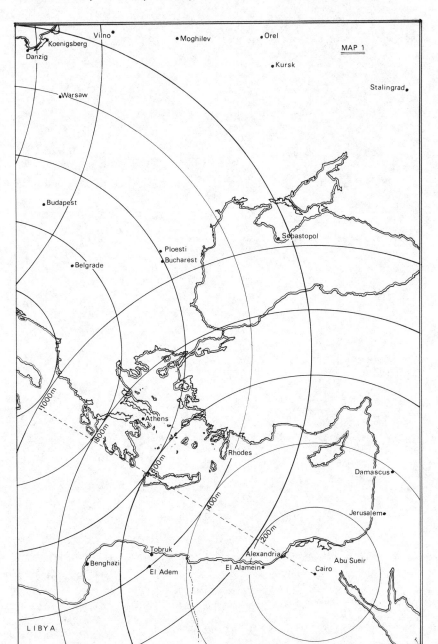

Part I

THE PREPARATION

"Qui desiderat pacem, praeparet bellum"
(Let him who desires peace prepare for war)

Vegetius

1 Beginnings

Marshal of the Royal Air Force Lord Trenchard retired from active RAF duty in 1929. By that time he had left a deeper personal mark on the British armed forces and on British Defence policy than any other senior officer of the First World War, in which he had achieved fame. The Royal Air Force which entered the 1930s, and very shortly had to gird its loins for the coming test of power, was the air force that Trenchard had made – and in so doing added an extra dimension to all Defence considerations. It was he who had ministered to the RAF's very survival in its cradle days, he who found it its first rôles and guided its first expansion, he who established its structure, governed its composition and breathed into it a great gust of his own fiery spirit.

Under Trenchard as Chief of the Air Staff, the RAF confirmed its basic squadron organization (inherited from the Royal Flying Corps); established its personnel functions and named its basic trades; set up its Apprentice School to ensure a flow of skilled technicians without whom a highly technical Service could not have carried out its duties; set up a cadet college to provide a flow of qualified entrants to the permanent force, and a staff college for their further education in it; created a second-line Auxiliary Air Force imitating the Territorial Army; and most important of all, developed the Short Service Commission system which, recognizing that military aviation is basically a young man's job, offered the necessary intake of young aircrew recruits without loading the Service with impossible numbers of candidates for higher rank. As one of its earlier historians said:

> The short service officers formed at any given time the bulk of the officers of the Royal Air Force . . . The Air Force was essentially a short service force. Its flyers were birds of passage.[1]

Like every British institution, the third Service had its curiosities. It liked to emphasize its newness, and not unnaturally lost no time in giving itself new titles, some sensible, others quite amazing. We have lived now for over sixty years with an air force in which the "airmen" are the ones who do not fly; we are used to this fact, but that does not make it less odd. However, we learned long ago that RAF language is not the same as others. A "flight-lieutenant" is not the lieutenant of a flight; he is – or generally was – its commander. A "squadron-leader" might or might not lead – or even command – a squadron; in the large squadrons of the heavy bomber force of the 1940s, that rank was more usually associated with commanding flights.

It is the upper reaches of the hierarchy that provide the chief amazement. "Marshal" is a word normally reserved for the highest military rank of all, but in the RAF marshals abound, in assorted sizes.[2] On May 19, 1804, Napoleon appointed eighteen officers of the French Army to the rank of Marshal of the Empire, fourteen of them on the active list.

"Allow me to congratulate you," said a friend to one of these.

"One of fourteen," was the tart reply.

But at least no one out-ranked him, or his thirteen colleagues; no one stood between them and the Emperor. An "air marshal", on the other hand, is out-ranked by two grades; an "air chief marshal" is not chief at all, because there is still another rank above him. And what possessed King George V to propose *that* title is a mystery, because the only proper "marshal of the Royal Air Force" is the monarch himself, who is also the "admiral of the Royal Navy", whose topmost serving officers are Admirals of the *Fleet*.

Logic was never a strong suit of the RAF which is just as well, because as we shall see in due course logic can be a dangerous tool. The very nature of the third Service led to illogicalities. Some of its officers clearly, from the first, performed functions similar to those of naval and army officers of comparable grades. A great many did not. In the Royal Navy, when it is fulfilling its ultimate function which is fighting at sea, officers and men, from the senior admiral to the most junior rating, share the same iron hulls, which may at any moment turn out to be their coffins. They are all at the "sharp end". This is less true in a modern army, but still substantially true. "Sooner or later," said Field-Marshal Lord Wavell, "the time comes when Private Snodgrass must advance straight to his front." This is the ultimate moment of a soldier's war; and when that time comes Private Snodgrass will (or should) see ahead of him his platoon or company commander leading the way. To lead their men in battle is what army officers are for – not the only thing, but a very important one. The RAF is different, and peculiar.

In the RAF the fighting is done chiefly by officers (together with that proportion of senior non-commissioned officers who are entitled to wear wings on their chests, though not rings on their sleeves). By 1945, according to one authority,[3] in an air force numbering over a million men, 17.5 per cent were aircrew; the function of the remaining 82.5 per cent was to project the aircrew (officers, warrant officers and sergeants) into battle, but rarely to accompany them. This fact clearly constitutes a major difference in officer-, or command-functions between the RAF and the other Services. Furthermore, aircrew had virtually no other function than combat. This meant, among other things, that that section of command for which the force as a whole would have the deepest respect and regard by virtue of its proven combat capacity was not the section normally handling the discipline, administration and welfare of the Service. These important duties (and, of course, a number of others) were in general performed by officers who did not wear wings, or wore wings earned in other wars at other times. Clearly, here was a potential source of discord. We shall return at a more appropriate time to the question of non-commissioned aircrew; at this stage let us simply remark that while, without doubt, this curious separation of officer-functions did cause ill-feeling and anger (exacerbated by the stresses of war: bleak and dismal stations, poor food, draughty huts, long working hours, inadequate transport for leave, etc.) there is no evidence that at any time it seriously impaired the efficiency of the force.

That this should have been so is a matter which has now been taken for granted for nearly four decades. To this author it does not appear as something which ought to be taken for granted. The very nature of RAF recruiting makes it remarkable. The technical character of the Service, referred to above, meant that for most of its ground-crew duties it had to seek and select men of a different type from those suitable for the needs of the Navy or the Army at that time – a type implicit in the very use of the words "trades" and "trades-men".[4] These were men with skills, and implicit in that was a generally higher level of education than one would normally expect to find in the mass of sailors and soldiers. Such men tend to have enquiring – or at any rate, questioning – minds; they do not take readily to discipline; they are impatient of "bull"; they grouse; they answer back. Most of them never enjoyed that "special relationship" between air- and ground-crew operating individual aircraft in the squadrons of the small peace-time Air Force. That happy and valuable intimacy virtually vanished after the Battle of Britain, except for special units performing special tasks. And that was a serious matter, because it was the one and only really close link between the skilled pilots who flew the machines and the skilled mechanics who made it possible for them to do so. Thenceforward ground-crew were commanded by men for whom they could not – except where rare personal qualities were displayed – have the same sort of regard. Many of them were long-service officers with totally different outlooks. Yet the RAF carried on, its efficiency perhaps curtailed in ideal terms, but never seriously impaired in practical terms, and steadily improving. This outcome can only be attributed to the fundamental good temper, good humour, good sense, professional pride and deep unspoken patriotism of the overwhelming majority of the men who put on the light blue uniforms.

2 Disarmers and bombers

The struggle for survival of the Services against the ferocious retrenchment and the political naïveté of the 1920s (supremely expressed in Churchill's "Ten Year Rule") is a story that needs no re-telling here. All three were severely damaged in the process, but the RAF's battle was hardest, because it was the newcomer. Merely keeping the infant Service alive was Trenchard's greatest victory; it was bought at a price. In that post-war atmosphere of miserly folly, cheapness was the word that worked the spells. Trenchard was able to demonstrate that an air force could be (comparatively) cheap, and this was generally a decisive consideration. But cheapness was a trap. Summing up Trenchard's ten years as Chief of the Air Staff (CAS), Sir Maurice Dean has said:

> One of the most serious failures was that over the period 1919–1934 the quality of the fighting equipment of the Royal Air Force steadily deteriorated. The equipment of the Royal Air Force in 1929 when Trenchard departed was not very different from what it had been ten years earlier.[1]

The names of the aircraft which thrilled the crowds at the Hendon displays as the new decade opened have an antediluvian sound to modern ears: the Vickers Virginia night bomber (which continued to appear at Hendon until 1937), or the Handley Page Hyderabad (whose last appearance was in 1931) and its successor the Hinaidi, or the Westland Wapiti, which continued in service in India until 1939; fighters such as the Armstrong Whitworth Siskin IIIA, or the Gloster Gamecock (in which Pilot Officer D. R. S. Bader performed an aerobatic display at Hendon in 1931). In that year the Hawker Harts of Nos. 12 and 33 Squadrons introduced the crowds to the beautiful lines of that sleek and prolific family. But this was still an air force of mainly wooden biplanes, heirs of a memorable past rather than pointers to the stern future which was in store.

As the decade opened, except for the Air Force itself and a growing body of air enthusiasts stirred by the feats of the air pioneers and the breathtaking performances of the Schneider Trophy competitors, the quality of the nation's military aircraft was not a matter of widespread concern. On the contrary, there was an influential body of opinion which would have liked nothing better than to abolish military aircraft altogether. Notable among these in 1931 was Stanley Baldwin, Lord President of the Council, and soon to be Prime Minister for the third time, and Sir Maurice Hankey, Secretary of the Cabinet and of the Committee of Imperial Defence.[2]

For the air force that Trenchard had fashioned there were ironies in store: fulfilments in unintended ways, disappointments in unexpected quarters, justifications for "wrong" or "illegitimate" reasons – reasons, that is, that one may never count upon, such as the enemy's error or folly. It is possible to detect, in the run-up to war, at least three strands, three threads of action affecting the RAF in different and sometimes conflicting ways. The first of these is that national frame of mind during the early 1930s of which the views of Baldwin and Hankey, referred to above, are clear reflections. This was, fundamentally, a nationwide mood of complete revulsion from the First World War, an event which was almost universally misunderstood and constantly misinterpreted. The only thing, it seemed, that could justify such a bloody occurrence, was that it must be a "war to end wars". Hope for the future, accordingly, must depend on the new League of Nations, and on general disarmament. As I have said elsewhere:

> Disarmament – the "general limitation of the armaments of all nations" envisaged in the Treaty of Versailles – became the great quest of the postwar years and nowhere was it pursued more wholeheartedly than in Britain, where dread of military commitment was linked to dread of military expenditure, and both were excused by constant reference to the "futility of war".[3]

It was in accordance with this mood that fifteen nations, including not only Britain, France and the United States, but also Germany, Italy and Japan, signed on August 27, 1928 the Pact of Paris ("Kellogg Pact") by which they condemned recourse to war, "and renounce it as an instrument of national policy in their relations with one another". Forty-five more states later proclaimed their adherence. Coming just ten years after the great holocaust, this seemed to many to be a firm position from which to launch the long-awaited World Disarmament Conference which would set humanity on the right road to everlasting peace and consign the First World War to deserved oblivion. It

7

certainly created a very poor atmosphere for demanding the prompt re-equipment of the Royal Air Force.

The Disarmament Conference assembled in Geneva on February 2, 1932, and its proceedings continued in spasms until November 1934. During that time there was no question of the RAF making significant headway against its serious problems of matériel; these were "the years which the locusts ate".[4] At times the very existence of the Service seemed to be threatened, as British delegates in Geneva put forward proposals which would have spelt its disappearance. It was saved, not by any act of its own Government (though the Prime Minister, Ramsay MacDonald, despite deep pacifist instincts, did have a soft spot for the Air Force), but by the sheer impracticability of the ideas being canvassed in the bland atmosphere of the world capital of internationalism, and by the harsh, discordant warnings from the world outside.

The Conference was intended to be about that general reduction and ultimate elimination of arms foreshadowed in the Treaty of Versailles, but the truth is that by 1932 the "civilized" world was already in the grip of an obsession with aerial warfare and especially aerial bombing. The obsession took two forms: on the one hand, extravagant enthusiasm as one after another the courageous men and women aviators set up and broke their records in the third dimension, and as the public cheered spectacular aerobatics and brilliant formation flying; on the other, panic, as prognosticators (factual and fictional) painted the scenes of future war. In Britain, the only country to have endured air attack on a considerable scale for any length of time, the subject discovered very raw nerve-ends, and the Air Staff did nothing to soothe them. In consequence, by 1932, Disarmament had come to mean chiefly air disarmament, and above all the abolition of bombing.

Since this obsession was to play a highly significant part in British Defence policy and in Royal Air Force thinking for a crucial decade, we need to inspect it at least briefly. Bombing from the air was first essayed by the Italians against the Turks in Tripoli, 1911–12. Doubtless it was disconcerting, for such Turkish soldiers as experienced it, to have things that exploded dropped upon them from aeroplanes, but the consensus of informed opinion was that as a means of conducting war the exercise was futile.[5] This assessment was confirmed by the Balkan Wars which immediately followed the Italian victory; a Bulgarian aeroplane dropped thirty bombs on Adrianople in one day – killing or injuring a total of six people. On August 31, 1914, a *Taube* aeroplane dropped two bombs on Paris, without effect. In December it was Britain's turn: on the 21st a German plane appeared off Dover and dropped a bomb presumably aimed at the harbour, but it fell into the sea. On the 24th another arrived, and this time succeeded in hitting English soil, but it did no harm. These were the warning examples, deceptively trivial.

The first strategic air offensive in history began on January 19, 1915: that evening two Zeppelin airships of the German Navy crossed the Norfolk coast and dropped bombs ("explosive devices" would be a better description) wherever they saw clusters of lights. They killed two men and two women and injured 16 people, 15 of them civilians. They did £7,740-worth of damage. Zeppelins returned to England nineteen times in 1915; the first raid on London was on the night of May 31, when seven people were killed and 35 injured (33 civilians). They came back in every year of the war, a total of 52 raids; in all they killed 556 people (58 military) and injured 1,357 (121 military). It was not, materially, a very impressive performance; the Zeppelin, in fact, was not a satisfactory weapon for a strategic offensive. Yet they did have certain assets, above all the ability to strike deep inland, at the Midland and Northern counties and as far across as Lancashire and Cheshire. This, and the alarming impression created by their monstrous size and surprising apparent invulnerability, at once established that aspect of air attack later summed up by Trenchard in the words: "The moral effect of bombing stands to the material in a proportion of 20 to 1."[6] The lesson was not forgotten.

Even more effective, both morally and materially, was the second strategic air offensive. This opened on May 25, 1917, when 21 Gotha bombers appeared over Folkestone, and in the space of ten minutes killed 95 people (18 military) and injured 192 (98 military). The Gotha, though it could not reach as far as a Zeppelin, was a much more powerful and accurate weapon; it carried a 500-kilogram bomb-load which could be placed with reasonable precision thanks to a Goerz bomb-sight, "the best German instrument of its type produced during the war".[7] A rearward-firing machine gun in the underside of the fuselage covering the notorious "blind spot" made it a difficult aircraft to shoot down. Its very first attack was a serious enough matter, but far worse was to come. On June 13, 14 Gothas penetrated to the centre of London in the middle of the day. Their bombs killed 162 people and injured 432, all but 11 of these casualties being civilians, including 46 children in one infant class in a Poplar school. Not one Gotha was lost. Naturally the alarm and indignation in Britain were very great, and soon reinforced when another attack on London on July 7 by 22 Gothas killed 57 and injured 193, all but five being civilians. In contrast with the broad picture of the Second World War,

9

a considerable degree of demoralization and hysteria possessed the population of London and the South-Eastern counties; production was affected; the Government, deeply disturbed, demanded the return of fighter squadrons from the Western Front. The Chief of the Imperial General Staff, Sir William Robertson, attending a Cabinet meeting on July 9, reported that "much excitement was shown. One would have thought that the world was coming to an end."[8] So for the first time we see an air offensive directly affecting the strategy of a war; the results were, as may be supposed, far-reaching – not least of them the creation of the Royal Air Force itself.

An important feature of twentieth-century war has been the manner in which every dramatic advance of technology has been quickly overtaken by some further development, itself soon to suffer the same fate. Nowhere is this more evident than in air warfare. The Zeppelins alerted Britain to the need for air defence; the early Gotha raids came as a surprise, but the defences soon rallied, and at the end of August 1917 the Germans abandoned daylight attacks as they did in November 1940. Their night attacks continued until May 1918; the twin-engined Gothas with their three-man crews were augmented by a small number of the even more formidable four-engined R (Riesen)-type "Giants" with a crew of seven, including a wireless-operator whose outgoing and incoming signals provided a novel navigational aid. In all, the German bombers made 27 raids on Britain between May 1917 and May 1918. During that time they killed 836 people (233 military) and injured 1,994 (381 military). All told, including the trifling losses caused by hit-and-run forays by single-engined aircraft, Zeppelins and bombers between them killed 1,413 people (1,117 civilians) and injured 3,407 (2,886 civilians).[9] The civilian total in four years of war (4,003) seems amazingly low by comparison with the Second World War: 60,595 civilian killed out of a total of 146,777 casualties. Indeed, the number of citizen casualties at home between January 1915 and November 1918 was less than those sometimes suffered by single divisions of the citizen army on the Western Front in *one day*. But the result was out of all proportion to the statistics.

The gunfire of the First World War had not long died away when Britain awoke to her first post-war air scare. In March 1922 *The Times* revealed to its startled readers what the Air Ministry had known for some time: that the French *Armée de l'Air* possessed a striking force of 300 bombers and 300 fighters, to which the RAF, virtually wrecked by the imbecile post-1918 disarming policies, could oppose only three squadrons, or less than 40 aircraft. Since relations between the wartime allies were by now very frigid, this caused a great shock – as may be supposed. Out of that shock was born the decision, in 1923, to create a Home Defence Air Force of 52 squadrons "with as little delay as possible". The good intention, however, was in turn nearly wrecked by the "Geddes Axe" and the paralysis of the "Ten Year Rule". But it is not the story of the RAF's first expansions that concerns us here; it is the bomber obsession.

In 1925 an inter-Service committee was set up to consider air-raid precautions; still under the influence of the 1922 scare and the supposed French threat, the committee asked the Air Ministry for an estimate of the probable effects of an attack by the *Armée de l'Air*. The Air Staff selected the statistics of the second German air offensive in 1917–18 as its basis of calculation. It did not regard the total figures for 1915–18, nor did it consider the figures for Trenchard's own strategic offensive against Germany in 1918. His "Independent Force" in that year had carried out 242 raids on Germany in the space of six months, causing the overwhelming majority of German civilian casualties by air attack during the war: 746 killed and 1,843 injured. The Air Staff, concentrating on the Gotha raids, and translating these into the expanded French offensive capacity, pronounced that casualties in London would be at the rate of 1,700 killed and 3,300 injured in the first twenty-four hours, 1,275 killed and 2,475 injured in the second twenty-four hours, and 850 killed and 1,650 injured in every subsequent twenty-four hours. This meant, in other words, a loss of more than twice the whole First World War total of casualties *in only three days*. Nor was that all; the Air Staff also stated:

> It is well known that the moral effect of Air attack is out of all proportion greater than the material results achieved. While, therefore, serious material damage may be expected from bomb attack, the most probable cause of chaos in the community will be the *moral* collapse of the personnel employed in the working of the vital public services, such as transport, lighting, water and food distribution.[10]

And for good measure the Air Staff added that no defence was possible against this form of attack. The War Office demurred; it challenged the estimate of casualties and pointed out that in 1917–18 only half the German aircraft sent out in daylight had reached London, and also that improved defences had taken a toll of 22 per cent of the attackers. But the Air Staff was adamant.

It is at this point that we may detect the coming together of two of the three strands of RAF history referred to above. First, revulsion from the First World War and all reminders of it, belief in universal

11

disarmament, and in the League of Nations as the instrument of international security, combined to produce an atmosphere hostile to all the Services, but especially dangerous to the new one, which remained for several years under "suspended sentence of death".[11] The second strand was the Air Force's own contribution to the national malaise, beginning with this firm prognostication in 1925; this was the start of that tenacious theory of the "knock-out blow" from the air which was to dominate Air Staff thinking and gravely influence Government decisions during the 1930s. By the time the World Disarmament Conference opened in February 1932, the dread of air bombardment had received certain powerful supports.

As far back as 1913 H. G. Wells had predicted atomic warfare, and had given the language the name, "atomic bomb".[12] Revolution was the chief bogey of the 1920s, and the flow of prophecies of future wars in the Wellsian manner did not begin until 1931. In that year appeared a novel entitled *The Gas War of 1940* by *"Miles"* (S. Southwold); it described to a ready public the destruction of London by air attack:

> And then, in a moment, the lights of London vanished, as if blotted out by a gigantic extinguisher. And in the dark streets the burned and wounded, bewildered and panic-stricken, fought and struggled like beasts, scrambling over the dead and dying alike, until they fell and were in turn trodden underfoot by the ever-increasing multitude about them . . . In a dozen parts of London that night people died in their homes with the familiar walls crashing about them in flames; thousands rushed into the streets to be met by blasts of flame and explosion and were blown to rags . . .[13]

To this electrifying material, reality offered instant confirmation. Just five days before the Disarmament Conference opened, fighting broke out between Japan and China in Shanghai, and rapidly escalated:

> A world not yet entirely hardened to the spectacle of repeated air attacks on densely populated towns was shocked by the vigorous bombing, by Japanese naval airplanes, of Chinese positions in the Chapei district of Shanghai.[14]

The news photographs and film, and the accounts by horrified witnesses, of what the Japanese bombers were doing appeared as precisely confirmatory footnotes to the texts of the novelists. Nor did "experts" offer any comfort: "There seems to have been little to distinguish between professional analysis of air attack in a future war and its portrayal in contemporary science fiction."[15]

12

Stanley Baldwin was among those who were deeply shocked by the Japanese action; "Shanghai is a nightmare," he said. It was a nightmare which did not fade. As the year went by, and the Disarmament Conference made no progress, he and those who shared his views became more and more despondent. It was on November 10, in the course of a House of Commons debate on Disarmament, that Baldwin made one of his most famous pronouncements – exercising, in Sir Maurice Dean's words, his "unhappy knack of coining memorable phrases remembered long after and often out of context".[16]

I think it is well also for the man in the street to realise that there is no power on earth that can prevent him from being bombed. Whatever people may tell him, the bomber will always get through. The only defence is offence, which means you have to kill more women and children more quickly than the enemy if you want to save yourselves.[17]

This was, of course, official Air Staff doctrine, the message brought down by Trenchard from the clouds and engraved on every loyal Air Force officer's very soul. The phrase "the bomber will always get through" was memorable indeed; it is just possible that it may not have been Baldwin's own – Hankey records that "I sketched out the lines of his speech";[18] but then, Baldwin was an accomplished politician, which is to say an accomplished phrase-maker. Whatever its origin, as Stephen Roskill says, the phrase as uttered by Baldwin "propagated the psychology of fear very widely among his countrymen [and] contributed to the British public's initial acclamation of the policy of 'appeasement' of the dictators".[19]

So we see, at this stage, the airmen, the alarmists and the disarmers, if not in agreement, all pulling in the same direction – a formidable crew. The British Government continued to press at Geneva for the abolition of military and naval air forces, despite the reluctance and dismay of the unfortunate Secretary of State for Air, Lord Londonderry, who had the distasteful task of putting forward arguments which in his heart he did not believe. "I feel most out of place discussing these fatuous doctrines every day," he wrote to his wife.[20] And well he might; the idea was fatuous indeed. It foundered, as might have been foreseen, on the rock of civil aviation. This obstacle had been clearly discerned as far back as 1921, when one of the British Government's advisers at the Washington Conference on Limitations of Armaments had flatly stated:

Speaking broadly, all aircraft will be of some military value no matter what restrictions may be placed upon their character.[21]

This meant, quite simply, that as long as there were aeroplanes there would be military air forces. The abolition of civil aviation being unthinkable, the only possible solution of the problem was control by an international air force under the auspices of the League (to which neither the United States of America nor the Soviet Union belonged). It is wholly unsurprising that the World Conference of 1932–34 proved unable to find a formula for such a thing.

So the Disarmament Conference foundered in futility; it went into liquidation in November 1934. The locust years had done their work. As J. M. Spaight wrote:

> The waste of time was more harmful to us than to other nations. We halted our re-arming. We should probably not have done so if there had been no Conference; we should have gone ahead with the fifty-two squadron scheme [NB of 1923!]. It is true that financial stringency was responsible also for our halting, but undoubtedly the desire not to prejudice the discussions at Geneva was a contributing factor. The halt would not have mattered if other nations had halted too; but they did not.[22]

Worst of all, while the men of high intent were debating at Geneva, a new and deeply disturbing element had come upon the European scene: in January 1933 Adolf Hitler became Chancellor of Germany. In October Hitler took Germany out of both the Disarmament Conference and the League of Nations. In that year and the next it became clear that Germany was rearming, in defiance of the Treaty of Versailles.

Britain awoke reluctantly to a familiar situation, the more distasteful by reason of its very familiarity. The last thing that British public opinion wished to be reminded of in the 1930s was the decade before the First World War. Yet it was precisely then that the realization had dawned that German naval armaments could only be directed against British security. Liberal Britain had had to adjust itself to understand that

> it was no use trying to turn Germany from her course by abstaining from counter measures. Reluctance on our part to build ships was attributed in Germany to want of national spirit, and as another proof that the virile race should advance to replace the effete over-civilized and pacifist society which was no longer capable of sustaining its great place in the world's affairs.[23]

On Trafalgar Day, 1904, however, the Royal Navy had found its response to the challenge:

> There now commenced an epoch of prodigious activity ... Under the stimulus of a master mind the whole machine was overhauled from top to bottom.[24]

Admiral Sir John Fisher became First Sea Lord on October 21, 1904, and at once set about converting an imposing Victorian navy into a great modern instrument of war. The half-decade 1934–39 was certainly no "epoch of prodigious activity" – and there was no Fisher, nor even another Trenchard to inspire swift and drastic reform. Yet all was not lost; fortunately, a silent, almost unseen transformation of the Royal Air Force was in hand.

3 A modern Air Force

We now encounter the third strand of RAF development. It is at such variance with the two already discussed that we seem to be dealing with a different race of men, existing even on a different planet. Their work was unseen and unrecognized outside a very limited circle within their own Service and its closest associates; outwardly, it expressed itself strikingly enough in the transformation of the air force of low- to medium-performance partly wooden biplanes of 1934 into the air force of medium- to high-performance all-metal monoplanes of 1939[1] – and that was all. Unknown to the public, to parliamentarians and largely to the Government itself, throughout the decline of national morale leading up to the Disarmament Conference, and throughout those "locust years", a small number of dedicated men, acting in apparent oblivion of all those sterile proceedings, were preparing the aircraft and the air force that would be required for modern war.

Most of the significant achievement in this direction was set in motion during the tenure of office as Chief of the Air Staff of Marshal of the Royal Air Force Sir Edward Ellington, 1933–37. Ellington is an officer who has received, if not a "bad press", at any rate one sufficiently lukewarm to make his name now virtually unknown. He flickers fitfully through the historiography of the period. Like many dedicated professionals, he was retiring and self-conscious when faced with the ordeal of public utterance, and this made him "less likely to impress the Cabinet or fellow Chiefs of Staff in a conference".[2] Lieutenant-General Sir Henry Pownall, who was at that time an

Assistant Secretary to the Committee of Imperial Defence, and Secretary to the Defence Requirements Committee,[3] described him in his Diary as "extremely weak in discussion and his utterances most confused".[4] He was, said Pownall a few days later, "a cheerless cove. In eleven meetings I have never once seen him smile nor heard him make a cheerful remark to anyone. And the use of the word 'Good morning' is unfamiliar. He and Londonderry must be a pretty bad half section."[5] Later still Pownall asserted that Ellington's subordinates "have no confidence in their own man and think he gets done down by the other two [Chiefs of Staff]. That is an exaggeration, but it is a fact that he is a poor representative of their own case."[6] Pownall connected this with "the latent 'inferiority complex' of the RAF", which may or may not have had something to do with Ellington, but certainly has to be taken into account in considering various inter-Service transactions, both before and during the war. Ellington was clearly a difficult person to understand – all inarticulate people are; and in the Services there is generally no lack of them. Haig was one, Robertson was one, Allenby was one, Wavell was one – and Trenchard was one. "I can't write what I mean, I can't say what I mean, but I expect you to know what I mean," Trenchard told his Personal Assistant, Maurice Baring, in the early days of their association.[7] Ellington had no Maurice Baring, so that even such normally acute an observer as Sir Maurice Dean could patronizingly say that "despite splendid qualities [he] knew little about aviation as it existed world-wide in the mid-Thirties"[8] – which is palpably untrue.

It is instructive, in the light of the above, simply to look at the list of major advances made in RAF (and national) preparedness for war while Ellington was Chief of Air Staff. The list (and I do not pretend that it is complete) reads as follows:

1934 Air Ministry Specification F.5/34, from which came the Hawker Hurricane and the Supermarine Spitfire
First steps towards the development of the RAF "Typex" Cipher Machine
The first of the eight expansion schemes by which the RAF prepared itself for war

1935 Establishment of a Committee for the Scientific Survey of Air Defence, under the chairmanship of Sir Henry Tizard
Construction of new airfields and redeployment on the East Coast
Two further expansion schemes

16

1936 Air Ministry Specification B.12/36, from which came the Short Stirling four-engined bomber, and P.13/36, from which came the Handley Page Halifax and the Avro Manchester, father of the Lancaster
Setting up of shadow factories to expand production
A revolution of RAF purchasing methods by "ordering off the drawing-board"
Placing of orders in the United States of America
Creation of the Command system with which the RAF fought the Second World War

1937 Creation of the Royal Air Force Volunteer Reserve

It is not being argued here that all these matters were the inspirations of Sir Edward Ellington. The placing of orders in the United States, for instance, is very much to the credit of Lord Swinton, Secretary of State for Air, 1935–38; other names, too, will be noted as we look more closely at each item. Yet Ellington presided over the whole, and the whole is impressive. He was not a personal originator, as Lord Fisher was, putting his immense drive behind his brain-children, the dreadnought battleships and battle-cruisers, and pushing forward the development of submarines. Ellington did not galvanize his Service with slogans such as Fisher's "Three R's" – "Ruthless, Relentless and Remorseless"; but then, he did not split it from top to bottom with feuds, either. For what he did, for what he permitted, for what he gave his blessing to, his country should be grateful.

Major breakthroughs in technology are rarely attributable to single individuals; in the evolution of a new type of aircraft many streams of thought must come together. The British fighter breakthrough of 1934, for example, could not have happened without some hard and gifted thinking in the firm of Rolls-Royce, which produced the PV-12 engine, later known as the Merlin, just at the right time (1933). Four names must here represent the teamwork which went into the design side: two civilians, Mr Reginald Mitchell, chief designer at Supermarine, and Mr (later Sir) Sydney Camm, chief engineer at Hawkers; two RAF officers, Wing Commander A. T. Williams and Squadron-Leader (later Air Marshal Sir) R. S. Sorley. The interplay between the Air Ministry, pronouncing the requirements of the Service, and the aircraft industry which had to supply them, was flexible and therefore fruitful. Ideas emerged "organically", and it is not rewarding to search for absolute points of origin; designers never "down tools", and private initiative counted for much; but to result in effective

17

production, an experiment had at some stage to be expressed in terms of an Air Ministry Specification. Specification F.5/34, issued in November 1934, was the product of such an interplay.

While the Disarmament Conference was giving its mind to the abolition of air warfare, some very deep thought was being given elsewhere to the nature of the beast. To appreciate what this was, it is helpful to look back. The last, and most up-to-date, fighter delivered to the RAF in the First World War (only eight weeks before the Armistice) was the Sopwith Snipe, which continued in service until 1927. The Snipe was a snub-nosed, radial-engined biplane whose maximum speed was 121 mph, whose initial rate of climb was 1,500 feet per minute, service ceiling 19,500 feet and range 310 miles. In its brief active-service life it showed itself to be an excellent performer. Less than fifteen years after the advent of the Snipe, and only five years after its "burial", air tacticians had to take into account the very different performances of modern aircraft displayed in the Schneider Trophy flights (Supermarine won the 1931 Trophy on September 13 with a course speed of 340 mph; on the same day Flight-Lieutenant Stainforth set up a world speed record of 379 mph, improved to 407.5 mph on the 29th). The tacticians concluded that at such speeds a fighter would only have one chance to destroy its prey – the first attack – and that that chance would last precisely two seconds. Ballistics experts showed that a battery of eight machine guns, firing 1,000 rounds a minute each, would be needed to destroy a bomber in two seconds. Senior officers, brought up on a standard of two synchronized forward-firing Vickers guns, raised their eyebrows; Williams and Sorley, however, took up the cause of the eight-gun fighter, and when Williams, "its original and very ardent champion",[9] died in 1934 it was Sorley who, more than anyone else, was responsible for its adoption by the RAF.

It was the confluence of this tactical need, the work already being carried out by Camm and Mitchell, the arrival of the Merlin engine, and the Browning machine gun, that bore fruit in Specification F.5/34 (revised later to F.36/34 and F.37/34). The American Browning was "a first-class weapon"[10] with a rate of fire of 1,260 rounds a minute. A perfect example of intimate collaboration between airman and designer was Sorley's test showing that in order to achieve a lethal density of bullets the Brownings would have to use their maximum rate of fire. This meant that they would have to be clear of the propeller, which in turn meant that the wings would require special strength and rigidity – which Camm and Mitchell promptly undertook to provide. So the Specification went forward, and bore fruit in May

1935 in mock-ups of aircraft by both designers which Sorley inspected; he reported:

> Both aircraft look to be excellent and in the hands of Mitchell and Camm I suggest that they are likely to be successes. I say this because I foresee in those two aircraft the equipment we should aim at obtaining for new squadrons and re-equipping . . .[11]

The Air Ministry accepted the Squadron-Leader's judgment. His further proposal, that jigs and tools should be ordered at once, before the prototypes had even been completed and tested, was rather too much for Ellington to approve all at once. He was already halfway through a revolution.

Hawkers were the first to produce results: the Hurricane made its first flight on November 6, 1935, and was "a winner from the start".[12] It entered service with No. 111 Squadron at Northolt in December 1937; this was the Mark I, whose maximum speed was 316 mph, initial rate of climb 2,520 feet per minute, service ceiling 33,200 feet and range 460 miles (or 970 with auxiliary tanks). In February 1938 a Hurricane startled and cheered the nation with an evening flight from Edinburgh to Northolt at an average speed of 408 mph. Admittedly, this was at optimum height and with benefit of a strong tail wind; but it revealed a different world from that of the Sopwith Snipe. Like most really good designs, the Hurricane lent itself to various improvements which took it from Mark I to Mark XIIA; in all, 12,780 were built in Britain, and another 1,451 in Canada. It was one of the world's great fighters.

Even greater, though a little slower in coming, was Supermarine's Spitfire, Mitchell's masterpiece. It made its maiden flight on March 5, 1936; Owen Thetford says:

> The Spitfire handled like a thoroughbred from the start, and its performance staggered everybody who saw it demonstrated.[13]

Group Captain Sir Douglas Bader flew both Hurricanes and Spitfires; he had great admiration for the former, but of the latter he said:

> . . . here was the aeroplane *par excellence* . . . in fact, the aeroplane of one's dreams.[14]

For a time, the Spitfire was only a dream; a considerable interval separated the maiden flight of the prototype in 1936 from production of the Mark I in 1937, and a further interval followed before the RAF

19

(No. 19 Squadron) received its first machines. The Spitfire Mark I had a maximum speed of 355 mph at 19,000 feet; its initial rate of climb was 2,530 feet per minute, its service ceiling 34,000 feet and its range 395 miles. In 1934 the splendid Rolls-Royce Merlin engine was replaced by the even more powerful Rolls-Royce Griffon. Thanks to this, the Spitfire could claim to be the only Allied fighter to remain in continuous production throughout the Second World War. It went from Mark I to Mark XIX, and in all (excluding the Fleet Air Arm's Seafires) 20,351 were built for the RAF. During its life the Spitfire's power increased 100 per cent, its maximum speed by 35 per cent and its rate of climb by 80 per cent. It remained one of the world's fastest piston-engined aircraft, with a final maximum speed of 454 mph. Reginald Mitchell died of tuberculosis in March 1937; he did not even live to see the first production Spitfire in the air, let alone the triumphs that were to come. It does seem only reasonable to remember him as he has been commemorated, "the first of the Few".

To have two fine fighter aircraft designed and put into production was one thing; to ensure that they would be an effective weapon in war was something else – something requiring the accomplishment of the second half of the revolution in thinking about air warfare that was quietly taking place. It must be remembered that from its earliest days the RAF had conceived itself to be an offensive instrument. This was a legacy from the Royal Flying Corps under Trenchard, who enunciated his doctrine with great clarity (thanks to Baring) in September 1916:

> The aeroplane is not a defence against the aeroplane. But the opinion of those most competent to judge is that the aeroplane, as a weapon of attack, cannot be too highly estimated.[15]

Trenchard had carried this doctrine over into peace, and it had been the core of RAF strategic thinking throughout the entire period. Only an offensive force, it was insisted, could win the next war. Consequently, by a considerable number of influential officers, every fighter squadron was grudged as a diminution of the decisive effort. The scare of 1923 forced some modification of this extreme view, but Trenchard fought like a lion for the pure doctrine:

> Fighter defence must . . . be kept to the smallest possible number. It was, in the view of the Chief of the Air Staff, in a sense only a concession to the weakness of the civilians, who would demand protection and cause the Cabinet and even the Secretary of State for Air to do so likewise. These demands, he insisted, must be resisted as far as possible.[16]

A natural outcome of this belief was a neglect of air defence. Nowhere was the dogma that "the bomber will always get through" supported more staunchly than in the RAF, which was determined that its own bombers *would* always get through. It required something in the nature of a miracle to bend RAF thinking to the notion that bombers must *not* get through, and could be prevented from doing so.

The miracle was forthcoming. Its origin lay in the lamentable condition to which the offensive doctrine had reduced air defence by 1934. A personal investigation of this question so impressed and alarmed A. P. Rowe of the Directorate of Scientific Research in the Air Ministry that he informed his Director, H. E. Wimperis, that unless science could come effectively to the rescue, any war in the next ten years was bound to be lost. Wimperis was in turn sufficiently impressed to propose to the Secretary of State, Lord Londonderry, that a scientific committee should be formed within the Air Ministry to survey air defence. He further suggested that the chairman of this committee should be H. T. Tizard, Chairman of the Aeronautical Research Committee and once a Royal Flying Corps pilot. The committee was duly formed, at the end of 1934, consisting of Professor P. M. S. Blackett, a Nobel Laureate who was then Professor of Physics at Manchester University, Dr A. V. Hill, another Nobel Laureate from University College, London, who had First World War experience of defence research, and Wimperis, with Tizard as chairman and Rowe as secretary. Its first meeting was on January 28, 1935. It was a moment of great significance in British military history; it marked, as Blackett later said, "the recognition that scientifically-trained research workers had a vital part to play not only (as of course was traditional) in the weapons and gadgets of war but also in the actual study of operations."[17] If, in the long term, this invocation of science made mankind a poorer insurance risk, in the short term it transformed the prospects of British survival.

Tizard very properly took the view that nothing, however improbable, should be ignored if there was the slightest chance of it being of use to repel an enemy air attack. Within every grotesque proposal there may lurk the germ of something practical. Marshal of the Royal Air Force Sir Arthur Harris recalls how during the First World War an imaginative man hawked round a method of freezing clouds in order to mount anti-aircraft guns on them.[18] In the Second World War a serious scientist devised a method of freezing stretches of sea to make floating airstrips; under the code-name "Habbakuk", this made powerful appeal to no less a person than Lord Mountbatten, who demonstrated it to the Combined (British and American) Chiefs of Staff at the Quebec Conference in 1943, causing some pain and considerable fright, as he would relate with unconcealed pleasure.[19] In the event, the idea, whose purpose was to facilitate air cover for the Allied assault on north-west Europe, was never put to practical test because it was ultimately not needed. In 1935 one of the first matters to come before Tizard's committee was that hardy perennial, the "death ray". One of these deadly devices was demonstrated to Field-Marshal Lord Haig in 1916; it was directed at two rabbits, which promptly expired. It later turned out that for the "ray" to be fully efficacious the victims had to be poisoned first. Science fiction, however, was very enthusiastic about death rays, and Tizard was too painstaking a researcher simply to brush the subject aside.

It was as well that he did not. Instead, Tizard decided to consult R. A. Watson-Watt, who was Superintendent of the Radio Department of the National Physical Laboratory. The result, as Denis Richards has said, was "nothing less than a revolution in the science of air defence".[20] Watson-Watt, with the aid of one of his staff, A. F. Wilkins, was able to dismiss the "death ray" once and for all; but he did not leave it at that. He pointed out that even if a "death ray" could be devised it would be useless unless its target could be accurately located. And in the matter of locating targets in the air, he thought he could be of some help. He took his clue from a Post Office Report of June 1932, in which it was mentioned that aircraft interfered with radio signals and re-radiated them; he considered the possibility of transmitting a radio pulse which would be reflected back by aircraft as a signal to the ground. Further calculations (by Wilkins) enabled Watson-Watt to submit to the Air Ministry on February 12, 1935 an historic document, "Detection and Location of Aircraft by Radio Methods". Thus was born "RDF" (Radio Direction Finding), the Air Force name for what the Press and the public, when they were permitted to know, called "radar".

To Wimperis and Rowe, whose alarm about air defence had prompted all this very brisk activity, Watson-Watt's paper suggested that very breakthrough by science that they knew to be urgently needed. Wimperis, accompanied by the Air Member for Research and Development, Air Vice-Marshal H. C. T. Dowding, met Watson-Watt, and asked if he could provide a demonstration of his proposed system. The story has been often enough and well enough told, of the caravan in the field near Weedon, the little group of men – Watson-Watt, Wilkins, A. P. Rowe and their driver, Mr Dyer – staring at a screen like that of a television set, with a bright green spot in the middle of it, connected to a radio receiver, the heavy Heyford bomber flying a straight course up and down a beam transmitted from the nearby BBC short-wave station at Daventry, the green spot elongating as the aircraft came nearer, contracting as it went away. The range of this primitive piece of locating equipment was only eight miles; it didn't matter. What it had shown was that Watson-Watt's system would work; there was a long way still to go – much more research, ever-improving equipment to be obtained, staff to be trained, masts and buildings to be erected, all with mounting urgency against the background of the increasingly ominous international scene, and all under a cloak of deepest secrecy. But between them, Watson-Watt's RDF and the eight-gun fighters meant that the revolution was a fact. It did not express itself in sudden transformations, as when the launching of Fisher's *Dreadnought* on February 10, 1906 made every existing battleship obsolete. The revolution over which Sir Edward Ellington presided advanced at a more measured pace;[21] it did not spell the immediate obsolescence of every existing bomber – that would have come about quite quickly in the normal progress of aviation technology; but as its implications sank in, they indicated the obsolescence of the RAF's whole existing theory of war.[22]

We are already well out of chronological sequence in the story of the RAF's preparation for war, and it is best to continue so, for there is yet another element in the great transformation to be considered: that which gave it, as it were, its frame. In 1935–36 the whole structure of the Royal Air Force began to take on a new look; there were important changes inside the Air Ministry – in 1935 what had been a Directorate of Supply and Research was divided for greater convenience into Research and Development (Dowding) and Supply Organization (Air Marshal Sir Cyril Newall). In May 1936 the organization for operations was completely changed; a "Training Command" was set up, under Air Marshal Sir Charles Burnett, followed on July 14 by a "Bomber Command" (Air Chief Marshal Sir John Steel), a "Coastal Command" (Air Chief Marshal Sir Arthur Longmore) and a "Fighter Command" (Air Chief Marshal Sir Hugh Dowding). All these officers were directly responsible to the Air Council through the CAS. This, with various additions, was the Command system with which the RAF fought the Second World War, the system which made possible the Battle of Britain. It was a clear advance upon the clumsy existing organization: a Commander-in-Chief of "Air Defence" with both fighters and bombers under him, standing in an indeterminate relationship to the Chief of the Air Staff.[23] What might be workable in a very small air force headed by a very large man was no longer practicable in an expanding force feeling its way into an uncertain but ever-more-complex future.

The new system of grouping by functions, however, does have its critics, most notably the Official Historians, Sir Charles Webster and Dr Noble Frankland, who say:

> It made still wider the gulf between attack and defence. The experience of one Command was not so easily transferred to another. Combined operations were made more difficult. Joint tactical planning was neglected.[24]

Sir Maurice Dean comments that while Fighter Command enjoyed the freedom to press ahead with sophisticated defence techniques, Bomber Command

> did not get the advantages they could have got from radar and lacking the training opportunities of a unified command they did not learn as quickly as they should have done how vulnerable bombers would prove to be in daylight against modern fighters.[25]

Certainly, as we shall see, some "great awakenings" were in store very shortly indeed after the outbreak of war. It is nevertheless, I think, fair comment that the criticisms, while perfectly correct, are counsels of perfection in the context of the expansion which is our next topic. And it is not easy to see what sort of alternative might have been preferred. The German system of self-contained *"Luftflotte"*, while very satisfactory for an air force conducting aggressive offensives in close collaboration with ground forces, was far less effective in defence – and, indeed, the German Air Force moved steadily towards functionalism as the war went on. Hindsight suggests that Fighter Command should have been seen from the first to be exceptional; except for a varying number of transport planes (convenient, but not absolutely essential) Fighter Command needed nothing but fighters. Both the others needed some variety – including, of course, fighters, for reconnaissance or long-range bomber escort. Hindsight is a wonderful thing, but it has to be patient with men in the midst of a profound revolution.

4 Expansion

We have seen (p. 10) that the first post-war expansion of the RAF was prompted by the French scare of 1923 – a scheme to form a

Metropolitan Air Force of 52 squadrons.[1] By the opening of the Disarmament Conference in 1932, 42 squadrons had been formed; nothing more was done between 1932 and 1934, so that when further expansion was decided upon in that year the original scheme was still incomplete. Yet in the view of the Air Staff the 1923 plan was "the foundation upon which the expansion of 1934–39 was built".[2] As the new schemes struggled to make progress in an uncongenial climate, the Air Staff remarked with understandable sourness:

> It may be said that the roots of our difficulties lie in the slowing down and then the stoppage of the 52-Squadron scheme. Under normal conditions it is impracticable to lay down a carefully thought out programme of development, slow it up, stop it for a year or two, and then resume not only at a rate calculated to overtake the delay but also to deal with a further expansion superimposed upon the original scheme.[3]

In all, eight expansion schemes between 1934 and 1939 have survived as identifiable stages of British air rearmament; they are lettered "A" to "M", the missing letters representing those which never achieved formal approval. They were all, in the strictest sense, failures. All had a double purpose: to enable Britain to overtake the lead in air power which Germany had stolen during the "locust years", and to deter Germany from policies which would embroil her with Britain by demonstrating "our ability to build 'keel for keel'" – a phrase with a very Fisherite ring.[4] There was no doubt in the collective mind of the Air Staff that this rearmament was directed against Germany and Germany alone; and, of course, it failed either to overtake the German lead or to deter her from the aggressive policies which brought war in September 1939. However, the schemes did provide Britain with an air force which was fit (just) to go to war in 1939, and fit (by a narrow margin) to win a decisive victory in 1940.

The first four schemes, "A", "C", "F" and "H", were all launched during Ellington's term of office as CAS. Scheme "H" (January 1937) was withdrawn and requires no further consideration; the others are interesting. Scheme "A" was promulgated in July 1934, prompted by a very sombre Annual Report by the Chiefs of Staff in October 1933, as the first year of Hitler's Chancellorship drew to an end. In November the Government set up yet another of the innumerable committees which served chiefly to brake and limit rearmament; this was the Defence Requirements Committee, chaired by Sir Maurice Hankey, and consisting of Sir Robert Vansittart, Permanent Head of the Foreign Office, Sir Warren Fisher, Permanent Secretary to the

Treasury, and the three Chiefs of Staff with General Pownall as secretary. This Committee reported in March 1934,[5] catching the Government at an awkward moment (it was a government whose moments varied only in the degree of their awkwardness). The disarmers of Geneva were performing their final contortions. At the end of January the Government had issued a Memorandum designed to rescue the sinking Conference. It proposed partial rearmament for Germany, partial disarmament for the powers already possessing arms (this to be ensured by a system of control – the ever-recurring fantasy); and it revived once more the idea of abolition of military and naval aircraft, together with "a thorough inquiry into the whole question of air power".[6] And while the Defence Requirements Committee was coming to grips with Britain's weakness and minimum needs, the Lord Privy Seal, Anthony Eden, was visiting Paris, Berlin and Rome to canvass this proposition of quite opposite import. The results of Eden's tour were inconclusive, and it is unsurprising that he wrote:

When I returned to England on March 1st I found the Government hesitant to take decisions and the outlook murky.[7]

When the Defence Requirements Committee report came in a week later, the Government's hesitancy touched paralysis; it did nothing for two months, and then referred the report to the Ministerial Committee on Disarmament (DC(M)), on which the most powerful voice was that of the Chancellor of the Exchequer, Neville Chamberlain. We shall return to a consideration of that significant personage in due course. What concerns us now is the attitude which he took in May 1934 towards the recommendations of the Defence Requirements Committee, and in particular towards its proposals for the RAF. *En passant*, however, we may note his claim to his sister Ida on May 12:

I have practically taken charge now of the defence requirements of the country.[8]

This would mean that he had supplanted the Prime Minister, the three Service ministers, the Committee of Imperial Defence, and all its associated sub-committees. One must not, however, permit oneself to be repelled into scepticism by the distasteful boastfulness of Chamberlain's statement; it came all too near the truth.

The recommendations of the Defence Requirements Committee take on, with hindsight, a very modest look. They seem scarcely related to the dreadful arms race with Germany that was now beginning – and, indeed, they were not intended to compete in such a manner. As Montgomery Hyde says:

> What the DRC recommended was not a programme of expansion but in its own words it was confined to remedying "the worst deficiencies in existing programmes that have accumulated during the régime of the Ten Years Rule, abandoned not a moment too soon: in other words, our recommendations all fall within the scope of approved Government policy".[9]

The last phrase reveals men (the Chiefs of Staff) schooled and disciplined by long experience of Government parsimony; they were accustomed to tightrope walking, with on one side the hazard of asking for what was really needed and having the whole report thrown out as ruinously expensive, and on the other the risk of asking for considerably less and having even that whittled down in the inevitable haggling with the Treasury. So they settled for minimum requirements: modernization of Britain's by now distressingly antiquated battle fleet, still regarded as the hard core of sea power; preparation for an Expeditionary Force at least equal in size (but unfortunately all too closely similar in composition if not in quality) to that of 1914; and the completion (at last) of the RAF's 1923 plan for 52 home-based squadrons, plus 10 new squadrons (chiefly to strengthen the RAF overseas), and 16 for the Fleet Air Arm (whose aircraft and pilots it was the Air Ministry's duty to provide). The Committee did add that "if we were to meet our responsibilities an additional 25 squadrons would be required" for the RAF.[10] But within its terms of reference – remedying "worst deficiencies" – the Committee did not feel justified in making this a definite recommendation.

All the DRC's proposals were joint; that is to say, there were no dissenting voices. And as regards the Air side, Ellington had the firm support of the Secretary of State, Lord Londonderry. Nevertheless, at the last moment, Vansittart became strongly critical of the Air demand, insisting that it ought to have included, then and there, the extra 25 squadrons. He blamed himself for not putting in a minority report to this effect, and still regretted not having done so when he came to compile his memoirs over twenty years later. Ellington himself seems to have been in two minds; he circulated a note of protest to his fellow committee-members on March 1 but, like Vansittart, he did not push it to the point of a separate report. Our awareness of the difficulties under which the RAF was to labour during the next five years gives Ellington's performance a somewhat feeble look, but in fact it is highly understandable. Other historians (Denis Richards, Montgomery Hyde, Stephen Roskill, J. M. Spaight) have pointed out the RAF's passionate attachment at all times to quality rather than quantity. A sudden increase of nearly 50 per cent in aircrew was no easy matter to provide; reserves for the existing force were slender enough; experience was to show that provision of *properly trained* reserves for an expanded one at short notice was impossible without extra facilities. Furthermore, there was a very proper horror in the Air Ministry of piling up large numbers of machines which were already or shortly to become obsolescent; this was, in fact, precisely what the French were doing, with disastrous results in the not-far-distant future. And this reluctance on Ellington's part was, of course, fortified by his knowledge of the transition of matériel which was taking place in the RAF at this very time, with a number of projects at critical stages requiring a little more time for correct evaluation.

A brief digression is here necessary to understand what is implied by a "transition of matériel". Civil aviation in Germany and America was making giant strides into the world of fast metal monoplanes as the decade began, while, unsubsidized and impoverished, the British firms could only gnash their teeth. Their obvious support, the Air Ministry and the RAF, was also always chronically short of funds. Since the Air Ministry, unlike the Admiralty, did not have its own constructors, it depended on the private firms and their designers; the latter were, indeed, the key men of all aviation, civil and military. To keep the designers going, the firms had to be kept alive – with the result that the Air Ministry's exiguous funds had to support no fewer than sixteen design teams. Outright competition was obviously ruled out; instead a cumbersome, slow process of enquiry, selection and ordering held sway.

> Anything from five to seven years might elapse between the date when the first enquiry was addressed to the firms and that at which the squadrons were in possession of their new operational aircraft.[11]

A perfect example of this slow motion was the famous Vickers Wellington bomber, whose specification, B.9/32, was issued in September 1932, but whose first flight was not until June 1936, and squadron delivery not until October 1938. A feature of the Wellington was its great strength, derived from the geodetic design of B. N. (later Sir Barnes) Wallis, already incorporated in its single-engined predecessor, the Wellesley, another example of slow development. This aircraft's specification is dated 1931, yet its first flight was not until June 1935, and squadron delivery in April 1937. Two others of 1932 vintage, and therefore already specified but untested while the Defence Requirements Committee was conferring, were the Fairey Battle (P.27/32) whose first flight was in March 1936 and delivery in March 1937, and the Handley Page Hampden (B.9/32) whose first flight was in June 1936 (like the Wellington) and delivery two months earlier, in August 1938. In addition to those innovations, already on order, in 1933, the Bristol Aeroplane Company, with the backing of the newspaper proprietor, Lord Rothermere (Secretary of State for Air for a short time in 1918), was working on a metal monoplane eight-seater civil transport which it was hoped would out-perform the latest American machines. And, of course, there was the work of Camm and Mitchell which led to the 1934 specifications for the Hurricane and Spitfire fighters. A degree of caution, and an inclination to tread warily for the time being, are understandable enough in the CAS and his advisers as 1934 came in.

Chamberlain's attitude in May took them all aback. Steadily, during the winter and early spring, his mind had been moving in the direction of some form of deterrent to the Nazis, by diplomacy or a show of force. The former – an extraordinary proposal for a "limited liability" mutual guarantee (as though there could ever be such a thing!) by Germany, France, Britain, Italy, Poland and Czechoslovakia – did not win Government approval; the Cabinet reluctantly resigned itself to contemplating at least a measure of rearmament, not, as the DRC had been viewing the matter, in order to give some reality to national defence, but as a war preventive. Hitler's announcement in April of a 33 per cent increase in German military expenditure reinforced this decision. Nevertheless, the gap in intention between the Cabinet and the DRC was serious, as Chamberlain's interventions soon revealed.

The DC(M) began its discussions of the DRC report on May 3. The proceedings were not hasty; it took until June 18 for Chamberlain to enounce firm proposals and until July 11 for the Cabinet to give final approval. The first hurdle was Japan, recognized by the DRC as the immediate threat, although Germany was "the ultimate potential enemy". Chamberlain made no trouble of Japan; he quickly concluded that:

> ... we cannot provide simultaneously for hostilities with Japan and Germany and that the latter is the problem to which we must now address ourselves ...[12]

He easily persuaded himself that Japan would not attack the British Empire unless Britain was preoccupied with hostilities in Europe, and therefore that a deterrent against Germany would also be a deterrent against Japan.[13] The question was, what would serve best against Germany?

> ... the air force seemed the best choice as a deterrent for the same reasons that had made it the prime target for disarmament; it was regarded as barbaric and terrifying in its destructive potential.[14]

In practical terms, this thinking took the form of proposals to make drastic cuts (in the region of 50 per cent) in the DRC recommendations for the Navy and the Army, but actually to increase the amount allocated to the RAF so as to produce 80 squadrons for the Metropolitan Air Force instead of the long-awaited 52. His brisk dismissal of the Japanese threat enabled Chamberlain to brush aside the DRC's intention to increase overseas RAF contingents, invoking public opinion for support:

> ... he did not think that arguments to increase our air forces at such places as Penang would carry much conviction.[15]

At this time, it may be noted, the strength of the RAF facing the Japanese in Singapore was three squadrons, one of them operating flying-boats.

The final recommendation of the DC(M), presented to the Cabinet on July 16, and approved two days later, was an expenditure of £20 million in five years, to produce a total Metropolitan Air Force of 84 squadrons (1,252 first-line aircraft) by March 1939.[16] It was, as Montgomery Hyde says, "a modest but none the less real expansion programme and not merely a programme for remedying accumulated deficiencies such as the DRC had proposed."[17]

It was, in fact, Expansion Scheme "A". It had its critics; as Chamberlain unfolded his ideas, the Air Staff became increasingly uneasy. Londonderry (June 26) had already described Chamberlain's plan for large RAF expansion as "better designed for public consumption than for real utility".[18] Hankey (June 29) had told Baldwin that the thing was a "panic measure", expressing also grave concern about the neglect of the Fleet Air Arm and the Far East.[19] As chairman of the DRC he had not failed to take the point of the Air Staff's hesitations, and finally stigmatized it as "without providing for the reserve machines and bombs, etc. – a politician's window-dressing scheme".[20] All this, however, though instructive as an example of the difficulties which democracies face in coming to grips with reality, was soon rendered academic by the hot pace of the running that the dictators were making.

The year 1935 was a bad one for democracy, and for peace. In January came the first rumblings of international consequences for a border incident between the Empire of Abyssinia and Italian Somaliland. For the next nine months this dispute would put to test the League of Nations as a peace-keeping organization, the remaining unity of the victors of 1918, Britain, France and Italy, and the true state of British defences, especially naval and air. When the Italians went to war in October, all three were seen to have failed: the League and its half-hearted sanctions were useless, Italy became an enemy of Britain and France, the Fleet had trembled for its safety in its Mediterranean bases, and the RAF had been quite unable to offer it protection – though Ellington startled his fellow Chiefs of Staff by proposing to send 13 squadrons to the South of France in order to attack Northern Italy.[21] The Abyssinian crisis seriously weakened what Correlli Barnett calls "the whole rickety and overstrained structure of imperial defence";[22] a disastrous long-term result was to offer German cryptanalysts "their first bite at the signal systems used by the British Fleet"[23] – an advantage gladly used by U-boats in the first years of the war. Yet all these omens were overshadowed by matters nearer home in 1935.

On February 26 the German Air Force, proscribed by the Treaty of Versailles, was reborn. Its Commander-in-Chief was Hermann Goering, ex-squadron commander in the famous *Richthofen Geschwader* of 1918; General Erhard Milch, Secretary of State for Air, was the effective controller of the new *Luftwaffe*. Its strength was 1,888 aircraft of all types, and some 20,000 officers and men – which was not a bad beginning. Conforming to his normal practice, Hitler picked his moment for announcing this portent with some care. He was not long denied a cue: the British Defence White Paper of March 4 drew particular attention to German rearmament and the consequent peril to peace. Anglo-German relations, momentarily curiously cordial, chilled abruptly, and on March 8 Hitler sprang one of his "Saturday Surprises"; he informed G. Ward Price of the *Daily Mail* as an "exclusive" of the rebirth of the *Luftwaffe*. When the paper came out on the Monday morning, releasing the half-guessed secret, its readers awoke to a new fact of power in a bleaker world. Six days later it became bleaker still: Hitler bluntly denounced the military clauses of the Versailles Treaty, and proclaimed the creation of an army of 36

31

divisions (some 550,000 men) and a return to conscription.

Neither of these matters need have been fatal. Air forces and armies do not arise overnight – it would be a matter of years before either of the two measures announced in 1935 could become militarily effective. All that was required was resolution on the part of Britain and France: resolution to enforce the Versailles Treaty, or at the very least to make such preparations as would ensure the continuation of their preponderance. No such thing took place; resolution was conspicuously absent in both countries. Instead, outright pacifism was reaching its zenith, just as Nazi power began its forward stride. In Britain, in June, a "Peace Ballot" organized by the League of Nations Union registered 11 million votes opposed to war, while in France more millions of signatures were being inscribed in a "Golden Book of Peace". The parallel with the upsurge of West European neutralism coincidental with Soviet aggression in Afghanistan in the 1980s requires no emphasis.

Meanwhile, from the air point of view, matters looked ominous indeed. In late March 1935 the Foreign Secretary, Sir John Simon, and Anthony Eden visited Berlin, where they were courteously received by Hitler, but made no progress with any discussion of the levels of arms and armament. There was a moment of shock for the English Ministers:

> Finally, Simon put . . . the question that to us mattered most: what was the present strength of the German air force? After a moment's hesitation, Hitler replied that Germany had reached parity with Great Britain. There was no triumph in his tone, but there was grim foreboding in my heart.[24]

"Parity" is a word with, in this context, depressing and confusing overtones and implications which we shall need to examine somewhat later. The immediate effect of Hitler's boast was to alarm the Government and the Air Ministry into a dramatic revision of its still new-born expansion scheme. In fact, Scheme "A" was scrapped; a cautious Air Staff amended version, based on the proposition that Germany would not be ready and did not intend to go to war until 1942, was put forward as Scheme "B". It was fiercely attacked by Vansittart, who stated flatly, on the basis of secret information:

> Anything that fails to provide security by *1938* is inadequate and blind.[25]

In a sharp memorandum to the DRC, he reminded his colleagues that Baldwin had pledged in March 1934 that Britain would "no longer be in a position inferior to any country within striking distance of our shores".[26] No one, said Vansittart acidly,

has ever before suggested either to the Foreign Office or to the public that we must wait four years, and even then run the risk of not attaining so simple and vital a requisite. And these four years may well be the most crucial in the history of Europe; indeed, they will probably decide its fate.[27]

Ellington was stung into one of those unanswerable retorts which normally uncommunicative men sometimes produce in moments of justified ire:

The Foreign Office must realize that still more extensive developments cannot be effected by merely expressing a desire for them.[28]

And he added: "What has been lacking is a clear long-dated policy which would have permitted careful and detailed planning." Which was, of course, only too true, as Vansittart recognized with chagrin. Nevertheless, Scheme "B" was brushed aside; instead, the Government took two characteristic measures. The first was to set up yet another committee, the Air Parity Sub-Committee of the DC(M), to recommend measures by which Baldwin's pledge might be redeemed; the second, when this body reported, astonishingly, in less than ten days, was Scheme "C".

If Scheme "A" had deserved the label "panic measures", Scheme "C" did so even more. It proposed a Metropolitan Air Force of 123 squadrons, containing 1,512 first-line aircraft by March 31, 1937 – which was clearly both a decided increase and a great acceleration. On the other hand, it made no further proposals for overseas establishments or the Fleet Air Arm, both of which were ridiculously weak, and it had even more serious defects:

It was one of the deterrent schemes and an unsound one when analysed ... it suffered from the same grave defect [as Scheme "A"] in that it made practically no provision at all for reserves ... It would have given us an air force which would have been unable to go on fighting for more than a month or so if, as was quite possible, severe losses were incurred at the outset ... The Air Staff were naturally apprehensive about the unsatisfactory position in regard to reserves which any expert analysis of Scheme "C" could not fail to detect. As a matter of fact it probably did not achieve its object of impressing the Germans. The finance of it gave it away. It was altogether too cheap . . .[29]

33

However, it didn't matter; like Schemes "A" and "B", and later Schemes "D" and "E", Scheme "C" soon found its way to the dustbin.

In this case the precipitant of dissolution and the propellant of the new idea was a General Election – a much healthier point of origin than panic reaction to hostile moves. The National Government won a crushing victory in the election of November 1935, and used it to bring out in February 1936 a Defence White Paper which, says Sir Maurice Dean,

> gave Britain its first coherent defence policy for twenty years ... By this act Baldwin deserved, but did not receive, the profound gratitude of Britain. So far as the Royal Air Force is concerned the result was Scheme "F". This provided for a Home Defence Air Force of 124 squadrons by March 1939, and it was the longest lived of all expansion schemes. Sir Kingsley Wood, then Secretary of State for Air, was able to tell the House of Commons in March 1939 that in a few weeks the Scheme would be completed as planned.[30]

Scheme "F" was, in fact, the only one of the 1934–39 expansion schemes which was actually completed. It had two significant features: the first was the elimination of the light bombers (Hawker Harts and Hinds, whose bomb-load was 500 lb) in favour of "mediums" (Blenheims[31] and Hampdens) and "heavy mediums" (Whitleys and Wellingtons).[32] Two points are worth adding here: first, that no specification was issued (nor would be until 1940) for a modern light bomber, a lack which war quickly made apparent. Secondly, we see here an acknowledgment of a tendency for all bombers to become heavy bombers (rather in the way that, in earlier wars, all cavalry tended to become heavy cavalry or all destroyers to grow into light cruisers). Later in 1936 this trend expressed itself very significantly indeed, with the issue of Spec. B.12/36 in July and P.13/36 in September (see p. 17). From the former sprang the Short Stirling, the first four-engined bomber to enter RAF service (August 1940), while from the latter came the Handley Page Halifax, the first four-engined bomber to attack Germany (March 1941) and the Avro Manchester which, although itself a failure, fathered the famous Lancaster of 1941–45. So it may be said that 1936 was the year in which the strategic bomber force (in the sense of aircraft possessing the requisite range and bomb load) was born.

The second important feature of Scheme "F" was that, for the first time, it provided for adequate reserves. The Metropolitan Air Force was to consist of 124 squadrons with 1,736 first-line aircraft, the overseas forces were to be built up to 37 squadrons with 468 first-line aircraft (not exactly a massive show of strength for an empire stretching from Hong Kong to Gibraltar!), and the Fleet Air Arm was to have 26 squadrons with 312 aircraft. The date of completion was to be March 31, 1939. This was true rearmament, because the equipment of this force would be almost entirely modern (as the word was understood in 1935), giving it much greater real strength. Furthermore, in addition to 75 per cent reserves of aircraft with the squadrons or in servicing or maintenance, a further 150 per cent was allotted to the RAF and 135 per cent to the Fleet Air Arm. This, it was hoped, would meet the likely wastage of four months of war, by which time industry should be able to expand production sufficiently to keep pace. Personnel reserves, both air- and ground-crew, were also catered for. Further schemes and greater expansion would be prescribed as the international scene darkened and the threat of war became more pressing. But Scheme "F" was where RAF policy began to touch firm ground, where "expansion" moved out of the cosmetic stage into reality.

Such, then, were the beginnings of conversion from a peacetime to a wartime air force – what would undoubtedly, in the hands of a more flamboyant and forceful character have been called the "Ellington Schemes". There is no doubt at all about what they would have been called if Trenchard had still been CAS. But Ellington was definitely not flamboyant, and gave no impression of being forceful (although he could be stubborn). Furthermore, after the departure of London-derry (a very able aristocrat, but lacking in political "weight") in June 1935, Ellington worked under Philip Cunliffe-Lister (soon Lord Swinton), a Secretary of State whose "name towers above those of all other ministers who have served the Royal Air Force".[33] Swinton was a man of great energy, impatient of red tape, and receptive to new ideas; not only that, but he was *seen* to be all those things – he had the reputation of "hustling" things along. Ellington, whose tempera-ment was quite different, was to serve with him for more than two years – years very fruitful for the RAF.

Theoretical expansions might read well as White Papers, enrage an Opposition still devoted (in the teeth of all daily evidence) to dreams of disarmament, and calm the fears of the excitable; but without the actual aircraft – which means the capacity to produce the aircraft – they would remain theoretical, mere paper tigers. When the Defence Requirements Committee presented its third report in November 1935, it grasped this nettle. Prompted by Lord Weir, the Government's industrial adviser,[34] it recommended the creation of a "shadow" armaments industry, the Government financing the construction of new factories which would be managed by existing firms. For the RAF, of course, such a project was heaven-sent and Swinton and the Air Staff pressed it forward. Without the shadow factories, it would not have been possible for British aircraft production to catch up with Germany's by the outbreak of war – a leap, in fact, from 158 aircraft a month in April 1938 to nearly 800 in September 1939. As Correlli Barnett says:

> It was not until 1937, when the new "shadow factories" came into production by fits and starts, that British rearmament really began to get under way.[35]

5 Rearmament under way

An expanding air force, new aircraft on the way, new productive capacity: these were the beginnings – late and slow, reflecting the Government's hesitations and dismay – of the RAF's preparation to meet the menace of Nazi Germany. The need was becoming more and more apparent: hot on the heels of the Defence White Paper (and heavily underlining the purpose of its recommendations) came Hitler's reoccupation of the Rhineland on March 7, 1936. Britain and France were caught unawares, thrown off balance by this bare-faced defiance. Militarily, they were still far stronger than Germany; as Churchill wrote:

> France alone was at this time quite strong enough to drive the Germans out of the Rhineland.[1]

Yet the French Commander-in-Chief, General Gamelin, told his government that Germany had nearly a million men under arms, with 300,000 already in the Rhineland – and fear prevailed, so that:

> With an investment of 19 battalions of infantry and 13 artillery groups, plus two anti-aircraft battalions and two groups of 27 single-seater fighter planes without reserves, a total strength of 22,000 men plus 14,000 local police ... Hitler had effectively destroyed the post-First World War security system.[2]

This was the first of the open humiliations of the democracies by Germany. Humiliation by Italy came to its fulfilment in May, when Mussolini's troops entered Addis Ababa. Two months later the Spanish Civil War broke out, and from the beginning the forces of the two dictators – especially their air forces – were seen in impressive action, while democracy was once more impotent. In November the Rome-Berlin Axis was proclaimed.

Clearly, the expansion of the RAF would be only just in time – if that. The Air Staff was never in doubt about what it was expanding against: the danger from Germany. Italy by herself could be dealt with; she was only dangerous by the sanction of German strength. And quite apart from numerical disadvantages, now apprehensively recognized both in the matter of first-line strength and production, the RAF perceived that it was ill-deployed. Born in the First World War, its airfields were naturally placed to support the Army fighting in northern France, with almost the entire action taking place over France and Belgium. Now, the advances in technology and its own offensive doctrine made Germany herself the designated field of action, and the approach lay across the North Sea. Once more, history was repeating itself: in the decade before 1914, the Royal Navy, having fought the Spanish and French for some 300 years from bases in southern England, had also had to give its mind to the North Sea, and build new bases as fast as it could at Scapa Flow, Rosyth and Cromarty. In 1935 the RAF faced an exactly similar problem:

> The natural bases for an offensive against Germany, given the fact, which we were bound to assume, of the neutrality of the Low Countries, would have been Yorkshire, Lincolnshire, Norfolk and Suffolk. It was in fact from bases in these counties that we did conduct our strategic air offensive of 1940–45. Yet in all the broad acres of those four counties there was only one solitary aerodrome from which squadrons were to operate – that at Bircham Newton (near King's Lynn) . . . The four counties were, one might also say, a demilitarized zone for the purpose of air warfare.[3]

Sites were selected and acquired – a statement easy to write and read, much less easy to interpret into fact. Huts and hangars were erected, living quarters laid out, runways laid down; the new air force of constantly larger and heavier machines could no longer make do with grass runways; now they had to be of concrete. The new stations came into being, seven in 1935–36, eight in 1936–37, six in 1937–38. The 52 home airfields of the RAF in 1934 increased to 89 in 1938, which seemed a lot at the time, but is less impressive by comparison with the *Luftwaffe*'s 400 airfields in 1939;[4] the 79 sites whose acquisition was inaugurated between 1934 and 1938 also look less impressive by comparison with the 389 of 1939–43. But it was not the numbers that mattered most:

As the expansion progressed, it was evident that our Air Force was not only re-forming, but re-forming on a new line. The line was one facing Germany. But no one in polite society alluded to the possibility of our starting from that line to bomb Germany. Such things were simply not said.[5]

In Eastern England, however, the pattern of RAF strategy was becoming clear to those who had eyes to see.

The Air Ministry's cumbersome purchasing procedures have already been alluded to (p. 28). A remarkable departure from those hallowed rituals took place while Ellington was CAS, and once again the originator was the very able Weir, though Swinton has generally received the credit. It was Weir who concluded:

> The technique of aircraft design and the capacity of the technical side of the industry has reached a stage at which the actual performance and qualities of design can be accurately predicted from the design.[6]

This took some swallowing; Dowding for one, Air Member for Supply and Research, while recognizing that in the circumstances of 1936 exceptional measures had to be taken, found it hard to approve of this proposal to "order off the drawing board". And, indeed, there were mistakes and consequent disappointments; conspicuous among them were the Blackburn Botha, the monoplane torpedo-bomber of 1939, whose failure seriously weakened Coastal Command at the beginning of the war, and the Manchester. The risk of some failure had to be accepted; it was better than the other – the risk of not having the new aircraft until it was too late.

It was the recognition of the probable need for very quick and urgent expansion that prompted Swinton, in September 1936, to make the suggestion that orders might be placed in America. He told Ellington to prepare a plan for two or three squadrons each of American fighters and bombers, "on the hypothesis that we were told to increase our first-line strength very rapidly in the next 15 months, before the shadow industry had got into production".[7] This was a revolutionary proposal which, not surprisingly, provoked loud cries of protest from British manufacturers. However, Swinton stuck to his guns, and the Government agreed: yet it is an indication of the still leisurely and hesitant pace of rearmament that the British Purchasing Commission was not actually set up until April 1938. As Denis Richards says, right up to the eleventh hour there was "a sense of time, if limited time in hand: a sense of urgency, but not of immediate and overpowering urgency".[8] Swinton was ahead of his time, and blamed accordingly.

One of the members of the Purchasing Commission in 1938 was Sir Arthur Harris, who gives us this revealing glimpse of the contrast between American and British production methods and attitudes. The Commission's chief (though not sole) interest was in reconnaissance and trainer aircraft, and Harris visited the then small Lockheed factory to inspect their Super Electra Airliner, which seemed highly suitable for the former rôle – with adaptations. Lockheeds offered a mock-up of this and invited Harris to come back and see it in a few days' time, but he said he could not do that because he had to go on and view flying-boats and the Boeing "Flying Fortress" bomber:

> To my astonishment, only twenty-four hours later a car arrived to fetch me out to the Lockheed works, and there I saw a mock-up of all our requirements in plywood, fitted complete in every detail, with two alternative noses hinged on to a real aircraft all ready for our inspection. The first alternative was our idea of our own requirements, and the second was Lockheed's idea of the same thing, but showing how it could be done better by themselves – and it was this second alternative that we chose. As I was well aware that at home we were never able to get a mock-up of any description produced in less than months, I was entirely convinced that anyone who could produce a mock-up in twenty-four hours would indeed make good all his promises – and this Lockheed's most certainly did.[9]

The result of this enterprise was an Air Ministry order for 200 of what the RAF called the "Hudson" maritime general reconnaissance aircraft. It aroused a storm of protest from the British Air industry lobby, but the arrival of the Hudsons was a great relief to Coastal Command. In all, some 2,000 Hudsons were delivered to the RAF; but more important was the stimulating effect of early British interest and orders on the military side of the American aviation industry, the small opening which later unleashed a vast flood.

We approach the tally of the significant changes brought about or set in motion during Sir Edward Ellington's tenure. Two remain to be considered, both of great value in very different ways. "Typex" is the name of the cipher machine adopted by the RAF and the Army before the outbreak of war which gave complete security to its users. Its story contains a number of teasing ironies. We have very briefly noted (p. 31) that the Abyssinian crisis enabled German cryptanalysts to penetrate the Royal Navy's codes and ciphers (by the simple process of relating coded signals to observable responses). An RN detachment based on Aden to observe Italian preparations used the Navy's wartime codes, and in so doing "they offered a cryptanalyst's feast. Call-signs were easily identified; key words and phrases regularly repeated."[10] Yet – this is the first irony – it was the Admiralty which had taken the original initiative towards the Typex machine which would have offered security – as far back as 1928.[11] In 1936 Lord Mountbatten, then a Commander in the Naval Air Division, urged the Admiralty to introduce the by now well developed Typex machines for the use of the Fleet. Yet, as Professor Hinsley says, "the Admiralty's earlier interest . . . had drained away".[12] No one has yet explained the reason for this; Lord Mountbatten told Donald McLachlan that it was "sabotage" of the experimental use attributable to the Board of Admiralty's innate conservatism. That may be so; in any case, Ronald Lewin's conclusion stands:

> The Silent Service has never been more tight-lipped than about the reasons for this terrible lapse.[13]

It was, in fact, the Royal Air Force which actually developed the Typex machine. One can only marvel at the leisurely pace of research and progress with such vital matters between the wars. In 1928, at the Admiralty's instigation, two cipher-machines marketed by a German company, "*Enigma Chiffriermaschinen*" *Aktiengesellschaft*, were purchased for examination by the Government Code and Cypher School. This, of course, is the second irony: for this was the now famous Enigma machine used by the Germans throughout the war which provided the raw material for Ultra. It did not, it seems, create much of a stir in London in 1928, because useful action only begins in June 1934; it introduces the name of another of those almost-forgotten RAF officers of the period who displayed, in the words of Sir Maurice Dean, "more than a touch of genius in his composition".[14] He was Wing Commander O. G. W. G. Lywood, of Air Ministry Signals, who became interested in the possibilities of Enigma and asked if he might borrow one of the samples. He received this reply from the Government Code and Cypher School:

25th June, 1934

Dear Lywood,

As regards the matter of the Enigma Cypher Machine, I have arranged that you may borrow this machine in order that it may serve as a model for your "engineers".

I feel, however, that I must point out that it is probable that this machine is covered by patents taken out in this country (they may have expired).

It may be advisable, therefore, that you should consult your patent experts before proceeding to make a direct copy of the machine.[15]

Unfortunately, the signature appears to have been torn off the document, which is a pity, because it is historic; for all practical purposes, Typex starts here.

It did not take long to establish that the *Chiffriermaschinen* company had indeed covered their product with no fewer than three British patents, all of them still valid – another irony, perhaps the best. But such formalities did not deter that small, invaluable band of men who were concerned with the realities of war while so many thought only of the unrealities of peace. Lywood was advised by the Air Ministry Contracts Directorate:

In view of Section 29 of the Patents and Design Acts, the Air Ministry may by themselves, or by their contractors authorised in writing by them, *make or use any patented invention for the services of the Crown, without any licence from the patentee* [my italics]. The Department do not require the permission of the inventor to make his invention, *but he would be entitled to payment if an invention covered by a valid patent is used.*

The terms for such making and using may be considered after the making or using of the invention.

It is suggested that the question of infringement be referred to this branch *after the apparatus has been made and used* in order that any payment due to the patentee may be considered, and put on record. Apparently no action to settle the matter could be taken while the apparatus is secret.[16]

The reader may agree that no cooler *carte-blanche* could have been offered; he may also savour the wonderland in which it was suggested that the German inventor might be paid after use – use which could only conclude either with his country's defeat in war, in which case his survival was problematical, or its victory, in which case the Air Ministry's capacity to pay might be severely reduced! At any rate, there the matter rested for the time being, while Lywood and his engineers, aided by the GC & CS, continued their work of adaptation.

When we next encounter it, the result of their endeavours is still known by its original (German) name: it is referred to as "the RAF Enigma". By March 1936 considerable progress had been made, and the War Office had expressed a very definite interest – rather too much, perhaps, because word of what was afoot appears to have spread. A Mr Sidney Hole was anxious to know whether the "RAF Enigma" infringed Patent No. 207257 which he had taken out in

February 1924 for "Improvements in or relating to coding or decoding machines". Air Ministry Contracts was not sure; it admitted that if so, "the action to be taken will require careful consideration", adding:

> At the moment the position is that two experimental sets incorporating the R.A.F. Enigma have been completed and are undergoing trial: no decision has yet been reached as regards adoption.[17]

Contracts also admitted the possibility "of the RAF Enigma infringing patents obtained in the name of *Chiffriermaschinen Akt. Gesell.*"; it recommended the War Office to send "a suitable non-committal reply" to Mr Hole. Next day, however, Signals came clean, informing Contracts quite frankly that:

> The machine made for us was copied from the German "ENIGMA" with additions and alterations suggested by the Government Code and Cypher School.[18]

This once again raised the question of the German patentees – against a background of progressively deteriorating Anglo-German relations. By the end of 1937 the name "Type X" had displaced "RAF Enigma"; twenty-nine machines had been produced with the original adaptation, and sanction was being sought for production of 238 sets of a Mark II for distribution to lower formations (the War Office requesting 25 for trials). It was candidly admitted that *Chiffriermaschinen* Patent No. 267472 was being infringed, and:

> difficulty arises in remunerating the patentees, in the near future at any rate, since this would entail a suggestion that the Department is using a cypher apparatus similar in some respects to that to which the patent relates.[19]

This has a sound of Queen Elizabeth I informing the Spanish Ambassador that "difficulty arises" in remunerating the King of Spain for damage to part of his beard owing to the suggestion that Sir Francis Drake might soon be attempting to singe the remainder also. Certainly it strikes a refreshing note amidst the general pusillanimity of the 1930s. Correspondence on this sensitive subject dies away at this point, probably because it was generally realized that the less said on paper the better. There appears to have been quiet agreement that "the question of remuneration to the patentees [be] deferred until such time as it is permissible to negotiate with them" – a delightfully convenient formula.[20]

So we arrive at the point, in September 1939, where Typex was in use at all RAF headquarters and remained completely secure throughout the war. The Army used it for communication between the War Office and both home and overseas commands, and down to divisional level within the commands, with equal security. It is the final irony that the Germans were never able to penetrate what was, in effect, their own system. It tells us something about the Third Reich that the nation which could produce astonishing aircraft such as the rocket-propelled Me 163 or the turbo-jet He 162, which could set up and bring to fruition a Peenemünde, was never able to create a Bletchley Park. But that apart, Britain had plentiful reason to be grateful for Wing Commander Lywood's initiative in 1934.

We come now, finally, to that vital aspect of expansion, personnel. During 1936 it became apparent to a number of reflective officers that the Regular Air Force even with its Reserve and the valued support of the Auxiliary Air Force squadrons, would not be enough for the purposes of war. It was the Director of Training at the Air Ministry, Air Commodore A. W. Tedder, who was most visionary in conceiving a new air reserve. He advocated a "Citizen Air Force" which would form a real second line of defence behind the Regulars, in the same way as Lord Haldane and Lord Haig in 1906 had urged the formation of "an army rooted in the people" – "an army complete in every respect".[21] This was the origin of the Territorial Army, the first step towards the mass Citizen Army with which Britain had fought the First World War. The Royal Air Force Volunteer Reserve, created in 1936, did not take the form that Tedder wished; nevertheless it, too, was a first step towards the mass Citizen Air Force which he perceived would be necessary for a second war. The RAFVR was, from the first, a true reserve for the whole Air Force; it did not have separate units of its own as the Auxiliary Air Force did. Its purpose was to teach young men with no previous Service experience to fly in their spare time. It had, for its day, a remarkably forward-looking feature:

> The new organization was essentially a democratic one. It was designed to appeal, and it did appeal, to the young men of our cities, without any class distinctions. The Air Council, it was stated in the letter submitting the scheme to the Treasury, "propose to open the new force to the whole middle class in the widest sense of that term, namely, the complete range of the output of the public and secondary schools". "In a force so

43

recruited," the letter went on, "it would be inappropriate to grade the members on entry as officers or airmen according to their social class; entry will accordingly be on a common footing, as airman pilot or observer, and promotions to commissioned rank will be made at a later stage in accordance with the abilities for leadership actually displayed.[22]

Entry into the RAFVR began in April 1937; the aim was to recruit some 800 potential pilots a year, and it was quickly apparent that this would be more than fulfilled. By 1939 the Secretary of State was able to announce that pilot strength had increased to over 2,500. By September 1 the strength of RAFVR aircrew stood at:

Pilots	6,646
Observers	1,623
Wireless Operators/Air Gunners	1,948
	10,217[23]

On September 1, 1937 Air Chief Marshal Sir Cyril Newall replaced Sir Edward Ellington as CAS. Ellington's four-and-a-quarter years had seen a veritable transformation of the RAF; the list of things done during his tenure (pp. 16–17) is formidable and unanswerable. It is not, of course, being suggested that he was personally responsible for all these developments; he was never the unquestioned "father" of an important weapon, as Fisher was for dreadnoughts, or Churchill and Sir Ernest Swinton for tanks. We have noted some of the men who have better claims in that direction: Sorley, Wimperis, Rowe, Tizard, Watson-Watt, Dowding, Swinton, Weir, Lywood, Tedder. We have noted also that distressing degree of shyness which caused Ellington to be misjudged and underrated. Indeed, Air Chief Marshal Sir Wilfrid Freeman, whose name may be added to the list above as the most legitimate "father" of the heavy bomber force, and who was to play an important part in the higher direction of the RAF during the war, told Trenchard that Ellington was "the worst [CAS] we ever had". He added:

He was not only a misanthrope, but he never made the least attempt to do his job and get to know politicians. He pretended to despise them but was, in fact, frightened of them.[24]

It seems likely that there was a clear clash of temperament between the two men – and Freeman was well known for forthrightness in expressing his views. Their ideas of the functions of a CAS obviously differed; to Ellington, the business of dealing with politicians was the

Secretary of State's job, and both Londonderry and Swinton brought powerful advantages to it. He probably over-stressed the separateness of their rôles; however, it was he who spanned their terms of office, he who presided over the full range of progress between 1933 and 1937. It is frankly impossible to see how he could have done this if he had not been in broad sympathy with what was being done. We may leave the last word on him to Sir Maurice Dean:

> What is rarely mentioned is Ellington's superb quality as a Staff Officer. He had an acute mind and a remarkable memory. He was quick to embrace new ideas. His faults, if such there were, did not include lack of understanding.[25]

At a time of revolutionary change in a large institution, understanding and receptiveness to new ideas are very great virtues.

The last word on the RAF itself, as Ellington retired from office, must nevertheless be equivocal. Great changes had taken place since 1933, great strides had been made towards preparedness for modern war – but some of the most significant innovations were still a long way down the pipeline. Meanwhile, the continuing time-lag in development and production of new types, and the consequent dragging pace of re-equipment, remained alarming. Years of penury leave their mark; cautious habits died hard, and it was not as though, during this period, the Treasury was being lavish with the great lubricant – money. The Air Estimates of 1933 (including extra expenditures) amounted to £16.8 million, a sum which, even allowing for subsequent devaluation, still appears ludicrous. In 1936 it had only risen to £50.1 million; it was not until 1937, as Ellington departed, that any really substantial amount was made available – £137.6 million. Only now could any real progress be expected. But what the last four years had seen was a major revolution in technique and technology, set within the framework of a simultaneous large expansion. It was a formidable combination of stresses, and the crises of the next two years would reveal the price that had to be paid for incurring it.

6 *The knock-out blow*

In the last year of Ellington's term and the first of Newall's, the general political and defence situation not only continued to deteriorate, but also became exceedingly confusing. The German menace remained, and no one in their senses could feel anything but apprehension as

Nazi energies were poured into the build-up of the armed forces: an army which the British Chiefs of Staff feared would be superior to the French by 1939, and an air force which already showed every sign of being stronger than Britain's. Hitler's foreign policy was quieter in 1937 than in the preceding and following years, but sharp-eyed observers took note of ominous Nazi activities in Austria and in the German-speaking Sudetenland of Czechoslovakia. In Spain the flyers and aircraft of the German Condor Legion had already established themselves as a major instrument in General Franco's bid for victory; on April 26 they gave the world a new lesson on the meaning of air power with the destruction of Guernica. Unfortunately, this lesson was so much taken to heart that equally important ones were disregarded. Off the Spanish coasts, the young German Navy was also flexing its muscles; the pocket battleship *Deutschland* was bombed at Ibiza on May 29 and two days later a German squadron shelled Almeria in retaliation. The realities of reborn German militarism were plain for all to see. Yet it was not Germany herself, but her friends, who held the centre of the stage in 1937.

This was the period when a determination to support good causes, even at the risk of making powerful enemies, went hand in hand with British military impotence. The British lead in promoting worthless sanctions against Italy during the Abyssinian war had had the natural effect of antagonizing that country; constant British pressure for the withdrawal of "volunteers" from Spain (the International Brigades on the Republican side, and on the Nationalist the Condor Legion and some 50,000 Italians in 1937) was another source of friction. British refusal to recognize Italian sovereignty in Abyssinia was a final straw; Mussolini countered with violent anti-British propaganda in the Middle East, exacerbating British difficulties in Palestine, and by substantially increasing the garrison of Libya, threatening Egypt and the Suez Canal. It was precisely at this moment of evidently mounting Italian hostility that Japan set the Far East once more aflame with her attack on China in July; Peking and Tientsin quickly fell, Japanese bombers ranged over Chinese cities, Nanking was heavily bombed in September, Shanghai was occupied two months later. Sir Maurice Hankey summed up the strategic dilemma:

We have our danger in the West [Germany], and our danger in the Far East [Japan], and we simply cannot afford to be on bad terms with a nation which has a stranglehold on our shortest line of communications between the two possible theatres of war . . .[1]

It is in such recognitions of the nation's weakness in the face of its increasing tests that we see the true significance of the "locust years".

The year 1937 was not of unrelieved darkness on the Defence front: in February the Treasury announced a *volte-face*, abandoning its adamant opposition to financing Defence by borrowing, with the flotation of a £400 million Defence Loan. To many at the time, this seemed a "vast sum";[2] the Chancellor would shortly refer to "stupendous sums" that he was being asked for for Defence;[3] to modern eyes, and in relation to war costs, the adjective "modest"[4] seems mild. More impressive, but still not measuring up to real needs, was the announcement in the White Paper on February 16 that defence expenditure could be expected to be not less that £1,500 million in the next five years. This did at least indicate that Britain was at last taking rearmament seriously, even if not yet seriously enough. Less encouraging was the quick inclination of the Treasury to treat the sum mentioned as a maximum; old habits die hard. And if a country unused to such measures was impressed by its own new-found virility, we may doubt whether, as some believed, "This vast programme of rearmament made an immense impression throughout the world."[5] More warships and more RAF squadrons in the Mediterranean would have made an even better impression.

The worst omen of 1937 was the ministerial change in May: Stanley Baldwin retired, and Neville Chamberlain became Prime Minister, with Sir John Simon as Chancellor of the Exchequer. Anthony Eden was Foreign Secretary. A new card had already been introduced into the political pack: a Minister for Coordination of Defence. Sir Thomas Inskip took up that office in March 1936, and held it until January 1939. Chamberlain, of course, was the dominant personality, as he had been as Chancellor; the personal pre-eminence of that strange man is an important element in the politics of the time. He had that strength which comes from a remarkable degree of self-assurance; unfortunately, this quality itself was in his case founded neither on deep knowledge nor on particular expertise, but all too often on pure ignorance. We have seen (p. 26) how in 1934 he unhesitatingly "took charge" of defence requirements. As Chancellor of the Exchequer he showed no diffidence whatever in challenging the opinions of the Chiefs of Staff on strategic and other military matters – indeed, he attached little weight to those opinions. Now, as Premier, he took the same position over foreign policy, ignoring, bypassing and brushing aside the Foreign Secretary. The consequences we know too well; the reasons continue to be disputed. I would suggest three main strands in Chamberlain's approach, and its outcome, the policy called "Appeasement".

The word itself has been subjected in recent years to sharp and sceptical scrutiny, yet as a political reality it does not readily lose force. Appeasement was, in fact, a disastrously effective political position, and since Chamberlain was its prime exponent he has been accordingly attacked with bitterness, and sinister motives have been attributed to him as leader of the "Guilty Men". Recent research presents a different picture; Chamberlain's personal attitude towards the dictators does not now appear all that different from Eden's or Churchill's. As regards the Nazis, as Dr Wrench says, "he regarded them with hatred and contempt";[6] such episodes as the brutal murder of the Austrian Chancellor Dollfuss sickened him no less than anyone else. Regarding Mussolini, he clung to the idea of keeping Italian Fascism and Nazism apart by friendly gestures long after any such possibility had evaporated. But fundamentally, the conflict between the appeasers and the resisters was one of method rather than intention.

Chamberlain's methods were dictated, first, by an attitude towards all things military which was far from common in men of his age and background. Neville Chamberlain was born in 1869; 31 years of his life had passed in the nineteenth century – the formative years. This, and his Birmingham business upbringing, were decisive:

> The school of thought which remained predominant throughout the great industrial epoch bitterly resented the assumption, made by certain classes, that the profession of arms was more honourable in its nature than commerce and other peaceful pursuits ... Inefficiency, indifference, idleness, trifling and extravagance were a standing charge against soldiers as a class ... The soldier ... according to Political Economy, was occupied in a non-productive trade, and therefore it was contrary to the principles of that science to waste more money on him than could be avoided.[7]

The experience of the First World War seemed, to men like Chamberlain, to underline every word of this text; it positively hurt to put large sums of money in the hands of military profligates of doubtful competence. And it hurt all the more because – this is the second strand – Chamberlain, all his supporters and above all the senior officials of the Treasury, had an immense, overwhelming respect for money itself. They really did believe, as Brian Bond says, that "economic stability was one of the cornerstones of the nation's defence structure and an integral part of the defensive strategy."[8] This would have serious implications for Defence planning, particularly affecting the RAF, as we shall see. Finally, in Chamberlain's make-up, and perhaps the decisive element, was sheer conceit, the self-assurance referred to above, which Dr Wrench calls "his unassailable belief in his own rectitude".[9] All in all, it was a formidable combination.

It was, then, with more money in its pocket than it would recently have dared to dream of, but still not enough, and under the eagle eye of a premier innately hostile to military spending, that the RAF approached the last crisis before the war. The key word, of ill omen, during this period was "parity". Ever since Hitler had made his startling boast of air equality to Simon and Eden in March 1935, the fear of German air power had been growing in Britain. Linked to the theory of the "knock-out blow" (p. 12), it had most serious effects in decision-making circles. In October 1936 the Joint Planning Committee of the Chiefs of Staff examined the probable course of a war starting in 1939, and pronounced:

> We are . . . convinced that Germany would plan to gain her victory rapidly. Her first attacks would be designed as knock-out blows . . . It is clear that in a war against us the concentration, from the first day of war, of the whole German air offensive ruthlessly against Great Britain would be possible. It would be the most promising way of trying to knock this country out . . .[10]

The Joint Planners then proceeded to draw a picture of casualties mounting to 150,000 within a week, internal security breaking down, and "angry and frightened mobs of civilians" trying to sabotage RAF aerodromes. The hysterical reactions of civilians to the air raids of the First World War were bearing poisoned fruit; fear of a breakdown of civilian morale was very strong at this time. One of the country's most famous military experts, Major-General J. F. C. Fuller, who was passing through a period of searching doubt about democracy's survival capacity, was writing of air power achieving victory "through terror and panic"; after even one air raid, said Fuller,

> London for several days will be one vast raving Bedlam, the hospitals will be stormed, traffic will cease, the homeless will shriek for help, the city will be a pandemonium. What of the Government at Westminster? It will be swept away by an avalanche of terror.[11]

The Joint Planning Committee has been taken to task for its "disgraceful estimate of the guts of their fellow-countrymen".[12] The Air representative on it was Group Captain A. T. (later Sir Arthur) Harris; the naval spokesman was Captain T. S. V. Phillips, who was to fall victim to Japanese air power in HMS *Prince of Wales*, and for the Army Colonel Sir Ronald Adam, Adjutant-General, 1941–46. Their prognostications seem unduly alarmist with the hindsight that 1939–45 was to bring, but in those last pre-war years they were in good company. And as Marshal of the RAF Sir John Slessor said, it must be remembered that "before 1939 we really knew nothing about air warfare".[13]

Slessor became Deputy Director (in effect Director) of Plans at the Air Ministry in May 1937. He very soon became alarmed at what he was able to discover on the subject of air parity with Germany, the more so in view of the limping progress of British industry with the production of new aircraft. Air Ministry Intelligence estimated that Germany already had "800 bombers technically capable of attacking objectives in this country from bases on German soil";[14] by September, 738 were identified in units, but the estimate of those actually serviceable was put at 500–600. In addition, Italy was credited with a long-range striking force of over 400 bombers.

> Against this we could mobilize in Bomber Command only ninety-six corresponding "long-range" bombers – thirty-six each of Blenheims and Wellesleys and twelve each of Battles and Harrows, pretty poor stuff compared with the Ju 86, He 111 and Do 17, of which we knew some 250 were mobilizable in Germany. Our nominal bomber strength was 816 in the Metropolitan Air Force; but the remaining 700 odd were mostly obsolete short-range types like Heyfords, Hinds, Audax and Ansons, and in any event over 30 per cent of the squadrons would have to be "rolled up" on mobilization to provide some reserves for the remainder.
>
> Here was something to keep one awake at night![15]

Slessor did not let grass grow under his feet; on September 3 (interesting date) he and his fellow Deputy Directors submitted a paper to the CAS in which they said:

> ... the Air Staff would be failing in their duty were they not to express their considered opinion that the Metropolitan Air Force in general, and the Bomber Command in particular, are at present almost totally unfitted for war; that, unless the production of new and up-to-date aircraft can be expedited, they will not be fully fit for war for at least two and a half years; and that even at the end of that time, there is not the slightest chance of their reaching equality with Germany in first-line strength if the present German programmes are fulfilled ...[16]

Newall and Swinton were impressed by this forthright language, and the Air Staff was requested to draw up a scheme to produce, in

Swinton's words, "what as a General Staff you consider is militarily the proper insurance for safety, leaving it to the Cabinet to decide the extent to which the programme should be carried out". The result was Scheme "J" (October 1937), "in many respects the best of all the schemes submitted".[17]

Scheme "J" proposed a bomber force of 90 squadrons (as compared with 70 in Scheme "F") of which 64 would be heavy and 26 medium (as compared with 20 heavy and 65 medium in the abortive Scheme "H"). The first-line strength (1,442) was actually slightly lower than that proposed in Scheme "H", but the aircraft were to be more powerful and the figure was real – not dependent on juggling with reserves or overseas Commands. There was also better provision for reserves within the scheme. Scheme "J" was due for completion by the spring of 1940 – if agreed. It had, however, two snags: first, it involved the mobilization of industry, and even with the lowering stormclouds of 1937 neither the Government nor the nation was yet ready to go that far. Secondly, the Minister for Coordination of Defence recoiled from the cost – and in doing so he used the argument of the knock-out blow to challenge the Air Staff's view of strategy:

> If Germany is to win she must knock us out within a comparatively short time owing to our superior staying power. If we wish our forces to be sufficient, to deter Germany from going to war, our forces – and this applies to the air force as much as to the other Services – must be sufficiently powerful to convince Germany that she cannot deal us an early knock-out blow. In other words, we must be able to confront the Germans with the risks of a long war, which is the one thing they cannot face.[18]

The RAF's rôle, argued Inskip, "is not an early knock-out blow . . . but to prevent the Germans from knocking us out". He was not, he insisted, arguing for nothing but fighters:

> That would be an absurdity. My idea is rather that in order to meet our real requirements we need not possess anything like the same number of long-range bombers as the Germans . . . the numbers of heavy bombers should be reduced.[19]

Pursuing this line of thought, he suggested substituting "a larger proportion of light and medium bombers for our very expensive heavy bombers". This, of course, flew in the face of all expert thinking; the whole development of modern aircraft – the very power of the new fighters themselves – was forcing bombers (except for specialized purposes) to become larger and larger. As it was, the outbreak of war

51

found the RAF with too many light bombers of practically no value; Inskip's suggestion would have compounded that disastrous condition. But Inskip was not really thinking about tactics and strategy; like too many of his Government colleagues, he was thinking above all of expense – and in this he received strong support from the Prime Minister, who stressed the need for economic stability once again. So Scheme "J" was referred back for cuts to make it cheaper – embodied in Scheme "K" of January 1938. But this never left the ground, because 1938 was the year when everything began to fall apart.

The first sign of the new bad times was the German occupation of Austria in March – once more in flat defiance of the Treaty of Versailles. More significant but not yet apparent was a German strategic advantage which became clearer as the Czech crisis developed only a few weeks later. Czechoslovakia's powerful frontier defences against Germany were now outflanked by the open 250 miles of what had been the Austrian frontier, a fatal weakening. More blood-curdling to British opinion, however, at this stage, was the bombing of Barcelona between March 16 and 18, chiefly by Italian aircraft; some 1,300 people were killed and about 2,000 wounded – a total not vastly different from Britain's in the whole of the First World War. And it was in London that the Barcelona raids made a significant impact; it was officially calculated, on the basis of these losses, that one ton of bombs would produce 72 casualties. Later, however, taking *all* raids on Barcelona into account, it appeared that the average number of people killed by a ton of bombs was three and a half. "This new casualty ratio was not apparently substituted in the British Home Office plans for the earlier and more drastic figures."[20]

This example of what air power could do in only three days seemed to bear out all the prognostications of the knock-out blow, and was prominent in the minds of public men and public opinion as the Czechoslovakian crisis built up through the summer of 1938. The Barcelona raids denoted a deep advance into the comfortless future, with every probability of worse to come. Yet calm examination of what history had already revealed about the subject of bombing could have offered some encouragement – if permitted. But just as the very small number of people killed by air action in Britain between 1915 and 1918 was ignored (as was the fact that even in 1917 improved techniques of air defence had made the Germans abandon daylight bombing), so now in 1938–39 there appears to have been no attempt to put Spanish air raid losses into any true perspective. Admittedly, this would not have been an easy task; but it *was* important. Hugh Thomas's calculations, which to the best of my knowledge have not been overthrown, indicate that probably some 14,000 people were killed by air action in the Republican zones during the whole war, and possibly another 1,000 or so in the Nationalist – out of a grand total of approximately half a million dead; in other words, air raids accounted for about three per cent. Even if interim figures pointing towards this conclusion had been discovered and proclaimed, however, it is doubtful whether they would have won any wide acceptance, running as they did absolutely counter to the prophecies of the most respected pundits and the most alarmist science-fiction writers. As Sir John Slessor said many years later:

> We may have been wrong about the knock-out blow; I still do not believe anyone is justified in saying we were *certainly* wrong there . . . And at least no one should judge the men of 1938 without understanding that that was the atmosphere in which decisions were made.[21]

7 Munich

It is not necessary to follow the stage of the Czech crisis once again, from its eruption in May to the miserable outcome of surrender at Munich in September. It is all too clear that neither in Britain nor in France was there any real intention of fighting the dictators in 1938. All that we need to concern ourselves with here, then, is whether or not ideas of air power made a correct or helpful contribution to the strategic assessment on which that frame of mind was founded.

Air marshals and writers on air power have naturally been acutely conscious of the very marked improvement which took place in British aircraft production in the year following Munich; they have been even more conscious, if possible, of the vital increase in modern types, and of the progress in radar development. There has consequently been a tendency among them to accept – certainly with distaste – the Munich policy. Sir John Slessor wrote:

> It is really a waste of breath discussing what Mr Chamberlain should or should not have done at Munich itself. That surrender was the inevitable Nemesis that overcame us as a reward for the follies of the years before.[1]

Sir Maurice Dean, who in the late 1930s was Private Secretary to the Chief of the Air Staff, lists the reasons for not fighting in 1938:

> . . . the re-equipment of Fighter Command had barely begun. The radar chain was half completed. Of the forty-five fighter squadrons deemed necessary at that time only twenty-nine were mobilisable and all but five

of these were obsolete. The five modern fighter squadrons could not fire their guns above 15,000 feet owing to freezing problems . . .

All of these are "knock-out blow factors", and Sir Maurice clearly still believed in 1979 that such a stroke would have been feasible in 1938; he concluded firmly, on the strength of this:

. . . there can be no real doubt that Britain was better placed to fight in September 1939.[2]

J. M. Spaight, in his official monograph written shortly after the war, is equally emphatic:

The Royal Air Force was simply not in a position to fight the *Luftwaffe* in the autumn of 1938.[3]

These are opinions with authority, and they are backed by others. But there is one powerful contrary voice which challenges their basic assumptions, dismisses the knock-out blow, and puts the RAF's disadvantages in a much less dismal light. Ironically, it is Churchill's; ironically, because for the last three years it had been he who sounded the most alarming notes on the subject of the relative RAF *Luftwaffe* strengths – in other words, parity, or the lack of it. We need not pursue the parity argument through all the cloudy realms of contradiction and unreality which it frequently traversed. Basically, it was a dispute between the more conservative Air Ministry view of Germany's real air strength, and a view which had strong Foreign Office backing (especially from Vansittart and Eden) and whose most formidable parliamentary and public mouthpiece was Churchill. According to them, Germany's advantage was already dangerously large, and increasing monthly.

The evidence of subsequent historical research is that the Air Ministry figures were closer to actual truth, though Slessor's memorandum quoted above (p. 50) shows that they were serious enough to rule out complacency. The Foreign Office figures were sounder in the matter of future development, though even there we see a constant tendency to exaggeration. The sombre fact remains that however alarmist Vansittart and Churchill may have been in the strictest terms, they were not alarming enough to galvanize the Government out of its life-time habits – as the fate of Scheme "J" shows. Churchill himself drastically revised some of his opinions, and in *The Gathering Storm* he wrote:

We might in 1938 have had air raids on London, for which we were lamentably unprepared. There was however no possibility of a decisive

Air Battle of Britain until the Germans had occupied France and the Low Countries, and thus obtained the necessary bases in close striking distance of our shores.[4]

In other words, London (and possibly other centres) might well have sustained damage and losses on the scale of Madrid in 1936 and Barcelona in 1938, but definitely not a knock-out blow as envisaged by the Joint Planners and the science-fiction writers. Furthermore, and this is crucial, any projection of air warfare over England in 1938 in the manner seen two years later is quite wide of the mark. The hard facts of aircraft performance and availability bear this out.

The three elements which cast such dire confusion over the parity discussions have been tersely summed up by Slessor as "the fallacy of mere numbers".[5] They are, first, a tendency to treat grand totals as real strength. (It is virtually certain that when Hitler made his boast to Simon and Eden in 1935, if he was not simply lying in his teeth, he was using a grand total figure quite unrelated to military facts.) In order to approach real strengths, we have to look, not at totals, but at front-line numbers; and in order to arrive at final truth we have to break these down again into front-line totals and serviceable totals. Nothing, perhaps, better illustrates the numbers fallacy and the serviceability aspect than No. 19 Squadron of the RAF in August 1938. At the beginning of that month it represented a front-line strength of 16 aircraft, equipped with Gloster Gauntlet fixed undercarriage, open-cockpit biplane fighters. During the month it began to re-equip with Spitfires; at the end of that process its front-line strength was still 16 aircraft – but of course they were aircraft which really belonged to a different world from the Gauntlets. However, during the whole period of the final 1938 crisis No. 19 Squadron's front-line strength was effectively nil, because the Spitfires only arrived one or two at a time, all would require careful inspection and some modification before they could properly "go on the strength" – and pilots and ground-crew would require to be trained with the new machines. For such reasons, all comparative figures are to some degree suspect; furthermore, they almost never agree. However, for what it is worth with these reservations, here is the 1938 reckoning.

Churchill himself gives us totals of German fighters and bombers only:

	Bombers	*Fighters*	*Total*
1938	1,466	920	2,386
1939	1,553	1,090	2,643[6]

Denis Richards offers a comparison of front-line strengths:

	German	British
September 1938	3,307	1,982
September 1939	4,161	1,911[7]

(The drop in RAF numbers was due, he says, to formation of reserves – long needed.) Using a German source, Derek Wood and Derek Dempster offer different figures and a further breakdown of German strength:

	Total	Serviceable
September 1938	2,998	2,542
September 1939	4,204	3,609[8]

The Rise and Fall of the German Air Force 1933–1945, provides a detailed table of the *Luftwaffe* strength as of August 1, 1938, which gives us:

Strength	Serviceable
2,928	1,669[9]

The last figure, which is the one that matters, is repeated in the latest authoritative work on this subject, Dr R. J. Overy's *The Air War 1939–45*:

Strength	Serviceable
2,847	1,669[10]

Happily, Wood and Dempster also accept the total of 1,669 serviceable aircraft as the *Luftwaffe's* real strength at the time of Munich, as well as (with minute variations) the Air Ministry "pamphlet's" breakdown of types including:

Bombers	582
Dive–bombers	159
Fighters	453[11]

So hindsight gives the mighty weapon of the knock-out blow a different aspect. What was so unfortunate at the time was that the calming influence of the Air Staff's more moderate and balanced assessments was offset by its own emphatic belief in the bombing offensive; the RAF was hoist with its own petard. As Stephen Roskill says:

> At the end of 1938 there was in fact little disparity between the *Luftwaffe's* effective bomber strength and that of the western allies . . .[12]

Dr Overy goes further; he states that Britain's serviceable front-line strength in September 1938 was 1,642, and comments: "the great disparity of forces believed to have existed in the air was a myth."[13]

When we turn to performance – a subject as vexed with contradiction as parity itself – this impression is reinforced. It is here that we perceive the force of Churchill's assertion that "there was no possibility of a decisive Air Battle of Britain" in 1938. It is a simple fact that no German fighter could have reached Britain from bases in Germany in that year. The image of Messerschmitt 109s making mincemeat of Gauntlets, Furys and Demons has to be dismissed; the Me 109 did not have the range, and the Me 110 was not yet in service. As regards bombers, range and speed are the key considerations, and at this stage the *Luftwaffe* possessed only two types capable of operating over England from German bases:

	Range	Speed
Do 17F	994 miles	220 mph
He 111E	745 miles	258 mph (maximum; 205 mph with full load)[14]

The hard core of British defence was Fighter Command, and fighters depend for effectiveness on a number of factors: rate of climb, endurance, manoeuvrability, armament – but above all on speed, because a fighter which cannot catch its prey is useless. At turning points of technology, speed becomes particularly significant, because of the possibility of a modern bomber actually outstripping the obsolescent fighter which has to try to shoot it down. As Sir Maurice Dean said, the state of Fighter Command in September 1938 was not encouraging:

Type	Squadrons	Speed (maximum)
8-gun fighters		
Spitfire I	1 (partially equipped; untrained)	355 mph at 19,000 ft
Hurricane	5 (but unable to fire guns above 15,000 ft)	316 mph at 17,500 ft

Type	Squadrons	Speed (maximum)
Others		
Gladiator	6 (biplane)	253 mph at 14,500 ft
Gauntlet	9 (biplane)	230 mph at 15,800 ft
Fury II	3 (biplane); obsolescent	223 mph at 16,400 ft
Demon	2 (biplane); obsolete	182 mph at 16,400 ft[15]

Clearly, Fighter Command would not have had an easy time, trying to deal with whatever proportion of Germany's 582 serviceable bombers appeared over England. Yet the example of the Fiat CR 32 biplane fighters on the Nationalist side in Spain, and the similar Polikarpov I-15s and I-16s for the Republicans, suggests that it could certainly have harried and taken a toll of the *Luftwaffe's* unescorted bombers. But the real question is, would they have been there at all? There is no escaping the impression of dire strategic confusion in the Air Staff at that time, caught in the trauma of having its most cherished beliefs profoundly shaken. When, for instance, it gave practical consideration to what Bomber Command might be doing, it quickly perceived that there was no point in trying to attack such western German airfields as British bombers could reach, because they would find no targets there. The reason was simple, and *clear at the time*: the German Air Force was not, as confidently expected, deployed for a knock-out blow at England, but "concentrated against Czechoslovakia".[16] As long as Czechoslovakia remained in the ring, Fighter Command would not be called upon for a life-and-death struggle.

Obviously, much that we can now say with firmness is due to the blessed quality of hindsight; yet as we consider the hard facts of this air equation, certain observations seem to be appropriate. As we reflect upon Cabinet minutes, the deliberations of the Committee of Imperial Defence and its sub-committees, or of the Chiefs of Staff, to say nothing of the opinion-forming organs and the reflectors of public opinion, we are drawn to the inescapable conclusion that the British people collectively, leaders and led, committed between the wars the cardinal error: they "made a picture" of future war – indeed, more than one. "A general should never paint pictures," said Napoleon, meaning that a general (and the same, of course, applies to a political leader) should never try to force facts into preconceived patterns. In what tone of voice Napoleon uttered this axiom we do not know; sorrowfully, we must suppose, since his own fall was in large part due to this very mistake – "painting pictures".

The British, in the 1930s, painted a picture of the German threat from which the centrepiece was strangely missing; no one, it would seem, ever asked the simple question, "What is the main element of German power?" On the contrary, they rushed in with answers before the question could be properly posed. Thus Sir John Simon, as far back as February 1933, had pronounced: "Germany will rely for her military power above all on military aircraft."[17] Shortly afterwards Baldwin echoed him: "The air was the first arm which the Germans will start to build up."[18] This belief became an almost universal article of faith, undisturbed by clear, prominent evidence to the contrary. When Hitler announced the rebirth of the *Luftwaffe* in 1935, he also announced Germany's return to conscription and the intention to form an army of 36 divisions (see p. 31). By 1937 this army had risen to 39 divisions; by the summer of 1938 the German standing army numbered 47 divisions of which three were armoured (with one more forming) and four were mechanized.[19] This was Germany's unquestionable main weapon – as her neighbours apprehensively understood, but the British only spasmodically and partially compre-hended. And failure to perceive this meant also a wrong estimate of the *Luftwaffe* whose rôle, whatever the intentions of its founders, proved to be to support these powerful ground forces.[20] It was, in other words, a tactical rather than a strategic weapon; Brian Bond rubs the point in:

> Recent research has confirmed that Germany had not made serious plans to bomb London before the Munich crisis and that she would in any case have been incapable of doing so with any hope of success . . . The *Luftwaffe* was unprepared for such a task in nearly every respect.[21]

Since these delusions are intimately bound up with the history and development of the Royal Air Force, it seems in order to digress briefly to see how they came about. How was it possible to "miss" such an object as the Germany Army? We may find the cause (as with many of Britain's misfortunes then and later) in the almost universal national misunderstanding of the previous war, only twenty years past. The United Kingdom's deathtoll of three quarters of a million (almost a million for the whole Empire) between 1914 and 1918 had shocked the British of all parties, creeds and classes more than anything in their previous history, and more than any other partici-pating nation. It was not only the casualties (though these affected people with a force which remained and remains quite impervious to comparisons with other belligerents, Allied or enemy); there was also the damage done to British concepts of freedom by national mobiliz-ation; and there was a sense of sacred island security having been

59

breached by the new frightening weapons, submarines and aircraft.

All these factors constituted grim warnings which remained fresh in the minds of men and women at all levels. In the political front ranks of the 1930s were men who had held office during the war, and were thus by association in part responsible for its horrors: Sir John Simon, who had resigned from the Home Secretaryship in 1916 in protest against conscription, the Liberal leader Sir Herbert Samuel, who had succeeded Simon at the Home Office, Neville Chamberlain, who was Director of National Service in 1917. Their revulsion from any repetition of the events with which they had been all too intimately concerned was intense. Others drew an equally vigorous revulsion from experience at the "sharp end" – "the trenches" (to use a favourite, but often misleading expression of the time). Among them was Anthony Eden who, as a young Rifleman officer, had seen "the destruction of the world as I knew it . . . Every single male member of the family, with whom I had spent my life before the war, was dead, wounded or captured."[22] Clement Attlee, Leader of the Labour Party, had served at Gallipoli; Sir Archibald Sinclair, the new Liberal leader, had been second-in-command in Churchill's battalion of Royal Scots Fusiliers in Flanders. On the benches behind them were men such as Sir Edward Spears, wounded four times in the course of his liaison duties, and many other ex-Servicemen, decorated or otherwise. To all of them, Britain's participation in another land-war of masses on the European continent seemed for a long time to be the ultimate and unthinkable disaster. Many chose to forget or ignore the "basically correct reasons"[23] which had caused Britain to enter that war, and refused to contemplate the possibility that equally sound (or sounder) reasons might compel her to do the same thing again. Not all were wilfully blind, but there were enough who, if the growth of the German Army pointed in a certain direction, preferred not to read the sign. And if the RAF played a prettier tune than the Western Front of 1914–18, they would prefer to listen to that.

Greatly fortifying this frame of mind was the output of certain prominent publicists of the 1920s and 30s. We have already noted the helpful contribution of Major-General J. F. C. Fuller to the knock-out blow theory. The writings of Captain B. H. Liddell Hart (military correspondent of *The Times* from 1935) lent a spurious "expert" authenticity to the "disenchantment" school of novelists and poets who painted the 1914–18 war, and above all the British contribution, as one vast exercise in stupidity, incompetence and futility. Chamberlain was much impressed by Liddell Hart's writings, but he was by no means the only one; as Brian Bond says:

... it was precisely because he articulated, albeit with more cogency and military expertise, the heartfelt feelings of a vast number of people in all walks of life – including the Army – that his writings made their immense appeal to public opinion.[24]

Important military leaders shared, in varying degrees, Liddell Hart's view of the First World War, and its lessons for the future. Thus, in 1926, in the euphoric aftermath of the Locarno Treaties, we find the Chief of the Imperial General Staff, Sir George Milne (commander of the British forces at Salonika, 1916–18) speaking of the First World War as an "abnormal" occurrence, and stating that another continental war was an extreme improbability. He recommended that only a small "Expeditionary Force" of about one infantry division with some cavalry and tanks was ever likely to be needed.[25] Before long the struggle for a viable Expeditionary Force became the touchstone of British defence policy; but the unfortunate truth is that in this matter, as Brian Bond has shown, the Army itself did not speak with a clear, united voice.

All too often, unfortunately, even when rearmament began, it resolved itself into a struggle between RAF requirements and the Expeditionary Force, as though these must always be mutually exclusive. It is characteristic that Inskip, in his note to Swinton urging reductions in Scheme "J" (December 8, 1937) should seek to soften the blow by saying, "I hope to obtain some reduction in the provision made by the War Office for the Expeditionary Force ..."[26] The baleful influence of the theory of the knock-out blow meets us at every turn; Inskip had to admit that even if he did manage to reduce the (virtually non-existent) Expeditionary Force, a proportion of the savings would be swallowed up by anti-aircraft defences. By now there was belated awareness of the very backward state of these in all respects – balloons, searchlights, shells, fuses, guns. The result, inevitably, was more hysteria; of the Home Secretary, Sir Samuel Hoare, General Pownall tartly remarked:

He has no thought in his head except AA guns – he'd put a million of them in if he could manage it.[27]

As the Army struggled for funds against a reluctant Treasury, the demands of Home Defence against the knock-out blow seriously conflicted with the need to build up a credible land force to oppose Germany's expanding army. Nevertheless, one senses in addition a hesitation, an enfeebling doubt about the Continental commitment within the Army leadership itself right up to the last (well after Munich) moment. For this two causes may be traced.

There was, first, and in particular among the rising generation who had been regimental or junior staff officers in 1918, a sense of the First World War on the Western Front having witnessed a nadir of generalship and command by which they felt professionally contaminated. Large armies, static warfare and huge losses seemed to go hand in hand, and were anathema. They were against British tradition, what Liddell Hart called "the British way in warfare". By contrast, General Allenby's swift-moving 1918 campaign in Palestine (certainly as depicted for Staff College consumption by such teachers as Colonel A. P. Wavell, for example[28]) seemed to offer the right alternatives. The critiques of Liddell Hart and others (Fuller, with his Tank Corps background, was prominent) supported belief in new styles of war. In the ranks of the older generals, conservatism delayed the development of armoured warfare doctrines; nowhere in the Army, however, was there sufficient conservatism to advocate – actually advocate – a return to 1914–18 trench warfare. And it was all too easy to represent plans for an Expeditionary Force as leading to precisely that.

False prophets of air war had misled their fellow-countrymen with the knock-out blow; false analysts of land war were equally misleading. None of them seemed to see that there had been nothing even odd, let alone unique, in the British experience of 1914–18. None asked whether phenomena identically affecting all the armies engaged, and generals reared at academies as different as St Cyr, Potsdam, West Point, Vienna, St Petersburg and Sandhurst, might have an explanation a little more plausible than universal simultaneous idiocy. Above all, nobody rammed home the lesson that trench warfare itself had been overtaken by technological progress and was already defunct, on the Western Front in 1918. But the war of masses was by no means defunct, and the "gurus" of the 1930s have much to answer for in helping to expose Britain to that test again in total unpreparedness, mental as well as material. Here, too, the image of the air force as the "cheap" weapon (see p. 6) played its sinister part. But worst of all was the "picture": the "picture" of a world which thought the same way about mass warfare as the British. It did not. The 47 divisions of the 1938 *Wehrmacht* were not for ceremonial parades.

Secondly, there was another "lesson" of 1914–18 which exercised a baleful effect on British soldiers throughout the inter-war years. In 1914 Britain's minuscule Expeditionary Force of four infantry divisions had found itself fighting beside French forces numbering 61 infantry divisions. The British Commander-in-Chief, Field-Marshal Sir John

French, soon reached a painful realization of where strategic control lay – inevitably, with the commander of the Army which enjoyed this great preponderance, General Joffre. In due course the BEF itself rose to a strength of 61 infantry divisions – a size never dreamt of in Britain's entire military history. But by then the French had 100 divisions on the Western Front, so they still dominated strategy. This was a fundamental fact of life which was clearly grasped by Sir John French's successor, General Sir Douglas Haig; very shortly after he took up his command, he showed the Head of the French Mission at GHQ the orders he had received from the Government:

> I pointed out that I am not under General Joffre's orders, but that would make no difference, as my intention was to do my utmost to carry out General Joffre's wishes on strategical matters as if they were orders.[29]

Between 1916 and 1918 (and never more so than in the final campaign of the war on the Western Front), despite the French preponderance in numbers, it was the British Army which bore the chief burden of the fighting by engaging the main body of the main enemy. This was inevitable, in view of the enormous French losses in 1914 and 1915, followed by the attrition of Verdun; and as 1939–45 would prove again, *somebody* had to engage the enemy's main body. Naturally, while this was happening, the status of the British C-in-C in the alliance was considerably enhanced, particularly in the triumphant last stages of 1918. But Haig, who was an admirable coalition war commander, was never in any doubt about where ultimate control must lie, and indeed, it was largely at his instigation that General Foch was appointed Allied Generalissimo in March 1918. But there were many in the British Army (and in the Government) who never understood the cause of this subordination and deeply resented it. After the war there was a marked tendency to blame much of Britain's loss and suffering upon it. The Army's dislike of the French alliance and the Continental commitment was in no small part due to a dread of once more becoming pawns on a French board; even air marshals were preferable to that. And in this, of course, the soldiers only reflected a national attitude whose vigour was startlingly revealed in the wave of lunatic relief when France fell in 1940 and Britain stood alone.

It has to be said that the delusions of the Air Staff fitted into these various "pictures" all too conveniently. Having convinced themselves from the earliest days of the separate Service that the air weapon was essentially strategic, the airmen could not see – let alone admit – that others (and most significantly their potential enemies) might think differently. Practical demonstrations did not convert them. In Spain, the Madrid and Barcelona air raids and the destruction of Guernica took the eye; they obscured the day-in and day-out activities of the air forces of both sides in close support of ground operations. Indeed, we find the incoming Chief of the Air Staff, Sir Cyril Newall, saying in 1937 that these close-support tactics were "a gross misuse of air forces".[30] The RAF fought every Army demand for squadrons to be allocated to Army cooperation tooth and nail; indeed, one reason for the Air Staff's powerful aversion to a strong Expeditionary Force was dread of the size of the Air Component that it would require. This led Newall into further dangerous courses.

An apparently unnoticed and certainly unregarded sentence in that Joint Planners' paper of October 1936 referred to above (p. 49), forecasting the knock-out blow at Britain, contained this plain warning:

> The success of a knock-out blow by Germany on the Continent would ultimately be as disastrous to this country as the success of an immediate attack on Great Britain.[31]

And the planners even went so far as to say that if "the greater danger" appeared to be land operations by the German Army, "all our resources should be directed against the rear organization and lines of communication of her advancing armies" – which would seem to suggest a long step towards Newall's "gross misuse" of the RAF. Yet Newall remained adamantly opposed to the Continental commitment, an attitude which he had displayed from the moment of becoming CAS.[32] The Munich crisis appears to have taught him nothing, because when the Chiefs of Staff met in December 1938, and Lord Gort (CIGS) and Admiral Backhouse (First Sea Lord) expressed grave misgivings of the consequences of German occupation of the Channel Ports, Newall

> remained unimpressed by any of his colleagues' arguments . . . He did not believe the allies could hold the Low Countries, but he did not regard German occupation of the Channel Ports as necessarily fatal.[33]

Yet it was precisely German occupation of the Channel *airfields* that would make the Battle of Britain possible in 1940, and the lack of it that had made such a thing impossible in 1938. But Newall was unrepentant; when the Chiefs of Staff next met, on January 18, 1939, he was as strongly opposed as ever to an Expeditionary Force which, he said,

> bound us to a land Continental commitment. Once we were launched on land in support of the French in France it might well be impossible to turn off the tap.

This imagery would soon be heard again.

It is quite clear, then, that in 1938 the British Government, most of Parliament, the Army and the Air Force had all "painted a picture" in sharp conflict with reality. It is small wonder if the general public was confused. But what *was* the reality? Unfortunately, it was no less confusing than the "picture". It is impossible to dismiss the air factor, but it has to be frankly confessed that the air factor was not fundamental. Thus Brian Bond:

> It is now clear that from a purely military viewpoint France should have been prepared to risk war by supporting Czechoslovakia in 1938. This was her last opportunity to fight Germany on favourable or at least even terms.[34]

Churchill is just as forthright:

> The German armies were not capable of defeating the French in 1938 or 1939.[35]

He goes even further:

> . . . the French with nearly sixty or seventy divisions could most certainly have rolled forward across the Rhine and into the Ruhr.[36]

Contrary views have been equally forcefully expressed; Sir John Slessor, for example, flatly disputes Churchill's last statement:

> I believe he always gravely overestimated the value of the French Army. That Army under Gamelin was useless in 1939, and . . . I do not believe [it] would have been so much better in 1938 that it could have "rolled forward across the Rhine and into the Ruhr", even against the relatively weak German opposition at the time of Munich.[37]

Eden was another doubter; writing in 1962, he said that even in December 1937 he "did not believe that France could sustain the effort on land by herself".[38] One does wonder, of course, to what

65

extent these post-war judgments were affected by what happened in 1940. However, very few senior British officers would have disagreed with them in 1938. General Gamelin, the French Commander-in-Chief, did not make a good impression, either on soldiers or civilians, when he expounded the French military view in London on September 26.[39]

We do not know, and we never shall, how well or badly the French Army would have performed in 1938. We do know, however, with disagreeable certainty, that it would have received no help worth talking about from Britain – nothing to compare with what it obtained in 1914, which many Frenchmen would say was little enough. But as regards the land warfare capability, which was what counted most, the French Army was still a powerful instrument of war. It had 68 infantry divisions facing Germany, and two "light armoured divisions". Each of the latter contained 87 Hotchkiss H-35 light tanks and 87 Somua S-35 mediums. A reliable authority on tanks informs us that the Somua, when it went into production in 1934 "was probably the finest of all armoured fighting vehicles" of its day.[40] In addition the French had some 800 Renault R-35 infantry tanks, distributed among the infantry divisions, and 400 Hotchkiss with the three horsed cavalry divisions – not a happy marriage. Renault also supplied two battalions (66 machines) of the heavy B-1s, the "Char-B"; in 1940 General Guderian, the famous German tank commander, called this "the best tank in the field". Finally, there was the garrison of the Maginot Line, the equivalent of another 11 divisions. In one arm the French definitely enjoyed a marked superiority: as late as 1940 they had more than 3,000 more artillery pieces than the Germans, and in 1938 their advantage was considerably greater. In anti-tank guns, however, they were already badly lagging.

In the air the picture was very different. The French Air Force had, for various reasons, been in decline since 1933, and by 1938 the overwhelming majority of its supposed 1,375 front-line aircraft were either seriously obsolescent or downright obsolete. The Chief of the Air Staff, General Vuillemin, said that he could put no more than 250 fighters and 320 bombers in the air, all of doubtful performance. He expected to sustain 40 per cent casualties in the first month, and 64 per cent by the end of the second, a cheerless prospect indeed.[41] Vuillemin told his government in September 1938 that he hoped to be supported by 120 British bombers after one week, and another 120 in 25 days. How helpful this would have been to him – even if realistic – has to be assessed in relation to the equipment of Bomber Command at that time:

Type	Squadrons	Speed	Bomb-load	First flight
Fairey Battle	17	241 mph	1,000 lb	1936; obsolescent
Bristol Blenheim	16	260 mph	1,000 lb	1936
Armstrong-Whitworth Whitley	9	222 mph	7,000 lb	1936
Handley Page Harrow	5	200 mph	3,000 lb	1935; obsolescent
Vickers Wellesley	2	228 mph	2,000 lb	1935; obsolescent

By September 1939 there would be six of the new Handley Page Hampden squadrons, and five of the excellent Vickers-Armstrong Wellingtons which remained operational in Bomber Command until October 1943 – a very distinct improvement. If the British airmen show little enthusiasm for going to war at the earlier date, it is understandable. General Vuillemin has been described as being "scared out of his wits";[42] the Royal Air Force was not scared out of its wits, but no thinking airmen could relish battle with a weapon 50 per cent of which was really unfit for combat.

And what of the Czechs, the third element in the anti-Hitler line-up of 1938, and standing at the heart of the storm? Unfortunately, there is no firm agreement among British authorities on the actual strength of either the Czech Army or Air Force. For the former, published figures vary from 17 divisions[43] to 42.[44] In between, Brian Bond speaks of "some 34 Czech divisions"[45] and Liddell Hart of 35.[46] Most historians agree that this army, whatever its precise size, was well equipped with the products of the great Skoda arsenal, and well-trained. Since, betrayed by those whom it thought of as its allies, it did not fight either in 1938 or in March 1939, when Hitler dismembered Czechoslovakia, we do not know what performance it might have offered. It enjoyed the benefit of powerful and well-planned fortifications along much of its frontier with Germany, but as we have seen, the *Anschluss* had turned the southern flank of this defence line. The Czechs did what they could to plug this gap, but there was a limit to what they could achieve between March and September. As regards their Air Force, once again there are substantial discrepancies: Correlli Barnett gives it a strength of 400 aircraft,[47] but Dr Overy says it had a first-line strength of 600,[48] and Telford Taylor quotes a Czech source stating that in 1939 "the Germans got from the Czechs some 1,600 aircraft".[49] The real military strength of Czechoslovakia in 1938 thus remains a mystery; one thing is certain – the presence of some 3¼ million disaffected Sudeten Germans (almost 25 per cent of the total population) cannot have failed to have a weakening effect.

So, on the side of democracy, we find a confused and contradictory balance sheet. It is only when we look at "the other side of the hill" that some degree of clarity emerges. Regarding the German air force, as we have seen, there were serious misapprehensions, but in other respects the British Chiefs of Staff were surprisingly well informed. Major-General Pownall, who was at that time Director of Military Operations and Intelligence, set down in his diary on September 25, 1938 what he believed to be the disposition of the German land forces:

Facing France	nine divisions, with two in immediate reserve
Facing Italy	none – all withdrawn
Facing Yugoslavia	none – all withdrawn
In E. Prussia	three normal divisions and two Cavalry (or Light) divisions
Round Czechoslovakia from Silesia – through   Dresden – round   to Vienna some twenty-eight divisions including their mountain divisions, all their armoured divisions, and two or three light divisions
In reserve	some six regular divisons and in various places *about* eighteen reserve divisions.[50]

Modern researches show this appreciation to have been substantially correct; thus Telford Taylor, in a chart showing the German Order of Battle in September, confirms Pownall's estimate of the number facing France, and places 30 infantry divisions (including mechanized and mountain) on the Czech front (compared with Pownall's 28) with 3 light and 3 armoured (as Pownall). However, he adds that the German Army had very small trained reserves. What strikes one immediately is, as Pownall said, "the comparatively lightly held Western front, implying that they do *not* believe the French will march".[51] What also strikes one is that Churchill was absolutely right when he said "the German armies were not capable of defeating France in 1938". This was certainly also the view of the German General Staff. What it meant was that there could not have been a 1940-style Battle of France in that year, and as we have already noted, it was only the outcome of the Battle of France that made the Battle of Britain possible. The Joint Planners had not been wrong in 1936, when they gave their warning of the disastrous consequences of a "knock-out blow on the Continent". They should have proclaimed it more loudly; there were a great many preconceived opinions to contend with.

One question remains: granted that British and French terrors about 1938 itself were not in full degree justified, how would a war have continued into the next year? Once again, there are widely divergent views: on the one hand there are those who insist that, so far from Munich giving a "breathing space" to the West, it was the Germans who profited most from the delay. By that reckoning, Germany might have won in 1939 the victory that she certainly could not have won in 1938. Others, on the other hand, find it hard to believe that Germany could have sustained war for any length of time; they point to

> . . . an inadequately mobilized war economy, an insufficiency of strategic stockpiles, an incomplete western line of fortifications, and an officer corps whose upper ranks lacked confidence in the chances of success . . .[52]

For the RAF, certainly, 1938 was the bad time, after which things could only get better. We have seen that new types did, in fact, begin to come into service during the next year; the numbers were inevitably small to begin with, but they were increasing. British aircraft production, in fact, was turning a corner, as this table shows:

	German	British
1938	5,235	2,827
1939	8,295	7,940
1940	10,826	15,049[53]

In 1938–39, however, the advantages were all in the pipeline.

It is generally pointless to speculate beyond the first stage of any potential military operation, and in the case of the Munich crisis it is also unnecessary. Clearly, France was not going to be attacked in 1938 – but that is not what mattered. What mattered was Czechoslovakia. As long as Czechoslovakia remained in the field, giving employment to the bulk of the German forces, land and air, the Allies would have a good chance which might get better; without her, their chances deteriorated very sharply. And there was only one thing that could keep the Czechs in the fight – a French Army not merely undefeated, but rolling, in Churchill's words, "across the Rhine and into the Ruhr". Materially, it is ridiculous to suggest that 68 French divisions could not have overcome the five regular and four reserve German divisions holding the incomplete "West Wall". A prompt, heavy offensive by, say, 40 French divisions was bound to make progress and pull substantial German forces away from the Czech front – and thus keep the Allied chance alive. But here we come full circle, and further speculation is needless. A "prompt, heavy offensive" by the French Army was not just a military consideration; it required political sanction – and everything that we know informs us that the French Government was resolved not to fight. So the verdict on 1938 must be that while the military balance was by no means as unfavourable to the Allies as is often suggested, the favourable military aspects were annulled by political cowardice, to which, it has to be said, the prognosticators of air warfare had contributed more than their share. The result, in Churchill's unshaken verdict, was "defeat without a war".[54]

8 Coming of age, coming of war

The Royal Air Force was born on April 1, 1918. History decreed that the year of its coming of age should also be the year in which it entered on its greatest test. And history decreed, too, that those who best knew the stripling Service could only view the imminence of that test with deep trepidation. The period leading up to and following the Munich crisis was one of truly agonizing reappraisal for the Air Staff and senior commanders. This was, of course, concealed from Parliament and the country at large, and also from the air and ground-crews for reasons of morale (though the more thoughtful and observant of them must have had their own apprehensions). Yet it is difficult to discover that anyone – anyone at all – took in the full measure of the disarray[1] of the RAF as it went to war – which was perhaps just as well.

The true position in September 1939 may be briefly summarized as follows: of the three operational Commands, one (Coastal) was an acknowledged Cinderella, weak in numbers and almost entirely equipped with obsolescent aircraft.[2] The second (Fighter) did actually possess – but in barely adequate numbers – two aircraft types which were fully capable of carrying out their intended rôles; but the Commander-in-Chief was locked in head-on dispute with the Air Staff over fundamental strategy. The third (Bomber) was the real core of the RAF, the embodiment of its offensive capability – indeed, of its very independence. Yet in May 1939 its Commander-in-Chief described Bomber Command as lacking the strength and efficiency to go to war "within any predictable period".[3] This very distinguished officer was also locked in head-on dispute with the Air Staff and the possibility of his dismissal was already under consideration.[4] So for the immediate purposes of war Britain possessed not so much an air force as an unformed embryo. The Official History says:

70

Bomber Command in 1939 was above all an investment in the future.[5]

The words might apply to the whole of the RAF.

It may seem strange that such grave hazards should go unremarked, but the circumstance is not unfamiliar. In September 1914 a handful of informed men (Churchill among them) would have been justified in concluding that Britain had already to all intents and purposes lost the First World War. Her only army was said to have been virtually shattered in a Continental disaster,[6] while her pride and pillar, the Grand Fleet, was driven to refuge on the western coast of Scotland by the new threat of underwater weapons. Fortunately, matters do not always appear to those taking part in the cold light in which historians later view them. That was very true indeed of 1939–40; as Churchill said of another of the many crises of that period:

> It is odd that while at the time everyone concerned was quite calm and cheerful, writing about it afterwards makes one shiver.[7]

Let us now examine the RAF's predicament in more detail. Coastal Command (Air Chief Marshal Sir Frederick Bowhill) need not detain us long; it would shortly claim the distinction of being the first to shoot down a German aircraft (see p. 228) – a feather in the cap, but not an indicator of combat capacity. More pertinent was the recognition that the Command was quite incapable of offensive action. As far back as January,[8] the Air Staff had transferred the task of attacking the German Fleet to Bomber Command – a decision with far-reaching results, as we shall see.

The position and status of Fighter Command (Air Chief Marshal Sir Hugh Dowding) had undergone a dramatic transformation. The last pre-war RAF expansion was outlined in Scheme "M"; this was announced by the new Secretary of State for Air, Sir Kingsley Wood (appointed in May) to the House of Commons on November 10, 1938, while Scheme "F" was still running (see pp. 34–5). Timed for completion on March 31, 1942, Scheme "M" planned to raise the Metropolitan Air Force to 163 squadrons (2,549 first-line aircraft) with an all-heavy Bomber Command of 85 squadrons, and Fighter Command increased from the 38 squadrons proposed in the short-lived Scheme "L" (April 1938) to 50. This new emphasis on the fighter arm was the scheme's distinguishing feature: "I propose," said Sir Kingsley Wood,

> to give the highest priority to the strengthening of our fighter force, that force which is designed to meet the invading bomber in the air.

So one of the revolutions initiated under Ellington came to fulfilment (see p. 23); Baldwin's dictum, "the bomber will always get through", was overthrown; the main business of the RAF, for the time being at any rate, would be to see to it that the German bombers did not get through.

This was no random conversion; it was a fruit of the revolutions of technology and technique which had made possible the fast eight-gun fighters and the now expanding chain of RDF stations which Fighter Command, under Dowding's tutelage, was weaving into a new instrument of defensive war. And in one area at least the habitual bottlenecks and logjams of production appeared to be breaking up: between February and May 1939 the output of fighters exceeded forecasts by 25 per cent. During those four months 467 Hurricanes, Spitfires and Gladiators were delivered, and by the end of June Fighter Command even had a reserve of 200 modern aircraft.[9] By August, with the addition of 14 Auxiliary squadrons, the Command attained a total of 39 – but it was now evident that the remaining 11 (and more besides) would be needed long before March 1942. And while the equipment aspect of Fighter Command offered some encouragement, others did not:

> From 1937 onwards the expansion programmes were not satisfactorily carried out. Peacetime conditions in the British aircraft industry and the voluntary system of recruitment could not provide the aircraft or the men required to complete the expansion schemes in full, and, towards the end of 1937, the Air Ministry were faced with the alternatives of maintaining first-line strength without adequate reserves, or of building up sufficient reserves for a smaller number of first-line squadrons than they were publicly committed to raise. It is doubtful if even this unhappy choice existed as far as Fighter Command was concerned. The scale of the home-based bomber effort could be controlled in wartime in the interests of economy, but not that of the fighters. *This would be dictated by the size and intensity of the enemy's attacks.* [My italics.][10]

This, too, was a familiar lesson of the First World War, now being painfully re-learned.

Dowding's quarrel with the Air Staff developed as realities thrust themselves forward. It was a three-pronged argument: first, there was the question of deployment, secondly, of German intentions, thirdly, of conflicting requirements of the RAF itself. The deployment scheme which Dowding inherited envisaged four defence zones, each containing a minimum force which could be reinforced from other zones when attacks developed. This already foresaw a need for 46 squadrons – seven more than Dowding possessed when war broke out. Still under the influence of the "knock-out blow" theory, it also envisaged attacks on a scale of 1,000 sorties a day for the first fortnight, and it assumed (among other things) that a concentrated attack on London by 1,000 aircraft would take three hours. Dowding became more and more sceptical of all this theorizing; he doubted whether squadrons could be switched in a crisis with the speed that would be called for. In October 1938 he told the Deputy Chief of the Air Staff (Air Vice-Marshal R. E. C. Peirse):

> The suggestion that a raid on London can be "held" for two hours, while fighters fly down from Scotland to intercept it, can only be described as fantastic.[11]

He accordingly abolished the four defence zones of the original scheme, substituting a linear deployment in three uneven Groups: the main strength in No. 11, in the south, about half as many in No. 12 in the centre, and fewer still in No. 13 in the north. He accepted the obvious risks beyond the London area, believing that that was where the initial battles were certain to be fought.

The second and third arguments were both, in different ways, related to the very late acceptance of the Continental commitment which the Air Staff under Newall had so bitterly resisted (see pp. 63–4). This was an emotional and doctrinaire attitude whose practical implications were fairly devastating:

> It was not until July 1939 that any attempt was made to assess in terms of fighters what a German occupation of the Low Countries would mean to the air defence of Great Britain. Ten more fighter squadrons were recommended to offset the German dive-bomber units, which could only operate effectively against Britain from bases in Holland and Belgium. No additions were recommended to deal with the increased effort which the long-range bombers would be capable of, nor to counteract the escort fighters which might accompany them.[12]

The Royal Air Force was awaking to a world of very bleak realities which became apparent most quickly to the Commanders-in-Chief. The Air Staff expectation – against which the 46 fighter squadrons had been prescribed – was attack by some 2,000 German bombers. For Dowding, directly facing that threat, duty, in the span of time between Munich and war, resolved itself into a fight for the 46 squadrons, which also meant a fight against any extra commitment unless extra provision was made for it. The bleak reality of having to meet dive-bombers and German fighters was an extra commitment which could not be avoided if the Germans obtained the necessary airfields – therefore there must be more squadrons in Fighter Command. Another bleak reality which was only perceived at the last moment was the need to protect convoys up and down the East Coast. In theory this should have been a function of Coastal Command; in practice, it meant a demand for four squadrons from Fighter Command. Dowding resisted; 46 squadrons, he stated flatly, was his minimum requirement to defend the country; he only had 39; he could do no more. The Navy suddenly awoke to the lack of any modern fighter defence for the Home Fleet at Scapa Flow (an amazing oversight); two more squadrons were required. They did not exist, said Dowding; nor, indeed, did they, until the spring of 1940, with the result that the Home Fleet was forced to adopt the same depressing expedients as the Grand Fleet in 1914 – seeking refuge off the West Coast of Scotland (see p. 71). At the same time it was realized that Northern Ireland, with the large industrial centre of Belfast, might need to be defended too, and one squadron would be required for that. Only one squadron – but it was a squadron that Dowding did not have. There was nothing in the slightest degree frivolous about the late demands for these seven squadrons, but Dowding had to resist them all. Yet there was one demand that he could not resist, and which alarmed him more than anything.

On March 15, 1939 Hitler seized the rest of Czechoslovakia, in mockery of the Munich "agreement". At that moment the prospect dreaded by so many for twenty years, and strongly opposed by the Air Staff, a commitment to another war on the Continent as part of a coalition in which the French would have the chief land force (and therefore the commanding voice in opposing the *Wehrmacht*), became a certainty. The truth is that it had been a certainty from the moment the *Wehrmacht* was born, and all those who averted their eyes from this obvious portent must bear a share of blame. But in 1939 what mattered was that another British Expeditionary Force was going to be needed, without the decade of preparation for its 1914 predecessor, and that it would clearly need an ingredient that the 1914 Force did not – air protection. This was something that Dowding could not refuse, though he could – and would – strive to limit the drain on Fighter Command. Too much of a realist, too honest – and patriotic – for subterfuge, Dowding saw and said that the only possible aircraft that could give the BEF the protection it required were fighters of the modern type – Hurricanes. Four Hurricane squadrons were accordingly taken from him for the purpose, reducing Fighter Command to 35 squadrons – 11 below the minimum defence requirement. Dowding, needless to say, was deeply concerned – and he was not the only one:

> ... the Air Staff took the line that the Army should not be allowed a fighter force the commander of which was subject to the orders of an Army general officer. It was regretted that even four squadrons had been specifically allotted to the Field Force ...[13]

Realities – those bleak realities – took little cognizance of the prejudices of the air marshals. Very soon (May 11) the Air Staff had to tell Dowding to earmark six more squadrons for probable attachment to the BEF Air Component.[14] Dowding was naturally much concerned, and a heated argument ensued; on July 7 he warned the Air Ministry:

> ... the air defence of Great Britain will be gravely imperilled ... If 10 Regular Squadrons are withdrawn, the remaining resources would be altogether inadequate for the defence of this country.[15]

Dowding launched his crusade for more fighter squadrons, but at this stage the Air Staff still pinned its faith to bombers and recoiled from any step likely to hold up the bomber programme. How nearly each Command's requirements affected others at that time may be seen from the fact that when the demand for coastal trade defence did have to be met (in the autumn) this could only be done by allocating Blenheims which would otherwise have gone to the medium bomber force.

To look forward a little further, in order to follow this vitally important argument, in July 1939 we find Newall putting up his last rearguard action against the Continental commitment:

> ... if the demands of the Admiralty and the War Office are to be pressed regardless of the effect on the air defence situation at home it becomes a duty to resist them.[16]

The ironies of this statement will shortly become apparent; meanwhile Dowding, of course, fully supported it. In his view the commitments to the BEF already undertaken constituted a serious threat to the efficiency of his Command. His thoughts on this subject were, in fact, hardening out into a doctrinal position which the Air Staff itself would find simultaneously difficult to accept in theory and impossible to reject in practice – a sure sign that its own thinking was faulty.

Anticipating still further, to complete this tale, with war less than a fortnight old, we find Dowding acknowledging that a "knock-out blow" against France, as contemplated by the Joint Planners in 1936 (see p. 64) was certain, and that it would create new pressing demands for fighters. The first instalment had begun the mischief:

> . . . the despatch of 4 Field Force squadrons has opened a tap through which will run the total Hurricane output.[17]

This echoed Newall's warning in January (p. 64) with even sharper point, because Hurricanes were not just another kind of aeroplane; they and the Spitfires were the life-blood of Fighter Command. And this drew Dowding to his fiercely-held conclusion:

> . . . in any clash of interests Fighter Command must be given priority.[18]

This now (September–October) drew him to what we may call "the Dowding Doctrine"; it was the very opposite of "the Trenchard Doctrine" which had hitherto held unchallenged sway. It was the doctrine of "the Fear of the Fighter".

> The best defence of the country is the Fear of the Fighter. If we are strong in fighters we should probably never be attacked in force. If we are moderately strong we shall probably be attacked and the attacks will gradually be brought to a standstill. During this period considerable damage will have been caused. If we are weak in fighter strength, the attacks will not be brought to a standstill and the productive capacity of the country will be virtually destroyed. The other components of the Metropolitan Air Force will then become a wasting asset and the preservation of their full numbers at the present time will prove to have been a fruitless sacrifice . . . I must put on record my point of view that the Home Defence Organisation must not be regarded as co-equal with other Commands, but that it should receive priority to all other claims until it is firmly secured, since the continued existence of the nation, and all its services, depends upon the Royal Navy and Fighter Command.[19]

"When a man knows he is to be hanged in a fortnight, it concentrates his mind wonderfully . . ." Dowding's lively apprehensions were not yet shared; they soon would be when the "hangman's" tread was heard. Meanwhile, as Denis Richards eloquently remarks:

> However many calls there might be on our resources, Dowding was convinced that one call – the safety of the base – was primary and absolute;

and till that was met, he proposed neither to understand other arguments, nor to compromise, nor even to accept with good grace the decisions that went against him.[20]

The Air Staff, tossed on a four-pronged pitchfork, found no comment that it cared to make – "and it is difficult to see what could have been said without entering upon a long controversy on the nature and application of air power."[21] The Air Staff was in no condition to discuss the nature of air power with Dowding, or anyone else, because as we shall now see its fundamental beliefs were in the melting-pot. On the other hand, it could not accept the "Dowding Doctrine" in all its starkness. It just had to put up with the position that the Commander-in-Chief of Fighter Command held a view of grand strategy that it could not share.

Hugh Caswall Tremenheere[22] Dowding was born in 1882; he was 21 years old when the Wright brothers demonstrated the first practical aeroplane at Kitty Hawk. Ten years later (December 1913) he was granted Royal Aero Club Certificate No. 711, and shortly afterwards was seconded from the Royal Artillery to the Royal Flying Corps Reserve. By 1917 he was a Brigadier-General; his post-war progress in the RAF was steady and continuous until he became the first Commander-in-Chief of the newly created Fighter Command in July 1936. In 1937 he reached the rank of Air Chief Marshal. In 1939 he was 57 years old, and due to retire that summer; in view of the international crisis, however, Sir Kingsley Wood wanted him to stay on for another nine months, and Newall concurred. It says much for the patience and good sense of the leaders of the RAF that Dowding's outspoken disputations did not make them change their minds; instead, his tenure as C-in-C was extended by another three months – months which would be crucial in the history of the world.

And so we come to Bomber Command, the RAF's "Holy of Holies". Since its very earliest days the belief in the offensive rôle of the Service had possessed religious force, with Bomber Command as the priesthood. Even at the end of the 1930s, with Defence a universal preoccupation, and fighters coming into the ascendant, it remained axiomatic that Bomber Command's reprisal capacity constituted a powerful deterrent. Strange as it may seem – but when what ought to be practicalities assume a religious content all things are possible – it was not until 1937 and 1938 that any real examination of bombing strategy and tactics took place. It was not until then that a serious attempt was made to translate the broad dogma of the offensive rôle into detailed plans and operation orders capable of being issued to the Groups and squadrons which would have to carry them out. It was a salutary exercise.

The Bomber Command 1938 table on p. 67 really contains the core of the matter; it requires closer examination. To begin with, there were the 17 squadrons of Fairey Battles; this aircraft was a disaster. It was a single-engined light bomber with a crew of three; it first flew in March 1936 and came into squadron service in March 1937. It was under-powered and it lacked both speed and defensive fire-power. Before it even reached the squadrons it was suspect, and in December 1936 Sir Edward Ellington directed that no more Battles were to be ordered.[23] Yet there it was – a convenient sort of aeroplane for an inexperienced shadow factory to construct, and no fewer than 2,184 were in fact built. How to fit it into an operational plan was a mystery which ended as a tragedy.

The Blenheim was better; it, too, was a light bomber with a crew of three. It was faster than the Battle – sufficiently faster, indeed, to take on an unexpected fighter rôle in 1939–40 – but it was also under-gunned. However, it remained usefully in Bomber Command service until August 1942, and longer than that in overseas theatres. The trouble was its lack of range; if Holland and Belgium remained neutral, it would only just be able to reach targets on the north-west coast of Germany. So the Blenheim, too, was difficult to fit into a strategic offensive plan.

The so-called heavy bombers were hardly more promising. The Handley Page Harrow was frankly a stop-gap; designed as a transport, it was pressed into service as a bomber in 1937 purely to meet the exigencies of expansion. In its original rôle it continued to do good service until 1944, but all the Bomber Command Harrow squadrons converted to Wellingtons in 1939. The Wellesley first flew in 1935; built to a Barnes Wallis design (see p. 28), this aircraft is credited with having won over the Air Ministry to monoplane bombers.[24] The Vickers Wellesley was a two-seat, single-engined aircraft capable of some surprising performances; in November 1938 two of them flew non-stop from Ismailia to Darwin (7,162 miles) in 48 hours. When war came, Wellesleys were active in the Middle East, East Africa, and over adjoining seas until 1942. But it took a long stretch of imagination to consider them as first-line bombers in 1938.

That left the Armstrong-Whitworth Whitley, and it is hardly too much to say that this sturdy old war-horse virtually *was* Bomber Command in the year of Munich. Built to Specification B.3/34, it first flew in March 1936 and delivery to the RAF began in March 1937. A feature of the Mark III was the retractable "dustbin" ventral turret; the Mark IV (squadron service commencing May 1939) featured a powered Nash and Thompson rear turret with four Browning .303 machine guns. We shall have more to say about the Whitley very soon; here we need only add that it was "one of the mainstays of Bomber Command in the early years of the Second World War",[25] that it also did most useful service with Coastal Command, and continued as a glider-tug and paratroop trainer with Airborne Forces well into 1943. Nine squadrons of Whitleys, however, did not make a strategic bombing force.

It was with these depressing considerations that the Air Staff (prominently Group Captain Slessor as Deputy Director of Plans) now began to think very seriously – and belatedly – about what Bomber Command could do, and what it could not. First, what might be called a "shopping list" of possible tasks was drawn up; these were known as the "Western Air" ("WA") Plans (see Appendix A). They covered a wide range of possibilities, from attacking the German air striking force to setting forests on fire, from attacking war industry to dropping propaganda leaflets. With these established, the next question was that of priority, and in establishing that the full limitations of Bomber Command became apparent.

By the time the Munich crisis was coming properly to the boil, three sets of priorities had been identified:

> The attack on the German Air Force in its own western bases, and on the German aircraft industry which supported it (WA 1)

> Attacks on the German Army's rail, canal and road communications to impede its advance in the west and delay invasion of the Low Countries and France (WA 4), in conjunction with the British General Staff and the French Staffs

> Attacks on German war industry, especially in the Ruhr, and also on German oil supplies (WA 5)

One by one, as these alternatives came under the frigid scrutiny of the planners, and above all of Bomber Command's able and realistic Commander-in-Chief, Air Chief Marshal Sir Edgar Ludlow-Hewitt, they had to be struck off.

The project of destroying the German Air Force on its airfields, and at the same time (with luck) rendering those airfields useless, was superficially very tempting. Only superficially; as we have seen (p. 58) the Munich crisis put it in a new light when it was realized that the *Luftwaffe* would not, in fact, be occupying the western airfields which

79

were within reach of the RAF. Even if it had been, however, the task became more daunting the more it was examined. It was known that the Germans were working on emergency airfields to which their aircraft could be dispersed, but these would have to be discovered, and when discovered could easily be changed. As regards their aircraft industry, it was calculated that unless the Germans contrived to lose 100 per cent of their force in the first month, and 50 per cent damage could be done to their factories in the first week, only very long-term effects could be expected from this form of attack. The same applied to fuel oil plants and the manufacture of such components as ball bearings. Sir Edgar Ludlow-Hewitt reported that to mount a really determined attack on these targets would mean the elimination of his medium (actually light) bomber force in three and a half weeks, and of his "heavies" in seven and a half. This, then, could clearly only be a course of desperation.[26]

Attacking the German Army (or its communications) was a course which had never held out any real appeal to the Air Staff. It fell firmly into Newall's category of "gross misuse"; furthermore, it presupposed a whole set of circumstances which no one had envisaged in any detail. It contained disagreeable implications – such as bringing a considerable part of Bomber Command under Army control, or worse still, French Army control. There was disagreement about method: the French preferred attacks on the German Army on the move, in direct support of ground forces; the RAF argued for strikes against fixed communication centres, in particular rail junctions, stations and locomotive sheds. The dense network of western European railways did not in 1938–39, give this a very promising aspect; nor were Bomber Command's aircraft suited to these tasks. In any case, it was not difficult to foresee that either course "would absorb practically the whole force, would result in heavy casualties and would be doubtful in result".[27]

This left the attack on German industry, which had always commended itself. The Ruhr seemed to be a particularly promising target:

This area, smaller than that of Greater London, concentrated within it 70 to 80 per cent of Germany's coal and coke supplies, and 67 per cent of her supplies of pig-iron, as well as 75 per cent of her steel capacity, and most of her basic chemical production. If an early attack were made, before the defences were fully efficient, a crippling blow might be struck at the outset. This view had long been held by the British staffs, together with the opinion that an attack on oil would effect an equally immediate reduction in Germany's capacity to wage war.[28]

80

In 1938 Bomber Command was sufficiently optimistic to predict that by concentrating on 19 power plants and 26 coking plants specified in the latest Intelligence reports, it would be able to bring German war-making capacity to a standstill in a fortnight, and it asserted that this could be done by 3,000 sorties in that space of time at a cost of 176 aircraft. Thereafter, however, the operational difficulties began to loom ever larger; to produce such a result obviously called for precision bombing; it was just beginning to be realized that Bomber Command was neither equipped nor trained for that. And at the same time certain other grave deficiencies in equipment, but above all in training, were becoming apparent, prompting the cruel question, what *was* Bomber Command equipped and trained for in 1939?

To no one did this question pose itself more sharply and insistently than to the Commander-in-Chief, Air Chief Marshal Sir Edgar Ludlow-Hewitt. Four years younger than Dowding (b. 1886), Edgar Rainey Ludlow-Hewitt had also spent the whole of his 1914–18 war in the air force. Commissioned into the Royal Irish Rifles in 1905, he transferred to the Royal Flying Corps on August 1, 1914, received his Flying Certificate (No. 887) later that month, and was seconded for flying duties on September 12. He soon became known in the RFC as a very good flyer; he was also a very good officer, whose steady promotion carried him, like Dowding, to the rank of Brigadier-General, but in his case ending by commanding the X Brigade of the RAF in the field. His post-war career included two Overseas commands (Iraq, 1930–32 and India, 1935–37) and a spell as Director of Operations and Intelligence at the Air Ministry (1933–35). He was the complete professional, with an unfaltering concept of the standards at which the RAF should always aim, and (also like Dowding) unhesitating frankness in identifying shortcomings. And of these there was no lack, he discovered.

Ludlow-Hewitt's appointment as C-in-C, Bomber Command, dated from September 12, 1937; he immediately set out on a tour of inspection to acquaint himself with his new Command, casting his sharp, enquiring eye upon the key aspects of its preparedness for war. He reported to the Air Staff on November 10; what he had to say must have come as an unpleasant shock, and since he was still saying much the same thing when war came two years later, it repays us to take some note of what he found. He admitted that he had expected to discover "a certain amount of confusion and inefficiency . . . as a consequence of the rapid expansion of the Force". He expressed himself as well pleased with the way all ranks, but especially the large number of very junior officers,[29] were coping with their difficulties and lack of experience. He paid tribute to the admirable training provided by the Flying Schools (always an RAF strong point). But when it came to his main interest, preparedness for war, he found "the present situation is most disquieting"; Bomber Command, he pronounced, was "entirely unprepared for war, unable to operate except in fair weather, and extremely vulnerable both in the air and on the ground".[30]

Every page, almost every line, of Ludlow-Hewitt's report contradicts the image of a highly professional, efficient pre-war air force with which the British comforted themselves at the time and continued to delude themselves in after years. Ludlow-Hewitt put forward a number of demands as a matter of urgency, but concentrated his attention on the first two, which were fundamental:

> The provision of the Navigational Aids, Safety Devices, and Safety Arrangements required to enable War Training to be carried out in all conditions of weather.

> A more realistic Aircraft Crew policy, with the object of providing efficient crews, adequate to the tasks required of them in War, without which the Air Force will never become an efficient War organisation."[31]

Ludlow-Hewitt certainly got his priorities right; the next two years saw him arguing undeviatingly that all war planning was hypothetical without operational efficiency, that navigation was central to this, and aircrew training more important than any other single factor. It was here that rapid expansion had had its worst effects (not unforeseen in the Air Ministry: see p. 28). Between 1935 and the outbreak of war, the RAF took nearly 7,000 men for initial flying training; in 1936 four new flying schools were added to the existing five, but they had only 247 pilots on their strength; eight more schools were planned for 1938, but the drain of competent flyers in order to staff them was considered too great. The burden of training was thus thrust upon the squadrons themselves, with the result that in early 1939 there was a deficiency of 1,200 pilots under training.[32]

Navigation, of course, was only partly a matter of training; it was to a large extent a matter also of equipment. It was accepted, said Ludlow-Hewitt, "that decisive air action will ultimately depend upon the power of the Air Force to maintain sustained attack"; this clearly meant that it must be able to operate in all weathers, by day and by night:

> A fair-weather air force is relatively useless and is certainly not worth the vast expenditure now being poured out on the air arm of this country.

And yet today our *Bombing Force* is, judged from a war standard, practically useless and cannot take advantage of the excellent characteristics of its new and expensive aircraft.

These were strong words, but there was worse to come:

> ... little real progress can be made in training Bomber units to operate under the conditions in which they must operate in War until adequate provision is made for the reasonable security of the aircraft and crews undertaking this training.[33]

As Ludlow-Hewitt then spelt out exactly what he meant by this, we begin to perceive the realities of the air force created by abrupt, belated and spasmodic expansion. Bomber Command, he said, would have to fly by day and night over great distances, making flights of 5 to 10 hours in the air, making maximum use of cloud as cover, in order to attack small, inconspicuous targets "in the heart of a strange and hostile country". The very least the crews would require would be the assurance of being able to find their way back to base when they had accomplished this testing mission. And this, after all, was not a far-fetched demand:

> In recent years Civil Aviation has made remarkable progress in providing for the navigation of aircraft through every kind of weather, and today the airline pilots of all the leading European and American airlines are capable and accustomed to flying their aircraft for long periods and for great distances through thick clouds, fog, snow and other adverse conditions. But these pilots depend upon navigational aids and homing devices, combined with an efficient and adequate D/F, meteorological and control organisation on the ground, which are at present far from being available to Royal Air Force pilots.[34]

That catalogue of necessities alone shows how far the RAF had lagged in the process of modernization, which was not simply a matter of introducing new types of aircraft. The high accident rate of Bomber Command emphasized the point: 478 forced landings in two years, due to pilots losing their way. No civil airline could have contemplated such a thing; nor could a civil airline ignore the problems of night-flying in the way that the RAF had (perforce) ignored them. The day- and night-flying hours of Bomber Command illustrate this:

	Day	*Night*
1936	41,644	2,990
1937	129,794	8,773
1938	148,458	14,615[35]

In 1937 only 84 pilots of Bomber Command were qualified for night flying, and of these only 13 were above the rank of Flying Officer. These are matters worth noting, if only to measure the magnitude of the achievement which in so short a time would make long-distance penetration by night a commonplace of air action. In 1937, however, though instrument panels were being introduced ("a very great step forward", said Ludlow-Hewitt), they were not yet complete with all requisite instruments, and lacked a reliable energizing medium. Hoods, for night-flying training in an unblacked-out country, were in short supply; night-flying over the sea for practice was ruled out because the aircraft of Flying Training Schools did not have life-saving equipment. Wireless equipment was carried only by formation leaders, and the layout of that equipment in such aircraft as possessed it was unsatisfactory.[36]

It was during Ludlow-Hewitt's tenure that Bomber Command's largest new problem came to the fore; it went beyond instrument panels, navigation aids and safety devices, important though all these were. Throughout this period there was a universal tendency, in both civil and military aviation, for aircraft to become larger (see p. 51); with bombers, this was enhanced by increasing range, increasing bomb-loads, and increasing requirements for defence against modern fighters. The inevitable effect of this was an increase in the crews. Two-man crews were a thing of the past: the new Hampdens had crews of four, the Whitleys five, the Wellingtons six.[37] Training them *as crews* was the new necessity, with which Ludlow-Hewitt grappled untiringly. In November 1937 he wrote:

> . . . we have been ready to go to great expense in providing highly skilled maintenance personnel, the best possible aircraft and equipment, and all the very costly overheads[38] required to maintain an efficient air force, and yet when it comes to the climax of the whole organisation, namely the crew of the aircraft, we have considered economy before efficiency. Consequently, our crews fall far short of practical war requirements, and are not well devised to carry out the very duties for which alone the force as a whole exists.[39]

Eighteen months later he was again pointing out that modern bombers needed "far higher qualifications in each member of the crew", and that this in turn needed "thorough specialised training of all members of bomber crews". It was no easy matter, he remarked, to train "five or six people to work together in the most perfect understanding, generally with inefficient intercommunication". Too frequent posting, he pointed out, did not help. He did not feel that this matter was sufficiently gripped in the Air Ministry; he felt "an acute sense of the inadequacy of the Force, as it exists today, for the purpose for which it was intended".[40]

How fresh all these considerations were is illustrated by the fact – difficult to grasp today – that the Air Ministry did not at that time consider any aircrew duties except the pilot's to be really full-time occupations. It has to be remembered that the Hawker Hind light bomber was still in front-line service in 1937, and in second-line service with Auxiliary squadrons until 1939. It was a fixed-undercarriage, open-cockpit two-seater biplane, with the observer also doing duty as air gunner. Even the monoplane Wellesleys of 1937–38 had two-man crews, with an open rear-cockpit for the observer/gunner. As Malcolm Smith says,

> The air observer was perhaps the epitome of the amateur status of aircrew at this time.[41]

This "amateur status" was not only a matter of a confusion of functions in the air; it was above all that observer/gunners were provided by volunteer ground-crew, whose air duties were regarded as "spare-time", and paid accordingly. The Air Ministry – though the real villain was no doubt the Treasury – fought a hard rearguard action against recognition of aircrew status. In 1939 1,000 out of 3,000 required Bomber Command observers were still officially observer/gunners. In April 1938 the Ministry did agree to the 10-week navigational course for observers that Ludlow-Hewitt had been demanding since January 1937, but as late as August 1939 he "still had to face the fact that over 40 per cent of a force of his bombers were unable to find a target in a friendly city in broad daylight".[42]

Ludlow-Hewitt was clearly ahead in diagnosing a serious weakness; he was right also in insisting that "the present policy of using highly skilled tradesmen as air observers should now be abandoned".[43] His recommendations, however, though perfectly logical, did not point in the direction that Bomber Command would have to follow. He argued that the contemporary bomber crew was vulnerable, "in that some of its essential functions are centralised in one individual and if this individual becomes a casualty the whole crew may find itself in great difficulty or danger, or at best be unable to fulfil its task". This led him to argue for "a regular standard crew trade" in which all members would be interchangeable in the rôles of air gunnery, bomb dropping, navigation, photography and wireless operator. Pilots and second pilots, he said, should be able to "(a) pilot (b) navigate (c) aim and drop the bomb (d) obtain a D/F bearing (e) work the rotating D/F coil, when provided, and (f) work a gun". This was, of course, a very tall order, reflecting Ludlow-Hewitt's very high standards of proficiency. Faced with the objection that the long training required for such interchangeable expertise would be impossible in war, his reply was:

> It is inevitable that unless we aim for a high standard in peace, we shall have no standard at all in war.[44]

He also flatly stated:

> I am convinced that the idea that we shall be able to fight the next war with mass-produced pilots and crews as we did the last war is fallacious.[45]

The vast wartime expansion of the RAF, which put all peacetime efforts into the shade, was something that no one as yet envisaged; the triumphs of the Training Commands and the Empire Air Training Scheme would have sounded like very wild dreams in 1939. But clearly they could not have been achieved by Ludlow-Hewitt's formula; it was, in fact, the coming of the four-engined bombers which finally rationalized the crew question, in 1942.[46]

Meanwhile, there was another aspect of it which gave him even more concern (indeed, Dr Smith calls it "a particular *bête-noire* of the C-in-C"):[47] air gunnery. This, also, was a victim of the "amateur status" – the situation of the observer/bomb-aimer/photographer/gunner in the rear cockpit, hugging a Lewis gun on a First World War Scarff Ring mounting, which continued well into the late 1930s. The mechanics or fitters who volunteered to serve these weapons earned no promotion advantages by doing so, nor did they become wealthy. Flying regular hazardous sorties over hostile territory (eg in the Near East, or on the North-West Frontier of India) brought a remuneration of sixpence (2½p) a day, with a further 18 pence (7½p) if there was an acknowledged state of war involving "operations". This was the "two-bob bonus". However, all crews did carry leaflets, printed in various local dialects, guaranteeing financial rewards for returning them unharmed if they crash-landed. These were known colloquially as "ghooly-chits"; their value among tribesmen who were considered to be 98 per cent illiterate, were renowned for their artistic cruelty, and usually worked up to a high degree of fanaticism by such leaders as the Fakir of Ipi, was dubious, to say the least. Such reflections help us to understand what Ludlow-Hewitt (and his crews) were up against.

Increasing altitudes, increasing speeds (both of the bombers themselves and of the fighters that would oppose them), new guns (the simple, reliable Browning[48] and the Vickers Gas-Operated (VGO) "M"), reflector sights (very slow in coming), and above all the power-operated turrets whose possession gave the RAF a clear lead over all other air forces,[49] all these developments spelt the demise of the old-fashioned observer/gunner. The Armament Training (114) Squadron's 1938 report revealed a most alarming situation: an average of 20 per cent hits in free gun tests in 1937 had dropped to 0 per cent in the following year. This, said the report, was due to "lack of qualified instructors, lack of proper training equipment and the simple inability of gunners to operate their turrets properly."[50] Ludlow-Hewitt, already aware of these deficiencies, was campaigning for a Central Gunnery School[51] and for proper recognition of air gunnery as a separate specialized function. It was Air Ministry Order (AMO) A.17/1939, dated January 19, 1939, and dealing with conditions of service for "Aircraft Crews (other than Pilots)", which began to tackle the status question. All air gunners were to be full-time, which was a large step forward, but doubling as wireless operators. AMO A.552, in December, gave them their famous half-wing "AG" badge and the rank of at least Sergeant. Not until 1942 were the wireless and gunnery functions properly separated. The Central Gunnery School was formed in October 1939. In other words, only war itself produced the real answers to this key problem.

As war approached, Ludlow-Hewitt perceived gunnery as the main threat to the effectiveness of his Command; in May 1939 he told the Air Ministry:

> There is little doubt that the weakest point of our bomber force at this moment lies in its gun defence . . . I fear that the standard of efficiency of air gunners and their ability to resist hostile attack remains extremely low. Throughout the Bomber Force great uneasiness is expressed on the whole subject of air gunnery . . .[52]

The Commander-in-Chief frankly admitted that the very thought of active operations gave him "most acute anxiety"; he continued:

> We have all this valuable equipment and highly trained personnel depending for its safety upon one inadequately trained and inexperienced individual, generally equipped with a single relatively inadequate gun in a very

exposed position in the tail of the aircraft. Here he has to face the full blast of the eight-gun battery of the modern fighter. The demands which will be made on the coolness, presence of mind, skill and efficiency of this single individual are, in existing conditions, almost superhuman, and in his present state of knowledge and training it is utterly fantastic to expect . . . the efficient defence of our aircraft . . .[53]

This was reality: bleak indeed. And with war only six weeks off, Ludlow-Hewitt had his last word on this subject:

As things are at present, the gunners have no real confidence in their ability to use this equipment efficiently in war, and Captains and crews have, I fear, little confidence in the ability of the gunners to defend them against destruction by enemy aircraft.[54]

It was, indeed, as well that this knowledge was confined to a very small number of men.

And still this was not all. "The bomb, after all," says Sir Maurice Dean, "is what bombing is all about,"[55] – and bombing was what Bomber Command was all about. It had little cause for satisfaction, either with its bombs or its proposed methods of delivering them. As regards the former, the short and bitter truth is that British bombs in 1939 were, generally speaking, awful, as British mines and torpedoes had been in the First World War. Often they failed to explode, and when they did they frequently produced negligible results. The basic reason for the continuation of a bad weapon is failure to test it in realistic conditions. For a variety of reasons, which include the procreative habits of cockles and the peace of mind of swans, the provision of ranges for the proper testing of bombs proved impossible in peacetime, difficult even in war. This was not unnatural in a small island, given the un-military prejudices of so many of its people, but as Sir Maurice Dean pertinently asks, "What about all those deserts to which the Royal Air Force of those days had almost unlimited access?"[56] The lamentable fact remains that they were not put to use – with the result that the RAF's bombs were for a long time little more than a liability, costing the lives of brave men to no good purpose.

The method question resolved itself into two elements: identifying the target, and hitting it. Both were beyond the capacity of Bomber Command to solve at this stage. Targets were classified as "precise" (airfield installations, railway stations, bridges, power stations, individual factories, etc.) or "group" (an area containing many targets of virtually equal importance close together, thus not requiring such pin-point accuracy; this would later be called "area bombing"). Bomber Command had no effective experience of either in European conditions; all its knowledge was theoretical, and the more closely it was examined the less helpful it looked. Tests at Armament Training Camps, says the Official History,

> were often made at levels which would be impossible in war time against defended targets. They took place in daylight and in good weather. There were hardly any tests as to what could be done at night or in cloudy weather . . . There was great difference of opinion as to the methods by which a precise target could be hit either by day or by night.[57]

In his "Readiness For War" Report in March 1939, Ludlow-Hewitt dwelt on this difficulty of identification in all kinds of visibility:

> . . . the mission may often be flying above cloud until close to its target, when they will come down and must pick up the target with as little delay as possible. The complicated and congested appearance of an industrial area is notoriously most confusing to crews of aircraft, and it is impossible to provide them with too much assistance in picking out their particular objective from the tangled mass of detail.[58]

Success, he said, would depend upon crews being provided "with every possible aid to the location and recognition of their targets". The compilation and distribution of this kind of Intelligence was still in its infancy; the Air Ministry was only just beginning to appreciate the significance of photographic reconnaissance. This was another of Ludlow-Hewitt's "crusades"; he pressed for the best photographic equipment and for fast reconnaissance aircraft specially for this purpose (but also capable of harassing attacks). He also urged the need for Intelligence Officers trained in photographic interpretation on the stations, and mobile equipment for the multi-reproduction of photographs which would clearly be needed.

If recognizing targets was difficult, hitting them was no less so. The ideal aimed at was to hit precise targets from high level, but it was widely accepted that this might be simply impossible, even by day, and certainly so by night. Dive-bombing was not a technique approved of by the RAF; dive-bombing from high level "was thought probably impossible in modern aircraft".[59] That left only low-level attack, which offered better opportunities of actually seeing the target and getting bombs near to it, but on the other hand exposed the attacker to the full force of anti-aircraft fire, to the hazards of balloon barrages, and the decreased performance of engines at low levels. There was, as

may be supposed, lively argument over all these matters, and suggestions flowed freely. The DCAS (Sir Richard Peirse) was one who
believed that good results might be obtained if crews deliberately
slowed up over their targets. Others said the ensuing casualty rate
would be prohibitive, and anyway it would be against human nature
to do such a thing. In the end Newall himself ruled:

> I do not consider it practical politics to *expect* a pilot to slow up in order
> to increase bombing accuracy.[60]

All this discussion, remarks the Official History, "revealed great
uncertainty on nearly all fundamental questions". It also brought out
some dire lacks: a really efficient bomb-sight (not corrected until
1942) and the poor performance of British flares, which remained a
matter of complaint for a long time; above all, a Bomber Development
Unit, for which Ludlow-Hewitt campaigned incessantly. The net
result of it all is summed up by the Official History in chilling words:

> Thus, when war came in 1939 Bomber Command was not trained or
> equipped either to penetrate into enemy territory by day or to find its
> target areas, let alone its targets, by night.[61]

This, then, was the distressing condition of the very vitals of the
RAF facing the test of war. For two years Ludlow-Hewitt had been
drawing it to the attention of the Air Ministry with indefatigable and
outspoken force which made him, as Denis Richards says, "almost too
clear-sighted . . . to remain an altogether comfortable colleague for
those in Whitehall". The British generally dislike contemplating
uncomfortable truths and look askance at those who announce them.
It would be no light matter to dismiss a man of Ludlow-Hewitt's
standing, but by August, having received yet another salvo which
suggested that the C-in-C was now in virtually "open revolt", Air
Chief Marshal Newall reached the point of saying that he was "not
at all sure how the letter should be answered".[62] He and Ludlow-
Hewitt were almost exact contemporaries; they had advanced up the
ladder of RAF promotion side by side; it must have been a painful
moment. For the time being, however, the coming of war itself
deferred the resolution of this conflict.

Such, then, was the reappraisal of capability as the Royal Air Force
came of age; as the Official History says, the sum of it "seems a
strange result after twenty years of devoted work".[63] But as it hastily
adds, it has to be borne in mind that "in no other country had the

problem of strategic bombing been solved or even formulated". This was the plain truth, and the RAF was paying the penalty of pioneering – and also of being caught at an interim stage of re-equipment, which is also a well-known hazard of war. What it amounted to, though, as the last hours of peace ran out – and this was certainly the most shattering part of the reappraisal – was that "it was difficult to find an adequate rôle for Bomber Command".[64] Sir John Slessor, who had had a part both in permitting this lamentable state of affairs to arise, and then in perceiving it and seeking a cure, frankly admits:

> We in Plans were too optimistic on many counts . . . it became more and more obvious as war came nearer that the force likely to be at our disposal in the next few years, before the new heavies could get into bulk production, was sadly inadequate to our needs, whether in technical performance, hitting power, training or ability to sustain operations in the face of war wastage of aircraft and crews. The expression "conservation of the bomber force" began to take its place in our thinking, and by the outbreak of war had become a determining factor in policy . . .[65]

So, for the time being, conservation – of aircraft, but above all of aircrews, against future need – became the guiding principle of Bomber Command. It was not a glamorous programme, but it was fully endorsed by Ludlow-Hewitt who accordingly, with characteristic realism, welcomed the Government's policy of "restricted bombing". The avowed object of this was inglorious: to avoid reprisals (the French enthusiastically agreed), but an unforeseen consequence was to save Bomber Command from attempting a kind of aerial Charge of the Light Brigade before certain harsh but essential lessons had been learned. In operational terms, the net result of all these conditions was that by September 1939 the only practical rôles remaining for the Command appear to be pinprick attacks on the German Fleet in its harbours by day, and the dropping of propaganda leaflets by night – both occupations being considered by many to be of very dubious value.

As Sir Charles Webster and Noble Frankland say, "it is surely remarkable that it was less than a year before war broke out" that the Air Staff realized that the RAF's most treasured instrument was incapable "of carrying out the operations on which the Air Ministry had based its strategy for the last four years".[66] But thus it was, and what made matters worse was the extent to which belief in that strategy (going back considerably more than four years) had diverted attention

91

from the realities of German power, centred in the *Wehrmacht*, and the need for the land forces (with air cooperation) which sooner or later would be required to defeat it.

Indeed, it can be said (and not simply with hindsight) that the fault of all British rearmament in the 1930s was that it was conducted, not in relation to the visible enemy, but in relation to theories of war: first, the broad theory (founded purely on emotion) that Britain would never again be heavily engaged on the Continent – which was ridiculous because that would depend on enemy intentions – and secondly, for the RAF, the narrower but still potent theory that air power should be developed independently of land or sea requirements – which would very quickly prove to be equally ridiculous, nearly fatal.

Part II

THE TEST

"The battle is the pay-off . . ."

9 North Sea tutorial

September 3, 1939: at 11.15 a.m. Neville Chamberlain became the first British Prime Minister to inform the people by word of mouth that they were at war – at war with Germany. At three minutes past twelve, a Blenheim of No. 139 Squadron took off from Wyton to make a reconnaissance of the German naval ports and so commence hostilities for the Royal Air Force and Bomber Command. The day was clear over the North Sea, and the Blenheim's naval observer was able to identify at 24,000 feet three capital ships with four cruisers and seven destroyers in the Schillig Roads leading into the naval base at Wilhelmshaven. This discovery was immediately reported by radio, but the signal was too corrupt for use. Not until the aircraft returned to base at 16.50 hours could its information be relayed. Eighteen Hampdens of No. 5 Group,[1] drawn from no fewer than four squadrons (Nos. 49 and 83, Scampton, 44 and 50, Waddington) and nine Wellingtons of No. 3 Group (No. 149 Squadron, Mildenhall, No. 37, Feltwell) had been standing by all day; at 18.15 they took off for the German coast. The long time-lag would probably have been fatal in any case; as it was, the weather had deteriorated, with severe thunderstorms and darkness closing in. No contact was made with the German ships, and both forces turned for home, the Wellingtons returning by 22.40 hours, and the Hampdens by two minutes past midnight.[2] It had been a spirited gesture on the first day of war, no more than that. And already a serious defect had been revealed – the unsatisfactory performance of the Blenheim's wireless equipment. But tomorrow would be another day.

So Britain was at war with Germany again, the second time in twenty-five years. It meant, as it had done in 1914, war against the most powerful land force in the world, and this time fully supported by a strong and efficient air force built and trained for that purpose. As in 1914, there was no conceivable way that Britain could even engage, let alone defeat, this force, except as part of a coalition. So once again Britain was entering a coalition war, and would be subject to the disciplines of such, the fundamental discipline being strategic subjection to the strongest member. In 1914, the supremacy of British naval power was unchallenged – which meant that no one disputed, even for a moment, the direction of the war at sea. On land, in the West, the preponderance of the French Army was massive – which meant that it was impossible to dispute French control of land strategy.

Until July 1916, indeed, France bore almost the entire burden of the Western war; the appalling losses she sustained in doing so meant that from then onwards, with two short intervals, it was the British Army, so painfully weak in 1914, so short of so many essentials thereafter, which had to engage the main body of the main force of the main enemy – the German Army. Yet even though the British Expeditionary Force was holding "the right of the line" between 1916 and 1918, it was still part of a coalition, with the French still preponderant in numbers, and America swelling in strength. The coalition disciplines held: fighting on French soil, beside a larger French Army, and depending on French facilities at all points, it was inevitable that the BEF should come under a French Generalissimo, when such an office was created.

Exactly the same considerations applied in 1939, as a direct result of policies based on a refusal even to contemplate such a thing. The new coalition was three-fold: Poland, France and Britain. But Poland was struck down in four weeks of a new style of warfare – the *Blitzkrieg*, combining the crushing weight of armoured onslaught with intense air activity (including, most spectacularly, the very dive-bombing against which the British Air Staff had so resolutely set its face). There was absolutely nothing that Poland's allies could do to save her. That scepticism about the French Army's capacity for war which may have been right or wrong in 1938 was well-founded in 1939. The poor impression which its Commander-in-Chief had made a year earlier (see p. 66) was confirmed. Only a massive French offensive could have saved the Poles, but the best the French could do was a token advance towards Germany's "West Wall"; nine divisions advanced a maximum distance of five miles on a 16-mile front, and occupied some twenty abandoned villages.[3] Casualties were negligible, but on September 12 the French halted, and when Warsaw surrendered on the 27th they began a withdrawal to the Maginot Line which was completed by October 4. It all looks ludicrous, and was undoubtedly pathetic, but it does not behove the British to dwell upon it; their own Expeditionary Force had not even completed its assembly.

As regards the air forces, the position was even worse. The French Air Force in September 1939 could only muster 285 bombers,[4] none of them capable of carrying out a daylight raid. Their best fighter was the Morane-Saulnier 406, "underpowered, lacking in performance and somewhat lacking in fire-power".[5] The RAF's condition we have seen. The 10 Battle squadrons of No. 1 Group of Bomber Command crossed to France actually before war was declared (September 2) to form the Advanced Air Striking Force. Commanded since February

1938 by Air Vice-Marshal P. H. L. Playfair, No. 1 Group (or AASF) had originally been conceived as "an outpost of Bomber Command"[6] – a force of short-range bombers pushed up closer to the enemy's frontier in order to be able to reach it, and always answerable to Bomber Command and the Air Staff. Indeed, from the Air Staff point of view, it was regarded as no more than a temporary expedient:

> It is not too much to say that they looked forward to a time when the performance of aircraft would have improved to such an extent that it would no longer be necessary to base squadrons on the Continent in order to carry out attacks on Germany. In those circumstances the need for an expeditionary force would, from the Air Force point of view, have disappeared.[7]

It was all part of the RAF's general awakening from such unrealities that the policy of restricted bombing at once abolished the strategic rôle. Though nominally still only taking orders from the Air Staff, Air Vice-Marshal Playfair's Group, if it was to do anything at all, would be doing what the Army required of it. So restricted bombing did at least bring the Battle crews a stay of execution, saving them to die in their "flying coffins" (as a fighter pilot called them) on a later day. The remainder of Bomber Command was also facing moments of truth.

On August 31, 1939 the Command consisted nominally of 55 squadrons with 920 aircraft. Three days later it had available for operations 25 squadrons, with 352 aircraft.[8] No terrible catastrophe had befallen, no sudden onslaught had wiped out machines and crews; but truth had asserted itself. The Battles had gone to France, taking 160 aircraft; two Blenheim squadrons of No. 2 Group were earmarked for the BEF's Air Component; one Whitley squadron had not yet completed its training for operational standards. Of the remainder, 17 squadrons – nearly 50 per cent – were non-mobilizable, having been converted on the outbreak of war into advanced training units. This constituted, as Sir Arthur Harris said, "a very serious drain on our front-line strength" – but it was the only way to ensure the building up of an adequate force to carry on the war.[9] Sir Charles Webster and Noble Frankland, understandably, describe the allocation of these Operational Training Units as "a clear, courageous and ultimately justified decision".[10] Denis Richards, however, suggests that though this step was in conformity with accepted policy, it may well have been one more cause of rift between the Air Staff and Sir

Edgar Ludlow-Hewitt. Faced with a reality which it should not have been difficult to envisage, "the resulting diminution of the available bombing force came as a surprise, and even a shock, in some political quarters."[11]

So, much reduced, and conscious of many defects, but undismayed, Bomber Command set about the tasks that it was able to perform. No one had any illusions about the Whitleys of No. 4 Group; their unsuitability for daylight bombing was obvious, and from the first they took on a night-time rôle – leaflet dropping, known to the RAF by the code-name "nickels". We shall return to that activity later. Meanwhile we may note the unfolding of the ironies referred to on p. 75: having fought tooth and nail for over a decade to free itself from any kind of shackle to the other Services, the RAF now found its Advanced Striking Force in effect reduced to Army cooperation, while, still smarting from the blow of yielding up the Fleet Air Arm to the Royal Navy (1937), it had already been forced to accept the relegation of its main bomber force to "a weapon of naval cooperation".[12]

Detailed plans for attacking the German Fleet in its harbours had been prepared as far back as January. Ludlow-Hewitt received a copy on the 27th, and "his reactions were not favourable".[13] With his habitual frigid realism, he pointed out that an attempt to surprise the Germans by a dawn attack "would require extreme accuracy of navigation at night over the sea with no previous landfall". We know already what his opinion of his Command's navigational capacity was. Nor did he think much of a daylight attack on the powerful defences of a major naval base. In March and April he held discussions with the C-in-C Home Fleet to examine the possibilities of forcing the German Fleet to sea so that the Royal Navy could engage it. Neither C-in-C was particularly struck with this proposal, but the Air Staff was insistent. A final plan emerged in July: "the Air Aim was stated to be to cause the maximum damage to warships lying in the harbour or roads of Wilhelmshaven and the Naval Aim was to bring to action any German ships putting to sea." Even the authors of the plan had doubts: the chances of doing much serious damage with the 500 lb bombs which would be the RAF's heaviest weapon were not brilliant; nor was the Navy likely to find another Trafalgar:

> The hopes that [the Germans] would put to sea also seemed unlikely unless [they] lost their heads as there were plenty of alternative ports nearby in the Weser or Elbe. On the whole the prospects of the plan achieving any real success were rather remote.

98

It was Flying Officer A. McPherson of No. 139 Squadron who had carried out the reconnaissance of Wilhelmshaven on September 3; at 08.35 hours on September 4 he was off again in the same direction. This time weather conditions were very bad, with what one pilot called "a solid wall of cloud" from sea-level to 17,000 feet with squalls of rain. McPherson nevertheless succeeded in photographing warships in Brunsbüttel (where the Kiel Canal reaches the North Sea), Wilhelmshaven and the Schillig Roads. Once again he reported by radio, and once again the signals were corrupt. As he made his oral report for the second time, he must have felt very frustrated; it is satisfactory to record that his efforts were rewarded with the Distinguished Flying Cross.

Twenty-seven Blenheims of Nos. 107, 110 and 139 Squadrons had been on standby all the morning; 15 (five from each squadron) took off in the afternoon for Wilhelmshaven.[14] Fourteen Wellingtons (Nos. 9 and 149 Squadrons) were also sent to attack the two German battleships reported in Brunsbüttel. The three Blenheim squadrons flew in independent flights; Flight-Lieutenant K. C. Doran of No. 110 Squadron led, flying in and out of cloud at 50-100 feet. By, in his words, "an incredible combination of luck and judgment" he made a correct landfall for the Schillig Roads; the cloud base lifted to 500 feet and there before him he saw a large merchant ship, and beyond her the pocket battleship *Admiral Scheer*. At this height, with bombs (500 lb General Purpose) fused for 11 seconds delay, only three of the five Blenheims were able to put in an attack. Despite their radar which, according to a trusted Intelligence report received not long afterwards,[15] detected the attackers when they were 120 kilometres away, the Germans appear to have been taken entirely by surprise. This may be due in some part to the weather, but is more likely to be the result of inexperience in the use of their warning system (the war was, after all, only two days old!). Whatever the reason, Doran and his companions saw washing hanging out around the stern of the *Admiral Scheer*, and sailors standing idly on deck. Doran came out of a shallow dive from 500 feet at masthead height and dropped his bombs "bang amidships". They bounced off the armoured deck into the sea. The second Blenheim's bombs fell short and also exploded in the sea. The third could not make it in 11 seconds, and attacked another target. Of the remaining two aircraft of No. 110 Squadron, the leader failed to return; he crashed on the fo'c'sle of the training cruiser *Emden*, killing nine of the crew and wounding several more. For this gallant but fruitless feat Flight-Lieutenant Doran was also awarded the DFC. One aircraft lost out of five – 20 per cent casualties;

No. 107 Squadron's experience was the exact reverse – only one of its five aircraft returned. There is no indication that there was anything to show for this alarming 80 per cent casualty rate. No. 139 Squadron was fortunate in having bad luck: it was unable to locate its targets and returned without loss. So the final figure for No. 2 Group was 5 Blenheims lost out of 15: 33⅓ per cent.

No. 3 Group's Wellingtons did not suffer so severely, but they did not achieve any more: "the majority turned back or failed to locate their objectives due to bad weather."[16] The leader of one section of three dropped four 500 lb bombs at low level, but they appeared to miss the battleship he was aiming at and hit the sides of the lock. His two consorts were not seen again. Another section of three sighted a naval force which it described as one battleship and five cruisers at sea, steaming due west at high speed. Just as the Wellingtons were about to attack, these ships made the Royal Navy's recognition signal of the day; "the aircraft therefore concluded that they were part of the British Fleet",[17] which seems reasonable, and continued to Brunsbüttel where they made as ineffective an attack as their predecessors. One Wellington is believed to have bombed the town of Esbjerg – a navigation error of 110 miles. All returning aircraft reported heavy and accurate anti-aircraft gunfire, and vigorous attacks by Messerschmitt Bf 109 fighters, though these were not credited with any kills. Thus Bomber Command's losses for the day amounted to seven out of 29 sorties.

The RAF's first "active" operation of the war is considered worth relating in some detail, partly because of the special atmosphere and interest which always attaches to "firsts", and partly because, as Denis Richards says, it "may be regarded as characteristic of our first attempts to damage the enemy from the air":

> The over-optimistic view of what might be achieved: the care taken to avoid harming the German civil population: the large proportion of aircraft failing to locate the objective: the ineffective bombs and inconsiderable results: the expectation that crews would be skilful enough to find and bomb in atrocious weather a precise and hotly defended target on the other side of the North Sea: and the unflinching courage with which the attacks were pressed home – all these were typical, not merely of September 1939, but of many months to come.[18]

The RAF was now back in school – the school of war. The lessons were not slow in coming, nor in being digested. September 4 taught that the best way to attack ships with bombs was along the fore-and-aft line, with aircraft in pairs at two to three second intervals. Nothing would ever make such attacks on the slender lines of well-defended warships easy, but this at least offered a better length of target. Another realization was the need for improved intercommunication inside the aircraft. The worst problem was clearly the time-lag between observation of a target and the arrival of the striking force. The real answer to this was obviously better wireless transmitters and receivers, and perhaps better training in their use. Until this technological progress could be made, however, the solution had to be tactical; since it appeared that German warships put to sea every day, it could be assumed that whenever there was clear weather there would probably be targets, and reconnaissance in force would permit these to be attacked immediately. Henceforward Bomber Command would periodically carry out such reconnaissances in squadron strength; the first was on September 26, by 12 Hampdens of No. 5 Group, but no contact was made with German ships. Three days later it was another story; once more 12 Hampdens (Nos. 61 and 144 Squadrons) went out, one turned back early, one section of three sighted two German destroyers near Heligoland and attacked without result, another section also sighted the destroyers but did not attack because they were broadside on. The remaining five were themselves attacked by fighters off the Frisian Islands, and all were shot down; it is possible, but not certain, that they accounted for two Me 109s. Five out of 11 (for No. 144 Squadron, five out of five): it was a portent, but Bomber Command was not yet ready to take in its meaning.

It was holy writ in the Command – but in view of what Ludlow-Hewitt had been reporting on air gunnery with such vehemence, Heaven knows why – that a section of three heavy bombers in tight formation could "see off" any fighter attack by their combined gunfire. It was, at this stage, considered most unlikely that either of the two Wellingtons lost on September 4 had been shot down by fighters; the Hampdens, with their weak armament,[19] were known to be vulnerable – "cold meat for a determined fighter in daylight,"[20] said their Group Commander, Air Vice-Marshal A. T. Harris. There seemed, therefore, to be no reason to doubt the doctrine, and as weather conditions now cut down the 85 sorties flown in September to 30 in October and 46 in November, with no losses to the heavy bomber force, no new reason arose for doing so. In December, however, the weather greatly improved; Bomber Command flew no fewer than 233 sorties – and met its moment of truth without mistake.

Three operations by No. 3 Group's Wellingtons during the month decided the future of the Command; indeed, Webster and Frankland describe them as "among the most important of the war".[21] The first was on December 3; 24 aircraft from Nos. 38, 115 and 149 Squadrons set off in the direction of Heligoland. Flying in sections of three at 10,000 feet, with the leading section ahead for reconnaissance, the formation reached Heligoland at 11.26 a.m., with a considerable amount of shipping visible through gaps in the clouds, in particular two cruisers between the islands. The Wellingtons attacked at once by sections through heavy anti-aircraft fire; two were hit, but their flying qualities were unimpaired. It was not possible to form any clear estimate of results, owing to the cloud. The significant thing, however, was the arrival of Me 109 and twin-engined Me 110 fighters; these made numerous attacks, coming in astern of the Wellingtons, facing the two-gun rear turrets of the bomber sections. The feature of this onset was that throughout the action

> the German fighters had shown a notable reluctance to press home their attacks in the face of the Wellingtons' rearward defences.[22]

They generally broke off their attacks at from 400 to 600 yards; four attacked one bomber which had become separated from its formation, but only one came in closer than 60 yards, and then appeared to be hit. The Wellington was not hit. Four others fell behind the main formation on the way home, but all returned safely. It was small wonder in the general euphoric mood of the time, if December 3 was interpreted as a complete vindication both of Bomber Command's aircraft and its tactics, to say nothing of the fighting quality of its crews.

On December 14 complacency was severely dented. Twelve Wellingtons of No. 99 Squadron left Newmarket for the Schillig Roads, again flying in sections of three, in two groups in line astern, the second echeloned to starboard. Flying conditions were bad: the squadron crossed the English coast at 1,000 feet, just below the cloud base; by the time it reached the Dutch coast it was down to 600 feet, and as it altered course for Wilhelmshaven it was at 200 feet, with visibility half a mile. What then took place is hard to understand, especially in the light of the policy of "conserving the bomber force". The Wellingtons had been ordered not to bomb from a height below 2,000 feet, which in the prevailing circumstances really ruled out effective action. Nevertheless, according to Webster and Frankland, Wing Commander Griffiths, the formation leader, held it "for more than half an hour" over the target under "almost continuous fire" from German naval anti-aircraft guns, despite the unfavourable attacking conditions. This was certainly believed at Bomber Command Headquarters, where Ludlow-Hewitt remarked that "he did think it had been rash for the formation to trail its coat for forty-eight minutes in such hazardous circumstances".[23] It was also believed that the squadron had been continuously attacked for 26 minutes by Me 109s and Me 110s. The German fighters on this occasion pressed their attacks right home, and one was seen to go down in flames; but five Wellingtons failed to return, and one more crashed on landing: 50 per cent.

It is a difficult scene to envisage, and the author was not greatly surprised to be told, by Wing Commander A. J. Payn of 99 Squadron in July 1982, that in his opinion the squadron was actually over the target for only about four minutes. Wing Commander Payn said that two Wellingtons were lost in the first minute (presumably by AA fire); the remainder then "did one horse-shoe round and out". He was emphatic that there was definitely no "coat-trailing", and no 26-minute battle with enemy fighters. This account certainly has a ring of likelihood.

Whatever the precise facts, at Command and Group Headquarters even now there was deep reluctance to recognize the true equation between bombers and fighters. Some believed that the damage had all been done by anti-aircraft fire; Air Commodore N. H. Bottomley, Senior Air Staff Officer (SASO) at Bomber Command, asserted:

> It is now by no means certain that enemy fighters did in fact succeed in shooting down any of the Wellingtons ... the failure of the enemy must be ascribed to good formation flying. The maintenance of tight, unshaken formations in the face of the most powerful enemy action is the test of bomber force fighting efficiency and morale. In our Service it is the equivalent of the old "Thin Red Line" or the "Shoulder to Shoulder" of Cromwell's Ironsides.[24]

Others (among them the Group Commander, Air Vice-Marshal J. E. A. Baldwin) were disposed to attribute the heavy loss to the tactics of Wing Commander Griffiths (though his personal gallantry was unquestioned).

December 18 settled the matter beyond reasonable doubt – though some unreasonable doubt persisted, as it usually does. Once more No. 3 Group's objective was the Wilhelmshaven area, this time to be attacked by 24 aircraft of Nos. 9, 37 and 149 Squadrons. And once more the sections of three were the basic unit, grouped in four sub-formations. On this day the North Sea sky was cloudless; two Wellingtons dropped out before reaching the enemy coast, the remainder continuing their stately progress towards the *"flak"*[25] and the fighters, sharply outlined at 15,000 feet in the clear blue, without a vestige of cover. The Germans who saw them come in called it "criminal folly".

Visibility on December 18 was about 30 miles, but the Germans did not depend on the naked eye to detect No. 3 Group's approach. Their "Freya" RDF installation at Wangerooge picked up the Wellingtons at 114 kilometres, enabling them to operate a controlled fighter defence for the first time.[26] The coordination between "flak" and fighters was noted by the British crews, but at the height at which the main action was fought there was no doubt that it was the fighters that did the damage. They tore into the British bomber formation without delay, the Me 110s, fresh from their triumphs in Poland, making a marked impression with their two 20-mm cannon. A proportion of 109s also had a cannon, firing through the propeller-hub, but there was a tendency to credit all cannon-fire to the larger machines. Even the stoutly-built Wellingtons were severely knocked about by this form of attack: N2983 of No. 9 Squadron had its intercommunication system and wireless wrecked by cannon-fire, and great pieces torn out of the geodetic fuselage; then the rear turret was smashed and the gunner killed; shortly afterwards the nose turret's side and bottom were ripped out ("I looked down and saw water below me," said the gunner, AC2 Charlie Driver); a shell sheared off the barrels of both guns, bullets were coming into the fuselage, wounding the second pilot, and virtually all the fabric was ripped off the wings; engine cowlings were battered and torn. Worst of all, the main petrol tank was holed, forcing the aircraft to ditch in the North Sea; fortunately a Grimsby trawler picked up the survivors and brought them home.[27]

They were among the lucky ones; of the 22 Wellingtons which had entered German territory, twelve were shot down and three more made forced landings on return. It was a disaster; as the Official History says:

> The loss of fifty per cent of the force despatched, and nearly fifty-five per cent of that engaged, was at least ten times the casualty rate which Bomber Command could ever afford as a regular drain on its crews and aircraft ... If this was the kind of punishment which daylight formations of bombers might expect to receive in general actions of the future, then clearly the whole conception of the self-defending formation, and with it, the most important among the Western Air Plans, particularly the Ruhr plan, had been exploded.[28]

The heart-searching was, as may be supposed, intense, and not much assisted by the habitual stoic cheerfulness of the surviving crews. All were convinced that they had taken a heavy toll of the fighters – 12 were claimed as definitely shot down.[29] Noting how the Germans had this time pressed home their attacks – in one case coming as close as 50 yards – and their new tactics of beam approaches to hit the Wellingtons where they were defenceless, there was a widespread conviction that crack *Luftwaffe* squadrons had been rushed to Wilhelmshaven for this occasion. Wing Commander R. Kellett, who led the bombers, displays the amazing buoyant mood of the aircrews in his immediate account of the action:

This was, in fact, the biggest aerial battle ever fought.[30] At a hazard I should think that there were about eighty to one hundred aircraft engaged. We were greatly outnumbered, and outmanoeuvred because of the higher speed of the fighters. The crews fired shot for shot and gave better than they got. Most of our crews were under fire for the first time and they have returned confident that on the next occasion the enemy will suffer a far heavier blow. The occasion they hope will not be too distant.[31] There is no doubt whatever that we were attacked by the best fighters of the German Command; ours was just a normal team. All of the crews were surprised at the performance of the German aircraft and their determination to press home the attacks. We felt they were worthy opponents.[32]

Wing Commander Kellett was correct about the fighters to this extent: owing to a wrong tactical and technical conception, the Me 110 squadrons were regarded as the *Luftwaffe*'s fighter élite, creaming off many of the best pilots. Known as *Zerstörer* (destroyers) their outstanding features were the heavy armament noted above (two 20-mm cannon and four forward-firing fixed machine guns, with a fifth manually operated facing rearward) and their long range (680 miles at 13,780 feet); they were certainly alarmingly effective against unescorted bombers. In other circumstances it would be a different story. The closing sentences of Wing Commander Kellett's report show that the World War I tradition of chivalrous mutual esteem between the two air forces was still very much alive, and many captured airmen of both nations would owe their life and limb to it.

It is, generally speaking, a literary and theatrical idea rather than historical that large decisions in war are suddenly taken or reversed. Nobody in Bomber Command on December 19 was ready to say that its entire theory of war would now have to be revised. On the contrary, attention concentrated on such matters as centrally sited guns to fight off the beam attacks, and the evident need for self-sealing petrol tanks. The Wellingtons, it was noted with dismay, "seemed to burn very easily",[33] and this was certainly something which could affect crew morale. It was also still believed that losses were due to failing to keep tight formation, while all Ludlow-Hewitt's earlier doubts about the proficiency of the air gunners were revived. He feared that they were still too ignorant of the nature and use of their equipment; he told Air Vice-Marshal Baldwin on December 24:

> Now that we are actually at war, we must, I think, take drastic action to ensure that crews do actually understand what is required and do organise themselves efficiently for active operations.[34]

Baldwin had already made his own views clear:

> There is every reason to believe that a very close formation of six Wellington aircraft will emerge from a long and heavy attack by enemy fighters with very few if any casualties to its own aircraft. A loose formation is however liable to suffer very heavy casualties under the same conditions.[35]

On January 2, 1940 Harris of No. 5 Group went so far as to say that "so long as three bombers were in company in daylight the pilots 'considered themselves capable of taking on anything' ". And this is definitely no senior officer's dream-world. His namesake, Squadron-Leader (later Group Captain, DFC) P. I. Harris of No. 149 Squadron, a survivor of the Wilhelmshaven attack, supports the official view absolutely. He makes the good point that No. 3 Group had, until immediately before the outbreak of war, been a night bomber Group (Handley Page Harrows):

> Our training then had been totally different, with none of the formation flying which was so vital to survival in daylight operations.

What is surprising, in view of the strong belief in it among senior officers, is that "Group Headquarters had laid on no Group Formation Training". Worse still, squadrons were sent into action without ever having flown together:

> It was like trying to form a football team of people who had never met each other before, had never played together as a team, and had different ideas about the rules.

In the event, of the nine aircraft of No. 149 Squadron and the three aircraft of No. 9 Squadron which did hold a tight formation under

Kellett's control, only one was shot down (with two severely enough damaged to come down in the sea near the English coast on return); of six more aircraft of No. 9 Squadron on the left, and the six of No. 37 Squadron who brought up the rear (they "seemed to be far away and running their own show in an independent, but dangerous sort of way") four and five respectively were shot down. Squadron-Leader Harris is quite clear about the reason for this contrast:

> We survived simply because Kellett's leading was immaculate, we kept in close formation, our guns worked and our two losses in 149 Squadron were almost certainly due to having no self-sealing tanks.[36]

December 18 can be looked upon as a turning-point; yet it was a combination of factors that now led Ludlow-Hewitt to a momentous reappraisal of the rôle of his Command. And by yet another irony the instrument of it was not any of the admired aircraft of his striking force, but the "sturdy old war-horse" (see p. 78), the Whitley, which was busily and fruitfully engaged in building up a whole new range of experience for Bomber Command. Air Vice-Marshal Coningham's No. 4 Group had been hard at work since the very first night of the war dropping leaflets designed, in Churchill's discontented words, "to rouse the Germans to a higher morality".[37] Sir Arthur Harris, on the other hand, considered that the purpose they chiefly served was "to supply the Continent's requirements of toilet paper for the five long years of war".[38] He also shrewdly suggested that the time to use resources to strike at enemy morale is when it is already severely dented by defeat, not when it is flushed with early victory at the beginning of a war. His first point gains force from the consideration that on the very first night alone Hamburg and Bremen were each in receipt of over a million leaflets, while the Ruhr received 3¼ million more.

Leaving aside all further consideration of the value of "nickels" for the purpose intended, one thing was evident to all at Bomber Command Headquarters: the contrast between the heavy cost of the daylight operations and the negligible losses inflicted on the Whitleys of No. 4 Group by enemy action at night. Government policy on "nickels" fluctuated, and the RAF's own belief in them was never high, but Ludlow-Hewitt and Air Vice-Marshal Coningham were increasingly aware of their value, both as training in the much-neglected art of night-flying, and as reconnaissance:

> . . . crews were under orders to observe the enemy territory beneath them, and to report on such interesting items as the effectiveness of the black-out,

the whereabouts of dummy towns, the degree of activity at various airfields, the position and accuracy of searchlights and anti-aircraft guns, and the trend of movements by road, rail and water.[39]

If this "shopping-list" was a lot to ask of hard-pressed crews in often diabolical conditions, there was one reward to which Ludlow-Hewitt definitely looked forward: as the Whitley crews steadily built up invaluable experience, it might be possible, he believed, to carry out "the major destructive part of our plans by precision bombing at night".[40] So Bomber Command's future was beginning to take shape.

It will not do to leave the Whitleys on that note, significant though it is; few flyers can have arrived at a deeper appreciation of the meaning of the words *"per ardua"* in the Royal Air Force motto than No. 4 Group's crews. As their elderly machines penetrated into Germany (No. 10 Squadron reached Berlin on the night of October 1, 1939), they were tested to the limit by the onset of a winter which was to be memorably severe. One night's experiences will have to stand for many: No. 51 Squadron's foray into South Germany on the night of October 27. The Official History, quoting personal experience reports, informs us:

> One of the aircraft engaged on the Munich operation experienced icing in cloud at 1,000 feet. It climbed to 20,000 feet, where it was still in cloud with severe icing conditions. Crystalline ice formed on the leading edges of the wings, over the gun turrets and on the cabin windows. The front gun was frozen up and rendered useless. The aircraft's trimming tabs were jammed by ice and the "dustbin" turret stuck about a third of the way down its travel. The ceiling of the bomber was reduced to 16,500 feet and it was forced to remain in cloud. After two and a quarter hours in the air the oxygen supply in the cabin was exhausted. Some of the crew occasionally banged their heads on the floor or navigation table as a relief from the feeling of frost bite and oxygen lack. On the return journey the icing became worse and the rear guns now also froze, lumps of ice flew off the airscrews, striking the sides and nose of the aircraft. Nevertheless, the Whitley successfully homed on a French base.[41]

A second Whitley had a (relatively) uneventful outward journey to Frankfurt, where it successfully released its subversive literature:

> After that the trouble began. First the mid-turret, lowered for the dropping of the leaflets, stuck fast in the down position. Eventually the combined strength of the crew got it up again, but the navigator fainted from the effort. Then, after five and a half hours' flying, the exhausted captain handed over the controls to the second pilot and collapsed. When he

recovered, flames were pouring from the starboard engine. This was at once switched off; but the second vacuum pump had now gone, the blind-flying panel was no longer functioning, and with six inches of ice on the wings the aircraft soon went into a steep dive. From this it was pulled out by a united effort on the part of both pilots. Then the captain gave the order to jump, only to cancel it when he got no response from the front and rear gunners, knocked unconscious during the dive. By this time the Whitley was heading down at a shallow angle towards a forest. By desperate coaxing the second pilot held it up over the first belt of trees, brushing the topmost branches, then "pancaked" in a clearing. The half-stunned crew crawled out as quickly as they could, extinguished the fire in the starboard engine, and sought help.[42]

That crew spent the night in their half-wrecked aircraft, and the next morning a Frenchman solicitously asked them what time they would be taking off. Another of the Munich-bound crews was even less fortunate. On the way out ice blanketed the windows and there was snow on the floor of the front turret. The crew kept up their spirits with songs like "Roll out the Barrel", and other popular numbers:

But when the "Nickel" dropping was done the "dustbin" remained frozen in the down position, and the effort to move it manually soon reduced the crew to complete exhaustion. Then the starboard engine gave trouble, and near the frontier a cylinder head blew off. As the Whitley lost height, it descended into thicker and thicker snow clouds, and the port engine began to fail. Finally, at 2,000 feet and with hills ahead, the captain ordered the crew to abandon aircraft.

One by one, with varying alarms, they did so, the captain trimming the aircraft to a slight descending angle before he baled out:

When all this was done the Whitley glided down, bumped heavily, and burst into flames; and from the rear turret stepped Sergeant A. Griffin, air-gunner. Blissfully ignorant of the parachute descents – his inter-communication point had failed at the last moment – he dashed to the front of the burning aircraft to save his comrades. The cockpit was empty. Dazed, cut, burned, and more than a trifle puzzled, the sergeant limped his way to the nearest village, where the sight of familiar figures taking refreshment in a café rapidly restored his full powers of movement and expression.[43]

Other hazards endured by Whitley crews that winter included sudden uncontrollable flat spins – a No. 10 Squadron aircraft, with all its anti-frost appliances in use, fell through 12,000 feet – inches of ice actually protruding from the engine cowlings – and above all the unspeakable, eternal numbing cold. For the air gunners in particular, this was a problem never satisfactorily resolved throughout the war; and in the Whitleys of 1939–40 there were no sophistications.

For the RAF 1939 ended on an uncertain note. Fighter Command used these first four months in training, and building up its strength, but still with all too few of the modern types which everyone knew it was going to need one day soon. Its only serious "operation" was a tragedy, on September 6, when a radar fault caused a false alarm of massive German attack. In the ensuing confusion, two Hurricanes were shot down by Spitfires (one pilot killed) and one Spitfire was shot down by anti-aircraft fire. This was a depressing way to start a war, but as Gavin Lyall says, it did have a compensation:

A loophole in the defensive system had been discovered – and was promptly plugged – without the enemy having slipped through it. Just suppose [it] had never happened; suppose the fault had waited, say, exactly a year to reveal itself? – until 6th September 1940.[44]

Fighters shooting down friendly planes are like artillery shooting short; it is not a thing that can ever be absolutely ruled out, but training and experience can reduce the chances of it happening to almost zero. As the new year came in, with four precious months already granted to it, Fighter Command was still to be presented with another three before it began to be seriously tested – which is no doubt why such episodes were so mercifully rare thereafter.

Coastal Command, hampered by what was quickly revealed to be a serious weakness in numbers (quite apart from the question of obsolescence) was also learning important lessons. It would be some time before the teaching could be effective, but meanwhile the Command could chalk up one useful victory. In addition to losses by U-boats, 59,027 tons of shipping were lost in British coastal waters in September and October by mines. Many of these were of the magnetic variety, and the quick defeat of the magnetic mine was one of the early triumphs of the "backroom war" of 1939–45. Between November 1939 and May 1940, one-eighth of the magnetic mines swept or detonated were dealt with by "DWI" Wellingtons of Coastal Command.[45]

As for Bomber Command, the Whitleys of No. 4 Group were pointing the way towards a future which no one yet clearly recognized. But the Group Commander had observed certain fundamental truths which the future would emphasize. In a report to Ludlow-Hewitt on December 9, Air Vice-Marshal Coningham stated:

> The real constant battle is with the weather . . . The constant struggle at night is to get light on to the target . . .

He foresaw "a never-ending struggle to circumvent the law that we cannot see in the dark".[46] And this would be crucial indeed, because what 1939 had taught was that

> if Bomber Command was to remain in the war it had no alternative but to fight in the dark.[47]

10 Night bombing; Ludlow-Hewitt

The turn of the year brought with it one of Europe's famous bad winters: frost conditions extended right down to the Italian Riviera; there was ice in the Channel; Britain experienced her coldest weather for 45 years. Frost and snow did not discourage the Russians from pursuing their attack on Finland (launched on November 30, 1939), nor the Finns from putting up a stubborn and surprisingly successful defence. In the West, however, cold and fog tipped the balance against the attack on France and Britain which Hitler had first planned for November, and then successively postponed – much to the relief of his generals. Misled by a prediction of clear days ahead, on January 10 he fixed the opening date as January 17, but the weather once more enforced delays, and on the 16th the winter offensive was finally ruled out; Hitler would await the spring. This meant that the "*Sitzkrieg*", or "phoney war" in the West, which had already confounded prognosticators and helped to demoralize public opinion, would continue indefinitely. The Germans were saving their strength, and the Allies, in the mood of the time, would do nothing that might provoke them. Air activity was at a minimum.

The first months of 1940, which were also the final months of Sir Edgar Ludlow-Hewitt's tenure, were a time of searching reflection about the future of Bomber Command. The wounds of December were fresh; what was their meaning? One conclusion, unwelcome but inescapable, was that the "Ruhr plan" (see p. 80) which had hitherto been the cornerstone of the Air Staff's strategic thinking, was evidently an operation fraught with appalling risks. In truth, Ludlow-Hewitt had been cooling towards daylight attacks on the German hinterland from the very beginning of the war. Now he had clear indications of

111

what the cost might be: 50 per cent of the attacking force, a figure which spelt not only an immediate tragedy, but dire future consequences. Bomber Command could not afford to lose, possibly at one stroke, half the crews who would be required to man the new generation of heavy bombers which it impatiently awaited. Furthermore, Ludlow-Hewitt had grave doubts about the likelihood of doing any damage commensurate with such a loss; at high level, Bomber Command was unlikely to achieve any worthwhile degree of accuracy, and at low level it would run into smoke screens, balloon barrages and anti-aircraft fire which had already shown itself to be disagreeably effective. On January 28 he wrote to the Air Ministry:

> I suggest the urgent necessity to reconsider the whole question and in particular to study the possibility of devising some other means of employing the bomber striking force to the best effect without committing the whole force to such grave risks of heavy loss as is involved in the plan under consideration.[1]

The Air Staff could only agree, and on February 22 the CAS ruled that the Ruhr plan should be relegated to the category of an emergency measure in the event of a German invasion of the Low Countries.

Deeply reluctant, as always, to make any significant retreat from the strategic rôle of Bomber Command, the Air Staff recommended attacks on specific oil targets (W.A.5c) as an alternative. This was not really much of an alternative, because a number of important oil targets were, in fact, located in the Ruhr; and the truth is that the attraction of the Ruhr itself never really faded in the minds of the RAF planners. The significant change lay rather in the matter of method; as Webster and Frankland say, Ludlow-Hewitt's misgivings had

> set in motion an even more important revolution than a mere change of strategic aim from the Ruhr power plants to the German oil industry. [They] had begun the conversion of Bomber Command from a predominantly day to a predominantly night force.[2]

This in turn raised another question of method: could precision bombing (e.g. of oil plants) be carried out by night? Which prompted yet another question: in Ludlow-Hewitt's own words, "whether *night precision* bombing training is being sufficiently carried out, & whether the urgent importance of maximum training in this subject is everywhere appreciated?"[3] An interim answer was about to be supplied.

On March 16, 15 German bombers attacked Scapa Flow, whose

112

defences had now been sufficiently improved for the Home Fleet to return there (see p. 74). The cruiser *Norfolk* and the depot ship *Iron Duke* (once the proud flagship of the Grand Fleet) suffered some damage, and a few civilians were killed – the first in Britain during that war. The Government demanded retaliation, and accordingly a night attack was ordered upon the seaplane base at Hörnum on the North Frisian island of Sylt. This was carried out on March 19 by 30 Whitleys and 20 Hampdens, spreading their strikes over six hours – the first four for the Whitleys and the last two for the Hampdens. Forty-three of the aircraft allocated succeeded in locating and attacking the target; seven made premature returns due to error or technical failures. For those which reached Hörnum, the hazard was anti-aircraft fire, which destroyed one Whitley and damaged two other bombers (both returned to base). An impressive (for March 1940) number of bombs was dropped: 59 500-lb, 132 250-lb and 1,360 4-lb incendiaries. Crews reported many direct hits, on hangars, living quarters, a slipway and a light railway, with various structures set on fire. It was not possible to verify these claims by photo-reconnaissance until March 27, when a Blenheim brought back photographs which revealed very little damage. German reports spoke of three men wounded by a hit on a sick bay, and a few aircraft damaged.

> It was the first object lesson on the ineffectiveness of night bombing, with the existing lack of navigation facilities.[4]

The Hörnum raid was Bomber Command's first night attack; it supplied a sadly equivocal note on which to end Air Chief-Marshal Ludlow-Hewitt's term as C-in-C. On April 3 he ceased to lead the bomber force, and became Inspector-General of the RAF. He was undoubtedly one of the most clear-sighted, wholly professional officers in the history of the Service. Marshal of the Royal Air Force Sir Arthur Harris says:

> He was a man with a minute and detailed knowledge of every aspect of his job. He was far and away the most brilliant officer I have ever met in any of the three services.[5]

If he had never been mistaken he would not have been human, and in fact he was wrong, as the war would show, on at least three very significant matters. The chief of these was bluntly stated in his memorandum of May 25, 1939 (see p. 86):

I am convinced that the idea that we shall be able to fight the next war with mass-produced pilots and crews as we did in the last war is fallacious.[6]

One of the most astonishing phenomena of the Second World War was the formation of the mass air force (see Appendix E). As Ludlow-Hewitt left Bomber Command the process was only just beginning; we have seen (p. xii) how the RAF's strength rose to well over a million men and women. Its more than 8,000 first-line aircraft could clearly not have flown without mass-produced crews. And it was this movement into mass which proved Ludlow-Hewitt wrong in another matter: his strong belief in interchangeable aircrew with a standard crew trade. It would have been simply impossible to train such paragons in the numbers required. He was also wrong, as much pain and grief would show, in believing that precision bombing could normally and regularly be carried out at night by ordinary crews – but here he was in good company.

Ludlow-Hewitt's qualities were vividly impressed on those who knew him.

> Never [says Harris] have I come across an officer in any of the services who so completely commanded and earned the faith and respect of his subordinates ... In losing Ludlow-Hewitt we lost the finest of commanders. But our loss in the end was the gain of the Service as a whole, because as an Inspector-General, with his immense technical ability and practical knowledge, Ludlow-Hewitt had an influence during the rest of the war on design, production, development and organisation which was of incalculable value through the service. Without him I am sure we should never have prevailed.[7]

Sir John Slessor confirms this, and adds a revealing touch: as Inspector-General Ludlow-Hewitt "did some eight hundred hours flying his own aircraft in almost all weathers during the war years, a record of which any man getting on for sixty has good reason to be proud".[8]

Montgomery Hyde says of Ludlow-Hewitt, "It was a pity he never became CAS." One can see what he means: such clear vision is a rare quality. On the other hand, there are moments in history when it is better not to see the truth too clearly, in case it proves too terrible. One cannot help wondering how what Denis Richards calls Ludlow-Hewitt's "mixture of percipience, persistence and pessimism" would have stood up in the higher rôle to the successive shocks of 1940–41. Yet he departs from the centre of the stage a most distinguished – if now too much forgotten – figure.

He was succeeded at Bomber Command by Air Marshal Sir Charles Portal.

11 *Norway, 1940*

Ludlow-Hewitt had not been gone a week when all traces of "phoneyness" vanished with brutal suddenness from the war. On April 9 Britain and France were harshly reminded of the realities of conflict with the world's most formidable land power: Denmark was over-run without a struggle and German forces, sea and airborne, landed in Norway. From the beginning to end the Allied operations in Norway – though planning, if that is what it can be called, had anticipated the German landings – display an amateurishness and feebleness which to this day can make the reader alternately blush and shiver. On March 28 the Supreme War Council (wretched legacy of a very low ebb of the First World War[1]) approved plans for landing three battalions at one place, two battalions at another, two more somewhere else "to forestall the Germans". "With regard to air forces it was decided that none should accompany the expedition in the first instance . . ."[2] It was as though Poland had never been, Spain had never been, the great air operations of 1918 had never been; but brutal reality would now teach that, in a large country with poor communications at any time, and still largely in the grip of that notorious winter, air power was decisive.

For the initial invasion, the *Luftwaffe* deployed 500 combat aircraft and another 571 Ju 52/3M transports. It was the latter which brought in the six companies of airborne troops who captured the Norwegian capital with its 250,000 inhabitants; it was Ju 52s again which dropped the 120 paratroops who captured Stavanger aerodrome shortly after eight o'clock on the morning of the very first day. By that evening, 180 Ju 52s, "arriving with clock-work regularity", had touched down at Stavanger. In the course of the whole campaign (but their chief use was in the early stages) these invaluable aircraft flew 3,018 sorties, carrying 29,280 personnel, 259,300 imperial gallons of fuel and 2,376 tons of supplies.[3] They were one of the most vulnerable aircraft in the sky – but in Norway they virtually had the sky to themselves.

The Allied troops did not often see the Ju 52s, whose work was generally elsewhere. What they saw altogether too much of was the German bomber force, some 330 aircraft, including 40 (rising to 50) Ju 87 dive-bombers. The *Luftwaffe* now proceeded to subject British

115

and French troops to the ordeal which had shattered the Poles just over six months before. Concentrated bombing is a shocking experience which familiarity does not readily improve; yet it is fair to say that first experiences are the worst. The ground crews of No. 263 (Gladiator) Squadron, trying to operate from the ice of Lake Lesjaskog on April 25, found it altogether too much when the Heinkel 111s came over, bombing and machine gunning, setting fire to aircraft and breaking up the frozen surface of the lake. They took cover in the neighbouring woods, and no example set by officers and sergeants, or the crews of two Royal Navy Oerlikon guns (special targets for the bombers) could move them to come out. Yet as one historian of the campaign says, it was no shame to them that they were not cast in a more heroic mould:

> Of course they should not have run, and of course it is reprehensible that they did . . . The truth is that they were even less prepared for what they had to face than the rawest and least stout-hearted man in any of the Territorial battalions. They were not truly even soldiers at all: they were tradesmen, theirs was the problem the R.A.F. has had to face as the only one of the three services in which only a small élite go into battle. The answer to this problem is squadron spirit – which these men could not possibly be expected to have, since they were strangers to the squadron.[4]

The soldiers – a mixed force of very uneven quality, displaying the British Army a considerable distance below its best – also found bombing not at all to their liking. An RAF liaison officer noted that while at first the braver men, officers, NCOs and privates, tried to ignore the bombs and carry on with their work,

> This was soon abandoned, and all ranks took to the woods and cellars as soon as the aircraft approached . . . I would say that the average man can stand no more than one week's bombing, as experienced at Aandalsnes, before his nerves are affected.[5]

It is an interesting observation, because it reveals the impact of this novelty of war. Before the year was out, airmen, soldiers, sailors and civilians would all display fortitude far beyond what this Squadron-Leader predicted. Nevertheless, the terrifying impact of bombing on men psychologically quite unprepared for it would shortly change the configuration of the war and the destiny of the world.

For the RAF the Norwegian campaign was largely a mixture of frustration and tragedy. Bomber Command was called upon first to attack German naval units escorting or covering troop convoys along the Norwegian coastline. In frequently atrocious weather, these proved to be elusive targets, and sometimes, when found, altogether too well protected. Twelve Hampdens of Nos. 44 and 50 Squadrons, attacking a warship in Kristiansand on April 12, were caught by German fighters and lost half their number – a gloomy reminder of the lesson of September 29 (see p. 101). Equally daunting (and if anything more frustrating, because of the weather which constantly made targets impossible to find) was the task of attacking German airfields. Sir Charles Portal had little faith in this activity, but the war demanded it; in his despatch he recorded that in 782 sorties between April 7 and May 10 his Command lost 31 aircraft. All one can say is, it might have been worse.

Coastal Command was also called upon by the exigencies of the Norway campaign; its Hudsons and Sunderland flying-boats were invaluable for reconnaissance, and the Sunderlands were generally reasonably able to look after themselves. Yet in such conditions, and above all in face of such unquestionable air superiority as the Germans possessed, even Sunderlands operated at grave disadvantage. But the tragedies were reserved for Fighter Command. No. 263 Squadron had its fill of them: at Lake Lesjaskog, on April 25, it was reduced to five serviceable aircraft; the next day it was down to three, and the day after that, nil. The surviving pilots were withdrawn to rebuild the squadron, and on May 22 it reappeared in Northern Norway as part of the force attempting to capture Narvik. Joined on the 26th by No. 46 Squadron (Hurricanes), No. 263 was now able to get some of its own back in the course of a strenuous fortnight. It operated on twelve days, flew 389 sorties and engaged the enemy in 69 combats; it claimed 26 enemy aircraft shot down. No. 46 Squadron, arriving later and leaving later, also operated on twelve days, flew 249 sorties and engaged in 26 combats, in which it claimed 11 shot down.[6] On May 28 the Allies took Narvik – their only victory in the whole Norwegian campaign. The air cover provided by the two fighter squadrons was undoubtedly a major factor in this success – but the success itself was hollow: the Allies were already planning the complete evacuation of Norway. This was completed on June 8, which was the day of final tragedy. No. 263 Squadron's Gladiators (reduced to eight) had already been flown on to the aircraft-carrier *Glorious*; about midnight on June 7, despite the fact that they had never done a deck landing (it was, in fact, considered impossible for aircraft such as Hurricanes) and despite a day of almost continuous combat flying, the 10 pilots of No. 46 took off to do the same. One by one they came low over the carrier, touched down, and braked to a heart-stopping halt:

Against all chances and all predictions, here were the Hurricanes safe on the deck, ten priceless machines saved for the Battle of Britain and an achievement that made the dead-beat pilots forget their weariness.[7]

Their jubilation was short-lived. The next afternoon the battle-cruiser *Scharnhorst*, on her way to attack the Allied sea communications with North Norway, cut across the evacuation routes and in due course sighted *Glorious*. She opened fire at 28,000 yards and hit with her second salvo – practice worthy of her predecessor, the crack gunnery ship of the Imperial German Navy. The helpless carrier, blazing and out of control, was sunk within an hour; 1,474 officers and men of the Royal Navy went down in her, and 41 of the Royal Air Force, including all but two of the pilots who had fought with such effect and flown on with such skill.

The loss of *Glorious* and all that she contained made a sickening end to what had been, from the beginning, a sickening story. A truly cold-blooded commentator could add that even this tragic climax had proved a point: that it was, after all, possible to fly fast modern aircraft off and on to an aircraft-carrier; it was a lesson for the future, but it was bought at an awful price. Meanwhile, both the tragedy and the fuller story had been eclipsed by the even more sickening dramas unfolding further south. What, finally, does the Norwegian Campaign remind one of? Surely it must be the equally ill-fated (but fortunately much smaller-scale) expedition to Antwerp in October 1914: another case of forces sent to the wrong place too late, too weak and ludicrously ill-equipped. On both occasions one of the most powerful guiding influences was Winston Churchill; these predilections for forlorn endeavour in remote places were high among his weaknesses as a war leader.

12 Crisis of battle: Fighter cover, bomber offensive

"The battle is the pay-off";[1] that short sentence encapsulates one of the vast simplicities which lie at the heart of great events in history. The Battle of France was a pay-off indeed: the pay-off of blindness, hysteria, dogma, credulity and at times sheer folly both in Britain and in France, spanning the whole period of two decades between the wars. The Ten-Year Rule, the balanced Budget, disarmament, appeasement, the Maginot Line, the "knock-out blow" – all the theories, all the doctrines, all the half-thought-out devices whereby a catastrophe like that of 1914–18 might be averted, now met their pay-off in a catastrophe even greater: the overthrow of France in six weeks, and the reduction of Britain to a fatal isolation which must have overthrown her also, but for an inconceivable accident.

Dawn on May 10, 1940 brought the great awakening to the true nature of the war and the true nature of the enemy. The huge land force of the *Wehrmacht*, with its formidable air component, the *Luftwaffe*, was set in motion for its most important venture to date. So far, its victories, dramatic though they were, had been at the expense of small nations, not even deserving to be called "powers". But France was definitely a power; her army numbered some 2,776,000 men in front-line units, with another 2,224,000 mobilized in the interior.[2] It possessed 11,200 field guns of all calibres, and some 3,000 tanks. The line of direct approach from Germany was protected by the most powerful fortified system ever seen. The idea that such a force as this could be disposed of in the manner of Poland or Norway seemed ridiculous – and there were German generals who shared that view. Everything, moreover, that hindsight has to teach us about relative numbers – numbers of men, of divisions, of guns, of tanks – indicates that the advantage was with the Allies. No one trying to stem what soon proved to be an irresistible German tide would have believed that; many could never bring themselves to believe it. But this was to be yet another of those battles which prove beyond doubt that counting heads is folly in war, and that mere numbers by themselves mean little. Only in the air was the story different – even there, the German superiority was not what it was made out to be – but it was sufficient.[3]

The twenty months between the crisis of Munich and the Nemesis of May 1940 had not sufficed to cure the serious ills of the French Air Force (see p. 66). New types were on order, but production was pitifully slow; orders had been placed in America, but these, also, were slow of fulfilment. A table[4] for February 1 repeats again the deception of numbers; it credits the French Air Force with these totals:

Fighters	2,671
Bombers	873
Reconnaissance and Observation	1,318

These impressive numbers, however, deflate immediately on inspection; we find that of front-line aircraft ("*en ligne*") what France really possessed was:

Fighters	614
Bombers	170
Reconnaissance and Observation	363

119

And this is still not the full truth; it turns out that "*en ligne* means ready and equipped to take off from an airfield, but it does not mean a 'modern' plane, that is, one built within at least the last two years."[5] For modern front-line aircraft, then, the February table reads:

Fighters	523
Bombers	37
Reconnaissance and Observation	118

So we see a global figure of 4,862 shrink to a reality of 678. By May this had somewhat improved; there were 790 fighters *en ligne*, but the vast majority were still the underpowered Moranes (see p. 96); the much faster Dewoitine 520 only achieved quantity production in May, and saw service with five *groupes*; of another excellent French fighter, the Bloch 152C, there were sufficient for eight *groupes*, and the Curtiss H75A equipped five *groupes*. These were the only French fighters comparable to the Messerschmitts, and a large question mark hangs over the H75As, though one authority says they "wrote a glorious chapter over France in May 1940".[6] The bomber force had 140 aircraft *en ligne*, but this low figure disguises an increase in value due to conversion of some *groupes* to the Martin 167F (Maryland) and the Douglas DB-7 (Havoc Boston); a new French bomber of merit, the Bloch 174, was too late to influence the battle. Realistic figures for reconnaissance aircraft are not readily available, but these units were "in general well below theoretical establishment".[7] It is evident that this air force, which nevertheless contained a large number of very bold and determined flyers, was fighting throughout at a serious disadvantage. This was compounded by the character of its Chief of Staff, General Vuillemin, "an elderly bomber pilot not over-endowed with dynamism"[8] whom we last encountered "scared out of his wits" in 1938 (see p. 66). His morale was not significantly improved in 1940. Worst of all was a clumsy command system, with a serious lack of liaison between the air force and an army whose High Command still had everything to learn about the meaning of air power on a modern battlefield.

If, for the French Air Force, May 1940 was the pay-off of a long period of at times unbelievable and inexplicable decline into inefficiency, for French and British Air Staffs alike it was also the pay-off for, in Guy Chapman's words, not having "given thought to the matter of war". He continues:

To be sure, they had prepared for fighting, but that is not the same thing. Neither air force was prepared for or had given serious thought to cooperation with the ground troops, and, by 1939, the soldiers had little respect for air force plans, which seemed to be confined to bombing factories in Germany and employing their fighters against similar enemy bombing attacks.[9]

The RAF, indeed, could be said to have fought the Battle of France looking over both shoulders at once – an awkward posture for a man, tending to blur his vision. Neither the Chief of the Air Staff nor the C-in-Cs of Bomber or Fighter Commands believed that the right place to fight was in the skies over France – and yet it was precisely in France that the course of the war and the future of the world were being decided, and the mastery of those skies was all-important. Thus years of penury and false doctrine (both political and strategic) had reduced the RAF to a condition of virtual irrelevance to this decisive battle.

Indeed, the penalties of late awakening were lying heavily upon the RAF, which now found itself faced with the price of other people's errors also. Right up to the eleventh hour, the Army, as we have seen (pp. 62–3) had dragged its feet over the Continental commitment. Then suddenly, in May 1939, came the announcement of the change of heart – a Field Force of 32 divisions to be overseas or ready to go in twelve months. May 1940 found the BEF 10 divisions strong, showing once more what all the experience of 1914–18 had already proved – the great difficulty of improvising effective forces in time of war. Meanwhile, however, the 32-division scheme had given the RAF a bad scare. On the basis of a War Office proposal (March 1939) for one Army Cooperation squadron per division (which cannot be called unreasonable) and one per army corps, it meant an immediate allotment of 39 squadrons. But it did not stop there: the Army also announced a requirement of six long-range reconnaissance squadrons, 24 "direct support" squadrons (i.e. close-range bombers performing similar functions to the German *Stukas* on the Spanish model), four intercommunication squadrons and an indeterminate (but obviously not small) number of artillery control, fighter and transport squadrons.[10]

The full "bill", by any reasonable (e.g. *Luftwaffe*) calculation, must have amounted to over 100 squadrons – roughly speaking, the combined strengths of Bomber and Fighter Commands. Since Coastal Command necessarily operated in close and increasing intimacy with the Royal Navy, what this glimpse of future military exigencies would have meant was quite simply the end of the RAF as an independent force, its surviving functions being mainly recruiting, training and aircraft procurement. Of course, the demand was unrealistic, but

121

reality was bad enough, and it is small wonder if there was alarm and despondency in Adastral House.

One – useful – effect of this alarm was the setting up of the British Air Force in France Command (BAFF) under Air Marshal Sir Arthur Barratt in January 1940. It was obviously sensible to make a single officer responsible for the RAF's affairs in France, and since his directive gave him specific responsibilities towards the BEF it was hoped that his appointment would enable him to "abate the more unreasonable military demands".[11] What neither Air Marshal Barratt nor anyone else could abate, of course, was the "unreasonable demands" of the war itself. Nor could he suddenly turn aircraft which, with one brilliant exception, were fundamentally unsuited to their rôles, into important weapons of war. Nor, furthermore, was Air Marshal Barratt (though he tried hard) ever able to overcome the initial disadvantage of never having a properly balanced force under command; both the AASF and the BEF Air Component (always referred to by the Air Force as the "RAF Component") over-emphasized their specialist rôles – bombing and reconnaissance, and found themselves from beginning to end chronically short of the fighters which alone gave security for all operations in daylight.

For the aircrews of the AASF there was very hard fighting and grim tragedy in store. By May 10, two of the 10 squadrons of Fairey Battles which had flown to France on September 2 (p. 96) had been replaced by Blenheims, and No. 67 (Hurricane) Wing had been added. This consisted of No. 1 and No. 73 Squadrons; No. 1 Squadron would have disputed anyone else's right to be known as "Pontius Pilate's Bodyguard" – if its cheerful, extrovert pilots had ever heard of Pontius Pilate, or cared about being a bodyguard. It was No. 73, however, which first encountered the Me 109s, on December 22. A section of three Hurricanes was surprised by four Messerschmitts, and two – both flown by inexperienced pilots – were shot down. Fortunately, this proved to be a deceptive start. No. 1 continued to chafe at not meeting German fighters, but its sensible CO, Squadron-Leader P. J. H. Halahan, made a virtue of caution and ordered "no fooling about, no 'dare-devil ace' stuff".[12] So No. 1 grew in wisdom and skill, picking up from the French the invaluable tactical rôle of "Arse-end Charlie", a pilot told off to weave above and behind a fighter formation to protect it from surprise (sometimes there would be two "Charlies") – with the result that "we always saw the enemy before he was in range and were never jumped".[13] On May 10 No. 501 Squadron (AAF) joined 67 Wing and was in combat within an hour.

The long-suspect[14] Fairey Battles had already been found wanting. On September 20, a formation of three belonging to No. 88 Squadron, having been first engaged by French AA guns, was then attacked by Me 109s, and two were shot down. Ten days later No. 150 Squadron had an even worse experience; six aircraft took off on a high-altitude photographic reconnaissance; one had to land with engine trouble; the remainder were attacked over Saarbrucken at 22,000 feet by 15 Me 109s; four were shot down and the fifth crashed on landing: 100 per cent. Not surprisingly, it was decided that daylight reconnaissances by Battles were not a good idea, and in October they were abandoned. A less fortunate conclusion was that it would be safer for Battles to operate at very low levels; no one can be blamed for not foreseeing the remarkable intensity and accuracy of German light AA fire, for which the Battles, with their 241 mph maximum speed, would be sitting ducks. What is amazing, however, is the spirit of the exceedingly brave young men who flew them, still, on the eve of battle, "pathetically confident in their tight formation with their fire-concentration tactics. We admired their flying and guts, but although we gave them as much practice and encouragement as we could, we privately didn't give much for their chances."[15]

A special tragedy awaited the BEF Air Component: in addition to the losses it would sustain in the heavy fighting that lay ahead, its achievement was to be largely lost to history by the destruction of its records. Some were burnt by units in the stress of hasty evacuation, others were stacked on the quayside at Boulogne and then, in the words of the AHB Narrative,[16] "dumped into the harbour, presumably from an absence of shipping, time or forethought". The historian looking for detailed information about the Air Component's battle is therefore

> regretfully referred to an indeterminate spot at the bottom of Boulogne harbour. The particular pity about this is that, though the RAF Component squadrons obviously flew and fought magnificently, it is in consequence quite impossible to do justice to their performance.[17]

As the great battle opened, the Air Component comprised four Blenheim squadrons for long-range reconnaissance (up to the Rhine), five squadrons of Westland Lysanders for tactical reconnaissance, and four Hurricane squadrons (two, Nos. 607 and 615, AAF, still in process of converting from Gladiators). For the whole Component, the supreme disadvantage, during the whole period of the "*Sitzkrieg*", was the interposition of neutral Belgium between them and their opponents. This meant that there was no active rôle at all for the Lysanders, which entered the battle as untested instruments of war, and virtually no practical experience of the enemy for the Hurricane pilots (in contrast to 67 Wing). As for the Blenheims, they had made 82 sorties since the outbreak of war, but what with the difficulties of geography and the dreadful winter, 44 of these were classified as "definitely unsuccessful".[18]

The great land battle – on a scale exceeding even the *Kaiserschlacht* ("Emperor's battle") of March 21, 1918 – did not immediately declare its character. On May 10, 1940 it had all the appearance of a massive air strike, as the *Luftwaffe* once more, and with even more convincing effect, showed what a powerful, well-balanced air force can do to influence decisive land operations. During the coming battle it would deploy some 3,530 operational aircraft out of a total first-line strength of 4,500, divided into the following categories:

Longe-range bombers	1,300
Dive-bombers	380
Single-engined fighters (Me 109)	860
Twin-engined fighters (Me 110)	350
Long-range reconnaissance	300
Short-range reconnaissance (Army cooperation)	340
	3,530

In addition, the Germans used 475 transports (the invaluable Ju 52s) and 45 gliders.[19] Virtually the whole of this array was flung into the fight on May 10, the long-range bombers striking at Allied airfields and road and rail centres, the reconnaissance machines prowling far and wide to find the Allied armies, and the fighters covering the movements of the German main bodies with an impenetrable screen. By the end of the day they had written a new chapter in the story of air power; half the minuscule Dutch Air Force (62 out of 125 aircraft) had been destroyed; the almost equally puny Belgian Air Force (24 Fairey Battles were counted among its "modern" planes) had also sustained heavy losses; in addition,

the Dutch airfields at Waalhaven, Rotterdam, Wassennaar, Volkenburg, Dordrecht and other places were occupied by German paratroops, and the bridges over the Maas [Meuse] at Moerdijk were in their hands . . . In Belgium, Brussels, Antwerp and Namur had been bombed, and the bridges over the Maas at Maastricht had been seized and parachutists had captured those over the Albert Canal at Briedgen, Weldwezelt and Vroenhoven, and had dropped on the fortress of Eben-Emael and captured it by vertical attack.[20]

"Quick to embrace new ideas": Marshal of the Royal Air Force Sir Edward L. Ellington, Chief of the Air Staff, 1933-1937.

"Prime architect of the wartime Air Force": Air Chief Marshal Sir Cyril L. N. Newall, Chief of the Air Staff, 1937-1940.

Crown Copyright

"Longmore's best fighter": the Gloster Gladiator, last of the biplanes, entered RAF service January 1937.

Above: "Hard core" of Coastal Command: the Avro Anson ("Faithful Annie") remained in RAF service from 1936 to 1956. Here we see an Anson I over France in 1940.

"Mitchell's masterpiece": the Supermarine Spitfire. The Mark I entered service in 1938; the improved Mark V came in 1941, the VC being a fighter-bomber; in 1942 the Mark IX appeared, the most widely used of all. The eight-gun Battle of Britain variant that we see here was the Mark IA. The Spitfire was the only Allied fighter to remain in continuous production throughout the war and flew its last operational mission in Malaya in 1954.

Below: The "only really modern aircraft" in Coastal Command in 1939: the Lockheed Hudson, ordered in 1938. It was the first American type to be delivered by air, and the first RAF aircraft to shoot down an enemy (October 1939); in August 1941 it became the first to capture a U-boat. In all over 2,000 were delivered.

"This invaluable machine": the Short Sunderland flying-boat, with its range of just under 3,000 miles, endurance of 13½ hours, 10 machine guns and crew of 13 entered RAF service in 1938 and continued to perform first-line duties in Coastal Command until 1955.

"Tireless workhorses": the Bristol Blenheim I entered service in 1937 and was already superseded by the Mark IV in 1939. Until 1942 Blenheims were the mainstay both of No. 2 Group, Bomber Command, and the Middle East bomber force. Fighter variants served in Fighter and Coastal Commands. These Mark Is are on their way to attack an Italian aerodrome.

"The finest of commanders": Air Chief Marshal Sir Edgar Ludlow-Hewitt, Air Officer Commanding-in-Chief, Bomber Command, 1937-1940.

"That sturdy old war-horse": the Armstrong Whitworth Whitley served the RAF well from 1937 to 1943. In Bomber Command Whitleys were the pioneers of night attacks on Germany. A variant with increased tankage, the GR VII, was also built for Coastal Command.

What had happened, in fact, was the saturation of a battle area by air power on a scale that had hardly been dreamt of, with results which were not merely deeply gratifying to Hitler, Goering and the *Luftwaffe* leaders on account of their tactical value, but also, as the following days would show, psychologically devastating. In addition, the *Luftwaffe* had seized for Germany an initiative which she never lost throughout the campaign, and gave her that "battle without a tomorrow" which a similar initiative in 1914 had failed to do.

The extent of this initiative is illustrated by the fact that whereas the *Luftwaffe* took off with first light, the Allied air forces made no significant riposte until after mid-day. When they did, the German initiative commanded their endeavours. In accordance with the famous (or notorious) "Plan D", the French and British ground forces at once began their rush to Antwerp and the Dyle line in Belgium, and their air forces were drawn in the same direction to give them cover and support. Ground and air forces were thus pulled, to the satisfaction of the German High Command, immediately into what only a few days would show to be an "off-balance" position – all the worse for the air forces, which had forfeited their flexibility. It is, unfortunately, almost impossible to give any reasonable account of the French Air Force, whose devoted efforts have been swept into oblivion by defeat. The First World War offers us ample documentation of a curious tendency of British observers not to notice vastly superior forces of Frenchmen fighting beside them on French soil; similar manifestations in 1940 must be qualified by the consideration that, although too weak, the French Air Force did outnumber the RAF in this battle, and although badly directed, did fight hard. But it is only the RAF that we can speak of with any certainty.

Within five days of the opening of battle, the BAFF were forced to make a radical revision of their fighting methods; within hours the inadequacy of the light bomber force was put beyond all doubt. Once again, first experiences may speak for many dismal repetitions. Beginning about mid-day, successive "waves" of Battles took off to attack German columns advancing through Luxemburg; one has to put the word "waves" in inverted commas, because what we are speaking of is four formations of eight bombers each – a ludicrous number, by comparison with the real waves which the *Luftwaffe* was sending over, of hundreds of aircraft at a time. Out of the 32 Battles sent, 13 were shot down and every one of the rest was damaged; nor could they even lay claim to any conspicuous results to compensate for this loss. The AASF reported:

Even at this early stage of operations, the difficulties of operating against fleeting targets became evident. The columns against which the raids had been despatched proved to have dispersed or to have moved elsewhere by the time the raid reached the area of operations.[21]

The Battles went in to attack at 250 feet, and it was noted that "the decisive factor in causing the losses was undoubtedly the low approach in the face of the enemy ground fire".[22] This was the first acquaintance with the German light AA (20-mm and 37-mm), totalling 6,700 guns, quite apart from the 2,600 heavy 88-mm. The Battle pilots were startled to find themselves greeted with intense fire from German vehicles on the roads, even from motorcycles, while static targets such as bridges were ringed by AA batteries.[23] For the obsolescent bombers of Britain and France, the storm of fire that came up from the ground made each of these missions tantamount to suicide – yet they continued until the squadrons were practically wiped out. And besides the losses of the Battles, there was another disagreeable portent when six Fighter Command Blenheims of No. 600 Squadron (Manston) attacked the captured Dutch airfield at Waalhaven. Engaged by Me 110s, five of the six were shot down: 83 per cent. Fortunately, attacks by Bomber Command on similar targets were, for one reason or another, if not notably effective at least much less expensive: 9 per cent.

The only gleam of light on this first of many dark days of a brilliant summer was the performance of the Hurricanes of both the AASF and the BEF Air Component. Both groups were "frantically busy" during the day, which was complicated for the AASF by having to pull back from the advanced positions which it had been occupying near the Franco-German border. It is not possible to give an exact profit-and-loss account of the fighters' day: the AASF flew 47 sorties, claimed six enemy aircraft shot down and lost two Hurricanes; the four squadrons of the Air Component flew 161 sorties, engaged in 81 combats and claimed 36 German bombers shot down for a loss of two Hurricanes destroyed and six damaged. But the claims cannot be verified. What is certain is that the Hurricane pilots, and they alone of the Allies, had the satisfaction of meeting the enemy with entirely adequate equipment and the ability to use it. They had an exhausting day, but at the end of it Group Captain Fullard, commanding the Air Component fighters, wrote:

I have never seen Squadrons so confident of success, so insensible to fatigue and so appreciative of their own aircraft.[24]

So the great battle opened with high drama in the skies above the northern flank in Holland and Belgium; the main ground forces had still to make contact. Further to the south, in the region of the Ardennes, protected from view by "an immense fighter umbrella", and quite unsuspected by the Allies, a movement was unfolding which presented to the *Luftwaffe* pilots flying above it

> ... the spectacle of a lifetime. Nose to bumper was the greatest concentration of tanks – between 1,200 and 1,500 of them – yet seen in war. Kleist's massive Armoured Group was moving forward in three blocks, one densely closed up behind the other ... Uneasily, the *Panzer* commanders, aware of what a superb target the dense, crawling columns presented, gazed up to the skies; but there they saw only the reassuring black crosses of the *Luftwaffe*.[25]

The next two days saw the pattern of events thus established alarmingly repeated for the BAFF, with a most unwelcome additional feature. At 05.45 hours on May 11 twelve Do 17s came low up the River Marne to deliver a 10-minute attack on No. 114 (Blenheim) Squadron's airfield at Condé-Vraux, at the end of which six aircraft were completely destroyed and all the remainder rendered unserviceable. The effect, remarks the AHB narrative, "was virtually to eliminate No. 114 Squadron from operations before it had even begun them".[26] Of eight Battles sent off in bad weather to attack German columns near Luxemburg only one returned, badly damaged: 100 per cent loss, and "there is no indication that the bombers ever reached their target area".[27] RAF losses on the 11th were 44 aircraft (BAFF, 35)[28] bringing the two-day total to 86. Haunted by a sense of paucity in all directions, the Air Staff was naturally disturbed, and the CAS repeated on the telephone to Air Marshal Barratt a warning (which he scarcely needed) to conserve his forces for the decisive moment, which was clearly not yet.

It was easier said than done; May 12 cost the RAF 48 aircraft, of which the BAFF accounted for 32. It was a bad day for Blenheims; the AASF, having lost one of its two Blenheim squadrons on the ground the day before, now had the second virtually shot out of the sky. Seven out of nine aircraft of No. 139 Squadron were lost in an attack on German columns near Maastricht. Not long afterwards 24 Blenheims of Bomber Command No. 2 Group attacked Maastricht itself, and 10 more were lost. But the feature of the day for the Royal Air Force was No. 12 Squadron's attack on the bridges over the Albert Canal to the west of Maastricht. These had already taken a toll of 10 out of 15 Battles of the Belgian Air Force; now it was the RAF's turn.

Volunteers for six crews were called for from No. 12 (Battle) Squadron, but the entire squadron stepped forward, so that in the event it was the first six on the duty roster who were taken. But only five took off, because one crew found the wireless in its aircraft out of order, and when it transferred to a second machine, the hydraulics proved to be unserviceable.

Two bridges were attacked, that at Vroenhoven by Flying Officer N. M. Thomas and Pilot Officer T. D. H. Davy, diving from 6,000 feet. Thomas was shot down and captured with his crew. Davy succeeded in bringing his Battle, riddled by AA fire, back to base and making a crash landing; he was the sole survivor of the whole formation. The second section under Flying Officer D. E. Garland (his No. 2 and 3 were Pilot Officer I. A. McIntosh and Sergeant Marland) went in at low level to attack the bridge at Weldwezelt. All were shot down, but at least one of their bombs hit the target, wrecking one of the trusses of the bridge. McIntosh and his crew, like Thomas's, were taken prisoner; the others were not so fortunate. But the extreme gallantry of No. 12 Squadron did not go unmarked; Flying Officer Garland and his observer, Sergeant T. Gray (an ex-"Halton brat") were both posthumously awarded the Victoria Cross, the RAF's first of the war. For one or other of the inscrutable reasons which govern such matters,[29] Leading Aircraftman L. R. Reynolds, the "part-time" air gunner, received no award.

Denis Richards, in his moving account of the foray against the canal bridges, speaks of "all that poignancy which surrounds the death of the young and the brave".[30] The poignancy is the more acute by reason of the fact that these devoted efforts on May 12 were misdirected. It was on that day that General d'Astier de la Vigerie, commanding the French air forces supporting the Allied northern group of armies (*Zone d'Opérations Aériennes Nord*: ZOAN), reported:

> Considerable motorized and armoured forces are on the march towards the Meuse round Dinant, Givet and Bouillon, coming respectively from Marche and Neufchâteau . . . One can assume a very serious enemy effort in the direction of the Meuse.[31]

This was, in fact, the main body of the German Army, Army Group "A", commanded by Colonel-General Gerd von Rundstedt, with seven *Panzer* divisions as its spearhead, aiming the deadliest thrust yet seen in history at the centre of the Allied line, Sedan, where Napoleon III had capitulated to the Prussians seventy years before. The whole northern involvement of the French and British was, in fact, a trap, and everything – tanks, vehicles, army units, air squadrons – used up in it would be sorely missed at the decisive moment and the decisive place. But deluded by the supposed protection of the "impassable barrier" of the Ardennes, the French High Command refused to credit the clear evidence of its own airmen. To General d'Astier's amazement and disgust, the commander of the northern Army Group, General Billotte, continued to allocate air priorities to the Maastricht sector, ignoring the threat on the Meuse. As in 1914, the French were permitting preconceived theories of war to blind them to realities; but in 1914 they had a Joffre to push prejudice aside and grip the real situation; in 1940 they found no such leader.

Shackled by his own Command, d'Astier appealed to Barratt for help, and 15 Battles accordingly attacked the advancing Germans near Bouillon; six were lost. This meant that by the end of the day the bomber strength of the AASF had been practically halved: 135 on May 10, now reduced to 72. Newall told Barratt: "I must impress on you that we cannot continue indefinitely at this rate of intensity . . . If we expend all our efforts in the early stages of the battle we shall not be able to operate effectively when the really critical phase comes . . ."[32] But "the really critical phase" *had* come, revealed by d'Astier's reconnaissances. And the very next day would display "the total failure of both Allied air forces"[33] attributable, certainly in part, to the chronic failure of communication and liaison in the French command system, but even more in both nations, and among soldiers and airmen alike, to an equally dire failure to appreciate the speed with which a modern battle would unfold. A generation of senior commanders which had passed through the First World War seemed only able to remember the great static battles of 1915–17; they forgot how fast things had often moved in 1918 and they ignored what had happened in Poland in 1939.[34] The battle which had begun on May 10 was only three days old; the main forces were not yet engaged, but the crisis was already imminent, and in three more days the whole issue would be decided. Yet when all is said and done, the ultimate reason why the Allied air forces failed on May 13 was that they were simply not strong enough.

For the BAFF, reinforcement had now become a major issue, and for the RAF – and, indeed, the nation at war – a strategic dilemma of dire importance. Two Hurricane squadrons (Nos. 3 and 79) had joined the Air Component on May 10; No. 504 Squadron, originally intended for the AASF, was diverted to the Component the next day, thus bringing the number of Hurricane squadrons in France up to the agreed maximum of ten (see p. 75). The demand for more and yet more, from the French, from the Army, from the bombers, from Barratt himself, never ceased until the battle was over. The "tap" which Newall and Dowding had long dreaded had been turned on (pp. 65, 76). Fighters alone could confer that air superiority which a 1940 battle required, but Dowding clung to his fighters as a miser clings to gold; of his 19 Spitfire squadrons he never let go. He was the first to see, and saw most clearly – had, indeed, by a quirk of his dour nature, always seen – that the battle in France might belong to that bleak area of military prognosis known as "the worst possible case". The worst possible case, he saw, would be if Britain's only fully effective, up-to-date instrument of war, Fighter Command, should be so weakened in waging – but not winning – the battle over France that it would be unable to wage and win a second battle over England: a battle for sheer survival. This was his nightmare, and the fact that he had been enduring it for a long time did not make it any better. On May 13, having reached what he had believed to be the limit agreed, his dismay can be imagined at having to send a further 32 Hurricanes and pilots (equivalent of two more squadrons) over to France; but still the demand for more continued.

May 13 was the day the Germans forced the Meuse, the first day of continuous, unchecked defeat for France and Britain, a crucial day of war, the last opportunity of doing some serious damage to the heads of the German columns while their main bodies were still winding through the Ardennes defiles. For the RAF it was a quiet day, with 14 aircraft lost – half of them, ironically, by Fighter Command itself, five (out of a flight of six) being Boulton Paul Defiants,[35] caught by Me109s in a sweep over the Dutch coast. According to General d'Astier, the French fighters made 250 sorties in the key sector (Second and Ninth Armies) on May 13; they claimed to have shot down 21 enemy aircraft for a loss of 12. How true this is we do not know; what we do know is that it is insignificant in relation to the battle that was taking place. Alistair Horne remarks:

> . . . considering the seriousness of the threat on the 13th, one does get the impression that the French fighter squadrons, whose pilots were already short on sleep, did not press home their attacks with every ounce of vigour.[36]

Yet this was a day of great significance in the history of air power, a chapter belonging to the *Luftwaffe*. Under the constant protection of its fighter swarms, the main thrust of the bomber force was now directed at the French rear areas – road and rail communications far behind the battle zone, to impede the movement of reserves and supplies (in fact to cripple French ability to manoeuvre), and to destroy installations immediately in rear of the fighting units. The effect of this (apparently quite unforeseen) onslaught was profound; during the course of the day,

> prolonged bombing had wrecked communications, isolated command posts and individual units, and left the various formation headquarters ignorant of what was happening in the forward zones, and unable to check information and exercise any control.[37]

We see here the beginning of a collapse of command which was never cured. Henceforward, whatever generals might plan or order, the actual movements of troops were determined by the extent to which they could escape the attentions of the *Luftwaffe* and avoid the scenes of destruction that it had already caused. And at the same time the demoralizing impression of German air supremacy on the troops themselves became a factor to reckon with; as a survivor tells us, it left "indelible memories which statistics and analyses cannot black out".[38]

Nowhere was demoralization more profound than in the battle zone itself. Here the false supposition of the French staffs, still thinking at the tempo of the artillery war of 1914–18 (and not the most impressive parts of that), and convinced that the Germans, despite all the obvious signs, could not be launching a major battle because their guns would not be ready, were cruelly exposed. The Germans now displayed a remarkable extension of artillery performance by air power: the Ju 87 dive-bomber – which was, after all, no novelty in May 1940 – was now brought into play to smash the French defence line and make a bridgehead long before the German guns (still largely horse-drawn) could reach the battlefield. Its impact was shattering; a sergeant of a signals unit of the 1st *Panzer* Division describes its arrival:

> Three, six, nine, oh, behind them still more, and further to the right aircraft and still more aircraft, a quick look in the binoculars – *Stukas!* And what we are about to see during the next twenty minutes is one of the most powerful impressions of this war. Squadron upon squadron rise to a great height, break into line ahead and there, there the first machines hurtle perpendicularly down, followed by the second, third – ten, twelve aeroplanes are there. Simultaneously, like some bird of prey, they fall upon their victim and release their load of bombs on the target. We can see the bombs very clearly. It becomes a regular rain of bombs, that whistle down on Sedan and the bunker positions. Each time the explosion is

overwhelming, the noise deafening. Everything becomes blended together; along with the howling sirens of the *Stukas* in their dives, the bombs whistle and crack and burst. A huge blow of annihilation strikes the enemy, and still more squadrons arrive, rise to a great height, and then come down on the same target. We stand and watch what is happening as if hypnotized . . .[39]

So the legend of the *Stuka*, hinted at in Spain, more clearly outlined in Poland and Norway, came to its full measure. For the remainder of the campaign, and in campaigns yet to come, the dread of the dive-bomber was to be an important element of battle. On May 13, in the infernal din of this new form of attack, the nerve of many French units gave way; contagious hysteria gripped them, and spread to the rear echelons:

Quickly, the rearward artillery command posts emptied: telephones to the front went dead; forward gunners – still manning their guns against the advancing Germans in the Sedan pocket – found themselves stranded. Without communication or firing instructions, these also decamped. The panic spread in widening circles . . .[40]

The collapse of the French artillery, traditionally (since the days of Napoleon) the crack arm of the French Army, has been noted by historians, and Alistair Horne contrasts it with the resolute response of the French gunners at Verdun, similarly smitten by a devastating surprise bombardment on February 21, 1916.[41] Even outside the area of *Stuka* attack, the legend spread its paralysis, and the phenomenon (soon to become all-too-familiar) of weeping French officers was shortly seen.[42] The legend quickly reached Paris, and from there, London; Sir Edward Spears records how, after a visit to the French Military Mission:

. . . the dive-bomber emerged in my consciousness as a really serious danger. I soon became accustomed to hearing it described as a nerve-shattering, irresistible weapon, attacking vulnerable points with uncanny pertinacity. Guns were helpless against it, so was infantry . . .[43]

The unfortunate men who endured *Stuka* attacks in 1940 would have been surprised to learn that they were being terrorized by an obsolescent aircraft. Design work on the Ju 87[44] began in 1933; pre-production models of the Ju 87A came off the assembly line late in 1936, and production started early in 1937. A *Kette* (section of three aircraft) manned by roster joined the Condor Legion and took part in the fighting on the Ebro and the Nationalist offensive in Catalonia. From the first, the Ju 87s were controversial, with enthusiasts in the *Luftwaffe* proclaiming them as war-winners – the Director-General of Equipment, ex-fighter "ace" Ernst Udet, was a strong supporter – while others expressed considerable doubts. The Ju 87B came into production in 1938, and five went to Spain, where they carried on the good work of the 87As. By September 1939 all nine of the *Luftwaffe*'s dive-bomber *Gruppe* were equipped with Ju 87Bs – yet already it was being planned to phase this machine out by the end of the year. It was success in Poland that saved it, and the fresh success in France naturally enhanced its reputation and extended its lease of life – with what has been called "a disastrous influence on the subsequent development of the German close support arm".[45]

The qualities and defects of the Ju 87B are not difficult to enumerate; first, the credit side:

It was an extremely sturdy warplane, with light controls, pleasant flying characteristics and a relatively high standard of manoeuvrability. It offered its crew members good visibility and it was able to hit its target in a diving attack with an accuracy of less than 30 yards.[46]

Against that was the simple fact of its great vulnerability, due to its very slow speed: maximum (at 13,410 feet) 238 mph, at sea-level (or bottom of dive) 211 mph, maximum cruising speed (at 12,140 feet) 209 mph, and economical cruising speed (at 15,090 feet) 175 mph. It was, in other words, a "sitting duck" for modern fighters, and required the fullest operation of air superiority in order to perform. In the dive, terrifying though this was, and above all at the bottom of it, the Ju 87 would also present an excellent target for AA fire, and if the French had been able to put up anything at all resembling the storm of German fire that met Allied low-level bombing the *Stukas* would have had a bad time. Their legend, in fact, was founded on ideal conditions, above all, absence of opposition. Even so, the actual casualties they caused were in no way commensurate with their psychological effect; but this, undoubtedly, became for a time a dominant feature of the war.

The contrast between the opposing methods and results was vividly seen the next day (May 14), which witnessed "the biggest series of daylight bombing attacks carried out by the Royal Air Force during the campaign".[47] It did not begin too badly: 10 sorties carried out by Nos. 103 and 150 Squadrons in the early morning cost only one forced landing. But now the French High Command, thoroughly alarmed, called for a maximum effort against the German pontoon bridges at Sedan and the armoured columns approaching them. All the AASF bombers available (77) were accordingly prepared, and 71 actually took off to attack between 1500 and 1600 hours on May 14. Some 250 Allied fighters were there to give them protection, a figure which is only impressive until one notes that the Germans had more than three times as many flying in that sector. And as ever, there was the "flak":

> With that extraordinary organizational brilliance which characterized the whole Sedan operation, Guderian had somehow disentangled his flak batteries from the columns still stretching across the Ardennes and rushed them forward so that they now ringed the pontoon bridges with an imposing concentration of firepower.[48]

What with this and the fighters, the result was like that of May 12, but on a very much more serious scale:

Wing	Squadron	Aircraft dispatched	Losses
No. 71	No. 105	11 Battles	6
	No. 150	4 Battles	4
	No. 114	2 Blenheims	1
	No. 139	6 Blenheims	4[49]
No. 75	No. 88	10 Battles	1
	No. 103	8 Battles	3 (perhaps 7)
	No. 218	11 Battles	10
No. 76	No. 12	5 Battles	4
	No. 142	8 Battles	4
	No. 226	6 Battles	3

Thus, out of the 71 sorties, 40 (or 44) aircraft were lost, a total of 56 per cent (or 62 per cent). The AASF fighters lost five Hurricanes, and another 11 were lost by the Air Component (against a claim of only 12 enemy aircraft destroyed). As Alistair Horne says:

> For the RAF the Meuse that day was an unimaginable hell, a real Valley of Death from which few returned.[50]

The RAF's total losses for the day were 71, making it a "black day" indeed. The number was less, of course, than on that other "black day", August 8, 1918 (see Note 30 to page 105) when 94 were lost, but it must be remembered that that figure has to be deducted from an Air Force at the peak of its strength, and participating in one of the classic victories of British arms, both circumstances very different from those of 1940. Heavy losses are bearable if they are compensated by important results; the most that one can say with any assurance of the efforts of May 14 is that they caused *some* damage to probably three bridges, possibly destroying one of them, and that this would have caused some degree of disruption and delay to the enemy, but nothing like enough to inhibit next day the exploitation of the decisive victory that his forces were winning on the ground.

May 15 was the climacteric. Winston Churchill had now been Prime Minister for five days, each one critical, but this one was special, and it began as it meant to go on. Churchill describes how the French Prime Minister set the tone:

> About half-past seven on the morning of the 15th I was woken up with the news that M. Reynaud was on the telephone at my bedside. He spoke in English, and evidently under stress. "We have been defeated." As I did not immediately respond he said again: "We are beaten; we have lost the battle." I said: "Surely it can't have happened so soon?" But he replied: "The front is broken near Sedan." . . . the idea of the line being broken, even on a broad front, did not convey to my mind the appalling consequences that now flowed from it. Not having had access to official information for so many years, I did not comprehend the violence of the revolution effected since the last war by the incursion of a mass of fast-moving heavy armour. I knew about it, but it had not altered my inward convictions as it should have done.[51]

He spoke for a generation.

The pay-off of false doctrines and false hopes on May 15 was seismic. At 11 o'clock that morning Holland surrendered. Betrayed by the false protection of neutrality, her puny forces had been swept away. But her spirit had also been crushed – by yet another blow from the air: the bombing of Rotterdam on May 14 had utterly broken the Dutch will to resist. Rotterdam ceased to be just a placename; it became a watchword, almost a slogan, joining Madrid, Barcelona and Warsaw, and soon to be joined in turn by the names of English cities, all transmuted into symbols of Nazi atrocity. The Dutch proclaimed that 30,000 people had been killed in Rotterdam in seven and a half minutes. Post-war investigation revealed that the true figure was 980; the damage, however, was very considerable – more than a square mile of the centre of the city set on fire, 20,000 buildings destroyed, and 78,000 people made homeless. The shock, to combatants and neutrals alike, was very great, but not unnaturally it was nowhere so great as in Holland herself. Rotterdam was the only city whose ordeal by bombing was a direct cause of national surrender until Hiroshima and Nagasaki.

Meanwhile the seven *Panzer* divisions of Army Group "A" had taken the bit between their teeth. They poured forward through the 50-mile gap in the French line, brushing aside small pockets of resistance, overtaking, capturing and disarming hordes of demoralized fugitives, constantly moving, constantly advancing, seemingly without fear or even thought for flanks and rear. The only thing that threatened to stop them was running out of petrol, and this they seized as they went along from the stunned French. It was the classic penetration manoeuvre of the war, aimed at the encirclement and total destruction of the Allied northern armies – a concept not quite, perhaps, as grandiose as Count von Schlieffen's 1914 plan, but far more practical, given the advantages of mechanical horsepower over horses and human legs. The bulk of the German Army, of course, was still dependent on horses and human legs (and would remain so), but the *Panzers* on May 15 thrust 60 miles beyond their starting line.

The BEF, by now, had taken up its positions along the River Dyle, east of Brussels. It had not been heavily engaged, and such encounters as it had had with the Germans had not alarmed it. On May 15 it stood fast, its commander, General Lord Gort, more concerned by the evident weakening of the Belgian Army on his left and some disconcerting symptoms in the French First Army on his right, and by the general lack of cohesion among the Allies, than by a threat to his own army. He knew that a big battle had developed on the Meuse, but he did not know very much about it; a sheer lack of knowledge of what was happening hobbled the Allied commanders throughout the campaign. Two things were worrying him a great deal, and the RAF accounted for both of them. The first was that although the fighter element of the Air Component had now been more than doubled – the four squadrons of May 9 increased to the equivalent of nine – representing an establishment of 144 aircraft on the basis of initial equipment, in fact only about 50 Hurricanes were serviceable. They were doing superb work, mostly out of sight of the troops, but appreciated by their commanders. The demands on them were not only unending but increasing: the Belgians wanted their help, they were supporting the AASF fighters over Sedan, the French Army was begging for more – M. Reynaud asked for ten more squadrons – and it was perfectly obvious that the BEF's own imminent battle would require strong air cover. The generals reflected bitterly on the "thirty-four squadrons at home where there is no attack. And here the decisive battle is being fought. But the Air Staff refuse to part with any more even 'on loan'."[52] The Air Staff was also responsible for Gort's second worry: at a moment when every professional soldier would be thinking in terms of "decisive force at the decisive point", not merely fighters but bombers too, not to waste their strength against fleeting targets such as columns on the move, as favoured by the French (see p. 81), but to pound the communication centres behind the German advance as the *Luftwaffe* was doing to the French railways and key roads, the Air Staff reverted with persistent emphasis to the plan of bombing the Ruhr. This held out no appeal to the French:

> ... they remained obstinately unconvinced on one point – whatever the merits of bombing Germany at some moments they entirely doubted whether the correct moment to begin was at the initiation of a great land struggle.[53]

With this the British General Staff cordially agreed; as the CIGS said:

> If the battle is lost, the bombing of the Ruhr means nothing at all to the fate of the Empire.[54]

Both of these matters were to receive the urgent attention of the War Cabinet on May 15.

The War Cabinet (No. 123) met at 11 a.m. with the Prime Minister in the chair. Among those present were the new Secretary of State for Air, Sir Archibald Sinclair, all three Chiefs of Staff, the Vice-CAS, Air Marshal R. E. C. Peirse, and Dowding. No fewer than fifteen subjects were discussed, ranging from operations on the Western Front and Norway (the Narvik attack was being prepared), to the likely attitudes of Italy and Japan, and the danger of parachutists and Fifth Columnists in Britain. Air policy was item No. 2 on the Agenda, under two sub-headings:

(1) Whether we should send any more fighter squadrons to France in response to M. Reynaud's appeal.
(2) Whether we should attack military objectives in the Ruhr and elsewhere in Germany east of the Rhine.

Some decidedly over-excited accounts of the War Cabinet's proceedings on May 15 have been presented. For some of these Lord Beaverbrook (who was not among those present) was responsible; he was never one to let mere facts spoil a good story. His admirer, A. J. P. Taylor, has written of Dowding,

> ... appearing in person at the war cabinet and threatening to resign. When argument failed, Dowding laid down his pencil on the Cabinet table. This gentle gesture was a warning of immeasurable significance. The war cabinet cringed, and Dowding's pencil won the battle of Britain.[55]

Dowding himself said later:

> I may have thrown down the pencil in exasperation, although I have no recollection of doing so. But of one thing I am absolutely sure, I should never have dreamed of resigning in such circumstances and the thought never for a moment entered my mind.[56]

Yet Dowding himself was responsible for a fair amount of the highly-coloured presentation of this undoubtedly significant moment in history. He later spoke of going to "beard Churchill in his den"[57] – as though a War Cabinet was some private amusement of the Prime Minister's that one might gatecrash. And describing how he moved from his seat to show Churchill a graph that he had prepared, he said, "I think some of the others thought I was going to shoot him."[58] These flights of fancy are not helpful.

Dowding found a deeply sympathetic biographer in his old staff officer, Robert Wright. Those who have read Wright's account of the May 15 War Cabinet (written before the Cabinet records became publicly available) will probably share my own surprise at finding that the only intervention by Dowding actually inscribed in the minutes of the meeting relates not to his own, but to Bomber Command:

> THE AIR OFFICER COMMANDING-IN-CHIEF, FIGHTER COMMAND, welcomed the proposal to attack the Ruhr. He considered that it was the soundest action which we could take in the present situation. We should not be deterred by the fear of attacks from Germany since these, in his opinion, were bound to come sooner or later.[59]

Group Captain William Elliot, of the War Cabinet Secretariat, described the May 15 meeting as "one of the most highly charged that he had ever attended".[60] No doubt it was; May 15 was a highly charged day. Group Captain Elliot's assertion that "discourtesy" was shown to Dowding by asking him to take a chair against the wall "while other business was discussed" would seem only to indicate Elliot's unfamiliarity with War Cabinet procedure, and masks the fact that Dowding's contribution would not be long delayed, since it was in Item 2 on the Agenda.

As may be supposed, it was Churchill who opened the discussion on air policy. Basing himself on Dowding's version,[61] Robert Wright says:

> . . . with Churchill emotionally influenced by what he felt was a paramount need to help the French, Dowding began to feel something akin to despair, and with that the need for firm action.[62]

The Minutes inform us, however, that, having indicated the two questions to be decided, Churchill "suggested that the War Cabinet would have little difficulty in deciding against the despatch of further fighter squadrons in view of the fact that no demand for these had been received from the Military authorities in France".[63] According to Dowding, "the Air Ministry representatives took no part in this discussion", but in fact Newall at once corrected the Prime Minister by saying that while no request had been received from General Gamelin, Air Marshal Barratt had emphasized the need for additional fighter support in a long telegram which the CAS then proceeded to read into the Minutes. Asked directly by Churchill,

> the Chief of the Air Staff said that he would *not*, at this moment, advise the despatch of any additional fighters to France.[64]

These two contributions are (with Barratt's telegram) recorded at some length; they take up the whole of the one and a half pages (compared with the five and a half on the question of bombing Germany) devoted to fighters. There is no record of any statement by Dowding, and given the tenor of Churchill's opening remarks it is clear that the idea of some "confrontation" is wide of the mark.

Not merely does the Cabinet record make no mention of a contribution from Dowding, but Churchill, who as the protagonist of the supposed confrontation might be expected to remember it clearly, makes no mention either. However, there is no doubt that Dowding *did* speak (that was what he was there for, after all), and to some effect. Lord Ismay, then Head of the Military Wing of the Secretariat, who was present on the occasion, refers in his *Memoirs* (p. 139) to the Prime Minister and the War Cabinet having been "solemnly warned" by Dowding of the dangers to the defence of the British Isles if more squadrons were sent to France. Sir Ian Jacob, another member of the Secretariat, says (according to Robert Wright, p. 106) that Dowding "spoke up clearly and well, and his case for retaining the whole of Fighter Command for home defence was very strong". Sir Ian presumably received this information from Ismay or another colleague, since he is not listed among the five members of the Secretariat who were present. Elliott *was* present, of course, and later contrasted Dowding's style with that of other speakers:

> He was factual and to the point, the professional airman stating expertly and concisely a case that had to be made. There was no room for rhetoric.[65]

And in the Minutes of the next day's meeting we find Sinclair referring to Dowding's "strong representations the previous day".

It is strange that the meticulous Secretariat did not record what was clearly an important statement; possibly, since in effect it only re-emphasized what the Prime Minister and the CAS had already said, the Secretariat decided that there was no need to load the Minutes further. In any event, the War Cabinet decided without difficulty

> that no further fighter squadrons should for the present be sent to France, and to invite the Prime Minister so to inform Monsieur Reynaud.

To Air Vice-Marshal Park, commanding No. 11 Group, Fighter Command, in south-east England, and therefore intimately concerned with this decision, Dowding reported that same afternoon in a tone significantly different from that of his later writings:

> We had a notable victory on the "Home Front" this morning and the orders to send more Hurricanes were cancelled. Appeals for help, however, will doubtless be renewed with increasing insistence and I do not know how this morning's work will stand the test of time.[66]

The rationality of that comment seems to display the lucidity of the man who won the Battle of Britain. The unreality of what Dowding said later perhaps displays the unhingeing bitterness of one who was scurvily treated in the moment of victory.

The War Cabinet then addressed itself to the bombing of Germany. It would be incorrect to say that it debated the matter; on the contrary, there was a remarkable degree of agreement, producing a unanimous decision. Since this led directly and immediately to the beginning of the RAF's long-awaited strategic air offensive against Germany, which was to absorb so much of its efforts for the next five years, and cost it such a heavy price in human life, we may appropriately spare a moment to see what was in the minds of the men who took the decision so unhesitatingly.

Churchill first called on Sinclair, who dwelt on the ruinous losses being sustained in daylight bombing in support of the land forces, and the extreme difficulty of effective night bombing in the battle zone:

> He therefore thought that the right course would be to extend the activities of our long-range night bombers. By contrast with the heavy losses sustained by our light bombers in daylight operations in France, our heavy bombers had gone out on the previous night 64 strong, and only one had failed to return.[67]

He suggested that it should not only be the Ruhr that was attacked; he also drew attention to the importance of oil targets, some "of enormous dimensions – and highly inflammable". He stressed the importance of taking early advantage of the waxing moon, which meant that "operations should begin within the next two days at the latest". He accepted that such attacks "would almost certainly provoke retaliation on this country", and mentioned threats that had already been broadcast on the German radio.

Newall followed, entirely endorsing Sinclair's statement, and strongly urging that the War Cabinet should give its approval. He was followed by Peirse, who was also in full agreement, and gave his opinion that "the attack on the oil refineries would unquestionably have the effect of retarding the land operations for which the Germans required large quantities of petrol for the use of their mechanised forces". Then came Dowding, whose views we have noted. (It may be added that it was steadily in Dowding's mind that Fighter Command would engage the enemy with much greater advantage in English skies, which was a reason for welcoming anything that would draw the Germans towards him, rather than having to go and find them.) The RAF, then, presented the argument for strategic bombing with absolute unanimity.

Churchill commented that one advantage of this strategy would be to relieve the pressure on France by drawing away German air strength (a remarkable misunderstanding of how the Germans waged war). The Chief of the Naval Staff, Admiral of the Fleet Sir Dudley Pound, backed the Air Staff view on strategic grounds and added that an attack on Germany would "provide a convincing and conclusive reason for refusing the request of the French for the diversion of British fighter squadrons to France" – an interesting demonstration of the subtleties that may lie hidden within the breast of a bluff old sea-dog. The First Lord of the Admiralty (the Right Honourable A. V. Alexander) was less Machiavellian; he thought that if Hitler was going all out for a quick win, "we also ought not to delay in counter-attacking with all the strength at our command".

It should have been the Army which provided the opposition – it was, after all, the Army that had been clamouring for the full weight of the RAF to be used in direct support. Instead, the CIGS, General Sir Edmund Ironside (now widely regarded as a spent force), confined himself to putting in a plea for raids on marshalling yards in the Sedan area. As regards the proposed attack on oil, "the War Office would prefer that it should be attacked in transit, but if, in the opinion of the Air Ministry, this was impracticable, he was prepared to agree to an attack on the refineries themselves". After this feeble performance, the Secretary of State for War (Anthony Eden) had little to say except that "in choosing those [marshalling yards] which were to be attacked . . . due regard should be paid to the selection of yards of which the interruption would be likely to have the greatest effect in delaying the movement of German reinforcements". The Army there rested its case.

Churchill voiced a doubt about how the bombing of industrial targets would be viewed by neutrals; would it produce a hostile reaction in the United States? The Foreign Secretary (Lord Halifax) thought not, provided the attacks "were directed against military objectives". The Minister of Information (the Right Honourable Alfred Duff Cooper) robustly added that "the proposed operations would in his view have an admirable effect on American opinion whose only complaint was that we were not doing more". The Lord President of the Council (Neville Chamberlain), admitting that he had been hesitant before, "now felt that this battle had reached so critical a stage that it would be useless to attempt to influence its course by continuing daylight bombing with the extremely heavy losses which this incurred, and that it would therefore be wrong to stay our hands any longer from the proposed night-bombing operations". The Lord Privy Seal (the Right Honourable C. R. Attlee) "considered that the moment had arrived when it was essential that we should counter-attack. The proposed attack on the German railways and oil refineries seemed to provide the best means of doing this, and he was accordingly in favour of our carrying out these operations forthwith."

It remained only for Churchill to sum up what was evidently a united Cabinet opinion in favour of delivering a hard blow at Germany:

> He considered that the proposed operations would cut Germany at its tap root, and was hopeful that they might even provide an immediate contribution to the land battle. They should dispel French doubts about our willingness to suffer and also have a salutary effect on Italy. Finally, he considered that this was the psychological moment to strike Germany in her own country and convince the German people that we had both the will and the power to hit them hard. He accordingly suggested that the operations should be carried out that evening.

Pausing only to ask Duff Cooper to arrange that "discreet reference should be made in the press to the killing of civilians in France and the Low Countries" by the Germans – without, of course, any reference to the possibility of British retaliation, Churchill then steered the War Cabinet

> to authorise the Chief of the Air Staff to order Bomber Command to carry out attacks on suitable *military* objectives (including marshalling yards and oil refineries) in the Ruhr as well as elsewhere in Germany; and that these attacks should begin that night with approximately 100 heavy bombers.

For the RAF representatives present, this was a moment of consummation; Ironside tells us:

> I never saw anything so light up as the faces of the RAF when they heard that they were to be allowed to bomb the oil refineries in the Ruhr. It did one good to see it. They have built their big bombers for this work and they have been keyed up for the work ever since the war began. Now they have got the chance.[68]

What the Cabinet records tell us is that the initiation of the strategic air offensive was unquestionably a collective, unanimous decision, shared by civilians and military alike, by Conservatives, Liberals and Labour equally. With hindsight, we can now see that this Cabinet meeting perfectly illustrates the "looking over both shoulders at once" posture of the RAF (see p. 121): Fighter Command preoccupied with Britain, Bomber Command preoccupied with Germany – and only the unfortunate Barratt really concerned with the war as it was being fought, in France. Hindsight tells us also – though the Hörnum raid had provided a strong enough hint – that this belief in the so-called "big bombers" was pathetically misplaced. The hard fact is that the Whitleys, the Hampdens and even the Wellingtons (fine aircraft though these were) were unsuitable both for the direct support rôle that the war required, and the strategic rôle that the Air Staff yearned for. Indeed, it could be said that what May 1940 showed was that the RAF itself was unsuited to the war that Britain was fighting: what was needed was not Whitleys and Hampdens, but twice as many Hurricanes and Spitfires and a good close-support bomber (the Hawker Henley, first flight 1937, but rejected in favour of the Battle, might well have been the one). But the RAF had set its face too resolutely against the idea of all forms of cooperation; this was the 1940 madness – itself all part of the 1920–40 madness, the folly of "never-againism" (never again a Continental commitment), and the triumph of the "futility"-mongers (the futility of mass land warfare; of whom Churchill had been – and remained – a conspicuous practitioner).

And the pay-off was that very night – though it took a while to recognize it. It will be convenient to follow this story through. First, the thinking, clearly expressed by Bomber Command's new C-in-C, Air Marshal Portal; it was Portal who had already prompted the withholding of No. 2 Group (originally designated as the Second Echelon of the AASF), on the grounds of "serious doubts whether the attacks of 50 Blenheims based on information necessarily some hours out of date are likely to make as much difference to the ultimate course of the war as to justify the losses I expect".[69] Portal was as bitter a foe of close Army cooperation by Bomber Command as Newall; he just did not believe that attacking troops and supplies in movement could be good business. He adhered firmly to the dictum that:

> Bomber aircraft have proved extremely useful *in support* of an advancing army, especially against weak anti-aircraft resistance, but it is not clear that a bomber force used *against* an advancing army, well supported by all forms of anti-aircraft defence and a large force of fighter aircraft, will be economically effective.[70]

The RAF's sense of history seems to have failed it again; it was correct to recall the good use of the air arm in the final Allied offensive of 1918; it was unfortunate to lose sight of the extremely valuable air contribution to the desperate defence against the crushing German onslaught in March and April of that year. The French air "ace", René Fonck wrote:

The massive air assault of 1918 will certainly remain a great date in the annals of our aviation. For the first time in the war, the airmen achieved an important tactical result by themselves . . . A wide gap had been opened in that part of the front where the French and British forces made their junction. The gap was growing wider by the hour . . . and it seemed as though the invasion could no longer be stemmed by ground forces. In that tragic moment, somebody thought of the aviators . . .[71]

Conditions were different in 1940, certainly, but the crisis was all too similar. In 1918 "somebody thought of the aviators" . . . but the aviators themselves had forgotten; all part of the 1920–40 madness.

Portal analyzed the air situation as "the root cause of the crisis on the ground" (incorrect, though it was certainly a major contributory factor; the "root cause" was 10 *Panzer* divisions and the frame of mind that created them) and he dismissed close support as incapable of affecting this air situation, "whereas the bombing of objectives in Germany was likely, not only to damage the German war machine in general, but to force the Germans to withdraw fighters and flak from the front to the rear, and to divert their bombing offensive to objectives in England".[72] He was making the same mistake as Churchill and Dowding (p. 141); the Germans did not regulate their system of war by casualties and damage, they regulated it by objectives. Both wars showed that it requires a very great many casualties indeed to make a German High Command change its mind, and the remainder of the Second World War would show the unbelievable amount of damage that a German High Command would accept *without* doing so. But on May 15, 1940 Portal, Bomber Command and the Air Staff proposed, with a force of 100 Wellingtons, Whitleys and Hampdens, to cause just that to happen.

The reader will not be surprised to learn that there is no certainty about the number of aircraft which took part in the first operation of the strategic air offensive. A table in Appendix K3 of the AHB Narrative, *The RAF in the Bombing Offensive Against Germany*, vol. ii, lists two groups of Wellingtons, one of 33 aircraft, the other of 12, 36 Hampdens and 24 Whitleys: a total of 105. Denis Richards, in his *Royal Air Force 1939–45*, vol. i, p. 124, says the total was 96. Webster and Frankland (*The Strategic Air Offensive Against Germany*, vol. i, p. 144) say 99. It appears that nine aircraft were directed primarily against marshalling yards, nine against blast furnaces, and 78 (equals 96) against oil targets. All were given marshalling yards as secondary or last-resort targets. Nevertheless, 16 crews were unable to find any target at all to attack. Out of the 78 directed against oil targets, only

24 even claimed to have identified and attacked these. One Wellington was lost – a proportion in gratifying contrast with the operations of the previous day.

Such was the beginning of a mighty conflict; it is laughable, with what we know of what was to come, that such puny fist-shaking was expected to deflect the German High Command and the *Führer* in the full flood of victory. Yet even the knowledge that 30 per cent of sorties against oil had proved abortive, and 16 per cent of all sorties totally abortive, did not discourage the Air Staff too much. Three days later, the Deputy Director of Plans (Group Captain J. W. Baker) was writing a memorandum to the effect that "the most vital and vulnerable objectives in Germany were some twenty-four oil plants, the great majority of which might very possibly be destroyed within the next few days if the whole effort of the heavies were concentrated against them."[73] So, while the *Panzers* rolled on, and the Heinkels, Dorniers and *Stukas*, covered by the ubiquitous Messerschmitts, continued their object lesson, Bomber Command continued with its private war. On 11 of the remaining 16 nights of May, it attacked Germany in lesser or greater strength: 77 aircraft on May 17, 36 on May 18, 48 on May 19, 76 on May 21, 60 on May 27, and so on, and continued this offensive into June, a total of 430 attacks on oil targets alone by June 18, with 535 tons of high explosive dropped. What was the result? Let Denis Richards sum up:

> ... the heavy bombers achieved none of their objects. Industrial damage was negligible; whatever delay was inflicted on the German Army was insignificant; not a single German fighter or anti-aircraft gun was withdrawn from the Western front to protect the Reich; and not a single German bomber was diverted from attacking the French armies and their communications to reply to the provocation from England. The assault on the Ruhr, most cherished of all Air Staff projects, was a failure. The conception had been admirable; the timing doubtful; the available means utterly inadequate.[74]

In his AHB Narrative, the same writer percipiently remarked:

> The united opinion of the Air Staff and of the AOCs-in-C of Bomber and Fighter Commands was a powerful factor: but it was not as potent as the pressure of events in France.[75]

This is as good a reminder as any that we still have unfinished business with May 15. It was on that traumatic day that Air Marshal Barratt decided that except in dire emergency the AASF bombers would not again be used in daylight. This meant that the only remaining daylight strike force was No. 2 Group of Bomber Command in England. Taken in conjunction with the enforced movement of the AASF to new airfields further back, it virtually meant that for any offensive purpose the British air arm was out of business, while the French *Zone d'Opérations Aériennes Nord* was reduced to 237 service-able fighters and 38 bombers. By mid-day on the 15th, partly due to German bombing of airfields, half this fighter strength had been knocked out. And still the *Panzers* tore on:

> Guderian's route westward lay open, with virtually no obstacles ahead of it. Of even more fundamental significance was the fact that, whereas the twenty-four hours previously the German bridgeheads across the Meuse had consisted of three isolated bulges, they now formed one continuous pocket sixty-two miles wide – with no bottom. It is thus perhaps hardly an exaggeration to say, as has more than one French historian, that 15 May was the day France lost the war.[76]

13 The pay-off; Dowding protests

So six days of battle had decided the war: six days during which the RAF had done the best it could, sometimes displaying astounding courage on suicidal missions, sometimes displaying also admirable skills in handling its better weapons. But always it was operating under the shadow of disastrous pre-war policies, begun in the very moment of victory in 1919, and prodigiously promoted by Churchill's "Ten-Year Rule", for which he – and the nation – now faced retribution.

The decision of the battle did not, of course, immediately proclaim itself on May 15, nor on May 16. To most participants and observers, it remained in balance for several more days; to super-optimists, there was always a chance, even if slight, right up to the very end. At the War Cabinet on May 16 Newall reported a telephone conversation with Barratt, who was certainly not envisaging outright defeat at that stage. On the other hand, he stressed the great strain upon the Air Component fighters:

> . . . our fighter pilots were very tired; they had had to deal all the previous day with waves of 40 bombers every hour, heavily escorted by fighters. Squadrons of fighters were the proper counter to this form of attack, but they had had to operate with flights of 3 or 5, always in great numerical inferiority. Every pilot was carrying out 4 or 5 sorties a day.[1]

This talk with Barratt had clearly had a considerable effect on Newall; he said he had decided now, on all the information at his disposal, to recommend that eight flights, the equivalent of four fighter squadrons, should be sent over immediately. Churchill said that it would be taking a very grave risk, at a time when we were most likely to be attacked ourselves in reaction to our attack on the Ruhr, "but it seemed essential to do something to bolster up the French". He suggested withdrawing the two squadrons stationed at Scapa Flow, and sending six in all; "more than that we could not do". Sinclair did not favour sending more than four, and warned the Cabinet that by sending even these they would be incurring a serious risk and acting contrary to the advice that Dowding had given them the previous day. The First Sea Lord (CNS) made a dignified protest at stripping the Scapa Flow defences. Mr Chamberlain said that it was not only Scapa that might need to be defended, but aircraft factories and other vital points. The CAS did not favour sending six squadrons, and said that if Scapa were stripped, it should only be for home defence at Dowding's discretion. Then Lord Halifax injected an alarming note: he had just received a message from Paris saying that the French Government feared the *Panzers* might reach the capital that night. The CIGS was inclined to disbelieve this. Churchill pointed out that one reason for sending the fighters was to give the French some moral support, in the hope that their defence would stiffen sufficiently to deal with the small advance guards of the German armoured forces. Thereupon the Cabinet agreed:

> That arrangements should be made for the immediate despatch of the equivalent of four fighter squadrons to France.

Little did it know what May 16 still had in store.

At three p.m. that afternoon Churchill flew to Paris, to encounter a succession of shocks of the utmost gravity. At the British Embassy he was told that the Germans were expected in a few days at most. He met the French Ministers at the Quai d'Orsay; "utter dejection was written on every face".[2] In the garden smoke rose from large bonfires where officials were burning documents by the wheelbarrow-full. Gamelin described how the mighty thrust of the German armour had completely separated the two wings of the Allied forces, overrunning all the lines of communication between them. This was another shock, quite bad enough; but the worst was to come. Recalling the crises of 1914 and 1918, Churchill asked the obvious question:

"*Où est la masse de manoeuvre?* (Where is the strategic reserve?)"

Gamelin shook his head, shrugged his shoulders, and made the unbelievable reply: "*Aucune.* (There is none.)"

148

Churchill comments:

> I admit this was one of the greatest surprises I have had in my life . . . It
> had never occurred to me that any commanders having to defend five
> hundred miles of engaged front would have left themselves unprovided
> with a mass of manoeuvre.

And finally, as the conference proceeded from these disastrous
premises, came the worst shock of all: the realization that the French
leaders, civilians and military alike, already believed that all was lost.

All of this translated itself very rapidly into a reopening of the fighter
reinforcement question. The theme of all French representations, says
Churchill,

> was insistence on their inferiority in the air and earnest entreaties for more
> squadrons of the Royal Air Force, bomber as well as fighter, but chiefly
> the latter.

He accordingly sent a telegram for urgent consideration by the War
Cabinet:

> I shall be glad if the Cabinet could meet immediately to consider following.
> Situation grave in last degree . . . the question we must face is whether
> we can give further aid in fighters above four squadrons, for which the
> French are very grateful, and whether a larger part of our long-range
> heavy bombers should be employed tomorrow and the following nights
> upon the German masses crossing the Meuse and flowing into the Bulge
> . . . I personally feel that we should send squadrons of fighters demanded
> (i.e. six more) tomorrow, and, concentrating all available French and
> British aviation, dominate the air above the Bulge for the next two or three
> days, not for any local purpose, but to give the last chance to the French
> Army to rally its bravery and strength. It would not be good historically if
> their requests were denied and their ruin resulted. Also night bombard-
> ment by a strong force of heavy bombers can no doubt be arranged. . . .
> I again emphasise the mortal gravity of the hour, and express my opinion
> as above . . .

The battle is the pay-off indeed.

The telegram was sent off at nine o'clock, and at about 11.30 p.m.
the reply was to hand. The War Cabinet had reversed all its previous
decisions: it would make six more fighter squadrons available (the last
six Hurricane squadrons in Fighter Command that had not already
been drawn upon); it would throw Bomber Command into the battle.
In the event, a sheer shortage of available airfields and infrastructure
in France modified the first decision to the extent that the Hurricanes

were concentrated in Kent; it was arranged that every morning three squadrons would fly over, operate from French bases until mid-day, then return while the other three replaced them. The decision meant that the equivalent of 16 squadrons were not actually in France; this represents an initial establishment of 256 Hurricanes, but with replacements the total sent by the end of the battle was to be far more. In addition, it was agreed that 20 tired pilots of the Air Component should be replaced by 20 experienced Hurricane pilots from Fighter Command. And it must be remembered that the Command was further weakened at this moment by the detachment of No. 46 (Hurricane) Squadron to Narvik. Dowding's worst fears were being realized, and were in the process a curious misunderstanding, or failure of communication, between him and Churchill comes to light; or possibly it was something else.

In his narrative of the terrible events of May 15/16, Churchill tells us:

> Air Chief Marshal Dowding, at the head of our metropolitan Fighter Command, had declared to me that with twenty-five squadrons of fighters he would defend the Island against the whole might of the German Air Force, but that with less he would be overpowered.[3]

This, he suggests, was his guideline. "Twenty-five squadrons" is not a mistake, a slip of the pen (and print) on one page of Churchill's book. On page 45 he says again that the request to the War Cabinet for a further six squadrons "would leave us with only the twenty-five squadrons at home, and that was the final limit." On page 130 he refers to "our last twenty-five fighter squadrons, on which we were adamant", and on page 137: "Twenty-five fighter squadrons must be maintained at all costs for the defence of Britain . . ." Asked later whether he had ever said anything to Churchill about twenty-five squadrons being his minimum requirement, Dowding said:

> The suggestion is ridiculous . . . there was no opportunity for me to have given any personal estimate of my requirements to Mr. Churchill before the Cabinet meeting and his departure from France. I had no contact with him at all.[4]

"Ridiculous" would certainly seem to be the word; as we have seen (pp. 72–3) ever since Munich Dowding had been struggling ceaselessly for a minimum of 46 squadrons. Now the deteriorating situation had forced him (and the Air Staff) to a new assessment. And here, fortunately, we can speak with assurance, because on May 16 Dowding put pen to an historic document; he addressed a letter to the Air Ministry:

I have the honour to refer to the very serious calls which have recently been made upon the Home Defence Fighter Units in an attempt to stem the German invasion on the Continent.

2. I hope and believe that our Armies may yet be victorious in France and Belgium, but we have to face the possibility that they may be defeated.

3. In this case I presume that there is no one who will deny that England should fight on, even though the remainder of the Continent of Europe is dominated by the Germans.

4. For this purpose it is necessary to retain some minimum fighter strength in this country and I must request that the Air Council will inform me what they consider this minimum strength to be, in order that I may make my dispositions accordingly.[5]

5. I would remind the Air Council that the last estimate which they made as to the force necessary to defend this country was fifty-two squadrons, and my strength has now been reduced to the equivalent of thirty-six squadrons . . .

9. I must therefore request that as a matter of paramount urgency the Air Ministry will consider and decide what level of strength is to be left to the Fighter Command for the defence of this country, and will assure me that when this level has been reached, not one fighter will be sent across the Channel however urgent and insistent the appeals for help may be.

10. I believe that if an adequate fighter force is kept in this country, if the Fleet remains in being, and if Home Forces are suitably organised to resist invasion, we should be able to carry on the war single-handed for some time, if not indefinitely. But, if the Home Defence Force is drained away in desperate attempts to remedy the situation in France, defeat in France will involve the final, complete and irremediable defeat of this country.[6]

The effect of this letter was powerful – far more powerful than Dowding's intervention at the War Cabinet the previous day – and the circumstances of the war reinforced it. A major result was that

from this point onwards the CAS appears as the chief protagonist of what can be called the Fighter Command point of view.[7]

We are left with the mystery of the twenty-five squadrons. *Their Finest Hour* was first published in 1949; it is the second volume of Churchill's great six-volume memoir of the war. Such works, packed with facts, statistics and documents, are not composed out of one man's memory in lonely splendour; they are the result of team-work, and their factual basis is subjected to severe scrutinies. Why is Dowding's letter not among the documents quoted? Did nobody remind Churchill of it? If not, why not? If he *was* reminded, why was the error, four times made, not corrected? Speculation is profitless, but it is fair to comment, in the words of Wood and Dempster, that if twenty-five squadrons *had* been accepted as the true minimum, "The Battle of Britain would have been lost before it began."[8]

14 Dunkirk

The Second World War teems with examples of the influence of air power on land operations, the activities of the *Luftwaffe* in May–June 1940 being an outstanding case. There is another side to the coin: that period offers an equally striking example of the influence of land operations on air forces. Scarcely had the decision been taken to employ the equivalent of 10 more fighter squadrons in France than the onrush of the *Panzers* forced it to be cancelled. The eight half-squadrons proposed by Newall on May 16 (it was hoped that by only sending halves the drain on Fighter Command would be less severe, but Dowding later said it simply resulted in "disorganisation and loss of efficiency")[1] joined the Air Component on the 17th, and were at once dispersed through it as replacements, rather than reinforcements. Retirement was already being mooted, and the units of the Air Component were warned to be ready to move at 30 minutes' notice. The AASF was already moving, and its bombing operations virtually ceased for three days (May 16–18).

This meant that at this height of the battle the only possible offensive operations in daylight were those that could be carried out by No. 2 Group of Bomber Command. These produced another tragedy. At 4.50 a.m. on May 17, 12 Blenheims of No. 82 Squadron (Watton) took off to attempt blocking the passage of German columns through Gembloux, south-east of Brussels. The plan was that they should circle round the target to attack it from the south-east, making a rendezvous with Air Component Hurricanes over Gembloux itself. The Hurricanes kept the appointment at the appointed time (0600 hours), but they looked in vain for 82 Squadron. Attacked by Me 109s, 11 out of the 12 Blenheims were shot down before they could even reach their objective; one, badly damaged, limped back to Watton. And so another tactical fallacy was exposed in the hard school of war. The self-defending tight formation had been found wanting over the North Sea in December; now it was the turn of the "clean sky" theory[2] – the belief that it was a waste of fighters to use them for close escort, but that their task should be to "fight the enemy out of the sky" and thus clear a "line of air" up to which bombers could operate with impunity. This, despite all evidence to the contrary, was firm Air Staff doctrine – until Gembloux. It may here be remarked that if the Air Staff under Ellington had been as obdurate against, say, the potential of the eight-gun fighter and radar, as the Air Staff under Newall against the demonstrated use of tactical bombing and the need for fighter escort, it is hard to see how Britain would have survived.

On May 17 Newall laid Dowding's letter before the Chiefs of Staff and declared his own hand: a note urging that no more fighter squadrons should be sent to France. It was not merely Dowding's forceful argument that had reconvinced him; it was the progress of the *Panzers*. "I do not believe," wrote Newall, "that to throw in a few more squadrons whose loss might vitally weaken the fighter line at home would make the difference between victory and defeat in France." Twenty-four hours of steadily worsening news had brought the conviction that "it would be criminal to compromise the air defence of Great Britain any further".[3] He was not alone in perceiving the crisis; on May 19 Churchill ruled:

> No more squadrons of fighters will leave the country whatever the need in France.[4]

By this time the whole of the BAFF was labouring under the confusion inevitable in hasty retirement and the ensuing breakdown of communications. It was on the 19th that the remains of the eight half-squadrons sent out two days earlier returned to England, "but in most cases only two or three aircraft appear to have rejoined their parent squadrons".[5] On the 20th the remaining fighters of the Air Component also returned, and by the 21st the only British fighter squadrons still in France were those of the AASF (Nos. 1, 73 and 501), very reduced in numbers of serviceable aircraft. Thereafter, all support for the BEF and neighbouring Allied forces (the French First Army fought hard to the bitter end) would have to come from England. As the Germans drove towards the Channel, an air umbrella extending from south-east England became more feasible and more effective, but never satisfactory. Thus twelve days of *Blitzkrieg* had sufficed to place the BEF in fearful peril and deprive it of close air support – a notable feat in itself. Now Fighter Command would have to pick up the remnants, and pass without perceptible interval to the new battles ahead.

The first of these was Dunkirk, the evacuation of the BEF, an event which has been as copiously written about in Britain as any aspect of the war (how the British savour their disasters!) and which remains to this day largely hazed in myth. For present purposes it is only necessary to stress the following points: first, in the words of one of the Official Historians, Dunkirk (and the Battle of Britain later),

> were not miracles. They were military events whose outcome was determined by military factors. No assistance from the weather could have enabled the British to ferry three hundred thousand men across the Channel under the noses of the Germans without sea power and air power ... The British were able to get their troops away from Dunkirk because they had overwhelming naval superiority and enough seamen to undertake the business at short notice, and the means of providing at least the bare minimum of air cover which seemed necessary to make the project feasible.[6]

Dunkirk was another landmark in RAF history: the first time it was able to bring its concentrated strength to bear for a single purpose in a single clearly-defined location (the next time would be in 1944). It was a "battle of all arms". Fighter Command was the one that the Army (and the public) looked to for protection of the evacuation against the massed attacks of Goering's *Luftwaffe*; but Coastal Command flew continuous daylight patrols from May 28, unhesitatingly exposing its Blenheims, Hudsons, Skuas and Rocs (borrowed from the Fleet Air Arm) to the swarming German fighters, even when no British fighters were present, while No. 2 Group's Blenheims (happily conserved by Portal) hit German troops around Dunkirk in daylight and Bomber Command's "heavies" attacked road approaches and rear communications at night. But it was Dowding's Command that held the limelight, and Air Vice-Marshal Park's No. 11 Group that would bear the brunt of this new battle.

Fighter Command had, of course, just profited to some extent by the return of the Air Component squadrons – not merely the half-squadrons and other reinforcing drafts, but (on paper) also the first seven full squadrons. In reality, these were far from "full" and Dowding characteristically commented to the Air Ministry on May 24:

> The withdrawal of seven squadrons from France has converted a desperate into a serious situation.[7]

It meant that Park would have at any moment some 200 serviceable aircraft with which to oppose the 300 assorted bombers with their escorts of Me 109s and Me 110s drawn from the 550 available to *Fliegerkorps* I, II, IV and VIII. Behind Park's 200 front-line fighters stood the full single-seater fighter strength of the Command as a reserve – at Dowding's discretion. What the C-in-C was not prepared to do, however, was to strip more distant parts of the country of fighters and leave them defenceless against a surprise attack. Nor would he willingly throw tired or incompletely trained pilots into the battle. Park's squadrons were therefore always outnumbered – a pilot of No. 213 Squadron said "the whole *Luftwaffe* seems to leap at us" – and it is still a matter of argument whether, by flinging in more squadrons at the start, Dowding might have sustained fewer losses, rather than the heavier losses that he feared. We shall never know.

As it was, by the end of the evacuation (Operation DYNAMO) on June 4, every squadron of Fighter Command except three in Scotland had seen action at some time or other since the beginning of the campaign; on June 3 twelve squadrons were going into line for the second time. This meant that for this action not only the doughty Hurricanes were in the fight, but the Spitfires too, in quantity for the first time. It would be agreeable to record a stunning immediate success for these superb aircraft, the pride of the Command; that, however, would be an exaggeration. In this high-speed, split-second combat, experience was probably the most important single factor. and those who had it fought at an advantage over those who lacked it. A fair number of Hurricane pilots now had some very useful experience, and in due course steps were taken to diffuse this throughout Fighter Command, but on May 27, when DYNAMO began, there was not yet time for this to happen. Nor had there been time for certain essential modifications adopted by the AASF and Air Component squadrons to become universal. No. 1 Squadron, for example, on its Squadron-Leader's initiative, and in the teeth of "expert" opinion, had proved in late 1939 that defensive armour behind the pilot did *not* decrease performance. The resulting modification was – ultimately – to save many lives in Fighter Command. Tests with a captured Me 109 had proved the need to change the fixed-pitch two-bladed wooden airscrew of British fighters for a metal three-bladed variable-pitch alternative giving improved climb and speed – but this conversion did not become general until June 9. Already by April, combat had taught No. 1 Squadron that the harmonization of guns for a range of 400 yards (the "Dowding spread") would not do against German fighters; they re-harmonized to 250 yards – with the result that "we had shot down every enemy aircraft we'd attacked".[8] This lesson, also, took time to be absorbed. But the Spitfire pilots were good learners.

So No. 11 Group gave battle over Dunkirk and the Channel. It was, effectively, a seven-day contest,[9] with the honours going to the *Luftwaffe* on two of those days – May 27 (the first full day) and June 1. The distinctive character of Operation DYNAMO was settled straight away. The surrender of the Belgians, a retreat by the French which brought Dunkirk itself under German artillery fire, and above all a massed attack by the *Luftwaffe* on the town and port, all combined to make May 27 indeed a day of crisis. It was on this day that the decision was taken to conduct the main evacuation from the neighbouring beaches (though the port was never entirely eliminated). Stretched to its limits,[10] No. 11 Group now faced the insoluble contradiction of its task: Park had 16 squadrons available for the battle and with these he was expected to provide continuous air cover for the beachhead, which could only be done by out-fighting the *Luftwaffe*. There was thus a direct conflict between the demands of continuity and strength.

The only possible (and evidently unsatisfactory) solution to this dilemma – which otherwise threatened to see the destruction of Fighter Command's squadrons in detail – was to increase the numbers of aircraft in the RAF patrols, but to make these less frequent. The hazards of this policy were seen on June 1, when the *Luftwaffe*, taking advantage of gaps in RAF patrolling, sank 31 ships, forcing the decision to restrict evacuation to hours of darkness. The result, of course, was a very sharp drop in the number of men brought away.[11] Furthermore, the policy of the stronger, but less frequent, patrols was the cause of a persistent and sad misunderstanding.

For the ordinary soldier, air support is the support that he can see: the fighter formation driving the enemy away, the bomb-line ahead of him, the supply-drop. An air battle out of sight is a battle that never happened; attacks on enemy communications or distant assembly points are equally non-events. At Dunkirk the cry went up, "Where was the RAF?" The soldiers were not to be persuaded by argument or statistics; they "never saw a British fighter" – and that was that. Feelings were very bitter between the Services. Thus Spitfire pilot Alan Deere (No. 54 Squadron), having been shot down some fifteen miles from Dunkirk, made his way through the confusion of the town to the mole, where destroyers were taking off soldiers in the teeth of *Luftwaffe* attacks. As he tried to board one, he was stopped by a major, who told him: "For all the good you chaps seem to be doing, you might as well stay on the ground."

When he did finally get aboard, "he was greeted in stony silence by a crowd of other army officers. 'Why so friendly?' he asked. 'What have the RAF done?' 'That's just it,' someone said, 'What *have* they done?' "[12]

It was a typical case.

It need hardly be said that when we do look at the statistics of the event, they tell a very different story. During the nine days' battle, Coastal Command reconnaissance aircraft flew 171 sorties, Bomber Command 651, and Fighter Command no fewer than 2,739 directly concerned with DYNAMO.[13] Even on May 27 (the first bad day) there were 287 fighter sorties, and the next day 321.[14] The losses tell the story. As usual, there are conflicting reports on these: Gregory Blaxland (*Destination Dunkirk*, p. 346) says, "The Royal Air Force lost 177 planes . . ."; the Official History (*The Defence of the United Kingdom*, p. 116) attributes to Fighter Command "the loss of rather more than a hundred machines" and "some eighty fighter pilots". But as we have seen, this was not just a Fighter Command battle, and a table in the Air Historical Branch Narrative (Appendix M) shows that in the nine days the home-based RAF lost a total of 145 aircraft (excluding casualties to those borrowed from the Fleet Air Arm). Of this total, Fighter Command accounts for 99, of which 42 were Spitfires. Churchill, no doubt alarmed at the bad feeling towards the RAF, which was being fed by the gloomy tales of BEF survivors, told the House of Commons on June 4:

> Wars are not won by evacuations. But there was a victory inside this deliverance, which should be noted. It was gained by the Air Force.[15]

He went on to paint a characteristic picture of "a great trial of strength between the British and German Air Forces". The Germans, he said, "were beaten back; they were frustrated in their task. We got the Army away; and they have paid fourfold for any losses which they have inflicted." It was firmly believed at the time (and long afterwards) that the Germans lost 262 aircraft over Dunkirk (Gregory Blaxland in 1973 says 240), but as the Official History shows, this claim was greatly exaggerated: the true figure was 132. This still gives an advantage of 33 "kills" to Fighter Command – but nothing like Churchill's "fourfold". And when the losses of the other Commands involved are taken into account, we see that it was in fact the RAF which suffered most severely at Dunkirk.

Statistics, however – especially casualty statistics – can be a misleading guide in war. Nothing alters the fact that over 338,000 Allied

157

troops were successfully evacuated from Dunkirk, against all the apparent odds, and that this constituted a definite disappointment for Germany, despite euphoric communiqués. The *Luftwaffe*, indeed, had suffered its first real setback of the war; for the first time it had the sense of having met an opponent of equal fighting capabilities, and Goering's boasts that his *Luftwaffe* alone could annihilate the Allies in the beachhead were proved hollow. It was an augury. Churchill, needless to say, made the most of it; he told the House of Commons:

> All of our types and all our pilots have been vindicated as superior to what they have at present to face.[16]

This was morale-boosting talk; he may have believed it – the British believed many strange things about the war – or he may not. But the extraordinary penetrative imagination which that remarkable man could sometimes display came a few moments later: remarking how "a few thousands of armoured vehicles" had overthrown the great French Army, he asked:

> May it not also be that the cause of civilisation itself will be defended by the skill and devotion of a few thousand airmen?

15 *1940 catastrophe: the reckoning*

In Britain, the effect of Dunkirk "was to stimulate a new interest in the war";[1] in the drama of this disaster all "phoneyness" was swept away. The British became angry; they had a strong sense of being betrayed by foreigners everywhere – the quick surrender of Holland, the Belgian surrender, the obvious collapse of France. It never occurred to them – it is only now becoming a commonplace – that the evacuation of the BEF had, in fact, left the French in the lurch. It was the French First Army that covered the BEF's evacuation from Dunkirk: 50,000 French troops standing between the Germans and the beaches. "The German records show that the French fought for every house and foot of ground."[2] The French authorities evacuated some 20,000 after the BEF had gone, and by a special effort the Royal Navy managed to collect some 30,000 more, but between 30 and 40,000 men of France's best Army were left to lay down their arms. There was little doubt then, and there is virtually none now, that this desertion of an ally in battle was the right thing to do in the appalling circumstances, but it is none the prettier for that: another pay-off for the years of madness.

Among those with knowledge, there was an undoubted sense of guilt; Churchill, who visited France four times during this tragic period, sought every means of giving aid that would not at the same time cripple England. Thus, with one BEF only just painfully extracted from the enemy's jaws, the decision was taken to try to build up another to support the French in their new fight south of the Somme. The only two formed divisions left in Britain were ordered to Normandy. "I wonder how we had the nerve to strip ourselves of the remaining effective military formations we possessed," wrote Churchill afterwards.[3] It was a gesture – but no more than that. The new battle flared up on June 5, and though it was remarked that the French soldiers were now fighting far better than in early May, within ten days the inevitable outcome was apparent. Paris fell on June 14; on the 17th the French requested an armistice. By June 18 a second evacuation had been completed from the French Atlantic ports: a total of 191,870, of whom 144,171 were British troops and airmen. But "wars are not won by evacuations".

The air story has a sadly familiar ring. The French Air Force had suffered heavy loss, but a surprisingly high proportion of it had been made good, by increased production and American deliveries. In particular, the excellent Dewoitine D 520, with its armament of one cannon and 4 machine guns, maximum speed 329 mph, was now being delivered at the rate of 10 a day. But it was the shortage of pilots that proved to be the most serious problem for the French. Even before the new phase of battle began (May 31) Vuillemin was asking Barratt for RAF support amounting to "at least a half" of Fighter Command operating from England, and preparations to send over at least 20 squadrons to France. Barratt reported to Newall:

> He was in a very depressed state of mind and said that unless the fighters in France were reinforced to the maximum extent possible, the German bombers would have their own way, with the result that the infantry would not hold their present positions, and that we would lose the war. I pointed out that it was up to the infantry to take action against the dive-bomber, that the British troops had done so with a certain amount of success and that the war was not going to be won by fighter squadrons but by the fight on the floor.[4]

The grim truth was, however, that it was already too late to win the fight "on the floor" – or anywhere else.

In this coming battle, Barratt's command was, effectively, just the AASF, six squadrons of Battles, and three (increased to five on June 8) squadrons of Hurricanes. He was all too well aware that such a force was altogether inadequate for the task that was looming up; he told the Air Ministry on June 3:

> It is suggested that only two logical courses remain open:
> (a) To withdraw the British Air Forces from France.
> (b) To bring the fighter squadrons up to a total strength of ten, with a group organisation for control, to permit the British Air Forces to sustain their effort.[5]

It was a hopeless request; on June 4 (the last day of Dunkirk) "British fighter defences were at the lowest point in the whole of 1940".[6] Such was the weakness of squadrons and deficiency of certain items of equipment that to send, say, four squadrons to France would have robbed Fighter Command of seven squadrons. Yet something had to be done, because on June 5, when the Germans struck again, the three fighter squadrons of the AASF were down to 18 serviceable aircraft, making as many as four sorties each during the day.[7] So No. 17 and No. 242 joined them, and that was the last reinforcement to be actually stationed in France.

However, it was not the last drain on Fighter Command. The decision was taken to bring the AASF squadrons up to strength (a reinforcement of 30 aircraft). And as long as the land battle was within reach of home-based squadrons, the Command would have to play a part. In the event, 17 squadrons belonging to Fighter Command saw action over France during this phase, the maximum on one day being 10, on June 11 and 12, giving aid to the unfortunate 51st (Highland) Division which surrendered at St Valéry-en-Caux on the 12th. And just as a reminder of what Fighter Command's ultimate purpose was, the Germans now mounted a series of distracting pin-prick night raids on Britain – 134 were plotted on the night of June 6/7 alone.

St Valéry was a fearful warning; with everything in flux as the French front crumbled once again, Air Marshal Barratt saw no point in holding his virtually useless Battle squadrons as hostages to fortune. They completed one last mission, and soon after mid-day on the 15th they departed for England, while the ground crews made their way as best they could through the confusion of the crowded roads towards the ports. By now the AASF was used to this sort of thing, but didn't enjoy it. The fighters remained to cover the Army's embarkations, which were not long delayed; there were five squadrons to cover seven ports, so it was as well that the evacuation was conducted promptly and efficiently, marred only by the sinking of the SS *Lancastria*, with a loss of probably some 5,000 lives.[8] The bulk of the ground-crews returned with the Army, Air Vice-Marshal Playfair leaving on the last ship to sail, and by afternoon on June 18 the Hurricanes themselves returned, the rear parties of the ground-crews coming back in transport aircraft. The battle was over.[9] Its 13 days had cost the AASF 31 Battles, two Blenheims and 15 Hurricanes. Fighter Command in the same period lost one Spitfire, 26 Hurricanes and three Blenheims. These figures do not in any way measure the disaster that had befallen.

France surrendered on June 22. Driven out of the Continent three times already, bereft of allies, her army virtually disarmed, her air force severely weakened, Britain now faced invasion by the strongest military power in the world; the pay-off was complete. It is pointless to blame particular men or particular policies except on particulars; the prime fault was national, and dates back to 1919 – to allowing the Entente Cordiale to fade away in the moment of victory. During the 1930s, when the dangers became apparent, only the combination of the strength of a great French Army and a powerful Royal Navy, both equipped with modern weapons and backed by modern air forces, could have held the dictators at bay. It was too late to try to put together such a combination in 1939. Britain was thus caught, from the beginning, in a position of inherent weakness perfectly illustrated by the dilemmas of Fighter Command.

At every stage of the battle, as we have seen, fighters were the key. This fact unfortunately, ran counter to the main stream of RAF orthodoxy; it was a fact nevertheless. Against a strong fighter force, the *Stukas* could not have operated to neutralize the French artillery and demoralize their infantry; fighters could have hindered, if not prevented, the bombing of communications which paralyzed the French Command; but to do both these things there would have had to be enough fighters also to defeat the German fighters which gave their bombers a free run. It is possible that, even with the deletion of the German Air Force, the French would still have been defeated by the *Panzers*; but it is certain that they would have had a better chance. So the question will always remain, should the full weight of Fighter Command have been thrown into the battle – say, another 400 modern fighters on the Allied side? To this question the Air Historical Branch Narrative (by Denis Richards) gives a clear answer. It recalls that the equivalent of 16 squadrons actually was sent to France during the first phase of the battle – an initial establishment of 256 aircraft (see p. 150) – and says:

> There can be little doubt that any considerable number of squadrons beyond these forces could not have been operated effectively in France: an effective administration and maintenance organisation would not have been there to handle them.[10]

This is fairly conclusive, and its force is undiminished by the argument that arrangements should have been made beforehand to switch fighters from British to French bases. Plans for providing such strategic flexibility by increasing the number of Fighter Wing Servicing Units were in hand, plagued by the normal shortages and the fear of tying up personnel in units that might not be needed. Yet this would only have been an expedient in lieu of long-planned arrangements for using French airfields. Similarly, the obvious need for an air transport service on the German model can only raise a sad smile in the light of the RAF's long list of deficiencies, and the same is true of the need for an organization for quick construction of landing-strips. These luxuries were for later – much later – in the war. Historically, the hard fact remains that in May 1940 it was impossible to operate the bulk of Fighter Command from France. And after May,

> To have acceded to [the French] request . . . would have been to reduce the fighter defences of this country far below the safety margin. At a time when the enemy was in possession of the Low Countries and Northern France, and when night activity by the enemy over this country had already begun, no British government mindful of its primary duty could have accepted this risk . . .[11]

It remains to count the cost of the RAF's first major test in battle. It was high; as we have seen (Chap. 12, Note 28) it is not possible to say with absolute exactitude how high – the two tables in the AHB Narrative show a discrepancy of 28 aircraft, 15 of which are accounted for by including 11 Swordfish and 4 Skuas of the Fleet Air Arm, on loan during the Dunkirk operation. We need not trouble ourselves overmuch about the remaining variation of 13. What matters is a total loss of well over 900 aircraft in six weeks; from the point of view of the immediate future, what matters most is that 453 of these were Hurricanes (386) and Spitfires (67). The Hurricane total has to be looked at with care; the Air Component accounts for 203 machines between May 10 and May 20, but of these only 75 were written off as a result of combat. The remainder were either destroyed on the ground, or were aircraft under repair which had to be abandoned – and to these the AASF added its own quota when its turn came. The Spitfires all belonged to Fighter Command and were combat losses. Next to Hurricanes, the chief sufferers were Blenheims, which served in all Commands; 200 were lost, viz.:

AASF	37
Air Component	41
Bomber Command	97
Fighter Command	11
Coastal Command	14

The AASF's loss of 137 Battles, and the Air Component's loss of 35 very vulnerable Lysanders will not surprise us. In Bomber Command, after the Blenheims, the highest losses were of Wellingtons (26) and Whitleys (26); in Coastal Command, Hudsons (20). Excluding those due to accidents, the RAF's personnel losses were 1,382, which is a low figure compared with the Army's 68,111, but it contains within it 915 aircrew, of whom 534 were pilots, killed, missing or wounded. And this was certainly a number that the RAF could ill afford. Newall and Dowding had not been wrong about the "tap" – just far too late to give it an effective "flow".

What was there to show for these losses? Fighter Command, which had borne the brunt, could view the event with some grim satisfaction. In the words of the AHB Narrative, "the British fighters in France could not possibly have done more".[12] Their claims are sometimes startling; Wing Commander Paul Richey, who kept the tally for No. 1 Squadron, put the squadron's at 114 enemy aircraft destroyed between May 1 and 19, which makes the Air Component's total claim of 201 between May 10 and May 20 look very reasonable – if he is to be believed. We shall return to the *Luftwaffe*'s losses shortly; here we need only remark that the Hurricane had proved itself as a robust, manoeuvrable fighter suited to modern conditions without doubt. The story of the light (or "medium") bombers – the Battles and Blenheims – is sadly different, as their losses show. And not only were these prohibitive, but their operations were, by and large, ineffective. For this there were many reasons: in the case of the Battles, sheer defencelessness; for both types, the strength of German AA fire and fighter defence; the elusiveness of the targets they were sent to attack; poor information from French sources; mistaken low-flying tactics; frequent movement of bases. And of course, above all, there was the ever-recurring numerical weakness: 17 squadrons altogether, an absolute maximum of 272 aircraft, but usually far fewer, to cover a front from the Channel to Luxemburg, with the aid of about 100 French machines. It is hardly to be wondered at, in all these circumstances, that daylight tactical bombing proved a failure. Tactical night bombing, by the "heavies", much frowned upon by Bomber Command (and certainly, *prima facie*, unappealing), achieved, to Portal's surprise, "unexpectedly good results".[13] Considering that this was so without any training for the task, one can only wish that the Air Staff had been less doctrinaire about this matter.

And what of the enemy? As usual, it is impossible to say anything with total assurance about *Luftwaffe* losses in the Battle of France, except that they were nothing like as high as people supposed at the time. Early estimates put them at about 2,000 aircraft; this figure was in due course whittled down to 1,469 (Wood and Dempster, p. 123) and then to 1,284 (Denis Richards, *R.A.F. 1939–45*, vol. i, p. 149). An official German table, supplied by the Air Historical Branch, gives a total of 1,279 lost or damaged owing to enemy action, May 10–June 20. This figure includes 184 transport aircraft (which would mostly have been incurred over Holland and Belgium in the very early days); of the remaining 1,095, 522 were bombers (411 destroyed) and 109 dive-bombers (89 destroyed). The fighter total is exactly 300, comprising 193 Me 109s (162 destroyed) and 107 Me 110s (87 destroyed). All these totals, of course, represent the joint achievement of the British and French Air Forces; what percentage is attributable to the French there is no knowing. (Nor do we know what French losses were; the latest authority puts them at 757.[14]) It is salutary, however, to compare the admitted German total of 1,065 actually destroyed by their two enemies, and the RAF's admitted 959.

One thing is certain: of all the aircraft which flew and fought in this battle, the one that emerged as really outstanding (confirming informed earlier impressions) was the Messerschmitt Bf 109E fighter. This was the descendant of the aircraft of which *Generaloberst* Ernst Udet, when he first saw it in 1934, said, "That will never make a fighter!"[15] He soon changed his mind; the Bf 109 proved itself in Spain, and again in Poland; it was, in fact "one of the greatest combat aircraft in history".[16] Production of the E-Series began in early 1939 and continued until 1942; this featured an armament of two 20-mm cannon in the wings and two 7.9-mm machine guns in the fuselage; powered by a Daimler-Benz DB 601A engine, the E-3 had a maximum speed of 348 mph at 14,560 feet, and a climbing rate of approximately 3,000 feet per minute. The Bf 109E-3 captured on May 2 (see p. 155) went to the Royal Aircraft Establishment at Farnborough for handling trials on May 14; these

confirmed the already widely-held opinion that the Hurricane, even when fitted with the Rotol three-blade constant-speed airscrew, was inferior to the German fighter in all respects with the exception of low-altitude manoeuvrability and turning circle at all altitudes. In so far as the Spitfire I was concerned, when fitted with the two-pitch airscrew – and at that stage of the war virtually all Spitfires *were* fitted with such airscrews as priority in the supply of constant-speed units had been allocated to bombers – this was also bested from virtually every aspect of the Bf 109E-3, although its inferiority was markedly reduced by the application of a constant-speed airscrew with which the average production Spitfire was only marginally slower than its German contemporary at rated altitudes. It was ascertained that the Messerschmitt could outclimb the Spitfire up to 20,000 feet, above which altitude the British fighter possessed an edge, but the German fighter could always elude the Spitfire in a dive, the float carburettor of the Merlin engine of the latter placing it at a distinct disadvantage. However, the Spitfire possessed a definite superiority in manoeuvrability at all altitudes as a result of its lower wing loading, a smaller turning circle, and enjoyed a distinct advantage above 20,000 feet.

The general consensus of opinion among RAF pilots who had an opportunity to evaluate the Bf 109E-3 in flight was that it provided a formidable opponent to be treated with respect.[17]

Thanks to the Messerschmitts – and to the Junkers, the Heinkels and the Dorniers which fought beside them – and thanks to the German Army with its ten *Panzer* divisions, Hitler was now the master of Europe, and the war was utterly transformed.

Part III

THE STRAIN

"The only plan is to persevere."

THE BATTLE OF BRITAIN

"...A Few Thousand Airmen..."

16 Britain alone

The fall of France was a catastrophe whose consequences can scarcely be measured. As time increasingly separates us from the event and the mood surrounding it, the "wave of lunatic relief" (p. 63) which possessed the British in June 1940 seems more and more incomprehensible. Yet it was an undoubted fact, a characteristic of the whole nation from King to commoner. King George VI wrote to his mother on June 27:

> Personally I feel happier now that we have no allies to be polite to & to pamper.[1]

At about the same time, the commissionaire of one of the Service clubs in London cheered a depressed member with the words:

> Anyhow, sir, we're in the Final, and it's to be played on the Home Ground.[2]

As Liddell Hart says:

> ...the British people took little account of the hard facts of their situation. They were instinctively stubborn and strategically ignorant. Churchill's inspiring speeches helped to correct the depression of Dunkirk, and supplied the tonic the islanders wanted. They were exhilarated by his challenging note, and did not pause to ask whether it was strategically warranted.[3]

They displayed, he says, and subsequently justified, "sublime stupidity".

The sentiments of the King and the commissionaire, and – let it be said – the overwhelming majority of their fellow-countrymen, were echoed with somewhat different motives by Dowding. Lord Halifax visited him at the end of June at Fighter Command headquarters in Bentley Priory, Stanmore; Dowding said to him:

169

Thank God we're alone now.[4]

It meant something more particular for him than for anyone else. He was thinking, no doubt, of the 453 Hurricanes and Spitfires that the French alliance had cost his Command, and its deficit of 362 pilots at the end of the Battle of France, a deficit whose quantity he could only very slowly remedy, and whose quality he might not be able to replace at all. Being alone, for Dowding, meant once and for all the end of those inescapable pressures on the Government and the Air Staff which had for the last six weeks been steadily draining away the life-blood of Fighter Command. For that he might well thank God; but there was precious little else in the situation of the nation and the RAF to give thanks for.

The immediate prospect was, of course, invasion. For Hitler, having reduced Denmark, Norway, Holland, Belgium and France to subjection in less than three months, it was a logical strategical sequence to reduce Britain similarly. Hindsight confirms what appeared as a natural progression at the time: failure to dispose of the British – which did not necessarily call for an outright attack – appears in history as the factor which, above all others, cost Hitler the war. However, it is now quite clear that in this vital matter, his mind was divided – indeed, according to one interesting analysis, his deterioration as a war leader (hitherto amazingly successful) dates from this very period immediately after the French collapse when, to his astonishment, the British made no overtures for peace. Instead, grand in tone and unmistakable in content, there came only the thunders of Churchillian defiance. Hitler was at a loss:

> The British refusal to give in when the French did disrupted the Führer's schedule. It also added a dimension to the war that he did not understand and could not master. The effect upon his strategy was disturbing and permanent. From now on it was marked increasingly by impatience, by plans that were ill conceived, implemented without conviction, and then abandoned, by profligacy in the use of human and material resources, and by an impulsive wilfulness that had disastrous results.[5]

It is clear that an attack on the Soviet Union was never very far back in his mind. Two events in June, often overlooked in the historiography of this time, brought it back sharply to the forefront. The first took place on the very day that France asked for an armistice, injecting an acid flavour into that otherwise delectable moment: the Soviet Union began the occupation of the Baltic States, Estonia, Latvia and Lithuania, which was completed a week later. And then, on June 26, the Soviet Government demanded from Rumania the provinces of Bessarabia and Northern Bukovina annexed in 1918, and the following day the demand was met. These evident signs of Soviet independence of purpose and warlike intention were unwelcome enough; coupled with the British attack on the French fleet at its anchorage at Mers-el-Kebir (Oran) on July 3, underlining the determination to carry on the war, they faced Hitler with a most disagreeable dilemma.

Mers-el-Kebir "wakened the Führer from his complacent dream of a quick settlement with England while emphasizing his own inability to either control the French fleet or checkmate the Royal Navy. He who was practically landbound was stunned by the shocking mobility of sea power."[6] Russia was prominent in his mind, but something would clearly have to be done about Britain – and quickly. It is quite true, as Liddell Hart has said, that for Britain

The course of no compromise was equivalent to slow suicide,[7]

and attention has also been drawn to a belief of Hitler's which contained

one of the basic concepts of Germany's conduct of the war, and one which came to the fore again and again, namely that Britain could be defeated by cutting her overseas supply lines.[8]

But if the Soviet Union was shifting her frontiers westward, and if Britain was going to lay about her in the manner of Mers-el-Kebir, Hitler would need to apply a quicker treatment than slow death by strangulation of supplies. But what? There was no doubt that his great Army, flushed with victory after victory, would make short work of the British – if it could get at them. There lay the rub. In the face of the Royal Navy's superiority, the German Fleet (much weakened during the Norwegian campaign) was quite unable to guarantee a passage for the *Panzers* and their supporting units. The only possible weapon against the superior strength of the Royal Navy was air power.

The *Luftwaffe* was also flushed with victory at the end of June. This bred a complacency which proved unfortunate in both the short and the long term. "There was," says the AHB Narrative, "a widespread inclination to relax and enjoy the fruits of a victory as good as won."[9] Air and ground-crew were given home leave in Germany in large numbers. There was no serious debate on the lessons of the

171

victorious campaigns (for which Hitler and Goering freely claimed credit), no new equipment was ordered, no new training instructions issued, and no expansion approved. All the effort that was made was directed towards making good the losses – which were considerable. Dr Karl Klee, citing the archives of the *Luftwaffe* Study Group attached to the *Führungsakademie* of the *Bundeswehr*, says that "in the months of April, May and June the *Luftwaffe* lost 2,784 planes".[10] This seems a high figure; as we have seen (p. 164), the likeliest figure for German losses in the Battle of France is 1,279 destroyed or damaged, to which we may add 388 aircraft lost on operations "but not due to enemy action", giving a total of 1,667. By subtraction, that would leave 1,117 to be accounted for in April – effectively, the 22 days of the campaign in Norway, in which the *Luftwaffe* encountered very little significant opposition. It may be true that losses were so high, but it seems unlikely. Dr Klee would appear to be on safer ground, however, when he tells us that a front-line bomber force of 1,102 aircraft on March 30 had fallen (even with replacements) to 841 on June 29, and at 949 when serious action against Britain began, was still below its March strength. It is clearly true to say that "the *Luftwaffe* was in no condition to mount an immediate assault against Britain"[11] after the French collapse. Goering, however, was undeterred. Ignoring the lessons of battle, ignoring his losses, and ignoring also the realistic studies of an attack on Britain made by his own Ministry in 1938 and 1939 (which concluded that air attack alone was unlikely to produce a British surrender), the newly-appointed *Reichsmarschall* promised Hitler that the *Luftwaffe* alone would break British resistance.[12] At the very least, it would create the conditions that would make invasion possible.

So, half hopeful, half doubting, and increasingly preoccupied with thoughts of Russia,[13] Hitler ordered a study of invasion of Britain to be made. That was on July 2, 1940; Goering had preceded him by two days with a *Luftwaffe* Directive. It is one of the extraordinary facts of the Third *Reich* that until these dates no plan or preparation for hostilities with Britain had been made. And Goering's operation orders (June 30) were confined to an initial phase of "nuisance raids by relatively minor forces on industrial and RAF targets".[14] The Directive did, however, prescribe the objectives:

When regrouped and in a full state of readiness the *Luftwaffe* will aim:
(a) to create the conditions necessary for a successful campaign against the enemy's war industry and supply lines by defeating his air force, destroying his ground organization, and disrupting his aircraft industry, thus defending Germany's own *Lebensraum*;

172

(b) to dislocate Britain's supplies by attacking ports and harbour installations, ships bringing supplies into the country, and warships escorting
them ... So long as the enemy air force remains in being, the supreme
principle of air warfare must be to attack it at every possible opportunity
by day and by night, in the air and on the ground with priority over other
tasks.[15]

On July 16 Hitler issued his own Directive No. 16, containing the
formal approval of invasion (Operation SEALION):

As England, despite her hopeless military situation, still shows no sign of
willingness to come to terms, I have decided to prepare, and if necessary
to carry out, a landing operation against her.
The aim of this operation is to eliminate the English motherland as a
base from which war against Germany can be continued and, if necessary,
to occupy completely.[16]

A target date of mid-August was indicated for the grand attack,
which allowed four weeks – precisely the period that Goering said
would be required to prepare the way.[17]

17 The Dowding system

The intimate connection between the intention to invade[1] and the
daylight duel between Fighter Command and the *Luftwaffe* (which
British sources consider to have begun on July 10 and continued until
October 31) is the true background of the Battle of Britain. It was not
simply a contest in British skies. It involved the whole apparatus of
Britain's Air Defence, including Lieutenant-General Sir Frederick
Pile's Anti-Aircraft Command, the Royal Observer Corps and Civil
Defence. It involved Coastal Command and Bomber Command. It
involved the Army, appallingly short of all essential equipment after its
Dunkirk losses.[2] And it involved the Royal Navy, which by September
accumulated a flotilla of some 800 light vessels in eastern and southern
ports. An authoritative German source informs us:

The German invasion craft were certain to suffer very heavy losses if these
small fast English warships got in amongst them in half-light or at night.[3]

But he adds: "The most alarming factor was the probable reaction of
the Royal Navy" – by which he means the Home Fleet. And we may
be quite certain that the Fleet would have displayed, if called upon,

the same sacrificial devotion in Home waters in 1940 that it displayed in the Mediterranean in 1941 and the Far East in 1942 and again in the South Atlantic in 1982. However, until necessity compelled, the Admiralty was understandably unwilling to commit itself to operations with capital ships south of the Forth in the face of unbroken German air power. Only one instrument could break that power – Fighter Command. The numerical odds against it would be considerable, but, says Churchill:

> I rested upon the conclusion that in our own air, over our own country and in its waters, we would beat the German Air Force. And if this were true our naval power would continue to rule the seas and oceans, and would destroy all enemies who set their course towards us.[4]

Fighter Command, by the end of the Battle of France, was in a seriously weakened condition in relation to what Dowding never ceased to consider its prime purpose – the defence of Britain against the "knock-out blow". Unreal for most of the time that it had haunted British imaginations, that threat was real enough now, and against all the ill consequences of the knock-out blow theory in the pre-war years one has to set in balance the fact that, thanks to it, detailed preparations to deal with the contingency of July 1940 had been in hand since 1937. What had not been foreseen was a heavy battle over the Continent in the course of which every squadron in Fighter Command except three in Scotland would be engaged (12 of them twice), and suffer more or less heavy losses.[5] On the other hand, thanks to the complete absence of any serious German plan for dealing with British opposition,[6] Dowding was permitted a few weeks in which to repair some of the damage. As a result, on July 7, as Goering and his men prepared themselves for battle again, Fighter Command's deployment comprised 52 squadrons in three Groups (No. 10 Group, forming since January, became operational later in the month); 19 squadrons were equipped with Spitfires, 25 with Hurricanes, two with Defiants and six with Blenheims; out of an establishment of over 800 aircraft, 644 were available for operations; an establishment of 1,456 pilots were represented by 1,259 nominally present for duty (a deficit of 197).[7] And backing them were the ground-crews of the squadrons,[8] the ground-staffs of the headquarters of the Command, the Groups, the sectors and the stations (RAF and WAAF), the operators of the radar chain, the personnel of the aircraft storage, repair and salvage units, and indeed, the whole array required to operate a complex, modern war machine, all probably, and those in the south certainly, soon to find themselves in the front line along with the famous flyers who, for obvious reasons, took the limelight.

Dowding was in his fifty-ninth year; he was due to retire on July 14, but on July 5 he received a letter from Newall asking him to defer retirement until the end of October.[9] This he readily (if testily) agreed to do, which was as well, because there was no-one who understood the true nature of Fighter Command and its battle system as well as Dowding, who created it. His assessment of his own, and the Command's, task in 1940 was clear:

> Mine was the purely defensive rôle of trying to stop the possibility of an invasion, and thus give this country a breathing spell . . . it was Germany's objective to win the war by invasion, and it was my job to prevent an invasion from taking place.[10]

As regards the actual conduct of the coming battle, Dowding was equally clear. The Germans would undoubtedly launch heavy bombing attacks against ports and industries (and the cities in which these were lodged) and whatever other targets they might think vital to Britain's war effort. Fighter Command, in Dowding's view, had not only to defend, but to protect these targets:

> Every effort had to be made to stop the enemy before he bombed, not afterwards.[11]

To this purpose and this method all the years of preparation would now be bent.

At the very centre of the Fighter Command system is the concept of control, and the technology on which it was based. There was no question, in the British skies of 1940, of the kind of "free-range" activity of the fighter "aces" of the First World War, Richthofen, Mannock, Guynemer, Ball and the rest. There was no question, either, in the minds of any of the responsible leaders of Fighter Command, that this battle, if it was to be won, could only be won by a narrow margin – so narrow that virtually any kind of gamble would be criminal, and only the tightest discipline of all ranks from the Air Chief Marshal downwards would serve. What made the narrow margin possible, and the exercise of sufficient control within it, was, of course, radar (RDF).

Churchill, in his history of the Second World War, speaks almost slightingly of radar, describing it as "in its infancy" (which was true, but it was a lusty infant), and saying that "the Battle of Britain was

175

fought mainly by eye and ear"[12] (which is also true, but misses the fundamental). What is more to the point is that from the primitive beginnings in 1935 (described on pp. 22-3), radar had developed by 1940 into a sufficiently effective instrument of war to transform air defence. This it did by offering just enough warning of an incoming attack and its general direction, and far less reliably its height and numbers, to enable a suitable response to be made. Supported, once the enemy was in view, by the invaluable and increasingly proficient "eyes and ears" of the Royal Observer Corps, what this meant, to the amazement of German listeners, was that

> The air was full of voices, calmly and systematically placing fighters here and there and guiding others back to base. It dawned on the listeners that this was part of a complex and smooth-running organization of great size.[13]

It was not that the Germans did not have radar of their own; they had been developing it since 1934, and by 1939 had achieved considerable sophistication (especially in the matter of anti-aircraft fire-control; see p. 104). But in these early days of the war there was a tendency on both sides to under-rate the technical advancement of the enemy. Thus a very detailed (and thoroughly misleading) report by the *Luftwaffe*'s *Chef (IC)* (Chief of Intelligence) in July 1940 made no mention of the British defence system and its radar stations. Yet by that time there were 21 operational (and very visible) "Chain Home" (CH) fixed mast stations capable of providing a long-range picture of the air situation, supported by 30 CHL (Chain Home Low) stations with rotating aerials capable of tracking the movements of shipping and low-flying aircraft. On their frail-looking trellises rested the main burden of Britain's security

Two other information sources must be mentioned, two more elements in a type of battle that had never been seen before. Radio monitoring itself was not new; in the First World War it had been developed to a point where, it was said, "the Germans could not move a picket-boat in harbour without the Admiralty in London knowing it". The most remarkable feat to date of radio interception was the one which produced the Battle of Jutland on May 31, 1916; it enabled the British Grand Fleet to set sail three and a half hours before the German sortie, which it was to counter, had even begun.[14] We have already seen (p. 39) how radio interception had allowed the Germans, in 1935–36, to break the Royal Navy's codes, with disastrous results. Strangely enough, the RAF, so well ahead in the matter of codes with its Typex machine, was slow to build up a monitoring service. It was not until December 1939 that serious investigation of German signals began, and not until February 1940 that Flight-Lieutenant (later Group Captain) Scott Farnie set up the first listening post at Hawkinge. Thus began the invaluable "Y Service", which held the Germans under permanent radio surveillance, one of the war's very well-kept secrets.

The ever-increasing requirement of fluent German linguists made it quickly obvious that women would have to be recruited for this work as well as men; one of the earliest intake was Section Officer Aileen ("Mike") Morris MBE, who tells us:

> By the end of the summer of 1940, the Air Ministry Intelligence had an almost complete picture of the *Luftwaffe*'s Order of Battle, particularly in Western Europe. With all this knowledge added to the information that we were amassing at Kingsdown[15] about the callsigns and frequencies used by the various German squadrons to which we were listening, we were able, for instance, to advise No. 11 Group that the enemy raid that was approaching Beachy Head was probably made up of Me 109s of II/ JG 51 based at St Omer. This would be most helpful for the Controllers, who would then be able to anticipate the probable return route of the enemy aircraft. Later, when we had direction-finding (D/F) facilities, we could pinpoint the transmissions and thus knew the exact position of the enemy formation whose messages we were hearing. But even in those early days of the summer of 1940, we could almost certainly confirm the height at which the formations were approaching, and we might also be able to give some indication, from what we were hearing, of their intended action.[16]

This is an impressive claim; it is sobering, however, to note Section Officer Morris's belief that the German equivalent of the "Y Service" (*Horchdienst*) "may at that time have been rather more efficient than ours".[17] Sobering, too, were the early limitations, especially when listening-in to the voice of battle itself, in a fashion that had never yet been done:

> There were occasions when we would intercept a message from a German formation approaching RAF fighters . . . having spotted our aircraft before they themselves were observed. We were then likely to hear: "*Indianer unten fuenf Uhr, Kirchturm 4, Aufpassen*" (Bandits below at five o'clock, height 4,000 metres, look out.)
> In those days we were unable to get this information through in time for it to be of tactical use, and would get hopping mad that we had no means of warning our fighters that they were about to be jumped.

177

Then *"Angreifen!"* (attack) the formation leader would yell, and we would know that the German fighters were diving on their target.

I would often hear one of the WAAF operators murmuring: "Oh God ... oh God ... please ... *please* look up ...", and I knew how helpless she felt.[18]

Eventually, says Aileen Morris, even this seemingly impenetrable communications block was overcome, and "we were able to bring the time-lag down to one minute".

"Everything," says Ronald Lewin, "began with the intercept."[19] The monitoring of all German signals "whether in low-grade or high-grade cipher, radio-telephony, or non-Morse transmissions, was the responsibility of the Y Service".[20] And utterly dependent upon "Y" was "Station X", Bletchley Park, the war station of the Government Code and Cypher School, with its astounding assembly of dedicated genius which broke the German Enigma codes and thus endowed the Western Allies with the priceless gift of Ultra. Throughout the whole critical – and at times nerve-racking – period of the invasion threat, Ultra played a significant part in permitting the British leadership to build up a "meaningful mosaic" (in Lewin's words) of German intentions. In the Battle of Britain,

> The early and authentic information that came from Bletchley about forthcoming raids was a strong buttress for Dowding in his conduct of the battle.[21]

"Buttress" would seem to be a well-chosen word: a useful support to a building, but not part of the main structure. It is possible to picture a strong building without a buttress, but a buttress without a building is nothing – and so it was with Air Intelligence in 1940. There are clear reasons for this: first, the Bletchley organization was still in its early days, by no means the comprehensive and streamlined system that it was soon to become; secondly, as the *Luftwaffe* settled down on its new French, Belgian and Dutch airfields, naturally the bulk of its signals traffic was carried by landline – impervious to Ultra. On the other hand – a most valuable *future* asset for Bletchley – the *Luftwaffe* proved to be the most careless and least secure of the German Services in the use of Enigma; the *Luftwaffe* cipher was the easiest way in for the British cryptanalysts. However, in 1940 Ultra was evidently not a major factor; Dowding received it from the beginning, at first via the Air Ministry, then direct from Bletchley by teleprinter through a Special Liaison Unit lodged in a sound-proof cubicle next to the Operations Room in Bentley Priory.[22] Dowding and Air Vice-Marshal Keith Park, commanding No. 11 Group, alone of the Fighter commanders, were in the Ultra secret. There is no record, however, of what its precise usefulness to them was.

These, then, were the particular Intelligence sources on which the Fighter Command organization was based in 1940 – one could say, its very sanction, the fabric of the Dowding system.[23] And this system had been carefully built up during five years entirely with a view to exploiting these particular sources in the most effective way. Obviously, for this purpose a most elaborate communications system would be required – a dense telephone network, backed by sufficient emergency lines, for the exclusive use of the Command, and in addition a Defence Teleprinter Network reserved for the Services. All this was provided in the last year of peace and during the respite of the "phoney war", a magnificently quick and secret achievement of the Post Office which has not gone unnoticed, but cannot be allowed to pass here without further recognition. And finally, the installation of high-frequency radio direction-finding equipment provided the means of putting the British fighters on an interception course with the incoming German bombers whose every move was being so closely watched. Intelligence and the communication of it were the sinews of the system; its "brain" was the control with which it was exercised.

At the heart of the whole complex was Bentley Priory, Dowding's headquarters, and at the heart of that the Operations Room, which had only been securely lodged underground and under concrete in March 1940. The image of that room is, to British readers, one of the most familiar of the Second World War; somewhat less familiar is the neighbouring filter centre (sharing the same concrete bunker), where all the information received from the two radar chains (CH and CHL) and the Observer Corps was cross-checked before appearing on the famous map in the Operations Room, attended by the WAAF plotters with their "croupier" rakes. There is no need for yet another detailed description of this nerve centre; it is reproduced with exactitude for future generations in the Battle of Britain Museum at Hendon, and its working is clearly described by Wood and Dempster in *The Narrow Margin* (pp. 84–90) and elsewhere. The point that cannot, however, be over-stressed, is that, as they tell us:

This was the only room where aircraft tracks over the whole of Britain and the sea approaches were displayed.[24]

It was, in other words, the only place where the whole battle, wherever it might flare up, could be – and was – centrally controlled. And there sat Dowding, with General Pile of AA Command, the Commandant of the Observer Corps, liaison officers from Bomber and Coastal Commands, the Admiralty, the War Office and the Ministry of Home Security: the chief brain-cell of the defence of Great Britain.

The essential information filtered and continuously plotted at Bentley Priory was disseminated outwards in "cones". At the tip of each cone was the Group[25] Operations Room, modelled on the "master" at Bentley Priory, but displaying on its key map only the Group area and immediately adjacent sectors. The only independent source of information in the Groups was that supplied by the Observer Corps, which it was their duty to pass to Fighter Command and other Groups. The cone then broadened out to embrace the sectors, and the sectors to the squadrons. The sector Operations Rooms were the final link in the control system; it was they who put the squadrons into the air, positioned them, fed them with essential information, and brought them back again. The sector Controllers were the key men; each one "retained executive authority over the aircraft he despatched until the fighters saw the enemy ... When combat was broken off the controller resumed command ..."[26] Heavy responsibilities lay upon these officers, generally of Squadron-Leader or at most Wing Commander rank. The duties of a sector Controller "needed a sense of judgment amounting to an intuition".[27] And they were unique to the RAF; in the Navy it would not be normal to entrust operational decisions of this significance to Lieutenant-Commanders and Commanders, nor in the Army to Majors and Lieutenant-Colonels. When the Operations Rooms first came into being, because their functioning depended on Signals equipment, it was thought reasonable that Controllers should be Signals Branch officers. Not surprisingly, this did not go down well with the fighter pilots, and despite protests from Signals, these officers were replaced by men who had flying (and preferably combat) experience. Their voices, calm, measured and friendly, brought support and reassurance to the young paladins in the sky; for their own part, the Controllers looked on themselves as being as much the servants as the commanders of the flyers whom they controlled. Such was the Fighter Command system, a delicately interlocking net of communications and responsibilities, comprising a carefully tuned instrument of war. That is why there was no place in it for "freerange" activity or for mavericks.

18 *"Contact Phase"; Sir Keith Park*

No attempt will here be made to offer yet another narrative of the often-told story of the Battle of Britain – the decisive victory of Dowding's system and of Dowding's "chicks", that light-hearted band of brave young men whose skills and devotion made it work. Thanks to them, the Royal Navy did not have to sacrifice its major units in the narrow seas; thanks to them, the virtually helpless Army did not have to face the overwhelming *Panzers*. Nor was that all:

> For the first time in history an attempt was made to use air power to cripple an enemy to such an extent that he would not thereafter be in a position to offer any serious resistance – in fact it was even hoped that air action alone could force him to sue for peace.[1]

Thanks to Dowding and his Command, that hope was comprehensively dashed, and Hitler's Germany met its first defeat in the war.

The chief instrument by which Goering hoped to achieve his triumph was the combined strength of *Feldmarschall* Albert Kesselring's *Luftflotte 2* and *Feldmarschall* Hugo Sperrle's *Luftflotte 3*, in Belgium and north-western France. As usual, it is not possible to give a sure, precise statement of their numerical strength. Totals – all from respectable sources[2] – vary from 2,422 to 2,600: a variation of approximately 7 per cent, which is no disaster. The Air Historical Branch Narrative offers this table:

Bombers	1,200
Dive-Bombers	280
Single-engined Fighters	760
Twin-engined Fighters	220
Reconnaissance	140
	2,600[3]

Other accounts put the bomber force at just below 1,000, but the single-engined fighters at 800 or more. Dr Overy, on the other hand, while crediting the latter with a strength of 893 on July 1, says that only 725 were serviceable[4] which is very close to the AHB figure.

British and German sources are in broad agreement about the shape of the Battle. Wood and Dempster divide it into five phases; in

Dr Klee's account these become three phases, but with subsidiary "stages":

KLEE	WOOD & DEMPSTER
Contact Phase End of the campaign in France – August 7 1940; fighter sweeps	**First Phase:** July 10–August 7
Main Phase I *Battle for Command of the Air* **Stage 1:** August 8–23 Attacks on targets near the coast in South and South-East England. Fighter battles; attacks on ground organization and aircraft industry.	**Second Phase:** August 8–23
Stage 2: August 24–September 6 Attacks extended as far as the London area.	**Third Phase:** August 24– September 6
Main Phase II *Attack on Britain's Economic Potential* **Stage 1:** September 7–19 Day and night bomber attacks on London and on targets in the London area.	**Fourth Phase:** September 7–30
Stage 2: September 20–November 13 Daylight fighter-bomber attacks, and night bombing raids, chiefly on London.	**Fifth Phase:** October 1–31 (October 31 is normally regarded in Britain as the close of the Battle.)
Stage 3: November 14, 1940 to start of campaign against Russia. Night bombing raids against targets throughout Britain, including London.[5]	(Known in Britain as "The Blitz".)

In those tense last days of June and early July, it clearly behoved Fighter Command to conserve and build up its strength as much as possible; to the *Luftwaffe* it appeared that the RAF was refusing battle, a circumstance from which some German observers drew correct conclusions, but others did not. In any case,

The result was that the *Luftwaffe* enjoyed command of the air by default in those areas it penetrated with reasonably strong forces, but it was unable to force a decision and make this permanent.[6]

From the RAF point of view, the stepping-up of air activity which became noticeable on July 10 really marks the moment when it took up its position "on the right of the line". As regards Germany, the main enemy in the war, for the next four years there would not be very much that Britain could seriously do to bring about her defeat except what the RAF could contribute. And Fighter Command would be the first to put its silver in the plate.

The "Contact Phase" brought sharp lessons for both sides. It became distressingly clear that the teaching of the Battle of France had not yet had time to sink in all through Fighter Command. In the early days some squadrons continued to engage the enemy according to pre-war doctrine, in tight V-formations of three aircraft, with disastrous results. The German fighter pilots, first schooled in Spain, and with their techniques well polished over the Low Countries and France, were more practical, more flexible. Their basic unit was the *Rotte*, a pair of fighters about 200 yards apart, free of all preoccupations of formation-flying, and giving all their attention to covering each other. Two of these made up a *Schwarme*, a formidable mutually-supporting group of machines. In due course the RAF adopted this style also, which it called "finger-four", because the aircraft flew in positions corresponding to the alignment of four fingers of a hand, seen from above, the leader represented by the longest finger. The essence of the thing was mutual support to guard against surprise, and absolute concentration on the combat, without frills.

For the Germans, too, the "Contact Phase" brought disagreeable awakenings. The first was the recognition, particularly displeasing to Goering, of the limitations of the Me 110, already suspect against modern single-seater fighters. Against Hurricanes over France, the Me 110s had been forced to form defensive circles; against undiluted Hurricane and Spitfire opposition, they were now seen to be useless as bomber escorts (soon they would be receiving escorts themselves). This meant a diminution of German fighter strength by upwards of 200 aircraft. Secondly, the Me 109s, on which everything increasingly depended, faced serious weakening in other ways: first was the realization that they would need to provide escorts roughly three times as numerous as the bombers they were to protect;[7] secondly, there was the ever-louder demand by the bomber crews that they should escort as closely as possible, thus sacrificing some of their best combat

183

qualities; thirdly, there emerged the need to hold back a certain number in order to protect damaged German bombers which were being pursued all the way back to the French coast by persistent Fighter Command pilots. Glancing forward, we may note that Dr Overy, in addition to his figure of serviceable Me 109s on July 1, quoted above, also supplies figures for September 1 (actually 7th) and October 1: 438 and 275 respectively. Evidently, the sense of being "the few" must at times have extended to the German single-engined fighter arm also. More significant, however, for the battle that was developing, was the recognition in the "Contact Phase" that its character was to be decided by the Me 109; where the Me 109 could go, there could the *Luftwaffe* also go; where the Me 109 could not go, the other *Luftwaffe* types would be ill-advised to try. The one weakness of this superb aeroplane was its lack of range; effectively, it could only spend about an hour in the air; this meant that

> operating from bases in the Pas-de-Calais area, it could spend only about twenty minutes over targets like Kenley which were some 95 miles away. And even that short time was possible only if the fighter pilots were permitted to make the most of their limited fuel; if they had to fly a zig-zag course to match their rate of advance to that of a formation of cruising bombers, the Messerschmitt's limited radius of action was further reduced.[8]

Why the Germans did not fit the Me 109 with drop-tanks remains a mystery; however, it is clearly the simple truth that "the combination of a fighter of this kind with medium bombers was the wrong recipe for the Battle of Britain".[9] It was, nevertheless the recipe which decided where it would be fought, how it would be fought, and who would have to fight it.

The fact that London marked, in effect, the limit of the range of the Me 109 signified where the fighting would be: in Southern England, the fief of No. 11 Group and (at the end of July) No. 10 Group. This meant that it would be fought according to the Dowding system, which was also the Park system; it could be said, for literary effect, but without straining the truth, that Dowding controlled the battle from day to day, Park controlled it from hour to hour, and the No. 11 Group sector Controllers from minute to minute. In Air Vice-Marshal Sir C. J. Quintin Brand of No. 10 Group, when it became operational, Dowding and Park found an unswervingly loyal subordinate and colleague. But it was Park who shared Ultra with Dowding, Park whose Group stood at the centre of the fight from beginning to end, Park who emerges as the outstanding practitioner of the Dowding-style battle.

New Zealand-born, 48 years old, quiet, devout, businesslike, Keith Rodney Park came up through the ranks of the New Zealand Artillery in the First World War (Gallipoli, 1915; the Somme, 1916) in which he was severely wounded; he then entered the Royal Flying Corps, and became a fighter pilot. Thus he had deep roots in the business. He and Dowding saw their task eye to eye; he completely shared Dowding's sense of the system, and the decisive factor of control. No fewer than 35 Instructions to his Group in the course of the battle show Park's sensitive awareness of every shift in enemy behaviour, his flexible response to every new tactic (and they were not few) that was thrown at him. Park was now to conduct (virtually in the orchestral sense) a decisive battle, and in doing so reveal himself a master tactician. Yet today, even among some who interest themselves in air matters, his name is hardly known, which is something of a national disgrace.

19 "Adler Tag"; The "Numbers Game"

On August 1 Hitler issued his secret Directive No. 17, in which he ordered:

> The *Luftwaffe* will use all the forces at its disposal to destroy the British air force as quickly as possible . . . August 5th is the first day on which this intensified air war may begin, but the exact date is to be left to the *Luftwaffe* and will depend on how soon its preparations are complete, and on the weather situation.[1]

So the word was given to launch the *Adlerangriff*, the "Attack of the Eagles", and a date offered for *Adler Tag*, "Eagle Day". Bad weather conditions in the Channel area, and some less than competent staff work by *Luftwaffe* Headquarters, both contributed to early delays, but the tireless eavesdroppers were not deceived. Bletchley Park responded to Directive No. 17 like a plucked violin:

> . . . as August started to move on, the number of German signals began to boil over. They mounted to one, two and three hundred a day; when we could break them each one had to be scanned, sorted, translated and edited.[2]

A final conference on August 6 disposed of the *Luftwaffe*'s problems, and on August 8 Goering issued his Order of the Day:

From *Reichsmarschall* Goering to all units of *Luftflotte 2, 3* and *5*. Operation *Adler*. Within a short period you will wipe the British Air Force from the sky. *Heil Hitler*.[3]

Goering's Order was in the hands of the British Chiefs of Staff and the Prime Minister within the hour; "Dowding had got his copy direct".[4]

When Goering made his broadcast, the intention was that *Adler Tag* should be August 10, but once more the Channel weather intervened; it was finally fixed for August 13, but even then there were confusions and delays which prevented the attack from being made until the afternoon, and restricted its scope. The *Luftwaffe* flew 1,485 sorties – its largest number to date; it succeeded in doing some serious damage to ground installations, and destroying a certain number of British aircraft on the ground,[5] and claimed a total of 88 (including 70 Spitfires and Hurricanes). Fighter Command's actual combat losses were 15 (against the *Luftwaffe*'s 39).[6] Significantly, a considerable proportion of the German losses consisted of Ju 87s. This aircraft still had a useful career before it, but never again would it be the terror weapon of May and June. Against strong fighter opposition, its helplessness was fully revealed (see p. 133); in the next six days 41 were shot down, and on August 19 the *Stukas* were withdrawn from the battle.

Meanwhile the test had reached its severity. August 13 had really only seen a "half-cock" *Adler Tag*; the big battle came on August 15. Once again, there was no surprise:

> The Ultra signal was precise. The attack would be made by *Luftflotten 2, 3* and *5*, and the orders sent to them warned us that their attacks were carefully timed so as to keep our defences fully stretched the whole day.[7]

There was no doubt whatever about the *Luftwaffe*'s objective on August 15: it was Fighter Command itself. A series of crushing blows against the Command's airfields (or what the *Luftwaffe* took to be its airfields) had the double object of destroying its ground organization, and at the same time pulling its squadrons into the air to be destroyed also. A particularly interesting feature of the day was the intervention of *Luftflotte 5*. Beginning shortly after mid-day, it put in two attacks aimed at the north-east coast, evidently with the aim of drawing Dowding's reserves away from the decisive point in the south. No. 12 and No. 13 Groups, however, were forewarned, and both attacks were repelled with heavy losses. And so it came about that, thanks to good

Intelligence from sundry sources and cool nerves, however few "the Few", somehow there were always a few more.

The *Luftwaffe* flew 1,786 sorties during the twenty-four hours of August 15; it claimed 99 British aircraft shot down in combat. Fighter Command's actual losses were 35; the Air Ministry News Service claimed 180 enemy aircraft destroyed by Fighter Command and AA gunfire, but the reality has proved to be less than half that figure – 76.[8] Already the Press and the BBC, and through them the British public, had formed the habit of following the progress of claim and counter-claim like a Test Match score. It was firmly believed that the British claims represented accurate, verified statements of German losses:

> and this they never were nor could be, so short was the interval between the end of a day's operations and the publication of figures . . .[9]

Even when the Air Ministry itself began to have doubts, as the battle wore on,

> it would have been next to impossible to have introduced a conditional or disclaiming element into their casualty figures, even though it became increasingly obvious that the published claims were at best only a guide to what the Germans had actually lost. Air Chief Marshal Dowding himself deplored to the Secretary of State for Air the impression that was being formed in the public mind . . .[10]

As the Battle was drawing to an end, Dowding told the Vice-Chief of the Air Staff (Sir Richard Peirse) that his personal view was that RAF claims were exaggerated by probably 25 per cent. The compiler of the AHB Narrative (T. C. G. James) shortly after the war, shrewdly gave his own opinion

> that they were at least that. If this proves to be so, there is likely to be a sense of deflation and disappointment amongst those who fought the battle and amongst the public at large. For it is true to say that the success that Fighter Command undoubtedly achieved has largely been measured by the casualties suffered by the German Air Force.[11]

It is certainly true that the "numbers game" had a baleful effect on the conduct of the battle in certain quarters, as we shall see. It is also true, however, that though the reality of 76 German aircraft destroyed (and, of course, an uncertain additional number badly damaged) looks poor against the grossly inflated claim, 76 is a substantial quantity of aircraft, the largest, in fact, lost by the Germans on any single day.

It is ironic that the best success of the Germans during the day was unrelated to their objective. Two strong forces attacked east Kent in the mid-afternoon, and at Rochester the Short Brothers factory was badly damaged, causing a severe setback to the production of the four-engined Stirlings which were an important ingredient of the eagerly-awaited "new generation" of Bomber Command. In all other respects the day went badly for the *Luftwaffe* – worst of all for *Luftflotte 5*, which was "to all intents and purposes finished in the daylight battle apart from reconnaissance".[12] The lesson of the decisive significance of the Me 109 was rubbed in once more – with all that that implied for Park and No. 11 Group. The Me 110 joined the Ju 87 among the rejects for this style of war – though it lived to fight another day in another rôle. The loss of at least 128 aircrew[13] – the only occasion when (known) losses were over 100 – was undoubtedly a factor in Goering's decision to forbid the presence of more than one officer in any crew. All in all, we may look upon August 15 as a triumph for Dowding's system: Ultra, radar, the indefatigable Observer Corps, cool handling by No. 11 Group – Park and his Group Controller, Wing Commander Lord Willoughby de Broke – and underpinning all these all the time, the skill and devotion of the undaunted young pilots who outfought their formidable enemies in the air.

20 August, the crunch; Beaverbrook

August was the crunch; August was when the *Luftwaffe* was supposed to win this battle and make invasion possible; August was when it failed. It was a hard month; the *Luftwaffe* was back in strength – 1,715 sorties – on August 16. The Ventnor CH station, knocked out on the 12th, received further damage which kept it out of action until the 23rd. (It was a personal serious error of Goering's that the *Luftwaffe* did not make the radar installations a prime target.) Tangmere suffered heavy damage, and at Brize Norton 46 trainer aircraft were destroyed. The Germans lost 44 aircraft, Fighter Command 24. The Command also gained its first VC (the only VC of the Battle of Britain): Flight-Lieutenant J. B. Nicolson of 249 Squadron. Two days later came what Alfred Price has called "the hardest day", the one which he considers most deserving of being remembered as "Battle of Britain Day"; on August 18, he says,

The *Luftwaffe* had 100 aircraft put out of action, 69 of them wrecked or damaged beyond repair. Fighter Command had 73 fighters put out of action, 39 of them wrecked or damaged beyond repair. A further 62 British aircraft of other types were destroyed or damaged during the attacks on airfields, 29 of them wrecked or damaged beyond repair. Never before during the battle, nor afterwards, would the two sides suffer such heavy material losses during a single day.[1]

Subsequent research marginally changes some of Price's figures: the 69 German wrecks become 67, Fighter Command's 39 fall to 33. But his conclusions stand, and his narrative of the day leaves one in no doubt about what the *Luftwaffe*'s attempt to smash Fighter Command's ground organization meant at the receiving end. Kenley, Croydon, Biggin Hill and Ford were conspicuous (but not alone) in the front line of battle that day, Kenley alone received 100 bombs. On the ground and in the air the strain of this battle was becoming critical; at Bentley Priory and at Uxbridge – and in Whitehall too – the margin between victory and defeat began to appear terribly thin.

It was fortunate that the eternal sanction of air warfare – the weather – now intervened to force a few days' lull; a few days in which to rest, recoup a little, rethink and reckon up. August, up to midnight on the 18th, had cost Fighter Command 106 pilots killed or died of wounds – and, of course, a number of others so badly wounded or injured that they would take no further part in the battle, or, in some cases indeed, the war. And apart from death, wounds and injury, there was increasingly to be reckoned with that everlasting enemy of the fighting man in prolonged operations, sheer fatigue, whose effects would shortly become depressingly apparent. In Fighter Command, during the same period, 208 aircraft had been lost in combat; in Coastal Command the wastage for the whole month would be 45, and in Bomber Command the losses sustained in direct anti-invasion operations (attacking naval targets, aerodromes in occupied territory, minelaying) would amount to 18.[2] In No. 11 Group, where losses in the air and damage on the ground were inevitably greatest, the strain on ground-crew as well as pilots was also a factor to consider:

Quick servicing had been developed to a fine art – refuelling, rearming, engine checking, including oil and glycol coolant, replacing oxygen cylinders, and testing the R/T set would go on simultaneously. On many occasions all the aircraft of a squadron formation were replenished with fuel and ammunition, and got ready for another battle, in eight to ten minutes after landing . . . Regular repair and maintenance were carried on day and night with all maintenance personnel pooled on each station

189

. . . Most of the maintenance work on the signals equipment of the fighters had to be carried out at night by the light of torches. Trouble was caused by damp, and extreme care was necessary to keep R/T sets dry in rain or dew . . . Dispersal of aircraft not only to satellite aerodromes, but over wide areas at each of them, combined with lack of transport, increased the labour requirement for a given job. The blackout, damage to power and water mains, and to the station organization, added to the difficulties. Initially bomb craters and building repairs were undertaken by the station works and buildings detachments. As the damage grew, these units could no longer cope, and works repair depots were called in. Manned by between 50 and 200 workmen . . . in many cases the depots performed sterling work, but often during an air raid a gang would retire to the shelters and refuse to budge . . . Invariably a lot of the crater filling and rubble clearing was carried out by the airmen of the station itself.[3]

German Intelligence was, as usual, well adrift from reality; a summary issued on August 16 confidently asserted that since July Fighter Command had lost 372 Spitfires, 179 Hurricanes, 9 Curtiss Hawks (none took part) and 12 Defiants. It calculated that there were now only some 300 serviceable British fighters left, which would have meant that the *Luftwaffe* was well on its way to fulfilling Goering's order to "wipe the British Air Force from the sky". The reality was alarming but nothing like as bad as that; there were still over 700 aircraft with the squadrons, and the danger was in the longer term, rather than immediate. For the week that ended August 17 saw an ominous trend beginning: for the first time losses of Spitfires and Hurricanes exceeded the number available in storage units, and during the next three weeks this excess mounted to formidable proportions. As Denis Richards says,

If this went on for many weeks there could only be one end – defeat for the Royal Air Force.[4]

Fortunately, the trend was reversed in early September, to recur for one week only at the end of that month, and never again. That this was so is attributable to an unfamiliarly large extent to the Civilian Repair Organization (CRO) set up in 1938 and transferred from the Air Ministry to the Ministry of Aircraft Production when the latter was created in May 1940. Thanks to the CRO and the RAF's salvage units, "miracles of repair were worked in 1940";[5] by July the weekly output of repaired aircraft was 160 a week. The contribution of CRO, the RAF's own repair depôts and the salvage units to the winning of the Battle of Britain, say Wood and Dempster, cannot be over-emphasized. Between July and December 1940 CRO put back into the line 4,196 damaged planes. Of the total number of aircraft issued to fighter squadrons during the Battle of Britain excluding the fly-in repairs, 35 per cent were repaired and only 65 per cent were new.[6]

The Ministry of Aircraft Production was Churchill's own creation, inspired by memories of the Ministry of Munitions between 1915 and 1918; he himself had presided over some of the finest feats of that Department in 1917–18. British aircraft production had long been one of his *bêtes noires*; as far back as 1936 he had referred to its "dark and confused landscape",[7] and as recently as June 3 he had scathingly written to Sinclair of "the muddle and scandal of the aircraft production branch".[8] His sovereign remedy for this state of affairs was the appointment of his old friend Max Aitken, Lord Beaverbrook, proprietor of the *Daily Express*, as Minister. It suited him, and it suited Beaverbrook's many vociferous supporters, to report thereafter that Beaverbrook had performed a vital miracle on behalf of Fighter Command:

> All his remarkable qualities fitted the need . . . He did not fail. This was his hour. His personal force and genius, combined with so much persuasion and contrivance, swept aside many obstacles. Everything in the supply pipe-line was drawn forward to the battle . . .[9]

One still reads how, thanks to Beaverbrook, a production shortfall of 282 aircraft in February 1940 was turned into an excess over the target of 291 in August.[10] The following table, however, presents a somewhat different picture; it must be read with the date of Beaverbrook's appointment firmly in mind: May 11, 1940:

1940	Planned production, all types	Actual production, all types	Planned production, fighters	Actual production, fighters
February	1,001	719	171	141
March	1,137	860	203	177
April	1,256	1,081	231	256
May	1,244	1,279	261	325
June	1,320	1,591	292	446
July	1,481	1,665	329	496
August	1,310	1,601	282	476[11]

It is quite clear from this table that the turning-point of production was in April, before Beaverbrook's appointment, and in that month fighter production, in particular, made its first dramatic progress, well maintained in May, before even Beaverbrook's great energies could bear fruit. Of the energies there is no doubt; he drew into his task all the "hustling" methods for which he was already famous as a newspaper magnate, and from that sphere he borrowed a flair for publicity which made the whole country aircraft-production-conscious to an unprecedented degree. He thus immensely fostered and stimulated the frame of mind in which long shifts would be worked, dangers braved, difficulties tackled and targets surpassed – in other words, he was part and parcel of the tonic which Churchill was administering to the nation in its crisis. "For a time, short but crucial," says Sir Maurice Dean, "he was the right man in the right job", but

> In the long run, of course, Beaverbrook's effect on aircraft production would have been disastrous.[12]

By November 1940, Air Vice-Marshal A. W. Tedder, on leaving the Ministry of Aircraft Production, wrote to the Secretary of State:

> I am compelled to state that . . . the present organization and working of the Ministry are such as gravely to threaten the efficiency of the Service and consequently the safety of the country.[13]

As we have seen (p. 72) 1940 was the year when British aircraft production turned the corner and exceeded German production by nearly 50 per cent. It was, in fact, the year in which certain processes, begun years before and at first slow to develop, began to bear their fruit.[14] And for that no single man could possibly be responsible; as Denis Richards says:

> the magnificent achievement of June, July and August was of course the achievement of the aircraft industry as a whole, not only that of the newly appointed Minister.[15]

Beaverbrook dazzled for a while with a display of brilliant plumage; fortunately, like some other birds of that description, he proved to be a passage migrant.

It was on August 20 that Churchill paid his unforgettable tribute to Fighter Command: "Never in the field of human conflict was so much owed by so many to so few." The question, ever more pressing in these days of hectic combat, was "how few?"; how much longer would Dowding be able to go on finding that vital "few more"?

By the time the August battles began in earnest, five new squadron numbers were shown on the Fighter Command Order of Battle. But since one of these (232) represents a half-squadron of Hurricanes at Wick in Northern Scotland, and another (247) a half-squadron of Gladiators in Cornwall, the growth is not quite what it seems. The return of 73 Squadron to operations (Church Fenton, No. 12 Group) and the accession of 605 and 607 AAF Squadrons to No. 13 Group were obviously cheering; but nothing could disguise the seriousness of the wastage of experienced pilots. And these were increasingly hard to come by. The Fleet Air Arm, over and above two squadrons lent to Fighter Command, seconded 58 pilots of high quality; Bomber Command, on August 17, contributed five volunteers from each of four Fairey Battle squadrons, and later combed the Battle squadrons again (reluctantly, because it was hoping to re-equip them). Coastal Command lent three Blenheim squadrons and transferred some of its best fighter pilots, while from Army Cooperation came three pilots from each of four Lysander squadrons, as well as a number of Lysanders for air-sea rescue work. The Dominions, as ever, lent much-valued aid, though in process of building up their own Air Forces: the South African, Squadron-Leader "Sailor" Malan of No. 74 Squadron, was one of the first "aces". Australia, New Zealand and Rhodesia made their contributions; No. 1 Squadron, Royal Canadian Air Force, appeared in the Order of Battle at the end of August. There were pilots from France, from Belgium, from Holland, even from neutral America; above all, there were the two Polish (302 and 303) and two Czech (310 and 312) squadrons which formed part of Fighter Command in the later stages. And yet the shortage of pilots persisted, a graver source of anxiety to Dowding than any other.

Fighter Command was, in fact, now paying the price of the RAF's disorderly pre-war expansion. We have seen (p. 82) with what difficulties the RAF faced the problem of its increasing demands for aircrew and how serious the general deficiency was at the outbreak of war. Its resources stretched to their limits, Training Command was hampered also by its own very high standards. Air Chief Marshal Ludlow-Hewitt's disbelief in mass-produced aircrew (see p. 86) was not confined to him; Training Command considered that to produce a pilot took about a year – which naturally restricted the flow. Fifty per cent serviceability of aircraft – if Churchill is to be believed[16] – cannot have helped. For Dowding, his Group commanders and his squadron leaders, looking round for replacements in August and September, the picture was bleak; all they could say was, with deep feeling, "Thank God for the RAFVR!"

21 The "big wing"; Leigh-Mallory, Bader

"The colossus of World War II seemed to be like a pyramid turned upside down," wrote Adolf Galland,[1] "and for the moment the whole burden of the war rested on the few hundred German fighter pilots on the Channel coast." It is only appropriate to add the few hundred of the same breed on the other side of the Channel – but there was a conspicuous difference between the two groups. Whereas the gay young men of Fighter Command knew that they were the country's heroes, enjoying the deepest admiration and affection of their Commander-in-Chief, their German counterparts were being accused by their chief, Goering, of lack of aggressiveness, on which he blamed the failure to drive the RAF out of the sky. It was a bitterly unfair accusation – but Goering knew next to nothing of modern air warfare. However, despite the *Luftwaffe*'s heavy losses (192 aircraft) between August 15 and 18, he was determined to proceed with the all-out attack on Fighter Command. His Directive of August 19 called for the infliction of "the utmost damage possible on enemy fighter forces"; restrictions on *Luftflotten 2* and *3* in the choice of targets were lifted, with two exceptions: "I reserve only the right to order attacks on London and Liverpool."

Dowding and Park were under no illusions; Park's Instruction No. 4 of August 19 stressed the need to avoid, as far as possible, fighter-to-fighter combat. "Our main object," he said, "is to engage enemy bombers . . ." There were to be four more days' respite, and then the August fighting entered its most taxing phase. As always, the *Luftwaffe* continued to display great tactical versatility (for which Kesselring and Sperrle and their junior commanders must take credit, since it clearly does not belong to Goering), taxing Park's wits and patience to the utmost. With the opening of the next phase (August 24) he found himself seriously perplexed by a new tactic: dawn to dusk patrols of the Straits of Dover by formations of varying size,

whose mere presence helped to conceal preparations for genuine attacks still further disguised by occasional feints towards the English coast.[2]

On August 24, honours were more or less even; Fighter Command succeeded in bringing down 41 German aircraft for a loss of 20; on the other hand, it was now forced to abandon Manston except as an emergency field; in the day bombing Ramsgate and Portsmouth were heavily hit, and, ominously, by night,

> For the first time since the Gothas of 1918, Central London was damaged in an air raid.[3]

Park's No. 4 Instruction (paragraph "e") may be taken as a starting point of a controversy which is not yet stilled. It stated:

> If all our [11 Group] squadrons around London are off the ground engaging enemy mass attacks, ask No. 12 Group or Command Controller to provide squadrons to patrol aerodromes Debden, North Weald, Hornchurch.[4]

But soon we learn, when battle resumes on the 24th, and 11 Group is hard pressed:

> No. 12 Group were called upon to assist over North Weald and Hornchurch, but the Duxford wing was flown in too late to have any major effect.[5]

August 26 was another heavy day (29 Fighter Command aircraft lost, 43 German), with Biggin Hill and Kenley the first targets. No. 11 Group, according to its practice, broke these attacks up well forward. In the afternoon, North Weald, Hornchurch and Debden were the targets; a powerful riposte by 11 Group disorganized the attacks on the first two, but at Debden

> a squadron sent from Duxford in No. 12 Group to guard the aerodrome saw nothing of the enemy, probably because they had been given too little time to reach the spot.[6]

As a result, Debden received over 100 bombs which did much damage and killed five ground personnel.

Park, as usual, responded promptly to the German initiatives. On August 26 he prescribed what became known as the "Tally Ho!" procedure – not a concession to the British passion for blood sports, but a formula whereby formation leaders on sighting the enemy would report back corrective information regarding their numbers, height and approximate position. The object was to "enable us to engage the enemy on more equal terms", and this became standard drill. On the 27th he issued another Instruction (No. 7) which "brought into the open the disagreements between himself and Air Vice-Marshal Leigh-Mallory at 12 Group over tactics".[7] It was this disagreement which constituted the controversy that unfortunately overhung the whole of the remainder of the battle, with sour aftermaths.

At this point two significant personalities have to be taken into account. Leigh-Mallory was the same age as Park, but he came comparatively fresh to fighter warfare and its problems. His professional background lay in the distinctly undervalued sphere of Army cooperation. As commandant of the School of Army Cooperation at Old Sarum in 1927, Leigh-Mallory had put his career somewhat at risk by giving his full support to that despised activity, at a time when the Air Staff (under Trenchard) had set its face severely against it.[8] Never a shrinking violet – his brother spoke of him in 1924 looking forward "without a doubt to success and promotion in the future",[9] and he has been referred to as "a man of driving egoism"[10] – he may have felt twinges of doubt in his new rôle, and it has been suggested that his habitual somewhat haughty manner was a mask for these.[11] By August 1940, however, it is clear that he had formed some very definite views – and a definite view held by Leigh-Mallory was very definite indeed. The most important of them may be summarized as follows:

1. According to Park,[12] as far back as March, after a difficult interview with Dowding, Leigh-Mallory had said that he would "move heaven and earth to get Dowding sacked". It would appear that he had little regard for his C-in-C from that time onwards.
2. From this it follows that he had also little regard for the "Dowding system". He appears to have laboured under some resentment at the rôle of his Group, which was to defend the Midlands, with their numerous important industrial complexes. And when his squadrons did participate in the battle to the south, "he was unwilling to see them confined to the minor task of guarding sector-stations north of the Thames Estuary while major actions were going on elsewhere".[13]
3. Chafing in his relative idleness while the spotlight of national attention played upon No. 11 Group, Leigh-Mallory became critical of the manner in which Park (with Dowding's blessing) was fighting the battle. The image of the outnumbered Spitfires and Hurricanes hurling themselves into exhausting combats with swarming enemies preyed upon his mind. He desired – understandably – to reverse the picture: let Fighter Command do the "swarming" in its turn. His thoughts were moving in the direction of the "big wings", and as they did so they were much fortified by one of his most distinguished juniors.

Squadron-Leader Douglas Bader, now 30 years old, first joined the RAF in 1930, and so swiftly demonstrated his exceptional ability as a flyer that he was performing aerobatics in the Hendon Display of 1931 (see p. 6). In December of that year, however, a dreadful tragedy appeared to have ended his career before it even began: his aircraft crashed in an unofficial exhibition flight, and both his legs had to be amputated. For many, such a catastrophe would have been crippling in every sense for the remainder of life; for virtually everyone, it would have spelt quite clearly the end of flying. How Bader overcame adversity, mastering the use of his artificial legs, refusing even to use a stick, was already a personal epic. In 1939 he added to it the well-nigh unbelievable: he returned to the RAF, to find that the modern fighters suited him perfectly, and to win once more the tribute "exceptional" for his ability to fly them.[14] In June 1940 he was appointed to command No. 242 Squadron (Hurricanes) at Coltishall in No. 12 Group.

At Coltishall, as the battle swelled just out of reach, Bader in turn chafed increasingly at an idleness which he found difficult to understand. It was intolerable, to a man of his eager temperament, to be held back while the 11 Group squadrons were fighting at such apparent disadvantage, and taking heavy losses. Unfortunately out of a natural impatience, he began to weave tactical theories which bore no relation to the battle that was being waged. Bader, like most interesting people, revealed himself a man of contradictions: on the one hand, a brilliant handler of the most modern aircraft; on the other, his theoretical ideas leaned on a past belonging to a different phase of technology. His heroes were the "aces" of the First World War (see p. 175); he firmly believed that their principles and methods must still apply. To a certain, but limited, extent, this was true; action over Dunkirk persuaded him that particular basic 1914–18 tenets still held good:

> He who has the height controls the battle.
> He who has the sun achieves surprise.
> He who gets in close shoots them down.[15]

This was an "A.B.C." of dog-fighting, learned over France and Flanders the hard way between 1915 and 1918, and still obviously valid – more valid than the "textbook" theories which, as we have seen (p. 183), were so soon found to be irrelevant. There was nothing wrong with these first principles of combat; where Bader was at fault was in not grasping the method by which, in 1940, combat was brought about – the Dowding system, based on techniques unknown to the

1915–18 generation. One says "Bader was at fault"; was it Bader? Was it not, perhaps, the case that in No. 12 Group the "Dowding system" had never been explained – for the simple reason that the AOC did not understand it himself, and clearly did not agree with it?

At all events, according to Bader's latest biographer,[16] this rage at enforced idleness translated itself into a whole alternative theory. Bader argued that the No. 12 Group squadrons should "be called off the ground as soon as the radar had begun to show that the Germans were building up in strength over the Pas de Calais and that a major raid was imminent". This, he said, would have enabled them to be at 20,000 feet over the Thames Estuary by the time the attackers were crossing the Channel:

> Another 15 minutes on a south-easterly course and the wing would be in position, well forward over East Kent . . . with all the height and freedom to manoeuvre into a good, tactical, attacking position as the first enemy formations crossed the coast. The wing leader and the 12 Group squadron commanders would then have had *control of a battle of their own seeking* – the overriding requirement for a successful defensive action . . . Meanwhile, the 11 Group squadrons . . . would have been airborne from their bases as the 12 Group force moved down from the estuary to the advanced patrol area. In this way they would have gained more than their customary time and room for manoeuvre . . . They could well have found, for a change, splintered formations of bombers and groups of deranged [*sic*] fighters to deal with . . . In a word, 11 Group might well then have confronted an enemy whose determination to press on to the primary target had been agreeably punctured. In this way, too, a significant tourniquet might have been applied to the alarming drain of squadron pilots.

It goes without saying that this style of intervention by No. 12 Group was not to be performed by "penny packets"; what Bader had in mind was a large formation of, say, three or five squadrons – the "big wing", generally known as the "Duxford wing", because Bader's No. 242 from Coltishall would rendezvous there with No. 19 and No. 310 (Czech).

The whole thing was, of course, an impatient junior officer's fantasy. Junior officers do have fantasies, in which they wield their batons in a manner to put their superiors to shame. What is unforgivable is that a less junior ex-officer (Lucas) should try to place blame where it does not belong. There was, he says, in Bader's mind, one governing prerequisite for the success of the plan. Control of the defence against the massed raids must come from the centre, from the headquarters of Fighter Command at Stanmore ... Hugh Dowding did not, however, see the need for comprehensive Command control until the third and last phase was too far spent.

In fact, of course, as will be apparent from all that has gone before, the exact opposite was true.

As we have seen (p. 175) the very essence of the Dowding system was control – at all levels. And it was an important part of central control (Command control) to allocate the areas and responsibilities of the Groups. The *primary* rôle of No. 12 Group was, as stated, to protect the Midlands; its secondary rôle was to act as a tactical reserve for No. 11 Group when the southern battle became critical. What Bader was proposing was, in effect, to ignore both of these, and have No. 12 Group committed to battle *before* No. 11 – the extraordinary notion, in other words, of engaging the reserve before the main line of battle! Certain further observations would seem to be in order: first, that it was clearly not the business of a Squadron-Leader to decide which Group should form the line, and which the reserve. It was perfectly proper, if the Air Vice-Marshal consented, for him to discuss the Group's rôle with its AOC, and if he succeeded in convincing Leigh-Mallory (which would not be difficult, in view of what we have noted above) that No. 12 Group had been given the wrong rôle, it was Leigh-Mallory's duty, and his alone, to raise the matter with Dowding. Unfortunately, the combination of Dowding's aloofness and Leigh-Mallory's contempt (plus, of course, the day-to-day pressures of a decisive battle) would appear to have made it impossible for them to talk it through. That being so, it was Leigh-Mallory's duty to tell Bader that there could be no further discussion, and that he must obey orders like everyone else.

Bader was, in fact (with Leigh-Mallory's tacit approval) kicking against the system at every point. It was not merely the Group rôle that infuriated him, it was also the method of committing squadrons to battle. It will be convenient to follow this subject through to its decidedly bitter end (if only to remind ourselves that historical events which now seem cut-and-dried had by no means that appearance at the time). Park's careful, regulated system, based on his Group and sector Controllers, now has such a rational look that it is hard to believe the intensity with which it was challenged by Bader (and obviously some others, too). Bader's style, according to Lucas, was "opportunist, creative play", and he describes one of the later actions

(September 18) as "a fine game of aerial Rugby, with the Duxford wing running the ball all over the London sky".[17] Whatever one may think of this wording, it does seem to catch the spirit of certain occasions. An earlier biographer of Bader[18] fills in some details of "creative opportunism" in action. This time the date is August 30; the attacks on No. 11 Group's airfields were at their height; a Duxford squadron ordered to cover Biggin Hill missed the raiders, with the result that the airfield was "reduced to a shambles";[19] besides the very heavy damage, there were 39 dead and 26 injured – a bad business. No. 242 Squadron was ordered to cover North Weald, and placed by the No. 12 Group Controller at 15,000 feet; to Bader,

> This was no damn' good. He wanted to be up-sun himself. Disregarding controller's words, he swung thirty degrees west. Might miss the enemy! One usually obeyed a controller.

One did indeed; but Bader was lucky. His squadron found an enemy formation south-west of North Weald, waded into it, and drove it off before it could bomb the airfield. When 242 returned,

> they totted up the score – twelve confirmed and several more damaged . . . not a single bullet hole in any of the Hurricanes.

Bader explained why he had disobeyed the Controller's instructions:

> If the controller will tell us where they are in time – direction and height – we'll sort out the tactics in the air, get up-sun ourselves and beat hell out of them before they can bomb.

It is small wonder, as Robert Wright says, that when this passage was shown to Dowding in later years he could find only one word with which to comment: "Monstrous!"

Just how monstrous, how very far distant Bader's "Hell's Angels" tactics were from the modern, scientific battle that Dowding and Park were waging, may be judged if we glance forward again. On September 7, ordered to orbit North Weald at 10,000 feet, he went at once to 15,000; on the 9th, over North Weald and Hornchurch, he translated the Controller's 20,000 feet into 22,000. This was "sorting out the tactics in the air". It was very precisely what Park did not want, and what, if practised freely in No. 11 Group, would have ruined the whole system. On September 7 Park drew attention to a tendency for both pilots *and Controllers*, having in the early stages sometimes been caught with insufficient altitude, to add a few thousand feet to the given height of enemy formations. Another Instruction accordingly followed:

> After pointing out that on one occasion the previous day only seven out of eighteen squadrons despatched engaged the enemy and on another only seven out of seventeen got into the right position, he commented that it was obvious that some controllers were ordering squadrons intended to engage enemy bombers to patrol too high. When Group ordered a squadron to 16,000 feet, sector controller added on one or two thousand, and the squadron added on another two thousand in the vain hope that they would not have any enemy fighters above them. The net result had been that daily some of the enemy bomber formations slipped in under 15,000 feet, frequently without fighter escort, and bombed their objectives, doing serious damage . . .[20]

So Bader was not alone. It was on August 30 that he suggested to Leigh-Mallory that all the standby squadrons of No. 12 Group should take off together when alerted, thus putting a formidable fighter formation – a "balbo"[21] – into the air. Leigh-Mallory, disregarding the whole battle experience and ignoring his duty to ensure the safety of the Group's own area, said "Sounds splendid!" On September 9 he offered Bader two more squadrons, and thus the Duxford "big wing" (5 squadrons) was born.[22] The Germans were busily deluding themselves that Fighter Command was on its last legs, and there can be little doubt, as Liddell Hart says,[23] that when they encountered the "balbo" it gave them a very unpleasant shock. And the justification, by contemporary battle arithmetic (the "numbers game"; see p. 187), seemed to be palpable. Between September 7 and 27 the Duxford Wing claimed 135 enemy aircraft definitely destroyed, apart from "probables" and those severely damaged. Its own losses during the period were seven pilots killed; Lucas comments:

> 135 to 7: it was quite a contribution to the month's victory.[24]

It has, of course, to be read in relation to what was firmly believed at the time. Air Ministry claims of definite kills, between September 7 and 27, amounted to 764. Deducting the Duxford claim, that would leave 629 to be divided between the 22 (September 7) or 24 (September 30) squadrons of No. 11 Group. The average is about right;[25] but, of course, the figures themselves are fiction. The latest statement of actual *Luftwaffe* losses during the period is 400[26] – just over half the claim. And there is now no way of establishing what proportion of the true figure is attributable to Duxford. What is quite clear, though, is that any tactical system based on the "scorecard" is deeply suspect.

This was the "baleful effect" of the "numbers game" that I have referred to above: it diverted attention from the true rôle of defence. In the eyes of Dowding and Park, a defence which did not protect was, if not an absolute failure, certainly not a full success. As one distinguished 11 Group pilot, Squadron-Leader J. H. ("Ginger") Lacey, put it:

> We believed that if you did not get to the enemy bombers before they bombed you were only doing half your job.[27]

Or, in the succinct summary of Group Captain T. P. Gleave:

> The prime purpose of a fighter defence is to prevent the enemy bombers reaching their targets.[28]

And to be fair to him, Bader, too, wanted to hit the enemy before he bombed. Inevitably, however, positioning and timing often meant that the Duxford Wing came in on the heels of a retreating enemy, to take their toll as he turned for home. Bader was not happy about this, but there were others who, rejoicing in the falsehoods of the "numbers game", were by no means unhappy. Among them, significantly, was the Deputy Chief of the Air Staff, Air Vice-Marshal Sholto Douglas, who declared "that 'it does not matter where the enemy is shot down, as long as he is shot down in large numbers'." Later Douglas pronounced that

> he had "never been very much in favour of the idea of trying to interpose fighter squadrons between the enemy bombers and their objective". He would rather, he said, shoot down fifty of the enemy when they had bombed their target than ten forward of it.[29]

The argument is a strong one; crippling losses would act as a deterrent, so that damage sustained on an occasion when the Germans did get through would have to be offset against later occasions when they did not even care to try. But the counter-arguments are stronger: first, once again, this was a misunderstanding of the German system of war. As I have said above (p. 145) it takes a very great many casualties indeed to make a German High Command change its mind. Secondly, when the targets in question were the very sinews of Fighter Command itself – its airfields and the aircraft factories which supplied it – as they were in September 1940, the risk involved was simply not acceptable. Finally, one wonders if Douglas himself would not have formed a different view if he had not been misled by the "numbers game". Five times, during the Battle of Britain, the Air Ministry claimed over 100 German aircraft destroyed on one day:

Date	Claim	Actual
August 15	180	76
August 18	153	67
September 7	103	41
September 15	185	61
September 27	133	57[30]

On no occasion did the Germans actually lose as many as 100 aircraft on one day; on only four occasions did they lose more than 50. These considerations would seem to remove the very keystone of the "big wing" theory. Yet such was its force at the time, and such was the influence of some of those who supported it (influence through political pressures sometimes invoked in a distinctly conspiratorial manner) that both Dowding and Park would rue the day they failed to perceive its menace.

At this distance in time it is perhaps permissible to round off this subject with some question marks. As regards Bader, there are no questions; he was definitely out of line, but what is more extraordinary is that nobody seemed disposed to tell him to get back into line. His biographer, Brickhill, draws frequently displeasing pictures of the latter-day Achilles:

> Day after day while the fights raged Bader alternately sulked and stormed ... he kept railing at the stupidity of keeping them on the ground while outnumbered squadrons had to engage a massed enemy ...
>
> No. 11 Group seemed to be hogging the battle. Intolerable! Bader said so repeatedly ... All day he railed ... demanding to be let off the leash ... etc., etc.

But one has to make allowances; one can imagine the fiery young leaders of Napoleon's Reserve Cavalry, held back for the *coup de grâce*, protesting in like manner as the long hours of battle thundered on.

With each day's newspaper and every BBC News bulletin marking the stages of the nation's crisis, the strain on someone of Bader's temperament must have been very great; so we may explain, if not entirely excuse, his extravagant behaviour by reference to his great gallantry, his skill as a pilot longing to be used, and a natural fighter pilot's dislike of waiting. The theories he evolved were no more than a dubious mantle for his admirable impulses.

Park was not "hogging the battle", nor did he base his complaints against No. 12 Group on "poaching". He was conscious that Dowding relied on him not to call for help until he had exhausted all his own resources. When he did call, however, he expected the help to materialize in the right place, not in the form of unheralded interventions in battles many miles away. And if the consequence was that his airfields were being bombed, his wrath is even more understandable than Bader's frustration. There is one question about Park, however, which seems worth pondering: did he circulate his 35 Instructions to his fellow Group commanders? Seen purely as up-to-date, authoritative information about the ever-changing problems of the battle being fought, this would surely have been helpful. If he did *not* circulate them, one wonders why not? And if he did, it would be helpful to know what happened to them. The contrast in attitude between Leigh-Mallory at No. 12 Group and Brand at No. 10 Group is definitely suggestive.

With Leigh-Mallory some of the questions answer themselves. He carried doubts about Dowding's tactics to the point of challenging Dowding's very orders, and of allowing political intervention in No. 12 Group. In terms of discipline, there can, of course, be no defence; in terms of strategy and tactics, since he felt so strongly, was it not his duty to overcome his reluctance and discuss his doubts with the C-in-C? Further to that, was it not his clear duty to let Dowding know about the discontents and frustrations that were being expressed by some of his pilots? At the end of the battle, we have the extraordinary situation of the Secretary of State himself visiting Duxford (late October) followed by the Under-Secretary (November 2), but never a visit by the C-in-C. Should Leigh-Mallory not have urged Dowding, as a matter vital to morale, to come and explain what was happening to the 12 Group Squadrons? And if this proved impossible in the press of battle, was it not his own very clear duty to explain Dowding's view to his pilots, whether he agreed with it or not? But finally, one is forced to wonder, did he *understand* it?

And then there is Dowding. There can be no disguising the fact that this was his failure. Why did he not *make* Leigh-Mallory and Park resolve their differences? As Sir Maurice Dean says:

> It is a serious criticism that Dowding failed to settle this squabble. Dowding states that he did not know. Commanders-in-Chief have to know. That is what it is all about.[31]

There is no arguing with this. And equally, if one asks why Leigh-Mallory did not urge Dowding to go to No. 12 Group – or Duxford, at the very least – one must also ask why it was necessary for him to make such a request. Why did Dowding not see the need himself? Wood and Dempster tell us:

> Dowding was not a familiar figure to the pilots he commanded. He was seldom seen in the squadrons and he did not mix easily with his subordinates. There was, in fact, an extraordinary contrast between the AOC-in-C and the pilots of Fighter Command . . . Nevertheless there existed between these two extremes a close bond of mutual respect and admiration.[32]

The last question is closely linked to this: since squadrons were constantly moving within the Command (as they became weakened or exhausted) why did he not move No. 242 into 11 Group? It remained in 12 Group throughout the battle. And if, for some reason, he did not wish to move the squadron, why did he not move Bader? It seems as certain as human affairs can be that a taste of No. 11 Group's normal daily activity would have cured Bader's ills in no time, and saved his superiors much grief. But as Dowding was unaware of the problem, he naturally did not apply the remedy; the brilliant scientific designer of battle fell down in the human area of command – by no means the first to do so, certainly not the last.

Such was the "big wing" controversy. Let us leave the last word to Dowding's Senior Air Staff Officer, Air Vice-Marshal Sir Douglas Evill:

> It is quite useless to argue whether wing formations are or are not desirable, both statements are equally true under different conditions.[33]

And with that cool zephyr of common sense we may close a debate which should never have been allowed to reach the pitch of bitterness that it did.

22 Battle of attrition; the climax

The period August 15–September 15, inclusive, marked the peak of the fighting in the Battle of Britain: Fighter Command had 201 aircrew killed, and lost 493 aircraft during that 32-day span; the *Luftwaffe* lost some 1,132 aircrew and 862 aircraft. And it was during this period, when things seemed to be at their most difficult and daunting, that the Germans made the fundamental alteration of strategy which gave a new lease of life to Fighter Command. It was prompted by the overall success of Park's policy of refusing battle, as far as possible, with German fighters and concentrating against their bomber force. These tactics, says Dr Klee, which

> were absolutely correct in the given situation, frustrated the efforts of the *Luftwaffe* to force a decision. Fighter Command had certainly suffered heavy losses, but it had not been put out of action.[1]

Meanwhile, summer was departing and the prerequisites of Operation SEALION remained tantalizingly out of reach. The destruction of Fighter Command became a matter of increasing urgency; attacks on airfields and radar stations were now pushed home relentlessly. August 31 saw Fighter Command's heaviest losses on any single day: 38 aircraft (nine pilots killed) as against the *Luftwaffe*'s 39. On September 1 Biggin Hill sustained its sixth and seventh attacks in three days, the Operations Room was wrecked, and only miracles of skill and devotion on the part of Post Office engineers and ground-crew kept the station going. The next day a low-flying attack hit Biggin Hill again, while other raids did heavy damage at Kenley, Brooklands, Detling, Eastchurch and Hornchurch. On September 3 it was the turn of North Weald, Debden and Hornchurch again. Lympne and Eastchurch were attacked on the 4th – and there was a significant extension of German target selection: a raid on the Vickers Armstrong factory at Brooklands virtually stopped production of Wellington bombers for four days, while the Short factory at Rochester, attacked on August 15 (see p. 188), suffered fresh damage. It was, indeed, as an RAF diarist said, "a war of attrition".[2] Yet even more than this was clearly needed if Fighter Command was to be quickly finished off:

> There was only one target which would quite certainly force Fighter Command to send all it had into the air in its defence, and that was London.[3]

206

At this point certain threads came together, as they often do at critical moments. The bombs which fell on London on the night of August 24/25 had immediate repercussions; 81 aircraft of Bomber Command attacked Berlin the following night. This was an act which deeply pleased the Prime Minister, the Government, the Press and the overwhelming majority of a public which was displaying unexpected reserves of belligerency. The Air Staff was less pleased; it had little faith in the effectiveness of pure reprisals, and still firmly believed that its slender bomber forces could do real damage to military targets.[4] How much damage Bomber Command actually did to Berlin on August 25/26 is uncertain; that it caused considerable annoyance to Hitler and Goering, who had boasted that such a thing would never happen, is obvious. And some damage was certainly done by attacks on other targets in Germany. Thus Hitler had more than one motive for rescinding his prohibition of deliberate attacks on the British capital, and Goering now ordered the matter to be put in hand with immediate effect. On September 5 the "Y" Service intercepted his order for an attack by over 300 bombers with massive fighter cover on the London docks on the afternoon of September 7.

Thanks to Ultra, Goering's signal was in the hands of the Prime Minister and of Dowding within minutes of its despatch.[5]

Foreknowledge enabled fire-engines and other appliances to be assembled and positioned, and other Civil Defence arrangements to be made in time. But foreknowledge by itself cannot repel a massive attack; and Ultra or no Ultra, Park would seem on this occasion to have been caught on the wrong foot. Understandably, he was preoccupied with the offensive on his airfields (this was the day he issued his Instruction on altitude) and four attacks on Hawkinge in the morning suggested that he was right. He had now ordered his squadrons to operate in pairs: Spitfires high, to engage the German fighters, Hurricanes low, to break up the bomber formations, and was hoping for good results from this. He also had the factories in mind, especially where his Group and No. 10 joined each other. And to fill his cup, during the morning he received from the Air Ministry Invasion Alert No. 1, signifying "an attack is imminent".

It was four o'clock in the afternoon when radar picked up the assembly of the big formation over Calais, where Goering with a large entourage watched its departure in person. It came in in two waves, at unusually high altitude, with the bombers at 16–20,000 feet, and it was some time before it was recognized for what it was. No. 11 Group could only intercept with four squadrons – a totally inadequate force in the face of practically the entire Me 109 strength of *Luftflotten 2* and *3*: some 600 fighters. Furthermore, the Germans were again using new escort tactics which, say Wood and Dempster, "were skilfully evolved and carried out, and they were extremely difficult to counter".[6] As well as a high escort group, the close escort flew above, below and behind, and on both sides of the bombers; the Messerschmitt pilots hated it, but Fighter Command found it extremely effective. Although 21 out of 23 squadrons ultimately committed managed to get into action, the losses inflicted, in relation to the large German force used, were disappointing: 41 aircraft (to Fighter Command's 25). As the Official History says, on the whole September 7 "amounted to a victory for the German bombers, most of which had reached their targets without much difficulty, dropping more than three hundred tons of high-explosive and many thousands of incendiaries on and round the capital within an hour and a half".[7] London "had had its first and last mass daylight raid",[8] but that night 247 bombers returned to stoke the fires, and by dawn on September 8, 306 civilians were dead, and 1,337 seriously injured.

It is not difficult to detect the results of the "war of attrition" in the poor results and sad happenings of September 7. Fighter Command was becoming very weary; indeed, "the command was literally wasting away under Dowding's eyes".[9]

Experienced pilots were like gold-dust, and each one lost had to be replaced by an untried man who for some time would be vulnerable, until he acquired battle know-how. Fresh squadrons, moved in to replace tired units, very often lost more aircraft and pilots than the formations they replaced.[10]

Thus 616 Squadron lost five pilots and 12 aircraft in a week (August 25–September 2) 603 Squadron lost 12 pilots and 16 aircraft in a similar time (August 25–September 5 – a most alarming rate); 253 Squadron lost nine pilots and 13 aircraft in seven days.

In contrast the experienced squadrons, while utterly weary and often flying over fifty hours per day, continued to show far better results. No. 54 Squadron when sent north from Hornchurch on September 3rd, had lost only nine aircraft and one pilot since August 24th. No. 501 Squadron in the Biggin Hill sector during the complete phase (August 24th–September 6th) had suffered the loss of nine aircraft and four pilots.[11]

As we have seen (p. 190) it was precisely at this stage that aircraft losses, for four frightening weeks, exceeded production and those available in store. At the same time squadron establishments dropped from 26 pilots to 16; yet, as Denis Richards says, "it was not so much the smaller quantity as the lower quality that gave Dowding so much anxiety".[12]

Dowding was now forced to adopt a depressing, but not unfamiliar, expedient. Napoleon, in the last years of his empire, when his army was badly worn down, creamed off the best of it into an *élite* that he could rely on: the Imperial Guard. The German High Command in 1918, faced with a similar situation, divided its forces on the Western Front into "attack divisions" ("Storm Troops") and "trench divisions"; Ludendorff tells us that it

> regretted that the distinction ... became established in the Army. We tried to eradicate it, without being able to alter the situation which gave rise to it.[13]

Later, when the March–April offensives had run their course, the British Expeditionary Force also had to have recourse to what it called "B Class" divisions. In September 1940 Fighter Command in turn made its concession to weakness: it was called (for some strange reason) "stabilization"; it adopted the categories of "A" class squadrons, chiefly in No. 11 Group and its immediate neighbours, which were kept up to strength in fully trained pilots; "B" class, also kept up to strength, and intended as reliefs for the "A" class; and "C" class, which were only permitted a few (five or six) experienced pilots for training purposes. Nobody likes such methods; they are demoralizing and divisive – but by September 7 Dowding had no more fresh squadrons to move, so he had no option.[14] As it turned out, however, Goering had solved his problem for him.

Unbelievably, the *Luftwaffe*, with Fighter Command distinctly "gasping on the ropes", now changed its objective to the cities of Britain. Indeed, the change ante-dated the attack on London; August 28/29 saw the first of four successive attacks on Liverpool which may be reckoned "the first major night attack on the United Kingdom".[15] After September 7 London was the main target for many nights, with Merseyside a good second. Meanwhile, invasion preparations, especially the assembly of barges and other shipping, continued, under incessant attack by Bomber and Coastal Commands. The coastline from Dunkirk to Calais became known as the "Blackpool Front" – for reasons clearly stated by a Blenheim pilot:

209

It was an amazing spectacle. Calais docks were on fire. So was the waterfront of Boulogne, and glares extended for miles. The whole French coast seemed to be a barrier of flame broken only by intense white flashes of exploding bombs and vari-coloured incendiary tracers soaring and circling skywards.[16]

By mid-September the Germans had assembled about 1,000 assorted invasion craft in the Channel ports, with some 600 more in the Scheldt.[17] RAF bombing crippled about 12 per cent of this armada; what remained was still sufficient for the first stage of invasion as planned, but the combination of the bombing, and a sharp riposte by Fighter Command to a renewed attempt at a daylight attack on London on September 9, forced Hitler to yet another postponement of SEALION. It was deferred until the 24th, which meant that a final decision should have been made on September 14 (ten days' notice was the German Navy's very reasonable stipulation). With Hitler, however, nothing was ever normal; the decision he actually took on that day was to bring *forward* SEALION to the 17th. He had been misled again by Goering, himself in turn misled by the *Luftwaffe*'s faulty Intelligence.

It was not so much the evidence that was at fault – rather the ability to interpret it correctly. The 9th had shown that Fighter Command was still very much a force to be reckoned with; the 11th and 14th, however, spoke with equivocal voices. On each of these days Fighter Command and *Luftwaffe* losses were equal,[18] though this was not appreciated by the Air Ministry at the time. On the 14th, particularly,

> To the *Luftwaffe* the opposition appeared scrappy and uncoordinated, and they felt that during the last few days Fighter Command had begun to collapse. This news was, of course, conveyed to the *Reichsmarschall*, and via the situation reports to Hitler. Both felt that the hour of destiny was approaching.[19]

The "hour of destiny" was September 15, a date thereafter commemorated as "Battle of Britain Day". The title has been disputed; Alfred Price, for one, says that September 15 "has singularly little to commend it . . . the day when the British victory claim was furthest removed from the truth . . ."[20] Yet, forgetting the "numbers game", it is hard to dispute Churchill's verdict that it was, in fact, "the crux of the Battle of Britain".[21] He made that judgment in the light of his knowledge of what happened to Operation SEALION – which was, of course, from beginning to end, what the Battle of Britain was really about. The Official History sums up with clarity:

If 15th August showed the German High Command that air supremacy was not to be won within a brief space, 15th September went far to convince them that it would not be won at all.[22]

It was a day in marked contrast to September 7. For Fighter Command, on the 15th, just about everything went right. Despite ominous signs, a few days earlier, of successful German jamming, the radar screen gave full warning of the coming attacks:

> The stupidity of large formations sorting themselves out in full view of British radar was not yet realized by the *Luftwaffe*.[23]

Astonishing – but, on this day at least, apparently true; better still, on the 15th there were no feints to distract the operators and worry the filter rooms. Park was able to alert his squadrons to give the enemy a warm reception the moment they crossed the coast. With 17 squadrons (11 of No. 11 Group, one of No. 10, and the five of the "Duxford Wing") opposing it, the first German formation was harried all the way to London, causing many bombers simply to unload at random – which did not, of course, prevent much damage being done, including two bombs on Buckingham Palace. Goering promptly ordered a second attack, to be pressed home with all energy.

> His signal was duly picked up and this was an occasion when the speed of the Ultra operation and the direct line to Dowding made history.[24]

The second attack, shortly after one p.m., despite Goering's exhortations, did no better than the first, being forced to jettison many bombs – some of which, obviously, scored lucky hits, but the overall damage was nothing like as heavy as on the 7th. Two diversionary attacks by *Luftflotte 3*, on Portland and Woolston, also failed to produce serious results. The Air Ministry, at the end of the day, in a state of exceptional euphoria claimed 185 German aircraft destroyed, for a loss of 25; the latest figures revise this to 61 German, 29 British (16 pilots killed). The "Duxford Wing" alone claimed 52 enemy aircraft destroyed and eight "probables"; Bader unrepentantly says:

> Frankly, those of us who were present at the time disagree most emphatically with the bureaucratic acceptance of German figures which had been proved unreliable in the U-boat campaign. My own view is that no one will know the correct assessment unless the English Channel and the Thames Estuary are drained.[25]

Few things are absolute in history, but one of them is the unwisdom of only believing what you want to believe.

To what extent Ultra really "made history" on the 15th, and to what extent the clear victory of Fighter Command on that day was attributable to the usual prescription, is not clear. Certainly the build-up of a cloud layer at 4–6,000 feet over Kent and Sussex during the afternoon (following a clear morning) cannot have helped ground observation; on the other hand, the main action was really over by then. Two days later, on September 17, Ultra spoke with perfect clarity: a signal was intercepted from the German General Staff to the officer responsible for the loading and turn-round of supply and troop-carrying aircraft in Holland. It authorized the dismantling of the air-loading equipment on the Dutch aerodromes; and without the air-loading equipment there could be no invasion. The signal, with appropriate gloss, was sent to the Prime Minister immediately, and it was discussed at the Chiefs of Staff Committee that evening. Churchill asked the Chief of the Air Staff to explain it:

> Cyril Newall had been well briefed; he gave it as his considered opinion that this marked the end of SEALION, at least for this year . . . There was a very broad smile on Churchill's face now as he lit up his massive cigar and suggested that we should all take a little fresh air.[26]

Ironically, a heavy air raid was in full swing; it did not dilute, for this handful of men who knew, the sweetness of the moment, the knowledge that, as far as 1940 was concerned, there was not going to be an invasion after all. This was the victory; this was what September 15 really meant.

"Few things are absolute"; the decision of September 17 (for which only Hitler could be responsible) was actually only another postponement of SEALION, but this time indefinite. Churchill reminds us that Hitler only accepted its impossibility in 1940 on October 12, when it was deferred until the next spring. After the launching of the attack on the Soviet Union, SEALION was postponed again, until the spring of 1942; it did not finally die until February of that year. The demise came as a deep relief to the German Navy, which had always (in contrast to the Army) taken a very clear, cold view of its chances. German naval officers were appalled (as Napoleon's admirals were, between 1803 and 1805) at the Army's over-confident approach – expressed in the phrase, "simply a large-scale river crossing". "I would like," says von Plehwe, "to lay great emphasis on the fact that the decisive deterrent to the operation was the expected large-scale intervention by the British fleet."[27] The achievement of Fighter Command was in keeping alive the possibility of that intervention. It was not exactly what Lord Trenchard had had in mind, in his fierce battles with Lord Beatty for the future of the RAF in the 1920s; history moves in a mysterious way.

After September 15, the weather deteriorated and the nature of the battle changed. Once more the *Luftwaffe* varied its tactics; the unpleasant phenomenon of the fighter-bomber had already been seen, but in the second half of September and in October it became the standard German daylight raiding method. Sometimes using Me 110s in the bomber rôle (with Me 109 escorts) and sometimes the Me 109s themselves, the *Luftwaffe* taxed Fighter Command's skills very severely. The new tactic took full advantage of the Me 109's excellent performance at high altitude, and gained also by freeing it from the constraints of close escort of slow bombers. Both the radar screen and the Observer Corps found the tracking of the fast-moving, high-flying Messerschmitts decidedly difficult. Pilots soon began to notice the extra strain of high-altitude operations.

Using this tactic, the *Luftwaffe* resumed its attacks on aircraft factories – Hawker's at Weybridge on September 21, Supermarine at Woolston on the 24th and 26th killing many workers, the Bristol Company on the 25th, when over 250 people were killed. There was no real sense of the battle truly easing up. On the 27th and 30th, indeed, there were more great daylight encounters, the former costing the *Luftwaffe* 57 aircraft and Fighter Command 28, the latter costing the *Luftwaffe* 47 and Fighter Command 21. Curiously, while on September 27 the Air Ministry made one of its more inflated claims (133), on the 30th it was very nearly right, claiming only 49. And this was "the last great daylight battle".[28]

23 Defeat for Dowding

In British accounts, the Battle of Britain is deemed to have ended on October 31; such tidiness is usually deceptive, but certainly by that date its nature had drastically altered. There was still daylight fighting on every day of the month – sufficient to cost Fighter Command 186 aircraft (120 pilots killed) and the *Luftwaffe* 379. But the reduction in intensity may be measured by the fact that only on two days did the Germans lose more than 20 aircraft, while only on six days did Fighter Command lose more than 10. The evidently decreasing German losses were worrying to Fighter Command and the Air Ministry, but in truth they were only a reflection of a far deeper cause for anxiety. The *Luftwaffe* had shifted the *Schwerpunkt* of its attack.

All through the second half of September and on every October night that weather permitted, the warning sirens wailed in London and selected British cities from Aberdeen to Wales. The Dorniers and Heinkels practically vanished from the daylight skies, reserving their effort for night raids, while the fighter-bombers maintained their damaging harassment by day. The contrast between the sort of performance by Fighter Command that the public and national (*and* Service) leaders alike had become accustomed to, under the impression of the Air Ministry's unfortunate communiqués, and the very obvious failure to match this in any way at night, was distinctly painful. The reasons for this were very simple, but not for public consumption: the effectiveness of ground defences in 1940 was reduced almost to zero at night, while Fighter Command possessed neither the aircraft, nor the equipment, nor the training for useful night air defence. Dowding was under no delusions; Fighter Command's task, he admitted, would not be finished until "we can locate, pursue and shoot down the enemy in cloud by day and by night".[1] As usual, he correctly foresaw the solution to the problem in scientific terms: interception by airborne radar (AI), which would have to "become a gunsight", and the laborious evolution of a system of night-fighting by trial, error and careful analysis. The public, alarmed, angry, and disposed to believe in "miracles", would not have cared much for this, even had it been aware (it was not even aware of radar itself yet). What the public wanted was another miracle, and it preferred to be told that this could be provided by such methods as nourishing selected pilots on a massive diet of raw carrot, rather than receive lectures on the hard grind of technological progress.

It is at this point, with his day battle showing every sign of being handsomely won (though still taxing enough to those who were fighting it), but a far more intractable problem now weighing upon him, that the final elements of the Dowding story begin to come together. Though he remained so strangely unaware of it, his disagreement with Leigh-Mallory over day tactics was still festering (its political ramifications now in full development), and at the same time he came into head-on collision with two of the RAF's most senior and respected officers over the night battle. On September 14 an exceptionally high-powered Night Air Defence Committee was set up at Beaverbrook's instigation; its chairman was Marshal of the Royal Air Force Sir John Salmond (commander of the RAF in France in 1918 and CAS 1930–33), and among its members was Air Chief Marshal Sir

Wilfrid Freeman, the senior RAF officer in the Ministry of Aircraft Production. The committee worked at lightning speed, reporting via Beaverbrook to Sinclair on September 18; a week later Dowding received a letter from the Air Council making certain recommendations based on the Salmond Committee's report. While accepting that a proper solution to the problem of night defence lay with airborne radar, as stated by Dowding, the committee also endorsed the view of one of its members, Sholto Douglas, that there was a rôle for single-seater fighters (which could not carry such equipment) as well. Douglas had already suggested that a Hurricane squadron should be allocated to night-fighting; Dowding had dissented. He continued to prove "difficult to move in his opinions".[2] The Air Council, however, was won over, and Dowding was ordered to allocate *three* Hurricane squadrons exclusively to night work; "he obeyed the order with great reluctance, conveyed to his superiors in a trenchant protest".[3] Since in any case "neither Salmond nor Freeman were friendly towards or admirers of Dowding,"[4] it is clear that his reputation in inner RAF circles as a difficult, obstinate old man was much enhanced.

With our applicable hindsight, not merely of the RAF's night-fighting problems, but also of Germany's at a later stage, it is clear that Dowding's approach was correct; night attacks would never be truly defeated or diverted, as the daylight assault had been, but such answers as would be found would be arrived at by the application of science; fortunate encounters by Hurricanes flown by keen-eyed pilots (with or without benefit of raw carrots) were *not* the way forward. Meanwhile the picture was bleak, and tempers became understandably frayed. The worst of it was the RAF's sheer lack of a suitable aircraft for this purpose. The now-despised Me 110, a complete failure in its *Zerstörer* rôle, would in due course have a valuable new lease of life as a night-fighter; the best that Fighter Command could manage was its two squadrons of Boulton Paul Defiants, backed by six squadrons of Blenheims which had space for radar equipment, but were too slow. The newcomer, the fast, twin-engined, heavily armed Bristol Beaufighter, which has been called a "historic, war-winning aeroplane",[5] and eventually equipped 52 operational RAF squadrons,[6] was at this stage most disappointing, being "abnormally beset by teething troubles".[7]

It was, then, against a disturbed and disturbing background of war that Dowding on October 17 attended a meeting at the Air Ministry which has gone down in history and legend. Although the tempo of the daylight battle was now much reduced,[8] while the tragedies and damage of the night "Blitz" were in the forefront of everyone's mind,

215

it was "Major Day Tactics in the Fighter Force" that the meeting came together to discuss. One has to bear firmly in mind that, although invasion was now no longer in prospect, the renewal of mass attacks on the lines of September 7 and 15 remained entirely possible, indeed probable. And with a painful awareness that the Germans were no longer suffering heavy losses, either by day or by night, it is not surprising if the meeting wanted to air Leigh-Mallory's "big wing" theory, and his claim that this was the way to hit the enemy hard.

In the absence of Newall, who was indisposed, the meeting was chaired by Sholto Douglas. Newall, in any case, only had another week to go in office; his successor-designate, Air Chief Marshal Sir Charles Portal, was present, but appears to have taken no part in the proceedings. Park, Brand and Leigh-Mallory were all present with Dowding, as well as Air Commodore Slessor (Director of Plans) and other interested parties. With a surprise which does not diminish with the long interval of time, one learns that Squadron-Leader Bader was also among those present, and *did* take part. No squadron-leaders from 11 or 10 Groups were invited, though the experience of those Groups in day fighting was comprehensive. The point is worth making, since the then Under-Secretary of State for Air, Harold Balfour (later Lord Balfour of Inchrye), is quoted as saying:

I cannot find it so reprehensible that a breath of reality from someone who was doing the job was wafted into Air Staff circles.[9]

Nobody had been "doing the job" more thoroughly than the squadron-leaders and pilots of 11 Group. And it was, after all, "major", not "minor" tactics that the meeting was convened to discuss.[10]

What actually took place at that meeting will never be known. Group Captain Haslam tells us: "The Minutes of the meeting do not suggest that it was a hard hitting discussion."[11] On the other hand, Sholto Douglas refers to "an unnecessarily heated argument" between Park and Leigh-Mallory, and says:

one had to see Leigh-Mallory and Park actually facing each other to realise how strong the clash was between these two forceful personalities.[12]

We cannot even be sure what Dowding said; Slessor wrote in a letter years later:

The curious thing is that I have no recollection of Stuffy ever saying a word – though I suppose he must have.[13]

216

It has been suggested (by Winterbotham and others, quoting Slessor's Foreword to *The Ultra Secret*) that Dowding deliberately and self-sacrificingly kept silence at the meeting to protect Ultra. This seems unlikely, on several counts; first, because there is no obvious reason why Ultra should have come into the discussion at all (it was a strategic, rather than a tactical instrument); secondly, if a leak had seemed possible for some reason, it was the clear duty of the DCAS, the CAS-designate and Slessor himself to steer the talk away from it or clamp down; and thirdly, Dowding did not lack means of defending himself (by reference to "the system") if he felt pressed. The question thus arises: did he really feel pressed?

As for Bader, his first biographer says that, for the most part, he "sat quietly, hands in lap"[14] amid the assembled "brass". Minute 16 simply records:

> Squadron-Leader Bader said that from his practical experience time was the essence of the problem; if enough warning could be given to bring a large number of fighters into position there was no doubt they could get most effective results.[15]

The outcome of the meeting is contained in Minutes 20 and 21:

> 20. The DCAS said he thought the views of the meeting could be summarized as follows:
> The employment of a large mass of fighters had great advantages, though it was not necessarily the complete solution to the problem of interception ...
> 21. The AOC-in-C said that it would be arranged for No. 12 Group "wings" to participate freely in suitable operations over the 11 Group area. He would be able to resolve any complications of control ...

For some inscrutable reason Wing Commander Lucas says that "For Bader and his AOC this was just about game, set and match."[16] At this distance, the conclusions thus stated look, on the contrary, decidedly tepid and *déjà vus*. Nevertheless, it amounted to defeat for Dowding; he, Park and Brand all filed protests when they received the Minutes. Requests for corrections were turned down.[17] All in all, October 17, 1940 must rank in RAF history, if not as a "black day", at least as a disagreeable and futile one.

24 *Victory for Fighter Command*

For Operation SEALION, for the Battle of Britain, for Newall, for Dowding and for Park the sands were running out. For Fighter

Command, though its losses substantially decreased, October provided "one of the most severe tests of the whole Battle".[1] The "hit-and-run" raids by the German fighter-bombers called for exceptional viligance; they also

> shattered one of the basic principles of Fighter Command organisation, namely economy of effort by keeping planes grounded until they were needed.[2]

Instead, with great reluctance, Fighter Command had to revert to the concept of standing patrols which was understood to have been exploded in the First World War; thus, like tight tactical "Vs", like dislike of escorting daylight bombers, like belief in the self-defending bomber formation, another shibboleth bit the dust. War is a hard school. But what it meant was that 12-aircraft squadrons were averaging 45 flying hours a day – sometimes 60. Added to the extra strain of high-level fighting, this meant that the weariness factor was now critical:

> It was estimated in the summer of the Battle that every pilot kept in action for more than six months would be shot down because he was exhausted or stale, or even because he had lost the will to fight. In terms of flying hours the fighter pilot's life expectancy could be measured at eighty-seven.[3]

With squadrons flying their October average, this meant that a pilot could only expect some four or five weeks of life. It cannot be disputed that

> although it is true that there were more squadrons in the Command at the end of October than at the beginning of July its fighting strength had fallen considerably.[4]

It was fortunate indeed for Fighter Command (and for Britain) that the German *Schwerpunkt* had shifted to the attack on cities. Fighter Command was stretched like the strings of a violin – but with characteristic opportunism the German High Command switched to the "soft target":

> The attraction of London was the German Air Force's undoing. Like an indestructible sponge it absorbed punishment and diverted what might have been the death blow from the sorely tried organism of defence.[5]

The outcome of the battle, whatever closing date one accepts, is quite clear:

The objective of the *Luftwaffe* in the Battle of Britain was not achieved. The Battle of Britain was lost by Germany.[6]

Thus, Dr Klee; *Luftwaffe* General Werner Kreipe adds:

. . . though the air battles over England were perhaps a triumph of skill and bravery so far as the German air crews were concerned, from the strategic point of view it was a failure and contributed to our ultimate defeat. The decision to fight it marks a turning point in the history of the Second World War. The German Air Force . . . was bled almost to death, and suffered losses which could never again be made good throughout the course of the war.[7]

Both German authorities agree that from all angles the Battle of Britain has to be viewed as a decisive battle of the war; in Klee's words:

. . . the invasion and subjugation of Britain was made to depend on victory in that battle, and its outcome therefore materially influenced both the further course and the fate of the war as a whole.

It was for this that the losses were endured – and they were heavy for both sides. Once again, sources disagree; the majority follow the figures given by Denis Richards in 1953: *Luftwaffe* losses, 1,733 aircraft; Fighter Command, 915. Wood and Dempster repeat this in *The Narrow Margin* (p. 269; published 1969); yet their daily "scores" add up to: *Luftwaffe*, 1,679; Fighter Command, 938. The latest figures, in the daily table on p. 707 of *The Battle of Britain Then and Now* (on which I have leaned throughout this account) are: *Luftwaffe*, 1,882; Fighter Command, 1,017. The same source informs us that Fighter Command had 537 pilots killed (Wood and Dempster: 415) while the *Luftwaffe* lost 2,662 aircrew (but this last figure is an admitted estimate). It will be noted that I refer constantly to "Fighter Command" rather than "the RAF". I consider it a serious blemish in existing accounts that British air losses in the fight for national survival almost never include those of Bomber and Coastal Commands. They are difficult to arrive at (especially for Bomber Command, whose losses have to be separated from those incurred in attacking Germany and other targets unconnected with Operation SEALION). My researches give these results (which should be treated as approximate, but better than nothing):

July–October   Bomber Command: 118 aircraft   Coastal Command: 130

These additions (or whatever the exact figures may be) evidently affect the balancesheet very considerably. It should be noted, in this connection, that the Roll of Honour in the Battle of Britain Memorial Chapel in Westminster Abbey, compiled as far back as 1947, contains the names of 718 aircrew of Bomber Command and 280 of Coastal Command, and amounts to a total of 1,494, which may be taken as a reasonable indicator of the RAF's full human loss.

25 Battle of Britain: Envoi

On November 24, 1940 Dowding ceased to be Commander-in-Chief of Fighter Command; he was replaced by Sholto Douglas. Park ceased to be AOC of No. 11 Group on December 18; he was replaced by Leigh-Mallory. The circumstances of these two departures cast a shadow over what is otherwise an entirely glorious occasion for the Royal Air Force. In the case of Dowding, it was not his going, but the manner of it, that spoils the story. It is not the case, as has been stated,[1] that Dowding was dismissed on the telephone, a *canard* for which he himself is responsible:

> I received a sudden phone call at my Headquarters from the Secretary of State for Air. He told me that I was to relinquish my Command immediately. I asked what was meant by "immediately", and I was told that it would take effect within the next day or so . . . and that was that, with no explanation for such a precipitate step being taken.[2]

The facts are that he was first informed that he was about to be replaced by Sinclair, in a courteous personal interview on November 13, during which he also asked Dowding to carry out an important mission in the United States. Dowding was (rightly) doubtful of his ability to carry out this mission, and asked to see Churchill. This he did the following day; Churchill, however, was insistent on the importance of the work, and sent a note to Sinclair saying:

> Personally I think he will perform the task very well, and I will give him a letter to the President. I have a very great regard for this Officer and admiration for his qualities and achievements.[3]

That night the country was deeply shocked by the German raid on Coventry, during which 554 people were killed and 865 seriously wounded;[4] 125 sorties by Fighter Command did not produce even a

"Nothing left to command": Air Marshal Sir Arthur Barratt commanded the British Air Forces in France in 1940. In November of that year he became AOC-in-C of the anomalous Army Cooperation command until its disbandment in 1943. His RAF nickname was "Ugly" – it is a matter of opinion; seen here with his personal Hurricane.

"Robust, manoeuvrable and versatile": the Westland Lysander, designed specifically for Army Cooperation, entered service in 1938. Not a conspicuous success in its designated rôle, it soon found others: Air-Sea rescue and Special Duties (carrying spies and agents into and out of Occupied Europe).

"A close bond of mutual respect": Air Chief Marshal Sir Hugh Dowding (centre) with Fighter Command pilots. Left to right: S/Ldr A. C. Bartley DFC, W/Cdr D. F. B. Sheen DFC, W/Cdr I. R. Gleed DSO DFC, W/Cdr M. Aitken DSO DFC, W/Cdr A. G. Malan DSO DFC, S/Ldr A. C. Deere DFC RNZAF, Dowding, Flight Officer E. C. Henderson MM WAAF, F/Lt R. H. Hilary, W/Cdr J. A. Kent DFC AFC, W/Cdr C. B. F. Kingcombe DFC, S/Ldr D. H. Watkins DFC, Warrant Officer R. H. Gretton.

"The essence of the Dowding system was control": the photograph shows the temporary filter room servicing the Operations Room at Fighter Command HQ, Stanmore, in early 1940. The clock, with its coloured segments, was part of the standard direction-finding equipment enabling controllers to keep constant check on aircraft positions.

"The Dowding system": the Station Operations Room seen here shows how much Fighter Command's control system leaned on the WAAF.

"Intolerable . . . to be held back": Squadron-Leader Douglas Bader of No. 242 Squadron (Coltishall) (centre) with Canadian pilots and a Hurricane, summer 1940.

"Brilliant defensive abilities": Air Vice-Marshal Keith Park, AOC, No. 11 Group in the Battle of Britain.

"Never a shrinking violet": Air Vice-Marshal T. L. Leigh-Mallory, AOC No. 12 Group.

single claim (indeed, only seven sightings of the raiders were reported) though AA Command believed it had destroyed two. Those who considered that it was time for new blood and new ideas at Stanmore were much reinforced, and on the 16th Dowding did indeed receive a telephone call telling him that his replacement would be carried out at once. It is entirely in keeping with his experiences of the Air Ministry that, after all, there was still another week's delay. The American mission was a failure; Dowding's career effectively ended in 1942.

It is a sad tale – saddest of all that Dowding, having brooded upon his wrongs, came to see it only through a distorting lens. Sir Maurice Dean sums up:

> He was fifty-eight years of age and he had borne the burdens of Fighter Command for four years. In truth, it was time for a change.[5]

Dowding did not depart without reward: on September 30 he had received the GCB, and in May 1943 he received a Barony. What was conspicuously lacking, however, was recognition at the time of his departure; as Sir Maurice Dean says,

> In the light of hindsight it is clear enough that Dowding should have been given a peerage and made a Marshal. But it is also fair to say that it didn't look like that at the time.[6]

It may not have looked like it in the inner circles of the Air Ministry and the Government; the instincts of the pilots and the public were (for once) more correct. They are expressed with precision in the words of one of "the Few", Squadron-Leader "Ginger" Lacey:

> Where would we have been if Stuffy had lost the battle?[7]

Park's story is quicker to tell and less depressing. In December, immeasurably tired by an exertion rarely matched by any other British commander of the Second World War, he was transferred to No. 23 Training Group. From this oblivion (though evidently valuable work; it is hard to think of a more suitable appointment for a man of his talents) he emerged late in 1941 to become AOC, Egypt. In July 1942 he became AOC Malta, and once again displayed the brilliant defensive abilities that he had shown in No. 11 Group. In February 1945 he became Allied Air Commander-in-Chief, South East Asia Command. The officer first designated for this post was Leigh-

221

Mallory; but he was killed in an air crash on his way to take up the appointment. Park had the satisfaction of being just in time to take a distinguished part in the Burma victory.

The last word on the Battle of Britain must be for the men who fought and won it in the sky, the pilots of Fighter Command – "the gayest company who ever fired their guns in anger".[8] They were a remarkable breed, not quite like any other set of British fighting men:

> [they] cultivated a rakish and light-hearted approach to life. They affected to despise the external manifestations of Service discipline and disregarded the more pompous conventions of King's Regulations whenever possible.[9]

But, adds Denis Richards,

> This lightness of heart, a lightness which defied even tired limbs and jangled nerves, only adds to the quality of the epic. It would not, however, have carried our pilots very far had their equipment or their skill been inferior to that of the enemy. But of that there was no danger.

The Battle itself, of course, was not like any other; its extraordinary quality, both for those (the many) who were so close to it but not in it, and for those who were all too certainly in it (the Few), is hardly to be better expressed than in the words of Squadron-Leader G. A. L. ("Minnie") Manton of No. 56 Squadron:

> I don't think any of us (and I was older than most) really appreciated the seriousness of the situation. When we could be scared to death five or six times a day and yet find ourselves drinking in the local pub before closing time on a summer evening, it all seemed unreal . . .[10]

> Speak for the air, your element, you hunters
> Who range across the ribbed and shifting sky:
> Speak for whatever gives you mastery –
> Wings that bear out your purpose, quick-responsive
> Fingers, a fighting heart, a kestrel's eye.
>
> Speak of the rough and tumble in the blue,
> The mast-high run, the flak, the battering gales:
> You that, until the life you love prevails,
> Must follow death's impersonal vocation –
> Speak from the air, and tell your hunters' tales.[11]

THE BATTLE OF THE ATLANTIC (I)

"Anxiety supreme"

26 Coastal Command: Rôle and equipment; U-boat war, wireless war

The first fight for survival had been won; it had lasted (officially) for 16 weeks. The second fight for survival lasted for four years; it, too, was won by a narrow margin, and it entered its first critical phase in parallel with the Battle of Britain. It cannot be said that in this fight the RAF alone occupied "the right of the line" as Fighter Command unquestionably did during those critical months of 1940, yet it is simple fact that involvement in the Battle of the Atlantic dated from the first moments of the war, that all three of the operational Commands took part, that the Air Force rôle was always immensely important, and that it became dramatically more so as time went on.

As so often, it is Winston Churchill who specifies the character of this battle with precision – speaking this time from the double standpoint of First Lord of the Admiralty at the beginning, and then Prime Minister:

> Amid the torrent of violent events one anxiety reigned supreme. Battles might be won or lost, enterprises might succeed or miscarry, territories might be gained or quitted, but dominating all our power to carry on the war, or even keep ourselves alive, lay our mastery of the ocean routes and the free approach and entry to our ports.[1]

In this long-drawn-out struggle, no less decisive than Fighter Command's crisp victory, the RAF's champion was the weakest of its components: Coastal Command, the "Cinderella" referred to above, with its pitifully small numbers and its antiquated aircraft.[2] In the posture of Coastal Command, as it approached its vital rôle, we may see in close-up the delusions and uncertainties which made the long tale of early defeats inevitable.

The C-in-C, at the outbreak of war, was Air Marshal (soon Temporary, then acting unpaid Air Chief Marshal) Sir Frederick William Bowhill, GBE, KCB, CMG, DSO. Fifty-nine years old, he

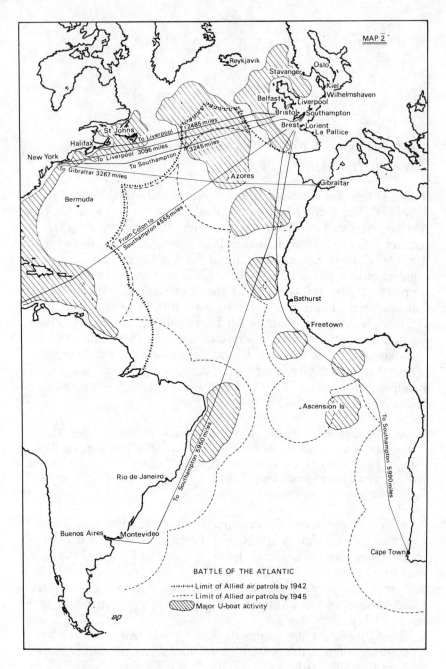

MAP 2

BATTLE OF THE ATLANTIC
..........Limit of Allied air patrols by 1942
- - - - - Limit of Allied air patrols by 1945
▨ Major U-boat activity

had joined the Royal Navy in 1904, gained his Royal Aero Club Flying Certificate (No. 397) in 1913, and then entered the Royal Naval Air Service. On Christmas Day 1914 he had commanded one of the Navy's first aircraft-carriers: HMS *Empress*, a converted cross-Channel steamer carrying seaplanes whose task was to attack the Zeppelin sheds at Cuxhaven. He took a permanent commission in the RAF with the rank of Wing Commander in 1919. He was, says Sir Maurice Dean,

> an ideal Commander-in-Chief for the early days of the war . . . he had seawater in his veins. He had an appreciation of naval needs based on a lifetime's experience.[3]

Bowhill's appointment dated from August 1937; there was still, at that stage, considerable doubt about what Coastal Command's function should be – and it is fair to say that that uncertainty was not cleared up until the Germans made the matter plain. His predecessor, Air Marshal P. B. Joubert de la Ferté, had been informed in March 1937 that the Command would have two main rôles:

1. Cooperation with the Bomber Command in the main strategic air offensive.
2. Cooperation with naval forces and such army forces as are allotted for coastal defence in countering enemy attacks on our coast and sea communications.[4]

Shortly after Bowhill's appointment, however, this directive was revised, and in December 1937 he was informed that the Command's primary rôle would be "trade protection, reconnaissance and cooperation with the Royal Navy".[5] The precise implications of this were then worked out; clearly they would be determined by the Admiralty's view of how the war at sea would develop. And here we need, as so frequently, to glance back at the teaching of the previous war.

In 1914 the German surface fleet was a serious threat to the supremacy of the Royal Navy and British security – indeed, it was this threat more than anything else that drew Britain into the Continental alliances which in turn drew her into war. In the event, the German battle-fleet and cruisers did not prove to be the menace that had been feared, but a maritime threat did develop which came near to bringing Britain to her knees: the submarine attack on commerce and supply. Sinkings by German U-(*untersee*) boats in 1917 reached the horrifying total of 6,623,623 tons, with a peak of 834,549 in the month of April alone. It was at that stage that the First Sea Lord, Admiral Jellicoe, told the American Admiral W. S. Sims that if this continued Germany would win the war. Sims asked:

"Is there no solution for the problem?"

"Absolutely none that we can see now," Jellicoe announced.[6]

In fact, however, the U-boat peril was overcome during the course of the next twelve months, not by the application of one "solution", but by a combination of many. The adoption of the convoy system was, of course, a highly significant step; but the Royal Navy always regarded convoys, no matter how effective, as a defensive device, and insisted that they must be matched by offensive measures. These took the form of anti-U-boat patrols; as depth-charges improved and projectors became available, the patrols naturally had more success. In the autumn of 1917 the introduction of the first (somewhat crude) Asdic underwater detection device provided a valuable new aid – and a pointer to the future.[7] Better mines, nets (more deterrent than destructive), gunfire, torpedoes (often fired by British submarines) all made their contribution; and so did the Air.

By November 1918,

> the strength of the purely maritime side of the RAF in Home Waters . . . was 43 squadrons and seven flights numbering about 685 planes and 103 airships. No less than 37 of these squadrons (285 flying boats and seaplanes, and 272 landplanes) were engaged on anti-U-boat duties, together with all the airships.[8]

Admiral Jellicoe informs us that in 1917 the Air Force sighted a total of 161 U-boats and attacked 100 of them; the fact that only seven U-boat sinkings are attributed to aircraft of all kinds during the war may look superficially disappointing, but there is no doubt that their deterrent effect (which cannot, of course, be precisely measured) was very great. Concerning convoy duties the AHB Narrative tells us:

> The conclusion of the Naval Staff in 1918 on the correct usage of air escort was that "a single escorting machine should keep close to the convoy as, for fear of being betrayed by the track of their torpedoes, the U-boat commanders refrain from attack on convoys with aerial escort. The ideal was that a convoy should be escorted by at least two aircraft, one keeping close and one cruising wide to prevent a submarine on the surface from getting into a position to attack. The rear of the convoy should not be omitted, for a submarine may be following on the chance of getting in an attack after dark.[9]

How familiar all this would sound again in the 1940s! How strange that it all had to be relearned!

Indeed, everything about anti-U-boat warfare had to be relearned. At the root of the matter lay a simple fact: the technical improvement in the Asdic device which had taken place since 1918. By 1937 the new version, in the hands of well-trained operators, was certainly very good indeed; the Naval staff felt able to state that "the submarine should never again be able to present us with the problem we were faced with in 1917".[10] This somewhat breathtaking pronouncement was more than a pity; it drew the Royal Navy back to an exaggerated belief in the efficiency of its offensive patrols, depreciating the value of convoys, although by 1918, as the AHB Narrative says,

> much confused reasoning had been clarified and experience had shown that the convoy system, with adequate surface and air escort, far from being defensive was highly offensive in character, for not only did it prevent ships from being sunk but the escorts destroyed more U-boats than any other method of direct attack. *Area patrol unrelated to convoy movements was useless.*[11]

It is not mere hindsight that makes the Naval Staff's devotion to the new Asdic so extraordinary; it is the fact that although undoubtedly potent against submerged submarines, it was virtually useless against enemies on the surface, and this was known to be so. Yet the very measures which had been carefully worked out to discourage surfaced U-boats in 1918 were now set aside; the effect of this on the young Coastal Command was bound to be serious, and verged on being disastrous.

Confident in its own ability to handle the underwater threat, the Navy anticipated a need for only relatively small air support in that task. The German battle-fleet presented nothing like the problem of 1914, and though it contained some fine ships, it did not cause the Admiralty real anxiety. On the other hand, the Naval Staff did envisage a serious potential threat from powerful commerce raiders (pocket-battleships, battle-cruisers) breaking out into the Atlantic via the northern exits from the North Sea. "From this it was clear that Coastal Command's primary task in war would be North Sea reconnaissance."[12]

Tedious and unglamorous as this rôle was, with the existing equipment it tested Coastal Command fully. It has to be noted that over and above the general shortage of aircraft affecting all Commands, Air Marshal Bowhill's was afflicted with particular sorrows. As we have seen (p. 38) the awaited new torpedo-bomber on which the Command was relying for its strike-capacity, the Blackburn Botha, proved to be a failure. This meant that the ancient Vickers Vildebeest biplane, first delivered to the RAF in 1933 (final delivery 1937), was all that was available for this rôle. Moreover the Saro Lerwick flying-boat, which was to have replaced the Short Sunderland (to free Short Brothers for production of the Stirling for Bomber Command), was also a failure, with incurable handling characteristics. The worst of this was that by the time the Lerwick's faults had become apparent (April 1940) the Sunderland order had lapsed and Shorts had dismantled the jigs; as a result, despite frantic efforts, renewed production of this invaluable four-engined machine, with its crew of 13, 10 machine guns, 2,980-mile range and endurance of 13½ hours, was for several months desperately slow.[13] The Lerwick failure meant that two squadrons were compelled to retain their biplane Saro London and Supermarine Stranraer flying-boats, adding to the antique appearance of the Command. Its only really modern aircraft was the Lockheed Hudson (No. 224 Squadron) ordered in America (see p. 39). And the early versions of this were insufficiently armed, lacking a rear turret; it was also regarded at first by aircrews as a difficult aircraft to fly. Nevertheless, it was a 224 Squadron Hudson which claimed the first German aircraft to be shot down by the RAF in the Second World War: a Dornier 18 flying-boat on October 8, 1939.

Nothing so vividly illustrates the weakness of Coastal Command as the fact that its hard core, in September 1939, was 10 squadrons of Avro Ansons. This was an aircraft which served the Royal Air Force well; in twenty years of service it earned its nickname, "Faithful Annie". Its career began on March 6, 1936, with No. 48 Squadron; six days later an Air Ministry Order (AMO A53) warned its recipients:

1. The Anson is a civil type of aircraft adapted for service purposes and is therefore restricted to the type of flying allowed within the normal civil category.
2. The following instructions are therefore to be observed in flying the Anson:
    (i) the aircraft must not be subjected to violent manoeuvres at any speed . . .
    (ii) An air speed indicator reading of 170 knots must not be exceeded in any condition of flight.
    (iii) No attempt to spin the aircraft is permitted.
    (iv) The engine speed for continuous cruising must not exceed 2,100 rpm . . .

Apart from these trifles, it had sterling qualities, as its long career showed; but in relation to Coastal Command's primary task in September 1939, it was the drawbacks which were more apparent. With an armament of only one fixed forward-firing .303 machine gun and another in a turret behind, it was clearly not suitable for combat. A bomb-load of only four 100-pounders made it a very weak weapon of attack. But worst of all was that its limited range prevented it from spanning the North Sea which it was to patrol; a gap of about 50 miles existed between the Anson's extreme flight limit and the Norwegian coast.

Such were the difficulties and discouragements which faced Air Marshal Bowhill's Command; almost all its work was routine – convoy escort and reconnaissance – and therefore monotonous. Gazing down at the sea for hours on end could induce a trancelike condition – but trance could well be fatal. With a continuing paucity both of aircraft and of trained crews, the Command had to operate from the very first at full intensity, "and as autumn deepened into winter to fly in the bleakest northern latitudes even in the severest weather".[14] By comparison with this day-in, day-out and all too often unrewarding effort, the tribulations even of Bomber Command's Battles and Blenheims and Whitleys, or Fighter Command's Gladiators, begin to pale. But the crews of Coastal Command stuck to their exacting task "with unflagging patience, vigour and resource".[15]

The task itself was changing significantly. The Germans lost no time in commencing their tutorial: in September 1939, 53 ships, totalling 194,845 gross tons of British, Allied and neutral shipping were sunk.[16] Mines, including the magnetic variety (see p. 110) accounted for 29,537, and commerce raiders for another 5,051, but there was no doubting who the real villains were: U-boats sank 41 of the ships, a total of 153,879 gross tons in the first month of war. In so doing they declared themselves the main enemy at sea, as they had been in 1917, and many ideas and beliefs, both in the Royal Navy and the RAF, had to be drastically revised.

There were, of course, special reasons for this success, which was only once surpassed in the first nine months of the war (February 1940: 169,566 tons). The first reason (constituting one of the war's superior ironies) was that it was precisely while the Royal Navy was conducting its last pre-war combined air/sea exercise (August 15–21, 1939) that 14 of Germany's 42 operational U-boats slipped through the North Sea to the Atlantic – which was just what the combination was designed to prevent. Coastal Command was fully occupied with the exercise, and unable to resume its routine patrols until August

24 – by which time two more U-boats had entered the Atlantic, and two pocket-battleships (*Admiral Graf Spee* and *Deutschland*) had passed unobserved into its wide waters. On August 25 the weather thickened, with dense fog in the North Sea, and 14 smaller U-boats took advantage of this to reach their patrol positions. Thus at the outbreak of war two pocket-battleships and 30 U-boats were ready to strike – all unknown to the British Admiralty. As the AHB Narrator (himself an ex-submariner, Captain D. V. Peyton-Ward) tartly remarks:

> Our Intelligence was not so much inefficient as totally inadequate.[17]

German Naval Intelligence ("*B-Dienst*",[18] under *Kapitän zur See* Kupfer), on the other hand, was in a very happy position; indeed, in these early days, as Ronald Lewin says, it held a "commanding lead" in the wireless war. We have seen (p. 39) how the Abyssinian crisis of 1935–36 had offered the German cryptanalysts their "first bite" at British naval signals. They had not wasted the intervening time. By the outbreak of war, *B-Dienst* was extensively reading the Royal Navy's low-grade Administrative Code. This proved to be most helpful in attacking the higher-grade naval ciphers. By April 1940, *B-Dienst*

> was reading without great delay 30 to 50 per cent of the traffic intercepted, though it should be added that the evidence suggests that it had no success with traffic encyphered in the tables used by Commanders-in-Chief and Flag Officers.[19]

In August 1940 the Navy replaced the Administrative Code with Naval Code No. 1, and simultaneously replaced Naval Cipher No. 1 by No. 2. This checked the Germans for about a year, but by September 1941 they were again reading the Navy's signals to a considerable extent, and continued to do so until January 1942. As we shall see, their success with Naval Code No. 3, which served Anglo-Canadian-US operations in the Atlantic, was even more marked.

Nor was it merely a matter of penetration of the Royal Navy's codes, though that was serious enough; *B-Dienst* had also discovered with satisfaction that one of the most vulnerable was that used by Merchant shipping.[20] In this combination lay the second reason for the success of the U-boats in September, and again in October (27 ships sunk, 134,807 tons). The third reason, of course, was that protected convoys cannot come into existence overnight, or even in days; the Germans enjoyed the benefit of meeting many sitting ducks, and Coastal

Command was much strained in trying to rescue them. Fortunately, despite appearances to the contrary, the German U-boat fleet was very weak in numbers. When the first strong concentration returned to port, numbers at sea dwindled drastically. Many had teething troubles, which kept them in dock for a long time because an insufficient labour force had been allotted to U-boat repair. Very few new boats were coming into service; all had to make a long northabout journey round Britain to reach their stations. This meant that

> there were rarely more than six or eight U-boats in the area of operations at the same time; usually there were between three and five, and sometimes even fewer.[21]

The result, naturally, was a sharp drop in sinkings by U-boats during the next seven months (with the ominous exception of February). Indeed, Churchill went so far as to say:

> Nothing of major importance occurred in the first year of the U-boat warfare.[22]

– which was, to say the least, euphoric.

27 The U-boat enemy; bombs and depth-charges

The truth is that a great deal happened during the first year of war at sea, and not least the fundamental fact that Captain Peyton-Ward singles out:

> The distinguishing feature of this early battle of the North Sea was that the enemy were able to seize and retain the initiative. This had the result that British naval and air policy evolved as a series of responses to changing and unexpected developments and also that the Air Ministry's plans for naval cooperation proved difficult to implement.[1]

This was in sharp contrast with 1914, when the Royal Navy itself had seized an initiative which, with the exception of the first part of 1917, it held throughout the First World War. The 1939 position was a consequence, partly of the unexpected vigorous onslaught of the U-boats, and partly of another manifestation of German air power.

On October 14, 1939, *U-47* (Lieutenant Prien) penetrated the defences of Scapa Flow and sank the battleship *Royal Oak*. No sooner was this severe shock digested than the *Luftwaffe* provided another: an attack on cruisers in the Firth of Forth (October 16). Only a small amount of damage was done, and four (out of twelve) German aircraft were brought down. But the next day Scapa was bombed; again only unimportant damage was sustained, but for a disagreeable reason – the Home Fleet had gone, driven out of its base to the west coast of Scotland, as in 1914. There it remained until March 1940, and in its absence the question arose whether there was any point in Coastal Command continuing its exhausting northern patrols – what, after all, could it do, even if it did sight German warships? Air Chief Marshal Bowhill decided that, on balance, it was best to maintain the patrols; he was certainly right, but it meant that the ordeal of the aircrews continued through the winter, while an unprecedented British weakness reigned in the North Sea.

It was during this bleak period that Coastal Command significantly changed its outlook. It was discovered – or rather, *re*-discovered – that U-boats could be located from the air far more easily than had been supposed in some quarters. With suitable tactics, and above all *better weapons*, enthusiasts pronounced that it was anti-U-boat warfare that would give the Command its place in history, and each passing day drew it further in that direction:

> From being concerned predominantly with reconnaissance the Command had become 60 per cent U-boat-minded, while an unlooked-for rôle – that of the long-range fighter – had been added to its functions.[2]

By the turn of the year, as Denis Richards says, Coastal Command was "developing an anti-U-boat offensive in its own right".[3]

The question was, how to carry it out. In no area of RAF armament was avoidable weakness so patent as in anti-submarine weaponry. By the end of 1917 it was the considered opinion of those concerned that the best weapon for air attack on a submarine was a bomb containing at least 300 lb of high explosive; with the casing this would give a total weight of 520 lb, and it should be fitted with an impact fuse or a delay fuse to detonate at about 40 feet below the sea surface.[4] In keeping with the general view that nothing that had happened in the First World War could be of any interest, this lesson was totally ignored, and in 1934 orders were placed for three sizes of bomb: 100 lb, 250 lb, and 500 lb. Six years of trial and tribulation followed. As we have seen, Coastal Command's most numerous aircraft could carry only 100-pounders; their usefulness was fully demonstrated on December 3, 1939, when by mistake HM Submarine *Snapper* was hit by one, at the base of the conning-tower; four light bulbs in the control room were broken. It was finally concluded that the 100-lb bomb would probably be ineffective even with a direct hit, that the 250-pounder would have to explode within six feet of the pressure hull to do serious damage, and the 500-pounder at about eight feet. Yet the Navy had specified the 100-lb bomb as its chief requirement, which meant that Coastal Command was saddled with it. Meanwhile the crews discovered that, lacking a proper bomb-sight, if they went low to hit their elusive targets, their bombs were as dangerous to themselves as to the enemy. At least one Anson and two Fleet Air Arm Skuas were destroyed by their own bombs in September 1939 alone.[5] A wilful blindness seemed to be at work; the AHB Narrative says:

> Although circles in direct contact with this problem were convinced of the uselessness of the existing anti-submarine bombs there was an influential body of fixed opinion which refused to admit this. The result was that attacks on U-boats developing out of intelligent design of anti-U-boat patrols and sweeps came to nought as regards inflicting any serious damage. All we could do was to harass and frighten.[6]

Not until 1940 was it accepted that the proper weapon for attacking submarines, by aircraft as well as by surface vessels, was the depth-charge. Even then tribulations did not end; there were (one need hardly say it) not enough depth-charges to go round; and until one suitable for air dropping could be devised, Coastal Command would face a new hazard. The maximum height for release was 300 feet – above this the depth-charge would break up on hitting the water. But with the very inaccurate altimeters of the period, this meant that to carry out a depth-charge attack by night meant a very real risk of flying into the sea.

One wonders, at times, whether "Cinderella" is the right name for Coastal Command in 1939–40; Cinderella *was* supposed to be beautiful, and she *did* have a fairy godmother.

It is not, in the end, surprising, after this list of deficiencies and drawbacks, that out of 85 attacks on U-boats by the Command between September 1939 and May 1940, only one resulted in a sinking. This was on January 30, 1940, when *U 55* was under attack by surface convoy escorts; a Sunderland of 228 Squadron kept track of all her attempts to escape until her batteries were exhausted and her captain gave orders to scuttle and abandon her. The "kill" was thus shared between the Navy and Coastal Command. The first "kill" by an aircraft alone came two months later – but it was carried out by a Blenheim of No. 82 Squadron, Bomber Command. Coastal

233

Command would have to wait until 1941 to make its own first "kill"; until then it could only "soldier on" and – had it only known – thank heaven for the paucity of U-boats.

28 The battle begins; The Dönitz system; ASV radar

The "sublime stupidity" of the British in 1940 (see p. 169) was nowhere more in evidence than in relation to the war at sea. By the end of June, Germany was in possession of the whole coastline of Western Europe from the North Cape to Bordeaux. It was just as well that the British public did not grasp the implications:

> Never before in her history had Great Britain found herself faced by enemy forces on all sides except the West, a loophole which the German Navy attempted to close and thus isolate this country from the rest of the world.[1]

Taken in conjunction with the threat of the Italian Navy and Air Force in the Mediterranean, this meant that Hitler's belief in defeating Britain by cutting the supply lines (p. 171) was all too credible. By July the French Atlantic ports were already in use as U-boat bases; airfields in Western France gave the *Luftwaffe* easy access to the shipping lanes west of Ireland. The Focke-Wulf FW 200C (Condor) made its appearance; known for a time as the "scourge of the Atlantic", this four-engined reconnaissance plane owed nothing to *Luftwaffe* forethought – it was an adapted air liner. With a standard range of over 2,000 miles, it could take off from Brest or Bordeaux, fly round the British Isles to westward, land in Norway, and make the return journey next day. Its four 550-lb bombs made it an effective low-level attacker of shipping, accounting for 90,000 tons in August and September.[2] Cooperation of aircraft with U-boats now became a menacing feature of the sea war; in answer, the efforts of Coastal Command and the Royal Navy would need to be increasingly integrated.

Meanwhile, Coastal Command – numbering only some 500 aircraft of all types – was stretched by a sudden load of new tasks. It was heavily involved (as we have seen) in anti-invasion operations, and lent valuable support to Fighter Command in the Battle of Britain. In addition, while continuing its North Sea patrols, it had now to attempt a close watch on the deeply indented Norwegian coastline with its maze of fjords and channels; it had to maintain long-range patrols north and south of Iceland; it was called on for reconnaissance of the now hostile coasts of Holland, Belgium and France; it had to provide some long-range fighter (Blenheim) protection for shipping in the Atlantic approaches; it faced increasing calls for air escort and anti-U-boat measures along the convoy routes, to distances recently unthought of; new overseas trade protection commitments also steadily increased. It will not be wondered at that the C-in-C's demands for reinforcement now became a constant refrain; nor, in this period of universal crisis and shortage, is it any surprise that these demands were slow and disappointing in fulfilment. Yet, as Denis Richards says, the keenness and skill of Bowhill's airmen were never blunted.[3]

The new complexion of the war declared itself immediately: sinkings of British, Allied and neutral ships in June 1940 amounted to 140 vessels – 585,496 gross tons. Of this frightening total, aircraft accounted for 105,193 tons, and U-boats for 284,113; in the stress and confusion of the evacuations from France, the Navy was not able to give normal protection to merchant shipping, and the U-boats took full advantage. The July total was 386,913 tons (105 ships) – a drop, but still serious. On August 17 Hitler proclaimed a "total blockade" of Britain and in that month the U-boats began to display new tactics; the monthly average of shipping losses (June–December) stood at over 425,000; the Battle of the Atlantic had begun.

We now have to take into account a remarkable German war leader: 49-year-old Admiral Karl Dönitz, *Führer der U-Boote*, later Grand Admiral and Commander-in-Chief of Naval Forces, and finally Hitler's successor as Head of State. A dedicated naval officer and a Nazi fanatic, he was determined and ruthless, but also highly professional and flexible. As Liddell Hart says, he showed himself "a very able strategist, always probing for the soft spots and concentrating to strike when the defence was weak".[4] He shared certain important characteristics with both Marshal of the Royal Air Force Sir Arthur Harris and Air Chief Marshal Lord Dowding. Both Dönitz and Harris placed great faith in a particular weapon; in Harris's case it was the heavy bomber:

> The surest way to win a war is to destroy the enemy's war potential. And all that I had seen and studied of warfare in the past had led me to believe that the bomber was the predominant weapon for this task in this war.[5]

If, for "enemy's war potential" we read "enemy's capacity to continue waging war", this was precisely how Dönitz regarded the submarine. And thanks to his affinity with Dowding, he came very close to proving his point; for the essence of the "Dönitz system", like the "Dowding system", was control. The "wolf-pack" tactics with which Dönitz is so intimately associated depended, like Dowding's, on a major advance of technology: in Dowding's case it was radar, in Dönitz's it was wireless telegraphy, which transformed the U-boat

> from a lone raider without communication with its fellows or its home command into an able, willing, gregarious puppet which a master named Karl Dönitz could manipulate and maneuver swiftly and ruthlessly at the end of an electronic string.[6]

Fortified by the admirable work of *B-Dienst* in penetrating the British naval and merchant shipping codes, Dönitz was able to exercise a degree of tight tactical long-range battle control unparalleled in the history of war. The irony, as we shall subsequently see, was that the very technology which made this system possible also became largely responsible for its downfall.

The heavy shipping losses which marked the first phase of the Atlantic battle – in practical terms beginning in June 1940, more formally in August – were indicators of what was to come. This phase lasted until June 1941, and because its end was marked by a distinct fall in losses, a degree of false optimism was engendered whose chief danger was the continued reluctance of the Air Staff to upgrade Coastal Command's priority in the use of new aircraft and technical devices as these became available. There was a tendency to self-congratulation which failed to take into account – indeed, it would scarcely have been credited – the true reason for the apparent failure of the U-boats: the extreme paucity of them already mentioned. This table, from Sir Maurice Dean's *The RAF and Two World Wars* (p. 153) contains the heart of the matter (once more, sources disagree on precise numbers, but the ratios and conclusions stand):

U-BOATS OPERATIONAL

	1939	1940	1941	1942	1943	1944	1945
January		33	23	89	214	170	155
February		34	22	101	221	167	156
March		31	30	111	231	164	156
April		31	30	119	237	161	150
May		23	40	128	239	157	126
June		26	47	130	218	181	
July		29	60	140	209	180	
August		28	60	152	178	151	
September	42	31	74	169	167	146	
October	49	26	75	192	177	139	
November	38	25	81	205	163	148	
December	38	22	86	203	163	152	

236

These figures include all six types under construction. The ocean-going "medium" Type VII, with its 6,500-mile range, which Dönitz favoured for convoy attack, constituted only 25 out of the 72 being built or completed in September 1939. And the Type VII itself was in many respects little different from the U 114 type of 1918. Furthermore, the U-boats in 1939 and 1940 were experiencing serious disadvantages through defects in their prime weapon – the torpedo.[7] These became particularly apparent during the Norwegian campaign, but several months earlier than that Dönitz had been moved to write in his diary:

> I do not believe that ever in the history of war have men been sent against the enemy with such a useless weapon.

As Alfred Price remarks, if he had known what Bowhill's aircrews were contending with, he might have felt inclined to moderate that remark.[8]

It was for all these reasons that the "wolf-pack" tactics which Dönitz had been enthusiastically developing since 1935, and now attempted to put into practice, proved a failure in 1939–40 – above all, of course, because the "packs" were just not big enough. Yet the morale of the U-boat crews, always high, soared with their spectacular successes in June. This was the time when their famous "aces" came into the limelight, building reputations which were seized upon by Dr Goebbels's propaganda machine, and which matched those of the flyers of 1914–18. As they went to work in the suddenly transformed situation of 1940, they gave the Battle of the Atlantic the evil name that haunts it to this day:

> It was a grim war, the war at sea . . . Once a torpedo hit a vessel, often without warning, chances of survival were few. Death might come with the first explosion, or a man might be trapped belowdecks. Burning oil often extended hundreds of yards from the stricken ship, cruelly weighting the odds of death. If there was time to man lifeboats before the last convulsive shudder of the vessel, survivors might find themselves face to face with the U-boat that had damned them, as it surfaced to survey the agony and sometimes to add to it by machine-gunning lifeboats and floating survivors. So few rescue craft were available in the early days that survivors often were prostrate from hunger, blistered by a merciless sun, or stiff from an icy sea before rescue came – if it came at all.[9]

It was in August that the U-boat tactics which Dönitz had so long prepared, but so far only disappointingly realized, started to become effective and recognizable. They consisted, basically, of these ingredients:

> First – clearly – Intelligence: knowledge of convoy movements and positions, sometimes derived from air reconnaissance (Condors), but more likely from *B-Dienst* and the penetration of the British and Allied Mechanical Ship (BAMS) code, supplied to U-boat HQ and relayed to the U-boats.
>
> Secondly, shadowing of the discovered convoy by one or more U-boats on the surface in daylight; it should be noted that in good visibility it was possible to see a convoy's smoke 30 to 40 miles away; in bad visibility a U-boat's hydrophones could pick up a convoy's sound up to 20 miles away.[10]
>
> Thirdly, on instruction from Dönitz's headquarters – but *only* on receipt of such instructions – a combined night attack by the whole "pack" of U-boats in the vicinity; this could be either a submerged or a surface attack, according to circumstance.

This was the "Dönitz system", which with minor variations remained standard until 1944. Its nerve centre was U-boat Headquarters, at first situated at Lorient, but moved to Paris in March 1942. It had one weak point, as the AHB Narrative remarks; this was "the volume of W/T signals necessarily passing between the U-boats or Focke-Wulf aircraft at sea and the shore based Command".[11] If the day should come when British Intelligence was able to read the U-boat ciphers as *B-Dienst* read the BAMS code, the tables could be turned; and thanks to the "Y" Service, Bletchley Park and a certain amount of luck, the day did come – but not yet.

Meanwhile, the Dönitz system was all too effective; the Royal Navy, like Coastal Command, was desperately short of vessels suited to the U-boat war – though the acquisition of 50 First World War-vintage American destroyers in September 1940 was certainly a help (and a gesture that America had cause to regret just over a year later). It would be some time, of course, before these ships were ready to take part in operations, and at the time the agreement was signed it was rare for a convoy to enjoy an escort of more than three naval vessels. Air escort in daytime was a help, but obviously of no avail against the tactic of night attack; and Coastal Command's own tactic was still one designed to combat submerged attack by day, consisting of the patrolling of a "box" 15 miles wide ahead of the convoy, and 15 miles across on either side of its bow. This form of escort, well in view, was considered essential for the morale of merchant crews, but with the Command's overall shortage of aircraft it meant that there was no long-range cover against the distant watchers. Night escort had never even been envisaged, but was attempted as a palliative on moonlight nights, naturally with disappointing results.

What was desperately needed was a form of radar as efficient as that which had enabled Dowding to perfect his system of daylight fighter defence. And indeed, research on airborne radar had begun in 1936, only a year after the beginning of the main RDF chain – which naturally took priority. Under the leadership of Dr Edward Bowen, a small but industrious team had by 1937 devised an airborne radar apparatus capable of detecting large ships at a distance of up to five miles. In September Bowen reported results which "encourage the hope that it will ultimately be possible to discover and locate ships at sea at distances up to about 10 miles from an aircraft".[12] This was good work in the time given, but in relation to the critical need progress remained slow. As Alfred Price says:

> During the spring of 1939 airborne radar was still a "hothouse flower", requiring the care of, and operation by, skilled scientists; and even with this treatment it often failed to give consistent results. As yet it was neither simple enough nor reliable enough to be introduced into service.[13]

"No virtue like necessity"; primitive as it was, Dr Bowen's apparatus went into production shortly after the outbreak of war "with a minimum of refinement; speed was of the essence".[14] This was the ASV (Air to Surface Vessel) Mark I model, so named to distinguish it from the model under development for night-fighters, AI (Airborne Interception). By January 1940, twelve Coastal Command Hudsons were thus equipped – and discovering that what they carried was no war-winner. The chief drawback of this equipment (apart from size and weight) was the volume of short-range signals which it picked up from the sea's surface – the "surface clutter" – especially in choppy weather. Only by very low flying (200 feet), with the hazards that we have already noted, could a real target be readily distinguished from the "clutter"; at that height a maximum location range of three and a half miles might be achieved, with observation of the target down to a minimum range of half a mile. But ASV I was always unreliable, and even when it worked there was no means of illuminating the located target. Yet the future potential was there.

It was a bold step, nevertheless, with the device still at this stage, to put ASV II into production as early as the spring of 1940, with an order for 4,000 sets. Bowen and his team had made certain significant changes:

A more powerful transmitter and more sensitive receiver promised an improved location range against submarines. Most important of all, however, was the fact that the new set had been engineered for mass production from the start; for this reason it was far more robust and reliable than its predecessor.[15]

Difficulties were never lacking: the demands of the Battle of Britain, and then of the night blitz, and the hazard of German bombing of factories, all combined to slow up production, so that by October only 45 out of the 4,000 sets ordered had been delivered. Once again, technology offered a future promise rather than a present benefit – but this time with a further, highly attractive, prospect. By this time Bowen's indefatigable "boffins" were already well advanced with a third ASV version, embodying the "magnetron" oscillator which made centimetric radar practicable; by the summer of 1940 this was already able – experimentally – to detect an aircraft at six miles and the conning tower of a submarine at four miles, and its performances steadily improved. So the future certainly looked brighter; but for the present there was nothing for Coastal Command to do but "soldier on" with its few ASV I sets, no illuminant, too few depth-charges, too few aircraft and too few trained crews: a hard war.

29 Lord Beaverbrook rushes in

At this juncture, the Command suddenly faced a threat to its existence which for a brief span looked more serious than anything the Germans had so far achieved. On November 4 the First Lord of the Admiralty, A. V. Alexander, wrote a memorandum in which he spoke of Coastal Command's need for "1,000 planes in operation at the earliest possible moment". He gave a considered estimate that a minimum of 826 shore-based naval cooperation aircraft was needed in home waters – which indicated a current deficiency of about 400 and an additional overseas deficiency of about 480. Like everyone concerned with the mounting strain of the Atlantic battle, A. V. Alexander was a worried man, and all he was trying to do was to obtain more resources for a part of the RAF which, he feared, was not getting all the help that it might from the Air Staff. He actually used the name, "Cinderella". Little did he know what a malign force he had activated.

The next day the Defence Committee,[1] with the Prime Minister in the chair, met to consider Alexander's memorandum. Sir Archibald Sinclair reminded the meeting of the dire effects of the failures of the Lerwick and Botha, and said that the request for 1,000 aircraft was exaggerated. He also pointed out that "any undue expansion of the naval cooperation force would inevitably hamper the building up of Bomber Command's strength and would sacrifice the possibility of its being employed effectively on offensive operations".[2]

At this point Lord Beaverbrook, who was present in his capacity as Minister of Aircraft Production (and enjoying Churchill's warm regard), made an intervention "which was entirely alien to the matters under discussion".[3] He suggested that Coastal Command should be removed from the Royal Air Force and handed to the Royal Navy to be run as part of a separate Naval Air Service. He said he thought the Navy should have its own training establishments, its own pilots and its own maintenance staff; as regards aircraft, he anticipated no difficulty in supplying all that would be needed. One imagines that there must have been a pause in the discussion while those present took this in.

Churchill was clearly caught in two minds; his admiration for Beaverbrook drew him to comment on the advantages of having all trade protection measures under a single operational control; he remarked that though he had opposed such an amalgamation in 1937, less serious consequences for the RAF were now likely, in view of the rapid expansion by which it was "forming itself into the leading element in bringing about our victory". And then came a flash of practicality and caution; he added that "it would be a poor economy to duplicate training grounds or to set up competition between the services in the market for aircraft".

The First Sea Lord, Admiral of the Fleet Sir Dudley Pound, then brought the meeting back to its original business: the need to strengthen Coastal Command. The crux of the problem, he said, "was how to safeguard our trade during the next few months" – and this was a matter of aircraft and air and ground-crews. Sir Archibald Sinclair said the Air Ministry was ready to consider any proposals for improving the efficiency of Coastal Command. The newly-appointed Chief of the Air Staff, Sir Charles Portal, well and truly pitched into the "deep end" of Whitehall warfare, drew attention to the difficulty of creating a unified control of trade protection, since the protection of naval bases, airfields and coastal shipping was the responsibility of Fighter Command. In any case, he said, "there was no evidence that the effective control of the day-to-day operations of Coastal Command did not rest in the hands of the local naval Commander-in-Chief". And finally, rather echoing Pound, he suggested that the only real test of the proposal to transfer authority was whether or not it would result in an increase of actual resources.

241

Fortified by these breaths of realism from the Service Departments, Churchill decided that an inquiry should be held on the merits of Beaverbrook's proposal, but he reminded the Defence Committee of the waste of resources in the previous war when the Royal Naval Air Service, engaged on purely defensive home duties, was allowed to expand at the expense of the Royal Flying Corps "fighting for its life in France". Such a thing, he said, must never be allowed to happen again.

Conferences were accordingly held between Admiralty and Air Ministry representatives on November 11 and 13; to guide their deliberations, Churchill circulated a questionnaire, in which he drew attention to certain key matters. He wanted to know exactly what complaints the Admiralty had against the present system (it was not the Admiralty, after all, that had raised the matter); he asked, if the suggested transfer were carried out, what would be the operational advantages? Would training of pilots and crews be better managed in Air Force or Navy establishments? Above all, he put the straight question: "What would be the effect of the change on the provision of men and aircraft? Would there be any net increase of resources?" How could overlapping of functions be avoided? And so on; this was, in fact, another of those Churchillian documents which may stand for a very long time as perfect examples of democratic control of war.

Beaverbrook, too, had not been idle; without waiting for Churchill's questions, he produced a memorandum which, as Captain Peyton-Ward says, "lacking both restraint and sound argument, virtually contributed nothing to the discussion and probably injured rather than promoted the policy of which he was a misguided advocate."

> It is not a satisfactory argument [said Beaverbrook], to say that the RAF can fulfil the task of supplementing the surface craft of the fleet. It has failed to do so. The Coastal Command of the RAF is quite inadequate.

In similar rhetorical vein he proclaimed: "Weeks only can be devoted to the strengthening of the naval air force. Time measured in months would be too long." How even Lord Beaverbrook could persuade himself that a major reconstruction of the maritime air forces could be accomplished, let alone bear fruit, in weeks, will remain a mystery. As we have seen the true solutions were, in fact, a matter neither of weeks nor months, but of the years required for technology to make its contribution.

In the interim, short- and medium-term programmes were agreed between the two Services. In the short term, Coastal Command was to receive a squadron of Wellingtons fitted with "long-range ASV" (Mark II), a squadron of Beauforts, the Bristol Company's new torpedo-bomber which was replacing the Vildebeests, and a long-range squadron of Beaufighters (still a doubtful quantity, as we have seen, but increasingly useful). The long-range fighter element was to be further increased by raising the establishment of the five existing squadrons from 16 to 20 aircraft. This represented the equivalent of a reinforcement of one and a half squadrons – the quick way of doing it. Furthermore, the anticipated arrival of 57 of the American PBY-5 (Catalina) flying-boats, whose distinguishing features were their range (4,000 miles) and endurance (17.6 hours), promised a further increase of the equivalent of four squadrons in 1941. The medium-term programme envisaged a total increase of 15 squadrons by June 1941.

When the considered responses of the two Ministries to Churchill's questionnaire came in, the Admiralty, in sharp contrast to Beaverbrook, paid tribute to "the already excellent cooperation which exists between Coastal Command and the Navy", and was unable to point to any likely gain in resources from the proposed transfer. Sir Archibald Sinclair drew attention to Coastal Command's vastly increased responsibilities since the fall of France, the special priority allotted to Fighter Command during the Battle of Britain, and the War Cabinet's decision to build up Bomber Command for a strategic offensive. Despite all this, he said, the strength of Coastal Command had increased by nearly 100 per cent during the last year – "a rate of expansion which exceeded that of the Air Force as a whole and which contrasted sharply with the rate of progress of Bomber Command . . ." But above all he dwelt on the duplication of effort and inevitable increase in "overheads" which would result from the abandonment of the system of common basic training – a system which had just demonstrated its value by the manner in which Coastal Command and Fleet Air Arm pilots had brought support to Fighter Command in its hour of need.

The Defence Committee met again on December 4 to settle this matter. By now Churchill's mind was made up – against the arguments of his old friend and admired colleague, Beaverbrook. It would be disastrous, he said, at that stage of the war, "to tear a large fragment from the Royal Air Force". It was generally agreed that this was not a suitable time to stir inter-Service controversy, and there the subject rested, on the understanding that operational control of the U-boat war must continue always to rest with the sailors. Since this was merely a re-statement of the *status quo* as indicated by Portal, it gave no offence. The conclusion was ultimately embodied (without significant further illumination) in a joint report on March 9, 1941, reaffirming "the predominance of the naval element in the existing operational partnership for the production of sea-borne trade", but preserving the right of direct command of Coastal Groups to their own officers and the C-in-C. The findings of this report became known as Coastal Command's "Charter".

This story has been considered worth telling, as an example of the "Whitehall war" which provided an eternal background to military events,[4] certainly, but chiefly because the relations of Coastal Command and the Royal Navy offer, from beginning to end, and despite political interference, an example of inter-Service cooperation at its best, a true integration of the Air arm into the fight for, first, survival, then victory, in a decisive battle of the war.

30   The Atlantic Gap: "The Crow and the Mole"; Western Approaches; False Dawn; Bismarck and others

The war against the Germans proceeded amid the Atlantic fogs and storms. By the end of 1940 it had cost 1,281 British, Allied and neutral ships, 4,745,033 gross tons of shipping, of which the U-boats accounted for 585 ships (2,607,314 tons). In the 16 months of war, only 32 U-boats had been sunk, a rate of two a month, which already pointed towards British disaster. Coastal Command's losses during the same period amounted to 323 aircraft, some 40 per cent being incurred in reconnaissance of German naval ports and units.[1] Its equipment now included Wellingtons and Whitleys, Beauforts and Northrop N3P-B seaplanes, in addition to its basic types listed above (p. 70, Chap. 8, Note 2). Its personnel, air and ground, numbered 28,000.[2] Still in the future – though now not far distant – were the awaited long-range aircraft on order from America, the Catalina flying-boats and the four-engined Consolidated Liberators.[3]

It was the latter which held out the highest promise of being able to do something effective at last in that dread area of ocean known as the "Atlantic Gap". All through the second half of 1940 and the first months of 1941, it was the constant endeavour of Bowhill and his Command to push their patrols and escorts further and further out from the coasts of Britain and Canada. The formation of No. 30 Wing in Iceland (Battles, Sunderlands and Hudsons; it was the addition of No. 330 Norwegian Squadron that provided the Northrop seaplanes) helped to narrow this fatal U-boat hunting-ground to some extent. The development of US bases in Newfoundland, Nova Scotia and later Greenland, was another step forward. But the "Gap" remained, and it was there that some of the bitterest battles were fought, right into 1943. The significance of the new aircraft will be appreciated when we recollect that while the Hudson could operate nearly 500 miles from base, and the Wellingtons and Whitleys could spend about two hours on station at that distance, the Sunderland could spend two hours at 600 miles and the Catalina the same amount of time at over 800 miles; but the Liberator, with its maximum fuel load of 2,500 gallons, could spend three hours patrolling over 1,100 miles from base.

During the whole of this period, however, pending the arrival of better locating devices (especially at night) and more effective offensive weapons, the anti-submarine rôle of Coastal Command was what was known, in the First World War, as "Scarecrow" – alarming the U-boat, and causing it to submerge. The best height for surfaced U-boat spotting was found to be 1,500–2,000 feet, but this meant that a vigilant look-out might see the aircraft before it saw the U-boat, or at the least simultaneously. Since a U-boat could submerge fully in 25 seconds from the sounding of the warning gong,[4] all the aircraft was likely to see was its diving "swirl" and once it was underwater there was nothing to indicate either its depth or its direction. It is hardly suprising that "kills" were few and far between; Admiral Dönitz, indeed, would boast in an interview with a Swedish journalist that "the aeroplane can no more eliminate the U-boat than a crow can fight a mole". The simile was ill-timed – August 1942, just as the "crow" was turning into an osprey. But in the early months of 1941, while ASV Mark II, with its 12-mile forward scan and 20-mile side scan, was still only for a favoured few, most Coastal Command pilots could do little more than sneak in and out of cloud and trust to luck. In one respect matters had improved: development of radio-telephony made for better communication and cooperation between surface and air convoy escorts. On the other hand, the strict wireless silence imposed on convoys made them frequently difficult for their protecting aircraft to find – and single ships even more so.

As promising for the future – but only for the future – as any of the technical advances that were being awaited, was an organizational measure adopted in February 1941. At the beginning of the war, Coastal Command had consisted of four Groups: No. 17 was a Training Group, with headquarters at Lee-on-Solent; the operational Groups were No. 15 (three and a half squadrons), headquarters Plymouth; No. 16 (five squadrons), Chatham; No. 18 (nine and a half squadrons), Rosyth. This distribution reflected the North Sea orientation of the Command at that time. After June 1940, it was no longer appropriate, and as the Battle of the Atlantic declared its true nature, it became increasingly obvious that the key sector faced the opposite way: it was the Western Approaches, leading to the estuaries of the Mersey and the Clyde. The signing away (in 1938) of British rights to the naval bases in southern Ireland, Queenstown (Cork Harbour), Berehaven (Bantry Bay) and Lough Swilly (Donegal), was not acutely felt; the question of pressure on the Government of Eire was naturally raised, but Churchill declared that "nothing but self-preservation would lead me to this", and the Defence Committee agreed.[5] The whole stress was thus thrown on the north-western approach via the North Channel, and it was recognized that Plymouth was hardly a sensible place from which to control operations in that area. The setting up of a new headquarters, with its operations rooms and elaborate communications networks, took time, but was completed in Derby House, Liverpool, by February 16, 1941, and the next day Admiral Sir Percy Noble was installed as Commander-in-Chief, Western Approaches. In this Command, cooperation between the Navy and the RAF would be brought to its highest pitch. No. 15 Group moved into the new Command area, and a new No. 19 Group took over Plymouth and the watch on the Bay of Biscay. Its day would come.

The Atlantic winter brought some relief; the gross total of sinkings dropped to 320,240 tons (76 ships) in January. But at the end of the month Hitler threatened a new sea offensive: "they will notice that we have not been sleeping", he said, and in February "they" did indeed notice – 403,393 tons sunk. The signs of a renewed U-boat attack were clear: "this mortal danger to our life-lines gnawed my bowels," wrote Churchill. He even questioned whether the increased sinkings might be due to "possible leakage of convoy routeing intelligence to enemy agents"[6]; it would be a long time yet before anyone suspected the real leakage – the penetration of the Naval Cipher and the BAMS code. On March 6 he drew up a directive entitled "The Battle of the Atlantic"; in the preamble he said "we must assume that the Battle of the Atlantic has begun" – recognizing a fact that was now some nine months old (in similar vein he attributes the beginning of the "wolf-pack" tactics to this period – and others have followed him[7] – which, as we have seen, was not the case; and even now only 30 U-boats were operational, which spells a high degree of proficiency in their captains and crews).

Churchill's directive laid down the guidelines for a defeat of the U-boats during the next four months, and this, too, proved misleading, because it was precisely four months later that the false dawn came, as we shall see. The directive was long and comprehensive; there is only space here for a few salient points:

1. We must take the offensive against the U-boat and the Focke-Wulf wherever we can and whenever we can. The U-boat at sea must be hunted, the U-boat in the building yard or in dock must be bombed. The Focke-Wulf and other bombers employed against our shipping must be attacked in the air and in their nests . . .

3. All the measures approved and now in train for the concentration of the main strength of the Coastal Command upon the North-Western Approaches, and their assistance on the East Coast by Fighter and Bomber Commands, will be pressed forward . . .

6. The Admiralty will have the first claim on all short-range AA guns and other weapons that they can mount upon suitable merchant ships plying in the danger zone . . .

7. We must be ready to meet concentrated air attacks on the ports on which we specially rely (Mersey, Clyde and Bristol Channel). They must therefore be provided with a maximum defence . . .[8]

In order, says Churchill, "to give timely directions which would clear away difficulties and obstructions and force action upon the great number of departments and branches involved", a Battle of the Atlantic Committee was set up, under his own chairmanship, which met weekly from March 19 until May 8 (then fortnightly; it was disbanded in October). It is not uncommon for the authors of directives and the members of committees to date whatever progress is made from their own deliberations; progress *was* made during the next months, but by the nature of things it could only have been the result of processes already in hand – increasing numbers of ships and aircraft, better weapons, longer-range patrols, increased proficiency. Yet Churchill's measures did have the valuable effect of concentrating attention on the greatest need – the decisive battle.

Meanwhile the U-boat offensive continued: 139 ships were sunk in March – 529,706 gross tons. What is interesting is that although U-boats claimed by far the largest share of the tonnage (243,020), they shared their tally of ships with aircraft (41 each); the Condors were doing well, and were now supported by He 111s. Seaborne catapult aircraft and escort carriers would provide the corrective; but as usual, the time was "not yet". However, March saw its successes for the defence: three of the outstanding German U-boat "aces" were eliminated. Radar improvements accounted, in each case, for the destruction of *U 47* (Prien), *U 100* (Schepke) and *U 99* (Kretschmer).

Denis Richards calls this a "turning-point"; unfortunately, it was only part of the false dawn.

April came, and it was indeed "the cruellest month", the worst month of the war at sea to date, a true reminder of that terrible April of 1917: the 1941 April tally was 195 ships sunk, 687,901 gross tons. For the first time, U-boats were eclipsed in the tonnage figures by aircraft, which accounted for 116 ships, 323,454 tons (U-boats sank 43 ships, 249,375 tons). Fortunately, the fearful total and the aircraft account were both freaks. This was the month of the British campaign in Greece, in the course of which 187,054 tons of shipping were sunk in Greek ports,[9] a prolonged "field day" for the *Luftwaffe*. Nor was it only Greek ports that were under attack; more material to the Atlantic battle were the shipping losses caused by three raids on Bristol, one on Belfast, two on Portsmouth and four on Plymouth. Churchill, in his directive, had referred to "the immense mass of damaged shipping now accumulated in our ports"; these blows added depressingly to it.

On the Atlantic "front" itself, the 1941 offensive presented a complication. Surface raiders, warships and armed merchantmen, much feared by the Admiralty at the outbreak of war, did not at first offer any serious threat: between them, they only succeeded in sinking 18 ships (74,504 tons) by the end of May 1940. Then there was a most alarming transformation: 68 ships sunk (450,844 tons) between June and December. In that month the cruiser *Hipper* broke out into the Atlantic and made her way to Brest. In January the battle-cruisers, *Scharnhorst* and *Gneisenau*, also came out, and in the course of a two-month cruise they sank 22 ships (115,000 tons) before entering Brest on March 22. *Hipper*, too, had emerged and taken her toll, including seven out of 19 ships of a Sierra Leone convoy, before returning to Brest. Needless to say, Coastal Command strained every nerve to keep watch upon these movements; however, "all attempts at the location of these enemy units were unavailing."[10] Thanks to weather conditions, the battle-cruisers were in Brest for six days before photographic reconnaissance established that fact. Once it had done so, pursuant to Churchill's directive, Bomber Command made the two ships a prime target (somewhat reluctantly, and subject, of course, to weather). In two months, 1,161 sorties were flown, and 829 tons of bombs were aimed at the battle-cruisers;[11] it is a depressing comment on the difficulty of such targets and the quality of Bomber Command's equipment that only four direct hits were made. As the AOC-in-C (Air Marshal Sir Richard Peirse) remarked,

We are not designed for this purpose and we are not particularly effective in execution.[12]

The four direct hits were damaging; some useful effect was produced by a number of the near misses; and damage to the docks and dockyard installations obviously played a significant part. But it was not a Bomber Command aircraft which produced the greatest individual result – that was reserved for a Beaufort of Coastal Command's No. 22 Squadron on April 6. With matchless courage the pilot, Flying Officer Kenneth Campbell, and his three-man crew, Sergeants J. P. Scott, W. Mullis and R. W. Hillman, came in below mast height to attack *Gneisenau*. The Beaufort was shot out of the sky by the storm of AA fire that greeted it – but not before it had dropped its torpedo on a true course to hit the battle-cruiser's stern below the waterline. Eight months later she was still under repair. Flying Officer Campbell received a posthumous Victoria Cross.

Bomber Command's efforts did not lack their reward, which became apparent in May. It was on the 18th of that month that the mighty battleship *Bismarck*, accompanied by the heavy cruiser *Prinz Eugen*, left Gdynia at the eastern end of the Baltic to make a dash into the Atlantic. It was the most serious surface threat yet, extending the Home Fleet to its limits (and shocking the nation with the sinking of the Royal Navy's pride, the battle-cruiser HMS *Hood*). But at least the combination of these two menacing vessels with *Scharnhorst* and *Gneisenau* had been ruled out by the RAF's bombing and mining. And in the tense nine-day chase that followed, with the German ships vanishing into the vast Atlantic spaces, it was Coastal Command that played a crucial part. When contact was lost on May 25, Air Chief Marshal Bowhill himself was responsible for redirecting the air search to intercept *Bismarck* on a south-easterly course, which was duly done next day by Catalina "Z for Zebra" of No. 229 Squadron, and when that aircraft was driven off by AA damage, by another Catalina of 240 Squadron. Later that day Fleet Air Arm Swordfish from *Ark Royal* inflicted the damage which enabled the Royal Navy to reach and sink its mighty enemy on May 27. And so ended the operations of heavy German surface units against the Atlantic convoys.[13]

Bowhill's tenure at Coastal Command was now drawing to an end. He left at a true turning-point, both of the war itself, and of the Command. Its main enemy, despite numerical weakness, remained grimly effective: out of a total tonnage of 511,042 sunk in May, U-boats accounted for 325,492 (58 ships).[14] However, there were hopeful signs; chief among them was the increasing involvement of the United States in the maritime war, beginning with the sale of the destroyers in 1940, continuing with the construction of Atlantic bases, and finally, in April, the extension of the American "Security Zone" to the 25th meridian. All this made life more difficult for the U-boats. In May, continuous escort right across the Atlantic was achieved. In addition, Coastal Command itself was now operating from Bathurst and Freetown on the West African coast (No. 95 Squadron, Sunderlands; No. 200 Squadron, with Hudsons, arrived in June). The Command had yet to make a kill by its own unaided efforts; on the other hand, as Denis Richards says,

> Its equipment had improved out of all recognition. The nineteen squadrons of 1939 had grown to forty. The average range of its aircraft had doubled. Efficient torpedo-bombers and long-range fighters[15] – though still all too few – had taken their place in the line of battle. More than half the aircraft of the Command had been fitted with . . . an improved ASV . . . Experiments in the camouflage of Coastal aircraft and the development of an airborne searchlight were about to be crowned with success. It was with the knowledge that many, though by no means all, of the basic problems and difficulties had been overcome that Bowhill handed over[16] to his successor, Air Marshal Sir Philip Joubert.[17]

Eight days after Bowhill's departure from Coastal Command, Hitler attacked the Soviet Union, creating his insatiable Moloch of the Eastern Front, and transforming the nature of the war.

THE STRATEGIC AIR OFFENSIVE (I)

"The leading element in bringing about our victory . . . "

31 Newall and Portal; the Growing Service; the Empire Training Scheme

Air Chief Marshal Sir Cyril Newall, KCB, CMG, CBE, AM,[1] ceased. to be Chief of the Air Staff on October 24, 1940, having held that high position for almost exactly three years and two months. When Newall took office, the RAF was smarting at what many of its senior officers considered to be a disastrous political defeat – the return of the Fleet Air Arm to the Royal Navy only a month earlier; the Secretary of State for Air, Lord Swinton, on the other hand, was one who was more disposed to welcome the compromise by which the Air Ministry held on to Coastal Command.[2] Newall's successor, as we have seen, was faced within a fortnight of his taking office with the threat of losing the land-based aircraft also, which must have prompted a wry reflection.

Defeated on one part of the Whitehall front, the RAF under Newall outwardly prospered on others. It was during his tenure that its most vigorous pre-war expansion took place, and his claim to fame lies chiefly in the manner in which he presided over this feverish and testing period. In the words of Sir John Slessor, Newall was "the prime architect of the wartime Air Force".[3] The task was sufficiently great to explain – if not excuse – failings in other directions. As commander of the 41st Wing, RFC, at Ochey in 1917, Newall had been Trenchard's forerunner as leader of an "independent" bombing force (and subsequently his deputy). Trenchard had referred to him as "one of the best generals in the air service", and strongly backed him for elevation to CAS in later years. But "generalship", in its normally accepted sense, is what we seem conspicuously to miss in Newall during these years when war loomed ever closer and finally burst upon an ill-prepared nation.

Deeply influenced by Trenchard, Newall accepted without challenge the theory of the "knock-out blow" and the bomber deterrent. He learned nothing from Spain (see p. 64); he resisted a Continental commitment which was daily becoming more obviously inevitable

251

(and with it, of course, the needs of army cooperation). He did not perceive that only airfields in France could make Bomber Command at all effective in 1939–40. He grudged the growth of the fighter force, even when it had become impossible to find a rôle for the cherished bombers (p. 91). The hard saying that neither the French nor the British Air Staffs had "given thought to the matter of war" before 1940 must stand as a professional reproach to the head of the British Staff (p. 120). And though, after May 18, Newall drastically revised his views and threw his weight behind Dowding's determination to conserve Fighter Command, in another respect he appears to have preserved what now strikes one as a deafening silence. In the "big wing" dispute, in which C-in-C of Fighter Command, the Deputy Chief of the Air Staff and two Fighter Group commanders reached a position of loggerheads amounting in one case practically to insubordination, we look in vain for any intervention by the professional head of the Service. It may be – indeed, it is more than likely and very understandable – that Newall was exhausted. Certainly, there was already afoot a surreptitious campaign (with obvious collaboration inside the RAF) to have him removed. An anonymous paper which reached the Secretary of State in August, referred to him as "a real weakness to the RAF and the nation's defence", and criticized him "on the score of inadequate mental ability, limited practical experience, weakness of character, lack of judgment and foresight, and reluctance to remove incompetent officers".[4] In particular Newall was accused of not having the strength of character to deal with Dowding – which suggests a possible source for some of the evidently inside information contained in the paper. However, it is the opinion of Lord Beaverbrook's biographer, A. J. P. Taylor, that "the opening and closing paragraphs are almost certainly Beaverbrook's composition, and that the intervening paragraphs were probably supplied by his staff".[5] This certainly fits Beaverbrook's frame of mind at that time; Robert Bruce Lockhart, dining with him on July 2, reports how he "Thundered against the Air Marshals – Newall especially – minds not elastic".[6] It would be characteristic of Beaverbrook to blow up any available fire into a great deal of smoke.

However, the more serious criticisms, many going back well beyond this anonymous poison, have to stand – though they apply equally, of course, to more than a few others. In mitigation, it must be said that few things can be more unnerving for a champion than to have his lance snatched away as he gallops into a joust – which was roughly the Air Staff's position when Bomber Command was found wanting at the very beginning of the war. And in this, as other crises, Newall performed a true service by preserving an unruffled front. Let Slessor offer the last word:

> I have seldom met a man who was so good for one's morale as Newall; when times were at their worst I could come out of his office feeling as though I'd just had a stiff whisky and soda.[7]

Neither Newall himself, nor his best friends, would have claimed for him high intellectual qualities. In this respect, his successor was a very different article. Air Chief Marshal Sir Charles Portal, KCB, DSO, MC, became Chief of the Air Staff on October 25, 1940. Lord Ismay, an intimate observer of the Chiefs of Staff Committee, wrote:

> Academically and scientifically he was probably the best educated of the Chiefs of Staff, and there was no aspect of Royal Air Force work in which he was not thoroughly versed.[8]

Churchill referred to him as "the accepted star of the Air Force",[9] and this is undoubtedly correct; the unanimity of support for Portal is impressive. Yet in one respect he and Newall were certainly alike; something that Slessor also said of Newall was even more true of Portal: he "took a bit of knowing".[10] Indeed, one wonders whether, outside his closest family circle, anyone ever did really know him.

Portal's "intelligence and efficiency"[11] are undisputed; so also are the "formidable will-power and astonishing physical stamina" which he shared with General Sir Alan Brooke, who became CIGS in December 1941, and which enabled both these officers to serve Churchill until the end of the war. The stress of this responsibility undoubtedly helped to kill their older colleague, Admiral of the Fleet Sir Dudley Pound, in October 1943.[12] Churchill's method of work, the hours he kept, and his trick of summoning his senior advisers either to his Whitehall headquarters or to Chequers at any hour of the day or night for consultations which could turn into long exhausting conversational exercises, sometimes supplemented by film shows, are well established in the lore of the Second World War. Sir David Fraser has given us a vivid impression of a day in the life of the CIGS;[13] Denis Richards does the same for Portal:

> The hard core of a Portal day was several hours' work on papers. This was broken by attendance at the COS meetings (and sometimes at those of the Defence Committee or the War cabinet as well), and by brief discussions with the VCAS, other senior officers, important visitors and his own personal staff. Telephone conversations – most frequently with

Churchill, his fellow Chiefs of Staff and senior RAF commanders – also occupied some part of every day. He rarely left London to visit a Command headquarters, still less an RAF station.[14] (Visit a few, and he might be expected to visit all) . . . With singularly little variation, and that mainly in connection with the great inter-allied conferences, he fought his war in Whitehall . . .[15]

"Work on papers", says Richards, may to some extent be measured by the 1,400 CAS folders which lie in the Public Record Office; "nearly all of them contain copies of letters and memoranda bearing Portal's name" – and this was only part of the paper burden. In addition,

> Portal himself reckoned that he attended about 2,000 COS meetings out of some 2,360 held between October 1940 and August 1945. The official minutes of a meeting often ran into twenty or more closely printed foolscap pages. These Portal had to read and check daily. But before each meeting memoranda were also circulated as a basis for the discussion. No fewer than 5,830 of these memoranda, averaging about eight pages each, were circulated during Portal's period of office . . . How many minutes from the Prime Minister Portal received in all as Chief of Air Staff is not readily ascertainable; but when Portal's staff were told, at the end of the war, to copy the important ones, the total came to over 500. It would not be possible to gather from Churchill's memoirs that Portal ever replied to a single one of these. He did, of course. Of the minutes which he addressed to Churchill, 765 are preserved in copy form in Portal's papers at Christ Church, Oxford.

Portal's 14- or 15-hour working day was, generally speaking (apart from formal occasions or the Chequers nights), broken only by his daily lunch at the Travellers Club, Pall Mall. But he did not go to the Club in search of any conviviality:

> One of the most familiar sights . . . was that of the Chief of Air Staff lunching alone at one of the small side tables, a newspaper propped up before him. Portal acted in this way not simply because he was hard-pressed but because despite his friendliness and courtesy he was at heart un-sociable.

It is this analysis which confirms that he was a difficult man to know.

There was, however, an exception to this rule. Ten days after Portal took office, he was joined, at his own insistence, by Air Chief Marshal Sir Wilfrid Freeman, in the capacity of Vice-Chief of the Air Staff.

Freeman, holding the same rank as Portal, was actually senior to him in the Air Force List (in 1922 he had been one of Portal's instructors at the first RAF Staff College course). Freeman offered to take a step down in rank in order to "regularize" their new relationship, but this did not prove to be necessary. Portal and Freeman worked together in perfect amity and concord, separated only by a green baize door dividing their rooms in the New Public Offices in King Charles Street. "That green baize door," says Sir Maurice Dean,

> deserves a second look. Propinquity plays a bigger part in human affairs than is sometimes supposed. On the shoulders of Portal and Freeman most problems of Air Force policy rested. A push on a gently resisting green baize door, a peep, and there they were. It meant much.[16]

Freeman, said Portal later, "virtually took charge of the internal policy governing the enormous wartime expansion of the Royal Air Force",[17] and this shouldering of the day-to-day running of the Service, according to Slessor, who served under them both, "left Portal far more free than would otherwise have been possible for his wider responsibilities in the Chiefs of Staff Committee".[18]

Portal's début as CAS was equivocal. We have seen how, with scarcely time to sit back in his chair, he was plunged into inter-departmental warfare over Coastal Command, and how well he acquitted himself against Beaverbrook at the height of his power. Thenceforward this formidable crony of the Prime Minister preserved a healthy respect for the new Head of the RAF, and treated him accordingly, which can only have been a national benefit. In another important respect, however, a large question mark hangs over Portal's head. It cannot have been at all pleasant to face, at the very beginning of his sufficiently onerous office, the question of the position of such a distinguished officer as Dowding, and the apparent disorder within his Command. Once again, as with Newall, we are deafened by the silence on high. It is as though these weighty matters were not the concern of either the outgoing or the incoming CAS – which prompts the question, *whose* concern were they? And it prompts the further question, if Dowding and Park were roughly treated (which is now hardly disputed) who must be blamed? Who *can* be blamed, except the man at the top? And here, perhaps, we may detect a weakness in Portal and a flaw in his relationship with Freeman. It was Portal's habit, continued throughout the war, even when Freeman had left the Air Staff, to consult him in the matter of senior appointments, and, says Denis Richards,

There was a refreshing absence of ambiguity in Freeman's verdicts on his fellow-officers and an abundance of sarcastic exaggeration which Portal, he was well aware, knew how to discount ... Portal clearly relished his friend's pungent style; and though he did not invariably follow Freeman's recommendations and in some cases could not, he undoubtedly found them a valuable supplement to those received from more official quarters.[19]

Freeman, as we have seen (p. 215) was no great admirer of Dowding in 1940 (though he later, to some extent, changed his mind[20]). It is hard to resist the conclusion that Portal was swayed by Freeman (and may also have been personally offended by Dowding's abrupt manner); an understandable desire to bring young men forward no doubt also played its part; anxiety about the night fighting could have done the rest. But two serious questions remain: first, even if Portal was personally convinced that Dowding must go (and even if he was quite right), why was the acknowledged victor of the daylight battle allowed to go in such a disrespectful fashion? And secondly, did Portal really think that the insubordination of Leigh-Mallory and the machinations surrounding the entire event were unimportant? The whole subject has an odour which refuses to die away.

What makes the "Fighter Command mystery" so especially puzzling is that Portal, in other respects, displayed a firm hand on the rudder of RAF affairs. On his very first day as CAS, he issued a Directive to Bomber Command (see below) – here, of course, he was on firm ground, as ex-C-in-C. We shall return to this subject shortly. First, however, it will be useful to glance briefly at the Service he took over after a year of war.

The great wartime expansion of the RAF, which was to be such a significant feature of the British war effort, was still in its early stages. In numbers of officers and men, however, it had already surpassed the large total of November 1918 (291,748). On September 3, 1939, its strength had been 175,692;[21] a year later it was nudging the half-million mark (437,473). But it would be during Portal's first year of office (and no doubt owing much to Freeman's ministrations) that it would make its greatest stride and approach the million: 836,916 on October 1, 1941, of whom 40,892 were officers.[22]

All through Portal's first year, a continuing shortage of aircraft would be felt, particularly of the heavier types wanted for long-range operations by Bomber and Coastal Commands. A total of 2,451 first-line aircraft at the outbreak of war had only increased to 3,106 by August 1941 – still substantially below the first-line strength of the *Luftwaffe* although British production was now well ahead of Germany's.[23] In 1941 British production almost doubled Germany's, but her first-line strength on December 1 was still below the *Luftwaffe*'s, and her increase was only 65 per cent. Worst of all was the very slow increase in the numbers of the new types. Lord Beaverbrook's rough and ready methods in the summer of 1940 had certainly produced a stimulating effect on fighter production for a short time, but it is in this persisting numerical weakness during the next 18 months (at least) that we perceive the significance of Sir Maurice Dean's remark that his influence "in the long run . . . would have been disastrous".[24]

Aircraft themselves, of course, are merely metal artefacts. Without bases and without crews (ground- as well as air) they cannot function; 1940 saw important progress in both these matters. In the five years since the beginning of RAF expansion in 1934 until 1939, the acquisition of 142 new sites for airfields had been inaugurated and largely completed; in 1940 alone the number was 126, the largest in any year.[25] As regards the servicing of aircraft on these new stations (and all others), there were, as may be supposed, serious problems. These were particularly apparent with the most highly skilled ground-crew trades, such as those of fitter, armament fitter, wireless and electrical mechanic, and instrument maker. Such people do not sprout on bushes; yet they are absolutely essential to an air force. As Air Member for Personnel in February 1939, Portal had come face to face with this very serious matter; the solution was not yet apparent, but as Denis Richards says, it is certain that

> but for some of the steps taken by Portal as AMP these deficiencies would have been worse in September 1939 and, more important, would not have been so readily overcome as the war progressed.[26]

The separation of Training Command into a Technical Training Command and a Flying Training Command in May 1940 was clearly another step in the right direction.

Flying training itself – the provision of the aircrews who alone could turn the metal artefacts into powerful weapons of war – was in the process of a transformation which Sir Maurice Dean has called "one of the most brilliant pieces of imaginative organization ever conceived".[27] This, too, owed something to Portal's energy and foresight before the war; it emerged as the Empire Air Training Scheme (later called the British Commonwealth Air Training Plan). The origin of this amazing enterprise – which was to be the very foundation of

257

the Empire's Air Forces for most of the rest of the war – was the
pre-war recognition of the dangerous limitations of a cramped, vulnerable island for training purposes (the fate of Brize Norton on August
16, referred to on p. 188, is a useful pointer). Overseas, however,
there were vast spaces available, and negotiations were set in train
with the Dominion Governments. These bore fruit in the agreement
signed on December 17, 1939, and in April 1940 the first training
courses under the scheme began. At its peak, in 1943, the Empire
Air Forces were served by no fewer than 333 flying training
schools,[28] distributed thus:

United Kingdom	153
Canada	92
Australia	26
South Africa	25
Southern Rhodesia	10
India	9
New Zealand	6
Middle East	6
USA	5
Bahamas	1

In all, between 1940 and 1945 the scheme trained and turned out[29]

from Canada	137,739	aircrew (including pilots)
United Kingdom	88,022	
Australia	27,387	
South Africa	24,814	
Southern Rhodesia	10,033	
New Zealand	5,609	
and from the United States	over 14,000.	

The benefits of the Empire Training Scheme could not be felt
at once; it came into its own when the RAF's wartime expansion
came to fruition in 1943–44. There was, indeed, an aircrew surplus
in 1941,[30] but it was for the wrong reasons – the shortage of aircraft
due to production failures, and an unwise shortening of training
periods in Operational Training Units which led only to reduced
efficiency on operations themselves, and increased wastage through
accidents, especially on return from operations.[31]

As Portal took up the reins, Bomber Command was just emerging
from its defensive phase (counter-invasion strikes) and resuming the
rôle for which it had always been intended – the offensive against

Germany. Coastal Command, as we have seen, was deep into a stern apprenticeship to the anti-U-boat war. Fighter Command, flushed with daylight victory, was finding success far more elusive at night. In 1941 it began making progress – bedevilled, once again, by the "numbers game", whose effect was as deceptive as in the Battle of Britain.[32] An attempt to find the Command a new, offensive rôle, which we shall shortly notice, did not produce the expected results. Meanwhile a new burden had fallen on the RAF, a drain on its slender resources whose rewards were all in the distant future: cooperation with the Army in the defence of the Middle East. The Chief of Staff would clearly not lack occupation.

32 Bomber offensive resumed; German morale; area bombing

So Bomber Command was embarked upon the strategic air offensive which, for so many years, had seemed to be the very *raison d'être* of the RAF. War had decreed otherwise. War had already shown that unprotected bombers could not operate in daylight; war had cast doubt on the effectiveness of night bombing with the Command's existing equipment; the war brushed aside the Command's feeble endeavours and strode forward to Germany's great victory in the West. And when the RAF took the right of the line in the summer of 1940, it was not with Bomber Command, but with Fighter Command; and with Fighter Command it won the first battle for survival. It participated in the second struggle for survival (which would not be won for a long time yet) with Coastal Command. But survival is never an absolute while war continues; survival can only be clinched by victory. The ardent spirit and resolution of the Prime Minister and the men around him never ceased to look beyond survival, to the winning of victory. But how?

Churchill had no doubts. Just as the Battle of Britain was about to begin, he wrote to Beaverbrook:

> ... when I look round to see how we can win the war I see that there is only one sure path. We have no Continental army which can defeat the German military power. The blockade is broken and Hitler has Asia and probably Africa to draw from. Should he be repulsed here or not try invasion, he will recoil eastward, and we have nothing to stop him. But there is one thing that will bring him back and bring him down, and that is an absolutely devastating, exterminating attack by very heavy bombers from this country upon the Nazi homeland. We must be able to overwhelm them by this means, without which I do not see a way through.[1]

Like so many of Churchill's wartime pronouncements, this goes to the heart of the matter. The path ahead may not have been as "sure" as he liked to think, but it was, without doubt, the only one. The only means – for several years ahead – by which Britain could carry the war to her main enemy was by Bomber Command, which would thus very shortly have to take its place on the right of the line and stay there, whatever might betide. Some two months later Churchill re-formulated his thoughts for the benefit of his Cabinet colleagues and the Chiefs of Staff:

> The Navy can lose us the war, but only the Air Force can win it. Therefore our supreme effort must be to gain overwhelming mastery in the air. The Fighters are our salvation, but the Bombers alone provide the means of victory.[2]

This is one of the terrible simplicities of the Second World War. It resembles closely the terrible simplicity – the over-riding demands of the French Alliance – which forced the BEF, between 1915 and 1917, into that series of vain and costly attacks (lacking numbers, equipment, training and experienced leaders) which left such an indelible imprint of horror on that war. The compulsions of 1915 and 1940 produced, as Sir John Slessor said, "two of the most unbelievable manifestations of human courage and endurance in the history of war – the infantry of 1914–1918 and the bomber crews of 1939–1945".[3] It is a compulsion which predominates over all considerations of material weakness or strength, good tactics or bad, immediate balances of profit and loss. There was no other way.

With that important analogy established, there are some equally important differences to be noticed. First, it bears pondering that while the compulsion of the first war was due to the discipline of having an ally, the compulsion of the second was obedient to the discipline of having none. Which serves at least to underline the grim truth that whether inside or outside an alliance, there is no substitute for strength. And secondly, there is the very important difference indeed that, while the 1915–18 BEF, for better or for worse, could only make its effort by combat with its mighty enemy, the German Army, for Bomber Command there was another option. Bomber Command could carry the war directly to the German civil population. Bomber Command could seek to realize the premises of the "knock-out blow". And it could attempt this, as Churchill so early perceived, by the method of "absolutely devastating, exterminating attack".

"Exterminating": the prospect of exterminating the civil population of Germany was distinctly remote in July 1940, and in the circumstances, let it be admitted, not unappealing. It was closer acquaintance, when it became a more practical proposition, and uneasy apprehension of what it might be meaning in terms of life and death and pain to very large numbers of people who might or might not be Nazis, or pro-Nazis, or privately anti-Nazi in varying degrees, which caused the extermination policy to be viewed askance by a not inconsiderable number of people at the time – and, of course, by many more in later years who have had the advantage of not being under the compulsions and the stresses of the war. The writer can assure them that the shriek of a descending bomb can strip the mind to some very stark essentials, and arouse some implacable sentiments.

It must be understood, too, that the sense of what bombing would actually mean was not confined to Churchill – though characteristically it was he who used the grim word that signifies it. Just over a week after the Prime Minister had written his letter to Beaverbrook, Portal, in his capacity as Bomber Command C-in-C, was writing to the DCAS (in the course of an Air Staff/Bomber Command debate on bombing policy). In his Command, he said,

> we have the one directly offensive weapon in the whole of our armoury, the one means by which we can *undermine the morale of a large part of the enemy people*, shake their faith in the Nazi régime, and at the same time and with the very same bombs, dislocate the major part of their heavy industry and a good part of their oil production.[4]

"Morale" is a cosmetic word. Attacking morale, whatever phrases it may be dressed up in, really means only one thing: putting the fear of death into individuals. On a collective scale, it means threatening a massacre. This is, of course, disputed; Denis Richards, whose wise and well-chosen words are frequently quoted in these pages must now be quoted in another sense. In his biography of Portal, agreeing that Portal was definitely an advocate of destroying German industrial towns, he says:

> ... his object was to demolish factories, communications, the homes of the workers, the apparatus and amenities of major urban life. It was not to massacre civilians, who, he hoped, would retreat from the urban areas to the countryside with consequent loss of production, or, if they remained, suffer loss of morale from hours spent in shelters and from the reduced amenities of life. To many, bearing in mind the weight and fury of Bomber Command's attacks from 1942 onwards, this distinction may seem unreal, or even hypocritical.[5]

Alas, it does. It has to be asked, what was it that would cause the German urban populations to "retreat to the countryside"? What would cause them to "suffer loss of morale" if they remained? Surely, it was the simple fear of being blown to bits. "Morale", in a bombing directive, means either the threat or the reality of blowing men, women and children to bits.

It may be noted – and remembered – that in July 1940, with the "Blitz" still in the future, this programme did not appeal to the Air Staff. It informed Portal that "moral effect, although an extremely important subsidiary result of air bombardment,[6] cannot in itself be decisive. There must be material destruction as a primary object." Effective material destruction, said the Air Staff, was the strategic objective, and other considerations "should not influence strategical factors to the point where moral effect is taken as the primary, instead of the subsidiary, object".[7] There the matter rested for a while; but by October the *Luftwaffe* had well embarked upon another course of instruction of the British people and their leaders in the nature of total war; anger and vengeance for German bombing raids had become significant motives – and Portal became CAS. Air policy, Bomber Command policy, the whole course of the strategic offensive, were drawn inexorably towards the method which not even Churchill now called "extermination", though "morale" would still be widely used, and even more generally, "area bombing".

Portal's draft Directive to Bomber Command on October 25 set the seal upon the new development.[8] It prescribed two primary objectives: oil and morale. Thus began a *pas-de-deux* of alternating targets which was to continue for the remainder of the war – and not always with the harmony and synchronization suggested on this occasion. Sir Richard Peirse (Portal's successor at High Wycombe), who was beginning to appreciate some of the limitations of his Command, and feared that the proposals of the draft Directive might have the effect of spreading its strength too thin, made some demur; but the final Directive, issued on October 30 "showed remarkably little change in form or emphasis".[9] With the invasion danger past, or at least in abeyance for the time being, and the invasion fleet dispersed, Bomber Command would resume its interrupted attack on Germany. Conscious of past errors, the Directive stated the aim of achieving "a more decisive effect, both in the material and moral spheres by a greater concentration of our offensive air attacks". The time, it said, "seems particularly opportune to make a definite attempt with our offensive to affect the morale of the German people when they can no longer expect an early victory and are faced with the near approach of winter and the certainty of a long war". The Directive stressed that "if bombing is to have its full moral effect it must on occasions produce heavy material destruction. Widespread light attacks, if there are never any heavy attacks, are more likely to produce contempt for bombing than fear of it." In the intervals between the heavy attacks, operations "should be spread over the widest possible area so as to take advantage of the fear induced by the concentrated attacks . . ."[10]

Oil is unquestionably a legitimate military target; as we have seen (p. 141) Bomber Command's first strategic attack made oil plants its primary objective. They continued to hold top or high priority until the Command was forced on to the defensive in July 1940. Inspired by Lord Hankey, a body of influential opinion constantly pressed the advantages of striking at the German oil industry.[11] In the final stages of the war, this strategy paid magnificent dividends. But in 1940 two disadvantages in attacking oil targets loomed large: first, they were difficult to hit, even in the best weather conditions, and secondly, a number of them were at a distance from heavily populated centres, so that only minimal side-effects could be anticipated from attacking them. It was, in other words, to a large extent a choice *between* oil and morale.

Morale, as an objective, offered great temptation, thanks to the complete misjudgment of the German character and situation which reigned in all sections of the British consciousness. Government, Services, Press and people shared the same self-glorifying delusions. Nowhere are these better expressed than in the memorandum which Lord Trenchard, from his backstage position, addressed to the Chief of Staff after deep cogitation in May 1941:

When we have surveyed the whole area of the struggle and the factors involved, what is the outstanding fact? It is the ingrained morale of the British nation which is nowhere more strongly manifest than in its ability to stand up to losses and its power to bear the whole strain of war and its casualties. Strategically it must be sound to hammer the weak points of the enemy . . . Where then is Germany's weak point? It is to be found in precisely the sphere in which I began this paper by stating that we had a great strength. All the evidence of the last war and of this shows that the German nation is peculiarly susceptible to air bombing. While the ARP services are probably organised with typical German efficiency, their total disregard to [*sic*] the well-being of the population leads to a dislocation of ordinary life which has its inevitable reaction on civilian morale. The ordinary people are neither allowed, nor offer, to play their part in rescue or restoration work; virtually imprisoned in their shelters or within the

263

bombed area, they remain passive and easy prey to hysteria and panic without anything to mitigate the inevitable confusion and chaos. There is no joking in the German shelters as in ours, nor the bond which unites the public with ARP and Military services here of all working together in a common cause to defeat the attacks of the enemy.

This, then, is their weak point compared with ourselves, and it is at this weak point that we should strike and strike again.[12]

There is little doubt that Trenchard, writing just as the first German night offensive ceased (London was attacked by 507 bombers on May 10; air raid casualties in Britain in just over four months of 1941 amounted to 18,007 killed and 20,744 injured), was expressing a British "gut-reaction". The comments of the Chiefs of Staff are interesting. Sir Dudley Pound agreed with Trenchard's general thesis, but said "the paper is a complete over-statement and it suffers from the dangers of all over-statement". General Sir John Dill was less critical:

With our existing strength, and allowing for inevitable diversions of effort on to other targets, it is unlikely that we could achieve results on a large enough scale to justify selecting morale as our primary aim *at present*. At the same time it will almost certainly be the most profitable target when our bomber force expands . . .

Sir Charles Portal agreed emphatically with Trenchard's views; taking into account the evident defects of Bomber Command at that stage, he said:

. . . we should concentrate our efforts against a limited number of objectives and aim at sustaining our attack on them. Even during the period of short summer nights, suitable objectives are to be found in the densely populated and industrially important Ruhr area.

He endorsed Trenchard's faith in the superior staying power of the British people, but added that it "should be fortified to the utmost practicable extent by material aids designed to alleviate the hardships that have to be endured".[13]

Trenchard had, of course, always been a believer in the moral effect of bombing (see p. 9); loud protests by burgomasters to the German Government at the activities of his own Independent Force in 1918 no doubt fortified this belief, and he would seem to have conveniently forgotten his own disgust at similar hysterical manifestations in Britain the previous year. The stoicism of Madrid and Barcelona did not alter his conviction – and there is no doubt that it was widely shared. Once more we face a damaging consequence of misunderstanding of the First World War. The growing tendency throughout the Twenties and Thirties to look upon 1914–18 as a great British tragedy, regardless of what it was doing to the enemy, led straight to serious incomprehensions of the Germans. Failure to realize that the British Army, despite the initial weakness, on the Somme, at Arras and at Ypres, was subjecting the Germans to what, in the least case, one of their generals called "the greatest martyrdom of the World War",[14] meant equal failure to appreciate the great fortitude with which the German Army endured its terrible ordeal. Some who observed it were less blind; Captain Cyril Falls, RA, later a distinguished historian, wrote:

> The commanders who had such troops to rely on in days of adversity were fortunate. It was almost impossible to ask or expect of them more than they were ready to give and capable of giving.[15]

The same tribute could be paid to the German Army between 1939 and 1945. But in each case it must be borne in mind that this great conscript force was really a cross-section of the nation from which it sprang. The qualities and defects of the Army reflected its parentage. And in both wars the German civilians also displayed great fortitude; in World War One, by their stoical endurance of privation – the grim "turnip winter" of 1916–17 when food supplies failed, and the Allied blockade which caused serious malnutrition whose effects were seen in the toll of the influenza pandemic; in World War Two by their amazing endurance of the rigours of bombing. Nothing could be more wrong than Trenchard's (and Portal's) diagnosis that German morale was a "weak point" and could be easily overthrown. Overthrown it definitely was in 1945 – by a combination of circumstances:

Shattering losses on the Eastern Front

The Soviet Army's remorseless advance into Germany

The intensification of bombing due to the defeat of the *Luftwaffe*

The advance of the Western Allies

These supply the context of the last, obviously intensely destructive phase of the final bombing offensive.[16] Even without that phase, stark defeat was staring Germany in the face, and nothing undermines morale so readily as that. But to assume in 1940–41, when Germany was still flushed with vast victories, and her strength undiminished, that her morale could be *easily* overthrown, was a very grave error.

It was an error, furthermore, which becomes even more difficult to understand when one considers the instrument with which it was

265

intended to achieve this goal. It was with a force composed of Wellingtons, Whitleys and Hampdens (and even sometimes some Blenheims) that the Air Staff convinced itself that it achieved such results that

> the population of Western Germany took to its shelters, cowered under an incessant rain of high explosive, and plotted rebellion against the hated Nazi régime.[17]

It could not have been more wrong.

We have seen above how the RAF was suffering from aircraft production failures; these were the more disturbing in the light of the expansion of Bomber Command which was so palpably necessary, and which was set in hand shortly after Portal's (and Freeman's) arrival. Two targets were set: "Target Force C", a total of 100 Heavy[18] and Medium squadrons, of which 50 per cent would be "Stirling" (i.e. four-engined) types by mid-1942; "Target Force A", 75 Heavy and 20 Medium squadrons by the end of 1941. This programme, taking into account the number of stations which would be required to operate it, represented "approximately 100 per cent increase in the size of Bomber Command".[19] An extra Group was contemplated for the operation of "A", and another later for "C". The production shortfall was making sad work of this plan. Even by mid-1941, against an initial establishment of some 700 aircraft, Bomber Command could only average about 400 bombers with operational crews a night.[20] (By comparison we may note that the *Luftwaffe*, though not designed as a strategic force, during the course of the "Blitz" attacked with over 400 aircraft on seven occasions: on London, October 15, 1940 (410), December 8 (413) and March 19, 1941 (473); on Coventry, November 14, 1940 (449); and on London again, April 16, 1941 (685), April 19 (712) and May 10 (507). The attacking force on April 19 was thus larger than the full initial establishment of Bomber Command even three months later.)

As disconcerting as the shortage of aircraft was the assessment of what they were actually doing when they reached Germany. In a striking phrase, Churchill, on October 20, 1940, urged the Secretary of State and the CAS that "a whole-hearted effort shall be made to cart a large number of bombs into Germany"; this was to be performed by a "second-line" bomber force, without prejudice to the "accurate bombing of military objectives" by the first line.[21] Only a few men in responsible positions were beginning to apprehend that even the first line was not doing much more than "carting bombs into Germany".

One of them was Sir Richard Peirse, and his demur to Portal's October 25 draft Directive was in part due to the conclusion that he had reached that "on the longer-range attacks only one out of every five aircraft which he despatched actually found the target. On the short-range attacks, he thought one in three found the target."[22] On November 12, the chairman of a Group Navigation Officers' conference in Bomber Command (Wing Commander L. K. Barnes) pronounced his conclusion that only 35 per cent of all bombers despatched were reaching their primary targets. These gloomy perceptions were not generally well received in 1940, and certainly not for wide consumption; in due course they would receive striking confirmation. Here we need only glance ahead to note that in May 1941 it was accepted that approximately 50 per cent of the Command's bombs were falling in open country.[23]

The effect of all these doubts about Bomber Command's performance was, of course, to make the doom of the German civilians more certain. It is, as normally in history, wrong to make cut-and-dried statements about attitudes and bombing policies. The Air Staff and Bomber Command itself were quite capable of pursuing two or more policies at the same time and of changing attitudes according to new circumstances or information (no fewer than 45 Directives to the Command between 1940 and 1945 are listed in the Official History). But from 1941 onwards, it is a fact that "the overwhelming majority of its attacks consisted of area bombing at night", and the chief reason for this was, quite simply, that "the only target on which the night force could inflict effective damage was a whole German town".[24] The AHB Narrative associates this recognition frankly with Portal, and a more pessimistic but at the same time realistic attitude which he brought to the Air Staff deliberations, with the result that

> ... due allowance was made for the inaccuracy of bombing, by ensuring that targets selected were not isolated, but if possible in large centres of population and industry. This was the reason for the initiation of area bombing and the selection of "industrial centres" instead of factories.[25]

"Normal" bombing of Germany continued in November and December 1940: 283 sorties in five attacks on Berlin between November 1 and December 24; 279 sorties (three attacks) on Hamburg in November (none in December); 205 sorties (six attacks) on Cologne; varying numbers on Düsseldorf, Gelsenkirchen (oil plants), Duisburg, Essen, Bremen, Kiel, Munich (November 8, coinciding with the Nazi Party rally), Magdeburg, Merseburg (oil plants) and Mannheim. All were intended to hit specific targets, indisputable military objectives; only one attack managed three figures – 131 sorties against Hamburg on November 16. Losses varied according to target, accident and weather; Germany was not yet formidably defended against air attack – the real development of defences came in the following year under the aegis of General Kammhuber. Yet sometimes there were shocks; on the day after much activity against different targets including Berlin, Churchill minuted to Sinclair and Portal:

> This amounts to a loss of eleven of our bombers in one night. I said the other day by Minute that operations were not to be pressed unduly during these very adverse weather conditions. We cannot afford to have losses of this kind in view of your very slow replacements. If you go on like this you will break the bomber force down to below a minimum of grave emergencies. No results have been achieved which would in any way justify or compensate for these losses. I consider the loss of eleven aircraft out of one hundred and thirty-nine – i.e. about 8 per cent – a very grievous disaster at this stage of our bomber development.[26]

While all this was going on, however, a quite different type of operation, conforming to Portal's own convictions and drawing inspiration from the damaging German attack on Coventry on November 14/15, was being planned. Under the codename ABIGAIL, one of three designated industrial towns was to be attacked in strength, "without specific objective other than an industrial centre".[27] The intention of the ABIGAIL raid was "'to cause the maximum possible destruction in a selected German town', and was therefore a radical departure from the previous policy of bombing industrial objectives only".[28] The towns selected were Bremen (ABIGAIL-JEZEBEL), Düsseldorf (ABIGAIL-DELILAH) and Mannheim (ABIGAIL-RACHEL); the original selection was DELILAH, but adverse weather reports brought a late change of plan on the afternoon of December 16. Such are the chances of life and death in air warfare: Düsseldorf was spared that night; the experiment would be made at Mannheim.

The original concept of an ABIGAIL was that not less than 200 bombers should take part – it was not a large number; the Germans sent more than 200 to Britain on 29 occasions between November 14, 1940 and May 16, 1941. However, on the night of December 16/17, Bomber Command was only able to muster 134 for ABIGAIL-RACHEL. Once more drawing on the lesson of Coventry, the advance guard of the attack was a detachment of 14 Wellingtons of No. 3 Group carrying their maximum load of four-lb incendiary bombs, whose fires would provide a beacon for the following waves. "This was the first instance of the use of a 'pathfinder' force."[29] In good weather conditions, with good visibility, 47 out of 61 Wellingtons, 33 out of 35 Whitleys, 20 out of 29 Hampdens and three out of nine Blenheims succeeded in finding and bombing Mannheim. "Results reported by all the successful aircraft were satisfactory".[30]

> Bombs were clearly seen to fall all over the target area and countless fires and many large explosions are referred to in all reports . . . In the southern part of the target area dense black smoke was observed as though from an oil fire. Aircraft arriving late in the night report that many blocks of buildings in the western and south-eastern areas of the target were ablaze and at Neckerstadt there was a continuous series of explosions thought to be from a munitions dump.[31]

Two Hampdens and one Blenheim did not return; three Blenheims crashed on return, two crews being saved; one Wellington crashed on take-off, three members of the crew being killed. The total loss was thus seven aircraft and 17 aircrew.[32] Sir Richard Peirse signalled his congratulations to all concerned in what was considered a highly successful operation.

Satisfaction was short-lived; on December 21 a Spitfire of the Photographic Reconnaissance Unit succeeded at the second attempt in photographing Mannheim in daylight.

> From the mosaic, it was immediately apparent to Sir Richard Peirse that the operation had "failed in its primary object . . ." Though "considerable damage" had been done, the photographs showed "a wide dispersal" of the attack.[33]

With area bombing and the terrorization of the German civilians thus making a highly dubious début, it is appropriate to break off the narrative of the strategic offensive at this point to consider what was undoubtedly one of its most important adjuncts and one of the RAF's outstanding successes throughout the war – the Photographic Reconnaissance Unit.

33 *Photographic reconnaissance*

Photographic reconnaissance is an element of air warfare whose necessity seems so self-evident that it is hard to grasp the initial difficulties which it had to overcome. First and foremost of these was the fact that until March 1938 photographic interpretation was in the hands of the Army, and the whole photography exercise was regarded as a survival of the trench warfare of 1914–18, when the RFC's aerial surveys had made possible the revolution in artillery techniques known as "predicted shooting". The RAF, with much else on its mind, neglected the subject; in 1939 it possessed neither special aircraft to take the photographs, nor special cameras for use at great heights, nor special developing apparatus, nor special techniques of interpretation – all of which proved to be absolute necessities. It was Air Chief Marshal Ludlow-Hewitt who directed serious attention to these matters in his "Readiness for War" Report of March 1939 (see p. 89) – but that was late in the day.

For Bomber Command, photography offered three vital gifts: important help in recognizing targets; firm evidence of damage done (or not done); and identification of the aircraft which had found their targets. The last of these was achieved by photographing during the run-up, and in September 1939 few perceived that this would have to be done at night, requiring many efficient night cameras; indeed, despite Ludlow-Hewitt's emphatic warnings, the value of air reconnaissance itself was only just being realized in the Air Ministry.[1] Lower down in the Command, even after war had begun, there was a perceptible indifference to it, amounting at times to outright scepticism. No. 2 Group's Blenheims were the chief agents of photographic reconnaissance; they were too slow and vulnerable, and lacked the altitude performance to be really useful. But even when Spitfires were introduced (against Dowding's sharp protests), the small-scale photographs which the Special Survey Flight brought back were often dismissed as useless by Bomber Command Photographic Interpretation. As late as mid-May 1940, a report on two reconnaissance sorties said:

> Sadly enough the scale of the photographs taken by both sorties defies interpretation, reduces the effort expended to futility and the writer to tears. There is absolutely nothing to be gained by the activities of these aircraft. The sole achievement is waste of petrol, time, energy and imagination.[2]

Two days later, with mounting frustration:

> On yet another occasion, excellent but completely useless photographs have been produced by this unit. A scale of 1/48750 or 1 inch to 1,350 yards on the photographs is utterly futile for the assessment of damage caused by bombing or for reporting of activity.[3]

What was lacking, of course, was the right equipment; improved

270

cameras, using a 20in lens (as against the 8in of the original F.24) were needed and in due course provided – but like every innovation or development, exasperatingly slowly at first; a small but forward-looking private firm, the Aircraft Operating Company at Wembley, placed its Swiss-made Wild photogrammetric machine and operators at the RAF's disposal, transforming the potential of interpretation. Above all, inspired by the inventive imagination of Wing Commander Sidney Cotton (aided by Flying Officer M. V. Longbottom) the Photographic Development Unit came into existence at Heston in April 1940. It was Cotton who first "charmed two Spitfires out of Dowding",[4] stripped and polished them to a sleek aerodynamic efficiency which took them to 35,000 feet and gave them (in the form of the "Type D") "a safe range of 1,700–1,800 miles, more than sufficient to reach Trondheim, Stettin and Marseilles and capable of reaching Toulon and Genoa".[5] The "Type D" not only carried 145 gallons of extra fuel, but unlike the "B", "C" and "F" types, it "involved a radically new construction of a peculiarly difficult nature". Originally ordered in October 1939, this aircraft did not become available until over a year later. An Air Ministry inquiry into the inordinate delay discovered that two machines on order had been taken off the priority list and no further work was being done on them. It took a month to regain for them equal priority with standard Spitfires for Fighter Command – another casualty of Ministry of Aircraft Production methods under Beaverbrook.

In July 1940 the Photographic Development Unit at Heston became the Photographic Reconnaissance Unit, while the semi-civilian Interpretation Unit at Wembley took the official title of Photographic Interpretation Unit as part of the RAF. Both were now part of Coastal Command, whose reconnaissance needs during the period of invasion danger were over-riding (not to say overwhelming). Even when that danger had passed, it proved convenient to keep the photographic rôle within this Command, where it served the whole of the RAF and was also immensely useful to the Royal Navy. The special needs of Bomber Command were recognized, however, and it enjoyed "a privileged position in relation to other users".[6] A casualty of this rationalization was Wing Commander Cotton; having pioneered photographic reconnaissance (with Group Captain F. W. Winterbotham) he now ceased to command the PRU. The Air Council paid tribute to "the great gifts of imagination and inventive thought which [he had] brought to bear on the technique of photography in the Royal Air Force". During the experimental stages of the Unit, the value of a "dynamic individualist" like Cotton was evident, despite the "many inconveniences" arising from his forthright methods and utterances. With its rôle well established, however,

> the smooth working of the Unit demanded first and foremost the qualities of command and organisation too seldom associated with the qualities of imagination and initiative needed in the initial stages.[7]

Cotton was succeeded by his second-in-command, Wing Commander G. W. Tuttle DFC, a former flying instructor and fighter pilot. Sir Maurice Dean remarks that it was lucky that the RAF, in 1939–40, was still a young and unconventional Service;

> But for this, the problem of coupling the genius of Cotton and the necessary rigidities of a disciplined service might well have proved unmanageable.[8]

With the return of Bomber Command to its strategic rôle, the importance of photography steadily increased, but it was a long time before full recognition was reached that "the camera was really the sole reliable means of judging the accuracy or otherwise of the Bomber Command attacks".[9] It would take some hard knocks to shift the prevailing Bomber Command view that photographs were "a useful adjunct to bombing, but not a vital necessity".[10] It is easy to be sarcastic about this frame of mind, but more profitable to try to understand it:

> It must be remembered that until the spread of night cameras over a sufficient part of the force to give representative results, crews' reports of what they believed they had accomplished were treated as reliable. Proved cases of error, usually revealed by daylight photographic reconnaissance, came as a great shock, and at first threw doubt on the efficiency of the photographic interpretation rather than on the visual reports.[11]

It was neither an easy nor an agreeable task to grill and cross-question exhausted, strung up crews as they returned from operations, or to confront them with evidence that they had never even reached their targets; nor did senior officers like it:

> At one Group headquarters, the intelligence officers found it was best not to say anything about the photographs which did not show the target area; at another an officer who passed to his chief an interpretation showing that an attack had missed its mark found it later on his desk with scrawled across it in red: "I do not accept this report".[12]

It is one of the curiosities, and unfortunate, that during this time when all was uncertain and unfamiliar, the overall drift of crews' claims tended to be borne out by other Intelligence sources – agents' reports, information from neutrals, study of the German Press:

> These told often of heavy damage and lengthy disruption of transport and other facilities; or bolstered up current belief in the effect of that imponderable weapon, the attack on morale ... There can have been no greater contrast imaginable than that between the enthusiastic reports received in bomber crew-rooms and the "travellers' tales" from Germany via Sweden or Switzerland on the one hand, and on the other hand the bleak pictures of scarcely-damaged towns brought back by PRU Spitfires and the tell-tale night photographs of fields and open country. Rarely can there have been a campaign in which Intelligence was so conflicting.[13]

The more realistic Group commanders came to the gloomy conclusion that, in the absence of navigational aids, most of their crews were bombing on ETA (estimated time of arrival – the most rough-and-ready system possible). We have already noted Sir Richard Peirse's misgivings about his Command's actual performance. As operations continued in 1941, as the AHB Narrative says,

> So adverse were the conditions in which the offensive was attempted that it might be thought the attack should have been called off completely until the difficulties were surmountable.[14]

The Narrative offers two reasons why this could not be so: first, the wide recognition that "the bomber force could only become proficient by constant effort, and that experience was necessary as well as more strength and better equipment". The explanation of "gaining experience" is familiar; it is to be met with as the sun sets on many stricken fields – *passim* between 1915 and 1917, again after setbacks in the Western Desert between 1941 and 1942, after the "bloody nose" of Dieppe, and many more such occasions. The layman is tempted to ask what profit experience is to the dead, and if there are a great many of them laymen and others ask the question with some vehemence. It is nevertheless a fact that the Army of 1918 *was* vastly more proficient, more adept in battle skills, thanks to the grim experience of its predecessors in the previous three years, that the Eighth Army of 1942/43 was a different animal from the one that had fought in BATTLEAXE, CRUSADER and Gazala – for the same reason; and that the D-Day landings were amazingly economical in life, largely thanks to Dieppe. Experience, even if hardly bought, *is* an asset in war.

Secondly, there was the Intelligence enigma, the rosy pictures contradicting the work of the PRU. And here national temperament plays a part. The reluctance to face unpleasant truths was nothing new; it was well-known between 1915–17, that to report uncut enemy wire, or impassable bog on the front of a forthcoming attack was not, generally speaking, the avenue to congratulation and promotion. The hard truth is that both the BEF of the earlier war and Bomber Command now *had* to go on attacking. The BEF had to maintain an "active front" to remind the French that it was in the war; Bomber Command had to go on attacking to remind the Germans that *it* was in the war. To dwell upon the difficulties (indeed, impossibilities) struck many of those in command as merely unhelpful and depressing. This is a not uncommon attribute of command, with a good side as well as a bad. Service leaders, sending their sailors, soldiers and aircrew into battle, tend to estimate their chances with courageous optimism. Others, including military historians, enjoying the fuller knowledge conferred by hindsight, are more prone to dwell upon the difficulties and the fault of under-estimating them. It is well that military historians do not often conduct wars. The author was made vividly aware of this during the Falkland Islands campaign of 1982. His own disposition, instructed by history, was to brood upon the immense problems of logistics and the dire consequences of defeat. The commanders on the spot, though well aware of these and the penalty of error, were more disposed to concentrate on the possibility of victory, and duly obtained it. They were fortunate; Bomber Command in 1941 was less so.

No sooner had Sir Richard Peirse digested the unhappy truth which photographic reconnaissance revealed about Mannheim, than the same source brought him more. Of all specific targets in Germany, the oil plants were regarded as the most important and received attention accordingly. The current assumption was that "an oil plant could be put out of action for four months by aiming four hundred 500-lb bombs at it, and that this could be achieved by two hundred sorties".[15] In late December the two oil plants at Gelsenkirchen, in the Ruhr, were subjected to what was supposed to be a devastating onslaught; 162 aircraft, carrying 159 tons of bombs (exclusive of incendiaries) were to attack one plant, and 134 aircraft, carrying 103 tons (exclusive of incendiaries) the other. The expectation, from such a weight of attack, was that serious damage had been done. But on December 24 the PRU Spitfires brought back excellent photographs of the two plants; when these were examined it was seen that neither had sustained any major damage.

There was no sign of any important repairs having been carried out and few bomb craters could be seen in the vicinity. It was obvious . . . that the greater part of the 260 tons of bombs, excluding incendiaries, which (the crews) reported as having fallen on them, had not done so, and, on the contrary, had missed by an immeasurable distance.[16]

This was a cruel blow for Sir Richard Peirse; at the top levels of the Air Staff, however, "the significance of this report was not immediately appreciated".[17] There were months still to go before Photographic Reconnaissance established its full authority.

34 Oil; "diversions"; heavy bombers; the Mosquito

The Gelsenkirchen photographs could hardly have been more tactlessly timed. Lord Hankey's master Committee on Preventing Oil from reaching Germany (POG), set up in October 1939, was reinforced by an Intelligence sub-committee (the Lloyd Committee) in January 1940. Headed by Geoffrey Lloyd, the Secretary for Petroleum in the Board of Trade's Mines Department, this included representatives of the Services and other departments, and the head of the Intelligence Branch of the Ministry of Economic Warfare. This Ministry was naturally a key adviser on all matters relating to the German economy, and thus played a very large part in shaping Bomber Command's plans. But the Lloyd Committee drew its information from other sources also, among them the technical staffs of the great oil companies. Its assembled talents were responsible for some of the more feverish prognostications in a campaign not lacking in what Marshal of the Royal Air Force Sir Arthur Harris would later contemptuously label "panaceas" (see p. 493).

One of the great surprises of the war would be the expansion potential and resilience of the German economy, viewed by orthodox "experts" as the Achilles' heel of Germany's military power, and no part of the heel more tender than oil supply. On May 31, 1940 the Lloyd Committee reported to the 20th meeting of the POG its belief that if the RAF could destroy some 350,000 tons of German oil by September 1, Germany "would then be on the danger list as regards her oil supplies".[1] This sort of language would recur; in December, encouraged by Bomber Command's own estimates of what it had been accomplishing, the Lloyd Committee concluded "that a fifteen per cent reduction in synthetic oil output had been achieved by the expenditure of only 539 tons of bombs or, in other words, no more than 6.7 per cent of the total effort expended by Bomber Command

275

against industrial targets, communications or invasion ports".[2] It stated that the oil position in Axis-controlled Europe was deteriorating rapidly, and spoke of a "quick death clinch". This was heady talk for December 1940.

Nevertheless, the Air Staff was impressed, and Portal drew up a memorandum for the Chiefs of Staff on December 29, arguing that the destruction of 17 major synthetic oil plants during the next six months would cause the loss of potential production of nearly 1½ million tons of oil.

> Such a loss, even though it would leave the Rumanian supplies uninterrupted, would, in the context of the Lloyd report, be a heavy and possibly fatal blow to Germany ... Sir Charles Portal thought that Bomber Command could, in fact, destroy these seventeen targets. "Assuming that we can hope for an average of nine clear nights a month," he told his colleagues, "this entails the employment of a minimum of 95 sorties on each of these nights, i.e., 855 sorties per month and 3,420 sorties in four months. On the basis of the present strength of our bomber force this effort should be within our capabilities.[3]

On January 7 the Chiefs of Staff accepted Portal's analysis, endorsing oil as the primary target for Bomber Command during the next six months, with morale as a secondary target. On January 13 the Defence Committee approved the COS proposals. London had been under attack the night before (141 bombers) and the night before that (137); this was the third attack already in 1941, with three in December, including one by 413 bombers on December 8. The War Cabinet was not in a mood to discourage ruthlessness by Bomber Command; the feeling was that the British people were entitled to know that they were giving as good as they were getting. On January 15 Sir Richard Peirse received what the Official History calls "the most pungent directive which had yet gone to Bomber Command".[4] Over the signature of Sir Wilfrid Freeman, he was informed "that the sole primary aim of your bomber offensive, until further orders, should be the destruction of German synthetic oil plants".

The degree of enthusiasm with which the Gelsenkirchen photographs were received in the midst of all this may be imagined. There is no evidence that they had the slightest effect upon the decisions of the CAS or the Air Staff. This may be taken as a sign of laudable resolution on the part of those officers; or it may be regarded in a quite different light. Similar manifestations of inflexibility on the part of the British High Command of 1914–18 have been castigated for many decades as indications of stubborn, bloodthirsty stupidity – and

276

few of the RAF's 1939–45 leaders would have dissented from that. The truth is, as stated above, that both the High Command of the first war, and the Air Staff of the second were operating under compulsion. The 1914–18 BEF and Bomber Command did what they had to do. What grates is the absolute assurance with which Sir Charles Portal and other Air Marshals announced their certainty that they could produce decisive results single-handed, when the inadequacy of their force was becoming daily more apparent, and they had clear evidence of its weakness in performance. Their position was unenviable; it was entirely understandable that the bomber commanders did not want to convey any impression to their gallant crews that they were no more than forlorn hopes; that would have been cruel indeed, and probably disastrous. But within the Air Staff itself, and in dealing with the leaders of the other Services, less doctrinaire assurance would surely have been helpful; it is the cocksureness that offends.

However, as so often happened, the war, in its various manifestations, supervened, and Freeman's "pungent" directive did not long hold sway. The first enemy was the weather: between January 1 and February 27 operations were only possible on 33 nights. Of these only three were devoted exclusively to attacking oil – as compared with 19 on naval targets, six on industrial towns and five on the Channel ports. "The selection of the two latter categories had been entirely the result of the weather."[5] The result was that only 221 sorties were flown against the oil plants in the first three months of 1941, as compared with 425 in the last quarter of 1940, and the 3,420 sorties in four months which Portal's optimistic mathematics required.[6]

The second enemy, of course, was Germany – in the form of the revived U-boat offensive (see pp. 246–7) which called forth Churchill's "Atlantic Directive" of March 6, over-riding all else. As stated above, Bomber Command's activities should never be regarded as entirely single-minded. In December 1940 it had stepped up its action against U-boat bases and Condor "wasp's nests" to 124 sorties; in January 1941, 269 sorties (five attacks) were flown against Wilhelmshaven, the objective being the battleship *Tirpitz*; a further 116 sorties were flown against her on February 28. All this was before the "Atlantic Directive"; conversely, during its reign, Cologne, Düsseldorf, Gelsenkirchen, Hanover and Berlin were among Bomber Command's targets. The Air Staff at the time, and the bomber "lobby" afterwards, never ceased to complain about the constant "diversions" of Bomber Command from its "rightful" – one might almost say "God-given" – rôle. A (probably incomplete) list of these "diversions" will be found in Appendix "B"; it will be seen that in effect they add up to the war itself. Indeed, it is at times difficult, taking into account the ineffectiveness of Bomber Command's "proper" activity, and its strong resistance to all "improper" activity, to decide whether it is more correct to say that Bomber Command was irrelevant to the war, or that the war was irrelevant to Bomber Command.

Throughout this winter, numerical weakness haunted Bomber Command; Churchill wrote to Sinclair, Portal and Beaverbrook on December 30:

> I am deeply concerned at the stagnant condition of our bomber force. The fighters are going ahead well, but the bomber force, particularly crews, is not making the progress hoped for. I consider the rapid expansion of the bomber force one of the greatest military objectives now before us ... The figures placed before me each day are deplorable. Moreover, I have been told on high authority that a substantial increase in numbers available for operations against Germany must not be expected for many months. I cannot agree to this without far greater assurance than I have now that everything in human wit and power has been done to avert such a complete failure of our air expansion programme.[7]

As ever, Churchill urged the "increase of our bomb deliveries on Germany", and he was disturbed to note that "some of the types and patterns most adapted to this are not coming forward as we had hoped".

This apprehension was all too correct. We have seen (p. 266) that it was in the heavier types that bomber production was so badly falling short; and we have seen also that the specifications for heavy bombers – the four-engined Short Stirling and the (originally) twin-engined Handley Page Halifax and Avro Manchester – dated back to 1936 (p. 34). The Stirling's maiden flight was in May 1939; ominously, it was disastrous – the prototype crashed and was completely destroyed. Squadron delivery was accordingly delayed until August 1940 (No. 7 Squadron, Leeming), but the first operation (against Rotterdam) was not until February 1941 – nearly five years after the order. Worse still, the aircraft was not a success. Its short wing-span (for accommodation in pre-war hangars), coupled with the Hercules II engine, gave the first models an operational ceiling of only 10,000 feet, which seriously limited the Stirling's value. The more powerful Hercules IX engine was then installed, which gave it a maximum of 17,000 feet (but effectively 15,000) – still low for offensive flying. And at such heights its wing structure made it liable to icing which caused it to become unstable – which also restricted its operational usefulness. Its bomb-load was unimpressive over long distances. A further defect in the tail-wheel led to more delays, frustrating to commanders and crews alike. The Stirling in due course took its place in the first line, but never possessed the qualities of a true first-line bomber like the Halifax or Lancaster.

It is not to be wondered at that Bomber Command clung jealously to the Halifax (see p. 243). Re-designed for four Merlin X engines, the Halifax prototype made its maiden flight on October 25, 1939, but it was practically a year later that the first production Mark I made its appearance; No. 35 Squadron (Leeming) received its first Halifax in November 1940, and the first operational sortie was on March 10/ 11, 1941, against Le Havre – three and a half years since the ordering of the four-engined version. Already a tail-wheel defect had been detected and overcome; but now hydraulic troubles and other minor faults appeared, which took the Halifax out of commission until June. On June 1 two squadrons (35 and 76) were theoretically operational – an initial establishment of 32 aircraft. Production, however, remained very slow, and continuing "teething troubles" meant that average serviceability right up to February 1942 was only 23 aircraft.[8] By the end of that year, Halifaxes would form "the bulk of the heavy bomber force",[9] and in the end 6,176 of them were built for the RAF. But it was a long, hard haul, with not much to show as the bomber offensive tried to make its mark in 1941.

Another four-engined disappointment was the Boeing Fortress I. This was the RAF designation of the modified B-17C, not to be confused with the B-17E, F and G, which were later the mainstay of the US Army Eighth Air Force. Twenty Fortresses were flown to Britain in the spring of 1941, and No. 90 Squadron (2 Group) was formed to fly them; service delivery began in May, but by July the squadron had only received seven, so many modifications being required. Even with these, the faults of the Fortress I were legion. They were worth naming, as a sample of the blighted hopes of Bomber Command in 1941:

> The Americans had had little experience themselves of flying the Fortress in operational conditions at heights near its ceiling; the Sperry bomb-sight was not fully automatic above 20,000 feet, and therefore bombing accuracy still depended on the human element; armament consisted of heavy, manually-operated machine guns, and to operate the beam guns large blisters had to be opened, reducing the internal temperature of the aircraft to the order of $-50°C$; armour was inadequate, but if augmented would lower the ceiling; its turbo-blown engines, though giving a higher ceiling than any other bomber, took it up to 35,000 ft., not to the stratosphere; it

279

made great demands on the physiology and mentality of its crew at such heights – and not even an American bomb-aiming expert had been able to place a single bomb in the town of Bremen; weather conditions limited its operational scope; it formed contrails, and would do so until it could exceed 40,000 ft.; its radius of action at 30,000 ft. was still only 500 miles; its engines developed defects in the rarefied atmosphere near its ceiling; and its atmospheric oxygen supply needed to be replaced by a pressure cabin system.[10]

Daylight operations by the Fortress I were abandoned in September 1941, after only 51 sorties, of which no more than 24 were even claimed to have been effective; in October 1942 the remaining Fortress Is were transferred to Coastal Command for reconnaissance.

As dismal as the Fortress story was that of the Manchester. Much had been expected of this aircraft and its supposed ability to carry a heavy bomb-load; in the event, however, it only demonstrated the risks of ordering off the drawing-board. Although in appearance a twin-engined machine, the Manchester rated as four-engined, inasmuch as its two engines were actually double. Called Vultures, each was, in fact, a pair of Rolls-Royce Kestrels, mated with a common crankcase. It was these engines which caused the Manchester's failure. It entered service in November 1940 (No. 207 Squadron, Wadding-ton), and its first operational flight was to Brest on the night of February 24/25, 1941. But steadily through the year its defects became apparent – above all the tendency to bearings failure in the engines, causing these to catch fire in the air. It was found impossible to cure this fault which, in conjunction with others, led to constant groundings; thus on June 1, though three squadrons were equipped with Manches-ters, giving an initial equipment of 48 aircraft (the largest number of any of the heavy types), none were operational. A year later the type was withdrawn, and remaining orders cancelled. It was a disaster.

During the whole of 1941 Bomber Command remained under the shadow of production failures, performance failures and, at times, shortage of aircrew also (due chiefly to the demands of the Middle East and the breakdown of the ferry pilot organization[11]). It was a discouraging phase of the war, with few agreeable prospects – very similar in this and other ways to the year 1915. But it was not unrelieved gloom; March 31 saw the first use of the RAF's new high-capacity bombs, 4,000-lb "block-busters", the leaders of a range of destructive weapons which, once the vehicles for them had been produced in sufficient numbers, would transform the power of bomb-ing. And the vehicles were on their way, a beam of light inside the dark cloud of the Manchester's failure. Marshal of the Royal Air

Force Lord Tedder tells us how, even in its earliest days, there were doubts about the Manchester. He and Freeman went to Avro's, and after a couple of circuits in a prototype, they retired to the office of the chief designer, Mr Roy Dobson. They learned that Rolls-Royce were unhappy about the Vulture engines:

> On the desk in Dobson's office there was a nice model of the Manchester. Before we got any farther on the subject, Dobson asked Freeman a direct question: "I am told you have plenty of Merlins coming in. Is this right?" to which Freeman answered "Yes." "Then what about this?" said Dobson, taking one of the wing tips off and adding an extra wing and an extra engine on one side and then repeating the process on the other side. "How's that?" he asked. "That" was the Lancaster – an afterthought that became one of the most successful and effective bombers of the war.[12]

The first prototype Lancaster made its maiden flight on January 9, 1941; a second prototype flew on May 13; the first prototype went to No. 44 Squadron (Waddington) for Service trials in September; the first production Lancaster made its maiden flight on October 31. It and its 7,365 successors held the hopes of Bomber Command.

And not only was the famous Lancaster on the way, but a bonus that the Command had not even hoped for. This was the realization at last of what Ludlow-Hewitt called a "speed bomber"; in his report of March 1939 he said that he had been pressing for its development for 18 months without success. He saw such a machine as performing the tasks of photographic reconnaissance (see p. 89) and harassing bombing; he repeated his conviction that the need was urgent. As it happened, a similar thought was in the minds of the de Havilland Company, which as a private venture began work on a twin- (Merlin) engined all-wooden aircraft with no armament, relying for protection entirely on its speed. This was in 1938; even to think of an all-wooden aircraft ran counter to all modern trends indeed, it appeared wholly retrogressive. The Air Ministry was thoroughly unimpressed – with one powerful exception: Freeman, then Member for Research, Development and Production on the Air Council. Thanks to him, de Havillands were instructed to commence design work for a light bomber which could carry a 1,000-lb bomb load to a distance of 1,500 miles. Work on "Freeman's Folly" began in December 1939, confirmed by Specification B.1/40 in March 1940, and the first prototype made its maiden flight in November of that year. Official trials took place in February 1941, and production began in July. This was the Mosquito Mark IV, and it so improved upon the original specification that it could carry four 500-lb bombs. However, Bomber

Command was not – as may be imagined – the only customer for this astonishing machine, with its ceiling of 36,000 feet, its range of 3,500 miles, its cruising speed of 315 mph at 30,000 feet and maximum speed of 425 mph at 30,500. Out of the first order for 250, the Photographic Reconnaissance Unit was to receive the first 10, Bomber Command the next 10, Fighter Command was to receive 180, and Bomber Command the last 50. Bomber Command's first batch was expected in September, but as usual there were delays; the first two Mosquitos were delivered in November, and a few more trickled in by the end of the year.[13] The priceless gift was withheld until 1942 – but it was priceless nevertheless; the Mosquito, the Lancaster and the Spitfire were the outstanding British aircraft of the Second World War.

35 New allies; "Rhubarbs" and "Circuses"; compulsions of alliance

1941 was the climacteric of the war – a climacteric in two parts. The first was in June, when Germany embarked on a course which would be fatal to her – the attack on the Soviet Union. It also restored to Britain a European ally, but an ally with whom cooperation was always peculiarly difficult, and whose sense of combination for a long time took the form of peremptory demands for aid which Britain could ill afford to give or which was downright impossible. The second part of the climacteric, in December, the Japanese attack on Pearl Harbor which drew America into the war, brought an ally of a very different kind, one that had already developed collaboration to a very remarkable pitch even before becoming a belligerent. As the military strength of both the Soviet Union and the United States grew, however, Britain's rôle would, by comparison with her vast allies, diminish. It would become a different kind of war: the military outcome more certain and hopeful, the long-term consequences less clear and less appealing.

Each part of the climacteric naturally affected the RAF immediately and profoundly. The immediate, and persisting, demand of the Soviet Union, reeling under the blows of its Nazi ex-ally, was for what its British acolytes and dupes called a "Second Front Now". This fell very securely into the category of the downright impossible. However, as the First World War had shown, the disciplines of an alliance demand something more than for one ally to do all the fighting and dying while the other makes admiring noises from the ringside. The approximately 2 million French casualties by the end of 1915 (when

Britain's were about half a million) put that coalition to severe strain; by the end of 1941 – that is to say, after only seven months of invasion – the Soviet Union's admitted casualties were 4½ million, and this figure was, according to an authoritative writer, "if anything an understatement".[1] Right up to the end of the year, as the German forces ploughed on into Russia, until their universally unexpected setback in front of Moscow, it appeared that the USSR was *in extremis*. A "second front" was absolutely outside Britain's power – except as a means of providing the Germans with another gratuitous victory; but *something* had to be done. The only available means of fulfilling this necessity was Bomber Command, which now took up the position on the right of the line which it was to hold until 1944. In September 1915, when the French were making their supreme effort, the weak and unready BEF was committed, for the same reasons, to the wretched Battle of Loos. It is difficult to view the Battle of Loos with anything but distress; Bomber Command was now entering the same sort of ordeal. The right of the line can be a very uncomfortable place.

Bomber Command received its new Directive on July 9, over the signature of the DCAS, Air Vice-Marshal N. H. Bottomley:

> ... The wide extension of [the enemy's] military activities is placing an ever-increasing strain on the German transportation system, and there are many signs that our recent attacks on industrial towns are having great effect on the morale of the civil population.
>
> Subject, therefore, to para. 7 below, I am to request that you will direct the main effort of the bomber force, until further instructions, towards dislocating the German transportation system and to destroying the morale of the civil population as a whole and of the industrial workers in particular.[2]

"Para. 7 below" recognized that "it will on occasions be necessary to make diversionary attacks on objectives, the destruction of which is of immediate importance in the light of the current situation". There was rather more to it than that.

No sooner had the defensive victory of the Battle of Britain been won than the more ardent spirits in and around Fighter Command began looking for new laurels. Air Marshal Sholto Douglas took over the Command on November 25, 1940; even before he did so, he informs us, Portal told him that Lord Trenchard had said that the time had come for Fighter Command to go on to the offensive. "He thought that we should now 'lean towards France', and he advocated a system of offensive sweeps of fighters across the Channel which was along much the same lines as that used by us in our operations over the Western Front in the First World War."[3] Douglas says that he at first felt considerable doubts about this policy, fearing that casualties "would be too severe for the results that we would be likely to achieve". However, he quickly changed his mind; and no such doubts vexed No. 11 Group's new commander, Leigh-Mallory. So the institution of "Rhubarbs" – sweeps of massed fighters – began; the Germans appeared to be largely unimpressed. They were more impressed when the fighters were accompanied by bombers; Bomber Command, however, did not greatly care for the rôle of bait. The joint operations were known as "Circuses". Between January and June 1941 they involved 190 bomber sorties and the "Rhubarbs" and "Circuses" together involved 2,700 sorties by fighters. In the course of these activities Fighter Command lost 51 pilots, and was only able to claim 44 German aircraft in return. Even this was an exaggeration; "the number of fighters shot down by our aircraft during offensive operations was probably not more than a score or so."[4] Sholto Douglas's initial trepidations were proved correct, but instead of claiming credit for this, he preferred to blame the historians![5]

It may well be that the evidently marginal effect of "Rhubarbs" and "Circuses" would have led to their abandonment, had it not been for the pressures arising from the German attack on the Soviet Union. Bomber Command's counter-action could, clearly, take two forms: direct attack on Germany, as prescribed in the July 9 Directive, and/ or an attempt to pull *Luftwaffe* formations back from the Eastern Front. Daylight bombing, abandoned in 1939 and 1940, was considered again – and "Circuses", with fighter escort, won a reprieve. Three things were now expected of them: damage to "valuable military objectives"; destroying enemy fighters ("an important blow in the battle for air superiority"[6]); and forcing the Germans to concentrate their fighters in the Pas-de-Calais area, thus permitting Bomber Command to make sneak raids on Germany herself. It was admitted that the last prospect could hardly be more than a stunt without possibility of repetition.

So "Circuses" were stepped up in the second half of 1941. *Pace* Sholto Douglas, Leigh-Mallory, the Air Staff and the brave men who performed them, they were not a success. What they did, in fact, was to transfer to the slender German defending forces precisely the advantages which Fighter Command had enjoyed during the Battle of Britain. If the Germans had then been surprised by British radar, the British fighter pilots now discovered that the German versions had improved "out of all recognition",[7] making the surprise always aimed at very difficult to achieve. The British fighters suffered the same disadvantages now as the Messerschmitts a year before, escorting bombers to their range limit. Worse still, the new Me 109F displayed a superiority over the Spitfire V which, in these circumstances, spelt a very hard time for Fighter Command. The advent, in September, of the superb new Focke-Wulf FW 190 compounded these penalties. However, the British had one sure card: the "numbers game". Thus, Air Vice-Marshal Leigh-Mallory claimed that between June 14 and September 3 his Group had destroyed 437 German fighters, with another 182 probables.[8] Since the *Luftwaffe* had no more than about 260 single-engined fighters in France and the Low Countries at any given time, of which only about 200 were serviceable, it is not surprising that the actual figure turns out to be 128 destroyed and 76 damaged. Fighter Command itself admitted the loss of 194 pilots during this period. For the six and a half months (June 14–December 31) to the end of the year, Fighter Command claimed 731 enemy aircraft shot down, for a loss of 411.[9] The actual German losses were 154, including 51 not attributed to British action, but with 11 more lost over the United Kingdom in quite other operations.[10] The combat balance sheet would thus appear to be about four to one in Germany's favour. Even on a lower count, Denis Richards remarks:

> It was for such results as these, together with the need to guard against a mass disengagement of German bombers from the east, that a force of seventy-five day-fighter squadrons were retained in this country throughout the latter part of 1941. Whether this was a wise allocation of resources at a time when there were only thirty-four fighter squadrons to sustain our cause in the whole of the Middle and Far East is, perhaps, an open question.[11]

Strategically, the main point was that 61 per cent of Germany's air strength remained, as before, on the Eastern Front.[12]

Bomber Command also suffered losses in these "Circus" operations, while at the same time pushing home its attacks on Germany against much strengthened defences[13] with a mounting rate of loss: 3.9 per cent in May, 4.4 per cent in June, 5.8 per cent in July and as high as 7.7 per cent in August. In the four months, April to July, no fewer than 776 bombers were written off from all causes; in August the figure was 525.[14] It was small wonder that anxiety grew in the Air Staff and beyond at the remoteness of the possibility of expansion in these circumstances. A sample of eight days at the end of June illustrates the fighting and the problem:

Date	Target		Sorties	Aircraft missing	Crew lost[15]
June					
29/30	Bremen Hamburg	}	137	6 Wellingtons (1 crew saved)	30
				4 Stirlings	28
				2 Hampdens	8
				1 Whitley	5
				13	71
30 (Day)	German coast N. France	}	55	2 Blenheims	6
				1 Halifax	7
				3	13
	24-hour total			**16**	**84**
30/July 1	Cologne Düsseldorf Duisburg	}	64	2 Hampdens 3 Whitleys (1 on return)	8 15
				5	23
July 1 (Day)	German coast N. France	}	46	2 Blenheims	6
				1 Stirling	7
				3	13
	24-hour total			**8**	**36**
1/2	Brest Cherbourg	}	57	3 Wellingtons	18
2 (Day)	Lille Merville	}	13	2 Blenheims	6
	24-hour total			**5**	**24**
2/3	Bremen Cologne Duisburg	}	161	1 Wellington 1 Whitley 2 Hampdens	6 5 8
	Düsseldorf Cherbourg			4	19
3 (Day)	Hazebrouck		17	1 Blenheim	3
	24-hour total			**5**	**22**

286

Date	Target	Sorties	Aircraft missing	Crew lost[15]
July				
3/4	Essen	} 163	5 Wellingtons	30
	Bremen		2 Whitleys	10
	Aerodromes		2 Hampdens	8
			9	48
4 (Day)	Bremen	} 32	6 Blenheims	18
	Chocques			
	Nordeney			
	24-hour total		**15**	**66**
4/5	Brest	} 150	3 Hampdens	12
	Lorient		1 Whitley	5
	Cherbourg		1 Wellington	
	West Germany		(on return)	6
			5	23
5 (Day)	German coast	} 21	Nil	Nil
	France			
	24-hour total		**5**	**23**
5/6	Munster		3 Hampdens	12
	Osnabruck		1 Whitley	5
	Bielefeld	} 208	4	17
	Magdeburg			
	Rotterdam			
6 (Day)	German coast	} 30	2 Blenheims	6
	Lille			
	24-hour total		**6**	**23**
6/7	Brest		3 Whitleys	
	Munster	} 215	(1 on return)	15
	Dortmund		4 Wellingtons	
	Rotterdam		(1 on return)	24
			2 Hampdens	
			(1 on return)	8
			9	47
7 (Day)	German coast	} 34	3 Blenheims	9
	Dutch coast			
	24-hour total		**12**	**56**
	8-day total		**72**	**334[16]**

287

It will be noted that three days out of the eight accounted for 43 aircraft and 206 aircrew; and these figures do not take into account damaged aircraft or aircrew alive but wounded more or less seriously. An example of what those statistics might mean is revealed by the daylight attack on La Pallice on July 24 launched by 15 Halifaxes (Nos. 35 and 76 Squadrons). The target on this occasion was the battle-cruiser *Scharnhorst*, which was naturally heavily defended by AA and fighters. Fourteen Halifaxes reached La Pallice and attacked. Every one of them was hit; five failed to return (16 aircrew killed, 19 taken prisoner); five more were so seriously damaged that they took three weeks to repair; in three of these there were further casualties amounting to two killed, four wounded and 15 injured – 100 per cent of the crews of these eight aircraft; two more were less damaged, and two only superficially – even so, there remains the possibility of casualties among their crews also. Five hits were obtained on the *Scharnhorst*, doing considerable damage, which was something. On the other hand, as the Official History says, these losses "did not augur well for daylight attacks on the interior of Germany".[17] Indeed, they underlined once more the impossibility of any such adventures – yet the wish died hard.

The compulsions of the new alliance were severe. They were not always sensibly interpreted; Churchill wrote to Portal on August 29:

> The loss of seven Blenheims out of seventeen in the daylight attack[18] on merchant shipping and docks at Rotterdam is most severe. Such losses ... seem disproportionate to an attack on merchant shipping not engaged in vital supply work. The losses in our bombers have been very heavy this month, and Bomber Command is not expanding as was hoped.[19] While I greatly admire the bravery of the pilots, I do not want them pressed too hard.[20]

Freeman reminded him that the attack formed part of the plan to try to bring relief to the Russian front by hitting the Germans in the West by all available means – which certainly conformed to his own definition of a "first-class strategic objective". Churchill replied:

> Good.
> The devotion and gallantry of the attacks on Rotterdam and other objectives are beyond all praise. The charge of the Light Brigade at Balaclava is eclipsed in brightness by these almost daily deeds of fame.
> Tell the squadrons and publish if you think well.[21]

What the squadrons thought of being compared with one of the classic unnecessary disasters of British military history is not recorded.

36 Four thousand bombers; euphoria and despondency; the Butt Report; air policy dispute

The Air Staff, under Portal and Freeman, certainly cannot be accused of any degree of timidity. It was during this dark period, when the strain on the RAF was mounting all the time, when production shortfalls constantly disappointed Bomber Command's expectation of expansion, when the failure of new types cheated it of the power to strike harder, and when nagging doubts about its effectiveness were beginning to grow, that the demand began to be aired for a force of no fewer than 4,000 heavy bombers. This was "Target Force E", a plan inaugurated in June 1941 to expand the Command to 250 standard-sized squadrons by the spring of 1943; it envisaged eight operational Groups, each having seven or eight "parent" airfields, each of those in turn having two "satellite" stations – a total of 168 airfields. The organizational problems involved were, of course, enormous, the command problems equally so; yet a force of approximately this size would continue to be the Air Staff's target for a long time to come, despite disrespectful comments by more realistic officers like Slessor (commanding No. 5 Group) who called it "an opium-smoker's dream".[1]

The penalty of the small peacetime forces to which (with the exception of the pre-1914 Navy) Britain has always been addicted is the extreme difficulty of effective quick expansion. Expansion itself is not so difficult; large numbers of men can be thrust into uniforms, substantial numbers of machines can be assembled. For the men to be trained and properly equipped, for the machines to be suited to their tasks, is something else again. RAF histories tend to dwell on the machines – understandably, since the very core of the Service is the aeroplane. But as stated above, the aeroplane depends upon the men. Expansion generally pulls the best men to the top quite quickly, which is good; it ensures the inflow of a wide range of talents further down, which is also good. The difficulty arises in the staffing of the important intermediate ranks, above all, in an air force, the squadron and flight commanders (equivalent of battalion and company commanders in the expanding Army of 1915–18 and 1940–44). Finding 250 good squadron commanders was a very real problem, especially as casualties mounted; finding 750 good flight commanders was just as bad. The experiment of three-flight squadrons (24 IE aircraft plus six IR) was tried in No. 5 Group in 1941, and worked reasonably

289

well.[2] It reduced the problem to that of finding 179 Wing Commanders, 537 Squadron-Leaders and 5,370 crews. Regarding the latter, any attempt to reach such a number would result, in Slessor's words, in the position that

> 40 per cent will be useless and will never catch up but deteriorate through being kept on the ground, will crash aircraft and get in the way of the chaps who will do the job.[3]

It need hardly be added that the provision of skills on the ground to support such a force in the air would also be well-nigh impossible. When the prototype Lancaster was demonstrated to No. 44 Squadron in September 1941, the squadron mustered 490 ground crew (128 Rhodesian, as were all the aircrew). It may be imagined what this figure translates into in terms of mechanics, fitters, armourers, radio mechanics, instrument repairers, electrical mechanics, and so on, for the whole Command.

Referring to the 4,000-bomber force, Sir Arthur Harris says:

> It was not, of course, in any way my decision to build up a force of this size; to put so large a part of the nation's war effort into the production of one weapon was a decision that could only be made by the War Cabinet advised by the Chiefs of Staff.[4]

This is clearly correct, and in considering the air policy of the period the attitude of the Chiefs of Staff requires attention. It has to be remembered that the Royal Navy was also engaged in belated large-scale expansion, especially of the escort craft so badly needed in the Atlantic, and that the Army was aiming at a force of not less than 55 divisions – it was awareness of these facts that heightened Slessor's scepticism.[5] The First Sea Lord and the CIGS, however, seemed not to see the conflict of purpose implied in the Air Staff's programme. On July 31, they drew up a remarkable document: a fresh statement on general British strategy for the guidance of the Prime Minister in his forthcoming interview with President Roosevelt and his advisers.[6] In this paper, the Chiefs of Staff asserted their reliance on bombing to provide the weapon which would overcome Germany; the bombing offensive, they said, must be on the heaviest possible scale, and

> we set no limits to the size of the force required, save those imposed by operational difficulties in the United Kingdom. After meeting the needs of our own security, we give to the heavy bomber first priority in production,

for only the heavy bomber can produce the conditions under which other offensive force can be employed.[7]

It would be difficult to find anywhere a more full-blooded advocacy of the strategic air offensive than this paper bearing the signatures of the professional heads of the Navy and the Army; their support for the attack on German morale is explicit:

As our forces increase, we intend to pass to a planned attack on civilian morale with the intensity and continuity which are essential if a final breakdown is to be produced. There is increasing evidence of the effect which even our present limited scale of attack is causing to German life. We have every reason to be confident that if we can expand our forces in accordance with our present programme, and if possible beyond it, that effect will be shattering. We believe that if these methods are applied on a vast scale, the whole structure upon which the German forces are based, the economic system, the machinery for production and destruction, the morale of the nation will be destroyed, and that whatever their present strength the armed forces of Germany would suffer such a radical decline in fighting value and mobility that a direct attack would once more become possible. When that time will come no one can with accuracy predict ... It may be that the methods described above will by themselves be enough to make Germany sue for peace and that the rôle of the British Army on the Continent will be limited to that of an army of occupation. We must, however, be prepared to accelerate victory by landing forces on the Continent to destroy any elements that still resist, and strike into Germany itself ...[8]

With hindsight, this paper almost defies comment. Even without hindsight, it failed to win universal applause. Churchill was sufficiently impressed to direct that it should be shown to the American Chiefs of Staff; they, however, were less enthusiastic. At this stage – there were still over four months to go before America herself was at war – they deprecated the attack on morale as a primary target; their views would be modified. That apart, they may be excused if they found the tone of the whole paper more liturgical than strategical. One thing it certainly displays: the strong influence of Portal on his older colleagues. One cannot help wondering whether the paper would have been couched in such uncompromising terms a few months later, when General Brooke became chairman of the Chiefs of Staff Committee. In the text as offered one observes a mixture of euphoria and despondency – neither of them characteristic of Lord Alanbrooke. The euphoria speaks for itself; the despondency is explicable in Pound and Dill at this point in the war. The Navy went through a bad time in 1941: the Battle of the Atlantic was a steady, heavy strain; the action against the *Bismarck* (including the shock of losing HMS *Hood*) had stretched resources very far; losses in the Mediterranean (especially during the evacuation of Crete) were heavy.[9] A "naval solution" was not easy to see, except in the negative terms of the battle which the Navy must not lose. The Army, too, was at a low ebb; its own expansion was proceeding with all the difficulty, referred to above, which normally besets that activity in wartime; its equipment problems were acute; its winter triumphs in Cyrenaica were turned into the ashes of defeat; it had been ejected ignominiously from the European mainland once again in Greece, and then from Crete also. With Operation BARBAROSSA[10] in full swing, the prospects of the Army engaging the main enemy effectively were faint indeed. Only the Air Force could permit itself euphoria in July 1941 – and that, too, was about to be rudely shattered.

The prime agent of this distressing circumstance was Lord Cherwell, previously Professor Sir Frederick Lindemann, Churchill's Scientific Adviser. Widely regarded as an *éminence grise* of the Prime Minister, Cherwell was also considered in some scientific circles as a *bête noire*; his influence was undoubtedly considerable, and across the span of Churchill's premiership its effects were variable. But when, in early August 1941, he asked D. M. B. Butt of the War Cabinet Secretariat to attempt a statistical investigation of the results of British bombing of Germany, he produced an effect akin to that of crude, old-fashioned dentistry: the patient's slow recovery might now begin, but the pain was awful.

Mr. Butt examined some 650 photographs taken during night bombing operations on 48 nights between June 2 and July 25, relating to 100 separate raids on 28 different targets. It is best to give his conclusions verbatim:

1. Of those aircraft recorded as attacking their target, only one in three got within five miles.
2. Over the French ports, the proportion was two in three; over Germany as a whole, the proportion was one in four; over the Ruhr, it was only one in ten.
3. In the full moon, the proportion was two in five; in the new moon it was only one in fifteen.
4. In the absence of haze, the proportion is over one half, whereas over thick haze it is only one in fifteen.
5. An increase in the intensity of AA fire reduces the number of aircraft getting within five miles of their target in the ratio of three to two.

6. All these figures relate only to aircraft recorded as *attacking* the target; the proportion of the *total sorties* which reached within five miles is less by one third.[11]

Mr Butt's examination of the photographs (carried out, of course, in collaboration with the Photographic Interpretation Section, which now saw at last a possibility of its work becoming truly valuable) was backed by investigation of operational summaries and other documents. He carefully explained the basis on which he had reached his devastating conclusion "that only about one third of aircraft claiming to reach the target area actually reach it". He insisted that two qualifications to this result should be made clear:

(a) This figure of one third . . . relates to the aircraft recorded as having attacked the primary target, not to the total aircraft despatched. In the raids considered in this analysis 6,103 aircraft were despatched but 4,065 attacked, i.e. 66 per cent. Thus of the total despatched not one-third but one-fifth reached the target area.
(b) It must be observed also that by defining the target area for the purpose of this enquiry as having a radius of five miles, an area of over 75 square miles is taken. This must at least for any town but Berlin consist very largely of open country. The proportion of aircraft actually dropping their bombs on built-up areas must be very much less, but what this proportion is, however, cannot be indicated by the study of night photographs.[12]

Such was the gist of the Butt Report, which marked the end of a chapter in the history of Bomber Command. This is not to say that there was immediate self-abasement and contrition on the part of the bombing prophets, Air Staff, Group commanders, or station commanders. Peirse summed up a widespread attitude with considerable moderation when he noted in pencil on his copy of the report:

I don't think at this rate we could have hoped to produce the damage which is known to have been achieved.[13]

Cherwell, presenting the report to the Prime Minister, conceded that Mr Butt's figures might not be entirely accurate, but he went straight to the heart of the matter when he added: "they are sufficiently striking to emphasize the supreme importance of improving our navigational methods". Churchill told Portal that the report was "a very serious paper and seems to require your most urgent attention". Portal, like Peirse, was doubtful and puzzled; both of them, and others in the same frame of mind, were victims of that unusual conflict of

293

Intelligence referred to above (pp. 273–4). Portal said he thought Mr Butt's figures might be "wide of the mark"; but he agreed with what Cherwell had said to Churchill. The Official History comments:

> Thus, for the first time in air force history the first and paramount problem of night operations was seen at the highest level to be not merely a question of bomb aiming, though this difficulty remained, but of navigation . . . By showing the need for the development of scientific aids to navigation, the scientific study of navigation, and the development of revolutionary tactics, the Butt Report . . . had rendered a service to Bomber Command which was second to none.[14]

In Portal's logical mind, one thing was at once apparent: if these were the sort of results that henceforward (until science came to the rescue) must be considered normal, then Bomber Command was going to need every one of those 4,000 frontline bombers that the Air Staff was dreaming of. But there was, of course, another way of looking at it, and one of the sharpest debates of the war on air policy now followed. One thing, however, was not in dispute: "the lack of any alternative means of attacking Germany"[15]–which meant that the issue at stake was scale. Bomber Command was now firmly clasped in the vicious circle which had been closing on it:

> Because of the limitation upon its bombing accuracy, imposed mainly by darkness, it required an immense force to achieve decisive results by imprecise means. But because of doubts about its effectiveness, arising mainly from its inaccuracy, it might never be given the necessary force.[16]

Portal addressed himself to the situation characteristically. At last the question of navigational aids was gripped with a sense of urgency; the "general inertia"[17] which had persisted in this matter for two years of war began to be dispelled. Less helpful was the continuing disposition to find ways of resuming day bombing, when really there was only one way that could make it effective – the introduction of a true long-range fighter to protect the bombers. Churchill had already perceived this necessity, but Portal firmly set his face against it. A long-range fighter, he believed, could never hold its own against a short-range fighter; it was an attitude which, as Churchill said, "closed many doors"[18] (see Appendix G).

On the main issue, Portal was undismayed and undeterred. From an examination of the effects of German bombing of Britain, the Air Staff concluded that with a force of 4,000 first-line bombers it would be possible to destroy completely forty-three German towns. These comprised the majority with a population of over 100,000, a total of some 15 million people, whose re-housing alone would put a great strain upon Germany's resources. Portal passed the plan on to Churchill, saying that the proposed force could obtain "decisive results against German morale . . . and that the time taken would be about six months".[19] He did not say *which* six months. Since the average daily availability of Bomber Command aircraft at this stage was 506 (250 Wellingtons) and fifteen months later the figure would only have increased by 9 (515),[20] it was clearly no prospect of quick victory that he was offering.

Churchill was certainly not impressed; always a firm supporter of the policy of bombing Germany – a conviction founded partly on his deep loathing of the Nazi *régime* and all its works, and also partly on the desire, universally shared, to bring retribution for the damage of the "Blitz" – he had now, in the light of a year's experience, lost some of his first assurance. He replied:

> It is very disputable whether bombing by itself will be a decisive factor in the present war. On the contrary, all that we have learnt since the war began shows that its effects, both physical and moral, are greatly exaggerated. There is no doubt the British people have been stimulated and strengthened by the attack made upon them so far. Secondly, it seems very likely that the ground defences and night-fighters will overtake the air attack.[21] Thirdly, in calculating the number of bombers necessary to achieve hypothetical and indefinite tasks, it should be noted that only a quarter of our bombs hit the targets. Consequently an increase in the accuracy of bombing to 100 per cent would in fact raise our bombing force to four times its strength. The most we can say is that it will be a heavy and I trust a seriously increasing annoyance.[22]

This communication cannot have been pleasant for Portal; it looked as though the leader who had hitherto been the bomber's best friend might be on the point of deserting it. Portal bent his mind to a considered reply which Sinclair, when he saw it, called "masterly" and "audacious": Sinclair was perhaps liable to regard any blunt reply to Churchill as an audacity. What Portal did, without difficulty, was to underline the unquestionable fact that ever since the Fall of France the bombing offensive had been "a fundamental principle of our strategy", fully backed by Churchill himself at every stage. He recalled the recent policy statement of the Chiefs of Staff, which Churchill had also endorsed (p. 291), giving first priority to heavy bombers. "Production," he said, "has been planned to conform with this strategic conception and we are already deeply committed to it." If it was now to be accepted that the best heavy bombers could do would be to cause "a heavy and increasing annoyance, then, as I see it, the strategic concept to which we have been working must dissolve . . ."

Portal stated firmly that he could "see no reason to regard the bomber as a weapon of declining importance". However, he said, it was not his present purpose to re-argue the bomber case:

> My object is to suggest the necessity for a clear picture of our aim. As I have said, existing directives afford such a picture and give a clear-cut definition of the kind of Air Force we must create if victory is to be won. But these directives rest on the assumption that – given the necessary production – the Royal Air Force is capable by itself of carrying the disruption of Germany to a very advanced stage. If that assumption is no longer tenable, we must produce a new plan. The worst plan of all would be to continue our present preparations after we had ceased to believe in the efficacy of the bomber as a war-winning weapon.
>
> It is my firm belief that the existing plan is sound and practical. But other plans could be drawn up. We could, for example, return to the conception of defeating Germany with the army as the primary weapon. I must point out with the utmost emphasis that in that event we would require an Air Force composed quite differently from that which we are now creating. If, therefore, it is your view that the strategic picture has changed since the issue of your original directive I would urge that revised instructions should be given to the Chiefs of Staff without a moment's delay.[23]

Portal's Minute may be said to display him at his best and worst. Its extreme lucidity and cogent marshalling of very strong fundamental arguments display all the highest qualities of a Chief of Staff. He clearly grasped a basic truth which had been well established in the First World War, but which is always easily forgotten, namely, that the abandonment of any really large-scale project in modern war amounts to a major victory for the enemy. It continues to be often asked why some of the great, costly offensives on the Western Front between 1914 and 1918 were not given up, either before they began or shortly after. This is the overwhelming reason. Each one represented an effort of production, of administration and of logistics which would be the main preoccupation of the army concerned for many months, perhaps a whole year; to give up could only be a grave defeat – without a battle. The same consideration applied in 1941. A total reversal of policy, as Portal suggested, could only be a major setback, indefinitely postponing Britain's ability seriously to affect the war. Here he is on sure ground. He is at his worst in the absolute assurance of his stance; in his genuine belief in such a thing as "a war-winning weapon";[24] in his unhesitating acceptance that "the consensus of informed opinion is that German morale is much more vulnerable to bombing than our own"; and above all in his polarization of issues. The war would proclaim – indeed, was already proclaiming – the need not only for the air force that Portal advocated, but for the one which he defined as "composed quite differently". We shall return to this.

Churchill's reply, framed that very day, contains no such contradictions. He was well able to recognize a sound argument when he heard one, and hastened to reassure a Service Head whom he greatly liked that there was no intention of changing the policy so firmly laid down. On the other hand,

> I deprecate . . . placing unbounded confidence in this means of attack, and still more expressing that confidence in terms of arithmetic.

Alluding to a hope and a vision which sustained him (without much objective warrant) at this low ebb of the war, he told Portal:

> If the United States enters the war, [bombing] would have to be supplemented in 1943 by simultaneous attacks by armoured forces in many of the conquered countries which were ripe for revolt. Only in this way could a decision certainly be achieved.

With this reminder that more than one strategy might be demanded, he also recalled the morbid effect of the claims made for the "knockout blow" before the war, warmly supported by the Air Staff, which "depressed the Statesmen responsible for the pre-war policy, and played a definite part in the desertion of Czechoslovakia in August 1938". If there was one thing that the "Blitz" had proved, it was the vast exaggeration of those claims.[25] Churchill then concluded:

> It may well be that German morale will crack and that our bombing will play a very important part in bringing the result about. But all things are always on the move simultaneously, and it is quite possible that the Nazi war-making power in 1943 will be so widely spread throughout Europe as to be to a large extent independent of the actual buildings in the homeland.
>
> A different picture would be presented if the enemy's Air Force were so far reduced as to enable heavy accurate daylight bombing of factories to take place. This however cannot be done outside the radius of fighter protection, according to what I am at present told. One has to do the best one can, but he is an unwise man who thinks there is any *certain* method

297

of winning this war, or indeed any other war between equals in strength. The only plan is to persevere.[26]

With this Portal had to be content – but it was enough. The prescription was not as inspiring as "blood, toil, tears and sweat", but it was the right one. For each and every Command in the Royal Air Force, the only plan was to persevere.

Part IV

THE VICTORY

"The Air must hold the ring"

THE MEDITERRANEAN

". . . Air warfare in its own right . . ."

37 Middle East Command; the Takoradi Route; Longmore's problems

As 1940 drew to its enigmatic close, the RAF began to discover other ways of making war than seeking an offensive system for Fighter Command, or pressing Whitleys, Hampdens and Wellingtons deep into Germany, hoping for the best. It began to take in yet another lesson, and as usual the instructors were the remorseless war itself – and its enemy.

It was a matter of almost universal pride that Britain fought the Second World War, like the First, not as a nation, but as an Empire. In the darkest days of all, one of the few gleams of light was the possibility of rallying the Empire at least on the scale of 1914–1918, in the hope of redressing some part of the adverse military balance. In the event, the deeply impressive First World War imperial response was substantially exceeded in the Second: 2,950,000 enlistments in the armed forces of the Dominions and Colonies (including India) between 1914–18, 4,104,000 between 1939–45.[1] The Royal Air Force was a notable beneficiary of this great effort: quite apart from the large number of men from overseas serving in RAF squadrons as air or ground-crew,[2] by mid-1944 out of 487 squadrons under command, 100 were provided by the Royal Canadian, Royal Australian, South African, Indian and Royal New Zealand Air Forces. Out of a total of 340,000 aircrew for the whole war, 134,000 were supplied by the various parts of the Empire. In addition there were the Allied Air Forces fighting as part of the RAF. These were formed from men who had, by one means or another, escaped from occupied countries and made their way to British territory – in other words, men "cast in the heroic mould".[3] By June 1944 there were 31 Allied Squadrons in the home Commands: 12 Polish, seven French, four Czechoslovakian, four Norwegian, two Belgian and two Dutch; a further 20 French, three Greek, one Dutch, one Polish and one Yugoslav squadrons were serving in overseas Commands. It is with great regret that the author of this volume admits that he can make no attempt to tell the

301

splendid story either of the Empire or the Allied Air Forces except in the most fragmentary fashion; this acknowledgment must be the salute to a wonderful gesture and achievement.

Empire, in 1940 however, with overseas forces still in the slow process of formation, meant chiefly another commitment, an extra strain which would swell into a major activity for the next three years. The hinge of the Empire was, of course, Egypt – an independent country in which the British forces enjoyed "squatters' rights": the great naval base at Alexandria, a considerable Army garrison[4] and the important (though still inadequate) RAF depôt at Aboukir with its satellites at Abu Sueir and Fuka. The strategic significance of Egypt was obvious:

> From the earliest days it had been a crossroads of the world's land routes. In 1867 de Lesseps made it an intersection of sea highways. Now it has become a vital staging post in air communications between Europe and the East . . .[5]

In addition, there was the fact that one-twelfth of the United Kingdom's oil supplies normally came through the Suez Canal from Iraq and Persia (Iran); the Nazi-Soviet Pact, German pressure on Rumania and the U-boat campaign led inexorably to greater dependence on Middle-Eastern supply:

> Egypt then was not only a main link in the chain of imperial communications but was also the southern protector of these oilfields.[6]

So, despite Egyptian "non-belligerence", under a King and ruling clique whose attitudes ranged from frankly anti-British to exceedingly luke-warm support, and with internal security always questionable, Egypt had to be recognized as an imperial base of prime importance, second only to the United Kingdom. From an air point of view, it possessed even greater significance.

For the still unschooled believers in naked air power, Egypt seemed to hold rich potential, representing "a central area where in peace the air force could be effectively trained and administered in a tolerable climate and good living conditions. In war its geographical position would enable air forces to operate in many directions."[7]

The idea of exploiting air "mobility" from Egypt was tempting and persuasive; in the light of British Middle Eastern commitments – facing the Italian Empire in the west and in the south, holding open the Suez Canal and the Red Sea, guarding Palestine and the

302

vital Iraqi–Iranian oil, reaching out towards the Balkans and the Levant – the idea of a centrally positioned balanced air force capable of operating in any direction had evident merit. It was accepted, first, that such a force would depend on the life-line of serviceable imperial air communications through the Mediterranean (Gibraltar and Malta) to be effective.

> The second condition was that the air force must not be tied down to the central area by inclusion in the local garrison. Squadrons on airfields in the Middle East were to be regarded in the same light as battleships in the Grand Harbour.[8]

It is here that the sceptic takes alarm; the ringing language strikes up echoes – for instance of the plausible talkers of the First World War who spoke of "the unity of the Allied front from Nieuport to Bagdad". In theory, tremendous; in practice, meaningless; in each case the war itself brushed the theory aside. In the context of 1940–41 realities, attempts to fulfil the grandiose dreams of "mobile" air power were invocations of disaster, and when the base itself came under mortal threat, the Air Force had to include itself in "the local garrison" or die.

The Italian entry into the war on June 10, 1940, just as France was in the last stages of collapse, was the moment of truth for the Middle East. It meant the effective closing of the Mediterranean as an artery of supply or reinforcement; it meant that the Fleet could not use Malta as a base (indeed, the island itself was in serious danger); the Army, facing some 250,000 Italian troops in Libya and another 350,000 in East Africa,[9] could only pray for time and pray that time would bring some increase of strength; the RAF met, full face, the implications of what its chief, Air Chief Marshal Longmore, AOC-in-C, Middle East and his staff knew only too well – that it was, even by 1940 standards, a second-line force. Indeed, the RAF in the Middle East reflected, with advantages, all the tribulations that the home Commands had been trying to overcome since the beginning of the war.

As always, the proof is in the aircraft. The most modern bombers in the Command were a single squadron of Blenheim IVs; otherwise the first-line bombing force consisted of Blenheim Is, supported on the Libyan front by Bristol Bombays (No. 216 Squadron); the twin-engined Bombay monoplane was basically a transport aircraft which made its first flight in 1935, but was capable of good work as a night bomber, as the squadron bravely showed. On the East African front, the chief bomber was the sturdy old Wellesley (see p. 78), also of 1935 vintage, backed by Vickers Valentia biplane transports whose RAF service had begun in 1934. The most modern fighters in the Middle East Command were Gloster Gladiators, of which there were 75 in Egypt (including one Royal Egyptian Air Force squadron, which could only be called upon for home defence) and the equivalent of one squadron facing East Africa. Behind these stood an array of names from the past: Gloster Gauntlets (see p. 58), the Hawker Audax (squadron service, 1932), Hawker Hardy (squadron service, 1935), Hawker Fury II (squadron service, 1931) – all biplanes, needless to say. For Army Cooperation, there was the Lysander. The Sunderlands of Nos. 228 and 230 Squadrons seemed to belong to a different world. Fortunately – very fortunately – the RAF's second-line air force was faced, for the time being, by one which was also second-line, though very much stronger in numbers.

Australian-born, Air Chief Marshal Sir Arthur Longmore, KCB, DSO, was 55 years old in 1940; he obtained his Royal Aero Club Certificate (No. 72) in 1911; he served with distinction in the RNAS throughout the First World War until the creation of the RAF, into which he transferred with the rank of Group Captain in 1919. Commandant of the RAF College, Cranwell, from 1929–1933, then Commandant of the Imperial Defence College, 1936–39, he became AOC-in-C, Middle East, in May 1940. Sir Maurice Dean says:

> He was intelligent, polished, highly competent and imperturbable, just the man for stormy days in 1940.[10]

Uncertain of the exact limits of his sphere of command, Longmore asked for clarification, which he received on June 11:

> He was to command "all Royal Air Force units stationed or operating in . . . Egypt, Sudan, Palestine and Trans-Jordan, East Africa, Aden and Somaliland, Iraq and adjacent territories, Cyprus, Turkey, Balkans, Mediterranean Sea, Red Sea, Persian Gulf" – an area of some four and a half million square miles.[11]

With some 29 squadrons, chiefly of assorted antiques, it was clear that this task would call for every particle of Longmore's "happy gift for 'bluffing a full house with a couple of pairs'."[12]

The worst of Longmore's position was that the closing of the Mediterranean put the Middle East forces to a considerable extent under siege from the very beginning. This had been foreseen, and all three Services had built up a 90-day stockpile of essential supplies; for the RAF, the chief of these were aviation fuel and explosives; in addition, it held a reserve of aircraft amounting to 140 per cent of first-line strength. The worrying problem was that, with so many obsolete types on charge, the availability of replacements and spare parts would in any case be liable to rapid decrease. For the trickle of modern aircraft, when it began to appear, there were, of course, no reserves at all. And round the Cape via the Red Sea it took 70 days for reinforcements to reach Egypt. So the dreaded word "conservation", whose ominous ring, as we have seen (see p. 91), had already been heard in the home-based air force, was heard again immediately in the Middle East.

Clearly, only exceptional measures could overcome the exceptional hazard of the RAF's position – and those measures were put in hand in July 1940, when Group Captain H. K. Thorold with a small advanced party of RAF technicians arrived at Takoradi in the Gold Coast (now Ghana) and began work on the installations necessary for a trans-Africa route which would be capable of handling a heavy (it was hoped) reinforcement traffic. The bare essentials already existed in the staging posts of the weekly passenger and mail service set up from Takoradi to Khartoum in 1936. Now, however, Takoradi itself had to be developed into a base capable of handling upwards of 120 aircraft a month, while along the route runways had to be extended, additional airfields built, new accommodation constructed, signal communications and meteorological facilities improved. The main RAF party arrived in August, and under Thorold's direction carried out what Tedder would later call "a first-class piece of improvization". All ranks, he says, "were clearly imbued with the urgency of passing every aircraft up the line as quickly as possible".[13] So well did they work that the first reinforcement flight (1 Blenheim and 6 Hurricanes) was able to take off from Takoradi on September 20. Flying via Lagos (378 miles), Kano (525), Maiduguri (325), via Fort Lamy (Free French from August 29) to Geneina (689), then to Khartoum (754), the RAF's aircraft then had another 1,026 miles to go to Abu Sueir. At the end of this 3,697-mile, six-day journey, says Denis Richards, a pilot's "airmanship would doubtless be all the better for the flight. Not so, however, his aircraft."[14] The wear and tear of the Takoradi route was formidable for all types; one of the original six Hurricanes did not complete the journey – just one unit of the 10 per cent wastage in delivery calculated by Middle East Command. Yet by the end of October 1943 over 5,000 aircraft had been despatched to Egypt via

Takoradi, and well might Philip Guedalla say that "victory in Egypt came by the Takoradi Route".[15]

Meanwhile, until the Takoradi stream swelled into a river, the sense of excruciating material weakness haunted Longmore's days and nights. It is not surprising; as we survey his museum of venerable aeroplanes, it is hard to recognize a combatant air force. What he tended to lose sight of, however, was the fact that (as we have amply noted) the whole RAF was to some degree in similar difficulty, and the Fleet Air Arm no less. It still makes one catch one's breath to reflect that the crippling of the Italian battle fleet at Taranto in November was carried out by a mere 21 Fairey Swordfish biplanes with a maximum speed of 129 mph.

For the RAF throughout the Command, the daily deadly enemies were distance, dust and sand. Distance stretched performance to its limits and placed repair and maintenance under extreme difficulty. Dust, in the form of vicious storms, was the enemy of machines and men alike. Tedder, who arrived as Longmore's Deputy in December, made an early acquaintance with "the Desert's own special brand of 'peasoup' " –

> blowing hard, and the dust drifting like snow; visibility often only a few yards. Everything was covered with a fine, very soft, yellow powder – though it did not feel soft with a thirty or forty mile an hour wind behind it. Eyes blinked and teeth gritted with the sand. Outside one had to wear goggles, and some people occasionally even used their gas masks. On one occasion I had the front mud wings of my car literally sand-blasted down to the bare metal in the course of an hour's drive against the dust.[16]

Dust and sand together were the maintenance nightmare. A sentence like "Sand was doing its worst"[17] held special meanings for an organization haunted by lack of servicing equipment and spares:

> Air cleaners for Blenheims had to be serviced every five hours' flying, a job which takes some three hours of maintenance work. A replacement cleaner takes only fifteen minutes to fit, but there were in January only six spares in the Command . . . Sand penetrated into the instruments, dust and dirt interfered with the variable pitch air screws so that the screw would not pass to coarse pitch in the air. The heat of the desert sun exceeded the plastic temperature applied when moulding Perspex sheets, which as a result blew out and cracked. These difficulties, when added to the normal task of repairing and maintaining the air force, taxed severely the engineer and equipment organisation. Improvisation was possible up

to a point but not to the extent of manufacturing some of the essential engine and machine repairs for modern aircraft.[18]

One begins to appreciate the magnitude of this problem, and the particular meaning of "conservation" in Middle East terms, when, after only five weeks of war, one finds Longmore telling the commander of his Advanced Group in the Western Desert:

> We are rapidly consuming available reserves of all types of aircraft in the Command and must in consequence exercise still greater economy in their employment as there is no immediate prospect of wastage replacements arriving from the UK.[19]

For a year and more, this was to be the "theme music" of the RAF, Middle East. Since it was also to be the course of a profound and persisting misunderstanding between Cairo and London, which would have dire consequences for Longmore personally, it will be as well to pursue the theme a little further. With every Middle East return and report confirming the grim facts of perpetual weakness in numbers and types, it comes as a shock to find Churchill, addressing the CAS on November 10, saying:

> Altogether, broadly speaking, 1,000 aircraft and 17,000 air personnel in the Middle East provide 30½ squadrons, with a total initial equipment of 395 operational types, of which it is presumed 300 are ready for action on any date ... In the disparity between the great mass of men and numbers of aircraft on charge, and the fighting product constantly available, which is painfully marked both here and at home, lies the waste of RAF resources. What is the use of the 600 machines which are not even included in the initial equipment of the 30 squadrons? No doubt some can be explained as training, communication, and transport. But how is it that out of 732 operational types only 395 play any part in the fighting? I hope that a most earnest effort will be made to get full value for men, material, and money out of this very large force ...[20]

This extraordinary missive, which appears to ignore completely the minimum but now unfulfilled need of 100 per cent reserves for a force operating over 11,000 miles (via Capetown) from its industrial source of supply, shows Churchill at his worst. The truth was (though neither Portal nor Longmore nor any other suffering air marshal was likely to know this) that Churchill was harping on an ancient theme. A strong backer of tanks in the First World War, as Minister of Munitions in 1918 he resented anything which impeded the develop-

307

ment of the powerful tank force with which he believed the war would be won in 1919 or 1920 – and one impediment was the RAF. On September 9, 1918 he wrote to the Prime Minister (Lloyd George):

> There is no doubt that the demands of the Air Force on men and material are thought to be much in excess of the fighting results produced . . . The reason is not that a man in the air is not worth more than a foot soldier, but that a man in the Air Force is not a man in the air, and that anything from 50 to 100 men are required in the Air Force for every one man fighting in the air.[21]

This compared poorly with some 25 men per vehicle for his beloved tanks, and Churchill never forgot it; always impatient of Service "tails", he remained convinced that the RAF was an especially wicked offender in this respect. The acerbity of some of Longmore's signals on the subject of his material weakness only annoyed the Prime Minister more – and incidentally also annoyed Portal and the Air Staff. What they disliked above all was his habit of invoking support from his fellow Commanders-in-Chief, Admiral Sir Andrew Cunningham, and General Sir Archibald Wavell – support which they freely gave him, because both were constantly asking him for help. But to the hard-pressed Air Staff in London, this looked like conspiracy; much goodwill was thus lost on both sides.

At bottom, the Cairo/London argument turned on the question of serviceability and unserviceability, and found its meat and drink in definitions of the latter. Apart from the necessary reserves, there were a number of reasons why aircraft listed as in general serviceable might not be available for operations at certain times:

> There were aircraft undergoing minor repairs or inspections, there were aircraft returned to maintenance units for complete overhauls, aircraft awaiting spares, aircraft waiting to be scrapped, aircraft used for training and communications, aircraft still in crates awaiting erection, aircraft on the high seas.[22]

Evidently, the potential of misunderstanding was considerable – the more so since Churchill found very great difficulty in imagining the realities underlying the figures he liked to hurl like javelins at commanders who fell into his disfavour. Longmore was the first to suffer; the Army commanders would shortly share his ordeal. Meanwhile Churchill followed up his complaint to Portal with a direct shaft; on November 12 he informed Longmore that he was trying to speed up arrivals of Hurricanes and other types, and continued:

Pray report daily what you actually receive, and how many you are able to put into action. I was astonished to find that you have nearly 1,000 aircraft and 1,000 pilots and 16,000 air personnel in the Middle East, excluding Kenya. I am most anxious to re-equip you with modern machines at the earliest moment; but surely out of all this establishment you ought to be able, if the machines are forthcoming, to produce a substantially larger number of modern aircraft operationally fit? Pray report through the Air Ministry any steps you may be able to take to obtain more fighting value from the immense mass of material and men under your command.[23]

It may be imagined with what emotions this offensive communication was received at Middle East Headquarters.

Unfortunately, once an idea took hold in Churchill's mind, it was liable to be tenacious, and impervious to ordinary reasoned discourse; this one was no exception. Thus we find him returning to the charge once more, in the "Action this Day" memorandum on the "stagnant condition" of Bomber Command addressed to Sinclair, Portal and Beaverbrook quoted on p. 278. Remarking on the drain of aircraft and especially crews to the Middle East, he said:

Even before the recent reinforcements there were one thousand pilots in the Middle East. Air Marshal Longmore must be told to send back an equal number of good men of the various classes, and not add to his already distended personnel.[24]

What lends an air of the positively grotesque to this suggestion is its date: December 30, 1940. By then, as Churchill (and the Air Staff) well knew, the Middle East Air Force was playing its sturdy part in bringing him Britain's first major offensive victory of the war and the last he would see for a distressingly long time.

Such, then, was the prevailing "climate" of the Middle East war in 1940–41.

38 War with Italy; war for aerodromes; Operation "Compass"

The saving grace, for the RAF in 1940, was the enemy – the Italian Air Force (*Regia Aeronautica*) which, as stated above, was no less second-line than Longmore's veterans. As the name of the Governor-General and Commander-in-Chief in Italy's Libyan colony – Marshal Balbo (see p. 201, Chapter 21, Note 21) – recalled, Italian aviation and design in the 1930s had commanded universal respect, and the air performance in Spain had done nothing to diminish this, although by the end of the Civil War the Italians were overshadowed by their German colleagues. In June 1940, however, they went to war with an air force hardly distinguishable from that which had fought in Spain. Their best bomber was still the Savoia-Marchetti SM79 which had so effectively attacked Barcelona in 1938 (see p. 52).[1] It has been described as "a fine and robust bomber that unfailingly operated in the most difficult conditions with great reliability".[2] It carried a heavier bomb-load than the Blenheim I, and had a longer range. With a maximum (Mark II) speed of 270 mph it could outfly Longmore's best fighter, the Gladiator. It was confidently expected at RAF HQ that the Italians, in accordance with the teaching of their famous prophet of air warfare, General Douhet (now instructing at their Air Force War College), would at once launch Barcelona-style attacks on Alexandria. In such a case, the performance of the SM79 would have created undoubted difficulties; it rapidly became apparent, however, that the air force which had produced the first theorist of strategic bombing was, in fact, the most reluctant to undertake it. Whatever its qualities, the SM79 was given little chance of displaying them. One solitary Hurricane, attached to the Western Desert Air Force in June, served as an effective deterrent in support of the outclassed Gladiators. Against the best Italian fighter, however, the Fiat CR42, the latter were evenly matched. When these two types clashed, the Desert skies witnessed "dog-fights" of biplanes exactly like those of the First World War. It has been said[3] that the Italians clung to their older types (like the CR42) because their pilots "tended to associate spectacular aerobatics with good airmanship". They quickly learned, in these early combats, that this was not necessarily so.

Where the Italian advantage was very clearly was in numbers. As ever, figures for the strength of the *Regia Aeronautica* vary, quite considerably. An estimate of comparative air strengths in the Mediterranean by the British Chiefs of Staff in April 1939 gave it 276 aircraft of all types in Libya and the Dodecanese, 138 in East Africa, and 1,393 in Italy herself, a total of 1,807.[4] Denis Richards says that in June 1940 the figures were 329 in Libya and the Dodecanese, 150 in East Africa and 1,200 at home, a total of 1,679.[5] Philip Guedalla offers a round total of "2,600 first-line aircraft".[6] The Official History[7] does not state a total, but says that the Italians had 313 aircraft in Libya and 325 in East Africa, of which 142 were in reserve. East Africa was, of course, very difficult to reinforce (especially for fighters); Libya could draw relatively easily on reserves from Italy. Whichever set of figures one chooses to accept, the Italian numerical advantage was substantial, especially when France dropped out of the war. In

Egypt and Palestine the RAF mustered no more than 205 serviceable aircraft, and in the Sudan, Aden and Kenya only 163.[8]

Longmore was undismayed; he was fully convinced of a truth which we have already seen in operation, namely, that numbers themselves mean little – what really counts is morale, training, experience, and the manner in which a force is used. Although his forces facing the Libyan frontier (No. 202 Group) comprised only six squadrons (four of Blenheims, one Gladiator, one Lysander), Longmore believed that the much superior fighting strength of the Italians opposite might "deteriorate rapidly in the face of a determined air offensive".[9] In this belief he was entirely supported by No. 202 Group's AOC, Air Commodore Raymond Collishaw, DSO, OBE, DSC, DFC, a Canadian, who had been the third highest-scoring British "ace" of the First World War; Collishaw, says Tedder, was "the very epitome of the offensive spirit". His plans for an immediate attack upon the enemy air force were fully prepared; on June 10 he moved his Group headquarters up to his forward airfields. He then paraded all ranks, warned them that hostilities were imminent, and ordered all aircraft to be made ready. After that it was just a matter of waiting for confirmation. Evening wore on into a sultry June night while 202 Group curbed its impatience; just before midnight Longmore signalled a warning that they must "await repeat await further instructions before initiating hostile act",[10] but in fact there was not long to go. At nine minutes after midnight the word came: "A state of war with Italy exists . . ." At first light the Blenheims were off.

Astonishingly, although it was Italy that declared war, the Italian Air Force was taken completely by surprise on June 11. The Gladiators of No. 33 Squadron, waiting to intercept the Italian bombers, found no business. The reconnaissance Blenheims of No. 211 found aircraft not dispersed and "every sign of unreadiness"[11] at the *Regia Aeronautica*'s main base at El Adem, and this was still the case when, shortly afterwards, eight more Blenheims of No. 45 Squadron came in to attack. Their low-level approach was met by some AA fire, but no fighter opposition; they were able to drop high-explosive and incendiary bombs on installations and machine-gun aircraft on the ground. And here, immediately, we once again find the "numbers game" in progress. Returning crews had the impression of having caused a lot of damage, and when Nos. 55 and 113 Squadrons also visited El Adem in the afternoon, they came away in the same belief. We now know that the day cost the Italians no more than 18 aircraft destroyed or damaged on the ground, despite their unpreparedness.[22] No. 45 Squadron's attack cost two Blenheims and crews lost and one aircraft

311

damaged, out of eight which took part; the second attack cost two aircraft damaged out of 18. These numbers may sound small, but they were significant:

> The experience of this first raid on the Western Desert showed that much caution would have to be exercised if our slender resources were not to be depleted by constant casualties.[13]

Thus the very first day's operations set a lasting pattern: though Italian material loss was less than supposed, a complete and unmistakable moral ascendancy had been obtained by the RAF by offensive action – but the steady drain of its own loss from such action was sufficient to cause Longmore grave alarm. Within a month he was telling Collishaw:

> Whilst fully appreciating the initiative and spirit shown by the squadrons operating under your command in the Western Desert, I must draw your immediate attention to the urgent necessity of conserving resources.[14]

Moral ascendancy is a potent force; despite Longmore's understandable fears, and what some of the more fiery spirits in 202 Group called his "muzzling orders", the Italians remained under the influence of their early loss of initiative for the next two months. It was not until the end of July that they showed signs of any recovery, and not until September that they plucked up the courage and energy to heave their greatly superior forces forward into Egypt. By that time the RAF order of battle did at least show the name "Hurricane" against the equipment of three of its squadrons (though the Gladiators were still there), and even boasted one (No. 70) squadron of Wellingtons. Marshal Graziani's[15] advance began on September 9, and by the 16th he had covered the 50 miles to Sidi Barrani against only token opposition by British ground forces – and there he stuck. The British fell back a further 60 miles to the stronger position at Mersa Matruh, but Graziani showed no disposition to follow them. He had, however, given them some food for serious thought.

Chiefly, what Graziani's half-hearted advance had brought about was a recognition (which would become enduring) of what the RAF's main rôle in the Middle East must be. In September 1939, in accordance with prevailing RAF doctrine, which was determinedly anti Army Cooperation, the primary rôle was defined as action against the Italian air forces, their bases and supply lines – in effect, a "strategic offensive",[16] necessarily on a small scale because of the Command's limited resources. It was conceded, however, that "if the situation demanded" support to the Army "should be given first priority for as long as necessary".[17] The Army's withdrawal over a distance of some 120 miles, occasioned by Graziani's offensive, meant the loss of the group of forward landing grounds around Sidi Barrani, which was a serious matter for the RAF. It hindered reconnaissance; fighters were unable to give customary protection to bombers; bombers could not refuel for long-distance raids; reinforcement aircraft flying in from Malta were deprived of a staging post. The intimate connection between air and land operations was perfectly illustrated; and Longmore wrote to Portal on September 19:

> You will appreciate that the consequences of the rapid and extensive retirement of our Army eastwards most seriously reduces the effectiveness of our air operations and any further retirement will hamper the operations of even my few long-range aircraft. I have therefore deemed it advisable to bolster up the Army defences to the full extent of my available air resources and I must continue to do so until such time as the GOC-in-C is better able to resist the Italian advance.[18]

So it began to emerge in the Middle East – the only place where it *could* emerge, because this was the only place where the Army was actually at grips with the enemy – "that modern war might take the form of a war for aerodromes".[19] And since aerodromes are not in the sky, but on land, what happened in the land battle was of direct and vital consequence to the Air Force. Cooperation with the Army, in other words, was not just a tiresome survival of a forgotten war, but – as in France – a present necessity.[20] To be fair, the men on the spot behaved as though there had never been any doubt of this. General Wavell had been a convinced believer in Army/Air Co-operation ever since he had witnessed what it could do in the Palestine Campaign of 1918. In the last pre-war combined exercise (March 1939) he had referred very sharply to the lack of it.[21] But with Longmore as a colleague (both Army and Air GHQs were in Cairo; Admiral Cunningham felt unable to move from Alexandria where his ships were) Wavell had no cause for complaint; indeed, "unstinted praise for [the] achievements of the RAF was frequently given by the GOC-in-C".[22] The Secretary of State for War, Anthony Eden, visiting the Middle East in mid-October, reported to the Chiefs of Staff:

> Liaison between the Army and Air Force is excellent and the RAF are giving support for which no praise can be too high within their limited resources.[23]

There lay the everlasting sting: "limited resources". Wavell backed Longmore's demands for reinforcement with absolute conviction but, as we have seen, this militated against, not in favour of the AOC-in-C – such is the perversity of "Official Man". But Eden's message continued:

> Reinforcement of the RAF is the pressing need of the hour here and will, I am convinced, prove to be the decisive factor.

These strong words were not without effect. Between September and the end of the year, the Middle East Air Force received 41 Wellingtons (to the lamentation of Bomber Command), 87 Hurricanes and 85 Blenheim IVs. This was at least a useful beginning of re-equipment: it meant that, including one at Malta, there would be four Hurricane squadrons; on the other hand, though three squadrons were rearmed with Blenheim IVs, there were only 19 of these in reserve, of which only six were serviceable – this was better than the Blenheim Is, whose seven squadrons had only 26 reserves between them, of which only two were serviceable. The two Wellesley squadrons in the Sudan were reduced to 10 aircraft each, and had no reserves left at all. And against his accessions of strength Longmore had to count 189 aircraft totally lost from all causes by December 2.[24]

Despite distractions – and these were becoming increasingly menacing – and despite continuing numerical weakness, Wavell and Longmore were about to preside over the first really satisfactory cooperative enterprise of their two Services in the war. This was Operation COMPASS, the offensive brilliantly conducted on the ground by Major-General R. N. O'Connor; Collishaw, at No. 202 Group, was once again in complete charge of the air operations, and the cooperation between these two ardent spirits was never less than admirable. Their two headquarters were side by side, and Collishaw, with his staff of thirty-two officers, now had under command two Hurricane squadrons (Nos. 33 and 274), one mixed Gladiator/Gauntlet squadron (No. 3 RAAF), and three squadrons of Blenheims (Nos. 45, 55 and 113). Administratively under Collishaw but operationally under O'Connor were a mixed Army Cooperation squadron of Hurricanes and Lysanders (No. 208) and another (No. 6) with just Lysanders. Robust, manoeuvrable and versatile, the "Lizzies" in the Middle East were flown with great courage and skill and gave a good account of themselves.[25] It is astonishing that after almost seven months of Desert war, by December 30, only five of these seemingly highly vulnerable aircraft had been lost. On the other hand, their preservation "tied up a larger proportion of the fighter force than the value of the reconnaissance normally justified".[26] Hence the mixture with Hurricanes; but it was coming to be realized more and more clearly that fighters themselves could do the job that was needed, and look after themselves at the same time. This was a valuable pointer for the future.

Under Longmore's command, but available to Collishaw at discretion, were four heavy bomber squadrons – three Wellingtons (Nos. 37, 38 and 70) and one Bombay (No. 216). This gave him a theoretical strength of 220 aircraft. Air Intelligence estimated Italian strength at 250 bombers and 250 fighters, but this proved to be a considerable exaggeration. The Italian Air Force was always hard to number accurately, because of its low level of serviceability. Whatever criticisms may be levelled at the RAF in the Middle East on this score should be substantially multiplied for the Italians – and with their home base so much nearer, they had far less excuse. The fault, in fact, lay largely with their aviation industry:

> For engines without air filters, which sang gaily over the grassy aerodromes of Italy, were sadly out of place in the dust-storms of Libya; a faulty sparking plug impaired one type of bomber; petrol of low octane value was freely used with bad effects; and in the absence of spare parts a temporary casualty tended to become permanently unserviceable.[27]

The miseries of the Italians were compounded on the night of December 7, when 11 Wellingtons from Malta attacked their airfield at Castel Benito and destroyed or damaged 29 aircraft. The next night Wellingtons and Blenheims from Egypt attacked Benina, and the Italians lost another 10. By December 9, the first day of COMPASS, they were down to 140 bombers and 191 fighters and ground-attack aircraft.

The operations of December 7 and 8 were the RAF's preliminaries; they included fighter cover for the 4th Indian Division's approach march of over 60 miles in daylight on the 8th, a move across the open which was completed without any interference. Collishaw's intentions were precisely what they had been on June 11: a full-scale offensive to establish complete air superiority. Once obtained, the evidence of experience was that it would not be too difficult to keep it; and so it proved. Nearly 400 sorties were flown in the first week, with some of Collishaw's fighter pilots making as many as four a day. "The superiority of the Hurricane over the Italian fighter CR42 was very marked."[28]

Italian airfields, ports, supplies, troops and transport were all attacked. At the end of the first week the RAF claimed 35 enemy aircraft definitely destroyed and 12 more unconfirmed. The "numbers game" alas! was not only played in the skies of Britain and Northern France. The RAF's own losses were only six aircraft (three pilots),[29] "but the intense activity had a big effect upon the number of fighters that could be kept serviceable ... [Longmore] felt obliged to warn Collishaw not to go on operating at this intensity because the reserves of Gladiators were practically exhausted.[30]

No doubt Collishaw and his young men found this restraint irritating, but the fact is that they had already done what they set out to do. Once again, they had established, from the outset, a complete moral ascendancy – so much so that, in the words of the Official History, their opponent, the *5th Squadra*, "made no effective contribution to the campaign".[31] General O'Connor's brilliant advance from Sidi Barrani to Beda Fomm could thus be planned and executed virtually without regard to the opposing air force – a rare luxury. The initial victory set the tone of all that followed: 38,300 Italian and Libyan prisoners, 237 captured guns, 73 tanks and an unknown, but certainly large, number of vehicles ("units were notoriously reticent on this theme"[32]). The operation, said Wavell "could not have been executed without the magnificent support given by the Royal Air Force and the Royal Navy."[33] For both Army and Air Force this had been a triumph of morale and skill over numbers; Wavell insisted that it had been a triumph of inter-Service cooperation also.

The capture of the little harbour of Sollum on December 16 marked the end of the first phase of COMPASS – but only the first phase. Wavell and O'Connor were determined to exploit their victory; Longmore and Collishaw were determined to give them full support. For the RAF, during the rest of the campaign, the chief enemy would no longer be the Italian Air Force, but distance, with its accompanying difficulties of maintenance as the battle-front moved away from the existing bases. Airborne, the RAF boasted its supreme asset of mobility; but when not airborne, as Philip Guedalla said, "there is nothing quite so immobile as a grounded aircraft".[34] Air forces, he added,

> are no more than idle masses of machinery in the absence of air bases and supplies. If they were to play their part in Africa, they must acquire a new mobility. The RAF, in fine, must learn to be nomadic.[35]

The long haul from Sollum to Benghazi was the school in which it was taught.

"Seawater in his veins": Air Chief Marshal Sir Frederick W. Bowhill, AOC-in-C, Coastal Command, 1937-1941, about to take off.

"Officers . . . who preside over bad times": Air Chief Marshal Sir Philip B. Joubert de la Ferté, AOC-in-C, Coastal Command, 1936-1937 and 1941-1942, the crisis of the Battle of the Atlantic.

"Roof-top level or below": low-level photo-reconnaissance provided some spectacular flying and astonishing photographs, but equally effective was the work of the high-level sorties. The Spitfire XI, operative from 1942 onwards, flew at 42,000 feet, at which height it was almost invisible. This photograph was obtained in preparation for the Dieppe raid in July 1942; unfortunately none revealed the well-hidden German fire-positions.

"Strength to withstand the pressures of the ocean depths": a Sunderland caught this U-boat on the surface and scored a direct hit with a depth-charge that rolled off before exploding; a second depth-charge exploded right alongside. The official caption claims a kill, but such was the strength of U-boat construction that even this degree of accuracy could not be relied on without further evidence.

"Five Mark I Liberators": the struggle to obtain Very Long Range aircraft was crucial in 1942. True VLR meant the Consolidated Liberator Mark I, but Liberators were conceived as bombers (as seen here) and there was great reluctance on the part of the US Army Air Force to release them for the maritime duties in which they proved invaluable.

"A rising star of the RAF": Air Marshal Sir John Slessor's wartime career was almost entirely spent in high staff posts or at AOC-in-C level. In 1938 he was Director of Plans at the Air Ministry; in 1940 he was sent to America on special duties; in 1941 he commanded No. 5 Group, Bomber Command, returning to the Air Staff as Assistant Chief (Policy) in 1942; in 1943 he became AOC-in-C, Coastal Command, just in time for the Atlantic victory; in 1944 he was appointed Deputy AOC-in-C, Mediterranean Allied Land Forces and C-in-C, RAF, Mediterranean and Middle East; in 1945 back to the Air Staff as Air Member for Personnel.

Christmas came and went cheerfully, as the British forces counted their gains and prepared for more; in the New Year the harvesting began. Bardia was taken on January 4, the important port of Tobruk on the 22nd. By now the *Regia Aeronautica* was in serious trouble – forced back on its last remaining airfields in Cyrenaica, reduced to some 46 bombers and 34 fighters, and finding the greatest difficulty in maintaining these. The RAF, too, was feeling the effects of this style of Desert war, but Collishaw unhesitatingly backed O'Connor's wish to push on without a halt. Apart from anything else, he coveted the air bases round Benghazi, whose possession would push the Italians out of range of the Nile Delta, bring closer support to Malta, and greatly ease the attack on targets in Italy;

> ... these considerations outweighed the shortage of petrol, ammunition and rations in the forward area.[36]

Longmore backed his decision, and everything the RAF had available was thrown into the last spurt, leaving the main bases in Egypt stripped to the very bone of their air defence. Boldness had its reward: Benghazi fell on February 6, and the first British Desert victory was an accomplished fact.

O'Connor's crowning victory was the Battle of Beda Fomm, the last round-up of Italians attempting to escape from Benghazi as the Australian 6th Division closed in. When the final count for COMPASS was made, it showed that 10 Italian divisions had been destroyed, some twenty generals and 130,000 soldiers captured, with 845 guns and nearly 400 tanks. The cost, to an army which never numbered more than 31,000, was 500 killed, 1,373 wounded and 55 missing. The air victory was, if anything, even more devastating: Italian records show that they lost 58 aircraft in combat during the COMPASS period; 91 more were captured intact on their airfields; no fewer than 1,100 damaged aircraft were also captured during the advance.[37] This total of more than 1,200 aircraft captured and counted is firm ground for once in the calculation of profit and loss, and their significance is unmistakable:

> These losses alone crippled the Italian Air Force ...[38]

Henceforward the *Regia Aeronautica*, despite many brave individual pilots and crews and some useful aircraft (particularly Mario Castoldi's fighter designs for *Aeronautica Macchi*, the MC200,[39] MC202 and MC205), flew with a broken wing. Forced back on the defensive from

317

the beginning, poorly led and abysmally maintained, the Italian air effort, from now until their surrender in 1943, would be no more than a fringe activity in the march of war.

In the COMPASS operations, from December 9, 1940 to February 6, 1941, the Operations Records of RAF, Middle East, show that aircraft totally lost from all causes (shot down, destroyed on the ground, missing, crashed) numbered precisely 26, as follows:

Hurricane	6
Blenheim	11
Gladiator	5
Wellington	3
Valentia	1[40]

This does not, of course, by any means represent the full RAF wastage; the extreme difficulty of maintenance meant that many aircraft, although strictly speaking only "damaged", had to be written off the squadron books for a very long time. The increasing use of explosive bullets by the Italians added to this problem; out of nine Blenheims which attacked Bardia on December 14, for example, while only one was lost, seven more suffered damage from this cause. Nevertheless, by any standard, the RAF's victory was overwhelming and amazingly economical.

39 East Africa; air support

It will here be convenient to abandon chronology for the time being, and follow this story through to the defeat of Italy. For although she did not actually surrender until 1943, the damage done to her in 1941 was decisive; the broken wing of the *Regia Aeronautica* thereafter was only an aspect of the broken arm of the would-be successor of Rome. Since this result was exclusively achieved by the forces of the British Empire, Churchill's altogether too-often quoted saying, "Before Alamein we never had a victory", seems singularly unfortunate.[1]

In June 1940 the disparity of strength between the forces of the Italian Empire in East Africa and the British facing them was outwardly overwhelming: on the ground, the Viceroy of Ethiopia and Supreme Commander, the Duke of Aosta, with his 350,000 men (see p. 303), was opposed by only about 19,000 British, divided between three widely separated theatres of war: the Sudan, Somaliland and Kenya. In the air, 325 Italian aircraft (142 in reserve or under repair) faced the 163 items of Longmore's museum catalogue (see p. 318, Chapter

38, Note 8). But as ever, numbers meant little; in Abyssinia, internal security was Aosta's major preoccupation; 70 per cent of his troops were Africans – who might or might not fight hard for Italy; many of his aircraft were suited only to Colonial operations, while all suffered from the usual Italian maintenance problems; above all, he was virtually cut off from supply and reinforcement.[2] Conscious of their own alarming weakness, the British commanders did not at once recognize the difficulties which beset their enemy; but by the end of 1940, penetration of Italian communication by Ultra had reached such a pitch of efficiency that

> ... the Cs-in-C in Cairo were able to read the enemy's plans and appreciation in his own words as soon as he issued them; indeed, they sometimes received the decrypts while the Italian W/T operators were still asking for the signals to be checked and repeated.[3]

The campaign in East Africa was, in fact, a "cryptographer's war", and as Ronald Lewin has said, "The record of that campaign will now have to be completely rewritten."[4]

If only for that reason, no attempt will now be made to narrate the campaign; only salient points can be mentioned – and perhaps a little of an atmosphere which, within the framework of electronic modernity, often partakes of the styles of the North-West Frontier, Biggles and the breezy yarns of the *Chums Annual* in the 1930s. Above all, East Africa was the scene of inter-Service enterprise, and the elderly aircraft commanded by Air Commodore L. H. Slatter in the Sudan, Air Commodore W. Sowrey in Kenya (East Africa Command) and Air Vice-Marshal G. R. M. Reid at Aden, no matter how out of place they may have looked in terms of the Battle of Britain or the attack on Germany, won heartfelt praise from the soldiers whom they loyally supported. It was, of course, not only the character of the aircraft that decided the Air Force rôle; it was also the virtual absence of "strategic" targets in this theatre. The nearest to such was the port of Massawa in Eritrea, which housed administrative buildings, barracks, port installations, the base of the Italian Red Sea naval squadron, an airfield and – most tempting – oil stores. Briskly off the mark, the Wellesleys of No. 14 Squadron (Sudan) attacked Massawa on June 11 and sent up 780 tons of fuel in flames. For both the Sudan and Aden squadrons, "Massawa could always provide something worthy of their attention".[5] Apart from that, and the Caproni factory at Mai Edega (also in Eritrea, near Gura) which was extensively damaged by bombing in February, the chief and most profitable targets for the RAF and the South

319

African Air Force were the Italian airfields. But attacking these was only another aspect of Army Cooperation which, for most of the time, was the most important activity of all.

In 1868, General Sir Robert Napier marched an Anglo-Indian army 400 miles from Massawa to Magdala, defeated the Abyssinian Emperor Theodore, released his European captives, and brought the force out again at trifling cost in life and limb – a triumph of Victorian preparation and organization. It would therefore be entirely wrong to say that successful campaigning in Abyssinia was impossible without air power; on the other hand, there can be no doubt whatever that air power and air superiority played a decisive part in the British victory in East Africa in 1941. The solitary occasion when it changed sides underlined the point.

Relying on distance – from the Kenya border to Addis Ababa is 500 miles as the crow flies – on poor or non-existent communications, making movement of large numbers of men impossible during the spring rains, and on the known weakness of the British forces on his southern flank, the Duke of Aosta concentrated the best of his army and air force in the north, to meet any threat from the Sudan. By the end of October, British reinforcements made this a reality, and the Italians were expelled without difficulty from the frontier posts which they had occupied in July. The attempt to advance from Gallabat to Metemma, just inside Eritrea, then ran into difficulties which precisely illustrate the intimate inter-connection of ground and air operations. This movement was entrusted to the 10th Indian Infantry Brigade with a squadron of (12) tanks and some artillery under the command of Brigadier W. J. Slim.[6] The air support consisted of:

6 Gladiators	(No. 1 Squadron, SAAF)
4 Gladiators	("K" Flight; No. 112 Squadron, RAF)
4 Hardys	(No. 237 "Rhodesia" Squadron)
6 Wellesleys	(No. 47 Squadron)
6 Gauntlets and Vincents	(No. 430 Flight; Army Cooperation)

Gallabat was seized in the early hours of November 6, and the attempt on Metemma was planned to follow at once, but the Italian Air Force reacted strongly. A defensive patrol over the battle area by three Gladiators of "K" Flight, operating for the first time in an area where enemy fighters were to be expected, appears to have concentrated on "watching the battle instead of searching the sky",[7] with the result that it was "jumped" by a formation of CR42s. Two

Gladiators were at once shot down, and the third had to make a forced landing deep in the Sudan.

This was a bad beginning, but worse was to follow. The army advance was delayed by damage to the tanks, partly due to Italian mines, but chiefly to the rocky ground. Meanwhile, the Italian Air Force was concentrating in the skies over Metemma. At 0830 hours No. 1 Squadron SAAF engaged eight CR42s, losing two more Gladiators. At 1430 the remaining Gladiators of No. 1 Squadron and the sole survivor of "K" Flight attacked Italian bombers over Gallabat; in the "dog-fight" with the escorting CR42s two of these were shot down, but the "K" Flight Gladiator was also destroyed. The British fighter force was thus reduced from 10 to four machines; heavily outnumbered, and also outflown by the CR42s (these Italian pilots all had Spanish Civil War experience and handled their aircraft "with dash and enterprise"[8]), the surviving British fighters were unable to prevent frequent attacks by the enemy bombers. One of these scored a direct hit on the lorry containing the spare parts for the tanks – a heavy blow. But the most serious effect was, as in Norway and in France, the damage to morale. It was the Essex battalion of 10th Brigade that was now affected, and Brigadier Slim was shocked to see truckload after truckload of gesticulating British soldiers, shouting that "The enemy are coming!" and making for the rear "driving as if the devil were after them".[9] What had happened was that "the Italians had secured – for the first and last time – local air superiority in East Africa".[10]

We may note that this was not the only Italian success; in East Africa they were not always feeble adversaries. Two days after No. 14 Squadron had set fire to the aviation fuel at Massawa, three Caproni 133 bombers[11] performed a like service for 5,000 gallons on the airfield of Wajir in Kenya. Then, on October 16, at Gedaref in the Sudan, eight Wellesleys and two Vincents, collected to assist the Abyssinian insurgents against Italian rule, were bombed, shot up and all destroyed by a bold attack by seven CR32s and 42s and an SM79.[12] Again, as the British 1941 advance developed, the CR42s struck at the airfield at Agordat, destroying six British aircraft on the ground and severely damaging four; the next day (February 9) they came back and destroyed a Hurricane and damaged two more. However, it must be said that in the first phase of the East African campaign, both the RAF and its comrade-in-arms, the South African Air Force, despite losses, "more than held its own against Mussolini's *Regia Aeronautica* . . . There can be no doubt that the spirit of the South African airmen was responsible for many of their successes and led them on occasion,

321

to take inordinate risks both with their lives and their machines."[13] It was remarked that

The advent of the Hurricane aircraft of No. 1 SAAF Squadron gave the RAF air superiority "to an astonishing degree", and full use was made of these aircraft in attacks on enemy aerodromes.[14]

The British offensive, soundly informed by Ultra, took the form of a pincer movement – the jaws of the pincer being the forces of Lieutenant-General W. Platt in the Sudan, and Lieutenant-General A. Cunningham in Kenya, 1,200 miles apart. Platt's first advance was to the strong hill-position of Keren in Eritrea. Here the Italians put up what was probably their best fight of the war; Savoy Grenadiers and *Bersaglieri*, well backed by artillery, made a hard, long-drawn-out battle of it on the ground, and were well supported also by the CR42s (and 32s), the Capronis and the SM79s. But while the army continued to struggle and give the British and Indian troops a hard time at Keren, the Italian Air Force found itself at an increasing disadvantage. The British advance

secured to the Royal Air Force the use of landing grounds so far advanced that many of the enemy's bases in Eritrea and northern Abyssinia were brought within range of our fighters and resulted in heavy destruction of enemy aircraft on the ground. There was also a very marked decrease in enemy air activity, and their bombing attacks became of almost negligible importance.[15]

So the tables of Gallabat were turned at Keren; despite a fine resistance for nearly eight weeks, the Italians were turned out of their very strong position at the end of March, and this victory proved to be decisive because, in the words of the Official History, "they never fought with the same determination again".[16] The rôle of air superiority in the victory cannot be doubted; as Air Commodore Slatter said,

... when it is considered that the deployment of both Indian Divisions[17] with all their artillery, ammunition and stores necessary for the operation was done down a single road in a valley which was under complete observation from posts situated on the heights to the west of Keren, it is safe to assume that without complete air superiority the preparations necessary for the battle could never have been made ...[18]

322

With the fall of Keren, Italian resistance crumbled rapidly. Eritrea was quickly occupied by the British forces; British Somaliland, overrun by the Italians in August 1940, had already been freed, enabling Cunningham's troops to push on to Addis Ababa, which they entered on April 5. The collapse of their northern army with the best of their air force completely undermined Italian resistance to General Cunningham's advance from Kenya. The Italian Air Force on the southern front was in any case weak – a total of only 95 aircraft, of which only 21 were fighters, and only nine of those were CR42s. Even the antiquated aircraft of the South African Air Force, in the hands of their bold pilots, were more than a match for this. Just *how* antiquated may be judged from the fact of Ju 86 bomber squadrons being "modernized" by rearming with Fairey Battles!

With complete air superiority, the advance from Kenya was, in fact, hardly more than a military promenade, with distance, terrain and climate the chief enemies. Two vignettes, however, may give us the flavour of the strange war that was waged by the SAAF[19] in East Africa in those early months of 1941. First, a scene from the advance into Italian Somaliland in February; armoured cars were attacking the frontier fort of Hobok, supported by Hartbees of No. 40 (Army Cooperation) Squadron, SAAF. The commander of the cars, Lieutenant A. J. T. Irwin, charged his car at the wire entanglements, where it stuck under heavy fire from Italian machine guns:

Lieut. J. D. W. Human, SAAF, flew his Hartbee to Lieut. Irwin's assistance and although the aircraft was holed twice he continued to circle over the enemy's fort so that his rear gunner, Air-Sgt. J. Jackson, could bring his gun to bear on the enemy's machine guns while Lieut. Human dropped bomb after bomb on the fort. This timely intervention distracted the enemy's attention from Lieut. Irwin until the rest of our armoured cars had raced up. The Hartbee was forced to make a crash landing in the bush but the pilot and his gunner escaped injury. For their gallantry Lieut. Human was awarded the Distinguished Flying Cross and Air-Sgt. Jackson the Distinguished Flying Medal.[20]

It is pleasant to record that Lieutenant Irwin was not left out; he received the MC for his part in this curiously intimate style of battle.

One more glimpse must suffice: the attack made by No. 3 (Fighter) Squadron, SAAF, on Diredawa on March 15. The squadron claimed 10 enemy aircraft destroyed, and eight damaged; but two of its Hurricanes were also shot down:

One of these was piloted by Capt. J. Frost [who had won the DFC on February 3]. Frost had already shot down two enemy aircraft when his own aircraft was hit and its engine seized. He managed to land on the enemy's satellite aerodrome and he then set fire to his machine. Lieut. R. H. C. Kershaw, piloting another Hurricane, saw Frost's predicament and landed close to him through a barrage of enemy fire. Frost climbed on to Kershaw's lap (there was no room for him in the cockpit) and in that position he operated the "stick" and the rudder while Kershaw operated the "flap" and the undercarriage levers.[21]

And in that fashion these two cool men came home. Kershaw received the DSO, the first to be won by a South African in the war.

Within these combats of antique types and deeds out of the old legends of air warfare there were serious lessons in which it is not the past that we see, but a future still several years off. Air Commodore Slatter's report on the operations of the Sudan-based Air Force has little to do with past glories and everything to do with things to come. He listed five lessons from the campaign: the first was the difficulty created by the virtual absence of transport aircraft; the second was closely linked – the need for further development of supply-dropping apparatus, and for much more of it. Burma, 1944–45, would say a hearty "Amen" to both of these. Thirdly, he urged the provision of long-range fighters (Portal's *bêtes-noires*); Slatter considered that they would be "the real answer to the destruction of enemy aircraft on their aerodromes". The Combined Bomber Offensive would show that they were also the answer to enemy aircraft in the daylight air. Fourthly, Slatter drew attention to the lack of Red Cross aircraft, and pointed out that in the heavy fighting at Keren this service had to be improvised. The developing war would see air ambulances revolutionize the handling of casualties and transform the chances of survival, in all theatres. Finally, like many others, Slatter wanted dive-bombers. They were essential, he said, for attacks on pin-point targets – and, of course, he was right, as Mosquitos, Mustangs and others would show in due course. But in mentioning those famous aircraft we have to concede that the Air Staff was also right not to be stampeded into hasty production of dive-bombers *per se*. Soon the truth emerged that good aircraft could handle this task and others as well, which was sound economics and tactically cheering too.

Air Commodore Slatter's Report was shrewd and far-sighted. Air Commodore Sowrey's forces, however, were also pointing meaningful fingers at the future. On April 1 the SAAF formed a Close Support Flight, consisting of four Gladiators and four Hartbees. General

Cunningham, who paid tribute to the complete cooperation which he had received from Air Commodore Sowrey throughout the campaign, made – understandably – special mention of this experiment:

> . . . its Air Force commander *with his own communications* advanced with the commander of the leading troops. The value of this arrangement from the Army point of view cannot be over stressed. Air support for the forward troops of the nature called for by the situation was "on tap", and engendered the greatest confidence amongst both commanders and men.[22]

The italics are mine, but in fact the whole passage could be given italics. Air support, by fighters and bombers, "on tap" – not just carrying out a prearranged cooperation programme – and controlled by an Air Force officer with his own communications net, but using the same command post as the Army commanding officer, was a preview of the Tactical Air Force "cab-rank" techniques which were brought to great fulfilment between 1943–45. The Gladiators and Hartbees of the SAAF in East Africa in 1941 were the forerunners. But at that time Army Cooperation was "nobody's baby", so there were no fanfares. It is time to make acknowledgment.

40 The Greek fiasco, 1941

Over a month before O'Connor and Collishaw brought down the curtain on their desert victory, and even longer before the pincers in East Africa began to close, a new and very different enemy made his début on the Mediterranean scene. By January 4, 1941, Air Ministry Intelligence was aware, from Ultra intercepts, that the *Luftwaffe* was assembling units in Sicily. It knew, also, what units these were; they were from *Fliegerkorps X*, hitherto stationed in Norway, where it had specialized in attacks on shipping. The initial threat was clear: it was to the Mediterranean Fleet. Unfortunately, at this stage there would appear to have been a breakdown of useful communication between the Air Ministry and the Admiralty. The Mediterranean Fleet was engaged in covering the movements of a number of convoys towards Malta and Greece; when 30–40 Ju 88s and 87s made their appearance on January 10 it came as a most unpleasant surprise:

> The attacks were made with great skill and determination and were quite unlike anything the fleet had experienced at the hands of the Italians.[1]

The aircraft-carrier *Illustrious* was hit six times and set on fire, with many casualties; with great difficulty she was brought into Malta, where she was heavily bombed again, but escaped at last to Alexandria. As an effective unit, however, she was out of the war for a long time. And on the day after this blow (January 11), the dive-bombers damaged the cruiser *Southampton* so severely that she had to be abandoned and sunk. The Germans wasted no time in casting a shadow which was going to lie over the Mediterranean for a long time to come.

What brought them there was the general incompetence and sheer military failure of their Italian allies. Vainglorious, but ill-informed, Mussolini had launched an attack on Greece at the end of October 1940. He expected an early Greek collapse, but instead met fierce resistance which turned into a vigorous counter-attack before a month had passed. From then onwards the Greek adventure proved to be yet another costly humiliation for Italy. For the British Commanders-in-Chief in the Middle East, however, it was the first of the series of distractions (see p. 314) which proved the foundation of much grief and frustration during the next two years. Furthermore, it threw a remorseless spotlight on the false appreciations and confused thinking which passed for strategy in the highest British circles in that dark stage of the war. We cannot here examine the Greek fiasco in detail, but some consideration of it is needed, because of the effect it had on the RAF in the Middle East, and its AOC-in-C, Air Chief Marshal Longmore.

As soon as the Italian invasion began, on October 28, the Greek Government invoked the British guarantee given to Greece on April 13, 1939. This, says Churchill, "we were bound to honour".[2] Bearing in mind that the guarantee in question had been given jointly with France, that France was now no longer combatant and the whole situation totally transformed, it is not easy to perceive, at this distance in time, the force of that contention. It must, however, be remarked that it was almost universally subscribed to at the time, drawing much strength from references to that everlasting enigma, the power of world opinion. A more cynical generation may observe that nothing is more likely to affect world opinion than the hard facts of defeat or victory. However, it was with wide and cordial backing that Churchill promised the Greek Premier:

> We will give you all the help in our power. We will fight a common foe and we will share a united victory.[3]

The truth is that the British gesture was not merely quixotic, nor was it just angry retaliation against the Italian tendency "to rush to the aid of the victor".[4] Its roots went deeper – to the great delusion with which the British comforted themselves in the second half of 1940, and which, as we have seen (pp. 275–6) largely inspired the bombing policy: the belief of the Chiefs of Staff and others that, for economic reasons, "Germany will be in danger of collapsing in 1941".[5] Proceeding from this treacherous foundation, in the very moment of French collapse and Italian hostility, the Chiefs of Staff concluded that "it would be a British interest that the Balkans should become a theatre of war".[6] This unfortunately, awakened Churchillian dreams which would have been better left sleeping, but instead roused strong responses, not least in the new CAS, Sir Charles Portal.

With considerable misgivings, but no prompting from London – it was his own reading of signals from the British Minister in Athens that inspired him – Longmore decided to support the Greeks against the Italians immediately with a mixed Blenheim squadron (No. 30) of bombers and fighters. Churchill told him: "You have taken a very bold and wise decision".[7] During November two more squadrons of Blenheim bombers (Nos. 84 and 211) and a Gladiator squadron (No. 80) followed, with a further Gladiator squadron (No. 112) in December. With COMPASS in preparation, and this distraction mounting, the emotions of the Middle East Cs-in-C may be imagined on being told the latest pronouncement of the London strategic oracle. Ultra was by now producing "incontrovertible evidence that Germany was actively preparing a large-scale Balkan campaign"[8] – the first occasion in the war when such a clear warning was possible. The Chiefs of Staff, calculating the probable consequences of such a German move, came to the curious conclusion that

> the defence of Turkey was more important than that of Greece. The War Cabinet accordingly decided to do everything possible to ensure that if Turkey were attacked she would resist, and to give her all the aid in our power . . .[9]

The conclusion was curious for two reasons: first, the extreme shortage of all kinds of war material; secondly, the aid promised to Greece, which was already at war with an Axis power. However, this was the unpalatable dish thrust before the Middle East Cs-in-C, and the Prime Minister himself spelt out the recipe

> by pointing out that the importance of going to the help of Turkey would far outweigh that of carrying out the Western Desert operations which General Wavell was planning; indeed, in Egypt he would be relegated to the very minimum defensive rôle.[10]

327

In vain did Wavell point to the lessons of history:

I am quite sure Germany cannot afford to see Italy defeated – or even held – in Greece, and must intervene ... Germany probably does not want, at present, to push Bulgaria into war or invade Yugoslavia, but may be forced to do so. As in the last war, Germany is on interior lines and can move more quickly to attack Greece or Turkey than we can to support them.[11]

But Churchill, too, was beginning to hear echoes of the First World War – though in a very different sense. Always, in that war, an opponent of the Western strategy, like his friend Lloyd George, he had ceaselessly explored the possibilities of any alternative theatre. Lloyd George, in February 1915, had urged that bringing in Bulgaria, Rumania and Greece to help Serbia "means throwing an aggregate army of 1,500,000 on the Austrian flank".[12] On that occasion, however, the glittering vision was rejected in favour of Churchill's Dardanelles project; now, as 1940 merged into 1941, he would in turn be urging a Balkan front of Greece, Yugoslavia and Turkey, giving, with British support "70 divisions in this area". It was a witching prospect:

If at the wave of our wand Yugoslavia, Greece and Turkey would all act together it seemed to us that Hitler might either let the Balkans off for the time being or become so heavily engaged with our combined forces as to create a major front in that theatre.[13]

On the spot, the strategy of magic wands was less appealing. On January 29 Longmore was warned by Portal to be ready to send 10–15 squadrons to Turkey. His reply was in character:

Your message received. Quite frankly contents astound me ... I cannot believe you fully appreciate present situation Middle East, in which Libya drive in full career and Sudan offensive into Eritrea progressing satisfactorily ... However strong advantages may be of impressing the Turks, can you afford to lock up squadrons you propose in Turkey where they may well remain for some time inoperative? Would it not be forsaking the substance for the shadow?[14]

To which Portal loftily replied:

It is not a question of impressing the Turks. It is a question of trying to deter Germany by fear of bombing of Rumania from absorbing Bulgaria, Greece and Turkey without firing a shot and then dominating the Eastern Mediterranean and Aegean as she now dominates the Narrows. If we can prevent or even delay this, the squadrons in Turkey will have pulled far more weight than in helping to beat Italians in Africa.[15]

Such unreality takes some beating. Even Churchill was startled:

Some time ago we asked Greece to prepare airfields for fourteen squadrons, and this work is still going on. Then, after various interchanges, you proposed sending ten squadrons to Turkey, which the Turks have not yet accepted, but which they may accept ... Suppose they do accept, and after that Greece demands further aid beyond the five squadrons allotted, what are you going to do? I am afraid you have got to look at this very seriously. I am in it with you up to the neck. But have we not in fact promised to sell the same pig to two customers?[16]

Taken in the round, it was a reasonable question, its force undiminished by the fact that, either way, it would be a very small pig. The matter, however, was conveniently resolved when Turkey showed no inclination to risk war with Germany unless attacked. And the same was true of Greece; although glad enough of any help she could get from Britain (which meant Longmore) against Italy, the Greeks refused the offer of ground forces, and even prohibited RAF officers from looking for airfield sites in Macedonia – for fear of provoking German action. As for the Yugloslavs, when their moment came they were caught in such an extremity of unpreparedness that, as Denis Richards says, they "were beaten almost before they could take the field".[17] So much for magic wands.

From bad beginnings, things went from worse to worse. It is only fair to record how Churchill, the most powerful personage concerned, and the most subject to strategic fantasies, belatedly but assuredly became the first to return to sanity about Greece.[18] In this Ultra (to which Churchill always paid very close attention) no doubt played its part: in February 1941 the breaking of the German Railway Enigma[19] confirmed beyond further doubt the German intention to attack Greece. With COMPASS now triumphantly concluded and both East African campaigns well under way, the Middle East seemed full of options: there was still hope of bringing in Turkey; partly with this in view (and partly to anticipate the *Luftwaffe*), an attack on the Dodecanese Islands was being planned (MANDIBLES); planning was also in progress for an invasion of Sicily (INFLUX); the presence of the *Luftwaffe* in the Mediterranean placed a serious question mark against Vichy-held Syria. To help and guide the Commanders-in-Chief through this maze, the Government sent out the Foreign Secretary, Anthony Eden, and the Chief of the Imperial General Staff, General

Sir John Dill. There was thus a powerful array of political and strategic talent on the spot in this crisis.

As Eden and Dill reached Cairo (February 20), Churchill signalled:

> Do not consider yourselves obligated to a Greek enterprise if in your hearts you feel it will only be another Norwegian fiasco. If no good plan can be made please say so. But of course you know how valuable success would be.[20]

Eden, however, had arrived to find that Wavell's mind was already made up; bearing in mind General Wolfe's dictum that "War is an Option of Difficulties", he had come to the conclusion that

> Provided that conversations with the Greeks show that there is a good chance of establishing a front against the Germans with our assistance, I think we should take it.

As John Connell says, "Wavell certainly did not have to be persuaded against his will".[21] The same was true of Longmore and Admiral Cunningham; reporting his first meeting with the Commanders-in-Chief to Churchill on the 20th, Eden said:

> We are agreed we should do everything in our power to bring the fullest measure of help to Greeks at earliest possible moment. If the help we can offer is accepted by the Greeks we believe that there is a fair chance of halting a German advance and preventing Greece from being overrun.[22]

Churchill offered the men in the Middle East further opportunities of changing their minds; they dismissed them all. As Tedder later wrote:

> I was under the impression that this was one of those cases of a politician (Eden) over-riding the military (Wavell). One can see now that nothing could be further from the truth. The boot was on the other foot. It was the military commanders as much as the politicians who felt that the political considerations were overriding.[23]

Hindsight, not long delayed, stands amazed; the Air Historical Branch Narrative of the Greek Campaign says frankly,

> As one reads the story, it is difficult to see how anyone expected anything but a complete and rapid German victory . . .[24]

Quite so; but in all respects Britain's war during this strange, lonely intermission between June 1940 and June 1941 had a definite touch of madness.

One facet of madness did, however, begin to recede; in his signal of February 20 Eden admitted:

> Limitation of our resources however, especially in the air, will not allow of help being given to Turkey at the [same] time if Greece is to be supported on an effective scale ... Extent of help which we can later give Turks must depend upon volume of air reinforcements that can reach Middle East and war wastage in African operations ... If we now split our small resources, especially in the air, we can effectively help neither Greece nor Turkey.[25]

At least Longmore had managed to persuade him that the RAF's resources *were* small – though Churchill was never quite convinced, and Portal disliked being reminded. As to being split, that was already the case and would relentlessly remain so.

By the end of March 1941, the RAF in Greece, under Air Vice-Marshal J. H. D'Albiac, mustered the equivalent of eight squadrons, some 80 serviceable aircraft (200 including reserves).[26] The air and ground-crews, doggedly getting on with the job they were set to do, rose above the disgusting conditions of a Balkan winter campaign: there were no all-weather airfields in Greece; low cloud and mist in the mountains made flying impossible on an average of 15 days per month; communications were almost non-existent; accommodation could be "cold, damp and evil-smelling";[27] hygiene and sanitation were appalling, food revolting. The Western Desert was a comparative paradise. But as long as the ground-crews could keep them in the air, the aircrews stuck to a task which at least had the reward of the "numbers game" – a satisfying "bag" of Italian aircraft: 93 "confirmed" and 26 "probables" by March 31, for a loss of four Hurricanes and six Gladiators (six pilots saved).[28] It was a brave endeavour.

As an institution, on the other hand, the RAF in Greece has a less admirable look; indeed, it appears as doctrinaire and uncooperative. It could scarcely claim to represent a powerful, decisive reinforcement; on the contrary, it was weak in numbers – only five squadrons by December, rising to a maximum of nine, with detachments of three Wellington squadrons operating in support in Egypt. In no way could this represent more than a contingent in the Greek struggle for survival; yet it presumed to dictate policy. The Greeks knew what they wanted, and made no bones about it. They wanted direct air support in the battle their army was gallantly fighting, and as their own minuscule and ancient Air Force withered away in the attempt to provide it, they very badly needed the help of the RAF. But the RAF knew better. Direct support to an army, D'Albiac maintained, was not a "proper use of air power"; just as in France, almost a year before, all the RAF's doctrine and training taught that it must never "waste" its magnificent flying machines in attacking battlefield targets. (It was fortunate that Collishaw, Slatter and Sowrey saw matters differently, or Britain's only victories of the period could hardly have happened!) What makes D'Albiac's attitude hardest to understand is the actual composition of his command: apart from the Wellington detachments, one and a half squadrons of Hurricanes and one of Blenheim IVs, it consisted entirely of Blenheim Is and Gladiators. In any case, as we have seen, nowhere at that time, not even in the most modern squadrons of Bomber Command, did the RAF possess the equipment needed to carry out really effective bombing of long-range targets – and this was the Balkan winter, with all that that implied in terms of reduction of operational efficiency. Yet D'Albiac was quite determined about how his force should be used: his task was not to join in the vulgar fisticuffs of the Greek Army, battling in the Albanian mountains; it was a "strategic" attack on the Italian bases at Valona (Vlonë) and Durazzo (Durrës) – with all the mighty weight of about a dozen Wellingtons and the Blenheim Is.

For a long time, all attempts to shift D'Albiac from this position proved vain. He complained of "what amounted to a conspiracy to bring unfair pressure to bear"[29] on himself, on Longmore and on the British Government. He accused the Reuter correspondent and "an unofficial but influential Greek syndicate", who had the effrontery to suggest that in leaving battlefield intervention to the Greeks, the RAF had left them the harder task. These critics were not alone, however. When the British Air Attaché told the King of the Hellenes that the RAF had only three aircraft available for such a purpose,

> The King was very disappointed. I have explained (after consultation with D'Albiac) difficulties owing to small number of aircraft here *and importance of using what we have against other targets*. His Majesty explained Greek aircraft doing five or six raids a day while ours are doing only one. His Air Force was harassing the enemy at all points in this sector, and some extra support would help to complete task. Yesterday Greek Air Force destroyed 10 aircraft in air and 16 on ground; their own losses were 5. Today they have destroyed 5 Italians and their own losses were 4. With these losses and no spares, His Majesty fears his own Air Force will

soon be inoperative and that we shall then have to take over all air operations . . .[30]

The Greek Premier and Commander-in-Chief added their voices
to the King's, but to no avail:

> It was, of course, the British view that the faulty tactics of the Greeks were
> themselves responsible [for losses]. "Tendency to employ Greek aircraft
> in close support has resulted in disproportionate casualties."[31]

The dispute did not run on purely national lines; it concerned the
truths about the application of air power, which is why it is important.
D'Albiac and the RAF purists were irritated to find that British
soldiers sided with the Greeks, pointing out that it was German
practice, during a battle, to concentrate all their resources (including
the Air arm) on it until it was won. The AHB narrator wryly remarks:

> And it seemed at that date an almost intolerable paradox to argue that the
> Germans did not understand the proper use of air power. Today [he
> inscrutably continues] the conclusion can be more readily accepted.[32]

It only remains to add that when the Germans entered the fray on
April 6, the *Luftwaffe* swiftly brushed aside doctrines and superstitions.
With habitual efficiency in such matters, it very rapidly assembled
overwhelming strength (over 1,000 aircraft[33]) from places as far distant
as the Atlantic coast, Sicily and Tripolitania. Once again the value of
its large fleet of Ju 52 transports was displayed. And once again painful
tuition was offered in the battle use of aircraft:

> For two days I have been bombed, machine-gunned, and shot at by all
> and sundry. German *Stukas* have blown two cars from under me and
> strafed a third . . . all day and all night there have been waves of Germans
> in the skies . . . The Germans are using a fantastic amount of aircraft,
> more than I ever saw in Norway under similar conditions of terrain.
> Goering must have a third of his air force operating here and it is bombing
> every nook and cranny, hamlet, village and town in its path . . .[34]

Like the Greek Army and the British forces trying to bring its weak
and belated support, the RAF was swept away in this tide of battle:

> Within a few days it was plain that our small air force in Greece had been
> swamped by overwhelming low-flying attacks on its virtually undefended
> aerodromes.[35]

So the "Norwegian fiasco" which Churchill had feared came about. After only a fortnight's fighting, it was clear that only another evacuation (in the teeth of the triumphant *Luftwaffe*) could save anything of the British land and air forces which had been offered by their leaders as hostages to fortune. The withdrawal was completed by May 2 with less loss among the soldiers and RAF ground-crews than anyone had the right to expect, but at a heavy cost to the Royal Navy. All told, the campaign cost the RAF 209 aircraft, 72 in combat, 55 on the ground, and 82 destroyed or abandoned on evacuation. Out of 163 officers and men killed, missing and prisoners, 150 were aircrew.

For this disaster (and its postscript, Crete) blame would seem to lie squarely with Eden, Dill, Wavell, Longmore and Cunningham, in that order. Taking into account the very high qualities of all five men, one can only explain it by the period madness referred to above.

41 *The* Afrika Korps *arrives; first Desert defeat*

For Britain – Government, Chiefs of Staff, media and people alike – the arrival of the German Army in Africa in early 1941 gave the war a new focus; it created, in fact, an obsession which endures to this day. It is sobering to recall that, in Sir David Fraser's words,

> For two years – between the evacuation of the BEF from France and the early summer of 1942 in Africa – only four British divisions fought the Germans.[1]

It is even more sobering to note that from Dunkirk until the landings in French North Africa in November 1942, the British Army never engaged more than four German divisions, out of an order of battle which, in June 1941, amounted to 205. The campaign in Libya, so engrossing to the British, was from the German point of view never more than a very small sideshow – for the General Staff purists, indeed, just a tiresome diversion of effort. For the British Army, on the other hand, it offered practical experience and training in war of inestimable value, and for the RAF it was the school of a system of air support which would have decisive significance. And that is the thread that we shall try to follow through the labyrinths of the familiar Desert battles.

The Greek diversion exposed the basic fragility of the brilliant victory which O'Connor and Collishaw had completed in February. When German forces began to assemble in Tripolitania,[2] the natural response would have been to strengthen both the British land and air forces in Cyrenaica; instead, the Greek commitment caused the withdrawal of battle-hardened formations, and a general (and disastrous) thinning down. Worst of all, however, was the almost universal failure to interpret the mounting omens of a German offensive correctly; despite a brilliant forecast of German intentions by his Director of Military Intelligence (Brigadier John Shearer),[3] General Wavell persuaded himself on logistical grounds that there was no reason to apprehend serious danger until May. Unlike Brigadier Shearer, he entirely failed to penetrate (and therefore gravely underestimated) the aggressive enterprise of the German commander, General Erwin Rommel, whose name was to sound like a curse on British military operations for the next nineteen months.

When Rommel launched his first offensive on March 30, both the Army in the Desert and GHQ in Cairo – including GHQ, RAF, Middle East – were taken badly by surprise. The RAF in Cyrenaica was more fortunate; forming his own estimate from reconnaissance reports, and reaching his own conclusion of the Army's likely reactions, the A.O.C., Group Captain L. O. Brown, warned his units on March 22 to be prepared to move back at short notice. It was a timely thought, but it did nothing to sweeten the pill of calamity soon to follow: by April 11 Rommel had cleared the British out of Cyrenaica and carried his army forward to Egyptian soil. All that remained of O'Connor's earlier triumph was Tobruk, grimly held by the Australian 9th Division; O'Connor himself, belatedly sent back to the Desert in an invidious rôle, was now a prisoner, captured in the confusion of the headlong retreat.

The air side of all this is soon told. Under the pressure of Greek necessities, Group Captain Brown's forces had been whittled down to a mere four squadrons – two of Hurricanes (Nos. 73 and 3 RAAF), one of Blenheim IVs (No. 55) and one of Lysanders (No. 6). It was fortunate indeed that the *Luftwaffe* in North Africa was also very weak: about 50 Ju 87 dive-bombers and 25 Me 110s.[4] The result was that the ground forces on both sides were little affected by air action. With only one bomber squadron, the RAF was quite incapable of holding up the Axis advance, while the *Stukas*, though active and alarming at times, produced negligible effects and inflicted insignificant casualties on the British troops.[5] Perversely, however, the soldiers on both sides seem to have been convinced "that it was the opposing air force that held the upper hand".[6]

Even on this limited scale, and with these disadvantages, some useful pointers nevertheless emerged from their depressing episode.

With the Army in full and undignified retreat, Air Marshal Tedder (Longmore being absent in Greece) concluded that the RAF must do *something* to stop the enemy, and urged Brown to use his fighters for machine-gunning Axis transport columns. The two available squadrons were already overworked and lacked the equipment with which Hurricanes and others later performed so well in this rôle. But it is interesting to see how quickly another shibboleth about "proper use of air power" collapsed when a British army was involved and direct British interests were at risk. Very soon, at Tobruk, Blenheims (now joined by No. 45 Squadron)

> made sustained and heavy attacks with hundreds of small bombs, against motorised infantry and supply columns. It was evident that the enemy plan was adversely affected by the heavy casualties he suffered during these attacks, and that this form of low-level bombing with small bombs, aided by the complete absence of enemy fighters, was producing very profitable results.[7]

The German *Afrika Korps* diarist noted on April 14 that

> During the entire period since the encirclement of Tobruk, the British had complete air superiority and daily attacked the investing force with successive waves of bombers . . .[8]

It was thus becoming once more apparent that air superiority was not an entire objective in its own right; nor was it wedded solely to the long-range purposes of an air force. It was also a condition of intervention on a battlefield in close and useful cooperation with the Army: this was, of course, the lesson of the *Luftwaffe's* victories, repeated by the British in East Africa.

It is normal, in circumstances of humiliating defeat, for there to be recriminations, and Libya in April 1941 proved no exception. The Army complained that it had been badly misled by "false air reports", especially a tactical reconnaissance on April 3 which reported a "large enemy force of armoured fighting vehicles" moving on Msus, where the British 2nd Armoured Division had its main supply and petrol dumps. The "large enemy force" turned out to be a patrol of the Long Range Desert Group; but before this could be established all the petrol in the dump had been destroyed, virtually crippling the British armour. Thus, remarks John Connell, "a single false report set in motion a great train of misfortunes".[9] The Army claimed that the fault lay with partially trained pilots and an ineffective signals system.

The RAF was, naturally, somewhat incensed; an inter-Service enquiry was held which led to considerable modification of the Army's allegations. Portal himself was much exercised over the matter, believing that "a question of principle was involved". He explained to Churchill that it was hitherto accepted (by both Services) "that an airman on reconnaissance reports only what he sees, and leaves it to the Army Intelligence Officer with the squadron, or to the Army Formation Headquarters to place an interpretation on it". He re-enunciated this principle with clarity; it was based, he said,

on the fact that recognition of ground forces from the air is a very difficult business under practical reconnaissance conditions: the difficulty was accentuated in Libya owing to the fact that we were using captured Italian tanks and Motor Transport. On the other hand the Army Formation HQ or Liaison Officer was informed from a variety of sources to assist in making an interpretation. The RAF pilot is at liberty to give his own views to the Army Liaison Officer, but the responsibility for recognition rests with the latter.[10]

It may seem strange that after twenty months of war such an elementary proposition had to be restated at that level; it indicates the base from which Army/Air cooperation had to be built. Well might Churchill comment that there appeared to be a need for "drastic reform".

April to September, 1941, was time in the classroom. The next eleven months showed that time in the classroom does not automatically confer degree status. But there has to be a classroom, and frequently some disagreeable time has to be spent in it.

42 Tedder in command; "Combined operation in the full sense"; a system of air support

On May 1, 1941 Longmore was summoned to London "for discussions". His stock at home had been falling steadily, and the Greek catastrophe did nothing to restore it. But even before the Germans pounced in Greece, Churchill – with Portal's concurrence – had turned against the AOC-in-C, Middle East. On March 29 he told Longmore:

I have been concerned to read your continual complaints of the numbers of aircraft which are sent you . . . We are as fully informed as you of what you are getting. A weekly report is submitted to me of all movement via Takoradi. Therefore, when I read a telegram from General Smuts in which he refers to "Beaverbrook being persuaded to disgorge from his hoard", or when I read the C-in-C Mediterranean's telegram to First Sea Lord stating that "Only one Hurricane was received during the month of March", and when I also read your A442 which seeks to justify this absurd statement, I fear there must be some talk emanating from your Headquarters which is neither accurate nor helpful.[1]

It was the old theme music (see pp. 307–9); at the root of it was a triad of misunderstandings arising from the three categories labelled "quota", "dispatches", "arrivals" – and never the three would meet.[2] To this, in March–April, was added a serious congestion at Takoradi, chiefly owing to the arrival of large numbers of American aircraft (mainly Curtiss Tomahawk fighters, of which there were over 200 by the end of April, lacking spares and tool kits). The discrepancy between totals and serviceable numbers, also referred to above, continued; we shall return to it again. The effect of all this, by May, was serious erosion of confidence in Longmore, and, in fact, he never returned. He was the first in a procession of Middle East commanders to be superseded; his chief fault would seem to have been a certain lack of tact.

Longmore left Cairo on May 3. It tells us something about the curious inner nature of Portal that on the morning of May 5 Tedder received a communication from him saying "that 'on taking over command' I should feel free, in view of the everchanging situation, to act as I saw fit despite any appreciation or directive issued before Longmore's departure".[3] So the RAF in the Middle East passed into "the strong hands, velvet-gloved, of Tedder".[4] And there is further (if conflicting) light on Portal in the fact that if Longmore, like Dowding before him, had some reasonable grounds for complaint about his treatment at the hands of the CAS, Tedder never did. The accord between him and Portal was close (and, significantly, enjoyed Freeman's full agreement); Portal, in difficult times, backed Tedder to the hilt (see pp. 354–6), and both the Service and the nation profited thereby.

When General Foch became Allied Generalissimo on March 26, 1918, the French Prime Minister said to him, "Well, you've got the job you so much wanted."

Foch replied, "A fine gift! You give me a lost battle and tell me to win it!"

When Longmore stepped aboard the aircraft that was to carry him to London, he gripped Tedder's elbow and said, "Good luck, Ted."

What Tedder replied, or thought, we do not know; it might well have been on the lines of Foch's comment. The position, on that day, was this:

Rommel was attacking at Tobruk
The evacuation of Greece was in its final stage
The pro-Axis revolt in Iraq had reached its crisis, with the attack on the RAF station at Habbaniya
There were ominous signs of German presence in Syria
The campaign in Abyssinia was still in progress
Malta – as ever – was under heavy pressure

Clearly, Tedder was going to need all the luck he could find.

Arthur William Tedder was almost exactly at his 51st birthday; he was a Cambridge history graduate (1912) and winner of the Prince Consort Prize for an essay on the Royal Navy of the Restoration. He entered the Colonial Service, but almost immediately, at the outbreak of war in 1914, joined the Army with a commission in the Dorsetshire Regiment. In 1916 he transferred to the Royal Flying Corps, and in 1919 he entered the RAF with the rank of squadron-leader. A highly practical bent and concern for the increasing technicalities of his always technical Service came to a natural fulfilment in 1938 when he took up the new post of Director-General of Research and Development; in 1940 he became Deputy Air Member for Development and Production in the Ministry of Aircraft Production. He could hardly have had a more thorough grounding in his profession – but it carried its penalty. To Churchill, he was a "nuts and bolts man", and it would not be long before Portal and Freeman had to defend him against the wrath on high. However, his appointment as AOC-in-C was confirmed on June 1.

The previous month saw the resolution – for better or worse – of most of his distractions: the lamentable end in Greece, the successful conclusion of the main campaign in East Africa, the suppression of the revolt in Iraq. This last contained a minor RAF epic – the defence of No. 4 Service Flying Training School at Habbaniya. Here, once more, the "museum pieces" performed with triumphant valour: four provisional "squadrons", one composed of Fairey Gordons and Airspeed Oxfords, two of Hawker Audaxes, and a "modern" squadron of Gladiators. There were also a few Blenheim Is and some visiting Wellingtons. With this array the AOC, Iraq, Air Vice-Marshal H. G. Smart, beat off a "siege" by a strong body of the Iraqi Army, and attacks by the Iraqi Air Force with aircraft in some cases of decidedly superior performance. In his memoirs, Tedder seems distinctly churlish towards a determined and able officer who had the misfortune shortly to be badly injured in a car crash. He had made "Habbaniya" a word of pride for the Royal Air Force.

The German capture of Crete, mainly by airborne forces – an innovation of the war – was a less happy story. Stretched to its limits, lacking airfields, short of modern fighters and facing overwhelming numerical superiority, there was very little the RAF could do about Crete. But to the bruised and battered Army, and the badly mauled Navy, the Air Force had "let them down" again. There were sharp recriminations and, as at Dunkirk, the men of the third Service passed through an uncomfortable time, from the AOC-in-C to the most innocent AC2, off duty in Cairo or Alexandria.

Just over one month after Tedder's formal appointment (July 5) came the next major Middle East displacement: General Sir Archibald Wavell was replaced as GOC-in-C by General Sir Claude Auchinleck. Tedder had always admired Wavell as a man and a soldier, though distrusting his staff; with Auchinleck the association was much closer – in the words of Sir Maurice Dean,

> He made an immediate partnership with Tedder ... and from that moment Army/Royal Air Force misunderstandings in the theatre were for practical purposes at an end ...[5]

This may be rather too strong a statement, but undeniably the Tedder/Auchinleck accord was good news for Army/Air cooperation. Unfortunately, as time went by, accord with Auchinleck proved to be less good news in Churchill's understanding, and by no means the surest path towards his admiration.

Churchill was a man of instinct and sometimes of prejudice; but at the heart of his quarrels there was often a perception or a knowledge which explains, if it does not always justify, his attitudes. At the heart of his discontent with the Desert General was his knowledge of Ultra, and dissatisfaction with the different interpretations of it in London and Cairo. At the heart of his nagging at the RAF in the Middle East was the sense of aircraft somehow – inexplicably – "vanishing without trace" between England and Egypt. He was not altogether wrong;[6] and the fault lay, as Tedder knew, in the sphere of Repair and Maintenance. An able officer, Air Commodore C. B. Cooke, arrived in the Middle East as Chief Maintenance Officer on April 1:

He found the whole repair organisation in a deplorable state. Accumulations of damaged aircraft were dotted about the vast Command, and there were practically no reserve machines complete in all respects.[7]

The fault was largely structural: despite its size and importance – to say nothing of its peculiar difficulties – Middle East Command had nothing comparable to Maintenance Command in the home-based force. Maintenance was one province of the huge responsibility of the Air Officer Administration, Air Vice-Marshal A. C. Maund. Cooke saw clearly that it needed to be separated; it was a major function, requiring independent status and its own impetus. But few things are more immovable than an established hierarchy; it would require the energy of a kind of Hercules to pull the RAF's command structure apart and redesign it. Fortunately – by one of Lord Beaverbrook's happier inspirations – a kind of Hercules was at hand.

It was at Beaverbrook's suggestion that Air Vice-Marshal G. G. Dawson, one of his assistants at the Ministry of Aircraft Production, was sent out to the Middle East in mid-May to investigate and advise on the whole question of maintenance and repair. This was welcomed by Tedder, who knew Dawson from his own days at the Ministry. And Dawson, as well as being an engineer specialist, was a "ball of fire". The impetus which he lost no time in imparting in all directions quickly transformed the repair and salvage arrangements of the Command. The Maintenance Units were expanded and increased; local resources and civilian labour was exploited; salvage units were given a long-needed mobility. Even the technology of the distant past was put to use: the honeycomb of caves in the hills near Cairo where the Pharaohs had quarried stone for the pyramids in the 3rd millennium BC was opened up and transformed into a vast bomb-proof store and aero-engine overhaul depôt. And most spectacular of all, Dawson even managed to overturn the hierarchy, establishing, in flat defiance of Air Ministry policy, a Chief Maintenance and Supply Officer (himself) independent of Administration and with direct access to the AOC-in-C. Cooke, his staunch backer, was given command of a new Group, with executive control of all maintenance units. This reorganization clinched the whole effort, but as Denis Richards and Hilary Saunders remark:

Dawson . . . would have been entirely powerless without Tedder's support . . . [while] Tedder enjoyed the full confidence of Portal, and the latter met his wishes.[8]

This was a turning-point for Middle East Command, a period of transformation into a powerful, increasingly modern force – "a far cry from the situation Longmore had faced only a few months earlier".[9] The aim of the Air Staff, when Tedder took over, was to increase the Command from 34½ squadrons in mid-June to 40½ squadrons with modern aircraft and then to 50. On July 3 this target was raised to 62½ squadrons; by mid-October the order of battle contained 52 squadrons, with 846 aircraft of which 780 were modern.[10] By November Tedder had "just over a thousand serviceable operational types in my Command".[11] This expansion, coupled with Dawson's admirable efforts, could give nothing but satisfaction – but, as ever, there was a darker side. As Tedder says, "aircraft by themselves are of little value",[12] and what worried him very much was the "desperate" shortage of trained personnel on whom the running of the Command depended – "not only squadron ground crews, but also men for operational control duties, repair, salvage, and other administrative tasks of all kinds".[13] The Takoradi route, for example, absorbed nearly 7,000 men; the RAF's signals staff numbered 6,500; the observer and warning systems (almost exclusively manned by the RAF) required another 3,700. All in all, over and above the squadrons, there was a need for some 160 units of one kind or another, representing an establishment of 4,536 officers and 64,700 airmen. Perhaps it was the inherent contradiction of this designation, which we have noted on the first page of this book, that so offended him, but Churchill was never able to accept with a good grace the RAF's ground staff requirements[14] – least of all in the Middle East, where their dispatch competed with all comers for shipping space on the long Cape–Cairo route. In the summer of 1941, in the light of its proposed expansion of the Command, the Air Staff recommended that 35,000 airmen should have priority over the Army's drafts and reinforcements. This was too much for Churchill, who promptly cut the number to 20,000. A fierce argument followed on familiar lines, with the Prime Minister challenging the necessity for "well over a thousand men for every squadron of sixteen aircraft first-line strength", etc., etc. He took no account of the civilian supporting organizations (e.g., to name but two, the Royal Observer Corps and the Post Office) which made comparisons with the metropolitan air force pointless. Nor did he consider the higher sickness rate which had to be expected in the Middle East and Africa. Reluctantly, he conceded that 25,000 airmen might go out by the end of the year – but in the event only 15,000 went. It was a strange way of trying to extract value from a large investment, but this is what Tedder and Middle East Command had to live with.

Even with serviceable aircraft in the squadrons, there were problems. Generally speaking, the quality of aircrews – British, South African, Australian, New Zealand, Rhodesian or Free French – was very high, their morale good, and all the better for being re-equipped with "real" aircraft. On the other hand, says Tedder

> Their fighting efficiency varied ... Certain squadrons were excellent, while others lacked experience and leadership. Most of them had suffered from the long series of defensive patrols over shipping, which had made the supply of Tobruk possible, but had inevitably reduced their offensive efficiency. All were intensively practising more flexible and offensive tactics recently evolved at home.[15]

The problem was the usual Middle East curse – shortage of facilities, this time for flying training, especially on the most up-to-date machines. A visit to the Command in August by the Inspector-General, Air Chief Marshal Ludlow-Hewitt, was very fruitful; Tedder recorded admiration of "his wide and detailed knowledge, his balanced criticisms and judgment".[16] The arrival, at Tedder's request, of Air Commodore B. E. Embry to be Senior Air Staff Officer to the Desert Air Force, brought an officer of great experience and knowledge of the latest operational techniques. This was just as well, because the Germans had just introduced the latest Messerschmitt fighter, the Bf 109F 2/Trop, and the RAF's aircrews would shortly be severely tested.

Under Tedder's calm ministration, relations with the other Services were improving; in June he had told his two colleagues at a Commanders-in-Chiefs' meeting that "the three Services were not really working together".[17] Since then he had encountered serious trouble with the Navy, under its redoubtable admiral, A. B. Cunningham. "A.B.C." argued for "something analogous to Coastal Command" in the Middle East[18] – pointing to the enormous reconnaissance requirements of his Fleet in a sea 2,000 miles long. He found the RAF, he says, "very touchy and difficult to approach" after criticisms of its performance during the Crete campaign. He also alleged "an unwillingness to admit that personnel working over the sea required special training". It was an old story; but Tedder's resistance was founded on more than the normal reluctance of the RAF to see its aircraft "alienated". He was moving towards that larger view of the war which later made him so natural a choice as a Deputy Allied Supreme Commander. He told Cunningham:

> In my opinion, sea, land and air operations in the Middle East Theatre are now so closely inter-related that effective coordination will only be

possible if the campaign is considered and controlled as a combined operation in the full sense of that term.[19]

For June 1941, this was far-sighted reasoning – a lot more to the point than most of the material emanating from the RAF at that time. Cunningham was unimpressed, however, and though the two men were personally on cordial terms, professionally they were at logger-heads. Fortunately, Portal's good relations with Pound, the First Sea Lord, came to the rescue once more, and the dispute was resolved by the sensible compromise of designating No. 201 Group as "Naval Cooperation", remaining under RAF control, but keeping together its units specializing in over-sea operations.

Army Cooperation, the other part of Tedder's "combined oper-ation", was also passing through a germinal period, after some bad experiences. These dated from the final phase of Wavell's tenure: operations BREVITY (May 15–17) and BATTLEAXE (June 15–17). Both aimed at the relief of Tobruk, and at regaining the initiative in the Desert, even (in the case of BATTLEAXE) destroying Rommel's forces. Both proved premature, inadequately mounted, and complete failures; as Wavell engagingly said to Tedder when he left, "It's probably a good thing to have a change of bowling – and I have had one or two sixes knocked off me lately!"

Such brief operations offered no scope for the practical development of techniques, either by Army, Air Force, or both in combination. However, all was not lost; there were lessons to be learned in retro-spect, and digested through the summer. Already, as we have seen (p. 316) the RAF had been learning about ground mobility, and the sway of battle from March to June rubbed that lesson in. Direct air support had come to the fore in the British retreat; in BREVITY a sharp argument between Collishaw (AOC 204 Group) and Brigadier W. H. E. Gott, commanding the land forces, brought further clarification. Gott wanted the RAF to concentrate against the enemy armour, acting as free-ranging artillery. This was a rôle and a concept that the RAF had never cared for; and Collishaw had extra reasons for disagreement. First, he pointed out that in the first British advance the Italian Air Force had dropped "thousands of bombs in intensified attacks on the 7th Armoured Division";[20] subsequent analysis had shown these to have been almost entirely ineffective. Tanks, the RAF concluded, were not good targets; they were small, they were well protected, and they were able to retaliate against low-flying aircraft. The excellent German use of anti-aircraft guns made vehicle parks and fixed de-fences difficult to attack also; on the other hand, thin-skinned vehicles in movement – especially the ten-ton petrol tankers and troop-carrying lorries – could be very effectively attacked with machine-gun fire or by Blenheims using small (20 lb) anti-personnel bombs. The Germans and Italians protected their main communications with well-spaced AA guns, which was disconcerting, but did not save them from losses on the long haul across Cyrenaica. Collishaw insisted that it was the attack on enemy communications, paralysing the armour (it was hoped) by depriving it of petrol and ammunition, that offered the best air contribution, and Gott finally agreed. But the battle was too short to prove anything.

BATTLEAXE brought fresh instructions: first, the fundamental importance of communication. Both Army and Air Force came out of BATTLEAXE in a mood of intense frustration; air support had obviously broken down, and once more there was a tendency to back-biting, but

> In the opinion of the Air Officer Commanding-in-Chief, the main difficulty in providing air support was the almost complete lack of information from the Army. This was caused by the failure of both the pre-arranged air-to-ground recognition system, brought about mainly by lack of response to aircraft signal by ground formations, and the Army signals communication system . . . Coupled with this, the failure of the wireless communications[21] between forward troops and their headquarters had meant a serious lack of information at headquarters regarding the dispositions of formations so that it was frequently impossible for Army Headquarters to give even a conservative bombline, although periodic reports were received from the Wireless Observer Unit posts.[22]

As though this sheer lack of information was not enough, another cogent reason for the breakdown of Army/Air cooperation was offered by Lieutenant-General Sir Noel Beresford-Pierce, the land forces commander, "who considered that a grave drawback had been the siting of his headquarters and Headquarters No. 204 Group some eighty miles apart".[23] It was conceded that he had a point.

It was also conceded that all the pupils in this class, whether wearing Army or Air Force badges, had a lot to learn and had better apply themselves to their work. An inter-Service committee was set up in July to investigate and rationalize the whole system of cooperation, or, as the RAF called it, "air support". It was a useful step forward merely to arrive at some clear definitions; these were hammered out at a joint conference in Cairo on September 4 and embodied in the Air Support Directive of September 30:

Direct air support was "intended to have an immediate effect on current land or sea operations". It included defensive support to impede the enemy's ground and air offensive, and offensive support to destroy the enemy's ground forces. It was divided into pre-planned (pre-arranged) and impromptu support. Close support was a form of direct support, and was "offensive air support in close proximity to our forward troops".

Indirect air support was "that support given to land or sea forces against objectives other than enemy forces engaged in the tactical battle". It included air action against land communications, base installations, etc., and was in fact air support directed against any target which had an effect, although not an immediate effect, on the battle between ground forces.[24]

Having established at last some degree of precision about the nature of the subject, the committee, with the aid of No. 253 Army Cooperation Wing, which carried out joint exercises throughout the summer, then addressed itself to the practicalities of recognition and communication. The great step forward was the creation of jointly staffed Air Support Control (ASC) headquarters. An ASC was to be provided for each army corps, and for each armoured division, and each ASC was to be linked by a two-way wireless telegraphy "tentacle" (normally carried in one or two 15-cwt trucks) to the brigades in the field. Each brigade would have an RAF team – a Forward Air Support Link (FASL) – equipped with two-way radio-telephony, to control the supporting aircraft and receive tactical reconnaissance reports. In this way the brigades would be able to make their requests for air support quickly heard; they would be evaluated at the ASC, which would then communicate with the airfields and landing grounds by two-way radio-telephony through a Rear Air Support Link (RASL). The process was sufficiently flexible for it to be initiated by reconnaissance aircraft actually in flight on becoming aware of targets – impromptu support. All this obviously marked a great stride forward – a large-scale projection of the miniature experiment which we have already noted in East Africa (pp. 324–5). It was a theoretically sound system – but mid-October (when the ASCs were set up) was late for teaching two Services to change the habits of a lifetime, with a major operation impending in November.

The fact that there was a flow of ideas, however belated, was nevertheless entirely satisfactory, and Tedder and Auchinleck were pleased. Tedder found particular satisfaction in the fact that, as well as the practical support of the committee, his own views on the use of air power received powerful endorsement from Churchill himself, in his capacity as Minister of Defence. On September 5 he issued a memorandum for the guidance of Army and Air Force Commanders-in-Chief; it referred to the dispatch of 250 Bofors AA guns[25] to the Middle East, and continued in unequivocal terms:

> Nevermore must the ground troops expect, as a matter of course, to be protected against the air by aircraft . . . Above all, the idea of keeping standing patrols of aircraft over moving columns should be abandoned. It is unsound to distribute aircraft in this way, and no air superiority will stand any large application of such a mischievous practice.[26]

It would take more than words to break the Army's fixed belief that only the aircraft it could actually see in the sky above it were really helping, but words as clear as these from such a source could only be beneficial. Churchill then proceeded to the most fundamental principle of all, as it expressed itself in command relationships:

> Upon the military Commander-in-Chief announcing that a battle is in prospect, the Air Officer Commanding-in-Chief will give him all possible aid irrespective of other targets, however attractive. Victory in the battle makes amends for all . . . The Army Commander-in-Chief will specify to the Air Officer Commanding-in-Chief the targets and tasks which he requires to be performed, both in the preparatory attack on the rearward installations of the enemy and for air action during the progress of the battle.
>
> It will be for the AOC-in-C to use his maximum force on these objects in the manner most effective. This applies not only to any squadrons assigned to army cooperation permanently, but also to the whole air force available in the theatre . . . the sole object being the success of the military operation. As the interests of the two Cs-in-C are identical it is not thought any difficulty should arise.

Churchill spelt out the rôles both of bombers and of fighters, and the significance of "local command of the air". Here, indeed, was authoritative definition of the "combined operation" to which Tedder looked forward; and as between him and Auchinleck Churchill was right – no difficulty *would* arise. Their accord was, and remained, excellent. From Churchill's pronouncement, says Tedder, there "emerged a new dimension in the Middle East struggle, air warfare in its own right".[27] Yet, as the war would shortly show, neither sound precepts nor the best intentions are guarantors of victory.

43 *Air support/Army cooperation*

Some digression is here required. The débâcle in France, culminating in Dunkirk, had forced the subject of Army/Air Cooperation to the

MIDDLE EAST (ARMY AND R.A.F.).
DIRECTIVE ON DIRECT SUPPORT.
(September 30, 1941)
Communications for Air Support Control.

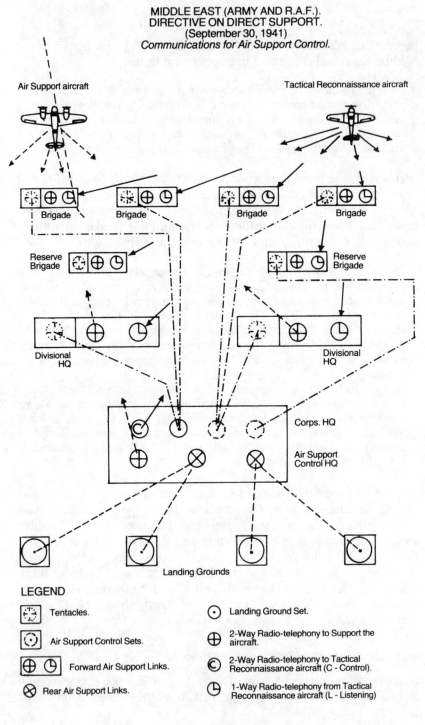

LEGEND

Tentacles.

Air Support Control Sets.

Forward Air Support Links.

Rear Air Support Links.

Landing Ground Set.

2-Way Radio-telephony to Support the aircraft.

2-Way Radio-telephony to Tactical Reconnaissance aircraft (C - Control).

1-Way Radio-telephony from Tactical Reconnaissance aircraft (L - Listening)

348

attention of both Services – and the general public; noisy voices in the press clamoured for dive-bombers and bitterly criticized the Air Ministry for not providing them (see p. 252, Chapter 31, Note 6). Rightly (as we have noted; see p. 324) the Air Staff set its face against such a step. Less forgivably, the subject of cooperation itself remained as unpopular as ever in Air Force circles. There was a strong tendency to equate it with tactical reconnaissance and artillery spotting, the functions of the Westland Lysander, designed specifically for those rôles (first flight 1936). Pre-war RAF doctrine frowned on other forms of battlefield intervention; the Air Force was expected to come into its own *beyond* the extreme range of the Army's artillery.[1] The true function of bombers, according to this creed, was

> to isolate the battle-movement of reserves, and generally create disorgani-
> sation and confusion behind the enemy front while the ground forces
> achieved their objectives.[2]

This had not worked out in France; worse still, the totally opposite German philosophy had been seen to work only too well – and did so again in Greece in April 1941.

It was not surprising that that year saw much debate (a good deal of it fairly acrimonious) and continual experiment in the field of Army Cooperation. This took place in three compartments. First, for obvious reasons, the Army's Home Forces, preparing to resist invasion, were much concerned. At Home Forces GHQ, Major (later Brigadier) C. C. Oxborrow was in charge of the Combined Central Operations Room (CCOR) where the Army's anti-invasion plans were coordinated with those of the Navy and the RAF. Army/RAF relations provided one of Oxborrow's permanent preoccupations:

> Resourceful and discreet, he made himself indispensable in the technical
> aspects of the little world of Army/Air cooperation, not without making
> some departmental enemies. His influence could be felt in every practical
> step forward and, without his persistence and ingenuity, many of the
> reforms that brought success to Army/Air in 1944 would never have got
> past the talking stage.[3]

With Fighter Command so palpably on top of its own anti-invasion procedures, the key to Army/RAF relations (and the chief source of difficulty) was Bomber Command. There, during the whole middle period of the war, the Army's Liaison Officer was Lieutenant-Colonel C. E. Carrington; Oxborrow and Carrington "formed the working link between the Army and Bomber Command".[4]

349

1941, of course, was precisely when Bomber Command was taking up its position on the right of the line of Britain's war-making, and painfully acknowledging its weakness in numbers, in types and in techniques. Invasion seemed distinctly fanciful, after the *Luftwaffe's* defeat in the Battle of Britain, and with the Royal Navy still intact. Cooperating with the Army accordingly came a long way down any Bomber Command agenda; the most it would concede was No. 2 Group, with its overworked Blenheims – as long as they were not pre-empted by aid to Coastal Command, "Circuses" and other bombing demands. With the best will in the world, No. 2 Group was quite unable to give the Army what it wanted – but no one would admit this:

> The real weakness of 2 Group, with its heavy casualties and poor rate of replacement, was a closely guarded secret. The Group Commander objected strongly when I told the truth to GHQ in a "most secret" message. What with losses in action and the drain to the Middle East, the strength of the Group was rarely over 60 serviceable aircraft with crews, in the summer of 1941, and once sank as low as 48.[5]

Production, it should be remembered, was switched from the Blenheim I to the Blenheim IV as early as 1939, which created serious difficulties in the matter of spares and replacements both in the Middle East and at home, and the Blenheim IV ceased to be operational in Bomber Command in August 1942. Obsolescent indeed, these tireless workhorses were all that Bomber Command had to offer in 1941; stony ground for the Army cooperation gospel.

The second compartment within which experiment and development was taking place (separate, but by no means hermetically sealed) was the RAF's own Army Cooperation Command. This had been set up, following the post-Dunkirk agitations, on December 1, 1940, under Air Marshal Sir Arthur Barratt, whom we last met as AOC, British Air Forces in France (see p. 122 ff.). From the beginning, says Charles Carrington, "there was an air of unreality in the rôle of Army Coop Command". It comprised two Groups; one of them, No. 71, consisted of the dozen or so AC squadrons distributed among the larger units of home forces – the familiar Lysanders. Over these Barratt, though titular AOC-in-C, had no operational control. The other Group, No. 70, "was to control the policy, training and administration of the units under [the Command]".[6] As Carrington says, "nothing was left for Barratt to command".[7] His anomalous position reflected that of the RAF itself. The basic truths of Army Cooperation were unpalatable; as much as possible the Air Staff preferred to push them into a corner, or disregard them, but the existence of a responsible AOC-in-C forced them into the open. Barratt's obvious rôle was that of Air colleague and chief adviser to the C-in-C, Home Forces (General Sir Alan Brooke), but this the Air Staff could not accept, because

> in the event of an invasion, Home Forces – charged with the defence of the United Kingdom – would have to make certain demands upon the other Royal Air Force Commanders-in-Chief, and the establishment of the AOC-in-C. Army Cooperation Command as adviser to the GOC Home Forces might well have provoked unnecessary difficulties.[8]

In other words, the RAF was tripping over its own Command system.

It was, nevertheless, in Barratt's deeply "underprivileged" Command that some of the most significant theoretical work on battlefield cooperation between the two Services (later translated into triumphant practicality) was done. It began even before the formal creation of the Command, with experimental exercises carried out in Northern Ireland in September 1940 under the aegis of Colonel (later Lieutenant-General) J. D. Woodall, who had been Barratt's Military Staff Officer at BAFF, and Group Captain A. Wann, who had commanded the ill-fated Fairey Battles of the AASF. Woodall, although a soldier, became Barratt's senior staff officer in the new Command, where the "Wann-Woodall report" was now expounded. It put forward, says Carrington,

> a plan that was far superior to anything possessed by the Germans then or thereafter, for coordinating the action of forward troops and supporting Bombers. It was a signals network which sent out what Woodall called "tentacles", army officers in light cars, who went forward to the leading troops and signalled back requests for support, by wireless links that avoided the normal channels, directly to a control centre, where they were monitored by Army and Air Force Staff Officers, sitting together. This shortened by several hours the time needed to lay on bomber action. The Woodall plan for what he called Close Support Bomber Control was almost at once adopted in principle, by both Services. After a period of trial and adjustment in England, the controls were established as Army Support Signals Units (ASSUs) . . . one of the outstanding successes of the war.[9]

The third compartment in which Army/Air cooperation was fruitfully developed was, of course, the Middle East; the reader will be

351

struck both by the similarities and the differences of the Wann/
Woodall system being preached in England, and the solutions which
were being simultaneously evolved in the fire of the battle in East
Africa and the Desert. There is no need to wonder at parallel
development taking place; the fundamentals of the subject, on examination, are common sense – so much so that the Germans, with their
Spanish experience behind them, saw little need to speculate or
theorize at all. The essentials, equally visible in England and in Egypt,
are:

(i) Intimate relations between the two Services at key points, i.e. at top
Command level (e.g. Tedder and Auchinleck), at important field
headquarters (significantly missing in BATTLEAXE) and at the very
front of battle (as in East Africa and projected in the FASLs; see
p. 346)

(ii) An independent signals network – vitally important, so that there
should be no competition for signals priorities and the minimum of
hierarchical delay

(iii) Recognition that at certain times and in certain circumstances Army
cooperation would be the function, not of "special" aircraft designed
and allocated for the purpose, but of *the whole available air power*,
using all its types: bombers, fighters, reconnaissance, transport, special
duties.

The most important difference between England and Egypt at this
stage was that the third principle, though perceived in England, was
not acted upon; in Egypt, under the stress of war, it *was* acted upon.
But Tedder did not have to struggle against the rigidities and dogmas
of the functional Command system; he could use the RAF in the
Middle East as a single unit. The day would come when the best of
both systems would be married together into one accepted drill; that
day was not yet – but it would be a bad one for Germany.

44 Churchill and Tedder; "Crusader"

Operation BARBAROSSA – the German attack on the Soviet
Union – was a catastrophe from the first: a catastrophe disguised by
brilliant outward successes, but a catastrophe nevertheless. It was, in
the first place, an elementary but appalling mistake to embark upon
such an adventure with an undefeated enemy in the rear. Only swift,
decisive victory in the East could have justified this, but as weeks
turned into months, and months brought the turn of the year and a
Russian winter campaign, though there were victories in plenty, they

were never decisive. Strong as they were, the German armed forces were simply not strong enough for the task that had been set them. And the political victory – the overthrow of the harsh Stalinist tyranny – which might have offset military insufficiencies, was denied them by the repulsive character of the dictatorship they served. The effects of Hitler's blunder were quickly felt in Africa.

Like his vigorous local commander, General Rommel (and like his arch-enemy, Churchill), Hitler was considerably affected by Tobruk; the resolute defence of this pettifogging harbour was for both Churchill and Rommel an irritant, a magnet, a temptation. For Rommel it was also the first block in the passage towards a triumphant invasion of Egypt and a vision of the eastern glories beyond, similar to that which had drawn the young and impressionable General Bonaparte in the same direction in 1798. Never doubting his forthcoming Russian victory, Hitler gave substance to Rommel's dream with his "Plan Orient" Directive of June 11, which envisaged a vast pincer movement from Libya on one side and down through the Caucasus on the other, to squeeze the British out of the Middle East. The "cool staff minds" of the German General Staff (OKH) viewed all these grandiose schemes with alarm and distaste; they were "wasteful distractions" on "a distant, irrelevant shore":

> it is fair to say that at no time were the heads of the Germany Army excited about either the strategical or the political significance of an absolute victory over the British in North Africa.[1]

Rommel never gave up his pursuit of the glittering prize, but Hitler – always a variable quantity in any case – became more and more absorbed in his own eastern tragedy. So from beginning to end Rommel conducted his campaigns on a "shoe string" – which was just as well from the British point of view, since even so he was able to test the full military strength of the British Empire to its limits.

For both sides the summer of 1941 was a time of very positive preparation for what was expected to be the decisive encounter of the Desert war; for both, Tobruk supplied the focus of attention – Rommel intent upon reducing it, Auchinleck determined to relieve it. And while the two land forces built up their strength and trained for battle, Tedder's airmen held the ring. Between June 1 and October 31, no less than 220,000 tons of Axis shipping was sunk on the convoy routes to Libya; of this total, the RAF and the Fleet Air Arm accounted for 115,000 tons, the Malta-based squadrons being responsible for at least three-quarters of it all. It probably amounted to "something between one-third and one-half of the entire enemy sailings to North Africa over the period".[2] The chief target of the Malta-based Wellingtons was Tripoli, attacked 72 times between mid-June and mid-October; the Egypt-based squadrons (37, 38, 70 and 148) concentrated on Benghazi, which they attacked 102 times. This was the famous "Mail Run", subject to a squadron song with a mournful refrain:

Seventy Squadron, Seventy Squadron,
Though we say it with a sigh,
We must do the ruddy mail run
Every night until we die.
Air: "Clementine"

For Rommel, however, the Benghazi "Mail Run" and associated activities were matters not to be relieved by any song; they spelt only delays and frustrations of his fixed intention to take Tobruk. Not until late October was he actually able to settle a date: preparations to be completed by November 15, advance on November 20. Even so, his planning would once again contain that "huge element of contingency, which might well have broken the nerve of some less buoyant commander".[3]

On the British side, the build-up for the offensive suffered no such setbacks – only the familiar long delay of deliveries round the Cape, and the serviceability problems on arrival which London found it so exceedingly difficult to comprehend. The Army now acutely suffered the hostile probes of the Prime Minister to which the RAF had always been subjected. Churchill was as angry and amazed at the impossibility of sending a consignment of tanks or motor transport straight into action as he was with aircraft. Auchinleck – like Wavell before him – had to fend off continuous prodding towards premature action all through the summer, forfeiting much of Churchill's esteem thereby; Tedder came close to losing his job by saying that the enemy would probably enjoy "numerical superiority" in the coming battle. What he did *not* say – for the simple reason that he did not believe it – was that the enemy would have "*air* superiority". He was quite confident that his aircrews, backed by their increasingly efficient ground-staff, would see to that. But Churchill was deeply incensed; even Portal thought that Tedder's statement was "most depressing". It was decided that a very senior officer must investigate the matter on the spot; one wonders why, at such a juncture (mid-October), Portal did not go out himself – Dill, after all, had spent some weeks in the Middle East earlier in the year. But in the event it was Freeman who went out. Churchill "introduced" him to Auchinleck in a letter in which he said that his confidence in Tedder had been shaken, and went on:

> You will find Freeman an officer of altogether larger calibre, and if you feel he would be a greater help to you and that you would have more confidence in the Air Command if he assumed it, you should not hesitate to tell me so ... Do not let any thought of Tedder's personal feelings influence you. This is not time for such considerations. On the other hand I am very glad to see that you and Tedder are in accord upon the tactical employment of the Air Force and that there is no danger of its being parcelled out among the various divisions, thus losing its power to make the characteristic contribution of its arm.[4]

By the time Auchinleck received this, Freeman had arrived, and no sooner had he done so than he heard from Portal that Churchill was clamouring for Tedder's head. Deeply disturbed, Portal persuaded Sinclair that if Churchill insisted, they must both resign, but first he wanted to know whether Freeman really believed that a change in the Air Command would improve the chances of the forthcoming offensive (CRUSADER), and secondly whether Freeman would accept Tedder's job. To these questions Freeman promptly replied: "(A) No (B) Certainly not repeat not." He added that he would be delighted to resign with Portal if pressed, and the next day (October 22) he added:

> You and S of S will understand that the rôle of Judas is one I cannot fill. Am convinced it would be a fatal mistake to change now. Obvious [Tedder] knows highest has no confidence in him which would certainly sap self-confidence if he felt he had lost yours. Your confidence is all he needs and wants. I gave him assurance.[5]

Auchinleck, for his part, confirmed this view; he told Churchill on October 23:

> I have confidence in the ability of Tedder and his subordinate commanders to do what we require of them and I am glad to be able to think that the confidence of the Army generally in the RAF in this theatre, which was somewhat shaken after the campaigns in Greece and Crete, is now restored. The cooperation between the two Services is very good and I hope they understand each other's capabilities and limitations much better than has sometimes been the case in the past.[6]

355

So the crisis passed; Churchill was mollified by revised figures of air strengths (at Freeman's suggestion). Characteristically, it is Tedder who quotes, with obvious enjoyment, the Prime Minister's minute on a note pointing out that the new figures and the old were not very far apart:

> The only difference was that the first version stated we should be inferior and the revised version that we should be superior. It is only the kind of difference between plus and minus, or black and white.[7]

Not all the auspices for CRUSADER were as bleak as this proposal to change the Air Commander-in-Chief on the eve of battle; they were, however, somewhat mixed. It looked very reasonable, after his Abyssinian victory, to bring in Lieutenant-General Sir Alan Cunningham to command the land forces, christened "Eighth Army" on September 18. Unfortunately, even very brief exposure to the stress of battle against the German *Afrika Korps* revealed that Cunningham was out of his depth. (A medical report *before* taking up his appointment might have saved him and the Army much grief.) On the other hand, the new commander of the Western Desert Air Force, Air Vice-Marshal Arthur Coningham (who replaced Collishaw in July), proved to have not only "immense energy and rare powers of leadership",[8] making him "one of the outstanding air commanders of the 1939–45 war",[9] but (with Tedder) one of the "main architects"[10] of inter-Service cooperation. A forty-six-year-old New Zealander, his first nickname, "Maori", had been corrupted into "Mary", in the manner of the British Services of that generation, but there was nothing in the slightest degree effeminate in this tall, impressive figure – "the airman born and bred", in Tedder's words.[11] His talent for cooperation was displayed at once: he and his like-sounding Army colleague set up their headquarters side by side for the coming battle, they and their staffs even sharing the same Mess – a good beginning. And, shrewdly, Coningham promptly revised what he saw as exaggerated decentralization in the new Air Support system. He perceived in good time that the true Air Support Control must be his own Advanced Headquarters; only at the centre, beside the Army Commander, could there be a picture of the whole battle which would make the Air rôle truly effective.

CRUSADER opened on November 18, to the accompaniment of ferocious thunderstorms like those which heralded the Battle of Waterloo – but there resemblances began and ended. This was going to be "a battle which both sides deserved to lose".[12] Rommel, hypnotized by Tobruk, allowed himself to be taken by surprise, and then indulged in spectacular but unprofitable manoeuvres when he might have been doing lethal damage. The British, with an unprecedented superiority of air power and in numbers of tanks, were thwarted by their sheer amateurism – like their fathers in 1915 and 1916. They suffered from

> shortcomings in tactics, equipment and organisation: particularly from a failure to combine the fire of all arms instantly and effectively, and to organise accordingly.[13]

No system of air support, however well designed, no will to cooperate, however sincerely held, can overcome faults which are so fundamental.

Coningham's will to cooperate was not in doubt; he had at his disposal a powerful force whose composition is interesting: 14 squadrons of short-range fighters (Hurricanes and Tomahawks), two of long-range fighters (Beaufighters and Hurricane IIs), eight squadrons of medium bombers (Blenheims and Marylands), three tactical reconnaissance squadrons (two Hurricane, one Boston).[14] What strikes one immediately is the great predominance of fighters (16 squadrons out of 27) at a time when air support in England was still being thought of as primarily bomber support. And within two days of the opening of the battle, the fighters revealed a new versatility: Hurricanes had already been used as bombers against shipping, from Malta in September, and in the English Channel in October; on November 20, No. 80 Squadron's Mark I Hurribombers made their début in land warfare. It must be admitted that their first bombing attack on enemy vehicles was not a success (though their subsequent "strafing" accounted for fifteen); yet, as the Official History says,

> This was an important step in the development of what proved to be a formidable weapon for supporting the Army.[15]

It was indeed – the real alternative to dive-bombers in view at last.

On November 18 Coningham was able to take advantage of the freak storms, which had waterlogged many of the *Luftwaffe's* airfields; the RAF's air superiority was quickly established, and German offensive air action during the first three days of battle was, in Tedder's words, "almost negligible". "It was clear," he remarks, somewhat tartly, "that the Army, for once, was pleased with the RAF."[16] Well it might be, for it was experiencing a very unusual favour:

the watchers on the Desert floor enjoyed the novel spectacle of a sky full of friendly aircraft.[17]

At last, it seemed, the miseries of the Battle of France and the disasters in Greece and Crete would be reversed. But it was an illusion.

Rommel quickly recovered from his surprise, concentrated his armour, and flung it into battle (despite all that Coningham's squadrons could do) with that tactical mastery which made him such a formidable opponent throughout the war. At Sidi Rezegh the Eighth Army suffered its first major armoured defeat; Cunningham – a sick man – lost his grip on the battle; by November 23 (less than a week from the brave beginning) there were all the makings of a collapse as damaging as earlier in the year. In this crisis, Auchinleck himself came to the front and took charge; he gave Cunningham a written order:

> The offensive would continue. The object remain unchanged. Tobruk would be relieved. Cyrenaica would be reconquered. By that firmness of decision when matters looked dark, Auchinleck saved the CRUSADER offensive . . .[18]

Cunningham was dismissed, and in his place Auchinleck appointed his Deputy Chief of Staff, Lieutenant-General Neil Ritchie. Everyone (including Auchinleck himself) regarded this appointment as temporary, and for the time being the GOC-in-C remained at Eighth Army Headquarters, controlling the battle. Rommel, having exhausted his *Panzers* in the extraordinary manoeuvre of the "dash to the wire" – a wild sally towards the Egyptian frontier in the worst manner of the Confederate cavalry under General J. E. B. Stuart in the American Civil War – was now on the defensive. Tobruk was relieved on November 28, and soon Rommel was in retreat. By Christmas Eve the British re-entered Benghazi; on Boxing Day Rommel was standing right back at Agedabia. CRUSADER was a victory after all.[19]

But there was a sting in the tail. For both armies, the supply position had become critical – for Rommel because of continued sinkings by the Royal Navy and the RAF, for Ritchie because of the long distances now involved, and the sound work of destruction which the RAF had already done to the port of Benghazi. It was Rommel who recovered first: a consignment of no more than 55 tanks and 20 armoured cars was sufficient to set him moving again, on January 21. He quickly devoured fresh, inexperienced, scattered British formations, and in a week he was back in Benghazi, the Eighth Army in full retreat to the

"Gazala Line", some 45 miles west of Tobruk. So the honours – such as they were – were even: a disappointing start for the Eighth Army, and for the new system of Army Cooperation from which much had been hoped.

Even under ideal conditions, it would have been a lot to ask, that a system so recently devised should work perfectly from the first. For both Services, the *finesse* of a systematized air support control was an absolute novelty, and for men struggling to master the basic grammar of their own trades, it was a new burden, a new examination tossed into an already crowded curriculum. For nobody was this more true than for the British armoured forces who, by comparison with their adversaries, were real beginners – yet it was on them that the success or failure of the land battle often depended. And it was the ill luck of all to be trying everything out in the face of a master of mobile warfare; fighting Rommel was not – in the jargon of the period, repeat, not – an "ideal condition".

Nevertheless – and despite obvious failings – CRUSADER was a victory for the new system. The planning and execution of the air operations both in the preliminary phase and during the battle "shaped the method of applying air power in support of a land campaign."[20] The battle experience had the particular advantage of throwing a merciless spotlight on deficiencies. First, disconcerting to all concerned, there was the relative failure of the day-bombing operations. They began well, on November 18, with a quick response by Blenheims and Marylands to a useful reconnaissance report (of mud-bound German armour and transport). But as each day brought greater and greater confusion on the ground in what is generally accepted as one of the most confusing battles ever fought, the light bombers found it ever harder to identify enemy and friendly forces. Thus deprived of targets, the crews endured the further frustration of long waits for "impromptu" support calls, as the Army itself endeavoured to tell friend from foe. Added to the normal difficulty of finding particular localities in a featureless desert, what this spelt was insuperable obstacles to effective day-bombing; by December "the light bomber effort was negligible, and for nine days in January the effort stopped altogether".[21]

Recognition of targets, identification of ground forces, both stood out as matters requiring still more thought and attention. And it was also quickly apparent that, for all its paper symmetry, the system itself still needed much streamlining. The *average* time-lag between a support call and the actual dropping of bombs on the target (if identified) was two and a half to three hours. This was average; from landing grounds near at hand the timings could be better – but clearly this was hardly "close" or "direct" support in the preferred meanings of those words. There were, it need hardly be said, good reasons for these delays; they were not simply the products of unfamiliarity or incompetence. There was, first, the inevitable slowing up in the relay of messages from Corps Air Support Controls to Coningham's Headquarters; if compensations outweighed this disadvantage (as they did) it remained a disadvantage nevertheless. Secondly – and chiefly – there was the distance between bomber airfields and the battle front – sometimes as much as 200 miles. Then there was the unavoidable delay caused by having to pick up fighter escorts. Fourthly, there was the briefing time for pilots, especially when ground movement made the briefings complicated. And finally, there was the time taken in actually finding the targets in a landscape without landmarks; if the target was moving (e.g. transport) or visibility poor, this could be the most difficult part of all.

To all of this, the fighters, and particularly the fighter-bombers, held the answer, even if it was not immediately one hundred per cent effective. They were, generally speaking, much closer to the battle than the bombers; their sweeps in pursuit of air superiority served also as valuable reconnaissances; their "strafing" attacks (practised earlier in the year) were visibly damaging. The Army noted with pleasure that a call to No. 80 Squadron for a bombing sortie rarely took more than half an hour to answer.[22] On the other hand, there were some serious problems here as well. The 40-lb bombs carried by the squadron were useless against tanks and only effective against "soft-skinned" vehicles in low-level attacks. But here a now familiar enemy was again encountered – the German light flak which, defending static targets, could make low-level attacks prohibitively costly. Not only did the Germans make far greater use than the British of their light AA guns, their methods of using them were sounder. They did not generally attempt to bring down individual aircraft by aimed fire; they chose rather to send up a thick barrier of shells virtually guaranteed at least to damage any aircraft that tried to fly through it. It was AA fire that accounted for four out of the 10 aircraft lost by No. 80 Squadron.

With the Germans learning lessons also – perhaps above all the lesson of dispersal on the ground – and with all the problems of movement to contend with as well as the problems of fighting, the Desert Air Force was fully stretched. The burden on the fighters was very heavy – no fewer than seven squadrons had to be withdrawn at the end of the year for lack of aircraft or to re-equip. Re-equipment was definitely due; Tedder had been inclined to believe at first that his fighters had laid the "bogey" of the Me 109F,[23] but by the turn of the year he accepted that the Hurricanes and Tomahawks were still outclassed in speed and climb, and remarked, "One squadron of Spitfire Vs would have been worth a lot."[24]

However, since it was considered that Spitfires were better employed in playing the "numbers game" over Northern France (see p. 285), and with Kittyhawks still unavailable for operations (32, still packed in crates, arrived in late December), Coningham's squadrons had to maintain air superiority by keeping larger numbers of fighters over the Army front. This practice offended air-power purists (as, indeed, did the whole field of Army Cooperation!), but Coningham found that it had its own rewards, which supplied a new gloss on air support. He told Tedder on December 17 that he did not merely regard fighter operations over the battle front as protection for the Army, but as a means of obtaining air superiority itself:

> In point of fact we use the ground forces purely as ground bait for enemy bombers and fighters. If the effect on our forces is one of protection, then all concerned, except perhaps the enemy, are happy, but I do not want our own tactical thinkers to be led astray into considering the operation as any more defensive than an ordinary offensive patrol.[25]

In other words, just as the Navy and Coastal Command had re-learned that the best place to find U-boats in order to destroy them was near a convoy (see p. 227), the Desert Air Force now learned that the best place to find and destroy enemy aircraft, to gain air superiority, was near the Army. Both propositions now have an elementary look; the lesson of history, however, is that such paradoxes do not yield themselves up easily.

For statistical purposes, CRUSADER is generally reckoned to have begun on November 18, 1941 and ended on January 20, 1942, Rommel's counterstroke being thus relegated to a limbo belonging to no particular battle. As regards air losses, this is, fortunately, not important. Between November 1 and January 31, the RAF's losses in the Middle East amounted to 539 aircraft of all types, of which 157 were destroyed on the ground, most of them in Malta. Subtracting estimated losses for November 1–18 and January 21–31, an approximate figure of 440 (excluding the Fleet Air Arm, but including Malta) "may be given for aircraft lost as a result of enemy action during the CRUSADER period".[26] This, of course, is the total for the whole of the Middle East, but since the action was virtually confined to the Desert and Malta, and since the total of serviceable aircraft in those two sectors on November 18 was no more than 616,[27] 440 is a high figure. It represents, in fact, a weekly rate of just under 49 aircraft, compared with a weekly rate of 63½ in the Battle of Britain. But since virtually all the aircraft lost in the Battle of Britain were single-seater fighters, while the Desert loss included bombers, reconnaissance aircraft and others, the aircrew casualties in the two engagements may well have been about equal. On each occasion, however, there was the consolation of the "numbers game": it was estimated that during the CRUSADER period the Germans and Italians had lost 982 aircraft destroyed, with another 83 probables, and of this total the offensive in Libya was believed to have accounted for 913 destroyed and 63 probables. German records, however, show that their total destroyed was 259; there is no exact figure for the Italians. However,

> accepting the figure of 259 German aircraft destroyed on operational flights and on the ground and the *conservative estimate* . . . of 204 Italian aircraft destroyed, we can accept 463 enemy aircraft destroyed in battle as the best approximate figure.[28]

So, once more, comparative records do not support the RAF's claim to a massive victory; on the contrary, the losses appear to have been roughly equal. However,

> None of this alters the fact that during "Crusader" the Army enjoyed the best air support it had ever had, and the diaries show how appreciative it was.[29]

This, at least, might have been a consolation for the loss, the effort, and the ultimate disappointment; but early 1942 was not a time for consolations.

45 *America in the war; a new strategy*

Churchill's reaction to the Japanese attack on the American fleet base at Pearl Harbor in December 1941 was characteristic – and uncommon. Shrugging aside the shock, and staring past the immediate havoc, he saw the essential: "the United States was in the war, up to the neck and in to the death." He bathed in the splendour of the long-term implications:

> We had won the war. England would live; Britain would live; the Commonwealth of Nations and the Empire would live. How long the war would

last or in what fashion it would end no man could tell, nor did I at this moment care. Once again in our long Island history we should emerge, however mauled or mutilated, safe and victorious. We should not be wiped out. Our history would not come to an end. We might not even have to die as individuals. Hitler's fate was sealed. Mussolini's fate was sealed. As for the Japanese, they would be ground to powder. All the rest was merely the proper application of overwhelming force.[1]

It was not given to everyone to see matters in that rosy light at that time. Indeed, the winter of 1941–42, and most of the following year, saw the Berlin/Rome/Tokyo Axis at its height, the anti-Axis powers at their lowest ebb.

A brief recapitulation of some – only some – of this period's dire events is here in order:

1941

December	7	Pearl Harbor
	7/8	Japanese landings in Malaya
	8	Japanese attack on Hong Kong opens
	8	Japanese landings in the Philippines
	10	*Prince of Wales* and *Repulse* sunk
	15	British withdrawal from Kowloon
	18	Japanese landing on Hong Kong
	19	battleships *Queen Elizabeth* and *Valiant* seriously damaged in Alexandria harbour
	25	fall of Hong Kong
1942		
January	2	Japanese enter Manila
	10	Japanese invade Dutch East Indies
	31	Japanese occupy Malaya
February	8/9	Japanese land on Singapore
	15	fall of Singapore; surrender of 85,000 British troops
March	7	fall of Rangoon
April	9	surrender of Bataan (Philippines)
May	6	surrender of Corregidor (Philippines)
	20	Japanese occupy all Burma, arrive at the frontier of India

Meanwhile, after a bad winter in the snow, the Germans were attacking again on the Eastern Front, Allied shipping losses were approaching their highest level of the whole war, *Scharnhorst* and *Gneisenau* derisively escaped up the English Channel – and on May 26 Rommel delivered his most telling blow of the Desert campaign.

It is an appalling catalogue of misfortune – yet Churchill is right. The entry of the United States – despite the train of disasters which immediately followed – was decisive. And the decision of the United States Government to treat Germany as the first enemy (despite the public outrage at Japan's surprise attack), taken at the "Arcadia" Conference in Washington, December 22, 1941–January 3, 1942, cast the war in a new mould. It is possible to see very clearly now what was far less clear at the time: that the whole thrust of the Anglo-American war effort from this time onwards would be towards a landing in north-west Europe, and a major campaign by the joint armies, directed at the *Reich* as broadly agreed at the conference. Henceforth, whatever contributed to this end would promote the prime intention; whatever impeded it would be, to a greater or lesser extent, harmful. This meant, inevitably, that sooner or later the main air effort would have to be in support of that campaign. It was not a matter of strategical niceties, or of abstract theories of war. This was an inter-Allied agreement – a foundation-stone, indeed, of the Alliance itself. It would be watched over by a new item of war-making machinery: the Combined Chiefs of Staff Committee (British and American Chiefs of Staff or their Deputies, sitting together in joint conclave and taking joint decisions), a body which Churchill suggests was "the most valuable and lasting result of our first Washington conference".[2] The decisions so taken would establish the discipline of the new coalition war. It was a discipline which, when the day came, would require the full value of Army Cooperation – indeed, of the whole air effort.

But that day was not yet. For the time being, there could be no possibility of a drastic revision of the war's immediate agenda. The United States had to repair the damage of Pearl Harbor and enormously expand her Navy, raise a mass army, and create a great air force. Meanwhile, somehow, the Japanese advance had to be held. In this the British must play a part – defending India and Ceylon, and building up some force for counterstrokes on the northern flank of the great Japanese salient in south-east Asia and the south-west Pacific. These were things that had to be done, whatever the main intention, and however great the current material weakness. Furthermore, unless the U-boats were decisively defeated, there would be no hope of fulfilling the main intention in any case – only a mid-Atlantic massacre with calamitous results. Yet some aid must, during all this, be given to the Soviet Union, struggling for its life and inflicting hard blows on Hitler's forces. So the immediate agenda remained depressingly familiar. In the Far East, sheer military weakness and unpreparedness repeated, for all three Services, a well-known pattern; once more the RAF found itself outnumbered and outclassed. In the Middle East its rôle was suddenly changed from helping the Army forward to saving it from disastrous rout.

46 Malta

One requires no strategic genius, nor profound instruction in warlike arts, to perceive the significance of Malta in the Mediterranean war. The island lies almost exactly in the centre of that sea, on a cross-roads of communication through it. It is right on the direct route from Italy to Tripoli, the capital and chief port of what was then Italy's empire in North Africa. A highly valued base of the Royal Navy since its occupation by the British in 1800, Malta's flotillas, both submarines and destroyers, were the scourge of Axis sea communications. Thanks to them, and to the RAF and Fleet Air Arm based on the island, Rommel fought most of his Desert war with a ball and chain at his ankle; as Ronald Lewin says,

> The Afrika Korps would always be a starveling, short of supplies, short of men, short of equipment.[1]

In August 1941, 35 per cent of Rommel's supplies and reinforcements were lost before they reached him; in October, the eve of CRUSADER, the figure was 63 per cent.[2]

It followed, as night follows the day, that Malta's offensive potential would draw down retribution, and the map shows how crushing this might be. The nearest point of Italy (Cape Passero, at the southernmost tip of Sicily) is only 55 miles away. The Italian fleet base at Taranto is 325 miles away; the island's vulnerability to air bombardment was absolute. At the outbreak of war with Italy, Malta's air strength was 10 aircraft, and its air defence consisted of four sea-Gladiators; one of these was soon wrecked, leaving three – the legendary, "Faith", "Hope" and "Charity". The first Hurricanes arrived in August – twelve of them, flown in off the aircraft-carrier *Argus*. A second attempt, in November, produced one of the RAF's more miserable disasters; for a variety of reasons, which would seem to have included somewhat careless planning, navigation errors, and sheer inexperience, out of two flights of six Hurricanes, each led by a Fleet Air Arm Skua, which flew off *Argus* just before dawn on November 17, none of the second flight were seen again, and two Hurricanes of the first flight crashed in the sea 34 and 25 miles from Malta respectively. One pilot was saved by a Malta-based Sunderland.

Malta survived through 1941 against all the probabilities. The arrival of the *Luftwaffe* in Sicily was obviously a bad omen, and the heavy attacks on Grand Harbour in what was known as the "*Illustrious* blitz", while the badly damaged *Illustrious* was receiving running repairs (January 12–23; see pp. 325–6), were a foretaste of what was to come. It was in the air raids of March and April, however, that the people and garrison of Malta first learned the difference between being attacked by the Germans and being attacked by the Italians. This was the first stage of Malta's ordeal. In the early months of 1942 the ordeal reached its height, and brought the threat, not merely of fierce bombardment, but of invasion and capture. And 1942 was when the intimate connection between Malta and the Desert campaign was heavily underlined.

The RAF had been aware of one facet of this intimacy for a long time; ever since General O'Connor's sweep through Cyrenaica at the beginning of 1941, the RAF's "theme song", according to Tedder, had been: "Give us the airfields of Cyrenaica and we can look after Malta."[3]

Here was a significant part of the "war for aerodromes" (see p. 313); but there was something else as well, something not altogether clearly perceived in London:

> It was held in London that it was essential to launch the Libyan offensive in order to relieve Malta; the truth was that it was essential to hold Malta in order to make it possible to launch the Libyan offensive. During the period in which Malta was pounded into uselessness, more than a quarter of a million tons of Axis munitions, armaments and oil were carried safely across the Mediterranean. This was why Malta mattered, but the authorities in London saw its significance the other way round.[4]

In November 1941 Malta actually caused a weakening of German forces on the Russian Front: the movement of *Luftflotte 2* from the sector before Moscow to Sicily. In December, *Feldmarschall* Kesselring, whom we last met commanding that same *Luftflotte* in the attack on Britain, took command of all German Air Force units in the Mediterranean, with orders "to obtain air and sea supremacy in the area between Southern Italy and North Africa", for which purpose it was clearly "particularly important to suppress Malta".[5] In the last week of December Kesselring commenced upon this task with his habitual energy; some 200 aircraft attacked the island, making the Royal Air Force their chief objective.[6] The ordeal had begun.

Facing Kesselring's forces, and dedicated to the proposition that Malta would not be suppressed, was another of that group of officers of Middle East Command whom it seemed that no apparent impossibility, no degree of material weakness, could ever daunt; Air Vice-Marshal H. P. (later Sir Hugh) Lloyd, AOC. Lloyd was a man possessed not only of "bulldog courage" (precisely the quality required in Malta's predicament) but also of an "unfailing determination not merely to keep Malta in being, but to use the island as an offensive base"[7] – which at the height of the ordeal was a vision indeed. Tedder considered Lloyd to be "the main driving force and inspiration of the defence of Malta",[8] and said of him at the time that "more than anyone he is the personification of Malta's resistance".[9]

The fight that followed was dominated by two considerations: first, the fact that Malta depended absolutely on supplies from outside, and secondly, that the island is virtually devoid of natural cover. It was thus a struggle of endurance, and a battle of wits. The cutting-off of supplies was the perpetual nightmare: a convoy from Alexandria delivered 21,000 tons in January; nothing at all came through in February; of two convoys attempted in March, one failed completely to get through, the other lost all its merchantmen either on the way or in Malta itself, only 5,000 tons of supplies out of 26,000 being saved – a substantial proportion of those only by the magnificent efforts of Lloyd's airmen. But "Malta got no more for another three months".[10] Not for the first, or last, time, the RAF's serious weakness (by comparison with the *Luftwaffe*) in transport aircraft became apparent.[11]

The battle of wits resolved itself around guns and fighters. In April – the worst month – Malta's heavy AA guns fired 72,053 rounds, and the light guns 88,176. When the Germans and Italians switched their main attack from the pulverized dock area to the RAF's landing grounds, much of this effort was for their protection; even so, there was a steady toll of RAF aircraft destroyed on the ground. How seriously the Air Staff viewed Malta's situation may be judged from the fact that on March 7 15 Spitfires were flown in from HMS *Eagle*; 16 more came in on March 21 and 29 – all these at a time when the Western Desert Air Force possessed none, and considered itself lucky to be at last obtaining some Kittyhawks. And yet it was Spitfires which experienced the full rigour of the battle of wits. On April 20, 47 flew in from the United States carrier *Wasp* – "spared from the many hundreds in Fighter Command".[12] Unfortunately, their arrival was observed, and within twenty minutes they were under attack; by the next morning, only 27 were serviceable, and by the evening, 17; on

April 23 the Governor of Malta reported that its serviceable fighters were reduced to six.

In April 1942 Malta's proud endurance was rewarded by the collective award of the George Cross. The hardships and tragedies which the island and its garrison were experiencing certainly deserved this acknowledgment. However, concealed within them, there were consoling features, not easily perceptible at the time. The chief of these was, undoubtedly, an enemy error. It was Grand Admiral Raeder, the German naval Commander-in-Chief, who first urged (in February) that Malta ought to be captured outright. Neutralization by bombing was a second best alternative, in his opinion. In March Kesselring came to the same conclusion. Then, on May 1, Hitler and Mussolini met and agreed on a Mediterranean programme: first, either in May or June, an advance by Rommel's forces to clear Cyrenaica (Operation THESEUS), to be followed in July or August by an assault on Malta – HERKULES. It is interesting, in the light of the easy optimism of the early SEALION planning, to note how cautiously both Germans and Italians now approached the problem of attacking Malta. It is interesting also that no attempt at an airborne *coup-de-main* was considered, and it is Tedder who remarks that this may be a neglected benefit of an otherwise wretched event:

> It has been well said that Freyberg and his troops, though they lost the battle of Crete, may have won the more important battle of Malta.[13]

It is an unquestioned fact that the Germans never, after Crete, attempted another major airborne assault, and that Malta offered a most tempting target for such an operation. What is also certain is that the low priority of HERKULES was a serious mistake, and that its subsequent steady downgrading was even worse. Rommel would rue the day that this opportunity was lost.

Also interesting, but unnoticed or disregarded in circles that should have been concerned, are the "vital statistics" of the air attack on Malta. In the grim month of April, the Axis air forces flew some 4,900 sorties against the island; the Valetta sirens sounded 275 times – "an average of once every 2½ hours throughout the month";[14] 6,278 tons of bombs were dropped. The damage, of course, was enormous. But the loss of civilian life under this massive onslaught was precisely 300, with another 330 seriously injured.[15] In other words, it took almost 22½ tons of bombs to kill a civilian, and about 10 tons to cause a serious or fatal injury. These were enlightening figures for the argument about air bombardment as a prime means of winning the war – had anyone cared to consider them. More satisfactory for the Axis, however, was the extinction of Malta's offensive power, reflected in the dramatic improvement in the quantity of supplies reaching Libya, referred to above. Yet even this success was only temporary,[16] and one can see that Admiral Raeder was certainly right in viewing air attack as second best to outright capture. HERKULES should have been permitted to put forth his strength.

47 *Gazala: the lowest ebb; "First Alamein"*

Even before CRUSADER was launched, optimists in London – and Churchill was always to be numbered among them – were thinking of its likely sequels: ACROBAT (a further offensive to clear Tripolitania) and WHIPCORD (a revised plan for attacking Sicily). The setback in early 1942 did not abolish these schemes; their promotion was a running refrain all through the spring, and a large factor in the evaporation of confidence between Churchill and Auchinleck, although the latter never lacked the support of his fellow Cs-in-C in urging delay. For each of the Service commanders, the sense of his own weakness was enhanced by awareness of the new enemy at his back: Cunningham, with his fleet "virtually destroyed by a series of disasters",[1] now faced the probability of a Japanese incursion into the Indian Ocean; Auchinleck saw promised reinforcements diverted to the Far East theatre; Tedder had to send nearly 450 of his own aircraft in the same direction, including four out of the six of the Desert Air Force's Blenheim squadrons. Churchill's impatient appeals for offensive action fell on understandably resentful ears.

Even without Japanese intervention, Middle East Command would have been in difficulty at this period. CRUSADER had brought heavy losses in fighters, and the replacement problem was serious; it was not just numbers – as we have seen, it was high time to replace the Hurricane Is, while Tomahawk supplies were in any case drying up, and Kittyhawks only dribbling in. Most serious of all,

> The loss of fighter pilots in casualties and through genuine fatigue was heavy, and only poorly trained replacements were available.[2]

The bomber position was little better: the remaining Blenheims were, quite simply, wearing out, and their serviceability rate was extremely low; the supply of Marylands was failing (like the Tomahawks); the new Martin Baltimore light bomber, built to British requirements, was slow in coming in (like the Kittyhawks); and the

Douglas DB-7s (Boston IIIs), the scheduled replacements for the Blenheims, were going through the phase of technical faults which appeared to be inevitable with the RAF's American acquisitions. This bad patch caused a temporary decline in operational efficiency and morale, but excellent work by the Middle East maintenance crews brought modifications to the Bostons which in due course "transformed them to some of the best aircraft in the Command".[3]

Despite these worries, while the Mediterranean Fleet, perforce, limited its activities, and the Army appeared to Churchill to be, inexplicably, dragging its feet, the RAF allowed itself no respite. Including Malta's few bombers, but excluding purely anti-shipping operations, Middle East Command flew nearly 14,000 sorties between February 7 and May 25 – an average of 130 a day. The cost of this steady, relentless effort was nearly 300 aircraft (from all causes)[4] – a high figure which, as the Official History says, has to be seen as "the price paid for an aggressive air policy and a fighter force composed for the most part of obsolescent aircraft".[5] In mid-April, however, extra point was lent to the RAF's activities by the growing indications that Rommel might be the first to strike; drawing chiefly on Ultra decrypts, Intelligence in London rightly gauged that the German attack would probably come "at any time after the third week of May".[6] Although Middle East Intelligence reached the same conclusion, Auchinleck and his colleagues were slow to agree; as late as May 17, Tedder was telling Portal that his "personal reading" of all the evidence pointed towards an attack on Malta. "He was at once informed that the CAS did not agree."[7] There were, in fact, only nine days to go; Rommel's target date was May 26.

The battle which followed, beginning on the Gazala "line", and ending at El Alamein, nearly 220 miles inside the Egyptian frontier, marked the nadir of Britain's military fortunes during the war. All the faults of her military system, all the weaknesses of her main field army (both lying outside the scope of this volume) were relentlessly exposed; and if, at the end, the rugged fighting qualities of her Commander-in-Chief, General Sir Claude Auchinleck, plucked fresh hope out of disaster against all the odds, that was the very most that offered itself by way of consolation to a very roughly handled army. For the RAF, however, the story was quite different.

As the battle opened, on May 26, Air Vice-Marshal Coningham's headquarters was still adjacent to that of the Army Commander, who was still, to the wonder of many, Lieutenant-General Ritchie. Apart from the various reconnaissance and other special duty squadrons under the direct control of Coningham's Western Desert Air Force

HQ, he had a wing (No. 3 SAAF) of light bombers (Nos. 12 and 24, SAAF, Boston IIIs; No. 223, RAF, Baltimores), and three wings (No. 211 Group) of fighters. In No. 233 Wing, two squadrons (Nos. 4 and 5, SAAF) had Tomahawks, two others (No. 2 SAAF and 260, RAF) had Kittyhawks. All four squadrons of No. 239 Wing (Nos. 3 and 450 RAAF and 112 and 250, RAF) also had Kittyhawks. In No. 243 Wing, three squadrons (Nos. 33, 274 and 80) had Hurricane IIs; a fourth squadron (No. 73) also had Hurricane IIs, but was designated and trained as a night-fighter squadron. No. 145 Squadron, which came into action after a week of fighting, enjoyed a special honour: a flight of Spitfire Vs, the first combat Spitfires (as opposed to Photographic Reconnaissance) in the Western Desert. Once again, we see how the stress of war gave fighters the preponderant rôle; it was now official policy that all No. 211 Group's aircraft should be equipped to act as fighter-bombers, but in fact by May 26 only one Hurricane and 3 Kittyhawk squadrons had been converted. Very shortly, yet another forward-pointing direct support rôle would be offered to them.

Numbers of tanks and numbers of aircraft are the statistics most commonly flourished in histories of the Desert War; both are often treated as decisive. And indeed, both are very important; but more important still, as the Battle of Gazala amply proved, were the quality of the machines, and the quality of the crews. In tank numbers the British advantage was impressive: 849, against 560 Axis tanks, of which only 330 were German. Yet the British lost all the tank encounters – and with them the battle itself. The air picture was startlingly different. Out of 320 aircraft in the Desert Air Force, some 290 were serviceable; against them the Germans and Italians had a total of 704, of which 497 were serviceable. Behind Coningham's squadrons stood, of course, the rest of Middle East Command – some 739 serviceable aircraft. But the Germans had another 215 serviceable aircraft available in Greece, Crete and Sicily, and the Italians some 775 in various locations:

> The British were therefore outnumbered in the whole theatre and also in the Desert. Moreover, in fighter aircraft performance, the Germans held the trump card in the Me 109F.[8]

Of these formidable aircraft, Coningham's opposite number, the *Fliegerführer Afrika, Generalleutnant* Otto Hoffmann von Waldau, possessed 120. Yet the RAF never lost the initiative, and was never defeated in the air.

But it was hard going. By May 31 the British fighters had flown over 1,500 sorties and had lost some 50 aircraft – about 20 per cent of the fighter force. This was the high price of army cooperation, of ceaseless attacks on Rommel's ground forces and above all his most vulnerable point – his supply columns. As ever, these were strongly protected by light AA and the German fighters also appeared in strength. On May 31 alone 16 British aircraft were lost (compared with three German fighters and two dive-bombers). The delusions of the "numbers game" saved Coningham and his pilots from too much discouragement, but there was no disguising the fact that squadron strengths were already down to seven or eight serviceable aircraft. The arrival of No. 145 Squadron's Spitfires on June 1 was more an omen for the future than a present reinforcement; but used as top cover for the Hurribombers and Kittybombers, "their mere presence in the battle meant that for the first time the enemy fighter pilot had to look over his shoulder".[9] Two days of dust storms which severely restricted flying brought even better relief, which was just as well because the reserves of Kittyhawks were running dangerously low. Coningham's squadrons now claimed to have destroyed some 200 Axis vehicles on the ground, which was direct support indeed, and of a kind that Rommel would not be able to stand for long. But neither could the Desert Air Force stand its own losses; from the beginning of June the fighters reduced this expensive exercise and applied themselves to trying to obtain air superiority by sheer numbers. Their losses dropped accordingly. At the same time, amid scenes of indescribable confusion, the Army's tank superiority was crumbling away, and the battle was being irretrievably lost.

These black days were constantly relieved by the glow of brave deeds; none was watched with more attention than the nine-day defence of the "box" at Bir Hacheim by General Koenig's First Free French Brigade. This was the first time that French troops had been engaged against the Germans since 1940, a fact which conferred a certain symbolism on the action. Such an attribute is not always an advantage in war, but this was indeed an occasion calling for special work. Coningham decided to "adopt" Bir Hacheim, and from June 3–10 his squadrons were heavily committed to what quickly became one of the fiercest engagements of the whole Gazala battle – "of extraordinary severity", Rommel's words. The Free French were highly appreciative of the work of the Desert Air Force, some of whose highlights took place in their full view. "*Bravo! Merci pour la RAF*", signalled General Koenig. "*Bravo à vous! Merci pour le sport,*" replied Coningham, courteously. If it was sport, it was a taxing one: the Desert Air Force flew 1,500 sorties in support of Bir Hacheim (950 by fighters[10]) and lost 20 aircraft; the Germans flew 1,400 sorties and lost 15, while the Italians lost at least five.

> Both sides felt the strain of such a prolonged effort, and the maintenance crews deserve a word of recognition for their work which enabled many aircraft to make four, and even six, sorties in a day.[11]

Bir Hacheim was evacuated on the night of June 10/11; the Free French Brigade had suffered heavy casualties, but its nine-day resistance had severely disrupted Rommel's schedule – "nine days of losses in material, personnel, armour and petrol. Those nine days were irrecoverable."[12]

It was during this period, which was also the period of the heavy fighting which defeated the Eighth Army in what was called "the Cauldron", that the second direct support innovation made its appearance. No. 6 Squadron arrived in the desert with 9 Hurricane IIDs – tank-destroyers, vulgarly labelled by the Army and the Press "tank-busters", armed with two 40-mm Vickers "S" guns.[13] In June 1942, No. 6 Squadron flew some 40 sorties against armour and soft-skinned vehicles, claiming 31 of the former and 42 of the latter. The tank claim is doubtful:

> With the intensive AA fire employed by the enemy in support of his armoured forces, attacks on tank targets in the battle area generally imposed too high a wastage of aircraft and could not be justified. Ideal targets were small groups of tanks away from the main armoured battle, and the squadron's activities were generally limited by the availability of such targets.[14]

The sheer weight of their guns and ammunition reduced the speed of the Hurricanes to 286 mph, but these pioneers were not easily deterred. Their aggressive spirit was well displayed by an action in July, when they claimed five tanks, five lorries and an anti-tank gun. One thrusting pilot, Flight-Lieutenant Hillier,

> after having destroyed a tank, accidently struck it with his aircraft as he pulled away from the attack, losing his tailwheel and the bottom half of his rudder. Notwithstanding the Hurricane responded to the controls and brought its pilot safely home.[15]

Once again, however, despite robust aircraft and determined pilots, the feats of No. 6 Squadron take their chief importance from the pointer they gave towards a future style of air warfare, rather than their immediate impact on the battle.

The battle itself, in the days immediately following the fall of Bir Hacheim, went from bad to worse. The Army, as in the worst days of CRUSADER, fell into great confusion, with commanders uncertain of the location of their own units, and intercommunication between units only fragmentary. In "the Cauldron" there was much inter-penetration with the enemy also – a combination of conditions which could scarcely be more unfavourable for Army/Air cooperation or direct support. It was usually impossible to determine a bomb-line; recognition also was often virtually impossible. Yet there were good days; June 16 is recorded as "undoubtedly a successful day for air support",[16] and the 21st *Panzer* Division on that day reported "contin-ual attacks at quarter-hour intervals by bombers and low-flying air-craft". It sent up a cry for fighter protection which would be heard again and again. Yet, once more, losses in the Desert Air Force were high: 10 aircraft on June 16, 11 on the 17th, which (added to one lost on the 15th) meant 22 in three days, or, in other words,

> that aircraft were being lost at a rate of two and a half per hundred sorties, or reckoning on an average daily strength of thirteen aircraft per squadron for thirteen squadrons, an optimistic assessment for this period, losses consumed thirteen per cent of the fighter strength.[17]

The work of the ground-crews during this first stage of the battle is beyond all praise, as these figures show:

	Average Daily Strength	Average Serviceability	Percentage
May 26 to June 1	15.3	10.3	67
June 2 to June 8	13.6	10.3	75.7
June 9 to June 15	13.3	10.9	82[18]

It seemed, however, that nothing could check the steady disinte-gration of the British armour, and in its train the overwhelming of the Army's other elements. Coningham's headquarters was still alongside Ritchie's Tactical Headquarters at Sollum when, on June 18, he was informed that no security could be given to his airfields against fast-moving enemy columns. It was fortunate indeed that he had already prepared a plan for the "worst possible case" – another retreat as head-long as that of January. It is that ability to look ahead, for ill as well as for good, that marks a real commander. But it was a bad moment, when the fighters left their forward airfields, and fell back to their prepared positions inside the Egyptian frontier. It was worse still when Advanced Air Headquarters accompanied them. The intimate link between the top echelons of the two Services which had taken so long to forge was broken, and would not be mended again while this battle lasted. This was a bad day for air support.

Coningham's move was timely, nevertheless. Two days later (June 29) Tobruk fell, to the vast consternation of Churchill and the whole Allied cause. On June 25 Ritchie was removed from the command of the Eighth Army, and Auchinleck, for the second time, took direct charge of operations. It was too late to avoid another disaster, at Mersa Matruh, on June 27/28 – "the last unqualified victory of the Afrika Korps".[19] These two brilliant successes – Tobruk and Matruh – apart from the heavy British losses in battle and the deep psychological effect, brought aid and comfort to Rommel precisely where he needed it most: 5,000 tons of supplies, 2,000 vehicles, 1,400 tons of fuel.[20] Fortified by this injection, against all logistical reason, and throwing all thoughts of Operation HERKULES to the winds, Rommel pressed his advance into Egypt with Alexandria his goal. But Auchinleck was not Ritchie:

> To his everlasting credit he was able in the next few weeks to produce a form of order out of chaos, and to exploit the flaws in the Axis situation created by Rommel's headlong advance – a situation which can only be described as brilliant but disastrous.
>
> During July 1942 Rommel came to a dead end.[21]

In the first Battle of El Alamein (July 1–22), Rommel was forced on to a defensive from which he was never able to escape, and Auchinleck repeated his record as the first British general to defeat a German general in the Second World War. "First Alamein" was the turning-point of the Desert campaigns: the first pale streak of dawn in the eastern sky.

There was already a strong hint that this might be so in the air action. By the time Rommel's ground forces entered Egypt, the *Luftwaffe* was practically exhausted. Its great effort at Bir Hacheim was followed by another, even greater, at Tobruk: 580 bomber sorties *in one day* (plus 177 Italian).[22] It was not combat losses that now crippled the German Air Force; it was the strain of these intensive operations on the crews and on the aircraft, whose serviceability dropped alarmingly. As a result, when Rommel decided to continue his advance, he did so "without the *Luftwaffe*",[23] a circumstance which he soon had occasion to regret bitterly. Not only were the retreating columns of the Eighth Army left "virtually unmolested", but the German ground forces were subjected to continuous harassment every mile of the way, by day and night. In this crisis, Tedder threw in everything that Middle East Command could raise: Hurricane IIs were taken from training units, Spitfires from Malta, Beaufighters from naval cooperation; more Hurricanes and Spitfires, intended for India, were held in the Middle East; Halifaxes and Liberators were ordered in. The United States Army Air Force lent encouragement and support, with the promise of a Medium Bombardment Group (57 B-25 Mitchells), a Heavy Bombardment Group (35 B-24 Liberators), a Light Bombardment Squadron (27 A-29 Hudsons) and a Fighter Group (80 F-40 Kittyhawks).[24]

In the first week of July, in sharp contrast with the *Luftwaffe*, the Desert Air Force flew 5,458 sorties. These included 60–70 sorties every night by the Wellingtons of No. 205 Group; in this work another new technique was further developed – "pathfinding", the marking of targets by special illumination before the arrival of the main bomber force (see pp. 268–9). This was done by the slow Fleet Air Arm Fairey Albacore biplanes of Nos. 821 and 826 Squadrons, whose good visibility and large flare-carrying capacity made them ideal for the purpose. Arriving 15 minutes ahead of the Wellingtons, the Albacores searched out the target areas and lit them at a specified time to coincide with the approach of the bombers; by July this had become standard – and profitable – practice.

It was still the fighters, however, which bore the brunt of the action, and their wastage was a serious matter. By July 7, in just six weeks of battle, the British fighter force had lost no fewer than 202 aircraft on operations. In some of the Kittyhawk squadrons, the losses amounted to 100 per cent of their original numbers.[25] It is in the light of these figures that one best appreciates the tribute of General von Waldau on July 25:

Although the enemy has lost a great many of his fighter aircraft during the last two months, there has been so far no apparent sign of a decrease in flying ability or combat performance. Combat effectiveness has been maintained, and indeed increased, by the assignment of new and excellently trained Spitfire squadrons from England. The employment of the Spitfires has given the enemy the confidence he needs to hold his own against our Me 109s.[26]

Yet the Spitfires were still few, and it was with aircraft outmatched in performance that the fighter force kept up its unremitting effort, refusing to be outfought.

For the RAF, then, there was no defeat; on the contrary,

> . . . the achievement of the Western Desert Air Force was to retain the initiative throughout, and to provide a strong defensive weapon with which to attack the *Panzerarmee* and delay its advance. Thus the Eighth Army was able to take up its positions at the Alamein Line in time to face the enemy successfully in a final stand. The Air Force, still unflagging, participated fully in the fierce battles of early July, in which Rommel's army was at last decisively checked and forced to go over to the defensive.[27]

What emerges from these two months of costly fighting, with all their humiliations, is an even greater emphasis than ever before on Army/Air cooperation – this time as a means, indeed, the *only* means, of staving off absolute disaster. If one tries to imagine subtracting the Desert Air Force effort from the crucial fighting of July one finds oneself at once in the realm of the unimaginable. And, indeed, throughout the whole battle, when it was given a chance, the air support system worked well – in fact, better and better:

> As the battle continued, the speed with which the Air Force answered calls for support steadily increased, until the average time of delay between a request from Eighth Army Headquarters and aircraft being airborne was eventually reduced to thirty-five minutes . . .[28]

This was clearly a great deal better than the two and a half to three-hour average of CRUSADER. But the key phrase is "when it was given a chance" – for it is equally clear that by July the system so carefully devised in 1941 had broken down. The Desert Air Force was by that stage acting virtually independently, with Coningham picking his own targets on the basis of his own reconnaissance. The separation of the two headquarters, which continued to the end (despite Auchinleck's sincere belief in air power) was the symbol of the breakdown, and Coningham's current method was simply a rough remedy for a thoroughly undesirable situation. It only worked because of the high degree of battle skill and understanding of the Force commander, and the proficiency and tireless, cheerful vigour of the aircrews. The cost of July alone to Middle East Command was 113 aircraft from all causes (compared with 80 German and 18 Italian). But its confidence was unimpaired, its sense of achievement was high, its experience much enhanced. If the system had broken, it was scarcely to be wondered at in the circumstances; it is hard to believe that any system could have stood up to the strain of the absolute defeat of the British armour in the early days of the battle, and all that flowed from that. If this defect could be repaired, there was hope yet.

48 *Montgomery and Coningham; Alam Halfa*

The procession that had begun with Longmore, had included Wavell and very nearly included Tedder, now took in Auchinleck. On August 15 he was replaced as GOC-in-C, Middle East, by General Sir Harold Alexander, and Lieutenant-General Sir Bernard Montgomery took over the Eighth Army. With the change of command came powerful reinforcement: new tanks (among them 300 American Shermans, the type which would become the Allied "work-horse" for the rest of the war), guns, vehicles; and on the air side, while the shortage of key types like Spitfires and Kittyhawks persisted, there was the beginning of the build-up of the United States Army Air Force in the Middle East which was planned to rise to a total of 24 squadrons. Once again, this was a promise of benefit chiefly in the future, and meanwhile posing the obvious problems of integrating an inexperienced air force with one that had acquired a lot of experience the hard way. Opportunities for friction were clearly plentiful; "fortunately, inter-allied relationship was Tedder's *forte*".[1]

A number of circumstances combined to bring about dramatic change at this juncture of the Desert War: reinforcements of men and material, the grave weakness of the Axis forces, exhausted by their great efforts, the renewal of the attack on Rommel's supply lines both from Malta and from Egypt. For all these reasons, August was a turning-point; but chiefly, and understandably, participants and historians have dwelt on the change of command. There can be no doubt that this factor was a great deal more than symbolic. General Alexander had displayed, in France and in Burma, rare qualities of imperturbability and reassurance; he was now, like Tedder, about to display an equally valuable aptitude for the new coalition war. Also, he had an excellent working relationship with his chief subordinate, Lieutenant-General Montgomery. Montgomery was not a good coalition general – indeed, he was a very bad one; and he was shortly to display certain unlovable attributes (notably a distressing boastfulness) which mar his record. But as a soldier, there is no doubt that he was outstanding:

No one in the [inter-war] years had studied the military art with such singleness of mind . . . He fought his battles according to sound and well-established principles, interpreted them into operational plans with great thoroughness, and pressed these through to victory with unrelenting authority.[2]

Montgomery's presence was immediately felt, with advantage, throughout the Eighth Army. It was also felt in the Desert Air Force; in Tedder's words, he "put cooperation with the RAF first in the order of priority".[3] This was no idle form of words; Air Marshal Barratt, from Army Cooperation Command, was visiting the Middle East at this time (August 27–September 9), and noted in his report:

On the arrival of General Montgomery, AOC Western Desert represented to him the difficulty of working in separate localities. General Montgomery was as fully insistent, as was Air Vice-Marshal Coningham, that they should both be together, and the former moved his camp back to the same location as that of A. V. M. Coningham. The senior officers mess together in the same Mess.[4]

This was, of course, simply a reversion to the sound system set up nearly a year earlier for CRUSADER, and sadly abandoned during the Gazala collapse. The difference, in 1942, was that now it was there to stay, with an important addendum which Barratt also noted:

Army "G" Operations Room and Air Operations Room were always sited adjacent and there was continuous liaison between BGS on the one hand and SASO on the other.[5]

Tedder commented:

It was most refreshing to find in Eighth Army Advanced Headquarters the embryo of a real operations room copied directly from our own mobile operations rooms. I took it upon myself to tell the soldiers that it was the first sign I had seen of their being able to collect and sift information about their battle, and consequently the first sign I had seen of their being able to control it.[6]

The results of all this would shortly be felt, but it will be as well to set down now the Montgomery philosophy of "Air Support", or "Army Cooperation", which was to inspire the remainder of the Desert War, the Tunisian campaign, the invasion of Sicily and Italy, and finally, but sadly less whole-heartedly, the campaign in North-West Europe. As stated by Montgomery himself in Italy in 1943, it was as follows:

I believe that the first and great principle of war is that you must first win your air battle before you fight your land and sea battle. If you examine the conduct of the campaign from Alamein through Tunisia, Sicily and Italy . . . you will find I have never fought a land battle until the air battle has been won. We never had to bother about the enemy air, because we won the air battle first.

The second great principle is that Army plus Air . . . has to be so knitted that the two together form one entity. If you do that, the resultant military effort will be so great that nothing will be able to stand against it.

The third principle is that the Air Force side of this fighting machine must be centralised and kept under Air Force command. I hold that it is quite wrong for the soldier to want to exercise command over the air striking forces. The handling of an Air Force is a life-study, and therefore the air part must be kept under Air Force command.

The next principle is that the Army Commander directs the military effort of Army plus Air, and the Air Force Commander who is with him applies the air effort in accordance with the combined plan. *There are not two plans, Army and Air, but one plan, Army-Air*, which is made by me and the Air Vice-Marshal together.

Next, the Army and Air Staff must sit together at the same headquarters. There must be between them complete mutual confidence and trust. Each has to understand the problems and difficulties of the other. My headquarters and the headquarters of the Air Support Force must be together. When I go forward with a small headquarters, there must be good telephonic communication back to our combined headquarters.

The confidence, trust, and integration of the two staffs is quite remarkable. The SASO and the Chief of Staff have to be great friends. If there is any friction there, you will be done. You have to be great friends, not merely to work together. And so it must go downwards. The machine is so delicate that it can be thrown out of gear very quickly. That mutual confidence and trust, starting with the Air Vice-Marshal and myself, must go right down . . .

Fighting against a good enemy – and the German is extremely good, a first-class soldier – you cannot operate successfully unless you have the full support of the air. If you do not win the air battle first, you will probably lose the land battle. I would go further. There used to be an accepted term of "army cooperation". We never talk about that now. The Desert Air Force and the Eighth Army are one. We do not understand the meaning of "army cooperation". When you are one entity you cannot cooperate. If you knit together the power of the Army on the land and the power of the Air in the sky, then nothing will stand against you and you will never lose a battle.[7]

The language is unmistakable; Lord Montgomery had a way of enunciating principles of war as though he had not merely personally brought them down, like Moses, from the high mountain, but had also had a large hand in inscribing them up there. The fact remains that no one had ever spoken and acted quite like this until Montgomery arrived. It is not to be supposed, of course, that every occasion of air support during the following year had gone with the clockwork precision that he suggests. That was not the case, nor likely to be, so long as war is conducted by fallible human beings. But it is certain that the potent system of land/air warfare hammered out so painfully in the desert between November 1941 and October 1942 was put to such good use thereafter that, from this point of view, the turning-point is as unmistakable as the fall and rise of the curtain between acts of a play. Unfortunately, Montgomery ignored his own precepts in 1944, but the system was strong enough to survive.

The new men, the new approach, were not long left untested. Montgomery assumed command of the Eighth Army on August 13; he moved his headquarters to join Coningham on August 16; the next day Ultra warned that Rommel would go over to the offensive on August 26.[8] On August 21 the Desert Air Force opened its own counter-offensive.[9] Ultra was meanwhile helping in other ways, including exact information about Axis shipping movements from which the Navy and the RAF derived great profit. During August, 25 per cent of the general military cargo despatched to Rommel was lost in transit, and 41 per cent of the fuel.[10] It was above all his chronic fuel shortage which compelled him both to limit his intended attack to a local operation,[11] and to delay the launching of it until August 30. By that time Coningham's counter-strikes had been in full swing for nine days, during which more than 450 tons of bombs were dropped on Rommel's forces – a taste of things to come.

The Battle of Alam el Halfa (August 39–September 6) saw Rommel's last attempt to break the defensive shackle imposed on him in July, and it was a complete failure. It was more than that:

> In many respects this little-known battle was the climax of army/air cooperation in the Western Desert and one in which, broadly speaking, the seal was set on the procedure and organisation for air support. The battle was a classic of its kind, exemplifying the use of air power on efficient and economical lines, when used in direct support of an army in the field.[12]

Air Marshal Barratt recorded:

> I had the good fortune to be present at Advanced Air HQ during the first three days of the battle, and I was able to watch the whole machine in

381

action. Each evening the GOC had a personal meeting with the AOC at which I was present. [Montgomery] gave him the clearest possible appreciation of the situation, the information as he knew it, what he intended to do himself, and what he expected the enemy to do. The AOC then said what he could do himself, and a general air plan was agreed upon. A further conversation took place the following morning as a result of events, ground and air, during the night. AVM Coningham subsequently informed me that never had he had such a clear and concise exposition of the military situation and needs during his experience in the Western Desert.[13]

Alam Halfa was a bombers' battle; in the words of the AHB Monograph, "practically the whole burden of offensive operations against the enemy devolved on the air force".[14] The Army's rôle, under Montgomery's judicious nursing, was strictly defensive; the fighters – 22 squadrons, including three of Spitfire Vs, but also 10 of Hurricanes and two of Tomahawks – cleared the way for the day bombers (Bostons, Baltimores and one squadron of USAAF Mitchells); No. 205 Group's Wellingtons (with the Fleet Air Arm's Albacores keeping constant company) gave the enemy no rest by night. On the night of August 31/September 1 the Wellingtons dropped over 90 tons of bombs; the next night, they and the Albacores dropped 112 tons, attacking transport and tank leaguers, sometimes from as low as 200 feet. "These enemy raids," says the *Afrika Korps* War Diary, "intensified night after night, are an effective battle technique." It was not merely the material damage, which the Germans found sufficiently impressive in itself, but there was a moral impact too; the *Afrika Korps* Diary recorded that

> officers and men were badly shaken and their fighting capacity considerably reduced by the enforced dispersal, lack of sleep, and the strain of waiting for the next bomb.[15]

On the night of September 1/2 No. 205 Group introduced them to 4,000-pounders – "with devastating effect".

The first three days of September contained the crisis of the battle, the complete defeat of Rommel's offensive intentions, and his decision to break off the action. Starting at first light on September 1, the day bombers flew 111 sorties, subjecting all concentrations of vehicles to intensive attack. In 372 sorties the fighters not only protected them, but also the Army from attempts at dive-bombing by Ju 87s. It made matters much easier, of course, that the Army was standing rigidly on the defensive, so that there was no doubt about where it was, no frustrating recognition problem. On September 2 "the light bombers were able to deal their most crushing blow at the enemy"[16] – 112 tons of bombs, dropped by 176 aircraft. It was on this day that Rommel gave orders for withdrawal to begin. In the course of that night and the next day, the RAF flew 957 sorties (nearly 600 by fighters) and dropped 230 tons of bombs – a record 24-hour total. In the whole critical 72 hours, fewer than 500 aircraft .

> had flown 2,500 sorties in support of the Eighth Army, which is equivalent to 35 aircraft in the air every hour, day and night. In addition, the United States Army Air Force had contributed nearly 180 sorties with its Liberators, Mitchells and Kittyhawk IIs.[17]

Air observers, on September 3, had the satisfaction of seeing the Axis forces in full retreat.

The battle of Alam Halfa, says the AHB Monograph, "stands out as a landmark in the development of air support organisation and technique during the war". No one was better able to comment on that estimate than Rommel himself; for him, says Ronald Lewin, it had been a revelation:

> It was the first time that he tried to fight an armoured battle with an absolute inferiority in the air. He realised that this lack was decisive, and that in the future it would be a permanent weakness for Germany. In his *Papers* there is a long passage which sets out his thoughts on this aspect of his defeat and ends, pessimistically, with the remark that "anyone who has to fight, even with the most modern weapons, against an enemy in complete control of the air fights like a savage against modern European troops, under the same handicaps and with the same chances of success".[18]

Rommel's tragedy began here, on the pitted, stony brown sands facing the Alam el Halfa Ridge, where his splendid, tempered instrument of war, the *Deutsches Afrika Korps*, was reduced to the level of a band of savages – by the application of air power. The tragedy reached its finale in Normandy in 1944, through the perfection of similar techniques.

49 *"Second Alamein"; advance to Tunisia*

"Between 1918 and 1939," wrote Sir Maurice Dean, "the Royal Air Force forgot how to support the Army."[1] By the end of 1942 it had re-learned the art, with advantages. "Henceforth," says Sir David

Fraser, "British soldiers seldom fought without the Royal Air Force masters of the air above." This was the crux, because at the heart of air support lies air superiority (see p. 336), and after Alam Halfa this was guaranteed by the swelling numbers and new types of the Allied Air Forces and the failure of the *Luftwaffe* to keep pace. The build-up of what was still, in October, known as the United States Army Middle East Air Force (US Ninth Air Force from November 12), under Major-General Lewis H. Brereton, was indicative: IX Bomber Command comprising two Heavy Bombardment Groups, six squadrons (one B-17, five B-24), a Medium Bombardment Group (four squadrons of B-25s) and a Fighter Group (three squadrons of P-40s). Overall control of the USAMEAF was vested in General Brereton in consultation with Tedder and the Middle East Cs-in-C. The Americans retained a measure of operational control of the Heavy Bombardment Groups,[2] but the day bombers and fighters were directly under Coningham. All told, the Allied Air Forces in the Middle East in October 1942 numbered 96 squadrons.[3]

The Second Battle of El Alamein has entered history and legend as the starting-point of the counter-offensive of the Western Allies which ultimately carried them into central Germany. The sum of that achievement has been rightly called a "mighty endeavour", and everything has to have a beginning. For perspective, however, it is well to recall that the Axis forces at El Alamein consisted of four weak German divisions and eight Italian divisions of varying but generally unimpressive quality (a total of some 50,000 Germans and 54,000 Italians). The Axis forces on the Eastern Front in 1942 amounted to 232 divisions, of which 171 were German (including 24 *Panzer* divisions) – a manpower total running into millions. Against the attenuated *Panzerarmee Afrika*, the British Eighth Army brought 11 divisions (four armoured), 195,000 men, with crushing superiority in guns and tanks. And the Desert Air Force immediately established its own crushing superiority in the air.

For the Army, the opening of the battle was marked by the flash and thunder of a barrage fired simultaneously by 456 guns on the main front, at 9.40 p.m. on October 23.[4] For the Desert Air Force, the battle had begun four days earlier, with a heavy bombing programme against enemy airfields. This was now a standard procedure: the preliminary air offensive taking the place of the long preparatory bombardments before attacks between 1915 and 1917. This was, of course, a use of air power which had been bitterly resisted, but defeat is a cruel teacher. And so effective did the procedure now prove that on October 23 Coningham's fighters were able to maintain a continuous patrol over the Axis forward airfields. This, also, was "against the book" but unorthodoxy was of the essence of the Desert Air Force. Air superiority, with Coningham's sure touch, was immediately established and firmly held (despite the fact that there were still only three Spitfire V squadrons to compete with the Messerschmitt 109Fs and 109Gs). This superiority, General Alexander later told Churchill, "had a great moral effect on the soldiers of both sides".[5] It meant, among other things, that the Bostons, Baltimores and Mitchells could operate effectively in daylight against Axis forces presenting attractive targets as they concentrated to meet the army's attacks – an admirable two-way cooperation. The light bombers generally flew in tight formations of 18 aircraft, and the Eighth Army took much pleasure in watching the "Eighteen Imperturbables" go over with their fighter escorts – seven times in the space of two and a half hours on one occasion (October 28). For the Germans and Italians it was rather different.

> All that Rommel had learned at Alam Halfa about the disabilities of a commander who, in modern war, lacks air superiority was once again proved to be true.[6]

The precious attribute is not to be obtained without loss. November 3 was certainly the busiest and probably the most successful day of air operations. In the space of 24 hours the RAF flew 1,208 sorties and dropped 396 tons of bombs on the now crumbling enemy (in addition to a further 53 sorties by US day bombers and 72 by fighters). However, British fighter losses that day amounted to 16, with 11 more damaged. In the whole battle, October 23–November 4, the RAF flew 10,405 sorties, and the Americans 1,181; the British lost 77 aircraft and the Americans 20. On the Axis side, the Germans (1,550 sorties) lost 64, and the Italians (estimated 1,570 sorties) lost an estimated 20. The result was a clear, unmistakable, and as it proved, irreversible victory; it was a victory for the air support system which had already shown its worth at Alam Halfa. But equally important to remember is that it was not

> simply the victory of the Eighth Army and the Western Desert Air Force. It was the victory of the Eighth Army and almost the whole allied air force in the Middle East.[7]

Once again, the war was driving home the lesson that when critical land operations are in progress, army cooperation is not simply a specialized activity of part of an air force. It is the function of the entire force, with all its available strength. Recognition of this was the most important contribution of the Middle East campaigns and from that recognition it is impossible to separate the name of Tedder.

And now the long march began which would carry both the Desert Air Force and the Eighth Army right out of the Middle East. To an important extent, this had been foreseen; as far back as September, Barratt, in his Middle East report, stated that Coningham "stressed the necessity for making plans in advance for movement either forward or back . . . Both the AOC-in-C and AOC Western Desert stressed the paramount need for mobility, and for all units being completely mobile."[8] Out of this foresight came Plan "Buster" – a detailed scheme for the "Operation of the Western Desert Air Force in Support of an Advance into Cyrenaica and Tripolitania", circulated a month before the battle began at El Alamein. For this purpose, the Desert Air Force was divided into two components:

Force "A" would provide direct support for the Eighth Army whilst Force "B" would act as a reserve and sustain the fighting strength of Force "A" by the transfer of aircraft and personnel and the exchange of squadrons, as required. Force "B" would also be responsible for protecting the line of communication. Arrangements were also made for the maintenance organisation to "leapfrog" their way forward, so that the air support would be continuous.[9]

Under this scheme, it was possible to get a complete fighter wing moving in fifteen minutes. A reconnaissance party moved ahead to select new airfields, linked by radio to Advanced Headquarters; an airfield construction party was positioned well forward in order to move immediately; detachments of Royal Engineers stood by to clear the mines and booby-traps which the Germans could be relied upon to sow lavishly, and the new RAF Regiment was at hand to guard the landing-grounds when occupied.[10]

As the Axis front crumbled, Tedder went forward to the Desert and found the "A" echelons already on the road; "all the squadrons were in magnificent form and out to kill". But he told Portal:

Coningham and I have repeatedly emphasised the importance of long swift moves to Army and am hopeful we shall get what we want. I think it is realised that this is a time when big chances must be taken.[11]

The "long swift moves" did not materialize; indeed, Correlli Barnett tells us:

On the morrow of its victory Eighth Army . . . lay at a standstill, paralysed by confusion as great as any seen under the predecessors Montgomery so despised.[12]

The first serious criticisms of Montgomery's generalship date from this failure to launch an immediate, all-out pursuit of Rommel's broken army. Fresh information confirms that judgment; in his revised edition of *The Desert Generals*, Correlli Barnett says:

> In accusing Montgomery of needless caution in his long pursuit of Rommel from Alamein to Tripoli, this book assumed that he could infer Rommel's weakness from the traditional sources of military intelligence. Now, however, Professor Hinsley's *British Intelligence in the Second World War*, Volume Two, puts Montgomery's caution in an entirely new light by telling us that throughout the pursuit "General Montgomery was fully apprised by the *Enigma*, by air reconnaissance and by Army "Y" of the state of Rommel's forces and, more important, the *Enigma* gave him advance notice of Rommel's intentions".[13]

Despite this priceless advantage, Montgomery's advance was, as Barnett adds, "a mere ghost of O'Connor's daring march of 1941". The reasons for this do not here concern us (they are discussed by Barnett and to some extent by Montgomery's official biographer, Nigel Hamilton); the consequences, however, were sadly significant. The air commanders were never able to lose sight of the fact that the Desert war was "a war for aerodromes" (p. 313) and their eyes were now firmly fixed on the Benghazi airfields. Tedder, certainly, knew what Montgomery knew, and was galled at his failure to profit by the knowledge;[14] and both Tedder and Coningham resented the boastfulness with which Montgomery claimed the victory as all his own. The breakdown of relations between the soldier and the air marshals, which was to have such evil consequences in 1944, seems clearly to date from the frustrations of this period.

In the Desert Air Force there was always a disposition towards bold action. It was a characteristic Coningham move (repeating a similar, but less successful operation with Fleet Air Arm Albacores in July) to place two Hurricane squadrons (Nos. 213 and 238) on a desert landing-ground far beyond the enemy's retreating army. The position selected was some 180 miles east of Agedabia; essential ground staff and supplies were air-lifted in on November 13. The Hurricanes followed the same afternoon, and immediately began operations against the long lines of unsuspecting Axis transport. In two days they claimed nearly 300 vehicles destroyed or damaged; when the surprise was spent, they withdrew on November 16. "Flexibility" could hardly have a better illustration.

The underlying truth, however, was less rosy; as Tedder told Portal in the signal quoted above:

> Hurricane squadrons doing magnificently loyal work, but are, of course, completely outclassed, and it is hard to tell them they cannot have modern aircraft yet.[15]

At the beginning of the Axis retreat, "by day and *particularly by night when the enemy's main movement took place*, a heavy toll of the enemy was taken by bombing, supported by low-flying fighter attacks".[16] The italics are mine: they express the only substance in the charge that had been made, that the Desert Air Force failed to make low-level attacks – for the simple reason that the efficacy of these depends entirely on being able to see the target. But as the advance continued, locating targets became increasingly difficult, and by November 9, says the Official History, the day bomber force "dropped right out of the battle"[17] for lack of them. On November 14 "the same fate befell the fighter-bombers" – with them the problems of bomb-supply were a major factor. But in any case, their limitations were becoming more evident as the advance progressed and a careful study was made of their results:

> Allowing for the fact that the enemy salvaged every available vehicle capable of being put in tow, inspection of the roads between Agedabia and Marble Arch led to the conclusion that, on the whole, the fighter-bombing had had disappointing results.[18]

Partly, this was considered to be a matter of training, which was accordingly stepped up, with useful effect later on. Partly also, as indicated above (p. 373), it was due to the continuing excellence of the German light AA.[19] This was the particular bane of the IID tank-destroyers, which had found little scope during the battle of El Alamein. But chiefly, as Tedder indicates, the problem was obsolescence; the Hurricane was too old for this work; a new type was needed. And new armament was also needed; the 40-mm cannon of the IIDs fired armour-piercing shot, which was reasonably effective at short ranges (at which the aircraft was extremely vulnerable). It was clear, says the AHB Monograph, "that although the attacks were generally successful, they would have been far more destructive if ammunition with an explosive charge could have been employed".[20] The way forward was already visible, for those who cared to look: the

Soviet Union's Ilyushin Il-2 ("Stormovik") single-seat close support and attack aircraft which entered production in March 1941 had an armament which "for the first time included effective ground-attack rockets".[21] The Il-2M3 of 1942 gave extra power to these (82-mm) rockets and added anti-armour bombs which proved very effective against the newest and toughest German tanks. The weakness of the Stormovik lay in its performance – a maximum speed of 281 mph, dropping to 231 mph with a full weapon-load. The way forward, clearly, lay in the combination of rockets at least as good as the Stormovik's with an aircraft of far better performance; and such a type emerged into limelight in November 1942 – the Hawker Typhoon, with its maximum speed of 412 mph and its battery of eight 60-lb rockets. In 1943 the Typhoon made its name in the skies of north-western Europe.

Meanwhile the great advance continued across Cyrenaica and into Tripolitania, Army and RAF alike haunted every inch of the way by the problems of supply, and the latter contemplating somewhat wryly the damage it had done to the harbours it now badly needed. And here, at last, came valuable aid indeed, in the form of the US 316th Troop Carrier Command, with its admirable DC-3s, the famous Dakotas which were to transform Allied air transport problems. It was impossible to carry inflammable high octane petrol in the "grossly inefficient" standard British four-gallon commercial tin inside an aircraft. "Any metal protuberance, any small nail, would puncture these tins and even a hefty jolt . . . would split them."[22] The alternative was 40–44-gallon steel drums, but the RAF did not have carrying capacity for these. The Dakotas could do it, and did, to the tune of 130,000 gallons lifted for the Desert Air Force for the El Agheila operation in mid-December, and 153,000 gallons of petrol as well as 9,500 gallons of oil lifted to Marble Arch landing ground alone during December and January – the equivalent of the total tank capacity of 1,575 Hurricanes, or 1,240 Kittyhawks, or 355 Bostons.[23] This, also, was a portent.

On January 23, 1943 the Eighth Army entered Tripoli. On February 1 Coningham handed over command of the Western Desert Air Force to Air Vice-Marshal H. Broadhurst, pending a new appointment. On February 4, "The Eighth Army crossed the frontier into Tunisia . . . thus completing the conquest of the Italian Empire by Great Britain."[24] So the two inseparables, Eighth Army and Desert Air Force, passed out of the aegis of the Middle East to play their part in the last of the African campaigns – the battles for Tunis, the first major essay in Anglo-American cooperation.

50 Operation "Torch"; the Casablanca Conference; victory in Africa

Operation TORCH, the British and American landings in Algeria and Morocco on November 8, 1942, should have crowned the break-through at El Alamein, but the "inter-allied machinery created at the 'Arcadia' conference[1] . . . creaked and groaned".[2] This is not to be wondered at in general; the machinery was new, the alliance untested, its nature unexplored. In certain particulars, however, one finds procedures which take a lot of explaining, and in some cases remain inexplicable; this is true especially of the air planning. To begin with, air operations in North-West Africa were conceived as taking place in two separate geographical and national compartments: Eastern Air Command (British) in eastern Algeria, and Western Air Command (American) in Morocco and Western Algeria, the two commanders (Air Marshal Sir William Welsh and Major-General James H. Doo-little) being directly responsible to the Allied Commander-in-Chief, Lieutenant-General Dwight D. Eisenhower. Such separatism is, of course, contrary to the very nature of air power, which is normally oblivious of frontiers or other demarcation lines on the ground. And the net result was that the British and American airmen "planned for 'Torch' in isolation".[3]

As if this was not bad enough, though one may just excuse it by inexperience, there is the further curiosity that although Tedder and his staff at Middle East Command knew the rough outline of the TORCH plan, "they had no share in drawing it up, and they were not informed of the moment for its execution".[4] The Middle East experience of the command (and command structure) of large air forces closely involved in major land operations "was not drawn upon".[5] This would seem to be an inexcusable omission on the part of the Air Staff and its Chief. Even taking into account the fact that the planning for TORCH coincided with the worst Middle East crisis and disarray, it is extraordinary that Portal did not make some use of Tedder's great knowledge. The relationship between them was close; as far back as May 1941, even before Tedder was confirmed in his appointment as AOC-in-C, Portal had told him:

> It would help me if you could send me from time to time very private repeat private and personal telegrams giving with complete frankness *your* view of the Middle East picture as it affects all three services.

This request "initiated a personal correspondence far more extensive than that between Portal and any other commander".[6] Yet now, when all the qualities in Tedder which Portal so obviously admired had been fully proved, he was not consulted. And Portal, after all, was in the best position to know that whoever else was taking a beating in Cyrenaica in the summer of 1942 – Italians, *Afrika Korps*, *Luftwaffe*, Eighth Army – it was not the Royal Air Force. So Tedder's opinion might have had special weight. And Portal also knew that, months before TORCH could take place, Tedder's Command was including Americans – the only available experience of the close cooperation of the two air forces. The omission is amazing; it comes as no surprise after this to learn that no attempt was made either to embody "the latest techniques in air support operations and organisation as practised in the desert"[7] in the TORCH air planning.

The consequences were soon felt. The Germans reacted with predictable speed and determination to the Allied landings; they began at once, behind a screen of skilful bluff, a lavish build-up in Tunisia which is in ironic contrast with Rommel's eternal penury of supplies and reinforcements. As the Allied forces began their advance eastward towards Tunis, one of the earliest lessons of the Desert war was distressfully relearned – this, too, was a "war for aerodromes" (see p. 391).

Almost from the first the race for Tunisia became a contest as much for the air as for the ground, for without close air cover to fend off the enemy's planes foot troops would be hard pressed to hold ground even when they arrived first. In this confrontation the Axis held all the advantages.[8]

The advantages were plentiful: ability to reinforce quickly from Sicily, Sardinia and Italy; convenient airfields, close to the front, in Tunisia itself; the first arrivals in Africa of the Focke-Wulf FW 190 fighter, superior to all Allied fighters except the Spitfire IX and the Mustang II; and without doubt above all, the lamentable regression of air support doctrine on the Allied side:

The policy at that time seems to have been to attempt to provide continuous fighter cover over any forward area which was being dive-bombed.[9]

This, of course, was in flat contradiction of Churchill's "Air Support Charter" of September 1941 (see pp. 346–7), and all subsequent Desert battle practice. Worst of all was the lack of liaison between the RAF and Lieutenant-General K. A. N. Anderson's First Army

Headquarters, with faults on both sides. Visiting Algiers at the end of November, Tedder pronounced himself "deeply disturbed by what I saw and heard". He told Portal:

> communications for all Services were practically non-existent except for the archaic French telephone system. The aerodromes were inadequate and heavy rains had bogged down two or three. Dispersal appeared to be non-existent, and the degree of congestion almost unbelievable. There seemed to be little drive to remedy the situation, which was to my mind dangerous in the extreme ... As for the control of operations, any semblance of a Combined Headquarters had gone ... The U.S. Air was running a separate war ...[10]

Tedder did not conceal his opinions from Eisenhower; he told the C-in-C frankly what he thought, "and he said he would so something about it. I expect he will." Thus began a long debate about the control of air operations – a debate which could, with advantage, have taken place before the operations began. Taking the large view, as he habitually did, Tedder already saw the problem (as he told Portal) as one requiring firm handling, "both from the point of view of the immediate conditions in Algeria and Tunis, and from that of the future control of the Mediterranean".[11] In other words, it was a problem which would require treatment from the very summit of Allied war-making. In the meantime, Tedder was adamant about one thing:

> I would most strongly oppose any suggestion that I should go there to advise. Advice without authority and responsibility is useless.

While this question simmered, soldiers and airmen endured miseries in North Africa. Both British and American armies now shared the sensations of Rommel's *Panzerarmee* during the last five months. General Eisenhower records hearing in the front areas those familiar cries of over-bombed infantry:

> "Where is this bloody Air Force of ours? Why do we see nothing but Heinies?" When the enemy has air superiority, the ground forces never hesitate to curse the "aviators".[12]

In the British sector the story was the same, and there was friction between the Services similar to that following the disasters in Greece and Crete over a year before. Tedder, visiting Algiers again in December, reported the general dissatisfaction to Portal, ascribing it "firstly to Anderson's fundamental misconception of the use and control of aircraft in close support and secondly his failure to appreciate almost hopeless handicaps in respect of aerodromes, communications, maintenance and supplies under which Lawson has been operating".[13] He considered that the RAF was doing magnificently in these circumstances, but it was clear that the position was no better than during his first visit. For the squadrons concerned, it was building up to a tragedy; on one day Eisenhower had to report the loss of six Spitfires, 10 Bisleys, five P-38s (Lightnings) and a Boston, "all of them lost because of the mastery in the battlefield area of German fighters". That was December 4, a grim day in RAF memory; the Spitfires were destroyed on the ground, attempting to use a forward airfield. The fate of the Bisleys recalled certain previous sickening occasions. This was the name given to the Blenheim V, the last of that loyal line, and, unhappily, a failure; underpowered and undergunned, this aircraft was, quite simply in naval parlance, "not fit to stand the line of battle", certainly in daylight. Nevertheless, it was in daylight and without escort that 10 Bisleys of No. 18 Squadron took off to bomb an enemy landing ground on December 4, most gallantly led by Wing Commander H. G. Malcolm. Attacked by a swarm of Me 109s, one by one they were shot down – the whole squadron. Wing Commander Malcolm received a posthumous VC – and Bisleys did not fly again by day. One recalls the 11 Blenheims out of 12 lost by No. 82 Squadron over Gembloux in May 1940 (pp. 152–3) and the same loss of the same squadron attacking Aalborg three months later. Overshadowed by the reputations of some more famous aircraft, the Blenheims and their crews are too often forgotten in the story of the RAF. Soon the Bisleys would be withdrawn, and it would have taken a very sentimental airman indeed to regret it. Meanwhile, "apart from a good meal, there was little cheer for our airmen that Christmas".[14]

Fortunately, the misery did not long endure. The first signs of improvement took the form of command changes – a matter of which the front-line soldier or airman is often surprisingly oblivious, though it affects him profoundly, and never more so than at this juncture in Tunisia. The first concerned Tedder; he was already designated as Vice Chief of the Air Staff (in succession to Freeman), and handed over Middle East Command on January 11, 1943 to Air Chief Marshal Sir W. Sholto Douglas. Three days later the Casablanca Conference convened, a full Allied "summit", with President Roosevelt and Churchill presiding over the deliberations of the Combined (American and British) Chiefs of Staff and the North African High Command, Tedder present among them. Under a mask of what seems at times excessive *bonhomie*, much critical business of far-reaching import was transacted at Casablanca, and sharp differences were apparent between the American and British strategic views. On January 17 (the fourth day) the CIGS wrote in his diary: "A desperate day! We are further from obtaining agreement than we ever were!"[15] But two days later there was a gleam of light, a break in the dark cloud of discord on future Allied policy and its priorities:

> The light was largely induced by a paper produced by Portal and drafted by Air Marshal Slessor . . . The Portal paper was ingenious in its wording. By deferring with the language of compromise all that did not need immediate action it won agreement on the latter.[16]

And what that meant was, specifically, that when the Allies had won in Tunisia they would go on to the occupation of Sicily – which, for the time being, was all that General Brooke wanted, because he could see quite well what must follow from it. We shall hear more of this.

Casablanca now takes its place in history chiefly as the occasion on which the notorious "Unconditional Surrender" policy was propounded – a formula from which it is not difficult to see many of the world's later ills proceeding. That matter lies outside our present scope; more cheering is the solution to the North African command – and above all, air command – problem laid down by the Conference potentates. On the broad front, it was a definite step forward to bring General Alexander over from Cairo as Deputy Commander-in-Chief under Eisenhower. More narrowly, the air command was totally reconstructed, abandoning its unpractical geo-graphical/national divisions in favour of functional descriptions. Most important of all, an entirely new top appointment was created, as suggested by Tedder: Mediterranean Air Command, taking in all the Allied air forces from one end of that sea to the other[17] – which was not unreasonable, since they were all fighting the same war; and since Tedder had long ago established that in such circumstances nothing less is required than the whole air resources, who better to rule over this great new Command than Tedder himself? His appointment as AOC-in-C dated from February 17; responsible to the British Chiefs of Staff for operations in the Middle East (Sholto Douglas) and Malta (now under Air Vice-Marshal Sir Keith Park), he was also responsible directly to Eisenhower for operations in north-west Africa, and accord-ingly set up his headquarters alongside Eisenhower's, in Algiers.

Under Tedder, the Allied air forces in north-west Africa were now united in a single command, headed by Major-General Carl Spaatz,

USAAF.[18] Under Spaatz came three sub-divisions: a North-West African Strategic Air Force, under Doolittle; a North-West African Coastal Air Force under Air Vice-Marshal Sir Hugh Lloyd (last seen splendidly inspiring the defence of Malta), and a North-West African Tactical Air Force, under Air Marshal (his promotion dated from February 8) Sir Arthur Coningham. "Tactical Air Force" – this was a name that was going to be conjured with, a name of most profound significance in the history of the war. It does not express what the RAF had alway believed itself to be about – indeed, the contrary – but it is scarcely open to doubt that in its broadest application (as well understood by Tedder and Coningham) it was one of the most important things that the RAF actually *was* about. Tedder thought hard about the name:

> Long experience determined me to avoid the use of the title "Air Support Command" for Coningham's charge. I found intense opposition to the title "Tunisian Command" and so came to the conclusion that the functional title "Tactical Air Force" was the right one.[19]

It was the right title and the right man. Coningham at once set up a joint headquarters with Alexander (who became operational land forces commander) – a move which "changed the whole atmosphere and outlook of the British and American land and air forces".[20] Indeed, as even Acting Lance-Corporals and AC2s may have noticed, "the effect of the air reorganization was profound and almost instantaneous".[21] It is therefore appropriate to set down here the natal date of TAF: February 18 1943, Coningham commanding.

NATAF (originally No. 242 Group RAF and the US XII Air Support Command) soon received powerful reinforcements; on February 23 the Desert Air Force came under its operational control. On March 2, Coningham issued his first directive; to his considerable surprise, he had discovered that air support arrangements in Tunisia in February 1943 were roughly speaking "the same as those he had found in the Western Desert in the summer of 1941".[22] He proposed to bring them up to date. The first objective, he insisted, was air supremacy:

> After this had been achieved it would be possible for land forces to operate practically unhindered by enemy air attack and the Allied air forces would be able to operate with increased freedom in the battle area and against objectives in the rear of the enemy.[23]

He dwelt on the need for training to this end, which was to be achieved by a continuous offensive against the enemy air force, in the air and on the ground. He dwelt also on the need – well established in the Desert – for the closest contact and communication between fighter and bomber units. In daylight operations, it would be the fighter leader's responsibility to decide whether the sortie was "on" or not, or at what stage to abandon it if necessary. All the light bombers were to be prepared to operate at night, in order to catch enemy ground forces on the move. Finally, characteristically, Coningham emphasized the need for mobility: with a 250-mile front, units must be prepared to shift from one sector to another at the shortest notice. For all of these requirements, as well as for small-unit tactics and marksmanship, intensive training was needed, and this became the chief preoccupation of the NATAF for the next month.

During this period the Axis forces made their last offensive forays, in the Kasserine area, against the US II Corps, and later against the Eighth Army. On the northern front, bad weather limited air operations in support of the Americans, but even so the advantages of unified command were felt – above all the ability to switch the Strategic Force at will against tactical targets. The Americans had a bad shock, at Kasserine, and were inclined to blame the air, but they held their front, and when the weather improved the airmen made life difficult for the retreating enemy. In the south, Rommel's last attack, at Medenine on March 6, proved to be an artillery battle, in which all his attempts to advance were crushed by the weight of Montgomery's massed gunfire. There was not a great deal of scope for the air at Medenine, but if Broadhurst's force felt cheated on the 6th, it found ample work to do on the 10th, the fighters and fighter-bombers bringing timely aid to General Leclerc's Free French forces from Lake Chad when these were attacked by a flying column of German armour and *Stukas*.

The great contribution of the Desert Air Force – and a peak of applied air power – came when Montgomery resumed his own advance, against the Mareth Line, on March 20. By now Rommel had departed from Africa, his *Panzerarmee* was renamed First Italian Army under General Giovanni Messe, and held strong positions in the old French fortified system, made even stronger by a substantial allocation of anti-tank and anti-aircraft guns. Montgomery enjoyed great superiority in tanks and artillery, while the Desert Air Force superiority was crushing: 535 fighters, fighter-bombers and tank-destroyers, 140 day-bombers, the equivalent of three reconnaissance squadrons, and 80 "heavies" of No. 205 Group, against 83 serviceable German aircraft and 40 Italian. Nevertheless, the opening stage of the battle, a frontal thrust on a narrow front, did not go well. While well-sited anti-tank guns took toll of the British armour, the habitual "flak" (including 88-mm guns in their original rôle) gave the Allied bombers an uncomfortable time; out of 125 British and 54 American day-bombers operating on March 21, about a quarter were damaged by German AA fire. On March 22 the Desert Air Force flew nearly 620 sorties, unquestionably effective, but still the army could not get forward. Montgomery decided to abandon his frontal push and try a wide left hook, relying heavily on the power of the Desert Air Force:

> The air plan originated with Air Vice-Marshal Broadhurst who, learning of the Army Commander's changed intentions formed the idea of concentrating his aircraft in a degree hitherto unknown, on a narrow front, in order to paralyse the enemy for long enough to permit the ground forces to break through. Montgomery enthusiastically accepted Broadhurst's plan.[24]

The first stage of Broadhurst's air offensive was the turning loose of the entire bombing force (including 205 Group) against the enemy's rear areas on the nights of March 24/25 and 25/26, with special attention to transport and telephone communications (clear echo of the *Luftwaffe*'s tactics in France in 1940). After this preliminary, the main attack was to go in in broad daylight, in order to obtain surprise; it was agreed with the Army that two and a quarter hours should suffice for the purpose of paralysis. Accordingly,

> At 1530 hours on 26 March, three formations of light and medium bombers launched a simultaneous pattern-bombing attack on the main enemy positions. The intention was to create disorganisation and particularly to disrupt telephone communications. This attack made a low and evasive approach and met no air opposition. Immediately afterwards, the first relay of fighter-bombers entered the area and began to bomb and machine gun from the lowest possible heights. A strength of two and a half squadrons was maintained in the area, fresh relays arriving at quarter-hour intervals. Pilots were briefed to bomb specific targets and then to attack gun positions with the object of killing the crews, particularly of those guns which were in a position to hold up our armour. Hurricane "Tank Busters" also attacked and broke up enemy tank concentrations. A Spitfire patrol of one squadron strength was maintained over the area to protect the fighter-bombers, while at the same time light bombers under the control of NATAF attacked enemy air forces as a diversion. The enemy were effectively surprised and no air opposition was encountered over the battle area . . .

397

Half an hour after the air offensive opened, infantry attacked under cover of a heavy barrage creeping forward at the rate of 100 feet a minute, thus automatically defining the bomb-line.[25] Aircraft bombed and attacked continually in front of this line and became, in fact, *part of the barrage*. The enemy defences were completely overwhelmed and this most difficult position was taken with relative light loss, and our armour was enabled to break through. The Western Desert Air Force made 412 sorties during the two and a quarter hour period at a cost of eleven pilots missing.[26]

The Mareth style displays Broadhurst as another commander in the Coningham manner: bold, original, creative, and entirely unawed by Service orthodoxy. Montgomery had re-introduced the Army to important elements of the war-winning tactics of 1918. Broadhurst unhesitatingly did the same for the Air Force. To use RAF bombing as "part of the barrage" (the italics are mine) was to step back twenty-five years in tactical thinking, but with all the advantages of new air technology. As Liddell Hart says, it was a "defence-stunning adaptation of the German 'blitz' method" which "worked very effectively – although frowned on by [Broadhurst's] distant RAF superiors as a breach of Air Staff doctrine".[27] However, nothing succeeds like success; Broadhurst may have been frowned on, but he had to be forgiven, because his style now became the Allied style of making war.

The remainder of the war in Africa can be quickly told. Pressed into an ever-contracting bridgehead, the Axis forces became more and more vulnerable to Allied air attack, in which the borderline between "strategic" and "tactical" became correspondingly blurred – a matter, in the end, of only a few miles. A remarkable feature of the final Allied advance was the close interlocking of artillery fire and bombing on the Mareth pattern, the two being treated as complementary facets of fire-power. And here we may note the introduction of a new air element, which found its first "stage" in North Africa. In a Royal Air Force order of battle, the novelty would appear as No. 651 Squadron; in the history of war it requires some further definition. Its other designation was Air Observation Post – the first of an honourable line, and the brain-child of Lieutenant-General H. C. Bazeley, RA. As far back as 1938, Bazeley, then a mere captain and secretary of the Royal Artillery Flying Club, had put forward the idea of providing

... batteries or brigades of the Royal Artillery with the same sort of small, low-powered aircraft that officers of the flying club flew for pleasure, able to take off from a meadow or a dirt strip close to the gun positions. The aircraft was to be merely a mount or a flying platform for artillery officers, who would use the ordinary artillery procedures for ranging a battery. They would not fly over enemy territory, but over their own guns or near them, gaining just enough height to see targets on ground dead to ground OPs.[28]

The RAF showed distinct lack of enthusiasm for this idea, but an experimental flight was formed in February 1940, using an American-designed light aircraft which was built under licence in England under the name Taylorcraft Auster. Although in France in May the flight took no part in that confused campaign, but was lucky (and skilful) enough to return intact to England. When Army Cooperation Command was set up at the end of the year, the Air OP seemed a natural ingredient of it, but this was one of Air Marshal Barratt's blind spots:

> Every objection was advanced . . .: artillery officers could not be trained to the necessary standards of airmanship, the aircraft would all be shot down, and so on. "Were these aircraft to be *armed?*" was a question revealing the Air Staff's fear that if the Army once got its hands on its own aircraft there would be a demand for more and better, the way opened for a resurrection of the Army air arm.[29]

However, thanks in large part to the intervention of the C-in-C Home forces, Sir Alan Brooke, himself a Gunner, the first Air OP, No. 651 Squadron, came into existence in July 1941, with Royal Artillery pilots and RAF ground-crews, still flying Taylorcrafts. In November 1942 the Squadron went out to Algeria as part of the First Army, at the insistence of the CRA, another distinguished artilleryman (later) Major-General H. J. Parham. It was followed in December by No. 654 Squadron, flying Auster Is. Fifteen RAF squadrons were formed as AOPs, using Austers Marks I–IV "by 1945 Auster light-cabin monoplanes had become an indispensable part of the military aviation scene".[30]

By late April, thanks to the ministrations of Tedder's Command and all parts of General Spaatz's North-West African Air Forces, "the German Air Force ceased to play any serious part in the battle".[31] In the final Allied attack, on May 6, the *Luftwaffe* made its last appearance, only to lose 20 fighters in three hours. It was quite unable to prevent an extraordinary manifestation of the new air power: 1,958 sorties between dusk, May 5, and dusk, May 6 – "a figure never before approached in Africa in 24 hours of direct support of troops."[32] The outstanding feature of this was what the Press soon called "Tedder's bomb-carpet", a moving barrage of air support along a line four miles long and three and a half miles wide, with concentrated artillery fire behind it. This demonstration of brute fire-power was irresistible; the Allies entered Tunis the next day, and by May 13 the last vestiges of Axis resistance in Africa had ended. Some quarter of a million prisoners were taken, 150,000 of them German, substantially more than those who had surrendered at Stalingrad on January 31. The damage done to the German Army by this double disaster made the spring of 1943 a turning-point of the war.

51 *The way forward*

Modern warfare resembles a spider's web: everything connects, longitudinally or laterally, to everything else; there are no "independent strategies", no watertight compartments, nor can there be. The entry of the United States into the war meant, as we have seen, that the lynchpin of Allied strategy would thenceforward be an assault on Hitler's "Fortress Europe". This was first envisaged as taking place in 1943, under the code-name ROUNDUP. It would be preceded by a massive build-up of US forces in the United Kingdom, code-name BOLERO. But if, as then seemed more than likely, the Soviet Union should show signs of crumbling under the heavy blows that rained upon her, it was thought that it might be necessary to mount a desperate diversionary cross-Channel attack in 1942, SLEDGEHAMMER. One by one all these propositions were ruled out. BOLERO was compromised first by the predictable difficulties of effectively mobilizing America's great latent power, and then by the persisting U-boat hazard. Victory in the Battle of the Atlantic was an essential precondition of a major operation in North-West Europe. Meanwhile, the best that could be managed was TORCH, which proved not to be at all a bad investment. SLEDGEHAMMER, fortunately (since it promised only catastrophe), could be dismissed, thanks to Hitler's strategic follies culminating in the Stalingrad surrender. But U-boats and stubborn Axis resistance in Tunisia, protracting that campaign until the summer, meant that there would be no ROUNDUP in 1943. And that meant, beyond dispute, that as far as carrying the war to the main enemy was concerned, Bomber Command would remain on the right of the line, though now no longer alone, as the United States Eighth Air Force fell in alongside, and Coastal Command came into its own.

THE BATTLE OF THE ATLANTIC (II)

". . . the dominating factor all through the war . . ."

52 Science and Intelligence; the Leigh Light; tasks of Coastal Command

Air Chief Marshal Sir Philip Joubert de la Ferté, KCB, CMG, DSO, belongs to a familiar category of unfortunates: those officers, in different Services and in different wars, who preside over bad times, weather the worst storms, but do not remain in command when the change of fortune comes and the reward of strain and effort can be collected. Joubert's period as AOC-in-C of Coastal Command (his second[1]), June 1941 to February 1943, saw the disappointment of a false dawn (see p. 248) and the terrors of a very dark night indeed. Shipping, wrote Churchill, "was at once the stranglehold and sole foundation of our war strategy".[2] Nearly eight million tons of British, Allied and neutral shipping were sunk by enemy action in 1942. That was the dark night of the war, when the possibility of losing it outright became very clear indeed; that is – in part – why Churchill also says:

> The Battle of the Atlantic was the dominating factor all through the war.[3]

It was, of course, a battle which was inseparable at any time from the heroic effort and achievements of the Royal Navy and the Merchant Marine – just as the Desert War was inseparable from the changing fortunes of the Eighth Army. There was an even more significant resemblance between the two sets of circumstances: in the Atlantic, as in the Desert, Britain was actually at grips with German forces. Both contests were – in the German fashion – *à outrance*; and if the stakes in the Middle East were high, in the Atlantic they were as high as it was possible to go. The battle in each case demanded – indeed, dictated – from the Air the maximum contribution, irrespective of inter-Service (or inter-Command) rivalries, or Service dogmas, those everlasting foes of sensible war-making. Coastal Command, in other words, would also have to make a place for itself on the right of the line.

In his first term of office, Joubert had made himself known by his promotion of the maritime uses of radar; in his second, radar in its various manifestations – ASV II and ASV III – provided a continuing theme. Yet it was only part of a much larger one: the "long, imaginative and productive alliance" of Coastal Command with the world of science.[4] This had begun, in fact, three months before Joubert's accession when Sir Frederick Bowhill had appointed Professor P. M. S. Blackett as his Scientific Adviser. Joubert accepted this legacy with enthusiasm, and under Blackett's leadership an Operational Research Unit grew up which in due course attained the power of no fewer than five Fellows of the Royal Society: Blackett himself, Sir John Kendrew, Professor E. J. Williams, Professor C. H. Waddington and Professor J. M. Robertson. Their function, collective and individual, was to subject every aspect of the work of the Command to scientific scrutiny, and because of its importance and its difficulty, the war against the U-boats claimed a very large measure of their attention. Since all scientific advance depends on sound and plentiful information, it is appropriate to mention here the work of Captain (then Commander) Peyton-Ward, the senior naval staff officer at Coastal Command Headquarters (and later AHB Narrator; see p. 230). "Though always loyal to his parent Service," wrote a later AOC-in-C, Sir John Slessor, "P.W." became "in all but uniform and rank an officer of the Royal Air Force."[5] It was in this very early stage of Joubert's tenure that Peyton-Ward

> commenced writing up each individual sighting and attack on U-boats as they took place using every scrap of first hand evidence obtainable and analysing the probable result from all the data available. Whenever possible the attacking crews came to the Headquarters which enabled personal corroboration, discussion of detail and practical experience to be effected while the event was still fresh.[6]

As Peyton-Ward himself remarks in a modest footnote, "by the end of 1941 this naval officer had become specialised in all aspects of Coastal Command's war against the U-boats"; he held a key position for the remainder of the war, working in close collaboration with the Admiralty Submarine Tracking Room.

The Operational Research Unit made every element of anti-U-boat activity its business: angles of attack, depth-charge settings, even the colour of the aircraft. The lookouts on the U-boat conning towers were generally vigilant men, and it was an important matter to make Coastal Command's machines as difficult to see as possible. Experiment showed that in normal conditions of sky and cloud in northern latitudes, plain white paint on all side and under surfaces of an aircraft conferred "a remarkable degree of invisibility . . . Thus started in the summer of 1941 the familiar 'White Crows' of Coastal Command."[7] Whatever the work, it was pressed forward with all proper speed; by July 25 it was possible to crystallize some of the conclusions that had been reached in a new Tactical Instruction (No. 15), which tells us much about the stage the Command had arrived at in its main sphere of action:

(i) The attacking approach was to be made by the shortest path and at maximum speed.
[Since U-boats could submerge completely in 25 seconds from the sounding of the warning-gong (see p. 245), it was necessary to emphasize this.]

(ii) The actual attack could be made from any direction relative to the U-boat.

(iii) The depth setting of all depth-charges was to be 50 feet, the spacing of depth-charges in a stick was to be 60 feet and all depth-charges carried were to be released in one stick.

(iv) *The ideal was to attack while the U-boat or some part of it was still visible.* Data was given, however, to enable pilots to estimate quickly how far ahead of the point of final disappearance their stick should be placed if the U-boat got under just before release was possible.

(v) *In cases where the U-boat had disappeared for more than 30 seconds it was pointed out that success was unlikely* owing to the progressive uncertainty of the U-boat's position either in plan or depth.
[Italics are mine. This grim conclusion was the fruit of lengthy and careful analysis of operations by Peyton-Ward and the scientists.]

(vi) The height of release must not be greater than 100 feet until an aiming sight was provided but the restriction against aircraft carrying depth charges at night was modified.
[See p. 233, radio altimeters were recognized as a basic need, not only at night but for any low-level attack in thick weather, by January 1942, but it would be a long time before Coastal Command received either officially approved aiming sights or radio altimeters.]

(vii) Great stress was laid on the need for training and constant exercises so as to attain a high standard of attack and aiming accuracy.[8]

Sighting a U-boat and killing a U-boat were two different things, but it was now recognized that the connection between the two was very intimate indeed; it was not just that without a sighting there would not be a kill, it was that there would only be a certain kill while the U-boat was in sight. So all through 1941 and the following years, the fight against U-boats was primarily a struggle to see them; and since their established habit was to remain submerged during much of daylight while within aircraft range, and travel fast on the surface at night, the need to see them at night was evident. Radar, as we have seen (pp. 239–40), offered some improvement on the performance of the human eye, but not that much; between September 1941 and August 1943, out of 1,112 sightings of U-boats in the Atlantic–Biscay–Gibraltar area, ASV radar was responsible for 125 – only 11.2 per cent. Yet ASV, in conjunction with another impatiently awaited device, was shortly to have a profound effect on the U-boat war; the development reveals Joubert at his worst and best. It was all part of what Sir Arthur Coningham had already called the RAF's "never-ending struggle to circumvent the law that we cannot see in the dark".[9] He had been referring to Bomber Command's difficulties in finding targets in Germany by night; in the first months of 1941, Fighter Command found itself in the same difficulty, trying to locate German bombers over Britain in the night "blitz". Coastal Command, when it joined the queue for the right equipment, thus found powerful competitors.

For Fighter Command, the solution to the problem of illuminating parts of the sky was approached through Group Captain W. Helmore's "Turbinlite" which, fitted in the nose of an aircraft, threw out a strong diffused light in which, it was hoped, a second aircraft would be able to detect and attack a bomber. It was an ingenious idea, full of difficulties of its own, and never properly tested operationally because the German attacks died away in May 1941. Coastal Command's approach was different; it had begun back in 1940, when Squadron-Leader H. de V. Leigh, a First World War pilot whose official duties at Command Headquarters were concerned with personnel, obtained Bowhill's consent to experiment with an airborne searchlight – a totally different concept from the Turbinlite. The searchlight was to be directed by ASV – and obviously, the longer the range of the latter the better. By January 1941 Leigh had succeeded in fitting a naval 24-inch searchlight into the under-turret of a Wellington, finding means of carrying away the dense fumes from the carbon arc lamp, and installing the ASV on which everything depended. On May 4, with Leigh himself operating the searchlight, the whole apparatus was tested against a submarine of the Royal Navy; an RN officer observing the test reported:

The aircraft was not heard by the submarine until it [the submarine] had been illuminated, and was able to dive and attack down the beam for 27 seconds before being pulled out at 500 feet. This effort was most impressive, and there seems no doubt that, given an efficient aircraft crew and good team work, this weapon would be invaluable in attacking U-boats on the surface at night and in low visibility.[10]

The Leigh Light was born.

It was very nearly strangled at birth; Bowhill, much encouraged by the May trials and some further refinements proposed by Leigh, wrote to Joubert, then ACAS (Radio) at the Air Ministry, suggesting that Leigh "should be officially entrusted with the task of bringing searchlight ASV aircraft to an operational condition".[11] But Joubert, at that stage, was a backer of the Turbinlite, and transferred responsibility for further technical progress to Helmore. Shortly afterwards he succeeded Bowhill as AOC-in-C, and since what immediately followed shows him in a poor light, it will be as well to hear his own account of it:

When I first took over at Coastal Command having been so closely associated with the Helmore Light I thought it might be given a general application by being used against U-boats as well. I thought that its wide beam and great illuminating power would be valuable. I therefore gave instructions that Squadron Leader Leigh was to return to his duties as Assistant Personnel Officer. After some two months I found, as I do not mind admitting, that I had made a mistake. I found out that the Helmore light was unnecessarily brilliant for use against U-boats and otherwise unsuitable. I then came to the conclusion that Leigh's light was preferable for use against the U-boat, and decided to drop the Helmore Light and concentrate on the Leigh Light.[12]

So there was the worst and best of Joubert: the high-handed assumption that the Air Ministry must know best – and the frank admission that he had been wrong. As Denis Richards and Hilary Saunders wrote:

Joubert, as befitted so acute and agile a commander, now changed his tack right about. He at once became Leigh's firmest supporter.[13]

It tells us more about that stage of the war, and about official thinking, that even with Joubert's complete support, it took nearly another year to give the Leigh Light its operational opportunity. By May 1942 there were still only five experimental Wellingtons (of No. 172 Squadron) equipped with the Light, and Joubert realized that if any further progress was to be made, these aircraft must prove the point once and for all. On June 3/4 he sent four of them out to patrol the Bay of Biscay:

> The result was highly gratifying. Three of the Wellingtons found no U-boats, but the ease with which they illuminated ASV contacts which turned out to be fishing vessels left little doubt of the merits of Leigh's invention. The fourth aircraft gave further witness in the best possible way. It contacted, "homed" on to, and successfully illuminated two enemy submarines.[14]

In fact, it was only one submarine – twice discovered. She was the Italian boat *Luigi Torelli*, and her attacker was flown by Squadron-Leader J. Greswell. His first run at her failed through a false setting of the pressure altimeter, placing the Wellington 100 feet too high. Amazed at this contact with an aircraft which carried a bright light but did not attack them, the Italians concluded that it must be German and fired recognition flares. This gave Greswell their position, quickly confirmed by his ASV, and with a reset altimeter he now came in again at the prescribed 250 feet and Pilot Officer Triggs switched on the light at a distance of three quarters of a mile – "and there, exactly where it should have been, lay the submarine".[15] At an altitude of only 50 feet, Greswell dropped four 250-lb depth-charges which so badly damaged the *Luigi Torelli* that she made for St Jean de Luz for emergency repairs – but instead found herself in danger of internment in the Spanish port of Aviles. Her subsequent adventures do not concern us, but they were amazing, including attacks by Sunderlands of No. 10 Squadron, RAAF, escape from internment in Santander, transfer to the Japanese Navy and capture by the Americans.[16] It was a month after this triumphant début that a Leigh Light Wellington scored the first U-boat kill, and the Air Ministry softened into sufficient approval to authorize a second squadron. By the end of the war Leigh Light aircraft had attacked 218 U-boats at night, and made 206 attacks on enemy shipping; 27 U-boats were sunk by this method, and 31 damaged.[17] The ratio of sinkings to attacks is not impressive – only 12.38 per cent; but the effect of the "*verdammte Licht*" was not to be measured merely by kills and damage. It forced the boats passing through the Bay of Biscay to remain submerged by night as well as by day, which was not merely bad for the comfort and morale of the crews, but reduced their time in the operational area by five days or more. Joubert's change of mind proved profitable indeed.

For Joubert's Command, most of his tour of office was a time of waiting with whatever patience the Group and squadron commanders and their crews could muster: the patience of long unrewarded hours of flight over empty seas, day after day in all weathers – that was taken for granted; there was also the more irksome patience of waiting for essential equipment to be produced and delivered. The Command's most pressing needs, in 1941, were summed up as "numbers of long range aircraft and lethal weapons"[18] – and nothing, it seemed, was harder to come by than either of these. In June, there were nine Flying Boat squadrons, with an initial establishment of 65 aircraft – but their average daily availability was 17. The 26 General Reconnaissance and Fighter squadrons had an establishment of 495, but only 281 could be reckoned available on any given day. The two attached Fleet Air Arm squadrons, with an establishment of 18, could provide seven. So Joubert's total available strength at any time was 305[19] – which could hardly be considered excessive in view of what his Command was expected to do. The U-boat war held the centre of attention, but besides that there was the "constant watch and ward over German warships",[20] wherever they might be. Separate from that was re-connaissance on behalf of the Royal Navy. There was the Command's own offensive against German coastal shipping, intended to do the maximum amount of damage and put the maximum strain on alternative forms of transport. There were attacks on ports and naval objectives; linked to this, but an "art-form" of its own (and immensely effective), was minelaying in enemy waters (see p. 422). Then, from August onwards, there was the new duty of support for the Arctic convoys carrying war supplies to the Soviet Union. In addition, also in August, a further "extra-mural activity" was transferred to Coastal Command; Photographic Reconnaissance was already under its wing – now it took control of all Air/Sea Rescue. This was becoming a highly specialized activity on an ever-expanding scale, and would ultimately save the lives of one in three of the aircrew forced to "bale out" over water or "ditch" their aircraft in the sea. Air/Sea Rescue brought a warm touch of humanity to what was generally a pretty inhuman trade. And finally, to fill the measure, in November Royal Air Force Gibraltar came into existence, directly under Coastal Command. In all of this work, as stated above (p. 244), liaison between the Command and the Royal Navy continued to be "an example of inter-Service cooperation at its best".

53 False dawn; defensive and offensive

Shipping losses in June 1941 showed a welcome further fall from May, but they were still high (109 ships, 432,025 tons), and the

U-boats accounted for over 70 per cent of them – 310,143 tons. And then, suddenly, there was a significant drop: a total of 120,975 tons in July, and 130,699 in August. This was the false dawn; these two months, according to Dr Rohwer, "saw the North Atlantic U-boat operations sink to their lowest level of effectiveness, and it looked almost as though the defence had won the race against the attack".[1] Such a dramatic change of fortune naturally prompted speculation at the time and afterwards. Some historians have, for obvious reasons, been tempted to explain it by the German invasion of the Soviet Union on June 22 – "an event which had an immediate effect on the Atlantic campaign . . . The German Navy was busy supporting operations on the Baltic coast."[2] That Operation BARBAROSSA had *some* effect can scarcely be doubted, but it would chiefly be in the long-term matter of diversion of materials and labour; there was no question of transferring U-boats from the Atlantic to the Baltic. As Denis Richards says,

> It was not for want of trying on the part of the enemy that the months following the fateful attack of 22nd June saw a great reduction in our shipping losses.[3]

And this is confirmed by no lesser authority than Grand Admiral Raeder himself, whose Directive of March 6 stated clearly:

> The main target for the Navy during the Eastern campaign still remains Britain.[4]

How, then, can we account for the false dawn? As usual, we have to consider a number of factors. There was certainly no fall in the number of operational U-boats – on the contrary, a slight rise from 47 in June to 60 in July and August and a steady increase through the remainder of the year to 86 in December. By comparison with the great packs of 1942 and 1943, however, these were still low numbers and insufficient to offset the advantages which were at last accruing to the defence. Among these we may note that the elimination of the German surface fleet threat had thrown the whole burden of the Atlantic battle on to the U-boats; and that these were simultaneously severely hampered by the extension of the American "Security Zone". There was also the "grotesque situation" created by the difficulty of distinguishing between neutral US destroyers sailing under their own flag and virtually identical craft lent to the Royal Navy. In the delicate state of US–German relations, this forced Dönitz in June to forbid any action against destroyers – which were, of course, the worst enemies of the U-boats – except in self-defence.[5]

On the purely British side, much was hoped for but far less achieved by what has been called the "first Bay of Biscay offensive" in June. The Bay was what Slessor later called the "trunk of the Atlantic U-boat menace" (the roots being the bases in the Biscay ports, and the branches being the distant packs in the North and South Atlantic and the Caribbean).[6] Through this "little patch of water about three hundred by a hundred and twenty miles", five out of six U-boats operating in the Atlantic had to pass within range of aircraft from England or Gibraltar –

> That was one place where we could be absolutely certain there would be U-boats to be found and killed.[7]

In June 1941, however, the means both of finding and killing were pitifully inadequate, and this first attempt to "stop" the Bay caused little but inconvenience. Far more to the point was the continuous escort of convoys which came in May (see p. 250). And to this, in June, the new Western Approaches Command added the refinement of the first use of what was to become a very effective system: a "Support Group" which enabled Convoy HX 133 to be brought through with a loss of only five ships, and two U-boats sunk in the process. And there was also the evident effect of evasive routeing, which enabled convoys to avoid the U-boats altogether.

What we now know is that both evasive routeing and the success of the Convoy HX 133 action were due to a sequence of successes in a very different manner on the Intelligence front. The Official History should here speak for itself:

> In the war at sea the situation was profoundly altered when GC & CS[8] began to read continuously and with little or no delay the wireless traffic in the Home Water (*Heimisch*) settings of the German naval Enigma that were common, as yet, to the entire German surface navy in the Atlantic area and to the U-boats. GC & CS's first substantial break into these settings had come in the second half of March 1941, when it read the traffic for February. By 10 May it had read most of the traffic for April. The traffic for the month of May was read with a delay of between three and seven days.[9]

Thus the code-breaking advantage which Admiral Dönitz had enjoyed for so long was beginning to crumble by May 1941; and in the early days of that month Bletchley Park had a windfall. On May 8 the destroyer *Bulldog*, escorting the convoy OB 318, drove to the surface *U 110* (*Kapitän-Leutnant* Lemp). The Germans set explosive charges and abandoned ship; but the detonators failed, and there was the empty U-boat, wallowing helplessly on the surface. A party from HMS *Bulldog* succeeded in boarding her (no easy matter in the heaving North Atlantic seas) and discovered her codebooks and her Enigma machine.[10] These captures, says the Official History,

> yielded the short-signal code books, which enabled GC & CS to read from May onwards the *Kurzsignale*, the short signals in which the U-boats transmitted their sighting reports and weather information. Captures[11] enabled GC & CS to read all the traffic for June and July, including "officer-only" signals, currently. By the beginning of August it had finally established its mastery over the Home Waters settings, a mastery which enabled it to read the whole of the traffic for the rest of the war except for occasional days in the second half of 1941 with little delay. The maximum delay was 72 hours and the normal delay was much less, often only a few hours.[12]

The sum effect of these gains, says Ronald Lewin,

> shifted the U-boat war into a new dimension. At last insight was possible into the whole life-cycle of a U-boat ... Months, indeed years had to pass before the Tracking Room could claim, with justice, to know more about the U-boats' deployment than Admiral Dönitz's own staff, but the summer of 1941 is the point at which Bletchley moved this process from the realm of guesswork into that of increasing authority.[13]

It was this knowledge of U-boat movements and positions, derived from Ultra, that enabled the Admiralty to re-route convoys, and it was this knowledge which enabled it to reinforce the escort of HX 133 by taking vessels from two outward-bound convoys to meet the attack.[14] So highly did British Intelligence rate this material that from June 1941

> no further operations were undertaken for the special purpose of capturing naval Enigma material. The wish to capture it gave place to apprehension lest even fortuitous capture, by alarming the enemy, should compromise the fact that GC & CS had now mastered the cypher.[15]

Clearly, any attempt to explain the false dawn in the Atlantic must take account of Ultra's contribution.

For Coastal Command, however, the depressing fact remained that until it could obtain better arms and equipment, no aid from Ultra, or anything else, could significantly improve its own contribution. And for the first half, at any rate, of Joubert's tenure, it must at times have seemed a very real question whether the worst enemies of Coastal Command were to be found abroad or at home. It became more obvious every day that the most pressing need was long-range aircraft, but as we have noted (Chapter 30, p. 244, Note 3); the Air Ministry remained "resolutely deaf" to any suggestion of allocating Halifaxes to Coastal Command. The solitary Liberator squadron (No. 120, formed in June) was afflicted by teething troubles which took a long time to cure. The flying boat picture was, as the AHB Narrative says, "not rosy"; out of 67 Catalinas delivered by September 1941, nine had been written off, three were under repair, and only 26 were operational in the United Kingdom, with nine more at Gibraltar and nine in the Far East; only 18 further deliveries were expected by December.[16] With Sunderlands the prospect was even worse; by October

> Labour troubles in Belfast coupled with a lack of interest in this type, as compared with "Stirling" aircraft, shown by the manufacturing firm had brought production almost to a full stop.[17]

The fact that six Stirlings could be manufactured with the same effort as three Sunderlands did nothing to ease the situation. What all this amounted to was that Coastal Command had to depend on aircraft which simply did not have the performance to close the fatal "Atlantic Gap" (see p. 000): a few squadrons of Wellingtons and the ever-faithful Whitleys. And in the cheerfulness of the false dawn, it nearly lost these also:

> Early in October 1941 the Prime Minister suggested to the First Lord of the Admiralty that, having regard to the fact that U-boats were, probably as a result of air operations, confining their activities to more distant waters and in view of the agreed plan for strategic bombing attacks on Germany which required the immediate building up of Bomber Command's strength, it would be desirable to transfer the Whitley and Wellington aircraft at present operating in Coastal Command.[18]

This would have meant the diminution of Joubert's exiguous strength by some 60 useful aircraft; fortunately the Admiralty reacted sharply, and Churchill was persuaded to defer decision on this matter until January 1942. The incident is an excellent sample of the prevail-

411

ing mood, the "mixture of euphoria and despondency" (see pp. 291–2) in which a bomber fleet of 4,000 aircraft was being contemplated and accorded absolute priority over all else.

Nor was it only a matter of extracting even small numbers of the most suitable aircraft from Bomber Command; there was also the question of that Command's rôle in the U-boat war. It kept up its attacks on the German surface vessels in the French Atlantic ports through the summer and autumn, at considerable cost but sometimes also with considerable effect;[19] further than that Air Marshal Sir Richard Peirse was not prepared to go:

> In a letter to the CAS, dated the 4 July, among proposals for cooperation between the three RAF Commands in the Sea War, [Joubert] put forward the suggestion that Bomber Command should take each U-boat operating base in turn and reduce it to the condition that Plymouth had been left in after the recent five days' raids by the GAF.[20] Sir Philip previously sent a draft of this letter to the AOC-in-C, Bomber Command, who had replied that he was firmly convinced that a better employment for his limited force was on objectives in Germany and, though he realised that his bombing effort must be deflected from their [sic] primary rôle in order to attack the major naval units in Brest, he could not agree to include the U-boat Biscay bases. These views were accepted by the CAS . . .[21]

Joubert recognized that there was no point in pressing this argument, but the glow of the false dawn filled him with further alarm. The idea seemed to be circulating that the Battle of the Atlantic had been won; "a number of official pronouncements and newspaper articles indicated the prevalence of this unjustifiable optimism".[22] He perceived a new threat to the build-up of his Command, and was not fully reassured by Portal's declaration that he, at any rate, did not share the rosy opinions. Joubert was convinced that it was only a question of time before the U-boats were reinforced and returned to their attacks where aircraft could not reach them:

> In a letter dated 5 September the AOC-in-C presented this point of view to the Air Ministry stressing that the U-boat Fleet was growing rapidly and, if no drastic steps were taken, we should have to reckon by the summer of 1942 with up to 150 U-boats operating at sea.[23] While a certain amount of harrying was inflicted on them at some points of their sea cruises they could count on complete quiet and rest in harbour. He again strongly recommended that these bases be bombed frequently (not necessarily with large numbers of aircraft) so that at least some interference could be made in the smooth working of the Biscay port facilities. The Air Ministry replied that, while fully appreciating the value of harassing

"Tackled an impossible task": Air Marshal Sir Richard Peirse, AOC-in-C, Bomber Command, October 1940 – January 1942, the period of the worst disappointments. Peirse did not have a happy war, but here we see one of the more pleasant moments, with the Queen at a Bomber Command fly-past.

"The sure touch of a leader": Air Chief Marshal Sir Arthur Harris, AOC-in-C, Bomber Command, February 1942 to the end. It was his firm belief throughout that "the bomber was the predominant weapon".

"The backbone of the Bomber Force": the specification of the Vickers Wellington is dated 1932; it entered service in 1938, and in 1942 was by far the most numerous type in Bomber Command. This excellent aircraft remained operational until 1943. Shown here are Wellington Is.

"Without exception the finest bomber of the war": here we see an Avro Lancaster with the men and women who put it in the air and flew it. Front rank: Flying Control officer, WAAF parachute packer, Meteorological officer, seven members of aircrew; 2nd rank: NCO fitter, mechanic, NCO fitter, five mechanics, electrical mechanic, instrument repairer, two mechanics; 3rd rank: bomb train with WAAF driver and bombing-up crew; 4th rank: corporal mechanic, four mechanics, engineer officer, fitter (armourer), three armourers, radio mechanic, two instrument repairers, three bomb-handlers, fitter; rear left: petrol bowser and crew; rear right: mobile workshop and crew. It is easy to see how the average 1,000 ground crew on a two-squadron station are accounted for.

"Freeman's Folly": the famous de Havilland Mosquito all-wooden "speed bomber" which also served as a fighter and in the Photographic Reconnaissance Unit. Conceived in 1938, the Mosquitoes began to reach the squadrons at the end of 1941; they were among the outstanding British aircraft of the war.

"The most brilliant feat of arms": Wing Commander Guy Gibson explaining the effect which No. 617 Squadron was expected to achieve, and which it so admirably performed on the Möhne Dam on the night of May 16/17, 1943, when Guy Gibson himself won the Victoria Cross.

"Captivity, a hard test": there was, generally speaking, great mutual respect between the air forces of both sides. This RAF aircrew member, brought down over German territory, is being interrogated by the *Luftwaffe*, who normally treated captured aircrew with respect and courtesy. With enraged civilians and the *Gestapo* it was another matter.

attacks on U-boat bases, such attacks would constitute a very considerable and unwarranted diversion from the present planned operations as approved by His Majesty's Government.[24]

Not content with this fairly crushing rejoinder, the Air Council then informed the CAS that

It considered that the AOC-in-C, Coastal Command, in common with the Admiralty, had overlooked the long-term indirect contribution which the bomber offensive had made and was still making to our security at sea by attacks, not only on the main German ports, but on the German industrial effort as a whole. This industrial effort supported their naval just as much as their military or other war effort. The Air Ministry had accepted that the bomber force should support the naval strategy more directly when the Battle of the Atlantic was in its earlier and critical stage *but there seemed no justification whatever for a return to this defensive strategy now when conditions at sea had so much improved and we were beginning to develop fully the air offensive to which we must look for winning as opposed to not losing the war.*[25]

No apology is here offered for recounting this exchange at length, including the mistaken but revealing final homily. It perfectly illustrates the implications of the "4,000-bomber" offensive doctrine, as interpreted by the purists at that time; it was one more element in the "1941 madness" to which we have alluded earlier (p. 331). And it is not mere hindsight that enables one to say that. Work had begun as early as January 1941 on the building of massive bomb-proof U-boat shelters ("pens") at Brest, Lorient, St Nazaire and La Pallice. Excavations for these were carried out between January and April, and more excavations for further groups of pens in July and August. All this had been duly observed and its progress monitored month by month by Photographic Reconnaissance. It was the sight of these massive preparations which had alarmed Coastal Command, and prompted Joubert's requests; they had this further point:

The foundation work, done behind caissons which kept the sea water out, was highly vulnerable to blast bombing and the subsequent erection was susceptible to grave delays by air attack until the massive roof was finally in place after which bombing became useless. At this stage (July 1941) few roofs were in position and much foundation work was still at the vulnerable stage. By January 1942 the pens at Brest and Lorient and the majority of those at St Nazaire and La Pallice had passed the stage at which interference by bombing was likely.[26]

The opportunity missed in 1941 was missed for good; but desperation is a cruel overlord, and by the end of 1942 the posture of the U-boat war was desperate indeed. On December 23 Bomber Command was ordered by the War Cabinet to bomb the U-boat bases

> In the five weeks from the middle of January 1943 Bomber Command's night attacks on Lorient and St Nazaire consumed half its total bombing effort; they destroyed almost everything except the pens.[27]

What doubles the depressing irony of all this is the transformation of the war which came about with the entry of the United States in December 1941 and the forging of the Grand Alliance. The American decision, declared at the Arcadia Conference (see p. 364), to dispose of Germany first, was fundamental to the Alliance from then onwards. Moreover, it gave a new meaning to the word "offensive". Until then, the only offensive that it was possible to envisage against Germany had been the bomber offensive; nothing else could touch that enemy. Now there was another: the assault on north-west Europe by Anglo-American forces which became the foundation-stone of Allied strategy. That assault could never take place without the BOLERO build-up (see p. 400); and BOLERO could never take place until the Battle of the Atlantic was won. This thus ceased to be a battle for survival only, a defensive battle; it became an intrinsic part of the main offensive strategy of the war. To the extent that Coastal Command could contribute to it, that contribution would be absolutely offensive in character, and required all the appropriate priorities. The proposition seems straightforward; yet neither at the time nor for long afterwards was it perceived.[28] The dogma of the "one true air offensive" persisted with blinding power, drawing strength from other live superstitions.

54 The dark night; anti-shipping operations; oil supplies; "an obstacle to victory"

The first shadow fell across the false dawn in September 1941, when sinkings suddenly increased again to 285,942 tons, over 70 per cent by U-boats. However, a fall to 218,289 tons in October, and then to the very low figure of 104,640 tons in November reassured some who occupied positions of power, though less convincing to the Admiralty and Coastal Command, where special circumstances were taken more seriously into account. Undoubtedly, the low November figure reflected, to some extent, the severe Atlantic autumn gales. But those intimately concerned with the U-boat war were aware, from Ultra, that there was a sharp drop in the number of U-boats operating in the Atlantic, which it was difficult to connect with any Allied action in that area. The sinking success of September[1] had been achieved by some 20 U-boats (excluding those on passage); on November 1 there were 10 in the North Atlantic and six more off Gibraltar; on December 8 there were only 12 in the whole Atlantic, all off Gibraltar, and by January 1, 1942 there were only six. All this was clearly revealed by the Ultra intercepts, and the Admiralty's Operational Intelligence Centre commented (with some surprise, one imagines) on December 20:

> ... the primary object seems, at least temporarily, to be no longer the destruction of merchant shipping.[2]

The development was, indeed, surprising, and requires further explanation, which Ultra could naturally not supply at the time. As Dr Rohwer says,

> For Dönitz, the ultimate and decisive criterion for the use of the U-boat weapon was the quickest possible sinking of the greatest possible enemy tonnage and tonnage that was potentially useful to the enemy.[3]

He recognized that the U-boat war was essentially – and with growing American involvement, increasingly – a race between Allied ship-building capacity and U-boat availability. His aim was 300 operational boats (fortunately he never achieved it), and the 81 of November and 86 of December were well below that target. He knew quite well that they should be used economically, that is to say, where they could find and sink the largest number of ships in the shortest time. All else was bad tactics.

> However, the German Naval Operations Staff thought it necessary to use U-boats for other tasks occasionally: to create a strategic diversion, for reconnaissance purposes, to protect blockade runners, and so on;[4] and to help in critical situations such as that in the Mediterranean towards the end of 1941 – where their intervention was not without tangible success.[5] But Hitler's intuition – he sensed the danger of a British invasion of Norway after a number of British Commando raids – led to what Dönitz regarded as a useless waste of U-boats on tasks not properly their own, at a time when they were urgently needed in the Atlantic ... It was certainly a blunder to withdraw such a large percentage [33 per cent] of the front-line U-boats from the supply war in which they were the only effective weapon left.[6]

As the hour appointed for the Japanese stroke at Pearl Harbor, and its inevitable consequence, American belligerency, approached, Dönitz warmly advocated greeting that event with what he called "a roll of drums" (*Paukenschlag*). And indeed, a "roll of drums" was heard in the war at sea in December 1941: 583,706 tons lost, 285 ships sunk. Dönitz himself, however, could claim little credit for this; less than 20 per cent of it was the work of his U-boats in the North and South Atlantic and British Home waters; virtually all the rest was attributable to the Japanese. However, Dönitz's day was not long delayed; by February the U-boats were back in force, with targets such as they had never dreamt of, to begin what Churchill calls "the terrible massacre of shipping along the American coast".[7] February cost a total of 679,632 tons, and this time it was the U-boats that claimed the lion's share: 476,451 tons.

February 1942 marked the beginning of the crisis of the U-boat war; it was the first of some very bad months indeed (see Appendix C). There is no surprise in this; the chronological table on p. 363 sufficiently illustrates the strain of this period of the war. The Royal Navy, suffering from what Churchill bluntly called a "series of major disasters",[8] was over-stretched everywhere. The same was true of almost every aspect of the work of the RAF, and Coastal Command perhaps above all; as Churchill says,

> The overwhelming demands for reinforcements in the Far East and the Mediterranean had made great inroads into its resources in aircraft and trained crews, which melted away to meet the harsh needs elsewhere.[9] Moreover, the expansion of the Command with new long-range squadrons, which had been eagerly expected, had perforce been temporarily arrested. Against this distressing background our airmen did their utmost.[10]

Perhaps, when he wrote that, Churchill was trying to make amends for some of his earlier unhelpfulness – trying to take away the Wellingtons and Whitleys, for example; or perhaps he had just forgotten.

It was unfortunate, to say the least, that the low ebb of Coastal Command and the Navy coincided with a significant rise in U-boat numbers: it was in February 1942 that the operational total for the first time went into three figures: 101. It rose steadily through the year, to 205 in November, dropped back to 203 in December and then mounted to its peak (239) in May 1943 (see p. 236). The 16 months now beginning saw the deployment and the apogee of the great packs whose operations brought sinkings by U-boats alone to a total of 7,721,486 tons (1,412 ships) during that period.

As though this combination of defensive weakness and increasing offensive strength was not enough, it was precisely at this juncture that the Intelligence war once more took a bad turn – indeed, two bad turns, offensive and defensive. The first concerned Naval Cypher No. 3, which was brought into use in June 1941 for purposes of inter-communication by the British, Canadian and US Navies in the Atlantic, but in some haste, without the protective devices used in connection with Naval Cypher No. 2 and Naval Cypher No. 4 (which replaced No. 2 in January 1942). It was in that month that:

> having realised that Naval Cypher No. 3 had become the most important cypher for communications concerning arrangements for convoys and stragglers in the Atlantic, the *B-Dienst* concentrated most of its resources against it. By February 1942 it had reconstructed the book, and from then until 15 December 1942 it read a large proportion of the signals – sometimes as much as 80 per cent. From 15 December 1942 a change in the indicator procedure created a setback for the *B-Dienst*, but it soon overcame this by increasing its staff. From February 1943 it was again reading a large proportion of the traffic, and was sometimes obtaining decrypts about convoy movements between 10 and 20 hours in advance. Throughout the period February 1942 to 10 June 1943 it frequently decrypted in this cypher the daily signal in which the Admiralty issued its estimate of U-boat dispositions.[11]

Once more Admiral Dönitz possessed a priceless secret advantage. By an evil chance, this offensive success of *B-Dienst* coincided with a most effective defensive measure:

> On 1 February 1942 the U-boat Command added a fourth wheel to the Enigma machine for the communications of its Atlantic and Mediterranean U-boats, and this step, though devised as a further measure against internal insecurity, was at last effective against GC & CS. Except for occasional days, GC & CS was unable to solve the U-boat settings until December 1942.[12]

It was a double victory: not only did it mean that Bletchley could no longer supply the necessary information about U-boat movements and numbers in the Atlantic, but also it was unable to perceive the extent to which Cypher No. 3 had been penetrated. It was, says the Official History,

> for these reasons, as well as because the U-boats exploited a new operational area off the North American coast from early in the year, that the first half of 1942 was to see a startling recovery in their performance and

417

that, despite continuous improvements in Allied defences and resources, there was to be no decline in the level of their successes until the beginning of 1943.[13]

These, then, were the multiple reasons for the dark night of the U-boat war in 1942. How dark it might become was perceptible in March, the first of three months during the year when sinkings totalled over 800,000 tons; on this occasion the figure was 834,164, with 537,980 (over 64 per cent) attributable to U-boats. The worst monthly total was in June, 834,196 tons, 623,545 in the North Atlantic, and no less than 700,235 by U-boats (nearly 84 per cent). But the largest U-boat contribution was in November: 729,160 tons out of a total of 807,754 (over 90 pert cent). Well might Churchill describe all this as "a terrible event in a very bad time".[14]

It is against this background that we must read the steady complaints and protests of Joubert during this period. He told the Air Ministry on February 19 that

> ... the prospect of Coastal Command being able to work at reasonable efficiency appeared to be becoming more and more remote. The promise of centimetric ASV fitted Liberators had come to nothing, the one Liberator squadron was being allowed to die out and there had been a continuous change of policy in regard to this long-range aircraft.[15]

It was at this point, deeply conscious of the inadequacy of his Command's equipment, that Joubert uttered the ultimate heresy:

> While fully aware of the importance of the sustained bomber offensive, it appeared to him that, if England was to survive this year, in which we were already losing shipping at a rate considerably in excess of American and British building output, some part of the bomber offensive would have to be sacrificed and a long-range type such as the Lancaster diverted to the immediate threat on our Sea Communications.[16]

It is not difficult to imagine the flutter that this request caused, especially with Churchill, master of the *volte-face*, now asking the CAS to report on proposals for compensating Coastal Command for long-range aircraft diverted to the Far East. Portal, in his reply, unveiled another discipline of the coalition war which is by no means immediately obvious:

> ... he deprecated any allocation of Liberators to Coastal Command on the grounds that the Americans were already restive about the use of

418

Fortress aircraft in Coastal Command on tasks other than high level bombing raids[17] and he considered there would be serious trouble with General Arnold[18] if Liberators were similarly diverted from the bombing rôle for which they had in the first instance been supplied to the RAF. Apart from the above reason the CAS said he was strongly opposed to the transfer of either Liberators or Lancasters from the bomber offensive as the former were earmarked for the Middle East where they would be the only aircraft capable of bombing targets in Tripoli, Italy and the Rumanian oilfields[19] while the latter was the only aircraft which could carry 8,000 lbs of bombs to Berlin. He proposed, therefore, to compensate Coastal Command by the transfer of Whitley aircraft until such time as the Catalina strength reached a figure of 45 aircraft . . .[20]

Portal would learn; meanwhile Joubert would continue to suffer. It was at about this time (March 1942) that he instigated a development within the Command of the greatest value, and from which we may learn an enormous amount about its daily work: the bi-monthly (later monthly) confidential periodical, *Coastal Command Review*. His successor tells us:

It was a serious professional review of the previous month's work and was a valuable medium for keeping the squadrons informed of what was going on throughout the Command and how the air/sea war was going, making generally known the tactical lessons that were constantly being learnt in the course of operations, and dealing with the whole range of professional activities of the Command in a way that would be interesting as well as instructive for the crews.[21]

Joubert's later well-developed sense of public relations here served him well; the *Review* covered a very wide spectrum of information, from the highly technical to matters of more general interest within the Command's experience, such as the characteristics of whales, or the phenomenon of St Elmo's Fire, which could disconcertingly sheath an entire aircraft in apparent flame – its nature clearly described, with reference to antiquity and its virtue as a sign of divine protection. It is from the very first issue of *Coastal Command Review* that we glimpse, for example, the manner of operation of Joubert's antique, over-worked and not very suitable Whitleys:

While engaged on an anti-submarine sweep from Reykjavik, the Whitley aircraft F/612 sighted a U-boat on the surface at 1125 on February 18th, in the position 63°15' N. and 24°30' W. The U-boat submerged when the aircraft had approached to 300 yards, and the swirl of its dive could be clearly seen at the moment of attack. Six depth-charges were dropped from 50 ft, each of 250 lb modified Mark VIII, with pistol modified Mark

X, which had been pre-set to 50 ft. They fell 90 ft ahead of the swirl across the track of the U-boat; two were thought to have exploded 15 ft from the track of the U-boat, two others at 75 ft, two at 135 ft and two at 195 ft. After a couple of minutes a large oil patch was seen, about 250 ft in diameter, and lines of air bubbles with thick streaks of oil. One minute later the U-boat surfaced again for a few seconds: a large patch of froth appeared 100 yards from the scene of the attack, then the conning tower of the U-boat showed on the surface and immediately submerged again. No wreckage or further signs of damage were visible, but there was a 35-knot wind at the time and the sea was rough. The aircraft circled round, getting a view over at least ten miles, and stayed an hour and a half. On the way home the port engine failed, and it was only just possible to reach land after reducing weight by jettisoning everything possible, including the camera with the photographs which had been taken. This is considered to have been an excellent attack which must, at the least, have shaken the U-boat very seriously, and should have prevented it from doing further damage on its cruise.[22]

Several things may be noticed; first, the factual, professional tone of the narrative, which adds to, rather than detracts from the drama of the episode; secondly, the great care not to make an unsubstantiated claim – owing, probably, a good deal to the methods of Peyton-Ward, but normal in Coastal Command. This contrasts very sharply with the "numbers game" of other Commands often referred to above, but the very different circumstances have to be taken into account: there is an enormous difference between attacking such an elusive enemy as a U-boat, whose chief asset is invisibility, and a free-for-all fighter battle in the air. Finally, we must note that the records show no U-boat sunk or missing on the day of F/612's attack, which indicates very clearly how robust they were; the great strength which enabled them to withstand the pressures of the ocean depths enabled them also to survive what looks like certain death at the hands of their enemies. This, also, was a problem which Coastal Command had to overcome. In this particular case, however, it seems a reasonable assumption that the U-boat would have had to break off its patrol and make for home and immediate repairs.

Such gallant work notwithstanding, Whitleys were not the answer to Joubert's problems, and the acquisition of another squadron (No, 58, from Bomber Command; Whitleys with ASV II) did little to ease his lot. His position, in fact, was rapidly becoming impossible, as he told the Air Ministry on March 30. He was, in the words of the AHB Narrative, being "metaphorically kicked by the Admiralty for not asking enough and blamed by the Air Ministry for demanding impossibilities'". The Air Council blandly replied that "occasions on which an AOC-in-C's views were at variance with Air Staff opinion were not abnormal and should not give rise to embarrassment in the case of Coastal Command".[23] As a sop, he received (on *loan* from Bomber Command) two more Whitley squadrons and two Wellington squadrons, while two Beaufort squadrons which had gone overseas were replaced by Hampdens.

Mention of Hampdens serves as a reminder of another area where Coastal Command's affairs were not prospering. In the last quarter of 1941, its anti-shipping strikes had succeeded in sinking 15 enemy vessels for the loss of 46 aircraft. The first four months of 1942, however, saw a depressing decline of effectiveness: only six ships sunk, at a cost of 55 aircraft. There was a brief improvement in May, when the Command claimed 12 ships sunk; 10 of these claims were subsequently confirmed, but the loss was high – 43 aircraft. The success was fleeting, the loss continuous; by June it was estimated that, during the last three months, one in four of all attacking aircraft had been lost. The war diary of No. 407 Squadron, RCAF (Hudsons), fills in the picture:

> Since this squadron became operational again on 1st April we have lost twelve crews, in all fifty persons either missing or killed. During the past month six crews have been designated missing or killed on operations with the loss of twenty-seven lives. This does not take into consideration the fact that after every major operation of this nature at least two or three aircraft are so very badly damaged that they are of no use to this, or any other squadron.[24]

The fault was, in large part, tactical: these anti-shipping strikes were carried out with amazing daring, at mast-head height. One pilot reported that he had gone in so low "that he struck a mast and hung one of the bomb-doors thereon";[25] another (of No. 455 Squadron, RAAF) actually returned with several feet of mast attached to his aircraft. With the departure of so many experienced crews to the Middle East, and increasingly powerful German anti-aircraft defence (what a running refrain this is!), it became clear that low-level attacks were prohibitively expensive. The reason for them was the continuing lack of a useful bomb-sight for medium-level attack; nevertheless, in July, Joubert was forced to order the abandonment of low-level strikes and adoption of medium-level bombing; casualties decreased at once; so did sinkings.

By the end of the year the tally of enemy ships sunk was 45, and the cost was 251 aircraft. No doubt something was achieved for this heavy outlay, but it is difficult to say exactly what. Denis Richards and Hilary Saunders say that it was a matter of keeping up necessary pressure on the enemy's transport system at all points – rather like the costly raiding policy on the British sector of the Western Front in the First World War when the BEF was too weak for major operations; and this construction is no doubt correct. But whereas the 1915–16 BEF had little option, a more profitable means of making war on enemy shipping did exist for Coastal Command. Between April 1940 and March 1943 it made 3,700 direct attacks, sank 107 vessels (155,076 tons) and lost 648 aircraft – just over six aircraft for each vessel sunk. Minelaying, on the other hand, a task which it shared with Bomber Command (enthusiastically supported by that Command's new AOC-in-C, Air Chief Marshal Sir Arthur Harris), in the same period accounted for 369 vessels (361,821 tons) at a cost of 329 aircraft – less than one aircraft per ship. Minelaying, in fact, was a most effective method which, says Harris,

> forced the enemy to divert more and more of his war-effort to anti-minelaying devices, and shipbuilding for replacements and repairs, and, before the end of the war drove him to engage 40 per cent of his naval personnel in minesweeping; it also put an immense strain on the enemy's alternative communications.[26]

Minelaying had the advantage of being perfectly practicable in conditions which made bombing of Germany impossible, so it in no way interfered with Bomber Command's main offensive. Unfortunately, its results could only rarely be seen and appreciated.

As so often happened, these hard times led to future advantages. Recognizing the unsuitability of the aircraft on which he was forced to depend (Hudsons and Hampdens), Joubert cast around for an alternative, and discovered it readily enough in the Beaufighters whose speed, fire-power and endurance were already serving the Command well. He persuaded the Air Ministry to authorize (June 1) the modification of some of these very adaptable aircraft as torpedo-carriers ("Torbeaus"); the intention was to form all-Beau "strike wings", with Torbeaus, Beau-bombers and cannon Beau-fighters. Slessor describes the tactics as later evolved; each strike, he says

> was a carefully planned, highly organized and hard-fought action involving up to thirty and more aircraft, each of which had its own particular rôle in the attack. The torpedo aircraft went straight for the merchant ships in the convoy while their escorts dealt with the enemy's escorting ships with bombs, cannon-fire and rockets.[27]

It was Slessor who reaped the benefit of Joubert's excellent device. As usual, there was a considerable time-lag between approval and action; the first Torbeau squadron (No. 254) did not become operational until November, and the first wing action, in bad weather on November 20, was a minor disaster. Joubert at once withdrew the wing for further training. In April 1943, after his departure, the Beaufighter wing showed its true quality with two highly successful operations against German convoys at the cost of only one aircraft. In due course, with Slessor's strong backing and despite contrary demands for their services, three Beaufighter strike wings were built up – a formidable offensive force.

All that, however, was in the future as Joubert grappled with his problems in mid-1942. This was a time of intense frustration, when it seemed as though "No" was the only word in the Air Staff's vocabulary. With German fighter strength increasing along the Dutch and Norwegian coasts, even normal reconnaissance was becoming costly and it was a very reasonable request that some Mosquito fighters might be spared for this essential work. The answer was that Mosquito production was entirely taken up in satisfying Fighter Command's prior need for night-fighters. April, May and June, it should be noted, were the months of the *Luftwaffe's* retaliatory "Baedeker raids" on historic centres such as Exeter, Bath, York and Canterbury; 1,637 civilians were killed and 1,760 injured, and public opinion was much incensed. So no Mosquitos for Coastal Command.[28]

And all the time the U-boats were inexorably swinging the pendulum of the war: a total of 674,457 tons in April, 132 ships, of which 74 sunk by U-boats; 705,050 tons in May, 151 ships, of which 125 by U-boats; and then in June the terrible total (834,196 tons, referred to on p. 418). The comparative immunity of convoys while the U-boats feasted on American coastal shipping was now over; the packs were back on the convoy routes in increasing numbers. If this went on unchecked there could be no BOLERO, no ROUNDUP, no riposte to enemy advances in the Middle East and the Far East; there would be starvation, breakdown and collapse. And high on the list of things that would not happen, if the U-boats kept up their stranglehold, was the bomber offensive; there would be no massive demonstration of strategic air power, because there would be no oil. Tankers were a prime U-boat target at all times, and British losses in the Atlantic in the first six months of 1942 amounted to as many as 68. The diversion of 49 more to the Indian Ocean for the war against Japan added severely to the strain. By the beginning of May, the combination of these factors brought the Oil Control Board to a state of deep alarm; the authorities

> calculated that their end-year stock level would be nearly two million tons below requirements unless they got tanker reinforcements. They put their need at seventy "notional" tankers (that is, ships capable of sailing in ten-knot convoys and carrying 10,000 tons of cargo).[29]

A request was made to America, and very handsomely acceded to: the Americans supplied 45 tankers, "among them vessels whose size and performance made the total contribution in terms of carrying capacity considerably more than seventy 'notional' tankers." The American gesture – for which Churchill expressed due gratitude – is the more remarkable inasmuch as, between January and June, they themselves lost no fewer than 73 tankers in the Atlantic. There was not much reason to doubt, in the summer of 1942, that it was here that the war would be lost or won.

The Admiralty had no illusions. It was, by now, very conscious of the value of Coastal Command's support, and most uneasy at the prospect of its continuing weakness. On June 23 the Naval Staff addressed a paper to Portal, with a copy to Joubert:

> It must be remembered that at this period of the war the U-boat fleet had been sinking an unprecedented tonnage of shipping in the Atlantic, our hold in the Mediterranean was precarious, surface raiders and U-boats were active in the Indian Ocean and the Japanese had been carrying all before them in the Far East and Pacific. A gloomy appreciation, therefore, formed the opening paragraphs of this survey in which it was stated that we had lost a measure of control over the sea communications of the world with all that this meant in the supply of raw materials and food for Great Britain *and the ability to take the offensive.*[30] Succeeding paragraphs outlined the conception of maritime strategy which the Admiralty considered necessary to rectify the situation ... One major point, it was claimed, stood out clearly – *ships alone were unable to maintain command at sea.*[31]

This frank admission by the senior Service marks an historic moment.

The Admiralty estimated, citing in support the Air Ministry's own targets, that the current deficiency of aircraft for the successful prosecution of the war at sea was about 800 of all types – of which the bulk, of course, related to Coastal Command. The Admiralty concluded that the only outstanding problem was to find a means of fulfilling the agreed requirements as quickly as possible for "we cannot await the fruition of a long-term programme when our hopes of even fulfilling that programme are being daily decreased by our lack of command of the sea."

Since the stated deficiency was roughly equal to the total *establishment* of Bomber Command as much as six months later,[32] the effect of this broadside upon the Air Staff may be imagined. Even Joubert was taken aback; he said there was general agreement with the Admiralty's arguments and figures

if there were unlimited aircraft available but, in the light of hard facts of shortage of aircraft in the RAF as a whole, he was against the demand for the immediate dissipation of RAF resources in order to strengthen Coastal Command alone. This view was shared by the CAS and the Air Ministry.[33]

The Air Ministry's position was not enviable; it was, says the AHB narrator "a striking example of having to cut a maximum coat out of a meagre amount of cloth." Everywhere, in 1942, the Allied war effort groaned under an acute shortage of aircraft. Joubert's broad view of the position, however, was in striking contrast to that of his colleague at High Wycombe. It was at precisely this juncture (June 17) that Sir Arthur Harris addressed a personal minute to Churchill, expounding his views on the conduct of the war and the proper use of air power which, he said, would ensure victory, "speedy and complete":

We are free, if we will, to employ our rapidly increasing air strength in the proper manner. In such a manner as would avail to knock Germany out of the war in a matter of months, if we decide upon the right course. If we decide upon the wrong course, then our air power will now, and increasingly in future become inextricably implicated as a subsidiary weapon in the prosecution of vastly protracted and avoidable land and sea campaigns.[34]

Fresh from the supposed triumph of Operation MILLENNIUM – the "Thousand-Bomber" attack on Cologne on May 30 – Harris continued:

It is imperative, if we hope to win the war, to abandon the disastrous policy of military intervention in the land campaigns of Europe, and to concentrate our air power against the enemy's weakest spots ... The success of the 1,000 Plan had proved beyond doubt in the minds of all but wilful men that we can even today dispose of a weight of air attack which no country on which it can be brought to bear could survive. We can bring it to bear on the vital part of Germany. It requires only the decision to concentrate it for its proper use.

To Sir Arthur Harris, in this enlarged frame of mind, the war was susceptible to simple remedies: the earliest possible return of all bombers from the Middle East; the return of all suitable aircraft and crews from Army Cooperation Command; obtaining every possible bomber from America while giving the highest priority to heavy bomber production in Britain; even a request to Stalin to transfer his bomber force to Britain. As for Coastal Command, he said it was "merely an obstacle to victory".

There is much that could be said about this breathtaking exposition of the philosophy of raw air power; we need only concern ourselves with a few points here. First, there is the extraordinary delusion that Britain, in June 1942, was "free, if we will" to prosecute the war in her own way. Britain was *not* free. She was already deeply dependent on America for many of the sinews of war, but over and above that, as more than once stated above, she was now subject to the disciplines of a coalition which had established its grand strategy and devised a machinery for the unrelenting pursuit of it – the Combined Chiefs of Staff. "Free", in Harris's sense of the word, could only mean "free of the alliance", which was really only another way of saying "sudden death". This unwillingness to accept the realities of coalition war had rung with steady discord right through the First World War, and unfortunately Churchill was one who had found those realities hardest to accept. It was unlikely that Harris would receive precise enlighten-ment from him. Fortunately Portal generally had a clear perception of American viewpoints, and Brooke never faltered in his understand-ing of the vital rôle of the Atlantic battle. Even Churchill, who did not much disguise his dread of a bloodbath on the beaches of North-West Europe on an even vaster scale than the one with which his name was already associated – Cape Helles in April 1915 – and had always hoped that the bomber offensive would provide a cheaper substitute, knew now that there was no other way. In his review of the war on July 21 he stated:

In the days when we were fighting alone we answered the question, "How are you going to win the war?" by saying "We will shatter Germany by bombing." Since then the enormous injuries inflicted on the German Army and man-power by the Russians, and the accession of the man-power and munitions of the United States, have rendered other possibilities

426

open. We look forward to mass invasion of the Continent by liberating armies, and general revolt of the populations against the Hitler tyranny.[35]

This did not, he hastened to add, imply any abandonment of the bombing programme – quite the contrary, since the Americans themselves were now keen supporters; but there was a new emphasis (which Harris clearly did not perceive). The relationship of the strategic air offensive to the Battle of the Atlantic Churchill wryly expressed in this way:

it might be true to say that the issue of the war depends on whether Hitler's U-boat attack on Allied tonnage or the increase and application of Allied air-power reach their full fruition first.

And this, also, was a loud, clear echo of the previous war – Colonel Repington's mordant comment as the unrestricted U-boat campaign of 1917 gathered momentum:

. . . in my view it was at present a question whether our armies could win the war before our navies lost it.[36]

Fortunately, in each crisis, the navies were able to make an eleventh-hour recovery, and in each case this owed no small amount to the intervention of air forces. The "obstacle to victory", throughout the year, was not Coastal Command (or any other); it was the sheer lack of escort vessels, aircraft (especially VLR), radar sets and suitable depth-charges – in other words, just about all the vital necessities.

Ironically, no sooner had Sir Arthur Harris made his astonishing pronouncement on Coastal Command than the precise opposite began to establish its truth.

55 *Turning point; the "Gap"; Liberators; U-boat reverses*

It is generally stated that the turn of the U-boat war came in 1943, and the month of May is cited for obvious reasons (which we shall shortly discuss); by that time Air Marshal Sir John Slessor had replaced Joubert at Coastal Command, but as he very reasonably says, "I hasten to disclaim any suggestion that this was cause and effect!"[1] Indeed, it was not; careful examination shows that a profoundly important change occurred in July 1942, while Joubert was still in command at Northwood. This is not to say that Joubert himself, any

427

more than Slessor, was personally responsible; it was a product of a number of factors simultaneously maturing, some having no direct connection with Coastal Command at all and some going back to Bowhill's time. But the essential fact is that in that month, July 1942, a highly significant fresh statistic begins to illuminate the U-boat war.

The stark numerical truths are these:

Between January 1 and June 30, 1942, only 21 U-boats were lost, one destroyed by a mine, one for unknown reasons.
Of the 21 lost, only six and a half[2] were attributable to air action.
Of the six and a half sunk by air action, three were attributable to the Americans.
Air action was therefore involved in 30.9 per cent of U-boat losses.
British air action – RAF, RCAF (whether in Coastal Command or flying from its own bases in Newfoundland and Nova Scotia), RAAF (such as the excellent No. 10 Squadron, with its Sunderlands at Mount Batten, and its sister, No. 461) and Fleet Air Arm – was involved in 16.6 per cent of U-boat losses.
Coastal Command was involved in none.[3]

This gloomy picture began to be drastically transformed in July; in that month 11 U-boats were lost, all through Allied action. Air forces accounted for five and a half of them – almost as many as the total for the whole preceding six months. American aircraft claim two and a half, the RCAF one (by a patrol off Nova Scotia), and Coastal Command (with its loaned support) the remaining two: these were its first "kills", the first of all being the Leigh Light kill by No. 172 Squadron on July 5.

This was the fresh statistic, and it was no flash in the pan. Ten U-boats were lost in August, 10 more in September; in October the figure rose to 16 – 10½ by air action. The second six months of 1942 cost the U-boat fleet 65 boats; air action accounted for 34½, the proportion thus rising from 30.9 per cent of a very small number to 53 per cent of a substantial number. Coastal Command's share was 15 U-boats (23 per cent); it was definitely in the game. Only once in the critical months of January to May 1943 did the air forces' share fall below 50 per cent (47.3 per cent in February). July 1942, in other words, saw the first gleam of the true dawn (see Appendix D).

So much for statistics; they are not merely essential for understanding what the campaign was about and the direction it was taking, they are also the accolade of some remarkable deeds. There is not space here to relate more than a few of these and even in doing so one has to remind oneself that each of them is matched by hours, days, even weeks of unrewarded flying. It has been said that "war is nine-tenths boredom", but in Coastal Command boredom was a luxury that none could afford; a Coastal crew had to be attentive and vigilant the whole time, not just – as with all air fighting – in order not to be surprised by the enemy, but in order also not to miss the tiny, probably distant, probably very indistinct sign on the monotonous surface of the sea which was often the only indication of a U-boat's presence. And when action came, it had to be swift, sudden and precise – thus:

At 1501 hours on 15th September, Whitley Q/58, flying at 6,700 ft, sighted a U-boat at a distance of 7 miles. It was making 10 knots. The aircraft turned and broke cloud at 3,000 ft, then attacked from the U-boat's port quarter with five Torpex[4] depth-charges released from 20 ft, while the U-boat was fully surfaced. The depth-charges straddled it; three fell short to port, one made a direct hit on the bridge, and one fell beyond to starboard. As the explosions subsided the bows were seen sticking out of the water at an angle of about 15°. The aircraft turned to make another attack. The bows of the U-boat slid under just before the release of the remaining depth-charge, leaving on the surface an oil-patch, about 90 yards long and 25 yards wide, in the centre of which were many bits of wood, which looked like broken up duckboard, a black object shaped like a drum, and pieces of orange-coloured stuff, a foot or two across, irregular in shape and curled up at the edges like scraps of orange peel (painted plywood?). The remaining Torpex depth-charge exploded in the centre of this oil and debris, 5 seconds after the bows had gone out of sight, but no further results were seen. The aircraft dropped a submarine marker, and flew away northward, returning to the scene twenty minutes later,[5] and then making a square search, without results. The wreckage and debris seen after the main depth-charge attack, together with the quantity of oil, indicate that total destruction is more than likely.[6]

It was indeed: post-war investigation shows that this marked the end of *U 261*.

September was an interesting month; scarcely had Admiral Dönitz uttered his bombastic statement about the crow and the mole (see p. 245) than he was forced to change his tune. "U-boat traffic round Scotland and in the Bay of Biscay," he lamented in September

is gravely endangered by daily, even hourly, hunts by aircraft. In the Atlantic the enemy's daily reconnaissance covers out as far as 20° W, which forces U-boat dispositions far out into the centre of the Atlantic with consequent higher fuel consumption, shorter operational periods, and greater difficulty in finding the enemy convoys in the open Atlantic . . . If development continues at the present rate, these problems will lead to irreparable losses, to a decline in ship sinkings, and consequently to reduced chances of success in the U-boat warfare as a whole.[7]

He drew attention to the effect already produced by even a small number of VLR aircraft in protecting convoys, quoting U-boat captains saying that successful attacks were possible "only as long as Allied aircraft were not in evidence". This was no more than the truth; the presence of, say, a Liberator, had not only defensive value in guiding surface vessels to the right areas, but a very positive offensive value in forcing U-boats to dive and stay under, preventing them from making an attack at all. To counter them in the Atlantic, Dönitz asked for reinforcement with Heinkel 177s, twin-engined heavy bombers which he considered "the only aircraft which have a range and fighting power capable of acting as a reconnaissance against the Atlantic convoys and of combating the English aircraft in the Biscay area".[8] The demands of the Eastern Front deprived him of He 177s until October 1943, and their performance proved disappointing.[9] However, in September 1942 he did receive a *Staffel*[10] of Ju 88C-6s, the very effective successors of the Me 110 in the *Zerstörer* rôle (see p. 215).[11] With a maximum speed of over 300 mph and powerfully armed, the Ju 88s (reinforced by a second *Staffel* in October and two more in November, to form *V/KG 40*) were bad news for Coastal Command's older and slower patrols. There were 44 combats over the Bay in September; Wellington U/311, well flown and bravely fought, was also a lucky one on September 11. It was attacked by four Jus and their first attack pierced the hydraulics of the rear turret, which thereafter had to be turned by hand. The second attack was made by three Jus together, two passing overhead, on either side:

The third opened fire at 300 yards as it approached from dead ahead of U 311, when it climbed steeply to avoid colliding. While its nose was pointing upwards, the Wellington's front gunner put a long burst into the belly; the Ju peeled off to port with smoke coming from both engines, and after flying level for a few seconds, crashed into the sea. The remaining three Jus then formated and repeated the manoeuvre, except that the third aircraft attacked from astern. These tactics were repeated three more times by the enemy aircraft, while the Wellington took evasive action by climbing from sea-level to about 300 ft and back to sea-level, and turning from port to starboard. Then one of the Jus made off for the French coast, leaving a thin trail of black smoke from the port engine. The two remaining Jus made two more attacks from the quarters, but came no closer than 600 yards. Finally, they took up positions above and to starboard, and shadowed for three minutes, till the Wellington ran into a patch of sea fog. The Wellington sustained many hits, but no member of the crew was hurt.[12]

In October the reinforced Ju 88C-6s destroyed 16 RAF aircraft, but already an effective counter was in operation against them – the Beaufighters of Nos. 235 and 248 Squadrons. Just *how* effective these could be was displayed on September 17:

At 1755 hours ... eight Beaufighters of 235 Squadron on interceptor patrol were flying at 200 ft in loose formation in the Bay of Biscay, when a Focke-Wulf 200 was sighted. It was flying one mile to starboard on a reciprocal course over an armed 300-ton trawler. The three leading Beaufighters (E, P, N) attacked the F.W. on the port side, while 0/235 dived from 2,000 ft to make a head-on attack, and the remainder attacked from the starboard quarter. The attack tactics given out at briefing were carried out perfectly by all aircrews. The trawler immediately opened fire and shot down C/235 into the sea. Beaufighter J/235 attacked the F.W. again from the port quarter, and E/235 delivered a third attack from starboard, broke away and attacked again from the port beam. The F.W. now burst into flames and dived into the sea with a series of explosions. A dinghy was released and seen in the sea half-inflated, with one man trying to climb in and three floating in the water. The Beaufighters re-formed and resumed their patrol at 1810 hours.

Ten minutes later the seven Beaufighters were flying in various positions, with six miles between the first and last aircraft, when three Ju 88s were seen ahead, circling at 1,000 ft above a fishing vessel with a French flag. The Beaufighters climbed to 1,000 ft and attacked simultaneously from various directions. One Ju was hit in the port engine and tail, and dived nose down into the sea. N, O and E attacked a second Ju; flames appeared in the cockpit and a large piece of cowling flew off. This Ju also dived into the sea, enveloped in flames. Meanwhile, A/235 followed the third Ju and attacked, but it took evasive action and disappeared in a cloud. A/235 flew through the cloud and re-sighted the Ju, delivering a second attack, but lost it again in cloud. When the Beaufighters left the scene of the action the tailplanes of two Ju 88s were still projecting from the water.[13]

This phase of the battle saw constant pendulum-swings of advantage to one side or the other. *V/KG 40* continued to be a menace, but at increasing cost to itself: so it was contained. The Torpex-filled depth-charges, linked to a reliable 25-foot pistol-setting, at last gave Coastal Command weapons of true lethality. On the other hand, it was in September that the Germans inflicted a serious setback on the ASV/Leigh Light squadrons with the introduction of the *Metox* receiver (so named after one of the French firms which produced it under orders). The *Metox* was

a simple receiver, to detect ASV transmissions from patrolling aircraft. In the submarine's radio room, the receiver operator heard the aircraft's radar transmissions as a buzz in his earphones. Thus warned of the approach of the aircraft, the submarine crews could dive to safety before the attack developed ... The German sailors commented favourably on the new receiver: it picked up transmissions coming from aircraft more than 30 miles away – more than twice the distance at which an airborne radar operator could detect a submarine ... By mid-September several German submarines had been fitted with the *Metox*, and often these would act as escorts for their less fortunate comrades during the crossing of the dangerous Bay of Biscay area. By the end of the year nearly all boats carried the device.[14]

So another round opened in the scientists' war on the radar front. And there remained the "Gap" (see p. 244), that area

several hundred miles wide in the north-east Atlantic, roughly south of the point of Greenland, in which convoys were beyond the range of shore-based air cover. The great majority of the terrible losses in the convoys occurred in this "Gap" which, of course, became the happiest hunting ground of the U-boat packs.[15]

This was where the VLR aircraft – or rather, the lack of them – were so profoundly important. Only they could operate in the "Gap" – and by "they", let us be quite clear what we mean. We mean the five Liberator Is of No. 120 Squadron in Iceland. It is to be noted that it was the Mark I Liberator which was truly VLR; it had an operational range of 2,400 miles, which meant that it could spend as long as three hours patrolling an area 1,100 miles from its base (see p. 245). The Mark II was a bomber variant, with a range of 1,800 miles; this, also, was part of 120 Squadron's equipment, but rated only as long-range, not VLR. The Mark III (range 1,680 miles) was also present in 120 Squadron; it, too, was designed as a bomber, and

extensive de-modification was necessary to prepare the Liberators for the very long-range, low-altitude, anti-submarine rôle: the self-sealing liners to the fuel tanks and most of the protective pieces of armour plating were removed, as were the turbo-superchargers for the engines, and the underneath power-operated gun turret. This weight pruning made it possible for the aircraft to take off carrying more than two thousand gallons of high octane fuel, in addition to its offensive load of eight 250 pound depth-charges.[16]

But as August 1942 began, VLR meant five Mark I Liberators: just five.

No. 120 Squadron, however, bears everlasting witness to the fact that in the end it is the man, not the machine, that counts. On its strength was Squadron-Leader Terence Bulloch, an Ulsterman who, by the end of July, had logged 2,300 hours' flying time and was officially assessed as "exceptional" as a pilot, and "above average" as a navigator. In addition, he was a dedicated U-boat killer. He was deeply interested in every part of his equipment; he imparted his enthusiasm to his crew, which became a close-knit professional team. Squadron-Leader Bulloch was a leader. And his leadership was not without reward: on August 16, while escorting a convoy (always the best place to find U-boats), he encountered *U 89*; only the lack of a proper 25-foot setting for his depth-charges saved her from destruction. Two days later he attacked *U 653*, and damaged her so severely that she had to return to base. He had to wait almost two months to be rewarded by a kill: 1223 hours on October 12, south-west of Iceland, when he sighted a wake eight miles away on the starboard bow; approaching down sun, he saw *U 597* travelling at 10 knots, 15 miles from a convoy:

Diving to attack from the U-boat's port quarter at 15° to the track, six Torpex depth-charges were released from 75 ft while the U-boat was still on the surface; two more depth-charges hung up. The U-boat was completely covered by the stick, both in line and range, from bows to stern.

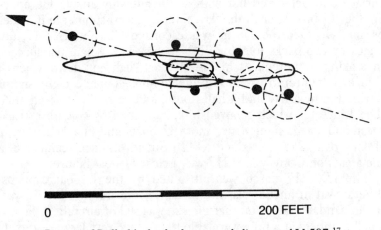

0   **200 FEET**

Pattern of Bulloch's depth-charges exploding round U 597.[17]

During the explosion of the first depth-charge right on the stern, three large and several small pieces of metal were thrown up in the air, and one large oval piece of metal flew past the Liberator's rear turret. As Nos 3 and 4 depth-charges were exploding amidships close up to the starboard side, the U-boat shuddered and lifted out of the water, leaving the deck clearly visible with the water pouring off it. As the spray subsided, the conning tower and one periscope appeared in the middle of the disturbed area; they hung there for about seven seconds, and then sank vertically with no forward movement. When the spray had settled, a white cylindrical object was bobbing up and down in the disturbance. Soon afterwards a patch of oil appeared at the leading edge of the explosion mark, and a greenish-grey cylinder studded with bolts, measuring about a foot in diameter and projecting about five feet out of the water, was seen floating in this oil; it was still there when the aircraft left half an hour later. Probably this was an airtight part of the exhaust system. Photographs confirm nearly all this visual evidence and show large air bubbles breaking surface. Judging by the amount of wreckage and oil, this very good approach and excellent attack were fully rewarded.[18]

U 597 and her entire crew had gone to the bottom.

For Bulloch, this was just the beginning of an exciting period; in the course of the next three weeks his crew sighted four U-boats and attacked two. November 5 was, for Bulloch, another day of triumph, though it followed a day of tragedy for Convoy SC 107, when 15 ships were lost. Bulloch's Liberator now came up in support, and at once forced a U-boat to dive; shortly afterwards he surprised *U 132* on the surface and destroyed her with another deadly attack. He attacked another U-boat later in the day, forcing her to submerge in order to escape. On December 8 he was escorting Convoy HX 217, under attack by two packs totalling 22 U-boats. These had just succeeded in sinking a merchant ship in the half-light of dawn when 120 Squadron's aircraft arrived. Bulloch himself made eight sightings during the next five and a half hours, and carried out seven attacks. The Liberator which relieved him, captained by Squadron-Leader Desmond Isted, sighted five more U-boats and attacked four. The sinking of *U 254* is credited to 120 Squadron on December 8, and the attack on Convoy HX 217 was a clear U-boat failure.

The HX 217 fiasco was attributed by the U-boat captains to "the arrival of air patrols in unusually large numbers".[19] It was an understandable delusion that the sky was full of aircraft; in fact, very small numbers at a time were able to produce very large results. One German Petty Officer prisoner told his captors that British air reconnaissance was particularly dreaded by U-boats. He said that if on the surface you see a plane, the plane has probably seen you and it is already too late: you are done . . .

Survivors of *U 501* complained about the insistent British air reconnaissance which forced them to spend much time submerged . . .

Prisoners of *U 131* stated that while in the Atlantic they were constantly forced to dive to avoid attracting the attention of aircraft patrols.[20]

There was no doubt about the effect of the air attacks – it was perfectly visible in the behaviour of the U-boats; but if any proof were needed, it came in the closing months of 1942, when the air menace had grown to such an extent that Dönitz tried the desperate expedient of ordering his crews to fight it out with aircraft on the surface. To enable them to do so, special gun platforms known as "bandstands" were constructed on the U-boats to carry single or (later) multiple 20-mm cannon, with a maximum rate of fire of 150 rounds per minute, and multiple machine-gun mountings.[21] This bulky armament, which included armoured shields for the gun-crews, cannot have failed to reduce the underwater performance of the boats. It certainly led to the shooting down or serious damaging of a number of aircraft, but the cold-blooded economics of the process were all against the U-boats. Even so large and complex a machine as a Liberator only cost, in those far off days, some £60,000, and carried a crew of 10; a U-boat cost upwards of £200,000 and carried a crew of 50. Coastal Command pressed home its attacks undeterred, and when (May 1943) it claimed six U-boats sunk for the loss of six aircraft the balance-sheet was plainly vastly in its favour. Long before that, however, a significant fact had been pointed out in *Coastal Command Review*,

namely that if a U-boat engages with gun or cannon fire she is obviously not going to dive. If the U-boat is not going to dive there is no longer any need to attack in the shortest possible space of time. The aircraft can break off the attack before getting dangerously close, then fly round the U-boat at about 800 yards range and bring all guns to bear. These tactics usually produce a high mortality rate among the gun-crews on the upper deck, resulting in a sudden decision on the part of the U-boat captain to *zum Teufel gehen*, i.e. "get the hell out of it", leaving the aircraft with a "sitter".[22]

So the tactical pendulum swung in 1942, with advantages first to one side then the other, but the basic message was coming clearly through: that a very strong new factor was now operating in the U-boat war: air power. Shipping losses continued to the end of the year to

435

reach dreadful levels – a total of 1,794,489 tons lost in the last three months. But at last they were being offset to some extent by serious losses to the U-boats. And the last months of the year witnessed another major defeat for Dönitz and his Command: the absolute failure of the U-boats to interfere with Operation TORCH. By November 19, having lost seven boats in 12 days Dönitz was forced to draw off his U-boat packs towards the west, a retreat which confessed the ominous reverse that they had sustained. But far worse than this was in store.

56 ASV III and H2S; Ultra breakthrough

1942, for all the progress that Coastal Command had made, closed with the usual see-saw of defeat and victory. Ironically, the defeat was not at the hands of the Germans, and the victory was not in battle.

For over two years work had been in progress at the Telecommunications Research Establishment on the centimetric radar first developed in the summer of 1940 (see p. 240). Exchange of information with the Massachusetts Institute of Technology in August of that year brought mutual benefits, and in 1941 the work bore fruit in experimental models of two systems based on the same technological principles: a sea version known as ASV III, and a land version called H2S.[1] It may be imagined with what hawk-eyed attention the RAF's Commands watched this progress and how sharply they competed for its benefits. As 1942 drew to an end, the performance of centimetric radar continued to improve; the ASV form proved able to detect convoys at 40 miles and surfaced submarines at 12 miles, with great clarity against the dark background of the sea. The problems were production and priority; the two more closely linked. In early 1942, when the bomber offensive still held the centre of the stage, the decision was taken to equip Bomber Command with centimetric radar, using the klystron valve. This produced much less precise results than the magnetron valve, favoured by Coastal Command, whose targets were small and elusive. Nevertheless, it was considered that the klystron's results

> would be good enough substantially to increase the proportion of bombs falling on built-up areas as opposed to open country, and the decision to develop Klystron H2S for Bomber Command was taken early in 1942.[2]

Flight trials in April, however, proved disappointing, and prospects of obtaining much improvement were seriously reduced in June, when

436

nearly half the scientific team working on H2S was killed in a Halifax crash.[3] Not long afterwards it was decided to use the magnetron valve, with priority still to Bomber Command. A personal appeal by Joubert to Harris in September did not persuade him to forgo his claim. By now, however, the acute peril of the Atlantic battle was well recognized, and when the *Metox* receiver began to prove its worth as a protector of U-boats against Coastal Command, the decision was reviewed again. The Air Staff decreed that forty H2S sets should be converted to ASV III, and the Americans agreed to install their equivalent apparatus (SCR 517) in all Liberators for Coastal Command.

None of this, however, could begin to take effect until February; and meanwhile there was another consideration, involving very fierce argument indeed. This centred around the question of which Command should have first use, Bomber or Coastal. If it was Bomber Command, then the absolute certainty had to be faced that sooner or later – and sooner *rather* than later – an aircraft carrying the highly secret new equipment would be brought down over enemy-held territory; if it was Coastal Command this would be most unlikely to happen, since the only aircraft so equipped would be operating over the Bay of Biscay or the Atlantic. The dilemma was very clearly stated in a paper sent on January 23 by Professor R. V. Jones (then head of the Scientific Intelligence Unit in the Air Ministry) to the Acting Vice Chief of the Air Staff, Air Vice-Marshal C. E. H. Medhurst:

> We may expect many months' life from 10 cms ASV, providing that we do not give the Germans a clue to the wavelength. The capture of H2S will not only do this, but also show them a satisfactory receiver design . . . The fact is obvious that should we try H2S first, and should it prove relatively unsuccessful, 10 cms ASV will have a spoilt chance, and we shall have lost every thing. Should we, however, reverse the order, we could test whether or not 10 cms ASV is an important factor in countering the mortal threat of the U-boats, and still be in a position to use H2S later, should we choose. The latter finessing course therefore appears correct, unless there is some overwhelming operational factor in favour of a precipitate use of H2S, or of any other application of 10 cms which is likely to fall into the hands of the enemy.[4]

This was one scientific opinion; others took the contrary view. Sir Robert Watson-Watt, the radar pioneer (see p. 22) discussed in a long paper the likely effect on the war at sea if the Germans captured H2S. There was, he considered

> a strong possibility that the Germans already knew about the new radar; if this was the case, the capture of an example of H2S would make little

difference to the U-boat war. If, on the other hand, the Germans knew nothing about this type of radar they could, in Watson-Watt's opinion, design and manufacture a simple receiver for submarines "within a period of two or three months at the most" of the discovery of the existence of an Allied centimetric-wavelength radar.[5]

The conclusion was that the bombers should use H2S as soon as possible, and this view was strenuously supported by Lord Cherwell; with this backing, Churchill ruled on December 22 that Bomber Command could use the new aid from the beginning of 1943 – with ASV III still not operational. This was Coastal Command's defeat.

As it turned out, both the eminent scientists quoted above proved to be wrong – though Professor Jones was right in principle. The feared misfortune was not long delayed: a Stirling fitted with H2S was shot down near Rotterdam on February 2.[6] The battered radar equipment was retrieved and its secret in due course revealed. Work began at once on counter-measures, and as time went by it became apparent that Sir Robert Watson-Watt was far astray in his belief that the Germans could solve their problems in "two or three months at the most". Professor Jones's caution was justified, but fortunately his prediction that "we shall have lost everything" was not borne out. The reason for this was, quite simply, that when the German scientists examined their treasure trove, they were astounded; their consternation is reflected in Goering's comment on the report which they submitted to him:

> I expected the British and Americans to be advanced, but frankly I never thought that they would get so far ahead. I did hope that even if we were behind, we could at least be in the same race.[7]

In the event, thanks entirely to the unforeseeable (and unforeseen) German backwardness in the field of centimetric radar, Coastal Command enjoyed some eight months[8] – considerably more than anyone dared hope – of operational immunity before the Germans produced an effective answer to ASV III: the *Naxos-U* receiver.

The consequences of Joubert's defeat were thus happily mitigated; the victory in the U-boat war at the turn of the year took longer to make itself felt, but it, too, began in December. The scene was Bletchley Park, where the GC & CS was locked in its struggle against the fourth wheel of the Enigma machine. After 10 months during which the only certainty was the enemy's ability to inflict terrible losses, the Admiralty was growing understandably restive; Rear-Admiral Clayton, the head of its Operational Intelligence Centre, remarked in November that the U-boat war was

> the one campaign which Bletchley Park are not at present influencing to any marked extent – and it is the only one in which the war can be lost unless B.P. *do* help. I do not think that this is any exaggeration.[9]

Less than a month later the GC & CS reported that it had broken the four-wheel key.

The significance of this victory was obviously very great – indeed, so great that some historians have seen in it virtually the whole explanation of the victory over the U-boats themselves which soon followed. The Admiralty, at the time, was deeply relieved at the breakthrough; it attached enormous importance to the decrypts of German signals – and not without reason:

> The great bulk of them consisted of immediate operational intelligence about the departure and return of U-boats, the numbers and types of U-boats at sea, the movements and dispositions of their patrol groups and their operational orders.[10] That the operational decrypts were so numerous and informative was a consequence of the U-boat Command's control of the north Atlantic offensive, a control which was even more rigorous now than in 1941. Not only did returning U-boats always signal their expected time of arrival; every outward-bound U-boat reported on clearing Biscay or, if leaving from Norway or the Baltic, after crossing 60°N ... No U-boat could deviate from its orders without requesting and receiving permission, and without requesting and receiving permission none could begin its return passage ... The control of the U-boat Command over the U-boats while they were searching for and attacking convoys was no less complete. It ordered the formation and re-formation of the patrol lines between specified geographical positions at regular intervals, addressing by name each U-boat commander who was to take a place in a line and giving him his exact position in it.[11]

This was the fatal weakness of the "Dönitz system" referred to above (pp. 236 and 238); the day had come at last when British Naval Intelligence "was able to read the U-boat ciphers as *B-Dienst* read the BAMS code". It was natural enough, both at the time and later, that this would seem to be the decisive factor in what followed. In fact, however, as one might suppose, the breakthrough was only a stage in a lengthy process. To arrive at a point where the vast mass of signal traffic involved could be read sufficiently fast for the decrypts

439

to be of operational value required a further effort, and in the event it was not until August that complete mastery was achieved, "from which time till the end of the war all the traffic for each day was read as a matter of course with little or no delay".[12] But by then the battle had been won. And for that there was no single reason but, as usual, a whole complex.

57 The last convoy battles; new weapons; Atlantic victory

Joubert departed in February, severing the links with Coastal Command forged by two tenures as AOC-in-C. He had presided over the worst of the dark night of the U-boat war – it still had a little while to run – and he had seen the turn in the Command's fortunes. It now had lethal weapons, and it knew how to use them; there were more to come – ASV III was almost ready, rockets were not far off, and the six-pdr anti-tank gun (57-mm) and other devices would follow. The foundation was firmly laid. The Command had also increased in numbers, after a fall in June 1942; it now had 43½ fighting squadrons fully operational, in addition to Photographic Reconnaissance, Meteorological and Air Sea Rescue and six squadrons forming, re-equipping or training – a total equivalent of 59½ squadrons with a strength of 839 aircraft and a daily availability of 469.[1] The weakness was still in VLR aircraft – only two Liberator squadrons, with some 14 aircraft available; the struggle to obtain more would be a preoccupation for Joubert's successor. Meanwhile he enjoyed the benefit of one of Joubert's most valuable contributions – "Planned Flying and Maintenance", described in *Coastal Command Review* as "the rationalization of war flying".[2] Instituted in August 1942, this meant the careful anticipation of operational needs so that maintenance could be carried out in the most economic and profitable manner (the *Review* pointed out that it was standard peace-time procedure in American civil airlines); the effect was to compensate some part of the weakness in numbers by increased use of resources that did exist. It was a legacy of continuing worth.

Slessor, generally considered a rising star of the RAF, took over on February 5, 1943. An "exceptionally violent" winter was at its peak, "the ice coming down almost as far as Newfoundland and hurricanes and severe gales prevailing throughout the north Atlantic".[3] The effect of this vile weather was largely protective: U-boats found extreme difficulty in sighting even convoys, let alone single ships; merchantmen were saved from attack by fog and thick veils of sleet. The total sinkings in January were thus reduced to 261,359 tons (50 ships), of which U-boats claimed 203,128 (37 ships). On the other hand, air operations were much hampered, with aircraft if not grounded virtually blinded; only six U-boats were sunk in the whole month, of which only two in the North Atlantic, one by unknown causes, one credited to No. 206 Squadron. Both counts showed a rise in February: 403,062 tons lost, with U-boats responsible for 359,328 (63 ships out of 73); the U-boats themselves lost 19, nine to air action, of which Coastal Command claimed seven.

Slessor came fresh to his new command from the Casablanca Conference (see p. 394), where the final report of the Combined Chiefs of Staff had roundly declared:

> The defeat of the U-boat must remain a first charge on the resources of the United Nations.[4]

The problem was to give effect to this impeccable sentiment. Belatedly – but, as we have seen, largely ineffectually – Bomber Command was now attacking the U-boat Biscay bases, hurling down a huge weight of bombs on to the 16-foot thick reinforced concrete roofs of the pens, where "they made no more than a slight indentation in the surface."[5] With more enthusiasm, pursuant to a Directive of January 21, Air Chief Marshal Harris sent his bombers to the construction yards in Germany with a view to choking the U-boat stream at its very point of origin. Neither form of attack, unfortunately, produced any worthwhile result; between January and March

> A total of 3,056 bomber sorties dropped 4,178 tons of high explosive on the main U-boat bases, losing 67 aircraft in the process; 1,825 sorties (2,848 tons dropped) against the U-boat yards cost 74 aircraft. Not a single U-boat was even damaged by any of these raids . . .[6]

However, Bomber Command was doing its best; the same could not be said of all parties to the Casablanca agreement. Joubert had been increasingly conscious, all through 1942, of the need for an Allied unified Atlantic command to match the advantage of Dönitz's single control. The obstacle, Joubert soon discovered, was the United States Navy, under its formidable Commander-in-Chief of the Fleet and the Chief of Naval Operations, Admiral Ernest King. King believed firmly that, for the United States, the Pacific was the theatre that mattered. The Pacific was, of course, pre-eminently a naval theatre of war, and there is no questioning the courage, the determination and the high degree of skill that the United States Navy and its admirals brought to the prosecution of that campaign with King's warm support and blessing. But as Slessor says,

> I'm afraid there is no disguising the fact that King's obsession with the Pacific and the Battle of Washington cost us dear in the Battle of the Atlantic.[7]

An Allied Atlantic Convoys Conference in March went some distance towards the unification of the Anglo-American effort. The system of convoy cover was reorganized, and, most important of all, VLR squadrons of the RCAF and the USAAF were established in Newfoundland. The US Navy even agreed to allocate escort carriers to the convoys, and these were shortly doing sterling work. At last the dreaded "Atlantic Gap" could be closed; at last there could be air cover for the convoys all the way. These were vital matters indeed, but in the other vital matter of unified command there was no progress. Slessor was as firmly persuaded as Joubert of the desirability of it; but, no doubt schooled by personal contact with Admiral King, he was shrewdly sceptical of its practicability. He knew that he was himself, in his capacity as AOC-in-C of Coastal Command,[8] a candidate for such a post as Ocean Air Commander, and that he would have American backers; but, as he told Portal, it would be meaningless without executive authority,

> which involved moving squadrons from A to B. I did not see King agreeing, for instance, to my coming to the conclusion on operational statistics that a US Naval squadron was not pulling its weight in the Caribbean and should be moved to Iceland. I think that's where it would break down . . .[9]

The fate of two somewhat lesser solutions showed how right he was: proposals for a joint system of operational intelligence and signals put forward by a Combined Procedure Board, were on the point of adoption when the US Navy Department closed the matter with a veto. An Allied Anti-Submarine Board made a number of proposals for better general cooperation; they remained stillborn. As Hilary Saunders says:

> it [is] difficult to escape the conclusion that Admiral King and his staff did not view the Battle of the Atlantic in the same light as General Marshall viewed the invasion of Europe in 1944.[10]

It was, then, with very mixed auspices that the fearful month of March came in – "like a lion" indeed, with "great storms sweeping across the Atlantic from west to east".[11] At the beginning of the month Dönitz (now Grand Admiral and Commander-in-Chief of the German Navy, but still personally controlling the U-boats) had 50 operating in the North Atlantic. They were formed into three packs and, thanks to *B-Dienst*, he was able to place them with precision. For the central drama of the month, the battle fought around convoys SC 122 and HX 229, *B-Dienst* supplied no fewer than 16 decrypts of "signals giving advance information of the movements of both convoys".[12] As a result, Dönitz was able to assemble 40 U-boats for the assault, which began on March 16. Even with such numbers and such good intelligence, the appalling weather almost defeated him; it was only when *U 653*, on its way home with engine trouble, found itself unexpectedly in the midst of HX 229 that the packs made contact. At the same time other U-boats, looking for HX 229, found SC 122. By the morning of March 17 twelve ships had been hit or sunk and the whole U-boat concentration was closing in. There can be little doubt, says Alfred Price,

> that such a force would have swamped the defences and caused great execution had not the "US Cavalry", in the form of No. 120 Squadron's Liberators, arrived in a nick of time.[13]

Three Liberators reached the area of SC 122; they sighted 11 U-boats and attacked six, largely as a consequence of which only one ship was lost that day. But not having Leigh Lights, the Liberators withdrew when darkness fell, and the convoy then lost two more ships; HX 229, without air protection, also lost two on the 17th. The next day, 120 Squadron was back with five aircraft over and around SC 122; they sighted seven U-boats and attacked five; the convoy suffered no loss that day. Less well protected, HX 229 lost two more ships. During the night of the 18th/19th HX 229, being the faster convoy,

> had closed up so rapidly that the two convoys made a very large collection of ships within a relatively small space, and in the meantime the escort had increased to a total of eighteen vesels.[14]

Better still, the Liberators were now joined by shorter-ranged aircraft: seven Fortresses and three Sunderlands gave cover to the convoys in addition to six Liberators. Two ships were sunk, but it was on this day that the U-boats suffered their first loss: *U 384* destroyed

443

(by a Sunderland of 201 Squadron) and *U 338* badly damaged. The next day, recognizing that prospects were now deteriorating, Dönitz called off his packs; as they withdrew *U 441* and *U 631* were bombed and damaged so badly that they had to return to base. So ended "the biggest and, from the standpoint of the U-boats, the most successful of all the convoy battles".[15] Twenty-one ships from the two convoys had been sunk; it was "the biggest convoy disaster of the war".[16] In the words of Captain Roskill, the naval Official Historian,

> the Germans never came so near to disrupting communications between the New World and the Old.[17]

March 1943 was a terrible month; conditions at sea were appalling, constant storms with heavy following seas were a major hazard in themselves: in HX 229 and SC 122, in addition to the 21 ships lost to U-boats, 10 more either foundered in the gales or had to put back to port and an escort anti-submarine trawler capsized. The U-boats themselves had difficulty in remaining afloat on the surface; in the hurricane on March 28 *U 260* reported five tons of water cascading through the conning tower hatch, voice pipe and diesel air intake. In all, during the month, 693,389 tons of Allied and neutral shipping were lost: 120 ships. This total was well up to the high level of 1942, and over 90 per cent of it (627,377 tons, 108 ships) was due to U-boats. U-boat losses dropped from 19 in February to 15, of which only 10 were sunk in the North Atlantic or the Bay of Biscay. Of the 15 sunk, nine were attributable entirely to aircraft, two in the Mediterranean, the rest to Coastal Command – a crumb of comfort. But the most menacing breakdown of statistics was that which showed that in the first 20 days of the month, out of 85 ships sunk by U-boats in all areas, 67 were lost while in protected convoys.[18] In the whole month, in the North Atlantic, 32 ships were lost while actually in convoy, and 10 more stragglers. In the attacks on these convoys only five U-boats were sunk. Dönitz's pack system seemed to have triumphed at last, and with the number of operational U-boats coming to its peak,[19] a dreadful thought occurred:

> It might be necessary to abandon the convoy system altogether, though in three and a half years of war it had been the backbone of Allied strategy in the Atlantic.[20]

As Captain Roskill pertinently asks:

> Where could the Admiralty turn if the convoy system had lost its effectiveness?[21]

The dark night was never darker than just before the dawn.

The Battle of the Atlantic between December 1942 and May 1943, says the Official History, "was the most prolonged and complex battle in the history of naval warfare."[22] The month of March well illustrates this complexity. The "surface" of the battle displays the U-boats at their most brilliantly successful; the deep tides were running all against them. Admittedly, Bomber Command's offensive against the Biscay bases and the construction yards was recognized to be a failure, and called off in April. On the other hand, the Atlantic Convoy Conference was taking the vital decision on VLR aircraft which soon became effective. By mid-April 41 were available, and by May there were 70; they played, in Dr Rohwer's words, "a leading rôle" during these weeks. It was at the end of March, too, that the first escort-carriers began to accompany the convoys, and the combination of these two elements (with the backing of ASV III) wrought a transformation in the air performance. In the naval escorts a somewhat similar effect was produced by the "Huff-Duff" (HF/DF; high frequency radio direction-finding) equipment which now became standard.[23] This, also, profited from the spate of signals required for the working of the "Dönitz system"; during one convoy action in early 1943, for example, over a hundred transmissions from U-boats in their area were noted by Allied escorts in a period of seventy-two hours. "Fixes" from these enabled ships or aircraft to pinpoint the U-boat, possibly sink it, at the very least to make it dive. At the same time, in March, Admiral Sir Max Horton, the new C-in-C of Western Approaches,[24] formed the first five of the Support Groups whose value had been established experimentally as far back as June 1941 (see p. 409). It was the abandonment of the Murmansk convoys during the summer that at last made destroyers available for this work; in addition, No. 4 Group contained the carrier *Archer*, and No. 5 Group the carrier *Biter*. When the US Navy supplied a sixth group, it brought with it the US carrier *Bogue*, which on March 26 was mistaken by the captain of *U 663* for a vessel "of the *Illustrious* class". The Support Groups, British and American, became an important element in the battle, working close to the convoys and in close conjunction with the RAF.

In weaponry, too, there were new movements afoot. At the end of 1942, Coastal Command Headquarters had recognized that, despite its much improved performance, the sad fact remained that only six per cent of depth-charge attacks proved lethal. Was this the fault of the weapon, or the aim? An exhaustive enquiry supported the weapon – the 250-lb Torpex charge – but intensive practice in marksmanship only improved the performance to seven per cent. The Naval

Staff (Peyton-Ward) and the Operational Research Section, then analysed some 300 attacks from every aspect, and came up with a report by which

> it was clearly shown that a universal stick spacing of 100 feet (in place of the existing 36 feet for large aircraft and 60 feet for Hudsons) was the optimum both for outright kills and infliction of damage. The spacing was therefore standardized at 100 feet from 14 March . . .[25]

The order was not popular at first with pilots and bomb-aimers, because it seemed to be a reflection on their efficiency, and an article in the March issue of *Coastal Command Review* carefully explained the reason for it, referring to an analysis of 43 36-foot spacing attacks for which there was photographic evidence taken at the time, and concluding:

> There is, therefore, absolutely no doubt that the 100-ft spacing is better than the 36-ft.[26]

But the proof was in the killing: in 83 attacks in May, using the 100-foot spacing, 14 U-boats were sunk and 13 damaged.

It was at this time, too, that Coastal Command received first deliveries of what was known for security reasons as the "Mark 24 Mine". This was, in fact, an air-launched torpedo with an acoustic homing head, developed in the United States – a handsome repayment on account for centimetric radar. By May, the Liberators of No. 120 Squadron and its sister, No. 86, were carrying this weapon, and it made its first kill on May 12. This evened the technological score, coming immediately upon the introduction by the Germans of their FAT (*Flächenabsuchender* torpedo), the "zigzag runner", liable to come in from all angles, and their new magnetic torpedo pistol. At this stage in the war science was excelling itself, its horrific wonders to perform.

And then there was Ultra. It was not until June that sufficient evidence accumulated from this source to persuade the Admiralty that its Atlantic cipher was compromised and to replace it at last – in the fourth summer of the war – by one that was secure. Not could Ultra yet supply operational intelligence with all the necessary immediacy. But amidst the general knowledge of the U-boat effort which it was now once more helping to build up were some very significant indications indeed. As early as February it had been noted that

Inexperienced U-boat commanders – a growing band – had . . . occasionally reported torpedo failures, made unsubstantiated claims and betrayed signs of timidity, particularly fear of air attack, and there had also been a noticeable increase in the occasions on which U-boats developed incapacitating defects during their outward passage of the Bay of Biscay.[27]

These signs of a crack in morale – ominous for the U-boat Command, but a bright gleam of hope for the Allies – were repeated even in March, the month of triumph, and still more distinctly in April. On the 4th of that month the *Löwenherz* pack of 14 U-boats sighted convoy HX 231; in the battle that followed it sank six ships, and lost two boats, *U 632* and *U 635*. Ultra recorded the Command's dissatisfaction with this result, and its reprimand to the U-boat captains for excessive use of wireless. On April 11 the *Lerche* pack sighted convoy HX 232 and sank three ships, all on the first night; after that there were no further losses, and the Command was heard voicing the suspicion that the U-boats were not pressing home their attacks. It called on them to display "the healthy warrior and hunter instincts". What it found particularly disturbing was that the U-boat reports

> contained increasingly frequent references to their fear of air attack and to the efficiency of the Allied surface escorts in following up aircraft sightings . . . By 19 April it was conceding that the U-boats could not effectively use pack tactics against convoys which had air support.[28]

So the tables were turned, and it was on this day that the Admiralty's Operational Intelligence Centre felt justified in drawing attention to an "incipient decline in U-boat morale". The action against convoys HX 234, ONS 3 and ON 178 on April 20–24 did nothing to improve it: only four ships were sunk – at a cost of three U-boats, with the Liberators of 120 Squadron once more prominent, sinking *U 189*. The month's final statistics reflected the abrupt change in the fortunes of the war at sea: the total tonnage lost was less than half the previous month's figure (344,680; 64 ships), and if U-boats were now responsible for 95 per cent of this, their own score was also virtually halved (327,943 tons; 56 ships). Their losses, on the other hand, equalled those of March: 15 boats, of which aircraft claimed eight, six of them falling to Coastal Command.

The "crunch" came in May, and it came quickly. The number of operational U-boats now reached its peak (see Note 19) and the number in the North Atlantic did likewise: a total of 60 boats. The weather – another hurricane, with snow squalls and enormous

447

seas – remained vile, hampering the U-boats, but causing even more difficulty for the convoys and their escorts. It was impossible to refuel the destroyers at sea; as their tanks emptied, all but two of those protecting ONS 5 were compelled to return to port. The stage was thus set for the last notable performance by the U-boats in a convoy battle: 13 ships sunk between May 1–5. But the cost was no fewer than six U-boats sunk and four badly damaged. This was considered to be "a very painful defeat"[29] – and there was worse to come.

Conditions dictated that in the ONS 5 battle all but one of the U-boat kills were carried out by surface vessels of the Royal Navy (an RCAF flying-boat accounted for the sixth). Thereafter it was a very different story: aircraft, land- or carrier-based, accounted for over two-thirds of the U-boats lost. In the battle of HX 237 and SC 129 (May 9–14), with Bletchley Park and *B-Dienst* bidding fiercely for advantages, 36 U-boats sank only five ships – for a loss of five of their own number. It was in this battle that the homing torpedo made its début; three Liberators of No. 86 Squadron were in action on May 12, each carrying two of these weapons in addition to their normal depth-charge load. The question was when and how to use them:

> Due to the homing torpedo's vulnerability to enemy counter-measures, there were rigid rules limiting its use in action: since it might conceivably run ashore and be captured, its use was forbidden close to enemy-held shores; it was, moreover, not to be used if its method of operation could possibly be observed from the target or any other enemy craft in the vicinity.[30]

As Flight Lieutenant J. Wright's aircraft approached *U 456* she dived, offering a perfect opportunity; he released his torpedo and circled to see what happened. For two minutes the answer was – nothing; then a small upheaval (as of a weak depth-charge) was seen about 900 yards from the U-boat's diving point. Soon afterwards, however, the crippled *U 456* (*Kapitänleutnant* Teichert) reappeared on the surface and defiantly engaged the Liberator with AA fire when it came in to make a second attack with depth-charges. Then Wright had to break off the action (his aircraft having reached the limit of its endurance) and the U-boat lay wallowing on the surface. From Teichert's report Dönitz concluded that she had been hit by "an aerial bomb". Early next morning a Sunderland of No. 423 Squadron, RCAF, found her again and forced her to dive, and shortly afterwards convoy escorts of the Royal Canadian Navy finished her off. Two days after Wright's attack, No. 86 Squadron by its unaided efforts destroyed *U 266* with another homing torpedo, and a Catalina of USN Patrol Squadron No. 84 disposed of *U 657* in the same way.

It was not the loss of U-boats, and it was not the homing torpedoes which caused the High Command to complain: "We can see no explanation for this failure."[31] What concerned Dönitz and his staff was the inability to sink more merchant ships, and the implication of a further decline in morale. The next two battles – "the last such battles of the whole war"[32] – were decisive; both were serious defeats for the U-boats, the first not merely a defeat but a disaster. This was the attack, by 33 boats, on convoy SC 130, May 17–19. Six U-boats were sunk and not one ship was lost from the convoy; four of the kills were the work of Coastal Command – two sunk by the Hudsons of 269 Squadron, two by the indefatigable No. 120. This fiasco was attributed by the U-boat Command to "inexperienced captains", a factor which certainly cannot be disregarded. But an intercept on May 21 reveals their fundamental diagnosis:

> If there is anyone who thinks that combating convoys is no longer possible, he is a weakling and no true U-boat captain. The battle of the Atlantic is getting harder but it is the determining element in the waging of the war . . .[33]

It was an amazing message, read with deep relief and satisfaction in the naval section at Bletchley and the Submarine Tracking Room. The battle next day – if it can be called a battle – against convoys ON 184 and HX 239 only confirmed it. On the 22nd a US naval aircraft sank *U 569*, and on the 23rd *U 752* was sunk by the Fleet Air Arm. No ship was lost in either convoy. On May 24 Dönitz, noting 31 U-boats lost already, wrote in his War Diary:

> Losses, even heavy losses, must be accepted if they are accompanied by proportional success in tonnage sunk. But in May one U-boat was lost for every 10,000 GRT [gross registered tons] sunk, where not so long ago one U-boat was lost for 100,000 GRT sunk. Thus our losses so far in May have reached an intolerable level.
> The enemy air force played a decisive rôle in inflicting these high losses.[34]

On that day, May 24, a notable date in history, Grand Admiral Dönitz called off the North Atlantic convoy battle.

It was done. The long martyrdom, the deadly peril were overcome. The Germans admitted:

The decision in the Battle of the Atlantic had gone to the enemy.[35]

The convoy battles alone in this astonishing month of May had cost the Germans 20 U-boats, eight sunk by surface vessels, three shared between surface and aircraft, nine sunk by aircraft alone, of which eight were due to Coastal Command. The full total of U-boats lost in that month was 41; of these, aircraft claimed 23 (56 per cent), and of those sunk by aircraft Coastal Command claimed 16 (69.5 per cent). Shipping losses during the month dropped to 299,428 tons (58 ships) of which U-boats still claimed the lion's share: 264,852 tons (50 ships). But this total would never be repeated and only once would it be even closely matched.[36]

The suddenness of the collapse lends it particular drama, but in fact, as Ronald Lewin says, to those who interpreted the Ultra decrypts,

who lived with them from hour to hour and day to day it was ... no surprise when Dönitz accepted defeat – indeed Winn[37] had predicted that a collapse would occur, and that it would be sudden. The conjunction, at last, of good Ultra, skilled escort groups with sophisticated equipment, aircraft carriers and Very Long Range Aircraft all working with the harmony of experience was put simply – too much for a U-boat fleet most of whose best men were dead.[38]

The U-boat war, of course, was not over; there could be no relaxation against enemies of such determination, no stand-down for the naval section at Bletchley, the Submarine Tracking Room, the escorts or for Coastal Command. But this was a turning-point of the war, far more significant than the battles of El Alamein, far more decisive than anything else that was happening at that time. It meant that Britain would not starve; British industry would not wither for lack of raw materials; Bomber Command's offensive would not halt for want of oil; armoured forces could be built up with the certainty of useful action; BOLERO would go on; OVERLORD would happen. It is hard to focus upon a battle fought for three years in an ocean over 3,000 miles wide in the same way as one can on one fought on an identifiable area of land for a matter of days or weeks. Yet of all the battles of the Second World War, it is impossible to think of one more momentous than the Atlantic victory.

There was, at the time, among those who knew the facts, an understandable sense of elation. At Western Approaches Command and at Northwood, relief and pride were well mingled. Slessor took pleasure in passing on, in *Coastal Command Review*, a message from Portal on June 1, in which he said:

> I wish to express to you and all under your command my admiration and warmest thanks for your achievements in the anti-U-Boat war during the month just ended. The brilliant success achieved in this vital field is the well deserved result of tireless perseverance and devotion to duty and is, I am sure, a welcome reward for the aircrews and others who have spared no effort during long months of arduous operations and training. Now that you have obtained this remarkable advantage over the U-Boats I know you will press it home with ever-increasing vigour and determination until, in conjunction with the Royal Navy, you have finally broken the enemy's morale.

It is a warm and perceptive message; one can only be sorry that Joubert, who had done so much to make all this possible, was not one of its recipients.

Slessor himself told his crews: "It is difficult to over-estimate the importance in Allied strategy of these results . . ."

He pointed out that Dr Goebbels had been promising the Germans a victory at sea, and he asked:

> what will happen when the Nazis at last hoist in the fact that their last hope of avoiding decisive defeat has disappeared largely through the efforts of Coastal Command?[39]

And yet it is difficult to escape the thought that Slessor himself had not properly "hoisted in" the nature of the victory that his Command had won. He went on to say:

> Many of us in Coastal no doubt sometimes envy our friends in Bomber and Mediterranean Air Commands their share in the shattering offensive which has been such a heartening feature of last month's news. But if we can keep up this rate of killing against the U-boats, or anything near it, we are doing as much as anyone to hasten the collapse of the Axis. If we could really kill the U-boat menace once and for all *many of us could be spared to take part in the more direct offensive against objectives on German and Italian soil.*

451

The italics are mine; Slessor, for all his shrewdness, was (like so many of his generation) a thoroughly indoctrinated believer in bombing, and also thoroughly imbued with dread of great land battles on the scale of the First World War (see p. 62). BOLERO, ROUNDUP and OVERLORD were names which he regarded with suspicion and some trepidation; Harris's mounting offensive, on the other hand, was "true air warfare". For these reasons, he under-rated his own victory – or rather, the victory that Joubert (and others) had prepared for him. Even at the end of the year, telling his Command that "1943 will have many claims on history", he continued:

> For us this has been primarily a defensive victory. The main object of the operations against the U-boat was to prevent us losing the war . . .[40]

This blinkered view has persisted down the years, even finding support in Official History; thus Hilary St George Saunders in Volume iii of *Royal Air Force 1939–45* (p. 62), published in 1954 and reissued in 1975, informs us:

> Coastal Command was essentially a defensive organization and should therefore draw as little as possible on limited resources which should be devoted to the offensive.

Such is the power of dogma. Let us spell it out just once more:

> Operation OVERLORD was the supreme offensive action of the Western Allies in the war.
> It could not have taken place without the Atlantic victory to which Coastal Command made such a magnificent contribution.

58 "Per Ardua"

The victory so handsomely won had to stay won. Against such an enemy as Germany, only actual surrender could guarantee this, and surrender was still some two years away. When it arrived, it revealed how frighteningly close the battle had come to being lost again. But at the end of 1943 there was every reason for the Allies to feel pleased with themselves and their performance; it had been a record year for destruction of U-boats – 219, of which Coastal Command (and forces under its direct control) accounted for no fewer than 84.[1] The crow was fighting the mole to some effect.

In 1944 the statistics of the war at sea show how well the work was kept up: a grand total of 1,045,629 tons of shipping sunk – a mere 13.4 per cent of the terrible total of 1942. Significantly, sinkings by U-boats fell to 773,327 tons (132 ships out of 205), and more significantly still, in the whole year sinkings by U-boats in the North Atlantic amounted to no more than 175,913 tons (31 ships).[2] It was during this period, without doubt, that Ultra proved itself; from August 1943 onwards, the ability to read the U-boat signal traffic currently made possible interception of returning boats by aircraft and naval offensive groups, just when they believed themselves to be relatively safe. Ultra also permitted the destruction of the U-tankers (the "Milchcows") with equal precision. It is remarkable indeed that in all this time *B-Dienst*, for all its brilliance, never diagnosed the fault. One reason must certainly be what has been called "trained incapacity":

Their minds had been dragooned and regimented into the belief that Enigma was totally secure: therefore they were incapable of assessing objectively any indications that it had become insecure.[3]

As Donald McLachlan succinctly puts it:

It is always difficult for experts to prove themselves wrong.[4]

But Professor R. V. Jones reminds us that the blindness of *B-Dienst* was much increased by certain deception ploys practised against it;[5] not least of these was the standard procedure of covering every Ultra-guided attack by ostentatious use of air patrols, so that a good reason for the ambush would readily suggest itself. Feints and decoys can be wearisome (and dangerous) work for those who have to carry them out; not least of Coastal Command's contributions was the long haul of tiring and apparently unrewarded (certainly unexplained) hours of flying simply to register a presence. Theirs was that kind of war.

The technological see-saw continued almost to the end; new weapons and new tactics made constant appearances. On the Allied side it is worth noting the advent of three-centimetre radar (Spring 1944) and sonobuoys; the combination of these with homing torpedoes proved fatal to over-confident U-boats. But it was the Germans who made the real breakthrough in submarine warfare – as one might expect. All submarines launched during the two world wars were, in truth, incorrectly named; their true designation was "submersibles". The true submarine, with unlimited underwater endurance[6] and underwater speeds equivalent to those of surface ships, did not appear until the atomic-powered craft of the 1950s. But it was in 1943 and 1944 that large strides were made towards this kind of vessel.

The need for a new type of boat, with much increased performance under water, and much reduced surface time or none at all, probably requiring a new system of propulsion, was recognized. The eminent German scientist and maritime engineer, Dr Hellmuth Walter, was working on such a vessel, but progress was slow; as a stop-gap, to enable existing U-boats to remain submerged for longer periods,[7] a pre-war Dutch device was introduced: the *Schnorkel*. This was an air pipe which could be extended above the surface when the U-boat was at periscope depth; it meant that "the air inside the boat could be kept fresh even though the rest of the craft was submerged; more important, a submarine could run virtually submerged on the diesel engines indefinitely, without the need to expend precious current from the batteries."[8] It had disadvantages: it limited the U-boat's speed to six knots; it caused much discomfort to the crew in rough weather; it could still be detected, both by the eye and by radar, but obviously with much more difficulty than a fully surfaced boat or even a conning tower.

> For all its limitations, however, the *schnorkel* was a large step in the right direction so far as the German Navy was concerned.[9]

A trial installation was tested in the summer and autumn of 1943, and by mid-1944 some 30 U-boats had been fitted with the device;[10] thereafter it became standard equipment and a great nuisance to the anti-submarine forces.

The real stride into the future, however, began at the same time as the adoption of the *Schnorkel*: a specification was finalized for a new kind of boat altogether, designated the Type XXI. This would have three times the battery capacity of a normal boat; its maximum underwater speed would be 18 knots (maintained for one and a half hours); it would be able to maintain 12–14 knots for 10 hours, or cruise at six knots for 48 hours – which meant a range of nearly 300 miles completely submerged. It would have to be a large boat – 1,500 tons, as compared with the 770 tons of the Type VII. The Navy placed orders for 290 Type XXI U-boats, expecting delivery of the whole number by February 1945. To expedite this programme, it was decided to pre-fabricate the boats in sections constructed in factories all over Germany; the completed sections were then to be moved to final assembly yards in Hamburg, Danzig and Bremen by canal – the only means by which such huge loads could be transported. Warned by Bomber Command's devastating attacks on the port of Hamburg in July and August (when heavy damage was caused to the Blohm *und* Voss U-boat construction yards) Otto Merker, head of the ship-building office, ordered the construction of a bombproof assembly factory at Bremen. The Germans were by now "artists at ferro-concrete";[11] the Todt Organization began work on an assembly bunker, code-named *Valentin,*

with walls 10 to 15 feet thick, measuring 1,350 feet long and 320 feet wide, covering an area about twice that of the Houses of Parliament in London, with an inside headroom of 60 feet, the whole covered by a roof of reinforced concrete 22 feet thick; to enable the XXI boats to test their *schnorkel* equipment while inside the bunker, the water level at the outer end was to be dredged to 60 feet.[12]

This massive structure was an even less promising target for bombers than the pens on the Biscay coast. However, there remained the canals, in particular the Dortmund-Ems, linking the Ruhr to the Ems River. On the night of September 23, 1944, Bomber Command (617 Squadron) attacked the aqueduct carrying this canal near Münster, wrecking it and causing a six-mile stretch to drain and bringing all traffic to a halt. When it was repaired in November, Bomber Command wrecked it again, and repeated the process twice more by the New Year. The Mittellands Canal, linking the Ems with Berlin, was similarly treated. The delivery programme of Type XXI U-boats naturally suffered, but it is yet another aspect of Germany's amazing resilience (to which we shall return) that, even so, 90 Type XXI boats had been launched, of which 60 were in service, by the end of December. In addition, 31 of the smaller Type XXIII had been launched, and 23 were in service. Fortunately, none were operational. In the event, six Type XXIII boats became operational in February 1945, and they sank six ships without loss to themselves. The first operational Type XXI boat put to sea on April 30; it succeeded in evading a Royal Navy submarine hunting group without difficulty, but before it could launch a torpedo in anger the signal came from Grand Admiral Dönitz announcing Germany's surrender, and ordering the U-boats to give themselves up in designated ports.

The end arrived none too soon in the maritime war:

after the war, trials established that even with the finest equipment available in 1945, against a *schnorkel* an aircraft radar search was on average only about 6 per cent efficient – that is to say, for every six *schnorkel* heads detected, a further *ninety-four* had come within radar range but had passed unnoticed in the general sea clutter ... Thus by 1945 the wheel had turned full circle: having evolved from a blunt and ineffectual weapon into a deadly killer of submarines, at the end of the war the anti-submarine aircraft was – for want of an adequate method of long-range detection of submerged boats – almost back where it had started. The fast *schnorkel* submarine had emerged from the Second World War technically, if not militarily, triumphant.[13]

What might have been, however alarming, in no way diminishes the quality of what was. Coastal Command's achievement stands for all time: starting with just two kills in 1941, by the end of the war its own unaided efforts had accounted for 169 German U-boats out of 326 destroyed by shore-based aircraft alone. Expressing it somewhat differently, shore-based aircraft had accounted for 41.5 per cent of all kills,[14] and of that number Coastal Command accounted for 51.8 per cent. In addition, another 40 kills were attributable either to US aircraft operating under Coastal Command control, or were shared with naval forces. The Command was also responsible for the sinking of four Italian boats (two in the Atlantic), with one shared.

For this, of course, there was a price to pay. In the final issue of *Coastal Command Review* in June 1945,[15] it was stated that, in the course of the whole war, 1,511 aircraft of the Command had been lost by enemy action or were missing. Adding fatal crashes on return from operations, Hilary Saunders makes this 1,777. He also tells us that 5,866 pilots and crew (1,630 from the Dominions) were killed.[16]

Slessor, writing in 1956, was convinced that

> The crews of Coastal Command certainly did not get their meed of public recognition at the time; nor have they since ...[17]

For this he is much inclined to blame Churchill, and the section of *Closing the Ring* which deals with the Atlantic victory does, indeed, seem distinctly meagre and cursory by comparison with other passages. Yet, as we have seen, Slessor himself was not entirely guiltless in this connection. His own tour of duty at Northwood ended on January 20, 1944; he was a popular commander, a hard-hitting professional with a clear mind (except when clouded by dogma); above all he was a leader. He was fortunate in arriving when the Command was on the brink of its long-awaited triumph. His successor, Sholto Douglas, arrived – as was his unlucky habit – too late for the great days. Yet it is fair to say that under all its chiefs – Bowhill, Joubert, Slessor and Douglas – Coastal Command, in its long fight not just against the enemy, but against inadequate equipment, the Atlantic storms and the tedium of endless miles and endless hours of empty sea, construed once more beyond any chance of error the motto, *"per ardua"*.

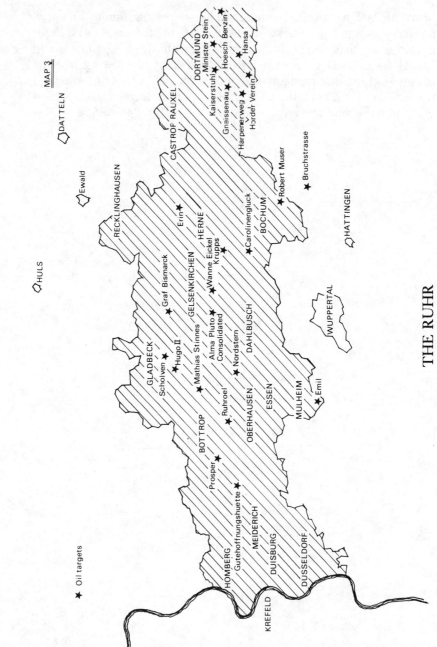

MAP 3

THE RUHR

★ Oil targets

HULS
Ewald
DATTELN
RECKLINGHAUSEN
CASTROF RAUXEL
DORTMUND
Minister Stein
Hoesch Benzin
Kaiserstuhl
Hansa
Gneissenau
Harperweg
Hörder Verein
Bruchstrasse
Erin
HERNE
Robert Muser
BOCHUM
Carolinengluck
Graf Bismarck
GELSENKIRCHEN
Wanne Eickel
Krupps
HATTINGEN
Scholven
GLADBECK
Hugo II
Mathias Stinnes
Alma Pluto
Consolidated
Nordstern
DAHLBUSCH
WUPPERTAL
Ruhroel
OBERHAUSEN
ESSEN
MULHEIM
Emil
Prosper
BOTTROP
Gutehoffnungshuette
HOMBERG
MEIDERICH
DUISBURG
DUSSELDORF
KREFELD

THE STRATEGIC AIR OFFENSIVE (II)

". . . they are sowing the wind . . ."

59 Bomber Command problems; aircraft and aircrew

The night of November 7/8, 1941 was disastrous for Bomber Command. Four hundred aircraft set out for North-Western Europe; they attacked Ostend and Boulogne, they mined the harbour at Oslo, they attacked the German searchlight belt, the Ruhr, Mannheim, Cologne and Berlin. Of the whole force despatched, 37 aircraft did not return – 9.25 per cent.[1] This high total was alarming in itself, but it concealed some far more startling statistics: in particular, the fact that all the losses occurred in five specific areas, involving a total of 267 aircraft, which meant a proportion of 13.85 per cent of the aircraft despatched, but far worse, a proportion of 25.87 per cent of the 143 aircraft which actually reached those targets. Worst of all was the attack on Berlin, to which 169 aircraft were sent (101 Wellingtons, 42 Whitleys, 17 Stirlings and 9 Halifaxes). Twenty-one aircraft were missing from this attack – 12.42 per cent of those despatched, but 28.76 per cent of the 73 which claimed to have attacked the city.[2] Very few bombs actually fell on Berlin that night; they caused nine deaths, injuries to 32 people, and loss of homes to 398 – at a cost of some 120 aircrew. This dismal result was, of course, only known after the war; but the sense of a tragic failure was very strong as soon as Bomber Command's report was received.

Sir Richard Peirse's immediate inclination was to lay the blame for the failures and the loss on Bomber Command's first and everlasting enemy – the weather, and insufficient warning of its treacheries by the meteorologists. He also considered that a number of pilots were insufficiently trained in long-range flying, and unable to cope with unexpected difficulties. There was no doubt that conditions had been very bad on the night of the 7th, with heavy cloud over most of the area attacked. Over Berlin it was reported as 10/10ths, causing severe icing *en route*, which especially affected the Whitleys (nine lost out of 42 despatched: 21.42 per cent). The Air Staff was at first disposed to accept Sir Richard Peirse's explanation.

Very soon, however, Portal and others became uneasy. It was

discovered that the meteorologists had in fact forecast thunderstorms, icing and hail, and as late as four o'clock on the afternoon of November 7 they warned of convection cloud over the North Sea with tops rising to between 15 and 20,000 feet and icy temperatures. To Portal it now seemed that

> ... the disproportionate losses during these operations were the result of failure to appreciate fully the extent to which icing conditions might affect endurance rather than to a faulty forecast in the weather.[3]

A sense of the issue being one of command, rather than of meteorology or technique, grew with the knowledge that one Group commander had proclaimed the conditions as unsuitable for long-range operations, and that one Station commander had only allowed his most experienced pilots to go out on that night, and though they had suffered no losses the amount of petrol left in their tanks showed that even they had been "near the bone". Peirse revised his report to some extent on December 2, but continued to insist that he had been inadequately warned by the meteorologists and that many of his crews were inexperienced. Freeman considered this response "objectionable", and the reference to the crews "a damning admission"; if they were insufficiently trained, he said, it was the commanders' duty to train them. However, with indications that morale in Bomber Command was in a somewhat delicate state (as well it might be at that gloomy stage of the war), it seemed both to Freeman and to Portal inadvisable to press further enquiries. At Sinclair's insistence, Churchill was shown the relevant papers in early January; to all concerned they suggested that Peirse had not gripped this operation firmly as Commander-in-Chief; that perhaps he was tired and needed a change, and that new blood was needed at High Wycombe. He departed to the Far East (and a depressing destiny[4]), and on February 22, 1942 he was succeeded as AOC-in-C, Bomber Command, by Air Chief Marshal Sir Arthur Harris, KCB, OBE, AFC.

The situation which Harris inherited was not exactly attractive. Nothing in the British war effort at the turn of 1941/1942 was encouraging – even the entry of America into the war meant, for the time being, only a reduction of supplies to Britain – and Bomber Command was no exception to this condition. It would be wrong to suggest that the Command was demoralized – it was never that; but it was undoubtedly at a low ebb. Churchill's reaction to what he called the "most grievous" losses of November 7/8 had been sharp, he told Sinclair and Portal:

We cannot afford losses on that scale in view of the shortfall of the American bomber programme. Losses which are acceptable in a battle or for some decisive military objective ought not to be incurred merely as a matter of routine. There is no need to fight the weather and the enemy at the same time. It is now the duty of both Fighter and Bomber Command to re-gather their strength for the spring.[5]

In other words, Bomber Command was back to conservation; Peirse had had to accept this, with its implications. The psychological factor worried him above all; the Command was sustained in bad times by the belief, constantly dinned in, that what it was doing was vital. If, he told Portal, "there is any hesitation in the handling of the Force, doubt must immediately arise in the minds of aircrews, and doubt spells irresolution . . . it is darned hard to fight a force like Bomber Command at a subdued tempo".[6]

The truth is that 1941 had been an unfortunate year, and if Peirse was, to some extent, the victim of circumstances and conditions far beyond his control, his successor inherited the cumulative sum of the year's misfortunes. Towering over all else was the failure of the expansion policy.[7] On the day he took command, Harris tells us,

there were 378 aircraft serviceable with crews, and only 69 of these were heavy bombers. About 50 aircraft in the force were not even medium bombers but the light bombers of No. 2 Group . . . In effect, this meant that we had an average force of 250 medium and fifty heavy bombers until such time as the Command really began to expand.[8]

It was not an impressive array, and its equipment, Harris grimly adds, was no more so than its numbers. The blame for this state of affairs can be squarely placed:

The failure of [the expansion] programme was due almost entirely to deficiencies in production, compared with the optimistic views held in spring 1941.[9]

For this one has to hold responsible the Ministry of Aircraft Production, under its "dynamic" chief, Lord Beaverbrook. The results were far-reaching, and for the Royal Air Force, disconcerting, not to say embarrassing. First, in order to man this flow of aircraft which did not materialize, the duration of courses at the Operational Training Units was reduced; in consequence,

Squadrons became diluted, during autumn 1941, with half-trained men, and became incapable of successful or sustained operations. This dilution

461

greatly aggravated the rate of wastage in the first line, owing to the high crash rate occurring on operational sorties. There were few bombers to replace this wastage, to expand the first line and to increase the OTUs.[10]

Not only that, but, at a time when sharp eyes were being directed at RAF demands of all kinds, "a large surplus of pilots began to appear".[11] Not surprisingly, this was accompanied by an equally awkward surplus of ground staff – no fewer than 52,000 men by November 1941, of whom half were in the fitter group. By March 1942 the surplus of fitters had risen to 42,000 – and this at a time when, as we have seen (pp. 341–2), there was an acute and continuing shortage of skilled ground staff in the Middle East. Small wonder that Dowding, called on to investigate this situation, "reported that the tremendous miscalculations which had been made in the recruiting department had been due to the gross inaccuracy of the estimates of aircraft production which the Manning staff had received from the Ministry of Aircraft Production . . ."[12]

In time, of course, both these surpluses would be absorbed by the intake of new aircraft, especially the heavy bombers; but, as Harris emphasizes, at the time of his takeover the flow of heavy bombers was the most disturbing aspect of the whole story. Every one of the heavy types had teething problems – in the case of the Manchester very soon, in the case of the Stirling rather later, fatal; in the case of the Halifax causing long delays in operational effectiveness (see p. 279). Up to the end of February 1942, the average number of serviceable Manchesters never exceeded 31, of Stirlings 21 and of Halifaxes 23. The gleam of light in this dark tunnel was the delivery of the first Lancasters to No. 44 (Rhodesian) Squadron at Waddington on Christmas Eve.

There was future promise, too, in certain changes which came to fruition as Harris appeared at High Wycombe. The problem of diluted training and the resulting half-trained aircrew was tackled and greatly eased by a bold stroke advocated and pushed through by Air Vice-Marshal MacNeece Foster, AOC, No. 6 (Training; later renumbered 91) Group: the abandonment of the hitherto statutory crew establishment of two pilots per aircraft. MacNeece Foster's reform was, not surprisingly, strongly opposed in some influential quarters, but when it went through with Harris's approval at the end of February it had the effect of immediately halving the pilot training requirement, which meant in turn that the course could be levelled up to 80 flying hours, at which it substantially remained until the end of the war.

It was also during Harris's first months of command that the RAF finally came to terms with the functions of members of aircrew themselves – the problem which had so much exercised Sir Edgar Ludlow-Hewitt as far back as 1937 (see pp. 84–6). After the dropping of the second pilot, the new designation of navigator was introduced, with navigation his sole responsibility. The single pilot was also to be assisted by a flight engineer. Bomb-dropping (previously one of the navigator's duties) was to be performed by an air bomber or bombardier – another new designation. The rôles of air gunners and wireless operators were separated; in an emergency wireless operators might man guns, but gunners were no longer required to take a wireless course. The Official History remarks:

> These changes had the effect of allowing each member of the crew to specialize,[13] and therefore permitted him to receive much more thorough training than had previously been the case ... Without these changes, Bomber Command would certainly never have approached the degree of efficiency which it ultimately attained ...[14]

Appropriate badges were in due course authorized for all the crew positions. It is no intended denigration of the other duties of a totally inter-dependent group of men to suggest that perhaps the insignia with the greatest emotional connotation for those who knew was the air gunner's "AG". Since December 1939, it had been accepted officially that the rank of gunners should not be lower than sergeant (though this did not rule out the continuing misuse of ground-crew volunteers, as a number of brave deeds demonstrate). The air gunner's rôle was intimately linked to the turret; his task, especially at the rear, was essentially solitary, calling for both deep moral reserves and great physical fitness:

> Sitting almost immobile in the cramped panoply of a metal and perspex cupola for six, eight, ten or even more hours, constantly vigilant, yet unable to relieve cramped legs, arms and back, called for frequent extraordinary feats of physical endurance.[15]

The most constant enemy of all aircrew was cold, with its inevitable serious reduction of efficiency. Chaz Bowyer says:

> Attempts to solve this general problem of crew comfort throughout the war were seldom fully successful; while the air gunner's job remained the coldest one in every bomber crew until the end.[16]

Electrically heated flying clothing was introduced early in 1942, but was only spasmodically useful, being obviously vulnerable to electrical faults in the aircraft, and also to careless stowage. It was a step forward, but still of uneven value:

> The problem of extreme cold suffered by all air gunners – whether inside gun turrets or, as in the case of the USAAF's Fortress and Liberator crews, waist gunners[17] – was never satisfactorily resolved during the war.

So the air gunner's prospects were a comfortless life and a lonely death – a combination calling for amazing fortitude.

It is perhaps appropriate here to look a few months ahead at another aspect of the matter of aircrew; it was in May 1942, at the United Nations' Air Training Conference in Ottawa, that the Canadians raised the highly debatable issue of the commissioning of all aircrew. The Canadian voice was by now one which had to be heard with attention,[18] and what it said made a great deal of sense. Canada's position was straightforward and clearly expressed:

> Rank commensurate with duties should be granted to all aircrew personnel, there being no justification for the commissioning of certain individuals whilst others are required to perform exactly the same duties but in N.C.O. rank. The responsibility resting upon the individual in aircrew capacity is sufficient justification for commissioned status. N.C.O. rank is not compatible with the heavy responsibilities imposed in commanding large and expensive aircraft.[19]

This was the nub of the argument, expressed with the bluntness of a young country. It was not, of course, by any means all there was to say. The Canadians drew attention to the sense of unfairness, "damaging to morale", at inequalities in pay, transportation, travel allowances and messing, and made a telling point by mentioning the effect of these inequalities on those unfortunate enough to become prisoners of war. They said it was unfair that an NCO training instructor should find himself serving under a former pupil, and equally unfair that an officer could be operationally under an NCO. They dwelt on the injury to the team spirit when "the crew, as an entity, is not able to live and fraternise, the one with the other, during leisure and off-duty hours." They believed that automatic commissioning on successful graduation would encourage aircrew enlistment. They said it was injurious to discipline (especially overseas) that aircrew sergeants should have a senior status in the Sergeants' Mess – whereas aircrew officers "are very junior members of the Officers' Mess and are aware of the fact". "All pilots, navigators and air bombers," they insisted, "are of equal importance, the one with the other, and all of them have an equal claim to a commission."

The RAF response also opened with its ace, and reflects the difference in the background of those concerned, and the differences of the two societies. It said:

> A commission is granted in recognition of character, intelligence (as distinct from academic qualifications), and capacity to lead, command and set a worthy example. Many aircrews, though quite capable of performing their duties adequately, have no officer qualities. The policy proposed by Canada would have the effect of depreciating the value of commissioned rank.

In support of this view, which embodies traditional beliefs going back into the distant pasts of the two older Services, the RAF spokesmen claimed that wholesale aircrew commissioning would have serious repercussions among long-service, highly skilled ground crew which would lead to "a general lowering of discipline". It would also, they said, cause trouble with the other Services. They rejected the proposition that all men undergoing the same risk should have the same status; pay "must be determined on the basis of the personal qualities . . . and not on the amount of risk incurred". Team spirit, they said, was essential, "but it is not agreed that this spirit can only be secured by granting the same status to all members of a team". They alluded (very perfunctorily) to the comparison with tanks and submarines, and insisted that

> it would be wrong to assume that flying and fighting in the air necessarily makes a man into a superman.

The RAF denied that more commissions were needed in order to attract men of the right type; it repeated that "officer-like qualities" were what mattered, and said in conclusion that the policy was that every aircrew member "who is suitable and is recommended for commissioning by the responsible authorities shall be commissioned."

The RAF reply does not speak the same language as the Canadian case. It certainly does not meet the Canadian objections to the existing system, which had both logic and humanity on their side. The RAF was still, in 1942, speaking the language of a small regular Service recruited in a country where inequalities found far readier acceptance than in the overseas Dominions. The Canadians used the terms appropriate to a modern, much larger and increasingly technical service, whose conditions of combat were unprecedented. Chief among these was the fundamental fact referred to at the very beginning (see pp. 4–5) of this book – that it was not an officer-function in the RAF to lead the other ranks in battle, as it was in the other Services. Battle was the aircrew-function, theirs alone, and their only one – which was what made the whole position unique.

It is easy to see and easy to say, at this distance, that what was needed was a complete reappraisal producing a quite different system which took this novel circumstance fully into account – the creation, in other words, of a force within a force, on a permanent basis, somewhat like Airborne Forces in the Army. The separation of air and ground functions in the RAF was very clear; it was no use trying to blur it. Wearing wings was not enough; there were a good many people wearing wings, fully earned, who were not operational flyers. The operational flyers were a "race apart", and this required formal recognition. Variations of personal quality within a crew could perfectly well be taken care of by grades of rank, without the insult of withholding commissions. Not least of the drawbacks of this palpably unfair practice was the absurdity of senior ranks sometimes being actually commanded by junior ranks, thus undermining the whole concept of rank itself, as the Canadians perceived.[20]

Bomber Command's style of war has also to be taken into account. As one reflects upon the situation of, say, a rear- or nose-gunner, or a bomb-aimer, at one o'clock in the morning somewhere over the middle of Germany, one is forced to question severely such concepts as a "capacity to lead, command and set a worthy example". Who did a rear-gunner ever lead or command? To whom could he "set a worthy example", frozen, frightened but ceaselessly vigilant in his isolated turret? In Bomber Command's night raids each aircraft, each crew, was very much alone from take-off until return, barring only the awareness that the sky was full of other aeroplanes with which one might collide, and which might (if one was in a lower layer) drop their bombs right through one's wings or destroy one utterly. This was not even like the operations of the American Eighth Air Force, which flew in daylight, in tight formations in full view of each other, and whose leaders obviously had very important functions and were required to exhibit high qualities. In Bomber Command, except on rare daylight occasions, each crew was on its own; "leading" and "commanding" was something that happened almost entirely inside the aircraft – it had to have a "skipper", who had to be implicitly obeyed; but beyond that all that was required from the crew was exceptionally high morale and sense of duty and an ability to conquer fear. That was "all"; not leading, not commanding, not setting examples – just continuing to do one's exacting, lonely duty as part of a mutually-reliant team in all circumstances, including some that defy description, even imagination.

However, in May 1942 it was the RAF's view that prevailed, not surprisingly, in view of the enormous preponderance of the RAF effort, and the Canadians (with whom Australians and New Zealanders must have considerably sympathized) had to swallow their irritation – which they nobly did.

It is all too easy to be critical forty years on, because now we can see that as well as being a very new problem (Ludlow-Hewitt was really the first to recognize it, in 1937), the aircrew-function was to a large extent also ephemeral; modern strike aircraft in the 1980s do not carry large, specialized crews, any more than the first combat aircraft did in the First World War and between the wars. So we are now able to pronounce that a temporary structural solution ought to have been found for this temporary problem – only, of course, nobody then *knew* that it was temporary. And the RAF is scarcely to be blamed for not wishing to overturn an established and working system, whatever its anomalies, at a critical moment in a war for survival.

So, complete with anomalies, and aware also of other depressing deficiencies, Bomber Command awaited its new commander in 1942; there was much to discourage:

> Bombing remained inaccurate; wastage remained high; expansion remained an unrealised ideal.[21]

On the heavy two-squadron bomber stations there would generally be about 1,000 ground-crew and staff, and some 200 aircrew. All were concerned in a single purpose, which was unremitting:

> ... even if it was possible to reduce the intensity of Bomber Command's operations ... it was not possible to withdraw the force from the line. The war in the air was necessarily continuous and through the dreary winter of 1941–42 Bomber Command continued to engage the enemy as best it could.[22]

For all it was a period of almost inexpressible stress:

> No one who was present at a bomber airfield before, during and after an operation could for a moment be unconscious of the unnatural and inhuman strain to which so many young men were being subjected; until all was over no one could feel the tension relaxed or forget what was at stake. A peculiar apprehension gripped all those on the ground who had even the smallest responsibility for the undertaking that was being carried

467

out at so great a distance and with only the most tenuous link between the base and the fighting force. For each bomber and its crew in the air there were at least ten times as many [men] on the ground; the prolonged effort of about sixty highly skilled technicians was required for each single sortie. It is not to be claimed that their work was in any way comparable to the task of the flying crews but it must be said that every decent man on the ground felt the heavy burden of his responsibility and experienced before and during each operation a most acute suspense. Suspense, indeed, was in the very atmosphere of the bomber station.[23]

The attack on Germany continued, even if reduced in weight, through January and February 1942: Emden, Hamburg, Bremen, Münster, Hanover, Mannheim, Cologne, Aachen and Kiel were not allowed to forget the RAF. The main preoccupation, however, was the German warships in Brest, Bomber Command's prime target on January 2, on five successive nights between January 5–9, again on the 11th, on three successive nights, 25th–27th, and on the 31st. There were two more attacks in February before the German ships escaped up the Channel, inflicting a national humiliation which shocked the British people and every part of the Services concerned. Indeed it was a bad time; "Grin and bear it" was the motto of the First World War; "Britain can Take It" was the proud slogan of 1940; Bomber Command set its teeth and "took it" at the turn of 1941–42. But it badly needed a fillip, a new atmosphere, a sign of its might for itself and all the world to see. It needed a victory. It needed a leader.

60 Harris; the Americans arrive; bombing aids; incendiaries

Arthur Travers Harris was born in 1892, not, as is sometimes confidently asserted, in South Africa or Rhodesia, but in Cheltenham, Gloucestershire. His father was in the Public Works Department of the Indian Civil Service, which meant that for much of his childhood he saw little of his parents, but was strongly aware of his family, which was distinctly military, with such an abundance of colonels that the young Harris conceived at a very early age a powerful aversion to the soldier's life and, indeed, remained a lifelong pungent critic of soldiers and their trade. Among many barbed statements that are attributed to him down the years we may find:

> In order to get on in the Army, you have to look like a horse, think like a horse and smell like a horse.[1]

He may well have said it; his first career, in Rhodesia between 1910 and 1914, had much to do with horses, and his first experience of the military life and war, in the 1st Rhodesia Regiment in south-west Africa, 1914–15, afforded him a close view of mounted men in action. It was this that enabled him to fire a broadside into a favourite British myth when he later wrote:

> I have ridden with colonial troops and shot with colonial troops and been shot at by colonial troops, and I have no hesitation whatever in saying that the dominion and colonial troops are on the average, with remarkably few individual exceptions, damned bad horsemen and damned bad shots unless and until they have been put through the standard riding school procedure in the days when horsemen meant something, and the standard musketry drill of the armed forces.[2]

This "blockbuster" forms part of the lead-in to one of the most impressive tributes ever paid to the United Kingdom aircrews of the Second World War, but it is quoted here because it is pure Harris, blasting ancient superstitions in set terms, letting in fresh ideas like a hurricane in a parlour.[3] With a C-in-C like this, Bomber Command, even if it scarcely ever saw his face except in a newspaper, would know that it was commanded, and all parts of the war effort would know that Bomber Command was being commanded.

This was just as well because, as Harris took over, ominous clouds of doubt were gathering over the Command. Coinciding with his own appointment, a reconstruction of the Cabinet took place, which brought in Sir Stafford Cripps (back from an exasperating and largely unprofitable ambassadorship in the Soviet Union) as Lord Privy Seal and Leader of the House of Commons. On February 25, when Harris had only been at High Wycombe for three days, Cripps wound up a Commons debate on the war situation and referred to the question that some members were asking,

> whether, in the existing circumstances, the continued devotion of a considerable part of our effort to the building up of this bombing force is the best use we can make of our resources.

He reminded the House that the policy of the bombing offensive had been adopted when Britain stood alone, "and it then seemed that it was the most effective way in which we, acting alone, could take the initiative against the enemy". But now both the Soviet Union and the United States were also in the war, and Cripps made what sounded like a solemn declaration:

Naturally, in such circumstances, the original policy has come under review. I can assure the House that the Government are fully aware of the other uses to which our resources can be put, and the moment they arrive at a decision that the circumstances warrant a change, a change in policy will be made.[4]

Cripps's speech served notice that Bomber Command's future rôle could not be taken for granted, and disquiet at High Wycombe was not entirely dispelled by Sinclair, when he told the House on March 4 that it was intended "to resume the bomber offensive against Germany on the largest possible scale at the earliest possible moment". The bombers were, he said, "the only force upon which we can call in this year, 1942, to strike deadly blows at the heart of Germany". But he also dwelt, at what some no doubt considered unseemly length, on the RAF rôle in the Battle of the Atlantic, and in the Middle East – both of which matters were anathema to Harris. His absolute *bête-noire* at this stage was what he saw as the grotesque dispersion of his already inadequate force. It must be admitted that he had a point:

> In terms of percentages of the whole effort of Bomber Command, the attack on German transport and industry[5] dwindled from 72 per cent in August 1941 to 40 per cent in January 1942; the attack on French docks and harbours rose from 6 per cent to 45 per cent in the same period. In February *only 20 per cent could be devoted to the offensive* while, on account of the movement of the battle-cruisers up Channel, 25 per cent of the effort was made on minelaying, 17 per cent on German shipyards and harbours, and 16 per cent on the naval vessels themselves – a total of 67 per cent of the whole effort for the month.[6]

Simultaneously with this heavy drain in support of the war at sea, Bomber Command was also feeding the Middle East with aircraft and crews to the extent which drew from Harris the strong protest to Tedder (see p. 269, Chapter 47, Note 2) which the latter tartly described as "three pages of hysterical verbosity".[7] It is not entirely surprising if Harris saw the Admiralty, Coastal Command and the Middle East as a flock of vultures tearing at the entrails of his Command. The effect of their demands was, as the AHB Narrative says, that "the offensive petered out owing to vastly overwhelming circumstances". Overwhelming indeed; what they added up to, as stated above (pp. 277–8 and Appendix "B") was the war.

This clash of interest – *national* interest, be it understood – was going to persist, and in it we see Harris at his worst. Of course it was distasteful to have his Command diverted to what in other circumstances would be called a "secondary front"; doubtless it was even worse, if anything, to see it used as a kind of reinforcement pool for other people. But the Battle of the Atlantic had to be won, for Harris's sake as well as everyone else's, and that battle needed long-range aircraft. And the Middle East had to have a bomber force – an effective bomber force, not antiques and rejects – as long as there was fighting to be done. And something had to be done, as well, to stave off utter disaster in the Far East. Where else did Harris think these aircraft could come from, if not from Bomber Command, and where else could the crews come from, if not from Bomber Command squadrons or OTUs? It was the extraordinary belief (see p. 425) that Britain was "free" to take unilateral decisions on how to conduct the air war that led him astray. He demanded the return of aircraft and crews from the Atlantic battle and the Middle East as though it was really possible to cease or reduce fighting in those theatres by unilateral action. In war, unilateral action is rarely possible so long as the enemy remains in the field, because he will have his own view of the matter; in coalition war it is never possible, because allies as well as the enemy will have views which can only be ignored at the peril of the coalition. For Britain in 1942, the only area where unilateral action was in any degree possible was the continuation or non-continuation of the night offensive of the bomber force against Germany, because no allied (American) forces were engaged in it and no German initiatives were involved – but even so the possibility of exercising this option was exceedingly faint. Wherever German forces possessed any initiative, unilateral suspension or reduction of hostilities was strategic nonsense. It would have meant, quite simply, defeat by the U-boats in the Atlantic, and Rommel in Cairo.

Nevertheless, what Sinclair had told the House of Commons was correct: Bomber Command *was* the only force the Allies possessed that could strike directly at Germany. It was essential to build up the offensive again, from all points of view; both the Russians, passing through their own lowest ebb, and the Americans, expected no less – and neither did the British public. The Americans, indeed, were determined to play their own – increasing – part in this offensive; this would be done by the US Army Eighth Air Force, whose advanced echelon and first commander, Brigadier-General Ira C. Eaker, arrived in England at the end of February. Sir Robert Saundby, at that time Harris's trusted SASO (and later Deputy), tells us:

> Harris and Eaker were firm friends, and they at once laid the foundations of a cooperation between the two long-range bombardment forces that was both admirable and enduring.[8]

There was, indeed, a warm and valuable friendship; yet the Official History adds that Harris and Eaker

> had quite different views from each other not only of the operational but also of the strategic prospects.[9]

1942 was, as we have seen, a grim year – the grimmest – for the Alliance. The Americans in particular found it unfolding in a maddening fashion – the British were more accustomed to trials and tribulations, delays, disappointments, hopes raised only to be dashed. It was in 1942 that the Americans became acquainted with the vast gulf between planning a large, lavishly equipped army, and actually raising and training one. They learnt, too, that even if the difficulties of doing this could be surmounted, they would not be much nearer to fulfilling the Grand Design if they could not get their army across the Atlantic – and there was no chance of this while the U-boats straddled the seaways. So they began to recognize, with resentment, that there was going to be no BOLERO worth talking about, and certainly no SLEDGEHAMMER, in 1942. Scarcely had they digested this, than they had to face the equally unpalatable fact that without a great deal of specialized equipment, above all landing-craft, there would be no cross-Channel attack in 1943 either. And while Admiral King clung to every landing-craft that he could lay hands on for the insatiable demands of the Pacific war, prospects even beyond that were scarcely bright. And while all these pills were being washed down they also had to come to terms with the recognition that the USAAF's cherished belief in daylight precision bombing, to which Eaker strongly subscribed, was no more possible with unescorted Flying Fortresses in 1942–43 than it had been for Bomber Command's unescorted Wellingtons and Hampdens in 1939–40. It was a lot to take in. And what it meant beyond a peradventure was that Bomber Command was going to have to keep on holding the right of the line for a long time to come. Only now it had a leader – and some interesting new tools for the job.

At the end of 1941, says the AHB Narrative,

> The four vital needs of the force . . . were (i) expansion (ii) better training (iii) the introduction of navigational aids, and (iv) a new attitude towards the incendiary bomb . . .[10]

Expansion, alas! was going to be a persisting disappointment throughout the year, partly for technical reasons (the failures among the new types) and partly because of the year itself, its crises and their demands. Certainly it was not something which was within any individual's province to transform. Training, as we have seen, was a matter that was being gripped. The last two items, navigational aids and incendiary bombs, were shots in Harris's locker, for him to find ways of using with effect.

The first of the navigational aids to come into use (and, indeed, the only one in sight for 1942) was "GEE", an invention of R. J. Dippy of the Telecommunications Research Establishment. In simple terms,

> It was a system by which the navigator could calculate the position of his aircraft by observing the time taken to receive pulse signals from three different ground stations.[11]

GEE promised, at the very least, that Bomber Command crews would no longer mistake open country for town targets; its weaknesses were its short range – a normal maximum of 400 miles, which effectively restricted its usefulness to western Germany – and the usual curse of slow production. The first service trials of GEE began in May 1941, and in July three Wellingtons of No. 115 Squadron (Marham) were fitted with the system. The crews concerned were enthusiastic, and on the night of August 11/12 two Wellingtons operated over Germany with what the Official History calls "very encouraging results".[12] "Of course," says Professor R. V. Jones, "it was only a matter of time before one of the aircraft was lost"[13] – and it proved to be a very short time indeed, the very next night, in fact, when No. 115 Squadron sent two Wellingtons to Hanover and one failed to return. Since no large-scale production of GEE was expected until March 1942, what this meant was that the system was compromised nearly eight months before Bomber Command could begin to use it fully. There was a one in three chance that the Germans now had the GEE receiver and could begin to probe its secret; nor was that all:

> Where the main danger lay was in the fact that 78 aircrew had been lost in the interval between the first GEE receiver being installed in a bomber at Marham . . . and the receiver being lost, and probably twenty or thirty of them would now be prisoners of war . . . If the Germans had twenty prisoners, it was quite likely that they might have overheard some reference to GEE, and this would have alerted them to investigating particularly the wreckage of any aircraft from the squadron involved.[14]

Professor Jones was called upon to display his recognized "spoofing" skills, and put deception measures in hand, while all GEE flights over occupied territory were prohibited until a substantial number of receivers had been delivered. Whether due to the deceptions, or to other causes, the Germans did not penetrate the mystery of GEE until May 1942, and their first jamming of it was not until August. But it was clear to the Air Staff in February that, if any considerable value was to be extracted from it, it had better be used at once.

The Directive which Harris inherited on taking over was only eight days old (February 14); it announced that conservation restrictions were now lifted so as to make the fullest use of GEE.[15] The Air Staff, it said, considered

> that the introduction of this equipment on operations should be regarded as a revolutionary advance in bombing technique which, during the period of its effective life as a target-finding device, will enable results to be obtained of a much more effective nature.[16]

Unfortunately, that effective life, it added, was not likely to be more than six months. In order, during that time, to extract the fullest value from GEE,

> it has been decided that the primary object of your operations should now be focused on the morale of the enemy civil population and in particular, of the industrial workers.

It was laid down that the "cardinal principle" in the use of GEE should be, from the very beginning, "the complete concentration on one target until the effort estimated to be required for its destruction has been achieved". To expedite this, it was pointed out that

> This is the time of year to get the best effect from concentrated incendiary attacks.

Harris later stated (1947) that "the idea that the main object of bombing German industrial cities was to break the enemy's morale proved to be wholly unsound".[17] He made a point which should not have eluded reflective minds five years earlier: that while, obviously, being heavily bombed would have a lowering effect on German workers' morale, it would not necessarily affect their conduct – in a ruthless totalitarian state ("with the *Gestapo* standing by") this was, after all, a reasonable conclusion! But he adds, rightly, that at the time the value of attacking morale in industrial centres "seemed quite a natural opinion", and there is no reason to suppose that he objected to this or any other part of the Directive when he perused it on February 22.

A technique for making the best use of GEE with the limited number of sets available had already been worked out at Bomber Command Headquarters; by March some 100–150 aircraft had been suitably equipped, and it was time to put the Directive into operation (bearing only in mind its warning not to try to fight the weather at the same time). The Air Staff advised that the initial attack should be upon Essen, "the supreme target",[18] and Harris did not dissent. It would provide, at the very least, an opportunity to try out the new bombing technique, known as SHAKER. For this, the attacking force was divided into three groups: the illuminators, the target markers and the followers. The illuminators, the most important, and providing, like the Middle East's Albacores (see p. 376), clear pointers towards the Pathfinder Force soon to be created, all carried GEE and would arrive in five waves at three-minute intervals:

> Each bomber was to carry twelve bundles of triple flares and was to run along the up wind side of the target, dropping them at ten-second intervals. The bomb load was to be completed with high explosives. Thus, it was hoped to illuminate the target at zero hour with lanes of flares approximately six miles long which would drift over the target and keep it so illuminated for twelve minutes.[19]

While the illuminators were still at work, the target markers, also using GEE, would begin to arrive, carrying "the maximum load of incendiary bombs". These, it was hoped, would create an unmistakable concentrated area of fire on which the followers, who did not have GEE, could home in, fifteen minutes after the first arrivals, with their high explosives. Harris, who had come to Bomber Command with a "profound faith in high explosive",[20] showed himself ready to be persuaded in this matter, and would soon be a champion of the required "new attitude towards the incendiary bomb".

The first trial of SHAKER was duly made against Essen, on the night of March 8/9; 211 aircraft were despatched, 82 of them equipped with GEE, of which 20 were illuminators. The weather was good, but, of course, there was the inevitable industrial haze to contend with; despite the "revolutionary" new aid, only 168 aircraft even claimed to have attacked the target. Of the twenty illuminators, it later transpired that only 11 dropped their flares on the GEE "fix". Out of 43 successful photographs taken during the attack, none "showed any recognizable feature of the target area".[21] Eight aircraft were lost. It was not a very good beginning.

More disappointment was to follow; the attack on March 8/9 was only the first of eight considerable operations against Essen during March and April (pursuant to the directive on concentration). The Official History bleakly sums up:

> . . . in none was any substantial success achieved.[22]

Out of 212 photographs taken, "only 22 proved to be within five miles of Essen". Conditions on the eight occasions varied so much (though the haze was always there) that evidently no blame could be directed at weather or cloud. In fact the crews, even the best of them, were finding GEE difficult to operate; many, though ordered to drop flares on the GEE "fixes", still preferred to use visual aim (14 out of 23 illuminators in the second attack). Incendiary bombs, once misdirected, created false aiming points for all who followed; bomb-aimers were dazzled by their own flares; and the Germans, always resourceful, were quick to supply dummy targets with fires burning temptingly fiercely in quite the wrong place. So it sadly appeared that

> What had seemed a device accurate enough for blind-bombing . . . was turning out to be simply an excellent aid to navigation.[23]

The Ruhr had always been a tough nut to crack, and would remain so. There were, however, other targets within the GEE range, or those for other reasons easier to find. Best of all were targets beside the sea, which in anything like reasonable conditions of visibility, gave clear geographical outlines for pilots and bomb-aimers alike. One such was Lübeck, once the capital of the Hanseatic League, standing only a short distance inland from its well-marked bay on the Baltic coast, whose Old Town on the River Trave, with its warren of ancient wooden houses, was, in Harris's somewhat blood-curdling words, "built more like a fire-lighter than a human habitation".[24] This made it, in the view of Bomber Command's Operational Research Section,

> a particularly suitable target for testing the effect of a very heavy attack with incendiary bombs.[25]

The only other notable attraction of Lübeck as a target being its comparatively light anti-aircraft defences, its choice showed, in the words of the Official History, the extent "to which a town might become a target mainly because it was operationally vulnerable".[26] Bomber Command, like Britain herself, had come a long way in two and a half years, from those first operations when it was forbidden to drop bombs even on German warships, if they were in dock and any risk thus arose of injury to civilians (see p. 100). War is a stern educator; some of its lessons are not nice to know.

"On the night of March 28–29th the first German city went up in flames," wrote Harris. 234 aircraft (Wellingtons, Stirlings, Manchesters) were despatched to Lübeck on that night, and 191 crews claimed to have reached the target. They dropped some 300 tons of bombs, including no less than 144 tons of incendiaries on the built-up area; photographic reconnaissance shortly afterwards showed "areas of total destruction amounting to probably 45–50 per cent of the whole city".[27] A factory making oxygen apparatus for submarine crews was completely destroyed, together with eight others of less importance. 1,425 houses were completely destroyed, 1,976 heavily damaged, and 8,000 more damaged to a lesser extent.[28] Goebbels, in his diary, reckoned that "eighty per cent of the old part of the city must be considered lost"; inevitably, "buildings of historic interest also perished in the general holocaust".[29] Lübeck, wrote Harris,

> was not a vital target, but it seemed to me better to destroy an industrial town of moderate importance than to fail to destroy a large industrial city . . . It was conclusively proved that even the small force I had then could destroy the greater part of a town of secondary importance.[30]

The Lübeck attack was greeted in Britain (hungry for news of any scrap of advantage in a bad time) with considerable satisfaction; nearly twenty years later the Official History still considered it an "outstanding success . . . which far exceeded anything previously attained by Bomber Command".[31] In Germany it came as a very bad shock; "The damage is really enormous." wrote Goebbels on April 4:

> . . . It is horrible. One can well imagine how such an awful bombardment affects the population. Thank God it is a North German population . . . we can't get away from the fact that the English air raids have increased in scope and importance; if they can be continued for weeks on these lines, they might conceivably have a demoralizing effect on the population . . .

However, as Richards and Saunders remark,

The German population, with its natural powers of endurance stimulated by fear of the *Gestapo*, was tougher than either Goebbels or the Air Staff imagined.[32]

No doubt, when the thunder of the bombing, and the accompanying terrifying sound-effects, had died away, the morale of Lübeck's citizens revived considerably with the discovery that out of a population of 120,000 (25 per cent in the Old Town), the total killed was 312, with 136 seriously wounded and 648 lightly wounded. 15,707 people were made homeless. Contemporary British reports claimed 2,600 dead, and German statements were disregarded, which naturally added to the current misconceptions. Damage to the German war effort was, as we have seen, very slight; the damage to the economy and social functioning of Lübeck, says the Official History (at some distance from its more euphoric verdict, quoted above) "was soon remedied by the vigorous action taken".[33] The historic buildings of the Hanseatic capital were, of course, irreplaceable. RAF losses in this operation were 12 aircraft, most of them on the way in.

One month later there was another "convincing demonstration of what could be achieved by the tactics of concentrated incendiarism".[34] Rostock, further along the Baltic coast, another old town, birthplace of Marshal Blücher, the Duke of Wellington's ally at Waterloo, and containing, like Lübeck, many highly inflammable medieval buildings, was now the target. And although Rostock did contain important war industries – shipbuilding works and aircraft factories, especially the Heinkel factory in the Marienehe suburb and the Arado works – like Lübeck it was also lightly defended.

It took four consecutive nights to inflict serious injury on Rostock; on each occasion the attack was divided, with a proportion of the force attempting precision bombing of the Heinkel factory at Marienehe. The Official History tells us:

> ... while Bomber Command was striving to perfect the tactics of concentrated incendiary area attack, it was simultaneously striving to test the possibilities of high-explosive precision attack ... This practice of accompanying the general area attack against the town with a rapier thrust against a particular target within, or near, that town was now becoming the standard procedure ...[35]

The precision work was entrusted to No. 5 Group (Slessor), which specialized in this style, and trained assiduously to cultivate navigational and bombing accuracy.

The first two attacks went in on April 23/24 (161 aircraft) and April 24/25 (125 aircraft); both were disappointing, despite a clear sky and a bright moon. On the third night (25/26), 128 aircraft were despatched, of which 110 claimed to have reached the target. Among these were 16 of No. 5 Group, looking for the Heinkel factory again, and including crews of No. 106 Squadron (Manchesters) commanded by Wing Commander G. P. (Guy) Gibson, bombing from a height of 2,000 feet or less.[36] Of 71 night photographs taken, 30 showed the centre of Rostock, 34 were within five miles of the centre, and three showed the factory itself. Daylight reconnaissance confirmed that heavy damage had been done; an "outstanding success"[37] had been achieved.

The "masterpiece" was reserved for the last night (26/27); 107 aircraft were despatched, 52 to the town and 55 to the factory. On this occasion No. 5 Group was supported in the precision attack by No. 3 Group. Ninety-two aircraft claimed to have reached the target, and of the 52 photographs taken every one showed the target area, including 13 showing the factory, where the attack had been made entirely below 6,000 feet, and in the case of the 5 Group aircraft, once more below 2,000 feet. Daylight reconnaissance showed "that Bomber Command had won another great victory".[38] What was truly remarkable was that the whole four-night operation, involving a total of 521 sorties, cost only 12 aircraft. If Harris could attain his object of "taking out" a German industrial town at a cost of no more than 12 aircraft, he had reason to be pleased; and there was every reason to suppose that this was what he had done. In Germany the reaction matched the satisfaction at High Wycombe; Goebbels called the situation, even after the first two relatively unsuccessful attacks, "pretty disastrous". There was a disposition to blame the *Luftwaffe*'s AA: Goebbels recorded:

> The *Führer* is in extremely bad humour about the poor anti-aircraft defence . . . the *Luftwaffe* wasn't adequately prepared, and this alone made the damage to the Heinkel works possible.

Hitler consoled himself to some extent with the effect of the Baedeker raids on England (see p. 423); Bath was attacked on the last two nights of Rostock's ordeal (April 25/26 and 26/27), and Hitler told Goebbels:

> that he would repeat these raids night after night until the English were sick and tired of terror attacks. He shares my opinion absolutely that cultural centres, health resorts and civilian centres must be attacked now . . . There is no other way of bringing the English to their senses. They belong to a class of human beings with whom you can only talk after you have first knocked out their teeth.

Unfortunately for the Nazis and the German people, when it came to "knocking out teeth", Bomber Command was already better equipped and would become far more so. By the time it had finished with Rostock, Goebbels was lamenting:

> The air raid last night . . . was even more devastating than those before. Community life there is practically at an end . . . The situation in the city is in some sections catastrophic . . . Seven tenths of the city have been wiped out. More than 100,000 people had to be evacuated . . . There was, in fact, panic . . .[39]

Nobody, not even the German leaders, yet grasped the amazing capacity for endurance and recovery of that formidable people (see p. 265); the Official History adds this footnote to the Rostock story:

> But the panic was soon over and the people hastened back to work, took energetic measures themselves to put the streets in order, much helped by the vigorous action of the Mecklenburg *Gauleiter* Hildebrandt. He could report on 29th April that the principal war factories, including the Arado aircraft works and Neptune works, were nearly back to hundred per cent production.[40]

Nearly 100 per cent production after only two days; and ultimately, when the reckoning of both Lübeck and Rostock emerged, it transpired that, for all the damage, they had "only lost a few days' full production".[41]

Harris, however, understandably saw it differently in 1942; taking the two towns together, and what was known of the damage done to them, he remarked that it "about squared our account with Germany in regard to bombing".[42] No doubt he had in mind that night in September 1940 when he called Portal up to the Air Ministry roof to see "St Paul's standing out in the midst of an ocean of fire – an incredible sight", and said:

> Well, they are sowing the wind.[43]

Now he and Portal, like the round-cheeked deities in the corners of ancient maps, were preparing whirlwinds beyond any previous calculation. As he said:

> There remained the problem of the first-class target . . .[44]

61 *"Millennium"; precision bombing in 1942; Pathfinders*

Bomber Command was much encouraged by the Lübeck and Rostock operations; at last it seemed to be getting somewhere, and the sense of a driving force at High Wycombe came down very strongly to the squadrons. Harris, like other air commanders (Portal conspicuously), fought his war at GHQ.[1] He tells us:

> I should have liked to have been able to see far more than I did of my air-crews, but it was quite out of the question for a Commander-in-Chief during the war to get round to most of the stations.[2]

The manner of communication between a commander whom few of them will ever see, and the soldiers or airmen who risk their lives in desperate actions at his bidding, is one of the great mysteries of war. Churchill ascribes it to "occult channels"[3] – and, indeed, he may be right; whatever the cause, it is a reality to which Bomber Command fully testifies.

It is not to be supposed that the operations particularly referred to in this text represent by any means the sum of Bomber Command's activities; quite the contrary. In March, besides Essen on the 8th/9th and Lübeck, there were three more heavy attacks on Essen, and Kiel and Cologne were also targets, as well as daylight raids on industrial targets and ports in France. And like a bass accompaniment to the high notes, there was always mine-laying (15 nights), there were anti-shipping strikes (in tandem with Coastal Command), leaflet-dropping (chiefly in France) and offensive patrols against airfields. During the month, 82 aircraft were missing from operations and 14 more crashed either on take-off or return, or in the sea; the aircrew losses (including those killed in crashes) amounted to 539. It was a strenuous existence, and became even more so in April, despite 14 days and nine nights of prohibitive weather. Besides the Rostock actions, and the "bass accompaniment", Essen was attacked three times, twice with over 200 bombers (10/11, 254; 12/13, 251); Cologne was also attacked three times (263 aircraft on the night of 5/6); Dortmund was attacked twice (208 aircraft on 14/15); Hamburg was attacked by 272 aircraft on the night of 8/9; and Bomber Command also visited Kiel, where *Scharnhorst* had taken refuge. On 17 nights there were operations against targets in France, and others roamed as far afield as Turin, Genoa, Pilsen in Czechoslovakia (the Skoda armament factory) and Trondheim in Norway.

By day, the Bostons of No. 2 Group (Air Vice-Marshal A. Lees) struck at targets in France with fighter escort ("Rhubarbs") on four-teen days. These must have been amazing spectacles; the Bostons never numbered more than 30 (divided between several targets); their escorts frequently amounted to 25, 26 or 27 squadrons of Spitfire Vs (over 300 aircraft) – on one day, April 30, no fewer than 38 squadrons were escorting 24 Bostons on four separate operations. Six Bostons were lost during the month, but Spitfire losses, in combat with Me 109Fs, FW 190s and (arriving at the end of April) Me 109Gs, were sometimes high: 11 on April 4, 15 on April 12, 12 on April 25 – a total of 59 for the month in "Rhubarbs", over and above the losses in Fighter Command's private "Circuses", which at times involved as many as 500 aircraft in a single sweep. (1942 cost the Command 915 aircraft in all.) Bomber Command's own losses for April were 150 aircraft missing from operations and another 22 crashed, a total of at least 871 aircrew on operations and another 58 killed in crashes, a perceptible wastage of trained personnel. Such was the pattern of offensive air action in 1942.

One operation especially, against a non-German target, gave great encouragement and whetted appetites for more of the same: the attack on the Renault factory at Billancourt, on the outskirts of Paris, on March 3/4. This was carried out by 236 aircraft, of which 223 claimed to have found their target; 470 tons of high explosive were dropped; the concentration of bombing during the attack was the highest yet achieved; all the evidence showed that very considerable damage had been done,[4] only one aircraft was lost, and it was learned with relief that loss of life among the French workers and population had been very low indeed.[5] Billancourt was an important factor in keeping alive the hope of precision bombing. But taken all in all, where training continued concurrently with operations (in No. 5 Group the aim was one day in three) there was not much rest during this period. Some Group Commanders believed that it was too much, that "the Com-mand was operating at an intensity which was too great for its health".[6] Harris was acutely conscious of a continuing need for a dramatic gesture to impress opinion both inside the Command and beyond it – something akin to Admiral Dönitz's "roll of drums".[7]

The question was what form it should take. There was a definite divergence of aim between Bomber Command and the Bomber Operations Directorate in the Air Ministry, and even the successes of March and April only served to underline this. We shall return to this subject, which was to have important effects on both the technique and the structure of the Command. In the meantime Harris, despite serious misgivings of his own concerning what was being achieved, clung to the idea of hitting a "first-class target", i.e. a large industrial city, which was bound to be heavily defended. His idea was to find a means of saturating these defences in order to produce, at one stroke, the kind of result that had finally been produced at Rostock; in other words, it was a matter of concentration in time and space. For this, evidently, numbers were of supreme importance, and numbers were what Harris did not appear to have. As we have seen (p. 461) the average daily serviceability of the Command in February was 378 aircraft; this rose to 421 in March, but dropped back to 416 by May.[8] But what it meant, on any particular occasion, as Harris says, was a maximum of something between 250–350 – which was very far from being a saturation. What he had in mind was 1,000 aircraft in action all at once against the same target. It was a very large idea, outwardly quite impracticable, obviously full of risks, but offering precisely the *coup de théâtre* that Harris desired. He mentioned it to Portal on May 18; Portal spoke to Churchill, and both warmly approved. It was then a matter of finding the machines.

Harris's first notion was to raise, by hook or crook, some 700 aircraft out of Bomber Command itself, and beg the rest from Coastal, Army Cooperation and Flying Training Commands. His request met a better reception from Joubert than he ever gave to the latter's pleas for help: an offer of no fewer than 250 aircraft of assorted types. However, this gallant gesture was vetoed by the Admiralty – and small wonder, with the curve of shipping losses rising towards disaster as it then was (see p. 424). Flying Training Command offered 30 Wellingtons, Whitleys and Hampdens, but owing to technical faults and lack of training this finally came down to only four Wellingtons. Fighter Command and Army Cooperation Command gave support to No. 2 Group in diversionary operations, but ultimately, when the count was made for the big attack, it was Bomber Command's own resources, front- and second-line (OTUs) that provided all but four of the 1,043 bombers which Harris was able to muster. It is interesting to note what they consisted of:

598 Wellingtons[9]	73 Lancasters
131 Halifaxes	46 Manchesters
88 Stirlings	28 Whitleys[10]
79 Hampdens	

What Harris had assembled was very nearly the absolute maximum of British bomber strength; it is sobering to reflect that in this third year of the war the 1936-vintage Wellington was still providing 57.33 per cent of the force, and the heavy bombers, planned in that same year, could only supply 32.40 per cent.

What takes the breath away, however, is not the composition of the force, but the manner in which Harris assembled it. All his first-line Groups were involved,[11] Nos. 1, 3, 4 and 5 putting in all they had, as might be expected; but this still left a considerable gap between Harris's intention and reality. The gap was filled by the two Operational Training Groups, Nos. 91 and 92, which provided no fewer than 367 aircraft manned by instructors and advanced pupil-crews. Harris was thus, says the Official History,

> committing not only his entire front-line strength, but also absolutely the whole of his reserves in a single battle. Such a bold action might produce a great triumph, but, if anything went wrong, the disaster might well be irremediable. The whole programme of training and expansion might conceivably be wrecked.[12]

The instructors, of course, men who had completed their tours of operations, were priceless; "the future of Bomber Command was in their hands and heavy losses among them would have had a paralysing effect".[13]

The great operation was code-named "MILLENNIUM"; every part of it was fraught with daunting risk. To the risk of committing the Training Groups – the "seed corn" – was added the eternal weather risk. Weather, at that time, says Harris, "had absolute power to make or mar an operation"; but good weather over England could well turn into heavy cloud over Germany, which would deeply compromise the plan, possibly with disastrous results. On the other hand,

> If I waited I might have to keep this very large force standing idle for some time, and I might lose the good weather over England; to land such a force in difficult weather would at that time have been to court disaster and for so many aircraft it was necessary to have a large number of bases free from cloud.[14]

He was determined that the attack should be made in bright moonlight, and the full moon came on May 30. Weather in England was good (after ten bad days), in Germany it was doubtful, but of all the German targets, the most hopeful was Cologne, though there was no certainty even about that. However,

I chose Cologne and dispatched the force. It was by no means the greatest risk that a commander in the field has had to take in war, but it was a considerable risk.[15]

His words reveal "a Commander endowed with exceptional courage and resolution".[16] This was the best of Harris, the power to decide and command, recalling (among other examples) the words of General Joffre in 1916, when called upon to decide quickly whether to abandon the right bank of the Meuse at Verdun, or hold on, risking the loss of much of the French artillery. Unhesitatingly, he decided to hold, and when his Deputy Chief of Staff remarked that his decision involved a great weight of responsibility, Joffre calmly replied, "I've taken plenty of others."[17]

There are not many occasions in the Second World War when Allied leaders were called upon to accept such risks and decide matters of such moment; Lord Gort's decision to evacuate the BEF in 1940, Wavell's decision to launch and push through Operation COMPASS against all the apparent odds in 1940–41, Slim's decision to go ahead with the Chindit Operation THURSDAY in 1944 when air reconnaissance seemed to show that the Japanese were forewarned and waiting, General Eisenhower's decision to launch OVERLORD on June 6, 1944 in despite of ambiguous weather forecasts – and how many more? Such instances do not crowd forward in the mind. Harris's calm, deliberate decision to stake his whole force and its future, on the night of May 30/31, showed the true quality of command.

The risks taken at High Wycombe were matched on the stations. Such a vast air armada had never been assembled before; merely to put it into the air was a risk, especially with crews whose training was incomplete. There was risk in routeing such a swarm to a single target, and the greatest risk of all when it got there. The attack was planned to take no more than 90 minutes from beginning to end – indeed, all aircraft were ordered to turn for home at zero hour + 90, whether they had bombed or not, to avoid having stragglers caught over Germany in daylight. The risk in such a degree of concentration was obvious to every member of every crew.

"The key to the success of this raid is saturation," said the briefing officer to No. 50 Squadron, and went on to explain the time-spread and the consequent need for very accurate timing.

"Now I'll come to the collision risk." Here the crews, already attentive, sat forward apprehensively, eager for reassurance. Ever since the figure of a thousand had been introduced at the start of the briefing, this was

485

the spectre that had haunted them. Mid-air collision was a hideous experience, one which few men had been known to survive.

"The boffins are confident," went on the briefing officer, "that the risk is negligible." There was a murmur of scepticism, which died away as the briefing continued. "They have assessed the chances" – here the briefing officer paused for a moment, to give full effect to his statement – "at one in a thousand."

They were being given the bull. That was the instant reaction . . .[18]

They might well be sceptical; with over 6,500 British airmen simultaneously in the sky and homing in on one German city, trying to avoid searchlights, flak and fighters, perhaps struggling with damage, the prophecy of only two aircraft being involved in collision sounded like lunacy. Out of so many men taking part, it is certain that there were some who viewed the whole prospect with deep alarm. However, there was nothing for it but to batten down disbelief and fear, wait for the appointed time, take up one's position in the aircraft – and take off. Which they did, and almost immediately ran into bad weather over the North Sea, with much cloud and heavy icing on the wings of some machines. But once over the Dutch coast and on the way to Germany, matters began to improve; there was only a little cirrus over Cologne, the moon was bright and visibility was good. The force was led in by GEE-equipped aircraft of Nos. 1 and 3 Groups – Air Vice-Marshal J. E. A. Baldwin, AOC of No. 3, accompanied his Group as a passenger in a Stirling – the leaders arriving seven minutes ahead of schedule at 0047 hours, and immediately starting fires on a scale which served as a beacon for the rest. All told, 898 crews claimed to have reached and attacked Cologne; they dropped nearly 1,500 tons of bombs, of which some two-thirds were incendiaries. Huge fires were seen blazing right through the target area, so large that they were still visible to returning crews 150 miles away. Since less than a quarter of the force despatched carried cameras, the night evidence of success was scanty, only 32 photographs being plotted within five miles of the central aiming point. It was the daylight photographs, taken when the smoke had cleared away, that gave the necessary proof:

> They showed that the damage was "heavy and widespread" and that it was "on a much larger scale than any previously inflicted on a German city". Six hundred acres of Cologne, including about three hundred acres right in the centre of the city, appeared to have been completely destroyed. There was no "considerable" part of Cologne which these photographs showed to be free of damage. Bomber Command had at last won a major victory against a major target.[19]

Harris had done what he had set out to do; he had captured the imagination of the British and American public, he had exhilarated his Command, and he had won the unreserved admiration of the Prime Minister, thus saving the bomber offensive for a yet more vigorous future. Churchill told him:

This proof of the growing power of the British Bomber Force is also the herald of what Germany will receive, city by city, from now on.

As Sir Robert Saundby says,

The last sentence of this message showed that the Government was firmly committed to the policy of reducing German military and industrial strength by means of air bombardment . . . in operation MILLENNIUM can be discerned the beginning of the end.[20]

So Harris had pulled off his *coup*; and the cost? Forty-one aircraft were missing from the operation (29 of them Wellingtons).[21] This represents 3.93 per cent of the force despatched (3.8 per cent is the figure normally quoted). However, four more Wellingtons crashed on landing, and two came down in the sea, while a Hampden and a Halifax collided on return, and another Hampden also crashed, raising the total of aircraft to 50 – 4.79 per cent. In addition, 116 aircraft were damaged to a greater or lesser extent, of which 12 had to be written off, so that the final count of aircraft completely lost as a result of MILLENNIUM was 62 – 5.94 per cent. And since a further 33 aircraft were seriously damaged – which meant that they would certainly not be available for the next operation, only two days later – it is not unfair to say that the full count for MILLENNIUM was 95, of 9.1 per cent.[22] The loss of aircrew, including those lost in two Blenheims in the diversion and killed in crashes, but not including any in the 116 damaged aircraft, was 291. From aircrew reports it was estimated that 22 aircraft had been lost actually over the target, due to the following causes:

Flak	16
Fighters	4
Collision	2

So the "boffins" were right after all – there *was* only one collision over the target, a matter at which one may still marvel. Away from the target area, it was considered that fighters accounted for twice as many aircraft as AA guns. It was noted that the proportion of losses of the

OTU Groups was "appreciably below" that of the operational Groups; on the other hand,

> the greater proportion of pilots lost . . . were Instructors (including seven from No. 91 Group alone) who could ill be spared from the Training organisation.[23]

When Goering received the first reports of MILLENNIUM by telephone the next day, he flatly refused to believe them; it was simply not possible for such a number of bombs to be dropped on a single night, he said, and he told the Cologne *Gauleiter*: "The report from your police commissioner is a stinking lie!"[24]

But there was no doubt in Cologne that a great deal of damage had been done on the night of May 30/31 – more, it turned out, than in all the previous 70 attacks on the city. The British estimate of between 1,000 and 6,000 deaths, however, was very wide of the mark; the real total was 474, and over 5,000 injured, of whom only 565 were admitted to hospital. 3,330 houses were destroyed, 9,510 damaged, and 45,152 people were rendered homeless – but this last figure is not very meaningful, since many were only homeless for a short time. Loss of production is hard to evaluate; 36 factories ceased production altogether, and 70 were reduced to half their normal output. But, again, it is practically impossible to set a time limit on this result. The Official History finally concluded that a loss of one month's production was probably a reasonable supposition.[25] Harris told Churchill in June that Cologne had been practically destroyed: "a leading asset to Germany turned in one night into a vast liability".[26] It was not so; the population of Cologne, contrary to Lord Trenchard's prognostications, did not fall "easy prey to hysteria and panic" (see p. 264); instead they displayed the same stoic qualities that the British civilians had shown in 1940–41, and like their compatriots in Lübeck and Rostock, they took swift measures towards recovery:

> Within two weeks the life of the city was functioning almost normally.[27]

So Harris's victory was in the minds of his beholders, rather than on the ground in Germany. This was not appreciated until long after – which was probably fortunate; those were dark days, and it would have been intensely depressing to know that Britain's most powerful weapon was so much less powerful than it seemed.

Not the least astonishing aspect of MILLENNIUM is that it was immediately repeated. If Harris had shown boldness in conceiving the idea of 1,000-bomber attacks he now displayed real audacity in keeping this great force together to maintain the offensive. On the night of June 1/2, 957 aircraft were launched at the most difficult of targets: Essen. All but two (from Flying Training Command) were Bomber Command machines, though Army Cooperation Command supplied 15 Blenheims to join in the diversionary attacks on German aerodromes. Of the main force, 767 pilots claimed to have reached the general Essen area, but, as the Official History says,

> Very few crews were ... prepared to assert with certainty that they had identified the target.[28]

Cloud over Essen was 5-10/10ths at 8,000 feet, in addition to the normal haze. Thus, in Harris's words, an "unforeseen change in the weather (had) given almost complete protection to Essen that night".[29] Only eight night photographs proved to have been taken within five miles of the target; daylight reconnaissance confirmed that very little damage had been done to the city, and none at all to the famous Krupp works. From the main force, 32 aircraft were missing, two crashed (one soon after take-off, one on return), and of 99 damaged five had to be written off – 4.07 per cent. Aircrew losses, including the crashes, were 212. In addition, three Blenheims were missing from the diversions.

This was disappointing, and what was worse, the disappointment was felt at the time. For public consumption, the pretence was made that Germany had again suffered a heavy blow, but Bomber Command Headquarters and the Air Staff knew better. Four more considerable attacks were made on Essen during June, a total of 651 sorties, generally referred to, for Press and radio, as attacks upon "the Ruhr", a convenient cover for further misfortunes. Harris, however, was undaunted; Cologne, in his mind, had been a triumph, and he wanted more of them. For the time being he had to disperse the 1,000-Force, the contingents from the OTUs returning to their normal (and essential) duties. But he had a "strong feeling", as he told Portal, that four "thousand-attacks" a month

> might prove to be very much more effective than one Thousand Plan a month plus ordinary everyday hum-drum operations in the interim.[30]

Harris was planning accordingly, and for his next "production", while accepting that nothing more should be expected from Flying Training Command, he took care to obtain a contribution from

Coastal. He persuaded Churchill to put pressure on the Admiralty, as a consequence of which Joubert (who would probably have done even more, left to his own devices) supplied 20 Wellingtons and 82 Hudsons. Army Cooperation Command supplied five Blenheims.

The target selected was Bremen where, as well as U-boat construction yards and important docks, there was also a Focke-Wulf aircraft factory; the date chosen was June 25/26. On this occasion, including the supporting contingents, and once more drawing upon its training Groups, Bomber Command was able to send out just over a thousand aircraft (1,003).[31] Once more the weather was treacherous and once again the results were considerably less than what had been hoped for. Some striking damage was done to the buildings of the Focke-Wulf factory, which offered consolation at the time, but post-war investigation showed that the effect on production was far less than the contemporary photographs suggested. Losses were high: 44 aircraft of Bomber Command were missing, four more crashed in the sea, and one Wellington and four Hudsons of Coastal Command also failed to return – 5.28 per cent. Aircrew losses, including those killed in crashes, were 291. In addition, 65 aircraft were damaged, 22 of them seriously. Disturbing considerations were the fact that over 40 per cent of the aircraft losses were sustained by No. 91 Group – 22 aircraft, of which 21 were manned entirely by pupil crews; also disturbing was the loss of eight Halifaxes out of 124, 6.45 per cent, and eight Whitleys out of 50, 16 per cent. Bremen was the last of the thousand-bomber operations; in mounting no fewer than three in the space of four weeks, "Bomber Command had achieved the seemingly impossible".[32] The question was, was it worth it? Seen as a propaganda exercise,[33] the answer was, with one reservation, undoubtedly "yes"; Bomber Command was right back "on the map" with government and public alike. The reservation is contained within that very fact:

> Despite specific warnings by the Prime Minister to Parliament and the general public that "thousand" raids must not be regarded as the general rule until the size of the bomber force had been considerably increased, there was already a growing tendency in both official and unofficial circles to regard the 200–300 sorties which were Bomber Command's normal effort at that time as mere chicken feed . . .[34]

Soon Harris found himself in the ironic position, having urged the large operations, of explaining why they were impracticable. In operational terms, there was not much doubt of it; every week that went by tended to weaken belief in the damage done to the enemy, while the cost of the three big attacks remained: 134 aircraft (15 crashed) and over 770 aircrew. These figures (apart from write-offs) represent just over a quarter of the aircraft total for the three months, April, May and June, and some 25.5 per cent of the aircrew.[35] It was a high proportion, contributing heavily to high totals; and worst of all, of course, was the wastage of training instructors and pupils from the OTUs.

In the second half of 1942 the tempo of the air offensive against Germany was markedly reduced. There *were* large-scale attacks, but far fewer of them; that on Düsseldorf on July 31/August 1, for example, involving 630 aircraft, while another attack on the same city on September 10/11 involved 476. These two operations did heavy damage, but did not prevent Düsseldorf's industrial production in the second half of the year from exceeding that of the first half by 1.8 per cent. The interesting feature of the second half, however, is not the weight of particular attacks, nor the amount of damage done by them. It lies in the renewed inclination of the Bomber Operations Directorate (see p. 491) to strike what it hoped would be mortal blows at precise targets. Inspired by what the Directorate believed to be Harris's notable success against Lübeck, it urged him in April to mount a similar operation against Schweinfurt, where two-thirds of Germany's vital ball-bearing production was believed to be concentrated.[36] This marked the opening round of a long contest between Harris and the supporters of what he tartly described as "panacea" targets –

> targets which were supposed by the economic experts to be such a vital bottleneck in the German war industry that when they were destroyed the enemy would have to pack up.[37]

For the time being Harris was able to fend off the Schweinfurt scheme; he considered it a very difficult target to locate, and the Air Ministry, on reflection, agreed. However, precision bombing was definitely on the agenda again, and April saw a very remarkable attempt to give effect to it.

From its first appearance, Avro's revised version of the Manchester, the Lancaster (see p. 282), had won golden opinions. Air Vice-Marshal N. H. Bottomley, commanding No. 5 Group in 1941, had expressed himself as "tremendously impressed by its performance". "I am sure," he said, "that our crews will be most enthusiastic about the aircraft when it reaches them."[38] Unfortunately, 14 months later, it was only reaching them in driblets; up to mid-April 1942, very few had taken part in Bomber Command operations, the maximum on any particular occasion being seven or eight. There was no doubt, however, that they were magnificent aircraft – Harris later called the Lancaster "without exception the finest bomber of the war".[39] It was a wonderful weight-lifter; it was easy to handle; it had the lowest accident rate – and in retrospect, according to Harris, "the casualty rate of Lancasters was also consistently below that of other types".[40] So in April 1942 there was a definite sense of the Lancaster being the aircraft of the future, and no doubt there was also a desire to know just what (now that trained crews were available) it could and could not do. There was only one way to find out. Even so, a daylight attack involving a round trip of 1,250 miles without escort seems to be pressing fortune to its limits.

Nevertheless, Harris decided to send 12 Lancasters to attack the *Maschinenfabrik Augsburg-Nürnberg Aktiengesellschaft* submarine diesel factory at Augsburg on April 17. Nos. 44 and 97 Squadrons were designated for this astonishing adventure, and went into special training for low-level, long-distance flying a week before. It is a tribute to the ingrained civilian mentality of the British people that, in the third year of war, this produced a spate of complaints from local authorities of "pranks by the RAF flying large four-engined aeroplanes low over the country".[41] On April 17 the ground-crews filled the tanks to capacity: 2,154 gallons of fuel,[42] and six aircraft of each squadron stood by, in sections of three, under Squadron-Leader J. D. Nettleton, a South African pilot of No. 44. Take-off was at 1500 hours, covered, it was hoped, by vigorous action by No. 2 Group's Bostons and Fighter Command. Unfortunately, this diversion proved to be counter-productive; it merely stirred up the *Luftwaffe*'s fighters, which began to engage the Lancasters almost as soon as they had crossed the Channel. Before they had even passed Paris, four were down in flames, including two piloted by Warrant Officers who already held the DFM.[43] The two remaining 44 Squadron aircraft pressed on across central France, beyond the range of the coast-based fighters, skirted Switzerland, and came up to Augsburg in the late afternoon sunlight. They were greeted by the inevitable storm of flak, and the Lancaster piloted by Flying Officer A. J. Garwell, DFM, having bombed at chimney-top height, was brought down. Then No. 97 Squadron's two sections came in; having missed the fighters they still numbered six aircraft – but not for long. Squadron Leader J. S. Sherwood, DFC, was hit over the target "and went down smoking to crash in a ball of flame"; shortly afterwards Warrant Officer Mycock also went down enveloped in flames.[44] The remaining five Lancasters, all damaged, made their way home aided by the gathering dusk;

Nettleton landed just before one a.m., having been ten hours in the air. He was awarded the Victoria Cross, and the other survivors received the DSO, DFC or DFM.

Seven out of twelve of Bomber Command's precious new aircraft: Harris says the loss

> was not excessive in proportion to the importance of the objective and the serious damage done to it.[45]

Even at the time, he was challenged on both counts. The Ministry of Economic Warfare was deeply angered that this attack on a specific "key" target had been made without any consultation; the Minister (Lord Selborne) told Churchill:

> The Air Ministry had long ago been informed that the vulnerability of the MAN plant was low and that there would be no sensible effect on the supply of engines even if it were destroyed completely. Surely the experts should have been consulted before the raid was made so that the sacrifice could have produced corresponding results.[46]

Harris, of course, challenged the very word "experts"; he distrusted such persons completely, placing them firmly in the category of "the panacea-mongers who were always cropping up and hawking their wares".[47] The remainder of the war witnessed a running battle between the Commander-in-Chief of Bomber Command and the Ministry of Economic Warfare.

As regards the damage done to the MAN works, Bomber Command's own Operational Research Section claimed no more than that there was "little doubt that work has been delayed", and *Bomber Command Quarterly Review*, while calling the operation "one of the outstanding raids of the war", only claimed that it had resulted in work being "very seriously delayed".[48] Post-war investigation shows that the Ministry of Economic Warfare was right in its assessment of the target: even a complete stoppage of submarine engine construction would not have been disastrous, since MAN had five other firms under licence throughout Europe for this work. The actual effect on production was "slight".[49] It is depressing, too, to learn that after such heroic endeavour, out of 17 bombs which hit the target, five failed to explode.

On one point there was almost no disagreement. As the Official History says,

... the action had convincingly demonstrated that this type of operation was not a feasible proposition of war for Lancasters in 1942.[50]

Harris agrees; the losses, he says,

did demonstrate beyond all question that daylight attacks on Germany could at that time only be carried out by Bomber Command at a prohibitive casualty rate.[51]

That was a lesson which he had firmly learnt; whether it should have required the loss of 49 gallant young men, mostly dead in horrible circumstances, is a question which is not easy to answer with assurance from an armchair forty years on. But Harris's emotions may be imagined when, just over a month later, he was told by Freeman (still VCAS) that "twelve specially armoured Lancasters would shortly be delivered to Bomber Command."[52] And as though this was not bad enough, Freeman added that an order for 100 of these armoured Lancasters had been placed, for delivery in September. He told Harris:

I know you do not like the specially armoured Lancasters, but I want you to give them a really thorough trial. The lessons which we hope to learn from them about daylight attack may be of enormous value and affect the whole range of tactical doctrine.

If, in some respects, the Augsburg operation displays again the worst of Harris (a ruthless contempt for opposing views, even if well-founded), we now see him once more at his practical best. He told Freeman that if this interesting experiment was going to be carried out in the face of the enemy, he did not think the crews would "survive long enough to develop anything". If a formation of Lancasters met a large number of enemy fighters in daylight, he said, there was no doubt

that very few, whether armoured or unarmoured, would survive. Their fate would depend, therefore, on chance – not armour.

And to this opinion he firmly adhered – so perhaps the young men of 44 and 97 Squadrons had not died in vain. Certainly, the whole weight of Bomber Command opinion was behind Harris. But Freeman, too, was a strong-willed man, and as time went by and Harris continued to stonewall, he went so far as to make the armour experiment an order. "When two strong men stand face to face ..." Harris remained obdurate; this was, as he saw it, a matter of the tactical handling of his force, and that was his responsibility and no one else's. He was fortunate in two circumstances: Freeman returned to the Ministry of Aircraft Production in November, with the matter still unresolved; and Portal, on the subject of daylight attacks by heavy bombers, mainly agreed with Harris.

Nevertheless, partly as a fruit of the revived quest for precision, and partly as a manifestation of what were called "Moling" and "Scuttle" activities, daylight operations continued to be a feature of 1942 in Bomber Command. "Moling" was the name given to sorties against specific targets in 8-10/10ths cloud, making full use of cloud cover and bombing on a GEE fix; "Scuttle" meant roving commissions by individual aircraft, bombing built-up areas seen through gaps in the clouds (or, as a last resort, on ETA or possibly a GEE fix). Both were manifestations of that entirely false estimate of the German character to which several allusions have already been made. Taking into account the German Air Raid Precautions regulations which decreed that, on the sounding of the alarm, everyone must take cover and remain in shelters until the All Clear, it was assumed that:

> The German mentality is not well constituted to withstand this sort of treatment. A crowd of Germans herded together in a communal shelter lacks the collective sense of humour which sustains a British crowd under similar circumstances of discomfort and there is no doubt that enforced confinement particularly in winter had a profoundly depressing effect on them.[53]

It was pure wishful thinking, of course; but it resulted in some 204 sorties being flown in daylight by the heavy and medium groups between March and September. Fortunately, owing to variable weather conditions, most of them were abortive, which saved many Wellington, Stirling, Lancaster and Mosquito crews from becoming sacrificial victims to the unpleasing national traits of arrogance and contempt for foreigners.

There were, however, some daylight operations in 1942 which cannot be brushed aside. On July 11, 33 Lancasters were sent to attack the submarine yards at Danzig, very near to the 800-mile radius, indicating a nearly 1,600-mile round trip.[54] This was Bomber Command's heaviest daylight attack to date against a German target. There were special circumstances which make it difficult to draw conclusions: the bombers had cloud cover all the way; they met no German fighters, and since they were mostly flying over the sea they were little troubled by flak on the approach and return; finally, the attack was timed to go in at dusk, which made it virtually a night operation (searchlights were in use by the defence). The result was a loss of only two Lancasters – but, as usual, no significant lasting damage to the target.

With the withdrawal of the Manchesters in June (Bremen on June 25/26 was their last operation with Bomber Command) and the Hampdens in September, the Lancasters were concentrated in No. 5 Group.[55] In the autumn of 1942 their latest "teething trouble" was in the fuel installation, which meant an average operational strength in the Group's nine squadrons of only 80 aircraft instead of a potential of about 175. Nevertheless, on October 1, crews began practising low-level, long-distance formation flying, as they had (belatedly) done before the Augsburg attack but with this difference, that after a spell of squadron practice, wings of three squadrons flew together, then the whole Group. They were about to carry out the largest – and most risk-laden – daylight attack yet carried out: on the great Schneider-Creusot armament factory, one of the largest steel works on the Continent. Le Creusot is in eastern France, not far from the Swiss frontier, and closely adjacent to that area whose placenames – Gevrey-Chambertin, Nuits-St Georges, Beaune, Meursault, Mâcon – read like a melodious passage of a favourite wine list. But it was a long way away; only Lancasters would have the necessary performance.

The date selected was October 17; 94 Lancasters were assembled to take part in the operation which some acutely security-minded person code-named "ROBINSON", presumably on the grounds that no German Intelligence Officer would ever connect that name with anything that sounded in the least like Crusoe. The formation was led by Wing Commander L. C. Slee of No. 49 Squadron; the other squadrons were to keep station by observation of 49 Squadron aircraft. The whole force assembled at Upper Heyford, flying from there to Land's End at under 1,000 feet in order to avoid radar observation, then swung out into the Atlantic, dropping to below 500 feet, then turning into the Bay of Biscay and crossing the French coast just south of the Ile d'Yeu at about 100 feet. The round journey, by this route, was about 1,700 miles.

The Germans, this time, were taken completely by surprise. No fighters were encountered, the hazards being those endemic in low flying. *How* low may be judged by one man's observation that the railway tracks leading to Le Creusot looked rusty and unused, while a pilot remarked that the cattle in the fields looked underfed, which was contested by another, who said that on the contrary they seemed well fed. The force reached Le Creusot at dusk (1809 BST); flak was negligible; some 120 tons of high explosive and nearly 40 tons of incendiaries were dropped from between 4–6,000 feet; the whole attack took seven minutes. Only one Lancaster was lost, and that, it was believed, not by enemy action, but by hitting a building after a very low-level approach to a special target, the electricity switching station at Montchanin. The crews had the impression of an extremely successful attack, and this seemed to be confirmed by immediate reconnaissance and intelligence reports. Alas! it was not so; very soon

the Operational Research Section at Bomber Command came to the conclusion that the accuracy of the bombing had been far less than was expected. They thought this was partly attributable to the failing light and the smoke which soon began to drift across the target, but they also thought that the tactics adopted had been inappropriate and that the bomb-sights had not been properly used. They suggested that the outcome was the penalty of employing night crews in complex daylight operations without giving them more than a few days' training.[56]

The quest for precision through daylight operations of heavy bombers was not a success; indeed, they only served to illustrate the virtually insuperable difficulties of quickly turning a night force into a day force. The only surprising thing is that anyone ever had any doubt about the matter. What is sad to relate is that the light bombers, which existed entirely for daylight purposes, hardly did any better. The idea of a very fast, very low-level attack on a pin-point target has always held out great appeal, and the Mosquito seemed to be exactly the instrument whereby it might be achieved. Yet even with such a high-performance aircraft as that, these operations proved to be far easier to talk about and write about than to perform. Four Mosquitoes took off on September 25 to knock out the *Gestapo* headquarters in Oslo, a precise target if ever there was one. One Mosquito was shot down by FW 190s, but the immediate impression was that this spectacular, roof-top level attack had been "highly successful".[57] Intelligence sources "reported the encouragement given to the Norwegians by this attack and stated that it was the main subject of conversation in Stockholm next day".[58] What the tenor of that conversation was, however, is not clear, because merciless photographic reconnaissance soon revealed that it was a house on the opposite side of the street to the *Gestapo* headquarters that had received most of the damage.

More satisfactory from that point of view, but depressing in other ways, was the large operation mounted by No. 2 Group against the

Philips Radio Works at Eindhoven on December 6. Among the 93 aircraft despatched were 47 of the new Lockheed Venturas (the remainder comprising 36 Bostons and 10 Mosquitoes). Bostons were to take the lead, bombing from the lowest possible altitude; more Bostons and the Mosquitoes would then bomb from 1–1,500 feet, and finally the Venturas from 200 feet or less. The reality was not so tidy; the approach to the target was ragged and the return even more so. However, over 60 tons of bombs were dropped, and this time the photographic reconnaissance evidence indicated that severe damage had really been done to the factory. The cost, however, was high: 13 aircraft lost in the attack and two more crashed; a further 53 were damaged, seven of them seriously.[59] Aircrew losses amounted to 62.

Clearly, if Bomber Command wanted precision, daylight alone was not going to offer it; the alternative was to improve the night-time performance. There were different ways of doing this, the most obvious being improved target-finding devices. GEE had disappointed; an excellent navigational aid (it remained in service for the rest of the war, and was valued by crews as a sure way of getting home after bombing) it was unable to provide accurate target location. It also lacked range, and by mid-year its jamming-free life was running out. New devices were on the way – but it was not an easy way; and we have noted the competition of Coastal Command, in its desperate straits, for ASV III, clashing with Bomber Command's need for H2S. For the rest of 1942 there was nothing for it but to wait for science and technology to mature.

There was, however, another way forward which had been coming increasingly into discussion during the early part of the year, especially among operational aircrews: the creation of a special force, using the best equipment available and consisting of the most efficient crews, to mark targets and so guide in the main body of bombing forces, which would necessarily consist of a cross-section of crews, good, bad and indifferent, and would most probably not be universally provided with up-to-date aids. As we have seen (see p. 475) the SHAKER technique, with its first wave of "illuminators" was already a pointer to such a procedure; indeed, the Official History says:

> ... some form of target-finding force had become inevitable from the moment that GEE was introduced.[60]

The question was, *what* "form" of force? How special should it be? The more junior the officers, and therefore the closest to current operational conditions, the greater the certainty seemed to be that it should be very distinctly special, a set of squadrons which should be given sole responsibility for this work, and cultivate expertise in it above all else. They found their champion in Group Captain S. O. Bufton, the Deputy Director of Bomber Operations at the Air Ministry, himself a squadron and station commander until November 1941. He suggested that the target-finding force should consist of six squadrons in "close proximity" to each other, one third of the crews to be drawn from the best crews of the whole Command. This worked out at about one crew from each squadron, and would be a once-for-all measure, all replacements or reinforcements coming direct from OTUs.

Bufton's proposal, which he upheld with great determination and no little courage, ran head-on into one of the RAF's deep prejudices: a strong, irrational distrust and dislike of anything smacking of a *corps d'élite*. The arguments for and against such formations have run steadily through military history; the answer would seem to be, as is often the case, that moderation serves best. It is certainly true, as the opponents of *élites* always insist, that creaming off the best men into them has a weakening effect on the main force. The British, in the Second World War, showed an alarming disposition towards such procedures, and the ill results became very apparent in the Army towards the end. On the other hand, the existence of such formations as the Guards, with their very high standards, so far from having a demoralizing effect on other units, has supplied an example and a level to aspire to of the utmost value. In the Navy, every keen captain has desired to make his ship a "crack" ship in some way – gunnery, torpedoes, cleanliness, general alacrity, or whatever it might be. The RAF did not like the idea of "crack" squadrons, any more than it liked the idea of "aces". So Bufton met powerful opposition, chiefly from the Bomber Group Commanders, firmly supported by their redoubtable AOC-in-C.

Once again, in the long-drawn-out controversy that followed, we see the two sides of Harris. He told Bufton in April that he had "a fairly open mind on the subject of the Target Finding Force", but as the Official History says, "he made it perfectly clear that he had no intention of creating one".[61] It is difficult to dismiss the thought that what he most rootedly objected to was the notion of what he would call a "junior staff officer" in the Air Ministry presuming to tell him and the distinguished officers commanding his Groups how to run their business. As the Official History points out, there was undoubtedly a fundamental difference between his approach to bombing and Bufton's:

Air Marshal Harris . . . regarded area bombing as an end in itself, and, if vigorously enough pursued, as a means of winning the war. Group Captain Bufton thought it was only a preparatory phase through which Bomber Command would inevitably have to pass before it could perfect the technique of precise attack. The whole future tactical development of Bomber Command hung between these two extremes of opinion, for it was, of course, the ultimate aim which conditioned the process of design, scientific investigation and production which resulted in the equipment, and of training which resulted in the operational aircrews.[62]

In more immediate terms, Harris and Bufton were not far apart. In correspondence with the Air Ministry, Harris was disposed to defend Bomber Command's record and argue that there was no need for a structural change. In private, and within the Command, he was as concerned as Bufton over some of the results that were coming to his notice. What worried both was an apparent lack of bombing discipline in the Command; Bufton worked out that in eight attacks on Essen in just under six weeks of March and April, as many as 90 per cent of aircraft had dropped their bombs between 5 and 100 miles from the target – an appalling conclusion. Harris himself considered that the attack on Mannheim on May 19/20 (197 aircraft despatched, 154 claimed to have attacked) had been "most disappointing". Photographs showed that practically no damage had been done to the town or suburbs; on the contrary, as Harris pointed out to the Group Commanders, "almost the whole effort . . . was wasted in bombing large fires in the local forests, and possibly decoy fires".[63] He pronounced:

> . . . somehow or other we must cure this disease, for it is a disease, of wasting bombs wholesale upon decoy fires.[64]

These were the considerations which were now building up a formidable body of opinion against the views of Harris and his Group Commanders – and, surely, helping to undermine the defence of those views. The Report on the Bombing of Germany by Mr Justice Singleton, presented to Churchill on May 20, provided another powerful voice against them. Having interviewed two operational officers "of great experience", Singleton said:

> They are both completely satisfied with the accuracy of TR 1335 (GEE) provided that it is used by a specially trained crew. In such conditions they say it will take you within four miles of the target longitudinally with a possible error of two miles laterally. They regard it as of tremendous help.

500

It is in the last few miles that the real difficulties arise, and they can only be overcome by determination and will power. The crews are not by any means all of the same calibre, and the officers to whom I refer are firmly convinced of the desirability of a specially trained Target Finding Force, which, they believe, would lead to greatly increased efficiency in combing.[56]

Bufton was winning, by the sheer logic of events as perceived by those most intimately concerned. By June, Portal had been won over; on the 14th he wrote to Harris, saying that "the problem confronting us is clearly so great that nothing less than the best will do"; various compromise solutions proposed by Bomber Command would not, he considered, be likely to supply a real answer, and he announced the opinion of the Air Staff

that the formation of a special force with a rôle analogous to that of the Reconnaissance Battalion of an Army Division would immediately open up a new field for improvement, raising the standard and thus the morale which could not fail to be reflected throughout the whole force.[66]

This settled the matter, and not before it was time; even now it took until August 11 for the Pathfinder Force (as Harris christened it) to be formally created. This was in part due to the better side of Harris asserting itself once more; having bitterly opposed the setting up of the Force, now that it was decreed he was determined that it should have its rights:

As the Pathfinder squadrons were to be asked to run even greater risks than the squadrons of the main force, to work longer tours and probably to miss promotion in their parent squadrons, I proposed that the men in them should get quicker promotion and wear some sort of distinguishing badge; as we were compelled by events to have a *corps d'élite* it seemed to me necessary to carry the principle through to its logical conclusion.[67]

In history it is not often recorded that "they lived happily ever after"; the coming of the Pathfinders did not bring about immediate, dramatic improvements in Bomber Command's performance. Their commander, Air Commodore D. C. T. Bennett, an Australian still in his early thirties, had "an understanding of the many problems of long-range flying which was probably unique in the Service. He was an acknowledged expert on the subject of air navigation and he knew intimately the job which each member of a bomber crew had to undertake."[68] "His technical knowledge," says Harris, "and his personal operational ability was altogether exceptional." However, so much ability had its drawbacks:

> He will forgive me if I say that his consciousness of his own intellectual powers sometimes made him impatient with slower or differently constituted minds, so that some people found him difficult to work with. He could not suffer fools gladly, and by his own high standards there were many fools ... he is, in fact, very much an intellectual and, being still a young man, had at times the young intellectual's habit of underrating experience and overrating knowledge.[69]

The Group Commanders were not among Bennett's warmest admirers; it was galling for them to be asked to part with their best crews for the benefit of a force whose work, they were sure, could equally well be done by squadrons in their Groups. Bennett made no friends in high places with remarks about senior officers who had not been "fortunate enough to be permitted to operate themselves".[70] One Group, No. 5 (now under Air Vice-Marshal W. A. Coryton), already had a reputation for accurate navigation and was generally singled out to supply leaders to difficult targets and make precise attacks. No. 5 Group did not relinquish one particle of this reputation, and the squadron most famous for combining these attributes, No. 617 ("Dam-busters"), remained part of that Group and outside the Pathfinder Force (later numbered 8 Group).

As regards equipment, the Pathfinder Force "was never more than a powerful competitor for what was available and it certainly never enjoyed absolute priority",[71] which may be considered curious, in view of all the trouble taken to set it up. It thus had, from the first, to struggle against substantial difficulties. Its first operation, against Flensburg on August 18/19, was not a success; 118 aircraft were despatched and 91 claimed to have attacked; but in conditions of extreme darkness and thick ground haze the Air Staff Operational Summary stated that "early arrivals (i.e. Pathfinders) were unable to identify definitely the aiming point". Only "scattered fires in the town and shipyards" were reported.[72] During the remainder of the year the Pathfinders led 26 attacks on Germany; on six occasions, in very bad weather, they completely failed to find the target; of the remainder, in better conditions, they found and marked three times out of four – and to everyone's surprise their losses, at less than three per cent, were considerably less than had been expected.[73] Yet the fact very obviously remained that, like so much else, the Pathfinder Force would have to await 1943 to find fulfilment. So precision bombing whether by day or night, continued to be outside the capability of Bomber Command, which left a choice between area bombing or nothing – which in war meant no choice at all.

62 *"Prescription for Massacre"; another strategic debate*

There was not much for the Allies to console themselves with until almost the end of 1942. The Japanese were triumphant in south-east Asia and over most of the Pacific; their tentacles reached as far as Sydney in one direction, the Indian Ocean in another, and Vancouver in a third. In the East, the Germans recovered from their winter setbacks, captured Sevastopol, swept forward to the Don and menaced the Caucasus; the Soviet Union's calls for help were a shrill often (understandably) bitter accompaniment to the strategic planning of her Western allies. What was happening in the Atlantic threatened at times to undo them utterly. And even when light broke through, and success began to shine upon them in the Desert and North Africa, it brought with it new perplexities, new arguments about strategy which threatened serious divisions within the alliance. It is not to be wondered at if the bombing offensive once more came under searching scrutiny while its supporters continued to stake out startling claims.

It is hard now, in view of what has been fairly common knowledge for a long time of the real results of the bombing programme, to understand the degree of optimism with which it was viewed in certain very influential quarters. What was it that led Portal, in August 1942, to tell Tedder that the attack on Germany "is really beginning to have great results"?[1] August was the month in which the Pathfinder Force was created precisely because the offensive was *not* having the results desired, and was also the month in which the Germans started jamming GEE, making those results yet more difficult to attain. One must assume that Portal's view was honestly held, in which case it amounts to a most disturbing degree of delusion – a degree which might just be acceptable in Harris at High Wycombe, but not in the Chief of the Air Staff. Yet it was contagious; in the next month we find Churchill himself telling Roosevelt:

. . . we know our night bomber offensive is having a devastating effect.[2]

It was clearly on this foundation that Portal constructed the proposal that he put forward in a note to the (British) Chiefs of Staff on

September 30 – a paper on which, says Slessor, "I always look back as one of the best I remember". In it Portal said there were three policies that the Allies might adopt:

> "A" was to build up the resources necessary to get a decision by invasion *before* German industry and economic power had been broken; "B" was to shatter German resistance by air and then put in the Army; and "C" was a compromise under which we tried to build up simultaneously strong land and air forces on a scale unrelated to any particular task, without any clear intention of attaining a definite object by a definite time.
>
> Course "C" appeared to him to be the one that the United Nations were then pursuing; the only argument that he could see in its favour was that it was largely non-controversial . . . For his part, he favoured course "B", for which he thought a combined heavy bomber force rising to a peak of between four and six thousand might be necessary.[3]

This Anglo-American aerial battering-ram, Portal told his colleagues, would make victory possible in 1944 with the intervention of only "a relatively small land force".[4]

Sir David Fraser, in his biography of Lord Alanbrooke, says that the other Chiefs of Staff (Brooke, Pound and Mountbatten) "disagreed", and "Portal's paper was rebutted".[5] This abbreviates an interesting story; the truth is that at first the British Chiefs of Staff accepted the Air view without apparent demur. On October 30 the committee circulated a strategic review in which it reaffirmed the proposition that the Allies must

> undermine Germany's military power by the destruction of the German industrial and economic war machine before we attempt invasion . . . The heavy bomber will be the main weapon . . . [with] absolute priority of Anglo-American production . . .

This review used a form of words which would make a significant reappearance:

> The aim of the bomber offensive is the progressive destruction and dislocation of the enemy's war industrial and economic system and the undermining of his morale to a point where his capacity for armed resistance is fatally weakened.[6]

The Official Historians remark:

> This declaration by the Chiefs of Staff represented an extraordinary victory for the Air Staff point of view and it was a tribute not only to the persuasive

powers of Sir Charles Portal but also to the prestige which Bomber Command had acquired in the course of 1942. It was, nevertheless, by no means a final victory.[7]

Scarcely had the Chiefs of Staff put signatures to their paper than the war itself, as was its habit, supervened. By November 4, General Montgomery had won his battle at El Alamein, and the pleasing spectacle was seen of Rommel in full and disastrous retreat. No sooner was that fact taken in than the TORCH landings followed, and a second major campaign in Africa (with attractive prospects) established its claim for attention and resources. Every week that went by also revealed the Germans stuck on the Eastern Front for another winter, with a whole Army in mounting difficulty at Stalingrad. Though sinkings by U-boats reached one of their highest levels (see p. 418), there was encouragement to be drawn from their total failure against the great TORCH convoys (see p. 436). In other words, there was a definite change in the texture of the war; new possibilities of obtaining victory suggested themselves. When they came to consider the detailed arguments by which Portal sought to support his plea for 4–6,000 bombers, the Chiefs of Staff changed their views considerably.

It is yet another of the war's curiosities that the Chiefs of Staff gave such powerful endorsement to the Air Staff prospectus before they even heard or saw the details. These came before them on November 3; they expressed the core of Portal's thinking with terrible clarity. Two points stand out at this distance in time: his statement of intention, and his assessment of its practicability. The first was based on a reasoned assumption that, in 1943 and 1944, it would be possible to drop 1¼ million tons of bombs on Germany. The effect of this, Portal reckoned, would be the destruction of 6 million houses, with industrial buildings, transport installations and public utilities in proportion.

Twenty-five million Germans would be rendered homeless, 900,000 would be killed and one million seriously injured.[8]

Taking a different yardstick, this meant that three-quarters of the inhabitants of all German towns with over 50,000 population would be made homeless, and at least one third of German industry would be destroyed. As regards the practicability of this programme, Portal said:

The heavy drain of the Russian war, the campaign in Libya, the existing air offensive and the blockade are all contributing to a progressive attrition.

Damaged resources, plant and stock of materials cannot now be adequately replaced; structural damage can no longer be adequately repaired; replenishments obtainable from the stocks of occupied countries are a waning asset. The output of German labour is falling through war weariness, food difficulties and other domestic problems, while that of foreign labour – whether in Germany or in the occupied territories – falls with Germany's diminishing prospects.[9]

Translating all this into yet another manner of speaking – the familiar subject of "morale", Portal said:

It is ... difficult to estimate the moral consequences of a scale of bombardment which would far transcend anything within human experience. But I have no doubt whatever that against a background of growing casualties, increasing privations and dying hopes it would be profound indeed.

He concluded,

I am convinced that an Anglo-American bomber force based in the United Kingdom and building up to a peak of 4,000–6,000 heavy bombers by 1944 would be capable of reducing the German war potential well below the level at which an Anglo-American invasion of the Continent would become practicable. Indeed, I see every reason to hope that this result would be achieved well before the combined force had built up to peak strength.

In view of what has already been said about the actual effects of Bomber Command's attack on Germany in 1942, and the fact that the USAAF had not, so far, even joined in that attack, Portal's view of the condition of Germany is nothing less than astonishing. It is a fearful proof of the power of faulty Intelligence and wishful thinking to misguide strategy. Unfortunately, by its very nature, the effect of the strategic air offensive was not a subject which could be expected to expose itself to Ultra penetration – in a country full of land-lines there was no need to use radio. And since the Germans had little to tell their allies, even the "other Ultra", the eavesdropping of reports from the Japanese Embassy in Berlin to Tokio, yielded nothing of value. Photographic Reconnaissance was, in this respect, actually misleading: it showed plentiful evidence of great damage to buildings, but could say nothing of the skilful improvizations taking place in the ruins, or the movement of vital plant to other localities. The result was, in the words of the Official Historians, that

506

In so far as it depended upon a diagnosis of the German war economy [Portal's], estimate was based upon a judgment of the situation inside Germany which completely failed to comprehend the economic, industrial and moral resilience of the country.[10]

Based, then, on a totally incorrect assessment of present reality, what can one say of Portal's statement of future intent? What is one to think of the calm proposal, set down in a quiet office, to kill 900,000 civilians, and seriously injure a million more? One thing emerges, with absolute clarity: this was a prescription for massacre, nothing more nor less. Here is the proof that the attack on morale did, indeed, spell "the threat or the reality of blowing men, women and children to bits", as stated above (p. 262). When the policy was put into effect (even on a lesser scale than Portal had envisaged) it marked another milestone on the road to Hiroshima, a destination which subsequent generations have viewed with scarcely diluted dismay. This is not to say that the strategic air offensive "led to Hiroshima"; there were many other factors in that progression, which owed much to the disposition of the enemy. Notable among them were the German air attacks on Warsaw, Rotterdam and the cities of Britain, Germany's known investigations of atomic energy, and the fanatical Japanese style of war to the death which promised massacres of a different kind. What the Allied policy of massacre by aerial bombardment more truly indicates is something pointed out by General Sir David Fraser:

That such kindly, sensitive men as Portal and Brooke believed in the policy bears simple witness to the brutal influence imposed upon the principal actors of all nations by the Second World War. Nor were the military men unsupported. Air Marshal Harris, the Commander-in-Chief Bomber Command, and the Air Staff were never discouraged by their superiors on moral grounds.[11]

This is not the place for exhaustive participation in the discussion of the morality of the bombing policy of the Allies between 1943–45, though the subject compels some attention, as will be further seen. Here, the author would like to make only two observations: first, an absolute agreement with what Dr Noble Frankland told the Royal United Services Institution in December 1961:

The great immorality open to us in 1940 and 1941 was to lose the war against Hitler's Germany. To have abandoned the only means of direct attack which we had at our disposal would have been a long step in that direction.[12]

507

Regrettably, for a variety of reasons, the same was true in 1942 and again in 1943, by which time the power of the offensive had greatly increased, producing the results which have horrified so many people. Yet – this is my second point – it is absolutely clear that there had to be a bombing programme. Until conditions were acceptable for a cross-Channel combined attack (the chief consideration being the outcome of the Battle of the Atlantic) there was still no other offensive option open to the western Allies. The only question was, what kind of bombing? In the event, more than one style was put into operation. The Americans certainly clung to their belief in precision, and they were not alone; precision bombing continued to have its supporters in the Air Ministry, and Portal himself never completely lost hope of it. It was unfortunate indeed that he so continuously blocked the path towards it by his absolute lack of belief in a long-range fighter. And it was at this juncture that another voice chimed in, with a challenge to the whole Portal prognosis. The First Sea Lord, Sir Dudley Pound, reflecting on Portal's ideas, now cast serious doubts upon the availability of aviation fuel imports for such a massive force – a very reasonable question (see pp. 423–4) which Portal tended to brush aside. But more serious still was Pound's questioning of the fundamental Air Staff proposition for the use of the great bomber force itself, which seemed to him to assume that "we cannot even then hope to win the war by defeating the enemy armed forces . . . but only by dehousing the German population and destroying industry".[13] Neither the Navy nor the Army was now in the despondent condition of a year earlier; 1942 had been dreadful for both at times, but both had come through it, and both could congratulate themselves on the latest turn of events in the Mediterranean. The chief lesson learned there was that the once-omnipotent German forces *could* be beaten; to Pound the way forward for the Air Forces was similarly to defeat the German fighter force and begin the bombing of real military targets by daylight. The RAF's disinclination to do this seemed "pessimistic and defeatist".[14]

Looking back, this judgment seems not far wrong; there was an undoubted vein of pessimism in the pronouncements of the chief bombing apologists, Harris and Slessor, who was at that juncture Assistant Chief of the Air Staff (Policy). In his trenchant memorandum to Churchill of June 17 (see pp. 425–6), Harris had strongly opposed a Continental campaign which, he said, would "play right into Germany's hand" and lead to a slaughter of the country's youth "in the mud of Flanders and France" – an image calculated at any time to make Churchill's flesh creep. Slessor had asked, as far back as November 1939,

"Played a weak hand with much finesse": Air Chief Marshal Sir Arthur Longmore, AOC-in-C, Middle East, May 1940–June 1941. Longmore's squadrons contributed handsomely to Britain's only two early victories: Operation COMPASS and the conquest of East Africa.

"The enemy of machines and men alike": a graphic impression of a Middle East dust-storm.

"Qualities which served their country well": in this galaxy we see (left to right) Air Chief Marshal Sir Arthur Tedder, a great coalition leader, Air Chief Marshal Sir Charles Portal, Chief of the Air Staff, October 1940-1945, "a brilliant staff officer", Air Vice-Marshal Sir Harry Broadhurst, the aggressive and inventive commander of the Desert Air Force and subsequently No. 83 Group in Normandy, and Air Marshal Sir Arthur Coningham, "the practical artificer of Army Cooperation" and the Tactical Air Force. The photograph was taken in Italy.

"A common touch, a nice informality": Tedder, about to leave Middle East Command, saying goodbye to aircrew in Tripolitania.

"Vulgarly labelled 'tank-busters'": Hurricane IIDs with their 40-mm cannon. They entered service with No. 6 Squadron in the Desert in June 1940 and produced some effect; however, they were far from being the last word in tank-destroyers and were withdrawn in March 1943 because of their high losses.

"Speed, fire-power and endurance": such were the outstanding characteristics of the Bristol Beaufighter. This aircraft was used with success by Coastal Command and in the Desert; the specimen seen here is in Malta, where they arrived in May 1941; it is somewhat masked by one of the island's precious Spitfires.

"One plan, Army-Air, made by me and the Air Vice-Marshal together": here we see Lieutenant-General Sir Bernard Montgomery in an unusual rôle – listening, while Air Vice-Marshal Coningham explains. The photograph may hold the key to the subsequent decline in relations between the two men; the Air Vice-Marshal to whom he was referring in the quotation was Broadhurst.

"Air superiority would bring all else in its train": the meaning of the phrase is well displayed in this photograph of a *Luftwaffe* "graveyard" in the Desert. Airborne, these machines were formidable enemies; air superiority had reduced them to so much junk.

Do we envisage winning the war in the same way as last time – a series of land battles over a period of years, a succession of Passchendaeles leading to military occupation of Germany? . . . I cannot feel any confidence that the method of military occupation is the right answer as to how to win this war . . .[15]

He did not depart from this view; in 1956 he still insisted that with higher priorities to Bomber Command "the soldiers could [have gone] back on a march-table as an occupation force instead of on the operation order that hurled them against the Normandy beaches".[16] Even Portal was now deploring "the folly of returning to '1918 ideas' by which was meant a frontal attack on the German Army before it was undermined from the rear".[17] The irony is, of course, that neither Portal nor any of the other Air Marshals was really thinking of 1918, with its ebb and flow of great mobile battles on reasonable ground through a dry, sometimes hot, summer, closely supported by large air fleets. While Coastal Command and the Middle East Air Force were correctly relearning the real 1918 lessons, Bomber Command turned its back; its thinking was firmly caught in the slough of 1916–17. And perhaps the supremest irony of all was that what it had to offer as an alternative amounted simply to a programme of grotesque destruction which would turn a whole country into a desert resembling the static war zone of 1914–18, which was generally considered to have been quite sufficiently awful.

These strategic doubts and qualms ran very deep; they touched the fundamentals of air warfare. They were to do with the question, as Dr Noble Frankland expressed it, whether strategic air power was a "revolutionary" weapon or "essentially classical", by which he meant whether "it conformed to the general principles which had governed the conduct and outcome of wars before the advent of air power".[18] In other words, was the successful exercise of air power, like land and sea power, dependent on the overthrow (or threat of overthrow) of the enemy's armed forces in battle? It is a question to which we shall return – indeed, it is the thread that we shall follow in considering the next stages of the bomber offensive. For the time being, however, we need only note how Dr Frankland and Sir Charles Webster saw it in relation to the debate in late 1942:

. . . the Air Staff believed that the victory could be won before the battle whereas the Admiralty inclined to the view that the battle itself would be decisive. It was because the plan for daylight bombing almost certainly involved a battle with the opposing air force that the majority of the British Air Staff tended to regard it as impossible or at least unnecessary.[19]

Sir Dudley Pound had thus called into question a significant sector of Air Force orthodoxy. Sir Alan Brooke confined himself to a more immediate and practical disagreement:

> ... he argued that the whole strategy would be self-defeating if the bomber programme, which was intended to pave the way for a continental invasion, prevented the creation of an army and supporting tactical air force adequate to carry out that invasion.[20]

Churchill, too, had grave doubts. Portal's demand (although two-thirds of the great combined force were expected to be supplied by America) would palpably put a heavy strain on the economy and on manpower. The RAF already numbered over a million men and women,[21] and the pinch of a national manpower shortage was beginning to be felt. This programme could only be fulfilled if other necessary expansions were cut down, or cut out. It came perilously close to putting all the eggs into one basket; too close for Churchill – "above all, he was anxious to preserve a freedom of choice".[22] So when the Chiefs of Staff put forward a revised review on November 24, Portal's proposals underwent marked modification:

> ... the proposed allied offensive policy was re-defined as being, firstly, rendering material assistance to Russia, secondly, preparing for the invasion of Europe and thirdly, softening up North-West Europe by bombing ... The changes of emphasis, wording and content which this memorandum showed by comparison with that of 30th October were most significant. The plan for a force of 4,000 to 6,000 heavy bombers by the beginning of 1944 was revoked, or at least thrown open to a future decision. The possibility of a continental invasion before 1944 was recognized and the importance of military campaigns in Russia and the Mediterranean area was stressed. Finally, the aim of the bombing offensive itself was significantly diversified.[23]

It now remained to take this prospectus to the Americans and see whether it would win the approval of the Combined Chiefs of Staff; this would constitute an early item on the Allied agenda in 1943.

So 1942 closed in some degree of doubt and unquestionable disappointment for Bomber Command. The United States Eighth Air Force was now operational; its daylight bombing techniques were impressive, but only within the range of fighter cover (chiefly supplied by Fighter Command); it had made no attack as yet on Germany. Bomber Command's own equipment was improving, but terribly slowly; GEE was jammed; its successor was only just appearing; the operational total of Lancasters was still only about 200.[24] Meanwhile the Whitleys, like the Hampdens and Manchesters, had left the Command, and it was clear that the days of the Wellingtons and Stirlings were also numbered. Losses during the year had been high: 1,404 aircraft missing and another 2,724 damaged in action.[25] The immediate prospects of expansion were thus as bleak as ever. Nevertheless, Harris looked at the bright side; it had been, he said,

> a year of preparation, in which very little material damage had been done to the enemy which he could not repair from his resources, but in which we had obtained or had in near prospect what was required to strike him to the ground and learned how to use it.[26]

This was a manner of speaking (and characteristic of his robust personality). It was equally true to say that the Germans had been well alerted, at relatively small lasting cost to themselves, to what might be in store; they might be depended on to strengthen even further their already formidable defences and improve on Air Raid Precautions and rescue and repair organization which was even now performing wonders. But as the prospects of any alternative Allied action against Germany herself faded for 1943, the certainty was that Bomber Command would remain firmly at the right of the line, and this would mean that

> the bombers would discharge at least something of the function which in the war of 1914–18, despite the blockade, had largely devolved upon the armies during their long-drawn-out and vastly costly ordeal in the trenches; that is the wearing down of the enemy's war potential and his will to war until the conditions for a break-through had been created.[27]

It was, in fact, to use the language of another Service and the earlier war, once more a case of "Soldier On!"

63 Air "battles" 1943; aids and opposition; the Ruhr

On November 15, 1864 General W. T. Sherman, commanding the Western Armies of the United States, began a march which has gone down in song and history, and which earned for him the title of "the Attila of the West". In the course of it,

> A corridor, 250 miles long and up to 50 miles wide, from Atlanta to Savannah, was swept almost bare of provisions and livestock, and the

systematic destruction of railroads, bridges, mills, workshops and many public buildings left a trail of twisted metal and smoke-blackened ruins behind the marching army.[1]

The object of this savage act was perfectly clear to Sherman:

If the Southern people persisted in the folly of rebellion after three years, they must take the consequences. As he swept across their land, he would seize or destroy their crops, their animals, their barns and mills and wagons, not as an act of destruction for its own sake, nor as an act of vengeance, but as a means of *destroying the Southern capacity, and above all the Southern will, to make war.*[2]

As I have said elsewhere, General Sherman "was a very modern soldier; Bomber Command Headquarters, 1942–45, would have understood him well".[3] To all the critics of his offensive against Southern morale Sherman would reply in two fashions: either he would tartly respond, "War is cruelty, and you cannot refine it", or he would point out that his intention had been to hasten the end of the war (in which there was evidence that he had succeeded), and ask whether that, also, was to be regarded as inhuman. What Bomber Command was setting out to do in 1943 was the logical extension of what Sherman had performed nearly eighty years before.

Unfortunately, in the context of the revival of total war in the period of the Industrial Revolution, a phrase like "logical extension" bears a wealth of terrible meaning. In 1864, on Sherman's orders, "few if any noncombatants were physically harmed".[4] In 1943 the leaders of civilized democracies at war could coolly contemplate the hideous arithmetic of Portal's massacre, and the cheerful, amiable, brave young men of the aircrews could as coolly carry out a large amount of it. It has been pertinently suggested that, if ordered to produce the same effect on civilians at close quarters, with flame-throwers and hand-grenades, that they produced with incendiary bombs and "block-busters" from heights of about 20,000 feet, the young airmen would have been far less cheerful.[5] Indeed, they would then have faced the dilemma of many young Germans of their own age. It needs to be remembered, as part of this context of total war, that out of some twenty million Soviet deaths caused by the war, about one-third were civilians – a number which puts even Portal's proposals in the shade. It has been asked, often enough, whether the German soldiers should not have refused to obey orders that produced such results. Gestures of that kind, however, are not in the nature of total war.[6]

So Bomber Command had no option; with its improved bombing

aids, and its ever-increasing force of heavy bombers, it would proceed with the destruction of German cities in 1943. For Germany in general, it was a bad year – the first really bad year of the war. Disaster at Stalingrad was followed by total defeat in North Africa. Almost simultaneously, the U-boats had to accept defeat in the Battle of the Atlantic. Italy collapsed, and then re-entered the war on the Allied side. The last German offensive on the Eastern front (the Battle of Kursk) was a failure; the Russians soon passed to the offensive which they steadily pursued to the heart of Berlin. And all the time, a melancholy running refrain to an already sufficiently gloomy theme, the air attacks pounded away. The great German ordeal had begun; what no one could guess was that, under its detestable régime, the German people would endure it for two more years. To the extent that the Allied ultimatum issued at Casablanca on January 23, "Unconditional Surrender", contributed to this, it has something to answer for.

It was in 1943 – or, to be more accurate, in the span of time contained within the period March 1943 to March 1944 – that "independent" strategic air power reached its peak in the Second World War.

At last the strategic theories which for a quarter of a century had been the inspiration of the Royal Air Force were coming to operational maturity.[7]

The offensive is generally described as taking the form of three "battles": the Battle of the Ruhr, beginning on March 5/6, 1943, and ending, according to taste, either in June or July; the Battle of Hamburg, July 24/25 – August 2/3, and the Battle of Berlin, November 18/19 – March 1944. But as the Official Historians say, "these names are only convenient labels".[8] At a longer distance in time, only Hamburg is recognizable as a self-contained battle – and even that was interrupted by another major attack on the Ruhr.[9] Nevertheless these "battles", fulfilling as they did the "manifest destiny" of the Royal Air Force, and characterized by all the virtues and defects of great air bombardments – a phenomenon never before witnessed – that is to say, the great fund of courage called for from those delivering the attacks, and the great fund of endurance called for from those receiving them, as well as the skills and sheer brutal drama in their display of destructive power, have attracted a whole copious literature of their own. For that reason, it is not now intended to trace their details once again. This narrative will content itself with some highlights, some reflections, and some matters arising.

As 1943 opened, Bomber Command was – not surprisingly – much concerned with the anti-U-boat war, and a good deal of its energy was consumed in vain attacks on the Biscay bases (see p. 441). Its main purpose, however, was laid down by the Combined Chiefs of Staff at their 65th meeting, at Casablanca on January 21. Harris was told:

> Your primary object will be the progressive destruction of the German military industrial and economic system, and the undermining of the morale of the German people to a point where their armed resistance is fatally weakened.

In other words, the mixture as before (see p. 504); and despite the listing of certain broad priorities, the committee-style wording, as Harris says,

> gave me a very wide range of choice and allowed me to attack pretty well any German industrial city of 100,000 inhabitants and above . . . The new instructions therefore made no difference.[10]

However, as he also says, the Ruhr, being Germany's greatest industrial area, "remained a principal objective". The concentration of heavy, and particularly armament, industry in the Ruhr makes it exceedingly difficult to look on it as anything but one huge military objective. For that reason it was powerfully defended, in addition to the protection of its everlasting haze, and over two years of attacks upon it had so far produced pitifully small results. But times had changed.

What distinguishes the air offensive of 1943 from that of preceding years is, above all, the introduction, one by one, of four new bombing aids. The first of these was OBOE, which made its operational début on December 20, 1942. This was a radar pulse, audible to a pilot on course as a musical note similar to that of the instrument of the same name. Variations from course were signalized by easily recognizable variations in the pulse. The novelty lay in a second signal, coming in as the receiving aircraft approached its target; this culminated in a series of dashes, and then a series of dots:

> When the dots ceased the bomb-aimer pressed his button. As far as the aircrew were concerned, it was as simple as that.[11]

OBOE, at last, offered a real bombing aid; if all went well, it meant that whereas GEE offered a margin of error measured by miles, this was now reduced to a matter of hundreds of yards. Heavy cloud, or the Ruhr's industrial haze, were no longer a protection; blind bombing could now be expected to produce what might even be called a degree of precision. The weakness of OBOE (like GEE) was its limited range, due to the curvature of the earth. To overcome this to some extent, altitude was obviously important, and the Mosquito, which had no difficulty in reaching 28,000 feet, thus performed yet another of its valuable services. It was the Mosquitoes of No. 109 Squadron which made the first essay of OBOE, and the same squadron which supplied the first markers in the first operation of the "Battle" of the Ruhr.

The second bombing and navigational aid was H2S, which went into action on January 30, 1943. This was, as we have seen, Bomber Command's version of ASV III. It was a radar scanner carried inside the aircraft, and giving an actual "picture" of the ground below. It had no limitation of range, and in theory offered the perfect solution to the navigator's (and possibly also the bomb-aimer's) problems. In practice, however, "it provided data of varying obscurity which not infrequently defied the most skilled interpretation".[12] And when the Germans developed their *Naxos* receiver, H2S served their night-fighters well as a means of homing in on the bombers. What with these three devices (GEE, OBOE, H2S), the aircraft interiors were filling up nicely; "even the escape hatches were often obstructed".[13] Fortunately, the other two novelties of 1943 could be accommodated elsewhere: they were the target-indicator bombs, whose pyrotechnic explosions were coloured red or green as guides to later-comers (introduced on Janury 16), and WINDOW, the short metal strips which so simply and effectively blanketed German radar (introduced in July). These were "the basic devices upon which the new tactics of the strategic air offensive were founded".[14] In this war of technology, change was continuous; modifications of existing systems and fresh novelties followed without pause, and as they appeared, they "transformed the operational capacities of Bomber Command".[15]

If Bomber Command's aids were now increasing in quantity and efficacy, its opponents, schooled by the battles of 1942, were also more formidable. The Kammhuber Line (see Ch. 35, Note 13 to p. 268) was extended to stretch from Denmark to south-east of Paris. Kammhuber's system was based entirely on ground-control interception (GCI); by the beginning of 1943,

The whole system was now supported by a network of early warning radar, and large central plotting rooms, which gave a picture of operations throughout the system, had been erected and elaborately equipped and staffed.[16]

Searchlights, guns, night fighters all operated under tight control. The German use of radar-controlled searchlights was aggressive; a good example was the attack on Warnemünde on May 8/9, 1942, when despite the efforts of a detachment whose whole task was to extinguish the lights, they had played a large part in frustrating the RAF. Dazzle from searchlights was a blinding factor as important at times as cloud or haze or the smoke-screens which covered special targets. The quality of German flak needs no further comment; we have noted it time and again. Its quantity was now enormous; by the end of 1943 70 per cent of the *Luftwaffe*'s flak personnel – no fewer than 900,000 men – was deployed in the West. Their armoury contained 75 per cent of Germany's heavy AA guns, principally the 88-mm dual-purpose guns which remained a terror to Allied tanks until the end of the war.

The German night-fighters consisted of variants of the Messerschmitt Bf 110F-4 and G-4 and the Junkers 88C-6c and Ju 88R-1. The Me 110, it will be recalled, had been a sad failure in its day-fighter rôle; as early as 1940 it began to be switched to night operations, and in fact made its first night kill (a Whitley) on July 19 of that year. As the RAF bombing offensive developed, the Me 110 "found its *forte* in the nocturnal skies of Europe".[17] In 1943, however, it was fated to go into another eclipse; it was always inferior to the Ju 88, one of the most versatile aircraft of the war.

German armament was usually powerful; the fighters of 1943–44 were no exception. Some Me 110s (Bf 110G-2/R1) were fitted with 37-mm anti-aircraft cannon in the autumn of 1942; a single hit from one of these would normally disable a Flying Fortress. On the other hand, they distinctly lowered the flying performance of the fighter. In 1943 rocket shells made their appearance, and once again the United States VIII Bomber Command was at the receiving end. RAF Bomber Command had no illusions about the night-fighters; they were regarded as its most dangerous enemies. In the summer of 1943 they became even more so, with the introduction of "*schräge Musik*" ("jazz music") in the Bf 110F-4; somewhat reminiscent of the "bandstands" mounted on the U-boats (see p. 435) this unpleasant device consisted (in the Messerschmitt version) of two 30-mm cannon, pointing forward and upward at an angle of 15° from the vertical. Later the same

system was fitted in Ju 88C-6cs, using 20-mm cannon. In either case the tactic was the same; homing in first on radar contact, once the target was in sight the fighter would come in below, with speed adjusted to match the bomber's. Coming in very close in the bomber's blind area, and aiming by a reflector sight on the roof of the cockpit, the fighter pilot loosed off a short burst which would normally be enough to wreck the bomber above. It was a dangerous game; some German pilots would return with parts of the bomber attached to their aircraft. But for Bomber Command crews it was one more unnerving factor in a business that was perilous enough. A striking passage in the Official History, written with obvious personal recollection,[18] may serve as a last word on this running battle between the German fighters and Bomber Command:

> Bearing enormous loads of bombs and petrol, these heavy aircraft, both because of their weight and on account of the need to conserve fuel for the long hours of endurance, travelled, by comparison with the German night fighters, very slowly, making an airspeed of perhaps 180 knots on the way out and 210 knots on the way home. Though they could perform the famous "corkscrew" manoeuvre by which they sought to evade or at least to present a more difficult target to the fighters, their manoeuvrability was, nevertheless, far inferior to that of their smaller and more speedy opponents. Restricted to .303-calibre machine-guns, they were substantially outshot and completely outranged by their cannon-equipped enemies. Their armour-plating was progressively removed, until little remained, to increase their bomb-lifting capacity. Belching flame from their exhausts as well as radar transmissions from their navigational and fighter warning apparatus made them all too apparent to those who hunted them. *Once engaged in combat, they had little chance of victory and not much of escape*, while the large quantities of petrol, incendiary bombs, high explosives and oxygen with which they were filled often gave spectacular evidence of their destruction. Outpaced, outmanoeuvred and outgunned by the German night fighters and in a generally highly inflammable and explosive condition, these black monsters presented an ideal target to any fighter pilot who could find them, and it was the night fighters which caused the overwhelming majority of the losses sustained by Bomber Command ...[19]

Such – with rare exceptions – were the prevailing conditions of Bomber Command operations during the great bombing actions of 1943–44. These began, as Harris says,

> ... at a precise moment ... the night of March 5–6th, 1943, when I was at last able to undertake with real hope of success the task which had been

517

given to me when I first took over the Command a little more than a year before, the task of destroying the main cities of the Ruhr.[20]

The first target in the "Battle of the Ruhr" was Essen, the magnet to which Bomber Command had been drawn from the earliest days of the war. On the night of March 5/6 the force despatched was 442 aircraft; the leaders were eight Mosquitoes of No. 109 Squadron, dropping red target indicator bombs purely on OBOE fixes; behind them came 22 heavy bombers, dropping green indicators. The main force[21] thus had two colour guides to aim at. 381 crews claimed to have attacked the target, and 293 brought back photographs. Though these were not as informative as could have been wished, the sub-sequent reconnaissance photographs revealed that "destruction was exceptionally severe and widespread", with a heavy concentration of damage right in the town centre which was "virtually devastated". Since this had been the aiming point for the OBOE fix, the new aid won general applause. Best of all was the perception that Krupp's, hitherto practically immune in spite of all Bomber Command's efforts, had at last suffered serious damage. For these satisfying results, the losses were no more than 14 aircraft missing (3.16 per cent) and 38 damaged. Bomber Command had "cracked" the Ruhr – at last.

So the "Battle" began on a note of very considerable success. It continued for four months, and it was not like any other battle ever fought. Even the long-drawn-out battles of the First World War had definite geographical locations from which they could be named; in this one,

> Bomber Command carried out major attacks on areas as widely separated from the Ruhr as Berlin, Stettin and Pilsen in the east, Munich, Stuttgart and Nuremberg in the south-east, Turin and Spezia in the south, and Lorient and St Nazaire in the west.[22]

Clearly "Ruhr" is a figure of speech; in the course of the "battle" there were forty-three major attacks on targets in Germany, of which just over half were in the Ruhr. Certainly the Ruhr targets were attacked very heavily; Essen received five visits from Bomber Command, as did Duisburg, while Cologne was attacked four times. The light casualties of the first operation were deceptive; in a total of 2,070 sorties against Essen, Bomber Command lost 92 aircraft (4.44 per cent), with 334 damaged. In the whole campaign, 18,506 sorties were despatched, from which 872 aircraft did not return (4.71 per cent),

while 2,126 were damaged, "sometimes so seriously as to be total losses both as regards the aircraft and its crew".[23] Some occasions were very bad: out of 327 aircraft despatched to Pilsen on April 16/17, 36 were missing (11 per cent), and out of 203 sent to Oberhausen on June 14/15, 17 were missing (8.37 per cent). On the other hand, there were occasions of amazingly light loss: 7 out of 335 against Nuremberg on March 8/9 (2.08 per cent), six out of 455 against Duisburg on March 26/27 (1.31 per cent), 12 out of 577 against Kiel on April 4/5 (2.07 per cent). What did become clear was that a big force, tightly concentrated behind its Pathfinders, could saturate and penetrate the Kammhuber defences with far less loss than large numbers of bombers making their straggling way towards a target on a wide front. Yet the fact remained that "Bomber Command was approaching perilously close to the unbearable, or at any rate, the insupportable sustained casualty rate during the Battle of the Ruhr".[24]

Sir Arthur Harris drew comfort from the fact that, losses notwithstanding, his Command was at last beginning to grow, and he looked forward to launching ever larger onslaughts as the year continued. Meanwhile,

> Nothing like the whole succession of catastrophes which overcame the cities of the Ruhr and North-West Germany in the first half of 1943 had ever occurred before, either in Germany or elsewhere. It was an impressive victory . . .[25]

The Official History professes to agree with this assessment; it cites the undoubtedly severe damage that was at last being sustained by the great German industrial centres, in particular Krupp's, "the symbol of German rearmament".[26] There is, indeed, no doubt at all that, by comparison with all that had gone before, Germany was now being severely hurt. But how severely? The Official History adds:

> . . . it was natural that first estimates should be too optimistic . . . It was not realised that even when the roofs and other parts of buildings had been destroyed the heavy machinery remained intact and production would soon be resumed . . .[27]

And it concludes:

> Perhaps, a reasonable deduction from all the evidence would be that there was a loss of from one to one and a half months' production in the Ruhr and Rhineland as a result of the battle, *spread of course over the whole ten months of 1943*.[28]

The italics are mine; it is unfortunate that the records have not made possible a more exact report on the damage done during the precise period of the "Battle of the Ruhr", but such is the case. We shall later have an opportunity of putting the 1943 damage in a wider context. For the time being, all that needs to be said – once more – is that the Germans now, and throughout the year, displayed extraordinary powers of organization and improvization which enabled them to recuperate even from this new scale of air bombardment in an amazing manner, and that this could not have happened if, in the words of the Official History, "German men and women had not displayed great endurance, energy and courage under most appalling conditions".[29]

64 Moral fibre

The conclusion of the 18,506 sorties attributed to the "Battle of the Ruhr" did not mark any intermission in the work of Bomber Command. Like the infantry on the Western Front between 1914–18, its task, from 1941 to 1945, was continuous, subject only to weather conditions. The strain was, except during the relatively brief peak of the great Western Front battles, even greater for Harris's aircrews, and of an unprecedented and peculiar nature:

> To be a member of a bomber crew required persistent fortitude at a time and in circumstances when the stoutest mind and heart would have every excuse to show a natural and normal weakness. The average operation was in darkness and in the early hours of the morning; everyone who took part in it knew that the odds were against the survival of any particular airman. It never was and never could be a mode of warfare to be conducted in hot blood; the bomber crew was engaged throughout a flight in a series of intricate tasks resembling those of a skilled craftsman in his workshop; calculations and minute adjustments of machinery had to be made all the time with a clear head and a steady hand. And a long flight by night is in itself no task for a weakling when a small navigational error may result in a forced landing at the best.[1]

Only by interpreting this very exact description of the task itself into the further context of penetrating the German defence system, encountering all the hazards over the target[2] and making the long, perilous journey home, night after night, can one arrive at any even remote sense of what was being demanded of Bomber Command during those years. Even the casualty figures and percentages do not express the human reality of the strain upon what the Official History nevertheless calls "the resilient morale" of the aircrews. The Command's two chief dangers, it says, were, first, the loss of experienced crews and potential leaders, and secondly, a loss of morale:

> In Bomber Command the latter problem was always less acute than the former.[3]

It was, nevertheless, a problem – inevitably; it is simply not possible to take large numbers of young men abruptly out of civil life and subject them to most unnatural stress for a long period, without problems (sometimes serious) arising. In the First World War, when over 8½ million men of the British Empire put on uniform, the two offences most clearly relating to morale were listed as Cowardice and Desertion. It is amazing that out of that enormous number of men, and over a statistical period of 68 months, only 551 court-martial charges of cowardice were brought, 18 of which resulted in death sentences being carried out. 7,361 charges of Desertion resulted in 266 death sentences being carried out. For officers – the broad equivalent of Bomber Command aircrews – the figures were: Cowardice, nine court-martial charges, no death sentence carried out; Desertion, 18 charges, two death sentences carried out. In addition, it may be noted that in the theatres of war 173 officers were cashiered and 670 dismissed the Service. The overwhelming impression of these figures – upon this author at least – is of the extraordinary degree of stamina and resolution (what used to be known as "grit") to be found in a very wide cross-section of people. The experience of the RAF in the Second World War displayed the same phenomenon. It is most unfortunate that it cannot be documented with the precision and detail of the earlier war; the requisite papers do not exist. The Office of the Judge Advocate General is only able to state that, between 1939–45, 5,240 Field General and General Courts-Martial of RAF personnel took place, and 10,880 District Courts-Martial.[4] No breakdown is available, even between air and ground-crew, no indication of the offences charged, nor the sentences passed. It is a most surprising state of affairs.

The existence of the problem of morale was acknowledged at the time. It was bound to be: flying itself, though an exciting and rewarding experience, is a stressful one (at least, it is for many people). Fear of flying was a factor to be reckoned with. Fear of *operational* flying was something that very few escaped. Bomber Command's 8,000 aircrew killed in training or accidents supply a sufficient reason. It was thus a question – as with the front-line troops of the First World War – of mastery of fear. And until the pattern of the war had hardened out, it was not easy to see how to ease the difficulty of achieving that. Each man had, by and large, to overcome it for himself, according to his temperament. According to one experienced officer, it was an advantage that

> ... the average aircrew personnel are simple and, to a certain extent, selfish. A large number of them boost up their morale by the simple but often effective saying "It won't happen to me". I must admit my own personal experience was that this somewhat unintelligent outlook was far more comforting while on the job than the rather saner course of taking a mathematical view of one's chances.[5]

The "mathematical view" is obviously of great significance; even a civilian pilot must have occasional qualms, as he reckons up his air-hours or air-miles, and wonders how long it will be before the laws of probability assert themselves. In 1939, and indeed, for a good deal of 1940, with modern air warfare in its infancy, and no real sense anywhere of the war's likely course, character or duration, there could be no valid yardstick of probability, any more than in 1914. It was only as a pattern of trench warfare formed in 1915 – a set rotation of front-line duty, then support-line duty, followed by a spell in reserve – that something emerged on the lines of a "tour". It brought with it, of course, the question for each man to ask himself, how many front-line spells, how many "tours" was he likely to survive – and how many could he stand? In the RAF, by the end of 1940, it was clear that operational flying must be broken up into manageable portions of time, and that these must offer a reasonable chance of survival. This was known as the "datum line"; it was generally accepted that it should be drawn at a point which offered a 50–50 chance.[6]

The next question was, where exactly to draw this line. This became a matter of urgent enquiry by the Air Ministry at the end of 1940, and at once a persisting confusion became apparent. All the Home Commands were consulted, and by the end of January the Air Ministry was in possession of their views; the Air Member for Personnel reported to the CAS and the VCAS:

> The replies ... are now in and show a rather unforeseen similarity of views with one exception, thus the recommendations for reliefs are:–
> (a) *Army Co-op. Command.* After 5 months in the face of the enemy or 200 hours' operational flying.

(b) *Fighter Command.* After 200 hours' operational flying with latitude both ways.

(c) *Bomber Command.* After 30 sorties not exceeding 200 hours' operational flying.

(d) *Coastal Command.* Unable to assess a limit and wish to deal with each case on its merits.[7]

Coastal Command was in difficulty from beginning to end over this matter, because of the extreme diversity of the tasks carried out by its various components, and the different sorts of hazards that its air-crews faced. Bomber Command's reference to "sorties" is of special interest.[8] It is customary to think of Bomber Command in terms of tours comprising sorties, and 30 is the usually accepted figure. It comes as a surprise, therefore, to find that officially (certainly as far as the Air Staff was concerned) there was no acknowledgment of this as the "datum line" until 1942, and that uncertainty still prevailed in 1943, as we shall shortly see.

The trouble, it is easy to see, was the continuing reference to "operational flying hours", and it is by no means as easy to understand what was so attractive (except possibly to bureaucrats) about this measure. It seems, in retrospect, obvious that 200 hours of operational flying, mostly over Germany, by a man in Bomber Command was likely to be quite unlike 200 hours in the life of someone in Coastal. Equally, a fighter pilot might, in 200 minutes, pack as much direct personal stress and danger as members of other Commands might encounter in as many hours. What is interesting is the evidence that within Bomber Command, among the crews themselves, already, before the end of 1940, it was not hours that counted but the number of "trips" one made – and that 30 sorties seemed to them to offer their 50–50 survival chance. It is thus surprising to find Harris himself, as late as August 1942, telling his Group Commanders that he was "considering the *possibility* of changing the basis of an operational tour in Bomber Command from that of hours flown to one of sorties completed . . ."[9] Harris did not take long to make up his mind, the whole question being at that stage intimately linked with the creation of the Pathfinder Force; it was only just over a fortnight later that Saundby informed the Groups:

The full operational tour is to consist of a maximum of 30 sorties and . . . aircrew members are to be transferred to non-operational duties on or before completing the maximum number of sorties . . .

523

> ... A completed sortie is one in which the crew satisfy their Squadron Commander that they have in fact bombed the aiming point or the target. In general, the proof as to whether this has been done will rest on a satisfactory night photograph, but it will be left to the discretion of the Squadron Commanders to decide, if for any reason the night photograph has failed to provide the necessary evidence, whether or not a crew have completed a sortie ...
>
> ... Less than 30 completed sorties may count as a satisfactory operational tour if the Group Commander is satisfied that the individual concerned has carried out his aircrew duties satisfactorily and is in need of a rest from operational flying or is to be transferred to non-operational flying to fill a normal posting ...[10]

In view of this clear instruction, it is indeed surprising to find that as much as six months later the Air Council and the Air Staff were still unclear about this matter. One reason for this was, evidently, doubt arising from the working out of the squadron commanders' discretion to which Saundby had so precisely referred. The leaders of squadrons were by now virtually all combat-experienced, and selected for the possession of at least some elements of the various attributes of leadership as well as their operational proficiency. But they were mostly young, their dashing quality mixed with a certain amount of youthful intolerance, and they did not have even the amount of managerial expertise that officers of the same age in the Navy and the Army could acquire from close daily contact with the other ranks. So we find such unfortunate situations arising as one which the Assistant Chief of the Air Staff (Air Marshal Sir Norman Bottomley) drew to Harris's attention on January 20, 1943. He referred to

> ... a crew which was engaged in combat over the North Sea on the outward flight of a sortie, resulting in the bombs being jettisoned at 52.23°N, 04.25°E. The aircraft was hit five times by cannon shell, but, owing to successful evasive action, the Captain was able to bring the aircraft back to Coltishall and land safely without further incident. It is felt that, on this occasion, the crew may have undergone more than the average stress and that it would be reasonable to count this flight an operational sortie; it was not so recognised by the Squadron Commander ...[11]

Air Marshal Bottomley's concern is understandable, but nevertheless does him credit since it is to be assumed that the ACAS had plenty to think about besides the injustice being done to one crew. What is less understandable is that he was still, at that late date, under the impression that "the operational tour in your Command has been fixed in general terms at 200 hours", and that the 30-sortie routine was no more than an *ad hoc* arrangement. "It is," he said, "accordingly of some importance that an authoritative definition of an operational sortie should be laid down and approved" – as though Saundby's instruction had never been issued.

It is quite certain that the Air Staff was, at this stage, confused about this matter. A fortnight before Bottomley wrote to Harris (January 7) an informal meeting had taken place in Portal's office, precisely to discuss the length of operational tours. Since the meeting displays both the RAF and the CAS in a revealing and attractive light, and also illuminates the subject, it will be as well to repeat its minutes in full. The attractiveness of the occasion lies in the *personae* who took part. They were:

The Chief of the Air Staff,
The Vice-Chief of the Air Staff (Acting: Air Vice-Marshal C. E. H. Medhurst),
Wing Commander Tait (Bomber Command HQ),
Wing Commander Elliott (83 Squadron),
Wing Commander Mahaddie (7 Squadron),
Squadron-Leader Casement (5 Group),
Squadron-Leader Holford (1 Group),
Squadron-Leader Daniels (Pathfinder Force)

It may be considered an odd way of doing business (especially business that had actually already been done), but there is something definitely pleasing in the spectacle of the two officers at the very top of the Service consulting three Wing Commanders and three Squadron-Leaders on a matter of such utter practicality. It is hard to imagine a similar meeting taking place in the Admiralty or the War Office, despite the high qualities of their top officers. The following questions were put on January 7, and the following responses made:

1. *What is the average number of sorties needed before a crew can be called operationally efficient?*
   Replies varied from between 10 to 20. It would be fair to say that an average of 15 is required for four-engined aircraft.
2. *What should be the length of operational tours?*
   There was a general consensus of opinion that the first tour should consist of 30 sorties, followed by nine months in an OTU, followed by a second tour of 20 sorties. There is a definite tailing-off towards the end of the second tour which is at present 60 sorties [sic.; it

525

means a *total* of 60 sorties, including the second tour]. The loss of
experienced crews towards the end of their second operational tour
has a lowering effect throughout the whole squadron. The proposal
to limit the number of operational sorties to 50 would partially avoid
this.

3. *Should ex-operational OTU Instructors be employed on operations during
   their OTU period?*
   Except for some particularly special operations this practice was
   universally condemned.

4. There was a strong feeling that a pilot, having completed his second
   operational tour, should not be asked to go back for a second OTU
   tour, and if possible not to a Conversion Unit. A change of Command
   was strongly evidenced [sic], preferably to such jobs as Ferrying or
   Transport.

5. The general feeling was that should political pressure be such as to
   demand the return of Dominion crews after one operational tour, the
   effect would be negligible on British crews; in fact it could give them
   a sense of superiority which at present Dominion crews assume at
   the expense of British.[12]

The present author suggests that it would be difficult to discover a
document that speaks with greater authority on the nature of this
problem; it is pleasing to record that virtually everything advocated by
this highly practical group of men received official approval. Another
(loftier) meeting took place, with Portal in the chair, in the Air Council
Room, on February 4. This time Harris was present, and when Portal
asked him what length of tours Bomber Command recommended, he
replied that

the first tour should consist of 30 sorties and the second tour should
normally not exceed 20 sorties. The Pathfinder Force should be on a
different basis and these should consist of 45 sorties, but crews could be
withdrawn at any time after the completion of 30 sorties.[13]

It was at this meeting that he finally disposed of the confusion about
flying hours as far as Bomber Command was concerned. Asked by
the Air Member for Supply and Organization "how many hours of
flying were represented by 30 sorties", Harris said "that the practice
of reckoning sorties by hours had now been stopped . . . The average
was probably about 5 hours per sortie."

So a matter that was considerably more complex than is generally
supposed came to its resolution.[14] It is not to be thought that everyone
"lived happily ever after" in this case, any more than in others.

Wing Commander Simmons, whom we have quoted above (p. 522), remarked in the same document that

> ... the vision of the average member of an aircrew was extremely short. While I commanded a squadron, we were told that aircrew personnel must expect to do two operational tours of 30 trips, divided by about eight months in an OTU, yet in practice it was difficult to make them realise that their operational flying would not be finished after their first tour. They all hungrily looked towards the goal of 30 trips and did not bother to look any further.[15]

No doubt this frame of mind was another psychological defence mechanism. What is most interesting is the manner in which the RAF came to terms with this matter of the utmost operational significance and formalized a workable solution. This was finally laid down in an Air Ministry Letter of May 8, 1943.[16] It stated the following rules:

> Bomber Command: first tour, 30 sorties; second tour, not more than 20 sorties.
> Pathfinder Force: a single continuous tour of 45 sorties.
> Fighter Command: Day Fighters, normal maximum 200 hours.
> Night Fighters, 100 hours or a maximum of 18 months.
> Army Cooperation Command: 200 hours.
> Coastal Command: Flying boats and four-engined land-plane crews, 800 hours.
> Twin-engined general reconnaissance squadrons (including meteorological squadrons and flights), 500 hours.
> Photographic Reconnaissance squadrons, 300 hours.
> Fighter, torpedo and other squadrons employed offensively, 200 hours.[17]

Overseas Commands were instructed on similar lines.

The tour of operations, with its definite promise of relief, was a sheet anchor of morale in Bomber Command. It made the unbelievable endurable.[18] Nevertheless, there would be some men who could not endure; it is now time to consider them. Military law, in 1914, was based on the necessities created by a long tradition of smallscale voluntary recruitment, drawing considerably on the rougher elements of the population. It did not take long to perceive that it was not at all appropriate to the needs of Citizen Forces. Thus we find that out of a total of 3,080 death sentences passed in accordance with military law between 1914–21, only 346 were carried out: 11.33 per cent – which may be expressed as an 88.67 per cent advantage to reason and compassion. By 1939 the lesson was well understood: Citizen Forces, raised by conscription, cannot – at any rate, in democracies – be treated like regulars. In the Second World War, there were only 40 executions following courts-martial, 36 of them for the crime of murder, including the solitary member of the RAF. However, the condition which in 1914–1918 was crudely termed "Cowardice", but which is more accurately defined as "inability to master fear", did still exist, and had to be dealt with. In the Royal Air Force, in the cases of aircrew who had "forfeited the confidence of their Commanding Officers in the face of danger in the air", it was known as "lack of moral fibre".

As we have seen (p. 500) there was already, by the summer of 1942, very real concern at Bomber Command Headquarters about "bombing discipline" and the disposition of crews to make sure that their bombs were aimed at a real target – it was this, in fact, that clinched the argument for the Pathfinder Force. This concern extended to the whole question of morale as affected by flying stress, a matter which would, if anything, increase in significance in 1943 and 1944 with the expansion of the bomber force and the stepping up of its operations, with consequent increasing casualties. An investigation of "Psychological Disorders in Flying Personnel" was conducted in Bomber Command in August 1942. It was carried out by Air Commodore C. P. Symonds and Squadron-Leader Denis Williams, and 44 General Duties officers and 37 Medical Officers were questioned in the course of it. The bulk of the ensuing report[19] is concerned with medical and administrative procedures, but its introductory section, "The Effects of Flying Stress", is of wider interest.

This section is divided into three parts:

A. Facts observed by others
B. Facts reported by the man
C. Facts noticed by the man himself but not reported by him

It is the first of these sub-sections that is most illuminating, most revealing of the character and behaviour of the Bomber Command crews. Nineteen observers said that early signs of stress in individuals "were increased excitability, restlessness, irritability or truculence . . . The contrasting signs of unusual quietness, with a desire for solitude, are equally evident . . ." Twenty-seven observers commented on changes in facial expressions: looking tired and haggard, or pale, worried, tense and nervy, miserable and depressed. Others noted fidgeting, sometimes even a tremor. Most significantly (another strong argument in the Canadian/RAF disagreement on commissioning of aircrews that we have noted on pp. 464–7):

One Medical Officer said that [symptoms] are difficult to assess unless one knows the man really well, so that, because of the difficulty of mixing freely with NCOs in their mess, he only felt confident in his opinion when dealing with the officers with whom he lived and mixed freely.

An important indicator of stress, it was agreed, was "Loss of Keenness for Flying Duties". One observer said:

The first evidence of the effects of flying stress is usually to be found in diminished enthusiasm. A keen man will react to the announcement of "a heavily defended target for tonight" with immediate professional interest, but if he is suffering from the effects of stress he will show his lack of keenness by immediate preoccupation with the defences . . .

In such cases, a man would be noted as asking unnecessary questions, displaying lack of enthusiasm in conversation (or alternatively, over-compensating by appearing wildly enthusiastic).

The effects of such a condition were definitely matters to cause concern:

. . . foolish errors of judgment, or gross carelessness, leading to bad landings or crashes. In operations, carelessness or recklessness may lead to catastrophe . . . When one particular aircraft is badly damaged in successive trips "this usually means that the pilot's judgment is going. He forces himself to go in regardless of risks because he is afraid that his nerve is getting shaky . . ."

Alternatively, again, it was remarked that "He may go to pieces over the target". The most common symptom remarked was when

an aircraft returns without reaching the target, a mechanical defect being blamed. The defect may be trivial or imaginary . . . These unnecessary failures are usually due to the captain of the aircraft. Once they occur they tend to be repeated, a different reason being found each time . . .

One squadron commander commented:

You can usually tell when a man has had enough, you can tell by the results of his trips . . . In the first five trips it is well to sum up what he is like. After that if he alters at all you must look out for trouble.

529

Twenty-four officers, not surprisingly, said that they had "at some time observed increased drinking as a result of stress in flying crews. Usually the symptom has a gradual onset".

In the category of "Facts reported by the man", we find a Medical Officer saying:

> There are two sorts of men. The first report sick with some trivial complaint which has no real physical basis. After a talk if you ask them why they have come to sick quarters they will say that they are afraid or that they panic in the air. The other sort never report sick. They show their signs and symptoms in the mess, but they keep on flying and in the end write themselves off, because they become inefficient through loss of judgment.

Among the "trivial complaints" with "no real foundation" most commonly reported were: nausea, mild dyspepsia, "stomach pains" and vomiting, diarrhoea, eye strain or "pain over the eyes" and blurring of vision, "sinus trouble", which could include nasal catarrh and ear trouble.[20] It was also commented that:

> The man who comes up complaining of inability to carry on is the honest type, and there is more chance of getting him back to flying than the others.

When a very large number of men habitually display remarkable degrees of courage and fortitude, as was the case with the First World War infantry and the Second World War aircrews, it is all too easy to take this for granted. There are men – not many, but some – who are, quite simply, unacquainted with fear. Whether they should be called "brave" or not is an open question. For most men, bravery consists in being afraid, but refusing to submit to one's fears. It is amazing how many men, in moments of crisis, are able to achieve this. To appreciate what it is that they are doing, what kind of an effort they must be making, in order to live with their stresses and perform their duties, it helps to consider those who fail, which is why the above passages have been given so much space. The fears that they reveal were typical; the responses were not. We now turn to the third category, the men who noticed alarming facts about themselves, but did not report them, found their own answers and carried on. The men interviewed in this category were all experienced squadron or Station commanders who had themselves completed one or more tours of operations; but they spoke for the overwhelming majority of Bomber Command. One said, referring to the failures:

If they are as afraid as I am they know what "wind-up" is. They are scared stiff and I don't blame them either . . .

Another said:

I judge these men entirely on my own reactions because I know what it is like both before a trip and when you start a second tour. Everyone is frightened and if they could stop reasonably they would, unless they were damn fools.

These officers described their own symptoms; one, after 40 hours in his second tour said that he

found himself tired, listless and slow in taking evasive action. He found that after a little while in the air his instrument panels invariably became double. He went on leave and the symptoms disappeared.

Another squadron commander also spoke of tiredness, and said that his fear became obvious and increasingly difficult to control. He reached the stage where he would jump whenever a gun opened up:

He completed his tour successfully.

Yet another squadron commander, of great distinction, said that he had lost a stone in weight during one period of intensive operations, but had regained it during his rest period. Another said that he had suffered from sleeplessness, and dreamed that he was flying.

It was noticeable that in describing their own reactions to stress these officers dwelt upon the primary symptoms – fear and fatigue – rather than those of secondary development, thus showing evidence of their superior intelligence and insight.

It is, indeed, a rare quality, to be able to stand outside oneself and make an objective assessment of what one sees.

It remains to consider, as best we can, how the RAF dealt with "lack of moral fibre". Max Hastings[21] has said that

in 1943 most cases of men relieved of operational duty for medical or moral reasons were treated by the RAF with considerable harshness.

He quotes an unnamed 1943 Station commander as having said to him:

531

I made certain that every case before me was punished by court-martial, and where applicable by an exemplary prison sentence, whatever the psychiatrists were saying.

Wing Commander J. Lawson, of the Air Ministry Personnel Department, who was intimately concerned with the handling of such cases, and who provides one of the few authentic commentaries on this deeply obscured subject, expresses it rather differently:

... it must always be that a number are harshly treated[22] and it has been our constant endeavour to reduce that to an absolute minimum and I believe this had been achieved.[23]

Max Hastings's witness would appear to have been a somewhat unusual individual, because Wing Commander Lawson tells us that, from the RAF's point of view, whenever a man "forfeited the confidence of his Commanding Officer", the most important thing was that he should be "got away from the Station at the earliest possible moment". He adds:

I have many times been asked why we did not resort to court-martial action but in the ordinary way of such action an individual must remain on his Unit for a considerable time both before and after the court-martial and this would have a most serious effect on the morale of others. There was also the difficulty of calling witnesses on account of casualties and postings.

According to Max Hastings, "There was great fear at the top of the Service that if an honourable path existed to escape operations, many men would take it." This is surely an overstatement; the assumption – the only possible assumption – was that the vast majority of men who opted for RAF aircrew did so out of a desire to fly and take part in air operations. Wing Commander Lawson says:

The majority of individuals were not worried about rank but there is no doubt that the [aircrew] badge was of the utmost importance. A large number of volunteers were actuated by a spirit of adventure and the urge for excitement and speed. Glamour has also played its part, but not, in my opinion, in so great a measure as is supposed. To these reasons we must add that the old idea of being a "foot slogger" was not very tempting and that the pay of aircrew was very attractive indeed. The latter point has probably played a much greater part than is thought.

Of course, there would be exceptions; as Lawson says, there was evidence "that a number of young men enlisted voluntarily or opted for the RAF on ground duties with the knowledge that such employment was the least dangerous in any of the Services". When ground-crew recruiting closed, "a proportion volunteered for aircrew duties not having the slightest intention of going on. They intended to fail in the initial stages and thus be transferred to ground duties."

The treatment of failures was standardized in a Memorandum (S.61141/S.7), first issued in 1940 and three times revised purely in the interests of clarity. At first, if after ten hours' flying experience a man was considered unsuitable, he was discharged by procedures laid down in this Memorandum:

> This allowed [such cases] to take up civilian employment in jobs which were scheduled and so when they came to be called up by the Ministry of Labour they were exempted on account of their employment and settled down to a well paid job in civilian life.

This was obviously an unfair and unsatisfactory state of affairs; but retraining them as ground crew was not much better:

> This was exactly what a percentage of them wanted. Eventually it was decided that they should be transferred to the Navy or the Army and later to the mines and whilst a number of them objected to this procedure, nevertheless they went.

In cases of transfer to other Services, the Air Ministry would only say that "we had nothing adverse to record and we had no reason to believe that they would make other than satisfactory officers on duties other than flying." Wing Commander Lawson records with obvious pleasure that to his knowledge a number of these men won commissions in the Services to which they were transferred.

As Lawson says, at the root of the whole matter, and of all the procedures laid down in the Memorandum for dealing with those who forfeited the confidence of their Commanding Officers, was the fact that

> The RAF is largely dependent on the maximum of self discipline as far as members of aircrew are concerned.

It is obvious, given the conditions of air warfare, that unless the assumption could be made with reasonable safety that aircrew would discipline themselves to carry out their tasks to their best ability, the whole exercise would collapse. In other Services there was a disciplinary hierarchy to hold a man to his duty if necessary; in a single-seater fighter there was no one at all; in a bomber there were only six or seven men, all of much the same age, and probably more or less equal in rank. Discipline had mostly to come from within. And here again, as with the stress symptoms mentioned earlier, NCOs were at a disadvantage. Aircrew officers were members of the Officers' Mess, where they would be under the eye of and in contact with the senior officers of a Station. "I am convinced," said Lawson, that this personal contact "is of the greatest value". NCO aircrew did not have this advantage. As we have seen (p. 464), they did not share Station amenities with officers even if they were members of the same crew; on the Station, contact was broken in off-duty periods (though frequently resumed off the Station in pubs, at dances or local sports, etc.). And in the Sergeants' Mess, aircrew NCOs enjoyed a privileged status; Lawson comments:

> It is my belief that these young NCOs who must of necessity be lacking in disciplinary training and service experience are not over-welcome in a Mess which contains a large proportion of senior NCOs who have had to work hard and long to obtain a high grade of efficiency to get their rank and indeed to retain it. This in itself must be a basis for dissension within the Sergeants' Mess, but with preferential meals and ability to get meals at any time of the day combined with extra leave and no Station duties, then there must be a certain amount of feeling even amongst those who do not mind the rank. This must play a part in the attitude of both aircrew and ground personnel whose morale is not at the highest pitch.

One certainly does have the feeling that the dice were loaded against non-commissioned aircrew in too many ways. When we examine what appears to be the only available statistical analysis of cases of forfeiture of Commanding Officers' confidence (or lack of moral fibre), we see the reflection of this circumstance. Lawson tells us that out of 4,059 cases submitted for this classification by the terms of the Memorandum, 746 were officers (18.37 per cent); 3,313 were "airmen" (NCOs). Out of the 4,059 cases submitted, 2,726 were actually classified (67.40 per cent); of these, 389 were officers (14.26 per cent); 2,337 were "airmen". Putting it another way, 52.14 per cent of the officers suspected or accused were classified as lacking in moral fibre, but 70.54 per cent of "airmen" fall into this category. Wing Commander Lawson adds this further information:

> It is of interest to note that during twelve months July 1943 to June 1944, the statisticians obtained the total percentage of all aircrew submitted from

the whole of Bomber Command including OTUs. This was less than 0.4 per cent. It will be realised that by nature of the operations and intensive flying carried out by Bomber Command during that period they submitted most of the cases under the Memorandum. Therefore, *the total percentage submitted from the whole of the Royal Air Force would be less than 0.4 per cent. It is, however, clear that less than 0.3 per cent of the total aircrew have been classified under the Memorandum.* This is indeed a grand record.

The italics are mine; and the passage italicized might serve as a suitable conclusion to this entire dissertation. It makes it abundantly clear that when one refers to "lack of moral fibre" in the RAF (the old Army's "Cowardice"), one is speaking of a very small number of men indeed; Bomber Command, by June 1944, contained 155,510 men and women,[24] while the RAF itself in October of that year contained 1,171,421 (including WAAF), of whom 98,853 were officers. The numbers of men who failed to pass the test are, by that comparison, trivial.

There is, however, one more facet of this subject which should be considered, and fortunately it is one on which it is possible to be reasonably precise for once. It concerns what the Army would call "Desertion in the face of the enemy", and in 1914–18 this accounted for 76.87 per cent of the capital sentences carried out. Clearly, it is far more difficult for Air Force personnel than for soldiers to commit this crime. The author knows of no single rumoured (let alone recorded) case of a pilot or a crew deliberately making for enemy territory in order to desert, as a soldier can do if he picks his moment carefully and crosses the line with his hands up. On the other hand, it is known that a number of Allied aircraft arrived in neutral Switzerland and Sweden, and the crews were there interned, taking them effectively out of the war. It appears that the number of American aircraft involved was large enough to cause grave misgivings about USAAF morale.[25] It is, happily, possible to describe the RAF contribution with some exactitude. Swiss records show that precisely 13 RAF aircraft landed or crashed in Swiss territory during the war (eight Lancasters, four Mosquitoes, one Wellington) involving 70 aircrew. Only one aircraft – a Mosquito, returning from reconnaissance over Venice – landed intact; one other landed, but in an unrepairable condition; all the rest crashed. Of the aircrew, 36 were killed or missing, one baled out over Germany and became a prisoner of war, 33 were interned.[26] For Sweden, the number of aircraft involved was much larger; the reason for this is proximity to Denmark and Norway, where the RAF was constantly operating in one fashion or another, and the fact that Sweden lies across flight paths both to Eastern Germany and Poland and to the USSR. Out of a total of 64 British aircraft which landed in Sweden, seven are civilian (ascribed to "BOAC"), either shot down by German night-fighters or crashed on flights to Sweden or in transit to or from Russia. Of the remainder, three belonged to the Fleet Air Arm (all wrecked), three to specifically Coastal or Photographic Reconnaissance types (two wrecked, one forced down undamaged by the Swedish Air Force), one was a Tactical Air Force Mustang which had lost its way (wrecked). In addition there were 17 Mosquitoes belonging to one Command or another; 11 of these were total wrecks, one was broken up for spares, and five were still sufficiently intact to be sold to the Swedish Air Force. There were 20 Lancasters, all wrecked or never recovered, and 13 bombers of other types, all wrecked. Details concerning the aircrew are unfortunately not available. The above analysis, together with such details as the Swedes are able to supply – "Crashed into mountain ferryflying to Russia", "Damaged by German AA and fighters. Crew parachuted", "Total loss due to flak hit over Denmark. Three of crew parachuted", "Engine failure and hit from Swedish AA. Crew parachuted", etc., etc. – seems flatly to contradict any suggestion of deliberately seeking to take refuge in a neutral country.[27]

It is not possible, in the face of the frankly expressed concern of the Air Council and the Air Staff, Bomber Command Headquarters and the Groups, at different times and in regard to particular circumstances and evidence, to endorse Sir Maurice Dean's hyperbole,

The quality of aircrew throughout was never less than superb.[28]

It will be clear from much that has already been said that, inevitably, in a force quickly raised, trained and committed to battle, quality was uneven – hence the Pathfinders and (despite traditional prejudice) other specialized *élite* formations. In his practical manner, Sir Arthur Harris has remarked that

The education of a member of a bomber crew was the most expensive in the world; it cost some £10,000 for each man, enough to send ten men to Oxford or Cambridge for three years.[29]

The economics recall a departed world, but the point is taken; and in regard to the overall performance, not only of the bomber crews, but also of all the other Commands, one can only say that the money was well spent. It is appropriate, in saying that, to pay tribute once more to the admirable Empire Air Training Scheme which produced such a magnificent result. And with that we must leave the subject of morale, and return to the swelling roar of battle, in which Bomber Command would need to call on every ounce of its "grit", its determination, and the skills implanted in it.[30]

65 The Dams Raid; master bombers

In 1943–44 Churchill had his wish; it was in October 1940 that he had urged Bomber Command "to cart a large number of bombs into Germany" (see p. 266) – and now it was doing precisely that. The tonnages mounted impressively: 8,000 tons in March 1943 swelled to double the amount (16,000 tons) in July and August, dropped back to an average of about 13,000 per month in the last quarter, rose again to 16,500 tons in January 1944 and about three quarters of the large total of 27,000 tons dropped on "enemy targets" in March 1944.[1] It was a terrible pounding – and still only a prelude to the great drama that was yet to come. As we contemplate the much increased scale of the Allied air operations in the big "battles" of 1943, it is hard to grasp that this was, in fact, only a beginning, and that 85 per cent of the final tonnage dropped on Germany was delivered *after* January 1, 1944, and 72 per cent actually after *July* 1 of that year (see p. 265, Ch. 32, Note 16). These statistics became intelligible, however, when we take in such facts as the dropping of 65,000 tons on enemy targets by Bomber Command alone in August 1944, 50,000 tons on Germany herself in October and 53,000 in November, rising to the incredible peak of 67,500 tons in March 1945. It was in 1943 that this vast "mincing" process began; unfortunately, it turned out that there was many a slip 'twixt the tonnage and the target. But well might Albert Speer say:

> The real importance of the air war consisted in the fact that it opened a second front long before the invasion of Europe. That front was the skies over Germany . . . every square metre of the territory we controlled was a kind of front line. Defence against air attacks required the production of thousands of anti-aircraft guns, the stockpiling of tremendous quantities of ammunition all over the country, and holding in readiness hundreds of thousands of soldiers, who in addition had to stay in position by their guns, often totally inactive, for months at a time.[2]

He refers here to nearly 20,000 anti-aircraft guns which, he says, "could almost have doubled the anti-tank defences on the Eastern

537

front". In addition, of course, there was a serious drain on labour resources, both skilled and unskilled, in creating and elaborating defences and repairing damage, the whole entailing an "untold industrial and military effort",[3] as Speer knew only too well.

Thanks to the new aids, a much smaller proportion of the bomb tonnages than ever before was deposited in fields or forests; and though the spectacular scenes of the 1943 battles relate to attacks on cities in the familiar Harris manner, this was by no means the only kind of attack carried out by Bomber Command in that year. Indeed, what has become its most famous single exploit was in an altogether different style. The breaching of the Möhne and Eder dams on the night of May 16/17 has acquired a literature of its own; the gallant leader of the attacking force contributed a superb account of it. The details are widely known, and need no retelling: Dr Barnes Wallis's famous bouncing bomb (or rather, depth-charge); the formation of No. 617 Squadron (an *élite* of *élites*, in the teeth of all RAF tradition); the intensive training, first in very low-level night-flying over water, then bomb-dropping from exact heights at exact speeds; the trials and tribulations, very nearly up to the last moment, with the bomb itself; the modifications of the Lancasters, the installation of VHF radio telephones (as used in Fighter Command) for clear communication between aircraft and with No. 5 Group Headquarters at Grantham ("Ground crews had to work as they had never worked before . . ."[4]); the dress rehearsals (six out of 12 aircraft seriously damaged in one of them); finally, the operation – which was an epic – and the heavy loss: eight out of 19 of the RAF's very best crews. Wing Commander Guy Gibson formed No. 617 Squadron and led the attack; he was awarded the Victoria Cross, and thirty-three other members of the squadron were also decorated.

What did this breathtaking exploit – which Dr Frankland has called "the most brilliant feat of arms which has ever been carried out by any air force"[5] achieve? It is with a sense of sickness, as one considers the high endeavour in every aspect, and the inexpressible degrees of skill and courage called for to bring it to fruition, that one learns that the effects produced "were not, in themselves, of fundamental importance nor even seriously damaging".[6] The sickness mounts with the realization that, in effect, 617 Squadron was attacking the wrong targets. The object of the whole exercise was to wreck the Ruhr economy at a blow by cutting off the water supplies. For this purpose, there was no need to attack the Eder dam at all – its function was almost entirely agricultural. As to the Möhne dam, the Ministry of Economic Warfare expert consulted by the Air Staff refused to commit himself to any prophecy that its destruction would bring about "a critical shortage of water supplies in the Ruhr".[7] For such a purpose, the dam to go for was the Sorpe, and this expert warmly advocated attacking that and the Möhne, saying:

> The destruction of both dams would be worth much more than twice the destruction of one.

The trouble was that Dr Barnes Wallis's amazing bomb was not suitable for attacking the Sorpe dam, whose construction was different from that of the others. All three were, in fact, attacked, but what with the unsuitability of the weapons, and the loss of four-fifths of the detachment attacking the Sorpe, the damage done there was only slight. In view of the advice received from the MEW, it is difficult to understand why the Air Staff allowed this whole elaborate and expensive operation to be mounted. Sir Robert Saundby correctly refers to the fact that an attack on the Ruhr valley dams had been on the RAF's agenda since 1938, but the fact remains that when the proposal was put to Sir Arthur Harris in February 1943 by Saundby, his response was:

> This is tripe of the wildest description. There are so many ifs & buts that there is not the smallest chance of its working.[8]

Yet, stage by stage, he allowed himself to be won over. All the evidence suggests that the prime mover throughout was Barnes Wallis himself, indomitable and ingenious in all difficulties, persistent and persuasive; and Saundby was ever a sympathetic interpreter at Bomber Command HQ. In the end, one concludes, the reason why the Barnes Wallis "bomb" was actually used against the dams was the often-remarked tendency in war for destructive weapons to be used for the same reason that Edmund Hillary climbed Mount Everest in 1953: "because it was there". It would happen again.

What, then, is the final reckoning of the wonderful performance of Guy Gibson and 617 Squadron? It has, says Noble Frankland, like so much else in war, tended pronouncedly to be the victim of mythology:

> Indeed, the impression . . . seems to be widespread that the important facts about the operation were, first, the ingenuity of the bomb which was specially designed for it and, secondly, the devastating consequences supposed to have been produced upon Ruhr industry by its success. In truth, neither the special bomb nor the resulting floods were of any great importance. What mattered in terms of historical significance about the

dams raid was simply the extreme bomb-aiming accuracy achieved.

This was so because, from the tactics devised and executed in May 1943, by Wing Commander Gibson and the crews of 617 Squadron, there were presently evolved the low level and master bomber techniques which, in 1944, were a prime factor in converting the main force of Bomber Command from a bludgeon into a rapier. This, in turn, meant that when, in the second half of 1944, conditions of air superiority began to arise, Bomber Command stood ready to exploit them with highly accurate and highly effective attacks upon immediately vital targets ... It was these precision attacks which injected the decisive element into the great campaign which was waged by Bomber Command throughout the war.[9]

That happy outcome, however, remained obstinately in the future. In 1943, despite the growing tonnages of bombs dropped and the appearances of devastating results – the Möhne dam photographs offer a striking example – neither area nor precision bombing produced the anticipated effects. But the pursuit of precision was not abandoned; Air Chief Marshal Harris, dedicated as he was to area bombing, could be extremely open-minded, as his ultimate championship of the Pathfinder Force and the formation of 617 Squadron itself show; now that the great attack was over, and the squadron very seriously weakened in the process, he refused to allow it to be dispersed – a decision, says the Official History, "of far-reaching importance".[10] He stated his intention to rebuild the squadron – no easy task[11] – "for the performance of similar tasks in the future".

Meanwhile, precision attacks continued: 541 heavy bomber sorties were despatched against three specific targets in June and July. Two of these were in France (Le Creusot once more, June 19/20, and the Peugeot works at Montbéliard, July 15/16) where it was always an important consideration to try to avoid killing French men and women while attacking buildings. The third was the original Zeppelin factory at Friedrichshafen on Lake Constance, which was believed to be playing a vital rôle in the manufacture of parts for radar equipment – another very small target. This attack, carried out by 56 Lancasters of No. 5 Group, headed by four more of No. 8 (Pathfinder) Group, took place on the night of June 20/21. It had a number of interesting features: first, complicated tactics to make sure that real damage was done to the factory. These included No. 5 Group's speciality of "indirect" or "off-set" bombing, whereby markers were placed at a distance from the target itself, in order not to become hidden by the smoke of earlier explosions, and bomb-aimers made calculated overshoots, aiming at these markers. This required a controlled attack, like Guy Gibson's at the dams – the first use of a "Master Bomber" by a larger force, but unfortunately without benefit of the VHF radio-telephone equipment that the "dam-busters" had been able to use. Finally, when the attack was completed (without loss) instead of returning to Lincolnshire, the force flew on to Maison Blanche, a USAAF base in North Africa; on the return from there, on the night of June 23/24, the Lancasters bombed the harbour of Spezia, but the naval base was hidden in a smoke screen, making the effect doubtful. The lesson was learned that taking Lancasters on to a strange base (a "shuttle"), though clever as a map exercise and for press consumption, was not a very good idea; it meant that they "would have to travel with something like their own maintenance unit".[12] Yet this was a lesson worth learning.

As was so often the case in 1943, the results of Bomber Command's three mid-summer precision attacks, though spectacular to observe, were disappointing; however, they had the merit of being economical – only seven aircraft lost out of the 541 despatched. The same could not be said for the year's two remaining important precision operations. The first of these was on the night of August 17/18, when 597 heavy bombers attacked the "Secret Weapon" (V1 but chiefly V2) experimental station at Peenemünde in the Baltic. Once more the "Master Bomber" technique was used, this time with radio telephone equipment as on May 16/17. It was a system calling for steely nerves and the coolest head from the "Master" and his crew; at Peenemünde he was Group Captain J. H. Searby, a Pathfinder squadron commander (No. 83), who circled the target throughout the whole attack. Another innovation in the hectic development of war technology was introduced: a much improved marker bomb, known as "red spot fire":

It burst and ignited at 3,000 feet and burnt on the ground as a vivid crimson fire for about ten minutes. Its appearance was easy to recognise and difficult to simulate.[13]

Once more, despite innovations, the results were far less brilliant than they seemed: "on the production of the V1 the effect of this attack was only slight", while research and development of V2 was resumed "after a short delay".[14] Possibly the most useful product of this massive operation was the killing (among some 700 other people in the residential area) of Dr Thiel, who directed development, and another important scientist. Forty bombers were lost, and 32 more damaged.

In September, 617 Squadron returned to the fray. Now under the command of Squadron-Leader G. W. Holden, who led the attack, the squadron sent out eight aircraft on the night of September 15/16 in an attempt to break the banks of the Dortmund-Ems Canal by the same tactics that had been used against the Möhne and Eder dams. Despite the utmost gallantry and perseverance displayed by Flight-Lieutenant Martin and two other surviving crews, the attempt failed; the canal banks did not burst. Squadron-Leader Holden, his deputy, Flight-Lieutenant Allsebrook, Flight-Lieutenant Knight (whose bomb had breached the Eder dam) and two others with their crews failed to return: five out of eight.

> 617 Squadron had again been shattered, this time in one of the most gallant failures of the war in the air.[15]

Sir Arthur Harris's firm opinion that low-level operations by heavy bombers were "almost without exception costly failures" had received powerful reinforcement.

66 The German fighter force; "Pointblank"

Sir Arthur Harris did not, in general, take kindly to directives. Just over three weeks after 617 Squadron's famous attack on the Ruhr dams, he received yet another, which cannot have greatly pleased him, though he had succeeded in fending off an even more distasteful first draft. This was POINTBLANK, whose final form was presented to Bomber Command HQ on June 10; its origins, however, went considerably further back, and reflected a surprising and significant new factor in the bombing offensive, a challenge by the *Luftwaffe* which changed its whole nature.

Not surprisingly, it was the Americans who first became aware of this, and first reacted to it. Over France, in 1942, the Eighth Air Force (often powerfully supported by Fighter Command) had pursued its policy of daylight bombing with encouraging results. Certainly, nothing had occurred to shake American belief in their style of war. And their first foray into Germany, the attack on Wilhelmshaven on January 27, 1943, was also encouraging: out of 91 unescorted bombers sent, 53 attacked the target, and only three were lost. To General Eaker and his staff, the great problem of the Eighth Air Force at this stage did not seem to be a matter of tactics, but simply of numbers. The build-up of the force was proceeding very slowly; in February, its average bomber availability was only 74 aircraft with crews, and it was not until May that substantial reinforcements arrived. In that interval, however, its operations took on a different aspect. The

Wilhelmshaven statistics proved to be a freak; in the first four missions to Germany, the losses of aircraft attacking their targets amounted to over 10 per cent, almost all being due to combat with German fighters.[1] By May the bomber losses over all enemy-held territory had mounted to 5.6 per cent, or 6.4 per cent of those attacking.[2] These were very serious figures which looked no better on analysis; flak had taken its usual toll (an important contribution being the crippling of bombers which could then be finished off by fighters), but one thing had become clear:

> Enemy fighters remained . . . the principal obstacle in the path of the day bombers.[3]

With Bomber Command coming to the same conclusion (see p. 516), it was clear that matters had taken a dangerous turn. Throughout the year, the Allied air leaders watched with concern the increase in the German fighter force in the West, and its increasing effectiveness, both by day and by night. Despite Bomber Command's numerous radar aids, despite the most disciplined formation flying by the Eighth Air Force and its heavier weapons, despite its own undoubted combat losses, the fighter force continued to grow: 635 single-engined fighters in the West in January 1943 mounted to 870 in January 1944; 410 twin-engined fighters mounted to 780 – the respective totals being 1,045 and 1,650. The latter figure represents 68 per cent of the entire *Luftwaffe* fighter strength, a proportion whose effects were very apparent on the Eastern and Mediterranean fronts. Furthermore, by 1944, 75 per cent of this array was concentrated inside Germany, leaving very little indeed to cover important targets in occupied territory – industry, V-weapon sites and the Channel coast. Strategically, though not what the bomber chiefs were intending, these effects were of very distinct importance; tactically, they were bad news for the bomber crews. The *Luftwaffe* was making a definite bid for air superiority; the Battle of Germany was turning into a return match for the Battle of Britain. The strategic air offensive for all its "revolutionary" appearance, was having to obey the classical dictates of warfare after all.[4]

It was General Eaker, whose force was in continuous dramatic confrontation with the German fighters, who, if not in precisely this form of words, made the first recognition of this fact. In April, he put forward a proposal, sometimes known as "The Combined Bomber Offensive from the United Kingdom", but more colloquially as the "Eaker Plan", which (with modifications) found its way into the structure of Allied strategy in June as the POINTBLANK directive. It reasserted the firm American Air Force belief that German military operations could be fatally weakened by attacks on six selected target systems, comprising some seventy-six targets in all. For this purpose the Eighth Air Force would require substantial reinforcement, to a total of over 2,700 heavy bombers by April 1944. In addition to the – he hoped – steadily rising American numbers, General Eaker expected the full cooperation of Bomber Command – hence the designation, "Combined". At the same time, he recognized that as far as his own force was concerned, air superiority was crucial:

> The ulterior, or strategic, object of destroying selected segments of German industry was seen to be dependent "upon a prior (or simultaneous) offensive against the German fighter strength", which was, therefore, designated as an *intermediate* objective second to none in priority.[5]

The first draft of the POINTBLANK directive on June 3 made this matter crystal clear: the two bomber forces were "to seek the destruction of enemy fighters in the air and on the ground"[6] – that is to say, through the airframe, aero-engine, aircraft component and ball-bearing industries and the repair depôts and storage parks on which the German Air Force depended. It was, says the Official History,

> a most significant document. It conceded that the German fighter force not only threatened the American day offensive but the British night offensive as well.

It was noticeable that

> There was not a single mention of the general area attack upon German morale.[7]

This directive, the Official History remarks, "was not likely to be welcomed by Sir Arthur Harris", and indeed, in his book he does not even refer to it by name, but airily treats it merely as an extension of his own plan to carry his offensive deeper and deeper into Germany. A week elapsed between the circulation of the draft and the issue of the final directive – a week during which the C-in-C of Bomber Command could marshal his arguments against it. This he did to such effect that while repeating that the "first priority" was the attack on the German Air Force and its supporting industries, the amended directive then added that the "primary object" of the bombers was still as stated by the British Chiefs of Staff in October 1942 (see p. 504) and by the Combined Chiefs of Staff at Casablanca.

> the progressive destruction and dislocation of the German military, industrial and economic system, and the undermining of the morale of the German people to a point where their capacity for armed resistance is fatally weakened.

Thus, behind a confusing screen of "primary objects", "main aims", "primary objectives" and "first priorities", Harris led Bomber Command neatly back to square one. What this meant, in effect, was that the "combined" bomber offensive was strangled at birth; by Harris's interpretation,

> The "intermediate objective" of German fighter strength ... [was] now specifically allotted to the Eighth Air Force and to the Eighth Air Force alone.[8]

Anglo-American misunderstandings, plentiful enough, thereby received a fresh addition, reflected in the words of the American Official History:

> POINTBLANK, the code name for the CBO, would come in the usage of the next few months to mean for most persons the attack on the GAF.[9]

"Most persons" did not include Sir Arthur Harris; yet the "Eaker Plan" and the draft directive were right: the German fighter force *was* a most serious threat to Bomber Command, as it and its C-in-C would soon discover.

67 *Hamburg fire-storm;* Luftwaffe *victory; Mustangs; Bomber Command defeat*

It was, then, with confused intentions that the Allied summer bombing programme of 1943 began. For the RAF, it swiftly produced one of the two most horrifying examples of what area bombing – "undermining the morale of the German people" – might mean. This was the ten-day Battle of Hamburg,[1] in which Bomber Command attacked the city four times, on the nights of July 24/25, 27/28, 29/30 and August 2/3, a total of 3,095 sorties of which some 2,500 claimed to have bombed the target. In addition, the United States Eighth Air Force also attacked Hamburg on July 25 and 26 (making this one of the rare occasions when the offensive did actually "combine") with a total of 626 sorties, of which 417 claimed to have arrived and bombed. Bomber Command's performances were much assisted by the belated introduction of WINDOW (see p. 515),[2] which threw the whole German defence system – searchlights, guns, fighters – into total confusion. In conjunction with electronic jamming of the early warning radar, WINDOW meant that the Kammhuber Line,

> on which untold industrial and military effort had been spent, became an expensive and useless luxury overnight, and it became necessary to reorganize the whole system of night fighter defence.[3]

The result was that, as regards the battle against the *Luftwaffe*, Round One had gone to the RAF; like so many others, it was a deceptive story.

The feature which lends the Hamburg story its exceptional horror was produced by the second attack, on July 27/28: the fire-storm. This was the first time that such a phenomenon had been seen, and it was unintentional; when its nature was grasped, another appalling weapon was added to the armoury of modern man. The fire-storms of Hamburg and elsewhere have been frequently described and there is no need to dwell upon them; but since this was the first, some description of it is necessary. It was entirely a product of the incendiary attack; on July 27/28:

> Before half an hour had passed, the districts upon which the weight of the attack fell . . . were transformed into a lake of fire covering an area of twenty-two square kilometres. The effect of this was to heat the air to a temperature which at times was estimated to approach 1,000 degrees centigrade. A vast suction was in this way created so that the air "stormed through the streets with immense force, bearing upon it sparks, timber and roof beams and thus spreading the fire still further and further till it became a typhoon such as had never before been witnessed, and against which all human resistance was powerless". Trees three feet thick were broken off or uprooted, human beings were thrown to the ground or flung alive into the flames by winds which exceeded 150 miles an hour. The panic-stricken citizens knew not where to turn. Flames drove them from the shelters, but high-explosive bombs sent them scurrying back again. Once inside, they were suffocated by carbon-monoxide poisoning and their bodies reduced to ashes as though they had been placed in a crematorium, which was indeed what each shelter proved to be.[4]

After such scenes it was impossible to reach exact conclusions about the casualties. Webster and Frankland conclude that

546

The total number of deaths was probably nearer fifty thousand than forty thousand.[5]

In addition, there were some 40,000 injured; two survivors, a woman and an old man, passing a great pile of corpses, burnt beyond recognition, paused to stare in sick amazement. The woman said:

"If there were a God, he would have shown some mercy to them. He would have helped us."
"Leave God out of this," said the old man sharply. "Men make war, not God."[6]

Once again, the reckoning seems to mock the efforts and the agony. For Bomber Command, thanks to WINDOW, the price of the Battle of Hamburg was by no means excessive: 86 bombers (2.8 per cent) missing, with another 174 (5.6 per cent) damaged. The Eighth Air Force lost 43 aircraft. From the missing alone, this represents a total of about 1,000 Allied aircrew casualties; there are no figures for the damaged aircraft, which may well have added another 50 per cent to that total, possibly more. Even so by comparison with Hamburg's civilian losses, it was a very small number indeed.

The damage, of course, was terrible: 61 per cent of Hamburg's living accommodation was destroyed; the labour force was reduced permanently by about 10 per cent; armaments and other industries were badly affected. Probably the worst effect of all was shock, which has been compared to that after a great earthquake. *Generalleutnant* Galland, who was at that time Inspector of Fighters in the German Air Ministry, says:

A wave of terror radiated from the suffering city and spread through Germany. Appalling details of the great fire were recounted . . . A stream of haggard, terrified refugees flowed into the neighbouring provinces. In every large town people said: "What happened to Hamburg yesterday can happen to us tomorrow" . . . After Hamburg in the wide circle of the political and the military command could be heard the words: "The war is lost".[7]

The attack on morale, in Hamburg, was clearly effective; but the trouble with morale is that it easily fluctuates. Nearly a million people fled from the stricken port, but it was not long before the majority of the workers returned, "and continued to work with undiminished vigour".[8] Albert Speer, making an immediate survey of the damage to Germany's war-making ability, agreed with Galland's assessment:

Hamburg had put the fear of God in me ... I informed Hitler that armaments production was collapsing and threw in the further warning that a series of attacks of this sort, extended to six more major cities, would bring Germany's armaments production to a total halt.[9]

But Hitler, whose dream-world was sometimes closer to fundamental realities than the thoughts of realistic people, merely said: "You'll straighten all that out again."

It was "straightened out". Hamburg, say the Official Historians, "made a remarkable recovery". The July damage was very great, but "it could easily be absorbed in the whole economy of the Reich". The post-war United States Bombing Survey calculated that about 1.8 months' production had been lost, "say forty-five to fifty working days in the larger firms".[10]

It was some time before any real picture of what had taken place in Hamburg during the fire-storm emerged in England. When it did (within a somewhat limited circle) the tendency was, not unnaturally, to take the line that "it was the precept and the practice of the *Luftwaffe* which ... had inspired the British Air Staff. Indeed, the Germans were now reaping the harvest of what they themselves had sown".[11] Real revulsion awaited fuller knowledge after the war, by which time the Western powers were themselves reaping a harvest from what they had sown, at Hiroshima and Nagasaki. The word "napalm" (current in the Korean and Vietnam wars) also helped to excite the public mind against incendiary warfare, which in fact dates back at least to the "Greek fire" employed by the Byzantines in the eighth century, and as a regular twentieth century practice to the flame-throwers of 1916. At no stage in its history has it ever been attractive – but then very little war practice is attractive. It must be said, however, that Sir Arthur Harris's defence is unconvincing:

> In spite of all that happened at Hamburg, bombing proved a comparatively humane method. For one thing, it saved the flower of the youth of this country and of our allies from being mown down by the military in the field, as it was in Flanders in the war of 1914–1918.[12]

Sir Arthur Harris's recoil from what he believed about the First World War led him into specious arguments, never more so than in this case. British (United Kingdom) military deaths, 1939–45, amount to rather more than one-third of those incurred in the First World War.[13] They accurately reflect the fact that the Army, always the chief sufferer numerically, did very little heavy fighting during the middle period of the Second World War, whereas between 1916–18 it had been almost continually (and successfully) engaged against the main body of the German Army. That fact alone is quite sufficient to account for the difference in casualties in the two wars. In no way did bombing "save the flower of youth"; on the contrary, it only ensured that the concentration of casualties would be in that section of the population – usually referred to as the "natural leaders" – which could least be spared. The truth is that in every war *somebody* has to deal with the enemy's main body; in the Second World War it was the Russians. But as we have seen, if Britain was to hit the main enemy with any effect at all, for a very long time Bomber Command would have to do the best it could by the only means available, however frightful. General Sherman was right: "War *is* cruelty . . ." *And* you cannot refine it.

Not pausing to reflect upon these niceties, the *Luftwaffe* lost no time in adjusting its tactics to the new situation. Already, during the Battle of the Ruhr, it had learned to abandon the Kammhuber "boxes" in which its night-fighters operated under tight control of *Würzburg* radar. Instead, returning to visual contact over the bomber target, "where target markers, searchlights and fires combined to afford near-daylight visibility",[14] they introduced what they called "*Wilde Sau*" ("Wild Boar") tactics; for these the Ju 88Cs and Rs proved more suitable than the Me 110s, and by early 1944 these aircraft were providing "the backbone of the *Nachtjagd*, equipping almost the entire night fighter force".[15] By then, too, airborne radar (*Lichtenstein*) made possible "*Zahme Sau*" ("Tame Boar") tactics against the incoming and outgoing bomber streams, leading to running battles which cost Bomber Command dear. Indeed, as the AHB Monograph says, "for a period it seemed as though the introduction of WINDOW by forcing the Germans to discard their rigid GCI system, had actually brought about an improvement in night fighter defence".[16] So air superiority asserted itself in the night battle, as it was doing by day.

July was a bad month for the Eighth Air Force; during the course of it, the Americans lost 109 bombers, of whom, as we have seen, 43 were the price of combining with the RAF over Hamburg. The total represented 3.85 per cent of the aircraft despatched, but its significance is perhaps better understood when we take into account that the Eighth, at this stage, was still only able to maintain an average of 257 aircraft per major operation. August was worse still; its total loss of 107 bombers represented 4.72 per cent of those despatched. This included the disastrous assault on Schweinfurt on August 17, when the Eighth Air Force lost 60 bombers out of 376 despatched (15.95 per cent), or out of 315 which actually attacked, 19.04 per cent (in addition, of course, to a considerable number damaged). Not unnaturally, after this experience, the Americans took things rather more quietly during September, confining themselves chiefly to targets in France, where they generally had the benefit of fighter escort. Even so, their losses amounted to 83 bombers, but this represented only 2.56 per cent of the force despatched; their average force available for major operations rose to 293. In October came what the British Official History calls "the high tide of American tribulation"[17]: a total of no fewer than 175 bombers missing from only seven operations, an average rate of 7.3 per cent. Within this were some very daunting reckonings indeed: 30 out of 399 despatched over Bremen on October 8 (7.51 per cent), 28 out of 278 over East Germany the next day (10.1 per cent), 30 out of 313 over Münster on the 10th (9.58 per cent). And then came the "crippling disaster"[18] on October 14: the second Schweinfurt attack. On this occasion, too, 60 bombers failed to return, but it was 60 out of 291 despatched, 20.61 per cent, or out of 229 attacking, 26.20 per cent; 17 more were "heavily" damaged (i.e. beyond repair), raising the overall percentage lost to 26.46, while another 121 suffered damage in some degree. "Thus from the original force of 291 aircraft, no fewer than 198 had been destroyed or damaged."[19] It meant a total of 68 per cent; this was, says Noble Frankland,

> a great victory for the *Luftwaffe* – a greater one it seemed than Fighter Command of the Royal Air Force had scored against the German bombers on 15 September 1940.[20]

The similarity with September 1940 was marked:

> On the morrow, the Americans curtailed their bombing programme . . . They had no alternative, for losses on the Schweinfurt scale were far in excess of what any air force intending to remain in being could afford to sustain.

In another respect, also, the Battle of Britain was recalled; it was not only the RAF that played the "numbers game". The Americans tried to console themselves with the belief that they had shot down 186 German fighters (as compared with the 185 bombers and fighters claimed by Fighter Command on September 15 1940 – p. 211). The truth, alas! was even more depressing than the RAF's awakening: German records show that at Schweinfurt they lost 38 fighters destroyed in combat and 20 more damaged. And – for the time being, at any rate – they had won air superiority. But here the similarities with 1940 end; Fighter Command, in that year, was able to deflect the Germans from their objective, which was what the German fighter force was trying to do to the Allies in 1943, and after Schweinfurt believed it had accomplished:

But the Americans did not abandon their aim.[21]

The heroism of the Eighth Army Air Force aircrews was not in vain; pressing home their attacks most gallantly in the face of these awful losses, they had done much damage to their targets, and awaited now only one thing to resume their swelling enterprise – the long-range fighter that Portal had proclaimed impossible, but which was about to make its *début*. Nevertheless, until this happened, there was no disguising the defeat that they had suffered, and similar medicine was also in store for Bomber Command.

The period between the Battle of Hamburg and the Battle of Berlin is called in the Official History "the campaign on the road to Berlin". It is not a fortunate title; it suggests an element of geographical advance which is not in the nature of air warfare unless supported by powerful and successful land forces. It also suggests a culmination of effective intensity which is quite misleading. An analogy from boxing may be helpful; the "straight left" is the boxer's long-distance punch, and it can be very effective indeed to the limit of its distance. Beyond that limit, however, the attempt to push it further only results in over-reaching, loss of balance, and reduced power. In order to deliver a second straight left at a longer distance, the boxer must shift his feet. Now, the proposal to attack Berlin was Harris's "straight left", but as it turned out, this target was at the very extremity of the "punch"; and Bomber Command could not "shift its feet" in the manner, for example, of the Mediterranean Air Forces, advancing up Italy. If it *had* been able to pursue a "road" to Berlin that brought it nearer to its target, the story would have been different; but it could not.

Nevertheless, whatever title it may deserve to be given, this interim period in 1943 was one of some vigour. It witnessed twenty-seven major attacks upon German targets, two by more than 700 aircraft, seven by between 600 and 700, and four by more than 500. The attacks were spread wide over Germany; a total of nearly 13,000 sorties was directed against targets as far apart as Munich, Hanover, Nuremberg and Leipzig; the Ruhr was re-visited; Berlin itself was attacked three times. In the first of these attacks on the capital, August

23/24, 1,700 tons of bombs were dropped. This onslaught was followed up on August 31/September 1, and again on September 3/4, when 727 bombers were despatched. All told, 1,719 sorties were flown against Berlin on these three nights, and they cost 123 aircraft missing (7.15 per cent), and 114 damaged (6.63 per cent); it was "not a happy augury for Bomber Command".[22] For the whole "interim" period, the Command's losses amounted to 609 aircraft missing and about 1,000 damaged. The human statistics are not available; the human experience was one of unrelenting strain.

The duel between Bomber Command and the German night-fighter force entered its climactic phase on November 18; it continued until the end of March 1944, this period offering, in fact, "the last opportunity for decisive strategic air action before the direct preparations for, and then the launching of, operation OVERLORD".[23] It was not intended as a duel with the night-fighters; on the contrary, its object was stated with utter clarity in the grandiloquent language which flowed so easily from Sir Arthur Harris's pen; he wrote to Churchill on November 3:

> We can wreck Berlin from end to end if the USAAF will come in on it. It will cost between us 400–500 aircraft. It will cost Germany the war.[24]

As we have seen, and shall see again, Sir Arthur Harris had by now conceived an out-and-out detestation of the idea of a major military enterprise on the European Continent. He appears to have become possessed with a conviction of the necessity of knocking Germany right out before the great combined operation could take place. Such obsessions are not unknown in war:[25] sometimes the reasoning behind them is acceptable, sometimes it is questionable. Sir Arthur Harris was, on his own admission, a devotee of strategic bombing; he also knew that once OVERLORD assumed top priority, a substantial part of his own marked independence in command would cease. And ending the war quickly was, from any point of view, highly desirable. If he had an acute sense of "now or never", it is not surprising; what *is* surprising is that he could postulate full American cooperation only three weeks after the traumatic experience of Schweinfurt. As for Churchill, whether he believed this was going to win the war outright or not, a proposal to do severe damage to Berlin could only please him greatly.

The four-and-a-half month battle called "Berlin" can, in certain important ways, be looked upon as the equivalent, for Bomber Command, of the three-and-a-half month battle called "Passchendaele" for the infantry in 1917. Each constituted the last great set-piece of its kind before a final victorious campaign in a quite different style. In each, for different reasons, an oppressive sense of time lay heavily upon the Commander-in-Chief. In each, great damage was evidently done to the enemy – but in spite of it all he remained obstinately undefeated. At the end of the Battle of Passchendaele a war correspondent – admittedly one not renowned for his cheerfulness – said that "for the first time the British Army lost its spirit of optimism".[26] Looking back on the Battle of Berlin in 1944 no less a personage than Air Vice-Marshal Bennett (referred to by the Official Historians as "the only Group Commander in Bomber Command who had any substantial personal experience of bombing operations in the Second World War"[27]) concluded

> that it represented the second occasion on which the aircrews had "baulked at the jump".

The first such occasion, he considered, was the repeated attack on Essen in 1942 (see p. 460), and the reasons were similar in each case:

> a long series of most unproductive and highly expensive attacks were carried out with virtually no results ... the opposition was intense, the casualty rate was high and the difficulties of hitting the target ... were enormous. Crews openly admitted that it was useless going on throwing away crews when there was little chance of success. Moreover, the continued nature of these raids under precisely the same conditions caused them to lose their enthusiasm in the majority of cases.[28]

The echo of Passchendaele is loud and clear: "there was a sense of deadly depression among many officers and men with whom I came in touch".[29] Air Vice-Marshal Bennett in 1944 even went so far as to say:

> There can be no doubt that a very large number of crew failed to carry out their attacks during the Battle of Berlin in their customary determined manner.

The Official Historians remark that these forthright views appear to have drawn no protest or denial from Sir Arthur Harris, but they add:

> Silence ... did not by any means amount to consent ...[30]

They conclude that, even on the worst days, there was never "any sense of defeat in the Bomber Command squadrons". Like their fathers at Passchendaele, the aircrews "soldiered on".

Like the "Battle of the Ruhr", the "Battle of Berlin" was a figure of speech rather than a precise appellation. Berlin was certainly the core, or "heart" of the battle, but in fact less than half the operations which comprised it were directed at the German capital. Nineteen out of the full total of thirty-five operations were against other cities, two of which (Frankfurt and Stuttgart) were each attacked as many as four times. These nineteen attacks involved 11,113 sorties in all, and 555 aircraft failed to return from them; the attack on Leipzig on February 19, 1944, produced the second highest loss of the whole battle, 78 aircraft out of 800 – 9.75 per cent.

Nevertheless, it was Berlin that mattered: 9,111 sorties were despatched against that city, and 492 aircraft did not return; but in addition 954 were damaged, of which 95 were in fact destroyed, which makes the total completely lost up to 587. The resulting percentage – 6.44 – was a very serious matter for Bomber Command; yet percentages are chilly facts beside the drama of over a thousand bombers hurtling to the ground ablaze, or blown to pieces in mid-air, or forced down in heaps of wreckage all the way across Europe, in the course of "the greatest battle that Bomber Command had yet fought".[31]

It began on a hopeful note; the first attack of all, on November 18, was carried out by 444 aircraft, and only nine failed to return. Four nights later, Berlin suffered again, 2,300 tons of bombs being delivered on the night of November 22/23. On the 26/27th Bomber Command returned, and again on December 2/3. The overwhelming majority of the sorties were by Lancasters: 7,256 of the total despatched to Berlin, 7,396 of the total sent to other targets. It would not be far from the truth to say that by now Bomber Command was, in effect, a Lancaster force; this was entirely satisfactory to Sir Arthur Harris, who had, as we have seen (p. 492) nothing but admiration for this remarkable aeroplane. So impressed was he by its performance that on December 7, with the battle only in its third week, he addressed an extraordinary letter to the Air Ministry. It stated that during the next three months he anticipated having just over 40 Lancaster squadrons operational; with these he expected to drop 13,850 tons of bombs per month, sufficient to destroy between 40 and 50 per cent of the principal German towns; he concluded:

554

From this it appears that the Lancaster force alone should be sufficient but only just sufficient to produce in Germany by April 1st 1944 a state of devastation in which surrender is inevitable.[32]

Even Admiral Dönitz (see p. 235) had not specified a particular type of U-boat as his war-winner; Sir Arthur Harris's claim for the Lancaster is large indeed. His date is also significant: April 1 was the designated end of the "Combined Bomber Offensive", operation POINTBLANK.

Ironically, it was precisely in December, when the USAAF was still smarting from its heavy October defeats, and Bomber Command was about to experience the full measure of its ordeal, that a new instrument made its appearance which would transform the whole character and outcome of the bomber offensive. This was the North American Aviation P–51B (Mustang) fighter. The story of the P–51 is familiar: the initial RAF order, in April 1940, which led to the first under-powered and unimpressive version; the extraordinary transformation, in May 1942, when Rolls Royce Merlin 61 engines were fitted; and finally the evolution of the P–51B in June 1943. This was an aircraft outstandingly superior to any existing German fighter; without drop-tanks,

> it could outpace a FW 190 by nearly fifty m.p.h. up to 28,000 feet and by about seventy m.p.h. above that height. It was superior in speed at all heights to the Me 109G. It could outdive both the FW 190 and the Me 109G. It could easily outturn the Me 109G and slightly outturn the FW 190. It had a similar rate of roll to the Me 109G, but in this respect was slightly inferior to the FW 190.[33]

Most important of all, in the crisis of POINTBLANK, was the range of this astonishing machine: with two 75-gallon droptanks it could operate 600 miles from base. A further 85-gallon tank gave it a round range of 1,474 miles; even when carrying two droptanks, it could achieve speeds of 400 m.p.h. and more.

> An aircraft with the range of a bomber and the performance of a fighter had been created.[34]

Despairing of ever receiving effective long-range fighter support from the RAF, thanks to Portal's obstinacy (see Appendix G), and disappointed by the results of all attempts to improve the range of the P–47s and P–38s (Thunderbolts and Lightnings) General Arnold gave absolute priority to the Eighth Air Force in the supply of P–51Bs. They made their operational *début* (without droptanks) on December 5, but it was during the next three months, escorting the Eighth Air Force bombers to their full distance, that these aircraft, virtually single-handed, reversed the decision of the battle for air superiority, which the *Luftwaffe* by then seemed bound to win. Not least of those who profited mightily from this turn of events was Bomber Command.

With the new year, the battle began to grow increasingly severe. January 1944 was a very bad month – indeed, the worst of the whole war – for Bomber Command. No fewer than 314 aircraft were missing from night operations, 136 of them due, it was thought, to fighters; in addition, 416 aircraft were damaged, 38 of them being written off. It is indicative of unusual strain that of the total damage, 142 are listed as not being due to enemy action – incurred, in other words, in training or through accidents. The total spelt a loss of at least 2,000–2,500 aircrew – in one month. And the most costly operations were yet to come.

In the course of the battle, Bomber Command used every device that it could muster to outwit the defence. WINDOW was freely distributed in vast quantities; airborne radar aids were used to detect night-fighters (but in fact this enabled the fighters to home in on the bombers) or to jam the enemy sets; feints and diversions were practised; roundabout routes were taken. But nothing, it seemed, could mitigate the effect of the sheer distance to be travelled – 1,150 miles to Berlin and back. This was far beyond GEE or OBOE range; and as it turned out, the sprawling city was a poor reflector of H2S; its geography offered no clear characteristic to show up on a screen. Too often, Pathfinders and other leaders had to identify targets visually – and too often these were covered by heavy cloud. Guns and searchlights, as might be expected with a target of such importance, were exceptionally numerous. Ground controllers now directed the fighters towards the bomber stream in groups, instead of individually, a far more effective tactic.

In February, the fighters began to come out halfway across the North Sea to meet the bomber stream; it would thus face the prospect of attack almost the whole way from England to Berlin and back, and by the time it got there the fighters would have ample time to concentrate against it from distant airfields. These were the ingredients of what turned steadily and unmistakably into a defeat for Bomber Command, and a mockery of Sir Arthur Harris's hope of defeating Germany outright by April 1.

The highlights of this gloomy period were the attack on Berlin on February 15/16, when 42 bombers were lost out of 891 (4.71 per cent), the attack on Leipzig on February 19/20, which cost 78 out of 800 (9.75 per cent) and the last attack of all on Berlin itself, on March 24/25, when 72 were lost out of 810 (8.88 per cent). This occasion is treated in some accounts as the close of the battle, but that seems pedantic in view of what happened only six nights later: the disastrous attack on Nuremberg on the night of March 30/31, the "black night" of the RAF, when 95 bombers out of 795 failed to return (11.94 per cent).[35] And that really was the end – fortunately, for such losses could not be borne.

"The Battle of Berlin," says the Official History, "was more than a failure. It was a defeat."[36] It is difficult to argue with this conclusion. Having forced the Americans to break off their daylight attacks in October, the German fighter force now constituted a "grave and increasing threat" to Bomber Command; indeed, this force "had interposed itself between Bomber Command and its strategic object. This is the pith of the matter; the losses (1,047 aircraft missing, 1,682 damaged in the course of the whole battle) were bad enough, but worse still was the lack of result. Damage was done, without a doubt – enormous, horrifying damage, which awed those who saw it. The Wilhelmstrasse and the Reich Chancellery were smoking ruins; huge areas of Berlin (and other cities) were laid waste. But in derision of these fearful scenes, the German war economy seemed to thrive. Two key areas tell the story: tank production, which was 760 a month at the beginning of 1943, mounted to 1,229 in December, and rose to its all-time peak of 1,669 in July 1944; the total of aircraft production, which was 15,288 in 1942, rose to 25,094 in 1943, and 39,275 in 1944 – more than doubled. Total weapon production increased two and a half times between January 1943 and December 1944. As for morale, the story is the usual one; it did not collapse. Berliners could still make jokes; an example which seems to belie all contemporary British estimates of the German situation and character being the café story of an encounter between Goebbels and Goering. Hitler, Goebbels told the *Reichsmarschall*, had hanged himself. "There you are," replied Goering, "I always said we should win this war in the air." It was not a particularly brilliant joke – wartime jokes seldom are; but the point is that according to British orthodoxy, Germans were supposed not to be able to joke at all,[37] still less to do so under devastating air bombardment, and least of all to joke at the sacred person of the *Führer*. It was not just the Battle of Berlin that had failed, it was the whole three-year assault on German morale. Lord Trenchard and his disciples had picked the wrong target – as the next year would show.

557

And so we come to the summary of operation POINTBLANK; Noble Frankland says:

> The harsh fact remains that Berlin, though wounded, was still a going concern, that Hamburg, though partly killed, had made a remarkable recovery, and that the Ruhr was still producing at a very high rate indeed. It cannot be doubted that the German military, industrial and economic system and the morale of the German people had not been undermined to the point at which the German capacity for armed resistance had been fatally weakened . . . The German Air Force in being had proved capable of protecting the German Air Force in production.[38]

This force had succeeded, first, in inflicting insupportable losses on the Eighth Air Force, and then in inflicting insupportable losses on Bomber Command. "Revolutionary" air warfare had, indeed, proved to be classical, after all, as it had been in 1940: the opposing air force had to be defeated. The main achievement of POINTBLANK in 1943 – and valuable indeed – was the massive diversion of German resources to air defence, repair and reconstruction. That, at least, supplied a gleam of light; but until the defeat of the German fighters could be accomplished, their presence "hung like a spectre over all the plans and preparations for OVERLORD".[39]

". . . The highest degree of intimacy . . .'

68 *Combined Operations, 1942–45: "Cossac"; Leigh-Mallory*

In March 1942 Air Marshal Lord Louis Mountbatten was appointed Chief of Combined Operations, a post which also attracted the ranks of Vice-Admiral and Lieutenant-General. He had, in effect, already been doing the work for nearly six months with the title of Adviser, in pursuance of the brief which he had received directly from the Prime Minister:

> my task, he told me, was twofold: I was to continue the Commando raids in order to keep up the offensive spirit, gain essential experience, and to harass the enemy; but, above all, I was to prepare in every possible way for the great counter-invasion of Europe . . . Winston summed up my job in one sentence:
> "I want you to turn the south coast of England from a bastion of defence into a springboard of attack."
> So from now onwards my main preoccupation was this vast Combined Operation which was to be the climax of the war.[1]

As it turned out, the first, ill-fated move towards an assault on the enemy-held coastline of north-west Europe was prepared under Mountbatten's aegis. This was the Dieppe Raid, on August 19, 1942, a date still well within the phase of "euphoria and despondency" which has been more than once alluded to above. The complicated pressures, partly political, partly psychological, partly practical, which brought about that sad event have been copiously discussed, and do not require further examination here. As regards Mountbatten, the practical aspect undoubtedly dominated; his whole cast of mind inclined him towards concentration on the problems and possibilities of technology. Interviewed twenty years after the event by the Canadian Broadcasting Corporation, he unhesitatingly accepted responsibility "for the inception of the idea of the Dieppe Raid", explaining,

At Combined Operations Headquarters our job was to create the machine which would eventually make the invasion of the Continent possible, and to devise the new techniques for the assault, as well as for the maintenance by sea of the great forces once they had been landed. New landing ships, craft and appliances were to be devised, designed, tested and produced, and hundreds of thousands of soldiers, sailors and airmen were to be trained together to act as a single entity in the assault.

The Chiefs of Staff Committee . . . decided that it would be very necessary to carry out a reconnaissance in force . . . In fact a large-scale raid would have to be made to learn more of the technique required to breach what Hitler called the Atlantic Wall . . .[2]

Mountbatten never abandoned this perspective, seeing in the relatively bloodless triumph of June 1944 the justification of what had all the appearances of a bloody fiasco in 1942. As a Canadian survivor expressed it, another twenty years on:

We paid a terrible price . . . but it wasn't all for nothing.[3]

The very heavy casualties of the Second Canadian Division at Dieppe – practically 68 per cent – have naturally focused attention upon their terrible ordeal under devastating unsubdued cross-fire on the open beaches, and there is nothing to be regretted in the attention that was subsequently paid to the beach problem, and the means of overcoming powerful defences. (It was not the least of the rewards of the raid that German attention was also drawn in that direction, seeing the beaches themselves as the decisive point.) The air side – as all too frequently – has become somewhat lost to view, yet its significance can hardly be exaggerated.

Unquestionably the most important lesson learned at Dieppe was the absolute need for massive fire support in amphibious operations. This was recognized in the initial planning of the raid – though it is certainly arguable that it was not recognized enough. The Navy being understandably reluctant at that stage of the war to risk battleships or heavy cruisers in off-shore operations, the only alternative source of such support was Bomber Command; "maximum intensity" bombing was accordingly written into the earliest planning for the raid in April, and was approved by the Chiefs of Staff in May. "Maximum intensity", in 1942, as we have seen, did not amount to much; the request of the Air Commander, Air Vice-Marshal Leigh-Mallory, for an attack by 300 bombers seems, in the light of 1944 and 1945 numbers, ridiculously small, but to Air Chief Marshal Harris, daily contemplating the inadequacy of his Command for its main task, it represented a diversion of his whole available force to what he could only regard as an exercise as hopeless as the bombing of U-boat pens. The request, it must be remembered, at that stage of planning, was for a precision night attack, regardless of weather conditions, on the buildings facing the sea-front, while taking all possible care not to hit the town behind. Harris could make no guarantee of such accuracy, and faced with the prospect of a blazing town, its narrow streets choked with débris and impassable to tanks, the Canadian Land Force Commander accepted the withdrawal of the bombers. The assault would thus go in with no more fire cover than that which could be provided by eight destroyers and Hurricanes firing 20-mm cannon. It did not require a full-scale operation with live soldiers in 1942 to prove that this was totally inadequate; Cape Helles, twenty-seven years earlier, had made that point. But as we have too often seen, it took a long time in the Second World War before responsible commanders recognized that any useful lesson could be learnt from the First World War. General Montgomery, then GOC South-Eastern Command, to which the Canadians belonged, and the Chiefs of Staff, as well as the Force Commanders concerned, all acquiesced in a virtually unsupported attack – and the rest followed. Air support, on the day, comprised 70 squadrons, of which 61 were fighters, two were fighter-bombers, and only two (Bostons) were actual bombers.[4]

The fighter performance on August 19 was acclaimed as a great victory – a consolation prize for the heavy losses of the Army and the not insignificant losses of the Navy. Fighter Command had looked forward – none more so than Leigh-Mallory – to a big air battle in which the *Luftwaffe* would be seriously damaged. The claim at the end of the day did full justice to this hope: 43 German bombers and 49 fighters destroyed, 10 bombers and 29 fighters probably destroyed, 56 bombers and 84 fighters damaged – a total of 271. Alas, this was the heyday of the "numbers game". The reality was very different: 25 bombers and 23 fighters destroyed, with 16 bombers and eight fighters damaged. And against this the RAF lost 106 aircraft, of which 88 were fighters; 71 pilots were killed or missing.[5] These losses, says the AHB Narrative, "were certainly heavy, although they were in fact not proportionately heavier than those sustained during our general offensive operations over the previous few months".[6] It is not much of a palliative; more to the point is the signal from the Military and Naval Force Commanders to the Air Force Commander at 0956 hours on August 19: "Air cooperation faultless".[7] Otherwise interpreted, it meant:

Our soldiers fought completely unmolested from the air.[8]

However, the lessons of Dieppe were, above all, the lessons of how not to do it; certainly, it was better to learn them in 1942 than in 1944, but some of them had been waiting for pupils since 1915.

This at least can be added to the credit side of the Dieppe ledger: that it displayed unmistakably the absolute impossibility of SLEDGEHAMMER in 1942, and also the very great difficulties of attempting ROUNDUP in 1943. By then, Montgomery had moved on to his African triumphs and, as we have seen, a considerable illumination of the whole subject of Army/Air cooperation. Mountbatten would shortly move on also, to an equally triumphant Supreme Command in South-East Asia, in which air power again played a crucial part. Meanwhile, another organization altogether had come upon the scene, presided over by a semi-fictitious figure: COSSAC, the Chief of Staff to a Supreme Allied Commander for OVERLORD in 1944 who did not yet exist, in other words, Lieutenant-General F. E. Morgan, who ascended to that precarious dignity on April 13, 1943. The largest part of his inheritance was the very substantial preliminary work that had already been done in Mountbatten's Combined Operations directorate, with in addition the experience of Dieppe and the further experiences of amphibious operations in the Mediterranean throughout that year and into the next.

As well as this formidable mass of sometimes contradictory and always growing knowledge awaiting digestion, COSSAC drew also on two parallel streams of very recent experience of Army Cooperation. In North Africa, Tedder was orchestrating the whole available air power to the single end of the total overthrow of the Axis forces. Coningham was forging an Allied Tactical Air Force with multiple ingredients. Broadhurst and the Desert Air Force were perfecting new techniques of applying devastating air power directly to the battlefield (see pp. 397–8). At the same time (March 1943), in England, Home Forces conducted their last grand-scale manoeuvres, Exercise SPARTAN, which "was in fact a rehearsal for the liberation of North-West Europe".[9] The assumptions for SPARTAN were that the "Allies" had gained "marked air superiority", had established a bridgehead, captured a number of airfields, and were now preparing a further advance. It was reasonable to insist that fundamental organization should be based on the requirements of what promised to be a testing and probably protracted land campaign, rather than those of the spectacular initial amphibious phase. The report on SPARTAN was drawn up by Air Marshal Barratt, AOC-in-C, Army Cooperation Command, who had, as we have seen (p. 379 et seq.), only a few months earlier visited the Middle East to report on the Army Cooperation system evolved by Coningham and Montgomery, and its highly successful *début* at Alam Halfa. Barratt's report on SPARTAN thus drew not merely upon the exercise itself, but on the practical experience of the Desert battles.

The details of the report – the value of Air Observation Posts (Austers), modifications of the rôle of ASSUs (see p. 351), problems of maintaining mobility, etc. – need not detain us. The basic principle, already revealed in the Mediterranean, and now confirmed, of a "composite" air force, with command centralized at the highest level, but decentralized further down, was highly important; it constituted a

> broader conception of air support, in which the fighter, the ground attack fighter, the fighter reconnaissance aircraft, the light bomber and the heavy bomber were all harnessed for army support. This made the old idea obsolete, in which army cooperation was considered a specialised and limited form of air assistance.[10]

It is here, in this recognition at home as well as in the Middle East that, in decisive operations, Army Cooperation is a function of "the whole available air power", that the foundation of the ultimate success of OVERLORD is to be found. This was the "bad day" for Germany foretold above.[11]

It was not, of course, as we shall further see, a cut-and-dried proposition; to bring it to fulfilment would be no easy matter. And in other sections of Barratt's SPARTAN report we may find the first signals of yet more controversy, some of it still very alive to this day. Thus:

> The capture and retention of airfields and the need for speed in movement were shown to be the primary factors affecting the operations of supporting air forces. Forward moves of 30 to 40 miles were practised by Royal Air Force units . . .[12]

In the disappointment of this expectation we perceive the origins of the worst ill feeling between Air and Army that was to arise in the initial OVERLORD period. Barratt continued:

> It was considered of the greatest importance that air action should be concentrated on objectives vital to the ground operations and this could be achieved by careful selection based upon a clear air plan of campaign.[13]

This sounded elementary and straightforward in the aftermath of SPARTAN and with the examples of the Desert and Tunisia; it ceased to look straightforward in Normandy. "Vital" is a word that can take on many shades of meaning in different circumstances, and thereby lead to much misunderstanding. And equally ominous (with hindsight) was Barratt's innocent precept that it was essential "that a request for assistance should state why it was needed and the results it was hoped to achieve in accordance with a single concerted plan".[14] It did not occur to Barratt in 1943, and came as a shock to airmen in 1944, that such a statement of intention might not, in fact, be strictly accurate – might, indeed, be distinctly disingenuous.

It was, then, with these three prime pieces – Mountbatten's "School of Amphibious Operations", the Mediterranean experience of Army Cooperation and the teaching of Exercise SPARTAN for the Home Forces – that General Morgan began to assemble his jigsaw puzzle. At once a clear motif emerged and stayed: the absolute necessity of establishing air superiority from the first. There would have to be, on a far larger scale and for an indefinite span of time, at least that degree of control of the airspace of the assault that had been achieved for a few hectic hours at Dieppe. From the point of view of Fighter Command (still unaware of the precise truths of the "numbers game"), that forlorn occasion had, indeed, an appearance of success:

> Although it was not faced by a numerically equal enemy fighter force, the Command had shown that it could provide effective daylight cover for naval and military forces over seventy miles away from the English coast. In the light of larger scale operations later in the war, this point may not appear of great importance. But in 1942 such a fact could not be taken for granted; nor could any invasion plans be prepared without such an assumption.[15]

Looking at it a year later, with practical planning in hand, this demonstration took on a decidedly less encouraging look. General Morgan wrote:

> How many of us remember those rather disheartening maps of the Channel at which we used to stare, superscribed with circles of distressingly small radius centred upon the fighter fields in the South of England.[16]

That was the nub of the matter – the "distressingly small radius" – and it was, of course, a characteristic of that superb aircraft which had been the mainstay and the pride of Fighter Command since 1940, "Mitchell's masterpiece", the Supermarine Spitfire.[17] By 1943 the chief combat variant was the Mark IX, whose outstanding features were its rate of climb, 4,000 ft/min ("fantastic for those days") and its ceiling of more than 43,000 feet. No fewer than 5,665 Spitfire IXs were ultimately built; according to one who flew them,

> They lived up to our highest expectations – they were thoroughbreds in every way.[18]

But they still belonged to the category of short-range fighters, and in 1943 this limitation proved severe, both for the US Eighth Air Force carrying its daylight operations into Germany at high cost, and for the OVERLORD planners. Dependence upon the Spitfire lent added stress to the need for early capture of airfields if the beachhead was to expand.

Dependence on fighters in general, in the quest for air superiority, led directly to another matter, which proved equally serious. It did not take General Morgan very long to realize that air matters were so closely interwoven with so much of his business that

> his plans could scarcely prosper without the cooperation of a responsible air officer. Since it was Sir Charles Portal's view that the most important aspect of the air contribution to OVERLORD would be the attainment of air superiority over the beachheads, it was decided, with the concurrence of the Americans, that this officer should be a fighter commander . . .[19]

This being so, it seemed not unreasonable that the choice should fall on Leigh-Mallory, recently (November 1942) appointed AOC-in-C, Fighter Command, and he accordingly, in the words of the Official Historians, "gradually began to assume the rôle" of Allied Air Commander. The decision was clearly closely linked to another, which had been taken on March 10: that the so-called "Composite Group" to support the land forces in the cross-Channel operation should be re-named a "Tactical Air Force" (as in Tunisia) which was to be formed *within* Fighter Command. This force would consist of:

No. 2 Group: the light bombers, transferred from Bomber Command
No. 83 Composite Group (fighters, fighter-bombers and fighter-reconnaissance) already part of Fighter Command
No. 84 Group, not yet formed
No. 38 Airborne Wing, transferred from Army Cooperation Command
No. 145 Photo-Reconnaissance Squadron[20]

The Tactical Air Force duly came into existence on June 1, on which date Army Cooperation Command, whose functions had been growing more and more uncertain, ceased to exist.[21] On June 10 Air

Vice-Marshal D'Albiac was appointed AOC, Tactical Air Force, and in August, at the Quebec Conference, Leigh-Mallory (now Air Marshal) was appointed Commander-in-Chief of the as yet non-existent Allied Expeditionary Air Force. When the time came for the review of these appointments, D'Albiac's was not confirmed[22] but Leigh-Mallory's was, and great were the ensuing discords. It is clear that at this stage Portal and the Air Staff had not fully taken in the lessons of the Middle East and North Africa; there was still a disposition to treat air support for OVERLORD as a "separate" activity for the RAF. But there was still time to learn, and further teaching was coming in.

69 Combined Operations: Pantelleria; Luftwaffe eclipse; Sicily blueprint

The decision taken at Casablanca in January 1943 to make Sicily the next objective of the Allies when victory was achieved in Tunisia (see p. 394), bore fruit in July. It is interesting – and indicative – to observe how the invasion planners in London and Algiers simultaneously faced and accepted the same fundamental disciplines. General Morgan and his staff at one headquarters, and General Eisenhower and his staff at the other, recognized immediately that

> The key to the seaborne assault was the effective range of fighter cover.[1]

In the case of Sicily, that meant that the key was Malta, because "only Malta was within single-seater fighter range of the southern part of Sicily".[2] By June, under the energetic direction of Air Vice-Marshal Sir Keith Park, no fewer than 600 first-line aircraft were based on Malta and Gozo, backed by the latest fighter control and radar installations. And so it came about that

> From a besieged island forced to devote its full efforts to defence, Malta had become an effective forward base for offensive air operations.[3]

This was the first reward of long endurance – a very far cry indeed from the distant days of "Faith", "Hope" and "Charity".

The invasion of Sicily – Operation HUSKY – set the pattern of amphibious operations for the future, both in the Mediterranean and in North-West Europe the following year. It was the opposite of Dieppe – a study not of what not to do, but of what should be done, with useful pointers at how best to do it. The first lesson, well taken, was that while for sailors, soldiers and the airmen concerned with

566

direct support the operation proper could be said to begin with the D-Day assault, for the strategic air forces it would begin very much earlier. The bomber offensive against Sicily, in fact, was already well under way long before the Axis forces surrendered in Tunisia, and continued without any pause. The B–17s of the US Twelfth Air Force, the B–24s of the Ninth, and the Wellingtons of No. 205 Group undertook three main tasks against the island: attacks on airfields with the aim of destroying the Axis air forces on the ground; attacks on ports; and attacks on mainland communications. On May 8, five days before the Tunisian surrender, supported by Coningham's Northwest African Tactical Air Force, they added another important target: the small island of Pantelleria, lying practically in the centre of the narrows between Tunisia and Sicily, some 63 miles from the nearest point of the latter. Pantelleria was bombastically referred to in the Fascist Press as the "Italian Gibraltar"; to the Allied planners its capture had a double significance – to eliminate its radar stations, observation posts and submarine and torpedo boat facilities, and to provide more airfields to support those on Malta.

The air assault on Pantelleria became somewhat of a legend for air power champions. Between May 8 and June 11, when the seaborne attack went in, the Northwest African Air Forces flew 5,285 sorties against Pantelleria, saturating its 42½ square miles with no less than 6,200 tons of bombs. On June 10 alone, 1,500 tons of bombs were dropped, and when the Allied landing parties appeared the Italian garrison, very thoroughly demoralized, surrendered promptly. The neighbouring even smaller island of Lampedusa did likewise after an air attack lasting only 24 hours.

> These successes led some exponents of air power to claim that no defensive position or ground force could stand up to prolonged and continuous air attack.[4]

Delusion about the true capabilities of air bombardment was not confined to Bomber Command, and would recur with sad results during the next twelve months. In the case of Pantelleria, it would seem that the Allies had been too gullible – they had believed the Italian propaganda. It turned out that Pantelleria was by no stretch of imagination a "Gibraltar". Its only feature which at all resembled "the Rock" was a huge underground hangar, some 1,100 feet long, which did, indeed, prove impervious to the bombing. Elsewhere, though some batteries were securely emplaced in rock, others were poorly protected and badly camouflaged, lacking nearby shelters for crews and ammunition. The Allies were amazed to find that much of the communication network had been laid above ground. When the analysis of the bombing was made, it was discovered that whereas the prediction had been 10 per cent within 100 yards of the gun positions, the actuality had been 6.4 per cent for mediums, 3.3 per cent for heavies and 2.6 per cent for fighter-bombers. Italian casualties amounted to fewer than 200 out of a garrison of over 11,000. It thus became apparent that although a great deal of damage had been done to the defences,

> In the final analysis the morale of the defenders was the determining factor in the failure of Pantelleria to put up a strong and prolonged resistance.[5]

The island thus became the one clear example of unquestioned success for an air attack upon morale.[6] From this the Allies derived much comfort, insufficiently taking into account the special surrounding circumstances, not least being an enemy within weeks of total collapse.

On the credit side, apart from the considerable value of Pantelleria as a site for fighter airfields within effective range of Sicily, the operation, when it was analysed (by Professor Zuckerman) had valuable lessons to teach, especially concerning the bombardment of strongpoints and fixed defences, the most suitable bombs and fuses, and so forth. It was noted again that, spectacular and unnerving as they are, low-level "strafing" attacks, even against an enemy as lacking in resolution as the Italians on Pantelleria, were only temporarily effective, and this, certainly, was significant – the misfortune being that soldiers, generally speaking, were in love with this form of air support because they could actually see it happening, and discounted other forms which, though far more effective, were out of sight. It was a constantly recurring theme. Nevertheless, Pantelleria, as the American historians say,

> had many of the characteristics of a laboratory experiment in its influence on the analysis of target information and the development of operational techniques . . . [It] provided an excellent test of the pattern of operations which the Allies would use as they moved northward in the Mediterranean: landings would be preceded by a period of intensive air attacks by land-based planes, the attacks constantly increasing in tempo. Such a system required time and a large expenditure of bombs and gasoline; and it placed a heavy strain on aircrews, planes, and maintenance personnel. But it greatly improved the odds in favor of establishing and maintaining a beachhead, and – under a more general application – it contributed materially to later successes on the ground by isolating the battlefield so

that the enemy was denied supplies, reinforcements, and freedom of manoeuvre. Thus, it saved Allied ground troops; and in the long run, it saved combat air personnel.[7]

General Alexander, Allied Land Forces Commander for HUSKY, is on record in his subsequent Despatch saying that the operations themselves were less interesting than the preliminary planning because the conventional formula applies: they "proceeded according to plan". This is, as may be supposed, an exaggeration; military operations, except on the smaller scale, very rarely go exactly according to plan, and Sicily was no exception. Furthermore, this assault, when it came on July 9/10, was anything but small-scale:

Nearly 2,500 naval vessels and landing craft were to carry 115,000 British Empire and over 66,000 American assault troops on the largest amphibious operation that had ever been mounted in the history of warfare. Indeed the number of troops and craft involved were only exceeded in the Normandy landing [in 1944] if the follow-up formations are taken into account.[8]

With such forces engaged, and an entirely new type of enterprise afoot, it would have been unbelievable if nothing had gone wrong – and, of course, things did go wrong. But in one important respect Alexander was perfectly correct: the air plan for the preliminary phase had worked brilliantly.

Presiding, in his capacity as Commander-in-Chief of Mediterranean Air Command, over all the air planning was Air Chief Marshal Tedder, for whom this period may be looked upon as an invaluable apprenticeship for the lofty rôle that he was to play the next year. To Tedder, as to Barratt at the end of Exercise SPARTAN, two things were crystal clear: the need for air superiority, which no one disputed, and the need for an early capture of enemy airfields if the momentum of the assault was to be maintained. This now became Air Force doctrine, and even so seemingly air-minded a general as Montgomery found its implications hard to accept. The Armies, now as always, not unnaturally focused their attention on the beaches, and demanded above everything that the Air should protect and aid them in capturing these. Montgomery, whose Eighth Army was to land at the all-important south-east corner of the island, never underrated the extent to which the Air could help him; when his headquarters moved to Malta in preparation for the invasion, he was insistent that Air Vice-Marshal Broadhurst and the headquarters of the Desert Air Force should accompany him so that their plans could be fully concerted. He was less clear about the reciprocal: the Air would help the Army ashore; the Army must then help the Air by seizing the airfields it would need. As we have seen, the whole Desert war, and the campaign in Tunisia as well, had been a "war for aerodromes"; so was HUSKY. In Montgomery's failure to perceive this, and the sharp exchanges that now took place between him and the airmen concerned (in particular Tedder and Coningham)[9] we may detect ominous rumblings of what was to grow into a dangerous clash of opinions and wills in 1944. In 1943 the disagreement was resolved by compromise – which worked; but the doubts and resentments lingered on.

The compromise worked because the rest of the air plan worked. Even if the Allies did not obtain enemy airfields in Sicily as early as they had hoped, those airfields could not be used against them to any extent that mattered after their treatment at the hands of the Allied bombers. The Axis forces here endured once again from the first the misery of trying to fight under a canopy of hostile air power; and this was to be the German soldier's hard lot for the rest of the war in the West. The manner in which he sustained it stands as his lasting memorial. By July 1943 he had learned to expect little effective aid from the *Luftwaffe*; that once mighty instrument of war was now entering the period of its eclipse. July was the month of the last major German offensive on the Eastern Front, the Battle of Kursk-Orel, the greatest clash of armour in history:

> German officers had never seen so many Soviet aircraft, while Soviet commanders – who had seen a lot – had never before seen such formidable massing of German tanks ... These were tank armadas on the move ... almost 4,000 Soviet tanks and nearly 3,000 German tanks and assault guns were being steadily drawn into this gigantic battle, which roared on hour after hour leaving ever-greater heaps of the dead and the dying, clumps of blazing or disabled armour, shattered personnel carriers and lorries, and thickening columns of smoke coiling over the steppe.[10]

For this titanic encounter, the *Luftwaffe* made its last great effort in the traditional style; the German tank onslaught was led and assisted by "at least 1,000 first-line aircraft"[11] (some authorities say 1,800[12]) out of some 2,500 on the Eastern Front. In the opening days German aircraft flew 3,000 sorties per 24 hours, the dive-bombers carrying out five or six missions a day; for the whole month the average was 1,000 sorties per 24 hours. In the course of the battle, on July 8, a remarkable episode took place, full of future meaning. A Soviet tank brigade (60 T-34s) with supporting rifle battalions was observed preparing to make a rear and flank attack on the *II S.S. Panzerkorps*;

it was at once attacked by four *Staffeln* of Henschel 129B "tank-destroyers",[13] coming in from astern and abeam to strike the tanks from their most vulnerable angle, while FW 190 fighter-bombers suppressed Soviet anti-aircraft fire. The bulk of the Soviet tanks were destroyed, and the infantry formations broken up. It was the first occasion in history that "tactical aircraft scored [a] significant victory over enemy ground armoured forces, without any assistance or contact with friendly ground troops".[14]

It did not avail; the German offensive at Kursk was a failure, and the Soviet forces passed to their counter-offensive which was to continue until they reached Berlin in April 1945. The *Luftwaffe*, despite its enormous efforts at Kursk, had "failed at any stage to secure decisive air superiority"[15]; its losses on the Eastern Front during July amounted to 911, nearly all in this great battle, and shortly afterwards the Chief of Air Staff, *Generaloberst* Hans Jeschonnek, committed suicide. Meanwhile, the *Luftwaffe* itself had become the target of POINTBLANK, with consequences which now began to make themselves felt:

> The extraordinary change in the balance of forces in the Mediterranean which was an outstanding feature of the period July 1943–July 1944, resulting in a decrease in German first-line air strength in that theatre from 1,280 to 475 aircraft, was the direct consequence of the launching of an all-out Anglo-American air offensive against German war industry.[16]

The full import of the air disparity may be judged when we learn that by the end of 1943 the Allied Mediterranean Air Forces had expanded to some 7,000 aircraft served by 315,000 air and ground-crew. Such was the price of the *Luftwaffe*'s last desperate victories in the skies over Germany, against the US Eighth Air Force and Bomber Command. And this grim outlook for the German Air Force supplies the background of the whole remaining Mediterranean war, making the air contribution, of necessity, almost entirely an exercise in army cooperation.

HUSKY operations began with an experiment: a glider-borne assault by elements of the British First Airborne Division in the sector of the Eighth Army, and a parachute drop by elements of the 82nd (US) Airborne Division in the sector of the American Seventh Army, further to the west, both on the night of July 9/10. For the gliders, the US Troop Carrier Command provided DC–3 tugs, and No. 38 Wing, RAF (296 and 297 Squadrons) flew Albemarles and Halifaxes. Distractions were provided by Wellingtons of No. 205 Group, and No.

571

73 Squadron's Hurricane night-fighters were present to deal with searchlights. It was the first time the Allies had used airborne forces on any scale worth noting, and it certainly did not bear out General Alexander's contention that everything "proceeded according to plan". Unexpected strong winds and insufficient training for the DC–3 pilots wrecked the First Airborne Division's attack: out of 137 gliders released, 69 came down in a rough sea, 56 were scattered along the south-eastern coast of Sicily, and only 12, all towed by the RAF, found their landing-zone. Less than 100 officers and men out of over 2,000 were effectively carried into battle; as Alexander's biographer says,

> . . . these two thousand men could have been landed much less wastefully from the sea. The sacrifice of the most highly trained soldiers in both armies by entrusting them to inexperienced aircrews still seems unpardonable.[17]

"Both armies" is unfortunately correct; out of nearly 3,000 paratroops of the 82nd Division, only 250 came down in the right place, the remainder being scattered as much as 50 miles apart:

> Only one battalion came to earth anywhere near intact, and it was twenty-five miles from the designated drop zone.[18]

Despite these lamentable failures, two more large airborne attacks were carried out, one American (July 11) and one British (July 13). On each occasion, navigational error again constituted a severe hazard, but now greatly increased by the heavy volume of Allied anti-aircraft fire which greeted the aircraft from the massive naval armada below. According to the American historians, "perhaps twenty-five out of the forty-two aircraft lost had been shot down by friendly naval and ground fire"[19] – a bitter pill, and one which naturally brought much further bitterness in its train. Much of this was directed against the US Navy; the Army Air Force took a very poor view of being shot at by its own side – and the practice persisted throughout the whole beachhead phase. The RAF had learnt long ago that it was axiomatic in the Royal Navy to shoot first and ask afterwards, such experiences as the Crete evacuation in 1941 and the loss of the *Prince of Wales* and *Repulse* later in that year strongly confirming this disposition. Yet very nearly half the aircraft lost belonged to the RAF, and 50 more were damaged from the same cause. For all the airborne soldiers and the pilots who took them in, it was a tragic moment and the emotion lives on:

Their quiet graves in the military cemetery at Catania, with headstones recording euphemistically that drowned men were killed in action, are a silent reproach, and to their sons and daughters the only memorials of fathers whom they never knew.[20]

Enquiry, however, established that

In point of fact the ships were entitled to shoot at the transport aircraft ... by an unfortunate chance a small number of enemy aircraft were in the vicinity at the time the Allied aircraft were approaching ... It was considered that only in very exceptional circumstances should ships be deprived of their right to open fire at low flying aircraft approaching them and that the solution must always be to route transport aircraft clear of Allied shipping.[21]

All in all, as Colonel Shepperd says,

The airborne operations were a great disappointment to the Allies ... Unlike the Germans, who after Crete never used their parachute troops in their prime rôle again, the Allies were not disheartened in their efforts to develop their airborne forces, although Eisenhower at one point seriously considered recommending that the airborne divisions should be broken up.[22]

It is a subject to which we shall return.

July 10 was Sicily's D-Day; it was a blueprint for those that followed. Even so, it did not pass without recriminations, and these pointed to further improvements. The fundamental fact of July 10 was that the *Luftwaffe* had already been defeated before the Allied invasion even began; the bombing offensive had entered its intensive phase on July 3, and during the following week it not only caused the loss of over 100 German aircraft, but rendered so many airfields unusable that the FW 190s had to be pulled back to the mainland, using such Sicilian airfields as remained as advanced landing-grounds only. The airfields in neighbouring Sardinia were similarly smitten, so that

When the invasion of Sicily began on the night of July 9th–10th, *Luftwaffe* defences were ... already seriously weakened. The withdrawal of fighter-bombers to the Naples area meant that this force, on which the *Luftwaffe* relied for attacks on landing craft and beaches, was based some 200 miles away from the scene of operations ... In these circumstances the *Luftwaffe* reaction to the Allied assault was hesitant and lacked coordination ...[23]

Air superiority was thus undoubtedly achieved, but it is a condition which requires consideration and understanding. It is, in fact, a general term, which cannot be held to apply absolutely, everywhere, all the time. What it meant, between July 10 and July 12, was that the *Luftwaffe* proved capable of only some 275–300 sorties per 24 hours (half of them by night), and thereafter even this slender effort was halved; by July 18 only 25 German aircraft remained on the island. The first effect of this weakness was experienced by the Allied navies. It was unfortunate that, in the earliest moments of the assault, a *Stuka* sank the US destroyer *Maddox* with the loss of most of her crew, and shortly afterwards another sank a minesweeper. A natural uneasiness resulted, causing the US Navy to complain sharply, saying that "close support by aircraft in amphibious operations, as they understood it, did not exist".[24] Yet the fact is that on July 10, out of that vast fleet of all types standing off-shore, instead of the 300 vessels which it was feared might be lost, only 12 were actually sunk by enemy action – air superiority indeed!

The story on the beaches was somewhat more complicated, but once again the bedrock fact is that both Allied armies got ashore far more easily and with far less loss than anyone had dared to hope – and this was unquestionably due to the fact that, as Richards and Saunders say,

> the *Luftwaffe* appeared to be paralysed and unable to exercise any effect on the course of events.[25]

In the broad perspective, this is undoubtedly true; in point of very precise fact it is not totally accurate. The *Luftwaffe* did make some appearances, and did cause consternation, especially in the American sector, where the Axis forces mounted a dangerous counter-attack on July 11; an American official historian says:

> Conspicuously missing during the two days of crisis was direct support from American planes. Although they continued their campaigns against Axis airfields and engaged targets of opportunity over the entire island – and in the process fired on many Axis tanks and troops – no planes were available on call from the hard-pressed men on the ground and in the ships.[26]

Again, this is not strictly accurate. Fighter cover for the Eighth Army was supplied by Desert Air Force Spitfires based on Malta (55 miles distant) and for the Seventh Army by the P–40s of the US 31 Fighter Group on Gozo and the 33rd Fighter Group on Pantelleria (63 miles). The control system was another blueprint; at the base of it, in the launching territories, there were Air Command Posts for the overall direction of air operations, with subordinate headquarters to supply tactical direction; afloat off-shore, in the landing areas, were:

Headquarters ships for each assault area ... fitted to accommodate Headquarters staffs and to operate as Forward Fighter Controls using information received from broadcasts and, when fitted, from their own radar.

A naval Fighter Directing ship with each main Headquarters ship to provide information from its long-range radar, but not to control ... It was considered necessary to limit the function of control to Headquarters ships as the naval controllers on the Fighter Directing ships were insufficiently briefed to be certain of keeping the few available fighters within the most important patrol areas. In retrospect, however, it was evident that there was no basic reason why controllers and Headquarters staffs should continue to be crowded together on one ship, with an over-complicated communications system, and, consequently the provision of separate Air Force Fighter Directing ships was recommended.

Three seaborne GCIs (lodged on Tank Landing Ships) were used for the control of night fighters.[27]

It would have been surprising if such a well-planned and elaborate system had produced no result at all, and in fact that was not the case. In the British sector there were few complaints; Admiral Cunningham spoke for most when he stated that "the navies and armies owed a great debt to the air forces for the effectiveness of the protection offered them throughout the operation".[28] Continuous fighter patrols were flown over the five main landing areas during the first one and a half to two hours of daylight and the last hour; throughout the whole 16 daylight hours there was fighter cover for at least one or two landing areas, with additional patrol at times when enemy attacks might be expected. For the rest, support would necessarily have to be only on call, and was restricted by the number and distance of airfields. It is recorded that

On 10, 11 and 12 July Desert Air Force flew more than 3,000 sorties, of which attached 31st and 33rd US Fighter Groups accounted for more than 1,000. Most of the planes flew three sorties a day.[29]

It has to be remembered that covering the ships and the beaches was by no means the only fighter commitment during this phase; there was also the matter of escorting the Allied bombers. Thus, precisely at the time when the Germans and Italians were making their last desperate endeavours to hold the Allies in their beachheads,

Almost 1,000 sorties flown by Twelfth Air Force day fighters and fighter-bombers on [July] 12th left the roads of Sicily blocked with burned trucks, seriously hampered the enemy's road movements, and helped the Allied ground forces to strengthen and enlarge their beachheads.[30]

This was "interdiction" – a word that would be heard increasingly. But by its very nature, much of it was out of sight and the Allied soldiers found it difficult to take into account the enemies they never saw because they never reached the battlefield.

After July 12 the issue in Sicily was a foregone conclusion – yet there were lessons still to learn. Virtually deserted by their crumbling and feeble Italian allies, and bereft of air support, the Germans displayed all their familiar resolution in adversity and developed new skills to meet their hopeless situation. Thanks to these, despite overwhelming Allied superiority on the ground as well as in the air, they were able to fight delaying actions so successfully that 39 days were required to complete the occupation of the island. Nothing that happened in that time altered the Air Forces' belief in quick seizure of airfields. In the Eighth Army area, a Station Commander's party of No. 244 Fighter Wing landed on D-Day itself, and at 0830 the following day it arrived at Pachino landing ground, accompanied by a Servicing Commando Unit, AA squadrons of the RAF Regiment, and a Signals detachment. During the course of the day General Montgomery himself put in an appearance, and ordered the landing ground to be operational by the 12th. On that day some DUKWs (American-built amphibious lorries – an invaluable adjunct) brought up a quantity of ammunition and petrol; sadly, this proved to have been wrongly packed, or wrongly marked, because the ammunition was for 4.7-inch mortars which were not an RAF weapon, and the petrol was army tank fuel. War was ever thus; for Norway in 1940 tactical loading was practically unheard of; for Gallipoli in 1915 most cargoes had to be unloaded and repacked at Alexandria; in the Crimea in 1854 an entire consignment of boots turned out to be for the left foot only. No doubt Air Vice-Marshal Broadhurst, who also turned up at Pachino on July 12 (characteristically flying his own Spitfire), made suitable comments. And on that day the main body of the Wing embarked from Malta. On the morning of the 13th the AOC arrived, followed by the squadrons: No. 1 SAAF, Nos. 92 and 145. It then turned out that the Servicing Commando Unit had not been trained to handle Spitfire IXs; this work had to be done by advanced ground-crew parties of the squadrons themselves. The main party arrived during the day, complete with all transport; No. 244 Wing was operational in Sicily. Six aircraft stood by through the day for local defence, but "were not required to go into action".[31]

As the month wore on, the wing became somewhat disappointed with the course the campaign was taking. The Operations Record Book on July 31 complained:

... the Sicilian campaign has been the reverse of our anticipations. We expected the Hun to come out of his lair in droves, but though when we were in Malta there were enticing stories of formations of forty plus lurking at judicious distances from the operations we covered and the sweeps we did, in the main he just refused to play. The conclusion is that for us the campaign was more or less over before we started.[32]

According to the same source, the Wing had by that time flown over 3,000 sorties since becoming operational in Malta, but had only engaged 131 enemy aircraft, of which it claimed 11 destroyed and 15 damaged. By the end of July the Spitfire Squadrons were concentrated in Sicily, freeing their Malta airfields for Kitty-bombers; 21 Sicilian airfields were in operation, and 40 Allied squadrons were based on the island.

By August 12, the campaign now in its very last stage, the Tactical Bomber Force, at first divided between Malta and Tunisia, was united in Sicily. Next to the airborne fiascos at the beginning, its story is the least successful of those of the Allied air forces. The reasons for this would seem to have been, as usual, multiple and complex. Physically divided command in launching areas at a distance from the battles played their unfortunate part; in theory, radio communication should have disposed of this problem; in practice it did not. There was no substitute for constant physical contact. The geography of Sicily was also a factor; this terrain

with its steep folded valleys was very different from the wide, stony spaces of North Africa and made cooperation with the army on the ground no easy task. The positions occupied by the German infantry were often hard to discover and harder still to hit . . .[33]

The armies, it must be said, were not always judicious in making their requests for bomber support; individual gun positions, well concealed, or single machine-guns, which in hilly country could hold up an advance for hours, are not the best targets even for light bombers at low level. Fighter-bombers and fighters using cannon (or, as later stages of the war showed, rockets) were far more suitable, and the Germans freely acknowledged the effect produced by these on the battlefield and on the supply routes, only remarking that they were "exceedingly sensitive to anti-aircraft fire".[34] Attacks by tactical bombers on localities, in particular communication centres, though frequently causing great damage to buildings and raising impressive clouds of smoke and dust, were less effective. One German divisional history recorded:

In no case did [the enemy] succeed in causing a prolonged blocking of the roads. Even after Randazzo had been attacked 21 times in one day by waves of twelve planes, it was possible to re-open this to through traffic after only four hours.[35]

German demolitions, on the other hand, along stretches of mountainside or coast road, proved extremely effective in delaying the Allies, especially in the rugged area around Catania and Mount Etna on the Eighth Army front.

It is hard to escape the conclusion that there had been some falling-away of proficiency in the inter-Service cooperation which had flourished so fruitfully in Africa. In part, this was clearly an attribute of growth; the relatively small, closely-knit air forces which had produced such excellent results in Africa, operating with a single Army, were now replaced by very large forces indeed (267 Allied squadrons were deployed for HUSKY: 146 American, 121 RAF), administered by a complex of Commands, and serving two armies of different nationalities with different attitudes and demands. Close liaison, always a tender plant, was very liable to wither in such circumstances. The tendency, already noted, of the armies to ask for the wrong thing, or quite simply, too much of the Air, was to remain a persisting (indeed, increasing) feature of Allied operations. On the American side, it reflected a national level of machine-mindedness, and a disposition to make machines do the work of men in all circumstances. Cost-effectiveness was not a consideration; in regard to "hardware", the Americans were not cost-conscious. For the less well-off British, it was a reflection also of a progressive dilution of the Army's front-line elements, arising out of a widespread misinterpretation of the nature of the war, and a consequently flawed manpower policy. The result would be, as we shall see, considerable damage to relations between the RAF and the Army, which airmen saw as, in Tedder's words, less and less "prepared to fight its way with its own weapons".[36] It was clear that some running repairs were required to the machinery of cooperation, and it was obviously helpful when the first Mobile Operations Room Unit (MORU) arrived in Sicily in late July. This was a joint Army/Air control devised in England in October 1942 and tested in SPARTAN; its name was subsequently changed to Group Control Centre; its value would be appreciated in the campaign in Italy and in Normandy. The lesson of Sicily was that both the spirit and the structure of cooperation need constant intensive care – by both parties.

These critiques are the historian's prerogative; they have to be set alongside the steady, remorseless crushing of Axis resistance in Sicily until, by August, the only remaining question was whether anything would be left of the German and Italian forces at all. As regards the latter, the answer proved to be: very little. Italian casualties in Sicily amounted to some 132,000, the vast majority of them prisoners of war; for Italy the end of the road was clearly in sight, its most obvious manifestation being the fall and immediate arrest of Mussolini on July 25. As regards the Germans, the story is, as usual, very different. Their resistance was skilful and obstinate to the last, and its final stage was rewarded by the successful evacuation of some 40,000 (according to some authorities, 60,000) men and nearly 10,000 vehicles with 94 guns and even 47 tanks. This was in the teeth of the huge Allied navies and overwhelming air superiority. What made it possible was another triumph of that always admirable branch of the *Luftwaffe*, its anti-aircraft batteries. The exit point for the remaining Axis forces was Messina, where Sicily and the mainland are less than three miles apart. The Allied air forces now made Messina a prime target, and by August 8 it was "reduced to a condition much the same as that in which it had been left by the earthquake of 1909".[37] Yet in and around the rubble the Germans – well supported for once by the Italians – established a "flak" barrier which threw up fire so intensive that it was described as "heavier than the Ruhr".[38] From a captured *Luftwaffe* "flak" map it would appear that between 112 and 168 88-mm guns were emplaced along the two sides of the Straits, backed by 148 37-mm or 20 mm guns, with Italian 90-mm, 75-mm and lighter guns mixed in amongst them.[39] On August 1 Coningham told Tedder that he "considered that the Messina area 'flak' was now practically prohibitive for all aircraft except the heavy bombers", and Broadhurst confirmed this on August 3:

> ... the exceptional "flak" on both sides of the Straits of Messina will need, I think, the use of Fortresses if we are to maintain continuous air action to defeat an attempt at evacuation.[40]

The heavy bombers, however, were otherwise committed, and they were not diverted:

> The Germans ... were completely mystified by the absence of heavy bomber attacks by day and made full use of the situation.[41]

If the Allied victory was to that extent less than absolute, that is the worst that can be said for it. In all other respects it was impressive, and nowhere more so than in its air aspect. As they occupied the

Sicilian airfields one by one, the Allies counted over 1,100 Axis aircraft destroyed or damaged on the ground, of which some 600 were German. Well may the AHB Air Support Monograph say that

> the most outstanding feature of operation HUSKY was the success which attended the attacks on enemy airfields.[42]

And in addition to this initial crippling damage, a further 740 aircraft were destroyed in the air – for a loss to the Allies of less than 400. It was an equation which augured well for the future, and for OVERLORD. The same could be said of HUSKY in general; in Sicily we may discern all the elements, if not the details, of the amphibious operations that were to come – Salerno, Anzio, OVERLORD and DRAGOON. With all acknowledgment to inescapable failures and short-comings, the example was full of promise.

70 Combined Operations: Mainland Italy; systems of air support

Across the Straits of Messina, the mainland beckoned: the mainland of Italy, the mainland of Europe. It was to fight on the mainland that the Americans had come to the European theatre of war; five times expelled from it,[1] for the British, too, whatever their individual hesi-tations might be, the mainland was a national objective. Yet in a list of all the unsuitable places at which to launch the long-desired return, the tip of the toe of Italy would rank high. Churchill, whose recoil from the thought of a direct cross-Channel assault on North-Western Europe was always powerful, had long ago called the Mediterranean shores "the under-belly of the Axis".[2] This unhelpful phrase was expanded by Press and radio into "the *soft* under-belly"; it turned out to be a hard spinal column – and the extremity of the spine was the tip of the toe of Italy opposite Messina. Yet that is where Montgomery's Eighth Army made its crossing, seventeen days after the clearing of Sicily, on September 3, 1943.

To be fair, this was a diversion. The main attack was in the Gulf of Salerno, where another large amphibious operation, by the American Fifth Army, was timed to coincide with Italy's surrender. The negotiation of this event, marking the first crack in the Axis, a significant milestone of the war, proved to be no easy matter – with strong German forces standing in Italy, how could it be? The Allied Air Forces during this period put pressure on the Italians: continuous attacks on airfields and communications by the Mediterranean strategic bombers and attacks on the cities of northern Italy by Bomber Command. Genoa was attacked on August 7, Turin three times during the month, and Milan four times. Bombing in Italy always had special connotations; these attacks on Milan indicate them clearly:

> Forty churches, ninety-nine schools, and some hundreds of factories were damaged or destroyed. About 1,500 houses were razed to the ground and 1,700 badly damaged. The raid of the 12th/13th August was the worst. The Duomo escaped, but the Basilica of San Ambrogio, where St Augustine was baptized, was ringed by fire, its northern aisle destroyed and its famous frescoes hideously defaced. Hard-by, the church of Santa Maria delle Grazie was hit, and when day dawned, of its Refectory only one wall remained. Upon it still mouldered, untouched by the blast of bombs and yielding only to the slow assault of time, the *Last Supper* of Leonardo da Vinci.
>
> Whether the object of these raids, which was to hasten the surrender of Italy, was achieved is hard to say.[3]

The surrender came on September 8; it was "unconditional". That unfortunate phrase was already working its mischief, contributing considerably to the delay, which in turn afforded the Germans some time to prepare for the blow that was obviously coming.[4] Under the *Luftwaffe*'s most able commander – albeit chiefly in a ground rôle, due to the sheer lack of aircraft – *Generalfeldmarschall* Albrecht Kesselring, they thus began one of the most remarkable defensive campaigns against all the odds in the history of war. The fundamental fact of the German campaign in Italy which was now about to begin was the "canopy of hostile air power" referred to above (p. 570), resulting from the progressive elimination of the *Luftwaffe*'s flying arm (as opposed to its invaluable AA arm and its ground divisions). Against all the "rules", against all reasonable expectation, the German soldier was now about to demonstrate that it is possible to exist, to fight, and even fight successfully, against air superiority which was, in Slessor's words,

> more complete than anything I had believed possible . . . Yet he fights, and fights like hell, not only in defence but in counter-attack. He is undoubtedly the world's finest ground soldier . . .[5]

Because the Italian campaign soon came to be overshadowed by a far larger and more dramatic enterprise, this lesson that even overwhelming air power can be resisted was lost to view. It was painfully re-taught to the Americans in Vietnam, between 1964–73.

So, under their nevertheless potent umbrella, the Allies went ashore, on September 9, over the wide curve of beaches round Salerno, some 25 miles south of Naples as the crow flies – and quickly learned once more what some armies had already learned, and others soon would: that soldiers are not crows and beaches are not everything. The Salerno landings by the Fifth Army (which included the British X Corps) followed the pattern of Sicily, with some amendments. As always, the key question was fighter cover, and therefore fighter range; the American P–51s had no problems, and the P–38s could manage 60-minute patrols over the Salerno beaches, but even with extra tanks the Spitfires flying from Sicily were only able to remain for 25 minutes. The inevitable intervals were covered by Seafires of the Fleet Air Arm, operating from escort carriers which had been sent to the Mediterranean especially for this purpose. Portal blandly claimed credit both for the availability of long-range tanks for the Spitfires,[6] and the proposal to use the carriers, which is somewhat breathtaking, since his own obdurate refusal to press for long-range fighters was a main reason for adopting these expedients. Slessor, schooled by his Coastal experience, took a less friendly view of this use of carriers, which he considered

> an example of the extravagant dangers of having two separate Air Forces, in view of the insignificant part that the British aircraft-carriers played in the Battle of the Atlantic, which one must be excused for thinking was more their proper rôle than land/air warfare in a theatre where Tactical Air Forces were already more than sufficient.[7]

An innovation more profitable for the future was the rocket assault-craft, with their ability to discharge shattering fire-power on selected points as the landing craft closed in.

The Germans, too, provided an innovation which was little to the taste of the Allies: the HS 293 and FX 1400 radio-controlled glider-bombs.[8] HS 293, the smaller of the two, looked like a miniature monoplane with a wing-span of 11 feet; it carried 1,100 lbs of explosive, travelled at over 550 mph, and had a range of three and a half miles. The larger FX 1400, with a range of eight miles, was designed for armour-piercing:

> If released at 18,000 feet, this bomb was travelling at 800 feet per second at the end of its trajectory and it could neither be shot down by gun-fire nor avoided by manoeuvring, especially in the congested waters of the assembly areas.[9]

The massed Allied shipping standing off-shore at Salerno provided excellent targets for these menacing weapons; the wonder is that they did not cause more havoc. As it was, the American cruiser *Savannah* suffered serious damage on September 11, and *Philadelphia* was badly shaken by a near miss; on September 13 the British cruiser *Uganda* was hit and seriously damaged, but managed to make her way to Malta. On the 16th it was the turn of the famous old battleship, HMS *Warspite*, which

> after completing her third successful bombardment that day, was hit by a radio-controlled bomb which burst below, to inflict severe damage and many casualties. She was narrowly missed by two others. She managed to struggle out of action at slow speed; but at 3 p.m. the last boiler filled with sea water and all steam failed. The old ship was taken in tow, and after an adventurous passage sideways through the Straits of Messina reached Malta on the 19th.[10]

The Germans reacted with all their habitual vigour to the Allied landings, throwing in everything available, including the attenuated *Luftwaffe*:

> There is no doubt that the German Air Force made an all-out effort to liquidate the Allied bridgehead at Salerno. For ten days the close-support forces maintained the high average of two sorties per serviceable aircraft, beginning with some 170 sorties on September 8th and rising to a peak effort on the 13th in support of a counter-attack by the German ground forces, which seriously threatened the bridgehead . . . Most significant of all, however, was the revival of the long-range bomber force. On the night of September 8th–9th approximately 155 bomber and torpedo-bomber sorties were flown, and a further effort of 100 sorties was attained on the night of September 10th–11th. This effort was stronger than anything attained since the operations against Malta in March, 1942.[11]

This was the *Luftwaffe*'s convulsive reaction to the return of the Allies to the European mainland. By September 15 the Battle of Salerno was over; it had cost the *Luftwaffe* 221 aircraft for an Allied loss of 89.[12] The comparative scales of the air effort in Italy at this stage may be judged when we compare the numbers of German sorties quoted immediately above with 17,500 Allied sorties and 10,000 tons of bombs dropped between September 1–15, or, for example, the 3,400 sorties flown in direct support of the land battle on September 14 and 15 alone.[13] The key to German air defence in Southern Italy was the group of airfields in the Foggia area; heavy daylight attacks on these on September 17 and 18 destroyed some 300 German aircraft and gliders on the ground. Meanwhile the advance of the Eighth

Army made their evacuation inevitable; completed by September 25, this

> rapidly eliminated *Luftwaffe* activity against the Salerno area. By September 21st all remaining fighter and fighter-bomber units had withdrawn at least as far as Rome and Viterbo areas and, fighting at extreme range, were unable to afford appreciable air support.[14]

The pattern of the war in Italy was quickly established: Salerno at once revealed the amazing ability of the Germans to resist in apparently hopeless situations. The slow progress made by both the Allied Armies proved to be a permanent feature of the campaign, attributable in part to the quality of the enemy and in part to the difficulty of the steep, mountainous terrain which, in the well-chosen words of the novelist Eric Ambler,

> ensured that the attackers, no matter how brave they were, no matter how well and skilfully led, had to suffer repeatedly the despair and frustration of having to pay exorbitantly for every minor success. And the reward for a minor success was always the same: your first glimpse of the next obstacle to a major one.[15]

The lure of the "soft under-belly", it must be added, had not ensnared everyone concerned. Tedder, on the eve of the first crossing, was noting a "tendency to count too much on the military value of an Italian collapse", and voicing grave doubts about the wisdom of an advance through Calabria which, he feared, "may affect the length of the war by a year".[16] In his belief that the set-piece crossing at Messina was Montgomery's brain-child, we may discern further injury (see p. 578) to the good air/ground relations at top level which he, Coningham and Montgomery himself had forged in the crisis of October 1942 – a period receding already into history and mythology. But Tedder's misgivings proved to have some firm foundation; by the end of 1943, despite the capture of the great port of Naples, and despite an Allied air effort amounting to 27,500 sorties and 10,500 tons of bombs dropped in December alone, any vision of quick victory in Italy had faded:

> The front line was now approaching the narrowest part of Italy, which the seasoned German Army could hold with less troops. The weather, the terrain, the high morale and applied science of the enemy would harden the position of stalemate. Rome was still distant. Casualties had been high. Build-up was not rapid enough. The three Services were tired and disappointed by the deferment of their hopes.[17]

As 1944 came in, the armies found themselves trapped on battlefields either deep in snow or deep in mud, or both, inescapably and ominously recalling the doomed landscapes of the Western Front in 1916 and 1917. Soldiers and airmen alike suffered the depression of feeling that they were now caught in a secondary theatre where they would have to go on fighting and suffering casualties, but no longer for prime purposes. They noted the departure of familiar leaders, and the arrival of newcomers, among them General Eaker, replacing Tedder as Commander-in-Chief of the Mediterranean Allied Air Forces, with Slessor as his Deputy.[18] Slessor tells us:

> The big names, the men who had led the Allied forces to victory in the Desert and in Tunisia, in Sicily and in the initial invasion of Italy, Eisenhower and Montgomery, Tedder and Coningham had all gone to prepare for OVERLORD, which we knew was coming before very long. It was because I had some apprehensions about the effect of this on morale that I had begged Portal to leave Harry Broadhurst in command of the Desert Air Force, at least until I had time to get the feel of my new command.[19]

For the British, in the air as well as on the ground, there was another dismaying factor: the increasingly obvious evidence of a marked decline in national status as the American effort became more and more preponderant. Already, at the end of only the first month of the campaign, the USAAF was contributing two-thirds of the sorties flown, more than 70 per cent of the bomb tonnage dropped – and needless to say, two-thirds of the enemy losses claimed.

Nowhere was the American preponderance more marked than in the Mediterranean Allied Strategic Air Force, commanded by Major-General Nathan F. Twining. This comprised a day-bomber element, the US Army Fifteenth Air Force (activated on October 22, 1943, and operational on November 1), and a night-bomber element, No. 205 Group, RAF. The whole object of this force, "the job for which it existed", was, as Slessor says,

> participation in the combined bomber offensive as laid down by the Combined Chiefs of Staff in the Casablanca directive. In fact, so far from MASAF being in Italy to assist the land forces, the object of the earlier operations of the land forces in that theatre was largely to seize and cover the Foggia complex of airfields for the use of the Strategic Air Force.[20]

This is no doubt perfectly correct, but it was asking a lot of the land forces to console themselves with this thought while they struggled in their muddy doldrums down below. As Richards and Saunders remark,

> From the point of view of General Alexander, the presence at Foggia of units of the Strategic Air Force was more a liability than an asset. They were engaged in carrying out the strategic bombing programme which had no direct relation to the military operations for which he was responsible. Yet they were based on Italy ... The problem of supplying the heavy bombardment groups stationed at Foggia put a severe strain on the supply services and on shipping, while "their maintenance requirements were nearly as great as those of the Eighth Army".[21]

The Fifteenth Air Force made great strides in 1944, when it became the second arm of Major-General Carl Spaatz's US Strategic Air Forces in Europe (USST AF) co-ordinating its activities with those of the Eighth Air Force in England. Backed when appropriate, by No. 205 Group, the Fifteenth Air Force attacked targets in South Germany, Austria, Czechoslovakia, Hungary, Rumania (the Ploesti oilfields in particular) and as far afield as Poland. But the disparity between its two elements steadily increased until, at the end, the American daylight force amounted to no fewer than 85 bomber squadrons and 22 fighter squadrons, compared with No. 205 Group's nine squadrons in all of Wellingtons, Liberators and Halifaxes.

It is not, of course, correct to say that the Strategic Force played no part in the Italian campaign itself – on the contrary, it was shortly to provide the campaign's most controversial event, and a most serious lesson for the future (unfortunately ill-learnt). Meanwhile, its part in POINTBLANK, and its continuing attacks on Germany made their undoubted contribution to the further stretching of the German fighter force which rendered the *Luftwaffe* well-nigh powerless in Italy from beginning to end. Secondly, in tandem with their attacks on Germany, the Strategic Forces kept up – as far as the appalling winter weather permitted – an unremitting offensive against the German lines of communication running down the Italian peninsula. Roads, railway lines, junctions, repair shops and marshalling yards were regular targets: "interdiction", first essayed in Sicily, under the tutelage of Professor Solly Zuckerman as technical adviser, was now brought to a very high pitch. Slessor, watching the development with interest, noted the emergence of another type of target which surprised him; he told Portal in April 1944:

One of the remarkable developments in the past three months to my mind has been the emergence of the bridge as a worthwhile bombing objective. At the present time, of the twenty-five clean cuts in the Italian railways, sixteen are bridges. I have always thought the bridge was a rotten objective for a bomber – and so indeed it was in the past.[22] The explanation of the change is twofold; first, the astonishing accuracy of the experienced medium bomber groups – particularly the Marauders; I think that the 42nd Bombardment Group in Sardinia is probably the best day-bomber unit in the world; secondly, the accuracy of the fighter-bomber in the low attack. I hope the value of the bridge as an objective in attack on communications is thoroughly realized by the Tactical Air Forces in U.K. – it is something rather new since Tedder's day out here.[23]

Nevertheless, the fact remained, as Slessor gloomily admitted, that:

We are now in mid-April and I am afraid we are not going to succeed in doing what I had hoped with some confidence we should do, namely, make it impossible by the end of April for the Hun to maintain an army of seventeen odd divisions south of Rome.[24]

Those early months of 1944 had, indeed, exposed in a startling manner the limitations of even overwhelming air superiority, both tactical and strategic.

The Allies enjoyed absolute air supremacy; they enjoyed a considerable superiority on land over their enemies;[25] and they enjoyed the blessing of Ultra:

... it is impossible to convey in words the wealth and variety of intelligence about German activities throughout the whole of the northern and eastern Mediterranean that poured into [GHQ] from Bletchley. If one takes the half-year from November 1943 to May/June 1944, as represented in the thousands of Ultra signals now available in the Public Record Office, one sees that no previous commander was informed so extensively and so accurately as Alexander.[26]

Despite all this, by the end of 1943, the Allies had only advanced 70 miles beyond Salerno; they were still 80 miles from Rome, and between them and the capital the Germans were standing fast on what was at first called their "Winter Line", later the "Gustav Line". This formidable obstacle ran along the courses of the Garigliano and Rapido Rivers, with its central bastion at Cassino, on the important Highway 6, overlooked by Monastery Hill, rising some 1,700 feet behind the town. An attempt to rush the Gustav defences by the Fifth Army in mid-January failed, and immediately afterwards (January 22) the Allies once more deployed their massive amphibious power to make another landing, at Anzio. The hope was to cut off the German forces holding the Gustav Line, or at the least to bustle them in confusion back to Rome, some 30 miles to the north. Once more, however, these miles proved to be "crows' miles", not soldiers' miles; once more the Allies in the beachhead found themselves fighting desperately for survival, and then firmly stuck, as they had been at Salerno – and all-too-reminiscently of the fate of Sir Ian Hamilton's army at Gallipoli in 1915. Meanwhile the fighting at Cassino had also taken a reminiscent turn, into a battle of attrition, with inching progress similar to that of the Western Front battles of the same war. This was not at all what the campaign was supposed to be about.

Whatever the purists of air power might say – and they were not backward in expressing themselves – it is not to be wondered at if, in this moment of deep frustration, the armies looked to the impressive striking power of the Strategic Air Force for direct aid. Their chief preoccupation, by mid-February, was the Abbey of Monte Cassino, crowning Monastery Hill. The Abbey was a cradle of Western civilization, founded by Saint Benedict in AD 529, birthplace of the Benedictine Order, and containing the tomb of the saint. Here, during the Dark Ages, ancient literature was lovingly copied and preserved, linking Europe's classical past to her medieval and modern future. Great craftsmen decorated the Abbey; its cathedral became an architectural wonder. But the Dark Ages had returned and in 1943 the Abbey took on a significance that would have astonished its founder. A British soldier wrote:

> Everybody has experienced the sensation, when walking alone past a house, that invisible eyes were watching from a darkened interior. Hostile eyes can be sensed without being seen, and the soldier develops an exceptional awareness of this. Monte Cassino projected this feeling over an entire valley, and the feeling was being substantiated all the time by gunfire that could only have been so accurate and so swiftly opportunist through being directed by quite exceptionally positioned observers ... To the soldiers dying at its feet, the Monastery had itself become in a sense the enemy.[27]

The pressures – from below – on General Alexander, the Allied Commander-in-Chief, for the destruction of the Abbey mounted. Nobody could relieve him of responsibility for deciding yes or no. Alexander, like his subordinates and his men, saw the bombing of the Abbey as a military necessity:

... when soldiers are fighting for a just cause and are prepared to suffer death and mutilation in the process, bricks and mortar, no matter how venerable, cannot be allowed to weigh against human lives ... the commanding general must make it absolutely clear to his troops that they go into action under the most favourable conditions he has the power to order ... The monastery had to be destroyed.[28]

On February 15 the thing was done. One hundred and forty-two B–17s of the Fifteenth Air Force and 112 B–25s and B–26s of the Twelfth Air Force, commencing at 0830, dropped 576 tons of bombs on the Abbey, reducing its interior to a waste of heaped-up rubble, though considerable sections of the massive outer walls still stood. Fortunately, the movable treasures had gone, taken to safety by the Germans. Fortunately the abbot, the monks and the refugees collected inside the Abbey acted on the warning issued by the Allied Command and left in time. Fortunately, by a miracle, the tomb of Saint Benedict was undamaged. But the great building which spanned fourteen hundred years of European history was just a huge pile of broken stones.[29] And in the end it proved that the Germans, commanded in this sector by a devoutly Catholic officer, General von Senger *und* Etterlin, had not been in military occupation of the Abbey after all; their observation posts were discreetly hidden some distance below the summit of the hill. Furthermore, although the whole operation stemmed from the request of the ground forces, liaison in the final stages broke down; the units which should immediately have moved into the smouldering ruins were unprepared; the Germans remained in occupation. So it transpired that

the bombing, when it happened, expended its fury in a vacuum, tragically and wastefully. It achieved nothing, it helped nobody.[30]

"Nobody" is not quite correct; as General von Senger wrote:

Now we could occupy the Abbey without scruple, especially as ruins are better for defence than intact buildings ... Now the Germans had a mighty, commanding strongpoint, which paid for itself in all the subsequent fighting.[31]

The lesson proved hard to learn. There was now an intermission on the Cassino front, while the main action shifted to Anzio, where the Germans made a powerful counter-attack. But planning went ahead for another thrust at Cassino town, accompanied by what the Allied Command hoped and still believed would be a trump card:

The attack was to be preceded by such a bombing as had never before been attempted in support of ground forces. For the first time in history an obliteration bombing of a small infantry objective was to be carried out by heavy bombers.[32]

The soldiers had been much impressed at the spectacle of the bombs bursting on the Abbey; their failure to occupy it was put down to a failure of staff work, which could be remedied. The senior airmen differed; General Eaker was definitely unenthusiastic, and Slessor was quite certain that this was no way to use the Strategic Force. Bad weather caused long, frustrating delays, but nothing altered the optimism of the ground commanders. Finally, on March 15, the attack went in:

> Promptly at 0830 B–25s launched the air assault, which then proceeded according to schedule (with a few exceptions) until noon, when the last formation of B–26s hit the target and turned away. In the three and a half hours of bombardment more than 275 heavies and close to 200 mediums dropped over 1,000 tons of 1,000-pound demolition bombs.[33]

A British war correspondent described the scene as Cassino slowly vanished in a darkening cloud:

> The enemy was strangely, horribly silent, and very eerie it seemed. A little half-hearted ack-ack had greeted the first wave or two. Then we heard it no more . . . I remember no spectacle in war so gigantically one-sided. Above, the beautiful, arrogant, silver-grey monsters performing their mission with what looked from below like a spirit of utter detachment; below, a silent town, suffering all this in complete passivity.[34]

This was a delusion. At the end of the air bombardment the town of Cassino was a ruin, like the Abbey; since it was in every respect a legitimate military objective, this provoked no moralising as the previous occasion had done, but it did arouse deep professional misgiving. Although the bombers had been backed by the fire of 420 guns, half of them of heavy calibre, on the front of the assaulting New Zealand Corps alone, the infantry found they could make little progress:

> The bombing and shelling of Cassino, although a surprise to the enemy, did not greatly overcome his resistance or considerably reduce his morale. It undoubtedly reduced many German strong points and caused some casualties, but it did not destroy his skilfully deployed observation system. His machine guns, mortars[35] and artillery were only partially neutralised and the heavily fortified area of the defending infantry, well dug in, was

not cleared. All routes for vehicular traffic were destroyed, blocked and cratered . . . This resistance at Cassino . . . was a model of mastery in military exploitation of terrain, and of offensive and defensive warfare.[36]

Theatrically impressive though it had been, professionally it was clear that the air bombardment, especially by the heavy bombers, contained serious flaws, not the least being that a fair number of bombs fell among the Allied troops, including those of a formation which caused 140 civilian casualties in a town 15 miles away, and a stick which straddled a Corps headquarters. General Eaker ordered an investigation which revealed that, as usual, a combination of circumstances was to blame:

> . . . poor air discipline on the part of the two new groups, malfunction of bomb-racks in one formation, lack of specific aiming points, and the heavy pall of smoke and dust which obscured the target after the first few attacks.[37]

General Eaker was not slow to conclude that "bombing at Cassino was from too high an altitude . . . There should be direct contact between heavy bombers and one of their own observers in the battle area."[38] Slessor went even further:

> Another lesson which I think has been, not learned perhaps, but confirmed in recent fighting in Italy is that the immediate battlefield is not the place to use the bomber, *even the fighter-bomber*.[39] I have made many bad shots in the past, but one thing I have always said (and have in the past year or two often been twitted for having said) is that *the bomber is not a battlefield weapon*.[40]

Events on all fronts would show that this was going too far – indeed, it is somewhat contradicted by Slessor's own simultaneous acknowledgement (see p. 587) of the usefulness of the fighter-bomber against such a difficult target as a bridge. In the form of a rocket-firing fighter, it was already demonstrating amazing proficiency in France in attacking locomotives, which would soon be translated on battlefields as tanks, or any other moving vehicle. And the bombers of the Tactical Air Forces, in Italy as in Tunisia and Libya, won golden opinions; at Cassino, according to the American Official History,

> Mediums . . . maintained fine discipline and achieved remarkable bombing accuracy in spite of the fact that the target was largely hidden. The B–26s . . . which put close to 90 per cent of their bombs on the target, "stole the air show at Cassino".[41]

Italy, indeed, saw significant development of the processes already well advanced in the Mediterranean theatre which, in Eaker's words:

> has been the primary crucible for the development of tactical air-power and the evolution of joint command between Allies. Ever since Alamein the Mediterranean has been a laboratory of Tactical Air Forces, just as England has been the primary testing ground of Strategic Air Forces.[42]

In 1944 this fact took on a special connotation: Italy, during that year, witnessed an increasing dependence of the ground forces, especially the British, on the air – which meant, virtually always, the Tactical Force. Cassino was only one illustration of the point. Certainly one's heart goes out to the New Zealand, Indian, British and Polish infantry, trying to make their way forward against the desperate resistance of the *Luftwaffe*'s First Parachute Division over mountains of rubble which deprived them of tank support, under torrential rain which rapidly turned the welter of bomb craters into deep ponds.[43] But Slessor, in his letter to Portal quoted above, put his finger on another consideration which was becoming increasingly important:

> ... the second simple explanation of the Cassino failure was that the killed ... on the 15th, the day of the attack, amounted to four officers and thirteen other ranks. I hope we shall have learnt by the time we attack again that five hundred casualties today often save five thousand in the next week.[44]

In a footnote he added: "I cannot vouch for the exact accuracy of these figures, but the total casualties on the 15th – killed, wounded and missing – were 82." The exact number does not matter greatly; what matters is the growing reluctance of British infantry to accept casualties, a circumstance which was shortly to be noted again in disagreeable fashion in Normandy. This was not, let it be noted, a matter relating only to the soldiers in the line; it affected their commanders also. When this phase of the Battle of Cassino finally "stuck", we learn that

> General Wilson [Supreme Allied Commander, Mediterranean] was in favour of continuing but Freyberg replied in one word: "Passchendaele", and Alexander agreed. The 1st Parachute Division and the Monastery had won.[45]

Lieutenant-General Sir Bernard Freyberg, commander of the Second New Zealand Division and the so-called New Zealand Corps at Cassino, had won the Victoria Cross and the Distinguished Service Order with two bars (as well as being wounded nine times) in the First World War. His personal courage was never open to the smallest degree of doubt; but he was a victim of the prevailing absurdities about that war, as were so many of his contemporaries. The soldiers, for their part, had been schooled to believe that battle casualties were lives "wasted". In the German Army, neither generals nor soldiers were afflicted by such demoralizing beliefs. The position is well summed up by Brigadier Shelford Bidwell:

> . . . it is impossible to avoid at least the suspicion that the British infantry of 1914–1918 had more staying power and a greater appetite for combat than their successors in 1939–1945.[46]

Certainly it is difficult to imagine Freyberg's predecessor, Major-General Sir Andrew Russell, whose First New Zealand Division actually fought at Passchendaele, taking such an attitude, or his division, having (as its successor did) lost 1,600 men in 62 days,[47] being "never quite the same again".[48] But what this meant in battle realities was that the army increasingly leaned on the air for all kinds of day-to-day support, and increasingly the Tactical Air Forces gave it what it asked – hence Tedder's stricture which we have quoted above (p. 578).

The extent of this dependence was seen in the aftermath of the Cassino failure. While the ground forces regrouped and prepared themselves for another major thrust against the Gustav Line, the Air Forces put into operation the not-very-subtly named Operation STRANGLE, whose purpose was precisely to strangle the German communication lines down the leg of Italy. While the Strategic Force maintained its offensive against the main rail centres in the north, the Tactical Force was given the task of interdicting the railway system between the Gustav Line and the new rearward German defence, the Gothic Line, between Pisa and Rimini:

> Whenever possible, main lines were to be cut at points more than 100 miles from the Anzio area in order to impose a maximum strain on motor transport and all lines across Italy had to be cut in order to prevent diversion of traffic. Medium bombers were to attack bridges, marshalling yards and repair shops, and fighter-bombers were to attack active trains, troops, major bridges under repair, and secondary bridges. In addition, fighter and night bombers were to operate constantly over the whole road-net of central Italy with the object of destroying motor transport and disrupting movement by day and night.[49]

By the end of March, the Tactical Air Forces were causing an average of 25 cuts a day in the enemy's railways, and by May this figure had risen to 71 a day:

> Photographic cover of every line was attempted every forty-eight hours (so that each block could be cut again as soon as it showed signs of repair) but the enemy, after neglecting a damaged area for days, could be very quick in effecting the simultaneous repair of several multiple cuts – and no stretch of line was completely abandoned until the opening of the (ground) offensive in May. Furthermore, the Germans devised ingenious systems of trans-shipment whereby motor and animal transport was impressed to carry goods from one train to another – on the side of a break – and to supplement rail transport. As the shuttling from trains to MT fell off, the road movement increased in sympathy, but owing to Allied air attacks and bombing the supplementary traffic [road and sea] had to travel as much as possible in darkness and the four Royal Air Force light bomber squadrons that were employed by night were hard pressed to maintain a 24-hour schedule of air attack.[50]

After this it is startling to meet the final sentence:

> On the whole, it is probable that the Germans suffered no serious shortages during the static phase before [the ground offensive].[51]

Had interdiction failed? it may be asked. Slessor, in his shrewd, perceptive letter to Portal on April 16, perhaps supplies the best answer; noting first the serious effect of Italy's winter weather on all flying activities, he continued:

> But apart from that, I personally underrated the unsurpassed capacity of the Hun's Q staff to keep him supplied in apparently impossible conditions. Since March 24, every single railway behind the enemy front has been cut and kept cut in several places between the front and the Pisa–Rimini line, and at the same time we have delivered a number of really heavy blows at the great marshalling yards, with their loco sheds and repair facilities, in the north. At the same time in the month of February we know we destroyed between eight and nine hundred MT vehicles, and in March probably more than half that number. I think we can say that we have now made it impossible for the Hun to act offensively, as he did against the beachhead in February. But we have not yet succeeded in making him pull out, and I don't think we shall by air action alone: what we have done, I think, is to make it impossible for him to resist successfully a determined and sustained offensive by the ground forces.[52]

This proved to be the case; when the next Allied offensive (DIADEM) was launched on May 11, it was immediately successful, and the Italian stalemate seemed to have been broken at last. Monte Cassino was encircled and taken without a fight on May 18; the Gustav Line was breached on May 23; two days later the Fifth Army joined hands with the Anzio beachhead forces; on June 4, 1944, the Allies entered Rome. In all this, the air effort was unremitting and decisive:

> Heavy and medium bomber attacks on headquarters had been reasonably successful in causing disorganisation behind the enemy's lines and for the first three days the medium and fighter-bombers had concentrated upon such targets as command posts, strong points, gun positions, main towns on the road net, bridges and defiles . . . Once the breakthrough had been accomplished the fighter-bombers began armed reconnaissance mainly against MT and troop concentrations and the light bombers began to attack dumps. The German Tenth Army was, in fact, subjected to a pulverisation from the air such as had never yet been experienced by a well organised army.[53]

Clearly, in all this, there were useful lessons for the OVERLORD planners, and it is tempting to push General Eaker's statement quoted on p. 592 further than it ought to go. Italy was, indeed, a "laboratory" of air support – up to a point: the point being the very short time available for the lessons of one theatre to be digested in another (with due allowance for such fundamental matters as terrain), and the continuation of useful experiment in both theatres *after* the launching of OVERLORD in June. One phenomenon, which was soon to excite much wonder and acclaim did, however, emerge from the Italian "crucible" in the course of the fighting on the Gustav Line: called a "Cab-rank" later in Normandy, in Italy it went by the name of "Rover".

"Rover" was probably the most important, though by no means the only, development of the Air Support Control system which we have seen taking place since September 1941 (see p. 346 ff.). It was a tentacle whose name derived from the simple fact that "it could be switched from one brigade to another, without interfering with normal air support communications".[54] It consisted of an RAF controller, an army Air Liaison Officer (ALO) and VHF R/T for communicating with aircraft. Working from good observation positions, preferably on heights, it acted as either a Visual Control Post or a Forward Control Post (blind, but acting on information received) whose whole function was to bring in air support against targets close to the front line, often fleeting.

A fundamental part of the organisation was the provision of a "Cab-rank" of aircraft timed to arrive in the area at regular intervals of about 30 minutes. These aircraft would be briefed at their airfields to attack pre-selected targets but, for a period of about 20 minutes before the attack, they would be required to orbit close to the forward line in order to give Rover an opportunity to call and brief them for the attack of priority "fleeting" targets. If no call was received the aircraft would attack their original targets and return to base.[55]

"Rover" was a family name: the standard British variety described above was known as "Rover David"; the Americans, who had been impressed by British Air Support Control at Salerno, now adopted this further refinement under the name of "Rover Joe". With their habitual efficiency in such matters, they soon mastered the techniques and added refinements of their own; "when all worked satisfactorily, calls for support could be answered by bombing in as little as seven minutes".[56] Another member of the British side of the family was "Rover Frank", and was concerned, in close liaison with the Royal Artillery, with the attack on enemy gun positions (generally regarded as poor targets for aerial bombing):

> The method of employment was in five stages. First, the Counter Battery officers at the AGRA[57] furnished the Army Air Support Control with the most up-to-date list of enemy heavy batteries which could be produced by 2359 hours each night: secondly, missions were briefed to attack one of these batteries: thirdly, they were briefed to "call in" on "Rover Frank" on their way to the target: fourthly, they reported to "Rover Frank" the guns they were briefed to attack: fifthly, "Rover Frank" checked to ensure that the guns were still active and, if they were, the mission carried out the attack; if not, or if some other battery had become particularly troublesome, "Rover Frank" cancelled the initial target and rebriefed the mission in the air from photographs. This helped to ensure that the batteries attacked by our fighter-bombers were the batteries which were troubling our troops.[58]

All this, of course, was in addition to the increasingly excellent work of the Air OPs (see p. 399); by 1943, the war on the ground had become very much an "artillery war", like its predecessor. In the British Army, the Royal Artillery became the largest element, containing 22 per cent of the Army's entire strength; its proficiency impressed friends and enemies alike – indeed, Sir David Fraser says,

> the artillery was perhaps the one Arm of the British Army professionally acknowledged by the German enemy as his superior.[59]

To this result the swift, accurate observation and fire-control supplied by the Air OPs made an invaluable contribution.

It is natural, especially in the light of what was soon to follow in Normandy, to view these (and other) sophistications with considerable satisfaction. It is in no way derogatory to the "Rover" system to recall that it was only made possible by the absence of the *Luftwaffe* in any effective strength from the battle areas:

> That such a system could be adopted and maintained in action from the late autumn of 1943 until the end of the war is one of the many proofs of the supremacy which the Allied air forces established. It had, however, its disadvantages, the principal one being the very large number of aircraft needed to keep it in operation. Only when the air forces of a country have very great resources on which to draw, and the virtual certainty that air opposition will be negligible and will remain so, can they afford the luxury of a "Cab-rank" system. Fortunately, as the war progressed, the Allies came to be more and more in that happy situation with every day that passed, and there can be no doubt that it proved of great value and saved many lives.[60]

The capture of Rome came as a long-looked-for reward for nine months of travail; spirits rose as Alexander's armies surged forward towards the north. But shadows soon fell again. First, there was the cruel luck of this fine victory being immediately pushed into the background by the vast events unfolding in North-West Europe – D–Day and the progress of OVERLORD. The Fourteenth Army in Burma grimly called itself "the forgotten army"; the armies in Italy understood the feeling. Worse still, just as the pace of their advance began to slacken in the face of mounting resistance by the indomitable Germans, their strength was severely drained by the removal of seven divisions and some 70 per cent of the Fifth Army's air component in order to mount Operation DRAGOON, the landings in the south of France in support of OVERLORD. Controversy has surrounded that decision ever since; this is not the place to enter into it. It is not difficult to see the lamentable effect that such a diversion of strength was bound to have on the forces in Italy; how it might affect the air can be judged from one single statistic – the 4,249 sorties flown by the Mediterranean Air Forces on the first day of DRAGOON alone (August 15). For the Desert Air Force it meant, inevitably, a greatly increased burden of air support, uncomplainingly borne and brilliantly handled. It was against this disappointing back-ground that the Allies in Italy approached the Gothic Line and prepared to face another winter. "For the next six months mud ruled the Italian front."[61] It had taken the Allies nine months to reach Rome; it took another eleven months of arduous campaigning and hard battles before the Germans came to the point of surrender to Field-Marshal Alexander,[62] on May 2, 1945.

For the forces concerned, winning in Italy was all that mattered; for others – including historians – there were examples and lessons, some to be absorbed and put to use, others not. It is unlikely that any clearer short summary of these exists than the Appreciation of "The Effect of Air Power in a Land Offensive" drawn up by Slessor on June 18, 1944 (and given by him to Generals Marshall and Arnold when they visited Italy in that month); in it Slessor said:

2. It may clear the issue to mention first the things that air-power *cannot* be expected to do in a land campaign of this nature:
(a) It cannot by itself defeat a highly organized and disciplined army, even when that army is virtually without air support of its own. The German will fight defensively without air support or cover, and does not become demoralized by constant air attack against his communications and back areas. The heaviest and most concentrated air bombardment of organized defensive positions cannot be relied upon to obliterate resistance and enable our land forces to advance without loss.
(b) It cannot by itself enforce a withdrawal by drying up the flow of essential supplies. The German's efficient Q organization, his policy of living on the country regardless of the interests of the inhabitants, and his extreme frugality and hardiness result in an unsurpassed capacity to maintain his stocks in apparently impossible circumstances at the essential minimum, *in circumstances when he is not being forced to expend* ammunition, fuel, vehicles, engineer stores, etc., at a high rate.
(c) It cannot *entirely prevent* the movement of strategic reserves to the battlefront, of tactical reserves from one part of the front to another, or of forward troops to fresh positions in rear.
(d) In short, it cannot absolutely isolate the battlefield from enemy supply or reinforcement.
(e) It cannot absolutely guarantee the immunity either of our forward formations or back areas, port installations, base depots, airfields, convoys at sea, etc., against the occasional air attack or reconnaissance.
3. What it can do, and has done in the present battle which, it must be remembered, began with the preliminary air offensive on about March 15, is to make it impossible for the most highly organized and disciplined army to offer prolonged resistance to a determined offensive on the ground – even in country almost ideally suited for defence; it can turn an orderly retreat into a rout; and virtually eliminate an entire army as an effective fighting force.

The converse of 2(a) is equally true. An army by itself cannot, in modern warfare, defeat a highly organized and disciplined army on the defensive.

The power of the defence on land has not been overcome by the tank or by improved artillery technique, but by air-power. It is doubtful whether anyone could be found to deny that, if there had been no Air Force on either side, the German Army could have made the invasion of Italy impossible except at a cost in national effort and human life which the Allies would have been unwilling to face . . .[63]

These were wise words indeed, but by the time they were uttered the final act of the war's great drama was proceeding, with all its own preoccupations, and little time to study fruitfully what hard experience had ascertained.

71 Combined Operations: "Overlord"; commanders; manpower; aircraft

As 1943 drew to its end, the threads of the great Allied Combined Operation – what Charles B. MacDonald aptly called "The Mighty Endeavour" – came together one by one. Most important of all was the announcement of the names of the senior commanders; as they took up their duties the last doubts about the reality of the project faded. OVERLORD was going to happen, whatever lingering misgivings and regrets might be harboured by individuals, and virtually everything that concerned it became a matter of urgency. On Christmas Eve it was announced that General Eisenhower would be the Supreme Allied Commander; that Tedder would be his Deputy; that Montgomery would command the Twenty-First Army Group (British Second and Canadian First Armies) and that General Spaatz would command the US Strategic Air Forces (see p. 586). On December 28 President Roosevelt gave notice of further American command changes: Eaker to command the Mediterranean Allied Air Forces, and Major-General James Doolittle to take over the Eighth Air Force. On the 29th came the announcement that Admiral Sir Bertram Ramsay would be Allied Naval Commander-in-Chief, and Leigh-Mallory was confirmed in his appointment as C-in-C, Air. Further notices would follow; meanwhile flesh and blood filled the previously empty spaces and work went forward apace.

From this time onwards, in the European theatre of war, operations were "combined" indeed, in two fundamental respects, to a degree that no one could have anticipated, and which still strikes the historian with wonder. First, there was the "combination" of the Allies. The extent of integration between the British and Americans at all significant command levels was remarkable, beginning at the top, the

Supreme Headquarters, Allied Expeditionary Force (SHAEF), where Eisenhower and Tedder presided. It would be absurd, of course, to pretend that there was no national rivalry, no friction between the strong personalities of two nations with totally different traditions and methods; that would suggest superhuman qualities which would be, to put it mildly, unlikely. But SHAEF and the inter-Allied commands under it (like the Allied Commands in the Mediterranean and South East Asia) unquestionably produced an extraordinary degree of co-operation and goodwill, and in all areas this has to be largely attributed to the admirable coalition commanders at the top: Alexander, Mountbatten and Eisenhower. Of the latter it has been well said that:

> Remarkable in Eisenhower from the day he set foot in London was his deep, visceral dedication and determination to make Anglo-American cooperation a living and working reality. He brought with him a simple conviction about this which was as basic and unshakeable as his own patriotism. Moreover he made it work. It was not easy, for he was dealing with Britain at its prideful finest hour, and at the same time American chauvinism was on the increase along with American might and power. But Eisenhower was probably the least chauvinistic American and the least chauvinistic military commander in history. He never lost his American patriotism or pride; he simply added another patriotism to it.[1]

Tedder was of a similar cast of mind, as Eisenhower had already perceived:

> his own partnership with Tedder was perhaps the most closely integrated of all.[2]

It is not to be wondered at if, under the inspiration of two such officers, coalition war in 1943–44 took on an unfamiliar guise, startling to those who were aware of the extreme difficulty of effective integration experienced in 1914–18, even between allies with such close linguistic and cultural ties as the Germans and Austrians. In the Second World War it is probably right to say that the highest degree of integration was reached in the Mediterranean; Eisenhower and Tedder were its first practitioners and guardians, and their successor, Alexander, recorded with a mixture of pride and wonder that his command contained allies of twenty-seven nationalities plus one co-belligerent. It is also a fact that air operations displayed this "combined" quality more and more. The Combined Bomber Offensive, as we have noted, did not at first live up to its name; but in Sicily and Italy, and very clearly in North-West Europe, the Tactical Air

Forces in particular mingled their efforts, adopted each other's methods and jargon, and shared each other's targets. As the war moved into its final phase, the same became true of the Strategic Forces, until Harris could say:

> If I were asked what were the relations between Bomber Command and the American bomber force I should say that we had no relations. The word is inapplicable to what actually happened; we and they were one force.[3]

National identities did not disappear: the main formations kept their proud names (with one exception): Desert Air Force, Bomber Command, Second TAF, Eighth, Fifteenth, Ninth, Twelfth US Air Forces, Coastal Command. But more and more the communiqués and the histories speak of "Allied" Strategic Forces, or "Allied" Tactical Forces, conducting joint enterprises in a fashion never seen before.

"Combined" between Allies, the OVERLORD enterprise was also, of course, combined between Services, the most spectacular of all examples of the inter-Service cooperation which Mountbatten had been so ardently preaching – and which he had often found so hard to achieve:

> ... it was still a very unfamiliar idea, and it met with a good deal of resistance. There were soldiers, sailors and airmen who really did seem to find it most difficult to discover any virtue in working with other Services than their own.[4]

He was not the only one to make this discovery; Tedder is on record in 1944 saying,

> I do not myself believe that any modern war can be won either at sea or on the land alone or in the air alone ... In other words, war has changed to three dimensional, and very few people realise that.[5]

The way that much history continues to be written in the 1980s suggests that very few people realize it even now; but every one of the great amphibious operations is a living proof, and though the naval presence is not very obvious to forces fighting deep in a continent, if they have come from overseas their dependence on naval power never ceases. And one matter was made absolutely clear in 1943 and 1944: the utter dependence of both Allied sea and land forces on the air. Only the German Army, it appeared, could do without it.

Within the inter-Allied and inter-Service combination, the RAF did not take long to discover that OVERLORD was also "inter-Command". Indeed, not for the first time (see p. 351), the RAF found itself "tripping over its own Command system". The most obvious – and startling – evidence of this was the scarcely credible disappearance of the name, Fighter Command, from the order of battle in November 1943. The reason is easy to see: the RAF at home was learning what it had learned two years earlier in the Middle East, the need to use "the whole available air power" (see p. 376) that Tedder was so clear about, but few other people perceived – and Tedder did not arrive until January 1944. So when it became apparent that Fighter Command must supply both air cover and tactical support for OVERLORD, but nevertheless retain all its responsibility for defending the home base, minds became confused. The name, with all its splendid connotations, disappeared; instead, there reappeared the old (pre-1936) designation, Air Defence of Great Britain, fulfilling one function, while the Tactical Air Force (Second TAF) took care of the other. It was, of course, a horrible psychological blunder, and soon recognized as such; Fighter Command returned to life on October 15, 1944.

The story, apart from its curiosity, highlights the mingling of activities and rôles that was now characteristic. By 1944, in the Mediterranean and in North-West Europe, it was clear that bombing required not only bombers, but fighters too. Fighters carried bombs, they used cannon and rockets against ground targets, they carried out reconnaissance, as well as offering aerial combat. In Coastal Command the proliferation of rôles and types requires no further mention. Almost all the types and, in their different ways, all the Commands played their essential parts in Army Cooperation. It took some getting used to; the war – and the world – were less tidy than they once had been.

Indeed, it could be said that the RAF itself was less tidy. Lord Trenchard, fighting for its survival as a separate Service in the 1920s, had made much of its economical attributes – economical in expenditure, economical in manpower. It had long ago ceased to possess either of these. Thus, taking the whole span of active rearmament from 1936–1945, we find that the proportion of fixed capital[6] expenditure due to the RAF and the Ministry of Aircraft Production is 37.31 per cent. In other words, the third Service was consuming roughly a third of the resources that were being made available; no economy there. As regards manpower,[7] by the autumn of 1942, even after drastic reductions,

602

the combined allocation of MAP and the RAF, at 750,000 was still as great as that of the Navy, the ship-building industry, the Army and the Ministry of Supply put together, while the allocation of MAP, at 503,000, was nearly 75 per cent of the combined quotas of the Ministry of Supply and the Admiralty.[8]

It was in October, 1942, that the RAF's total numbers passed the million mark: 1,042,015. A year later the total was 1,168,735, of whom the WAAF accounted for 180,339 (5,880 officers); the overwhelming majority were serving at home – the contingents abroad totalled 330,946 in all theatres (339 women). It was in July 1944 that the RAF reached its highest total: 1,185,833 of all ranks and both sexes.[9] By that time it contained 487 squadrons, 100 of which were provided by the Dominions;[10] the ground-crew were mustered in 190 trades; its front-line strength was 7,300 aircraft.[11]

These figures look impressive, as indeed they are; but what they reflect, unfortunately, is a fault in British manpower policy, reflecting a fault in the national war-making disposition, which already, by the end of 1943, was producing some serious results. We have noted (p. 592) a growing reluctance in the Army to accept casualties, and a reluctance of commanders to incur them; underlying these frames of mind throughout was a mounting difficulty in obtaining adequate replacements and reinforcements which, in 1944, began to affect OVERLORD almost as soon as it was launched. The error was deep-rooted, and national; it stemmed back to the baleful rejection in the 1920s and 1930s of any suggestion of another European commitment, another Western Front. It was, in fact, the working of the poison of "Disenchantment" which has been pumped out so persuasively by "gurus" of all sorts (see pp. 60, 62) – and not the least of them was Churchill himself. His own views on manpower priorities were clearly expressed; thus, early in 1941, Roosevelt's confidential emissary, Harry Hopkins, reported to the President after an interview with Churchill:

He looks forward with our help to mastery in the air and then Germany with all her armies will be finished. He believes that this war will never see great forces massed against one another.[12]

A month later, on February 9, Churchill made the broadcast famous for the slogan "Give us the tools and we will finish the job". Less well remembered is this passage:

In the last war the United States sent two million men across the Atlantic. But this is not a war of vast armies, firing immense masses of shells at one another. We do not need the gallant armies which are forming throughout the American Union. We do not need them this year, nor next year, nor any year that I can foresee. But we do need most urgently an immense and continuous supply of war materials and technical apparatus of all kinds.[13]

It was, of course, in precisely that year, some four months after Churchill's euphoric prognostication, that the war became once more a war of massed manpower. Both the American and the Soviet armed forces reached peaks of over 12 million men; in Britain, the RAF topped the million and the Royal Navy nearly reached it, but a persisting inclination to deploy men anywhere but in the arm which always bore the brunt of casualties – the infantry – ensured that the Army's strength on the battlefield remained low, though its total numbers were high. By 1943, it was becoming clear that though the level of British mobilization for war was unmatched and unprecedented, it was by no means discreet. Production targets – above all, aircraft production – had been set for which Britain's population was simply unable to provide a sufficient workforce, and actually *fight* the war at the same time. There was, in other words, an acute manpower crisis[14] – exacerbated by such circumstances as the following, revealed in a letter from the Secretary of State for Air to the Air Member for Personnel of the Air Council:

Your statement . . . that some 2,000 aircrew (officers and NCOs), and this number increasing by 200 or more a month, are now idling reveals a serious situation . . . It is surprising to me that this situation should have been allowed to develop . . . It is particularly disconcerting that these facts should have emerged just at the time when, as US of S points out, it has also come to light that we have something equivalent to the manpower of two divisions locked up in our deferred lists . . .[15]

The full savour of this communication is in the date: April 1, 1944. Within a few weeks OVERLORD would be launched, and within a few months the War Office would be disbanding two divisions for lack of replacements.[16]

1943 saw a determined attempt to bring realism into the aircraft production scene: realistic re-assessments of the numbers of aircraft that British industry could actually manufacture, and realistic assessments of the size of the work force that could be allocated. Soon the dramatic turns in the course of the war itself would give added force

"The unnatural and inhuman strain": no moment was more tense on a bomber station than the final briefing at which the squadrons learned what was to be their "target for tonight".

"The resilient morale of the aircrews": this Pathfinder squadron, led by its CO, celebrates a "Stand Down" night at Downham Market. It is not to be assumed that their gesture indicates defiance of the enemy.

"What was left of the *Luftwaffe* pushed further and further away": constant attacks on German airfields paralysed the weak remnants of *Luftflotte 3* in 1944. This photograph shows the landing area of the Brussels Melsbroek ground after a Bomber Command attack on August 15.

"Air history was being made": the Hawker Typhoon entered RAF service in 1941. After an unpromising start, it came into its own as a fighter-bomber and rocket-firing tank destroyer in Normandy in 1944, and "made history" in the defeat of the last German counter-offensive at Mortain on August 7.

"The range of a bomber and the performance of a fighter": the astonishing North American Aviation P51B Mustang which transformed the daylight bomber offensive against Germany and was largely instrumental in destroying the German fighter force.

"A war for aerodromes": the failure of the 21st Army Group to capture the airfield country south of Caen was a main ingredient in the sharp clash between Field-Marshal Montgomery and the air marshals in 1944. The photograph shows one of the Normandy landing-strips used by No. 83 Group.

"A thousand bombers hurtling to the ground": this scene marks the end of a Halifax and its crew – a small fraction of the 47,268 Bomber Command aircrew killed on operations.

"A prescription for massacre": a pile of bodies awaiting burning in Dresden, February 1945.

to these considerations. In 1944 there was an actual cut-back in the strength of the RAF. The first sign of it was in May, when 2,000 airmen were transferred to the Army and the Royal Navy; the chief beneficiary was the hard-pressed infantry. Of the men transferred, 1,500 came from the RAF Regiment (making the shock somewhat less severe), the rest were Group V tradesmen; the hope was that all 2,000 would be volunteers for transfer, and there was surprise in official circles when only 691 men did come forward. In July the Air Ministry agreed to transfer another 5,000 ground staff to the Army, and in December 20,000 more, while some thousands more went to the Navy. These measures were never popular, for reasons which are not difficult to comprehend:

> Although the reasons for the transfer were fully explained to the men concerned, complaints were numerous. The most frequent causes of complaint were unwillingness to leave the RAF for another Service (particularly in the case of ex-ATC and volunteer entrants); dismay at the prospect of retraining after long service in the RAF; loss of opportunity to use trade experience; and anxiety regarding the relative rates of release of the two Services.[17]

This analysis is no doubt correct, but there was another – very human – consideration too: implicit in becoming a replacement in the arm suffering the highest proportion of casualties is the strong probability of becoming a casualty oneself. Never particularly attractive, this prospect becomes far less so in what can clearly be seen to be the last stage of a war. In any case, these transfers – and the requisite training – took time to become effective; of the last 20,000, only 10,000 transfers had been completed by June 1945, when the war in Europe had been over for a month. Incorrect long-term policies are not cured by last-minute patch-work.

As regards aircraft, the RAF was happy at last. Bomber Command was now relying almost entirely on Lancasters (I and III), the Halifax III (with some VI and VII) and Mosquitoes of various marks. The only notable newcomers were fighters, in Second TAF and for home defence. The Hawker Typhoon (see p. 389) was another of those aircraft which survived an unpromising start in life to achieve distinction later. Its first flight was in February 1940, and first delivery to the RAF in July 1941. Then came a long period of disappointment, due to constant engine troubles and structural defects, and the type was very nearly withdrawn from service. Fortunately it was reprieved, and began to show its promise against tip-and-run FW 190 fighter-bombers at the end of 1942. In 1943, with its rocket armament, it became famous as a "train-buster", destroying as many as 150 locomotives a month on French and Belgian railways. In 1944 there were 26 squadrons of Typhoons; their part in OVERLORD began before D–Day, with highly successful attacks on German radar stations on the French coast. In Normandy and after, Typhoons were "the backbone of the Second Tactical Air Force's fighter-bomber wings".[18] Their successor in the long, distinguished Hawker line was already present; Nos. 3 and 486 Squadrons (Newchurch) were equipped with Tempest Vs in April 1944. They were just in time to meet the menace of the V–1 flying bombs:

> The fastest of defending fighters, the Tempests destroyed 638 V–1s out of the RAF's total of 1,771 between 13 June and 5 September 1944.[19]

The Tempests proved, in fact, to be precisely what the Typhoons had originally been intended to be: high-performance interceptor fighters, and in that rôle performed with much distinction, though never entirely displacing the Spitfire IX.

There were two weak points in the RAF's armoury, neither of them, fortunately, fatal to operational effectiveness. The lack of long-range fighters has been commented on frequently in this narrative; it was possible to remedy this to some extent by acquiring P–51Bs and Cs from the Americans; as Mustang IIIs they served Second TAF well, but the Americans needed all the P–51s they could get, and Second TAF could only equip six squadrons. Even these were viewed with jealousy by Bomber Command, and taken away to escort daylight bombing in the autumn. Good relations with the US Ninth Air Force averted the worst consequences of this lack in the tactical forces.

The second weakness was the slow development of jet propulsion. Sir Frank Whittle's first jet engine roared into life in April 1937; an experimental research aircraft (Gloster E.28/39) made its first flight at Cranwell on May 15, 1941. Nearly two years elapsed before the first flight of a Gloster Meteor (March 5, 1943); squadron delivery (No. 616; two aircraft) was on July 12, 1944. In ordinary times, this rate of progress towards a major technological advance might even have seemed impressive; but this was wartime, and the redoubtable firm of Messerschmitt was very soon pursuing the same goal. Their progress took the form of the Me 262, whose design development may be dated to the late autumn of 1938. Despite considerable production difficulties and damaging political interference (by Hitler himself) the German jet was first in the field, with the establishment

of a Test Detachment (EKdo 262) in April 1944 which began intercep-
tions of high-flying Allied photo-reconnaissance aircraft in June. On
July 25 a Mosquito photographed an Me 262 while being attacked by
the latter; two days later No. 616 Squadron received operational
clearance for the Meteor I. Like the Tempest, it was quickly in action
against V–1s, and it was a Meteor pilot, Flying Officer Dean, who on
August 4 succeeded in tipping a V–1 into a dive to the ground by a
flick of his own wing tip. Meteors joined Second TAF in January
1945 and flew their first operational sortie on April 16. They were
the only Allied jet aircraft to see action in the Second World War, but
they never encountered German aircraft, and there was no tournament
contest between them and the Me 262s. Both were, in effect, too late
for the war.

72 *"Overlord": Command problems; a question of airfields*

Air Marshal Sir Arthur Coningham, KCB, DSO, MC, DFC, AFC,
was appointed to command the Second Tactical Air Force on January
21, 1944. It was a natural progression from his Mediterranean commands; he was the obvious choice. The appointment, however, proved
to be fraught with discord, because it underlined an unsatisfactory
state of affairs concerning the top Air appointments for Operation
OVERLORD – and Coningham, with his clear mind and frank Antipo-
dean tongue, was not the man to gloss over such matters. The chief
problem was Leigh-Mallory.

Tedder assumed the duties of his new post the day before Coningham's appointment, and he came to them well aware that this problem
was serious. His own position was affected:

> The post of Deputy Supreme Commander had been deliberately given to
> me because of the vast part the Air was to play in the battle for Europe,
> and Churchill insisted that I must have all the inherent powers:
>
>> "Tedder with his unique experience and close relation as Deputy to the
>> Supreme Commander, ought to be in fact and in form the complete
>> master of all air operations. Everything is then quite simple. There need
>> only be one Tactical Air Force which Leigh-Mallory can command.
>> Spaatz will come directly under Eisenhower as his senior officer, and can
>> be told to obey Tedder. There will be no difficulty in arranging between
>> Tedder and Harris. I do not like the idea of Tedder being an officer
>> without portfolio."[1]

It was by no means so simple as Churchill, convalescing at Marrakesh after a serious illness, allowed himself to believe. Coningham's appointment had already been decided, and Leigh-Mallory's position was becoming more and more invidious as each day went by. As Coningham perceived, and no doubt said, "the establishment of an extra Headquarters in the Air Force chain of command caused constant difficulties".[2]

The essence of the problem, as the Combined Chiefs of Staff discovered, lay in the fact that whereas in the Mediterranean Supreme Command meant exactly what it said – authority over all the Allied forces in the area – this could not be the case with an operation mounted in Britain. OVERLORD was, indeed, the supreme effort of the Allies; but it was not the *only* effort based on these islands. Coastal Command, for example, would certainly be called upon to give assistance to OVERLORD, but it would never cease, in concert with the Navy, to have other work to do. As regards Bomber Command and the US Strategic Air Forces, these were to remain under the POINTBLANK directive (however they might interpret it) until March 31. When they did become available for OVERLORD, it was not at all clear, in January 1944, in what rôle this would be, or how they would fit into the organizational pattern. In this matter General Spaatz made his influence felt in no uncertain fashion; he had two preoccupations. First, there was his absolute belief in the power of the bombing offensive:

> . . . in the early months of 1944, when he was fighting against the diversion of his bomber forces from their onslaught against Germany, Spaatz on several occasions expressed his belief that full-scale use of the air forces – including the tactical air forces – for strategic bombing would eliminate the need for the "highly dangerous OVERLORD operation".[3]

Sir Arthur Harris forcefully expressed similar views (see p. 552); they were discouraging. And Spaatz's second preoccupation was equally so; this concerned the status of the United States Army Air Force itself which, with the example of the RAF in its light blue uniforms and with its separate organization constantly before the eyes of American airmen, was becoming more and more jealous of its own position. As Professor Zuckerman has said, it was a question of prestige:

> As [Spaatz] put it, he might sink sufficiently low to accept orders from Tedder; he certainly was not going to accept any from anybody else since

he had the biggest Air Force. The second point was the fear that if they did come under the cloak of the AEAF they would be subordinated to Army operations and in that way the fight for independence would be set back.[4]

From all of which it became ever clearer that Leigh-Mallory, though officially commander of the Allied Expeditionary Air Force, was in fact only going to exercise real command over Coningham's Second TAF, Major-General Lewis H. Brereton's Ninth Air Force, Air Marshal Sir Roderic Hill's "Air Defence of Great Britain", whose fighters would be called upon to help protect the passage over the Channel and the beachhead and two Transport Groups for Airborne operations. Thus what should have been a significant coordinating function was indeed reduced, as Coningham said, to a tiresome "extra Headquarters in the chain of command" – and as the difficulties multiplied, eyes turned increasingly to Tedder to resolve them. In the meantime, however, the unsatisfactory position was characteristically tersely summed up by Churchill:

As Tedder is only to be a sort of floating kidney, we shall be wasting him and putting more on Leigh-Mallory than in my opinion he can carry.[5]

There are phases of Sir Trafford Leigh-Mallory's career which it is hard to view with favour: in the Battle of Britain his rôle had at times been distinctly unpleasing (see p. 204); his attempts to press a fighter offensive across the Channel in 1941 ánd 1942 smacked of wilful blindness. His manner was not well suited to cooperation with Allies, especially Americans. But in this predicament in 1944 he does command some sympathy:

Poor Leigh-Mallory, he could not have derived much pleasure or satisfaction from being Commander-in-Chief of the AEAF. He did not stand a chance either in the jungle where Commanders brought in from the Mediterranean knew all the call-signs, nor in the higher, more rarefied atmosphere where the Commanders of the heavy bombers mused about the destruction of Germany. His job seemed to me lonely and friendless . . . I always felt that L-M bore himself with dignity in the adverse currents of the impossible situation to which he had been appointed. It simply was not his world.[6]

His appointment proved not to have been one of Portal's best inspirations. It is not unusual, in such circumstances, to see a man's best qualities actually operating against him; and so it was with

609

Leigh-Mallory. In his earlier career he had been noticed for his interest in and helpfulness towards Army Cooperation – attitudes unlikely to win warm approval from the Air Staff at a time when the RAF was very sensitive about its separateness. In 1944, however, these could have been useful qualities – but Leigh-Mallory found himself once more trapped by the false position into which he had been put. On March 10 General Montgomery was appointed Commander-in-Chief of all the Allied ground forces in the assault phase of OVERLORD, a position matching Admiral Ramsay's and Leigh-Mallory's. About a month later, according to the Official History, Leigh-Mallory

> delegated to the Commander of the British Second Tactical Air Force, Air Marshal Sir Arthur Coningham, operational control of the planning and operations of both the British and American tactical air forces.[7]

Coningham was thereby designated Commander, *Advanced* Allied Expeditionary Air Force, with his headquarters at Hillingdon House, Uxbridge. The whole point was to match the unified command of the ground forces with a unified command of the tactical air forces that would be working closely with them in this critical stage of the campaign. The Official History then continues:

> It was indeed understood and written into the plan that Air Marshal Coningham would be the only air commander with whom General Montgomery would normally have to deal. The opening tactical air battle would thus be directed by Air Marshal Coningham, to whom all requests for air action would be made.[8]

This is not how matters worked out; the arrangement simply ensured that the Army Commander, Montgomery, unless he took very deliberate steps to avoid such a thing, would have, in Coningham's words, "to deal with more than one air authority".[9] This, one might suppose, would seem unsatisfactory to everyone – but apparently it was not so to Montgomery. He did not see Coningham as an opposite number ("equal partner" in his words) at all; he cheerfully remarks:

> Not only did I have two badges in my beret: I was wearing two berets. I was at once C-in-C 21 Army Group and the Ground Force Commander in Normandy. So I had two Air Force opposite numbers: Leigh-Mallory, who was Air C-in-C, and "Maori" [sic] Coningham in command of 2nd Tactical Air Force working with 21 Army Group.[10]

And this was, in fact, how Montgomery chose to play the hand. It is clear that Leigh-Mallory's intentions, as the Official History states them, were never fulfilled, and it is hard not to blame him for this. If he genuinely saw Coningham as Montgomery's "partner", he completely failed to insist that this was so. Some blame must also attach to Tedder for not ensuring that the position was made unmistakably plain. In the absence of such clarification of the command structure,

> Montgomery himself doomed it to failure by dealing directly with Leigh-Mallory on heavy bomber support and with Air Vice-Marshal Harry Broadhurst on tactical air matters.[11]

It is clear that something had gone very drastically wrong with Army Cooperation at this critical juncture, and very drastically wrong with personal relations between the two men most responsible for making it work so well in the past. The probability is that this was due to a combination of factors, but among them we may clearly discern a failure (with faults, no doubt, on both sides) to nurture the "tender plant" of close liaison (see p. 578). As we have seen, there were already difficulties in the aftermath of the Alamein triumph itself, when Tedder and Coningham both considered that Montgomery was unduly slow and cautious in pressing his advance on Rommel's heels (see p. 387). Chester Wilmot says bluntly that it was during the advance to Tripoli that the Army/Air "honeymoon" ended:

> Because the nature of the campaign made it necessary for him to be well forward at his Tactical HQ Montgomery left it largely to his staff to deal with the Air Force. Thus he appeared to treat the air commanders . . . as advisers, not equals. It was his battle. They were supporting him. This was resented, and so was the personal publicity which he deliberately courted as a means of advancing the pride of the Eighth Army in itself. This resentment had grown more bitter after Montgomery's return to England in 1944.[12]

This is true enough; it was not only airmen who found Montgomery's publicity-seeking profoundly irritating. But there is also a curious ambivalence in Montgomery's words and deeds from Desert days onward. It must be remembered that that remarkable statement on Army/Air cooperation quoted on pp. 379–80 ("There are not two plans, Army and Air, but one plan, Army–Air . . . You have to be great friends, not merely to work together . . . mutual confidence and trust, starting with the Air Vice-Marshal and myself, must go right down . . .") was uttered by Montgomery, not in Libya, or in Tunisia, or in Sicily, but in Italy, as late as the last quarter of 1943. And in 1944 he could still use the same style; on May 4 he wrote to the Army Commanders who would be working under him in Normandy, Generals Bradley, Dempsey and Crerar, drawing their attention to Army/Air relations:

> I feel very strongly on the whole matter, and I know that we can achieve no real success unless each Army and its accompanying Air Force can weld itself into one entity ... The two HQ have got to set themselves down side by side, and work together as one team; that is the only way.[13]

It is hard to believe that this is the same man who, instead of cultivating the best relations with his Air colleagues in the interests of "confidence and trust",

> went off on a "morale-raising" tour of camps and factories (a tour which the Air Force regarded as a personal publicity stunt), and nearly all the detailed negotiations with the airmen were handled by de Guingand, his Chief of Staff. Montgomery seldom attended conferences, and when he did deal direct with the Air Force, he turned to Leigh-Mallory.[14]

It was this personal distancing – an increasingly noticeable characteristic of Montgomery's command system – that probably did the most harm. He forgot his own precept, "My headquarters and the headquarters of the Air Support Force must be together" (p. 380); a most unfortunate physical separation reigned, as Coningham describes:

> The C-in-C 21 Army Group was located at Fort Southwick, near Portsmouth; the Air C-in-C was located at Stanmore; my Headquarters was at Uxbridge, though I stayed with the Army Group Commander at certain important periods.[15]

Both Tedder and Coningham, with Mediterranean experience in mind, found this separation and aloofness not only disagreeable, but alarming; it would have evil consequences.

Within these personal differences which, at such a time, were serious enough, another thread may be discerned which played a significant part in the ravelling of Army/Air relations. Here we go back to the planning of HUSKY and the disputes which then arose; for Tedder and Coningham, the Sicilian airfields had been all-important:

The salient fact ... was that without early possession of these airfields the entire plan would prove abortive. *Provision for their speedy capture therefore became the guiding principle of our operational plans.*[16]

As we have seen (p. 570), this was where the airmen seriously parted company with Montgomery. In January 1944, it looked as though this breach had been mended. Montgomery's most valuable contribution to British military history, in the minds of many competent judges, was his swift revision of the original COSSAC plans for OVERLORD. He wanted much greater strength and a wider front; Eisenhower entirely agreed. At his first conference as Ground Forces Commander, at St Paul's School, Hammersmith, on January 7, Montgomery outlined his thinking on the actual assault, which he then saw as being conducted by five British and three American brigade groups:

In discussion, he stated that his reasons for wanting five British brigade landing groups and only three American was the urgency of securing airfields, which were in the British sector.[17]

So far so good; it appeared that Montgomery had taken in the message. Then, on January 21, came the first Supreme Commander's conference, held at Norfolk House, St James's Square, where the Supreme Headquarters, Allied Expeditionary Force (SHAEF) then was. Montgomery explained his proposed alterations of the COSSAC ground plan; he wanted landings on a front of five divisions, supported by airborne forces; the Americans would be on the right, landing between Bayeux and the Cotentin peninsula, the British on the left, between Bayeux and the River Orne. Everyone understood clearly the need to capture a substantial port as soon as possible; the Americans were to aim at Cherbourg, at the northern end of Cotentin. The British would protect their eastern flank. It is essential to understand his projection of how this was to be done:

Throughout that day he constantly stressed the need for quick success in seizing key objectives in the British sector. It was his main reason for revising the plan and became the foundation of his post-landings strategy ... Only with rapid movement, combined with the hoped-for surprise of the invasion itself, could this quick success be achieved.[18]

It was now that a short placename began to assume a large significance. Facing the British left flank, some seven miles inland, is the ancient city of Caen, where William the Conqueror was buried. In

1944 it possessed an aerodrome, at Carpiquet. Caen was to be taken by the British Second Army on the first day of the assault. Beyond Caen, to the south and east, towards Falaise and Argences, lies wide, empty French farmland with vast horizons, entirely suitable country for constructing airfields – whereas, facing the British right and the Americans, the country was hilly, wooded, enclosed by high hedges and cut by narrow sunken lanes, the dreaded *bocage*, very difficult to fight in, and quite unsuitable for airfields. As the January 21 exposition proceeded, air commanders began to perceive that their own objectives were closely linked with the taking of Caen and the advance from there. But there seemed to be no reason to doubt that this was what the Army would be aiming for with all its available strength.

The first draft of the assault plan, the amphibious phase (Operation NEPTUNE) was delivered on February 1, and it was quite clear:

> ... the immediate postinvasion mission of the Second Army was to penetrate south of the line Caen–St Lô to gain airfield sites, as well as to protect the First Army's Cherbourg drive.[19]

The deeper the planning went, the clearer the central fact became to the air commanders; to Tedder it was Sicily all over again:

> If our strongest card, overwhelming air-power, was to be played effectively and promptly, we had to have airfields in France . . .[20]

It was necessary, also, to look beyond the beaches; Leigh-Mallory considered that the heaviest air fighting would probably occur along the Seine when the German counter-strokes came in. At another conference on March 10 he stated that

> We must, therefore, have enough airfields around Caen and the areas west of Paris to operate over the Seine in strength.[21]

In the original COSSAC plan that need had been fully recognized, and its timetable had called for the capture of the Caen airfields in the fortnight after D–Day, and a further group west of Paris by about a month from D–Day. Tedder was not sure that the revised plan was so firm, but at that stage he need not have worried. Montgomery told his Army Commanders on March 20:

> As we secure airfields and good areas for making airfields, so we get increased air support – so everything becomes easier. It is very important that the area to the south-east of CAEN should be secured as early as 2nd Army can manage.[22]

He could scarcely have been plainer; and in early April he supplied further confirmation. April 7 was Good Friday, and the day selected for Exercise THUNDERCLAP, a top-level conference at St Paul's School at which Churchill himself would be present. Montgomery opened the proceedings, and stated unequivocally:

> The intention is to assault simultaneously: immediately north of the Carentan estuary and between the Carentan estuary and the River Orne with the object of securing as a base for further operations a lodgement area which will include airfield sites and the port of Cherbourg.[23]

Leigh-Mallory, when his turn came, emphasized the need for "early seizure of the 'good' airfield area beyond Caen".[24]

The usual criticism of Montgomery, at the time and later, was that he was over-cautious, unwilling to take risks. Churchill, who had been deeply perturbed by the failure of the Allies to make a quick penetration from the Anzio beachhead in January,[25] was one who feared this; Tedder and Coningham never forgot the slow advance from El Alamein. Yet the evidence is that they – and many subsequent analysts – were wrong; on the contrary, Montgomery's planning was very bold – indeed, as the event would prove, too bold. A week after THUNDERCLAP (April 14) he wrote again to Generals Bradley and Dempsey; like everyone else, faced with a commander of the known talents and disposition of Field-Marshal Rommel, he had in mind the probability of a powerful armoured counter-stroke against the Allied landings. He told the Army Commanders,

> [we] must not get our main bodies so stretched that they would be unable to hold against determined counter-attack; on the other hand, *having seized the initiative by our initial landing, we must insure that we keep it.*
>
> The best way to interfere with the enemy concentrations and counter-measures will be to *push forward fairly powerful armoured force thrusts on the afternoon of D–Day.*
>
> If two such forces, each consisting of an Armd Bde Group, were pushed forward on each Army front to carefully chosen areas, it would be very difficult for the enemy to interfere with our build-up; from the areas so occupied patrols and recces would be pushed <u>further</u> afield, and this would tend to delay enemy movement towards the lodgement areas.
>
> The whole effect of such aggressive tactics would be to retain the initiative ourselves and to cause alarm in the minds of the enemy. To be successful, such tactics must be adopted on D–Day; to wait till D plus 1 would be to lose the opportunity, and also *to lose the initiative . . .*
>
> . . . I am prepared to accept almost any risk in order to carry out

these tactics. I would risk even the total loss of the armoured brigade groups – which in any event is not really possible . . .

Army commanders will consider the problem in the light of the above remarks, and will inform me of their plans to carry out these tactics.[26]

All this, of course, was first-class thinking from the point of view of seizing Caen and the "airfield country". It disposes completely of the argument that Montgomery

knew his difficulty would lie in getting beyond Caen; privately, he thought that the air forces could operate efficiently from home bases.[27]

One thing is certain: General Dempsey took his Army Group Commander perfectly seriously. On April 21 Dempsey issued his Second Army Operational Order No. 1, stating his objectives:

After the assault the intention of the Second British Army was to secure and develop a bridgehead south of the line from Caumont to Caen and south-east of Caen in order to obtain airfield sites and to protect the flank of First US Army while Cherbourg and the Brittany ports were taken. Operations were to be carried out in four phases, with maximum offensive action by mobile armoured forces . . . In Phase 3 (D+7–8), I Corps was to secure the high ground immediately east of Argences and north-east of Bretteville-sur-Laize for the purpose of permitting airfield construction . . .[28]

It may be noted that Argences is some ten miles south-east of Caen, and Bretteville is also about ten miles south-south-east; it may be noted also that airfields do not sit happily in the front line – if there were to be airfields near these localities, the front would need to be well ahead of them; and all this was to be done, according to Dempsey, in about a week – a decidedly bold and aggressive plan.

The final OVERLORD conference, once more at St Paul's School, took place on May 15; Carlo D'Este says:

If there were still suspicions about Montgomery's attitude after THUNDER-CLAP they were certainly removed at the great dress rehearsal for OVERLORD . . . on 15 May.[29]

It was an historic moment; the AEAF Official Record sets the scene:

If the occasion had not been a unique and solemn one in itself, there was nothing in the setting to make it so. There was a singular absence of ceremony, and the room where the meeting took place was a dark and uninspiring lecture room in the huge barrack-like school building ... General Montgomery himself and several of his officers wore battledress. The Prime Minister arrived smoking a cigar which he did not lay down when the King arrived. There were no cheers, no applause ... The audience looked down from their crescent-shaped auditorium upon a vast coloured map, on a scale of about 6 inches to a mile, of the NEPTUNE area ... With the help of this great map and with charts and maps hung upon the walls, the exposition of OVERLORD plans went forward.[30]

An observant witness of the scene was Leigh-Mallory, who dictated his impressions shortly after the event. Montgomery, he noted,

looked trim and business-like. He spoke in a tone of quiet emphasis, making use of what is evidently a verbal trick of his, to repeat the most important word or phrase in a sentence more than once ... [His] demeanour was very quiet and deliberate. He was not at all showy and seemed cautious, for he made no attempt to minimise the difficulties of the task.[31]

Nevertheless, Montgomery was thinking "big"; he told his audience:

We must blast our way ashore and get a good lodgement before the enemy can bring sufficient reserves up to turn us out. *Armoured columns must penetrate deep inland, and quickly on D–Day*; this will upset the plans and tend to hold him off while we build up strength. *We must gain space rapidly*, and peg out claims well inland. And while we are engaged in doing this *the air must hold the ring*, and must hinder and make very difficult the movement of enemy reserves by train or road. The land battle will be a terrific party and *we will require the full support of the air all the time*, and laid on quickly. Once we can get hold of the main enemy lateral GRANVILLE–VIRE–ARGENTAN–FALAISE–CAEN, and the area enclosed in it is firmly in our possession, then we will have the lodgement area we want and *then can begin to expand*.[32]

The southern penetration indicated was shown on Montgomery's great map by a coloured line, which also proclaimed that it was to be reached by D+17. Granville is about 45 miles as a very lucky crow might fly from the American Utah Beach; Vire, by the same conveyance, is just under 40 miles from the Omaha Beach; and Argentan is about the same distance from the British Sword Beach. And this was where the lodgement would "*begin* to expand". Needless to say, within such an area as that there would be space for airfields in plenty, so for the air commanders the prospects looked rosy – providing only that the armies could live up to the expectations that Montgomery now aroused.

One thing is certain: both Montgomery's words and his manner showed that he had no inclination to underrate the part the Air would play in the great operation and his dependence upon it. It is just not possible, in view of all the occasions indicated above when Montgomery made his opinions absolutely plain, to accept the view which is here concisely put by Richard Lamb:

> Montgomery and de Guingand were still having difficulty in keeping Tedder, Leigh-Mallory and Air Vice-Marshal Arthur Coningham . . . happy, so they again glibly promised the air force commanders the airfields beyond Caen which, in their heart of hearts, they knew were unlikely to be taken for some time after the landings.[33]

If Montgomery really *was* making glib promises which he knew to be doubtful of fulfilment – as he undoubtedly did later – his unfitness for his high command is obvious. It simply was not "command quality" to acknowledge with one breath that he would be needing the "full support" of the Air, and with the next to be deceiving the air commanders. All the evidence is that he was doing no such thing. Yet it is Montgomery himself who has done most to make the accusation plausible:

> "Maori" [*sic;* Coningham] was particularly interested in getting his airfields south-east of Caen. They were mentioned in the plan and to him they were all-important. I don't blame him. But they were not all-important to me. If we won the battle of Normandy, everything else would follow, airfields and all. I wasn't fighting to capture airfields; I was fighting to defeat Rommel in Normandy. This Coningham could scarcely appreciate: and for two reasons. First, we were not seeing each other daily as in the desert days, for at this stage I was working direct to Leigh-Mallory. Secondly, Coningham wanted the airfields in order to defeat Rommel, whereas I wanted to defeat Rommel in order, only incidentally, to capture the airfields.[34]

The more one examines this piece of prose the more specious and ridiculous it becomes. Here we obtain a good view of the Field-Marshal at his worst: conceited, condescending, prevaricating. The only charitable supposition is that he was feeling out of sorts on the day he wrote it. Most absurd of all is the proposition that he and Coningham were pursuing different aims – Coningham's, needless to say, the lesser one. If true, one may ask what had become of the "one plan, Army/Air" that Montgomery himself had so emphatically extolled? But of course, he was merely contradicting himself; as he then says, he and Coningham had exactly the same aim – to defeat Rommel.

There is, however, one point in Montgomery's weird apologia that does have significance: the fact that he and Coningham had not been in daily contact. His excuse for this is nonsense; he was only "working direct to Leigh-Mallory" in relation to the Strategic Forces, and it was not the Strategic Forces that required airfields south-east of Caen. It was Coningham who needed the airfields, and the only reason why Montgomery did not have daily contact with the Commander of the Second Tactical Air Force was that he did not want to. It was a sad business, because it meant that when things went wrong – as they very quickly did – there was no trust, no confidence. Montgomery's aloofness created a breeding-ground for suspicion and ill-feeling which even the diplomatic de Guingand could not dispel. If Montgomery had been able to turn frankly to his Air colleagues and say, "Look, we've got a dog's breakfast on our plates. What are we going to do about it?" the ill-will might have evaporated. But that was not his way; he insisted, at the time and for ever more, that everything had transpired according to his "master plan", and a tribe of worshippers have followed him. So "Montgomery the omniscient" laid open Montgomery the bold and resourceful general to bitter recriminations and sharp historical judgments.

History insists that the last word, in regard to the Battle of Normandy, must be that the quarrels did not, finally, matter: Allied air power was so overwhelming that the defeat of Allied intentions on the ground never threatened disaster, only delay, and that only in the early stages, well compensated later. But let us be quite clear about it: what made the ultimate victory possible was crushing air power. It is not pleasant to contemplate what might have happened without it.

73 Air supremacy; interdiction; Tactical Air Forces; "Bodyguard"

The outstanding feature of D–Day (June 6) and the whole of the remainder of the war in the West was Allied air supremacy. As Chester Wilmot, who, as a war correspondent, observed it in operation, later said:

The value of this air supremacy can hardly be overrated.[1]

It came, suddenly and unexpectedly, in the early months of 1944, and it is convenient (but also reasonable) to date it from the heavy fighting over Germany between February 20 and 25, what the Press called "Big Week". This may be considered the high peak of Operation POINTBLANK, the attack on the German fighter force whose successes were already having such serious effects on the Combined Bomber Offensive. During those six February days, 1,000 bombers and 900 fighters (notably the P-51Bs) of the Eighth Air Force carried out thirteen major strikes against fifteen centres of the German aircraft industry. The Fifteenth Air Force from Foggia joined in on the last four days:

> As Spaatz had foreknown, the enemy came up to fight, and the cost over the five days of operations was two hundred ten heavies and thirty-eight fighters against claimed totals of more than six hundred German interceptors.[2]

This, of course, was the "numbers game" again, but precise figures do not matter; it was quite clear to all concerned that the Americans had won a big victory in the air combats, "and it was this which made the 'Big Week' battle one of the most decisive of the war in the air".[3] Subsequent operations over Germany repeated the pattern; the *Luftwaffe*

> lost about 800 day fighters in the West during February and March and began to run out of competent pilots. Thereafter the German Air Force declined rapidly in effectiveness. The Americans had won air superiority. This can hardly be overemphasized, for it was the foundation of practically all of the later Allied successes in both air and ground offensives.[4]

General Galland reported that between January and April the day fighter force had lost over 1,000 pilots, including some of the best commanders:

> Each incursion of the enemy is costing us some fifty aircrews. The time has come when our weapon is in sight of collapse.[5]

The absence of the *Luftwaffe* on critical occasion after occasion, which was so remarked upon throughout the campaign in north-west Europe (as well as in Italy) was thus attributable to the great American air victory at the end of POINTBLANK – a fitting and fine reward.

With this inestimable benefit in hand, it was possible for the Allied Air Forces, Strategic and Tactical, to undertake their OVERLORD tasks with great freedom. What those tasks were to be was a matter calling for a fair amount of noisy paper and more or less metaphorical table-thumping. Harris was strongly opposed to what he called

> the irremediable error of diverting our best weapon from the military function for which it has been equipped and trained to tasks which it cannot effectively carry out. Though this might give a specious appearance of supporting the Army, in reality it would be the greatest disservice we could do them. It would lead directly to disaster.[6]

As we have seen, this was precisely Spaatz's view, and USSTAF officers were heard saying that "they only wanted another twenty or thirty clear operational days and they would finish the war on their own".[7] This desirable result could, said Spaatz, definitely be achieved if the Strategic Forces concentrated their attacks on German oil production. The RAF, of course, had "been there before" (see pp. 276–7); it had launched the attack on German morale by area-bombing mainly because of the recognition that hitting small, often isolated targets like the synthetic oil plants on which Germany relied, was far beyond the powers of Bomber Command in 1941 and 1942. Harris was by no means certain that his Command could do it now, in 1944; he urged a return, as rapidly as possible, to an all-out attack on German cities. Neither he nor Spaatz viewed with any favour the alternative that was put to them.

This alternative was the brain-child of Professor Zuckerman, who had begun his advocacy while still at Combined Operations Head-quarters under Mountbatten. The "Zuckerman plan" emerged in full plumage with his report on bombing in Sicily and Southern Italy; Tedder, in particular, was impressed, and not slow to extract a lesson for the future:

> It was this: that concentrated, precise attack upon railway targets scien-tifically selected would probably produce a degree of disruption and immobility which might make all the difference to the success or failure of the long awaited invasion of France. The clear and detailed reports submitted by Professor Zuckerman convinced me that this was the right method of attack.[8]

Zuckerman, according to Sir Maurice Dean, had "one of the best minds in operational research", and much credit goes to Tedder for perceiving this; as Tedder himself says,

> I had complete confidence in Zuckerman's knowledge and judgment . . . I therefore suggested to CAS that he get Zuckerman home and put him in touch with the Planners in London.[9]

So Zuckerman joined the AEAF Bombing Committee set up by Leigh-Mallory in January under the chairmanship of Air Commodore E. J. Kingston-McCloughry, another of the RAF's very valuable Australians. Leigh-Mallory became a firm supporter of the Zuckerman, or "Transportation" Plan. The opposition was powerful; it was not limited to Harris and Spaatz, whose scepticism remained profound, but gathered support in Government circles, especially the Foreign Office. There was understandable dread of causing heavy casualties among French civilians by the bombing of densely populated railway centres, and of what the German propaganda machine might make of such acts. Churchill was much swayed by this; he said:

You will smear the good name of the Royal Air Force across the world.[10]

Against these powerful considerations of humanity, there were the military arguments: no one doubted the importance of hitting the German oil industry, as Spaatz urged, but the effect of that could only be felt over a lengthy period. The Army needed immediate help to make its lodgement and consolidate it. As early as January 10, Montgomery had said that

it was essential to put the French railways out of commission for a radius of 150 miles from D–Day to D plus 14, and he wanted no bombing of the area itself before D minus 1, but then "everything possible on area with daylight bombing at communications and later railways".[11]

Montgomery did not change his view. The campaign began in March, beginning with Bomber Command's highly successful attack on the railway yards at Trappes, south-west of Paris, on March 6/7; eight more attacks were launched during that month, and the Eighth Air Force joined in in April. French casualties appeared to be far fewer than expected, but the protests if anything gained weight as each report of damage and destruction came in. Finally, it was President Roosevelt who settled the matter; Churchill told him on May 7:

. . . I ought to let you know that the War Cabinet is unanimous in its anxiety about these French slaughters, even reduced as they have been, and also in its doubts as to whether almost as good military results could not be produced by other methods. Whatever is settled between us, we are quite willing to share responsibilities with you.[12]

Roosevelt replied on May 11:

I share fully with you your distress at the loss of life among the French population . . . However regrettable the attendant loss of civilian lives is, I am not prepared to impose from this distance any restriction on military action by the responsible commanders that in their opinion might militate against the success of OVERLORD or cause additional loss of life to our Allied forces of invasion.[13]

This, says Churchill, "was decisive" – which was just as well, since there was less than a month to go.

Meanwhile, the work of the heavy bombers was bearing fruit:

. . . with the approach of "D–Day" a rapidly spreading paralysis was creeping over the railway network of the *Région Nord*. When that day dawned, 21,949 British and American aircraft had cast down a total of 66,517 tons of bombs on eighty chosen targets . . . The movement of German troops and material by rail had thus become a matter of very great difficulty and hazard, and this well before any landings had been made. Such trains as still ran moved very slowly, were forced to make long detours and travelled only at night. The enemy had no freedom of movement in a large part of France and Belgium . . . The "Transportation Plan" had proved singularly successful.[14]

It was Zuckerman who noted the (fairly characteristic) contradiction in the attitude of Bomber Command's formidable Commander-in-Chief:

The amazing thing is that Harris, who was even more resistant than the Americans to the idea of AEAF domination, has in fact thrown himself whole-heartedly into the battle, has improved his bombing performance enormously, and has contributed more to the dislocation of enemy communications, etc., than any of the rest.[15]

There was, in fact, an unexpected bonus for Bomber Command in the diversion of its strength from the routines and "drills" of the offensive against Germany. As the Official Historians note, the diversity of the targets that it had to attack in support of OVERLORD, so far from blunting the effectiveness of the Command, as Harris feared, actually increased its efficiency:

New technical aids were introduced, old ones were improved and put to wider and to different uses, remarkable developments occurred in the techniques of marking and bombing different kinds of target, and, in some cases, more powerful and more effective bombs were provided. Thus, Bomber Command became more powerful, more accurate and more versatile . . .[16]

Probably the most striking example of this accuracy and versatility, combined with the use of an amazing new weapon, was (glancing only a little way ahead) the attack on the Saumur railway tunnel on the night of June 8/9. This was carried out by the Lancasters of the famous No. 617 Squadron (now commanded by Wing Commander G. L. Cheshire VC), supported by four more Lancasters of No. 83 Squadron. The target was the main railway line running from south-western France to the Normandy battle area, where it crossed a bridge and ran into a long tunnel at Saumur. The aircraft of No. 83 Squadron were to mark the target with flares, then "take out" the bridge with 1,000-lb bombs. 617 Squadron carried another Barnes Wallis novelty, the so-called 12,000-lb "Tallboy" bomb (actually 14,000-lb):

> It was an extraordinary weapon, an apparent contradiction in terms, since it had at one and the same time the explosive force of a large high-capacity blast bomb and the penetrating power of an armour-piercing bomb ... On the ground it was capable of displacing a million cubic feet of earth and made a crater which it would have taken 5,000 tons of earth to fill. It was ballistically perfect and in consequence had a very high terminal velocity, variously estimated at 3,600 and 3,700 feet a second, which was, of course, a good deal faster than sound so that, as with the V-2 rocket, the noise of its fall would be heard after that of the explosion.[17]

Nineteen aircraft of 617 Squadron carried these bombs on the night of June 8/9. No. 83 Squadron was unlucky, both with its marking and its bombing; the H2S equipment did not display the target well, so that flares went wide, and the bridges never were the best of aiming points for heavy bombers. No. 617 Squadron also had difficulty; Wing Commander Cheshire, however, found the cutting leading out of the south-west end of the tunnel and marked it with a red spot flare. It was then found that the Tallboys made a great deal of smoke, concealing the markers, so that each aircraft had to wait for this to clear and make several runs before dropping the great bombs. The pilot of the nineteenth aircraft was never sure enough, and took his bomb to the bridge at the further end of the tunnel. Nevertheless, the squadron scored a direct hit on the roof of the tunnel, which fell in; hits were also registered on the cutting, and the overall damage was so great that the Germans never succeeded in clearing the line. This was "interdiction" indeed – and part of a significant transformation of Bomber Command from a force condemned to massed area bombing by inability to do effective damage otherwise into a force capable of great precision, and practising economy of force in the achievement of it.

While all this was going on, the Tactical Air Forces were not idle. In the Transportation Plan, their rôle was to attack the smaller, pin-point targets, locomotives and rolling-stock and, in particular, bridges. It may be that Slessor's hint to Tedder through Portal (see p. 586), on the strength of bridge-wrecking experience in Italy, was bearing fruit; but equally likely is the probability of separate evolution from the experience of the OVERLORD forces themselves. In any case, their contribution to interdiction was impressive: General Brereton's Ninth Air Force destroyed 18 out of 24 bridges over the Seine between Rouen and Paris, and blocked the remainder. And this was only a part of their programme. No. 2 Group, in Second TAF, was equally active.[18] It was commanded by one of the "characters" of the RAF: Air Vice-Marshal B. E. Embry who, as a Blenheim pilot in 1940, had been taken prisoner and escaped by sheer audacity, and by the end of the war, as well as collecting three bars to his DSO, had nineteen operations to his credit in the rank of Air Vice-Marshal, which was not commonplace. His Group was in process of shedding its Boston IIIAs in favour of Mitchells (B–25s); the Mosquitoes specialized in such exacting targets as individual buildings housing military and *Gestapo* headquarters, with some spectacular results. Meanwhile Typhoons (and others) were demolishing radar stations – all six of the long-range stations south of Boulogne were destroyed before D–Day, and fifteen others rendered unserviceable, so that "large stretches of the Channel coast . . . were desolate of radar cover".[19] Mustangs and Spitfires maintained continuous photo-reconnaissance, much of it daringly and skilfully pressed home at rooftop level or below. German airfields were attacked, and steadily what was left of the *Luftwaffe* was pushed further and further away from the beachhead area.

These were the real preparations, in all their breadth and scope, for the real Operation OVERLORD. What has to be borne in mind is that, in parallel with this intense and unprecedented activity, there was an even more demanding air contribution to the complete deception of the enemy, the creation of convincing delusions to divert German strength and attention from the real point of attack. For this purpose, air forces were the primary weapon:

> For every reconnaissance mission over Normandy, two were flown over the Pas de Calais. For every ton of bombs dropped on coastal batteries west of Le Havre, two tons were put down on batteries north of it. In the bombing of railways 95 per cent of the effort was directed against targets

north and east of the Seine. The impression created by these operations was confirmed by information which came from the English side of the Channel – from air reconnaissance, wireless interception, and the reports of spies who were surreptitiously provided with appropriate data.[20]

In many respects – its subtlety and complexity, its thoroughness, the exactitude required in its execution, the sheer effort involved – the Allied deception ploy ranks as one of the most amazing features of OVERLORD. The comprehensive name for it was BODYGUARD (from Churchill's saying, "In war-time, truth is so precious that she should always be attended by a bodyguard of lies"); it took various forms: ZEPPELIN, intended to make the Germans think a heavy attack was coming in the Balkans (by no means ineffective), FORTITUDE NORTH, playing on Hitler's incessant "intuitive" dread of an attack in Norway, and FORTITUDE SOUTH, most important and most effective of all, drawing German eyes steadily towards the Pas de Calais. This was the purpose of the elaborate, unceasing air cover within which the real plan developed; it was, in Ronald Lewin's words, "the greatest orchestration of deception ever achieved in military history".[21] He reminds us that:

> The historic fact is that without Ultra the weapons employed so successfully in BODYGUARD could not have been forged and sharpened.[22]

It was, perhaps, the operations of the RAF above all that profited from this priceless gift.

And, of course, all these activities, whether promoting the real OVERLORD or deceiving the enemy with feints or false ones, were the fruit of air supremacy. It was, says Chester Wilmot,

> undoubtedly the most important single factor in the success of the invasion, for its influence penetrated to almost every aspect of the enemy's plans and operations. German strategy and tactics, fortifications and armament, logistics and psychology were all adversely affected by the dominance of Allied air power. It had played the decisive part in the campaign against the U-boat, the essential prelude to the concentration for OVERLORD; it had protected the invasion base from interference by the enemy's bombers or V-weapons and had denied him the opportunity of discovering through reconnaissance the state of Allied preparations or the start of the cross-Channel movement. Through air power the Allies were able not only to surprise the enemy but to mislead him. The FORTITUDE plan could never have been carried through without the technique of radar deception and radio counter-measures which Bomber Command had developed ... The long arm of the strategic bomber left its fingerprints in unexpected places.

Finally, there was the successful interdiction of the Seine bridges, the threatened tactical isolation of the battlefield and the general undermining of German morale in France. Compared with all this, the actual bombing of the coast defences was perhaps the least important part of the air force contribution to the success of the landings.[23]

The total effort was immense; excluding the work of Coastal Command, it amounted to some 195,200 sorties by aircraft of all types, in the course of which some 195,400 tons of bombs were dropped. The RAF's share of the sorties was 71,800, of which Second TAF accounted for 28,600, and Bomber Command 24,600. This total was substantially below that of the American Eighth and Ninth Air Forces, but Bomber Command's great weight-lifting ability made the bomb tonnage totals very nearly equal: RAF, 94,200; USAAF, 101,200.[24] Losses were on a commensurate scale: an Allied total of 1,953 aircraft (in just over nine weeks), of which 1,251 were American. The bombers of the Eighth Air Force were the chief sufferers, with a loss of 763 aircraft. In human terms, says Tedder, the full total meant a loss of "more than 12,000 officers and men". This was before the great Allied armada even sighted the shores of Normandy.

74 *"Overlord": U-Boat fiasco; airborne assault; air effort*

The greatest amphibious operation in history displayed its awe-inspiring power on June 6, 1944. For Operation OVERLORD the Allies assembled a fleet of just under 7,000 ships and craft of all types, 1,213 of them being combatant vessels, of which 79 per cent were supplied by the Royal Navy and the Royal Canadian Navy.[1] Here, says Chester Wilmot,

> was the fulfilment of Britain's destiny at sea. It was the full turn of the wheel. Four years earlier, almost to the day, the Royal Navy under the direction of Ramsay as Vice-Admiral, Dover, had rescued the BEF from the beaches of Dunkirk. Since then under his command other expeditionary forces had been successfully landed in North Africa, in Sicily and Italy, but none of these could compare in power or purpose with the vast armada that now sailed in full flood of confidence back to France.[2]

Of course, not all of this great throng of shipping was involved at the same time, but at any given moment enough was present to offer a target beyond the wildest dreams of a U-boat captain or an E-boat flotilla commander. As we imagine the lines of ships and landing-craft making their way from the ports of Southern England towards Normandy, we must spare a thought for the 51 squadrons and three flights of Coastal Command whose duty it was, in company with the Royal Navy, to guard the western and northern flanks of this immense seaborne array. Ultra had revealed that the Germans planned to deploy about 40 U-boats against the Allied D–Day shipping; with the aid of this source, and air-reconnaissance,

> the Allies had no difficulty in blanketing the whole of the threatened area with ten naval attack groups while covering the western approaches to the Channel so generously with aircraft that every square mile of the sea was investigated every thirty minutes by day and by night.[3]

It was the South-Western Approaches that faced the greatest menace, from the U-boat bases in the Bay of Biscay, and here no fewer than 30 squadrons (Liberators, Sunderlands, Catalinas and Wellingtons, supported by Beaufighters, Fleet Air Arm Swordfish and some Mosquitoes) were assembled under No. 19 Group. Ultra served it well:

> Since Bletchley ... could decipher a U-boat's homing report and the instructions to the escorts which helped an incoming craft through the swept channels in the German minefields, 19 Group could estimate the exact moment when its aircraft ought to swoop from the skies and catch a U-boat on the surface, its crew relaxed and off guard at the end of a taxing cruise.[4]

It was an effective tactic, even more as a deterrent than as a killer, though valuable in that rôle also: Ultra Intelligence supplying the time and roughly the location, ASV III supplying the exact location, the Leigh-light illuminating it by night, and depth-charges or cannon finishing the job.[5] On June 6 there were 35 U-boats available to attack the Allied convoys, nine of them fitted with *schnorkel* apparatus; 16 were ordered to the Channel, but No. 19 Group harried them all the way. One was sunk on the night of June 6, three more on the 7th, and one each on June 9 and 10. On that day the U-boat war diary records that

> on account of the large number of air attacks and the extensive damage suffered, above all on U-boats without *schnorkel*, all further sailing of these boats has been stopped for the present.[6]

Unbelievably, the U-boat weapon had achieved precisely nothing.

The story of D–Day has been told and re-told; it is only possible here to pick out special features in it. Coastal Command's work was in the background, and its very effectiveness helped to make it unnoticed. Amid the vivid pyrotechnics of the assault, quieter but highly effective proceedings are too often ignored. Among such we may notice an ingredient of the FORTITUDE deception carried out while the main forces were on their way to France. Under the unappealing code-name TAXABLE, it supplies another view of the quality and versatility of No. 617 Squadron. On the night of June 5/6 the squadron took time off from its normal bombing activities to display its skills in another manner; its task was to make the Germans believe that a large convoy was crossing the Channel towards the Pas de Calais at a speed of seven knots on a 14-mile front. For this purpose, one German radar installation had been left intact, in order to be deceived by WINDOW at the appropriate time. Sixteen Lancasters of 617 Squadron, together with the Stirlings of 218 Squadron, flying at 3,000 feet, were to carry out this delicate task, after some 50 hours of intense rehearsal:

"The tactics," Cheshire explained later, "were to use two formations of aircraft with the rear formation seven miles behind the leaders, each aircraft being separated laterally by two miles. Individual aircraft flew a straight course of seven miles, turned round and flew on the reciprocal one mile away. On completion of the second leg it returned to its former course and repeated the procedure over again, advancing far enough to keep in line with the convoy's speed of seven knots." The task set the navigators was one of extreme difficulty. A ship cannot suddenly alter its position on the sea, but an aircraft, flying at three miles a minute or more has only to maintain its course for ten seconds too long for it to be seen much too far forward on the screen and thereby ruin the deception. WINDOW had to be discharged with the same accuracy and twenty-four bundles were thrown overboard on every circuit at twelve second intervals. Operation TAXABLE began soon after dusk and "went steadily and mercilessly on through the night".[7]

It is said that war is nine-tenths boredom, which is bad enough; but there are times when the ordeal consists in not permitting oneself, whatever the temptation, for one moment to be bored.

The story of D–Day is full of memorable incidents, none more so than its very beginning, which may be taken as the moment when, after a series of daunting forecasts by his meteorological experts (backed by a current howling gale and heavy rain), the Supreme

629

Commander gave the word to "go". The occasion has been described often enough[8] and has already been referred to in this text (see p. 485). It nevertheless serves as the best point of origin for consideration of the first act in the great drama. There is no need to dwell upon the pangs of doubt that possessed all the responsible commanders as they received the bad weather news about an operation which might live or die by weather conditions. Leigh-Mallory, being responsible for airborne operations, felt his position acutely. He had already expressed serious misgivings about the plan to drop three airborne divisions on the flanks of the seaborne landings, going so far as to say that 80 per cent losses in aircraft and troops would be likely.[9] He had been overruled by Eisenhower on the promptings of Montgomery and Bradley; but now, in face of forecasts which offered nothing better than a gamble, his doubt revived. However, Eisenhower's ruling stood, and Leigh-Mallory loyally stood by it, suppressing his trepidations.

So it came about that while Group Captain Cheshire and his crews were performing their TAXABLE rôle, and Bomber Command prepared for a direct attack on the German coastal defences, some 17,000 soldiers took to the air in gliders or powered transports. The American 82nd and 101st Airborne divisions were carried or towed by 56 squadrons of the US Ninth Troop Carrier Command. The British Sixth Airborne was lifted by four squadrons of Albemarles, four of Stirlings and two of Halifaxes belonging to No. 38 Group, and five squadrons of Dakotas of No. 46 Group.[10] The Ninth Troop Carrier Command on June 6 had 900 powered aircraft, and 100 or more Waco gliders, each carrying 15 soldiers. The British leaned more heavily on gliders; the two RAF Groups consisted of 460 aircraft with 1,120 gliders, including 70 Hamilcars which could carry 40 soldiers or eight tons of freight, the rest being Horsas, whose load was 29 soldiers or three tons of freight. It was six of the latter, towed by Halifaxes, which are credited with the first landing on French soil at 0020 hours: six platoons of the 2/Oxford and Buckinghamshire Light Infantry, the old 52nd Foot, out in the forefront of battle, as they had been in the Light Division throughout the Peninsular War and at Waterloo. In both the American and British zones experiences were similar: navigational errors (the Americans suffering particularly from pilots' lack of experience), high winds, and that everlasting enemy, German *flak*, causing pilots to swerve and "jink" with dire consequences for their passengers. Both American and British drops tended to be spread wide over the landscape; there was much confusion on landing, and many casualties as well as considerable loss of equipment before the airborne units could even begin to operate. Gallant deeds were done, the enemy was much confused, and the Allied land commanders, only too glad to have the airborne divisions in action, were by no means disposed to criticize; yet as regards the military casualties (though aircraft losses had been light) Leigh-Mallory was proved not far wrong after all. And despite the brave achievement and the apparent modernity of this method of waging war, the sad truth is that its future was very limited:

> Like the dreadnought fleets of 1910–20, the sight of which manoeuvring in close formation in the narrow waters of the North Sea left ever after in those who had witnessed it something of the fascinated awe felt by travellers stumbling unawares on an elephants' graveyard, the great airborne armadas were to prove obsolete almost as soon as conceived. The naval pachyderms, nearly invulnerable to each other's attack, had been withered out of existence in a few years by the appearance of the fragile but lethal carrier-borne aeroplane. Massed troop-carrying aircraft were to enjoy an even shorter life-span.[11]

Sir Arthur Harris has a disconcerting habit of denouncing in set terms any diversion of Bomber Command from its divinely-appointed mission, and then asserting its incomparable aptitude for other, very different tasks. It is therefore without surprise, but possibly with a slight sensation of throbbing at the temples that we read:

> It was obvious to me that the heavy bomber offered the only conceivable means of breaching the Atlantic Wall . . .[12]

Accordingly, on June 5/6, 1,056 Lancasters, Halifaxes and Mosquitoes set out to drop 5,267 tons of bombs on ten coastal batteries forming part of the Atlantic Wall defences in which Field-Marshal Rommel hoped to be able to resist and defeat the Allied landings. The first Bomber Command attacks took place early in the night, in order not to interfere with the airborne landings, the remainder between 0300 and 0500. Guns, sited individually and protected by immense thicknesses of concrete are not good bombing targets. The only possible method, as Harris says, was to drench the battery site, and with luck put the command posts and signals equipment out of action. Since all these targets were later also attacked by naval gunfire and the Tactical Forces, it is impossible to make any exact statement about the effect of Bomber Command's contribution at the shoreline; one thing is certain – it cannot have made the Germans happy. Eleven aircraft and 70 men were lost.

With Coastal Command, Transport Groups and Bomber Command

already committed, as daylight came the medium bombers, fighter-bombers and fighters of Second TAF, with heavies and mediums of the Eighth and Ninth US Air Forces, joined the fray. Below them, the Navies and the Armies made their landfall. The Combined Operation, OVERLORD – "the largest and most complex single military operation the world had ever seen"[13] – was a fact, taking its place in history. The Allied aircraft involved, of all types, numbered 11,590, of which 5,510 belonged to the RAF and its associated Air Forces. Despite a cloud base below 2,000 feet, the Allies flew 14,674 sorties (RAF 5,656); their losses during the day, chiefly caused through *flak*, were 113 – 0.77 per cent. So complete was the defeat of the *Luftwaffe* that during the whole day it flew only 319 sorties. As Sir Maurice Dean says,

> It is fearful to contemplate what would have happened to the Allied armies if these figures had been reversed.[14]

It is indeed, and it is also exceedingly difficult not to accept his conclusion that

> On D–Day the Allied armies would have faced disaster but for the Allied Air Forces.[15]

This was air supremacy.

It was Churchill, as usual, who found the exact phrase for the mighty endeavour:

> It involves tide, winds, waves, visibility, both from the air and the sea standpoint, and the *combined employment of land, air and sea forces in the highest degree of intimacy* . . .[16]

75 Tactical air supremacy

The "degree of intimacy", at the operational level, remained high – astonishingly high – throughout the Battle of Normandy; indeed, it is perhaps the best-known feature of the campaign. It was now that the once-neglected art of Army Cooperation reached its peak of effectiveness, which is not to be wondered at, since the whole OVERLORD campaign was an exercise in army cooperation, and North-West Europe became the magnet which attracted the bulk of Allied resources. The lessons – and the equipment – of the Mediterranean landings were embodied in the NEPTUNE planning and execution: a Headquarters Ship for each of the five beaches (four of them, *Ancon, Bulolo, Largs* and *Hilary*, had been present at HUSKY almost a year earlier), each containing an Air staff which was, broadly, responsible for directing all air operations in its sector. Linked to each ship was a Fighter Direction Tender, a seaborne control centre mounted in a Tank Landing Ship, suitably modified to contain the requisite communications equipment. This, also, was a "Sicilian" invention. By these means the air supremacy which made the landings possible was wielded; it was the work of the Tactical Air Forces:

> With the withdrawal of the heavy bombers, the fighters and fighter-bombers took over the area in and around the bridgehead. The plan called for what was virtually an air umbrella stretching from England to the beaches. Such a plan envisaged the employment of six squadrons of Spitfires on low cover, and three squadrons of P–47s on high cover throughout the hours of daylight. This commitment embraced the whole area of the five beaches and the area five miles inland and fifteen miles seaward. Patrols of the area were necessarily limited to fifty minutes for the low cover squadrons and an hour for the high cover squadrons.[1]

There are points to be noted in this paragraph: first, the low cloud ceiling mentioned above meant that the differences between low and high cover no longer applied; both groups had to operate at the same heights, sharing them with the naval fire-spotting aircraft, as well as with passing fighter- and medium bomber formations and reconnaissance flights, so that "the sky was congested with aircraft".[2] Secondly, we see that another wheel had come round full circle: the RAF had spent most of the war combating the idea of an "air umbrella" – yet here it was in full operation, fully accepted. The contradiction is resolved, however, by the simple but overwhelming fact of vast superiority. "Umbrellas" without supremacy were, indeed, a trap – a wasteful and incorrect use of air power; but with unchallenged supremacy all things are possible – as the Royal Navy once knew. Thirdly, we may observe how, as in the Mediterranean, air support at a distance was again introducing the time factor into tactics; on D–Day and during the first days in the bridgehead, this was not critical; but it is not hard to understand that the sooner it ceased to be operative the better the air commanders would like it.

Once ashore, the now well-understood and tested Army Cooperation techniques began to function at once. Air Vice-Marshal Broadhurst's No. 83 Group Control Centre (see p. 565) was ashore and operating by nightfall on June 6; Coningham reported:

Once the initial echelon of 83 GCC had started to operate ashore, the control of fighters over the bridgehead was gradually transferred from the fighter control ships to 83 GCC, which became the master control for the bridgehead in conjunction with the Ninth Air Force fighter control squadron which was set up in the American area ... The two Control Centres were ... able to operate as effective parts of a single machine, thanks to excellent teamwork between the Commanders of the British and American Control Centres.[3]

Quickly, all along the Allied front, the apparatus of tentacles, Air Liaison Officers, ASSUs, Forward and Visual Control Posts, now so well developed, came into action. Other developments were soon added: "Contact" and "Tentacle" tanks, with signals equipment in place of guns, carrying an RAF Controller and wireless operator, for armoured liaison; Contact Cars (half-tracks) acting as fast-moving Forward or Visual Control Posts came later; a "Horsefly" control placed in a light aircraft, tried out in Italy, was not favoured. On the other hand the AOPs, with their Austers, were impressively effective from the first:

> Not only did they help to economise in air effort, which would otherwise have been demanded on a lavish scale and thus reduce the air effort available to attack his soft spots deep in enemy territory, but these light unarmed aircraft earned such a reputation for directing retaliatory artillery fire on active hostile batteries that it was possible, on occasions, to reduce enemy artillery fire by merely flying Air OP sorties along a defensive front which contained practically nothing of our own artillery. The sight of these aircraft in the air was reported by prisoners to have caused enemy batteries to stop firing.[4]

This says much for the proficiency of the AOP squadrons – and also for that of the Royal Artillery which they served. Indeed, as the campaign proceeded, it became apparent that it was in the artillery that the British Army's real strength resided.

Also assisting the Royal Artillery, in areas where the highly vulnerable Austers could not go, were the Mustang Is of No. 39 (RCAF) Reconnaissance Wing. A Canadian pilot wrote:

> We were happy with our reliable fighters ... the Mustang had satisfied everyone with its ruggedness, reliability and comforting high speed. The only disappointments were its lack of dogfighting manoeuvrability and its inability to operate effectively at high altitudes. It was a big, impressive fighter, a much larger machine than the Spitfires of the day. Painted in

the dark greens of RAF camouflage and polished with loving care, the Mustang I was a sleek, beautiful aeroplane.[5]

If the Germans learned to respect the British artillery, all Allied flyers respected the German anti-aircraft batteries; the same pilot describes how a section of three Mustangs, somewhat later in the battle, would carry out a reconnaissance:

> We flew . . . with about two hundred yards between the lead aircraft and the two of us with him, one on each side. Each of us had begun flying as if we were on a rollercoaster swinging from side to side, then up and down, changing altitude in a range of some five hundred feet. We had learned that without this constant change of line and altitude, those incredible German 88 anti-aircraft guns would be putting their vicious black shells either into our aircraft or close enough that we would hear them explode. The rule was: "If they're close enough that you can hear them explode you're in real trouble." Even so, as we crossed the enemy lines either going out or coming back in that dense, heavily defended sector, the rollercoaster movement was no guarantee against being hit.[6]

So, by a variety of old and new methods, all bearing the stamp of fully-fledged professionalism, the Tactical Air Forces waged their war; from the first they produced some striking effects. German reactions on June 6 were slow; key commanders were away from their headquarters; FORTITUDE and the weather which had so alarmed the Allied leaders combined to give their enemies a bad surprise. On June 7, however, German reinforcements began to move towards the bridgehead, and in doing so received a sharp lesson in the meaning of air power:

> The experience of *Panzer Lehr* was typical. One of the best divisions in the German Army (led by the able Lieutenant-General Fritz Bayerlein, who had been Rommel's *Afrika Korps* chief-of-staff) *Panzer Lehr* was savaged during its move on 7 June from the Chartres area to the Seulles Valley . . . His objections overruled, Bayerlein had been ordered by the Seventh Army commander (Dollmann) to move his division by daylight; as a result *Panzer Lehr* suffered serious losses before their nightmare journey ended.[7]

The Germans learned what they should have known – Desert veterans certainly did – that moving in daylight in the face of over-whelming Tactical Air superiority was simply not "on". The cost to the *Panzer Lehr* Division (the only German division at full strength in

Normandy) on June 7 was 130 trucks and fuel tankers, five tanks and 84 self-propelled guns, half-tracks and other vehicles.

Three days later, Ultra made a useful contribution to the same style of war. The cryptanalysts located the mobile headquarters of General von Schweppenburg's *Panzer* Group West at La Caine Château, 12 miles south of Caen. There the Second TAF duly discovered it on June 10, the wireless trucks and office caravans parked in an orchard, uncamouflaged. Forty Typhoons of No. 83 Group[8] promptly attacked; then came 61 Mitchells of No. 2 Group, dropping 500-lb bombs from 12,000 feet.[9] The orchard was saturated, and everything in it destroyed; 18 staff officers were killed, advertising their presence by standing with field-glasses, and resplendent in red-striped trousers, watching the Typhoons come in. Among the dead was von Schweppenburg's Chief of Staff; the remains of the headquarters had to be pulled back to Paris to be reconstituted, a serious blow to German hopes of organizing an armoured counter-attack.

These, of course, were special occasions; it would be some time before the Germans obliged by offering such tempting targets again. And all the time, all through June and virtually all through the summer of 1944, they enjoyed the help and comfort of what Hilary Saunders calls their "only ally"[10] – the miserable weather. Day after day brought, instead of sun and blue skies, low cloud, rain (sometimes torrential) and heavy ground mists – exactly what the aviator least desires. In a campaign which saw ground action, from first to last, heavily dependent on the air contribution, it is not difficult to see that this must have had most serious effects – exactly how serious one cannot say, but it is interesting to note that just at the moment in the Passchendaele campaign in October 1917 when it appeared that the German line must give way, their Commander-in-Chief used words almost identical with those of Hilary Saunders:

Most gratifying – rain; our most effective ally.[11]

In 1917 such conditions were absolutely prohibitive to air activity; in 1944 they only made it a great deal more difficult and more dangerous. Yet "day by day and every day", as the Official History says,[12] "while the Army fought on the ground the air forces fought from the sky". It is unfortunate in a way that the famous "cab-rank" technique, introduced in Italy (see p. 595) and now brought to a high pitch of effectiveness, has become a sort of symbol of the whole tactical air effort; in truth, it was only one system among a number:

"Cab-ranks" were only used when it was clear that a rapid concentration of aircraft was needed for a restricted period in order to assist the Army either in an attack or in repelling an enemy counter-attack.[13]

It is the Official History that reminds us that

for the air forces the battleground reached out over a far larger area than the ground being fought over by the armies and that their work included the constant attack on railways, roads and bridges which was doing so much to prevent or hamper the enemy's operations.[14]

It is appropriate to permit a distinguished enemy to describe the absolute success with which this was achieved from the first days of the campaign; on June 12 Field-Marshal Rommel signalled to Field-Marshal Keitel:[15]

The enemy is strengthening himself visibly on land under cover of very strong aircraft formations . . . Our own operations are rendered extraordinarily difficult and in part impossible to carry out [owing to] the exceptionally strong and, in some respects overwhelming, superiority of the enemy air force. The enemy has complete command of the air over the battle zone and up to about 100 kilometres behind the front and cuts off by day almost all traffic on roads or by-ways or in open country. Manoeuvre by our troops on the field of battle in daylight is thus almost entirely prevented, while the enemy can operate freely . . . Troops and staffs have to hide by day in areas which afford some cover . . . Neither our *flak* nor the *Luftwaffe* seem capable of putting a stop to this crippling and destructive operation of the enemy's aircraft. The troops protect themselves as well as they can with the means available, but ammunition is scarce and can be supplied only under the most difficult conditions.[16]

That was on June 12; the picture could hardly be clearer – and it would persist throughout the battle. Very shortly air power would give Rommel himself his *coup-de-grâce* – severely wounded when his car was wrecked by marauding Spitfires.

76 *Command relations*

To No. 144 Wing of 83 Group (Nos. 441, 442, 443 Squadrons, RCAF) fell the distinction of being the first RAF unit to operate from French mainland soil since 1940. Four Servicing Commandos and Constructions Wings came ashore on June 7, and by that evening they had created an emergency landing strip; the next day another was added, and work was pushed forward on a proper airfield (completed on June 10). It was on the 10th that No. 144 Wing (Spitfire IXs, operating from Ford airfield, near Arundel in Sussex) put down at one of the emergency strips after a sweep, refuelled and repeated the sweep from the strip and then returned to England, thus obtaining its historic distinction. The Main Headquarters of 83 Group was already in France, but

> the congestion in the restricted area of the bridgehead made it difficult to find the ten airfields required to accommodate the Group. However, by 30 June 11 airfields had been completed and work begun on a further two. But it was not until the first week of August that No. 84 Group found it possible to move across to Normandy owing to the restricted nature of the beachhead. It was fortunate that the Air Forces already installed on the Continent proved sufficient to deal with the effort made by the GAF. Had the latter been more effective the position in the narrow beachhead might well have become serious.[1]

As the campaign unfolded, the "degree of intimacy" so admirably displayed at the "sharp end", where Broadhurst and Dempsey did their business and their pilots and soldiers battled together, became conspicuously absent at the high command level. A difference of opinion and of strategic emphasis became apparent between the air commanders, Tedder and Coningham, on the one hand, and Montgomery (with spasmodic but significant support from Leigh-Mallory) on the other. Since the air marshals have been, and continue to be, cast in the rôle of villains in this hidden drama, it needs to be considered now. Obviously, as we have seen, some personal elements and antipathies played their part in it, but as we have also had reason to expect, the question of airfields was at its root.

The crux of the matter was Caen. That city was an objective for the first day of the landings,[2] and we have seen the compelling reasons for that: to obtain the airfield space that RAF and Army alike would need for further advances, and to give the Second Army a strong point from which to cover the flank of the Americans. General Dempsey wrote in his notes for the May 15 conference at St Paul's School: "*I must have Caen.*" Nothing had happened to change his mind; Army and Air leaders alike had their eyes fixed on the city on D–Day with confident expectation. It came as a shock to find that, despite the relative (and surprising) ease of landing in the British sector, at the end of the day Caen was still in German hands; equally shocking, and more serious, was the fact that it remained so the next day, and the day after and the day after that – in fact, despite all the superiority of strength in numbers, tanks, guns and air power that the Allies brought to bear upon them, the Germans continued to hold Caen for over six weeks.

There were several reasons for the D–Day failure; heavy casualties were not one of them. Out of the 75,000 men in the British assault, 3,000 fell on June 6.[3] Nor was the Second Army held back by lack of equipment: by evening, 900 tanks and armoured vehicles were ashore, with 240 field guns (supported by the heavy artillery of the warships). But tanks and vehicles are only effective if they move, and this *was* a problem. An unusually high tide had left a very narrow beach which soon became congested; the exit routes were under fire and took longer to clear than had been supposed. They were, in any case, few, and the jam of vehicles on the beach only translated itself into long nose-to-tail stationary files reminiscent of Bank Holiday frustrations. German strongpoints checked the advance inland; the bold armoured thrusts and deep penetrations promised at the conferences did not materialize. Worst of all – a serious failure to respond to Intelligence warnings – was the presence of the 21st *Panzer* Division in the Caen area, threatening the lightly equipped Airborne troops east of the River Orne, and (late afternoon) counter-attacking the British 3rd Division whose task it had been to take Caen that day. The division has been sharply criticized for its performance; Chester Wilmot says that it had "lived too long" with the prospect of assaulting the German beach defences:

in all their training their attention had been fixed upon the strip of sand which would lie ahead when the landing-craft ramps went down.[4]

Having got ashore far more easily and with far less cost than they had ever dreamt possible, "their inclination was to dig in, consolidate, and defend what they had gained". Major-General R. F. K. Belchem, Montgomery's Head of Operations, confirmed this view thirty years later:

A more dynamic formation would not have dug in . . . This should not be taken as criticism of the troops but rather a comment on the lack of training and battle experience of some of the officers.[5]

There seems to be substance in the assessment, but the fault would seem to lie with the division as a whole, not just its officers, and reflects a condition of the 21st Army Group, as we shall now see. General Belchem is on sure ground, however, when he remarks that

The division had made few calls on the air forces for direct support, which was of course a mistake . . .[6]

Fortunately, General Dempsey had asked for continuous air attack on all German movements in the vicinity of Caen, which resulted in the 21st *Panzer* being unable to concentrate and greatly lowered its effectiveness. Matters might otherwise have gone very badly awry. As regards the 3rd Division, Chester Wilmot himself admits that "the capture of the city on D–Day had only been an outside chance", and this is a verdict which has also been confirmed thirty years on, by Carlo D'Este who points out that on D–Day "almost nothing other than the assault on the beaches went according to plan".[7] So much for Montgomery's "master plan"; what faced him now, from the very beginning of the battle, was the "dog's breakfast" (see p. 619).

We must return here – and it is not a digression – to the unhappy state of affairs in the Army already referred to on p. 578 ("progressive dilution of the Army's front-line elements") pp. 592–3 ("the growing reluctance of the British infantry to accept casualties") and pp. 603–4 ("this is not a war of vast armies"). The evidence of the deterioration of the British infantry in 1944 is very strong; in the words of Lieutenant-General Horrocks, it "seemed to have lost the sharp edge of its offensive spirit". Major-General Hubert Essame wrote:

> Their stock of courage could soon be exhausted, leaving them bankrupt and bereft of bravery. After the first few weeks in Normandy about 10 per cent of Second Army casualties in June and nearly 50 per cent in the case of one of the veteran divisions were classified as battle exhaustion.[8]

Those who have read pp. 528–32 of this work with attention will particularly note that

> Essame, in common with many other Great War veterans, thought that there was a *lack of moral fibre* in the younger generation of soldiers.[9]

Desertions increased; even before D–Day ominous tendencies had been noted, especially in the veteran formations which had fought in Africa. A New Zealand officer attached to the 50th (Northumbrian) Division, one of the three in the June 6 landing, noted:

> There was a strong feeling among the men while in England that the Div should not be asked to do the assault on D–Day . . . Absence Without Leave became very prevalent in the New Forest area amounting to well over 1,000 and there was considerable unrest.[10]

The new Commanding Officer of the 6/Duke of Wellington's Regiment in the 49th Division reported on June 30 that the battalion

> is not fit to take its place in the line. Even excluding the question of nerves and morale [it] will not be fit to go back into the line until it is remobilised, reorganised and to an extent retrained.[11]

The battalion was, in fact, disbanded. Montgomery himself, on July 15, sent a highly secret cable to the CIGS saying:

> Regret to report it is considered opinion Crocker,[12] Dempsey and myself that 51st Division is at present not – NOT – battleworthy. It does not fight with determination and has failed in every operation it has been given to do. It cannot fight the Germans successfully . . .[13]

Montgomery considered sending the 51st Division home for retraining, but in the end it did not come to that; however, the divisional commander was removed. There was no disguising the unpleasant state of affairs in responsible circles; a Second Army Intelligence summary in July went so far as to quote a *Panzer Lehr* Division report which said bluntly:

> The enemy is extraordinarily nervous of close combat. Whenever the enemy infantry is energetically engaged they mostly retreat or surrender.[14]

The German view, which examples support, was that the British infantry in 1944 sought "to occupy ground rather than fight over it".[15]

All this, of course, was based on the strong but wishful belief that there would be no protracted heavy infantry fighting (pp. 603–4). Thus a clearly alarming morale situation was compounded by a serious lack of reinforcements; by June 30 the infantry reserves in the United Kingdom (for all purposes) numbered 6,373 officers and 109,251 other ranks – a staggeringly low figure only three weeks from the beginning of the decisive campaign of the war.[16] It is well known that unfilled gaps in the ranks make for low morale; but worse still was the quality of replacements for the infantry Arm: it was at the bottom of a long list of priorities in manpower selection. At the top of that list, without doubt, stood the RAF. Not only did it hive off the equivalent of two divisions against its future needs (see p. 604), but the general quality of its intake, skilled, educated and self-reliant, was precisely what was now lacking in the infantry. Furthermore, within the Army itself there were vicious policies at work calculated to wreck the infantry. The Royal Armoured Corps and its adjunct, REME, for example, had now enormously expanded, making similar demands to those of the RAF. The Royal Artillery, the strongest Arm of all, was another competitor, and so were the Royal Engineers, also very numerous and requiring mechanically minded men of skill and initiative similar to RAF ground crew. All these were legitimate demands, foreseeable from the experience of the previous war. What was not legitimate, or even sensible, was the creaming off of the qualities that make good NCOs and Warrant Officers into various "private armies" by means of which, it was naively supposed, set-piece battle with its heavy loss could be avoided. Most famous of these were the Commandos, consisting entirely of men of high courage and combativeness who were encouraged to volunteer out of their units for their valorous deeds. In the Middle East, "Jock Columns", the Long Range Desert Group and the SAS, though few in numbers, helped to "compound the felony"; in Burma General Wingate's extraordinary "Chindit" aberration was allowed to spoil a whole division. In his 1944 operation, battle casualties were not remarkably high, but over 50 per cent of the survivors emerged medically unfit for further action. Field-Marshal Slim pronounced acidly on the cult of special forces:

> Any well-trained infantry battalion should be able to do what a commando can do; in the Fourteenth Army they could and did ... I would lay it down, that any single operation in which more than a handful of men are to be engaged should be regarded as normal, and should be carried out by standard formations.[17]

Worst of all the "offenders", it must be said, were the Airborne Forces, with their exacting physical and psychological requirements. There is an awful irony in the spectacle of the line infantry divisions in Normandy struggling to perform their ordinary duties, while beside them the 6th Airborne, first into battle when June 6 was only twenty minutes old, and consisting entirely of the type of men that the line infantry so palpably lacked, fought on *as line infantry* for 82 days. The 6th Airborne Division came out of the line on August 27.

These are matters which, so far from being the private business of the Army, affected the RAF very closely throughout the campaign. The difficulty experienced by the Army in carrying out its tasks threw ever-increasing burdens on the airmen, and made their own tasks more difficult. It was a process that began at Caen, and centred upon that sector of the front throughout. In view of the very considerable ill-feeling that later grew up, it is important to note that in the early stages there was no divergence of aim whatever between Montgomery and the air marshals. The general was as determined and eager to get Caen as they were, and the regrettable truths about his army outlined above had not yet emerged; all that had emerged was that the Germans were, as usual, fighting obstinately and well, and that the country to the west of Caen, the *bocage*, was horrible. But by June 10 everyone was becoming impatient, and Montgomery determined to pinch out Caen with a two-pronged attack, to the east and to the south – Operation PERCH. His first intention was to support this with a drop of the First Airborne Division in support of the southward thrust, but Leigh-Mallory, habitually hesitant about airborne operations (D–Day conditions no longer applied), demurred; Montgomery commented to de Guingand:

> Obviously he is a gutless bugger who refuses to take a chance and plays for safety on all occasions. I have no use for him.[18]

He would soon change this tune. And events showed that Leigh-Mallory was almost certainly right; when PERCH took place on June 12 the eastward thrust proved to be the first of the 51st Division's conspicuous failures, while the southward movement, headed by the Seventh Armoured Division, after a good beginning, came to grief and an ignominious retreat. The seventh Armoured Division was born in the Desert, and won fame as the "Desert Rats"; now fighting in the enclosed *bocage*, it found conditions little to its taste and its performance was disappointing.

It was, however, not so much the tank crews and their supporting infantry and gunners who were defeated in this battle, as their corps and divisional commanders; General Dempsey said afterwards "the whole handling of that battle was a disgrace".[19] The action was abruptly broken off for no very apparent reason on June 14, and this, says Carlo D'Este, was "the spark which ignited the airmen's criticism".[20]

Tedder, certainly, was so disturbed by events around Caen on June 14 that he told the Allied Air Commanders' Conference that the situation

> might become critical at any moment, and he felt that they ought to be prepared to hold the Air Forces in readiness to give all-out assistance as and where necessary.[21]

The reactions of the leading airmen varied according to their temperaments; Tedder was alarmed at what he saw as the violation of an important principle:

> As the days slipped by, I could not help being worried about Montgomery's methods of conducting the battle. The principle which we had proved after painful experience in the Mediterranean – that the Army and Air commanders should live side by side, and decide their policies together – had been allowed to lapse. The reason in this case was the lack of suitable communications in Normandy which would permit Coningham to control the air forces from Montgomery's headquarters.[22]

So Coningham, like the bulk of his force, was stuck in England; he did not like it and being a forceful personality with New Zealand outspokenness, he made that fact quite clear. At the Air Commanders' Conference on June 16, according to D'Este, he "unleashed a savage attack" on the Army's performance, and demanded that Montgomery should frankly admit that his plan was not working. The demand itself was not unreasonable; this was a time for frankness and a joint reappraisal, now that the "master plan" had failed – as it undoubtedly had. But as we have seen, there was no frankness forthcoming from Montgomery. We do not know the terms in which Coningham expressed himself; they were probably impolite. But it is to be noticed that it was not only air marshals who were becoming critical of Montgomery:

> From this point on the Americans began to criticize Montgomery for lack of drive.[23]

Obviously, Montgomery could not advertise the shortcomings of his Army, and its critical lack of reinforcements; nevertheless it seems a most serious fault that he did not discuss the matter fully with his American Supreme Commander and the airman who was also Deputy SAC. Much unnecessary friction might have been avoided.

Leigh-Mallory's reaction to the PERCH failure was different; without prompting, he flew to Normandy to meet Montgomery on June 14. The interview got off to a sticky start:

> Monty was not in a good temper for I had sent him a signal shooting down an airborne operation he wanted mounted. When I met him, therefore, he was not very kindly disposed . . .[24]

Leigh-Mallory brought soothing balm; when Montgomery had simmered down and explained his own view of the situation – not "in any way a critical one", but admittedly "something like a stalemate around Caen" –

The Air C-in-C proposed that to "unfreeze" the situation an air bombardment might be launched by medium and heavy bombers on a front of say, 5,000 yards, behind which the Army might advance.[25]

Not surprisingly, Montgomery "brisked up a bit" at this proposal:

When I made it he just swallowed it up, though even now I am not sure that he will choose the right area. We shall see.[26]

Leigh-Mallory was acting in perfectly good faith; he confided his philosophy to his diary not long afterwards:

I want to help the Army all I can, because that is what I am convinced the Air Force should now do. I have always been of that opinion . . . we must do our utmost as an Air Force to give them every possible assistance and to try to unstick them.[27]

Tedder, an architect of practical air support, was dubious of this all-out commitment; as he would later express himself:

The Army having been drugged with bombs, it is going to be a difficult process to cure the drug addicts.[28]

The Air, he insisted (see p. 578), "could not, and must not, be turned on . . . glibly and vaguely in support of the Army, which would never move unless prepared to fight its way with its own weapons". It was a fundamental difference of approach, and Tedder was the man with the experience. He was not alone; when Leigh-Mallory reported what he had proposed at the next Air Commanders' Conference, "Someone murmured 'Cassino'."[29] We may pause to wonder why it was only some*one* – and why they only murmured!

It would be some time before Leigh-Mallory's controversial formula could be applied, and during the interval OVERLORD went through a depressing period. On June 19 a great storm blew up which caused catastrophic damage to the Mulberry artificial harbours, the most exposed one in the American sector being wrecked beyond repair. The consequences, reported Eisenhower, were "so serious as to imperil our very foothold on the Continent".[30] It was three days before the gale blew itself out, by which time, in Chester Wilmot's words, its impact "upon operations ashore was direct and profound". Some 800 craft were stranded on the beaches, ferries were in short supply, reinforcements had to remain in their transports, and the Allies' ammunition stocks sank to dangerously low levels. It was a very serious setback indeed – though Coningham, now distinctly disenchanted, somewhat unreasonably called it "an excuse but not a reason for inaction on the left flank".[31]

Further – and more legitimate – disenchantment soon followed. It was now that Montgomery began to make significantly different noises from those he had uttered before. Knowing full well (none better) that his "master plan" had failed – his deep penetrations had not materialized; he did not possess the large lodgement area that he had envisaged – he had had to recast his strategy. There was nothing wrong with that; the ability to do so is a hallmark of generalship. As the Duke of Wellington said,

> I made my campaigns of ropes. If anything went wrong, I tied a knot, and went on.[32]

Montgomery now "tied a knot"; the War Diary of the First Canadian Army (now coming into action on the left flank of the 21st Army Group) records his review of past and future operations on June 23; the campaign, he announced, was founded on four principles:

> The first was to keep the initiative. This had been accomplished. The second object had been rapidly to improve our build-up. This, owing to the weather, had not been successful. The third object had been to damage and delay the enemy build-up. This, generally speaking, had been successful. *His fourth intention had been to pull the main enemy weight on the British Army*, in order to ease the pressure against the First US Army. In this the object had been attained. *This last aim had been in accordance with the strategy of the campaign* which was to get early possession of the Cherbourg and Brittany peninsulas. *To succeed in this, the main German forces required to be brought against the British Army, holding the eastern sector of the bridgehead, and that Army must hold firm.*[33]

What a contrast with the strong, unambiguous statement of intention on May 15! No longer "gain space rapidly . . . peg out claims well inland . . ."; instead, only "hold firm"! No wonder Montgomery found the constant reminders of the air marshals about the need for inland airfields so irritating. For this new plan, which had been forced upon him by failure, was now and for ever more proclaimed the "master plan" – what he had intended all along. It is now fixed in the mythology of OVERLORD that the British, from the first, were to have a holding rôle, pinning down the German armour, so that the Americans could make the great break-out. It is, as we have seen, quite simply not true; nor could it ever have been true. At his very first OVERLORD conference, on January 7, Montgomery had announced that "the British have reached the limits of their manpower";[34] what kind of a strategy would it have been for the weaker army, at the limit of its strength, deliberately to undertake the hardest and costliest fighting? Would Churchill have accepted this? Would Brooke? The idea is absurd; and equally absurd is the myth that this attrition was undertaken in order to enable the Americans to break out through France. The American goal was, first, Cherbourg, and secondly, Brittany – both *westward*; but victory lay eastward – requiring in due course yet another change of plan. It is sad indeed that Montgomery was never able to admit these very straightforward and unobjectionable matters, preferring to risk a breakdown of relations with important colleagues at a critical moment of the war.

77 *"Race-meetings"; V-weapons; "Had for Suckers"*

Montgomery's next operation, EPSOM (another poor choice of code-name), began on June 25; it was another attempt to encircle Caen from the west, the main thrust being supplied by Lieutenant-General Sir Richard O'Connor's VIII Corps. O'Connor had returned from captivity in a fire-eating mood; for this operation he had some 60,000 men, over 600 tanks and more than 700 guns under command. The advance began in thick ground mist, delaying air support; on June 26, flying weather was so bad that the whole air programme had to be cancelled ("for the first time since D–Day, practically no aircraft based in England left the ground"[1]); on the 27th there was again no air support from England, though all this time No. 83 Group was active and effective; it fought alone again on the 28th, claiming 26 enemy aircraft and many vehicles; only on the 29th did the weather clear – cruel luck for the Germans, because this was the day when they attempted a major counter-attack, but met the full weight of Second TAF by day, and endured 1,000 tons of bombs on their armoured concentration from Bomber Command that night. But the Second Army did not take Caen.

Montgomery's language exacerbated misunderstandings; EPSOM, he had stated, was "the showdown stage". It is scarcely surprising that the airmen should have become impatient and sarcastic when they saw what the "showdown" amounted to. Coningham was chiefly affected, and EPSOM admirably illustrates his difficulties:

My main problem at this stage was to ensure the maximum possible build-up of squadrons based on Normandy. The continued location of short-range squadrons in England involved much wasted flying. Unless I moved my short-range squadrons to the Continent within seven weeks [from D–Day], the rate of effort which could be maintained would be insufficient for my requirements to maintain air superiority, to harass enemy communications and delay the build-up of enemy ground forces which could otherwise concentrate in superior numbers against the bridge-head.[2]

In view of its own account of EPSOM, it is extraordinary that the Official History while admitting that the failure to obtain airfield sites was "regrettable", should add:

it is impossible to show that at this stage of the fighting air operations were seriously curtailed or their effectiveness impeded by shortage of airfields.[3]

It is more extraordinary still that Broadhurst should later say that he thought "too much emphasis" had been placed on their capture:

I never felt myself short of any aeroplanes; we could call on enormous reinforcements if we wanted them.[4]

There were clear reasons why air support did not completely fail: Broadhurst's own determination; an overcrowding of fields in the British sector (some often still under artillery fire); and an increase in the American sector despite its unsuitability, both Services, as Coningham says, "thus showing what can, in emergency, be done by taking risks. Performance went far beyond planned anticipation."[5] But it *was* an emergency; what makes Montgomery's statement, "I wasn't fighting to capture airfields", sound such a very poor joke is the reflection that he was only able to carry on without them because his plan had failed, and his army was stuck near the coastline. If he had made the deep penetrations that he had advertised, Coningham's requirements would have been seen by all as an obvious and pressing necessity.

The acerbity of the air marshals is not to be wondered at; the first twenty-five days of Operation OVERLORD witnessed a gigantic air effort by the Allies. In that time, a total of 163,403 sorties was flown against all targets, including Germany proper, V-weapons and sites, and maritime operations. Of that total, no fewer than 131,263 were in direct or indirect support of the ground operations (80.33 per cent), and of those the largest number were by Second TAF and ADGB (45,952). For comparison, and to underline once more the immensity of Allied superiority, we may note that in the same span of time *Luftflotte 3* in France could manage no more than 13,829 sorties. Proportionately to sorties, the Allied cost was light – 1.14 per cent; but the actual number of aircraft lost was 1,508, almost exactly divided between the Tactical (740) and Strategic (768) Forces. The aircrew losses were also very evenly distributed: RAF, 3,083; USAAF, 3,170. Of these casualty totals, however, the overwhelming majority (5,006) were sustained by Bomber Command and the Eighth Air Force. Here again there is an interesting contrast: the losses of *Luftflotte 3* were 808 aircraft – 5.84 per cent.[6]

Conscious of the magnitude of the air effort, and their losses, the air leaders were thoroughly dissatisfied with the reciprocal support they were receiving. In reply to a question on June 27, Tedder told Churchill that on that day there were 35 fighter and fighter-bomber squadrons of Second TAF in France, plus three Ninth Air Force squadrons, operating from 13 strips (five in the British sector), instead of the planned 81 squadrons using 27 airfields; "our progress was well behind schedule".[7] He had a strong sense of things being far from well in Normandy, despite Montgomery's bland assurances, and the latter was now complaining sharply of Coningham's critical tone, accusing him in turn of being "unco-operative",[8] an accusation which the figures quoted above make it difficult to justify. Tedder himself was convinced "that the matter would not be satisfactorily settled until the Army and the Air commanders lived side by side". A crisis was clearly brewing up, for on July 1,

> Eisenhower told me that he also was worried at Montgomery's dilatory behaviour outside Caen, and at the frankness of Coningham's criticisms of the Army. I was given to understand that Montgomery and his Chief of Staff, de Guingand, would not be unduly upset at the removal of Coningham. I replied that this would be a disaster, and that Coningham's frankness was justified.

Eisenhower, behind the beaming grin which he seemed able to summon up at will for public consumption, was a worried man. He was concerned about the Allied build-up: British resources were drying up, and the Americans were almost at the limit of the capacity of the available ports to maintain their forces. The capture of Cherbourg by the American First Army on June 26 was obviously a help, but not a present help; German demolitions and mines ensured that nothing came in through that harbour until July 16, that for another three weeks cargo ships would not be able to tie up alongside the quays, and even after two months the port would only handle as much daily tonnage as came in over the open UTAH beach. Eisenhower feared that the Germans would be able to take advantage of this cramping of Allied growth to increase their relative strength; there was evidence that this was happening. He was worried by the extreme difficulties encountered by the US First Army in the *bocage*, and worried above all by the static condition of the Second Army. He told Montgomery on July 7:

> On the left we need depth and elbow room and at least enough territory to protect the SWORD beach from enemy fire. We should, by all means, secure suitable airfields . . . We have not yet attempted a major full-dress attack on the left flank supported by everything we could bring to bear. To do so would require some good weather, so that our air could give maximum assistance. Through Coningham and Broadhurst there is available all the air that could be used, *even if it were determined to be necessary to resort to area bombing in order to soften up the defense* . . . What I want you to know is that I will back you up to the limit in any effort you may decide upon to prevent a deadlock . . . The air and everything else will be available.[9]

Montgomery was now well embarked on the business of re-fabricating his master plan and his reply (the next day) makes curious reading:

> I am, myself, quite happy about the situation. I have been working throughout on a very definite plan, and I now begin to see daylight . . . [there follows a long recapitulation of the campaign to date, concluding with the First Army's problems] . . . I then decided to set my eastern flank alight, and to put the wind up the enemy by seizing Caen and getting bridgeheads over the Orne; this action would, indirectly, help the business going on over on the western flank. These operations by Second Army on the eastern flank began today; they are going very well; they aim at securing Caen and at getting our eastern flank on the Orne river – with bridgeheads over it . . . Of one thing you can be quite sure – there will be no stalemate.[10]

No one was more pleased than the airmen to learn that Montgomery was setting his "eastern flank alight", and no airman more than Leigh-Mallory, whose brain-child was now coming to life. The meaning of Eisenhower's reference to "area bombing" was that Leigh-

Mallory's offer of heavy bombers on June 14 was being taken up; Bomber Command was now going to be used for the first time in tactical support of the Army. Operation CHARNWOOD had begun.

It was 2150 hours on July 7 when a stream of 450 Lancasters and Halifaxes, with a strong Spitfire escort even at that late hour, passed over the British front line to drop over 2,000 tons of high explosive on the outskirts of Caen in under 40 minutes. Some soldiers were much impressed; one officer said:

> the noise and sight of the bombardment was a tremendous morale boost. Officers and soldiers were jumping out of their slit trenches and cheering.[11]

Montgomery asserted later that the bombing had had a "tremendous effect" and "played a vital part in the success of the operation". He was one of a very limited number of people who considered the operation a success. Harris says that the effect on German morale was "shattering"; he had a predilection for shattering German morale, and always tended to ignore evidence that it had not happened – in this case, the fierce resistance with which the Germans greeted the British advance when it came. "When it came . . ."; Harris makes a better point when he says "the army unfortunately did not exploit its opportunities".[12] The truth is that the CHARNWOOD air plan was a mess. So great was the fear of bombing short and causing British casualties that the bombline was fixed "*6,000 yards ahead of the nearest troops.* This meant that the bombs would fall on the enemy's rearward defences on the northern outskirts of Caen, some three miles behind the strongly defended forward area which the infantry and tanks would have to capture".[13] From this initial mistake, by some extraordinary lapse of reason, stemmed the further decision that the actual attack should not take place until the morning of July 8, over six hours after the bombing had been completed. Small wonder that when Zuckerman and Kingston-McCloughry conducted an enquiry immediately afterwards, they found themselves interviewing officers and men who said:

> Apart from the enormous lift to their morale which the appearance of the heavy bombers had given, their view was that the bombing had made no material difference to the whole operation. They could not understand why heavy bombing had been called for and . . . said that not a single dead German or any enemy equipment had been found in the area that had been bombed.[14]

Caen itself, of course, had been thoroughly smashed; fortunately, as did happen, there were miraculous survivals of some particularly precious buildings. The centre of the city, however, was reduced to the too-familiar picture – mountainous rubble of huge stone blocks, interspersed with enormous craters, in places blocking the advance. It was Cassino all over again.

Curiously, the map of Operation CHARNWOOD in the Official History is entitled "Capture of Caen", yet the map itself shows clearly that only the northern part of Caen actually was captured in this action; as Chester Wilmot says,

> The city of Caen was in British hands, but by their continued defence of the suburbs and factories of Vaucelles beyond the river, the Germans were able to deny Montgomery the through routes he needed so that Second Army could maintain its threat to Paris.[15]

There were no bridgeheads over the Orne, and with amazement the air leaders (among others, who included the Supreme Commander and the Government) learned that the "light" which Montgomery had lit on the 7th was allowed to die out on the 9th. CHARNWOOD was over; there was stalemate after all.

It is not difficult to imagine the mounting frustration, anger and distrust with which Eisenhower, Tedder and other officers of both nations at SHAEF, the air marshals and their American opposite numbers, and the Government, were now viewing the progress – or lack of progress – of events in Normandy. For the Government, in particular, there was a complicating factor: the V–1 attack on London which began on June 13. By July 15, 2,579 of these unpleasant devices, variously known as "pilotless planes", "flying bombs", or "doodlebugs", reached England, of which 1,280 fell in the London area. They caused many casualties and, as Tedder remarks, "a good deal of heart-burning"; the author can vouch personally for their alarming characteristics. Churchill writes in his *History* as though Londoners and the nation's leaders brushed this menace aside; they did not. The V–1s caused a great deal of "alarm and despondency", and excitable ideas of retaliation were ventilated. Among these were threats to wipe out named German towns, which Portal considered would be a confession that the V–1s were effective, as well as a diversion of strength. Churchill himself asked the Chiefs of Staff to examine the pros and cons of threatening to use poison gas ("principally mustard", though only in a case of "life or death", or if it were certain to shorten the war by a year).[16] Eisenhower minuted on this suggestion:

Let's, for God's sake, keep our eyes on the ball and use some sense.[17]

Yet Eisenhower himself, concerned also about the dangers of V–1 attacks on south coast ports, had to give first priority in air operations to attacks on V-weapon sites, an activity known as CROSSBOW. During the next two months, this consumed about half the energies of Bomber Command. The sites were difficult, elusive and unrewarding targets for any type of aircraft (as were those of the V–2 rockets which were known to be in preparation); in all some 3,000 Allied aircrew would lose their lives in CROSSBOW operations. Against the "flying bombs" themselves, as we have seen (see pp. 606–7), Tempest and Meteor fighters played a distinguished part; a barrage of 2,015 balloons was also effective, but the best weapon proved to be anti-aircraft guns of all types, using the new proximity fuse. The details of the campaign – or of the V–2 campaign which followed in September – do not concern us now; what we do have to note, however, is the extra load on RAF resources, and the impatient mood which these weapons engendered. As Coningham later wrote:

> The chief lesson which can be drawn from the campaign is that the only way in which long-range weapons, such as super long-range guns, rockets or flying bombs can be effectively neutralised is by capture of the sites by ground forces.[18]

This proved to be entirely correct, and constituted another powerful pressure on Montgomery to "get a move on".

This, to be fair, he had every intention of doing, if he could only find a way. Apparently well pleased with the results of CHARNWOOD, he looked again to the heavy bombers as the key that would unlock the barriers in front of him; he told his friend, Major-General Frank ("Simbo") Simpson (Director of Military Operations at the War Office):

> We must definitely keep Leigh-Mallory as Air Commander-in-Chief. He is the only airman who is out to help us win the land battle and has no jealous reactions.[19]

This was the heyday of what Tedder would soon acidly call "Leigh-Mallory's flirtation with Montgomery at Coningham's expense" or "cashing in on the discomfiture of his own subordinate", a posture which Tedder did not admire.[20] Leaving this aside, however, as a separate matter, it is to be noted that Montgomery was not the only senior soldier to be deeply impressed by the spectacle of air power that had been displayed at CHARNWOOD. Dempsey, who had witnessed it at very close quarters as a passenger in Broadhurst's personal Fieseler *Storch* aircraft (piloted by the Air Vice-Marshal), was – at any rate for the time being – a convert, and wanted to use it again, taking certain lessons into account. Bradley, too, was revolving in his mind how the formidable strength of the heavy bombers could be made to fit usefully into a major land operation. And so, at a juncture when Montgomery, now seriously concerned with the British manpower crisis, was leaning towards switching the main offensive thrust to the American First Army on the western flank, it was Dempsey who suggested another large-scale attack by the Second Army in the east, preceded by saturation bombing, and using a huge mass of tanks to carve a way past Caen to the open country. Montgomery was quick to see the possibilities of Dempsey's suggestion, in combination with a strong thrust by the First Army, using a similar technique. Dempsey's attack was timed for July 18, with Bradley's two days later, and Montgomery accordingly requested Eisenhower:

> Grateful if you will issue orders that the whole weight of the airpower is to be available on that day to support my land battle . . . My whole eastern flank will burst into flames on Saturday. The operation on Monday may have far-reaching results . . .[21]

It is strange that neither Montgomery himself nor any of his staff officers could see dangers in using exactly the same imagery as he had used for the CHARNWOOD fiasco; equally strange, after EPSOM, that he should pick on another racing name for his next attempt: GOODWOOD. By any name, however, it was good news at SHAEF; to Tedder, who had been very tart about what he called Montgomery's "company exercises", it

> seemed to give evidence of a change of mind. We gathered that Operation GOODWOOD would soon be launched, its purpose being to break into the area south-east of Caen. Eisenhower and I decided that the reply should be worded in such a way as to make it clear that we expected Montgomery to go ahead, even if the weather ruled out full air support. Eisenhower sent off an enthusiastic message on 13 July. He assured Montgomery that all possible air support would be given. All the senior airmen were in full agreement because the operation would be "a brilliant stroke which will knock loose our present shackles. Every plane available will be ready for such a purpose."
> I signalled to Montgomery the same day that I fully endorsed Eisen-

hower's message. All the air forces would be full out to support the GOODWOOD plan to the utmost of their ability. Both Eisenhower and I were immeasurably happier at this turn of events.[22]

Eisenhower's "happiness" may be judged from the letter he wrote to Montgomery:

I am confident that [GOODWOOD] will reap a harvest from all the sowing you have been doing during the past weeks. With our whole front acting aggressively against the enemy so that he is pinned to the ground, O'Connor's [armoured] plunge into his vitals will be decisive. I am not discounting the difficulties, nor the initial losses, but in this case I am viewing the prospects with the most tremendous optimism and enthusiasm. I would not be at all surprised to see you gaining a victory that will make some of the "old classics" look like a skirmish between patrols.[23]

It is, then, with a certain sickness that we learn from one of Montgomery's most recent eulogists:

One of his chief difficulties with GOODWOOD was that in order to persuade the air marshals to give him another dose of carpet bombing, he had to infer that this was an all-out attack leading to a break-out. The air commanders had told him that they would not take their aircraft off the strategic targets in Germany for a limited attack;[24] *Montgomery, therefore, had to bluff that he would break the German front.* As a result he was criticised.[25]

He was indeed. For whether or not one can really accept the proposition that Montgomery was bluffing – and the evidence that he had so far taken leave of his senses is thin – the impression created by the exaggerated language he had used is much the same. For the sad truth is that GOODWOOD was another fiasco. Despite the 7,700 tons of bombs dropped on the outskirts of Caen by 1,570 heavy and 349 medium bombers of Bomber Command, the Eighth Air Force and the Tactical Air Forces on July 18, the great attack foundered once again, and halted with only marginal gains on July 20. The reasons for this have been copiously analysed, and require no further rehearsal here, except to remark once more what had already become a main feature of the Normandy battle, as it had been in Italy and Sicily: the magnificent courage, determination and skill of the German Army in what deserved at times to be called an extremity of adversity.

Whatever the true causes of Montgomery's allowing the battle at Caen to halt may have been – and they were certainly plural – the effect at SHAEF was what one might expect: an acute sense of having been not merely let down, but deceived. Eisenhower was described as being "as blue as indigo", and according to a biographer with a fairly vitriolic style,

> He thundered that it had taken more than seven thousand tons of bombs to gain seven miles and that the Allies could hardly hope to go through France paying a price of a thousand tons of bombs per mile.[26]

Tedder summed up a general feeling in a letter to Lord Trenchard on July 25; they all felt, he said, that they had been

> had for suckers. I do not believe there was the slightest intention to make a clean breakthrough. Moreover, as has happened before, deliberate and cold-blooded endeavours are being made in high quarters in Normandy to hide the facts.[27]

It was at about this time that, as he records,

> I am reported as saying that the British Chiefs of Staff would "support any recommendation that Ike might care to make with respect to Monty for not succeeding in going places with his big three-armoured division push".[28]

It is certain that Montgomery's position was very vulnerable at this stage, because he had aroused widespread anger and dismay at a nervous moment. Tedder was, however, disinclined in later years to believe that he had ever said such a thing, for the very good reason that

> although I strongly disapproved of Montgomery's action, it was quite beyond my powers to speak in the name of the British Chiefs of Staff. Indeed, the chairman of the Chiefs of Staff Committee, Alan Brooke, gave Montgomery strong support.[29]

This is reasonable, but there is no doubt that a nadir of RAF/Army relations had been reached.

It would be agreeable to record that, from this point onwards, matters improved, and good relations at the top were restored. Such, however, was not the case. It was not long before Montgomery was involved in a dispute with Eisenhower himself, and the SHAEF staff, as fundamental and acidulous as his quarrel with the air marshals, and very damaging to inter-Allied relationships. Tedder, as Deputy

SAC, naturally had a position which brought him once more into conflict with Montgomery; so the idea took root that there was a personal enmity at work between them. The conflict with Coningham, also, was never really mended; on August 1 we find the Secretary of State for war, P. J. Grigg, with whom Montgomery conducted a private, intimate and mischievous correspondence, writing to him:

> I am convinced that Conyngham [sic] is continuing to badname you and the Army and that what he says in this kind is easily circulated in SHAEF via Tedder . . . If I am right then you will have no comfort until you have demanded and obtained the removal of Conyngham from any connection with OVERLORD whatever. He is a bad and treacherous man and will never be other than a plague to you.[30]

It would be hard to think of worse – or more disgraceful – advice. Not long afterwards (September 14) when victory had carried the Allies forward, the headquarters of 21st Army Group and Second TAF were to share a single building in Brussels, which should, in theory, have restored if not good relations, at least working relations. And in fact it did improve them considerably, but as Coningham says, there still remained a stumbling-block:

> In order to ensure efficient direction of the air forces under me I found it necessary to live at my Main Headquarters . . . C-in-C 21 Army Group, on the other hand, made it a rule to live permanently at his Tactical Headquarters to enable him to be close to his Army Commanders and to show himself to his troops, to keep himself clear of details, to give himself some security from visitors and to ensure that he had time for quiet thought and reflection . . . The deliberate dissociation of C-in-C 21 Army Group from his Main Headquarters meant that a minor duplication of levels of command for the day-to-day conduct of the war was bound to occur. He and I used to meet at his Tac Headquarters at intervals to discuss and to decide upon our joint plan for the conduct of the battle by the Army and Air Forces in the British sector. At these meetings we were able to formulate the directives to the forces under our command, which defined the general policy for the period under review. The difficulty came, however, in the day-to-day implementation of these policies.[31]

It was a long way from "Army plus Air . . . so knitted that the two together form one entity" (see p. 380). However, as stated above, "with unchallenged supremacy all things are possible"; victory was obtained despite the breakdown of a good system. It has been thought useful to discuss this matter in some depth because too many accounts unfairly dismiss the air contribution, and it is thus easy to suggest that the whole question was merely one of personal hostility, petty jealousy or, at best, foolish misunderstanding on the part of the RAF. It was no such thing; serious professional considerations affecting the conduct of the war were at stake; without the unchallenged supremacy, this breakdown of relations could have been fatal; at bottom, it was a question of trust, on which "the highest degree of intimacy" always depends.

78 Making air history; Normandy: triumph of air power

GOODWOOD foundered in a drenching downpour which kept aircraft on the ground and delayed the start of the American First Army's advance, Operation COBRA. This was unfortunate for Montgomery; if Bradley had been able to start on time it is likely that the furore over GOODWOOD would have been less intense. For when the Americans did begin to move, on the 25th, it was soon seen that, whether originally intended or later improvised, Montgomery's strategy of holding and wearing down the German armour was now, at last, paying good dividends. The German forces, always practically devoid of air support, were now very weary, very discouraged, and very thin on the ground. Carpet bombing by the American strategic bombers on July 24 and 25 produced a tragedy – a total of 136 American soldiers killed and 621 wounded through bombing errors. This made for a bad start, but the Americans did not falter for long, and it quickly became apparent that if they had had a bad time at the hands of the bombers, the Germans had had far worse. Their new Commander-in-Chief, Field-Marshal von Kluge, summed up the heavy bombers' intervention:

> Whole armoured units . . . were attacked by terrific numbers of aircraft dropping carpets of bombs, so that they emerged from the churned-up earth with the greatest difficulty, sometimes only with the aid of tractors. The psychological effect on the fighting forces, especially the infantry, of such a mass of bombs, raining down on them with all the force of elemental nature, is a factor that must be given serious consideration. It is not in the least important whether such a carpet of bombs is dropped on good or bad troops. They are more or less annihilated by it, and above all their equipment is ruined. It only needs this to happen a few times and the power of resistance of these troops is put to the severest test. It becomes paralysed, dies; what is left is not equal to the demands of the situation . . . the troops have the impression that they are battling against an enemy who carries all before him.[1]

The effect of this began to be felt on July 27; at last, after weeks of costly, inching progress in the *bocage*, the Americans felt the enemy crumbling in front of them. The next day the process was even more perceptible; Bradley told Eisenhower:

To say that personnel of the First Army Headquarters is riding high tonight is putting it mildly. Things on our front look really good.[2]

Now began the American dash to Avranches, the "corner" turning into Brittany; four armoured divisions moving as armoured divisions were intended to move – at high speed over long distances into the enemy's rear areas, breaking up all resistance, sowing unlimited confusion. And at the same time,

Overhead, in a sun-drenched sky which dulled the memory of long days of rain earlier in July, flew fighter-bombers of the IX Tactical Air Command,[3] constituting a fast-moving, far-ranging aerial artillery which pounced on anything German that moved. Roads were soon lined with wrecked and abandoned guns, tanks, wagons, command cars, and assorted flotsam and jetsam. While the leading [Allied] tanks wore brightly coloured fluorescent panels atop their decks, in each command tank rode an air support control officer in constant touch with the pilots by radio. In the months between Tunisia and Normandy close air support had come to mean something the world had never known before.[4]

In some British eyes the Americans had been slow to learn; but when they did, they learned thoroughly and applied the lesson thoroughly. The effect of this triumphant cooperation of air and armour, like its German predecessor in 1940, transformed the campaign. No sooner had Avranches fallen (July 30) and the way to Brittany became clear, than it began to be evident in some quarters that Brittany no longer held the significance that had been credited to it throughout the campaign. Montgomery was quick to see this; he was, says a percipient American historian:

a commander of greater audacity than the Americans sometimes liked to admit. He was the first senior Allied commander to recognize enough to define them the full opportunities opened by the collapse of the German left ... Encouraged by their chief ... the 21 Army Group planners in late July weighed the OVERLORD plans' emphasis on the Breton ports against the new strategic situation created by COBRA. Montgomery and his planners decided that the latter had made the former obsolete.[5]

From now onwards the concept of trapping and destroying the German Seventh Army in front of the Seine became the guiding motive of Allied strategy. On August 3 Bradley ordered General George Patton, now commanding his newly-formed Third Army, to turn, not westwards into Brittany, but eastwards towards Paris.

Before this highly promising project could be put into effect, the Germans, under impulse from Hitler (who never seemed able to see any merit in saving beaten forces to fight another day), made their last attempt at a counter-stroke in Normandy. In doing so, they presented the Allied Tactical Air Forces with a wonderful opportunity, of which they took full advantage. On August 7 the Germans launched their attack westwards from Mortain to cut off and destroy the American spearheads; four *Panzer* divisions were collected for this final thrust, and even the *Luftwaffe* offered a contribution: some 300 fighters were promised to give air cover, as well as bomber support. But Ultra revealed all, and the Allied commanders had time to prepare a terrible welcome. The day opened with summer mist and haze, which meant that for a time the American ground forces had to fight alone, which they did with great determination. Then, shortly after mid-day the day cleared, and another impressive victory for air power went on record, as Coningham describes:

It was agreed . . . that the Typhoons, armed with rocket projectiles, of the Second Tactical Air Force, under the local control of AOC 83 Group, should deal exclusively with the enemy armoured columns, while the American fighters and fighter-bombers should operate further afield to prevent enemy aircraft from interfering with our air effort and, in addition, to destroy the transport and communications leading up to the battle area . . .

. . . It was the first occasion in Normandy when the air forces had the opportunity of striking at a German armoured concentration. It was also a situation which required speed and flexibility of air striking power. A fluid battle was imminent; in it the use of carefully planned concentrations of heavy bombers would not be practical. No fixed positions for planned obliteration existed; it was a battle of armoured columns striking with speed in what might be a decisive concentration against our ground forces. The fighter-bombers of the Second Tactical Air Force adopted a "shuttle service" of attacking formations, and as the day developed *it was obvious that air history was being made.* As the tempo of the attacks increased, so did the morale of the tank crews diminish, and at the height of the battle it was observed that the enemy were not waiting to stand our fire. The action of the Typhoons made many of them abandon their tanks and take cover away from them. The interception of the enemy fighters by the

Ninth Air Force was perfect, and left the ground attack Typhoons undisturbed ...

... This was to date one of the best demonstrations of the tactical use of air power which had been given in this war. It proved that a Tactical Air Force may be a decisive battle winning factor, and it showed the smooth coordination of air effort which could be achieved at short notice by the team work which had been perfected between the Ninth Air Force and the second Tactical Air Force.[6]

Coningham missed few opportunities of paying tribute to the excellent relations between his own Force and Lieutenant-General Hoyt Vandenberg's Ninth Air Force, which continued with mutual benefit for the remainder of the war. His historical sense in writing about the Mortain action did not betray him; air history *was* being made, and the next ten days brought universal recognition of its meaning. They began less happily, with two further interventions of the Strategic Forces on the battlefield where, as Slessor had remarked months earlier, and Coningham never doubted, they did not really belong. On the night of August 7/8, Bomber Command undertook the bold experiment of tactical bombing in support of an army advance by night; over 1,000 bombers were despatched, and the actual bombing most skilfully performed, two great "brackets" of bursting bombs enclosing the assault area of the Canadian First Army at Caen. Smoke and dust, however, built up to such a density that the Master Bombers had to order back about a third of the force with bombs undropped. The Canadians then endured the familiar experience: good progress at first, progressively slowing up as the Germans recovered from the first shock. On the 9th the US Eighth Air Force entered the action, but with sad results similar to those of the opening of COBRA; over 300 casualties were inflicted on Canadian, British and Polish troops. It is not to be supposed that the Americans had a monopoly of this type of error. On August 14 Bomber Command, attacking by daylight, caused nearly 400 British casualties, including 65 killed. It appears that someone had omitted to inform Bomber Command that the Army's standard colour for marking its positions was yellow; this was also Bomber Command's target-indicating colour, and 77 aircraft which had gone astray proceeded to bomb on yellow marks – "the more the troops burnt yellow flares to show their position the more the errant aircraft bombed them".[7] It was a further proof, if any were needed, that close support and cooperation are a skilled trade in which it is dangerous to improvize.

The Tactical Forces made no such mistakes; their proficiency was now of a very high order indeed, and they were about to attain their apotheosis. As the German Seventh Army belatedly tried to extract itself from what was clearly becoming a deadly trap, with the 21st Army Group pressing south towards Falaise, and Patton's Third Army advancing northwards to Argentan, the Tactical Forces hastened to turn retreat into dreadful rout. What went down into history as the "Falaise Gap" now became, in the words of Group Captain (later Air Vice-Marshal) J. E. ("Johnny") Johnson, "one of the greatest killing-grounds of the war".[8] As the gap narrowed, forcing the retreating German columns into a smaller and smaller space, but at the same time drawing the British and American armies into increasingly dangerous proximity, the air commanders pronounced firmly against any use of big bombers against the amazing targets that were daily presented. This action became a heyday for the mediums, the Mitchells and Mosquitoes, and above all for the fighter-bombers and fighters, Typhoons, Mustangs, Spitfires and P–47s. The image of the utter destruction of men and machines that they caused on the ground with rockets, cannon and bombs, is one of the most familiar pictures of the air war, described over and over again in graphic detail. No one who saw it would ever forget it. It was, in fact, the end of the Seventh Army. As ever, the German soldiers met disaster with stoic courage; thanks to them, there was no absolute encirclement, and no outright surrender, which certainly diminished the Allied victory. Nevertheless, as C. B. MacDonald says, "for the Germans it was a catastrophe of epic proportions".[9] The Allies took 50,000 prisoners, and another 10,000 Germans were killed; the exact figure for those who escaped the net is not known; authoritative German accounts say "between 20,000 and 40,000 men", "disproportionately non-combat troops".[10] No one will ever know the exact tally of vehicles burnt out, wrecked, smashed into scrap-iron by the tactical aircraft; but it is indicative that out of 2,300 German tanks and assault guns committed in Normandy, according to von Kluge's Chief of Staff, "only 100 to 120 were brought back across the Seine".[11]

So ended the Battle of Normandy: an outstanding triumph of air power. It was air power that paved the way into Europe; air power covered the landings and made it impossible for the Germans to concentrate against them; air power maintained interdiction, and pressure on the enemy when the "master plan" failed; air power completed the overwhelming victory. 1940 was avenged; the Greek and Crete catastrophes were avenged; calamities in the Desert were avenged; this was the right of the line.

It had been a mighty effort: the Allied Air Forces, between June 6 and August 31 flew nearly half a million sorties – the exact figure was 480,317.[12] Of these, the four RAF Commands concerned – Air Defence of Great Britain, Second Tactical Air Force, Bomber Command, Coastal Command – accounted for 224,889. Altogether, in those three months of action at maximum intensity, the Allies lost 4,101 aircraft and 16,714 aircrew.[13] These losses were divided very evenly: RAF, 2,036 aircraft; USAAF, 2,065; aircrew casualties were: RAF, 8,178; USAAF, 8,536. For the four RAF Commands, the details are:

	Sorties	Aircrew killed and missing	Aircraft lost
Second TAF and ADGB	151,370	1,035	829
Bomber Command	54,687	6,761	983
Coastal Command	18,832	382	224

No one would dispute that the Army did a great deal of hard fighting in Normandy – the 83,825 casualties of 21st Army Group are sufficient proof of that; but equally, it is exceedingly hard to deny that those losses would have been much greater, and the victory substantially less, without that great air contribution.

79 *"Bagration"; advance to the Rhine; Arnhem*

By the end of August, 1944, Germany was palpably defeated; on June 22 Marshal Zhukov launched Operation BAGRATION against the German Army Group Centre on the Eastern Front.[1] By the time this offensive was over, one month later, the Soviet forces had achieved their greatest single military success:

> For the German Army in the east it was a catastrophe of unbelievable proportions, greater than that of Stalingrad, obliterating between twenty-five and twenty-eight divisions, 350,000 men in all.[2]

Instantly, on top of this, came the Normandy disaster. It is a curiosity of that great passage of arms that to this day no certainty, even approximate, exists about German losses in the West. Estimates vary from about 200,000 to "little short of half a million men".[3] A senior German staff officer says that up to August 14 they totalled 158,930;[4] with the Falaise Gap losses added, this gives a total of about 220,000. Taking into account other fronts in the East and Italy, it is clear that Germany's losses, in three months of fighting, were not less than 600,000, probably 650,000 or more. This was a scale matching her fearful losses in 1918, and as in 1918 it spelt defeat and surrender; the only question was, how long would it take for her to admit it? With "Unconditional Surrender" staring her in the face, the moment would obviously be delayed as long as possible. It has been powerfully argued that Allied strategic errors also contributed to delay; this does not concern us now. In the event, as we know, it took just over eight months from the breakout from Normandy to accomplish the collapse of Hitler's Germany.

From the air point of view, nothing fundamentally new happened during that time, though processes well advanced came to amazing fulfilments, and the progress of technology, already touching the borders of belief, never stopped. It was, of course, absolutely fundamental that there was no effective revival of the *Luftwaffe*; indeed, the last citadel of German air power had fallen by August – it was in that month that the night fighters "ceased to operate as an efficient force".[5] With the Allied advance to the Rhine, the whole of the German early warning radar system as well as their forward bases were overrun; heavy daylight losses caused the diversion of experienced pilots; even the fighters themselves were in some cases diverted to ground-strafing rôles in Germany's extremity. A shortage of fuel was already affecting operations by July. The decline was abrupt, continuous and absolute; in operational terms, it meant confirmation of that happy state of complete air superiority which had stood the Allies in such good stead in Normandy and would continue to do so all the way to the Elbe. Coningham graphically describes it:

A noteworthy feature of the whole campaign was the way in which the Army accepted our state of air supremacy. Our own transport was allowed to move head to tail closely packed along all the roads which were outside enemy artillery range. Within Second Tactical Air Force I ordered the return of all camouflage netting to the Base Depot, since it was unnecessary and interfered with the mobility of units, and I authorised the withdrawal of the heavy AA for the close defence of our airfields. We accepted a larger number of aircraft, often as many as six squadrons, based on each airfield, with a consequent loss of dispersal. It also became a common sight to see a large number of defenceless communication and transport aircraft flying freely within our area. When our forces reached the Meuse, unarmed aircraft were allowed to proceed as far forward as Eindhoven and Antwerp without special fighter escort. On the other side of the line, however, except when the enemy was in full retreat, it was very unusual for our pilots to observe any large movement of enemy vehicles by day or, except when they were congested by damage to the roads, for enemy vehicles to move at all by day except when they were widely spaced.[6]

Air superiority itself is never absolute; as long as the enemy has any aircraft at all (and any fuel), he is able to make occasional surprise forays and sometimes score successes. But Coningham's picture is, in essence, correct; the air force which had once ruled the skies of Europe was now hardly to be seen outside Germany. In mid-August, the fighter component of *Luftflotte 3* in the West was down to 75 serviceable aircraft; in September, the total number of fighters in the whole *Luftwaffe* was about 1,900 of all types and in all conditions, the overwhelming majority of them reserved for home defence. That month saw German production of single-engined fighters reach its peak, and units were able to build up to strengths never before achieved; by November, the grand total had reached 3,300. Regrouping resulted in a much improved concentration of force,

> which should, theoretically, have added flexibility and effectiveness in the defence of Germany, but in practice this advantage was offset by the desperate fuel shortage, the steady decline in fighting value, and congestion and increased vulnerability of airfields.[7]

The defeat of the *Luftwaffe* was already an accomplished fact; but the German Army had learned to do without it.

On the Allied side, by contrast, dependence on the air, if anything, increased. The German garrisons, trapped by the Allied advance in the Biscay and Channel ports, amounted to some 140,000 men whose orders were to fight to the last. They turned their positions into fortresses whose capture was likely to cost the Army a great many casualties; it was reasonable to call on Bomber Command for aid, which was, as usual, handsomely supplied. Le Havre was attended to by 1,863 aircraft, chiefly Lancasters and Halifaxes, which dropped 9,500 tons of bombs between September 5–11. Twenty-four hours after the last onslaught the garrison surrendered. In one raid on Boulogne, 3,391 tons were dropped; a survivor of that garrison said after the bombing:

> It seems as if all fighting is useless, and all sacrifices are vain.[8]

Calais, bombed on the 20th, 25th and 27th of September, surrendered on the 30th. The Army was, on the whole, well pleased.

Others, however, were less enchanted by some aspects of these activities; Coningham noted

> a marked tendency for the ground forces to submit demands for concentrated disruptive air attacks against centres of road communications,

ranging in size from large towns to insignificant villages. Until we reached the German border such attacks entailed the wasteful destruction of habitations and the unavoidable heavy loss of life of friendly nationals in the occupied areas.[9]

It was a policy which opened up once more the controversy which had arisen over interdiction, but with the difference that the Allies were not now on the threshhold of a critical venture into unknown perils, but in the full flight of triumphant success. Coningham disliked this tactic greatly:

> In many instances I rejected requests for ploughing up of villages in open country by heavy bombers. I am of the definite opinion that concentrated area attacks by heavy bombers against small towns and villages away from the main roads leading to the battlefield are wasteful, because they do not achieve their object, which is to delay movement of enemy reserves ... Furthermore, when considering the wholesale destruction of large towns to assist their capture by the Army, it does not always make such objectives any easier to capture by the soldiers.[10]

He remarked on the phenomenon encountered in Sicily and repeated with emphasis at Cassino: "the damaged areas are actually improved as centres of defence by snipers and special detachments of the enemy". Examples supporting his argument against the massive destruction of towns, he said, were afforded by Caen, St Lô and Villers Bocage in Normandy, Le Havre and Boulogne (whatever the Army might say), and Nijmegen and Arnhem in Holland. German towns, of course, he viewed differently; his thoughts on this matter, as usual firmly expressed, are worth following to their conclusion because they strike a note not very frequently heard at that time:

> The bombing of friendly towns during the campaign, and the insistence by the Army Commanders that it was a military necessity caused me more personal worry and sorrow than I can say. My resistance, apart from humanitarian grounds, was due to a conviction, since confirmed, that in most cases we were harming Allies and ourselves eventually more than the enemy. *I thought, also, of the good name of our forces, and particularly of the Air Force.* It is a sad fact that the Air Forces will get practically all blame for destruction which, in almost every case, was due to Army demands. On many occasions, owing to the organisation of command, I was over-ruled and then came the "blotting" by strategic bombers who, on their experience with German targets, tended to over-hit. Ample factual evidence will now be forthcoming, and I hope that, in future, it will not be thought that the sight and sound of bombers, and their uplift effect on morale, is proportional to the damage they do to the enemy.[11]

Comment seems superfluous, except to note that bad habits die hard, and that Coningham's Despatch might, accordingly, have made instructive reading in Vietnam in the 1970s.

In September 1944 the atmosphere throughout the Allied forces in the West was heady and impatient; a very natural desire to finish the war by Christmas mingled with an equally natural belief that this was well within their powers. It would have been astonishing if there had been no dispute about how to do it; in fact, of course, there was plenty. Dispute had surrounded, from first to last, the Allied landing in the South of France (Operation DRAGOON) which took place on August 15, with effects on the campaign in Italy that we have noticed (p. 597), and which was now in full cry towards the north. Good idea or bad, the operation itself was entirely successful, more like a parade than a warlike advance, and on September 11 these Allied forces made contact with the main body of General Eisenhower's command, into which they were now integrated. The advance of the main body itself was performed to the accompaniment of more dispute, which in due course swelled to dangerous proportions. It centred around a divergence of strategic view which could not be reconciled by any compromise; and this, in turn, centred around a single factor – supply. By the end of August, the Allies had over two million men ashore in Europe, with nearly half a million vehicles; they did not have a single major port in working order on the Atlantic and Channel coasts. From this Montgomery argued that only one really powerful thrust was possible, and it should be made on the left flank, striking across the lower Rhine at the Ruhr and straight on to Berlin. However, strategy, like politics, is usually "the art of the possible", and it was very clear at SHAEF that this proposal – which included taking the American First Army from Bradley's just formed 12th Army Group[12] and placing it once more under Montgomery's command, while Patton's Third Army was deliberately reined in after a magnificent dash through France – whatever its strategic merits was simply not practical politics. The American forces were now preponderant and swelling; the British were in decline. Neither the American Government nor the American people would have accepted a strategy which flew in the face of such a fundamental fact. Leaving aside detailed pros and cons of Montgomery's proposal, it is to be remarked, however, that since his first bold, and excellent, plan for the Battle of Normandy had failed because his army was not able to carry it out, a serious question-mark hangs over this next daring proposal for the same reason. Even if, by some miracle of abnegation, the American Government had sanctioned the plan, is there any evidence that the 21st Army Group could

667

have performed it? It is Chester Wilmot, who observed it at close quarters and with considerable affection, who says that "the gravest shortcoming of the British Army" at that stage of the war was

> the reluctance of commanders at all levels to call upon their troops to press on regardless of losses, even in operations which were likely to shorten the war . . . [13]

The truth of these words was shortly to be seen again (during the attempt to relieve Arnhem), and they constitute a fairly devastating commentary on the Montgomery plan.

The truth is that the Field-Marshal (he was promoted on September 1) was at this juncture a considerable distance below his best. His faith in the "single thrust" impelled him to make what Richard Lamb has called "the two worst military decisions of his career".[14] The first was his extraordinary neglect of Antwerp, the great port whose capture and clearance promised immense alleviation of the logistical difficulties which beset the Allies. Antwerp to Montgomery, like Crete to Wavell, was in Ronald Lewin's words,

> his blind spot . . . a damning error of oversight by a normally alert commander whose attention was otherwise engaged.[15]

Instead of being fixed on the precious prize of Antwerp, Montgomery's eyes were looking across the Rhine – and towards a large, hazardous airborne operation which would give him his bridgehead. We cannot here examine in detail the endlessly recounted story of Operation MARKET GARDEN which took the British First Airborne Division to Arnhem in September 1944. It has to be said, however, that there is no aspect of the preparation of that tragic fiasco that does not fill one with dismay. The idea of pushing a vulnerable force far out on a limb only approachable along the defiles of exposed Dutch roads between the dykes; the lack of liaison between 21 Army Group and the First Allied Airborne Army; the defiant neglect of Intelligence about German concentrations, especially of armour; the failure to coordinate Tactical Air action; the gamble on the autumn weather – all add up to a recipe for disaster which could only have one result in the face of the German Army, even in September 1944. Even the choice of Arnhem as a target, says Lamb, was wrong – Montgomery's second fatal decision. Wesel, just across the German frontier, in the opinion of qualified officers, was the place to go to.

It was thus under a shadow of doom that MARKET GARDEN, the greatest airborne action of the war, was launched. And it would be deeply unfair not to state at once that two-thirds of the operation, the seizing of the bridgeheads over the Rivers Maas and Waal by the American 101st and 82nd Airborne Divisions, were a clear success. But what mattered was the Rhine, and Arnhem, and what happened there is all too familiar history. In Richard Lamb's words:

> Montgomery's decision to take the Arnhem option, in despite of warnings from his staff and of evidence of enemy strength, resulted in resounding defeat. He wasted the Allies' strategic reserve, a force which could have brought victory in 1944, and sacrificed the cream of the British Army . . . [16]

We return here to the bitter lesson of D–Day – the sheer wasteful-ness of the airborne style of war. The superb First Airborne Division had seen no action in its proper rôle since Sicily in July 1943; in 1944 no fewer than seventeen operations were planned, then cancelled; at Arnhem its losses were nearly 7,000 (1,300 killed); and the division never fought again. This was not sensible. And in addition to the waste of *élite* troops, there was the diversion of air effort in these ambitious actions, especially air transport, of which the RAF certainly did not have any to spare. Coningham is scathing on this subject:

> The plans of the First Allied Airborne Army . . . entailed tying up a great deal of transport aircraft which would otherwise have been available for the ground and air forces during the advance . . . I am of the opinion that a review will show that the "freezing" of air transport during a week of fine weather, with ample ground suitable for landings, when the American and British armies were only halted through lack of fuel and ammunition supply, was the decisive factor in preventing our armies reaching the Rhine before the onset of winter. [17]

This is blunt criticism, but it must be added that in Coningham's own department there were curious deficiencies, fatal to MARKET GARDEN. His own headquarters was in the process of moving to Brussels while the plans were being finalized in great haste at First Allied Airborne Army Headquarters in England. The Official History tells us:

> Second Tactical Air Force's representative missed an important planning conference for this operation when bad weather prevented his flying from Belgium and his point of view was not represented. [18]

It is extraordinary that Coningham was prepared to accept this situation – especially in view of what the Airborne Army plan contained. It is equally astonishing, of course, that General Brereton, that Army's commander, and an ex-Tactical Air Force commander himself, should also have accepted it. It is astonishing that Montgomery and the 21st Army Group Staff accepted it. For what was laid down was this:

> In the final plan the local tactical air group (83 Group) was ordered to be grounded during the time of airlifts and resupply. When these were postponed for several hours because of bad weather in England, 83 Group's aircraft remained grounded till released from England. During those hours the whole Arnhem operation had no close air support from Second Tactical Air Force.[19]

It remains only to recall that the entire Arnhem battle was dogged by bad weather, and that out of 95 calls for air support the RAF, for one reason or another, could only respond to 49,[20] and the lineaments of tragedy are clearly drawn.

It was not only a tragedy for the First Airborne Division in its gallant ten-day struggle against hopeless odds. It was a tragedy for Allied hopes and expectations. With the Arnhem failure died all prospects of ending the war in 1944. The Allies, shocked at their setback after such excellent progress, now concentrated on setting their logistical house in order – clearing the ports and building up supplies. Of these, petrol was the most important; in the 21st Army Group, at the end of August, there was a vehicle to every four men (every five men in the US armies) – an enormous petrol requirement, to say nothing of the aviation spirit required for the air forces. The build-up was a necessary task, but until it was completed active operations naturally died away; Montgomery was disgusted to see the SHAEF policy of a side-by-side advance of all armies to the Rhine being implemented, and his "single thrust" relegated to the "ifs" of history. The penalty of the pause, and the "broad front" strategy, needless to say, was that it gave the Germans a badly needed breathing-space, a chance to regroup and rebuild their forces which they seized with both hands. Montgomery's vociferous protests did permanent damage to his personal relations with Eisenhower, and considerable damage to Anglo-American relations during the final stage of the war.

80 Portal and Harris; Dresden; the final acts

It was against a general background of disappointment and dissension that certain significant command changes now took place. It will be convenient, for once, to deal with these in reverse chronological order. In October, Leigh-Mallory was appointed to the command of the Allied Air Forces in South-East Asia (SEAC); he departed from SHAEF on October 16, and it was decided not to replace him. As we have seen, his position had frequently been anomalous, never happy; as Coningham said (see p. 608), the "extra Headquarters in the Air Force chain of command" had, indeed, caused constant difficulties. Sir Trafford Leigh-Mallory's end was in keeping with this whole sad phase of his career; on November 14 he and his wife were killed when the York that was taking him to the Far East crashed in bad weather near Grenoble.

> So perished one of the most experienced officers of the Royal Air Force
> . . . his loss was one which [it] could ill afford.[1]

Coningham now came directly under Tedder, who acted as coordinator of air operations for the Supreme Commander. Coupled with the move of Second TAF HQ to Brussels, this should have eased Coningham's relations with Montgomery; as we have seen, it did not, and we have seen why (p. 657).

These were bad days for the "highest degree of intimacy" which Churchill had applauded on June 6 – intimacy between Allies, and intimacy between commanders, even in the same Service. The clear division of opinion between Eisenhower and Montgomery was now to be matched by one between Portal and the Commander-in-Chief of Bomber Command. This resulted, not altogether surprisingly, when in mid-September the Combined Chiefs of Staff decided to resume direct control of the Strategic Bomber Forces, nominating Portal and General Arnold as their executive officers. The decision terminated Air Chief Marshal Harris's subordination to the "direction" of the Supreme Allied Commander for OVERLORD, the only period, according to Webster and Frankland, when he "did really subordinate himself".[2] The new command structure was decreed in a Directive of September 14, shortly followed (September 25) by a second, stating Bomber Command's new priorities:

First priority
(i)   Petroleum industry, with special emphasis on petrol (gasoline) including storage.

Second priority
(ii)   The German rail and waterborne transportation systems.
(iii) Tank production plants and depôts, ordnance depôts.
(iv) MT production plants and depôts[3]

To General Spaatz, this was music; he had from the first advocated an all-out attack on German oil production, and had, indeed, begun his own campaign against that target system as far back as March, with some effect, as we have seen. Harris, however, was very far from pleased.

To Harris, the release (though it was never absolute) from commitment to helping the ground forces spelt a long- and erroneously delayed return to the destruction of German cities which he unfalteringly believed to be the best and quickest way to end the war. The Air Staff, on the other hand, after initial scepticism founded on bad memories of 1940 and 1941,[4] had warmed towards Spaatz's oil plan; by the autumn of 1944, recognizing how different conditions, weapons and equipment were from those of 1941, the Air Staff considered oil to be "a fundamental and potentially war-winning target system".[5] It is difficult, now, to challenge this; what, after all, was the value of Germany's soaring tank and aircraft production (see p. 557) if neither could move? There was, however, another suggestion to offer, which did not rule out a powerful and sustained offensive against oil; it came from Tedder.

It was Tedder's outstanding characteristic that he could generally take a broader view of any given situation than most of his contemporaries. He believed as firmly as ever what he had told Admiral Cunningham in June 1941, that modern war was "a combined operation in the full sense of that term" (see pp. 343–4 etc.). He saw land, sea and air rôles as mutually supporting; on October 25 he told Portal:

> As I see it, there are two methods of ending this war, one is by land invasion and the other is by breaking the enemy's power and control behind the lines. *I, myself, do not believe that these two courses are alternative or conflicting. I believe they are complementary.* I do not believe that by concentrating our whole Air effort on the ground battle area we shall shorten the war. Nor do I believe that we would shorten the war by putting our whole Bomber effort against industrial and political targets inside Germany ... The various operations should fit into one comprehensive

672

pattern, whereas I feel that at present they are more like a patchwork quilt.[6]

In essence, while agreeing that the oil plan constituted a decisive threat to German communication by road and by air, Tedder wanted to broaden the target to attack *all* communications, railways, rivers and canals as well, thus strangling industry, governmental control, life itself. Concentrated upon such an area as the Ruhr, and linked to a powerful ground offensive, he was convinced that this would be decisive and again it is hard to disagree. Obviously, there was no fundamental conflict between the oil plan favoured by Portal and the Air Staff, and Tedder's larger concept which would include it. The odd man out was Harris.

To Bomber Command's formidable commander-in-chief, the oil plan was another blatant example of the "panaceas" that he detested. It was not, he remarked, the only one; the Special Operations Executive was pressing him with urgent demands; the Admiralty was once more in a state of considerable (and, as we have seen, justifiable) alarm about U-boat developments; the armies still had a call on his resources. And meanwhile his true task awaited a completion which appeared to him to be temptingly close, but which he was now being instructed to ignore. It was a sore trial. The great qualities of Sir Arthur Harris were his power of command, "the fearless conviction with which he approached his tasks and the single-minded courage with which he carried them out".[7] These very attributes now impelled him into what became a distinctly unedifying collison of wills with the Air Staff, and Portal in particular as its Chief, sadly continuing into 1945. The net result of it was not even an agreed compromise, which held dangers enough, but the perpetuation of Tedder's "patchwork quilt". And in the course of it the tempers of the two main contestants were severely tested, and relations between them damaged, though not, perhaps, to the degree of those between Eisenhower and Montgomery.

To some extent, it has to be admitted, a "patchwork" was inevitable; harnessing the whole heavy bomber effort to a single target system was always a pipe dream. Bomber Command, it should be noted, never ceased to attack German cities, even at the height of its commitment to OVERLORD; Harris, indeed, alleged that during that "diversion" he had still succeeded "in maintaining a destruction rate of two and a half cities per month".[8] In August, with some reluctance (again founded on past experience, particularly Augsburg in April 1942), Harris had permitted the trial of large-scale daylight operations against

Germany. In the new conditions of complete air superiority, they were at once successful; bombing was shown to be accurate and well concentrated, casualties were few, and almost entirely due to *flak*. The diversity of calls on Bomber Command was well illustrated in September. This was the month in which Operation PARAVANE was mounted, probably the most remarkable of all the Command's activities, in that it involved operating two squadrons (9 and 617) from the Soviet Union against the battleship *Tirpitz*.[9] On September 11, 379 bombers made three separate daylight attacks on oil targets in the Ruhr, all successful, at a cost of nine aircraft. On the 17th, the Command attacked *flak* positions and airfields in support of MARKET GARDEN. On the 23rd, No. 617 Squadron was again active with "Tallboys", breaching the Dortmund-Ems Canal (see p. 455). They were exciting days for the aircrews as well as their commander:

> Tremendous striking power was available. Undreamt-of versatility had been acquired. Command of the air had been won. Huge armies stood ready to exploit the injuries which could be inflicted. Already, even after the limited effort which had been devoted to it, the German oil position was one of acute crisis.[10]

On all targets, in the last three months of 1944, Bomber Command dropped 163,000 tons of bombs – an amazing total, which would be surpassed in 1945. Indeed, so heavy was the bomb deluge by now that an unexpected crisis arose. The maid-of-all-work of Bomber Command operations was the 1,000-lb medium capacity bomb; in 1944 alone more than 200,000 of these bombs were dropped:

> As a result of this enormous and steadily increasing consumption it was not long before we were faced with the bogey of the limited industrial capacity of this country ... By the spring of 1945 the supply of high-explosive bombs for the joint air forces was critical in the extreme. At the end of March we in this country were scraping the bottom of the locker for these weapons. There were only three weeks' supplies in stock. The success of the whole campaign was in jeopardy.[11]

During the last six months of the war, Bomber Command had, as Harris says, "to live all the time from hand to mouth".[12] It was thus even more important than immediately appears that the bombs should be directed at the most profitable targets; it is instructive to note what the distribution of Bomber Command's effort was in the last three months of that momentous year, 1944:

674

Attacks on cities	53 per cent
Attacks on railways and canals	15 per cent
Attacks on oil targets	14 per cent
Attacks on enemy troops and fortifications	13 per cent
Attacks on naval and other objectives	5 per cent[13]

It is apparent from this table that Portal and the Air Staff were not winning their argument with Sir Arthur Harris.

December 1944 saw the last flicker of German military strength in the West: the Ardennes offensive which opened on December 16 and continued into January. Its initial success was the price the Allies paid for their failure to complete the destruction of the enemy's forces in the autumn; it is also one more tribute, if any were needed, to the resilience, stubborn skill and courage of the German Army. Yet it must be noted that this success was very largely dependent on the bad December weather which prohibited air reconnaissance and air support. The moment the weather turned, the tide of battle turned – one of the most vivid demonstrations of the decisive quality of air power. The fact that by the end of the battle the German forces were running out of oil merely underlines the point. Allied airmen were quick to point out another feature; particularly interesting from the British point of view, says Coningham, was the fact that

> the plan of attack, which we later captured, followed closely the plan which was put into effect in 1940 by the same German commander, von Rundstedt, using approximately the same ground forces and the same faulty tactics in using his air forces primarily in direct support of his Army instead of ensuring first that he established air superiority in the tactical area of the battle.[14]

The complete failure to concentrate the *Luftwaffe's* remaining strength over the battlefield, he says, was "due to the long-range tactics which our Tactical Air Forces employed in neutralising as many as possible of the enemy air bases". Undoubtedly this played an important part; yet it is very doubtful whether the German Air Force, at that stage, could by any means have achieved more than the smallest flash in the pan. Such, indeed, was precisely what it did achieve in its surprise attack on Second TAF's overcrowded airfields on New Year's Day, 1945. For this occasion the Germans assembled, in great secrecy, between 750–800 fighters drawing them from as far afield as Vienna and Prague and, like Harris for his "Thousand Plans", using training units to make up numbers. Preserving complete radio silence, they achieved absolute surprise over 16 Allied airfields in Belgium and Holland and one in France. As a result, they were able to destroy 150 Allied aircraft, and damage 111 more; personnel losses were 145 wounded and 46 killed, of whom only six were pilots in combat. But German losses, due almost entirely to inexperience, were catastrophic: 270 aircraft destroyed and 40 damaged, and 260 aircrew lost.[15] As General Galland said, this was "the final dagger thrust in the back of the *Luftwaffe*",[16] "in this forced action we sacrificed our last substance".[17] He writes the epitaph of the weak, once all-too-familiar to Germany's enemies:

> The *Luftwaffe* received its death blow at the Ardennes offensive.[18]

Portal and Harris did not compose their differences. By mid-January these were so acute, and the prospect of reconciling their views so remote, that Harris asked the Chief of the Air Staff to

> consider whether it is best for the prosecution of the war and the success of our arms, which alone matters, that I should remain in this situation.[19]

This suggestion, as the Official History says,

> confronted Sir Charles Portal with a most delicate decision. If he replaced Sir Arthur Harris he would be sacrificing a Commander-in-Chief with greater prestige than any other in the Royal Air Force. If he did not, he would undoubtedly experience much difficulty in pressing his views further . . .[20]

And always, of course, when the question of removing a very senior officer comes up, there is the question of replacement, and the effect upon the morale of the Command concerned (factors which undoubtedly weighed against critics of Montgomery). How Portal would have answered those questions is not easy to see. He replied to Harris on January 20, saying

> We must wait until after the war before we can know for certain who was right and I sincerely hope that until then you will continue in command of the force which has done so much towards defeating the enemy and has brought such credit and renown to yourself and to the Air Force.[21]

The Official Historians comment:

> No other course at this stage of the war was open to Sir Charles Portal which would not have been a remedy worse than the disease.

This is undoubtedly correct; Portal, like others before him, had fallen foul of the prestige which builds up in democracies around military commanders in war. It is the reverse face of the savagery with which they are pursued when they fail, even when that is no fault of their own. And, of course, commanders who do not have prestige are unlikely to be much sought after. Nevertheless, the end product of this defeat of the Air Staff – for such it was – as the Official History adds, "was neither success nor satisfaction either for Sir Arthur Harris or for Sir Charles Portal".[22] For Portal, the acceptance of what he knew to be a wrong emphasis in bombing policy could only mean a loss of authority (from whose consequences he was only saved by the swift end of the European war); for Harris and his Command, it meant that their prolonged and valiant effort would fall at the last under a shadow which, in future decades, would sadly diminish recognition of their high endeavour. For amid the list of cities on Bomber Command's agenda, awaiting the Harris treatment, was Dresden.

Dresden, capital of Saxony, was another of those ancient German towns which were, in Harris's depressing words, "built more like a fire-lighter than a human habitation" (see p. 476); that is to say, its centre was a maze of narrow streets with old timbered houses. Its normal population of over 600,000 was, in February 1945, swollen with refugees from the bombing of other towns, and from the remorseless advance of the Soviet armies. There were, in addition, a certain number of Allied prisoners of war in the city. As a military centre it would appear to have had no outstanding significance – but Harris's area attacks were not concerned with military centres; they were concerned with morale, which, as we have seen, was a cosmetic word for massacre. Drawn by what Portal had apprehensively called "the magnetism of the remaining German cities",[23] Dresden found its place in the fatal schedules of city destruction by Bomber Command on the night of February 13/14, with follow-up action by the Eighth Air Force on February 14 and 15. The Bomber Command attack was carried out in two waves, totalling 805 aircraft, which dropped 2,659 tons of high-explosive and incendiary bombs. The two American attacks involved over 600 bombers:

> These blows, and particularly the Bomber Command night attack, proved utterly ruinous to the city where, on an even more fearful scale, scenes reminiscent of the Battle of Hamburg were re-enacted.[24]

The recoil from the destruction of Dresden began early, long before the details of it were known; Churchill, on March 28, 1945, told

677

Portal that it "remains a serious query against the conduct of Allied bombing".[25] The Official Historians call this "perhaps the least felicitous" of Churchill's war-time minutes, and he did in fact withdraw it, substituting another on April 1 which simply called for a review of area bombing "from the point of view of our own interests".[26] But the blaze started in the fire-storms of Dresden did not die down; the reverberations of the cataclysm continue to this day. In 1963, David Irving's book *The Destruction of Dresden* appeared, and electrified a large readership with a "best estimate" of the death-roll in Dresden in the region of 135,000 – which he compared with "71,379 at Hiroshima" on August 6. Revulsion against the whole Allied bombing policy of the Second World War was much stimulated by this, and by accompanying photographs, and not extinguished when Mr Irving himself candidly admitted his error in 1966 in a letter to *The Times*; in this, he quoted a report of the Dresden area police chief, of whose authenticity he said there was no doubt, giving a death-roll of 25,000 dead, and 35,000 "missing". This was the best information that could be extracted from East Germany; it means that Dresden's ordeal was on roughly the same scale as Hamburg's – a similar tragedy. Mr Irving, having "no interest in promoting or perpetuating false legends", hastened to publish this. Sharp and special criticism of the Dresden attack nevertheless continues,[27] some of it far from temperate, and clearly fuelled by Nuclear Disarmament postures which have nothing to do with history. At this juncture it will suffice to point out that in February 1945 the war had been going on for five and a half years; only the luxury of hindsight and the detachment of non-participation can undervalue the enormous sense of that weight of time, the intense desire to bring the whole business to an end as quickly as possible, that possessed not merely Bomber Command, or the Royal Air Force, but virtually the whole nation. The argument, sometimes heard, that it was "unnecessary" to bomb Dresden because the war was nearly over anyway is absurd. That was a thought that could only have reality after May 7; in February it was an unfact, and what mattered above all else to most people was to end the war as soon as possible by any and every means.[28]

It is very sad that this shadow should lie over Bomber Command's final efforts, for it seriously distorts their true sense. They were, as usual by now, close to the borders of fantasy. Certainly there must have been a strong sense of fantasy in the minds of 1939 survivors, surveying this vast force with its daily average availability of 1,420 aircraft, 1,305 of them being four-engined heavy bombers. In the four effective months of 1945, they dropped over 181,000 tons of bombs, which was in fact *nearly one fifth of the aggregate for the whole war* (see p. 537). In order to do so, they flew 67,483 sorties, from which 608 aircraft failed to return – less than 1 per cent. Such was the transformation of the war by total supremacy. And once more it is instructive to see how this immense effort was divided up:

Attacks on cities	66,482 tons	36.6 per cent
Attacks on troops and defences	26,081 tons	14.4 per cent
Attacks on transportation	28,102 tons	15.4 per cent
Attacks on naval targets	11,140 tons	6.1 per cent
Attacks on oil	47,510 tons	26.2 per cent
Attacks on the German Air Force	637 tons	0.4 per cent
Attacks on specific industries	1,236 tons	0.7 per cent
Miscellaneous	552 tons	0.2 per cent[29]

From this it is clear that Harris, while continuing to give priority to attacks on cities – 29 are listed as targets of "major area attacks" besides Dresden – had accepted some degree of compromise in the case of oil, and still divided or "diverted" his force amongst a selection of other tasks, "panaceas" or otherwise.

The truth is that comparison of percentages is here somewhat misleading; area bombing was now, in fact, obsolete. It represented only a third of the whole effort, and in terms of war-winning was far less significant than the 26 per cent now allocated to oil (added to the American contribution). With the diversification of Bomber Command's operations came certain changes: the Pathfinder Force lost importance, each Group now having to devise its own methods, its own expertise, in the light of its current task. With the resumption of daylight attacks, a wheel came full circle: this was what the Command had believed in implicitly in 1939–40, only to be proved dreadfully wrong; now, despite the basic unsuitability of the Lancasters and Halifaxes (lack of altitude, as compared with B–17s and B–24s), despite the lack of training in formation flying, and the weak .303 armament, Bomber Command could operate as freely by day as by night – thanks to air superiority and the ability to fly fighters from bases near to Germany. The irony was that the advantage of daylight bombing was much reduced by the increased value of new aids, especially OBOE, H2S III and G–H, and the great efficiency of the crews using them, which meant that precision and concentration could be achieved as well by night, or through ten-tenths cloud, as on a clear day.

The second full circle of the wheel was the return to an early Air

Staff choice with the oil attack – Plan WA5(c) of September 1, 1939. In 1945,

> Bomber Command carried out seventy-four operations against forty-nine oil targets, which involved the despatch of 12,588 sorties, from which 11,849 sorties resulted in 46,636 tons of bombs being aimed at the targets. Thirty-eight of these operations were carried out at night and thirty-six of them in daylight.[30]

The oil offensive constituted a haemorrhage which drained the life-blood of German industry and armed forces alike. It was a Combined offensive at last in the full sense, with the American Eighth and Fifteenth Air Forces taking their full (and larger) share; and it brought the German war machine virtually to a halt. Characteristically, after all his fulminations, it was Harris who paid it one of its most handsome tributes:

> In the weeks just before the end of the war all the German armed forces were immobilised by lack of fuel. The amount of oil produced by the synthetic oil plants and other factories was so little that it would not have paid the enemy to use up fuel in conveying it to the armed forces. The triumph of the offensive against oil was complete and indisputable.[31]

The 14.4 per cent of Bomber Command's final effort devoted to "troops and defences" included the last great set-piece of the OVER-LORD campaign: the Rhine crossing on March 23. This was a Combined Operation indeed, involving the full strength of 21st Army Group (including the American Ninth Army), landing-craft of the Royal Navy, Commandos, the 6th Airborne and American 17th Airborne Divisions, Bomber Command, Second TAF and the American Eighth and Ninth Air Forces. Once again, as for June 6, the Strategic Forces carried out an interdiction programme to isolate the Ruhr area, while the Tactical Forces, under Coningham, performed the full gamut of supporting operations according to the practice now so fully understood. Profiting by the Arnhem lesson, this time there was no division of responsibility in connection with the airborne operations; and these were on a scale to ensure immediate concentration in the dropping area: 1,500 aircraft and 1,300 gliders lifted 17,000 soldiers with 800 vehicles and guns and 600 tons of ammunition. It took this vast aerial swarm two and a half hours to pass a given point. On this occasion, in close proximity to the main ground forces, the airborne operation was a complete success – but so was the whole crossing, against a German resistance which was now visibly at its last gasp.

The end was not long delayed. American tanks reached the River Elbe on April 11, and by the 14th they had bridgeheads over the river and were poised for the last dash to Berlin. It never happened. On that day the astounded forward troops received Eisenhower's command to halt. The enormous implications of that simple statement constitute the fundamental theme of world history ever since that day. For by now Soviet preparations were complete; two and a half million men, under Marshals Zhukov and Koniev, stood poised for the last assault on the German capital where a, by now, crazed Adolf Hitler still played "the grandiose war game with arrows stabbing the maps and lines coiling round supposed positions, where none but the dead now lay".[32] The assault opened on April 16; in three and a half weeks of unimaginable warfare – in which 100,000 civilians became casualties, the Russians themselves lost 300,000 men, and the Germans 134,000 taken prisoner in Berlin alone, to say nothing of their dead and wounded – the thing was done. On May 7 Nazi Germany surrendered unconditionally to the Allies. The Nazi Empire was dead, like its creator, but the capitals of Europe – Berlin, Vienna, Prague, Budapest, Bucharest and Sofia – now passed behind an iron curtain guarding the frontiers of yet another tyranny.

The RAF did not give much thought to such matters on May 8; VE–Day was a day of relief and rejoicing. The last "op" in Europe was over, the last bomb gone; now the Royal Air Force could quit with honour the arduous, illustrious station it had so long held on the right of the line.

81 The right of the line

On May 1, 1945, the Royal Air Force had on charge 9,200 aircraft; it numbered, in all theatres, 1,079,835 officers, men and women, including those from the Dominions and the Allied forces serving with it (see p. 301). Of this total, 193,313 were aircrew – a greater number than its whole strength in 1939. Forty-six per cent of the pilots came from the Dominions; the total Dominion aircrew contribution for all theatres, 1939–45, was 134,000, out of a grand total of 340,000. The WAAF had reached its peak of recruitment to the other ranks in 1943, but its officer recruitment came to its peak in January 1945: 6,355; they were distributed across 15 types of duty, ranging from catering to meteorology, codes and ciphers, Intelligence, Security and Operations Rooms.[1]

From first to last, 1939–45, the Royal Air Force lost 70,253 officers, NCOs and airmen killed or missing on operations, the overwhelming majority of them being aircrew. This was the price of its victory, and of it by far the largest share fell to Bomber Command between September 1939 and May 1945: 47,268. This great number is the grim total of those lost on operations; it was the unique hazard of the airman's trade that a further 8,305 Bomber Command aircrew lost their lives in non-operational flying – training or accident. In addition, 1,570 ground crew (RAF and WAAF) were killed or lost their lives from other causes during that period, making a full total of 57,143. The aircrew total, 55,573, has special significance; in the First World War the officer losses of the British Empire included 38,834 killed, and this slaughter of the nation's *élite* was widely regarded as the most tragic and damaging aspect of that war. It was to avoid such a thing ever happening again that Britain turned her back on a Continental policy, and looked to the Air Force rather than the Army for salvation. Yet, as stated earlier, by and large RAF aircrew were exactly the same type of men as the officers of 1914–18; it is salutary to see how the pursuit of a "cheaper" policy brought in its train only a much higher cost.[2]

Of necessity, this account of the RAF's part in Hitler's war has been thematic, and therefore selective, and the author feels keenly how much has been left unsaid. To those who find their own individual, and probably invaluable, parts dismissed without mention, he can only offer the most sincere regret. Let us just recall the themes that have been developed. First, the belated and somewhat frenzied expansion of the RAF in the last few years of peace; here we recollect the astonishly far-sighted and effective measures taken under the aegis of Marshal of the Royal Air Force Sir Edward Ellington, including the development of radar, the specifications of the Hurricane and the Spitfire (with which we should couple the name of Air Marshal Sir Ralph Sorley) and the four-engined bombers. Secondly, Fighter Command's decisive defensive victory in 1940 which, like the Battle of the Marne in 1914, made sure that Hitler's short war would be a long one, thus giving time for the follies that would lose it. Thirdly, the equally decisive victory in the Battle of the Atlantic, reaching its climax when Coastal Command became the chief U-boat killer. These two triumphs stand at the top of the roll. In the long ordeal of the Desert and the Mediterranean we have seen the methods of air support and Army Cooperation forged which came to the thunderous conclusion of OVERLORD. And in OVERLORD, thanks to air superiority, we see the greatest contribution of the Western Alliance to Hitler's overthrow. It is inevitable and right that we should end with Bomber Command, whose operations began at three minutes after noon on September 3, 1939, and ended on the night of May 2/3, 1945, when 16 Mosquitoes of No. 608 Squadron dropped their bombs on Kiel.[3]

It was Bomber Command's task, at the cost that we have seen, to wage war against Germany when no other forces of the British Empire could reach her. Bomber Command, in the days of Britain's weakness, was her only offensive weapon. No one could foresee how long that weakness would last, or how grave it would become; but while it did last – for three arduous years – Bomber Command had no option but to "soldier on", like the infantry in France and Flanders in the First World War, irrespective of what we can now see to have been crippling weaknesses of its own. During that time it learnt again the truth of Lord Kitchener's sorrowful saying in 1915:

We cannot make war as we ought; we can only make it as we can.[4]

Bomber Command fought with the weapons and equipment that it had, by the methods that those weapons and equipment dictated. At first its efforts, though they seemed great to those making them, were puny in relation to the task. As they improved, the bomber offensive did huge damage to the German war machine, and if it never broke German morale as it had set out to do, it unquestionably sowed deep discouragement; and steadily, as Speer admitted (see p. 537), it caused such diversion of German resources, especially in anti-aircraft defences and labour on shelters and reconstruction, as to constitute in effect a "second front" of its own. It is a happy, not a cruel irony, that in the end the military operations which Harris so derided proved to be of the utmost value to his Command by gravely weakening Germany's night defence, and so drastically reducing the losses of his crews. As to the morality of the methods adopted in the bomber offensive, it will be apparent that to this author among others area bombing provides a most displeasing spectacle; but equally clear to me is the force of what Dr Noble Frankland told his audience at the Royal United Service Institution on December 13, 1961:

The great immorality open to us in 1940 and 1941 was to lose the war against Hitler's Germany. To have abandoned the only means of direct attack which we had at our disposal would have been a long step in that direction.[5]

We have followed in these pages the development of the winning aircraft; let our last thoughts be of the men. First there was Ellington, presiding over farsighted policies; then Newall, whose cheerful courage proved a great help when the bad times came. And then Portal, who remained as Chief of the Air Staff to the end; few officers have won such general and continuous praise as he. Cool consideration shows him not to have been quite the paragon often presented to our view. Brought up on the bomber doctrine with which Trenchard launched the RAF, it was Portal who espoused the utterly unreal 4,000-bomber policy in 1941; later he frigidly propounded the outright killing of 900,000 civilians and the injury of a million more – this frank proposal must surely be unique in modern history; his obstinate resistance to the idea of a long-range fighter was a serious disservice; his handling of people at times left much to be desired – one thinks of Dowding, Longmore and Harris; but his support of Tedder was first-class. Cold, remote, enigmatic, but obviously of very high intelligence, down the years he does not warm the heart. Yet there is no question that his cool, analytic sanity was a strong support to the Chiefs of Staff Committee, who all looked on their young colleague with great respect. He won the admiration – and, indeed, affection – of Churchill, which was a victory in its own right. Possibly his greatest successes, however, were with the Combined Chiefs of Staff; at a time when this was immensely important, he won the confidence and respect of the Americans also. They trusted him as a colleague, and acknowledged a quality of greatness in him. He was, in fact, a brilliant staff officer, a brilliant Chief of Staff. The Service that does not have one is poor indeed.

We come to Commanders – a different type of person – and great are the differences between each one of them. It would be hard to name a greater contrast than that between Dowding and Harris. Dowding was the unquestioned victor of the Battle of Britain, which, it could be said, he had begun to win years before it was fought. As we have seen, it was the "Dowding system" that defeated the *Luftwaffe* – with Park's able backing. Dowding goes down in history as the one airman with an indisputable victory in a recognizable battle of decisive importance to his name; it is a very special accolade. Harris does not possess one like it; his one very clear victory is the Battle of Hamburg, but no one could call that decisive. Yet no one, either, can doubt his quality of command; his handling of his great force was always with the sure touch of a leader, recognized by everyone in it. Portal told him, when it was all over, and the dust settling on their sharp dispute,

For the support you have always given me, and for your tremendous personal contribution to the achievement of the RAF in this war I can never adequately thank you . . .[6]

It is not possible to list truthfully the great British commanders of the Second World War without including the name of Marshal of the Royal Air Force Sir Arthur Harris; he reincarnated the qualities attributed to (and readily acknowledged by) Admiral Fisher in a previous generation – "ruthless, relentless, remorseless" – but punctuated their revelation with the display of a warm and magnanimous heart.

It is only possible to mention a few names out of a long list with qualities which served their country well. Three successive C-in-Cs of Coastal Command, Bowhill, Joubert and Slessor, must be among them. Theirs was a victory indeed. It is right to acknowledge Longmore, who played a weak hand with much finesse, and received poor reward for doing so. Sir Richard Peirse, whatever may have happened later in another place, had the unenviable rôle in 1941 of guiding Bomber Command through the very darkest of its valley of shadow; history is rarely kind to the men who meet the bad days; let us acknowledge the robust spirit with which Peirse tackled an impossible task. We come to the two whose names have shone in this narrative: Coningham, the practical artificer of Army Cooperation, who never lost sight of the factor decisive in it, and which could make it decisive in battle: air superiority. Flamboyant, outspoken, often a difficult colleague with a sharply critical mind and tongue, Coningham was one of the makers of victory. During the last year of the war, the forces under his command mounted to about 1,800 aircraft and 100,000 men, drawn from seven nations.[7] There was hardly a day when some – usually large – part of this great force was not actively promoting the victory which it is impossible to see as being feasible without it.

And finally, there was Tedder. Again, no particular decisive victory attaches to his name – such is the fate of most airmen. Harris, who clashed with him on more than one occasion, and stood for a totally different system of war, says that Tedder had "one of the most brilliant minds in any of the Services", and this was a common view among those who met him. It was, says Harris, "a genuinely scientific mind with all the detachment of the scientist".[8] The affinity between Tedder and Portal is revealing: it was a matching of two very clear, fine minds. But Tedder had what Portal did not have: he had a common touch, a nice informality which helped him greatly in an informal Service to

685

keep contact with his air and ground-crews; and he had the experience of dealing with a situation calling for the total commitment of all his forces to a continuous combined operation in what soon became a coalition war. Combination and coalition were matters not too well understood in any Service; each one, however, produced a name outstanding in this regard: Mountbatten, from the Navy, Alexander, from the Army – and from the RAF, Marshal of the Royal Air Force Lord Tedder. Broad vision, long sight, complete professionalism – such were the ingredients of Tedder's undoubted greatness.

When we look below the ranks of the highest commanders, amid so much heroism, so much military virtue, it becomes invidious to start naming names. The overwhelming majority of the RAF's million were to be found in the ground crew – that assembly of skilled, educated, individualistic, irreverent, dependable men without whose untiring labours the aircraft would not have flown, the operations would not have happened, the victory could never have been won, and this book would never have been written. The off-hand diffidence of their generation still causes many of them to brush aside their war service with comic or sardonic anecdotes, an attitude reflected in their scurrilous joyful songs, and summed up in what may almost be called the anthem of the "erks" – "Bless (or otherwise) 'Em All":

> Bless all the sergeants and WO1s,
> Bless all the corporals and their bleeding sons –
> We're saying good-bye to them all . . . etc., etc.

Many of them would rather die than admit to any pride in their part in what they like to present as a most almighty "eff-up" from beginning to end. "Binding" every inch of the way, they made victory possible; they were splendid.

And what of the aircrew, the flyers, the ones who left their burnt bones scattered over all of Europe? In those young men we may discern the many faces of courage, the constitution of heroes: in lonely cockpits at dizzy altitudes, quartering the treacherous and limitless sea, searching the Desert's hostile glare, brushing the peaks of high mountains, in the ferocity of low-level attack or the long, tense haul of a bombing mission, in fog, in deadly cold, in storm . . . on fire . . . in a prison camp . . . in a skin-grafting hospital . . . My title shows what I think of them: there is no prouder place, none deserving more honour, than the right of the line.

Empty your pockets, Tom, Dick and Harry,
Strip your identity; leave it behind.
Lawyer, garage-hand, grocer, don't tarry
With your own country, your own kind.

Leave all your letters. Suburb and township,
Green fen and grocery, slip-way and bay,
Hot-spring and prairie, smoke-stack and coal tip,
Leave in our keeping while you're away.

Tom, Dick and Harry, plain names and numbers,
Pilot, observer, and gunner depart.
Their personal litter only encumbers
Somebody's head, somebody's heart.[9]

APPENDIX A

Western Air Plans, September 1, 1939

Number	Task	Action by	Remarks
W.A.1	Attacking German Air Force	Air Ministry	Targets plotted; Operation Orders in draft form
W.A.1(b)	Attacking aerodromes in N.W. Germany	Air Ministry	Operation Orders prepared
W.A.2	Reconnaissance of Home Waters and E. Atlantic	Air Ministry Admiralty	Coastal Command war stations agreed with Royal Navy
W.A.3	Convoy protection in Home Waters and E. Atlantic	Air Ministry Admiralty	Coastal Command war stations agreed with Royal Navy
W.A.4	Attacking German military communications (rail, canal, road)	Air Ministry	Subject of close study by Air Ministry with War Office, British and French General Staffs
W.A.4(a)	Attacking communications in W. Germany during concentration period		
W.A.4(b)	Attacking German invasion of Low Countries and N. France		Discussion proceeding between British and French Staffs on rôle of Bomber Command
W.A.5	Attacking German manufacturing resources	Air Ministry	
W.A.5(a)	Attacking German war industry		Operation Orders issued to Groups
W.A.5(b)	Attacking Ruhr		As 5(a) but Operation Orders for night attack in preparation

W.A.5(c)	Attacking oil production		Operation Orders issued to Groups
W.A.6	Attacking Italian manufacturing resources		Plans to be prepared
W.A.7	Attacking enemy naval forces and bases operating against trade	Air Ministry Admiralty	
W.A.7(a)	Naval/Air attack on Wilhelmshaven		Operation Order issued to Groups
W.A.7(b)	Air attack on Wilhelmshaven		Operation Orders being prepared
W.A.8	Attacking German depôts and stores	Air Ministry	No preparation pending reconnaissance
W.A.9	Attacking Kiel Canal	Air Ministry	Plan prepared, but awaiting 1,000-lb bomb delivery
W.A.10	Attacking German shipping and ports in Baltic	Air Ministry Admiralty	Impracticable without more long-range aircraft
W.A.11	Attacking forests	Air Ministry	Embodied in W.A.5
W.A.12	Attacking German Fleet (or part) at sea	Air Ministry Admiralty	Standing Instructions prepared and agreed between Bomber and Coastal Commands
W.A.13	Attacking German Headquarters and Ministries in Berlin	Air Ministry	No appreciation prepared
W.A.14	Dropping propaganda leaflets	Air Ministry Foreign Office Stationery Office	Operation Orders issued to Groups
W.A.15	Operations against enemy shipping by "M" Mine	Air Ministry Admiralty	Plans prepared in concert with Naval Staff
W.A.16	Mining of German waterways	Air Ministry Admiralty	Political repercussions under discussion

APPENDIX B

"Diversions" of Bomber Command

Year	Activity	Cause
1939	Attacks on German Fleet	None other possible
	"Nickels"	Political decision
1940	Attacks on Norwegian airfields	Enemy action
	Battle of France	Enemy action
	Attacks on Italy	Enemy action
	Anti-invasion bombing	Enemy action
	"Blitz" retaliation	Political decision
1941	Battle of the Atlantic (1st Phase)	Enemy action
	"Circuses"	Fighter Command cooperation
	Middle East build-up	Enemy action
1942	Far East build-up	Enemy action
	Battle of Atlantic (2nd Phase)	Enemy action
	Attacks on U-boat construction	Enemy action
1943	Mediterranean: N. Africa, Italy	Allied agreement
1944	OVERLORD	Allied agreement
	V-Weapon sites	Enemy action
1945	Cooperation with ground forces	Allied agreement

APPENDIX C

The Crisis of the U-boat war: British, Allied and neutral shipping sunk, January 1942–May 1943

Month	Total Tonnage	Total Ships	Tonnage by U-boats	Ships by U-boats
1942				
January	419,907	106	327,357	62
February	679,632	154	476,451	85
March	834,164*	273*	537,980	95
April	674,457	132	431,664	74
May	705,050	151	607,247	125
June	834,196**	173**	700,235	144
July	618,133	128	476,065	96
August	661,133	123	544,410	108
September	567,327	114	485,413	98
October	637,833	101	619,417	94
November	807,754†	134†	729,160	119
December	348,902	73	330,816	60
Date not known	2,229	2		
Total	7,790,717	1,664	6,266,215	1,160

*North Atlantic: 534,064 tons, 95 ships
**North Atlantic: 623,545 tons, 124 ships
†North Atlantic: 508,707 tons, 83 ships

Month	Total Tonnage	Total Ships	Tonnage by U-boats	Ships by U-boats
1943				
January	261,359	50	203,128	37
February	403,062	73	359,328	63
March	693,389*	120*	627,377	108
April	344,680	64	327,943	56
May	299,428	58	264,852	50
Total	2,001,918	365	1,782,628	314

*North Atlantic: 476,349 tons, 82 ships

APPENDIX D

Sinkings of U-boats, January 1942–May 1943

Date 1942		Boat No.	Area	Killer
January	9	577	E. Mediterranean	**aircraft (230 Sqdn); patrol**
	12	374	E. Mediterranean	Royal Navy
	15	93	N. Atlantic	Royal Navy
February	2	581	N. Atlantic	Royal Navy
	6	82	N. Atlantic	Royal Navy
March	1	656	Newfoundland	**aircraft (US); convoy escort**
	14	133	Aegean	mine
	15	503	Newfoundland	**aircraft (US); convoy escort**
	24	655	Arctic	Royal Navy
	27	587	N. Atlantic	Royal Navy
	29	585	Arctic	Royal Navy
April	?	702	North Sea	unknown
	14	85	US east coast	US Navy
		252	N. Atlantic	Royal Navy
May	1	573	W. Mediterranean	**aircraft (233 Sqdn); patrol**
	2	74	W. Mediterranean	RN & **aircraft (202 Sqdn); patrol**
	9	352	US east coast	US Coastguard
	28	568	E. Mediterranean	Royal Navy
June	2	652	E. Mediterranean	**aircraft (203 Sqdn & Fleet Air Arm); patrol**
	13	157	Cuba	US Coastguard
	30	158	Bermuda	**aircraft (US); convoy escort** (6-month total: 21; 6½ by aircraft)

Date 1942		Boat No.	Area	Killer
July	3	215	US east coast	Royal Navy
	5	502	Bay of Biscay	**aircraft (172 Sqdn); patrol**
	6	153	Caribbean	**aircraft (US); patrol**
	7	701	US east coast	**aircraft (US); patrol**
	11	136	N. Atlantic	RN & French Navy
	15	576	US east coast	**aircraft (US); convoy escort** & ship
	17	751	Bay of Biscay	**aircraft (61 & 502 Sqdns); patrol**
	24	90	N. Atlantic	Royal Canadian Navy
	31	213	N. Atlantic	Royal Navy
		588	N. Atlantic	Royal Canadian Navy
		754	Nova Scotia	**aircraft (RCAF); patrol** (11; 5½ by aircraft)
August	1	166	Gulf of Mexico	**aircraft (US); convoy escort**
	3	355	Shetlands	Royal Navy
	4	372	E. Mediterranean	RN & **aircraft (203 Sqdn); patrol**
	6	612	Baltic	accident
		210	N. Atlantic	Royal Canadian Navy
	8	379	N. Atlantic	Royal Navy
	10	578	Bay of Biscay	**aircraft (311 Cz. Sqdn); patrol**
	20	464	Iceland	**aircraft (US); convoy escort**
	22	654	Caribbean	**aircraft (US); patrol**
	28	94	W. Indies	RCN & **aircraft (US); convoy escort** (10; 5 by aircraft)
September	1	756	N. Atlantic	**aircraft (US); convoy escort**
	2	222	Baltic	accident
	3	705	Bay of Biscay	**aircraft (77 Sqdn); patrol**
	9	446	Baltic	mine
	12	88	Arctic	Royal Navy
	14	589	Arctic	RN & **Fleet Air Arm**

Date 1942		Boat No.	Area	Killer
September	15	261	Faroes	aircraft (58 Sqdn); patrol
	16	457	Arctic	Royal Navy
	23	253	Arctic	aircraft (210 Sqdn); convoy escort
	27	165	Bay of Biscay	mine (10; 4½ by aircraft)
October	2	512	French Guiana	aircraft (US); patrol
	5	582	Iceland	aircraft (269 Sqdn); convoy escort
	8	179	Cape Town	Royal Navy
	9	171	Bay of Biscay	mine
	12	597	N. Atlantic	aircraft (120 Sqdn); convoy escort
	15	661	N. Atlantic	aircraft (120 Sqdn); convoy escort
		619	N. Atlantic	Royal Navy
	16	353	N. Atlantic	Royal Navy
	20	216	Bay of Biscay	aircraft (224 Sqdn); patrol
	22	412	Faroes	aircraft (179 Sqdn); patrol
	24	599	N. Atlantic	aircraft (224 Sqdn); convoy escort
	27	627	N. Atlantic	aircraft (206 Sqdn); convoy escort
	30	520	N. Atlantic	aircraft (RCAF); convoy escort
		559	E. Mediterranean	RN & aircraft (47 Sqdn); patrol
		658	Newfoundland	aircraft (RCAF); convoy escort
	?	116	Atlantic	unknown (16; 10½ by aircraft)
November	5	132	N. Atlantic	aircraft (120 Sqdn); convoy escort
		408	Iceland	aircraft (US); convoy escort
	12	272	Baltic	accident
		660	W. Mediterranean	Royal Navy

Date 1942		Boat No.	Area	Killer
November	13	605	W. Mediterranean	Royal Navy
	14	595	W. Mediterranean	**aircraft (500 Sqdn); patrol**
	15	259	W. Mediterranean	**aircraft (500 Sqdn); patrol**
		411	Gibraltar	Royal Navy
	16	173	N. Atlantic	US Navy
	17	331	W. Mediterranean	**aircraft (500 Sqdn & Fleet Air Arm); patrol**
	19	98	Gibraltar	**aircraft (608 Sqdn); patrol**
	20	184	N. Atlantic	Royal Navy
	21	517	N. Atlantic	**Fleet Air Arm** (13; 7 by aircraft)
December	8	254	N. Atlantic	**aircraft (120 Sqdn); convoy escort**
	10	611	N. Atlantic	**aircraft (US); convoy escort**
	15	626	N. Atlantic	US coastguard
	26	357	N. Atlantic	Royal Navy
	27	356	N. Atlantic	Royal Canadian Navy (5; 2 by aircraft)

Six-month totals: January–June: 21;   6½ by aircraft (30.9%)

July–December: 65;   34½ by aircraft (53%)

Date 1943		Boat No.	Area	Killer
January	6	164	Brazilian coast	**aircraft (US); convoy escort**
	13	224	W. Mediterranean	Royal Canadian Navy
		507	Brazilian coast	**aircraft (US); convoy escort**
	16	337	N. Atlantic	**aircraft (206 Sqdn); convoy escort**
	21	301	W. Mediterranean	RN submarine
	?	553	N. Atlantic	unknown (6; 3 by aircraft)

Date 1943		Boat No.	Area	Killer
February	3	265	N. Atlantic	**aircraft (206 Sqdn); convoy escort**
	4	187	N. Atlantic	Royal Navy
	7	609	N. Atlantic	French Navy
		624	N. Atlantic	**aircraft (220 Sqdn); convoy escort**
	10	519	Bay of Biscay	**aircraft (US); patrol**
	12	442	Gibraltar	**aircraft (48 Sqdn); convoy escort**
	14	620	Portugal	**aircraft (202 Sqdn); convoy escort**
	15	529	N. Atlantic	**aircraft (120 Sqdn); convoy escort**
	17	201	N. Atlantic	Royal Navy
		69	N. Atlantic	Royal Navy
		205	E. Mediterranean	**RN & aircraft (SAAF); convoy escort**
	19	562	E. Mediterranean	**RN & aircraft (38 Sqdn); convoy escort**
		268	Bay of Biscay	**aircraft (172 Sqdn); patrol**
	21	623	N. Atlantic	**aircraft (120 Sqdn); patrol**
		225	N. Atlantic	US Coastguard
	22	606	N. Atlantic	US Coastguard & Polish Navy
	23	443	W. Mediterranean	Royal Navy
		522	N. Atlantic	Royal Navy
	24	649	Baltic	accident (19; 9 by aircraft)
March	4	83	W. Mediterranean	**aircraft (500 Sqdn); patrol**
		87	N. Atlantic	Royal Canadian Navy
	7	633	Iceland	**aircraft (220 Sqdn); supporting convoy**
	8	156	W. Indies	**aircraft (US); patrol**
	11	444	N. Atlantic	RN & French Navy
		432	N. Atlantic	French Navy
	12	130	N. Atlantic	US Navy
	19	5	Baltic	accident

Date 1943		Boat No.	Area	Killer
March	20	384	N. Atlantic	**aircraft (201 Sqdn); convoy escort**
	22	665	Bay of Biscay	**aircraft (172 Sqdn); patrol**
		524	Canary Is.	**aircraft (US); patrol**
	25	469	Iceland	**aircraft (206 Sqdn); patrol**
	27	169	N. Atlantic	**aircraft (206 Sqdn); patrol**
	28	77	W. Mediterranean	**aircraft (48 & 233 Sqdns); patrol**
	?	163	Bay of Biscay	unknown (15; 9 by aircraft)
April	2	124	N. Atlantic	Royal Navy
	5	167	Canary Is.	**aircraft (233 Sqdn); patrol**
	6	635	N. Atlantic	Royal Navy
		632	N. Atlantic	**aircraft (86 Sqdn); convoy escort**
	7	644	Arctic	RN submarine
	10	376	Bay of Biscay	**aircraft (172 Sqdn); patrol**
	14	526	Bay of Biscay	Mine
	17	175	N. Atlantic	US Coastguard
	23	602	W. Mediterranean	unknown
		189	N. Atlantic	**aircraft (120 Sqdn); convoy escort**
		191	N. Atlantic	Royal Navy
	24	710	N. Atlantic	**aircraft (206 Sqdn); convoy escort**
	25	203	N. Atlantic	**Fleet Air Arm**
	27	174	Nova Scotia	**aircraft (US); convoy escort**
	30	227	Faroes	**aircraft (455 Sqdn RAAF); patrol** (15; 8 by aircraft)
May	2	332	Bay of Biscay	**aircraft (461 Sqdn RAAF); patrol**
	3	659	N. Atlantic	accident (collision)
		439	N. Atlantic	accident (collision)

Date 1943		Boat No.	Area	Killer
May	4	465	N. Atlantic	aircraft (86 Sqdn); convoy escort
		630	N. Atlantic	aircraft (RCAF); convoy escort
	5	192	N. Atlantic	Royal Navy
		638	N. Atlantic	Royal Navy
	6	125	N. Atlantic	Royal Navy
		438	N. Atlantic	Royal Navy
		531	N. Atlantic	Royal Navy
	7	447	Gibraltar	aircraft (233 Sqdn); patrol
		109	Bay of Biscay	aircraft (10 Sqdn RAAF); patrol
		663	Bay of Biscay	aircraft (58 Sqdn); patrol
	11	528	N. Atlantic	RN & aircraft (58 Sqdn); convoy escort
	12	186	N. Atlantic	Royal Navy
		89	N. Atlantic	RN & Fleet Air Arm
	13	456	N. Atlantic	RCN & aircraft (86 Sqdn & RCAF); escort
	14	266	N. Atlantic	aircraft (86 Sqdn); convoy escort
		657	N. Atlantic	aircraft (US); convoy escort
	15	753	N. Atlantic	unknown
		176	US east coast	aircraft (US); convoy escort
		463	Bay of Biscay	aircraft (58 Sqdn); patrol
	16	182	N. Atlantic	US Navy
	17	128	Brazilian coast	US Navy & aircraft (US); convoy escort
		640	N. Atlantic	Royal Navy
		646	Iceland	aircraft (269 Sqdn); patrol
	19	273	Iceland	aircraft (269 Sqdn); convoy escort
		209	N. Atlantic	Royal Navy
		954*	N. Atlantic	aircraft (120 Sqdn); convoy escort

Leutnant zur See Peter Dönitz, 21 years old, was lost in this boat.

Date 1943	Boat No.	Area	Killer
May	381	N. Atlantic	Royal Navy
20	258	N. Atlantic	**aircraft (120 Sqdn); convoy escort**
21	303	W. Mediterranean	RN submarine
22	569	N. Atlantic	**aircraft of US Navy**
23	752	N. Atlantic	**Fleet Air Arm**
25	414	W. Mediterranean	Royal Navy
	467	N. Atlantic	**aircraft (US); convoy escort**
26	436	N. Atlantic	Royal Navy
28	304	N. Atlantic	**aircraft (120 Sqdn); convoy escort**
	755	W. Mediterranean	**aircraft (608 Sqdn); patrol**
31	563	Bay of Biscay	**aircraft (58, 228, 10 RAAF Sqdns); patrol**
	440	Bay of Biscay	**aircraft (201 Sqdn); patrol** **(41; 23 by aircraft)**

Total sinkings, Jan.–May: 96; 52 by aircraft (54.17 per cent)

APPENDIX E

A Mass Air Force

Date	RAF		WAAF		Total		
	Officers	*Other Ranks*	*Officers*	*Other Ranks*	*Officers*	*Other Ranks*	
September 3, 1939	11,519	162,439	234	1,500	11,753	163,939	175,692
October 1, 1940	23,636	396,473	1,170	16,194	24,806	412,667	437,473
October 1, 1941	37,880	734,727	3,012	61,297	40,892	796,024	836,916
October 1, 1942	54,483	846,065	5,379	136,088	59,862	982,153	1,042,015
October 1, 1943	74,034	914,362	5,880	174,459†	79,914	1,088,821	1,168,735
October 1, 1944	92,577	907,600*	6,276	164,968	98,853	1,072,568**	1,171,421††
September 1, 1945	100,107*	840,760	5,638†	135,891	105,745**	971,013	1,076,758

*RAF: Officer maximum: July 1, 1945: 103,023
       Other Ranks maximum: January 1, 1944: 924,481
†WAAF: Officer maximum: January 1, 1945: 6,355
       Other Ranks maximum: July 1943: 175,861
**Total: Officer maximum: July 1, 1945: 109,256
       Other Ranks maximum: January 1, 1944: 1,095,261

††Grand total maximum: July 1, 1944: 1,185,833
Source: AHB/II/116/14 (*Manning Plans and Policy*) Appendix 3

APPENDIX F

Secretaries of State and Chiefs of Staff, 1933–45

Date	First Lord Admiralty	First Sea Lord	S. of S. for War	CIGS	S. of S. for Air	CAS
1933	Eyres Monsell	Adml. Chatfield	Ld. Hailsham	FM Montgomery-Massingberd	Ld. Londonderry	M/RAF J. Salmond ACM G. Salmond M/RAF E. Ellington
1935					Ld. Swinton	
1936	Sir S. Hoare		A. Duff Cooper	FM Deverell		ACM C. Newall
1937	A. Duff Cooper		L. Hore-Belisha	FM Ld. Gort	Sir K. Wood	
1938	Ld. Stanhope	Adml. R. Backhouse	O. Stanley			
1939	W. S. Churchill	AF D. Pound	A. Eden	FM Ironside		
1940	A. V. Alexander			Gen. J. Dill	Sir S. Hoare Sir A. Sinclair	ACM C. Portal
1941				Gen. A. Brooke		
1942			Sir J. Grigg			
1943		AF A. Cunningham				
1945	B. Bracken A. V. Alexander		F. Lawson		H. Macmillan	

Note:
AF = Admiral of the Fleet
FM = Field-Marshal
M/RAF = Marshal of the Royal Air Force
ACM = Air Chief Marshal

Ministers of Defence:
1936 Sir Thomas Inskip
1939 Lord Chatfield
1940 Rt. Hon. W. S. Churchill

APPENDIX G

Sir Charles Portal and the long-range fighter question

My repeated assertion of the direct involvement of Sir Charles Portal, while CAS, in the question of long-range fighters for the RAF, and his personal opposition to such a weapon, has been questioned. Yet it is strongly documented in the Official History (The Strategic Air Offensive Against Germany; Webster and Frankland). As is so often the case, it is a long story, not to be comprehended purely in terms of the POINTBLANK difficulties of 1943.

The question first arose in connection with the "circus" operations of 1941. Webster and Frankland inform us (i, p. 239):

> Only increased range could confer the operational initiative upon the British fighters, but it was Sir Charles Portal's conviction that "increased range can only be provided at the expense of performance and manoeuvrability. 'The long range fighter', he told the Prime Minister [on May 27] 1941, 'whether built specifically as such, or whether given increased range by fitting extra tanks, will be at a disadvantage compared with the short range high performance fighter.'"
>
> In this crucial judgment, which was supported by much experience, Sir Charles Portal was eventually shown to have been wrong.

A week later (June 3) replying to Churchill's urging that fighter range must be increased, Portal repeated his conviction

> that long-range fighters could never hold their own against short-range fighters and were suitable for "regular employment only in areas where they will not be opposed by enemy short range fighters" (ibid, pp. 177 and 296 above).

In 1942 there was serious consideration of daylight bombing of Germany, and this was, of course, the favoured strategy of the US Army Air Force. It was, say Webster and Frankland (ibid, p. 449), viewed pessimistically by the Air Staff, "and *especially Sir Charles Portal himself*" (my italics). They continue:

> The clear realization of the limited offensive potential of Fighter Command did not result in efforts to extend the range of that force. Indeed, Sir Charles Portal was convinced that the production or modification of an aircraft with the range of a heavy bomber and the performance of an interceptor fighter was a technical impossibility.

703

This attitude led, as might be expected, to sharp disagreements with the Americans in 1943, and it is not open to doubt that, as far as General Arnold was concerned, Portal's responsibility for the effectiveness or otherwise of Fighter Command was unquestionable. He found the spectacle of a fighter force which Portal stated to consist of 1,461 aircraft with crews remaining inactive while his bombers were being shot out of the sky both incomprehensible and unacceptable. His direct correspondence with Portal on this subject in October is quoted freely in Webster and Frankland, ii, pp. 42–5. He even, at one stage, in order to demonstrate his point, "caused some Spitfires to be specially equipped and to fly the Atlantic" (p. 44, f.n. 1). Portal, however, was unmoved; the Official Historians conclude:

> Certainly, Sir Charles Portal saw no prospect of engaging the Royal Air Force Fighter Command effectively in the POINTBLANK campaign. He had never accepted the proposition of a long-range fighter which could effectively engage opposing short-range, or interceptor fighters . . .

The advent of the P-51B in December 1943 settled the matter; it is clear that it constituted a blind spot in Portal's war direction in what Webster and Frankland rightly call a "crucial" area. Once more (see p. 153) one remarks that if Sir Edward Ellington had responded to the advent of Hurricanes and Spitfires with similar scepticism, Britain's plight would have been serious indeed.

Notes

Part I: The Preparation

1. *Beginnings* p. 3–p. 6

1. Air Historical Branch Monograph. *The Expansion of the RAF 1934–1939*, Index No. AHB/II/116/17. The AHB monographs and narratives, covering every aspect of the Service in World War II, were compiled soon after the war, with access to official documents, Cabinet papers, etc., then restricted and available only to Official Historians. This particular monograph was written by J. M. Spaight, a noted authority on air power in the 1920s and 1930s.
2. Lord Templewood, in *Empire of the Air*, Collins, 1957, p. 49, attributes this to "Churchill's flamboyant preference for the title of Marshal". Sir Winston Churchill was Secretary of State for Air and War, 1919–1921. Lord Templewood, as Sir Samuel Hoare, was Secretary of State for Air three times: 1922–1924, 1924–1929, and for one month in 1940.
3. Sir Maurice Dean, KCB, KCMG; he became Private Secretary to the Chief of the Air Staff in 1934 and subsequently Head of the Air Staff Secretariat. In *The Royal Air Force and Two World Wars*, Cassell, 1979, p. 77, he says: "By May 1945 the strength of the Royal Air Force, including Dominion and Allied officers and airmen, amounted to some 1,080,000 of whom over 190,000 were aircrew."

   Let this serve as our introduction to a general lack of statistical consistency which makes research in this field unusually difficult. Thus the AHB Monograph, *Manning Plans and Policy* (AHB/II/116/14), in Appendix 3 gives a table showing:

RAF other ranks maximum reached, Jan. 1944	924,481
Officer maximum reached, July 1945	103,023
Grand total maximum, July 1944	1,185,833

   The same source shows:

Grand total, May 1945	1,113,315
of whom Women's Auxiliary Air Force	157,286

   On the other hand, Cmd. 6832, *Strength and Casualties of the Armed Forces and Auxiliary Services of the United Kingdom 1939 to 1945* (June 1946) shows:

Peak strength, June 1944	1,012,000
declining in June 1945 to	963,000

   Similar discrepancies and contradictions will recur.

4. AHB/II/116/14, op. cit., p. 172, says: "Altogether, the number of RAF trades, including those introduced especially for the Women's Auxiliary Air Force, increased from less than 50 on the outbreak of war to 190 by the middle of 1944."

The WAAF was formed in June 1939; by July 1944 it had 79 trades (see page 178, Chapter 17, note 16).

2. *Disarmers and bombers* p. 6–p. 15

1. Dean, op. cit., p. 39.
2. In Captain Stephen Roskill's *Hankey: Man of Secrets*, iii, p. 61, Collins, 1970 quoting Lord Hankey's diary, October 23, 1932, we read: "it would be worth a lot to get rid of submarines and aircraft (which I have advocated for a long time)."
3. Terraine, *The Mighty Continent*, Futura edition, 1974, p. 139.
4. AHB/II/116/17, pp. 30–1: "Reckon back 2½ years from January 1934 and one covers the whole active life of the Conference. Go on 2½ years, to mid-1936, and we were to be found already engaged in a fight with time. We lost that fight. How gladly should we have recalled, if we could, those two sterile years at Geneva. They were indeed the years which the locusts ate."
5. See *The Times History of the War (1914–1918)*, ii, pp. 180–2.
6. Quoted in the Official History, *The War in the Air*, vi, p. 136.
7. Major Raymond H. Fredette, *The First Battle of Britain 1917–1918 and the Birth of the Royal Air Force*, Cassell, 1966, p. 43.
8. Field-Marshal Sir William Robertson, *Soldiers and Statesmen 1914–1918*, ii, Cassell, 1926, p. 17; Robertson to Field-Marshal Sir Douglas Haig, July 9, 1917.
9. Once more we are in an area of statistical variation. All the figures quoted here are from the official compilation, *Statistics of the Military Effort of the British Empire During the Great War 1914–1920*, Part XXIV: "Airship and Aeroplane Raids over Great Britain and Bombardment of the Coast, with resulting Casualties", HMSO, 1922.
10. Quoted in the Official History (OH), *The Strategic Air Offensive Against Germany 1939–1945* by Sir Charles Webster and Noble Frankland, i, pp. 62–3; HMSO, 1961.
11. Templewood, op. cit., p. 37.
12. I. F. Clarke, *Voices Prophesying War 1763–1984*, p. 102, OUP, 1966.
13. Ibid, p. 169.
14. Richard Storry, *A History of Modern Japan*, p. 191, Pelican, 1960.
15. Uri Bialer, *The Shadow of the Bomber: The Fear of Air Attack and British Politics, 1932–1939*, p. 12, Royal Historical Society, 1980.
16. Dean, op. cit., p. 59.
17. Quoted in Dean, ibid.
18. Roskill, op. cit., p. 64.
19. Ibid, p. 43.

20. Quoted in *British Air Policy Between the Wars 1918–1939* by H. Montgomery Hyde, p. 283, Heinemann, 1976.
21. Royal United Service Institution *Journal* (RUSI), November 1966, p. 308, "The Problem of Civil Aviation in British Air Disarmament Policy, 1919–1934" by David Carlton.
22. AHB, II/16/17, pp. 30–1.
23. Churchill, *The World Crisis*, i, Odhams ed., 1938, p. 24.
24. Lord Hankey, *The Supreme Command 1914–1918*, i, p. 27, Allen & Unwin, 1961.

3. *A modern Air Force* p. 15–p. 24

1. See Denis Richards and Hilary Saunders, *Royal Air Force 1939–45*, i, p. 19, HMSO, 1974. (Denis Richards wrote Vol. I of this work, Richards and Hilary Saunders wrote Vol. II and Hilary Saunders Vol. III.)
2. Liddell Hart, *Memoirs*, i, pp. 150–1, Cassell, 1965.
3. The Defence Requirements Committee (DRC, not to be confused with the Defence Policy and Requirements Committee, DPRC, which replaced the Ministerial Committee on Disarmament, DC(M) as the reviewing body in July 1935) was set up in November 1934.
4. *Chief of Staff: The Diaries of Lieutenant-General Sir Henry Pownall*, i, p. 341, ed. Brian Bond, Leo Cooper, 1972.
5. Ibid, p. 36.
6. Ibid, p. 98.
7. Montgomery Hyde, op. cit., p. 57.
8. Dean, op. cit., p. 54.
9. AHB/II/116/17, p. 84, fn 2.
10. Derek Wood and Derek Dempster, *The Narrow Margin* (Arrow edition), p. 37, 1969. I owe much of the information in this section to this admirable book, which does much more than provide an authoritative blow-by-blow account of the Battle of Britain; it also thoroughly explores the technical context of that great victory, without which it would be incomprehensible.
11. AHB/II/116/17, p. 85.
12. Owen Thetford, *Aircraft of the RAF since 1918*, p. 306, Putnam, 1957. This, too, is an invaluable mine of information.
13. Ibid, p. 418.
14. Douglas Bader, *Fight for the Sky*, p. 12, Sidgwick & Jackson, 1973.
15. Andrew Boyle, *Trenchard*, p. 186, Collins, 1962.
16. OH (Webster & Frankland), i, pp. 54–5.
17. Dean, op. cit., p. 60.
18. Marshal of the RAF Sir Arthur Harris, *Bomber Offensive*, p. 59, Collins, 1947.
19. Churchill's *The Second World War*, iv, *The Hinge of Fate*, pp. 808–9, Cassell, contains a characteristic memorandum (December 7, 1942) to Lord Ismay on "Habbakuk": "I attach the greatest importance to the prompt examination of these ideas . . ." Volume v, *Closing the Ring*,

pp. 80–1, contains his account of the scene at the Quebec Conference when Lord Mountbatten demonstrated the qualities of "Pykrete", the ice mixture invented by Geoffrey Pyke, which was to be the basis of the floating ice field.

20. Richards and Saunders, op. cit., i, p. 23.
21. It is salutary to recall that the Gloster Gladiator, the RAF's last biplane fighter, did not enter squadron service until January 1937.
22. See pp. 72–94 for fuller treatment of this.
23. OH (Webster & Frankland), op. cit., i, p. 62, describe the pre-1936 system.
24. Ibid, p. 83.
25. Dean, op. cit., p. 66.

4. *Expansion* p. 24–p. 36

1. It is to be noted that, in discussing the RAF, it is almost exclusively the Metropolitan Air Force, that is to say, the RAF at home, that is meant. This is another significant difference between the RAF and the other two Services at that time. The Royal Navy had its home bases, of course, but these only gave a partial view of its strength and efficiency; of the Army it used to be said that whoever only knew the Army in England did not know the British Army.
2. AHB/II/116/17, p. 1.
3. Air Staff Note, March 10, 1935, AHB Folder V/5/1.
4. Ibid, pp. 36–7.
5. See Brian Bond, *British Military Policy Between the Two World Wars*, pp. 195–8, Clarendon Press, 1980, for details of the Defence Requirements Committee and its personalities.
6. Lord Avon, *The Eden Memoirs: Facing the Dictators*, p. 54, Cassell, 1962.
7. Ibid, p. 84.
8. Chamberlain to his sister Ida, May 12, 1934; quoted by Dr David J. Wrench in his important article, "The Influence of Neville Chamberlain on Foreign and Defence Policy, 1932–35", RUSI *Journal*, March 1980, p. 51.
9. Hyde, op. cit., p. 298.
10. Roskill, op. cit., p. 103, fn 7.
11. AHB/II/116/17, pp. 90–1. It is Sir Maurice Dean, op. cit., pp. 305–6, who tells us that 16 design teams were operating.
12. Chamberlain Diary, May 9, 1934; see Wrench, RUSI *Journal*, op. cit., p. 52.
13. Wrench, ibid.
14. Wrench, ibid.
15. Chamberlain, Cabinet, June 7, 1934; see Wrench, op. cit., p. 51.
16. Hyde, op. cit., Appendix VII: Table of RAF Expansion, 1934–39.
17. Hyde, op. cit., p. 306.
18. DC(M), June 26, 1934; see Wrench, op. cit., p. 53.
19. Roskill, op. cit., p. 108.

20. Hankey Diary, August 9; see Roskill op. cit., p. 119.
21. Pownall Diaries *(Chief of Staff)*, pp. 90–1, December 4, 1935; Pownall writes with some indignation of "the RAF going off on a 'private' war of their own".
22. Correlli Barnett, *The Collapse of British Power*, p. 352, Eyre Methuen, 1972.
23. Donald McLachlan, *Room 39: Naval Intelligence in Action 1939–45*, p. 76, Weidenfeld & Nicolson, 1968.
24. Eden, op. cit., p. 141.
25. See Hyde, op. cit., p. 337.
26. Debate on the Air Estimates, March 8.
27. Memorandum to DC(M), April 24, 1935. See Hyde, op. cit.
28. April 27; hard-pressed Chiefs of Staff are prone, from time to time, to favour their "superiors" with devastating glimpses of the obvious. Thus Field-Marshal Sir William Robertson (op. cit., i, p. 88), who was constantly having to rebuff impracticable schemes urged by politicians, tartly remarked: "There is seldom any lack of attractive-looking schemes in war. The difficulty is to give effect to them."
29. AHB/II/116/17, pp. 45–6.
30. Dean, op. cit., p. 55.
31. The Blenheim twin-engined light bomber (bomb-load 1,000 lbs) was the outcome of the Bristol Aeroplane Company's plan to build a civil transport faster than the new American models (see p. 28). The resulting aircraft was known as the Type 142; it was the first modern stressed-skin monoplane with retractable landing gear to be built in Britain. The prototype made its first flight in April 1935 and astounded all beholders, including its designer (Barnwell), reaching 307 mph on Air Ministry test. Lord Rothermere, who had sponsored the project, then presented this aircraft (christened "Britain First") to the RAF, and the Air Ministry ordered a military version off the drawing-board. The prototype Blenheim I first flew on June 25, 1936, and the first production Blenheim left the factory in November. Blenheims entered squadron service (No. 114, Wyton) in January 1937. They remained for several years the RAF's fastest bomber, and even did duty as day- and night-fighters in 1939–41. As usual, there are differences of opinion about numbers; Owen Thetford says that 1,552 Mark Is and 1,930 Mark IVs (the RAF's main combat version) were built, a total of 3,482; Bill Gunson (*The Encyclopaedia of the World's Combat Aircraft*, Salamander, 1976) says 1,134 Mark Is and 3,297 Mark IVs, total 4,431.
32. We have noted (p. 28) the long gap between the specification of the Wellington (September 1932) and squadron delivery (October 1938). The intermediate stages serve as a warning not to take approval of expansion schemes as markers of immediate change. The Wellington prototype first flew on June 15 1936; it was exhibited at Hendon (where it attracted considerable attention) and the Air Ministry ordered 180 Mark Is to Specification 29/36 in August. The prototype crashed and was

709

destroyed in April 1937, but the first production Mark I made its first flight on December 23. Marks Ia, Ic, II and III all followed before the outbreak of war. The early history of the Hampden tells a similar story.

33. Dean, op. cit., p. 85.
34. Lord Weir of Eastwood (1877–1959); engineer and businessman. Secretary of State for Air, April 27, 1918–January 13, 1919; unofficial adviser on air rearmament, May 1935–May 1938.
35. Barnett, op. cit., p. 415.

5. *Rearmament under way* p. 36–p. 45

1. Winston Churchill, *The Gathering Storm*, p. 175, Cassell, 1948.
2. Gordon A. Craig, *Germany 1866–1945*, p. 691, OUP, 1978.
3. AHB/II/116/17, p. 137.
4. See Air Ministry pamphlet, *The Rise and Fall of the German Air Force*, p. 38; AHB/II/116/19, published by Arms & Armour Press, 1983.
5. AHB/II/116/17, p. 142.
6. Quoted in Hyde, op. cit., p. 359.
7. AHB/II/116/17.
8. Richards & Saunders, op. cit., i, p. 15.
9. Harris, op. cit., pp. 27–8.
10. McLachlan, op. cit., p. 77.
11. See Hinsley, *British Intelligence in the Second World War*, ii, p. 631 (Official History) HMSO 1981; an Inter-Departmental Committee (3 Services, Foreign Office, Colonial and India Offices) was set up in 1926 to consider replacing existing book ciphers by cipher machines.
12. Ibid.
13. Lewin, *Ultra Goes to War*, p. 196, Hutchinson, 1978.
14. Dean, op. cit., p. 81.
15. PRO: AIR 2/2720.
16. Ibid; this letter is signed "W. J. Pryce for Director of Contracts"; it is dated 2.6.34, which is clearly an error, since it is pursuant to the late June correspondence.
17. Ibid; Air Ministry Contracts to War Office, 24.3.36.
18. Ibid, 25.3.36.
19. Ibid, 3.12.37.
20. Ibid.
21. Haig to Sir Gerald Ellison, October 1906; Ellison, article, May 1936.
22. AHB/II/116/17.
23. AHB/II/116/14, p. 137.
24. Quoted in Hyde, op. cit., pp. 494–5; Freeman to Trenchard, February 23, 1948.
25. Dean, op. cit., p. 88.

6. *The Knock-out blow* p. 45–p. 53

1. Roskill, op. cit., p. 270.

2. Stephen King-Hall, *Our Own Times 1913–1938*, p. 753, Nicholson & Watson, 1938.
3. Eden, op. cit., p. 498.
4. Bond, op. cit., p. 248.
5. King-Hall, op. cit., p. 754.
6. Wrench, op. cit., p. 53.
7. F. S. Oliver, *Ordeal by Battle*, pp. 403–9, Macmillan, 1915.
8. Bond, op. cit., p. 243.
9. Wrench, op. cit., p. 56.
10. Bialer, op. cit., p. 130.
11. Quoted in Barnett, op. cit., pp. 436–7; see also A. J. Trythall, *'Boney' Fuller: The Intellectual General*, pp. 193–9, Cassell, 1977.
12. D. C. Watt, reviewing *The Shadow of the Bomber* by Uri Bialer in the *Daily Telegraph*, 6.11.80.
13. Marshal of the Royal Air Force Sir John Slessor, *The Great Deterrent*, p. 138, Cassell, 1957.
14. Slessor, *The Central Blue*, p. 157, Cassell, 1956.
15. Ibid, pp. 157–8 (Ju = Junkers; He = Heinkel; Do = Dornier)
16. Quoted in Slessor, ibid, p. 158.
17. AHB/II/116/17, p. 51.
18. Aide-Memoire by Sir Thomas Inskip, Minister for Co-ordination of Defence, for the Secretary of State for Air, December 9, 1937; in full in Appendix 5 of Webster & Frankland, *The Strategic Air Offensive Against Germany*, iv, p. 96.
19. Ibid, p. 197.
20. Hugh Thomas, *The Spanish Civil War* (Penguin revised edition, 1965), p. 771, fn 1.
21. Slessor, op. cit., p. 152.

7. *Munich* p. 53–p.70

1. Ibid, p. 224.
2. Dean, op. cit., p. 58.
3. AHB/II/116/17, p. 74.
4. Churchill, op. cit., p. 303.
5. Slessor, op. cit., p. 164.
6. Churchill, op. cit., p. 303.
7. Richards & Saunders, op. cit., i, p. 410.
8. Wood & Dempster, op. cit., pp. 317–18.
9. AHB/II/116/19, p. 19.
10. Dr R. J. Overy, *The Air War, 1939–1945*, Europa Publications, 1980, p. 23.
11. Wood & Dempster, op. cit., p. 12.
12. Roskill, op. cit., p. 263.
13. Overy, op. cit.
14. These figures are from Gunston, op. cit.; see Appendix A. Needless to say, the value of a bomber depends on more than range and speed, but

these are the decisive qualities, since it can only reach its target if it has sufficient range, and speed is what is most likely to enable it to survive having done so.

15. Extracted from AHB/II/116/17, pp. 77–9.
16. OH (Webster & Frankland), op. cit., i, p. 99.
17. Bialer, op. cit., p. 23. He also quotes Vansittart in 1932: "Aviation in particular offers Germany the quickest and easiest way of making her own power effective."
18. Ibid, pp. 20–1.
19. Taylor, Telford, *Munich: The Price of Peace*, p. 706, Hodder & Stoughton, 1979.
20. Professor Williamson Murray of Ohio State University, in his article "Force Strategy, Blitzkrieg Strategy and the Economic Difficulties: Nazi Grand Strategy in the 1930s" (RUSI *Journal*, March 1983, p. 40), informs us: "Historians have ascribed the *Luftwaffe's* ultimate failure to its disregard of the importance of strategic bombing for the coming war. In fact the documents do not support such a contention . . . Unfortunately for the argument, virtually every single air force article in the 1930s in major German military journals stressed strategic bombing as the *raison d'être* of the *Luftwaffe* . . . The *Luftwaffe* did not live up to such high pre-war expectations, because in fact like the airmen of other nations German air force officers had considerably over-estimated the effectiveness of their weapon."
21. Bond, op. cit., p. 283.
22. Eden, op. cit., p. 60.
23. Bond, op. cit., p. 2.
24. Bond, *Liddell Hart: A Study of his Military Thought*, p. 91, Cassell, 1977.
25. Bond, op. cit., pp. 81–2.
26. See p. 51, Ch. 6, Note 18.
27. Pownall Diaries, op. cit., p. 166.
28. See *The Palestine Campaign* in the series "Campaigns and Their Lessons", edited by Major-General Sir C. E. Callwell, Constable, 1928.
29. Haig Diary, January 1, 1916; see Terraine, *Douglas Haig: The Educated Soldier*, p. 182, Hutchinson, 1963.
30. Bond, op. cit., p. 322.
31. OH (Webster & Frankland), op. cit., iv, pp. 90–1.
32. Bond, op. cit., p. 241.
33. Ibid, p. 295.
34. Ibid, p. 288.
35. Churchill, op. cit., p. 304.
36. Ibid, p. 311.
37. Slessor, op. cit., p. 146.
38. Eden, op. cit., p. 498.
39. See Guy Chapman, *Why France Collapsed*, pp. 42–3, Cassell, 1968.
40. Col. H. C. B. Rogers, *Tanks in Battle*, p. 94, Seeley, Service, 1965.
41. Chapman, op. cit., pp. 33–4.

42. Ibid, p. 43.
43. Eden, op. cit., p. 146; Chapman, op. cit., p. 41; Barnett, op. cit., p. 506.
44. Barnett, op. cit., p. 511.
45. Bond, op. cit., p. 288.
46. *History of the Second World War*, p. 22, Cassell, 1970.
47. Barnett, op. cit., p. 506.
48. Overy, op. cit., p. 23.
49. Taylor, op. cit., p. 992 fn.
50. Pownall Diaries, op. cit., p. 159.
51. Ibid, p. 160.
52. Craig, op. cit., p. 706.
53. Dean, op. cit., p. 76.
54. Churchill, *The Gathering Storm*, p. 294.

8. *Coming of age, coming of war* p. 70–p. 92

1. "Disarray" is the word used by Dr Malcolm Smith in his article, "Sir Edgar Ludlow-Hewitt and the Expansion of Bomber Command, 1939–40", in the RUSI *Journal*, March 1981, p. 55: "the disarray to which the RAF had been reduced by the hectic expansion of the last five years."
2. On August 27, 1939 Coastal Command's equipment was:

Anson (first flight, 1935)	10 squadrons
London (flying-boat, 1934)	1 squadron
Stranraer (flying-boat, 1935)	1 squadron
Vildebeest (torpedo-bomber, 1928)	2 squadrons
Hudson (general reconnaissance, 1938)	1 squadron
Sunderland (flying-boat, 1937)	2 squadrons

    (AHB/II/117/3(A): *The RAF in Maritime War*, Appendix V)
3. Ludlow-Hewitt to Air Ministry, May 25, 1939; Ludlow-Hewitt Papers, Air Historical Branch; Box 2, Folder 7.
4. Smith, RUSI *Journal*, op. cit., p. 55.
5. OH (Webster & Frankland), op. cit., i, p. 134.
6. See Terraine, *Impacts of War, 1914–1918*, pp. 56–62, Hutchinson, 1970.
7. Churchill, op. cit., p. 370.
8. AHB/II/117/3(A), p. 246.
9. AHB/II/117/2(A): *The Air Defence of Great Britain*, pp. 77–8.
10. Ibid, p. 64.
11. Ibid, pp. 100–2.
12. Ibid.
13. Ibid, pp. 85–6.
14. Generally referred to as the "Field Force Component"; ibid.
15. Ibid, p. 86.
16. Ibid, pp. 88–9.
17. Ibid, p. 113.
18. Ibid, pp. 112–14.
19. Ibid.
20. Richards & Saunders, op. cit., i, p. 63.

21. AHB/II/117/2(A), pp. 112–14.
22. Dowding's grandmother's maiden name was Maria Caswall, his mother's was Maude Tremenheere.
23. AHB/II/116/17, pp. 96–7.
24. Gunston, op. cit., p. 213.
25. Thetford, op. cit., p. 26.
26. OH (Webster & Frankland), op. cit., i, pp. 94–5.
27. Ibid, p. 97.
28. AHB/II/117/1(B), *The RAF in the Bombing Offensive Against Germany*, ii, p. 36.
29. Ludlow-Hewitt noted that no fewer than 38 Pilot Officers were commanding flights at this time.
30. Ludlow-Hewitt to Air Ministry, November 10, 1937, para. 4; AHB, Box 2 Folder 7.
31. Ibid.
32. Smith, RUSI *Journal*, op. cit., p. 53.
33. Ludlow-Hewitt, op. cit., para. 6.
34. Ibid.
35. OH (Webster & Frankland), op. cit., i, p. 113 fn 1.
36. Ludlow-Hewitt, op. cit., para. 8.
37. The Short Sunderlands of Coastal Command had crews of 13.
38. Subject, of course, to the deficiencies which he had already listed.
39. Ludlow-Hewitt, op. cit., para. 18.
40. Ludlow-Hewitt, May 25, 1939, op. cit., paras. 1 & 11.
41. Smith, RUSI *Journal*, op. cit., p. 53.
42. Ibid, p. 54.
43. Ludlow-Hewitt, November 10, 1937, op. cit., para. 13.
44. Ludlow-Hewitt to Air Ministry, "Readiness for War Report", March 10, 1939, para. 29; AHB, Box 2 Folder 7.
45. Ludlow-Hewitt, May 25, 1939, op. cit., para. 11.
46. See p. 463.
47. Smith, RUSI *Journal*, op. cit., p. 54.
48. Armstrong Whitworth acquired the British manufacturing rights of the Browning; the British Government made its first order (6) in 1926; by July 1939 the RAF possessed some 20,000 Brownings, and by mid-1941 production was nearly 2,000 per week.
49. The Frazer-Nash powered turret was adopted by the RAF in 1935; it was produced by Nash & Thompson Ltd. (Archibald Frazer-Nash and Esmond Thompson were both ex-RFC pilots.) Other firms put forward their own designs, and in 1939 Hampdens, Blenheims, Whitleys and Wellingtons were all using different types of turret.
50. Smith, RUSI *Journal*, op. cit., p. 54.
51. In his memorandum of May 25, 1939 Ludlow-Hewitt said: "Air gunnery needs to be raised to the level of a distinct science requiring its own centre where its problems can be properly studied and its technique and operational doctrines fully developed" (Para. 9).

52. Ibid, para. 8.
53. Ibid, para. 9.
54. Ludlow-Hewitt to Air Ministry, July 17, 1939; quoted in OH (Webster & Frankland), op. cit., i, p. 116.
55. Dean, op. cit., p. 306.
56. Ibid.
57. OH (Webster & Frankland), op. cit., i, p. 117.
58. Ludlow-Hewitt, March 10, 1939, op. cit., para. 13.
59. OH (Webster & Frankland), op. cit., i, p. 118.
60. Ibid, p. 119, fn 1.
61. Ibid, p. 125.
62. Smith, RUSI *Journal*, op. cit., p. 55.
63. OH (Webster & Frankland), op. cit., i, p. 125.
64. OH (Webster & Frankland), op. cit., i, p. 104.
65. Slessor, op. cit., pp. 205–6.
66. OH (Webster & Frankland), op. cit., i, p. 101.

Part II: The Test

9. *North Sea tutorial* p. 95–p. 111

1. The organization of Bomber Command at the outbreak of war was: HQ High Wycombe

No. 1 Group	A. V-M Playfair	HQ Reims	10 Battle Sqdns
No. 2 Group	A. V-M Maclean	HQ Huntingdon	10 Blenheim Sqdns
No. 3 Group	A. V-M Baldwin	HQ Exning	6 Wellington Sqdns
No. 4 Group	A. V-M Coningham	HQ York	5 Whitley Sqdns
No. 5 Group	A. Comm. Gallaway	HQ Grantham	6 Hampden Sqdns
	A. V-M Harris (Sept. 11)		

No. 6 Group: Training Group, non-operational, HQ Abingdon, 16 sqdns.
2. AHB/II/117/1(B), ii, p. 56.
3. Alistair Horne, *To Lose a Battle: France 1940*, p. 83, Macmillan, 1969.
4. AHB: Air Ministry War Room Summary No. 40, September 23, 1939.
5. Gunston, op. cit., p. 166.
6. Basil Collier, *The Defence of the United Kingdom*, p. 72, HMSO, 1957 (OH).
7. AHB/II/117/2(A), i, pp. 94–5.
8. AHB/II/117/1(B), p. 5.
9. Harris, op. cit., pp. 34–5.
10. OH (Webster & Frankland), op. cit., iv, p. 26.

11. Denis Richards, *Portal of Hungerford*, pp. 139–40, Heinemann, 1977.
12. AHB/II/117/3(A), i, p. 248.
13. Ibid, pp. 246–8 for this quotation and the rest in the paragraph. The final plan of attack on Wilhelmshaven in cooperation with the Navy was designated W.A. 7(A) (see Appendix A).
14. The use of detachments instead of complete squadrons was no doubt partly in order to give as many squadrons as possible some early operational experience. Another factor, however, is to be found in para. 33 of Ludlow-Hewitt's "Readiness for War" report of March 1939:
    "The fact that we have been unable to maintain a higher average than 50 per cent service ability in units is most disquieting . . . The whole basis of the calculations of our operational degree of effort is at present the expectation that we can maintain 75 per cent serviceability in peace time. The reduction of serviceability to 50 per cent automatically reduces our effort by one third. In war it is probable that this will be still further reduced, and if these figures are accepted we shall have to reduce our scale of effort by 50 per cent."
    This condition probably improved considerably during the following six months, but it is unlikely that it was wholly cured.
    Hampdens of No. 83 Squadron (Scampton) also took off on September 4, but were unable to locate their targets due to the poor visibility. They dropped their bombs in the sea and came home.
15. R. V. Jones, *Most Secret War*, p. 106, Coronet edition, 1979.
16. AHB/II/117/1(B), p. 56.
17. AHB: Air Ministry War Room Summary No. 4, Para. 64.
18. Richards, op. cit., p. 40.
19. They carried one fixed and one movable .303 gun forward, and twin .303s in dorsal and ventral positions; no turrets.
20. Harris, op. cit., p. 39.
21. OH (Webster & Frankland), op. cit., i, p. 192.
22. Ibid, p. 193.
23. Quoted in ibid, p. 195.
24. Ibid, p. 194.
25. *Fliegerabwehrkanonen* = German anti-aircraft artillery; in RAF usage, AA-fire.
26. OH (Webster & Frankland), op. cit., i, p. 199 fn 2.
27. Chaz Bowyer, *Guns in the Sky: The Air Gunners of World War Two*, pp. 64–7, J. M. Dent, 1979.
28. OH (Webster & Frankland), op. cit., i, p. 197.
29. As is now well-known, reports of losses inflicted by both sides, made and accepted in all good faith, were usually wildly unrealistic. On December 18 the Germans believed that they had accounted for 36 Wellingtons, 34 shot down, one landed in the sea, and one destroyed by naval AA fire (OH [Webster & Frankland], op. cit., i, p. 200).
30. At the Battle of Amiens, August 8, 1918, the RAF component of General Sir Henry Rawlinson's Fourth Army consisted of no fewer than 800

aircraft. The French First Army, which cooperated in the battle, had 1,104, an Allied total of 1,904. August 8 was described by General Ludendorff as "the black day of the German Army in the history of the war"; it was certainly the "black day" of the young RAF. It sustained a loss of 42 aircraft shot down and 52 more so badly damaged that they had to be written off – 13 per cent of the total engaged, but 23 per cent of the bombers. Surely there must have been *one* senior officer at No. 3 Group HQ, or Bomber Command HQ, who could have gently corrected Wing Commander Kellett without hurting his pride?

31. This is a real Balaklava touch. When Lord Cardigan, just after the calamitous charge of the Light Brigade, said to some survivors: "Men, it is a mad-brained trick, but it is no fault of mine", a voice from the ranks replied: "Never mind, my lord; we are ready to go again."

32. Bomber Command report (BC/S.21688/2), "The Big Air Battle over Wilhelmshaven", December 22, 1939; AHB, Ludlow-Hewitt Papers, Box 2 Folder 8.

33. OH (Webster & Frankland), op. cit., i, p. 199.

34. Quoted in OH (Webster & Frankland), op. cit., i, p. 198.

35. Quoted in ibid, p. 199.

36. Air Vice-Marshal Harris from OH (Webster & Frankland), op. cit., i, p. 200; Squadron-Leader Harris from *Fly Past* No. 23, June 1983.

37. Churchill, op. cit., p. 376.

38. Harris, op. cit., p. 36.

39. Richards & Saunders, op. cit., i, p. 49.

40. OH (Webster & Frankland), op. cit., i, p. 208.

41. Ibid, pp. 202–3.

42. Richards & Saunders, op. cit., i, pp. 51–2.

43. Ibid, pp. 52–3.

44. In his anthology, *Freedom's Battle: The War in the Air 1939–45*, pp. 7–8, Hutchinson, 1968, Gavin Lyall himself supplies an account of what he calls "The Battle of Barking Creek", with a clear explanation of the radar fault.

45. DWI = Directional Wireless Installation, a deliberately misleading name. The aircraft were fitted underneath with a great hoop containing a magnetic coil; they flew at 25–40 feet above the sea and so activated the mines. It was not uncommon for aircraft to be struck by fragments.

46. OH (Webster & Frankland), op. cit., i, p. 202.

47. Ibid, p. 212.

10. *Night bombing; Ludlow-Hewitt* p. 111–p.115

1. OH (Webster & Frankland), op. cit., i, p. 139.

2. Ibid, pp. 139–40.

3. Ludlow-Hewitt to Group Captain, Training, March 8, quoted in OH (Webster & Frankland), op. cit., i, p. 140 fn 1.

4. AHB/II/117/1(B), pp. 72–3.

5. Harris, op. cit., p. 35.

6. Ludlow-Hewitt to Air Ministry, 25.5.39, para. 11; Ludlow-Hewitt papers.
7. Harris, op. cit., pp. 35–6.
8. Slessor, op. cit., p. 114.

11. *Norway, 1940* p. 115–p. 118

1. See Terraine, *The Western Front*, pp. 101–8, Hutchinson, 1964.
2. AHB/II/117/4, *The Campaign in Norway*, pp. 31–3.
3. William Green, *Warplanes of the Third Reich*, p. 410, Macdonald & Jane's, 1970.
4. Bernard Ash, *Norway 1940*, pp. 178–9, Cassell, 1964. On the previous page Ash says: ". . . for some unfathomable reason the ground staff were not sent with the aircraft and flying personnel. The staff who were sent instead were strange to the squadron and unfamiliar with Gladiators."
5. Squadron-Leader Whitney-Straight, quoted in AHB/II/117/4, p. 68.
6. These claims are unverified.
7. Ash, op. cit., p. 303.

12. *Crisis of battle: Fighter cover, bomber offensive* p. 118–p. 147

1. This phrase is the title of the Prologue of Ronald Lewin's *Ultra Goes to War*, Hutchinson, 1978 and supplies a text to which he preaches effectively.
2. Peter Young, *World War 1939–1945: A Short History*, p. 50, Arthur Barker, 1966.
3. General Vuillemin later stated: "Our Air Force ran into an enemy which outnumbered it by five to one." Other French writers have made even more exaggerated comparisons. But the truth would seem to be that the German superiority was about two to one.
4. It appears in Chapman, *Why France Collapsed*, Cassell, p. 71, 1968.
5. Ibid, pp. 370–1.
6. Gunston, op. cit., p. 46.
7. AHB/II/117/5(A), *The Campaign in France and the Low Countries*, p. 160.
8. Horne, op. cit., p. 71.
9. Chapman, op. cit., p. 70.
10. AHB/II/117/5(A), pp. 72–3.
11. Ibid, pp. 45–6.
12. Paul Richey DFC, *Fighter Pilot*, p. 42, Jane's Publishing Company, 1980 (first published 1941).
13. Ibid, p. 66.
14. The Fairey Battle was built to Spec. P.27/32. Before it even took shape, Sir Edgar Ludlow-Hewitt, then Deputy Chief of the Air Staff, declared that it would never make a high performance bomber. As we have seen (p. 78) Sir Edward Ellington prohibited further orders in 1936, but a penalty of hasty expansion is that you have to use what is there. Eleven months later the Air Member for Research and Development, Sir Wilfrid Freeman, was saying that the Battle was a mistake that ought not to be

perpetuated. Wood and Dempster (op. cit., p. 37) comment on "the anomaly of ordering multi-gun fighters and a large day bomber with only one fixed gun firing forward and a single Vickers gun firing aft". In the Battle of France, 137 Fairey Battles were lost.

15. Richey, op. cit., p. 58 (on a visit to No. 12 Squadron).
16. *The Campaign in France and the Low Countries, September 1939–June 1940*, which was, in fact, written by Denis Richards himself.
17. Ibid, "Foreword".
18. A particular hazard, due to the weather, was freezing of the camera-shutters, and this proved by no means easy to overcome (AHB/II/117/5(A), p. 147).
19. AHB/II/116/19, p. 66.
20. Major-General J. F. C. Fuller, *The Decisive Battles of the Western World*, iii, p. 392, Eyre & Spottiswoode, 1956.
21. Quoted in AHB/II/117/5(A), p. 191.
22. Ibid.
23. Quantity of German AA from Horne, op. cit., p. 159. Anti-aircraft, it should be noted, was a *Luftwaffe* function, whose personnel accounted for nearly two thirds of the *Luftwaffe*'s total strength of about 1½ million in September 1939.
24. AHB/II/117/5(A), p. 194.
25. Horne, op. cit., pp. 182–3.
26. AHB/II/117/5(A), p. 200.
27. Ibid, p. 196.
28. Two tables of RAF losses in France, May 10–June 20, are offered in AHB/II/117/5(A): Appendix M, which gives a daily breakdown of losses by types and by Commands (from which these figures are taken), and a footnote on p. 474 which gives a breakdown by types and Commands, but not on a daily basis. The total in Appendix M is 931 aircraft of all types, that on page 474 is 959 (which is the total which Denis Richards selected for his official *Royal Air Force 1939–45* in 1953). Wood and Dempster (op. cit., p. 101) give a total of 944 – one more example of the impossibility of making exact statistical statements about the air war.
29. One recalls the "six VCs before breakfast" won by the 1/Lancashire Fusiliers at "Lancashire Landing", Gallipoli, April 25, 1915; this was in despite of the War Office, which wanted to cut the number to four – presumably regarding the number as more significant than the deed.
30. Richards & Saunders, op. cit., i, pp. 116–18.
31. Horne, op. cit., p. 213.
32. Richards & Saunders, op. cit., i, p. 119.
33. Horne, op. cit., p. 246.
34. There is a most marked and depressing resemblance between the battle of the Meuse in May 1940 and the Battle of the Aisne which opened on May 27, 1918. On that day the French were surprised and shattered by the most intense artillery bombardment of that war. In theory it should have been quite impossible for the Germans to assemble over 4,000 guns

on a narrow front in Champagne without being detected – just as, in theory, it was impossible to take armoured columns through the Ardennes. On each occasion the Germans showed that "the impossible" is often a delusion and a snare. On May 27, 1918 the German bombardment lasted two hours and forty minutes; the French (and British) defences were crushed, and the Germans made the deepest one-day advance of the war – about 10 miles, crossing three rivers in the process. All of which might have been worth remembering in May 1940.

At Amiens on August 8 – a day which started a tide of battle flowing which was as decisive as May 10, 1940 – the action began, with no preliminary bombardment, at 4.20 a.m. and nine hours later the decision of what Ludendorff called "the black day of the German Army in the history of the war" was a fact. There really was no excuse for supposing tha. armies would lumber about at 1916 speeds; modern artillery techniques had already given them a key to unlock battle fronts by 1918, and by 1940 there were even better ones, as the Germans showed.

35. The Boulton Paul Defiant was a failure. Built to Specification F.9/35, this two-seater fighter had the strange feature of no forward-firing armament, its entire battery of four Brownings being carried in its power-operated turret behind the pilot. Flown as a day fighter solely by No. 264 Squadron, it had some early successes but was withdrawn from daylight operations in August due to its severe losses.
36. Horne, op. cit., p. 247.
37. John Williams, *The Ides of May*, p. 151, Constable, 1968.
38. Patrick Turnbull, *Dunkirk: Anatomy of Disaster*, p. 66, Batsford, 1978.
39. Quoted in Horne, op. cit., p. 247.
40. Williams, op. cit., p. 151.
41. Horne, op. cit., p. 263.
42. This is treated in Brian Bond's *France and Belgium 1939–1940*, pp. 101–3, Davis-Poynter, 1975.
43. E. Spears, *Assignment to Catastrophe*, i, p. 142, Heinemann, 1954.
44. It is incorrect to equate the Ju 87 with *Stuka*, which is simply an abbreviation of *Sturzkampfflugzeug*, the generic term for dive-bomber, of which the Ju 87 was only one variety, but in 1939–40 the favoured one.
45. AHB/II/116/19, p. 73.
46. Green, op. cit., p. 428.
47. AHB/II/117/5(A), p. 219.
48. Horne, op. cit., p. 286.
49. These were flown by crews drawn from No. 114 Squadron (AHB/II/117/5(A)).
50. Horne, op. cit., p. 287.
51. Churchill, *Their Finest Hour*, pp. 38–9.
52. Pownall Diaries, op. cit., p. 311.
53. AHB/II/117/5(A), p. 177.
54. *The Ironside Diaries 1937–1940*, ed. Col. Roderick Macleod and Denis Kelly, p. 304, Constable, 1962.

55. Quoted in Robert Wright, *Dowding and the Battle of Britain*, p. 105, Macdonald, 1969.
56. Ibid.
57. Wright, op. cit., p. 106.
58. Horne, op. cit., p. 323.
59. Cab. 65/13: Confidential Annex to the Minutes of War Cabinet No. 123, 11 a.m., May 15. The Minutes of that meeting itself (Cab. 65/7) contain no record of the air policy discussion.
60. Wright, op. cit., p. 103.
61. In Wood & Dempster, *Twelve Legions of Angels*, Jarrold, 1946.
62. Wright, op. cit., p. 104.
63. Cab. 65/13.
64. Ibid.
65. Wright, op. cit., p. 103.
66. AHB/II/117/2(A), p. 138 fn.
67. Cab. 65/13.
68. Ironside, op. cit., p. 309.
69. AHB/II/117/5(A), pp. 173–4.
70. Ibid, p. 174.
71. René Fonck, *Mes Combats* (Paris, 1920), quoted in *The First World War* by Richard Thoumin, p. 450, Secker & Warburg, 1960.
72. AHB/II/117/5(A), p. 276.
73. Ibid, p. 277.
74. Richards & Saunders, op. cit., i, p. 124.
75. AHB/II/117/5(A), p. 278.
76. Horne, op. cit., p. 317; for French Air Force statistics, ibid, p. 321.

13. *The pay-off: Dowding protests* p. 147–p. 152

1. Cab. 65/13.
2. Churchill, op. cit., pp. 40–6.
3. Ibid, p. 38.
4. Wright, op. cit., p. 119.
5. It need hardly be said that the Air Council never acceded to this request; Dowding himself was, of course, the only man able to advise with authority on the matter.
6. The original of this letter, framed, now hangs in a place of honour in the RAF College, Cranwell.
7. AHB/II/117/2(A), p. 141.
8. Wood & Dempster, *The Narrow Margin*, p. 99.

14. *Dunkirk* p. 152–p. 158

1. Wright, op. cit., p. 113.
2. Churchill, op. cit., p. 45. He told General Gamelin on May 16: "The business of fighters is to cleanse the skies *(nettoyer le ciel)* over the battle."
3. AHB/II/117/2(A), pp. 141–2.

4. Ibid.
5. AHB/II/117/5(A), p. 291.
6. Basil Collier, *Barren Victories: Versailles to Suez 1918–1956*, p. 284, Cassell, 1964.
7. AHB/II/117/2(A), Appendix 16.
8. Richey, op. cit., p. 53.
9. The Admiralty ordered: "begin Operation DYNAMO" at 1857 hours on May 26. Bad weather, including thick fog, seriously interfered with flying. No. 72 Squadron, on June 4, lost four aircraft trying to land at Manston in fog.
10. A complication was the request to give fighter protection to Air Component Lysanders attempting a supply-drop to the 30th Brigade in Calais. It was not yet known that the brigade had surrendered the previous afternoon. Three Lysanders out of 21 were lost.
11. Figures for the last six days of evacuation were:

May 30	53,823
May 31	68,014
June 1	64,429
June 2	26,256
June 3	26,746
June 4	26,175

(Young, op. cit., p. 65).
12. A. J. Barker, *Dunkirk: The Great Escape*, p. 184, Dent, 1977.
13. Richards & Saunders, op. cit., i, p. 142.
14. AHB/II/117/5(A), pp. 320, 323.
15. Churchill, op. cit., p. 103.
16. Ibid.

15. *1940 catastrophe: the reckoning* p. 158–p. 165

1. Barker, op. cit., p. 228.
2. Nigel Nicolson, *Alex: The Life of Field Marshal Earl Alexander of Tunis*, p. 114, Weidenfeld & Nicolson, 1973.
3. Churchill, op. cit., p. 130.
4. AHB/II/117/5(A), pp. 364–5.
5. Ibid, pp. 367–8.
6. Wood & Dempster, op. cit., p. 101.
7. AHB/II/117/5(A), p. 381.
8. Gregory Blaxland, *Destination Dunkirk: The Story of Gort's Army*, p. 386, William Kimber, 1973.
9. When Italy entered the war on June 10, an attempt was made to chastise her by operating No. 99 Squadron (Wellingtons) from Salon in Provence. This did not meet with French approval, nor did it prove to be a practicable mode of waging war. Attacks on Genoa and Turin met violent storms over the Alps which made it impossible for most aircraft to find their targets. This operation was called HADDOCK; a clear, succinct account of it may be found on pp. 145–7 of Denis Richards's volume in

RAF 1939–45, including his conclusion that the French armistice on June 17 "ended a singularly unprofitable venture".

10. AHB/II/117/5(A), p. 468.
11. Ibid.
12. Ibid, p. 466.
13. Note on conference between C-in-C Bomber Command and Air Staff, May 28; AHB/II/117/5(A), p. 461.
14. Jeffrey A. Gunsberg, *Divided and Conquered: The French High Command and the Defeat of the West*, Greenwood Press, 1979. The Germans claimed a total of 1,841 enemy aircraft.
15. Frank Howard and Bill Gunston, *The Conquest of the Air*, p. 185, Paul Elek, 1972.
16. Gunston, *Encyclopaedia of Combat Aircraft*, p. 146.
17. Green, op. cit., pp. 541–2.

Part III: The Strain
The Battle of Britain

16. *Britain alone* p. 169–p. 173

1. Sir John Wheeler-Bennett, *King George VI*, p. 460, Macmillan, 1958.
2. Churchill, op. cit., p. 228. The story is possibly apocryphal; Wheeler-Bennett quotes it, with slightly different wording, but attributes it to "an office-keeper in a Government department to a senior civil servant" (p. 461). It is entirely true in spirit.
3. *History of the Second World War*, p. 142.
4. Wright, op. cit., p. 129.
5. Craig, op. cit., p. 721.
6. John Toland, *Adolf Hitler*, p. 621, Doubleday (NY), 1976.
7. Liddell Hart, op. cit., p. 141.
8. Dr Karl Klee in *Decisive Battles of World War II: The German View*, edited by Dr Hans-Adolf Jacobsen and Dr Jürgen Rohwer, p. 75, André Deutsch, 1965.
9. AHB/II/116/19 *(The Rise and Fall of the German Air Force)*, p. 73.
10. Klee, op. cit., p. 81.
11. Green, op. cit., p. 543.
12. Craig, op. cit., p. 722; Klee, op. cit., pp. 76–7. Goering was appointed *Reichsmarschall* on June 20.
13. Lieutenant-General Siegfried Westphal says: "It was specifically the Russian threat to Rumania, which imperilled Germany's oil supplies from that country, that worried Hitler most." (*The Fatal Decisions*, ed. William Richardson & Seymour Friedin, trans. Constantine Fitzgibbon, Michael Joseph, 1956; Ace Books edition, 1959, p. 26.)
14. Klee, op. cit., p. 79.
15. Ibid, p. 80.
16. Wood & Dempster, op. cit., p. 119.
17. See Craig, op. cit., p. 723: "Goering had predicted that four days of

intensive bombing would knock out the air defences of southern England and that four weeks of more generalized attacks would destroy communications and morale and open the way for a triumphant and bloodless crossing of the Channel."

17. *The Dowding system* p. 173–p. 180

1. The sincerity of Hitler's intention to invade Britain has been called into question inside and outside Germany. Major-General J. F. C. Fuller, in his *Decisive Battles of the Western World* (iii, p. 411), says bluntly: "The truth is, with the possible exception of Goering . . . nobody believed in Operation SEALION." Wood and Dempster, on the other hand, state equally firmly: "If, as has been postulated, the SEALION invasion plan was purely an exercise to frighten and put pressure on Britain, then it must have been the most expensive exercise ever." Germany, they insist, "had every intention of invading if Britain did not sue for peace" (*The Narrow Margin*, p. 118). This view is strongly supported by Herr von Plehwe who, in 1940, was posted as assistant to the Head of the German Army's liaison staff at Naval Headquarters. The Navy's chief preoccupation was the assembly of the requisite shipping, which it estimated to be over 3,800 vessels of all types. Von Plehwe says: "To all those in the know the mass of work put into creating and marshalling this invasion fleet was irrefutable proof that preparations for Operation SEALION were being taken seriously." The "almost total requisitioning of all inland water transport in Germany" had, he says, very serious effects on the German economy; "many large German towns could only be supplied with food 'with the greatest difficulty'". None of this dislocation, he says, "would have been necessary had the preparations for SEALION been nothing but a bluff" (RUSI *Journal*, March 1973). This would seem to be conclusive.

2. According to Churchill (op. cit., p. 226) there were hardly 500 field guns in the whole country, the majority being 1918 Mark IV 18-pdrs; production of the modern 25-pdrs was still painfully slow. There were hardly 200 "medium or heavy tanks".

3. Friedrich-Karl von Plehwe, "Operation Sealion 1940", in the RUSI *Journal*, March 1973, p. 51.

4. Churchill, op. cit., p. 249.

5. Wood & Dempster, op. cit., p. 101.

6. Wood and Dempster draw attention (p. 115) to a proposal by *Generaloberst* Erhard Milch, the German Secretary of State for Air, to Goering on June 18 for immediate landings by paratroops and airborne forces in southern England with a view to seizing key fighter airfields in the confusion of the aftermath of Dunkirk. "The plan involved considerable risk, but it might have succeeded . . . Goering's reaction was one of blank amazement and he described Milch's suggestions as nonsense . . . One of the most unusual opportunities in German military history had been thrown away."

7. All these figures are from Wood and Dempster. The 52 squadrons are

identified and located by Groups, sectors and stations on p. 124 of *The Narrow Margin*; the figure for aircraft appears in a table on p. 306, and that for pilots in a table on p. 310. I am indebted to Group Captain T. P. Gleave, of the Battle of Britain Fighter Association, for reminding me with some emphasis that the last two of these have to be treated with reserve. It would be quite wrong to suppose that there were 1,259 pilots ready and able to spring into a cockpit, take off and do battle. Group Captain Gleave says he doubts whether there were as many as 700; a large part of this discrepancy is accounted for by new pilots "with the down still on their cheeks", fresh from training schools and units, and in no way ready for battle with the *Luftwaffe*. Regarding aircraft, Group Captain Gleave also has doubts, and considers that about 500 would be nearer to the true figure for those actually operational.

8. At the outbreak of war the establishment of a single-seater fighter squadron in the United Kingdom was 13 officers and 132 other ranks. By July 1940 it was somewhat larger, ground-crew numbering about 180. Group Captain Gleave suggests that the ground-crew total in Fighter Command at that date (men and women) would probably be in the region of 12,000.

9. This was the fifth alteration of Dowding's retirement date in under two years, a matter which caused him some understandable anger, and obviously added to the already great strain of impending battle. His reply to Newall (July 7) repays study, and may be found at length in *Flying Colours* by Laddie Lucas, p. 166, Hutchinson 1981.

10. Wright, op. cit., p. 146.

11. Ibid, p. 215.

12. Churchill, op. cit., p. 338.

13. Wood & Dempster, op. cit., p. 84.

14. See Terraine, *White Heat: The New Warfare 1914–1918*, pp. 251–4, Sidgwick & Jackson, 1982 for the curious interventions of radio in the Battle of Jutland.

15. Hawkinge was very much a front-line position, and the decision was rightly taken to remove the precious "Y Service" to a less exposed locality, West Kingsdown in the North Kent Downs.

16. Aileen Clayton: *The Enemy is Listening*, p. 49, Hutchinson, 1980. The Women's Royal Air Force of the First World War was disbanded in 1920. In 1938 the Auxiliary Territorial Service was formed to train women for war service; No. 20 (County of London) Company was formed at Kidbrooke under Miss (later Dame Jane) Trefusis-Forbes to enrol women specifically for duties with the RAF. The need for a separate organization quickly became apparent, and by Royal Warrant the Women's Auxiliary Air Force was formed on June 28, 1939. Miss Trefusis-Forbes was appointed Director, with the rank of Senior Controller later changed to Air Commandant; Her Majesty Queen Elizabeth became Commandant-in-Chief. At the outbreak of war there were 48 WAAF Companies, containing 230 officers and 7,460 airwomen; at its

peak strength the WAAF numbered 181,909 women (1943). By the end of the war, they were employed in over 80 trades, including 21 concerned with the maintenance and servicing of aircraft. In 1940, apart from the "Y Service" in which Mrs Clayton served, the WAAF played an essential part in the radar chain, in filter rooms and Operations Rooms, in photographic interpretation and other forms of Intelligence and in code and cipher work. They had, in fact, become an integral part of the RAF.

17. Ibid, p. 33.
18. Ibid, p. 48.
19. Lewin, *Ultra Goes to War*, p. 115.
20. Clayton, op. cit., p. 18.
21. Lewin, op. cit., p. 84.
22. See F. W. Winterbotham, *The Ultra Secret*, pp. 44–5, Weidenfeld & Nicolson, 1974.
23. In addition, of course, there were the normal sources of RAF Intelligence: interrogation of prisoners of war, examination of captured documents, reports of secret agents, information from neutrals.
24. Wood & Dempster, op. cit., p. 86.
25. *No. 10 Group: AOC:* Air Vice-Marshal Sir Christopher Joseph Quintin Brand, *KBE, DSO, MC, DFC*
      HQ: Rudloe Manor, Box, Wiltshire
      4 sectors (as at 0900 hours, September 15, 1940)
   No. 11 Group: AOC: Air Vice-Marshal Keith Rodney Park, MC, DFC
      HQ: Hillingdon House, Uxbridge, Middlesex
      7 sectors
   No. 12 Group: AOC: Air Vice-Marshal Trafford Leigh-Mallory, CB, DSO
      HQ: Watnall, Nottingham
      6 sectors
   No. 13 Group: AOC: Air Vice-Marshal Richard Ernest Saul, DFC
      HQ: Blakelaw Estate, Ponteland, Newcastle-on-Tyne
      6 sectors
26. Wood & Dempster, op. cit., p. 87.
27. AHB/II/117/2(B) (*The Air Defence of Great Britain*, ii), p. 52.

18. *"Contact Phase"; Sir Keith Park* p. 181–p. 185

1. Klee, op. cit., p. 74.
2. Wood & Dempster (p. 123) say:

Bombers	998
Dive-Bombers	261
Single-engined Fighters	805
Twin-engined Fighters	224
Reconnaissance	151
	2,439

(+ 31 "ground attack" and 80 coastal reconnaissance, = 2,550 total);

Klee's (incomplete) reckoning (p. 86) is:

Bombers	949
Dive-Bombers	336
Single-engined Fighters	869
Twin-engined Fighters	268
	2,422

A similarly incomplete (and approximate) reckoning is offered by Christopher Dowling in *Decisive Battles of the Twentith Century*, ed. Dowling and Noble Frankland, p. 116 (Sidgwick & Jackson, 1976):

Bombers	"nearly 1,000"
Dive-Bombers	"some 260"
Single-engined Fighters	"about 800"
Twin-engined Fighters	220
	"some 2,500 serviceable aircraft"

3. AHB/II/116/19, p. 76. In addition, *Luftflotte 5* in Norway had a striking force of:

Long-range bombers	130
Twin-engined fighters	30
Long-range reconnaissance	30
	190

4. Overy, op. cit., p. 33.
5. Klee, op. cit., p. 85.
6. Ibid, p. 82.
7. AHB/II/116/19, p. 81.
8. Alfred Price, *Battle of Britain: The Hardest Day, 18 August 1940*, Macdonald & Jane's, 1979, Granada edition, pp. 29–30.
9. Peter Calvocoressi and Guy Wint, *Total War*, p. 134, Allen Lane, The Penguin Press, 1972.

19. *"Adler Tag"; The "Numbers Game"* p. 185–p. 188

1. Klee, op. cit., pp. 83–4.
2. Winterbotham, op. cit., p. 46.
3. Ibid, p. 47.
4. Ibid.
5. Among others, wrongly identified, heavily bombed and severely damaged was the Coastal Command airfield at Eastchurch; superb efforts made it operational again 10 hours after the raid. The extremely poor quality of *Luftwaffe* Intelligence is noteworthy throughout the battle.
6. *The Battle of Britain Then and Now*, ed. Winston G. Ramsey, p. 707; "After the Battle Magazine", 1980.
7. Winterbotham, op. cit., pp. 47–8.
8. *The Battle of Britain Then and Now*, p. 707.
9. AHB/II/117/2(B), App. 36.

10. Ibid.
11. Ibid. As may be supposed, there was more than "a sense of deflation and disappointment amongst those who fought the battle" when the truth came out. The biographer of one of them wrote: "RAF pilots who fought in the battle flatly and vehemently disbelieve the German total" (Paul Brickhill, *Reach for the Sky*, Collins, 1957). We shall return to this subject.
12. Wood & Dempster, op. cit., p. 169.
13. *The Battle of Britain Then and Now*, p. 707.

20. *August, the crunch; Beaverbrook* p. 188–p. 194

1. Price, op. cit., p. 240.
2. Coastal Command figures extracted from AHB/II/117/3(B), App. XIV; Bomber Command from AHB/II/117/1(B) App. "U".
3. Wood & Dempster, op. cit., pp. 181–3.
4. Richards & Saunders, op. cit., i, p. 103.
5. Wood & Dempster, op. cit., p. 103.
6. Ibid, p. 104.
7. House of Commons Defence debate, November 12, 1936.
8. Churchill, op. cit., p. 561.
9. Ibid, pp. 286–7.
10. See essay on Beaverbrook in *Who's Who in World War II* by David Mason, p. 24, Weidenfeld & Nicolson, 1978.
11. Richards & Saunders, op. cit., i, p. 3.
12. Dean, op. cit., pp. 137–8.
13. *With Prejudice* by Marshal of the RAF Lord Tedder, p. 14, Cassell, 1966.
14. As Sir Maurice Dean says (op. cit., p. 137): "Sophisticated munitions of war cannot be conjured up in days, weeks, months or even in years." Churchill should have been well aware of this; a revealing chronological table of First World War tank production will be found on pp. 238–9 of the author's *White Heat* (1982).
15. Richards & Saunders, op. cit., i, p. 154.
16. Memorandum to Sinclair, 14.12.40, op. cit., p. 621.

21. *The "big wing"; Leigh-Mallory, Bader* p. 194–p. 205

1. *The First and the Last* by Adolf Galland, p. 36, Fontana, 1970.
2. OH (Collier), op. cit., p. 204.
3. Wood & Dempster, op. cit., p. 189.
4. Ibid, p. 176.
5. Ibid, p. 188.
6. OH (Collier), op. cit., p. 209.
7. Wood & Dempster, op. cit., p. 195.
8. Bond, op. cit., pp. 144–5.
9. Wright, op. cit., p. 41.
10. Lewin, op. cit., p. 89.
11. See Lucas, op. cit., pp. 99–100.
12. Wright, op. cit., p. 94.

13. OH (Collier), op. cit., p. 246.
14. Lucas relates how, serving in No. 19 (Spitfire) Squadron in March 1940, Bader felt the urge to carry out the very manoeuvre which had cost him his legs in 1931: "two carefully fashioned, very deliberate, straight and level slow rolls – one to the right followed by another to the left – right down on the deck." They worked beautifully, and Bader walked away from his Spitfire feeling rather pleased, but was perhaps slightly less pleased to encounter his station commander, who said to him: "Oh, Douglas, I *do* wish you wouldn't do that. You had *such* a nasty accident last time."
15. Lucas, op. cit., p. 95.
16. Lucas, op. cit. The following quotations are from pp. 128–9.
17. Ibid, p. 138.
18. Paul Brickhill; see Chapter 19, Note 12. Quoted in Wright, op. cit., pp. 176–9.
19. Wood & Dempster, op. cit., p. 199.
20. Ibid, pp. 215–16.
21. In July 1933 the Italian Marshal Italo Balbo set off on a formation flight of 24 Savoia Marchetti S 55 twin-hull seaplanes from Italy to Chicago and back. Twenty-three of them completed the flight, amidst hysterical enthusiasm in Fascist Italy. This should not disguise the fact that, as Howard and Gunston (op. cit., p. 141) say, the performance "was a supreme aeronautical achievement. It marked the development of aircraft up to a point when a large formation could make a controlled and well regimented long flight." Hence "balbo".
22. Wright, op. cit., p. 194.
23. Liddell Hart, op. cit., p. 106.
24. Lucas, op. cit., p. 138.
25. The claims, with 11 Group at 22 squadrons, work out at 28.5 "kills" per 11 Group squadron, 27 for a Duxford squadron; with 24 squadrons in 11 Group, their average drops to 26.2. One should not be hypnotized by these mathematics; they are mere indicators.
26. Statistics taken from *The Battle of Britain Then and Now*, p. 707; on a proportionate basis, they would reduce the Duxford claim to 70 or 74 "kills" according to the strength of 11 Group.
27. Wright, op. cit., p. 201.
28. Ibid, p. 172.
29. OH (Collier), op. cit., p. 267.
30. Extracted from *The Battle of Britain Then and Now*, p. 707.
31. Dean, op. cit., p. 144.
32. Wood & Dempster, op. cit., pp. 271–2.
33. Lucas, op. cit., p. 142.

22. *Battle of attrition; the climax* p. 206–p. 213

1. Klee, op. cit., p. 87.
2. Wood & Dempster, op. cit., p. 202.
3. Klee, op. cit., p. 87.

4. Very occasionally the belief was justified, as on the night of August 12/13 when five Hampdens of Nos. 49 and 83 Squadrons attacked an aqueduct of the Dortmund-Ems Canal. Two were shot down, but Flight Lieutenant R. A. B. Learoyd succeeded in placing a bomb to such effect that the canal was blocked for 10 days, "with the result that the movement of barges and motor-boats from the Rhineland to the invasion ports fell seriously behind schedule" (Richards, p. 182). He received the Victoria Cross for his night's work.

5. Winterbotham, op. cit., p. 54.

6. Wood & Dempster, op. cit., p. 216.

7. OH (Collier), op. cit., p. 237.

8. Wood & Dempster, op. cit., p. 219.

9. Ibid, p. 213.

10. Ibid, p. 212.

11. Ibid, p. 212–13.

12. Richards & Saunders, op. cit., i, p. 192.

13. General Ludendorff, *My War Memories*, ii, p. 583, Hutchinson, 1919.

14. The Battle of Britain was the "Verdun" of the RAF in the Second World War. Attrition, in the First World War, began when General Falkenhayn decided to attack an objective "for the retention of which the French General Staff would be compelled to throw in every man they have. If they do so the force of France will bleed to death . . ." (*General Headquarters and its Critical Decisions*, p. 217, Hutchinson, 1919). This was matched by Goering's Directive of August 19 (see p. 194) to "do the utmost damage possible to the enemy fighters". The French at Verdun in 1916 adopted the practice of *"roulement"* – quick replacement of divisions before they became worn out. By the end of the battle practically every division in the French Army had served at Verdun. Fighter Command did the same; by November only 13 squadrons had not, at some stage, passed through No. 11 Group. As "Laddie" Lucas says, "it was an unrelenting turnover".

   In November the categories were: "A", 26 squadrons; "B", 2 squadrons; "C", 22 squadrons, and 11 squadrons allocated to night duties.

15. OH (Collier), op. cit., p. 211.

16. Richards & Saunders, op. cit., i, p. 187, quoting Flying Officer R. S. Gilmour.

17. None of the specialized landing-craft used by the Allies in 1942–45 were available to the Germans, nor did they attempt to construct any. It may be noted that among the Army's requirements were 4,500 horses to be landed in the first wave.

   Sergeant John Hannah of No. 83 Squadron became the first air gunner to win the VC in an attack on invasion craft at Antwerp on the night of September 15/16.

18. Equal losses were sustained on seven days of battle:

July 13	6 each
July 31	7 each
August 6	6 each

August 22	4 each
September 11	29 each
September 14	13 each
September 20	8 each

On four days the *Luftwaffe* had the advantage:

	Luftwaffe	Fighter Command
July 19	5	10
August 7	3	4
September 28	12	17
October 30	8	9

19. Wood & Dempster, op. cit., p. 230.
20. Price, op. cit., p. 161.
21. *Their Finest Hour*, p. 297.
22. OH (Collier), op. cit., p. 242.
23. Wood & Dempster, op. cit., p. 231.
24. Winterbotham, op. cit., p. 58.
25. Bader, op. cit., p. 122.
26. Winterbotham, op. cit., pp. 58–9.
27. RUSI *Journal*, op. cit., p. 53.
28. Wood & Dempster, op. cit., p. 241.

23. *Defeat for Dowding* p. 213–p. 217

1. Wood & Dempster, op. cit., p. 262.
2. Group Captain E. B. Haslam, "How Lord Dowding Came to Leave Fighter Command", p. 182 (*Journal of Strategic Studies*, June 1981).
3. OH (Collier), op. cit., p. 255.
4. Haslam, op. cit.
5. Gunston, op. cit., p. 36.
6. Thetford, op. cit., p. 140.
7. OH (Collier), op. cit., p. 252.
8. In the first 17 days of October, Fighter Command lost 68 pilots killed, a daily average of four.
9. See Lucas, op. cit., p. 151.
10. Leigh-Mallory is said to have told Bader: "I don't know whether I can get you in. It's rather high-level stuff" (Wright, op. cit., p. 218). Air marshals, summoned to a "high-level" conference on major tactics, do not surreptitiously introduce squadron-leaders. Bader, whether he knew it or not, was Leigh-Mallory's "fast one".
11. Haslam, op. cit., p. 180.
12. Sholto Douglas (with Robert Wright): *Years of Command*, pp. 88 & 90, Collins, 1966.
13. Haslam, op. cit., p. 180.
    Dowding gained the nickname "Stuffy" at the Staff College, Camberley, in 1910. Virtually a non-drinker, he "was never particularly interested in the social aspects of the life of a young Army officer" (Wright, p. 29). The name clearly suited him, and stuck. As a squadron commander in

731

France, 1915–16, he was known to some of his irreverent juniors as "Old Starched Shirt" (see *Wind in the Wires* by Duncan Grinnell-Milne, Hurst & Blackett, 1933, Panther, 1957).

14. Wright, op. cit., p. 218.
15. Lucas, op. cit., p. 151.
16. Ibid, p. 153.
17. Wright, op. cit., p. 222.

24. *Victory for Fighter Command* p. 217–p. 220

1. Wood & Dempster, op. cit., p. 269.
2. Ibid.
3. Ibid. One is reminded of the last letter of Captain Albert Ball VC, RFC, to his father two days before he was killed: "Oh, it was a good fight, and the Huns were fine sports . . . but oh! I do get tired of living always to kill, and am really beginning to feel like a murderer . . ." (May 5, 1917).
4. AHB/II/117/2(B), p. 573.
5. Wood & Dempster, op. cit., p. 48.
6. Klee, op. cit., p. 91.
7. Richardson & Friedin, *The Fatal Decisions*, p. 24 (see Chapter 17, Note 13, p. 176).

25. *Battle of Britain: Envoi* p. 220–p. 222

1. Eg Robert Wright, Len Deighton (*Battle of Britain*, Cape, 1980).
2. Wright, op. cit., pp. 241–2.
3. Haslam, op. cit., p. 184.
4. OH (Collier), op. cit., p. 263. As Ronald Lewin says (*Ultra Goes to War*, p. 103) it is a "monstrous distortion" to say, as some have alleged, that Coventry was "sacrificed to save Ultra". A full account of the rôle of Air Intelligence is contained in the RUSI *Journal*, September 1976: "Air Intelligence and the Coventry Raid" by N. E. Evans. This makes clear that the defence failure was in no way attributable to strategic intention or planning, but to execution – for reasons succinctly stated by Lewin: "Britain was not ready for a Blitz. But the real disaster was the clear moonlight night." As Sir Maurice Dean says, irrespective of Intelligence, in the existing state of night defence, "Given the weather, Coventry or some larger West Midlands city was a dead duck from the start" (p. 196).
5. Dean, op. cit., p. 144.
6. Ibid, p. 145.
7. Wright, op. cit., p. 280.
8. Richards & Saunders, op. cit., i, p. 196.
9. Wood & Dempster, op. cit., p. 272.
10. Quoted in Price, op. cit., p. 252.
11. C. Day Lewis: "Airmen Broadcast"; *Word Over All*, p. 32, Jonathan Cape, 1943.

Battle of the Atlantic (I)

26. *Coastal Command: Rôle and equipment, U-boat war, wireless war*
    p. 223–p. 231

1. *The Grand Alliance*, p. 98.
2. See Chapter 8, Note 2, p. 70.
3. Dean, op. cit., p. 158.
4. AHB/II/117/3(A), i, pp. 158–60.
5. Ibid, p. 209.
6. W. S. Sims and B. J. Hendrick, *The Victory at Sea*, pp. 6–7, Murray, 1927.
7. The name derives from the *A*llied *S*ubmarine *D*etection *I*nvestigation Committee of 1917. The Committee evolved an entirely new system of submarine detection – in effect, as Alfred Price says, a kind of "underwater radar". A beam of electrical energy was directed into the water in front of the searching ship; any object encountered by this beam would reflect the energy back in the form of an echo. It was known at the time as the "Electrical Submarine Detector", and Admiral Jellicoe (*The Crisis of the Naval War*, p. 96, Cassell, 1920) tells us that "it was brought to perfection" in the late autumn of 1917. That is not precisely the case; it was only able to indicate range and direction. Depth was a matter of guesswork – hence the depth-charge "patterns", set to explode at varying depths.
8. AHB/II/117/3(A), p. 44; in my book, *White Heat* (p. 262), following Sir William Jameson (*The Most Formidable Thing*; Hart-Davis, 1965) I said that 2,949 flying-boats, seaplanes and aeroplanes were in naval use in 1918. It is a very large discrepancy; unfortunately, Sir William Jameson now being dead, I have not been able to trace the reason for it. The AHB Narrative, however, has Official History status, and must be taken as authoritative.
9. Ibid.
10. Roskill, *The War at Sea*, i, p. 34, HMSO, 1956 (Official History).
11. AHB/II/117/3(A), p. 44 (my italics).
12. Ibid, pp. 220–1.
13. AHB/II/117/3(B), ii, p. 49.
14. Ibid, p. 3.
15. Ibid.
16. OH (Roskill), op. cit., Appendix R.
17. AHB/II/117/3(A), pp. 252–4.
18. *"Beobachter Dienst"* = Observation Service.
19. Official History: "British Intelligence in the Second World War", i, p. 381, by F. H. Hinsley *et al.*; HMSO 1979.
20. This was the British and Allied Merchant Ship Code (BAMS); it was, says Donald McLachlan (*Room 39*, pp. 84–5), "a typical victim of the government parsimony and the mood of 'no more war' which ensured that our great merchant fleet faced the U-boat campaign with no sure method of concealing its communications".

21. Jurgen Rohwer, "The U-Boat War Against the Allied Supply Lines", in *Decisive Battles of World War II*, p. 262.
22. *The Gathering Storm*, p. 371.

27. *The U-boat enemy; bombs and depth-charges* p. 231–p. 234

1. AHB/II/117/3(B), p. 4.
2. Ibid, p. 50.
3. Richards & Saunders, op. cit., i, p. 62.
4. AHB/II/117/3(A), Appendix VIII.
5. See Price, *Aircraft Versus Submarines*, p. 44, William Kimber, 1973.
6. AHB/II/117/3(B), p. 48.

28. *The battle begins; The Dönitz system; ASV radar* p. 234–p. 240

1. AHB/II/117/3(B), pp. 120–1.
2. Green, op. cit., pp. 225–6.
3. Richards & Saunders, op. cit., i, p. 228.
4. Liddell Hart, op. cit., p. 385.
5. Harris, op. cit., p. 31.
6. Charles B. MacDonald (US Official Historian), *The Mighty Endeavour: American Armed Forces in the European Theater in World War II*, p. 225, OUP, 1969.
7. U-boat torpedoes had been fitted with a new magnetic pistol whose working proved to be erratic. In addition, during the long daylight hours experienced in the Norwegian campaign, U-boats remained submerged for much longer periods than they normally would. This meant that small air leaks from the high pressure air system built up considerable pressure inside the hull, which affected the depth-keeping mechanism, which in turn affected not only the new pistols but also the older type. These failures were rectified by June 1940. (AHB/II/117/3(B), p. 9.)
8. Price, op. cit., pp. 44–5.
9. MacDonald, op. cit., pp. 49–50.
10. AHB/II/117/3(B), pp. 270–1.
11. Ibid, p. 293; W/T = Wireless Telegraphy.
12. Price, op. cit., p. 37.
13. Ibid, p. 38.
14. Ibid, p. 54.
15. Ibid, p. 55.

29. *Lord Beaverbrook rushes in* p. 240–p. 244

1. This is the Defence Committee (Operations). Lord Ismay tells us that besides Churchill the committee "always included the Deputy Prime Minister, the three Service Ministers, and later the Foreign Secretary. In addition, other Ministers, such as the Minister for Home Security, and the Minister of War Transport, were invited to meetings at which problems affecting their Departments were to be discussed. The Chiefs of Staff were always in attendance." (*Memoirs*, p. 159, Heinemann, 1960.)

2. AHB/II/117/3(B), pp. 276–9.
3. Ibid; this is the source of all quotations in this section.
4. A shrewd observer of the interior scene, Robert Bruce Lockhart, wrote in his diary on November 25, 1940: "The battle of Whitehall is far more important to civil servants than the battle of Britain." (*Diaries 1939–1965*, ed. Kenneth Young, p. 84, Macmillan, 1980.)

30. *The Atlantic Gap: "The Crow and the Mole"; Western Approaches; False Dawn;* Bismarck *and others* p. 244–p. 250

1. Only 19 aircraft were lost on anti-U-boat patrol during the 16 months. Other tasks were: convoy escort; attacks on enemy shipping; reconnaissance of enemy shipping; reconnaissance of German Navy; attacks on German Navy; air mining; attacks on land targets (79 lost); fighter protection. In addition, Photographic Reconnaissance for the whole of the RAF (PRU) was placed under Coastal Command administration on June 18, 1940. Seventeen aircraft were lost on this duty.
2. In the course of the debate on the transfer of Coastal Command, the CAS stated "that such a change would affect 28,000 men" (AHB/II/117/3(B), p. 283). As regards aircraft, it should be noted that establishments and operational numbers could vary sharply. The AHB Narrative points out that 28 Coastal squadrons in September 1940 had an initial equipment of 461 aircraft, but only 226 available with fully trained crews; 100 more aircraft were serviceable, but the crews were incomplete. The training problem was acute for the whole of the RAF at this stage.
3. As Denis Richards says, the Air Staff "remained resolutely deaf" to any suggestion of allocating some of the new long-range Handley Page Halifaxes to Coastal Command. The Halifax came into squadron service in November 1940, and its first operation was in March 1941; teething troubles then kept it out of action until June. It became a great standby of Bomber Command, for which it was now being jealously preserved. The Air Staff was concerned lest, in the tart words of Air Marshal Harris (DCAS) "twenty U-boats and a few Focke-Wulf in the Atlantic would have provided the efficient anti-aircraft defence of all Germany."
4. AHB/II/117/3(B), p. 305, fn 4.
5. Churchill, *Their Finest Hour*, p. 530; AHB/II/117/3(B), p. 272: Defence Committee meeting, October 31, 1940: "Regarding bases in Eire, it felt that negotiations with de Valera would be difficult; that seizure and maintenance of naval and air bases against the will of the government and people of Eire would involve a grave military commitment, but that it might have to be done if the threat on our Western Approaches became mortal."
6. AHB/II/117/3(B), pp. 300–2.
7. See Liddell Hart, op. cit., p. 376.
8. Churchill, *The Grand Alliance*, pp. 107–9: full text.
9. Royal Institute of International Affairs, *Chronology and Index of the Second World War*, p. 56; Newspaper Archive Developments Ltd., 1975. Chur-

chill (*Grand Alliance*, p. 196) describes the air raid on the Piraeus, April 6, in which SS *Clan Fraser* blew up with 200 tons of TNT: "This attack alone cost us and the Greeks eleven ships, aggregating 43,000 tons."

10. AHB/II/117/3(B), pp. 300–2.
11. Richards & Saunders, op. cit., i, p. 236 (sorties); Richards also says that "1,655 tons of bombs were aimed at the German battle-cruisers in two months". However, Sir Richard Peirse complained to the CAS on April 15 of having been compelled, since January 10, "to throw 750 tons of high explosive into Brest harbour". This figure was later amended to 829 tons. (Webster & Frankland, op. cit., i, p. 167 & fn 2.)
12. OH (Webster & Frankland), op. cit., i, p. 168.
13. Rohwer, op. cit., p. 265.
14. All the above statistics of shipping losses, and those to follow, as well as statistics of sinkings of U-boats (with causes) are from Captain Roskill's admirable Official History, *The War at Sea*, in its copious appendices.
15. The Beaufighter began operations in Coastal Command in March 1941 (252 Squadron).
16. June 14; Bowhill went to form the new RAF Ferry Command on July 18. This increasingly important task was absorbed into Transport Command in 1943.
17. Richards & Saunders, op. cit., i, p. 227.

The Strategic Air Offensive (I)

31. *Newall and Portal; the Growing Service; the Empire Training Scheme* p. 251–p. 259

1. Later Marshal of the Royal Air Force, Governor-General of New Zealand and Baron. AM denotes the Albert Medal which he won for conspicuous gallantry in extinguishing a fire in a bomb store, while commanding No. 12 Squadron, RFC, in France in 1916.
2. See Roskill, *Hankey: Man of Secrets*, iii, op. cit., pp. 291–3.
3. Slessor, *The Central Blue*, op. cit., p. 241.
4. Richards, *Portal of Hungerford*, op. cit., p. 168.
5. Ibid; A. J. P. Taylor supplied this information to Mrs Elizabeth Hennessy, researching for Denis Richards.
6. Bruce Lockhart, *Diaries*, p. 65. Beaverbrook (among many others) was deeply agitated at this time by the RAF's lack of dive-bombers and manifest reluctance to invest in such a weapon. The abject failure of the seemingly almighty *Stuka* was yet to come.
7. Slessor, op. cit.
8. Lord Ismay, *Memoirs*, p. 318.
9. *Their Finest Hour*, p. 19.
10. Slessor, op. cit., p. 240.
11. Richards, op. cit., p. 182.
12. Portal was 47 in 1940; Pound was 63; General (later Field-Marshal) Sir

John Dill CIGS, was 59; General (later Field-Marshal Lord) Sir Alan Brooke, who succeeded Dill in December 1941, was then 58.

13. Fraser, *Alanbrooke*, Ch. I, Collins, 1982.
14. The senior staff officers' penalty, often held against them by the unthinking; a conspicuous example was Field-Marshal Sir William Robertson, CIGS, 1915–1918, of whom the Prime Minister of the day thought it appropriate to write that he "never saw a battle".
15. Richards, op. cit., p. 173; the following quotations are from the same source.
16. *The RAF and Two World Wars*, p. 183.
17. Richards, op. cit., p. 219, quoting the Portal Papers in West Ashling House.
18. Slessor, op. cit., p. 41.
19. Richards, op. cit., p. 220.
20. On March 18, 1944 Freeman wrote to Portal: "Why did we get rid of Dowding, who did something, and retain a number of inefficients a little junior to him who have nothing whatsoever to their credit?" He went on to suggest that it might be time to "get rid of Sinclair". The phrase "*we* get rid of Dowding" is interesting: who are "we"? The great collective Air Ministry "we" – or is the meaning rather more personal? (See Richards, op. cit., p. 221.)
21. AHB/II/116/14, App. 3; the 1939 total includes 234 officers and 1,500 other ranks of the WAAF. Just under 14,000 officers and men (no women) were serving overseas.
22. Ibid, and App. 4. By this time the WAAF had expanded to 3,012 officers and 61,297 other ranks. A total of 103,982 (12.4 per cent), including 30 women, were serving overseas.
23. Dean, op. cit., p. 112.
24. See p. 192.
25. AHB/II/116/17, pp. 145–6; in 1941 another 106 sites were added, and in 1942 a further 91, whereafter this process virtually ceased.
26. Richards, op. cit., pp. 130–1.
27. Dean, op. cit., p. 77.
28. Ibid, p. 77.
29. Richards & Saunders, op. cit., iii, pp. 371–2.
30. AHB/II/117/1(C), pp. 24–6.
31. Ibid.
32. From September 1940 to May 1941, Fighter Command claimed to have destroyed 186½ enemy aircraft. The claims were taken as actual figures (and are reproduced as such in Lord Douglas's *Years of Command*, p. 127). The German records, needless to say, do not support this. Thus we find that in April 1941 Fighter Command and AA Command between them claimed 90 enemy aircraft destroyed at night, but the German records show only 75 destroyed over the United Kingdom in night *and* day operations, and in attacks on shipping. On the night of the last great raid on London (May 10), 19 victories were credited to single-engined

fighters, four to twin-engined fighters, four to anti-aircraft guns and one
to an intruder – a total of 28. "In fact, the Germans lost only eight aircraft
destroyed (including one which crashed on take-off) and three damaged"
(OH (Collier), pp. 278–80). Lord Douglas writes with bitterness of the
"pallid summaries" of the Official Historians, Denis Richards and Basil
Collier. But it is the bounden duty of the historian to seek out the truth to
the best of his ability, and set it down, however displeasing, without fear or
favour, which is what both of these writers do.

32. *Bomber offensive resumed; German morale; area bombing*
    p. 259–p. 269

1. *Their Finest Hour*, p. 567: Churchill to Beaverbrook, July 8, 1940.
2. Ibid, p. 405; Memorandum, "The Munitions Situation", September 3.
3. Slessor, op. cit., p. 366.
4. AHB/II/117/1(B), p. 151; Portal to DCAS, July 17, 1940; my italics.
5. Richards, op. cit., p. 166.
6. See pp. 9–10.
7. OH (Webster & Frankland), op. cit., i, pp. 150–1.
8. The Directives to Bomber Command normally appear over the signature
   of the Deputy CAS (in this case Air Vice-Marshal Sholto Douglas), and
   usually with the opening words: "I am directed to inform you . . ." The
   authority behind them, if not the actual authorship, is always, of course,
   that of the CAS.
9. OH (Webster & Frankland), op. cit., i, p. 157.
10. Ibid, iv, p. 129.
11. "The Germans waged World War II with oil, chemicals, rubber and
    explosives made largely from coal, air, and water . . . Less than 15 per cent
    of their aviation fuel and only a fourth of all their oil products made early
    in 1944 came from crude oil. The rest came from coal as did also nearly all
    of Germany's rubber, explosives, and other war chemicals . . . The oil,
    chemical, rubber, explosives, and other industries, in short, were inter-
    locked not only by their mutual dependence on coal but also historically,
    geographically, and mechanically. They were so closely and intricately
    woven together, in fact, that they were needlessly vulnerable to strategic
    bombing – but Hitler did not complain until too late." (US Strategic
    Bombing Survey, Oil Division Final Report, p. 10.)
12. OH (Webster & Frankland), op. cit., iv, pp. 194–5.
13. Ibid, pp. 198–200 (all COS extracts).
14. General von Kuhl, *Der Weltkrieg, 1914–1918* (Berlin), p. 113.
15. *The First World War*, p. 200, Longmans, 1960.
16. According to the US Strategic Bombing Survey, 85 per cent of all bombs
    dropped on Germany was subsequent to January 1, 1944, 72 per cent
    subsequent to July 1.
17. AHB/II/117/1(C), p. 65.
18. Wellingtons, Whitleys and even Hampdens still counted as "heavies"
    (though Hampdens were usually reserved for special functions, especially

mine-laying). "Mediums" were Blenheims, later downgraded to "light", and their replacements, Bostons, Mosquitoes and (briefly) Venturas.

19. PRO: AIR 2/8069: AOA, HQ Bomber Command (Air Commodore F. J. Linnell): Memorandum on Expansion of Bomber Command November 1940 to December 1941, November 14, 1940.
20. AHB/II/117/1(C), pp. 26–7; four reasons are offered for this low average: 1) the heavy squadrons were far below strength, 2) only 60 per cent of crews were fit for operations, 3) serviceability stood normally at about 65 per cent, 4) it was impossible to transfer surplus crews in one squadron to surplus aircraft in another.
21. *Their Finest Hour*, p. 604.
22. OH (Webster & Frankland), op. cit., i, p. 156.
23. AHB/II/117/1(B), p. 165.
24. OH (Webster & Frankland), op. cit., i, p. 233.
25. AHB/II/117/1(B), p. 122.
26. November 15, 1940; Churchill, op. cit., p. 611.
27. AHB/II/117/1(B), pp. 153–4.
28. Ibid.
29. Ibid.
30. Ibid.
31. Air Staff Operations Summary (ASOS) No. 27, December 18.
32. Ibid.
33. OH (Webster & Frankland), op. cit., i, p. 226.

33. *Photographic reconnaissance* p. 269–p. 275

1. OH (Webster & Frankland), op. cit., i, p. 122.
2. AHB/II/116/16 (Monograph: *Photographic Reconnaissance*, i), pp. 113–14.
3. Ibid.
4. Dean, op. cit., p. 169.
5. This and following quotations from AHB/II/116/16, i, pp. 198–201.
6. Ibid, pp. 196–7.
7. Ibid, p. 196.
8. Dean, op. cit., p. 170.
9. OH (Webster & Frankland), op. cit., i, p. 221.
10. Constance Babington Smith, *Evidence in Camera*, Chatto & Windus, 1958.
11. AHB/II/117/1(C), pp. 64–5.
12. Babington Smith, op. cit.
13. AHB/II/117/1(C), op. cit.
14. Ibid.
15. OH (Webster & Frankland), op. cit., i, p. 163.
16. Ibid, p. 228.
17. Ibid, p. 164.

34. *Oil; "diversions"; heavy bombers; the Mosquito* p. 275–p. 282

1. Roskill, op. cit., p. 476.
2. OH (Webster & Frankland), op. cit., i, p. 159.
3. Ibid.
4. Ibid, p. 162.
5. AHB/II/117/1(B), p. 146.
6. OH (Webster & Frankland), op. cit., i, p. 164.
7. Churchill, op. cit., pp. 635–6.
8. AHB/II/117/1(C), p. 15.
9. Harris, op. cit., p. 101.
10. AHB/II/117/1(C), pp. 17–18.
11. This meant that all Groups of Bomber Command had to ferry their own replacements. The maintenance units were, in many cases, as far away as Scotland or Northern Ireland; with winter causing further delays, this could mean a crew being away from its squadron for as much as a fortnight. At the beginning of March, for example, No. 3 Group was awaiting collection of 20 aircraft. With 10 sorties as a squadron average, this was equivalent to the loss of two squadrons from the order of battle. (AHB/II/117/1(B), pp. 147–8.)
12. Tedder, op. cit., pp. 9–10.
13. AHB/II/117/1(C), pp. 21–2.

35. *New Allies; "Rhubarbs" and "Circuses"; compulsions of alliance* p. 282–p. 288

1. Alexander Werth, *Russia at War 1941–1945*, pp. 401, 403, Barrie & Rockliff, 1964.
2. OH (Webster & Frankland), op. cit., iv, p. 136.
3. Douglas, op. cit., p. 114.
4. OH (Collier), op. cit., p. 292.
5. See p. 259, Chapter 31, Note 32.
6. OH (Webster & Frankland), op. cit., i, pp. 175–6.
7. Ibid, p. 236.
8. Ibid, p. 237.
9. AHB/II/117/2(D), App. (V)F.
10. OH (Collier), p. 294, fn 2.
11. Richards & Saunders, op. cit., i, p. 387.
12. Klee, op. cit., p. 90.
13. General Josef Kammhuber was given the task of organizing the new Night Fighter Division (later *Fliegerkorps* XII) in July 1940. In October, he set up three night-fighter zones, positioned to lie across the path of RAF bombers attacking the Ruhr. Each zone contained a searchlight battalion and two of the new *Würzburg A* radar sets, as well as night fighters. Each fighter was contained in its own "box", circling a radio beacon until directed towards British raiders by the central control. The idea of a tight, even overlapping, chain of such boxes, covering the Ruhr (and later other

740

sensitive areas), soon followed; this was the beginning of what the RAF (but not the Germans) called the "Kammhuber Line". In conjunction with the always very effective German AA fire, this system of defence, with ever-improving radar equipment, won the sincere respect of Bomber Command.

14. AHB/II/117/1(C), pp. 30–1, 10A. The same source informs us that between April and July 1941, 108 medium and 312 light bombers were sent overseas.

15. It is a curiosity of the AHB Narratives that the word "casualties" is generally used in reference to aircraft (though "wastage" is also sometimes used). Aircrew losses are not regularly stated; these figures are therefore an extrapolation from the standard crew establishments of the various types. It need hardly be said that the actual aircraft often carried passengers on special duties, who would naturally be lost with the aircraft itself.

16. Air Staff Operational Summaries Nos. 221–9.

17. OH (Webster & Frankland), op. cit., i, p. 241. Casualties supplied by AHB research.

18. On August 28.

19. British bomber production in August was only 331 machines (AHB/II/117/1(C), p. 32).

20. *The Grand Alliance*, p. 729.

21. Ibid, p. 730; August 30.

36. *Four thousand bombers; euphoria and despondency; the Butt Report; air policy dispute* p. 289–p. 298

1. Slessor, op. cit., p. 385.

2. The three-flight squadron did not become universal; in March 1945, for example, the Bomber Command Order of Battle shows that in No. 1 Group (Lancaster I, III), nine squadrons had two flights, five had three; in No. 4 Group (Halifax III, VI), five had two flights, six had three; in No. 5 Group (Lancaster I, III) 14 had two flights and only one (the famous 617 "Dam-Busters") had three.

3. Slessor, op. cit., p. 386.

4. Harris, op. cit., p. 53.

5. Slessor wrote: "I was convinced – and so remain – that the Air Ministry programme was far beyond our reach, and moreover more than we needed for the job in hand" (op. cit., p. 386).

6. The meeting in Placentia Bay, Newfoundland, on August 9, 1941, at which the Atlantic Charter was drawn up.

7. AHB/II/117/1(C), p. 85.

8. Ibid.

9. In the Crete evacuation the Royal Navy lost three cruisers, six destroyers and 29 other craft; one battleship, four cruisers and seven destroyers were damaged.

10. Codename for the German attack on the USSR.

11. OH (Webster & Frankland), op. cit., iv, p. 205.
12. Ibid, pp. 206–7.
13. Ibid, i, p. 179; Max Hastings (*Bomber Command*, p. 108; Michael Joseph, 1979) says Peirse "had already achieved a reputation for almost arrogant overconfidence about the work of his Command", but as we have seen (p. 267) Peirse had been doubtful for some time, though not to the extent warranted by the Butt Report. In *The Destruction of Dresden* (p. 32, William Kimber, 1963) David Irving refers to "what the neutral free press abroad had been proclaiming for a year about the impotence of the British bomber force". Yet, as we have also seen, neutrals were in considerable part responsible for over-optimism (p. 274).
14. OH (Webster & Frankland), op. cit., i, p. 180.
15. Ibid.
16. Ibid, pp. 177–8.
17. Ibid, pp. 204–5.
18. Churchill, June 8, 1941; Webster & Frankland, op. cit., i, p. 117.
19. Portal to Churchill, September 25; ibid. p. 182.
20. Admittedly 178 of these were Lancasters, giving a much higher bomb-load; but 128 were still Wellingtons.
21. A characteristic example of Churchill's vision.
22. Churchill to Portal, September 27; OH (Webster & Frankland), op. cit., i, p. 183.
23. Portal to Churchill, October 2; Richards, *Portal of Hungerford*, pp. 189–90.
24. If such a thing could have existed, it would most likely have been the U-boat, especially the Type XXI, which came very close to being a true submarine, virtually impossible to hunt. But it cannot be called a "war-winner", because by the time it appeared Germany had lost the war. No weapon can escape its content.
25. The Air Staff admitted that its pre-war prognostications had been "crystal-gazing".
26. Churchill, op. cit., pp. 451–2.

Part IV: The Victory
The Mediterranean

37. *Middle East Command; the Takoradi Route; Longmore's problems* p. 301–p. 309

1. *Statistics of the Military Effort of the British Empire During the Great War*, p. 740; *Strength and Casualties of the Armed Forces and Auxiliary Services of the United Kingdom 1939 to 1945*, p. 2; Cmd. 6832; HMSO, 1946.
2. One may cite as examples No. 44 (Rhodesian) Squadron (the first to receive Lancasters in 1941) whose aircrew were Rhodesian, as were 128 of the 490 ground-crew; also No. 1 Squadron, Southern Rhodesian Air Force, which was reformed at Nairobi on April 22, 1940 as No. 237 (Rhodesia) Squadron, RAF.

3. Hilary St George Saunders, *Royal Air Force 1939–45*, iii, pp. 370–1. Richards & Saunders, iii, op. cit., pp. 370–1.
4. 36,000 men in Egypt, 27,500 in Palestine, with another 19,000 in the Sudan, Somaliland and Kenya, facing Italian East Africa; (Official History, *The Mediterranean and Middle East*, i, pp. 93–4, by Major-General I. S. O. Playfair with Commander G. M. S. Stitt, RN, Brigadier C. J. C. Molony and Air Vice-Marshal S. E. Toomer; HMSO, 1954).
5. AHB/II/117/8(A), *The Middle East Campaigns*, i, p. 1.
6. Ibid.
7. Ibid, pp. 1–2.
8. Ibid.
9. There is general acceptance that the Italians in Libya numbered about 250,000. On East Africa, opinions vary: Captain B. H. Liddell Hart (*History of the Second World War*) says "more than 200,000 men"; Ronald Lewin (*The Chief*) says "some 300,000"; Brigadier Peter Young (*World War 1939–45: A Short History*, p. 79) says 350,000. He has good authority for this: "On 30th May Mussolini informed Hitler that there were 350,000 Italian and native troops." (OH (Playfair), i, p. 93, fn 2.)
10. Dean, op. cit., p. 204.
11. Richards & Saunders, op. cit., i, p. 242.
12. Philip Guedalla, *Middle East 1940–42: A Study in Air Power*, p. 157, Hodder & Stoughton, 1944.
13. *With Prejudice*, op. cit., p. 36. Tedder flew in via Takoradi to take up his post as Deputy AOC-in-C.
14. Richards & Saunders, op. cit., i, p. 248.
15. Guedalla, op. cit., p. 192.
16. Tedder, op. cit., p. 47.
17. AHB/II/117/8(A), p. 15.
18. Ibid.
19. Longmore to Air Commodore Collishaw, July 17; AHB/II/117/8(A), pp. 44–5.
20. *Their Finest Hour*, p. 609.
21. Martin Gilbert, *Winston S. Churchill*, iv, Companion Part I, Heinemann 1977, p. 388.
22. AHB/II/117/8(A), p. 71.
23. Churchill, op. cit., p. 610.
24. Ibid, p. 635.

38. *War with Italy; war for aerodromes; Operation "Compass"*
p. 309–p. 318

1. The Italians also used the SM81 as a night bomber. Contrary to the normal practice of aircraft designation this was older, not younger, than the SM79. It was, in fact, merely a military version of the civil SM73. Its maximum speed was 210–211 mph, and its bomb-load was 2,200 lb at a range of 1,030 miles, or 4,400 lb at 895 miles (see Richards, op. cit. App. VIII).

2. Gunston, op. cit., p. 194.
3. Guedalla, op. cit., p. 72.
4. AHB/II/117/8(A), App. XII.
5. Richards & Saunders, op. cit., i, p. 243; but NB on p. 410 Richards gives an "official Italian total" of 1,529.
6. Guedalla, op. cit., p. 72.
7. OH (Playfair) op. cit., i, pp. 95–6.
8. Ibid; the roll-call of types in East Africa is impressive: 85 Wellesleys and Blenheims, 9 Vincents, 24 Hartbees (SAAF), 15 Junkers 86 (SAAF), 30 Gladiators and Furies.
9. OH (Playfair) op. cit., i, p. 97.
10. AHB/II/117/8(A), p. 31.
11. OH (Playfair), op. cit., i, p. 112.
12. Ibid.
13. AHB/II/117/8(A), p. 33.
14. Longmore to Collishaw, July 5; AHB/II/117/8(A), 44.
15. He replaced Marshal Balbo, shot down and killed by Italian AA over Tobruk on June 28. "Sir Arthur Longmore caused a note of respectful regret to be dropped, which was acknowledged with gratitude" (OH (Playfair), op. cit., i, p. 113).
16. Even so, the demands of the other Services weighed heavily; thus, "The Navy would require air cooperation in interrupting supplies to Eastern Libya. For this air reconnaissance of enemy ports and seas would be needed. Enemy warships and transports would have to be attacked, convoys protected and troops and bases defended from air attack" (AHB/II/117/8(A), p. 26).
17. AHB/II/117/8(A), p. 7.
18. Ibid, p. 59.
19. Guedalla, op. cit., p. 100.
20. As we have seen, this had been the lesson of Norway and of France, but it was too early for it to have been absorbed; and the drama of the Battle of Britain directed attention to a quite different quarter.
21. John Connell, *Wavell: Scholar and Soldier*, pp. 204–5, Collins, 1964.
22. AHB/II/117/8(A), p. 67.
23. Eden to Chiefs of Staff, October 16; ibid. p. 68.
24. AHB: Middle East Operations Records; this total includes two Skuas and seven Swordfish of the Fleet Air Arm.
25. Thus on November 16 a Lysander of No. 208 Squadron was intercepted by three CR42s. "Although out-gunned and out-manoeuvred, the Lysander fought off the fighters for some time and shot down one of them before it was itself destroyed, the pilot and gunner escaping by parachute to be picked up later by our forward troops" (AHB/II/117/8(A), p. 68).
26. Ibid.
27. Guedalla, op. cit., p. 99.
28. OH (Playfair), op. cit., i, p. 272.
29. AHB/II/117/8(A), pp. 77–8.

30. OH (Playfair), op. cit., i, p. 272.
31. Ibid, p. 362.
32. Connell, op. cit., p. 295; it is to be supposed that the RAF contributed to this reticence.
33. AHB/II/117/8(A), p. 80.
34. Guedalla, op. cit., p. 63.
35. Ibid, p. 98.
36. AHB/II/117/8(A), p. 90.
37. Ibid, pp. 91–2; a large number of these, of course, were victims of the Italian Air Force's inability to maintain its aircraft.
38. Ibid.
39. Gunston (op. cit., p. 136) says of the MC200 that "in combat with the lumbering Hurricane it proved effective", and adds that it "saw more combat than any other Italian type".
40. The aircrew involved numbered 68, but this is not the casualty total, since fortunately a number survived unhurt.

39. *East Africa; air support* p. 318–p. 325

1. *The Hinge of Fate*, p. 541; what he actually wrote was: "It may *almost* be said 'Before Alamein we never had a victory. After Alamein we never had a defeat.' Italics are mine; the word "almost" is usually forgotten – which is why memorable phrases can be unfortunate.
2. It was possible to fly in bombers from Libya, but not fighters. However, the Italians were able to maintain a bi-weekly mail service between East Africa and Italy. This carried personnel, mail and stores; 30 CR42s were brought in from Italy by this service. The aircraft timed their arrival in Eritrea for dawn, and took off at night (AHB/II/117/8(E): *The Campaign in East Africa*, p. 103).
3. OH (Hinsley), op. cit., i, p. 381.
4. Review of the above in the RUSI *Journal*, September 1978 (p. 73).
5. Richards & Saunders, op. cit., i, p. 252.
6. 10th Indian Brigade consisted of a battalion of Garwhalis, a battalion of Baluchis and a battalion of the Essex Regiment.
7. AHB/II/117/8(E), pp. 66–71 (Gallabat narrative).
8. Ibid, p. 101.
9. Field-Marshal Sir William Slim, *Unofficial History*, p. 140, Cassell, 1959. In this splendid collection of vignettes of that great soldier's career, his account of Gallabat appears under the heading, "Counsel of Fears".
10. AHB/II/117/8(E), pp. 66–71.
11. The Caproni Ca 133 was a three-engined "Colonial" type bomber and transport. Its maximum speed was 174 mph, range 839 miles, bomb-load 2,200 lb and characteristic armament three 7.7 mm machine guns.
12. This happened within the "bailiwick" of a detachment of No. 1 (Fighter) Squadron, South African Air Force, which was much annoyed. The following morning, three pilots of the Squadron took off without permission, found the Italians by a shrewd guess (three CR42s and some SM79s

and Ca 133s), attacked them on the ground, destroying the CR42s and damaging the bombers.

13. AHB/II/117/8(E), pp. 43–4.
14. Ibid, p. 80, quoting Air Commodore Slatter's report.
15. Ibid, p. 85.
16. OH (Playfair), op. cit., i, p. 439.
17. 4th and 5th Indian Divisions.
18. Air Commodore Slatter's Report ("Air Operations in the Sudan, etc.").
19. Air operations from Kenya were conducted entirely by the South African Air Force, with eight squadrons (three fighter, three bomber, two Army Cooperation). When the campaign opened, among the fighters were to be found Hawker Fury IIs (open-cockpit biplane, first flight 1936) and Gloster Gauntlets (the last of the RAF's open-cockpit fighters; entered service May 1935); among the bombers were the Junkers Ju 86Z-7 (adapted civil transports) and Hartbees, South African-built versions of the Hawker Audax Army Cooperation biplane which had entered RAF service in 1930.
20. AHB/II/117/8(E), pp. 123–4.
21. Ibid, p. 152, fn 2.
22. Lieutenant-General Cunningham's despatch.

40. *The Greek fiasco, 1941* p. 325–p. 334

1. OH (Playfair), op. cit., i, p. 319.
2. *Their Finest Hour*, p. 472.
3. Ibid.
4. This was a French jibe: *"courir au secours du vainqueur"* (see C. R. M. F. Cruttwell, *A History of the Great War 1914–1918*, p. 135; Oxford, 1934).
5. AHB/II/117/8(F), *The Campaign in Greece*, p. 1.
6. Ibid.
7. *Their Finest Hour*, Churchill, op. cit., p. 473.
8. OH (Hinsley), op. cit., i, p. 259.
9. OH (Playfair), op. cit., i, p. 239.
10. Ibid.
11. Ibid; Wavell to Chiefs of Staff, November 17.
12. Gilbert, op. cit., iii, Companion Part I, p. 545.
13. *The Grand Alliance*, p. 84.
14. Richards & Saunders, op. cit., i, p. 278; Longmore to Portal, January 31.
15. Ibid.
16. Churchill, op. cit., p. 649.
17. Richards & Saunders, op. cit., i, p. 294.
18. This point is made with great clarity in Ronald Lewin's *The Chief*, Hutchinson, 1980, pp. 92–112.
19. OH (Hinsley), op. cit., p. 357.
20. Churchill, op. cit., p. 63.
21. Connell, op. cit., p. 336.
22. Churchill, op. cit., p. 63.

23. Tedder, op. cit., p. 32.
24. AHB/II/117/8(F), p. 79.
25. Churchill, op. cit., pp. 63–5.
26. AHB/II/117/8(F), pp. 54–5.
27. Richards & Saunders, op. cit., i, p. 256.
28. AHB/II/117/8(F), pp. 43–4.
29. Ibid, p. 13.
30. Ibid, pp. 13–15; my italics.
31. Ibid.
32. Ibid, pp. 10–12.
33. AHB/II/116/19, p. 123.
34. Australian Correspondent in *The Times*, April 19, 1941.
35. Tedder, op. cit., p. 73.

41. *The* Afrika Korps *arrives; first Desert defeat* p. 334–p. 337

1. Fraser, *And We Shall Shock Them*, p. 113, Hodder & Stoughton, 1983. There were, as he says, other British troops engaged: "independent brigades, army and corps troops, and British units in Indian formations". But the division, although not an exact measure, was the unit of calculation throughout the Second World War.
2. OH (Hinsley), op. cit., i, p. 386, says: "Despite their knowledge of the arrival of the German Air Force in Libya, the intelligence authorities were slow to conclude that the German Army would follow." Ronald Lewin (*The Chief*, p. 95) adds that "the service of Ultra intelligence to Cairo in early 1941 was of a most rickety character".
3. See Lewin, *Ultra Goes to War*, pp. 160–1.
4. AHB/II/117/8(A) p. 111. The Official History adds that the Italian Air Force at this stage was "now almost negligible".
5. AHB, ibid, pp. 132–3.
6. OH (Playfair), op. cit., ii, p. 31.
7. AHB/II/117/8(A), pp. 128–9.
8. Ibid.
9. Connell, op. cit., p. 396.
10. AHB/II/117/8(A), pp. 133–5.

42. *Tedder in command; "Combined operation in the full sense";
a system of air support* p. 337–p. 347

1. AHB/II/117/8(F), App. "J".
2. AHB/II/117/8(A), pp. 193–6 offers these two tables to illustrate:

	Hurricane	Blenheim	Wellington	Maryland	Tomahawk
Total quota (to end of April)	316	408	112	143	465
Total arrivals	244	239	110	29	25
Arrears	72	169	2	114	440

Takoradi arrivals (to end of April)	251	197		51	195
Dispatches	235	164		19	39
Outstanding	16	33		32	156

3. Tedder, op. cit., p. 83.
4. Richards & Saunders, op. cit., i, p. 311.
5. Dean, op. cit., p. 212.
6. As AHB/II/117/8(A), says, "there were a number of aircraft which may be termed 'unaccounted for', after arrivals, losses and strength had been added up"; it offers this table:

	Arrived, June 1940– May 1941	Wastage, June 1940– May 1941	Serviceable (early May)	Unaccounted for or unserviceable
Hurricane	244	90 (inc. 18 to Malta)	80	74
Blenheim	239*	138	110	91
Wellington	110	25	80	5
				170

*includes 100 already in the Middle East.

7. Richards and Saunders, op. cit., ii, p. 163.
8. Ibid, p. 167.
9. Tedder, op. cit., p. 190.
10. OH (Playfair), op. cit., ii, p. 290.
11. Tedder, op. cit., p. 189.
12. Ibid, p. 139.
13. OH (Playfair), op. cit., ii, p. 291.
14. Perhaps his most insulting remark on this subject was in a note to Sinclair and Portal on June 29, 1941, on the question of the defence of airfields: "Every airfield should be a stronghold of fighting air-groundmen, and not the abode of uniformed civilians in the prime of life protected by detachments of soldiers."
15. Tedder, op. cit., p. 146.
16. Ibid, p. 163.
17. Ibid, p. 124.
18. Admiral of the Fleet Viscount Cunningham of Hyndhope, *A Sailor's Odyssey*, pp. 415–16, Hutchinson, 1951.
19. Tedder to Cunningham, June 27; Tedder, op. cit., p. 148.
20. AHB/II/117/8(A), p. 155.
21. Such failures were one of the hazards of the desert war. As Ronald Lewin says (*Ultra Goes to War*, p. 165): ". . . reception conditions over the Western Desert were notoriously unreliable . . . The difficulties of transmitting from Cairo up to the front may be illustrated by the fact that it was often more effective for a signal to be sent from Abbasia to Whaddon

[Hall], by 'bouncing' it off the Heaviside layer in the upper atmosphere, and for it then to be re-transmitted immediately from England to the Liaison Unit with the Desert Army, rather than for the message to be sent by radio over a few hundred miles of wilderness to the battle-front."

22. AHB/II/117/8(A), p. 174.
23. Ibid, p. 175.
24. AHB Monograph, "Air Support", p. 7; AHB/II/116/22.
25. The 40 mm Bofors gun was developed in Sweden in the 1930s. Its outstanding feature was its rate of fire: 120 2-lb shells per minute – "devastating against aircraft of 1940 vintage" (Alfred Price). It, or its derivatives, became the standard light AA gun of most combatant nations in the Second World War.
26. OH (Playfair), op. cit., ii, pp. 287–8, for this and following quotation.
27. Tedder, op. cit., p. 170.

43. *Air support/Army cooperation* p. 347–p. 352

1. See Shelford Bidwell and Dominick Graham, *Fire-Power: British Army Weapons and Theories of War 1904–1945*, p. 263, Allen & Unwin, 1982.
2. AHB/II/116/22, p. 11.
3. C. E. Carrington, "Air Liaison Officer", unpublished MS, Chap. II, pp. 8–9.
4. Ibid.
5. Ibid, Chap. V, pp. 8–9.
6. AHB/II/116/22, p. 24.
7. Carrington, op. cit., Chap. III, p. 3.
8. AHB/II/116/22, p. 25.
9. Carrington, op. cit., Chap. I, pp. 15–16.

44. *Churchill and Tedder; "Crusader"* p. 352–p. 362

1. Lewin, *The Life and Death of the Afrika Korps*, p. 30, Batsford, 1977.
2. Richards & Saunders, op. cit., ii, pp. 169–70.
3. Lewin, op. cit., p. 26.
4. Connell, *Auchinleck*, p. 316, Cassell, 1959.
5. Richards, *Portal of Hungerford*, p. 236.
6. Connell, op. cit., p. 322.
7. Tedder, op. cit., p. 184.
8. Guedalla, op. cit., p. 162.
9. *Royal Air Force Quarterly*, April 1948. Air Marshal Sir Arthur Coningham, a passenger on a Tudor IV airliner, was lost on a flight from the Azores to Bermuda on January 30, 1948.
10. *The Times*, February 10, 1948.
11. *Royal Air Force Quarterly*, op. cit.
12. Lewin, op. cit., p. 82.
13. Fraser, op. cit., p. 175.
14. These were the forward units of the Western Desert Air Force; behind them, under the direct control of Coningham's Headquarters, were

squadrons and detachments doing the work of Air Ambulance, Survey Reconnaissance, Strategic Reconnaissance, Torpedo-Bombers, Air Transport, Bomber Transport, Communications, etc. Six squadrons and two flights were South African, two squadrons were Australian, one Rhodesian and one Free French.

15. OH (Playfair), op. cit., iii, p. 43.
16. Tedder, op. cit., p. 193.
17. Guedalla, op. cit., pp. 163–4.
18. Fraser, op. cit., p. 185.
19. Correlli Barnett (*The Desert Generals*, p. 121; William Kimber, 1960) says: "In terms of courage and resolution, *Crusader* was the greatest achievement of British Commonwealth soldiers in the desert."
20. AHB/II/116/22, p. 60.
21. Ibid, p. 61.
22. It may be noted, for perspective, that on September 21, 1917, the Battle of the Menin Road Ridge (part of the third Battle of Ypres), on a day which particularly suited air cooperation and reconnaissance, with 394 air messages received, all German counter-attacks were crushed before they could take place. In one case the artillery responded to signals within half a minute, and the machine-gun barrage came down in a matter of seconds.
23. Tedder, op. cit., p. 195.
24. Ibid, p. 202. It must be remembered (see p. 285) that the Me 109F had already shown itself superior in climbing and diving to the Spitfire V, in the "Rhubarbs" and "Circuses" over France.
25. Tedder, op. cit., pp. 206–7.
26. AHB/II/117/8(B), p. 293, quoting figures supplied by the Central Statistical Branch.
27. OH (Playfair), op. cit., iii, p. 15.
28. AHB/II/117/8(B), p. 293; my italics.
29. OH (Playfair), op. cit., iii, p. 99.

45. *America in the war; a new strategy* p. 362–p. 365

1. Churchill, *The Grand Alliance*, p. 539.
2. Ibid, p. 608.

46. *Malta* p. 365–p. 369

1. Lewin, op. cit., p. 39.
2. Young, op. cit., p. 112.
3. Tedder, op. cit., p. 49.
4. Connell, op. cit., p. 485.
5. Richards & Saunders, op. cit., ii, p. 182, quoting Hitler's Directive to Kesselring of December 2.
6. Malta's air bases were: fighters, Hal Far and Takali; bombers, Luca; seaplanes, Kalafrana.
7. Richards & Saunders, op. cit., ii, p. 192.

8. Tedder, op. cit., p. 264.
9. Tedder to Sir Walter Monckton, acting Minister of State in the Middle East, April; qu. op. cit., p. 269.
10. Churchill, *The Hinge of Fate*, p. 267.
11. In January, when Rommel launched his counter-offensive, the *Luftwaffe* had only enough fuel for two weeks' intensive operations. "Had not air transport carried enough fuel to meet daily consumption, the GAF units would probably have been grounded within a fortnight" (AHB/II/117/8(B), pp. 290–1). "Even after the attacks from Malta upon the sea route to North Africa had dwindled almost to nothing, the Germans made great use of their numerous transport aircraft to carry men and stores from Crete to Cyrenaica" (OH, Playfair, op. cit., iii, p. 211).
12. Richards & Saunders, op. cit., ii, p. 194.
13. Tedder, op. cit., p. 106.
14. Richards & Saunders, op. cit., ii.
15. OH (Playfair), op. cit., iii, pp. 184–5.
16. In April and May only 13 Axis ships were sunk in the whole Mediterranean; less than one per cent of Rommel's supplies were lost at sea in April. The May figures would have been just as bad, but for the sinking (with the aid of cryptanalysis) of a 7,000 ton ship off Tripoli by Malta-based aircraft. This "marked the recovery of Malta's strike capacity, the beginning of a period in which that recovery was combined with anti-shipping intelligence to produce another sustained *and decisive* attack on Rommel's supplies" (OH) Hinsley, ii, p. 349; my italics).

47. *Gazala; the lowest ebb; "First Alamein"* p. 369–p. 378

1. Churchill, *The Grand Alliance*, p. 512.
2. AHB/II/117/8(C) p. 91. We may here note that it was during this trying period for Middle East Command that Air Chief Marshal Douglas, AOC-in-C Fighter Command, remarked to Tedder that he was sending out 200 fighter pilots per month to the Middle East, and added:
   "While he was most anxious to help in every possible way he wanted an assurance that such large numbers were really required in ME Command as he had heard rumours of fighter pilots kicking their heels for months at a time with no aircraft" (March 23, 1942; AHB/II/117/8(C) p. 85).
   Tedder begged Douglas to ignore the "poison tongues" which were apparently active at home. At the same time (the simultaneity is striking) Bomber Command's new AOC-in-C, Air Chief Marshal Harris, told him that in the last year "the best part of a thousand crews, all trained at immense cost in labour and material in our OTUs, have been sent to you ... The bare fact that ... practically none return here, speaks for itself. We either alter this hopeless state of affairs, and at once, or we perish." Tedder told him: "Your information is fantastically incorrect ..." However, the Air Staff was drawn into these disputes, and Middle East Command was ordered to return 60 Wellington crews. (Tedder, op. cit.,

pp. 253–5.) There then ensued a shortage of Wellingtons in the Middle East in the vital month of October.

3. AHB/II/117/8(C), pp. 213–14.
4. OH (Playfair), op. cit., iii, p. 213; German losses during this period were 89, Italian 60.
5. Ibid.
6. OH (Hinsley), op. cit., ii, p. 362.
7. Ibid, p. 363.
8. OH (Playfair), op. cit., iii, p. 221.
9. AHB/II/117/8(C), p. 152.
10. Ibid, p. 161.
11. OH (Playfair), op. cit., iii, p. 237.
12. *Luftwaffe* Historical Section, quoted in Richards & Saunders, ii, op. cit., p. 202.
13. This was the heaviest ordnance used in aircraft until Coastal Command mounted 57 mm (6-pdr) guns in Mosquitoes in 1944, and the Germans put Pak 40 high-velocity 75-mm tank guns into the Henschel 129B on the Eastern front.
14. AHB/II/117/8(C), p. 217.
15. Francis K. Mason, *The Hawker Hurricane*, p. 108, Macdonald, 1962.
16. OH (Playfair), op. cit., iii, p. 256.
17. AHB/II/117/8(C), p. 180.
18. Ibid, p. 192.
19. Lewin, op. cit., p. 141.
20. Martin van Creveld, "Rommel's Supply Problem", 1941–42, in the RUSI *Journal*, September 1974.
21. Lewin, *Rommel as Military Commander*, p. 133, Batsford, 1968.
22. OH (Playfair), op. cit., iii, p. 266.
23. AHB/II/117/8(C), p. 224.
24. OH (Playfair), op. cit., iii, pp. 282–3.
25. Ibid, p. 374, fn 4.
26. Qu. ibid, p. 337.
27. AHB/II/117/8(C), p. 226.
28. Ibid, pp. 211–13.

48. *Montgomery and Coningham; Alam Halfa* p. 378–p. 383

1. Richards & Saunders, op. cit., ii, p. 227.
2. Fraser, op. cit., p. 233.
3. Tedder, op. cit., p. 347.
4. PRO AIR 37/760: "Report on Visit to Middle East by Air Marshal A. S. Barratt, KCB, CMG, MC: A.M. 27th August–P.M. 9th September", Para. 5.
5. AHB/II/116/22 Appendix 8: Notes compiled from Air Marshal Barratt's Report and Air Commodore Elmhirst's Memorandum on the Organization of the Western Desert Air Force for Cooperation with Eighth Army.
6. Tedder, op. cit., p. 355. The operations room referred to relied heavily on

the "J" Service, described by Montgomery as "an organisation for intercepting the signals sent out by our own forward units and relaying them to Army and Corps HQ . . . It had the overall effect of tightening the entity of the Army; bringing it all closer together. Wireless links became intimate links between men engaged on the same enterprise. It ended the remoteness of the staff." (*Memoirs*, pp. 137–8, Collins, 1958.)

7. Guedalla, op. cit., pp. 207–9; unfortunately, he does not tell us the occasion when the Field-Marshal made this statement. Montgomery himself says that at the time his army was "700 miles up" the Italian peninsula. The italics are mine. (The Air Vice-Marshal referred to was Sir Harry Broadhurst.)

8. OH (Hinsley), op. cit., ii, p. 412.

9. AHB/II/116/22, p. 70.

10. OH (Playfair), op. cit., iii, p. 327. It is one of the bitterest ironies of the Desert War that such effort was expended and loss sustained in bringing or preventing the bringing of oil to a country which rests upon a sea of it.

11. OH (Hinsley), op. cit., ii, p. 420.

12. AHB/II/116/22, p. 69.

13. Barratt Report, Para. 29.

14. AHB/II/116/22, p. 70.

15. OH (Playfair), op. cit., iii, p. 387.

16. AHB/II/116/22, p. 71.

17. OH (Playfair), op. cit., iii, p. 390.

18. Lewin, op. cit., p. 162.

49. *"Second Alamein"; advance to Tunisia* p. 383–p. 389

1. Dean, op. cit., p. 151.

2. They included the "Halverson Detachment" of USAAF Liberators which attacked the Ploesti oilfields in Rumania on the night of June 11/12. It is considered improbable that any significant damage was done, and four aircraft landed in neutral Turkey on the way back. But the remainder of the Detachment remained in the Middle East; these Liberators, with five more of No. 160 Squadron, were the first long-range bombers to appear in that theatre. General Brereton became a member of the Middle East Commanders-in-Chief Committee in December.

3. Richards & Saunders, op. cit., ii, p. 233.

4. As recently as October 23, 1982 the "Peterborough" column in the *Daily Telegraph* quoted the Royal Artillery Institution saying that the Second Battle of El Alamein was "one of the greatest artillery battles ever to be fought". In fact, the total British artillery used amounted to 592 guns, including 48 "mediums" (OH, vol. iv, p. 36). For comparison, we may note 1,295 guns (575 heavy) on a front of 4,000 yards in General Plumer's Battle of the Menin Road Ridge on September 20, 1917; the 6,473 guns and howitzers used by the Germans on the Somme on March 21, 1918 (2,435 heavy and 73 "super-heavy"); the 2,070 (684 heavy) in General Rawlinson's attack at Amiens on August 8, 1918; and the 24,000 guns and

mortars used by the Russians in their attack on Army Group Centre in 1944. As important as numbers at Alamein, however, was the revival of the neglected art of predicted shooting first used by the British at Cambrai on November 20, 1917, and brought to a high pitch of efficiency in 1918.

5. OH (Playfair), op. cit., iv, p. 78.
6. Lewin, op. cit., p. 171.
7. Richards & Saunders, op. cit., ii, p. 238.
8. Barratt Report, Paras. 12–14.
9. AHB/II/116/22, pp. 74–5.
10. The Royal Air Force Regiment was formed in February 1942 primarily for the purpose of defending airfields. It was the sensible outcome of the sharp Churchill/Portal exchanges referred to above (see p. 342, Chapter 42, Note 14). The Regiment did not form in the Middle East until September, when it took in some 7,800 "ground gunners" and trained them to clear airfields of remaining enemy, protect them, and guard RAF convoys. In October it provided detachments for Coningham's "A" Echelon.
11. Tedder, op. cit., p. 359; characteristically, he added: "Cooperation between fighters and bombers and between British and Americans in Desert is first-class, and the operational organisation is working like clockwork, with excellent mutual confidence."
12. Barnett, *The Desert Generals*, revised edition (Allen & Unwin, 1983), p. 288.
13. Ibid, p. 310.
14. Tedder, op. cit., p. 354.
15. Ibid, p. 359.
16. AHB/II/116/22, p. 75.
17. OH (Playfair), op. cit., iv, p. 99.
18. AHB/II/116/22, p. 76.
19. It should be recalled that AA was a function of the *Luftwaffe*. In September 1939, out of a total personnel of about 1½ million in the German Air Force, about 1 million were concerned with AA. In 1942 Speer speaks of "the barrels of ten thousand anti-aircraft guns pointed towards the sky" (*Inside the Third Reich*, p. 278, Weidenfeld & Nicolson).
20. AHB/II/116/22, p. 74.
21. Gunston, op. cit., p. 120.
22. Lieutenant-General Sir Francis Tuker, *Approach to Battle*, p. 17, Cassell, 1963; the distinguished commander of the 4th Indian Division speaks with warm approval of the admired and coveted German "Jerrycan", a significant feature of the Desert War. General Tuker estimates that about half the petrol transported in British containers was lost in transit.
23. OH (Playfair), op. cit., iv, p. 216 and fn 3.
24. Churchill, *The Hinge of Fate*, p. 645.

50. *Operation "Torch"; the Casablanca Conference; victory in Africa*
    p. 390–p. 400

1. Washington, December 22, 1941–January 3, 1942.
2. Keith Sainsbury, *The North African Landings 1942*, p. 133, Davis-Poynter, 1976.
3. OH (Playfair), op. cit., iv, p. 310.
4. Richards & Saunders, op. cit., ii, p. 246.
5. OH (Playfair), op. cit., iv, p. 114.
6. Richards, *Portal of Hungerford*, p. 232.
7. OH (Playfair), op. cit., iv, p. 313.
8. MacDonald, op. cit., pp. 106–7.
9. AHB/II/116/22, p. 83.
10. Tedder, op. cit., pp. 369–70.
11. Ibid.
12. Dwight D. Eisenhower, *Crusade in Europe*, p. 134, Heinemann, 1948.
13. Richards & Saunders, op. cit., iii, p. 254; Air Commodore G. M. Lawson commanded the forward squadrons.
14. Ibid, p. 257.
15. Fraser, *Alanbrooke*, p. 320.
16. Ibid, pp. 320–1.
17. Except for Gibraltar, which remained under Coastal Command until July 1943.
18. General Spaatz was in fact appointed C-in-C of the Allied Air Force in North-West Africa on January 5 (OH (Playfair), op. cit., iv, p. 265, fn 2), but his command did not become effective under its right title until February 18 (ibid, p. 271, fn 2).
19. Tedder, op. cit., p. 397.
20. Ibid, p. 404.
21. Richards & Saunders, op. cit., ii, p. 261.
22. OH (Playfair), op. cit., iv, p. 310.
23. AHB/II/116/22, p. 87.
24. OH (Playfair), op. cit., iv, p. 346.
25. It is interesting to see the revival of these further First World War techniques; the creeping barrage dates back to 1916; by 1918 it was normal to fortify it with smoke which helped the infantry to keep direction by defining a "shell-line" like the bomb-line of 1943. Coloured smoke, used for identifying ground units, was also a First World War innovation (AHB/II/117/8(C), pp. 211–13.
26. AHB/II/116/22, p. 79.
27. *History of the Second World War*, p. 419. It should be noted that it was not "Air Staff doctrine" that was being breached. That had been widely breached already, by the Tedder doctrine of committing the whole available air force in support of land operations, and the development of tactical air under Coningham. But Coningham was now among the "distant superiors" (not far distant!) who "frowned on" Broadhurst. The

reason is not far to seek: as we have seen, Coningham's first task had been to wean the armies away from the old desire to see the sky full of supporting aircraft. His struggle was for the air superiority which would bring all else in its train; this was being achieved, and he obviously viewed with trepidation Broadhurst's total commitment to direct support.

28. Bidwell & Graham, op. cit., p. 262. A further account of the development of Air OPs is to be found in *The Eye in the Air*, by Peter Mead, pp. 157–8 and 162–3, HMSO, 1983.
29. Bidwell & Graham, op. cit., p. 263.
30. Thetford, op. cit. (1968 edition), p. 36.
31. AHB/II/116/22, p. 89.
32. OH (Playfair), op. cit., iv, p. 451.

The Battle of the Atlantic (II)

52. *Science and Intelligence; the Leigh Light; tasks of Coastal Command*
p. 401–p. 407

1. Joubert had been AOC-in-C, Coastal Command, from September 1, 1936 to August 18, 1937.
2. *The Hinge of Fate*, p. 176.
3. *Closing the Ring*, p. 6.
4. Dean, op. cit., p. 156.
5. Slessor, op. cit., p. 486.
6. AHB/II/117/3(C), p. 43.
7. AHB/II/117/3(B), p. 306.
8. AHB/II/117/3(C), p. 42.
9. See p. 111.
10. Quoted in Price, *Aircraft Versus Submarine*, p. 64.
11. Richards & Saunders, op. cit., ii, p. 102.
12. Quoted in Price, op. cit., p. 65.
13. Richards & Saunders, op. cit., ii.
14. Ibid, p. 103.
15. Price, op. cit., p. 87.
16. For further details of this astonishing career see Price pp. 87–9; the *Luigi Torelli* survived until 1946, when she was scuttled by the Americans.
17. Dean, op. cit., p. 155.
18. AHB/II/117/3(B), p. 310, referring to a report of the Admiralty/Air Ministry Committee on Anti-Submarine Warfare, May 6.
19. It is interesting to note the types in use in the Command at that time: Anson, Battle, Beaufighter, Beaufort, Blenheim (Fighter and GR), Catalina, Empire Flying Boat, Hudson, Hurricane, Liberator, London (FB), Northrop (seaplane), Spitfire, Sunderland, Swordfish, Wellington, Whitley.
20. Richards & Saunders, op. cit., ii, p. 77.

53. *False dawn; defensive and offensive* p. 407–p. 414

1. Rohwer, op. cit., p. 267.
2. Young, op. cit., p. 136.
3. Richards & Saunders, op. cit., i, p. 343.
4. Ibid.
5. Rohwer, op. cit., p. 268.
6. Slessor, op. cit., p. 512.
7. Ibid.
8. Government Code and Cypher School (see p. 178).
9. OH (Hinsley), op. cit., ii, p. 163.
10. This story is graphically told by Ronald Lewin in *Ultra Goes to War*, pp. 204–7.
11. This refers to captures of other useful information from German trawlers. *U110* was the first to provide a complete Enigma machine; it is believed that the U-boat captain committed suicide when he realized what had happened.
12. OH (Hinsley), op. cit.
13. *Ultra Goes to War*, p. 207.
14. OH (Hinsley), op. cit., ii, p. 171.
15. Ibid, i, p. 338.
16. AHB/II/117/3(C), p. 5.
17. Ibid.
18. Ibid, p. 4.
19. Eg the five hits scored on *Scharnhorst* by the Halifax raid of July 24 (see p. 288).
20. Plymouth had, in fact, been attacked six times: March 20/21 and 21/22, April 21/22, 22/23, 23/24 and 28/29.
21. AHB/II/117/3(C), p. 24.
22. Ibid, p. 29.
23. Actual figures for the summer of 1942 were:

	Total Fleet	*Operational*	*Atlantic*	*Mediterranean*	*Norway*
May	296	128	89	20	19
June	313	130	90	19	21
July	331	140	101	16	23
August	342	152	113	16	23

24. AHB/II/117/3(C), pp. 30–1.
25. Ibid, p. 31, fn 1; my italics.
26. Ibid, p. 24, fn 1.
27. OH (Hinsley), op. cit., ii, App. 20.
28. See p. 452.

54. *The dark night; anti-shipping operations; oil supplies; "an obstacle to victory"* p. 414–p. 427

1. What Rohwer calls "the biggest convoy battle so far" (*Decisive Battles of World War II*, p. 267) took place during that month: SC 42, which lost 20 ships out of 63.

2. OH (Hinsley), op. cit., ii, p. 176.
3. Rohwer, op. cit., p. 269.
4. Rohwer gives examples of all of these uses in his Note 35.
5. A modest reference to the sinking of the carrier *Ark Royal* and the battleship *Barham* in November.
6. Rohwer, op. cit., pp. 269–70.
7. *The Hinge of Fate*, p. 107.
8. Ibid, pp. 14–15; Churchill to the Prime Minister of Australia, January 19, 1942.
9. Between the end of October 1941 and the beginning of January 1942, 166 crews were sent overseas, of whom only 21 were from OTUs, the remaining 145 coming from operational squadrons.
10. Churchill, op. cit., p. 111.
11. OH (Hinsley), op. cit., ii, p. 636.
12. Ibid, p. 179.
13. Ibid.
14. Churchill, op. cit., p. 110.
15. AHB/II/117/3(C), p. 10.
16. Ibid.
17. This was a future fear rather than a present reality. Fortresses did not become operational in Coastal Command until August 1942 (No. 59 Squadron). By then the education of both American and British air leaders in the realities of the U-boat war had advanced considerably.
18. General Henry ("Hap") Arnold, US Chief of Air Staff, a firm believer in the power of precision strategic bombing. Born 1886, d. 1950.
19. See p. 384, Chapter 49, Note 2.
20. AHB/II/117/3(C), p. 11.
21. Slessor, op. cit., p. 471.
22. *Coastal Command Review*, No. 1, January and February 1942, p. 29.
23. AHB/II/117/3(C), p. 12.
24. Quoted in Richards & Saunders, op. cit., ii, p. 95.
25. Ibid.
26. Harris, op. cit., p. 39.
27. Slessor, op. cit., p. 547.
28. Except, of course, those allocated to the Photographic Reconnaissance Unit (see p. 282).
29. OH: *Oil: A Study of War-Time Policy and Administration* by D. J. Payton-Smith, p. 298, HMSO, 1971; the following quotation from the same source.
30. This passage echoes April 1917, when Lord Derby, Secretary of State for War, having just come away from a Cabinet meeting, told Sir Douglas Haig: "We have lost command of the sea."
31. AHB/II/117/3(C), p. 15; my italics.
32. Churchill to Sinclair and Portal, January 7, 1943 (*Hinge of Fate*, p. 825); he quotes the establishment as 808 aircraft, with 547 serviceable.
33. AHB/II/117/3(C), p. 15.

34. OH (Webster & Frankland), op. cit., i, p. 340.
35. Churchill, op. cit., p. 783.
36. *The First World War 1914–1918*, i, p. 421, Constable, 1920.

55. *Turning point; The "Gap"; Liberators; U-boat reverses* p. 427– p. 436

1. Slessor, op. cit., p. 465.
2. "Half" means a kill shared with surface vessels; six and a half thus implies seven U-boats actually sunk.
3. All the kills by British aircraft were in the Mediterranean; Italian submarines are not counted in this total.
4. Torpex was a new explosive developed in 1941; it was 30 per cent more effective than the Amatol in previous use. When production commenced, absolute priority was given to torpedo warheads, and then to the projectiles of the Navy's new multiple anti-submarine mortar, the "Hedgehog". Filling of the RAF's Mark VIII depth-charges began in April at the rate of 150 a week, and Coastal Command received its first batch at the end of that month.
5. This tactic (already familiar in 1918) was known as "baiting". After an inconclusive attack, the U-boat having vanished into the depths, the aircraft would fly away from the scene and stay away for sometimes an hour or more, then return quickly, preferably through cloud cover or down sun. It was not unusual to catch the U-boat on the surface again, and so renew the attack.
6. *Coastal Command Review* No. 5, September 1942, p. 14.
7. Quoted in Richards and Saunders, op. cit., ii, p. 106.
8. The He 177 is sometimes referred to as a four-engined aircraft, but this is only correct to the extent that the same could be said of the Avro Manchester (see p. 281). The power plant of the He 177A-5 was two 2,950 hp Daimler-Benz DB 610A-1/B-1 engines, each being in fact two 12-cylinder engines geared to one propeller. Like the Manchester, the He 177 was never really satisfactory, its chief fault being, as with Avro's failure, a tendency of the engines to catch fire in the air. Much used on the Eastern Front, two interesting occasions in the He 177's western career were an attack by 20 of them on convoy SL 139 on November 21, 1943, using HS 293 guided flying-bombs (only one ship was sunk and one damaged for a loss of three He 177s), and the "Little Blitz" on Britain in 1944. For this the He 177s climbed to 23,000 feet in Germany and made their approach in a shallow dive at 423 mph, at which speed neither fighters nor AA were able to deal with them. However, they did little damage. Their rôle steadily diminished throughout 1944.
9. Dönitz also obtained a few Blohm und Voss BV 222 six-engined flying-boats. Their career was also disappointing.
10. The smaller organizational units of the *Luftwaffe* were:
    Rotte: a tactical formation of two aircraft
    Kette: a formation of three aircraft

Schwarm: two *Rotten* (see p. 183)

Staffel: the smallest self-contained unit (nine aircraft), equivalent to an RAF squadron

Gruppe: the basic fighting unit (equivalent to RAF Wing) usually containing three *Staffeln*

Geschwader: equivalent to RAF Group; normally containing three *Gruppen* (about 90 aircraft).

KG (Kampfgeschwader) = bomber group

JG (Jagdgeschwader) = fighter group

11. The Ju 88C-6 was conceived and built as a fighter (with photographic reconnaissance potential). It was a true *Zerstörer*, with a very heavy armament: three 20-mm cannon and three 7.9-mm machine guns fixed for forward firing, two fixed up-firing 20-mm cannon, and one flexible aft-firing 13-mm machine gun. The Ju 88C-6c night-fighter appeared late in 1943, and proved a serious opponent of Bomber Command thereafter.

12. *Coastal Command Review*, No. 5, September 1942, pp. 13–14.

13. Ibid, p. 14.

14. Price, op. cit., pp. 92–3.

15. Slessor, op. cit., p. 498.

16. Price, op. cit., pp. 123–6.

17. This diagram is taken from Price, op. cit., p. 97.

18. *Coastal Command Review*, No. 7, November 1942, p. 5.

19. Rohwer, op. cit., p. 280.

20. *Coastal Command Review*, No. 6; October 1942; p. 8. *U 501* was sunk on September 10, 1941, and *U 131* on December 17 of that year.

21. In May 1943 the Germans introduced the "submarine aircraft-trap". *U 441* was converted to carry two armoured "bandstands", one forward and one aft of the conning tower; her armament consisted of two quadruple-barrelled 20-mm guns and a semi-automatic 37-mm gun, with an increased crew of 67. She made only two cruises; in both she was so badly damaged that the "aircraft-trap" experiment was abandoned. Heavily armed U-boats, however, continued to appear.

22. *Coastal Command Review*, No. 7, November 1942, p. 12.

56. *ASV III and H2S; Ultra breakthrough* p. 436–p. 440

1. It is often stated that Lord Cherwell himself was responsible for the name, "H2S". Professor R. V. Jones, however, tells us that the origin was somewhat different: Cherwell, having appeared distinctly unenthusiastic at first, the team working on centimetric radar did not push the work. When he later asked them why not, they made various excuses which irritated him so much that he exclaimed, "It stinks! It stinks!" This prompted the thought of H2S, the formula for Hydrogen Sulphide (sulphuretted hydrogen), a gas with a powerful smell of rotten eggs: "But they had not foreseen his obvious question: 'Now why did you call it that?' There was an awkward silence until someone who deserved to go far came

up with, 'Please sir, Home Sweet Home!'" (*Most Secret War*, Coronet edition, p. 408; 1979).
2. OH (Webster & Frankland), op. cit., iv, p. 14.
3. Ibid.
4. Jones, op. cit., pp. 409–10.
5. Price, op. cit., pp. 113–4.
6. Ibid, p. 113; Webster and Frankland, op. cit., iv, p. 12 (Annex I) say "early in the following March the Germans recovered a set from a Bomber Command aircraft which came down near Rotterdam". The discrepancy may be accounted for by the lapse of time between shooting down the Stirling and recovering the set.
7. Quoted in Price, op. cit., p. 116.
8. Webster & Frankland, op. cit., iv, p. 12, fn 2 inform us that *Naxos-U* came into operation in October 1943, and the anti-bomber version in January 1944 (p. 13, fn 2).
9. Quoted in OH (Hinsley), op. cit., ii, p. 548.
10. Ibid, p. 549: "Except when a U-boat sailed for a special task or a distant area, it received its destination point and its operational orders by W/T after it had put to sea."
11. Ibid, pp. 549–50.
12. Ibid, p. 552.

57. *The last convoy battles; new weapons; Atlantic victory* p. 440– p. 452

1. *Operational Squadrons:*

Type	Establishment	Strength	Daily availability
12½ flying-boat sqdns (inc. 1 USN)	126	118	49
18 anti-U-boat GR sqdns (inc. 2 Bomber Command and 2 USAAF)	304	293	161
13 anti-shipping GR and LR fighter sqdns	238	260	145
	668	671	355
6 PR sqdns	91	85	54
1 Met sqdn + 4 flights	68	49	34
2 Air Sea Rescue sqdns	40	34	26
	867	839	469

AHB/II/117/3(C), App. I.
2. *Coastal Command Review*, No. 6, October 1942, p. 27.
3. OH (Hinsley), op. cit., ii, p. 556.
4. Qu. Churchill, op. cit., p. 619.
5. Harris, op. cit., p. 137.
6. Richard Humble, "Battle of the Atlantic", in *Military History*, April 1983

p. 180. OH (Hinsley) ii, p. 755 adds that "no U-boat was destroyed in a yard until April 1944 and that no bomb penetrated the roof of an assembly yard until just before the end of the war."

7. Slessor, op. cit., p. 499.
8. A large part of the trouble was, as Churchill says (*Closing the Ring*, p. 7) that "The United States had no organization like our Coastal Command, through which on the British or reception side of the ocean air operations were controlled by a single authority."
9. Slessor, op. cit., p. 490.
10. Richards & Saunders, op. cit., iii, p. 38.
11. Rohwer, op. cit., p. 289.
12. McLachlan, op. cit., p. 86.
13. Price, op. cit., p. 127.
14. Rohwer, op. cit., p. 292. On departure, HX 229 contained 40 ships, SC 122 contained 60.
15. Ibid., p. 293.
16. OH (Hinsley), op. cit., ii, p. 562.
17. OH (Roskill) op. cit., p. 367.
18. Rohwer, op. cit.
19. See p. 236: 231 U-boats operational in March, 237 in April, 239 in May.
20. Rohwer, op. cit.
21. OH (Roskill) op. cit., p. 368.
22. OH (Hinsley), op. cit., ii, p. 549.
23. Ibid, p. 564; ship-borne (as opposed to shore-based) DF entered service in 1942.
24. Appointed in November 1942.
25. AHB/II/117/3(D), p. 89.
26. *Coastal Command Review*, No. 11, March 1943, p. 8: article, "Depth-Charge Stick Spacing". Of the 43 attacks analysed, photographs showed that "owing to errors in range, 18 sticks overshot completely and four sticks undershot completely. Based on this analysis, the odds against straddling a U-boat (when near enough to the surface to be vulnerable to the 25-ft depth setting) with a stick of six depth-charges spaced at 36 ft proved to be roughly four to one against in beam attacks, three to one against in attacks close to track."
27. OH (Hinsley), op. cit., ii, p. 567.
28. Ibid, p. 569.
29. Rohwer, p. 302.
30. Price, op. cit., p. 134. The torpedo homed in on cavitation – the sound of the popping of bubbles caused by the rapid rotation of the submarine's propellers under water. The degree of cavitation varies; at great depths it ceases altogether. In order not to drown the cavitation, the torpedo itself moved at a low speed, and against a U-boat moving fast just below the surface it could home in from three-quarters of a mile. An unsuspecting captain would always try to get away from his diving swirl as fast as possible, thus offering ideal conditions for the torpedo. If he knew what

was coming, he would slow down or dive very deep, thus neutralizing the weapon.

31. OH (Hinsley), op. cit., ii, p. 570.
32. Ibid, p. 571.
33. Ibid.
34. Qu. Rohwer, op. cit., p. 306.
35. Ibid, p. 307.
36. That was in July 1943: U-boats accounted for 252,145 tons (46 ships) out of a total of 365,398 tons (61 ships). But of the U-boat total only 123,327 tons (18 ships) were sunk in the North Atlantic. 97,214 tons (17 ships) were sunk in the Indian Ocean. It may be noted also that "by July more Allied merchant ships were being built than were being sunk. That was the crux of the matter . . ." (Liddell Hart, op. cit., p. 389.)
37. Commander (later Captain) Rodger Winn, RNVR, a successful barrister before the war who became a Lord Justice of Appeal before his death in 1972. He triumphed over the disabilities of poliomyelitis to become the brilliant head of the Submarine Tracking Room. Donald McLachlan remarks: "To appoint a civilian to such a responsible post so early in the war [January 1941] was a daring decision" (op. cit., p. 103). It was one that earned a due reward.
38. Lewin, op. cit., p. 219.
39. *Coastal Command Review*, Vol. II, No. 1; May 1943.
40. Ibid, December 1943; Slessor's review of the year is reprinted in full in *The Central Blue*, pp. 472–80.

58. *"Per Ardua"* p. 452–p. 457

1. Slessor, op. cit., p. 465.
2. The greatest shipping losses during the year (266,442 tons; 65 ships) occurred in British home waters, mostly after the launching of Operation OVERLORD. They serve as a reminder of the slaughter that might have been if the Royal Navy and Coastal Command (and their allies) had done their work less well.
3. Lewin, *Ultra Goes to War*, p. 214.
4. McLachlan, op. cit., p. 89.
5. Jones, op. cit., pp. 410–11.
6. "Unlimited", that is to say, except for psychological and physiological factors affecting the crews.
7. The two chief reasons for U-boats spending long periods of time on the surface were the necessity of re-charging the batteries, and the wish to move fast (e.g. in order to catch up with a convoy).
8. Price, op. cit., p. 180.
9. Ibid, p. 181.
10. McLachlan, op. cit., p. 401.
11. Price, op. cit., p. 184.
12. Ibid.
13. Ibid, p. 235.

14. The total number of U-boats lost from all causes during the war was:
    German   784
    Italian   85
    Japanese   130
    Statistics are from *The War at Sea* and from Richards & Saunders, op. cit., iii, Appendix VI (pp. 403–4); Coastal Command losses are from Richards & Saunders, iii, p. 276.
15. It is interesting to note that the *Review*'s claim of 209 U-boats sunk and probably sunk (including those shared) tallies exactly with the final official count. It also claimed 346 merchant ships; the final count was 343.
16. Richards & Saunders, op. cit., iii, p. 276.
17. Slessor, op. cit., p. 468.

The Strategic Air Offensive (II)

59. *Bomber Command problems; aircraft and aircrew* p. 459–p. 468

1. Viz.:

Aircraft	Crew
19 Wellingtons	114
10 Whitleys	50
5 Hampdens	20
2 Stirlings	14
1 Halifax	7
37	205

Air Staff Operational Summary No. 353, November 9, 1941.
2. The missing aircraft comprised 10 Wellingtons, 9 Whitleys and 2 Stirlings. Comparison of percentage losses shows:

	Percentage of force despatched	Percentage of force attacking
Mannheim	12.42	16.7
Essen Area	16.66	25
Sea-Mining*	23.07	50
Offensive Patrols†	33.33	40

*13 aircraft despatched, 6 laid mines in the prescribed area, 3 missing.
†6 aircraft despatched, 5 attacked, 2 missing.
3. Portal to Peirse, November 23, 1941; quoted in Webster & Frankland, i, p. 255.
4. Depressing, that is to say, professionally. Peirse became AOC-in-C, India at a difficult time, on March 6, 1942, and Allied C-in-C, Air, South-East Asia Command, on November 16, 1943. While serving in the latter capacity, he eloped with the wife of General Sir Claude Auchinleck, C-in-C, India. This act, in the midst of war, drew universal condemnation and abruptly ended Peirse's career. He died in 1970, aged 78.
    See Philip Warner, *Auchinleck: The Lonely Soldier*, pp. 263–4; Buchan & Enright, 1981.
5. November 11, 1941; *The Grand Alliance*, p. 748.

6. Peirse to Portal, November 10; quoted in Webster & Frankland, i, p. 186.
7. *Bomber Expansion*

to end of	Squadrons planned: Heavy	Medium	Squadrons achieved: Heavy	Medium	Deficiency: Heavy	Medium
July 1941	12	46	8	40½	−4	−5½
August	18	49	10	40	−8	−9
September	21	54	9	41	−12	−13
October	27	60	9½	40½	−17½	−19½
November	32	68	11	40½	−21	−27½
December	35	72	15	38	−20	−34
January 1942	41	77	17	37½	−24	−39½

AHB/II/117/1(C), pp. 15 & 18.
8. Harris, op. cit., p. 73.
9. AHB/II/117/1(C), p. 15.
10. Ibid, pp. 24–6.
11. Ibid.
12. Manning Plans and Policy, p. 183.
13. See p. 84; it was on May 25, 1939 that Ludlow-Hewitt pressed upon the Air Ministry the need for "thorough specialised training of all members of bomber crews".
14. OH (Webster & Frankland), op. cit., iv, p. 27; however, we should note that Bruce Robertson, in his well-researched *Lancaster – the Story of a Bomber*, p. 16 (Harleyford Publications, 1964), says that from the spring of 1942: "the normal crew stations were pilot, navigator, flight engineer, two wireless operators/air gunners, and two air gunners."
15. Bowyer, op. cit., p. 39.
16. Ibid.
17. See pp. 279–81 for Fortress conditions; quotation from Bowyer, p. 40.
18. The increasing Canadian participation in the work of the RAF (Fighter and Coastal, as well as Bomber Commands) brought about the formation of an all-Canadian Group (No. 6) in Bomber Command on January 1, 1943. Even so, some 37 per cent of the pilots in Bomber Command at that time were Canadians, Australians or New Zealanders, and of those about 60 per cent were Canadians. By January 1945, 46 per cent of Bomber Command's pilots were from the three Dominions, 55 per cent of these being Canadians. In addition, as we have seen, there was a direct Canadian participation in the Battle of the Atlantic, operating from bases in Canada and Newfoundland.
19. Both sides of the aircrew controversy are set out in AHB/II/116/14, Appendix 18.
20. It is interesting to note that the more egalitarian society of Nazi Germany produced an entirely different system which appears to have worked perfectly well. Thus, on August 18, 1940, which Alfred Price calls "The Hardest Day" of the Battle of Britain, the *Luftwaffe*'s personnel losses

amounted to 38 officers and 37 other ranks; 19 officers and 18 other ranks were killed. In the bombers (Ju 87 and 88, He 111 and Do 17), it is known that 23 of the other ranks lost were piloting the aircraft, nine of them holding a rank equivalent to corporal in the RAF.

21. AHB/II/117/1(C), p. 46.
22. OH (Webster & Frankland), op. cit., i, p. 383.
23. Lawrence, W. J., No. 5 Bomber Group RAF (1939–1945), p. 18, Faber and Faber, 1951.

60. *Harris; the Americans arrive; bombing aids; incendiaries* p. 468–p. 480

1. Jones, op. cit., p. 227.
2. Harris, op. cit., p. 64. This passage strikes a sympathetic chord in the author, who once made the following analysis of the South African War, 1899–1902, in which the British Army was pitted against a race of "crack shots" who were "born in the saddle". During that war, 5,774 British officers and men were killed in action; the maximum strength of the Boer armies (Transvaal, Orange Free State and Cape rebels) may be put at some 60,000. If, for the sake of rough calculation, we call the British loss 6,000, it then appears that it took 10 "crack" Boer shots a year to kill one British soldier; but the war lasted about three years, and as one cannot kill one third of a soldier, we must take the yearly loss average – 2,000 – from which it appears that it actually took 30 "crack" Boer shots to do the job. Sir Arthur Harris is the only authority I know to reach a similar conclusion. (By contrast, on a single day of the First Battle of Ypres, October 1914, *one platoon* of the 2/Gordon Highlanders counted 240 German dead on its front.)
3. A hurricane in a parlour is not, of course, always a favoured circumstance; one is reminded of the words of Sir Pelham Wodehouse: "No hostess wants a Hamlet on the premises."
4. Hansard, Parliamentary Debates, quoted in OH (Webster & Frankland), op. cit., i, pp. 328–9.
5. Transportation and Morale were the "basic" Bomber Command targets of 1941.
6. AHB/II/117/1(C), pp. 134–5; my italics.
7. Tedder, op. cit., p. 253.
8. Air Marshal Sir Robert Saundby, *Air Bombardment: The Story of its Development*, p. 130, Chatto & Windus, 1961.
9. OH (Webster & Frankland), op. cit., ii, p. 5.
10. AHB/II/117/1(C), p. 186.
11. Richards & Saunders, op. cit., ii, p. 117. Probably the best account of the radar aids to navigation is Alfred Price's *Instruments of Darkness* (William Kimber, 1967); Webster & Frankland, op. cit., iv, pp. 3–17, give a clear account of GEE, OBOE, H2S and G–H in their Annex 1, and a briefer description in vol. i, pp. 316–17; Sir Robert Saundby (op. cit., pp. 263–4) also supplies a short account in his Appendix D, but is not always reliable

on operational use. Needless to say, Professor R. V. Jones has much to say of value.

12. OH (Webster & Frankland), op. cit., iv, p. 6.
13. Jones, op. cit., p. 284.
14. Ibid, p. 285.
15. Referred to in *Most Secret War*, as TR 1355 (actually TR 1335); this was one of Professor Jones's deception ploys (op. cit., p. 286). "TR", it was hoped, would make the Germans think of transmitter/receivers.
16. OH (Webster & Frankland), op. cit., iv, pp. 143–4.
17. Harris, op. cit., pp. 78–9.
18. OH (Webster & Frankland), op. cit., i, p. 389.
19. Ibid, p. 386.
20. Richards & Saunders, op. cit., ii, p. 131.
21. Ibid, p. 125.
22. OH (Webster & Frankland), op. cit., i, p. 389.
23. Richards & Saunders, op. cit., i.
24. Harris to Freeman, April 29, 1942; quoted in OH (Webster & Frankland), op. cit., i, p. 391, fn 3.
25. Ibid, p. 392.
26. Ibid, p. 324.
27. Ibid, p. 392.
28. Ibid, p. 483–4.
29. Richards & Saunders, op. cit., ii, p. 127.
30. Harris, op. cit., p. 105.
31. OH (Webster & Frankland), op. cit., i, p. 393.
32. Richards & Saunders, op. cit., ii; Goebbels quotation from same source.
33. OH (Webster & Frankland), op. cit., i, p. 484.
34. Ibid, p. 393.
35. Ibid.
36. Lawrence, op. cit., p. 69.
37. Webster & Frankland, op. cit., i, p. 394; next quotation ibid.
38. Ibid.
39. All German quotations are from Richards & Saunders, op. cit., ii, p. 129.
40. OH (Webster & Frankland), op. cit., i, p. 485.
41. Ibid, p. 488.
42. Harris, op. cit., pp. 107–8.
43. Ibid, pp. 51–2.
44. Ibid, p. 108.

61. *"Millennium"; precision bombing in 1942; Pathfinders* p. 481–p. 503

1. This, of course, has been a constant reproach against First World War generals, who are accused of living in comfort in *châteaux* while their men endured the misery of the trenches. What was not (and frequently still is not) understood is the increasing size of staffs with increasing specialization, and the need for a large building to house them – especially their

communications centre. The home-base RAF headquarters of the Second World War were obeying the same compulsion.

2. Harris, op. cit., p. 72.
3. *Great Contemporaries*, Macmillan, 1942, pp. 170–1: "The qualities of mind and spirit which Douglas Haig personified came to be known by occult channels throughout the vast armies of which he was the Chief. Disasters, disappointments, miscalculations and their grievous price were powerless to affect the confidence of the soldiers in their Commander."
4. M. Louis Renault reported to the Germans that "apart from one or two shops that might be at work again in fifteen days, three months or more would be needed before production could be resumed". (See Richards & Saunders, op. cit., ii, p. 123.) This may have been pessimistic; the final estimate of the US Strategic Bombing Survey was a loss of 2,272 trucks.
5. Richards & Saunders, op. cit.
6. OH (Webster & Frankland), op. cit., i, p. 428.
7. See p. 416.
8. OH (Webster & Frankland), op. cit., i, p. 402, quoting Harris's Despatch.
9. Throughout 1942 the Wellingtons were the backbone of the Bomber Force: 598 took off for Cologne on May 30/31, 547 for Essen on June 1/2, 472 for Bremen on June 25/26, 175 (out of 325) for Bremen again on July 2/3, 308 (out of 630) for Düsseldorf on July 31/August 1, and so on. The Wellington continued to be operational in Bomber Command until October 1943.
10. This is the total stated in the Air Staff Operational Summary (No. 557, June 1). The AHB Narrative (and the Official History) put the total at 1,046, the difference being accounted for by three Whitleys. Almost certainly these are the three belonging to No. 1 Group, in addition to its 151 Wellingtons. They may have been omitted by oversight from the return made to the Air Staff, or they may have dropped out at the last moment. Harris (p. 110) says the total was 1,047.
11. No. 2 Group carried out diversionary "intruder" attacks on German airfields, supported by Army Cooperation Command and 37 fighters of Fighter Command.
12. OH (Webster & Frankland), op. cit., i, p. 404.
13. Ibid.
14. Harris, op. cit., pp. 111–12.
15. Ibid.
16. OH (Webster & Frankland), op. cit.
17. *"J'en ai pris bien d'autres."*
18. Ralph Barker *The Thousand Plan*, pp. 191–5 (Chatto & Windus), quoted in *Freedom's Battle*, ed. Lyall, pp. 191–3.
19. OH (Webster & Frankland), op. cit., i, p. 407, quoting Bomber Command Operational Research Section.
20. Saundby, op. cit., p. 141.
21. ASOS No. 557.
22. In an army battle, all wounded treated at a Casualty Clearing Station

would be recorded as casualties, even if they returned immediately to their units.

23. AHB/II/117/1(D), pp. 170–1; it offers the following table:

	Staff	Pupils
Pilots	10	7
Others	30	42

24. Speer, op. cit., p. 279.
25. OH (Webster & Frankland), op. cit., i, p. 486.
26. Ibid, p. 341.
27. Ibid, p. 486.
28. Ibid, p. 411.
29. Harris, op. cit., pp. 120–1.
30. Harris to Portal, June 20; quoted in Webster & Frankland, op. cit., i, p. 413.
31. ASOS 583; Webster & Frankland say 1,006.
32. AHB/II/117/1(D), p. 185.
33. See Anthony Verrier, *The Bomber Offensive*, Batsford, 1968, p. 148: "The '1,000 plan' was seen, as Harris admits, not only as a means of heavily damaging urban centres and of testing new material and tactics, but as a propaganda exercise."
34. AHB/II/117/1(D), ibid.
35. The quarter's operational totals were:

	Aircraft missing	Crashed	Crew total
April	150	22	562
May	117	13	754
June	199	25	1,303
	466	60	2,619*

*This total assumes Stirling crews to have numbered seven; eight-man crews would make the total 2,660.

36. Air Commodore J. W. Baker, Director of Bomber Operations, to Harris, April 7; quoted in Webster & Frankland, op. cit., i, p. 347.
37. Harris, op. cit., p. 220.
38. OH (Webster & Frankland), op. cit., i, p. 254, fn 3.
39. Harris, op. cit., pp. 102–3.
40. Ibid.
41. Robertson, op. cit., p. 16.
42. Robertson (ibid) says: "These figures were to be quoted significantly by crews for the next three years – 'I hear they're filling up 2,154' portended a long run."
43. W/O H. V. Crum and W/O J. F. Beckett.
44. Robertson, op. cit., p. 17.
45. Harris, op. cit., p. 141.
46. OH (Webster & Frankland), op. cit., i, p. 463; Appendix 15 (vol. iv) sets out the arguments.

47. Harris, op. cit., p. 223.
48. OH (Webster & Frankland), op. cit., i, p. 443. The unfortunate word "raid" is perhaps justifiable here. It was really a hangover from the First World War, when air operations with the types available did amount to little more than raids. It is not in any way appropriate to the sometimes massive operations of Bomber Command between 1941–45, which were full-blooded attacks, often resulting in full-blooded battles. It will be noted that "raid" is a word used very sparingly in this text.
49. United States Strategic Bombing Survey, quoted in OH (Webster & Frankland), op. cit., i, pp. 464–5, fn 3.
50. Ibid, p. 443.
51. Harris, op. cit., p. 141.
52. OH (Webster & Frankland), op. cit., i, pp. 451–4, which is also the source of succeeding quotations on this subject.
53. Bomber Command Instruction, quoted in AHB/II/117/1(D), pp. 198–9.
54. Bombing radii are taken from Lincoln as the centre point (see Map 1).
55. The Lancaster squadrons were: Nos. 9, 44, 49, 50, 57, 61, 97, 106, 207. No. 83 Squadron now formed part of the Pathfinder Force.
56. Webster & Frankland, op. cit., i, pp. 446–7.
57. ASOS 674, September 26.
58. AHB/II/117/1(D), p. 292.
59. The losses comprised nine Venturas, five Bostons, one Mosquito. The total was over 16 per cent of the force despatched.
60. OH (Webster & Frankland), op. cit., i, p. 418.
61. Ibid, p. 421.
62. Ibid, pp. 422–3.
63. Ibid, pp. 423–5.
64. Harris to Group Commanders, May 22, 1942; qu. Webster & Frankland, op. cit., i, p. 425.
65. Singleton Report; text in OH (Webster & Frankland), op. cit., iv, pp. 231–8.
66. OH (Webster & Frankland), op. cit., i, p. 431.
67. Harris, op. cit., p. 129. Harris's proposals were bitterly contested by the Treasury – headed by a former Secretary of State for Air, Sir Kingsley Wood. It took fierce argument to beat down this resistance; a strong weapon against it was the idea that Pathfinder crews should serve a continuous tour of operations twice the length of that of normal crews.
68. OH (Webster & Frankland), op. cit., i, p. 432.
69. Harris, op. cit., pp. 129–30.
70. OH (Webster & Frankland), op. cit., i, p. 433.
71. Ibid.
72. ASOS 637, Aug. 20.
73. Richards & Saunders, op. cit., ii, p. 150.

62. *"Prescription for Massacre"; another strategic debate* p. 503–p. 511

1. Tedder, op. cit., p. 342.
2. Churchill to Roosevelt, September 16; qu. Webster & Frankland, op. cit., i, p. 355.
3. Slessor, op. cit., pp. 438–9.
4. OH (Webster & Frankland), op. cit., i, p. 366.
5. Fraser, op. cit., p. 265.
6. OH (Webster & Frankland), op. cit.
7. Ibid, p. 367.
8. Ibid, p. 369.
9. Note by the Chief of the Air Staff for the Chiefs of Staff on an Estimate of the Effects of an Anglo-American Bomber Offensive Against Germany, November 3, 1942; Webster & Frankland, op. cit., iv, Appendix 20. The following two quotations are from the same source.
10. OH (Webster & Frankland), op. cit., i, pp. 370–1.
11. Fraser, op. cit.
12. "Some Reflections on the Strategic Air Offensive, 1939–1945"; lecture to the Royal United Services Institution, December 13, 1961; RUSI *Journal*, May 1962, p. 94.
13. Qu. OH (Webster & Frankland), op. cit., i, p. 372.
14. Ibid.
15. *Strategic Policy for the Conduct of the War* (Note by director of Plans, Air Ministry), 4.11.39; PRO AIR 20/235.
16. Slessor, op. cit., pp. 389–90.
17. OH (Webster & Frankland), op. cit., i, p. 377.
18. Frankland lecture, op. cit.
19. OH (Webster & Frankland), op. cit., i, p. 372.
20. Ibid, p. 373.
21. 1,042,015 on October 1, 1942; AHB/II/116/14, Appendix 3.
22. OH (Webster & Frankland), op. cit., i, p. 374.
23. Ibid, pp. 374–5. In November 1942 it was not possible to foresee how the hope of a cross-Channel attack in 1943 (ROUNDUP) was going to be eroded, first by the protracted German resistance in Tunisia, then by the decision to attack Sicily, and all the time by the struggle to overcome the U-boats in the Atlantic. Pound, obviously, and also Brooke, were more affected by this than Portal; Brooke, in Sir David Fraser's words (p. 530) "was absolutely convinced of the primacy of the Battle of the Atlantic".
24. Robertson, op. cit., p. 23.
25. OH (Webster & Frankland), op. cit., ii, p. 91.
26. Harris, op. cit., p. 143.
27. OH (Webster & Frankland), op. cit., i, p. 377.

63. *Air "battles" 1943; aids and opposition; the Ruhr* p. 511–p. 520

1. Peter J. Parish, *The American Civil War*, pp. 479–80, Eyre Methuen, 1975.
2. Ibid, p. 455; my italics.

3. *The Smoke and the Fire*, pp. 26–7, Sidgwick & Jackson, 1980.
4. R. E. Dupuy & T. N. Dupuy, *The Compact History of the Civil War*, p. 372; Hawthorn Books (NY), 1954.
5. This is the gist of a letter (Lieutenant-Commander D. W. Waters; p. 157) in a large correspondence in the RUSI *Journal* in May 1962, following an editorial in the February issue. Commenting on the fact that, both in Dr Frankland's lecture on December 13, 1961, and in the review of the Official History (by Air Vice-Marshal E. J. Kingston McCloughry) in February "the question of morality was not raised", the editor added: ". . . purposely to adopt heavy attack upon a civilian population as a deliberate policy of war is to degrade it into a bestiality that one had hoped had come to an end with the horrors of the Thirty Years' War in Europe." Coming from such a source (the editor at that time was a retired naval officer and a distinguished naval historian), this comment naturally aroused some vigorous controversy.
6. The French journal *Miroir de L'Histoire* in September 1961, in an article comparing the death-roll of the two World Wars, quoted a Colonel Kalinov of the Soviet Headquarters in Berlin, saying that the Soviet military dead between 1941–45 had numbered 13,600,000 (which is more than the military dead *of all combatants* in World War I), and the civilian dead had numbered 7,000,000. Of these, some 2,000,000 were Jews, rounded up and shot in batches by the *Einsatzkommandos* of the SS. "The personnel of these Extermination Squads . . . was sometimes replenished by *Wehrmacht* volunteers, attracted to the unvarying routine of butchery by the promise of a threefold increase in pay, special leave and the prospect of loot" (Richard Grunberger, *Germany 1918–1945*, p. 169; Batsford, 1964).
7. OH (Webster & Frankland), op. cit., ii, p. 95.
8. Ibid, p. 256.
9. Essen, July 25/26, when 2,000 tons of bombs were dropped.
10. Harris, op. cit., p. 144.
11. Richards & Saunders, op. cit., ii, p. 155.
12. OH (Webster & Frankland), op. cit., i, p. 95.
13. Ibid, p. 103.
14. Ibid.
15. Ibid, p. 94.
16. AHB/II/116/19, p. 188.
17. Green, op. cit., p. 589; this is the source of all the accompanying information.
18. Dr Noble Frankland was himself a navigator.
19. OH (Webster & Frankland), op. cit., ii, pp. 201–2; my italics.
20. Harris, op. cit.
21. The main force consisted of 140 Lancasters, 89 Halifaxes, 52 Stirlings and 131 Wellingtons.
22. OH (Webster & Frankland), op. cit., ii, pp. 108–9.
23. Ibid, pp. 110–11.

24. Ibid, p. 136.
25. Harris, op. cit., p. 148.
26. OH (Webster & Frankland), op. cit., ii, p. 257.
27. Ibid, p. 258.
28. Ibid, p. 260.
29. Ibid, p. 243.

64. *Moral fibre*, p. 520–p. 537

1. Lawrence, op. cit., p. 17.
2. Including being hit by bombs from friendly aircraft above.
3. OH (Webster & Frankland), op. cit., ii, p. 111.
4. Information supplied to the author, 21.10.83.
5. Wing Commander D. G. Simmons, Staff Officer to the VCAS, to the Head of Training Progress Staff, November 14, 1942; PRO AIR 20/ 2859.
6. Memorandum, Air Member for Training to Air Member for Personnel, November 16, 1942; PRO AIR 20/2859.
7. PRO AIR 2/8038; January 27, 1941.
8. It is not the first such reference; Air Marshal Barratt, replying to the Air Ministry enquiry on December 22, recommended "150 hours' operational flying, or 50 sorties" in the case of medium bombers of Army Cooperation Command acting in close or direct support.
9. OH (Webster & Frankland), op. cit., i, p. 427; my italics. Harris added that "the majority of [sorties] would have to be photographically proved".
10. Saundby to Headquarters, Nos. 1, 3, 4, 5 Groups, August 20, 1942; PRO AIR 2/8039.
11. PRO AIR 2/8039.
12. PRO AIR 20/2859.
13. PRO AIR 2/8039.
14. It never ceased to cause problems. The second tour remained a thorny matter; Portal never wavered in the belief (despite much pressure) that "we must retain the right to demand more than one operational tour of any individual" (CAS to Secretary of State, December 2, 1944; PRO AIR 20/2861). In March 1945, with the war evidently in its last stage, and casualties dwindling with Germany's decreasing power of resistance, Bomber Command found itself faced with an acute shortage of trained crews, and Harris asked for an extension of the tour to 35 sorties. This at once led to strong dissent from the Canadian Government.
15. Simmons, op. cit.
16. PRO AIR 20/2859. The Letter also dealt with some other important matters: "As regards the disposal of aircrew withdrawn from operational flying . . . the Council have decided that requirements for operational training units and conversion units will be given first priority . . . It is very desirable that aircrew personnel who are relieved from operational duties on account of excessive war strain should not be sent immediately to training units where their temporary lack of freshness and zest might have

a depressing effect ... [a 'reasonable period of leave' was medical treatment] ..." It was also laid down that, in the interests of efficient instruction, a duty tour at an OTU should be not less than six months. The Air Council also decided "that the present obligation on personnel for a second operational tour should remain".

17. The Pathfinder tour of 45 sorties was queried by the (Acting) VCAS in December 1942; Harris reminded him that the original idea had been "that Pathfinders did only one operational tour of *60* sorties. I have since had to reduce it to 45 owing to lack of volunteers". (PRO AIR 20/2859)

18. The following table, worked out by the Air Member for Training and sent to the Air Member for Personnel on November 16, 1942 (PRO AIR 20/2859) is of interest.

Type of Squadron	Percentage Chance of Survival	
	One Tour	Two Tours
Heavy & Medium Bombers	44	19½
Light Bombers	25½	6½
Day Fighter	43	18½
Night Fighter	39	15
Long Range Fighter	59½	35½
Torpedo Bomber	17½	3
Heavy GR Landplane	71	50½
Medium GR Landplane	56	31½
Light GR Landplane	45	20
Sunderland Flying Boat	66	43½
Catalina Flying Boat	77½	60
Fighter Reconnaissance	31	9½
Bomber Reconnaissance	42	17½

"The wide difference between Sunderlands and Catalinas is due to the longer average duration of sortie of the Catalina."

The figures for Torpedo Bombers and Catalinas will be noted.

19. In battered condition in PRO AIR 2/8038.

20. With unpressurized aircraft (as those of 1939–45 were), nasal catarrh or ear trouble could cause agonizing pain, sometimes in the air, almost certainly on landing, as the author can testify.

21. Harris, op. cit., p. 214.

22. Sir Edgar Ludlow-Hewitt (in his capacity of Inspector-General) visited Air Crew Disposal Centres at Blackpool, Uxbridge and Brighton in December 1942. He drew attention to the case (among others) of Sergeant P. Rake, Wireless Operator/Air Gunner in an aircraft which crashed in June 1941. Sergeant Rake lost a leg as a result of the crash; his skull was fractured and a portion had to be removed; his left arm and part of his left side were paralysed for a considerable time; he was discharged from hospital in November 1941 and convalescent until June 1942. He was then posted back to his unit; despite his disability, he expressed keen desire to remain in the RAF and a Central Medical Board recommended him for ground instructor or flying control. His Station Commander, who

considered him "above average in keenness and intelligence", concurred and "strongly recommended him for training accordingly". He added: "I feel that he is deserving of much consideration since he was so gravely injured in circumstances over which he had no control, and has, in spite of these injuries, retained his great keenness to give of his best." Sergeant Rake was, however, suddenly posted to an Air Crew Disposal Centre, and abruptly notified that he was to lose his aircrew badge and revert to his ground-crew rank of AC2. He said: ". . . I could not help feeling that I had been treated like a criminal . . . I was therefore forced to ask for my discharge . . ."

Air Chief Marshal Sir Edgar Ludlow-Hewitt commented in his report: "It is gravely unjust that a man of this type and character should forfeit his flying badge . . . I understand that the regulations on this matter have now been changed and that he will be entitled to retain his badge. I further suggest that although it is fully recognised that the stripes are given only for classification as aircrew it is, under the circumstances, unduly severe to reduce this man, or others like him, right down to AC2 . . . I urgently recommend that Sgt Rake should immediately, by telegram preferably, have his badge returned to him, and that he should be considered for employment as a flying controller with retention of rank or possibly promotion to commissioned rank." Sergeant Rake's case (set out in PRO AIR 20/2859) was evidently extreme; but there were, undoubtedly, numerous cases of larger or smaller injustice in the RAF, as with all Services and large organizations. They naturally stick in men's minds and colour their attitudes, sometimes for ever more. Thus the whole Service may be blamed for a situation which it abhors, and which is really the fault of a purblind bureaucrat applying regulations without feeling or discretion.

23. Wing Commander Lawson tells us that he "dealt with all cases submitted under the Air Ministry Memorandum [S.61141/S.7; see p. 533] for the disposal of members of air crew who have forfeited the confidence of their Commanding Officers". He wrote a paper in 1945, embodying the fruit of his experience; this is to be found in the Air Historical Branch, and is here quoted extensively.
24. Richards & Saunders, op. cit., iii, p. 29.
25. See Hastings, op. cit., pp. 214, 269.
26. Statement supplied by the Swiss Government to the Air Historical Branch.
27. *Swedish Aviation Historical Society Review*, Special Issue, Nov. 1976; Air Historical Branch.
28. Dean, op. cit., p. 307.
29. Harris, op. cit., p. 98.
30. The final word on RAF morale must be a reference to morale in captivity, a hard test indeed. When Germany surrendered, 13,022 members of aircrew of the RAF, RCAF, RAAF, RNZAF and SAAF were released from the prisoner of war camps (4,480 officers, 8,542 Warrant Officers

and NCOs). This does not, of course, take into account those who died in captivity, or who succeeded in escaping. The Air Force prisoners earned a reputation as persistent potential escapers; as Hilary Saunders says (op. cit., p. 390), "escape became a duty to be pursued in deeds of fantastic ingenuity and determination". This is, in itself, an indication of high morale; but it could lead to tragic consequences. On March 24, 1944 there was a mass escape of officers from *Stalag Luft III*; 76 got out, of whom only three reached Britain, the rest being recaptured. Hitler, in a rage, ordered 50 to be shot, and this was done by the *Gestapo*. The *Luftwaffe* was in no way responsible for this brutal deed; when the news of it reached Bomber Command, it inspired an even deeper sense of personal motivation in the aircrews than before.

65. *The Dams Raid; master bombers*, p. 537–p. 542

1. *Chronology and Index of the Second World War*, Royal Institute of International Affairs; Newspaper Archive Developments, 1975.
2. *Spandau: The Secret Diaries.*
3. AHB/II/116/19, p. 188.
4. Lawrence, op. cit., p. 121.
5. RUSI *Journal*, May 1962, p. 103.
6. OH (Webster & Frankland), op. cit., ii, p. 168.
7. Ibid, p. 289.
8. John Sweetman, *Operation Chastise – The Dams Raid: Epic or Myth*, Jane's, 1982.
9. *The Dams Raid*; RUSI *Journal*, May 1964. The technique of long-distance control of military operations, used with startling effect in the Falklands Islands campaign of 1982, almost certainly owes its origin to the Dams raid.
10. OH (Webster & Frankland), op. cit., ii, p. 179.
11. "Air Vice-Marshal Cochrane informed Sir Arthur Harris on 2nd June 1943 that a fortnight's endeavour to reinforce 617 Squadron had ended in failure. In 5 Group, he said, only two crews suitable for the Squadron could be found and the other Group Commanders had told him that, between them, they could find no crews at all for 617 Squadron. The difficulty was that after two tours of operations with the main force, most men were 'tired and not fit to continue'." (Ibid, fn 1.)
12. Lawrence, op. cit., p. 144.
13. OH (Webster & Frankland), op. cit., ii, p. 159.
14. Ibid, p. 284.
15. Ibid, p. 182.

66. *The German fighter force; "Pointblank"* p. 542–p. 545

1. W. F. Craven & J. L. Cate, *The Army Air Forces in World War II*, ii, p. 326; University of Chicago Press, 1949 (henceforth US OH).
2. Ibid, p. 341; these are the rates for the five months, January–May 1943 (inclusive).

3. Ibid, p. 342.
4. See Noble Frankland's questions on p. 509. Statistics of the growth of the German fighter force are from AHB/II/116/19, p. 274.
5. OH (Webster & Frankland), op. cit., ii, p. 20.
6. Ibid, p. 28.
7. Ibid.
8. Ibid, p. 29.
9. US OH, op. cit., ii, p. 573.

67. *Hamburg fire-storm;* Luftwaffe *victory; Mustangs; Bomber Command defeat* p. 545–p. 558

1. Ten days reckoned from 0100 hours on July 25, zero hour for the first attack, to a.m., August 3. The second horrifying example of the potential of area bombing in Germany was the attack on Dresden on the night of February 13/14 1945.
2. The introduction of WINDOW had been under discussion since April 1942; it was opposed on the grounds of the possible effect on British air defence if revealed to the Germans, the Home Secretary, Herbert Morrison, being particularly adamant on this score. In fact, the Germans were well aware of this jamming method, and refrained from using it for the obvious reason that they had far more to lose.

   Sir Arthur Harris (op. cit., p. 134) wrote: "There can be little doubt that if we had been able and allowed to use this weapon in the first months of 1943 we should have saved hundreds of aircraft and thousands of lives and would have much increased the accuracy of our bombing."
3. AHB/II/116/19, p. 188.
4. Richards & Saunders, op. cit., iii, p. 9; this quotes the official report (dated December 1, 1943) of Major-General Kehrl, Police President and Air Protection Leader of Hamburg.
5. OH (Webster & Frankland), op. cit., ii, p. 261, fn 1.
6. *Hausfrau at War* by Else Wendel, Odhams Press, 1957.
7. Adolf Galland, op. cit., pp. 166–7.
8. OH (Webster & Frankland), op. cit., ii, pp. 260–1.
9. *Inside the Third Reich*, p. 284.
10. Qu. OH (Webster & Frankland), op. cit.
11. Ibid, p. 155; the Official Historians echo Harris's words (see p. 483).
12. Harris, op. cit., p. 176.
13. The comparative figures are: World War I (United Kingdom only): 704,803 (Official History, "1918", p. 597); World War II (UK): 264,443 (*Strength and Casualties of the Armed Forces and Auxiliary Services 1939–1945*, Cmd. 6832, 1946, p. 7).
14. Green, op. cit., p. 465.
15. Ibid, p. 466.
16. AHB/II/116/19, p. 277.
17. OH (Webster & Frankland), op. cit., ii, p. 39.
18. Ibid.

19. Ibid.
20. Frankland & Dowling, *Decisive Battles of the Twentieth Century*, p. 240, Sidgwick & Jackson, 1976.
21. Ibid.
22. OH (Webster & Frankland), op. cit., ii, p. 163.
23. Ibid, p. 198.
24. Quoted, ibid, p. 190.
25. A striking instance of obsession in war is the case of Colonel d'Alençon, Chief of Staff to the French C-in-C, General Nivelle, in 1917. He was convinced that the French Army was only capable of one more major effort, and he knew that he was dying of consumption. His resulting obsession with time helped to propel Nivelle into the disastrous April offensive whose costly failure shortly led to widespread mutinies.
26. Sir Philip Gibbs, *Realities of War*, p. 396; Heinemann, 1920.
27. OH (Webster & Frankland), op. cit., ii, p. 195.
28. Ibid, pp. 195–6; Bennett to Bomber Command, November 3, 1944.
29. Gibbs, op. cit.
30. OH (Webster & Frankland), op. cit., ii, p. 196.
31. Ibid, p. 198.
32. Ibid, pp. 54–7 (full text).
33. Ibid, p. 80, fn 6.
34. Ibid, p. 82.
35. See p. 105, Ch. 9, Note 30, for the RAF's "black day" on August 8, 1918.
36. OH (Webster & Frankland), op. cit., ii, p. 193.
37. See p. 264: Trenchard's Memorandum of May 1941, "There is no joking in the German shelters . . ."
38. RUSI *Journal*, May 1962, p. 102.
39. OH (Webster & Frankland), op. cit., ii, p. 54.

Victory in Europe
68. *Combined Operations, 1942–45: "Cossac"; Leigh-Mallory*
    p. 559–p. 566

1. Terraine, *The Life and Times of Lord Mountbatten*, p. 85, Arrow, 1980.
2. Record of statement made by Admiral of the Fleet Earl Mountbatten of Burma to the Canadian Broadcasting Corporation on July 12, 1962.
3. William Whitehead & Terence Macartney-Filgate, *Dieppe 1942: Echoes of Disaster*, p. 187, Richard Drew, 1982.
4. There were in addition three smoke-laying squadrons (two Blenheim, one Boston) and two intruder squadrons (Boston). The bomber element was supplied by No. 2 Group.
5. AHB/II/117/2(E), p. 124.
6. Ibid, p. 125.
7. Ibid.
8. Richards & Saunders, op. cit., ii, p. 145.
9. AHB/II/116/22, p. 38.
10. Ibid, p. 43.

11. See p. 352.
12. AHB/II/116/22, p. 41.
13. Ibid, p. 42.
14. Ibid.
15. AHB/II/117/2(E), p. 126.
16. Lieutenant-General Sir Frederick Morgan, *Overture to Overlord*, p. 51, Hodder & Stoughton, 1950.
17. See pp. 19–20.
18. Group Captain W. G. G. Duncan Smith, DSO, DFC, *Spitfire into Battle*, p. 94, John Murray, 1981.
19. OH (Webster & Frankland), op. cit., iii, p. 15.
20. AHB/II/116/22, p. 44, fn.
21. Air Marshal Sir Arthur Barratt became AOC-in-C, Technical Training Command, on this day, *vice* Air Marshal Sir John Babington. This appointment appears to be somewhat of a waste of Barratt's specialized knowledge and experience just at the time that they should have been most useful. Most probably he was a victim of seniority problems within the context of a functional Command system.
22. At the end of 1943, as OVERLORD came closer, the senior positions had to be filled as a matter of urgency, and this period naturally saw a large influx of Army and Air Force officers with the prestige of their Mediterranean experience. At the same time Admiral Sir Andrew Cunningham, Allied Naval C-in-C, Mediterranean, came home to the post of First Sea Lord.

69. *Combined Operations: Pantelleria;* Luftwaffe *eclipse; Sicily blueprint* p. 566–p. 580

1. G. A. Shepperd, *The Italian Campaign 1939–45*, p. 22, Arthur Barker, 1968. On retirement from the Army in 1947 Lieut-Col Shepperd became Chief Librarian at the Royal Military College, Sandhurst.
2. Ibid.
3. US OH, op. cit., ii, p. 437.
4. Shepperd, op. cit., p. 23.
5. US OH, op. cit., p. 432; the narrative of the air attack on Pantelleria (pp. 419–34) is full of interest.
6. In pre-nuclear warfare it thus joins Rotterdam in unenviable singularity (see p. 136).
7. US OH, op. cit., pp. 433–4.
8. Shepperd, op. cit., p. 27.
9. In *With Prejudice* (p. 433) Lord Tedder tells how in April he "arranged for 'Mary' Coningham" to discuss these differences personally with Montgomery: "Coningham's first report on their meeting was not, however, promising. He said that Montgomery was obstinate . . ." It is sad to reflect that only six months had passed since Montgomery and Coningham had established their close and fruitful accord at Alam Halfa (see pp. 380–2).
10. John Erickson, *The Road to Berlin*, p. 101, Weidenfeld & Nicolson, 1983.
11. AHB/II/116/19, p. 235.

12. Among them John Erickson, op. cit., p. 97.

13. The twin-engined single-seat Hs 129B did not make its mark until late in 1943. It was the *Luftwaffe*'s "only aircraft really suited to and designed for close-support and anti-tank tasks" (Green, p. 390), and thus increasingly valuable against the massed Red Army tank attacks. It provided a platform for some amazing weapons in this rôle. One of these was the SG 113A which "comprised a rhomboid-shaped container in which six individual mortars were mounted vertically, each mortar accommodating a single shell with a 77-mm soft metal jacket and a 45-mm armour-piercing core. A photo-electric cell attached to the nose of the aircraft triggered the mortars which fired their shells vertically downwards, the cell being actuated by the electro-magnetic field created by the enemy tank" (ibid, p. 396). This fearsome instrument proved unreliable, but in 1944 the BK 7.5 cannon was introduced, a huge 75-mm calibre gun, with 12 26-lb rounds which could be fired at a rate of 40 per minute. At 550 yards from a tank, the pilot could loose off four of these in one burst, with effects that can be imagined when we recall that only one shot was required to knock out the massive *Josef Stalin* tank of the Red Army.

14. See RUSI *Journal*, June 1977: "Air Power at Kursk: The Confrontation of Aircraft and Tanks – A Lesson for Today?" by Captain Lonnie O. Ratley III, USAF.

15. AHB/II/116/19, ibid.

16. Ibid, p. 273.

17. Nigel Nicolson, *Alex: The Life of Field-Marshal Earl Alexander of Tunis*, p. 201, Weidenfeld & Nicolson, 1973.

18. MacDonald, op. cit., p. 144.

19. US OH, op. cit., p. 455.

20. Nicolson, op. cit., ibid.

21. AHB/II/117/10 (*The Sicilian campaign*), p. 60.

22. Shepperd, op. cit., p. 71.

23. AHB/II/116/19, p. 260.

24. AHB/II/117/3(G), vii, p. 176.

25. Richards & Saunders, op. cit., ii, p. 306.

26. MacDonald, op. cit., p. 150; Charles B. MacDonald was Deputy Chief Historian of the Department of the Army when he wrote *The Mighty Endeavour*. Prior to that he had headed the European branch of the Office of the Chief of Military History, and in that capacity, as well as his supervising rôle, he wrote two of the official histories of the European campaign.

27. AHB/II/116/22, p. 95.

28. AHB/II/117/3(G), p. 178.

29. US OH, op. cit., p. 453.

30. Ibid.

31. AHB/II/117/10, p. 65; this is the source of all the above statements.

32. Ibid, p. 77.

33. Richards & Saunders, op. cit., ii, p. 320.

34. AHB/II/117/10, p. 77; record of the Hermann Goering *Panzer* Division.
35. Ibid; Randazzo was an important road junction north of Etna.
36. Tedder, op. cit., p. 558.
37. Richards & Saunders, op. cit., ii, p. 322.
38. Shepperd, op. cit., p. 69.
39. AHB/II/117/3(G), pp. 197–8.
40. AHB/II/117/10, p. 80.
41. Shepperd, ibid.
42. AHB/II/116/22, p. 97.

70. *Combined Operations: Mainland Italy; systems of air support*
    p. 580–p. 599

1. From Norway and twice from France in 1940, from Greece in 1941, and from Dieppe in 1942.
2. E.g. in a Note on strategy dated November 25, 1942; see *The Hinge of Fate*, p. 586.
3. Richards & Saunders, op. cit., ii, p. 325.
4. For a succinct account of the surrender negotiations see Liddell Hart, *History of the Second World War*, op. cit., pp. 451–3. On October 13 Italy declared war on Germany, and became a "co-belligerent" of the Allies.
5. Slessor (to Portal, April 16, 1944), op. cit., p. 575.
6. Tedder, op. cit., p. 463.
7. Slessor, op. cit., p. 585. Aircraft carriers were one of Slessor's bêtes-noires; he referred to the carrier era as an "appallingly expensive but short phase in the history of warfare". He appears not to have seen, or not to have been prepared to admit, that the carrier was the capital ship of World War II, and as such played a decisive part in the only major campaign fought between surface fleets – in the Pacific.
8. The very first use of HS 293 was almost a fortnight earlier, on August 25, in the Bay of Biscay (see p. 432, Ch. 55, Note 8). HMS *Bideford* was damaged by a near miss. Two days later the destroyer HMS *Egret* was sunk by a glider-bomb, and the Canadian destroyer *Athabaskan* also hit. But Salerno saw the first large-scale use against suitable targets.
9. Shepperd, op. cit., p. 125.
10. Cunningham, *A Sailor's Odyssey*, p. 570.
11. AHB/II/116/19, p. 262.
12. Shepperd, op. cit., p. 134.
13. Ibid, p. 132.
14. AHB/II/116/19, op. cit.
15. *Send No More Roses*, p. 86, Weidenfeld & Nicolson, 1977.
16. Tedder, op. cit., pp. 463, 458.
17. AHB/II/117/11(A), (*The Italian Campaign*, i), pp. 235–6.
18. He also performed the duties of Commander-in-Chief, Royal Air Force, Mediterranean and Middle East.
19. Slessor, op. cit., p. 561.
20. Ibid, p. 567, fn.

21. Richards & Saunders, op. cit., ii, p. 348.
22. For example, the disastrous attacks of the Fairey Battles on the Albert Canal bridges on May 12, 1940 (see pp. 127–8).
23. Slessor, op. cit., pp. 572–3.
24. Ibid, p. 570.
25. This was not so much in numbers of divisions as in actual strength; Liddell Hart (op. cit., p. 536) says that in June 1944 there were 30 Allied divisions in Italy, as against 22 German – "about two to one in actual troops".
26. Lewin, op. cit., pp. 286–7.
27. Fred Majdalany, *Cassino: Portrait of a Battle*, p. 121; Longmans, Green & Co, 1957.
28. *The Alexander Memoirs* (ed. John North), p. 121, Cassell, 1962.
29. The Abbey had been twice destroyed by human hands before: by the Lombards when it was only 50 years old, and by the Saracens 300 years later. Five centuries after that it was wrecked again by an act of God – the earthquake of 1349. Today, once more, it is miraculously restored.
30. Majdalany, op. cit., p. 125.
31. General von Senger und Etterlin, *Neither Fear Nor Hope*, pp. 202–3; Macdonald, 1963.
32. Majdalany, op. cit., p. 166.
33. US OH, op. cit., iii, p. 367.
34. Christopher Buckley, quoted in Majdalany, op. cit., p. 177.
35. The much-dreaded German multi-barrelled mortars *(Nebelwerfer)* "were deeply dug into the hillside, with clearance space for their projectiles cut out of the slope. The observer directing their fire was also provided with a deep hole, and did his observing through a narrow notch chipped out of the rock" (Majdalany, op. cit., p. 88).
36. AHB/II/117/11(A), p. 303.
37. US OH, op. cit.
38. AHB/II/117/11(A), p. 204.
39. My italics.
40. Slessor to Portal, April 16; op. cit., p. 573; last seven words in Slessor's italics.
41. US OH, op. cit.
42. Mediterranean Allied Air Force pamphlet, February 1945, quoted in Slessor, op. cit., p. 566.
43. It is one of the great curiosities of the Second World War that men who had personal experience of the previous war were constantly surprised when identical circumstances produced identical results. It was one of the most obvious lessons of 1915–17 that heavy bombardment by large-calibre high-explosive projectiles tore up the ground to such an extent that advances were impeded rather than aided by this method. When rain was added, the result was the virtually impassable swamps seen on the Somme and at Passchendaele. No one should have been surprised at this in 1944.

44. Slessor, op. cit., pp. 573–4.
45. Majdalany, op. cit., p. 193.
46. Letter to the author, November 27, 1979.
47. Majdalany, op. cit., p. 194.
48. Ibid.
49. AHB/II/116/22, p. 111.
50. Ibid, p. 112.
51. Ibid.
52. Slessor, op. cit., pp. 570–1.
53. AHB/II/116/22, pp. 111–12.
54. AHB/II/117/11(A), pp. 158–9.
55. AHB/II/116/22, p. 115.
56. Ibid.
57. Army Group Royal Artillery; this meant the collected medium guns of an Army, plus field batteries not allocated to divisions.
58. AHB/II/116/22, pp. 117–18.
59. Fraser, *And We Shall Shock Them*, p. 360.
60. Richards & Saunders, op. cit., ii, p. 352.
61. Richards & Saunders, op. cit., iii, p. 221.
62. Alexander's promotion was effective from the capture of Rome, June 4, 1944.
63. Slessor, op. cit., pp. 580–1; this important document also appears as an appendix in AHB/II/117/11(A). Slessor's italics.

71. *Combined Operations: "Overlord"; commanders; manpower; aircraft* p. 599–p. 607

1. Don Cook, essay in *The Warlords*, ed. Field-Marshal Lord Carver, p. 514, Weidenfeld & Nicolson, 1976.
2. Air Chief Marshal Sir Christopher Foxley Norris in *The Warlords*, p. 495.
3. Harris, op. cit., p. 246.
4. Terraine, op. cit., p. 88.
5. Press Conference, October 23, 1944; AHB/II/117/1(F), p. 245.
6. Government expenditure on installations, accommodation, production plant, etc.
7. Including womanpower.
8. OH *British War Production* by M. M. Postan, pp. 304–5, HMSO 1952. The fixed capital expenditure percentage referred to above is extrapolated from a table on p. 448 of that work.
9. AHB/II/116/14, Appendices 3 & 4.
10. 42 from Canada, 27 from South Africa, 16 from Australia, nine from India, six from New Zealand (Richards & Saunders, iii, op. cit., p. 370, fn).
11. Dean, op. cit., p. 112: table.
12. Joseph P. Lash, *Roosevelt and Churchill 1939–1941*, p. 277, André Deutsch, 1977.
13. Ibid, p. 284.

14. The same, of course, applied to Germany; Ultra intercepts revealed that the German Air Force began to feel the manpower shortage, especially in its fighter arm, as early as March 1942. By the end of that year the general German shortage compelled it, nevertheless, to give up a considerable percentage of its strength to ground fighting divisions (Hinsley, op. cit., ii, p. 238).
15. PRO AIR 20/2859: Sinclair to Air Marshal Sir B. E. Sutton, April 1, 1944.
16. 59th Division, August, 50th Division, November.
17. AHB/II/116/14, pp. 191–3.
18. Thetford, op. cit., p. 316.
19. Ibid, p. 320.

72. *"Overlord": Command problems; a question of airfields* p. 607– p. 619

1. Tedder, op. cit., p. 499; Churchill to Portal or (more probably) Sinclair, undated.
2. Coningham's Dispatch, "Operations Carried Out by Second Tactical Air Force Between 6th June 1944 and 9th May 1945, p. 3; unpublished; PRO AIR 37/876.
3. Alfred Goldberg in *The Warlords*, p. 577.
4. Carlo D'Este, *Decision in Normandy: The Unwritten Story of Montgomery and the Allied Campaign*, p. 215, Collins, 1983. It is ironic that at this stage the United States Army Air Force was less willing to cooperate with the army to which it belonged than the separate air Service, the RAF, to cooperate with another Service altogether.
5. Tedder, op. cit., p. 501.
6. Professor Zuckerman, *From Apes to Warlords*, pp. 348–9, Hamish Hamilton, 1978. Leigh-Mallory's unpopularity with the Americans is well attested. High-ranking Americans told Bruce Lockhart in 1945: "We could not stand Leigh-Mallory – too much of this high-hat and Oxford accent business" (*Diaries*, ii, p. 431).
7. OH (Ellis), *Victory in the West*, i, p. 73.
8. Ibid, p. 75.
9. Coningham, op. cit.
10. Montgomery, *Memoirs*, pp. 256–7; the two badges referred to were the General Staff badge and the badge of the Royal Tank Regiment, to which, strictly speaking, Montgomery had no right.
11. D'Este, op. cit., p. 219; Broadhurst now commanded No. 83 Group, working with Dempsey's Second Army.
12. *The Struggle for Europe*, pp. 340–1, Collins, 1952. Wilmot relates that the Air Force and its officers deeply resented the fact that public acclaim concentrated on Montgomery and the Eighth Army with "but a passing round of applause for Coningham and the Desert Air Force. The headlines stung. Speaking to war correspondents one day, Coningham burst out, 'It's always "Monty's Army", "Monty's Victory",

"Monty Strikes Again". You never say "Coningham's Air Force".'"

13. D'Este, op. cit., pp. 221–2; Lieutenant-General Omar N. Bradley commanded the US First Army, Lieutenant-General Sir Miles Dempsey the British Second Army, and Lieutenant-General H. D. G. Crerar the Canadian First Army.
14. Wilmot, op. cit.
15. Coningham, op. cit.
16. Tedder, op. cit.; my italics.
17. Richard Lamb, *Montgomery in Europe 1943–1945: Success or Failure?*, p. 65, Buchan & Enright, 1983.
18. D'Este, op. cit., p. 65.
19. Russell F. Weigley, *Eisenhower's Lieutenants*, p. 117, Sidgwick & Jackson, 1981.
20. Tedder, op. cit., p. 549.
21. Ibid, p. 550.
22. D'Este, op. cit., p. 81, fn 1.
23. Ibid, p. 75.
24. Lamb, op. cit., p. 80.
25. Churchill's mordant comment on Anzio was: "I had hoped that we were hurling a wild cat on to the shore, but all we had got was a stranded whale" (Wynford Vaughan-Thomas, *Anzio*, p. 88, Longmans, 1961).
26. Full text in D'Este, op. cit., pp. 80–1; my italics (except for underlining).
27. Lamb, op. cit., p. 80.
28. D'Este, op. cit., p. 78.
29. Ibid, p. 82.
30. Ibid, p. 83, quoting AEAF Historical Record, PRO AIR 37/1057.
31. Ibid, p. 84.
32. Ibid, p. 86, quoting Montgomery's address (Eisenhower Presidential Papers in the Eisenhower Library, Abilene, Kansas); my italics.
33. Lamb, op. cit., p. 84. Major-General Sir Francis de Guingand was Montgomery's Chief of Staff.
34. *Memoirs*, op. cit., p. 257.

73. *Air supremacy; interdiction; Tactical Air Forces; "Bodyguard"*
    p. 619–p. 627

1. Wilmot, op. cit., p. 189.
2. DeWitt, S. Copp, *Forged in Fire: Strategy and Decisions in the Air War over Europe 1940–45*, p. 460; Air Force Historical Foundation, Doubleday 1982.
3. OH (Webster & Frankland), op. cit., iii, p. 131.
4. Alfred Goldberg, *A History of the United States Air Force 1907–1957*, p. 66; D. Van Nostrand Co. Inc. (New York), 1957.
5. Copp, op. cit., p. 461.
6. Quoted in Tedder, op. cit., p. 504; undated.
7. Ibid, p. 509.
8. Ibid, p. 489.

9. Ibid, pp. 503–4.
10. Ibid, p. 530; the whole controversy over attacking French railways is set out very dispassionately by Tedder, pp. 516–33.
11. Lamb, op. cit., p. 66.
12. *Closing the Ring*, p. 467.
13. Ibid, pp. 467–8.
14. Richards & Saunders, op. cit., iii, pp. 88–9.
15. Zuckerman diary, July 9, 1944, quoted in D'Este, op. cit., p. 214.
16. OH (Webster & Frankland), op. cit., iii, p. 124.
17. Lawrence, op. cit., pp. 192–3; the first use of Tallboys was the highly successful attack carried out by 617 Squadron on February 8, 1944 on the aero-engine factory (Gnome et Rhône) at Limoges.
18. In June 1944 No. 2 Group comprised:

No. 88 Squadron	Boston IIIA
No. 342 (French) Sqdn.	Boston IIIA
No. 226 Sqdn.	Mitchell II
Nos. 98, 180 Sqdns.	Mitchell II
No. 320 (Dutch) Sqdn.	Mitchell II
Nos. 107, 613 Sqdns.	Mosquito VI
No. 305 (Polish) Sqdn.	Mosquito VI
No. 21 Sqdn.	Mosquito VI
No. 464 Sqdn. (RAAF)	Mosquito VI
No. 487 Sqdn. (RNZAF)	Mosquito VI

19. Richards & Saunders, op. cit., iii, p. 95.
20. Wilmot, op. cit., p. 200.
21. Lewin, op. cit., p. 315.
22. Ibid, p. 316.
23. Wilmot, op. cit., pp. 289–90.
24. Bomber Command's share was 87,200 tons; all figures from the table in OH (Ellis), op. cit., i, p. 109.

74. *"Overlord": U–Boat fiasco; airbone assault; air effort* p. 627–p. 632

1. OH (Ellis), op. cit., i, Appendix II, Part IV.
2. Wilmot, op. cit., p. 227.
3. Lewin, op. cit., p. 232.
4. Ibid.
5. "Cannon" includes the 6-pdr gun (57-mm; see p. 440) mounted in the "Tsetse" Mosquitoes. A pilot of one of these, about to attack a U-boat, found a covering Ju 88 right in his sights. "Instinctively he pressed the gun-button and, to his astonishment, saw the Junkers disintegrate before his eyes under the direct impact of a six-pounder shell. With Ultra even the improbable became possible – for it was Ultra . . . that had laid the basis for this extraordinary strike" (Lewin, p. 233).
6. OH (Ellis), op. cit., i, p. 241.
7. Richards & Saunders, op. cit., iii, p. 109.

8. A good short account, based on the recollections of the head of the British Meteorological team, Group Captain J. M. Stagg, is to be found in Richards & Saunders, op. cit., iii, pp. 103–5. There are also the narratives of the chief participants, Eisenhower, Tedder and Montgomery.
9. Lamb, op. cit., p. 90. Leigh-Mallory had been doubtful of the effectiveness of airborne operations ever since their failure to materialize at Dieppe in 1942.
10. For the information in this section see *Prelude to Overlord* by Humphrey Wynn and Susan Young, p. 127, Airlife 1983.
11. John Keegan, *Six Armies in Normandy*, p. 81; Jonathan Cape, 1982.
12. Harris, op. cit., p. 196.
13. Wynn & Young, op. cit., p. 130.
14. Dean, op. cit., p. 238.
15. Ibid, p. 237.
16. *Triumph and Tragedy*, p. 5; Churchill to the House of Commons, June 6, 1944; my italics.

75. *Tactical air supremacy* p. 632–p. 637

1. AHB/II/116/22, p. 148.
2. Richards & Saunders, op. cit., iii, quoting Air Commodore A. J. W. Geddes, Deputy SASO, Second TAF, who photographed the whole length of the beaches from a Mustang at a height of between 800 and 1,000 feet.
3. Coningham, op. cit., p. 4.
4. Ibid, p. 24.
5. Major-General Richard Rohmer, *Patton's Gap: An Account of the Battle of Normandy 1944*, p. 37, Arms and Armour Press, 1981.
6. Ibid, p. 103.
7. D'Este, op. cit., pp. 162–3.
8. From Nos. 245, 181, 182 and 247 Squadrons.
9. Nos. 98, 180, 226, and No. 320 (Dutch) Squadrons.
10. Richards & Saunders, op. cit., iii, p. 126.
11. Brigadier-General Sir J. E. Edmonds, *Military Operations France and Belgium 1917*, ii, p. 234, HMSO, 1948.
12. OH (Ellis), op. cit., i, p. 287.
13. AHB/II/116/22, p. 149.
14. OH (Ellis), ibid.
15. Field-Marshal Wilhelm Keitel was the head of OKW, *Oberkommando der Wehrmacht*, the central Command of the Armed Forces.
16. Quoted in Wilmot, op. cit., p. 313.

76. *Command relations* p. 637–p. 647

1. AHB/II/116/22, ibid.
2. I Corps Operational Order No. 1, May 5, 1944, stated: "The task of 3 Br Inf Div is to capture Caen and secure a bridgehead over the River Orne at that place."

3. Fraser, op. cit., p. 329. This excludes losses in Sixth Airborne Division.
4. Wilmot, op. cit., p. 278.
5. Belchem, *Victory in Normandy*, p. 109, Chatto & Windus, 1981.
6. Ibid, p. 110.
7. D'Este, op. cit., p. 145.
8. Quoted in Lamb, op. cit., p. 108.
9. Ibid, p. 109; my italics.
10. Quoted in D'Este, op. cit., p. 278.
11. Quoted in Lamb, op. cit., p. 111.
12. Lieutenant-General J. T. Crocker, commanding I Corps.
13. Quoted in D'Este, op. cit., p. 274. The original 51st (Highland) Division had won considerable fame in the First World War. Its successor, as we have noted (p. 160), came to a tragic end in 1940 – in Normandy; it was forced to surrender at St Valéry-en-Caux. A new 51st was formed by renumbering the 9th (Scottish) Division; it went out to Egypt in August 1942, took part in Montgomery's victory at El Alamein and the advance to Tunisia, and the campaign in Sicily. It was then brought back for OVERLORD and regarded as a "crack" division.
14. Quoted in Lamb, op. cit., p. 106.
15. Quoted in Wilmot, op. cit., p. 519; he was here referring to the hesitant performance of the 43rd Division, ordered to take "all risks" to reach the First Airborne, beleaguered in Arnhem.
16. See D'Este, op. cit., p. 268.
17. Field-Marshal Sir William Slim, *Defeat into Victory*, pp. 547–8, Cassell, 1956.
18. Quoted in D'Este, op. cit., p. 166.
19. Quoted, ibid, p. 196.
20. Ibid, p. 224.
21. Quoted ibid.
22. Tedder, op. cit., pp. 553–4.
23. Lamb, op. cit., p. 113.
24. Leigh-Mallory diary, June 14; quoted in D'Este, op. cit., p. 225.
25. AEAF Record, quoted ibid.
26. Leigh-Mallory diary, op. cit.
27. Early July, quoted in D'Este, op. cit., pp. 217–18.
28. Tedder, op. cit., p. 606. He was referring to Canadian calls for air support in the attack on Walcheren in October.
29. Ibid, p. 552.
30. Wilmot, op. cit., p. 322.
31. Tedder, op. cit., p. 554.
32. Philip Guedalla, *The Duke*, p. 272, Hodder & Stoughton, 1946.
33. Quoted in D'Este, op. cit., pp. 238–9; my italics.
34. Lamb, op. cit., p. 64.

77. *"Race-meetings"; V-weapons; "Had for Suckers"* p. 647–p. 658

1. OH (Ellis), op. cit., i, p. 277.

2. Coningham, op. cit., p. 5.
3. OH (Ellis), op. cit., p. 358; the author is much inclined to agree with Col. D'Este's comment (op. cit., p. 195) that "the British official history is not forthright in its discussion of important issues, particularly of those which might in any way reflect unfavourably upon Montgomery's generalship."
4. Interview with D'Este, November 22, 1979; op. cit., p. 223.
5. Coningham, op. cit.; he adds: "During this period there appeared a new disadvantage, unexpected in a Western theatre of war. The soil on which our airfields had to be constructed in Normandy was found to contain a very high proportion of abrasive silica dust, which lowered the life of engines, particularly those in the Typhoons which, at that time, were not fitted with any air cleaning devices. After intensive effort by MAP and the adoption of various impromptu expediencies such as pumping oil or sea water on to the landing and taxying surfaces, and the reduction of warming up time to a minimum, the crisis was successfully passed."
6. All figures from OH (Ellis), op. cit., pp. 305–6.
7. Tedder, op. cit., pp. 555–6.
8. Ibid (and the two following quotations).
9. Lamb, op. cit., pp. 420–2; my italics.
10. Ibid, pp. 422–5.
11. Major-General (then Lieutenant-Colonel) Sir Nigel Tapp, quoted in D'Este, op. cit., p. 316.
12. Harris, op. cit., p. 211.
13. OH (Ellis), op. cit., p. 132; my italics.
14. Quoted in D'Este, op. cit., p. 316.
15. Wilmot, op. cit., p. 351.
16. Professor R. V. Jones; letter in *The Daily Telegraph*, June 11, 1981.
17. Quoted in Tedder, op. cit., p. 582.
18. Coningham, op. cit., p. 25.
19. Quoted in Lamb, op. cit., pp. 126–7.
20. Tedder, op. cit., p. 562, and diary, July 19, quoted in D'Este, op. cit., p. 394.
21. July 12; quoted in D'Este, op. cit., p. 361.
22. Tedder, op. cit., p. 561.
23. Quoted in D'Este, op. cit.
24. This is fantasy; out of 180,000 tons of bombs dropped by Bomber Command in June, July and August, only 32,000 (17.77 per cent) were dropped on Germany (Webster & Frankland, iii, p. 45).
25. Lamb, op. cit., p. 125.
26. Stephen E. Ambrose, *The Supreme Commander*, quoted in D'Este, op. cit., p. 394.
27. Tedder, op. cit., p. 571.
28. Ibid, p. 563.
29. Ibid.
30. Quoted in Lamb, op. cit., p. 154.
31. Coningham, op. cit., pp. 16–17.

78. *Making air history; Normandy; triumph of air power* p. 658–
    p. 663

1. AHB/II/116/22, p. 157.
2. Bradley to Eisenhower, July 28, quoted in D'Este, op. cit., p. 405.
3. Commanded by Brigadier-General Elwood R. Quesada, an outstanding
   American fighter commander. Lieutenant-General Hoyt Vandenberg
   became Commander-in-Chief, Ninth Air Force, on August 1, in succession to Lieutenant-General Brereton, who went to command the First
   Allied Airborne Army.
4. MacDonald, op. cit., pp. 307–8.
5. Weigley, op. cit., p. 175.
6. Coningham, op. cit., pp. 10–11; my italics.
7. OH (Ellis), op. cit., i, p. 430.
8. Quoted in Lyall, op. cit., p. 351.
9. MacDonald, op. cit., p. 318.
10. Weigley, op. cit., p. 214.
11. Wilmot, op. cit., p. 434.
12. OH (Ellis), op. cit., p. 487.
13. Ibid, p. 488; these totals do not include the effort made and losses
    sustained in preparation for OVERLORD before June 6 (see p. 627).

79. *"Bagration"; advance to the Rhine; Arnhem* p. 663–p. 670

1. General Prince Peter Ivanovich Bagration commanded the Russian
   Second Army in the 1812 campaign against Napoleon. Operation BAGRA-
   TION in 1944 involved Russian forces amounting to 1,254,000 men, with
   2,715 tanks and 1,355 self-propelled guns, 24,000 guns and mortars,
   2,306 *Katyusha* rocket-launchers and four air armies with 5,327 aircraft.
2. Erickson, op. cit., p. 228.
3. E.g. Fuller, op. cit., iii, p. 577, following Wilmot, op. cit., p. 434; General
   Eisenhower, in his Report (p. 62) gives round figures for German losses:
   killed and missing, 200,000, prisoners of war, 200,000. Field-Marshal
   Montgomery (*Memoirs*, p. 263) says: "Total enemy losses: Difficult to
   estimate accurately. Probably about 300,000 but some German authorities would put the total at under 200,000."
4. Lieutenant-General Bodo Zimmerman, Chief Operations Officer of
   Army Group "D" (von Rundstedt); in *The Fatal Decisions*, op. cit.
5. OH (Webster & Frankland), op. cit., ii, p. 136; though numbers increased, loss of territory during this period was fatal: "Whereas, in July,
   the line of night-fighters extended from Denmark to Paris, in October it
   ran from Denmark to Switzerland, thus enabling Allied bombers to
   approach German territory without interception on the way" (*Rise and
   Fall of the German Air Force*, p. 367).
6. Coningham, op. cit., p. 33.
7. AHB/II/116/19, pp. 339, 365.
8. Richards & Saunders, op. cit., iii, pp. 190–1.

9. Coningham, op. cit., p. 73.
10. Ibid.
11. Ibid; my italics; the Despatch was written in 1945 or 1946.
12. The 12th Army Group was activated on August 1.
13. Wilmot, op. cit., p. 527.
14. Lamb, op. cit., p. 216.
15. Lewin, *The Chief*, p. 131.
16. Lamb, op. cit., p. 227.
17. Coningham, op. cit., p. 23.
18. OH (Ellis), op. cit., ii, p. 53.
19. Ibid, pp. 53–4.
20. Wilmot, op. cit., p. 527.

80. *Portal and Harris; Dresden; the final acts* p. 671–p. 681

1. Richards & Saunders, op. cit., iii, p. 200.
2. OH (Webster & Frankland), op. cit., iii, p. 80.
3. Ibid, iv, p. 172.
4. See pp. 263, 275–6.
5. OH (Webster & Frankland), op. cit., iii, p. 71.
6. Ibid, iv, p. 290; my italics. Tedder's Note is on Air Policy to be Adopted with a View to Rapid Defeat of Germany.
7. Ibid, iii, p. 80.
8. Ibid, p. 82.
9. *Tirpitz* was in Altenfjord, North Norway; she was attacked by 27 Lancasters, flying from Yagodnik near Archangel, with "Tallboys" and "Johnny Walker" anti-shipping bombs, on September 15. Though heavily damaged, she did not sink. When sufficiently repaired, she was moved to Tromso, and there finished off by Nos. 9 and 617 Squadrons (again using "Tallboys") on November 12.
10. OH (Webster & Frankland), op. cit., iii, p. 75.
11. Air Commodore P. Huskinson, *Vision Ahead*, pp. 176, 178, Werner Laurie, 1949.
12. Harris, op. cit., p. 236.
13. OH (Webster & Frankland), op. cit., iii, p. 184; p. 110, fn 1, of the same work says that 58 per cent of the effort was allocated to cities, and confirms 14 per cent to oil.
14. Coningham, op. cit., p. 42.
15. Extracted from OH (Ellis), op. cit., ii, p. 190, and Richards & Saunders, op. cit., iii, pp. 208–10.
16. Quoted in Coningham, op. cit., p. 43.
17. Galland, op. cit., p. 249.
18. Ibid.
19. Harris to Portal, January 18, 1945; qu. OH (Webster & Frankland), op. cit., iii, p. 93.
20. Ibid.
21. Ibid.

22. Ibid, p. 94.
23. Portal to Harris, November 12, 1944; ibid, p. 84.
24. Ibid, p. 109.
25. Ibid, p. 112.
26. Ibid, p. 117.
27. A recent impassioned denunciation is *Dresden 1945: The Devil's Tinderbox* by Alexander McKee, Souvenir Press, 1982; David Irving's *The Destruction of Dresden* was published by William Kimber.
28. When wars are long over, people tend to forget how compelling was the desire to finish them. The generals of World War I are often spoken and written about as though they engaged in murderous battles for their own sake. The truth is that General Joffre's costly battles of 1915 were inspired by the desire to end the war in that year, and thus staunch the flow of his country's life-blood. The Allied offensive in 1916 had the same aim. General Nivelle, in early 1917, was trying to end it with a single mighty stroke in 48 hours; Field-Marshal Haig was also trying to end the war, in his Flanders ("Passchendaele") offensive. Field-Marshal Montgomery's object, with his single-thrust strategy in 1944, was similar. It is by no means a wicked motivation – the contrary, in fact. But it is not often easy to accomplish.
29. OH (Webster & Frankland), op. cit., iii, p. 198, fn 1.
30. Ibid, p. 199.
31. Harris, op. cit., p. 233.
32. Erickson, op. cit., p. 579.

81. *The right of the line* p. 681–p. 687

1. All figures, and those for casualties which follow, are extracted from Richards & Saunders, op. cit., iii, pp. 371–2, Webster & Frankland (especially vol. iv, pp. 440–4, which contain a detailed breakdown for Bomber Command), and AHB papers. Regarding the WAAF, see also p. 176, Ch. 17, Note 16.
2. For more on this see Terraine, *The Smoke and the Fire*, pp. 206–8. It is to be noted that the aircrew losses of the United States Army Air Force were 120,000.
3. Thetford, op. cit., p. 166.
4. Quoted in Churchill, *The World Crisis: The Eastern Front*, p. 271, Thornton Butterworth, 1931.
5. See p. 537.
6. Quoted in Dean, op. cit., p. 286.
7. *Biographical Dictionary of World War II*, by Christopher Tunney, p. 37, Dent, 1972.
8. Harris, op. cit., p. 197.
9. John Pudney, *Ten Summers: Poems 1933–1943*, p. 48, Bodley Head, 1944. The poem is entitled "Security" – pre-take-off precautions on Bomber Command airfields.

Bibliography

Air Historical Branch (AHB) Specialist Monographs (/116)
AHB/II/116/14 Manning Plans and Policy
AHB/II/116/16 Photographic Reconnaisance
AHB/II/116/17 Expansion of The Royal Air Force, 1934–1939
AHB/II/116/19 The Rise and Fall of The German Air Force (published by Arms & Armour Press, 1983)
AHB/II/116/22 Air Support
Air Historical Branch (AHB) Narratives (/117)
AHB/II/117/1(B) The Bombing Offensive Against Germany (C)(F)
AHB/II/117/2(A) Air Defence of Great Britain 2(B)(D)(E)
AHB/II/117/3(A) The Royal Air Force in the Maritime War (B)(C)(D)(G)
AHB/II/117/4 The Campaign in Norway
AHB/II/117/5(A) The Campaign in France and Low Countries
AHB/II/117/8(A) Middle East Campaigns (B)(C)(E)(F)
AHB/II/117/10 The Sicilian Campaign
AHB/II/117/11(A) The Italian Campaign
Official Histories (OH)
British Intelligence in the Second World War, F. H. Hinsley, HMSO, 1981
British War Production, M. M. Postan, HMSO, 1952
The Mediterranean and Middle East (4 vols), I. S. O. Playfair, HMSO, 1954
Oil: A Study of War-time Policy and Administration, D. J. Payton-Smith, HMSO, 1971
The Strategic Air Offensive Against Germany 1939–1945 (3 vols), C. Webster and N. Frankland, HMSO, 1961
The Defence of the United Kingdom, B. Collier, HMSO, 1957
The War at Sea (3 vols), S. Roskill, HMSO, 1956
Victory in the West (2 vols), L. F. Ellis, HMSO, 1968
US Official History
The Army Air Forces in World War II, W. H. Craven and J. L. Cate, University of Chicago Press, 1949

Ambler, E., *Send No More Roses*, Weidenfeld & Nicolson, 1977
Ash, B., *Norway 1940*, Cassell, 1964
Avon, Lord, *The Eden Memoirs: Facing the Dictators*, Cassell, 1962
Babington Smith, C., *Evidence in Camera*, Chatto and Windus, 1958
Bader, D., *Fight for the Sky*, Sidgwick & Jackson, 1973
Barker, A. J., *Dunkirk: The Great Escape*, Dent, 1977
Barker, R., *The Thousand Plan*, Chatto & Windus, 1965
Barnett, Correlli, *Collapse of British Power*, Eyre Methuen, 1972
    The Desert Generals, William Kimber, 1960 (revised edition: Allen & Unwin, 1983)

Belchem, R. F. K., *Victory in Normandy*, Chatto & Windus, 1981
Bialer, Uri, *The Shadow of the Bomber*, Royal Historical Society, 1980
Bidwell, S. and Graham, D., *Fire-Power: British Army Weapons and Theories of War 1904–45*, Allen and Unwin, 1982
Blaxland, *Destination Dunkirk: The Story of Gort's Army*, William Kimber, 1973
Bond, B., *British Military Policy between the Two World Wars*, Clarendon Press, 1980
    France & Belgium 1939–40, Davis Poynter, 1975
    Liddell Hart: A Study of his Military Thought, Cassell, 1977
    (Ed), *Chief of Staff: The Diaries of Lieutenant General Sir Henry Pownall*, Leo Cooper, 1972
Bowyer, C., *Guns in the Sky: The Air Gunners of World War Two*, Dent, 1979
Boyle, A., *Trenchard*, Collins, 1962
Brickhill, Paul, *Reach for the Sky*, Collins, 1957
Bruce Lockhart, R., *Diaries 1939–1965*, Ed. Kenneth Young, Macmillan, 1980
Callwell, Sir C. E. (Ed), *The Palestine Campaign*, Constable, 1928
Calvocoressi, P., and Wint, G., *Total War*, Allen Lane Penguin, 1972
Carver, Lord (Ed), *The Warlords*, Weidenfeld & Nicolson, 1976
Chandos, Lord, *From Peace to War*, Bodley Head, 1968
Chapman, G., *Why France Collapsed*, Cassell, 1968
Churchill, W. S., *Great Contemporaries*, Macmillan, 1942
    The World Crisis, Thornton Butterworth, 1932
      The Eastern Front, Odhams, 1938
    The History of the Second World War:
      The Gathering Storm, Cassell, 1948
      Their Finest Hour, Cassell, 1949
      The Grand Alliance, Cassell, 1950
      The Hinge of Fate, Cassell, 1951
      Closing the Ring, Cassell, 1952
      Triumph and Tragedy, Cassell, 1954
Clarke, I. F., *Voices Prophesying War 1763–1984*, Oxford University Press, 1966
Clayton, A., *The Enemy is Listening*, Hutchinson, 1980
Coastal Command Review, Nos. 1 (Jan–Feb 1942), 5 (Sept 1942), 6 (Oct 1942), 7 (Nov 1942), 11 (March 1943), vol II, No. 1 (May 1943), vol II, No. 8 (Dec 1943), (June 1945)
Cole, H., *The Black Prince*, Hart-Davis, MacGibbon, 1976
Collier, B., *The Defence of the United Kingdom*, HMSO, 1957 (official history)
    Barren Victories, Versailles to Suez 1918–1956, Cassell, 1964
Cmd. 6832, *Strength and Casualties of the Armed Forces and Auxiliary Services 1939–45*, HMSO, 1946
Coningham Despatch: "Operations Carried Out by the Second Tactical Air Force Between 6th June 1944 and 9th May 1945", PRO AIR 37/876
Connell, J., *Wavell: Scholar and Soldier*, Collins, 1964
    Auchinleck, Cassell, 1959

Bibliography

Cooper, D., Haig, Faber, 1935

Copp, DeWitt, S., *Forged in Fire: Strategy and Decisions in the Air War over Europe 1940–45*, Doubleday, 1982

Craig, Gordon A., *Germany 1866–1945*, Oxford University Press, 1978

Craven, W. F., and Cate, J. L., *The Army Air Forces in World War II*, University of Chicago Press, 1949 (official history)

Cruttwell, C. R. M. F., *The History of the Great War 1914–1918*, Oxford, 1934

Cunningham, A. B., *A Sailor's Odyssey*, Hutchinson, 1951

Daily Telegraph, "Peterborough" column, October 23, 1982

Day Lewis, C., *Word Over All*, Cape, 1943

Dean, Sir Maurice, *The RAF and Two World Wars*, Cassell, 1979

D'Este, Carlo, *Decision in Normandy*, Collins, 1983

Douglas, Sholto, *Years of Command*, Collins, 1966

Dowling, Lord: *Twelve Legions of Angels*, Jarrold, 1946

Dowling, C., and Frankland, N., *Decisive Battles of the Twentieth Century*, Sidgwick & Jackson, 1976

Dupuy, R. E., & Dupuy, T. N., *Compact History of the Civil War*, Hawthorn Books (NY), 1954

Edmonds, Sir J. E., *Military Operations in France and Belgium 1917*, HMSO, 1948

Eisenhower, D. D., *Crusade in Europe*, Heinemann, 1948

Ellis, L. F., *Victory in the West*, HMSO, 1968 (official history)

Erickson, J., *The Road to Berlin*, Weidenfeld & Nicolson, 1983

Falkenhayn, General, *General Headquarters and its Critical Decisions*, Hutchinson, 1919

Falls, C., *The First World War*, Longmans, 1960

Flypast (No. 23) June 1983

Frankland and Dowling (Eds), *Decisive Battles of Twentieth Century*, Sidgwick & Jackson, 1976

Fraser, D. *Alanbrooke*, Collins, 1982
  And We Shall Shock Them, Hodder & Stoughton, 1983

Fredette, R., *First Battle of Britain, 1917–1918 and the Birth of the Royal Air Force*, Cassell, 1966

Fuller, J. F. C., *Decisive Battles of the Western World*, Eyre & Spottiswoode, 1956

Galland, A., *The First and the Last*, Fontana, 1970

Gibbs, P. *Realities of War*, Heinemann, 1920

Gilbert, M., *Winston S. Churchill*, Heinemann, 1977

Goldberg, A., *A History of the US Air Force 1907–1957*, D. Van Nostrand Co. Inc., 1957

Green, W., *Warplanes of the Third Reich*, Macdonald & Jane's, 1970

Grinnell-Milne, Duncan, *Wind in the Wires*, Hurst-Blackett, 1933

Grunberger, R., *Germany 1918–1945*, Batsford, 1964

Guedalla, P., *Middle East 1940–42: A Study in Air Power*, Hodder & Stoughton, 1944
  The Duke, Hodder & Stoughton, 1946

795

Bibliography

Gunsberg, Jeffrey A., *Divided and Conquered: The French High Command and the Defeat of the West, 1940* (ii/7), Greenwood Press, 1979
Gunston, B., *Encyclopaedia of Combat Aircraft*, Salamander, 1976
Hankey, Lord, *Supreme Command 1914–1918*, Allen and Unwin, 1961
Harris, Sir A., *Bomber Offensive*, Collins, 1947
Haslam, E. B., "How Lord Dowding came to leave Fighter Command", *Journal of Strategic Studies*, June 1981
Hastings, M., *Bomber Command*, Michael Joseph, 1979
Hinsley, F. H., *British Intelligence in the Second World War*, HMSO, 1981 (official history)
Horne, A., *To Lose a Battle: France 1940*, Macmillan, 1969
Howard, Frank, and Gunston, Bill, *Conquest of the Air*, Paul Elek, 1972
Humble, R., "Battle of the Atlantic", *Military History*, April 1983
Huskinson, P., *Vision Ahead*, Werner Laurie, 1949
Hyde, H. Montgomery, *British Air Policy Between the Wars 1918–1939*, Heinemann, 1976
Irving, D., *The Destruction of Dresden*, William Kimber, 1963
Ismay, Lord, *Memoirs*, Heinemann, 1960
Jacobsen, H. A., and Rohwer, J. (Eds) *Decisive Battles of World War II*, André Deutsch, 1965
Jameson, Sir William, *The Most Formidable Thing*, Hart-Davis, 1965
Jellicoe, Admiral, *Crisis of the Naval War*, Cassell, 1920
Jones, R. V., *Most Secret War*, Coronet, 1979
Keegan, J., *Six Armies in Normandy*, Cape, 1982
King-Hall, S., *Our Own Times, 1913–38*, Nicholson & Watson, 1938
Kuhl, General von, *Der Weltkrieg 1914–18*, Berlin
Lamb, R., *Montgomery in Europe 1943–45*, Buchan & Enright, 1983
Lash, I. P., *Roosevelt & Churchill 1939–1941*, André Deutsch, 1977
Lawrence, W. J., *No. 5 Bomber Group RAF (1939–1945)*, Faber & Faber, 1951
Lewin, R., *Ultra goes to War*, Hutchinson, 1978
The Chief, Hutchinson, 1980
Life and Death of the Afrika Korps, Batsford 1977
Rommel as Military Commander, Batsford 1968
Liddell Hart, B., *History of the Second World War*, Cassell, 1965
Memoirs, Cassell, 1965
Lucas, Laddie, *Flying Colours*, Hutchinson, 1981
Ludendorff, E., *My War Memories*, Hutchinson, 1919
Lyall, Gavin (Ed), *Freedom's Battle: The War in the Air 1939–1945*, Hutchinson, 1968
MacDonald, C. B., *The Mighty Endeavour*, OUP, 1969
Macleod, Col. R., and Kelly D. (Eds), *The Ironside Diaries, 1937–40*, Constable, 1962
McKee, A., *Dresden 1945: The Devil's Tinderbox*, Souvenir Press, 1982
McLachlan, Donald, *Room 39: Naval Intelligence in Action, 1939–45*, Weidenfeld & Nicolson, 1968

796

Bibliography

Majdalany, F., *Cassino: Portrait of a Battle*, Longmans, Green & Co., 1957

Mason, D., *Who's Who in World War II*, Weidenfeld & Nicolson, 1978

Mason, F. K., *The Hawker Hurricane*, Macdonald, 1962

Mead, P., *The Eye in the Air*, HMSO, 1983

Miroir de L'Histoire, September 1961

Montgomery, Field-Marshal, *Memoirs*, Collins, 1958

Morgan, F., *Overture to Overlord*, Hodder & Stoughton, 1950

Nicolson, Nigel, *Alex: The Life of Field Marshal Earl Alexander of Tunis*, Weidenfeld & Nicolson, 1973

North, J. (Ed), *The Alexander Memoirs*, Cassell, 1962

Oliver, F. S., *Ordeal by Battle*, Macmillan, 1915

Overy, Dr R. J., *The Air War 1939–1945*, Europa, 1980

Parish, P., *The American Civil War*, Eyre Methuen, 1975

Payton-Smith, D. J., *Oil: A Study of War-time Policy and Administration*, HMSO, 1971 (official history)

Playfair, I. S. O., The Mediterranean and Middle East, HMSO, 1954 (official history)

Postan, M. M., *British War Production*, HMSO, 1952 (official history)

Price, A., *The Battle of Britain: The Hardest Day*, Macdonald & Jane's, 1979
Aircraft versus Submarines, William Kimber, 1973
Instruments of Darkness, William Kimber, 1967

Pudney, J., *Ten Summers: Poems 1933–1943*, Bodley Head, 1944

Ramsey, W. G. (Ed), *The Battle of Britain Then and Now*, After the Battle Magazine, 1980

Repington, Colonel, *The First World War 1914–1918*, Constable, 1920

Richards, D., *Portal of Hungerford*, Heinemann, 1977

Richards, D., and Saunders, H., *The Royal Air Force 1939–1945*, HMSO, 1974 (Denis Richards wrote Vol I of this work; Richards and Hilary Saunders wrote Vol II and Saunders Vol III)

Richardson, W., and Friedin, S. (Eds), *The Fatal Decisions* (trans. Constantine Fitzgibbon), Michael Joseph, 1956

Richey, Paul, *Fighter Pilot*, Jane's Publishing Co, 1980

Robertson, Bruce, *Lancaster: The Story of a Bomber*, Harleyford Publications, 1964

Robertson, Sir W. R., *Soldiers and Statesmen, 1914–18*, Cassell, 1926

Rogers, Col. H. C. B., *Tanks in Battle*, Seeley, 1965

Rohmer, R., *Patton's Gap: An Account of the Battle of Normandy 1944*, Arms and Armour Press, 1981

Roskill, S., *Hankey: Man of Secrets*, Collins, 1970
The War at Sea, HMSO, 1956 (official history)

Royal Air Force Quarterly, April 1948

Royal Institute of International Affairs, *Chronology and Index of the Second World War*, Newspaper Archives Development Ltd, 1975

Royal United Services Institute *Journal*, May 1962, "Some Reflections on the Strategic Air Offensive", Noble Frankland
May 1964, "The Dams Raid", Noble Frankland

November 1966, "The Problem of Civil Aviation in British Air Disarmament Policy", D. Carlton

March 1973, "Operation SEALION 1940", von Plehwe

September 1974, "Rommel's Supply Problem", M. van Creveld

September 1976, "Air Intelligence and the Coventry Raid", N. E. Evans

June 1977, "Air Power at Kursk", Captain Lonnie O. Ratley III, USAF

March 1980, "The Influence of Neville Chamberlain on Foreign and Defence Policy", D. Wrench

March 1981, "Ludlow-Hewitt and the Expansion of Bomber Command", Dr M. Smith

March 1983, "Nazi Grand Strategy in the 1930s", Prof. Williamson Murray

Sainsbury, K., *The North African Landings, 1942*, Davis-Poynter, 1976

Saundby, Sir Robert, *Air Bombardment: The Story of its Development*, Chatto & Windus, 1961

Shepperd, G. A., *Italian Campaign 1939–44*, Arthur Barker, 1968

Sims, W. S., and Hendrick, B. J., *The Victory at Sea*, Murray, 1927

Slessor, J., *The Central Blue*, Cassell, 1956

   The Great Deterrent, Cassell, 1957

Slim, W. J., *Defeat into Victory*, Cassell, 1956

   Unofficial History, Cassell, 1959

Smith, D., *Spitfire into Battle*, John Murray, 1981

Southwold, S., *The Gas War of 1940*, London, 1931

Spears, E., *Assignment to Catastrophe*, Heinemann, 1954

Speer, A., *Inside the Third Reich*, Weidenfeld and Nicolson, 1970

   Spandau: The Secret Diaries, Collins, 1976

Statistics of the Military Effort of the British Empire, HMSO, 1921

Storry, Richard, *A History of Modern Japan*, Pelican, 1960

Sweetman, John, *Operation Chastise – The Dams Raid: Epic or Myth*, Jane's, 1982

Taylor, Telford, *Munich: The Price of Peace*, Hodder & Stoughton, 1979

Tedder, Lord, *With Prejudice*, Cassell, 1966

Templewood, Lord, *Empire of the Air*, Collins, 1957

Terraine, John, *Douglas Haig*, Hutchinson, 1963

   Impacts of War, 1914–1918, Hutchinson, 1970

   The Life and Times of Lord Mountbatten, Arrow, 1968

   The Mighty Continent, Futura, 1974

   The Smoke and the Fire, Sidgwick and Jackson, 1980

   The Western Front, Hutchinson, 1964

   White Heat, Sidgwick and Jackson, 1982

Thetford, Owen, *Aircraft of the RAF since 1918*, Putnam, 1957

Thomas, H., *The Spanish Civil War*, Penguin, 1965

Thoumin, Richard, *The First World War*, Secker & Warburg, 1960

Times History of the War (1914–18), The Times

Toland, John, *Adolf Hitler*, Doubleday (NY), 1976

Trythall, A. J., *'Boney' Fuller*, Cassell, 1977

Tuker, F., *Approach to Battle*, Cassell, 1963
Tunney, C., *Biographical Dictionary of World War II*, Dent, 1972
Turnbull, P., *Dunkirk: Anatomy of Disaster*, Batsford, 1978
US Strategic Bombing Survey
Vaughan-Thomas, W., *Anzio*, Longmans, 1961
Verrier, A., *The Bomber Offensive*, Batsford, 1968
von Senger und Etterlin, General, *Neither Fear Nor Hope*, Macdonald, 1963
Warner, P., *Auchinleck: The Lonely Soldier*, Buchan & Enright, 1981
Wavell, A. P., *The Palestine Campaign*, Constable, 1928
Webster, C., and Frankland, N., *The Strategic Air Offensive Against Germany 1939–45*, HMSO, 1961 (official history)
Weigley, Russell F., *Eisenhower's Lieutenants*, Sidgwick & Jackson, 1981
Wendel, Else, *Hausfrau at War*, Odhams Press, 1957
Werth, A., *Russia at War 1941–45*, Barrie & Rockliff, 1964
Wheeler-Bennett, J., *King George VI*, Macmillan, 1958
Whitehead, W., and Macartney-Filgate, T., *Dieppe 1942: Echoes of Disaster*, Richard Drew, 1982
Williams, J., *The Ides of May*, Constable, 1968
Wilmot, C., *The Struggle for Europe*, Collins, 1952
Winterbotham, F. W., *The Ultra Secret*, Weidenfeld & Nicolson, 1974
Wood, D., and Dempster, D., *The Narrow Margin*, Arrow, 1969
Wright, R., *Dowding and the Battle of Britain*, Macdonald, 1969
Wright, R., and Deighton, L., *Battle of Britain*, Cape, 1980
Wynn, H., and Young, S., *Prelude to Overlord*, Airlife, 1983
Young, P., *World War 1939–45: A Short History*, Arthur Barker, 1966
Zuckerman, S., *From Apes to Warlords*, Hamish Hamilton, 1978

INDEX

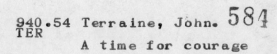